"Given that the Bible is from another time and another culture, all of us need help in understanding the Bible, its culture, and its intent. This *Companion* will be a valued friend to Bible readers. It is easily accessible and is packed with information and insight from the very best scholars. It provides helpful articles on crucial topics and a pathway through the entire Bible by showing the layout of each book and giving brief explanations of each section in the book. Lay readers of the Bible will love this reference work."

— KLYNE SNODGRASS
North Park Theological Seminary

The Eerdmans Companion to the Bible

Edited by

Gordon D. Fee
and
Robert L. Hubbard Jr.

with Commentary by

Connie Gundry Tappy

WILLIAM B. EERDMANS PUBLISHING COMPANY

GRAND RAPIDS, MICHIGAN / CAMBRIDGE, U.K.

Published 2011 by

Wm. B. Eerdmans Publishing Co.

2140 Oak Industrial Drive N.E., Grand Rapids, Michigan 49505 /

P.O. Box 163, Cambridge CB3 9PU U.K.

Printed in the United States of America

17 16 15 14 13 12 11   7 6 5 4 3 2 1

Library of Congress Cataloging-in-Publication Data

The Eerdmans companion to the Bible /

   general editors, Gordon D. Fee, Robert L. Hubbard, Jr.

       p.   cm.

    Includes index.

    ISBN 978-0-8028-3823-0 (cloth : alk. paper)

    1. Bible — Introductions.

    I. Fee, Gordon D.   II. Hubbard, Robert L., 1943-

  III. Title: The Eerdmans Companion to the Bible.

    BS475.3.E34 2011

    220.6'1 — dc23

                  2011032174

www.eerdmans.com

Contents

WELCOME TO THE BIBLE

THE OLD TESTAMENT

THE NEW TESTAMENT

Maps

Preface

We are proud to present this new *Companion to the Bible* to readers and students of the Bible. By its very nature as a *Companion,* this volume is by no means intended as a substitute for reading the biblical text itself. Rather, we envision the reader approaching Scripture with the Bible in one hand and the *Companion* in the other. In this way the *Companion* may serve as a guide to the Word, a practical resource for studying and reflecting on the biblical account. It may be used with any translation of the Bible.

The editors and contributors to this book have garnered a vast array of useful information and presented it in clear, reader-friendly fashion. Recognizing that some readers may be new to the Bible, with no previous background in biblical studies, contributors have kept technical matters to a minimum. Rather, the focus is on the content and meaning of the Bible, sensitively reflecting readers' concern for issues directly relevant to the quest for greater understanding and appreciation of what the Bible has to convey. Because the biblical text may at times appear difficult or puzzling, separated from the modern world over many centuries by language and culture, our goal has been to enable modern readers to benefit from the fruits of recent discoveries and the insights of responsible, current biblical scholarship into the lives and times of the inspired biblical writers and their setting.

In keeping with its aim of stimulating and guiding the Bible reader who seeks to grow in understanding what the text has to say, the *Companion* opens with an introductory essay, "What Is the Bible?" by the General Editors. Further setting the scene for studying the Bible as a whole are discussions of inspiration and authority, the formation, transmission, and translation of the biblical text, and surveys of the physical world of the Bible and aspects of daily life in its ancient setting.

The main focus of the *Companion* is the Bible itself. Each section dealing with the Old and New Testament begins with an introduction to the individual collections or genres—for the Old Testament, the Five Books or Pentateuch, the Historical Books, Poetry and Wisdom Literature, and the Prophets; for the New Testament, the Gospels and Acts, the Letters, and Revelation. The knowledgeable and lucid commentary by Connie Gundry Tappy summarizes and explains each book of the Bible, section by section, with fascinating insights into customs, natural phenomena, words and phrases, and more as recorded in the accounts. Articles by a host of foremost biblical scholars provide additional information on the setting and use of the Bible, with details of important historical, literary, and cultural interest that the student may encounter in reading or discussion.

Concluding the *Companion* are articles applying the sacred text to Christian faith and Christian living today. Handy reference tools include glossaries of terms, people, nations and groups, and places mentioned in the Bible.

A comprehensive work of this type depends on many talented persons who have generously shared their knowledge of the riches of the Bible, and the publishers wish to express gratitude to all who have directly or indirectly helped to make this *Companion* possible. Particular appreciation is due the General Editors, Robert L. Hubbard Jr. and Gordon D. Fee, distinguished scholars whose editorial expertise in shaping the volume is evident throughout. Thanks also to the consulting editors, T. Desmond Alexander, Joel B. Green, Richard N. Longenecker, Tremper Longman III, Marianne Meye Thompson, and Willem A. VanGemeren for their introductory articles and for vetting the respective articles. Connie Gundry Tappy has provided with precision and clarity a wealth of information and practical interpretation in the Commentary. John R. Kohlenberger III and Mike Peterson of Multnomah Graphics made significant contributions in the early stages of the project, and Richard Cleave graciously provided access to the resources of the Pictorial Archive.

We send forth this volume with the heartfelt desire that it bring new appreciation to the power and relevance of Scripture and its manifold riches. May this book truly prove a treasured companion, serving its readers in fruitful understanding of what the Bible has to say to our age.

THE PUBLISHERS

Contributors

General Editors

Robert L. Hubbard, Jr. Professor of Old Testament, North Park Theological Seminary, Chicago, Illinois. *(What Is the Bible?; The Law in Israel and in Judaism; The Historical Books; Entering the Land)*

Gordon D. Fee. Professor Emeritus of New Testament, Regent College, Vancouver, British Columbia. *(What Is the Bible?; The Holy Spirit in the New Testament)*

Consulting Editors

T. Desmond Alexander. Senior Lecturer in Biblical Studies and Director of Postgraduate Studies, Union Theological College, Belfast, Northern Ireland. *(The Five Books; The Tabernacle; The Calendar of Israel's Worship)*

Joel B. Green. Professor of New Testament Interpretation and Associate Dean, Center for Advanced Theological Studies, Fuller Theological Seminary, Pasadena, California. *(How to Interpret the Bible; The Gospels and Acts; The Trial, Death, and Resurrection of Jesus)*

Richard N. Longenecker. Professor Emeritus of New Testament, Wycliffe College, University of Toronto, Toronto, Ontario. *(The Course of Paul's Ministry; The Letters; The Question of Pseudepigraphy)*

Tremper Longman III. Professor of Old Testament, Westmont College, Santa Barbara, California. *(The Divine Warrior; Poetry and Wisdom Literature; The Divine and Human Kings in the Psalms; The Psalms in Worship; Israel and Its Enemies in the Psalms)*

Marianne Meye Thompson. George Eldon Ladd Professor of New Testament, Fuller Theological Seminary, Pasadena, California. *(The Johannine Literature; Revelation; Apocalyptic Literature in Judaism and Christianity)*

Willem A. VanGemeren. Professor of Old Testament and Semitic Languages, Director of the Doctor of Philosophy in Theological Studies, Trinity Evangelical Divinity School, Deerfield, Illinois. *(Languages, Writing, and Alphabets; Prophets and Prophecy)*

Commentary

Connie Gundry Tappy. Free-lance author and editor. Allison Park, Pennsylvania.

Articles

Bill T. Arnold. Paul S. Amos Professor of Old Testament Interpretation and Director of Hebrew Studies, Asbury Theological Seminary, Wilmore, Kentucky. *(The Patriarchs and Their Neighbors)*

Hector Avalos. Professor of Religious Studies, Director, Latino Studies Program, Iowa State University, Ames, Iowa. *(Disease, Disabilities, and Healing)*

Richard Beaton. Associate Professor of New Testament and Principal of De Pree Leadership Center, Fuller Theological Seminary, Pasadena, California. *(Use of the Old Testament in the New Testament)*

Daniel I. Block. Gunther H. Knoedler Professor of Old Testament, Wheaton College, Wheaton Illinois. *(The Temple)*

Craig L. Blomberg. Distinguished Professor of New Testament, Denver Seminary, Denver, Colorado. *(Women in the Early Church)*

Gerald L. Borchert. Senior Professor of New Testament, Carson-Newman College, Jefferson City, Tennessee, and Doctoral Thesis Advisor, The Robert E. Webber Institute for Worship Studies, Jacksonville, Florida. *(Jesus, His Disciples, and the Christian Today)*

Robin Gallaher Branch. Professor of Biblical Studies, Victory University, Memphis, Tennessee. *(How Was the Bible Passed Down to Us?; Women in the Old Testament)*

George J. Brooke. Rylands Professor of Biblical Criticism and Exegesis, University of Manchester,

United Kingdom. *(Exile and Return; Apocrypha/Deuterocanonical Books)*

Michael Joseph Brown. Associate Professor of New Testament and Christian Origins, Emory University, Atlanta, Georgia. *(Measuring Time)*

Roger A. Bullard. Professor of Religion and Philosophy, Retired. Barton College, Wilson, North Carolina. *(The Bible in English)*

Theodore W. Burgh. Assistant Professor of Philosophy and Religion, University of North Carolina at Wilmington. *(Music and Musical Instruments)*

Cottrel R. Carson. Assistant Professor of New Testament, McAfee School of Theology, Mercer University, Atlanta, Georgia. *(Acts and History)*

Stephen B. Chapman. Research Professor of New Testament and Greek, Duke Divinity School, Durham, North Carolina. *(Why Are These Books in the Bible?)*

Mark W. Chavalas. Professor of History, University of Wisconsin-La Crosse. *(Worshippers of Other Gods [Part 1])*

Steven L. Cox. Associate Professor of New Testament and Greek, Mid-America Baptist Theological Seminary, Memphis, Tennessee. *(The Use of Imagery in the Apocalypse)*

David A. deSilva. Trustees' Distinguished Professor of New Testament and Greek, Ashland Theological Seminary, Ashland, Ohio. *(Nations, Peoples, and Empires [Part 2])*

Craig A. Evans. Payzant Distinguished Professor of New Testament Studies, Acadia Divinity College, Wolfville, Nova Scotia. *(Jesus' Teachings)*

Wayne S. Flory. Associate Professor of Biblical Studies, Emeritus, Biola University, La Mirada, California. *(Worshippers of Other Gods [Part 2])*

Susan R. Garrett. Professor of New Testament Studies, Louisville Presbyterian Theological Seminary, Louisville, Kentucky. *(The Temptations of Jesus)*

Robert H. Gundry. Scholar-in-Residence, Westmont College, Santa Barbara, California. *(Heresies)*

G. Walter Hansen. Associate Professor of New Testament, Director of the Global Research Institute, Fuller Theological Seminary, Pasadena, California. *(Ancient Letter Writing)*

Joseph H. Hellerman. Professor of New Testament

Language and Literature, Talbot School of Theology, Biola University. *(Society in New Testament Times; Daily Life in the New Testament)*

Richard S. Hess. Earl S. Kalland Professor of Old Testament and Semitic Languages, Denver Seminary, Denver, Colorado. *(Other Ancient Accounts of Creation)*

Craig C. Hill. Research Professor of New Testament Pedagogy, Duke Divinity School, Durham, North Carolina. *(Jews and Gentiles in the Church; The Goal of Faith)*

Harold W. Hoehner. Distinguished Professor of New Testament Studies (deceased), Dallas Theological Seminary, Dallas, Texas. *(World of the New Testament)*

Michael M. Homan. Associate Professor of Hebrew Bible, Department of Theology, Xavier University of Louisiana, New Orleans. *(Weights, Measures,Money)*

Edwin C. Hostetter. Professorial Lecturer, George Washington University, Washington, D.C. *(Nations, Peoples, and Empires [Part 1])*

David M. Howard, Jr. Professor of Old Testament and Dean, Center for Biblical and Theological Foundations, Bethel Theological Seminary, St. Paul, Minnesota. *(Judges and Kings of Israel and Judah; The Two Histories)*

Barry A. Jones. Associate Professor of Old Testament and Hebrew, Campbell University Divinity School, Buies Creek, North Carolina. *(Beginnings of Apocalyptic Literature)*

John McRay. Professor of New Testament and Archaeology Emeritus, Wheaton College, Wheaton, Illinois. *(Paul's Cities)*

Calvin L. Marion. Candler School of Theology, Emory University, Atlanta, Georgia. *(Measuring Time)*

Claude F. Mariottini. Professor of Old Testament, Northern Baptist Theological Seminary, Lombard, Illinois. *(Old Testament History and History Writing)*

I. Howard Marshall. Emeritus Professor of New Testament Exegesis and Honorary Research Professor, King's College, University of Aberdeen, Scotland. *(The Last Supper)*

Ralph P. Martin. Distinguished Scholar in Residence, Fuller Theological Seminary, Pasadena, California; Professor of New Testament, Azusa Pacific University, Azusa, California; Professor of New

Testament, Logos Evangelical Seminary, Los Angeles, California. *(The Early Churches and Their Worship)*

Kenneth A. Mathews. Professor of Divinity, Beeson Divinity School, Samford University, Birmingham, Alabama. *(Holy, Clean, and Unclean)*

Victor H. Matthews. Dean, College of Humanities and Public Affairs, Professor of Religious Studies, Southwest Missouri State University, Springfield, Missouri. *(Society and Daily Life in the Old Testament)*

John Monson. Associate Professor of Old Testament and Semitic Languages, Trinity Evangelical Divinity School, Deerfield, Illinois. *(Lands of the Bible)*

James C. Moyer. Professor of Religious Studies, Head, Department of Religious Studies, Southwest Missouri State University, Springfield, Missouri. *(Weapons and Warfare)*

R. Scott Nash. Columbus Roberts Professor of New Testament, Mercer University, Macon, Georgia. *(Christianity in the Eyes of Non-Christians; New Testament Attitudes toward the Roman State)*

R. Steven Notley. Distinguished Professor of Bible, Alliance Theological Seminary, Nyack College, New York City, New York. *(Judaism in the Time of Jesus)*

Alan G. Padgett. Professor of Systematic Theology, Luther Seminary, St. Paul, Minnesota. *(Divine and Human)*

Christine D. Pohl. Professor of Church in Society and Associate Provost, Asbury Theological Seminary, Wilmore, Kentucky. *(The Guide for Christian Living)*

Kandy Queen-Sutherland. Professor of Religious Studies, Stetson University, DeLand, Florida. *(Sacrifices and Offerings)*

Brian M. Rapske. Associate Professor of New Testament, Northwest Baptist and ACTS Seminaries, Trinity Western University, Langley, British Columbia. *(Travel in the Roman Empire)*

Stephen A. Reed. Professor of Religion and Philosophy and Department Chair, Jamestown College, Jamestown, North Dakota. *(The Exodus)*

Sandra Richter. Professor of Old Testament, Wesley Biblical Seminary, Jackson, Mississippi, and Affili-

ate Professor of Old Testament, Asbury Theological Seminary, Wilmore, Kentucky. *(Covenants)*

Leland Ryken. Professor of English, Wheaton College, Wheaton, Illinois. *(The Bible as Literature)*

Charles J. Scalise. Professor of Church History, Fuller Theological Seminary, Seattle, Washington. *(The Guide for Christian Faith)*

Klyne Snodgrass. Paul W. Brandel Professor of New Testament Studies, North Park Theological Seminary, Chicago, Illinois. *(In Parables)*

J. Paul Tanner. Professor of Hebrew and Old Testament Studies, The Jordan Evangelical Theological Seminary, Amman, Jordan. *(Interpretations of the Song of Songs)*

Lynn Tatum. Senior Lecturer in Religion and Associate Director of Middle East Studies, Baylor University, Waco, Texas. *(Archaeology and the Bible)*

Frank Thielman. Presbyterian Professor of Divinity, Beeson Divinity School, Samford University, Birmingham, Alabama. *(Paul's Gospel)*

Michael B. Thompson. Vice-Principal and Lecturer in New Testament Studies, Ridley Hall, Cambridge, United Kingdom. *(From Jesus to Paul)*

Richard B. Vinson. Visiting Professor of Religion, Salem College, Winston-Salem, North Carolina. *(Jesus and History)*

John H. Walton. Professor of Old Testament, Wheaton College, Wheaton, Illinois. *(Flood Stories in the Bible and the Ancient Near East)*

Rikki E. Watts. Professor of New Testament, Regent College, Vancouver, British Columbia. *(Miracles)*

H. G. M. Williamson. Regius Professor of Hebrew, The Oriental Institute, Christ Church, University of Oxford, United Kingdom. *(Priests and Levites)*

Davis A. Young. Emeritus Professor of Geology, Calvin College, Grand Rapids, Michigan. *(Creation and Modern Science)*

Mark Ziese. Professor of Old Testament, Cincinnati Bible Seminary, Cincinnati, Ohio. *(Plants and Animals)*

Abbreviations

ABD	*Anchor Bible Dictionary*, ed. David Noel Freedman
BA	*Biblical Archaeologist*
BAR	*Biblical Archaeology Review*
BASOR	*Bulletin of the American Oriental Society*
CBQ	*Catholic Biblical Quarterly*
HSM	Harvard Semitic Monographs
JBL	*Journal of Biblical Literature*
JSNT	*Journal for the Study of the New Testament*
JSNTSup	Journal for the Study of the New Testament: Supplement
JSOT	*Journal for the Study of the Old Testament*
JTS	*Journal of Theological Studies*
KJV	King James Version
LEC	Library of Early Christianity
NEB	New English Bible
NICNT	New International Commentary on the New Testament
NIDOTTE	*New International Dictionary of Old Testament Theology and Exegesis,* ed. Willem A. VanGemeren
NIV	New International Version
NovTSup	Supplements to Novum Testamentum
OEANE	*Oxford Encyclopedia of Archaeology in the Near East,* ed. Eric M. Meyers
OTL	Old Testament Library
par.	and parallels
RSV	Revised Standard Version
SBL	Society of Biblical Literature
SBLDS	Society of Biblical Literature Dissertation Series
SNTSMS	Society for New Testament Studies Monograph Series
TEV	Today's English Version
TNTC	Tyndale New Testament Commentaries
WBC	Word Biblical Commentary
WUNT	Wissenschaftliche Untersuchungen zum Neuen Testament

Welcome to the Bible

What Is the Bible?

Welcome to the wonderful world of the Bible! Some first enter it as children hearing Bible stories told by teachers or parents, while others first experience it as verses to memorize from flash cards. Some first hear of it as young adults taught by youth pastors or campus ministers, but some first discover it as adults adopting the common practice of daily Bible readings. And some have spent only a little time inside its world, while others who have heard about it have not yet ventured there. Whatever your relation to the Bible — whatever your favorite story, Bible character, or biblical book — this *Companion* aims to help you understand and enjoy the Bible's wonderful world.

Why Study the Bible?

Why should we study the Bible at all? What is it about the Bible that demands our attention, just as it did hundreds of generations before us? The answer is surprisingly simple: we should study the Bible because it introduces us to God. Indeed, God is its leading character. Most of the Bible consists of narratives starring God. Thus the Bible is not simply another version of humankind's age-old search for God but the account of *God's* own story — the report of God's persistent search for *us*. Put differently, the Bible's narrative "history" is essentially "his story" — the "Great Story" that underlies all of human history, the story that ultimately gives history a purpose. The Bible tells this great story in four chapters: Creation, Fall, Redemption, and Consummation. In this grand, cosmic drama, God plays the divine protagonist, Satan the antagonist, God's people the deuteragonists or foils — and sometimes also the antagonists! It is an amazing drama whose narrative tension redemption and reconciliation resolve, and whose denouement the consummation achieves. This large "forest" comprises the context for all the Bible's "trees" — its verses, paragraphs, chapters, books, and testaments. Thus, to help Bible readers find how their stories intersect with God's own story, the Great Story bears telling again.

The Biblical Story

Creation The creation marks both the first chapter in God's story and God's debut as protagonist. Surprisingly, he debuts not as a hidden God whom people must seek — in the end led to God by Jesus — but as a compelling, majestic figure standing alone at center stage. The narrator's introduction, "in the beginning God," signals that God alone existed *before* all things, that God alone is the *cause* of all things, that therefore God alone rules *above* all things, and that God alone is the *goal* of all things. His opening scene, with its seven-day structure, presents God as the sole Creator of both the whole, vast, intricate universe and of history itself (Genesis 1). All creation and all history have the eternal God, through Christ, as their final purpose and consummation.

God's own words, "Let us make humankind in our image" (Gen. 1:26), stamp humanity as the crowning glory of the Creator's work. We are beings made in God's likeness, with whom he could commune, and in whom he could delight; beings who would know the sheer pleasure of God's presence, love, and favor. Created in God's image, humankind thus uniquely enjoyed a clear *vision* of God and lived in intimate fellowship with God. But our being *created* in that image implies that God intended humans to be dependent on the Creator for life in his world. Genesis 1–2 first voices the Story's dependence theme, but in scores of ways other voices throughout the whole narrative echo and reprise it.

The Fall The fall comprises the second chapter in the biblical story, a long and tragic one. It begins in Genesis 3 and weaves a dark, ugly thread through the whole Story almost to the very end (Rev. 22:11, 15). It narrates how man and woman, suspicious of God's goodness, coveted God's divine status, and how in one awful moment in our planet's history they acted to become gods themselves, thus rebelling against their creatureliness, with its dependent status. They chose *in*dependence from the Creator, but that choice violated God's intention, so a fall resulted — a colossal, catastrophic, and tragic fall. (Granted, this is not a popular part of the Story today; but its rejection is symptomatic of the fall itself and the root of all false theologies.)

The truly tragic result was that we humans — created to enjoy fellowship with God, to thrive in dependence on him, and to find our ultimate meaning in being his creatures — fell under God's wrath and came to experience the terrible consequences of our rebellion. Three specific calamities afflicted our fallenness:

First, we lost our *vision* of God. Our perception of his nature and character blurred. Guilty and hostile ourselves, we projected responsibility for that guilt and hostility on God. *God* is to blame for this mess: "Why have *you* made me thus?" "Why are *you* so cruel?" Such plaintive but foolish cries echo throughout the history of our race. We thus became idolaters, reconstructing every grotesque expression of our fallenness into a god. As Paul writes," They exchanged the truth about God for a lie" (Rom. 1:22-25).

In swapping the truth about God for a lie, we viewed God as full of caprice, contradictions, hostility, lust, and revenge — all projections of our fallen selves. But God is *not* like our grotesque idolatries. Indeed, as Paul says, if God seems hidden it is because we have become slaves to the god of this world, who has blinded our minds, so that we are constantly seeking God but are never able to find him (2 Cor. 4:4). In essence, we persist in living out one grand self-deceptive delusion.

Second, the fall caused us to distort — to blur, really — the divine image in ourselves, preferring to roll it in the dust rather than revel in it. We were made to be like God — loving, generous, self-giving, thoughtful, merciful — but we became spiteful, miserly, selfish, thoughtless, unforgiving. We were created to image God in our personhood and conduct, but instead with pleasure learned to image God's implacable enemy, the Evil One. Brief glimpses of our original divine image appear occasionally, but sadly, the Evil One's image dominates.

Third, in the fall we lost God's presence; we forfeited the relationship that bound us in joyful fellowship to God. Rather than commune with the loving Creator and serve our wonderful purpose in his creation, we became rebels, lost and cast adrift in an unfriendly world. We became creatures who broke God's laws and abused his creation; and we paid a terrible price for our fallenness — brokenness, alienation, loneliness, and pain. Worse, we are enslaved under the cruel, tyrannical grip of our sin and our guilt. That slavery renders us both unwilling and unable on our own to return to the living God for life and restoration. As Genesis 4–11 attests, our fallenness also ruins our relationships with others, a brokenness we pass on to our children.

The Bible tells us that an awful distance lies between us and God — and that it is our fault. It compares us to sheep going astray (Isa. 53:6; 1 Pet. 2:25) or to a rebellious, know-it-all son who chose to live in a far country, among hogs, reduced to eating their food (Luke 15:11-32). In our better moments, we squarely face that this is true about ourselves, not just about the murderer, rapist, or child abuser. We candidly admit that *we* are the selfish, the greedy, the proud, and the manipulative. It is no surprise to us that people think God is hostile to us; in our occasional honesty we know we deserve his wrath for being the kind of slimy stinkers we really are.

Redemption But the Bible tells us that the holy and just God — the God whose moral perfection burns against sin and creaturely rebellion — is in fact also a God full of mercy and love — and faithfulness. The reality is that God pitied — indeed, *loved* — these cranky creatures of his whose rebellious rejection of their dependent status dragged them down into the terrible degradation of sin, with its consequent pain, guilt, and alienation.

The Bible's third chapter narrates how God sought to get through to us to rescue us from ourselves, our wrongheaded views about God, and the tragic despair of our fallenness; how God sought to show us that he is *for* us, not *against* us (Rom. 8:31); how God sought to get us rebels not just to run up the white flag of surrender but willingly to change sides and, thereby, to rediscover the joy and meaning God intended for us in the first place. This chapter tells how God sought to redeem and restore these fallen creatures of his so he might renew our lost vision of him and remake the divine image in us. But two thematic threads drive this chapter's plot — the narrative tension between God's steps of intervention and our continuing resistance.

The first thread narrates how God came to a man, Abraham, and made a covenant with him to bless him and, through him, the nations (Genesis 12–50). He later came to Abraham's offspring, Israel, who had become an enslaved people (Exodus), and through the first of his prophets, Moses, freed them from slavery and made a covenant with them at Mount Sinai. God, whose name is Yahweh, promised that he their Rescuer would from that point on be their Savior and Protector forever. But God also stipulated that they would have to keep covenant with him by letting him reshape them back into his likeness. He gave them a gift — his law — both to reveal what he is like and to protect them from each other while the reshaping proceeded (Leviticus–Deuteronomy).

But the contrary, dark thread narrates that Israel rebelled over and over again and mis-read God's gift of law as a way of taking away their freedom. As shepherds being brought into a fertile land (Joshua), they weren't sure their God was up to helping the crops grow, so they turned to the gods of the peoples around them (Baal and Astarte). As a result, they experienced a round of oppression and rescue (Judges), even while some of them were truly taking on God's character (Ruth). Finally, God sent them another great prophet (Samuel), who anointed for them their ideal king (David), with whom God made another covenant: one of David's offspring would rule over his people forever (1-2 Samuel). But alas, those offspring rebelled (1-2 Kings; 1-2 Chronicles), so in love God sent them proph-ets (Isaiah–Malachi), singers (Psalms), and sages (Job, Proverbs, Ecclesiastes) to keep the reshaping process alive. In the end, their unfaithfulness proved constant, so God at last imposed judgment — the curses promised in Deuteronomy 28. But for all that, God left the door open for his people to return (Deuteronomy 30) and even promised great things for their future (Isaiah 40–55; Jeremiah 30–32; Ezekiel 36–37) — a new "son of David" and an outpouring of God's Spirit into people's hearts to transform their lives back into God's likeness. This final "blessing" would also fall on people from all nations (the "Gentiles").

But God reserves his greatest surprise for the Story's next-to-the-last scene, the one preceding the final curtain and Epilogue. This scene narrates the greatest event of all: the great, final "son of David" is none other than God himself! The Creator of all the cosmic vastness and grandeur around us presents himself on earth, amid the human scene, and in our own likeness. He was born to a carpenter's wife and was a member of an oppressed people, among whom he lived and taught. Finally, he suffered a horrible death, followed by a death-defeating resurrection. Through those events, he grappled with and finally de-feated the "gods" — all the powers that opposed God and enslaved us — and himself bore the full weight of the guilt and punishment for his creatures' rebellion.

Here is the heart of the Story: a loving, redeeming God, whose incarnation restored our lost *vision* of God, banishing the sinful blur so we could see clearly what God is truly like;

whose crucifixion and resurrection made possible our restoration to the *image* of God (Rom. 8:29; 2 Cor. 3:18); and whose gift of his Spirit restored his long-lost *presence* with us in ongoing fellowship. The Story is a marvelous, well-nigh incredible, revelation of God's redemption.

But the true genius of the biblical Story is what it tells us about God himself. It is about a God who willingly took on our earthly human form and sacrificed himself in death, all out of love for us, his enemies. It is about a God who preferred to experience our own death himself rather than be apart from the people he created for his pleasure. It is about a God who carried our sins to his cross, that he might provide us with pardon and forgiveness. It is about a God who would not let us go but pursued even the worst of us in order to restore us to joyful fellowship with himself. It is about a God who in Jesus Christ has so forever identified with his beloved creatures that the redeemed later came to praise him as the "God and Father of our Lord Jesus Christ" (2 Cor. 1:3; Eph. 1:3; 1 Pet. 1:3). It is about a God who lovingly gathers his followers together, wherever they may be on the planet, into "the church" and meets with them in worship.

This is, indeed, *God's* story, the story of his unfathomable love and grace, mercy and forgiveness. And that is also how it becomes *our* story. According to the Story, we are spiritually bankrupt, void of any claims on God, and our hands empty of anything with which to impress God. But surprise! In the end, we get everything: we deserve hell but get heaven; we deserve annihilation but get God's tender embrace; we deserve rejection and judgment but get acceptance as God's own children — get to bear his likeness and call him Father. Through faith in Jesus, we become part of God's story, and it also becomes our story, too. Indeed, God even gave some of us human creatures a part in writing it up!

Consummation God's story has not yet ended, because the final chapter is still to play out. Of course, we know how it turns out because of what the Bible teaches: the ultimate outcome, set in motion by what God did through the incarnation, death, and resurrection of Christ, and the gift of the Spirit, will finally be fully realized. This is what distinguishes the Story from other similar stories: it is full of hope. The present story has an End — a final, glorious climax. Standing at the tomb of his friend Lazarus, Jesus explained this hope: "I am the resurrection and the life. Those who believe in me, even though they die, will live" (John 11:25). Because Jesus is both the *resurrection* and the *life,* Jesus himself was Lazarus's hope for life now and for life forever. And his raising of Lazarus from the grave dramatically validated his claim to be the source of hope.

The final verification of his words came in Jesus' own resurrection from the dead. The wicked and the religious killed him because they could not tolerate having him around. His life and teaching utterly contradicted all of their own petty forms of religion and authority, forms based on their own fallenness. Worse, Jesus had the gall to tell them that he was the *only* way to the Father. But since he himself *was* Life — indeed, the very author of the life enjoyed by all others — the grave could not keep him in its grip. Jesus' resurrection not only validated his own claims about himself and vindicated his own life on our planet, it also spelled the beginning of the end for death itself. Jesus' resurrection forever provided the guarantee of life everlasting for all who are his.

This is what the final episode (the Revelation) is all about: God finally wraps up the Story, his justice bringing an end to the Great Antagonist and all who continue to bear his image (Revelation 20), his love restoring the creation (Eden) as a new heaven and a new earth (Revelation 21–22).

This is the Great Story of which the Bible's various "books" are part. We have shown briefly how each "book" fits in, and as you read the various books, you will want to ponder yourself how they fit into the larger Story — and how you yourself fit into it.

ROBERT L. HUBBARD JR.
GORDON D. FEE

Lands of the Bible

The message of the Bible cannot be separated from its geographical and historical setting. Climate and terrain determine agricultural potential, settlement patterns, and trade routes, all of which are used providentially in the biblical story. Most events in the Old Testament are set within the Fertile Crescent, a region that extends from the Persian Gulf, along the edge of the Mediterranean Sea, to the Nile Delta. The Land of the Bible occupies the midsection of this vast tract of habitable land. It is there, a short distance inland from the Mediterranean, that most of biblical history unfolds. This region — also known as Israel, Palestine, the Promised Land, or simply the Holy Land — is an area of great geographical and climatic variety. And yet it is very small, measuring ca. 150 miles from north to south and 60-90 miles from east to west. With the spread of the Jewish Diaspora and the gospel, many New Testament events occur outside the Land of the Bible in the regions of Anatolia, Italy, and the shores of the Aegean Sea, a northern bay of the Mediterranean.

Regions of the Ancient Near East

Several geological features and dominant weather patterns mark the geographical regions of the Near East. The massive Zagros mountain range winds its way from the heartland of Persia north toward eastern Anatolia. In the northeast it gives way to the smaller Taurus range that extends southward toward Cyprus. Plentiful precipitation from Europe falls upon these mountains and empties into the Tigris and Euphrates Rivers, which define the broad basin of southern Mesopotamia. This "Land between Two Rivers," which receives minimal rainfall, is bordered on the northeast by the steppeland of Aram or northern Mesopotamia and on the south by the barren deserts of the Arabian Peninsula. Egypt lies at the opposite end of the Fertile Crescent. Like Mesopotamia, it receives virtually no rainfall and is watered by a mighty river. After meandering through the desert, the Nile fans out into a lush delta and empties into the Mediterranean. Both Mesopotamia and Egypt have access to the Mediterranean Sea, which enables transport to Cyprus, Greece, and Italy as well as up and down the eastern seaboard of the Mediterranean.

Two important landmasses lie west of these areas. Anatolia is a large, well-watered plateau bordered by mountains on the east and south. It was home to the ancient Hittites and

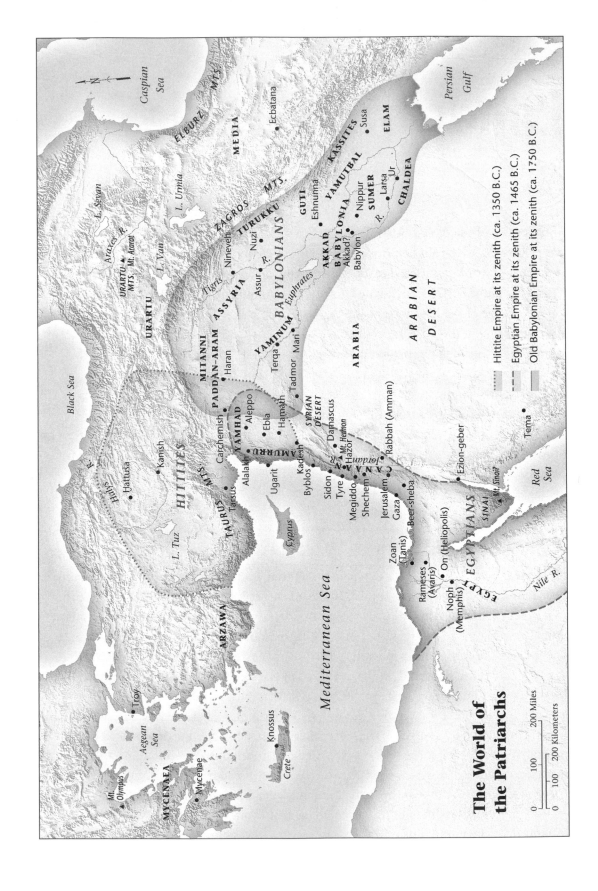

The World of
the Patriarchs

Hittite Empire at its zenith (ca. 1350 B.C.)

Egyptian Empire at its zenith (ca. 1465 B.C.)

Old Babylonian Empire at its zenith (ca. 1750 B.C.)

Caspian Sea

Persian Gulf

ELBURZ MTS.

MEDIA

Ecbatana

L. Sevan

Araxes R.

URARTU MTS. Mt. Ararat

L. Urmia

L. Van

URARTU

ZAGROS MTS.

TURUKKU

GUTI

Eshnunna

AKKAD

KASSITES

YAMUTBAL

Susa

ELAM

Nineveh

Nuzi

R.

Akkad?

BABYLONIA

Babylon

Nippur

SUMER

Larsa

Ur

R.

CHALDEA

Tigris

Assur

ASSYRIA

BABYLONIANS

Euphrates

MITANNI

YAMINUM

PADDAN-ARAM

Haran

Terqa

Mari

Tadmor

ARABIA

ARABIAN DESERT

Black Sea

R.

Hattusa

Kanish

HITTITES MTS.

Carchemish

YAMHAD

Aleppo

Ebla

Hamath

SYRIAN DESERT

Damascus

Rabbah (Amman)

Tema

Tarsus

TAURUS

Alalakh

AMURRU

Kadesh

Ugarit

Mt. Hermon

Byblos

Sidon

Tyre

Hazor

Jordan R.

CANAAN

Megiddo

Shechem

Jerusalem

Gaza

Beer-sheba

Ezion-geber

L. Tuz

ARZAWA

Cyprus

Mediterranean Sea

Zoan (Tanis)

Rameses (Avaris)

On (Heliopolis)

EGYPTIANS

SINAI

Mt. Sinai

Red Sea

Noph (Memphis)

EGYPT

Nile R.

Troy

MYCENAEA

Mt. Olympus

Aegean Sea

Mycenae

Knossus

Crete

0   100   200 Miles

0   100   200 Kilometers

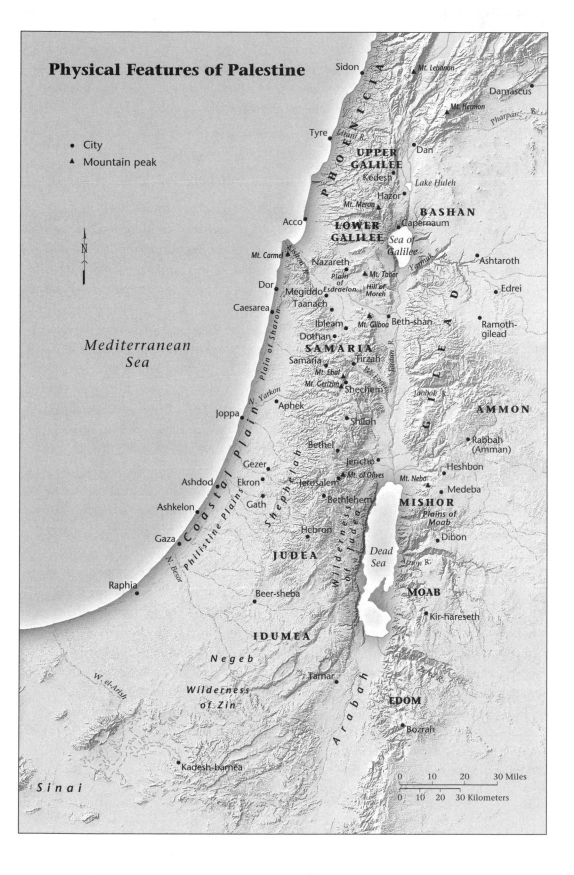

Physical Features of Palestine

- • City
- ▲ Mountain peak

N

Mediterranean
Sea

Sidon
Mt. Lebanon
Damascus
Mt. Hermon
PHOENICIA
Tyre
Litani R.
Pharpar R.
UPPER
GALILEE
Dan
Kedesh
Lake Huleh
Hazor
Mt. Meron
BASHAN
Acco
LOWER
GALILEE
Capernaum
Mt. Carmel
Sea of
Galilee
Yarmuk R.
Ashtaroth
Nazareth
Mt. Tabor
Dor
Plain
of
Esdraelon
Hill of
Moreh
Edrei
Megiddo
Caesarea
Taanach
Ibleam
Mt. Gilboa
Beth-shan
Ramoth-
gilead
Dothan
SAMARIA
Tirzah
Samaria
Mt. Ebal
Mt. Gerizim
Shechem
Jabbok R.
AMMON
Plain of Sharon
N. Yarkon
Aphek
Shiloh
Joppa
Rabbah
(Amman)
Bethel
GILEAD
Gezer
Jericho
Heshbon
Ashdod
Ekron
Jerusalem
Mt. of Olives
Mt. Nebo
Medeba
Coastal Plain
Gath
Bethlehem
MISHOR
Ashkelon
Shephelah
Plains of
Moab
Gaza
Hebron
Dead
Sea
Dibon
Philistine Plains
JUDEA
Wilderness of Judea
Arnon R.
Raphia
N. Besor
Beer-sheba
MOAB
Kir-hareseth
IDUMEA
Negeb
Tamar
Arabah
W. el-Arish
Wilderness
of Zin
EDOM
Bozrah
Sinai
Kadesh-barnea

0   10   20   30 Miles
0 10 20 30 Kilometers

several of the early churches visited by the apostles. Greece is a large peninsula extending southward from Macedonia and Eastern Europe. It gave birth to Classical Greece and its philosophies, as well as Hellenism and many Greco-Roman communities mentioned in the New Testament, such as Galatia, Ephesus, Colossae, and Corinth.

The Land of the Bible and Its Regions

In the land of the Bible competing geologic forces and weather patterns have created subregions that offer dramatic contrasts in terrain and climate. The most dominant feature is a central range of hills running NE-SW, whose westward erosion formed the coastal plain along the same orientation. The eastern, backside of this range gives way to a chalky wilderness and the Jordan Valley, part of the great Rift that extends southward to eastern Africa. Most scholars divide the land into distinct longitudinal zones. These include the relatively flat coastal plain; the low-lying hills of the Shephelah (or lowlands); the central range (with forested mountains as high as 2600 ft.); the narrow Judean Wilderness and the Jordan (Rift) Valley (1200 ft. below sea level); and the Transjordanian Plateau (ca. 3000 ft. above sea level). Precipitation in these areas varies widely, from plentiful rain on the coastal plain to virtually none in the Jordan Valley. Rainfall also decreases dramatically as one moves from the lush vegetation of Galilee to the desert conditions of the Sinai.

South of the central range is an open region called the Negev. Though it has limited rainfall and poor soil quality, it was farmed during the Judean monarchy and has always been an important link for the spice trade between Arabia and the commercial centers of the Mediterranean. The vast Sinai Peninsula lies to the south of the Negev. With massive granite mountains in the south and arid highlands in the north, it separates Egypt from the Land of the Bible.

If one adds geopolitical considerations to the patterns of climate, geography, a three-part division of the land into north, center, and south may be more useful. The north, comprising Galilee and Samaria, is well watered and easily accessible from all directions, which makes it vulnerable to conquest. Dominating the north is the Jezreel Valley with its choice agriculture and easy trade routes in all directions. The south, which includes the Negev and southern Judah, has limited rainfall and is more isolated due to the difficulty of desert travel. The central region encompasses the middle of the hill country, including the biblical territory of Benjamin and the vicinity of Jerusalem. It is a somewhat remote area that is accessible to the coastal plain and Jordan Valley through a series of strategic ridge routes that give life to biblical episodes such as the conquest (Joshua 24), the Benjamite civil war (Judges 19–21), the reign of Saul, and the kingdom of David.

The Significance of Biblical Geography

The Land of the Bible is best described as the "playing board of biblical history." As historians have shown, geographical realities determine the ebb and flow of human history. Like the stage in a drama, the geography of the Near East serves to enliven and clarify the message of God's redemptive work. This can be seen in two primary ways. First, the lands of the Bible provide the context and explain the pattern of biblical events. Throughout history the Land of the Bible has been an arena for competing political and cultural forces. Though limited in natural resources and hard to unify under one government, it is a narrow land bridge that offers convenient routes of trade and conquest between Arabia and the Mediterranean and between the cradles of civilization in Mesopotamia and Egypt. More often than not its political fortunes have therefore oscillated between the competing civilizations of Egypt to the south, Mesopotamia to the distant northeast, and Syria-Aram immediately to the north. Thus the Egyptian empire of the 2nd millennium B.C. dominated the land during the periods of the patriarchs, exodus, and conquest. On the other hand, the Mesopotamian empires of Assyria and Babylon dominated the 1st millennium during the days of the divided kingdom and most of the biblical prophets through the exilic period. During the opening years of the 1st millennium, David and Solomon offered the land a rare and short-lived period of local unity free from outside domination.

A second way in which the lands of the Bible animate its message is through imagery and metaphor. This is best seen in the regional perspectives of biblical authors and events. The text of Isaiah 40, which mentions valleys, crooked ways, and "preparing a highway for our God," is best understood in the setting of the rugged wilderness east of Jerusalem. The prophet Micah speaks of coming disaster for Judah from the perspective of the Shephelah, the primary invasion route used by the marauding armies of Assyria and Babylon. Jesus' ministry in Galilee is set within competing foreign influences that would culminate in the destruction wrought by Rome.

The biblical authors no doubt assumed that their readers were familiar with the world as it was in their day, including the lands of the Bible and surrounding regions. If the first rule of interpretation is to study the context of Scripture, the first step in such an approach is to gain an appreciation of biblical geography.

FOR FURTHER READING

Aharoni, Yohanan. *The Land of the Bible.* 2nd ed. Philadelphia: Westminster, 1979.

Baly, Denis. *The Geography of the Bible.* Rev. ed. New York: Harper & Row, 1974.

Barton, John, ed. *The Biblical World.* London: Routledge, 2002.

Hoerth, Alfred, Gerald L. Mattingly, and Edwin M. Yamauchi, eds. *Peoples of the Old Testament World.* Grand Rapids: Baker, 1994.

Monson, James M. *The Land Between.* Jerusalem: Institute of Holy Land Studies, 1983.

Orni, Efraim, and Elisha Efrat. *Geography of Israel.* 4th ed. Jerusalem: Israel Universities, 1980.

Rainey, Anson F., and R. Steven Notley. *Carta's New Century Handbook and Atlas.* Jerusalem: CARTA, 2007.

JOHN MONSON

Divine and Human

The Bible is a human document, written by people, for people, using human language. The church does not claim that its Holy Scriptures were dictated by God or angels or written by supernatural beings. At the same time, the Holy Scriptures were inspired by God the Spirit and encompass God's very message of salvation and truth for a hurting world — a world much in need of divine light and grace. How can both of these statements be true at the same time? That is the chief question when considering the nature of Holy Scripture in Christian thought.

The church has long affirmed both the authority and inspiration of the Bible and the full and complete humanity of the authors and editors. The roots of this idea go back to the New Testament attitudes toward the Old Testament. Jesus himself had a very high view of the authority of the Hebrew Bible. "Do not think that I have come to abolish the law or the prophets; I have come not to abolish but to fulfill. For truly I tell you, until heaven and earth pass away, not one letter, not one stroke of a letter, will pass from the law until all is accomplished" (Matt. 5:17-18). While Jesus certainly was willing to go beyond what Moses (the Law), David (the Writings), and the prophets taught, he accepted their full authority as Holy Scripture. Moses, David, the prophets, and scribes were human beings who were, nevertheless, inspired by God. 2 Peter expresses this viewpoint: "No prophecy ever came by human will, but men and women moved by the Holy Spirit spoke from God" (2 Pet. 1:21). Hebrews affirms, "Long ago God spoke to our ancestors in many and various ways by the prophets" (Heb. 1:1). With its own moral and educational emphasis, 2 Timothy proclaims, "All scripture is inspired by God and is useful for teaching, for reproof, for correction, and for training in righteousness" (2 Tim. 3:16). From the New Testament attitude toward the Old Testament, then, we learn that the authors and editors of the Bible were real human beings, but they were also inspired by God to speak and to write.

The early church transferred this attitude to the books of the New Testament without denying the authority of the Old Testament. For example, the oldest complete sermon from the early church, 2 Clement (ca. 150 A.D.), cites the Gospels as "Scripture" (ch. 6), introduces an Old Testament quotation with "the Lord says," and calls the Bible "the words of God" (ch. 13). So, while the authors and editors of Scripture were real human beings, they were nevertheless inspired to speak and write by the Holy Spirit; therefore, the accepted and canonical books of the Bible, taken as a whole, can be relied upon to teach

St. Matthew and the Angel, Michelangelo Merisi da Caravaggio (1602), Contarelli Chapel, Church of San Luigi dei Francesi, Rome. *(Scala / Art Resource, NY)*

God's message. The Bible is the word of God, not because God spoke it, but because it teaches God's message delivered through inspired speakers and authors. What is more, it is God's word because the Christian community has collected these sacred writings into a canon. From these books, and from these alone, do we preach God's word in our worship today. Thus, in both theology and practice, the Bible is the highest written religious authority for the Christian church.

One important point must be emphasized. Jesus Christ is superior to his Book. Hebrews clearly teaches that Christ is greater than the prophets of the Old Testament (Heb. 1:1-4), and one can safely add that Christ is also superior to his own apostles and to the writings of the New Testament. The primary importance of the Bible for Christians is that in it we learn of God and of the Messiah, Jesus. The Bible is important because it is the Book of Christ, and it can be trusted to convey the truth of God for salvation. The Bible is inspired for the purpose of "teaching" and "training in righteousness" (2 Tim. 3:16); it is given to us by the Spirit to bring us to Christ and keep us in the Christian way.

The church has long developed analogies to the word of God in Scripture to help us understand its divine-human character. For example, Jesus Christ and the Bible are both called "the word of God," and Christians have long found parallels between Christ and Scripture. Jesus is the word made flesh, while the Bible is the word made text. This common analogy is found throughout church history in Protestant, Catholic, and Orthodox writers; however, the correspondence must not be pressed too hard. Jesus is the living Word and is fully divine. We are right to worship Jesus as God in the flesh. On the other hand, the Bible is not the fullness of deity in textual form. We do not and should not worship the Bible. The correspondence between the Scriptures and Christ would be closer only if we abandoned a "high" interpretation of Christ's person and nature. If, for example, Jesus were just an inspired prophet, then the connections between Scripture and Jesus would be much closer. Both would be human and inspired by the Spirit. On the other hand, as long as we hold to a high Christology in which Jesus is very God, then this analogy will break down at important points.

Catholics and the Eastern Orthodox churches have in their traditions two rich analogies for the divine-human nature of Scripture: the sacrament of the Lord's Supper (Holy Communion or the Eucharist) and the icon. For many traditional churches Holy Communion is much more than a mere ritual or a symbolic memorial. The bread and the wine, in the mystery of grace, are media for the very presence of Christ. This understanding of the sacrament provides a good analogy for the divine-human Scriptures. In the church, by the power of the Spirit the bread and wine are physical means for the spiritual body of Christ to be present to the faithful. In this analogy, the Bible is a kind of sacrament, because its words are the physical media by which the living Word is present by the power of the Spirit. This view also has its limitations, since bread and wine are not inspired human products.

It is part of Orthodox Christian worship to venerate icons, sacred images of a saint, angel, or the living God. Like the sacrament, an icon is a physical and artistic medium for the communication of grace and spiritual presence. Icons help the church and the believer to focus on the saint, angel, or the living God. Through icons, the community in worship participates in the worship of God in heaven with all the angels and saints. At the same time, the icons make present — symbolically and spiritually — the angels and saints in the worship of the local church. This kind of spiritual communion is possible only through faith and the gracious activity of God. Orthodox Christians believe that the artists who create icons are inspired. In this view, then, the idea that the Bible is an "icon" of the word of God becomes a powerful analogy. The Bible, created by the inspiration of God, mediates the spiritual and living word of God, just as the icon conveys a spiritual and personal presence. In the reading of Scripture and biblical preaching in Christian communal worship, God's own word is known in and through the human words of Scripture.

Many evangelicals will be uncomfortable with the analogies of sacrament and icon. Protestants do not venerate icons, and many do not have a strong doctrine of the presence of Christ in his Supper. This is probably why the first comparison, that of the word with Christ, remains popular. Still, whatever analogy or metaphor we may find helpful, the Christian faith has long confessed the special character of the Bible.

The Holy Scriptures, written by fallible human beings in ordinary language, are the word of God. They are cherished, read, obeyed, and preached wherever Christ is Lord. As long as history endures, until at last the living Word returns to claim his own, Christians will read the Bible as authoritative revelation. The divine-human Scriptures will continue to guide Christian life and faith until the coming again of Christ. Only then will the authority of the Bible cease, for then we shall know him fully, and be fully known.

FOR FURTHER READING

Bloesch, Donald G. *Holy Scripture.* Downers Grove: InterVarsity, 1994.

Pinnock, Clark H., and Barry L. Callen. *The Scripture Principle.* 3rd ed. Lexington: Emeth, 2009.

Work, Telford. *Living and Active: Scripture in the Economy of Salvation.* Grand Rapids: Eerdmans, 2002.

ALAN G. PADGETT

Why Are These Books in the Bible?

The word "Bible" comes from Greek *ta biblia*, "the books." Although the Bible now commonly exists as a single volume, it is properly a collection of many different individual works, each with its own history of composition and literary development.

The Christian Bible is divided into two main parts: the Old Testament, those Scriptures Christianity inherited from Judaism; and the New Testament, which preserves the apostolic legacy of the early church. The two-part structure developed from the idea of a "new covenant" within the Bible itself (Jer. 31:31-34; Luke 22:20; 1 Cor. 11:25). Latin *testamentum*, "testament" or "will," translates the earlier Greek term for "covenant," *diathēkē*.

For both testaments, a central core of written books came to exist first through custom and usage, in effect postponing more formal discussions about the boundaries of those collections. In addition, early Jewish and Christian communities were sometimes separated by great distances and therefore often unable to possess in their local collections every book thought to be authoritative. Jewish Scripture was usually written on separate scrolls, making discussions of the scope and order of the entire scriptural collection both less urgent and more complex. Christian Scripture appears from very early on to have been transmitted in book or codex form, which required more consideration to the length of the total material. (The number of pages had to be planned in advance.) Also, occasionally there was genuine disagreement between individuals or communities about the authenticity or religious merit of particular books.

A few substantial differences in the scope and order of the biblical books exist to this day. Catholic, Orthodox, and Protestant traditions all accept the same 27 books of the New Testament. The Syrian church, however, does not fully recognize 2 Peter, 2-3 John, Jude, or Revelation. The Ethiopian church possesses a wider 35-book collection, including in its New Testament other ancient Christian texts such as the Shepherd of Hermas, 1-2 Clement, and the Apostolic Constitutions.

Broader disagreement exists in Christian tradition about the books of the Old Testament. Protestants hold to the same books as in Jewish tradition (arranged and counted

---

A Library of Books

PENTATEUCH
- Genesis
- Exodus
- Leviticus
- Numbers
- Deuteronomy

HISTORICAL BOOKS
- Joshua
- Judges
- Ruth
- 1 and 2 Samuel
- 1 and 2 Kings
- 1 and 2 Chronicles
- Ezra
- Nehemiah
- Esther

POETRY AND WISDOM LITERATURE
- Job
- Psalms
- Proverbs
- Ecclesiastes
- Song of Songs

PROPHETS
- Isaiah
- Jeremiah

- Lamentations
- Ezekiel
- Daniel
- Hosea
- Joel
- Amos
- Obadiah
- Jonah
- Micah
- Nahum
- Habakkuk
- Zephaniah
- Haggai
- Zechariah
- Malachi

APOCRYPHA/DEUTEROCANONICALS
- Tobit
- Judith
- Additions to Esther
- Wisdom of Solomon
- Sirach
- Baruch
- Letter of Jeremiah
- Additions to Daniel
- 1 and 2 Maccabees

GOSPELS AND ACTS
- Matthew
- Mark
- Luke
- John
- Acts

LETTERS
- Romans
- 1 and 2 Corinthians
- Galatians
- Ephesians
- Philippians
- Colossians
- 1 and 2 Thessalonians
- 1 and 2 Timothy
- Titus
- Philemon
- Hebrews
- James
- 1 and 2 Peter
- 1, 2, and 3 John
- Jude
- Revelation

---

differently, however). Catholics subscribe to an expanded 46-book collection, including seven "deuterocanonical" books also known as the Apocrypha. These books, together with 1 Esdras, 3 Maccabees, and the Epistle of Jeremiah, are also accepted in the 49-book Orthodox collection, but (unlike in Catholicism) with a lesser degree of authority. The Ethiopian Old Testament includes a few additional books (Jubilees, 1 Enoch, 4 Ezra, and Pseudo-Josephus) among those otherwise known as the Pseudepigrapha, a loose collection of ancient writings that did not find a lasting place in Jewish Scripture.

Although the early church in the West followed the lead of Augustine (A.D. 354-430) in recognizing the wider Old Testament collection (including the Apocrypha) as authoritative, the Eastern church favored the narrower scope of Jewish Scripture. A significant scholarly minority within both branches of the church continued to urge the superiority of the shorter 39-book collection, whose foremost advocate early on was Jerome (347-419). In the Reformation, the work of Wycliffe, Luther, and others led to the rejection of the apocryphal books, a move that still typifies Protestant opinion today, although Anglican tradition does commend the use of the Apocrypha for instruction (but not for doctrine). Modern Protestant Old Testaments follow the basic order of the Greek Septuagint, grouped in a fourfold pattern of law, histories, poetry, and prophets rather than in the three-part division of the Hebrew Bible, Law, Prophets, and Writings.

Despite such continuing variety, there are good reasons to speak of one Bible shared by the entire Christian church. The vast majority of the biblical literature has been agreed upon for many centuries. Christian tradition considers the Bible to be something all Christians share, despite any differences in its precise form, language, or interpretation. Variations in the number or order of the biblical books do not necessarily make for a material difference in interpretation or doctrine.

The process of Christian biblical formation can be said finally to have concluded at the end of the 4th century A.D., not because all Christians were then completely in agreement, but because a broad consensus did exist by this time and, more importantly, because a theoretical understanding of the whole collection as a "canon" had emerged. "Canon," from a Semitic root meaning "reed," can indicate both "norm" and "list." Until recently, the biblical canon was understood primarily as a list, a collection of writings which was "closed," or to which nothing else could be added or subtracted. From this perspective, the date for canonization would be correspondingly late, since the canon's precise delineation occurred only gradually. But when the authority of the biblical books already for ancient writers and sources is recognized (as "norm"), a functional, more *inclusive,* aspect of canon emerges, leading to an earlier date for canonization.

Critical biblical scholarship in the 19th century tended to assume that a canon was a nationally observed, legally binding, exclusive list of books that had been ratified in a public ceremony, similar to church councils such as the Council of Trent (1546), which reaffirmed the wider Catholic canon against the Reformers. On this basis, a reconstruction of the Old Testament canon developed in which 2 Kings 22–23 was interpreted as describing an initial act of canonization during the reign of King Josiah (639-609 B.C.) and the final "closing" of the entire canon was attributed to a rabbinic council in Jamnia (Yavneh), sometime after the fall of Jerusalem in A.D. 70.

The Pentateuch as a whole was usually thought to have been canonized in Ezra's time (ca. 440 B.C.), an act memorialized in Nehemiah 8. The Prophets were believed to have been "closed" sometime before 200, because the apocryphal book of Sirach (ca. 180) appears familiar with the prophetic corpus and refers to the Minor Prophets as a unified collection (Sir. 49:10). In addition, the later prologue to Sirach (ca. 120) refers explicitly to "the law and the prophets and the other books of our fathers." The place of Daniel in the Writings rather than in the Prophets was thought to provide further evidence for the closure of the prophetic corpus by the beginning of the 2nd century.

More persuasive is an organic view of canon formation in which the various books of all three collections — the Law, the Prophets, and the Writings — were edited and grew in authority roughly at the same time. Rather than a three-stage process, a more inclusive notion of "canon" seems to have preceded the exclusive understanding that most scholarship has assumed as original and standard.

The first page of the book of Luke in the Gutenberg Bible, the first substantial book printed with movable type (1454 or 1455, Mainz, Germany).
(Library of Congress)

A historical reconstruction based upon such an inclusive understanding produces the following alternative: the Law and the Prophets appear as twin scriptural authorities already within the biblical literature itself. In late conclusions to the Pentateuch (Deut. 34:10-12) and the Prophets (Mal. 4:4-6), the figures of Moses and the prophets serve together as a symbolic summary of scriptural faith. Although the roots of the Pentateuch reach back to the 9th century and ultimately to the time of Moses himself, and although core material from the prophetic books may be traced back to the 8th-century prophets (Hosea, Amos, Isaiah) and the 7th- and 6th-century Deuteronomistic writers (Deuteronomy–Kings), both collections probably reached a stable form *simultaneously* in the period following the exile (5th/4th centuries). Editorial work continued on each collection, including additions to both (especially to the prophetic collection because of the nature of prophecy), but by the time the Septuagint was begun in the 3rd century B.C. both collections were firmly established as twin expressions of Israel's scriptural identity.

Critical opinion about the "closing" of the Old Testament canon is currently split between two positions. According to the older consensus, the contents of the canon were finally delimited and fixed in Jamnia at the end of the 1st century A.D. It has become clear, however, that the rabbinic "council" in Jamnia was actually a religious school and court, and not a canonical decision-making body, thus suggesting a date considerably *later* for the canon's "closure." This view regards the processes of canonization within Judaism and Christianity as separate and distinct from each other.

Books of Scripture actually were debated at Jamnia, the discussions turning on whether certain books already accepted as authoritative should be retired from public use (not whether books that had never possessed authority should be granted "canonical" status). Josephus states clearly that a canon of Jewish Scripture had already been in existence for quite some time by the end of the 1st century A.D. The canon's contents are likely to have been stable and authoritative by the time of Judas Maccabeus in 164 B.C. (cf. 2 Macc. 2:14-15), although the reorganization of the canon into three-part form continued into the 1st century A.D., resulting in different canonical arrangements.

Central to the difference between these two positions is the role of the Old Testament for Jesus and the early church. Where the first view regards the Old Testament as not yet fully authoritative until *after* the completion of the New Testament writings at the end of the 1st century A.D., the second view insists that the early church inherited from Judaism a coherent and stable scriptural collection to which it granted a theological authority greater than its own experience but also viewed as ultimately consonant with its encounter with God in Christ Jesus.

For Jesus and the apostles, "Scripture" meant a particular body of *texts,* not a wide and uncertain variety of written traditions. In this sense, the Old Testament canon was already recognized in the New Testament period. In fact, in the New Testament "Scripture" usually refers to the Old Testament rather than to the entire Bible, for the simple reason that the New Testament only gradually took written form and found its place beside the Old.

The Christian "gospel" consisted at first of oral traditions (cf. 1 Cor. 11:23-26; 15:3-7). Already within the New Testament literature, however, a functional New Testament canon is becoming evident. Colossians 4:16 tells how Paul's letters were to be read aloud in other churches (cf. 2 Thess. 2:15). 2 Peter 3:15-16 regards Paul's letters as established tradition (Scripture). The Gospels are quite straightforward in their intention to provide a selective (and thus authoritative) version of the traditions about Jesus, in the hope of fostering faith within the postapostolic church (Luke 1:1-4; John 20:30-31; 21:25).

When Paul wrote to particular congregations, he was not attempting to write "Scripture," but rather to address particular theological and practical concerns on which those congregations needed pastoral guidance. Conveying a keen sense of what it meant to be a follower of Jesus, his writings claimed a certain status for themselves from the outset. The later two-testament format of the Bible is deeply implied within Pauline theology (2 Cor. 3:6, 14).

Paul sent his letters mostly during the decades A.D. 50-70. Based on Col. 4:16, it seems likely that early collections of the letters were created by individual churches for the purpose of sharing Paul's writings with other Christian communities. An edition of Paul's letters may have been made even within his own lifetime, however. By the first half of the 2nd century evidence exists of at least two different letter collections that were becoming standard.

If the Pauline Letters represent the earliest books of the New Testament canon, they did not precede the Gospels by long. Already in 65-100, the four canonical Gospels were written. It is possible that some written material containing sayings of Jesus (termed "Q" from German *Quelle,* "source") and an early account of the events surrounding his crucifixion may have circulated already in the period 50-65. Mark is usually considered to have been the first Gospel, written perhaps between 65-75. Both Matthew and Luke were composed between 75-90, basing themselves upon Mark and "Q." The Gospel of John was probably authored between 90-100. At some point most Christian communities chose to include in their canon four different versions of the story of Jesus' life rather than a single exhaustive account. But the Syrian church's use of the *Diatesseron* (until the 5th century) indicates that the choice between these two alternatives was both real and intentional.

The basic two-part conception of the Old Testament ("the Law and the Prophets") probably exercised a strong influence on the shaping of the New Testament into a collection of Gospels and Epistles. Another contributing factor was probably the structure of Luke-Acts, designed to be a continuous account about Jesus and the apostles, but in two parts (Luke 1:1-4; Acts 1:1-2).

The middle of the 2nd century emerges as the time at which the contents and scope of the New Testament became increasingly defined. The heretic Marcion may well have compelled an increasingly Gentile church to remember and commit itself unswervingly to the Jewish heritage of its faith and to a two-part Bible. Other controversies and events (Montanism, Gnosticism, Roman persecution) probably also precipitated discussions about the shape of the emerging Christian canon. Some books that gained early acceptance, at least in certain communities, were later excluded from the mainstream canon (Shepherd of Hermas, Wisdom of Solomon, Enoch). Other books were hotly debated early on and only gradually came to be admitted in most quarters of the church (Hebrews, 2 Peter, Revelation). By the end of the 2nd century, however, a stable collection of 20 books (the four Gospels and 13 Pauline Letters, together with Acts, 1 Peter, and 1 John) was recognized in the East and the West and called "the New Testament" (a term first used by Tertullian ca. 200). But it required another two centuries to reach broad agreement on the remaining seven books.

Even into the 4th century a strict consensus was lacking, although the general outline of the New Testament canon had long been clear by then (cf. Eusebius, *Ecclesiastical History* 3.25.1-7). The first list of the entire canon that gained widespread acceptance throughout the church is found in Athanasius's *Festal Letter for Easter,* 367. His list was taken up and in turn ratified by the North African church in the Councils of Hippo (393) and Carthage (397), and by the Western church in the Council of Rome (392).

As the early church sought to reach complete consensus regarding the boundaries of its canon, criteria such as apostolic attribution, orthodox content, and a tradition of widespread use within the church were employed in decisions about particular books. For the most part, however, these criteria were developed after most of the writings had already been recognized as authoritative and represent an effort to explain the rationale of a canon that already largely existed.

Since the use of Scripture has therefore always preceded its formal definition, neither Judaism nor Christianity can be said to have "created" the Bible. The authority of the biblical books has arisen out of their content, rather than being imposed by ecclesiastical mandate. By calling these books "canon," Christians confess further that a unique authority inheres in their biblical legacy. This is not to suggest that they cannot or do not hear God speak elsewhere, but that in harmony with their forebears they continue to hear God's word persistently and reliably *here.* The Christian canon of Scripture is thus a fact of history, and a gift to the present church by past generations of the faithful in order to ensure that future Christians will preserve their identity, ground their activity, and rightly frame their common vision.

FOR FURTHER READING

Barr, James. *Holy Scripture: Canon, Authority, Criticism.* Philadelphia: Westminster, 1983.

Barton, John. *Holy Writings, Sacred Text: The Canon in Early Christianity.* Louisville: Westminster John Knox, 1998.

Chapman, Stephen B. *The Law and the Prophets: A Study in Old Testament Canon Formation.* Tübingen: Mohr Siebeck, 2000.

Metzger, Bruce M. *The Canon of the New Testament: Its Origin, Development, and Significance.* Oxford: Clarendon, 1987.

Trebolle Barrera, Julio. *The Jewish Bible and the Christian Bible: An Introduction to the History of the Bible.* Grand Rapids: Eerdmans, 1998.

STEPHEN B. CHAPMAN

How Was the Bible Passed Down to Us?

The 66 books of the Bible didn't just happen. The processes of writing, editing, placement, copying, canonization, translation, and distribution involve thousands of people over millennia.

The word "Bible" comes from Greek *ta biblia,* which means "the books" and pointed to Scripture as a collection of books of great importance. The singular word *biblion* may come from the name of the Syrian port city Byblos, which was known to be an exporter of papyrus. In ancient Greek, *biblos* originally meant the inner bark of a papyrus plant. The title "Bible" began to catch on in the 5th century A.D.

The Jewish Bible *(TaNaK)* is composed of 24 books, the same as the 39 books of the Protestant canon of the Old Testament. The Hebrew Bible is made up of the Torah (Pentateuch), Nevi'im (Prophets), and Kethubim (Writings). The Jewish canon combines Ezra-Nehemiah, has one book of Chronicles and one book of Kings, and groups the 12 Minor Prophets together. The Christian canon divides the Old Testament into four sections: Pentateuch, History, Poetry and Wisdom, and Prophets.

The Beginnings

In common with other literature of the ancient Near East, the Bible does not give much information about the authors of its individual books. Instead, it concentrates on the messages of the books. Scholars have become detectives in piecing together biographical portraits of authors (and/or editors). Clues can come from the words they employ, their ideas, their styles of writing, the themes of their books, the times in which they lived, and what they wanted to say or emphasize about God. Luke is believed to be the only NT author born a Gentile; it is thought that all the writers of the Old Testament were born into the covenant or became converts. The most productive writer of the New Testament was Paul, with 13 books attributed to him or his "school," disciples, or others under his influence. Tradition associates Moses with the five books of the Pentateuch, and Jeremiah with the book bearing his name and Lamentations.

The people who wrote the books that comprise the Bible were not professional writers in the modern sense; they were instead committed individuals who wrote to specific people with a particular purpose in mind. For example, Obadiah wrote of a vision, what the Sovereign Lord was saying to Edom. Luke wrote for Theophilus an orderly account of events about Jesus that were taken from the testimony of eyewitnesses (Luke 1:1-4).

There is general agreement that most of the events recorded in the Bible span from ca. 1900 B.C. to A.D. 65. Jewish tradition credits Moses with writing the first five books of the Bible, but modern scholarship suggests that the final version of these books and perhaps even their initial writing took place hundreds of years later. Scholars also argue that some of the writing of the New Testament took place after A.D. 90.

The Old Testament was written in Hebrew and Aramaic. The Aramaic sections are in Daniel (2:4b–7:28) and Ezra (4:8–6:18). The New Testament was written in Koinē (everyday) Greek, the common, earthy language of the Roman Empire in force when Christianity began.

A Greek version of the Old Testament, the Septuagint (abbreviated LXX), dates to the 3rd century B.C. It was used by Jews scattered throughout the Roman Empire and was a source consulted by writers of the New Testament. According to legend, six translators from each of the 12 Israelite tribes (72 in all) worked independently of each other for 72 days, and when they were finished discovered that their translations were identical. The Septuagint was used extensively by Jews outside Palestine, but when Christians started using it as their Old Testament it fell into disfavor with the Jews.

Preserving the Word

The books of the Old Testament were written originally on papyrus and animal skin. Writing implements were reed pens, and ink was made from soot combined with gum. Clay or stone tablets and wooden writing boards were used for manuscripts of short length. The Jews favored animal skins, a longer-lasting material than papyrus, for synagogue copies of the Torah.

The books of the New Testament were written on scrolls and codices; a codex, a single book, was made by folding sheets of papyrus down the middle and stitching them together. Codexes gradually became more popular than scrolls, largely because they were easier to carry. Furthermore, scribes could write on both sides of the papyrus sheet. The oldest surviving New Testament texts are called uncials, because they were written in the Greek form of capital letters and without punctuation. These earliest manuscripts have no title pages and no paragraph or sectional divisions.

The Jews had strict rules about copying. The Torah had to be copied one manuscript

Remains of the Qumran scriptorium, a large hall where the Dead Sea Scrolls are believed to have been copied. In addition to copies of biblical books themselves, the Scrolls include commentaries interpreting Scripture in view of the Qumran community's own situation. *(Phoenix Data Systems, Neal and Joel Bierling)*

at a time from another scroll. Until A.D. 70, when the Romans destroyed the temple, all copies were made from a master copy. By ca. 250, Caesarea and Alexandria (Egypt) became major centers for teaching and study. At Caesarea shorthand was used for some texts and women were employed as scribes. Scrolls that became worn with age were put in a *genizah,* a hiding place, and not thrown away. One *genizah* discovered in Cairo in 1890 contained texts dating back 1000 years, a major find.

The Dead Sea Scrolls, containing nearly 100 complete or partial biblical books, were first discovered at Qumran in 1947, providing the earliest available Hebrew texts. For example, copies of the book of Isaiah dating from the 1st century A.D. can now be compared with the previously oldest surviving version, a codex copied ca. 895.

Scribes known as Masoretes (from Hebrew *masorah,* "tradition") carefully copied and controlled the transmission of the Hebrew text in the period ca. A.D. 600-900. Their methods were so thorough that little alteration can be found in the texts over the centuries. By 1000, the Masoretes had standardized the Hebrew text; their edition contained notes at the beginning and end of the books and in the margins. Hebrew was written only with consonants, and the Masoretes added vowel signs and other textual markings, thereby preserving the pronunciation and giving sense to the sentence structure. Corrections and variant readings were documented in the notes.

Ancient Texts

Some 13,000 manuscripts of the New Testament or sections of it have been discovered. Some early nonstandard texts made by nonprofessional scribes contain numerous minor variations. New Testament scholars compare the oldest and best versions of the books with nonstandard texts to arrive at the closest reading possible to what the New Testament writers indeed wrote. Probably 99 percent of the original text can be accurately reconstructed.

Surviving New Testament texts include 85 papyri (codices or books, not scrolls); 268 uncials (capital letter texts with no punctuation); 2792 cursives (texts with smaller, joined writing); 2193 lectionaries (texts divided into sections for reading in worship). By the second half of the 2nd century, the Gospel of John was known in Egypt. A fragment of a copy from that period is stored at the Rylands Library in Manchester, England.

A section of the Great Isaiah Scroll (1QIsaᵃ). The only one of the Dead Sea Scrolls to survive virtually complete, the scroll contains many variant readings that provide greater understanding of the biblical text. *(Courtesy of the Israel Antiquities Authority)*

Five main codices are used in reconstructing the New Testament text: Codex Sinaiticus, Codex Vaticanus, Codex Alexandrinus, Codex Bezae, and Codex Ephraemi Syri.

Codex Sinaiticus (symbolized as Aleph, the first letter of the Hebrew alphabet) dates from the 4th century A.D. Constantin Tischendorf discovered this Greek manuscript in 1844 at the remote monastery of St. Catherine on Mount Sinai and saved some 43 sheets of vellum from fire; these he gave to the king of Saxony. Tischendorf returned to the monastery in 1853 and was shown another 199 leaves that contained parts of the Old Testament, a complete New Testament, the Letter of Barnabas, and the Shepherd of Hermas.

Codex Vaticanus (B), containing the Greek text of both Old and New Testaments, has been in the Vatican Library in Rome since 1481. The combination of Codex Vaticanus and Codex Sinaiticus provides the best translation of the Greek New Testament.

Codex Alexandrinus (A) is an early 5th-century Greek text of both Testaments, copied and corrected by four scribes. It was acquired in 1757 by the British Museum. Alexandrinus contains chapter divisions and headings called *titloi* in Greek.

Codex Bezae (D), an important representative of the Western Text of the New Testament, dates from the end of the 3rd century and contains both the Greek text and the Old Latin version. Presented in 1581 to Cambridge University, the codex contains thousands of unique readings in the Gospels, yet includes many additions to Acts. Many scholars think this puzzling text may be based on a 2nd-century Syriac manuscript.

Codex Ephraemi Syri (C) is a recycled codex, a palimpsest, meaning that part of the original text has been scraped and then written over. In the 12th century, the sermons of St. Ephraim were written down, replacing the New Testament portion of the codex.

The complete Hebrew Bible was first printed in Italy in 1488, and a Greek New Testament was printed in 1514 in Spain.

Translations

The major Latin translation of the Bible was made by Jerome while living in Bethlehem from 390 to 405. His sources were the Hebrew and Greek rather than the existing Old Latin Text. Known as the Vulgate ("in common use"), this translation became widely accepted in the Catholic Church and by the Council of Trent in 1545 was termed the only suitable version. Stephen Langton introduced chapter divisions into the Vulgate in the 13th century. Robert Estienne, a Paris printer, introduced the verse divisions now commonplace in 1551.

Largely, translations were for use in the monasteries. Lay people did not have the Bible in their own languages until after the Middle Ages. Strange as it may seem today, ecclesiastical resistance to translations in the vernacular was strong. Those in state and ecclesiastical power thought that if common folk read the Bible, they would get ideas about changing the social structure. The powers felt that the Bible in the wrong hands could produce dangerous results, and so many of the courageous translators were seen as controversial and rebellious.

Around 700 the Psalms were translated into Anglo-Saxon by Aldhelm, bishop of Sherborne. A monk known as the Venerable Bede also translated part of the New Testament. In the 9th century the West Saxon king Alfred translated some of the Psalms and parts of Exodus.

John Wycliffe (1330-1384), master of Balliol College, Oxford, believed the Bible should be made accessible for the English people. At Wycliffe's inspiration, his friends and supporters translated and hand-copied the Scriptures. Known as Lollards, many were burned at the stake.

In 1408 it was forbidden to make English translations of the Bible. But English versions persisted. William Tyndale (ca. 1494-1536) produced a New Testament translation in 1525, the first to be printed in English. For his efforts, he was sentenced to be strangled and then burned at the stake.

Miles Coverdale (1488-1569) produced an English edition of the Bible in 1537. Soon a copy of the Bible was placed by law in each parish church.

In 1604 King James commissioned a new version of the Bible. Six panels of 47 men translated both testaments into English. This Bible, known as the Authorized Version of 1611, was the work of panels meeting at Oxford, Cambridge, and Westminster and was influenced greatly by Tyndale's work. (See "The Bible in English" [39-42])

Of the more than 6000 languages in the world today, more than 300 have a complete Bible, about 700 have the entire New Testament, and around 1000 have at least one book of the New Testament. Modern translations take into account local customs and conditions. For example, in cultures where a lamb or a chariot is nonexistent, other images are found to convey the meanings. Bible translation involves people trained not only in the three biblical languages but also in the customs and languages of the indigenous peoples. (See "The Bible in English.")

FOR FURTHER READING

Copley, Terence. *About the Bible: Questions Anyone Might Ask about Its Origins, Nature, and Purpose.* Swindon: Bible Society, 1990.

ROBIN GALLAHER BRANCH

Languages, Writing, and Alphabets

Languages

The Bible is written by people using the language of their contemporaries: the Old Testament in Hebrew and to a small extent in Aramaic, the New Testament in Greek.

Hebrew and Aramaic are Semitic languages, one of a group of languages whose literary accomplishments go back at least 5000 years and that includes languages that no one speaks today (Akkadian, Phoenician, Moabite) and languages that are still spoken (Hebrew, Arabic).

Abraham may have spoken a form of Akkadian (the language of Ur) and Aramaic (the language of Haran). The Israelites adopted a form of the language of Canaan which has come to be known as Hebrew. Hebrew and Aramaic are very close in structure and vocabulary. The Aramaic portions of the Old Testament are Dan. 2:4b–7:28; Ezra 4:8–6:18; 7:12-26; Jer. 10:11.

New Testament Greek is quite different from Classical or Attic Greek. Everyday or *Koinē* Greek was commonly used throughout the Roman Empire.

At the time of Jesus the Jews of Palestine spoke Aramaic and probably also Mishnaic Hebrew and Greek. Fewer would have used Latin, the language of the Romans.

The study of biblical languages for interpretation of the Bible is very important in helping the reader to inch closer to the original meaning. But most beginning students of biblical languages do not gain the competence to bridge the gap between the ancient text and the modern reader, because this requires both a competence in the language and in the world of the biblical text, as well as a willingness to step outside one's own cultural context. Fortunately, very good translations are available in English and most other languages. These translations should aid the reader in approximating the experience of reading the original text within a modern context, even when it is admitted that any translation is, to some degree, an interpretation. The human aspect of the Bible occasions the necessity of interpretation, implies a willingness to consider alternative ways of hearing the text, and demands the wisdom to assess competing interpretations.

Writing

As early as the 4th millennium B.C. people had developed elaborate systems of written communication in both Egypt and Mesopotamia. Writing was for official administrative purposes rather than private communication. Scribes were schooled from an early age for the purpose of copying, writing, and reading administrative, religious, and literary works. Often the profession was hereditary, passed on from father to son. The office of scribe was a privileged position, and much power belonged to the literary elite.

Literacy was on the rise, especially among the Hebrews. The use of the short alphabet (see below) furthered the spread of literacy in Canaan. The encouragement to reflect on the law of the Lord motivated many godly Hebrews to listen to and even to read the sacred text for themselves.

The ancients used various kinds of writing materials, often whatever was readily accessible, including broken pieces of pottery (ostraca). It was easy to use soft clay and imprint characters with a stylus or reed. The clay, when hardened in the sun or an oven, produced a lasting document of political, administrative, and business records. Archaeologists have retrieved many fragments of pots (sherds) with such writing marking ownership or contents of various items.

A more enduring record was left on rocks or stone tablets. By chiseling in a stone surface, the ancients produced records that have endured for millennia (e.g., Egyptian stelae, the Siloam inscription). Inscriptions on tombs (funerary inscriptions) provide such information as the person buried, his profession, and an occasional warning to grave robbers (who probably could not read!).

Similarly the engraving of metals (gold, silver), though less frequent, was effective. Less enduring were records left on wood coated with plaster or wax. Plaster could be smeared on any material and provided a ready medium for writing.

Tanned hides were also employed and were a common material on which to transcribe the sacred Scriptures of Israel. A refinement in leather production produced parchment, a thin, paperlike material that could be used and reused.

The use of common reeds growing at the edge of the Nile River in paper production made writing materials more accessible. A page was produced by layering sections of the pith of the reed horizontally and vertically, then pressing or beating the pith to make it strong. "Papyrus" designates such a page or collection of pages glued together into a scroll. A page would typically have two to four columns. A scroll resulted from connecting pages together and keeping them in proper order. The codex, a binding of pages into a book, developed around the time of Jesus and was popularized by Christian scribes (e.g., Codex Vaticanus). A palimpsest is a page of papyrus or parchment that was reused by a later scribe erasing the original contents and writing over it.

Scribes used whatever tools suited the writing materials: flint or hard metal for stone, a stylus for plaster and clay, and a fine brush and a pen for leather and papyrus. Black ink was made by mixing carbon with water.

Little of the vast written materials in Canaan, Egypt, and Mesopotamia has been found. Some materials were reused for other purposes, others were lost, and others perished in the poor conditions in which the materials were stored. The ancient inscriptional evidence that does survive is the best witness to the authenticity of the historical records in the Old Testament.

Alphabets

Assyrian tablet showing pre-alphabetic writing.
(Schøyen Collection)

A generalized portrayal of the development of writing in the ancient Near East takes us from pictographs and ideograms to sounds, which in Phoenicia and Canaan came to be written as alphabetic signs. Pictographs were originally pictures representing persons, animals, or things and later would represent activities (verbs) and eventually sounds. For example, in Egyptian hieroglyphics many signs (pictures) represent either words (ideograms) or multiconsonantal sounds. Other signs serve to differentiate between words (determinatives) or to mark consonantal sounds. In Akkadian cuneiform, named for its wedge-shaped form of writing, some 600 signs represent various syllabic sounds. Because of the complexity of both hieroglyphic and cuneiform writing, trained scribes were essential for the perpetuation of writing as well as reading.

A great advance came when a limited number of signs were used to create an alphabet. Two such systems developed in Canaan ca. 1500 B.C. The Ugaritic alphabet has 30 cuneiform signs, including several signs for vowels. Words were written from left to right. A shorter system, written from right to left in Phoenician/Hebrew script, has 22 signs, none for vowels, and extended beyond Canaan to Phoenicia and Moab.

A consonantal sign was originally a pictograph, but the sign came to designate the sound of the first letter. For example, the sign ✗, signifying a bull *(eleph)* in Hebrew, was the designation for *aleph,* the first letter of the Hebrew alphabet. Similarly, the letter

The Qeiyafa Ostracon, one of the oldest known examples of Hebrew writing, in Proto-Canaanite script. *(Khirbet Qeiyafa excavations, the Hebrew University of Jerusalem)*

Drawing of the ostracon by Haggai Misgav. *(Khirbet Qeiyafa excavations, the Hebrew University of Jerusalem)*

beth ("house," **ᗺ**) originally represented a house and later became the second letter in the Hebrew alphabet. The Greeks took over the Phoenician alphabet (*aleph* became *alpha*, *beth* became *beta*), changed the orientation of the letters (**ᗄ** to "A"), adapted it to include vowel signs, and changed the orientation of the writing (from left to right).

Much inscriptional evidence reveals the extensive use of paleo-Hebrew script in Canaan and beyond, but the Samaritan Pentateuch and some archaizing tendencies in the Dead Sea Scrolls are the only evidence of biblical texts written in paleo-Hebrew. By the 8th century the Hebrews adopted the script employed for Aramaic, the international language of diplomacy in the Persian Empire. Now the letters no longer suggested pictures but were squared off (e.g., *aleph,* א; *beth,* ב). This script is still used in Modern Hebrew.

As Hebrew writing continued to develop, consonants were used to indicate vowels in order to clarify meaning. For example, the two-letter word 'š ('sh) could represent 'esh ("fire"), 'ishsheh ("offering made by fire"), 'ish ("man"), or 'isha ("woman"). The addition of a *yodh (y)* clarified this word as reading 'ish, and the addition of the letter *he (h)* after 'sh helped the reader to read 'ishsheh or 'isha. Such developments help in dating Old Testament texts.

FOR FURTHER READING

Driver, G. R. *Semitic Writing from Pictograph to Alphabet.* 3rd ed. London: Oxford University Press, 1976.

Gelb, I. J. *A Study of Writing.* 2nd ed. Chicago: University of Chicago Press, 1963.

Millard, Alan R. "Writing." *NIDOTTE* 4:1286-95.

WILLEM A. VANGEMEREN

How to Interpret the Bible

Readers of the Bible are confronted by a sometimes dizzying array of challenges. Biblical texts originated in times distant from us, refer to places and persons personally unknown to us, and represent forms of communication increasingly alien to us. Although we possess no meaning-making machine or interpretive technique guaranteed to bring clarity for readers of Scripture, we cannot escape the reality that these books are our Scripture, that our understanding of God and his purpose are tied to how we interpret Scripture. The task of reading the Bible and making sense of it belongs to us.

Undoubtedly, for those genuinely interested in interpreting the Bible, the single most important practice to adopt is to get involved in reading the Bible with others who take its message seriously and who meet regularly to discern its meaning for faith and life. The best interpreters of the Bible are those who are actively engaged in communities of biblical interpretation. If such a group is multigenerational and multicultural, this is even better. There are two reasons for this. First, the books of the Bible have their genesis and formation within the community of God's people; therefore, they speak most clearly and effectively from within and to communities of believers. No interpretive tool, no advanced training can substitute for active participation in a community of Bible readers.

A second reason to read the Bible with others is our inclination toward self-deception. One of the most tragic effects of Bible reading can be that we read our lives into it in such a way that we find in the pages of the Old and New Testaments divine license for those of our attitudes and practices that are more base than biblical. We are too often quick to apply challenging messages to the lives of others and to assume that the Bible supports our ways of thinking and acting. We read Scripture in order to be addressed by God and formed by his Word. Other people set on the same purpose can serve to keep us honest so that we might hear more faithfully God's voice at those moments when we are tempted to substitute our word for God's.

Beyond this starting point, how we interpret the Bible is largely dependent on the mode we adopt in our approach to Scripture. The Bible can be read profitably in various ways —

especially as revealed history, as inspired literature, and as Christian Scripture — and each suggests its own conventions for faithful reading.

When we read the Bible as *revealed history* we take into account that much of the Old and New Testaments contains books that narrate the story of God's engagement with his people. Whether we are reading episodes related to Joseph or Hannah or Mary or Jesus, we understand that we are reading more than "just the facts." The biblical writers were not interested in recording for posterity a dispassionate chronicle of events. They select the episodes they record precisely because they see at work in these events a significance that surpasses the events themselves. They see the hand of God at work, bringing to fruition his redemptive purpose. Moreover, in narrating these episodes, the biblical writers have woven these events into the grand narrative of God's overarching purpose, which runs from creation (Genesis) to new creation (Revelation). Reading the Bible as revealed history, then, entails asking how these events, these stories, fit within the grand story of God's creation and redemption. It means taking seriously the implicit claim of historical narratives within the Bible to provide God's perspective on what historical events are most important, and why they are important.

Of course, reading the Bible as revealed history does not mean opening a great chasm between biblical times and our own. After all, we are a part of the grand story of God's work too. As we read the Bible as revealed history, we come better to understand that this story is our story. As we read the narrative of Scripture, we come to understand the events and progress of our own lives.

Historical approaches to biblical texts serve another purpose. We now understand how all aspects of communication — the words we use, the language we speak, the gestures that accompany our speech, and more — arise from and gain their particular significance in relation to particular cultural contexts. Historical study of the Bible can help to expose us to habits of communication, ways of relating, and turns of speech that we would otherwise miss in our reading of Scripture. In an important sense, we show respect to those who wrote the biblical books and to those about whom they wrote, when we take the time to hear, as well as we are able, what they would have heard and to see what they would have seen. Sometimes, our hearing and seeing are helped by reference books, such as this one, which provide background material that would otherwise be unavailable to us. At other times, our hearing and seeing are helped by bringing to the biblical texts the same sort of good listening skills and cross-cultural sensitivities we seek to develop in our everyday lives.

Some possible questions that arise from this approach to reading the Bible include:

- What purpose does this text serve when read against the backdrop of God's purpose in creation and redemption?
- What social or cultural issues does this text raise for us? What customs or practices does it mention that we need to investigate further?

- Does this text mention *persons* (such as King Nebuchadnezzar or Caesar Augustus), *places* (such as Jericho or Megiddo), *institutions* (such as the synagogue or temple), or *religious practices* (such as circumcision or the Jewish celebration of Pentecost) we might need to investigate further in order to understand better?
- What is God doing in this text?
- What does this text tell us about the character of the people of God?

We can also read the Bible as *inspired literature*. Although we refer to the Bible as a "book," it is actually a collection of books, an anthology of literature, that contains a number of different kinds of literature. Leviticus is a different sort of writing from Galatians, just as the Psalms differ from the Gospel of Matthew, and each makes its own demands on the reader.

Writers such as those who penned the biblical books chose particular literary forms as they wrote, drawing on forms already present in their cultural contexts. Forms, or genres, reflect ways of representing reality within particular cultures. "Letters," for example, are vital in historical contexts in which persons need to be present to communicate a message but cannot be. In such instances, the letter serves as a kind of "stand-in" for its writer or writers. The choice of a particular genre, then, is like an offer of a contract on the part of the writer. This agreement is shared when readers (or hearers) recognize and take seriously the form of the work before them. Taking seriously the literary shape of the Bible requires that we learn as much as we can about the nature of each kind of writing in the Bible, so that we are able to read it in ways consistent with its own character.

Reading the Bible as literature means other things as well. It means taking seriously such elements of writing as the use of symbolism and imagery and other literary devices. It means tuning our ears to different literary styles and the use of rhetorical conventions in the Bible. It means taking note of a document's structure and how such notice may enlarge our understanding of its message. And, perhaps most importantly, it means reading each book of the Bible as a whole document, each on its own terms, allowing the particular emphases of each voice within the Bible to be heard within the choir of voices found here.

Some possible questions that arise from this approach to reading the Bible include:

- What is the literary form of this book?
- What reading conventions govern the interpretation of books such as this one?
- Can we discern a structure within the book as a whole that helps us to understand the meaning of its parts within the significance of the whole?
- Do we recognize particular literary devices or instances of symbolism that affect how we make sense of this passage?

We may also read the Bible as *Christian Scripture*. This means at least three things. First, we approach the Bible from an explicitly Christian position, one that affirms that the Old and New Testaments are inseparable in their witness to God the Savior and that the coming of Christ is the point of orientation that gives all biblical books their meaning as Scripture. Even if Christians have long pushed the Old Testament to the margins, the reality is that we cannot know Jesus Christ genuinely apart from the God of Jesus Christ revealed first in the Scriptures of Israel, the Old Testament. The Christ proclaimed in the New Testament cannot be grasped apart from an understanding of the God who raised Jesus from the dead, and this God is the one who revealed himself in many and various ways within ancient Israel. The Old Testament is thus more than a preface to the good news of Jesus Christ. It is the revelatory narrative of God's dealings with Israel, the story of God's saving purpose, which culminates in the advent of Jesus. The Old Testament prepares the way of the Lord, and the New Testament proclaims that the Word became flesh and dwelt among us.

Second, even though each book of the Bible was written to people and in places far removed from us in time and culture, when we approach the Bible as Scripture we take seriously the faith statement that this book is our Book, these Scriptures are our Scriptures. We are not reading someone else's mail — as though reading the Bible had to do foremost with recovering an ancient meaning intended for someone else and then translating its principles for use in our own lives. When we recall that *we* are the people of God to whom the Bible is addressed as Scripture, we realize that the fundamental transformation that must take place is not the transformation of an ancient message into a contemporary meaning but rather the transformation of our lives by means of God's word. This means, third, that reading the Bible as Scripture has less to do with what tools we bring to the task and more to do with our own dispositions as we come to our engagement with Scripture. We come not so much to retrieve facts or to gain information, but to be formed. Scripture does not present us with texts to be mastered but with a word, God's word, intent on mastering us, on shaping our lives.

Some possible questions that arise from this approach to reading the Bible include:

- What commitments as Christian believers do we bring to this text? In what ways does this text support or challenge those commitments?
- How is the message of this text set within the whole biblical story of God's engagement with his people? How does it add to or direct that story?
- Does this text cite or allude to other biblical texts that help to give it significance?
- Understood within the whole biblical story of God's engagement with his people, what does this text expect of its readers? What transformed allegiances? What behaviors? What attitudes? What practices?

JOEL B. GREEN

The Bible in English

The effort to make the Bible available to the English-speaking reader has always involved an interplay between scholarship and technology. While fragments of Scripture were put into English in earlier centuries, John Wycliffe's Bible (1382) was the first entire Bible in English. Since every copy was made by hand, copies were scarce and expensive, and access to them was very limited. William Tyndale's New Testament (1525) was the first portion of English Scripture to be printed. The development of the printing press and the concomitant development of paper-making technology helped to make Bibles available to the public, not simply to well-endowed churches or wealthy individuals. But access was still limited, since few speakers of English were literate, and few were wealthy enough to afford even a printed Bible. Because of the limitations of the printing process, binding, and the quality of available paper, Bibles were large, cumbersome objects.

The Geneva Bible (1560) was conceived not only as a translation, but also as an edition that would be available to larger numbers of people. It was still a large, heavy book by modern standards, but it was smaller than previous Bibles and was printed in Roman type, making it easier to read for newly literate people than the traditional block-letter type. The Geneva Bible, produced by Puritans within the Church of England, spread widely and became the Bible that might be owned by a family and read in the home, although one would never have thought of carrying it to church.

Meanwhile, churches in England used in their services the Great Bible (1539), a revision of Miles Coverdale's Bible (1535), itself a revision and addition to Tyndale's work. The Great Bible was revised in turn as the Bishops' Bible (1568).

The Authorized or King James Version (KJV) appeared in 1611. It was a creative revision of the Bishops' Bible, keeping in its wording a great amount of material that went all the way back to Tyndale. At first it appeared only as a very large and heavy volume, but as it became available in a variety of editions it gradually became more popular, eventually supplanting the Geneva Bible in homes and the Bishops' Bible or Great Bible in churches. By the time of the American Revolution the KJV had become the version most English-speaking Protestants meant when they thought of "the Bible."

While the 19th century was not without creative attempts at Bible translation, the main advances in making the Bible accessible were accomplished by technology and business. From an early date, book buyers bought printed pages, which they would then take to a professional binder. In the early 19th century Bible publishers introduced a new concept of placing printing and bookbinding under one roof, so that the buyer could purchase a finished product. Printing itself became more efficient as stereotyping came into use, doing away with the need to set type into frames letter by letter, and as rotary presses took the place of hand presses. Technology developed to make paper thinner. All this contributed to making Bibles that were small enough to be held in the hand and read conveniently. Still, Bibles are books, and books are heavy. Only with the coming of the railroads did it become possible to transport Bibles in large quantities to all parts of the country economically. Riding the rails were Bible salesmen, whether wholesalers making Bibles available to distant bookstores or retailers walking dusty roads and streets selling door-to-door. By the end of the 19th century Bibles were common possessions in Protestant households, widely read and now often carried to church. Virtually all of these were the King James Version.

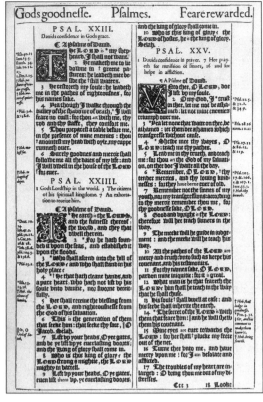

Psalms 23–25 in the Authorized (King James) Version of the Bible (Robert Barker, first edition 1611, London). *(British Library)*

The first half of the 20th century was a time of advance in translation. New discoveries and critical techniques had made it possible to have a Hebrew or Greek text much closer to the original writings than were available to King James's translators, and the English language itself had changed so dramatically that the KJV text was often not understood, or, more dangerously, misunderstood. The American Standard Version (1901) was an attempt to make the text of the Bible more accurate, but it was so lacking in literary grace that it was seldom used for worship, although it often served as a text in seminaries. Among other translations of the early 20th century, all of which found a readership, were James Moffatt's Bible (1913-24), the American Translation of J. M. Powis Smith and Edgar Goodspeed (1931), J. B. Phillips's rendering of the New Testament (1947), and Charles B. Williams's New Testament (1937). The Revised Standard Version (RSV 1952) was a conscious attempt to provide a realistic alternative to the KJV, not only bringing scholarship up to date, but also writing in a pleasing English style, sticking as closely as possible to the cadences of the KJV.

The RSV was not just another in a long series of Bible translations. It was a major undertaking, recognized by conservative American Protestants as a serious challenge to the King James. Slowly the RSV won its way among liberal and more moderate churches. During the second half of the century, however, it became more and more evident to conservative Christians that the King James Version had seen its day, and a variety of translations began to appear that were done under safely conservative auspices. Among the more recent have been the New American Standard Bible (1971, 1995), the New International Version (NIV, 1978), the New King James Version (1982), and the Living Translation (1996). The NIV shows signs of becoming widely accepted among a theologically conservative readership. A revision of the RSV as the New Revised Standard Version (NRSV, 1991) seems to be establishing itself as a norm among church people willing to accept a Bible translated by nonconservative scholars.

From developments in translation theory came the dynamic equivalent model, less concerned to reflect the sentence structure of the original language as to convey the meaning, even when it meant a drastic breaking down and reconstruction of the original syntax. An early attempt at this was the Twentieth Century New Testament (1902). More ambitious efforts were the New English Bible (NEB, British, 1970) and, at a simpler level of vocabulary, Today's English Version (TEV, 1976). The Contemporary English Version (1995) goes far beyond both the NEB and TEV in choice of vocabulary and freedom of restatement. A revision of the NEB in 1989 as the Revised English Bible was notable for being less venturesome and somewhat more traditional in its translation technique, while at almost the same time the NRSV was willing to venture into a freer translation style than its predecessor, the RSV.

American Jews throughout the 20th century used the Jewish Publication Society Version (1917). More recently, English-speaking Jewish scholars have made available for their readership (and Christians as well) the New Jewish Publication Society Version completed in 1985. Roman Catholic Christians, long accustomed to using the Douai-Rheims version (1582-1610; translated from the Latin Bible but thoroughly revised by Richard Challoner in 1750), have produced two notable versions, the Jerusalem Bible (1966; revised as the New Jerusalem Bible, 1990) and the New American Bible (1970), both translated from the original Greek and Hebrew, and both freely used by Protestant scholars as well. Most modern Catholics are also quite comfortable with most Protestant translations.

Social change has led to a series of revisions of existing versions so as to use inclusive language. Among these are the RSV (as NRSV, 1991), TEV (1992), and NEB (as Revised English Bible, 1989). A move so to revise the NIV was originally halted, largely from pressure by new leadership in the Southern Baptist Convention, but resulted in the publication of Today's New International Version (2002).

In recent years the attempt to make the Bible accessible has turned once again to technology and business. Many fine translations are available, but there is an increased desire on the part of Bible lovers and biblical scholars to access these texts on computers, where search engines and other aids open up new possibilities for studying the text. To business has fallen the task of making the Bible a desirable object. Whereas people once considered possession of a Bible to be a precious privilege, today increasing numbers do not care whether they own one or not. Publishers increasingly turn not to fresh translations, but to novel ways of marketing existing translations, often offering the same translation with different covers, under different titles, and with notations, directed at specific markets, such as teenagers, men, women, or children.

FOR FURTHER READING

Bratcher, Robert G., and Harry M. Orlinsky. *A History of Bible Translation and the North American Contribution.* Atlanta: Scholars, 1991.

Comfort, Philip W. *The Essential Guide to Bible Versions.* Wheaton: Tyndale, 2000.

Gutjahr, Paul C. *An American Bible: A History of the Good Book in the United States 1777-1880.* Stanford: Stanford University Press, 1999.

ROGER A. BULLARD

The Bible as Literature

The idea of the Bible as literature became prominent during the last two decades of the 20th century and produced a paradigm shift in biblical scholarship. But the idea is actually as old as the Bible itself. Biblical writers refer with technical precision to such genres as song, lament, history, gospel, proverb, apocalypse, and many more. Furthermore, the writings that these writers produced show their awareness of style and technique. One writer, moreover, presents a theory of the author as self-conscious artist that applies to the entire Bible: the writer of Ecclesiastes describes himself as "weighing and studying and arranging many proverbs with great care," and as an author who "sought to find pleasing words " (Eccl. 12:9-10).

Three main impulses come together in the writings that make up the Bible — the historical, the theological, and the literary. These three intermingle, but usually passages are dominated by one of them. In other words, while much of the Bible is *predominantly* literary in nature, literary *features* can be discerned throughout the entire Bible.

To speak of the Bible as literature implies that there are qualities of discourse that make a text literary, different from nonliterary texts. Current thinking about the Bible as literature applies the ordinary criteria of literature to the Bible. While the exploration of these features of the Bible can be conducted by placing the Bible into its original, ancient literary context, to speak of the Bible as literature usually means discussing the Bible in terms of the familiar literary criteria of English and American literature. When we make such application, four qualities stand out.

(1) The subject of literature is human experience concretely portrayed. Literature does not primarily express ideas or propositions but aims instead to re-create the very nature of human experiences and external reality. Instead of stating propositions about virtue and vice, for example, literature presents stories of good and evil characters in action. The command "you shall not murder" asserts truth by means of propositional statement; the story of Cain's murder of Abel is a literary embodiment of the same principle.

The type of truth that literature is particularly adept at conveying is therefore truthfulness to human experience. Accordingly, an appreciation of the literary nature of the Bible and a literary approach to it begins with an acknowledgement of the prevalence of recognizable human experience in it. The Bible is not only or even primarily a book of ideas. It is a portrayal of life as people live it. To read the Bible as literature is first of all to relive a biblical text as vividly and experientially as possible.

The literary parts of the Bible possess a universal quality, based on the fact that while history tells us what *happened,* literature tells us what *happens.* (The Bible tells us both.) Because writers of literature aim to convey to us the very quality of experiences, there is a certain irreducible quality to what they have written, so that a propositional summary of a text never does justice to the literary re-creation of an experience that the author intends.

(2) A second quality of literature is artistry of expression. Literature is self-consciously crafted. Writers and readers of literature are interested not only in *what* is said but also in *how* it is said. The key ingredients of artistic form have traditionally included unity, pattern or design, theme or central focus, unity-in-variety (or theme and variation), coherence, balance, contrast, symmetry, repetition or recurrence, and unified progression. It is the artistic impulse that leads biblical poets to balance their statements in parallel lines and to structure their poems skillfully. A love of artistry leads biblical storytellers to construct shapely plots, to choose telling details that make characters and settings come alive, and to infuse such things as dramatic irony and poetic justice into their stories. Biblical proverbs possess the qualities of conciseness and memorability.

(3) Literature is definable by certain types of writing that people through the centuries have agreed are literary genres. The Bible is mainly a literary book because literary genres make up by far the largest share of the Bible. All genres have their distinctive features and conventions, and to read the Bible as literature partly means applying the correct generic considerations to biblical texts. The two dominant genres are narrative and poetry, and together these comprise at least 75 percent of the Bible.

Narrative is the primary form of the Bible, characterized by the plot pattern of beginning, middle, and end organizing the details. A host of narrative subgenres make up the bulk of the Bible: story of origins, hero story, epic, comedy, tragedy, gospel, parable. The historical narratives of the Bible become literary (as opposed to expository or merely informational) to the degree to which they recount not only what happened but also how it happened and to the degree to which they fall into the narrative genres noted above.

Biblical poetry is differentiated by two chief features. One, poets write in a poetic idiom, consisting chiefly of image, metaphor, simile, hyperbole, personification, apostrophe, and paradox. Second, poetry is written in a verse form, which in the Bible is parallelism — saying something in varied but similar form in two or more consecutive lines.

Most poems are lyric poems — short poems expressing the thoughts or feelings of a speaker. Within that umbrella, numerous specific lyric forms appear in the Bible, including (but not limited to) lament poem, praise psalm, nature poem, psalm of worship, love poem, epithalamion (wedding poem), and Christ hymn. In addition to lyric poems, vast parts of the prophetic books are poetic in form.

A number of additional literary genres make up the remaining 25 percent of the Bible. These include drama, oratory, proverb, satire (an attack on human vice or folly), epistle, and visionary writing.

(4) A fourth trait of literature is the presence of special resources of language. Even if the genre of a passage is not literary, the prevalence of literary features of style requires literary analysis. The most obvious of these resources is figurative language, including metaphor, simile, symbolism, connotative language, allusion, pun, paradox, irony, and wordplay. Such language is of course the very essence of poetry, but it appears throughout the Bible, in narratives and even in parts that might be considered predominantly expository rather than literary, such as the discourses of Jesus and the epistles.

In addition to possessing literary features of vocabulary, a text can become literary by its arrangement of sentences or rhetorical patterning. Any arrangement of clauses that strikes us as unusually patterned might qualify as an example of literary rhetoric — series of questions or statements that follow a common pattern, rhetorical questions, imaginary dialogues, and (especially important in the Bible) a terseness that produces an aphoristic quality. In other words, style is one of the things that makes the Bible literary. Biblical writers frequently manipulate the resources of language, syntax, and rhetoric to produce a literary effect.

To sum up, in format the Bible resembles an anthology of English and American literature more than anything else. It is a kaleidoscope of literary genres. Virtually every part of the Bible invites stylistic analysis. Artistry of expression is everywhere evident, as is the experiential concreteness embodying the authentic voice of human experience as it is known in all places and times.

FOR FURTHER READING

Ryken, Leland. *Words of Delight: A Literary Introduction to the Bible.* Grand Rapids: Baker, 1992.

————, and Tremper Longman III, eds. *A Complete Literary Guide to the Bible.* Grand Rapids: Zondervan, 1993.

Leland Ryken

Archaeology and the Bible

"Archaeology" is "the study of ancient things." All cultures leave behind material remains — the debris of our living processes: pottery, clothing, houses. These physical remains are called "material culture." Archaeology is the discipline devoted to the study of the "material culture" of the ancients. By studying their material culture, archaeologists try to reconstruct the nature of the societies that produced it.

What Is Biblical Archaeology?

Over the last century, archaeology has become one of the major tools available to illuminate the peoples and cultures of the biblical world. The work of those archaeologists that focus on the world of the Bible has been termed "biblical archaeology," though this term has generated a great deal of discussion and debate.

The primary concern has been to clarify what excavators do in their fieldwork. Excavators should not focus only on the biblical era material. They should be careful to treat all remains, whether Byzantine, Crusader, Islamic, or Stone Age, with the same thoroughness and attention. In the excavation trenches, the excavator acts not as a "biblical archaeologist," but as an archaeologist of the "Syro-Palestinian" region interested in all remains from all eras.

Biblical archaeology is the work done after the excavation ends. It is the "armchair" work performed by the biblical scholar in his or her study in examining the results of Syro-Palestinian excavations. Biblical archaeology is the examination of the field reports and excavation summaries in order to discover what they say about the world of the Bible.

Does Archaeology "Prove the Bible"?

The most common question asked of biblical archaeologists is: "Does archaeology prove the Bible?" The short answer is: "archaeology *cannot* prove the Bible." All the major and most important assertions in the Bible are theological; they are not concerned with material culture. Archaeology, on the other hand, focuses only on material culture. It can tell us who the Israelites were, how they built their houses, what their farms were like. It cannot provide for the Christian proof that Jesus was the Son of God, or that his death has redemptive power. Archaeology can show that Nebuchadnezzar destroyed Judah in 586 B.C.; it cannot show that this destruction was the punishment for breaking a divine covenant. Archaeology does not *prove* the Bible; it *illuminates* the Bible.

History of Biblical Archaeology

Archaeology has an ancient pedigree. Already in the time of the biblical prophets, Assyrian emperors knew that primeval kings had ruled a thousand years earlier. We know also that Babylonian monarchs were "excavating" and then restoring ancient, abandoned temples in order to connect themselves to rulers of old.

In postbiblical times, pilgrims and crusaders alike traveled to the Holy Land to find relics of the world of the Bible. Queen Helena, mother of the Byzantine emperor Constantine, claimed to have found the "true cross," the site of Jesus' burial (now the Church of the Holy Sepulchre), the site of Jesus' birth (Church of the Nativity), as well as Mount Sinai (at the foot of which today stands St. Catherine's Monastery). The whole medieval trade in relics was an attempt to locate and identify "material cultural," remains, from biblical times.

This "treasure hunt" mentality began to change at the start of the 19th century. Napoleon's 1798 expedition to Egypt must first be noted, for along with his soldiers the French emperor brought a band of scholars to the Near East. The expedition's most important result was Jean Francois Champollion's deciphering of the Rosetta Stone's Egyptian hieroglyphics. The Egyptians were meticulous record keepers, but knowledge of their ancient writing system had been intentionally eradicated by Christian rulers. With hieroglyphics deciphered, the history of Egypt could now be read by modern scholars. In 1851, a British scholar, Charles Creswicke Rawlinson, accomplished a similar feat with cuneiform, the writing system used in Mesopotamia. He deciphered the cuneiform Behustin inscription, thus providing scholars the key to understanding Akkadian, the official language of both the Babylonian and Assyrian Empires. Now the records of Mesopotamia were open for examination.

Heinrich Schliemann is most famous for his discovery of ancient Troy. But equally important was his realization of the fundamental nature of a "tell" (see "Chronology" below). For biblical archaeology, few developments have been more important than the work of

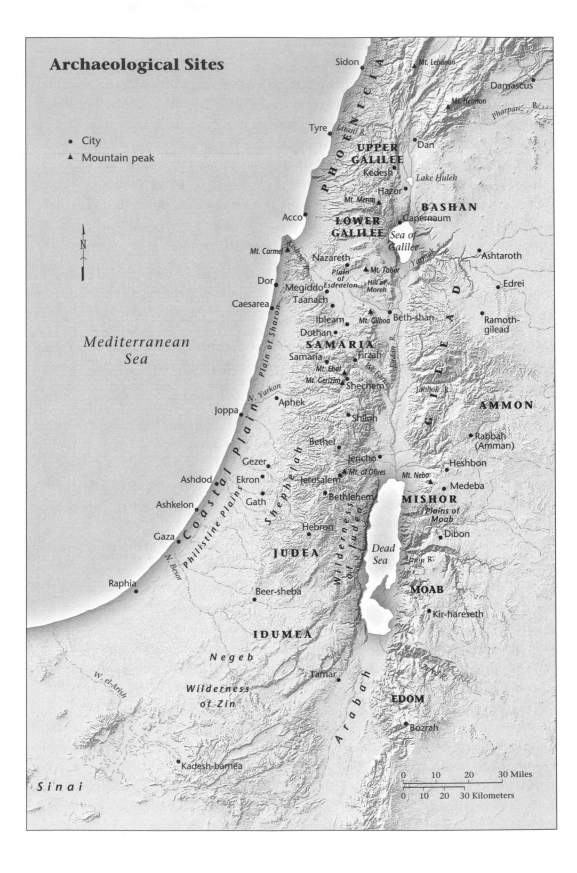

Archaeological Sites

- • City
- ▲ Mountain peak

Sidon

▲ Mt. Lebanon

Damascus

PHOENICIA

Tyre

▲ Mt. Hermon

Litani R.

Pharpar R.

UPPER GALILEE

Dan

Kedesh

Lake Huleh

Hazor

▲ Mt. Meron

BASHAN

Acco

LOWER GALILEE

Capernaum

Sea of Galilee

Ashtaroth

Mt. Carmel

Nazareth

▲ Mt. Tabor

Plain of Esdraelon

Hill of Moreh

Yarmuk R.

Edrei

Dor

Megiddo

Taanach

▲ Mt. Gilboa

Beth-shan

Caesarea

Ibleam

Ramoth-gilead

Mediterranean Sea

Dothan

Jordan R.

SAMARIA

Samaria

Tirzah

Mt. Ebal

Mt. Gerizim

Shechem

Jabbok R.

GILEAD

AMMON

Plain of Sharon

N. Yarkon

Aphek

Joppa

Shiloh

Rabbah (Amman)

Bethel

Heshbon

Gezer

Jericho

Mt. of Olives

▲ Mt. Nebo

Ashdod

Ekron

Shephelah

Jerusalem

Medeba

Ashkelon

Gath

Bethlehem

MISHOR

Plains of Moab

Gaza

Hebron

Dibon

N. Besor

JUDEA

Wilderness of Judea

Dead Sea

Arnon R.

Raphia

Beer-sheba

MOAB

Kir-hareseth

IDUMEA

Negeb

Tamar

Wilderness of Zin

W. el-Arish

Arabah

EDOM

Bozrah

Kadesh-barnea

Sinai

| 0 | 10 | 20 | 30 Miles |

| 0 | 10 | 20 | 30 Kilometers |

the American scholar Edward Robinson. Using a compass, his Bible, and his knowledge of Semitic languages, Robinson traveled throughout Palestine identifying a vast roster of long-lost sites mentioned in the Bible. At the start of the 20th century, Egyptologist Sir Flinders Petrie laid the theoretical background for establishing an archaeological dating system: ceramic dating. William F. Albright took up Petrie's theory and developed the basic ceramic chronology that, with minor adjustments, is still used today.

The last half of the 20th century witnessed several new developments in archaeology, including a refinement of field methodology. More important was the emergence of the so-called "new archaeology," which shifts its focus away from the traditional emphases on the great battles, large cities, important events, and dominant political characters of antiquity. Instead, the new archaeology concentrates on reconstructing the ancient "life-ways" of the biblical peoples. Instead of excavating the great tells and palaces, new archaeology focuses on farmsteads, domestic architecture, agricultural remains, and the means for acquiring the very necessities of life. It is a "social archaeology" that makes the daily life of the average ancient Israelite the object of study.

The new archaeology has also broadened the requirements for professional expertise. While Petrie and Schliemann could do their excavations without any support staff, current excavation teams include a broad range of specialists: geologists to study water supplies, paleo-botanists to study ancient ecology, biologists to study bones and reconstruct ancient diets, physicists to develop and monitor remote sensing techniques such as underground radar, and more.

Chronology

Two key issues face the archaeologist of the biblical world: establishing a basic chronology and correlating the biblical and archaeological material to that chronology.

Chronology (the establishment of a basic time frame) is the most fundamental concern of any archaeologist. There are two types of chronology: relative and absolute. Relative chronology is the placing of artifacts in chronological order "relative" to each other (e.g., stratum III at Lachish is older than Gezer V). Absolute chronology pins an artifact, event, or archaeological stratum to an absolute date (e.g., Lachish stratum III dates to 701 B.C.).

Establishing a relative chronology is the first and most basic step of the two. It is also the easier one due to the most common type of Near Eastern archaeological deposition, the "tell." A tell is a "layer cake" of archaeological remains. The establishment of a settlement, town, or city always requires certain geographic criteria: a reliable water source, agricultural land to produce food, and a defensible location. Whenever an ancient city or town was destroyed or captured, the newly arrived conquerors would look for suitable places to settle. Noting that the recently vanquished city had the necessary elements for settlement, the new

Unexcavated tell, north of Mount Sartaba and the Alexandrium fortress in the Jericho Valley. *(Phoenix Data Systems, Neal and Joel Bierling)*

conquerors would typically either rebuild and reoccupy the conquered city or they would simply level off the exposed rubble and build directly on top. Over the millennia, this produced the phenomenon of the tell, a "stack" of superimposed archaeological remains.

Naturally, this configuration enables the establishment of a relative chronology. The lower strata of a tell are older than the upper strata. Correlation between tells also becomes possible. If the artifacts in the stratum of one tell are similar to artifacts from a stratum in another tell, we can assume these two strata are contemporary. If there is an occupational gap at one tell, it can be "filled-in" by examining the stratification at other tells. As archaeologists excavate more and more tells, the relative chronology becomes more and more precise. Comparisons can even be made across international boundaries. Because of trade and military activity, archaeologists can discover Egyptian jewelry or Babylonian weapons in strata at Palestinian sites. These sites can then be dated by correlating them to Egyptian, Assyrian, Babylonian, or Persian sites.

The Bible itself provides a framework for relative chronology. Various biblical books contain occasional references to chronology. For example, in 1-2 Kings the kings of Israel and the kings of Judah are listed in chronological order with the lengths of their reigns. These references are not without problems, however; for example, the years given for the reigns of the kings of Israel do not exactly correspond to, or "add up" to, the years given to the reigns of their Judean counterparts. Nevertheless, beginning with the reign of David, biblical references provide a reasonably detailed, "relative" chronological scaffold.

A more difficult task is establishing an absolute chronology. Ultimately all biblical chronology is derived from the Mesopotamian empires of Assyria and Babylon — and, to a lesser degree, Egypt. Fortunately for chronology, these Mesopotamian societies were both good record keepers and immersed in astral religions. As a result, their military and political records contain occasional references to astronomical phenomena. For example, the annals of the Assyrian emperor Ashur-dan refer to a solar eclipse in the summer of the ninth year of his reign. Because eclipses occur with predictable regularity, we can now date that eclipse to the morning of 15 June 763. From this starting point, we can date not only Ashur-dan, but also all the Assyrian emperors. Since these Assyrian emperors were constantly interacting with Babylonians, Egyptians, and Israelites (usually by military campaigns), we can derive dates for these events as well. For example, we have an Assyrian account of Emperor Sennacherib's destruction of the Judean city of Lachish in the summer of 701. 2 Kings 18 describes the same event and dates it to the 14th year of King Hezekiah of Judah. Thus we can date Hezekiah's reign and, by extension, the other kings of Judah and Israel. Lachish has also been excavated, and its stratum III can be confidently correlated with the destruction of 701. In other words, from Lachish III we now have a "snapshot" of what the material culture of Judah looked like in the summer of 701. We can then relate the Lachish excavations with other sites and can thus begin to construct an absolute chronology from our relative chronology.

In summary, our archaeological and biblical chronology is fairly precise back to the reign of David (ca. 1000). Earlier dates are more tenuous.

Ceramic Dating

Certainly for archaeologists of the biblical periods the most helpful tool in establishing a chronology is ceramic or pottery dating. All societies are concerned with "fashion," and the ancients were no different. No 18th-dynasty pharaoh wanted to be seen riding in a 15th-dynasty chariot. No 8th-century Israelite woman wanted to use 9th-century pottery. While the stylistic changes in music, art, and even clothing are not well preserved in the archaeological record, changes in pottery styles are. Petrie had noted in his work in Egypt that tombs from different eras contained different pottery forms; tombs from the same period contained the same forms. Moreover, pottery is virtually indestructible; it may break into smaller pieces (sherds), but unlike clothing and other organic material, it does not disintegrate; therefore, pottery sherds are found throughout ancient tells.

Since we now know, for example, how 8th-century storage jars differ from 9th- or 7th-century types, an archaeologist can use this knowledge to date a stratum. Moreover, archaeologists do not need to have intact or complete pots. A trained archaeologist, even from a broken sherd of pottery, can "reconstruct" mentally the whole pottery form and thereby date the associated archaeological material.

Chronological Terminology

One of the most difficult problems for the nonarchaeologist is the mastering of the relevant chronological terminology. Two different systems of nomenclature are often used: "biblical" and "archaeological." The "biblical" terminology references the relevant biblical period: e.g., the period of the conquest, the united monarchy, the Babylonian exile.

"Archaeological" terminology, in contrast, labels eras based on the dominant technology in use. Thus the earliest era of stone tools is called the Stone Age — subdivided into the Paleolithic, Mesolithic, and Neolithic eras (the Old, Middle, and New Stone ages). The earliest metal to be widely worked was copper (Gk. *chalkos*), so the next era is labeled the Chalcolithic. Next, bronze was mastered (the Early, Middle, and Late Bronze ages). Next emerge the Iron ages (Iron I, II, and III). Within these periods, various changes occur in material culture, so that a variety of subdivisions has been introduced (the Middle Bronze [MB] era is often subdivided into MB I, IIA, and IIB). A great deal of scholarly debate occurs over the demarcation of these various periods, as well as the precise absolute dating assigned to them. Following the Iron Age, we have such complete historical sources that we begin to label by culture: the Hellenistic era, the Roman era, etc.

When Does "History" Begin?

Perhaps the most vexing problem facing archaeologists of the biblical world is the correlation of the Bible to the archaeological record. There is a broad consensus among biblical scholars that the Bible's "Primary History" (Genesis to 2 Kings) reached its final written form around the 6th or 5th century B.C. But the events it claims to describe often occurred centuries, even millennia, before the final editing. This raises the question about historiographic accuracy: to what extent do texts from the 6th century reflect precise knowledge of events a thousand years earlier? And how can this knowledge be connected with the archaeological material? In other words, at what point do the biblical narratives begin to reflect, in some sense, actual historical events; when does biblical "history" begin?

The proposed answer to this question has exercised scholars ever since the rise of modern biblical scholarship. At one end of the spectrum is the naïve assumption that all the texts are written with the same attention to historical detail that a modern historian would exercise. At the other extreme, some biblical scholars (not archaeologists) have argued that the Primary History is a Persian or even Hellenistic era "novel."

Contemporary archaeologists have rejected both extremes. Among professional archaeologists is a broad consensus that the first 11 chapters of Genesis (the Creation and Flood accounts) are not historiographic in the modern sense. They view these accounts as theological narratives parallel in form (and sometimes in content) with narratives found in other ancient Near Eastern cultures. Stories of paradisaical gardens, talking snakes, tree-fruit that gives immortality, peoples whose lives spanned hundreds of years, and accounts of great floods and half-divine giants are similar to stories from other Semitic cultures. So archaeologists are not in the quest to find these magic gardens or half-human giants; rather, they seek similar narratives in other cultures and study these stories in the context of ancient parallels.

A much more serious debate has revolved around the historicity of the patriarchal material. Albright and his followers argued that the patriarchal era could be tied to the Middle Bronze era (ca. 2100-1550). A significant debate has ensued concerning whether, or to what extent, these narratives should be considered historical at all.

In recent decades, the focus of the historical debate has shifted toward the exodus and whether it can be linked with the archaeological record. While it is clear that no specific Egyptian archaeological datum can be conclusively connected with the biblical accounts, many scholars have argued that the exodus account fits in reasonably well with the archaeology of the end of the Late Bronze era (1550-1200). While few archaeologists would accept a Cecil B. DeMille–type exodus with millions of former slaves leaving Egypt, many scholars feel comfortable with a more modest exodus measured in thousands rather than millions. But many scholars question even this more limited reconstruction.

As to the conquest and settlement/judges era, archaeologists are much more comfortable connecting these biblical narratives with the archaeological record of Iron Age I (1200-1000). It is clear that *something* was happening in Palestine in this era. New settlements were emerging in areas that would in later centuries be the heartland of the Israelite kingdoms; new housing forms (the four-room or Israelite house) were beginning to dominate; new pottery forms (the collar-rim store jar) were beginning to appear; the old Canaanite city-state system of the Late Bronze Age was collapsing; and a new Philistine population was beginning to take hold along the Mediterranean coast. These developments can all be correlated quite nicely with the biblical narratives of Joshua and Judges. Problems with this correlation do remain, however. For example, the two cities featured most prominently in the conquest narratives, Jericho and Ai, were not destroyed in this era (nor is it clear that they even existed as walled cities at this time).

As for the period of the Israelite and Judean monarchy, archaeologists agree that this can be dated with complete confidence to the Iron II era (1000-586). The connections between the biblical narratives and the Assyrian, Babylonian, and Egyptian records are solid, and for the most part these can be firmly associated with archaeological remains. The question of the extent of the Davidic and Solomonic kingdoms continues to be debated, for very little in the archaeological record can be firmly attributed to these kings. But this archaeological "uncertainty" can largely be attributed to two factors. First, Jerusalem, the center of David and Solomon's activities, has been destroyed and rebuilt numerous times and thus its archaeological history is extremely muddled. Second, the ceramic chronology of the Davidic era (and the demarcation between Iron I and Iron II) is still somewhat confused and uncertain.

Excavation Methodology

How do archaeologists *do* archaeology? There are two commonly used procedures: excavation and survey. The most commonly used method of excavation today is the baulk/debris method. A site (often, a tell) is selected. The site is then surveyed into a grid (usually 5×5 m.). The excavation crew moves inside these grid lines one-half meter. The crew then begins to excavate the remaining 4×4-m. square. As the crews in adjoining squares "go down," this procedure leaves a 1 m.-wide baulk of unexcavated material standing between the squares. By going straight downward, the team encounters the successive layers of the tell; by leaving the standing baulk, they can see in the side of the baulk the record of the layers they have already encountered. Pottery and other artifacts (animal bones, jewelry, organic materials) are collected, dated, and analyzed. Careful records, including photographs, survey drawings, architectural plans, baulk drawings, pottery analyses, and excavation notes, are kept. Ultimately, often after several seasons of excavations, a final report is issued describing the stratification, special finds, architectural remains, animal bones, metal finds, burials, ceramics, and any other items of interest.

A second, widely used procedure is the survey. Here a team of archaeologists grid off an entire geographical area. (Depending on the size of the team, it can be several hundreds

Excavation of adjacent squares at the iron-age site at Khirbet Qeiyafa, Israel. *(Khirbet Qeiyafa excavations, the Hebrew University of Jerusalem)*

of square miles.) Members of the team then either "walk" over the entire survey area or "sample" a predetermined subset of the survey area. They note any archaeological remains, gather sherds from the surface (thus determining the date of the remains), map the location of any sites, and try to determine the general nature of the sites (e.g., farmstead, fortress, threshing floor). Surveys are particularly helpful in determining the general settlement pattern in an area, what eras show population increase or decrease, and the forms of ancient political organization.

Both methods provide valuable information for the archaeologist. Excavations are obviously more site-specific; surveys reveal more regional, intersite relations.

Conclusion

Archaeology has emerged in the last century as one of the primary methods scholars can use to understand the Bible more fully. It can provide information about ancient life-ways, settlement patterns, and social organization. It can tell us about the different peoples present on the biblical stage and how they interacted. It can occasionally provide the discovery of ancient texts so that we can see what the biblical peoples said about themselves (e.g., the Dead Sea Scrolls). While archaeology does not and cannot "prove" the theological assertions of the Bible, it does illuminate and elucidate the lives of those who bequeathed to us the Scriptures.

FOR FURTHER READING

Cline, Eric H. *Biblical Archaeology: A Very Short Introduction.* Oxford: Oxford University Press, 2009.

Meyers, Eric M., ed. *The Oxford Encyclopedia of Archaeology in the Near East.* 5 vols. Oxford: Oxford University Press, 1997.

Stern, Ephraim, ed. *The New Encyclopedia of Archaeological Excavations in the Holy Land.* 4 vols. New York: Simon & Schuster, 1993.

Lynn Tatum

Plants and Animals

The biblical text swarms with life. Goats, trees, bees, and bears form part of the background against which prose narrative tells stories and poetic passages draw inspiration. Occasionally, the created order occupies a more central role: a lion mauls, an oak tree snares, a donkey speaks! Such moments are brief, though, and nature returns to a more comfortable functionary or descriptive position: familiar images are pressed.

Hundreds of different words in the Bible refer to plants and animals. These are named and ordered along lines that appear ancient, pastoral, descriptive, and utilitarian. No modern ranking system of genus and species is found here. Animal life is conceived between the poles of domesticated and wild, the clean and the unclean. The ordering of plant life is less obvious but may be surmised; Gen. 1:11 contrasts the low-lying grasses (Heb. *deshe*) and herbs (*'eseb*) with the overarching trees (*'ets*). Elsewhere, edible grains are contrasted with undesirable thorns and thistles (e.g., Job 31:40; Heb. 6:7-8). Other categorical terms include the wild *(nepesh hayyah)*, the creeping *(remes)*, and the swarming *(sherets)* creatures of the creation account, or herds of sheep and goats *(behemah)*, unfortunately translated by some as small cattle, (e.g., Eccl. 2:7). The term "beasts" (Heb. *hayyah*; Gk. *therion*, *theriomacheo*) metaphorically describes persons or forces hostile to God (e.g., Dan. 7:1-12; 1 Cor. 15:32; Rev. 11:7).

Some fairly specific terms are also found. Examples include the turtle-dove (Lev. 5:7), whose name in Hebrew *(tor)* possibly resembles the sound it makes, the eerie howler *(tannim)*, believed to be the jackal, or the almond tree, literally, the waker (Jer. 1:11), whose early blossoms announce the coming of spring. No classification of fish may be discerned, yet eight different Hebrew terms are translated as snake. Words that appear only once and without description are often very difficult to identify, although occasionally, as with the *liwyatan* (Job 41:1-34), additional description only adds to the mystery.

A Necessary but Challenging Study

These examples suggest why it is a challenging task to draw links between the text world of the Bible and the natural world to which it refers. It is a necessary study because it reveals how ancient people viewed, organized, and interacted with their natural environment. Interpreting and applying the text in a fair manner demands it. Yet it is a challenging study for several reasons. First, the natural world is enormous. Biblical texts address a space that sprawls from Spain to India, a distance of more than 4000 miles. Not surprisingly, an extraordinary range of habitats may be encountered. Second, habitats and populations change with time: urbanization, extinction, cultivation, and denudation limit the view from the present to the past. Third, until recently, archaeological excavation has often ignored material remains that help reconstruct past patterns of flora and fauna. This challenge is being met by new archaeological approaches that are more landscape-oriented and take into account ecofacts (seed, pollen, and bone) as well as artifacts. Finally, barriers of language and culture hinder hasty links and force confrontation with issues of local dialect and classification, poetic usage, and slang. As these challenges are met through personal experience, scientific research, and linguistic study, the identification of many plants and animals appearing in the Bible may be approached.

Four Biomes

Scientists classify into "biomes," ecological areas where climate, soils, plants, and animals are relatively uniform. While many distinct or blended biomes may be identified within the lands where biblical events occurred, these may be broadly organized into four groups for discussion: highland forests, Mediterranean shrublands, short grasslands, and warm deserts. A brief survey of these four biomes reveals not only a startling diversity of climate and landform, but also a departure point for identifying some of the more prominent plants and animals mentioned in the Bible.

Highland Forests Needle-leafed forests extend the length of Northern Europe and Asia. In the lands of the Bible, however, parallel conditions exist in subalpine areas of high ranges (e.g., Lebanon, Troodos, Pontic, and Zagros Mountains). The climate here is damp and cool to cold, with distinctive floral and faunal communities.

Climax vegetation in these forests includes coniferous trees of pine, fir, cedar, and juniper. In many cases, these were cleared in antiquity; only limited stands remain today. Biblical references allude to the height, strength, and value of the cedars of Lebanon (*Cedrus libani*; Heb. *'erez*), while the Aleppo pine *(Pinus halepensis)* and the highland juniper *(Juniperus phoenicia)* have yet to be positively identified in the Bible. At lower elevations these needle-leafed forests mix with and give way to broad-leafed forests.

Mixed broad-leafed forests exist in areas of southern Europe and press southward into the Levant as well as the Italian, Balkan, and Anatolian peninsulas. These regions resemble areas of eastern North America; temperatures and rainfall fluctuate and give rise to a biome rich in life. Climax vegetation includes the maple, beech, and oak. The latter

(*Quercus;* Heb. *'elon*), is noted in the Bible as a specimen or landmark tree (e.g., Gen. 13:18; 35:8) or part of a dense forest (2 Sam. 18:8, 9).

Wild animals of these needle-leafed and broad-leafed forests mentioned in the Bible include carnivores such as the bear (*Ursus syriacus;* Heb. *dob*), leopard (*Panthera pardus;* Heb. *namer*), and wolf (*Canis lupus;* Heb. *ze'eb*). Herbivores such as the chamois or ibex (*Capra ibex;* Heb. *aqqo?*) and wild sheep (*Ovis musimon;* Heb. *zemer?*) are also found and have been prey for humans and beasts alike.

Mediterranean Shrublands Mediterranean shrublands ring the Mediterranean seaboard from the Levant to Spain and create the most familiar landscape to the reader of the Bible. Here winters are short, mild, and wet, while summers are long, dry, and hot. These conditions both foster and isolate an enormous variety of life forms and encourage the dynamics of localization, or endemism, that complicate the task of identification. But these forces also offer enormous opportunities for food production and help explain the attraction and intensity of human settlement.

Apart from the high oaks that continue intermittently from the highlands, trees and shrubs found here tend to grow in dense thickets or maquis. These often include the pistachio or terebinth (*Pistacia palaestine;* Heb. *'elah, 'allah*), carob (*Ceratonia siliquia;* Gk. *keration*), myrtle (*Myrtus communis;* Heb. *hadas*), fig (*Ficus carica;* Heb. *te'enah;* Gk. *sykon, syke*), pomegranate (*Punica granatum;* Heb. *rimmon*), fig-sycamore (*Ficus sycomorus;* Heb. *siqma;* Gk. *sykomorea*), and other companion species, often with drought-resistant features. Prickly thorns, thistles, nettles, and brambles also grow readily but are difficult to identify with certainty. Some 70 species have been identified within the borders of modern Israel alone.

Mediterranean shrublands have been regularly occupied and cultivated. Many vegetables, herbs, and fruits thrive here and are mentioned in the Bible. Lentils and beans are attested (Heb. *'adashim, pol,* and possibly *'edom;* Gk. *keration*), as are onions (Heb. *batsal*), garlic (Heb. *shumim*), melons (Heb. *'abattihim*), cumin (Heb. *kammon;* Gk. *kyminon*), dill (Heb. *qetsah;* Gk. *anethon*), and mint (Gk. *hedyosmon*). Beyond these, the olive (*Olea europeae;* Heb. *zayit;* Gk. *elaia*) and grape (*Vitis vinifera;* Heb. *'enab;* Gk. *staphyle*) have been intensely propagated and exploited. The wood, fruit, and oil obtained from olive trees are key products for understanding human ways of life in Mediterranean shrublands. Similarly, the grape was domesticated at an early date and eaten directly or processed as raisins, vinegar, and wine. Oil and wine were viewed as blessings from God (Deut. 7:13) and formed an integral part of sacrificial and celebratory activities.

Animals facilitated trade, traction, and transport and supplemented diet in Mediterranean shrublands. The donkey is well known (*Equus asinus;* Heb. *hamor, 'aton*), as are the horse (*Equus caballus;* Heb. *sus*), or mule (Heb. *pered, pirdah*), ox (*Bos taurus;* Heb. *shor*), pig (*Sus scrofa;* Heb. *hazir*), sheep (*Ovis orientalis;* Heb. *kebes*), and goat (*Capra hircus;* Heb. *'ez*). Camels (*Camelus dromedarius;* Heb. *gamal*) also moved across the land in packed caravans.

Wild animals explicitly associated with Mediterranean shrublands include the fox (*Vulpes palaestinus;* Heb. *shu'al*), the striped hyena (*Hyaena hyaena;* Heb. *tsabu'a*), the dog (*Canus familiaris;* Heb. *keleb;* Gk. *kyon*), and the lion (*Panthera leo;* Heb. *'ari*). The crocodile (*Crocodylus niloticus;* Heb. *tahash*?) may also be mentioned here as part of a unique wetland community.

Short Grasslands Short grasslands are temperate zones dominated by short-grass prairie, steppe, or veld. These areas are transitional, positioned between Mediterranean shrublands and warm deserts. Short grasslands are found in stretches of modern Jordan, Israel, Syria, central Turkey, Iraq, and Iran. Here soil moisture in the dry season is insufficient to support a high canopy; hence, trees are widely scattered or focused in drainage systems. Despite the challenging climate, however, flora in the short grasslands is extremely diverse.

From a biblical perspective, wheat (*Triticum;* Heb. *hittah*) and barley (*Hordeum;* Heb. *se'orah*) are most significant. Winter grasses were domesticated at an early date and regularly planted, harvested, and eaten throughout the biblical period. Kernels of wheat and barley were used for bread, gruel, or beer.

Many flowers are found in short grasslands but are difficult to identify precisely in the Bible. Hebrew *shoshan*, literally whiteness, is translated lily (e.g., 1 Kgs. 7:26; Song 2:2) but may refer to any number of plants, including the narcissus *(Narcissus tazetta)* or the daisylike chamomile *(Anthemis nobilis)*. Interestingly, a good candidate for the rose of Sharon (Heb. *habatstselet*) may actually be the tulip *(Tulipa sharonesis)*.

Nubian Ibex *(Ester Inbar, Wikimedia Commons)*

If Mediterranean shrublands are characterized by the presence of farmers, short grasslands may be characterized by the presence of herders. Here flocks of sheep and goats moved regularly in season, plying the edges of this zone of possibility. Flocks devoured the stubble of harvested grain fields and left valuable fertilizer in their wake. Undoubtedly, other grazers and browsers also took advantage of these grasses, including deer (*Cervus capreolus;* Heb. *'ayyal*) and gazelle (*Gazella gazella;* Heb. *tsebi*). The cheetah *(Acinonyx jubatus)* is also home to this area but is not clearly identified in the Bible.

Warm Deserts Semidesert or desert regions of the Bible lands extend across North Africa and the Arabian peninsula and include broad areas of Jordan, Iraq, and Iran. Extremely arid conditions limit resources and encourage competition that may challenge or elimi-nate life in this unique biome.

Few large animals are found here, with the notable exception of the camel and perhaps the ostrich (*Struthio camelus;* Heb. *bat ya῾anah*). More common are small creatures like the jerboa (Heb. *῾akbar*), the hyrax (*Procavia capensis;* Heb. *shapan*), or a variety of lizards and snakes (cf. Lev. 11:29-30).

As with fauna, adaptive strategies allow flora to survive in the harsh desert environ-ment. Water management techniques and the ability to tolerate saline soils allow the date palm tree (*Phoenix dactylifera;* Heb. *tamar;* Gk. *phoinix*) to grow abundantly and produce shade and fruit. Branches and leaves from this tree were used for building booths (Lev. 23:40) and were waved by the people when Jesus entered Jerusalem (John 12:13). The aca-cia tree (Heb. *shittim*) is another hardy desert plant; acacia wood was used in constructing the tabernacle and other sacred objects (Exodus 25–26). Finally, gum resin trees (*Boswellia sacra* and *Commiphora myrrha*) of the dry heights of South Arabia were carefully harvest-ed for frankincense (Heb. *lebonah*) and myrrh (Heb. *mor;* Gk. *murra, smyrna*).

Conclusion

Biblical writers demonstrate a keen awareness of the natural world and view it as a wonder of creation (cf. Psalm 104). Flora and fauna are regularly mentioned and integrated into the text. Exotic and imported items, such as peacocks or baboons (1 Kgs. 10:22), the "balm of Gilead" (Gen. 37:25), or cinnamon (Exod. 30:23) from the Far East, testify to far-flung trade connections and demonstrate the continuing challenge of this necessary study.

FOR FURTHER READING

Borowski, Oded. *Agriculture in Iron Age Israel.* Winona Lake: Eisenbrauns, 1987.

———. *Every Living Thing: Daily Use of Animals in Ancient Israel.* Walnut Creek: Altamira, 1998.

Hareuveni, Nogah. *Nature in Our Biblical Heritage.* Kiryat Ono: Neot Kedumim, 1980.

Wagstaff, J. Malcolm. *The Evolution of Middle Eastern Landscapes: An Outline to A.D. 1840.* Totowa: Barnes & Noble, 1985.

MARK ZIESE

Weights, Measures, Money

Goliath towered at six cubits and a span, and his spear's head weighed 600 shekels of iron (1 Sam. 17:4, 7). Nineveh's size is calculated as a three days' journey across (Jonah 3:3). Hosea buys his wife for 15 shekels of silver, a homer of barley, and a lethech of wine (Hos. 3:2). Jesus speaks in a parable about a man who while traveling entrusts his servants with one to five talents (Matt. 25:15). The biblical authors assume their readers' familiarity with a variety of measurements of distance, mass, and capacity, and an understanding of these ancient weights and measures illuminates the Bible.

While fixing exact standards to biblical weights and measures is quite tentative, approximations can be derived from three sources: (1) the Hebrew Bible and New Testament, (2) other ancient Near Eastern sources (notably Egyptian and Mesopotamian metrologies), and (3) archaeology. Excavations have revealed architecture from which linear measurements can be deduced, weights inscribed with their value, and standardized pottery forms and storage areas that quantify volumes.

Strict regulations controlled the uniformity of weights and measures throughout the ancient Near East. Thus Lev. 19:36 dictates, "You shall have honest balances, honest weights, an honest ephah, and an honest hin."

Linear

The cubit is the most common form of linear measurement in the ancient Near East, calculated by the average length of a person's forearm, from the elbow to the tip of the finger. While this length varies considerably, evidence from both archaeology and literature suggests an average length for the common cubit of 17.5 inches (44.5 cm.). For smaller linear measurements, the cubit is divided into two spans, which represents the maximum distance between the thumb and the little finger in an outstretched hand (Exod. 28:16). Thus Goliath's stature of six cubits and a span converts to 9.5 feet (2.85 m.), although the Septuagint

Units of Weight and Measure with approximate metric and English equivalents

Biblical Name[1]	Biblical Weight or Measure	Metric Weight or Measure	English Equivalent
WEIGHT			
Old Testament:			
gerah	—	0.57 g.	0.02 oz.
beka	10 gerahs	5.7 g.	0.2 oz.
pim	1.33 bekas	7.8 g.	0.27 oz.
shekel	2 bekas	11.4 g.	0.4 oz.
New Testament:			
mina	50 shekels	571.2 g.	1.26 lb.
talent	60 minas	34.27 kg.	75.6 lb.
pound[2]	—	340 g.	12 oz.
LINEAR			
Old Testament:			
finger	—	1.85 cm.	0.73 in.
handbreath	4 fingers	7.4 cm.	2.92 in.
span	3 handbreaths	22.2 cm.	8.75 in.
cubit	2 spans	44.5 cm.	17.5 in.
long cubit	7 handbreaths	51.9 cm.	20.4 in.
reed	6 cubits	2.7 m.	8.75 ft.
New Testament:[3]			
cubit	—	42-48 cm.	17-19 in.
fathom	4 cubits	1.8 m.	6 ft.
stadion	400 cubits	183 m.	200 yds.
mile	8 stadia	1480 m.	1618 yds.
CAPACITY (Dry and Liquid)			
Old Testament:			
kab	4 logs	1.2 l.	1.3 qt.
omer	0.1 ephah	2.2 l.	2.3 qt.
seah[4]	2 hins	7.3 l.	2 gal.
ephah	3 seahs	22 l.	5.8 gal.
lethech	5 ephahs	110 l.	29 gal.
cor/homer	10 ephahs	220 l.	6.25 U.S. bu.
New Testament:			
modios	—	7.4 l.	.5 U.S. bu.
Old Testament:			
log	—	0.3 l.	0.63 pt.[5]
hin	12 logs	3.6 l.	1 gal.
bath	3 seahs	22 l.	5.8 gal.
homer	10 baths	220 l.	58 gal.
New Testament:			
choinix	—	.95 l.	1 qt.
modios[6]	—	38-115 l.	10-30 gal.

[1] NRSV terminology except where NRSV transposes into modern units.
[2] Gk. *lítra* also represents a unit of capacity equivalent to ca. 0.5 l. (1.13 gal.).
[3] NT linear measures differ according to whether Roman, Greek, or Palestinian units are used.
[4] Also referred to as a "tenth" (i.e., of an ephah).
[5] English units of capacity are U.S. liquid units.
[6] NRSV transposes into gallons.

and manuscripts from the Dead Sea record a height of four cubits and a span, a more reasonable 6.5 feet (1.95 m.). The cubit is further divided into six handbreadths (Exod. 25:25; 2 Chr. 4:5), and one handbreadth consists of four fingers or 2.9 inches (Jer. 52:21).

For linear measurements larger than the cubit, a fathom represents the distance covered by outstretched arms (Acts 27:28), approximately four cubits, while a reed consists of six cubits (Ezek. 40:3, 5-8; 42:16-19). Consequently, the common cubit yields the following conversions: ⅙ reed = ¼ fathom = 1 cubit = 2 spans = 6 handbreadths = 24 fingers. The picture is complicated by the fact that just as there were two cubits in Egypt and Mesopotamia, we learn from Ezek. 40:5 and 43:13 that a longer cubit existed which measures seven handbreadths as opposed to six. This longer measurement is frequently referred to as a "royal cubit."

Longer distances in the Hebrew Bible are approximated by a "bowshot" (Gen. 21:16), a "furrow's length" (1 Sam. 14:14), a "day's journey" (1 Kgs. 19:4; Jonah 3:4; Luke 2:44), and a "three days' journey" (Gen. 30:36; Jonah 3:3). A day's journey has been estimated in the 10- to 20-mile (16-32 km.) range. In the New Testament, the stadion represents 400 cubits, about 200 yards (183 m.; Luke 24:13; John 6:19; 11:18; Rev. 14:20; 21:16). The "Roman Mile" in Matt. 5:41 represents 1620 yards (1481 m.).

Weights and Money

Small objects were most often weighed through the use of handheld balances in the ancient Near East. Such devices usually were constructed by a beam supporting two pans. These balances are referred to in several passages in the Hebrew Bible (Lev. 19:36; Isa. 40:12; Ezek. 5:1; 45:10; Ps. 62:9; Job 6:2; 31:6; Prov. 11:1; 16:11; 20:23; Dan. 5:27; Hos. 12:7; Amos 8:5; Mic. 6:11). The Israelite system of weights was largely borrowed from their Mesopotamian neighbors, as the benefits created by a standard system of measurement greatly enhanced commerce for all participants. Nevertheless, while the Israelites maintained the Mesopotamian terminology for their weights, they seem to have reassigned their values. The Mesopotamian system was sexagesimal, that is, the number 60 served as its base. Contrarily, the Israelites incorporated a quinquagesimal system, in which the base was 50. Thus in the Mesopotamian system one talent consisted of 60 shekels, whereas in ancient Israel the talent was composed of only 50.

References to money in the Hebrew Bible designate measures of value in goods, including grain, oil, or wine, or in precious metals, primarily silver. Accordingly, the terminology for monetary values reflects that used for weights and measures. Literary evidence suggests that coinage originated in Asia Minor in the second half of the 7th century B.C.

The shekel was by far the most common weight in the Bible, and shekels of silver were the most frequent method of payment. The Hebrew word "shekel" is derived from a root meaning "to weigh." Yet, just as there were two cubits employed for linear measurements,

A collection of ancient Israelite weights. *(Hecht Museum, University of Haifa)*

there were at times two separate weights assigned to the shekel. The "shekel of the sanctuary" (Exod. 30:24; 38:25-26) and the "shekel by the king's weight" (2 Sam. 14:26) seem to be slightly larger than the average weight for the common shekel of 11.405 grams.

The largest weight in the Bible is the talent, consisting of 50 shekels. The word "talent" is derived from Greek *talanton,* meaning "weight." The Hebrew term is *kikkar,* literally a "round object," in reference to the frequent circular shape of the weights. For smaller weights, there is one reference to a *pîm,* the price for sharpening iron (1 Sam. 13:19-21). A *pîm* averages 7.8 grams, or roughly ⅔ of a shekel.

The shekel is further divided into two *beqaʿ,* a word meaning "to split" (Gen. 24:22; Exod. 30:13-15; 38:26). Finally, 20 gerahs compose a shekel (Exod. 30:13); nevertheless, archaeology provides evidence that through most of the Israelite period, there were 24 gerahs in the average shekel.

Far fewer references to weight exist in the New Testament. The Greek talent equaled 6000 drachmas (Matt. 18:24; 25:15-28). The drachma was roughly equivalent to the Roman denarius, or ¼ of a silver shekel. The exact weight of the mina (Luke 19:13-25) is

A variety of silver coins from the region of Samaria. *(Phoenix Data Systems, Neal and Joel Bierling)*

uncertain. Last, the pound (Gk. *litra*) of ointment was equal to 12 ounces (336 g.; John 12:3; 19:39).

Area

The measurement of surface area is poorly attested to in the Hebrew Bible and completely absent in the New Testament. In the Hebrew Bible, two references approximate land area by a yoke (1 Sam. 14:14; Isa. 5:10; cf. Ps. 129:3). The yoke probably represents the amount of land that a team of oxen might plow in a day, or just under an acre. The only other method of determining land area in the Hebrew Bible is by estimating the amount of seed necessary to sow it (1 Kgs. 18:32; Isa. 5:10).

Dry Capacity

The homer serves as the standard expression of dry capacity in the Hebrew Bible. The word "homer" is cognate to "ass" and serves as an approximation to the normal load carried by this animal. The cor is of equal value to the homer, both measuring approximately 6.25 U.S. bushels (220 l.; Ezek. 45:14). The homer/cor standard is divided into 2 lethechs (Hos. 3:2), 10 ephahs (Ezek. 45:11-14), and 30 seahs (Gen. 18:6). The omer represents a day's ration of grain, or $\frac{1}{100}$ of a homer (Exod. 16:16-18). The smallest unit seems to be the kab, referred to only once in the Hebrew Bible (2 Kgs. 6:25). The kab measures only $\frac{1}{180}$ of a homer. Thus we arrive at the following conversions for Hebrew Bible measures of dry capacity: 1 homer = 2 lethechs = 10 ephahs = 30 seahs = 100 omers = 180 kabs.

In the New Testament, the bushel (Gk. *modios*) represents approximately ¼ U.S. bushel (Matt. 5:15; Mark 4:21; Luke 11:33).

Liquid Capacity

The standard measure of liquid capacity in the Hebrew Bible is the "bath," converting to about six U.S. gallons (23 l.; 1 Kgs. 7:26, 38; 2 Chr. 2:10; 4:5; Isa. 5:10). The word "bath" derives from the Hebrew word "daughter" and presumably represents the capacity of water jars carried from the well (cf. Gen. 24:15, where a young Rebekah carries out this task). Larger measurements are again expressed by the homer, the same term used for dry capacity (Ezek. 45:11, 14). The liquid homer is composed of 10 baths. Units smaller than a bath include the hin, ⅙ of a bath (Exod. 29:40; 30:24; Lev. 19:36; 23:13; Num. 15:4-7, 9-10; 28:5, 7, 14). The hin is further divided into 12 logs (Lev. 14:10, 12, 15, 21, 24), a log consisting of approximately 0.3 quarts/liters. Thus the following conversions for liquid capacity for the Hebrew Bible are arrived at: $\frac{1}{10}$ liquid homer = 1 bath = 6 hins = 48 logs.

In the New Testament, the metretes (John 2:6) has been estimated to contain anywhere from 10 to 30 gallons. A less tentative value may be ascribed to the choinix (Rev. 6:6), which equals 1 quart (.95 l.).

FOR FURTHER READING

Measuring and Weighing in Ancient Times. Haifa: Hecht Museum, 2001.

Powell, Marvin A. "Weights and Measures." *OEANE* 5:339-42.

Scott, R. B. Y. "Weights and Measures of the Bible." *BA* 22 (1959): 22-40.

MICHAEL M. HOMAN

Measuring Time

Basic Terms

Day and Watch The Hebrew word *yom* can be used to express "time" in general, but it was regularly used to mean "day" in the sense of a period of light and darkness, or the time of light alone. It is probable that a day in the Old Testament was the period of time from evening to evening (e.g., Passover, Exod. 12:6, 8, 10, 18; and the Day of Atonement, Lev. 23:32). A day was divided into four watches, each constituting a three-hour period (first watch from 6 to 9 a.m.). Finally, the Old Testament is clear that from early times a week equaled seven days. Six days were days in which work could be performed, but on the final day of the week labor was forbidden (Exod. 34:21; Lev. 23:3; Deut. 5:12-15). The seventh day was the only day that received a name, the Sabbath; in the New Testament the day before the Sabbath is called the day of Preparation (Matt. 27:62; Mark 15:42; Luke 23:54; John 19:31, 42). In some places the Hebrew word "week" actually refers to a period of seven years (e.g., Lev. 25:8; Dan. 9:24-27).

Month The Hebrew year was divided into 12 months, but their names are not consistent throughout the Old Testament. Some scholars argue that three distinct systems of month names are recorded in the Bible. (1) Some Canaanite months are named in the Bible: Abib, the first month (Exod. 13:4); Ziv, the second month (1 Kgs. 6:1, 37); Ethanim, the seventh month (1 Kgs. 8:2); and Bul, the eighth month (1 Kgs. 6:38). (2) In the parts of the Old Testament describing the schedule of festivals, usually only the number of the month is used. For example, Passover is on the 14th day of the first month (Exodus 12; Lev. 23:5; Num. 9:1-5) and the Festival of Tabernacles occurs from the 15th to the 21st of the seventh month (Num. 29:12-38). (3) The Hebrew equivalents of Babylonian months are named, once in Ezra, as well as in Nehemiah, Esther, and Zechariah. All these books were written after the Babylonian exile, and the Jews brought these names back from Babylon. The Babylonian months were lunar, and each new year began in the spring.

Year The basic year in the Old Testament did not consist of 365 days. Our present calen-

Israel's Calendar

March			• Tishri (Ethanim)	
Month 1			**October**	
• Nisan (Abib)	Barley harvest		Month 8	
April			• Marchesvan (Bul)	Early
Month 2			• (autumn) rains	
• Iyyar (Ziv)	Grain harvest		**November**	
May			Month 9	
Month 3				Grain planting
• Sivan			• Kislev	
June			**December**	
Month 4	Grape harvest		Month 10	
• Tammuz			• Tebet	Rainy season
July			**January**	
Month 5			Month 11	Late planting
• Ab	Summer fruit harvest		• Shebat	
	Summer heat		**February**	
August			Month 12	
Month 6			• Adar	Later
• Elul			• (spring) rains	
September				
Month 7	Olive Harvest			

dar is based on a solar cycle, but the Old Testament calendar follows a lunar cycle. The Old Testament does not record how long a year lasted, and the date for the beginning of the year is difficult to determine. Scholars have argued from different sets of facts that the year began in either spring or autumn. It may be that the northern kingdom (Israel) began its year in the spring while the southern kingdom (Judah) began its year in autumn. By the time of Jesus, Jews were following a 364-day calendar, which was a combination of both lunar and solar cycles. This had made dating difficult at times. For example, the Last Supper occurs at sundown on Friday in Matthew, Mark, and Luke, but on Thursday evening in John; in John, Jesus was crucified at the time when the Passover lambs were being slaughtered.

Jubilee The Year of Jubilee always began in the fall. It occurred every 50 years, and was considered a year of restoration. Hebrew slaves were to be released, debts were to be forgiven, and there was to be no planting or harvesting of crops. The Israelites were normally prevented from planting and harvesting every seven years, but the 50th year was considered special — the end of a period of seven seven-year periods.

Special Measurements of Time

Occasionally in the Bible, certain numbers or methods, when used as a means of measuring time, are significant.

Forty Forty appears to have special significance in the measurement of time, and many important biblical events revolve around it. In general, 40 is the Bible's figurative way of saying "a lot." (1) Days. During the flood it rains for 40 days and 40 nights (Gen. 7:4, 12, 17; 8:6). Moses is on the mountain for 40 days and nights (Exod. 24:18; 34:28; Deuteronomy 9). The spies spend 40 days in the land of Canaan (Num. 13:25; 14:34). The prophet Elijah takes 40 days and nights to reach the mountain of God in Sinai (1 Kgs. 19:8). Jesus fasts 40 days and nights in the wilderness (Matt. 4:2; Mark 1:13; Luke 4:2). Jesus spends 40 days with his disciples prior to his ascension (Acts 1:3). (2) Years. Both Isaac and Esau marry at the age of 40 (Gen. 25:20; 26:34). The Israelites eat manna in the wilderness for 40 years (Exod. 16:35), the time of the entire wandering in the wilderness (Num. 14:33-34; 32:13; Deut. 2:7; 8:2; 29:5; Josh. 5:6). The Israelites are subject to the Philistines for 40 years because of their sinfulness (Judg. 13:1). Many of the kings are said to have reigned for 40 years (David, 2 Sam. 5:4; Solomon, 1 Kgs. 11:42; Jehoash/Joash, 2 Kgs. 12:1; 2 Chr. 24:1; Saul, Acts 13:21).

Three The third day appears to have been understood as a day of deliverance. Isaac is saved from death at Abraham's hand on the third day (Gen. 22:4). Jonah is delivered from the belly of the fish on the third day (Jonah 1:17). Paul's sight is restored after three days (Acts 9:9), and Jesus was raised on the third day (Matt. 16:21; Mark 8:31; 1 Cor. 15:4). Other instances of the third day are also important. The Lord appears at Sinai to deliver the commandments on the third day (Exod. 19:11, 16). Jesus feeds 4000 on the third day (Matt. 15:32). In general, three represents completeness (e.g., Gen. 40:13, 20; 42:18; Exod. 15:22; Josh. 1:11; 2:16; Ezra 6:15; Esth. 5:1; Hos. 6:2; Matt. 12:40; Mark 8:2; Luke 9:22; Acts 27:19).

Luke Unlike some other Gospels, Luke appears to be especially interested in measuring time. Luke is the only Gospel that gives Jesus' age at the beginning of his ministry (Luke 3:23). In addition to the traditional ways of measuring time in the Bible, Luke reckons time according to the method used by the Roman government. For example, we are told that the census was conducted during the reign of the Emperor Augustus and the governorship of Quirinius (2:1-2). Again, in the 15th year of the reign of the Emperor Tiberius, John began his ministry (3:1-3).

Indeterminate and Eschatological Time

Periodically, indefinite measures of time are important. For example, the word "immediately" is important to the narrative of Mark (e.g., 1:12, 18, 20; 5:30; 6:25, 27, 45; 8:10; 9:24; 14:43). It is less important in the other gospels. Likewise, the phrase "the next day" is used 53 times in the Bible to measure time's passage.

Eschatology is the doctrine regarding the end of time. With respect to this way of measuring time, the Bible uses several phrases. (1) Many scholars associate the day of the Lord (or Yahweh) with the religious practice of the re-enthronement of the king. Others say that this day has only to do with the end of time. In the prophets, the day of the Lord is seen as a day of judgment and deliverance (Isa. 13:6; Jer. 46:10; Ezek. 13:5; 30:3; Joel 2:1-2, 11, 31; Obad. 1:15; Zeph. 1:14; Mal. 4:5). In the New Testament this day is associated with the second coming of Christ (1 Cor. 5:5; 1 Thess. 5:2; 2 Pet. 3:10). (2) An aeon is a long, distant, uninterrupted period of time, either in the past (Luke 1:70) or the future (John 4:14). As a Greek adjective, it means "eternal" (2 Cor. 4:18; Heb. 9:12, 15), but nowhere is a clear distinction made between a limited and unlimited duration of time. The time between Easter and the second coming acquires importance as the aeon between "no longer" (Gal. 3:25) and "not yet" (Phil. 3:13). (3) *Kairos* is the decisive point of time, also known as the fullness of time (Gal. 4:4). It can also be used as a technical term (Luke 21:8; Rev. 1:3; 22:10).

FOR FURTHER READING

Cullmann, Oscar. *Christ and Time.* Philadelphia: Westminster, 1964.

Dentan, Robert C., ed. *The Idea of History in the Ancient Near East.* New Haven: Yale University Press, 1955.

Marsh, John. *The Fulness of Time.* London: Nisbet, 1952.

Pedersen, Johannes. *Israel, Its Life and Culture,* I-II. London: Oxford University Press, 1926, 487-91.

Thiele, Edwin R. *The Mysterious Numbers of the Hebrew Kings.* Rev. ed. Grand Rapids: Kregel, 1994.

Michael Joseph Brown
and Calvin L. Marion

The Old Testament

The Five Books

The five books of Genesis, Exodus, Leviticus, Numbers, and Deuteronomy provide the foundation upon which the rest of Scripture builds. Their full significance, however, is generally not well appreciated by most Christians, who have but a very limited knowledge of their contents. Moreover, much in these books seems far removed from life in the 21st century, given that they were composed at least 2500 years ago. If we are to understand them, we need to appreciate not only the unique features of the ancient culture and history reflected in them, but also the distinctive way in which these things are described. The contents of these five books are more alien than we often imagine.

Unlike modern books, these books were originally given no titles, either individually or as a whole. Although it has been customary to refer to them collectively as the Pentateuch, this title originated long after they were composed. The English word "Pentateuch" derives from Greek *pentateuchos* ("five-volume work"), a title first used in the 2nd or 3rd century A.D. In Jewish tradition, the designation Torah, a Hebrew term meaning "instruction" although often translated "law," has long been applied. While "law" is used within the Pentateuch itself, it clearly refers there to only part of the book of Deuteronomy (Deut. 4:44-49; 27:2-8; 31:9-13; 31:24-26). Through time the name Torah gradually became associated with the whole of the Pentateuch, and, indeed, occasionally came to denote the whole of the Old Testament as "law" (cf. John 10:34; 1 Cor. 14:21).

This gradual process by which titles were given to the five books together may mean that they were not intended to be viewed as a self-contained work when first composed. As they stand, Genesis through Deuteronomy narrate an unfinished story. While the whole movement in Exodus to Numbers is toward the Israelite occupation of the land of Canaan, by the end of Deuteronomy this remains unfulfilled. Only in the book of Joshua, which follows, do we learn of the people's successful progress across the River Jordan into Canaan. Without the books of Joshua to Kings the Pentateuch is incomplete.

At first sight, it may seem that the Pentateuch does not hang together and is inconsistent in form and purpose. The short, episodic nature of the narrative, broken up by other literary forms (e.g., genealogies, poetry, laws, census lists), can be disconcerting and confusing. While modern works may be compared to a finely woven tapestry, the Pentateuch resembles a large collage formed from a wide variety of materials. The product of a very different age and culture, it is clearly a masterpiece of composition, for on closer inspection the Pentateuch displays a much greater degree of unity and structure than is often appreciated.

We encounter this literary collage first in **Genesis,** where major narrative blocks are separated by genealogies. Although two very different types of material are found here, they are cleverly bound together by the use of almost identical headings, traditionally translated "These are the generations of . . ." (Gen. 2:4; 5:1; 6:9; 10:1; 11:10, 27; 25:12, 19; 36:1, 9; 37:2). More important, both types of material are intimately linked by the overall purpose of Genesis. By carefully positioning narratives and genealogies side by side, Genesis traces a unique family line that moves from Adam down through many generations to the sons of Jacob.

The family history recorded in Genesis, especially in chapters 12 to 50, forms the basis for what follows. Central to this family history is a series of divine promises that focus on two main issues: nationhood and the blessing of the nations. The promise of nationhood (see Genesis 15) is made up of two elements: the promise of numerous descendants and the promise of land. Although intimately connected to the promise of nationhood, the divine promise of *international* blessing is linked to a future royal descendant of Abraham.

Nationhood

The divine promises of land and numerous descendants form the background to the book of **Exodus.** On the one hand, they explain the remarkable growth of the Israelite population and the threat that this in turn poses to the Egyptians. On the other hand, God's earlier commitment to the patriarchs Abraham, Isaac, and Jacob provides the motivation for his intervention to deliver the Israelites from bondage to Pharaoh.

Although the exodus from Egypt is essential for the divine promise of nationhood to be fulfilled, this is only part of a much larger process described in the Pentateuch. Centered on Mount Sinai, the Israelites enter into a unique covenantal relationship with God which results in his coming to dwell in their midst. To make this possible, the Israelites construct a special tent or tabernacle, which will become God's earthly dwelling place.

While the final chapters of Exodus describe the construction of the tabernacle, **Leviticus** addresses the complex issue of how to maintain the newly established relationship between God and the Israelites. Exceptional measures need to be taken to enable a holy God to live among people who are prone to sin. A specific family of priests is appointed and a new sacrificial system is introduced, by which the people may atone for their sins. Other customs are also inaugurated, all intended to ensure that the Israelites maintain a standard of holiness acceptable to God, something vital for their future well-being.

The whole process of covenant-making and tabernacle-building is undertaken in order to establish Israel as a holy nation, their holy status coming from God's presence among them. While this separates the Israelites from other peoples, the Pentateuch reveals that their priestly status is not entirely successful. Surrounding and interspersed throughout the account of the Israelites' stay at Mount Sinai is a series of events that highlight their tendency to disregard and disobey God. Foremost is the construction of a golden calf (Exod. 32:1-8), which is undertaken in spite of a specific warning against such activities (20:23). This, however, is no isolated incident, for the theme of Israel's rebellious nature dominates the book of **Numbers,** resulting in God's decision to destroy the entire adult generation that came out of Egypt. To underline the tragedy of this, the Pentateuch emphasizes that only after a delay of some 40 years are Joshua and Caleb permitted to enter the promised land; even Moses, the great champion and leader of the people, dies outside the land of Canaan.

In spite of the Israelites' rebelliousness, God remains committed to the promises that he made to the patriarchs. The final chapters of Numbers and the whole of **Deuteronomy** look forward with hope toward the successful entry of the Israelites into Canaan. Before this can happen, however, a new generation of Israelites must affirm their covenantal relationship with God. Deuteronomy is devoted to urging them to embrace it again or to remain faithful to it.

While Deuteronomy prepares the reader to expect that the Israelites will soon enter the promised land, its concluding chapters are less than optimistic about Israel's long-term future in the land. In a variety of ways, attention is drawn to the possibility that the Israelites, due to their own waywardness, will be exiled from the land of Canaan. Various warnings against neglecting God in the future have an ominous tone. In Deuteronomy 28, for example, the list of curses for disobedience (vv. 16-68) is much longer than the comparable list of blessings for obedience (vv. 3-14). Similarly, Moses is instructed to teach the Israelites a song (Deut. 32:1-43) that will be a "witness" against them for rejecting God and breaking the covenant (Deut. 31:19-22). These warnings eventually come to fulfilment when, as recorded in the book of Kings, first the northern kingdom of Israel is decimated by the Assyrians and then later the southern kingdom of Judah is conquered by the Babylonians.

The manner in which Deuteronomy anticipates both Israel's occupation of Canaan and her eventual exile is striking. With good reason, scholars have argued that the books of Joshua to Kings cannot be easily separated from Deuteronomy. The promise of nationhood and its fulfillment link the book of Genesis to those of Kings to form a continuous story that needs to be read and understood as such. Some even call this the Primary History.

The Blessing of the Nations

Although the blessing of the nations is the second major divine promise given to the patriarchs in Genesis, and may appear at first sight to be less important, such is not the case. It forms the climax to the divine call of Abraham in Gen. 12:1-3, is central to the covenant of circumcision in Genesis 17, which affirms that Abraham will be the father of many nations, and is repeated in the divine oath sworn by God to Abraham in 22:16-18. Moreover, it looks to make amends for the alienation of humanity from God that follows Adam's and Eve's rebellion in the garden of Eden.

Through these passages and others, the book of Genesis gradually develops a fuller picture of the promise of blessing. One of the most significant factors to emerge is this: the fulfillment of the promise is linked to the "firstborn" descendants of Abraham, through whom a future monarchy will be established. Remarkably, the patriarchal narratives in Genesis focus particular attention on the fact that this line does not always proceed through the one who is born first. Isaac takes precedence over Ishmael, Jacob over Esau, Joseph over his 10 older brothers, and Ephraim over Manasseh. As a result, Genesis concludes by focusing attention on Joseph's lineage traced through Ephraim. In this way the expectation is created that through the tribe of Ephraim God will fulfill his promise to bless the nations. With each generation in the patriarchal sequence royal expectation surfaces (e.g., Gen. 17:6; 23:6; 27:29), Joseph's dreams being part of a much larger motif (37:5-10).

Yet, although Genesis associates royalty with the lineage of Joseph traced through Ephraim, the story of Joseph is interrupted in Genesis 38 by an unusual story involving Judah and his daughter-in-law Tamar. The location and content of this incident are important to the development of the Genesis narrative. Focusing on the continuation of Judah's family line, and especially Tamar's unconventional role in this, the chapter ends by describing the birth of twins, Perez and Zerah — yet another example of a younger brother taking precedence over a "firstborn" brother. The extraordinary account of the birth of Perez is especially significant because he is the father of the royal line of David (cf. Ruth 4:18-22).

While the Genesis narrative as a whole gives greater prominence to the idea that Joseph's line through Ephraim will become a royal line, Jacob's blessing of Judah (Gen. 49:8-12), viewed together with the events described in Genesis 38, suggests that royalty may later be associated with Judah. Significantly, as Ps. 78:67-72 emphasizes, it was in the time of Samuel that God passed over the lineage of Joseph in favor of Judah. This major new development also coincides with the rejection of Shiloh, in the region of Ephraim, as the location for God's temple. The transportation of the ark of the covenant to Jerusalem confirms God's choice of David as the head of the dynasty through which the earlier divine commitment to bless all the nations of the earth will now be fulfilled.

Any attempt to understand the Pentateuch must take into account the agenda set by the divine promises of nationhood and international blessing. While nationhood becomes a reality at Mount Sinai and through the conquest and settlement that follow, the promise of international blessing remains basically unfulfilled throughout the Old Testament. But as the New Testament writers confidently assert, with the coming of Jesus Christ God's blessing begins to be imparted in a unique way to all the nations of the earth.

T. DESMOND ALEXANDER

Genesis

The book of Genesis (Greek for "origin, source") gets its name from its opening verse ("In the beginning . . ."), which introduces the account of God's creating the world. Yet Genesis focuses on many more beginnings: the beginning of the sin of humankind; the new beginning of the world through Noah; the beginning of separation into nations; the beginning of the chosen nation of Israel; and, encompassing all these beginnings, the beginning of God's redemptive work in the world. Genesis does not simply describe the past, therefore; it also anticipates the future: God's triumph over sin through Jesus Christ and the final renewal of God's original creation. Indeed, the overarching concern of Genesis consists in conveying the theological message that not even human sin will thwart God's ultimate purposes — a message made even clearer by a presentation not only of the faith but also of the foibles of the chosen nation's patriarchs.

More substantive evidence exists for locating the events of chapters 12–50 (the patriarchal narratives) in history than for the earlier chapters of Genesis. The names of the patriarchs, certain of their social customs (such as adopting a slave as one's heir), and their marriage practices argue that Abraham and his descendants lived in the early 2nd millennium B.C. Yet the primary concern of the book as a whole remains theological, not historical or scientific, in the modern sense, and the central theme of chapters 12–50 emerges clearly: God keeps his promises.

By the end of Genesis, however, God has only begun to fulfill the promises of land, progeny, and blessing that he made to Abraham. But by concluding with the death of Joseph, the last of the patriarchs, Genesis sets the stage for the emergence of the nation of Israel, which will both embody them and realize them fully.

Content

Genesis does not attempt to prove God's existence; rather, the book assumes it. By narrating creation, the fall, the flood, and the Tower of Babel, chapters 1–11 tell why God's actions in the rest of Genesis — and in the rest of biblical history — are necessary in the first place. Called the "prologue" to Genesis, these chapters deal with proto-history, events that took place long before the invention of writing. Undoubtedly passed down orally for many generations before being gathered and written down, the stories in Genesis 1–11 display many parallels with other ancient Near Eastern tales. Yet certain distinctives make the Genesis accounts stand out as unique in the ancient world: their insistence on a single, all-powerful God; their portrayal of God's loving concern for humans and his faithfulness to them; and the moral regression (not progression) of humankind.

Authorship

Genesis does not claim for itself a particular author or time of writing. The traditional view asserts that Moses authored Genesis, as well as Exodus through Deuteronomy (the "Five Books of Moses"), in the late 2nd millennium. Beginning in the 19th century A.D., scholars viewed Genesis as a compilation by three editors: the Yahwist (10th century B.C.), who used the name "Yahweh" for God; the Elohist (9th century), who used the name "Elohim" for God; and the Priestly writer (6th century), who added the "priestly" or "cultic" material. In more recent years, scholars have criticized and revised this "Documentary Hypothesis," but they have not reached a consensus concerning the date or authorship of Genesis.

Creation and Modern Science

The uniform and pervasive teaching of Scripture is that God, for his own glory, in a creative act of perfect freedom effected by his omnipotent word, brought into being out of nothing everything that exists, whether spiritual or material, invisible or visible, and that he has assigned to all of his creatures their distinctive attributes, behaviors, and relations. Scripture also uniformly and pervasively teaches that God, by his omnipotent word, upholds and sustains all of his creatures moment by moment in all of their attributes, behaviors, and relations. The regular patterns of the world are, in the view of Scripture, evidences of God's covenantal faithfulness toward creation and his people.

These twin biblical doctrines of creation and providence provide one of the foundations on which the modern scientific enterprise rests. For science even to be possible, the world to be investigated scientifically must be characterized by order, structure, and regular patterns of behavior, because science is the ongoing process of detecting by observation, experiment, and measurement, and of understanding through theoretical reflection, the patterns of composition, structure, behavior, and history in the natural world. It is in the biblical conceptions of creation and providence that we are given a worldview that accounts for the universe as an orderly cosmos.

Other worldviews provide no satisfactory grounds as to why the world should be orderly or why the world may not at any moment dissolve into disorder or even nonexistence.

Scripture also teaches that human beings are created and sustained by the triune God. It regards them as God's image-bearers, capable of intimate fellowship with the Creator, and also as representatives of God placed on earth with the task of ruling and developing it. The assignment of this status and task implies that humans possess the capacities for coming into fruitful contact with the world and developing an understanding of the observations made about the world. Although Scripture further teaches that the human race has rebelled against the Creator, that it stands in need of redemption through Christ, and that all human faculties have been marred and tainted by sin, it denies that we have altogether lost the capacity for careful observation and reasoned thinking about our surroundings.

The biblical doctrine of humanity, therefore, provides the other foundation on which the scientific enterprise rests. In order for science to function, the orderly world must be investigated. The world to be investigated needs to be observed, apprehended, and understood by those in the role of knowing investigators. Just as there is no science in a world of chaos, there is no science in a world without intelligent observers. It is the biblical worldview that accounts for human beings as potentially careful observers and reasoned thinkers. Other worldviews provide no satisfactory grounds as to why we should be able to make intelligible contact with our surroundings or even why there should be humans in the first place.

Modern theoretical science began to flourish during the 15th through 17th centuries, in part because the prevailing culture of western Europe gradually liberated itself from unbiblical modes of thinking that had strongly shaped the medieval worldview. That culture also began to work out the implications of the biblical conception of a cosmos freely created by God. The scientific achievements of the last five centuries have been breathtaking. Ever since Copernicus, Galileo, Kepler, and Newton led the way to an understanding of the motions of the solar system, scientific knowledge has grown at breakneck pace. Physicists have unraveled the structure of matter, detecting a host of exotic particles and determining the nature of their interactions. They have discovered the relationship of matter to various forms of energy, and both matter and energy have been interpreted in terms of quantum theory. The laws of thermodynamics, gravitation, relativity, and electromagnetic radiation rank high among the triumphs of physics.

By training increasingly

sophisticated instruments on the skies, astronomers have discovered billions of galaxies, gaseous nebulae, and untold numbers of stars in various stages of development, from main-sequence stars to black holes. They have begun to understand the formation of galaxies and planetary systems. Cosmologists have discovered that the universe is expanding, developed an understanding of the formation of the chemical elements in stars and novae, and worked out many details of the initial stages of the historical unfolding of the universe.

Chemical investigation led to the atomic theory of matter and establishment of the periodic table of the chemical elements. Chemists have discerned the principles of chemical bonding, chemical equilibrium, and reaction kinetics. In addition, they have determined the physical conditions of a wealth of chemical reactions and unraveled the internal structures and properties of a staggering number of crystalline solids, liquids, solutions, and gases.

Biological studies have led to an awareness of the geographical distribution of much of the world's fauna and flora, and microscopes have disclosed the existence of a vast array of one-celled organisms and viruses. Great progress has been made toward an understanding of the interrelationships among living creatures in space and time. Biochemists have unraveled many of the functions of structures within cells and the chemical behavior of the organic compounds that compose them. The basic principles of genetic inheritance have been discovered, and the functions of individual genes, human and otherwise, are presently being worked out.

Geological investigation has disclosed the broad outlines of the earth's internal structure, the physical processes that occur on earth's surface and in its interior, and the modes of origin of a vast array of rock types and minerals. Geologists have determined the age of the planet and deciphered the broad outlines of its very complex and dynamic 4.55 billion-year history that includes the formation of earth's crust and its transformation through episodes of mountain building, magmatic intrusion, volcanism, seismicity, erosion, sedimentation, metamorphism, ore and petroleum formation, continental drift, and sea-floor spreading. The rich storehouse of fossils preserved in the earth's sedimentary rock cover contains a record of the progress of life on earth from its beginnings, with prokaryotic organisms at least 3.5 billion years ago to the appearance of eukaryotes at least 2 billion years ago, to the first appearance of multicellular life forms about 700 million years ago, to the appearance of dinosaurs about 130 million years ago, to the appearance of hominids a few million years ago, and, finally, to the climactic appearance of anatomically modern humans within the past several tens of thousands of years.

The scientific view of the universe that has been developed through several centuries of research has been the fruit of the cooperative labors of both Christians and unbelievers. The fact that our picture of the world has been shaped in part by the contributions of outstanding Christian scientists such as Copernicus, Kepler, Maxwell, Faraday, Buckland, Dana, Gray, Kelvin, Pasteur, and a host of others serves as a warning against the cavalier dismissal of the scientific enterprise as though it were inherently opposed to Christianity and against the rejection of scientific conclusions that are incorrectly viewed as contradicting Scripture. Although many Christians reject the concept of an ancient universe or the evolution of life, these concepts are not inconsistent with the Genesis account of creation. Genesis 1 is not an eyewitness, journalistic report but a theological statement of God's creative work presented in a stylized ancient Near Eastern literary form that is full of imagery and numerological symbolism and that is consciously directed against the mythological notions of Israel's polytheistic neighbors.

Scripture is silent regarding the history of life. Although there remains much discussion about the mechanisms of change, the fossil record makes it clear that life has changed through time. Moreover, Scripture teaches neither a young earth nor creation of the world in six literal days. The idea of a young earth and a theory of flood geology are not demanded by the biblical text, and they are hopelessly incompatible with the wealth of physical evidence that God has placed on earth and that has been critically scrutinized in great detail by tens of thousands of geologists, including a host of Christians, for more than two centuries.

Centuries of scientific endeavor have resulted in a picture

of a very dynamic, almost inconceivably complex, magnificently varied, and gradually developing universe that is staggeringly vast both temporally and spatially. Rather than reject the modern scientific picture of the universe, the Bible-believer ought to rejoice that that picture provides overflowing warrant for sensing the incomprehensible greatness of God, praising him for this "theater of his glory," and appreciating and protecting his spectacular achievement.

DAVIS A. YOUNG

1:1–2:3 The Creation

Genesis begins with a theological account of the one, sovereign God's creation of the world. In this account, God first creates the heavens and the earth and then brings order to their originally chaotic state.

God needs only to speak, and his word is accomplished (cf. Ps. 33:6; John 1:1-3). As he reviews each new creative act, God declares it "good." The opening verses of Genesis thus "introduce" us to God. They tell us not only of his great power but also of his interest in order and goodness and of his relationship to his creation.

This opening section serves as a prologue to the book as a whole by setting the stage for the Creator's continued involvement throughout history. Not only does God create light, but also the lights — the sun, moon, and stars (days one and four); not only the sky and sea, but also the creatures that live in them — birds and fish (days two and five); not only land and vegetation, but also those that live on them and are sustained by them — animals and humans (days three and six).

The recounting of creation in this order is not meant to convey events chronologically so much as it serves as a literary device highlighting the final, seventh day, which God declares "holy" and on which he rests. Day seven stands alone as the culmination of God's work and later becomes associated with the Sabbath day of rest.

God's creation of humans emerges as the crowning event of his creative activity. He begins by addressing the angels in his heavenly court, "Let us make man in our image," implying humans' likeness to these supernatural beings as well as to God. Then, in addition to creating both male and female "in his own image," he blesses them and charges them to rule over the rest of creation. This unique relationship to the world around them and to God himself not only brings privileges but also the responsibility of relating to the world and functioning in it as God does (both imitating his creative and caring acts on the human level and resting from them; cf. Proverbs 8).

Further, God's command that humans "be fruitful and multiply" contrasts with other ancient Mesopotamian stories wherein the gods curtail human fertility to prevent their becoming too numerous. Not so the God of Genesis, who thus from the beginning makes sexual intercourse between husband and wife an integral part of his good plan. See "Other Ancient Accounts of Creation" (83-84).

The repeated phrase, "and there was evening, and there was morning," accounts for each "day" of creation according to the ancient Hebrew understanding in which a 24-hour day begins at sunset and ends with the following sunset. But "day" here may refer more generally to the periods of God's creative activity, not to 24-hour days, as the Hebrew word for "day" can connote differing lengths — and even indefinite periods — of time. Indeed, God created time itself, but according to the creation account not until the fourth "day."

The reader of Genesis — and of the rest of the Bible — should bear in mind that these God-inspired texts (see "Divine and Human" [15-17]) have primarily theological purposes and were not intended to reflect the discoveries of modern science, nor do they always give adequate information to answer the questions modern science poses (see "Creation and Modern Science"[78-80]). Rather, they reflect the social and religious beliefs and practices of the times during which they were composed. For example, the creation account in Genesis implicitly attacks polytheism, which deified the sun, moon, stars, sea, land, and animals, by declaring all of nature a mere creation of the one true God.

2:4–3:24 The Fall

Creation complete, the narrative quickly moves on to describe how this "good" world went bad. The writer first revisits day six by giving more details about the creation of humans. God first makes Adam (akin to the Hebrew word for "ground," used to refer to humankind throughout the Old Testament) from the "dust of the earth" and breathes life into him. God provides sustenance for Adam in a garden called Eden ("delight") but forbids him to eat the fruit of one of its trees — the tree of the knowledge of good and evil — for doing so would represent rebellion and lead to independence from the Creator.

Two of the rivers said to have branched out from Eden are the Tigris and Euphrates, which flow alongside and through modern Iraq, respectively, and empty into the Persian Gulf. But we cannot pinpoint an exact location for the originally idyllic garden.

After bringing all the rest of the creatures for Adam to name, God sees that Adam does not have a "suitable helper" — a situation God declares for the first time "not good." So he sets about providing a creature that would complement Adam. God creates a "woman" as Adam's equal in status (he creates both in his image), and by naming her, Adam also discerns and affirms her created uniqueness.

But the woman falls prey to the deceit of the serpent, the craftiest of the wild animals God has made. Significantly, she knows about God's restriction concerning eating from the "tree which is in the middle of the garden," but it is the serpent that tells her that its fruit would make her "like God, knowing good and evil." "Knowing" here does not denote the ability to *discern* between good and evil, but rather *choosing* either good and evil. Accepting the serpent's denial of the "death penalty" for the disobedience that God has warned of, the temptation proves too much, and the woman succumbs, with Adam soon to follow. Thus it comes out that God granted free will to humans from the start.

The serpent's deceit does not negate the humans' responsibility for disobedience, however, nor does it lessen its consequences. Knowing full well what has happened, God visits Adam and his wife in the garden and elicits their confession of sin, of which they are now fully aware. He then pronounces judgment — by cursing first the serpent (foreshadowing God's ultimate triumph in Christ over Satan and also offering redemptive hope for humankind), next the woman, and finally Adam — before evicting them from Eden, lest they also eat from the tree of life and live forever.

The serpent proven wrong, Adam and Eve (now finally named, meaning "living" or "life") find that the real curse does not lie in toiling "by the sweat of your face," or in suffering pain in childbirth, or in feeling the tension that sin introduced into their husband-wife relationship. Rather, the curse reaches a deeper level: loss of the intimate fellowship with their Creator that they had enjoyed in the garden. Yet though God "drove the man out" and stationed cherubim (ancient Near Eastern guardians of holy places) to guard against Adam and Eve's reentry into Eden, he did not forsake them. Indeed, before banishing them from the earthly paradise, God himself "made garments of skin" to clothe them.

4 The Spread of Sin

Now outside Eden, Adam and Eve begin to fulfill God's command to "be fruitful and multiply." Eve gives birth to two sons, Cain and Abel, who become a farmer and a shepherd, respectively. Both brothers present offerings to God from the fruits of their labor, but God accepts only Abel's. This rejection angers Cain, so God helps him to recognize what has made his offering unacceptable (perhaps lack of faith or the failure to give God the best of his yield), as well as what to do to correct the situation ("do well," v. 7).

But not even God's counsel prompts Cain to change his heart. His bitter resentment only intensifies, and he kills Abel. Thus the destructive effects of sin spread from the human-divine and husband-wife relationships to break down the bonds of brotherhood also. As with Adam and Eve in the garden, God queries Cain concerning the sin that he knows Cain has committed. But unlike Adam and Eve, who at least acknowledged their wrong action, Cain tries to evade the question. God confronts him with the facts and then sentences Cain to a life of vagrancy and nomadism.

God answers Cain's protest that the punishment is too harsh by again showing continued care for his rebellious creatures. He sets a "mark" on Cain as a sign of God's protection from those who might seek to kill him (the earth now appearing populated beyond the immediate family of Adam and Eve). Cain then proceeds even farther from Eden to the land of Nod (from Hebrew "wandering").

The genealogy of Cain's line in verses 17-26 portrays the development of human creativity in city building, music, and metalworking. But it also shows the intensification of the effects of sin by recounting the boast of Cain's descendant Lamech that he has "killed a man." Adam and Eve shifted the blame for their sin; Cain avoided confessing his altogether; and now Lamech actually takes pride in wrongdoing.

Yet hope for humankind's redemption appears again through the God-fearing line of Seth, the third son of Adam and Eve, whose genealogy appears in chapter 5.

5:1–6:8 The Line of Adam

Chapter 5 traces the beginnings of the genealogical line through which God will redeem fallen humanity. It mentions 10 fathers from Adam to Noah and gives similar information for each: his age at the birth of his first son, his life span thereafter, a mention that he had other children, and his age when he died. Only the verses about Enoch depart from this formula. Presumably because Enoch "walked with God," he did not die as the others did. Rather, God "took him" (cf. Elijah, 2 Kgs. 2:11).

The ages of the patriarchs mentioned here range from 777 to 969 years (for Methuselah) and seem incomprehensible today, although compared to other ancient Near Eastern documents (e.g., the Sumerian King List) these ages appear quite modest. Scholars have made various attempts to reconcile these numbers with a modern understanding of human life span. They include the suggestion that one "year"

meant a shorter period than 12 months; that the ages refer not to the life span of the father himself but to that of his clan; or that the numbers symbolize astronomical periods. Although the preciseness of the ages given may seem to argue for a literal accounting of years, numbers in the Bible often convey importance or symbolic significance rather than actual quantity.

Verses 1-8 of chapter 6 tell of spirit-beings (or angels; Job 1:6; 2:1) marrying human women, and these women bore them children who became "mighty men" (Nephilim, v. 4). This account parallels other ancient Near Eastern stories of divine-human marriages that produced superhuman progeny and implies the practice of sacred prostitution for the purpose of ensuring fertility (both of the soil in farming and in normal human marriages). But this grieves God greatly, and because humankind seems bent on pursuing wickedness, God resolves to destroy not only humans but also all other creatures that inhabit the earth and sky. As the extent of sin intensifies, so does the degree of God's judgment.

Once again, however, God appears willing to redeem, for in noticing one man's righteousness — Noah's — he plans an alternative to the total destruction of his originally good creation. Yet the balance of initiative-taking in the redemptive process continues to shift from God to humans to an even greater degree with Noah. God takes complete initiative in clothing Adam and Eve without any request on their part; Cain must protest before God "marks" him as protected; but Noah himself does the "finding" of "favor in God's sight," and in the verses to follow he must also in effect save himself (by building the ark), despite no mention of any particular sin on Noah's part. This shift may provide the first clue that by this point Noah shares the sin of humankind in general.

6:9–8:22 Noah and the Flood

Familiar today as a children's Bible story, the account of Noah and the flood finds a number of ancient parallels, the closest of which come from Mesopotamia. Although the stories appear to share some basic elements (e.g., survival of one family in a boat, the boat's coming to rest on a

Other Ancient Accounts of Creation

Accounts of creation occur among most peoples throughout the world. Culturally and chronologically, those closest to the biblical accounts may be found in written sources from ancient Egypt, Canaan, Anatolia, and Mesopotamia.

Egyptian sources are widely scattered, especially in coffin texts and pyramid texts. They generally represent the principle of water as original and the divine Atum as generating the earliest created gods, who then reproduce and create the world. The material principle is represented by Atum, who generates through masturbation, spitting, his own speech, or other physical techniques and thereby evolves into creation's diversity. The earliest created deities, Shu and Tefnut, represent life and order in the universe. Although there is significant variation, these principles occur repeatedly throughout the narratives of creation. They focus on the unity and harmony of life as part of the created order. They have little resemblance to the biblical account of creation.

No Canaanite accounts of creation have been found as yet in the archaeological excavations of the region, even at Ugarit, the site of so many myths dating from the Late Bronze Age. Several motifs associated with biblical creation accounts do occur in the myths, however. Foremost is the conflict between Baal and the monsters and forces of the sea, which some have compared with the God of Israel's victory over the sea and its monsters, but this is clearly not an account of creation. A fragment of the Babylonian Atrahasis Epic has been found at Ugarit (see below).

In the 4th century A.D. Eusebius of Caesarea copied excerpts from the work of Philo of Byblos (ca. 100), who claims to have translated from Phoenician ancient accounts of the Canaanite religion. In what may be an eclectic source with strong Hellenistic influence, the creation of the universe is ascribed to a gaseous chaos from which wind produced a moist matter. Creatures were produced or awakened as a result of a combination of rain, wind, thunder, and lightning. Figures identified as wind and night brought about people who settled in Phoenicia. The fragmentary material describes the building of a city, the introduction of various forms of culture, and especially the origins of the worship and cult of different deities.

From Anatolia, the older myths of Illuyanka present two versions of a battle between the storm-god and a serpent. While this shares some motifs with the Canaanite tradition of the struggles of the storm-god and the biblical accounts as discussed above, it falls short of a full creation story.

Mesopotamia produced the largest collection of creation stories yet found and also includes some stories featuring one or more parallels with the biblical stories of creation. The best known of these is Enuma Elish, which describes how Marduk achieved leadership among the gods and cut up the watery monster, Tiamat. From her body he created the heaven and the earth. A form of this myth, in seven tablets, represents a Neo-Babylonian account of the exaltation of their chief god, Marduk. No recognizable form of this story predates 1100 B.C., however.

The closest parallel with

Fragment of Enuma Elish, the Babylonian creation epic. *(British Museum)*

Genesis 1-11 and its account of the creation of humanity and the whole sweep of genealogy and narrative occurs in the Old Babylonian Atrahasis Epic, itself derived in part from the earlier Sumerian story of Enki and Ninmah. It says that people were created to do the work of obtaining food for the gods, thus allowing the gods to rest. Despite repeated claims by scholars, the Babylonian creation accounts and their predecessors have little in common with the Genesis accounts of creation, and they share few details (unlike the flood stories). Nevertheless, these accounts are closer than other ancient mythologies and point in some measure to a common heritage in West Semitic Amorite culture. The international period of the Amarna Age (14th century B.C.) remains a possible time for the exchange of such texts, although shared motifs date much earlier.

For Further Reading

Attridge, Harold W., and Robert A. Oden, Jr. *Philo of Byblos, The Phoenician History.* CBQ Monograph Series 9. Washington, D.C.: Catholic Biblical Association of America, 1981.

Day, John. *God's Conflict with the Dragon and the Sea: Echoes of a Canaanite Myth in the Old Testament.* University of Cambridge Oriental Publications 35. Cambridge: Cambridge University Press, 1985.

Hallo, William W., and K. Lawson Younger, Jr., eds. *The Context of Scripture,* 1: *Canonical Compositions from the Biblical World.* Leiden: Brill, 1996.

Heidel, Alexander. *The Babylonian Genesis: The Story of Creation.* 2nd ed. Chicago: University of Chicago Press, 1951.

Hoffner, Harry A., Jr., and Gary M. Beckman. *Hittite Myths.* SBL Writings from the Ancient World 2. Atlanta: Scholars, 1990.

Lambert, W. G. "A New Look at the Babylonian Background of Genesis." In *"I Studied Inscriptions from before the Flood:" Ancient Near Eastern, Literary, and Linguistic Approaches to Genesis 1–11,* ed. Richard S. Hess and David T. Tsumura. Sources for Biblical and Theological Study 4. Winona Lake: Eisenbrauns, 1994, 96-113.

RICHARD S. HESS

---

mountaintop after the rains had ceased, sending out of a bird to determine whether dry ground had reappeared), the biblical account may actually be intended to correct a number of notions in these extrabiblical tales. See "Flood Stories in the Bible and the Ancient Near East" (86-87).

The Mesopotamian epics of Atrahasis and Gilgamesh portray multiple gods causing a flood — which they appear unable to control — in an attempt to curb the population growth of humans, who are creating too much noise. Their discovery of survivors surprises them, and they therefore devise other ways of preventing humans from reproducing (miscarriage and female infertility).

Genesis, however, describes the saving act of the one and only God in intentionally preserving a remnant of his creatures through his own destruction of creation for its rebellion against him. God remains in control of the flood throughout and afterward charges Noah to "be fruitful and multiply, and fill the earth" (cf. 1:28). These examples comprise only some of the differences in detail and theological perspective between the biblical account and ancient Mesopotamian parallels.

Theologically speaking, the flood represents an opportunity to "begin again." God returns the earth (or at least that region familiar to Noah) to a nearly primeval state by eliminating all but a remnant of the creatures that inhabit land and sky, as well as by making land and water indistinguishable from one another again (the floodwaters covered even the mountaintops). God then "re-creates" the earth by causing a wind to pass over it; this wind stops the rain and allows the waters to recede from the land once again (cf. 1:1, where God's Spirit moves over the surface of the waters while the earth was still "formless and void"). The righteous Noah emerges from the ark as an Adam figure charged with repopulating the world born anew.

In 6:13-21 God informs Noah of his plans to destroy the earth and its inhabitants because of humankind's corruption. God gives Noah specific (but not complete) instructions for building an ark as a means of escape for Noah, his sons (Shem, Ham, and Japheth), the wives of all four, and male and female representatives of each species of bird, animal, and "creeping thing." Righteous man that he is, Noah follows

God's instructions to the letter; the group enters the ark, and the rains begin after seven days.

The 40-day deluge that follows, as well as the parallel Mesopotamian flood stories, may recall local flooding attested in the archaeological record of the area ca. 4000-3000 B.C. Alternatively, the stories may relate to the end of the Ice Age (ca. 10,000), when heavy rains combined with melting ice to cover previously dry land. The "forty days and forty nights" may symbolize a lengthy period of time rather than an exact number.

Having accomplished his purpose of blotting out "every living thing that was upon the face of the land," God remembers the remnant of his original creation in the ark, and he "restrains" the rains. As the waters recede, the ark comes to rest "upon the mountains of Ararat" (ancient Urartu). This designation refers to the general area of modern Armenia and bordering areas in Turkey and Iran, not modern Mount Ararat.

Despite determining on his own that habitable land has reappeared, Noah waits for God's command to exit the ark. His first act thereafter consists in building "an altar to the Lord" and making animal sacrifices. The offerings please God so much that he promises never again to destroy the earth's inhabitants. Thus it appears that Noah's sacrifices atone for the sins of humankind in general, not only sins specific to Noah himself.

9:1-17 The Covenant with Noah

The Noahic covenant is the first of several formal "agreements" between God and humans in the Old Testament. The basic covenantal formula finds parallels in ancient Near Eastern literature (particularly from the Hittites) wherein an overlord establishes a legal relationship with a vassal. In the biblical covenants with Noah and later Abraham, the nation of Israel (through Moses), and David, God establishes the terms of the agreement — his requirements, the blessings for fulfilling them, and the curses for not fulfilling them. Jesus introduces the new and final covenant (or "testament") — one of grace through faith in him. See "Covenants" (141-44).

The beginning paragraphs of chapter 9 restate God's command to Noah that he and his family repopulate the earth, as well as God's promise never again to destroy his creatures with a flood. Several new elements also appear here. First, God "gives" all other living creatures to Noah as food. The requirement that humans show respect for animals' God-given life by not consuming their blood, however, later becomes an important Hebrew food law (Lev. 3:17; Deut. 12:16-25).

At the same time, God makes clear the punishment for taking the life of a human: the death of the killer. While God allows humans to kill other creatures for food, he protects the unique status of those made in his image by pronouncing the severest of sentences for their murder.

Finally, God pledges to remember his promise (not only to humans, but also to "every living creature of all flesh") never again to destroy the earth with a flood, and he establishes the rainbow as the sign of his covenant.

9:18-29 The Sin of Ham

This short note reveals the continued presence of sin in the postflood world. For the first time we hear of personal shortcomings in Noah (drunkenness and self-exposure). His youngest son, Ham, outdoes his father in sin by failing to honor him. (Not only does Ham view his father naked, but he also tells his brothers about the scene.) Yet Noah curses Ham's offspring, Canaan, for the infraction, rather than Ham himself. The immoral Canaanites later emerge as one of the peoples whom God instructs the Israelites to annihilate when they enter the promised land. In contrast, the honorable action of Shem and Japheth in covering "their father's nakedness" meets with Noah's blessing.

10

The genealogies of Noah's sons are intended to account for the development of the separate nations and languages of the biblical world after the flood (although not all nations known in ancient Israel appear in them). Some of the relationships this "Table of Nations" lists

Flood Stories in the Bible and the Ancient Near East

The story of the Genesis flood featuring godly Noah, the ark, and animals captures the imagination of every Sunday-school child. This is so even if they are sheltered from the impressive aspect of judgment that is the account's purpose to reveal. The overwhelming magnitude of this act of judgment also imprinted the tale indelibly in ancient literature. Beginning centuries before the book of Genesis took shape, the story of a massive, destructive flood was circulating in written form in Mesopotamia. As the tale was read or, more often, recounted through long centuries of family and community gatherings, transformations occurred that shaped the details of the telling to the culture of the audience. Like Nathaniel Hawthorne adapting the myths of classical Greece to his 19th-century audience in the *Wonder Book,* or Walt Disney reshaping the *Arabian Nights* in the movie *Aladdin,* ancient audiences interpreted the epic event to reflect their particular worldview. Comparing the versions tells us more about the cultures in which they were preserved than about the trail of their literary evolution. Whether or not the Bible is related to the ancient Near Eastern material through exchange of literary or oral traditions, the similarities make it difficult to dissociate them. Most telling is the fact that both include the episode of birds being sent to determine when it is safe to leave the ark.

Because of the stature accorded the Bible among Christians, and its long history in Western thought, it generally serves as the standard against which other accounts are measured. Those who accept the Bible as God's word have no difficulty attributing reliability to the version preserved in Genesis. Nevertheless, study of the other versions can also offer windows of illumination into the ancient world.

Sources

The earliest flood story, originating before 2000 B.C., is in Sumerian and recounts the story of Ziusudra. The oldest Babylonian account is found in the Atrahasis Epic, dating to early in the 2nd millennium. The best-known version from Mesopotamia is imbedded in the Gilgamesh Epic and explains how Utnapishtim (the flood hero) gained eternal life (which Gilgamesh was seeking). These three accounts mark stages in a single tradition, as the similarities clearly indicate.

Comparisons

What Is God Like? In the biblical flood story God is distressed with the behavior of the people he has created. In the monotheistic setting of Genesis, it is his decision alone to send the flood and his decision to preserve Noah and his family alive. He is portrayed as sadly resigned to this course of action, the only appropriate response. The Mesopotamian versions derive from a polytheistic culture and therefore portray the gods deliberating in a council. The decision to send the flood is portrayed as a reaction of angry frustration. As the story progresses, the gods are seen to be deceptive, short-sighted, and absorbed in petty squabbles.

Why Was the Flood Sent? Genesis documents the downward slide of humanity from the idyllic garden to the chaotic anarchy that introduces the flood story. Violence has become an incorrigible way of life, and the waters are sent as an act of justice. In the Mesopotamian tradition, Atrahasis preserves most clearly the reasons for the flood. People had been created to do the work that the gods had tired of doing. But the growing population and the inevitable internal strife that resulted had made even more work for the gods, as people were constantly disturbing them with their troubles, demands, and requests. All of this is captured as the "noise" of humankind that led the gods to embark on a course of total destruction.

Why Was It That Someone Survived? Righteous Noah attracted God's attention as one who should not share in the fate of the rest of the population. Special provision was therefore made for Noah to be spared. Mesopotamian accounts agree among themselves that the plan of the gods was that no one should survive. Despite the fact that they were sworn to secrecy concerning the plans of the assembly, one of their number, Ea, successfully carried out a scheme to inform his favorite human of the coming flood. He then instructed him secretly how to keep his knowledge a secret from the gods and the rest of the people and survive the seven days of the flood. His boat resembled a temple and saved not just his family but also various skilled workmen so that the arts of civilization could be preserved.

What Was the Outcome of the Flood? When Noah disembarked from the ark, he offered a sacrifice of thanksgiving and received covenantal promises that God would preserve a certain order in the cosmos rather than opposing the chaos of human sin by the chaos of flooding waters. When the Mesopotamian flood heroes emerged, they offered a sacrifice of appeasement to calm the anger of the gods. The gods had forgotten how much they were dependent on humans to supply them with food (sacrifices) and gathered around hungrily, wondering how such a foolish decision (the flood) could have been made. The hero is grudgingly granted eternal life by the head of the gods, who remains miffed that word of the flood leaked out.

The flood stories from the ancient Near East and from around the world offer persuasive evidence that a flood of significant magnitude did in fact occur and was remembered. The accounts from the ancient Near East are closest to the biblical account and help us to see how the Israelites would have understood the entire event differently from their neighbors.

JOHN H. WALTON

may represent treaty partnerships rather than strict bloodlines. The generations of Japheth and Ham appear first, and then those of Shem, from whom God's chosen line develops. (A fuller account of Shem's genealogy appears in 11:10-26.)

11:1-9 The Tower of Babel

These verses represent a flashback to the time before the nations of the world became distinct from one another. They present the geographic scattering of peoples and the development of different languages as purposeful acts of God to prevent humans from trying, like gods, to ascend into heaven itself. Since all people speak the same language, they can and do cooperate in an effort to build a tower that will help them achieve this goal. But instead, God *descends* from heaven and foils their plans. In seeking self-reliance apart from God (by making a "name" for themselves), they lose the very thing they seek to protect — geographic solidarity (v. 4).

This story takes place in Shinar (ancient Sumer, or Babylonia), whose inhabitants achieved notoriety for the *ziggurat,* a multisto-

The main stairway of Ur-nammu's ziggurat at Ur, a temple "stair-tower" resembling the biblical tower of Babel. *(Wikimedia Commons)*

ried tower topped with a temple where humans supposedly met with the gods. Babel itself means "gate of god," but here the one true God turns the plan of humans to achieve semidivine status into a disaster of "confusion" (Heb. *balal,* perhaps a pun). Here again is a refutation of

Old Testament History and History Writing

History is a sequential and systematic reconstruction of the past. The Old Testament presents a continuous history of the people of Israel from its earliest beginnings until the events leading to the rise of Judaism. Until recently, the biblical books were universally accepted as presenting an accurate description of the history of Israel; but two issues have been raised regarding the biblical account. The first is whether the Old Testament is a reliable source for reconstructing the history of Israel. The second is whether the text provides an accurate record of Israel's past.

Modern-day historians make a genuine effort to present an accurate account of the events of the past. With the invention of the printing press, the preservation of records became easier, allowing more accurate reconstruction of historical events; but in ancient societies writers had fewer written records, which made critical evaluation of their sources more difficult. For this reason they simply passed on what they had received from others or reworked their material in order to communicate their particular message.

Historiography is the presentation of history based on the examination, evaluation, and selection of past historical events in order to communicate a message to a specific audience. In studying the history of Israel, the reader must understand the manner in which the writers selected, combined, and arranged the written and oral traditions of Israel in order to express theological concerns and religious emphases. Thus, in writing their history, the writers first selected the material that would provide support to their ideological views, evaluated their material in the light of their intended aim, and produced their work to communicate their views. This combination of the written and oral traditions, which gave birth to the narratives of the Old Testament, is the result of the theological purpose of the writers that shaped the collection of the material and the conclusions of their work. Thus the writer or writers are the interpreters of their material, and they selected and put together as a literary unit only those materials that gave meaning to their concern.

In the English Bible the books of Joshua, Judges, Samuel, and Kings are classified as historical books, but the Hebrew Bible regards them as prophetical books. These are commonly known as the Deuteronomistic History. The Deuteronomistic History is a good example of historiography. First, the writer or writers had a purpose: The Deuteronomic History is a prophetic interpretation of Israel's life from the period of the settlement in Canaan in the days of Joshua until the fall of Jerusalem in 587 B.C. The purpose of this history is to show that Israel was in exile as a result of their violation of the demands of the covenant (Deut. 28:47-52, 63-64). Second, the writers of this history used several written sources: the Book of Jashar (Josh. 10:13; 2 Sam. 1:18), the Book of the Acts of Solomon (1 Kgs. 11:41), the Books of the Chronicles of the Kings of Israel (1 Kgs. 14:19), and the Books of the Chronicles of the Kings of Judah (1 Kgs. 14:29). In employing these sources, the writers used only the material that was relevant to their purpose and that proved their position.

Third, the writer or writers of the Deuteronomistic History desired to communicate a particular message. This should be understood as history seen from prophetic eyes, the eyes of faith. It does not report national and international events for the sake of recording history for posterity. The Deuteronomistic History seeks to penetrate the meaning of events and explore their religious significance. The writers sought to provide a theological explanation for the destruction of Israel and Judah. The Deuteronomistic History shows that from the conquest of Canaan through the end of the monarchy Israel had violated the covenant, and that violation demanded divine punishment. According to the writers, the political destruction of the nation did not indicate divine weakness but rather demonstrated the power of Yahweh. Yahweh had sent his prophets to warn the people of their failure to keep the covenant (Deut. 28:15, 36-37, 49-52, 63-65; 2 Kgs. 23:26-27), but the people did not listen, and as a result Israel was was carried into captivity in 722 and Judah in 587 (2 Kgs. 17:7-23; 24-25).

The book of Deuteronomy serves as an introduction to the Deuteronomic History and provides the theological and ideological foundation for the proper understanding of the history of Israel. According to the Deuteronomistic historians, Israel's rejection of Yahweh brought the nation to its tragic end. Israel had violated the two requirements of the covenant: they had abandoned Yahweh to serve the gods of Canaan and had oppressed members of the community in violation of the demands of the covenant.

Since historiography represents the ideological views of the writers, many scholars wonder whether a true history of Israel can be written today. In some circles, the ideological presuppositions of the writers become more important than the historicity of the text or of the sources used. The tendency among some scholars is to deny the historicity of most biblical narratives unless they are backed by external evidence, such as archaeology or extrabiblical documents. This skepticism derives from reconstruction of the archaeological evidence or from theories based on literary analysis or social-scientific models. The writers of the Old Testament may have had their theological and ideological biases, but this does not necessarily mean that they were fabricating history or that their writings are without any factual basis.

CLAUDE F. MARIOTTINI

the polytheism prevalent in the ancient Near East.

11:10-26 The Generations of Shem

The text now returns to the chosen line of Shem and traces in abbreviated form the generations from Shem to Abram (Abraham). The form of the genealogy appears similar to that of Adam in chapter 5. It lists the patriarchs' ages (now much younger) at the time their first sons were born, the number of years the fathers lived subsequently (now far fewer), and the fact that they had other children. Beyond the generational details, however, the genealogy serves the broader purpose of linking the life of Abraham and the subsequent patriarchal narratives (Genesis 12–50) to the preceding theological history of the world.

11:27-32 The Generations of Terah

A descendant of Shem and the father of Abram, Terah receives the greatest individual attention in the genealogical record of Genesis 11. Here we learn that Terah's family lived in "Ur of the Chaldeans" (in modern southern Iraq), that Abram married Sarai (Sarah) but that she could not conceive a child, and that Terah set out from Ur with Abram, Sarai, and his orphaned grandson Lot to live in Canaan. In view of Sarai's barrenness, Abram may have adopted Lot with the intent of making him his heir. The group travels 560 miles northwest through the Fertile Crescent along the Euphrates River as far as Haran (eastern Syria), where they settle and where Terah later dies. The family's situation in Haran sets the stage for the patriarchal narratives that follow and that include stories from the lives of Abram (Abraham), Isaac, Jacob, and Jacob's 12 sons (roughly dated to the Middle Bronze Age, ca. 2000-1550; see "The Patriarchs and Their Neighbors" [104-5]).

12:1-9 The Promise to Abram

Well before his father dies, Abram receives a call from God to leave his father's house for a land that God does not initially specify. For Abram to obey this command meant forfeiting his rightful earthly inheritance (Terah's animals, household possessions, and, most important, land), in addition to Terah's blessing before he died. God promises to supply Abram with all that Terah could bequeath to him and more: land, children (particularly significant in view of Sarai's barrenness), and blessing. In particular, the promise of nationhood implies that

Abram will have numerous descendants and occupy a particular land. God's words reach a climax in the statement that through Abram/Abraham all the nations of the earth shall be blessed. This theme of blessing is especially important throughout Genesis and beyond. New Testament writers will later hold Abram up as an example for his faith in trusting God for his future (Romans 4; Galatians 3; James 2).

Abram departs from Haran with Sarai, Lot, the rest of his household, and all of his possessions bound for Canaan (modern Israel, Lebanon, and southern Syria), 450 miles southwest of their home. Upon arriving at the site of Shechem, God declares Canaan (inhabited by and named after the descendants of Ham's youngest son) to be the land he has promised to Abram and his descendants. Although he has not yet seen the complete fulfillment of God's promise, Abram honors God by building altars and worshipping him at Shechem and near Bethel before continuing toward the Negev ("south").

12:10-20 Abram's Deception

Already inhospitable terrain for farming, the Negev and presumably the rest of Canaan are in the midst of a famine. This further test of Abram's faith for God's provision does not result in such commendable behavior, however, and Abram leaves the promised land for Egypt in his search for food. His faith wavers even more when he fears the Egyptians may kill him to take his beautiful wife, and so he convinces Sarai to reveal only their brother-sister relationship (according to 20:12, Sarai and Abram were half-siblings). Pharaoh himself takes Sarai into his harem and gives Abram a wealth of servants and animals as a dowry.

God must again intervene to stop human sinfulness; this time, however, he corrects the situation by punishing not the deceiver but the deceived. The "great plagues" God sends upon Pharaoh and his household result not only in the release of Sarai from Pharaoh's harem, but also in Abram's and his family's escorted exit from Egypt as a far wealthier household than when they had arrived.

This entire episode, from the famine in

Canaan to Abram's descent into Egypt and his subsequent departure with a wealth of possessions, foreshadows the great exodus of Abram's descendants under Moses.

13 Lot Separates from Abram

Abram leads his household back to the Negev and ultimately back to Bethel, where again he worships God at the altar he had built. But the land there cannot easily support all of Abram's and Lot's flocks, herds, and household members. As a result, strife between their herdsmen develops, so Abram proposes that they separate. Although Abram's position as family patriarch would have entitled him to take the best for himself, he shows renewed faith in God's promises by allowing Lot first choice of the surrounding territory. Predictably, Lot chooses to move eastward to the fertile Jordan Valley, and Abram settles in Canaan proper. Lot's selfish choice brings him to live in the midst of the "exceedingly wicked" people of Sodom. But God rewards Abram's selflessness and faith with an intensification of his promises: he will give Abram and his descendants "all" the land Abram sees; they will possess it "forever"; and God will make Abram's descendants as innumerable as "the dust of the earth."

14 Abram Rescues Lot

The archaic personal and place names recorded here hail mostly from Abram's former homeland north and east of Canaan. In this narrative, four kings from these areas join forces to quell a rebellion of their vassals who live in the "cities of the plain" (possibly on the eastern shores of the Dead Sea, according to archaeological evidence). The cities include Sodom and Gomorrah, whose fleeing vassal kings fall into the tar pits of the valley of Siddim (the Dead Sea valley, perhaps at its southern end, where petroleum oozes to the surface). The invading armies capture Lot and his household and transport them north (apparently with the rest of Sodom's defeated population; cf. v. 21) on their march homeward.

A survivor of the invasion alerts Abram to the fate of his nephew. In keeping with clan loyalties, Abram leads a meager army of his own 318 "trained men" on a mission to rescue Lot. The group pursues the invaders to Dan (the northernmost city of ancient Israel) and then even farther past Damascus, where they defeat the entire northern coalition and return home not only Lot and all of his possessions, but the rest of Sodom's inhabitants as well.

And now the theological point of relating this story emerges. Melchizedek, the king of Salem ("peace"; probably Jerusalem), who also serves as "a priest of God Most High" (his name means "my king [is] righteous"), honors Abram with a feast and pronounces a blessing on him for defeating his enemies. As God promised Abram in 12:3, Melchizedek can thus expect a blessing from God. (Indeed, Abram gives Melchizedek one tenth, or God's portion, of what he had taken from his enemies; cf. Ps. 110:4, which remembers Melchizedek as a forerunner of the Davidic line, and Hebrews 5–7, which venerates him as a forerunner of the Messiah.) But the king of Sodom, who clearly owes Abram the greater thanks, shows only disdain for him, a curse that will come back on him in chapter 19.

15 God Seals a Covenant with Abram

Up to this point, Genesis has emphasized Abram's obedience to God's commands and his faith in God's promises. Chapter 15 now portrays Abram's relationship to God in a more personal light. In a vision, God acknowledges Abram's fears. Ten years have elapsed since Abram responded to God's call in Haran, yet his adopted slave, Eliezer of Damascus, remains Abram's only heir-apparent, and Abram does not possess "all the land" as God promised he would. God reassures Abram that he will indeed father an heir from whom his descendants will become innumerable as the stars. Abram's response, "[Then] he believed [= 'continued believing'] in the Lord; and the Lord reckoned it to him as righteousness" (v. 6), will later become central in Paul's message of salvation by faith (Gal. 3:6ff.), not works.

God answers Abram's request for confirmation concerning his possession of the land by sealing the covenant in a ceremony involving sacrificial animals (cf. Jer. 34:18), which represent Abram's descendants, as well as smoke and fire, which represent God's presence with these children of Israel (cf. the pillars of fire and cloud in Exod. 14:24). In addition, God makes more specific his promise regarding the land by designating its geographical boundaries. Yet he also reveals his own patient nature — and the patience he expects Abram to display — when he speaks about the fulfillment of his promises. God indicates that he will allow Abram's descendants to live as oppressed strangers in a foreign land for 400 years but that he will indeed deliver them from their enslavement. Still he will not permit them to take possession of the promised land until he has given all Canaan's inhabitants due time to repent from their sinfulness against him.

16 Sarai and Hagar

In the story of Sarai's complaint against God concerning her barrenness and her consequent suggestion that Abram father a child for her by her Egyptian servant Hagar (accepted practice in the ancient Near East), Sarai appears more concerned with her own cultural disgrace as a childless wife than with the fulfillment of God's promise of descendants to Abram. When Hagar conceives, Sarai discovers that her plan does not produce the results she had hoped for (Hagar "despises" her), and her selfish motives become more obvious in her harsh treatment of Hagar.

The maltreated Hagar flees toward home ("the road to Shur" [v. 7] leads to Egypt), but God short-circuits this plan too. Through an angel, he instructs Hagar to return to her mistress and promises innumerable descendants to her as he has to Abram. Hagar obeys and bears a son, Ishmael ("God hears"), who will not be given to Sarai but who will remain her own.

17 An Everlasting Covenant

Several characteristics of this chapter mark it as an important turning point in the story of Abram. These include the number of God's speeches and the fact that they not only detail but also ratify God's promises to Abram; the careful attention paid to dating this episode

(vv. 1, 17, 24); God's giving new names both to Abram (Abraham, "father of many") and Sarai (Sarah; both mean "princess"); and the introduction of a permanent sign of the covenant.

Thirteen years have passed since the birth of Ishmael (cf. 16:16) — ample time for the now 99-year-old Abram to believe that Ishmael represented the fulfillment of God's promise to him of progeny (cf. 17:18). But now God establishes a new covenant focused on international blessing, which will require a deeper faith on Abram's part. The intensification of God's promises comes first. (Abraham will become not simply a great nation but father of "many nations," and God will extend the covenant to Abraham's descendants; v. 8.) Then God establishes the covenant's permanence by requiring Abraham and all the males of his household (including all relatives, slaves, and freemen) to undergo circumcision (common practice in the ancient Near East, but here given unique significance as a sign of God's covenant). Finally, God requires Abraham to trust him for a miracle — Sarah's conceiving at age 90 and bearing Abraham the son through whom God will fulfill his promise of innumerable descendants. Despite Abraham's incredulous laughter at this thought, he obeys God promptly and completely by submitting himself and all males of his household to the rite of circumcision.

18:1-15 Abraham Hosts God Himself

God demonstrates his increasingly intimate relationship with Abraham by visiting him at his home. Initially, the Lord does not make himself known to Abraham, but Abraham extends him and the two other "men" (angels; cf. 19:1) with him the kind of generous hospitality typical in ancient Near Eastern culture (and of modern Middle Eastern nomads). Verse 9 gives the first clue that these strangers were not mere men: they inquire after Abraham's wife by name. After specifying when God will fulfill his promise to Abraham concerning Sarah's bearing him a son (cf. 17:16), the Lord gives another clue to his identity by showing that he knows of Sarah's laughter upon overhearing the announcement of her impending pregnancy. Then the Lord reveals himself to Abraham and Sarah, and she

becomes so fearful that she denies her doubtful response.

18:16-33 Abraham's Plea on Sodom's Behalf

Although God has promised never again to destroy all living creatures (cf. 9:11-17), he has not pledged to refrain from destroying sinful humans he deems deserving of harsh judgment. Here God determines to find out just how sinful the inhabitants of Sodom and Gomorrah have become, and he shares his purpose with Abraham, whom he has "chosen" to uphold righteousness and justice. Apparently aware of Sodom's reputation for wickedness, Abraham immediately concludes that God plans to destroy this city for which God's two angels have now departed. Presumably out of concern for his nephew Lot and in further demonstration of his intimate relationship with God, Abraham begins to question God's justness (v. 23) and even rebuke God for the action he presumes God will take against the Sodomites without distinguishing between the righteous and the unrighteous (v. 25). Abraham's assumptions about God's plans for Sodom turn out to be correct, but God responds favorably to Abraham's pleas by agreeing not to destroy the city if at least 10 righteous people are living there.

19:1-29 The Fulfillment of the Curse on Sodom

The two angels who had accompanied the Lord on his visit with Abraham now arrive in Sodom to ascertain the truth about the conduct of its inhabitants and carry out God's judgment, if necessary. They first encounter Lot, who extends the same generous hospitality Abraham had offered them previously and who persuades them to lodge with his family for the night. But soon all the men of the town gather at Lot's home with the intent of gang-raping Lot's guests. This violates the almost sacred rules of hospitality (evidenced by Lot's offer that the mob have their way with his own virgin daughters instead of with his guests) and raises the issues of homosexuality and nonconsensual sex (rape). The participation of all the men in the city combined with the gravity of their intended offenses gives the angels all the evidence they need to carry out God's judgment on the wicked city.

Lot's refusal to comply with the Sodomites' demand angers them greatly, and the angels must rescue Lot from the mob before whisking him away from the doomed city. After forcibly removing Lot, his wife, and daughters from Sodom in an act of compassion, the angels give Lot and his family permission to flee to the town of Zoar rather than escaping to the mountains. The means by which God rains down "brimstone and fire" on Sodom (the judgment of which ch. 14 anticipates) and Gomorrah (presumed to deserve the same fate; cf. 18:20) sounds like a natural disaster, perhaps caused by exploding gases released by seismic activity common all along the Great Rift Valley, wherein the Jordan River Valley and the Dead Sea lie. Apparently still longing for her home in Sodom, Lot's wife disobeys the angel's command not to "look back" and so becomes a "pillar of salt," reminiscent of salt-rock formations typical around the Dead Sea.

19:30-38 Lot's Disgrace

Like the righteous Noah, Lot realizes deliverance by God from sure death; but also like Noah, he suffers disgrace at the hands of his children. Childless and without husbands, Lot's daughters dishonor him by ignoring incest taboos in an effort to become pregnant by their father. Both meet with success and give birth to boys, whose descendants later become the Ammonites and Moabites of Transjordan.

20 Abraham Repeats a Deceit

In keeping with his seminomadic lifestyle, Abraham once again moves south and settles for a time in Gerar, a city in the Negev near the Mediterranean coast. Fearful that the Canaanites here will kill him in order to obtain Sarah, he reveals only his (half-)sibling relationship to her (v. 12), and Abimelech ("my father [is] king"), king of Gerar, takes Sarah for his wife. But God reveals to Abimelech in a dream that Sarah and Abraham are married, and the God-fearing king returns Sarah to her husband without having "touched her." In addition,

Crystalized salt formation near the southern end of the Dead Sea. *(Phoenix Data Systems, Neal and Joel Bierling)*

Abimelech gives Abraham money, animals, servants, and an offer that the household settle in any part of his domain that Abraham pleases. The story recalls 12:10-20, which took place in Egypt; yet rather than Abimelech's expelling them from his territory (as did Pharaoh), the king welcomes Abraham to continue his sojourn there. Once again, Abraham's doubt in God's protection proves unfounded, and again God not only overlooks Abraham's lack of faith but also blesses Abraham despite the deceit he has perpetrated.

21:1-21 Isaac's Birth and Ishmael's Dismissal

Now God begins to fulfill concretely his covenantal promises of land and progeny to Abraham. No literary fanfare attends the announcement of Isaac's birth — a surprising omission considering the suspense built up over this event in the previous chapters. Instead, verses 1-5 succinctly underline God's miraculous fulfillment of his promise (by emphasizing Abraham's and Sarah's advanced age) and Abraham's consistent obedience to God (by naming his new son "Isaac" [17:19] and by circumcising him in accordance with the covenant God established with Abraham).

As for Sarah, anger replaces her joy over Isaac's arrival when after some time she observes Hagar's son, Ishmael (now a young teenager), mocking Isaac. (Ishmael is essentially "laughing at" Isaac, whose name means "he laughs.") As a result, Sarah refuses to tolerate any notion that Ishmael will share in her own son's rights as Abraham's heir, and she demands that Abraham "drive out" Hagar and Ishmael (cf. 16:6). God relieves Abraham's initial distress over sending the two away by promising to "make a nation" of Ishmael's descendants also; yet God makes clear that Isaac's line will represent the fulfillment of his covenantal promise.

Hagar and Ishmael find themselves in dire straits wandering in the southern wilderness, where they have run out of water. But the angel of the Lord repeats to Hagar the promise God made to Abraham concerning Ishmael, and God responds to Ishmael's crying by revealing to his mother a source of water. Verse 20 confirms God's faithfulness to Ishmael as he grows and continues to live in the southern desert. (The wilderness of Paran extends south into the Sinai Peninsula.)

21:22-34 Abraham Secures Water Rights

At first, Abraham's dispute with Abimelech over a well might seem trivial. But even today a reliable source of water proves essential to the life and livelihood of a herdsman dwelling in the dry desert of southern Israel, so Abraham's complaint that Abimelech's servants have seized his well actually constitutes a matter of great significance. Though Abraham and Abimelech settle the problem in a friendly manner, the situation foreshadows the many troubles with the Philistines that Abraham's descendants will encounter from the time of the judges onward.

Yet the story's real significance is theological, for Abraham's securing of water rights in a legal, covenant-bound agreement with Abimelech represents the first step in the fulfillment of God's promise of land to Abraham. For Abraham to own the well at Beer-sheba ("well of seven," for the seven lambs Abraham gave Abimelech to seal the oath) officially meant that he could now claim a part of Canaan, however small, as his. Abraham recognizes the importance of acquiring the well legally by com-

memorating the agreement with a monument (a tamarisk tree) at Beer-sheba and by worshiping God there.

22 God Tests Abraham's Faith

Chapter 22 straightforwardly portrays both God's shocking command that Abraham sacrifice his beloved "only son" (the only son through whom God will fulfill his promise to Abraham) as well as Abraham's unquestioning obedience. God calls, and Abraham answers — immediately and completely, just as he had obeyed God's command to leave Haran for the "land that I will show you" (12:1). He now travels with Isaac to the land of Moriah ("the Lord will provide") in search of the mountain "of which I will tell you" (according to tradition, the Temple Mount in Jerusalem; cf. 2 Chr. 3:1) full of fear and dread — not only of the impending death of his son at his own hands, but also of the dashing of his hope in God's promise of descendants through Isaac. Yet in the story Abraham appears unwavering in faith and unflinching in courage.

God rescinds his own order in the nick of time. With Isaac lying bound on the altar atop the wood arranged for the burnt offering and with Abraham's hand poised to kill his son with a knife, the angel of the Lord issues an urgent call for Abraham to abort the plan. The angel then announces that Abraham has passed this supreme and final test of his "fear" of God. On his own initiative, Abraham offers a "ram caught in the thicket" as a burnt offering in place of Isaac, and God reconfirms his promises to Abraham for the last time.

The story also shows that God requires more of himself than he did of Abraham. For Abraham, obedience to the command to sacrifice his son constituted a test of faith (cf. Heb. 11:17-19); God's provision of the ram, a costly sacrifice, foreshadows God's real sacrifice of his Son on the cross to meet his own righteous requirement to implement fully the covenant of grace with humankind.

Foreshadowing God's fulfillment of his covenantal promise to Abraham regarding making him a "great nation," the chapter ends with a short genealogy of Rebekah, who later becomes

Isaac's wife and bears him the son (Jacob) from whom the nation of Israel receives its name (32:28).

23 Abraham Buys a Tomb for Sarah

Sarah's death in Hebron (20 miles south of Jerusalem) occasions Abraham's acquisition of additional land rights in Canaan (cf. 21:22-34). Abraham himself acknowledges that he remains "a stranger and a sojourner" among the inhabitants of the land God promised to him (v. 4). After grieving for Sarah, Abraham negotiates buying a burial site for her in a bargaining process that parallels Hittite legal proceedings. The locals (probably not Hittites from Asia Minor, but Semites, as indicated by their names) generously offer Abraham his choice of their graves, and Abraham responds with a request that he buy the cave of Machpelah. The cave's owner, Ephron, offers to give to Abraham not only the cave but also the field in which it lies, but Abraham insists that he purchase them (probably so that he can lay legal claim to them). Ephron eventually names his price, and with no further bargaining Abraham pays the hefty sum of 400 shekels of silver, after which he receives the deed to the property.

Certain elements of this story confirm the legally binding nature of the purchase: the location at which the parties made the agreement (the city gate), the presence of witnesses (v. 18), the weighing out of money, and the type of currency exchanged ("commercial standard"; v. 16). After establishing Abraham's legal ownership of the field and specifying that Abraham also owned everything that fell within the "confines of its border," Abraham buries Sarah in the cave of Machpelah (which becomes their family tomb; 49:31). Together these elements establish the certainty of God's continuing to fulfill his promise of land to Abraham.

24 Isaac Marries Rebekah

With the fulfillment of God's promises of land and progeny in progress, the narrative emphasizes that God has also been fulfilling his promise of blessing to Abraham "in every way" (v. 1). Abraham is now nearing the end of his life, so the focus begins to shift to Isaac, through whom God will extend his covenantal promises to Abraham.

Abraham instructs his eldest and most trusted servant to take an oath (signified by the servant's placing his hand under Abraham's thigh; cf. 47:29) that he will find a wife for

Interior of the Dome of the Rock built on the site of the Jerusalem temple and considered the place where Abraham was prepared to sacrifice Isaac. *(Richard Cleave, Pictorial Archive)*

Isaac, but several restrictions apply. First, she must come from among Abraham's relatives back in Mesopotamia, not from among the Canaanites. Second, she must consent to marry Isaac sight unseen, for Abraham forbids his servant to take Isaac on the journey. Third, she must agree to leave home and family to make her home in Canaan (i.e., she must display a faith similar to Abraham's when he received God's call to leave Haran).

Faithful to his master's charge, the servant travels to Nahor (perhaps Haran or a town near it). Also faithful to God, the servant first prays that God will grant him success in his mission. When Rebekah (Isaac's distant cousin) shows herself to embody the answer to his prayers, it becomes clear that God himself has orchestrated the search as another step toward fulfilling his covenantal promise to make Abraham a great nation.

Rebekah's brother Laban (who serves as chief host and negotiator) and her father Bethuel agree to the arranged marriage between Rebekah and Isaac in acknowledgment that God has guided the process and ordained their union. Abraham's servant recognizes God's faithfulness and seals the betrothal agreement by giving bride-price gifts to Laban, Rebekah, and her mother. Yet Rebekah still has some say in her own future (cf. v. 58). Demonstrating that she indeed represents God's choice of a wife for Isaac, Rebekah agrees to depart for Canaan without delay, and when the two finally meet, not only does Isaac marry Rebekah, but he loves her as well.

25:1-11 The Death of Abraham

Verses 1-4 tell of Abraham's descendants through his third wife, Keturah. Their marriage may not necessarily have taken place after

the events recorded in chapter 24, but possibly many years prior. In any case, these verses show the relationship of the (later) Israelites to neighboring peoples (such as the Midianite traders who lived in the Sinai Desert and in Transjordan) and underscore that Abraham (as also Sarah) would give rise to many nations, as God promised in chapter 17.

Before he dies, Abraham not only bequeaths to Isaac "all that he [has]," but he also sends away any potential rival heirs to his estate and to the covenantal promises God made to him. Isaac and Ishmael join together in honoring their father by burying him in the family tomb in Hebron, but verse 11 makes clear that it is Isaac on whom God's covenantal blessings subsequently fall (cf. 17:20-21). After his father's death, Isaac settles in the south by Hagar's well (cf. 16:14).

25:12-18 Ishmael's Descendants

This account of Ishmael's descendants shows God's fulfillment of his promises both to Hagar (to "greatly multiply" her descendants [16:10])

Tomb of the Patriarchs at Hebron, encompassing the cave of Machpelah, burial place of Abraham and Sarah, Isaac and Rebekah, Jacob and Leah, and Joseph. *(Phoenix Data Systems, Neal and Joel Bierling)*

and to Abraham (that his son Ishmael would "become the father of twelve princes" [17:20]), as well as the angel's prophecy that Ishmael would struggle against his relatives and live apart from them (16:12).

25:19-34 Isaac's Descendants

A much more detailed account of Isaac and his descendants (God's chosen line) follows that of Ishmael. At the beginning, this section notes Rebekah's barrenness (cf. Sarah's), Isaac's prayers on her behalf (cf. Abraham's faith), and God's finally allowing her to conceive (as he did Sarah). Rebekah's double blessing of twins meets with problems from the start, however, and the struggle between the two boys in her womb continues at birth and afterward in accordance with the prophecy that "the older shall serve the younger" (v. 23; cf. Ishmael's subservience to his younger brother Isaac). The elder Esau grows into an outdoorsman, while the younger Jacob prefers sticking close to home. True to his prenatal personality and to his apparently calculating nature, Jacob the "supplanter" bargains a bowl of soup for his brother's birthright, and so he acquires the rights of a double portion of the inheritance and blessing normally bestowed by a dying father on his eldest son. Esau's later tears over the consequences of his shortsightedness cannot correct his earlier mistake (27:38).

26:1-33 Isaac's Sojourn with the Philistines

The events recorded here parallel closely those involving Abraham during his sojourn in the south (ch. 20; 21:22-34). For example, Abimelech and Phicol again appear as king of Gerar and commander of the army, respectively; Isaac lies about his relationship to his wife out of fear for his life; God blesses Isaac despite the deception; and a dispute between Isaac and the herdsmen of Gerar occurs concerning water rights. Despite these similarities, the details of these snapshots into Isaac's life make clear that this account reflects different events, as when verse 1 distinguishes the current famine from the one that occurred in Abraham's days; Isaac travels north to Gerar rather than south to Egypt; and

Abimelech never takes Rebekah into his harem. At least some of these events may have taken place before Rebekah gave birth to Jacob and Esau (ch. 25).

God promises Isaac that, through him, he will continue to fulfill the "oath" he swore to Abraham (vv. 3-4; cf. 22:17-18). Indeed, Isaac's great prosperity leads Abimelech to acknowledge God's presence with him (v. 28), and Isaac's growing power prompts Abimelech first to send him away (v. 16) and eventually to enter into a peace treaty with him (vv. 28-29).

Although Abraham had acquired legal rights to a well at Beer-sheba (21:22-33), the Philistines took the opportunity to stop up Abraham's wells upon his death; therefore, Isaac's digging them out again sparks more disputes with the Philistines over water rights. Isaac finally pitches his tent at Beer-sheba, where the Lord confirms his presence with and promises to Isaac. Isaac responds as Abraham did, by building an altar to the Lord and worshipping him.

26:34–28:9 Isaac Mistakes Jacob for Esau

Although Esau marries two Canaanite women, who cause problems for Isaac and Rebekah, he remains Isaac's favorite son, and so the dying Isaac determines to bestow his blessing upon his eldest. Having overheard the plan, which leaves the now rightful heir (Jacob, 25:33) out of the picture, Rebekah concocts a scheme to ensure that her own favorite receives the birthright blessing. Jacob cooperates reluctantly, apparently because he fears Isaac will find him out and curse rather than bless him. But Rebekah's plan works, and despite his suspicions concerning the true identity of the son before him, Isaac blesses Jacob. His blessing includes the prophetic statement that Jacob will "be master of [his] brothers" (cf. 25:23).

Upon discovering Jacob's deception, both Isaac and Esau become greatly distressed, but not even Isaac can revoke Jacob's blessing. Although of his own accord Esau had taken an oath sealing the sale of his birthright (which included a double share of the father's property) to Jacob, Isaac's announcement of his plan to bless Esau had apparently raised Esau's hopes for regaining it. A murderous grudge against

Jacob for claiming what Esau had sworn to give him now replaces those hopes. Ironically, had Isaac followed the current custom (rather than the preference of his heart for Esau) of summoning all his sons to his deathbed and bestowing a blessing on each, he would not have left Esau out entirely.

Nevertheless, Rebekah's realization that Esau now plans to kill Jacob once Isaac dies prompts her to persuade Isaac to send Jacob away in search of a wife among her relatives in Haran. Abraham had made certain that Isaac himself did not return to Mesopotamia in search of a bride, but Isaac sends off his own son readily (to Paddan-aram; 28:2) and with a blessing that fully recognizes Jacob's rights as heir to God's covenantal promises. Rebekah will never see her favorite son again. As for Esau, still eager to please his father (and perhaps hopeful of receiving a greater inheritance from Isaac with Jacob bound for foreign lands), he marries a more acceptable wife — one of his uncle Ishmael's daughters.

28:10-22 Jacob's Dream

Jacob's journey toward Haran takes him through Bethel ("house of God"), 12 miles north of Jerusalem, where he beds down for the night with a rock for a pillow. God extends his covenantal promises to Jacob in a dream and adds a guarantee of his presence wherever Jacob goes, as well as a promise to bring him back to Canaan. Jacob turns his rock-pillow into a monument commemorating the dream and signifying God's presence in that place. Then he makes a vow of his own — if God fulfills his promises, Jacob will tithe from everything God gives him (cf. Abram in 14:20). Jacob's conditional vow does not express a lack of faith in God's promises but thankfulness for them.

29:1-30 Jacob Marries

When Jacob arrives in his mother's homeland in search of a wife, he immediately falls in love with Rachel, daughter of Rebekah's brother Laban. With no material possessions to offer as a marriage gift, Jacob works for Laban for seven years in order to win Rachel's hand. But following custom (and unbeknownst to Jacob!), Laban substitutes his eldest daughter Leah for Rachel on the wedding night. After the bridal week, Laban also gives Rachel to Jacob in exchange for Jacob's promise of seven more years of service, but the marriage of one man to two sisters produces resentment and frustration for all three.

29:31–30:24 The Birth of Jacob's Children

Jacob's love for Rachel does not prevent him from becoming angry with her for her jealousy of Leah, whose unloved status initially led God to allow her to bear Jacob four sons (including Levi, from whom the priestly line descended, and Judah, from whom the royal line came). But Leah's hopes to win Jacob's love through childbearing seem to fail. As for Rachel, she demands that Jacob give her children through her maid, Bilhah (cf. Sarah and Hagar, 16:1-2). Determined to stay ahead of the game, Leah does the same with her own maid, Zilpah.

Still dissatisfied at not having borne children of her own, Rachel offers one of her nights with Jacob to Leah in exchange for some mandrakes (thought to enhance fertility; cf. Song 7:13). The "medicine" does Rachel no good; instead, Leah bears two more sons and a daughter, Dinah. The failure of Rachel's own plans for offspring underscores the underlying control of God in fulfilling his original covenant with Abraham. God finally "remembers" Rachel by allowing her to become pregnant with the son (Joseph) who will eventually save God's chosen line from starvation in Canaan (cf. 21:1-2; 25:21). God's eventual answer to Rachel's prayer for another son (Benjamin; 35:16-18) completes the line of patriarchs (borne by four women) from whom the tribes of Israel descend.

30:25-43 Jacob Positions Himself to Return to Canaan

The birth of a son to Rachel prompts Jacob to gain independence from Laban. Jacob requests to take only his family away, but Laban recognizes that God has blessed him through Jacob, and he hesitates to see Jacob go. Jacob agrees to continue tending Laban's flocks if Laban will give him any sheep and goats with white

(Hebrew "Laban") markings. Jacob then outwits his uncle by causing Laban's animals to produce spotted and speckled lambs and kids by mating them within sight of branches peeled to expose white streaks. Laban's sons become increasingly jealous of Jacob's growing wealth and power.

31 Jacob Departs for Canaan

After 20 years in Mesopotamia (14 served to marry Rachel and Leah, and six more in building up his own flocks; vv. 38, 41), Jacob responds to God's instruction (given in a dream; cf. 28:12-15) to return to Canaan. Fearing retribution from his relatives over his prosperity, Jacob gathers his family and flees without informing Laban, but not before Rachel steals her father's "household idols" (perhaps to help Jacob lay claim to inheritance rights from Laban, or perhaps to ensure protection on the journey). Despite Jacob's three-day head start (v. 22) and a river (Euphrates; v. 21) separating them, Laban catches up with Jacob in the "hill country of Gilead" (east of the Jordan River between the Sea of Galilee and the Dead Sea). But God has warned Laban not to harm Jacob (v. 24). After a verbal confrontation, in which Laban claims that Jacob has, in effect, stolen children and flocks that belong to Laban's household (v. 43), and in which Jacob points out that he has served Laban beyond normal and reasonable requirements (vv. 39, 41), the two make a peace treaty witnessed to by a pillar (cf. 28:18) and a cairn. They seal their agreement by eating together, and then Laban departs the next morning. Neither Laban nor Jacob discovers Rachel's possession of her father's household gods.

32-33 Jacob and Esau Meet Again

The confrontation with Laban behind him, Jacob focuses on the fearful situation ahead in the person of his brother. The servants Jacob sends to Seir to pave the way of peace with Esau return to him with the unsettling news that Esau and 400 men are on their way to meet Jacob. Fearing an attack, Jacob divides his household so at least some may survive, and he prepares a generous present to appease Esau's presumed anger, but not before humbling himself before God and reminding God of his covenantal promises.

The night before the encounter with Esau, Jacob finds himself wrestling with "a man," who turns out to be God. Although God injures Jacob's hip in the struggle, Jacob refuses to call a truce until he receives a blessing from the mysterious attacker. This blessing God gives in the form of a new name — Jacob becomes Israel ("he who strives with God"). The incident both recalls the adversarial relationship Jacob and Esau perpetuated from their conception in the womb and at the same time foreshadows the imminent overcoming of the brothers' enmity.

Jacob's fears concerning Esau's intentions prove unfounded, as Esau welcomes him with open arms and only reluctantly accepts Jacob's gifts. After this happy reunion, Esau returns home to Seir, while Jacob journeys to Succoth (in the Jordan Valley) and then east across the Jordan River to Shechem (40 miles north of Jerusalem), where he purchases property (the second parcel of land in Canaan bought by Israel's patriarchs; cf. 23:16-20).

34 Dinah's Defilement

The story of Dinah's rape by a Canaanite man and the violent response of two of her brothers evidences both the continuation of the sign of the covenant among God's chosen line and the extent and pervasiveness of sin among them. Jacob's sons clearly recognize circumcision as a sign of the covenant (cf. 17:10), but they impose this requirement on the Canaanites of Shechem in a deceitful plot to exact revenge. Not only do Simeon and Levi punish the guilty party by murdering him, but they also kill the city's entire male population and loot everything. Neither do they show mercy on the women and children left. Simeon and Levi may have been less concerned for Dinah herself than for the family's honor, for the fact that Dinah was (at least temporarily) living with her would-be husband (v. 26) hints at the possibility that they were using her in their ruse to trick the Shechemites. And Jacob himself seems more concerned about living in peace with the locals than about Dinah's disgrace (v. 30), although

Jacob does rightly chastise Simeon and Levi for their action (cf. 49:5-7).

God intervenes to ensure that Jacob and his line avoid the tempting implications of intermarriage with the Canaanites, perhaps the most appealing of which consists in the Shechemites' invitation that they "acquire property" in the promised land (v. 10). Yet once again, God overlooks the deceit (and now even worse sins) of his chosen line and allows them to prosper still more (cf. chs. 20 and 26). Later, God will himself bring judgment on the Canaanites for their wickedness (Deut. 9:1-4; cf. Gen. 15:16) as he continues fulfilling the Abrahamic covenant.

35 Jacob Returns to His Father's House

Now that God has brought Jacob back to Canaan safely, it becomes Jacob's turn to fulfill his own vow of making the Lord his God (28:21), so he puts away all the "foreign gods" of his entire household before returning finally to Bethel. God appears to Jacob again at Bethel (cf. 28:12-17), repeats the blessing of 32:28, and restates and expands the covenantal promises to Jacob (now Israel). This happy occasion contrasts with the tragedies that follow: Jacob's beloved wife Rachel dies giving birth to her second son, Benjamin; Jacob's eldest son Reuben commits incest with Bilhah (surrogate wife to Jacob); and Jacob's long-awaited reunion with his father Isaac is cut short by Isaac's death. As did Isaac and Ishmael with their father Abraham, so now the reconciled Jacob and Esau join in burying their father in the family grave at Machpelah (49:31).

36 Esau's Descendants

A list of Esau's descendants precedes the fuller account of God's chosen line (Jacob's, which extends through Joseph) beginning in chapter 37. Not surprisingly, this list appears quite extensive, for the prophecy to Rebekah indicated that "two nations" would emerge from the children in her womb (25:23). Esau's departure from Canaan for economic reasons (cf. Lot in 13:10-11) left the promised land clear for Jacob's descendants to occupy and led to the development of separate peoples (Edomites and Israelites). Although Esau's numerous descendants, many of whom became chiefs and kings, controlled much of the King's Highway, the strategic north-south trade route which extended through Edomite territory on the hilly plateau east of the Dead Sea, Jacob's descendants would later rule over Esau's as further fulfillment of the prophecy that "the elder shall serve the younger" (25:23).

37 Jacob's Descendants

From chapter 37 on, Genesis centers on Jacob's sons — especially Joseph and his brothers' relationship to him. In addition to Joseph, Judah also figures prominently. From the start, Jacob's unabashed favoritism of Joseph becomes apparent, fueling the brothers' jealousy (cf. 25:28 for favoritism among Jacob's parents and 27:1–28:5 for the jealousy it spawned). (The special multicolored tunic Jacob gives to Joseph in v. 3 may recall Egyptian paintings depicting Asiatic attire, or it might represent a "long-sleeved" leisure, as opposed to work, robe.) Indeed, Joseph (the eldest son of Jacob's favorite wife) was treated and viewed as the firstborn and thus Jacob's intended heir (cf. 48:21-22; 1 Chr. 5:1). (This situation fits the pattern throughout the Old Testament of a younger brother's receiving the right of the firstborn.) Joseph's tattletale behavior and his brashness in relating to his family his dreams that they would one day serve him further feed his brothers' resentment of this teenaged braggart. Even Jacob rebukes Joseph for appearing to think too much of himself, yet the dreams remain in the back of Jacob's mind, as he perhaps recalls his own personal history of ruling over his older brother, Esau.

Yet Jacob shows that he cares not only for Joseph but also for his other sons by sending his 17-year-old favorite on a lengthy, if not perilous, 60- (turned 75-) mile journey north to determine the siblings' welfare. Taking advantage of the geographical distance between them and their father, the brothers conspire to kill Joseph. Reuben (who had formerly sinned against his father by committing incest with Jacob's surrogate wife) wants to save Joseph's neck (perhaps simply in assumption of his responsibilities as eldest son, but perhaps also to make amends with Jacob; v. 22), and he convinces his brothers to throw Joseph into a dry well (or cistern) instead of doing him in. But with Joseph down in the pit and Reuben off somewhere else (v. 29), Judah devises an alternative plan that would both remove Joseph from the scene and also profit himself and his brothers handsomely. (Here the father of the kingly line perpetrates the crime, as Levi, father of the priestly line, did in ch. 34.)

So the brothers (not the Midianites of v. 28) sell Joseph to a passing caravan of Ishmaelite (used here interchangeably with "Midianite"; v. 36) traders, who were probably carrying spices back and forth between Damascus and Egypt via a major caravan road that passed by Dothan on its way to the coastal route. The sale gains the brothers three years' worth of shepherd's wages and sends Joseph on a journey to Egypt. But it also creates a quandary for the unsuspecting Reuben, whom Jacob would hold responsible for Joseph's welfare. To protect Reuben, the brothers take the tunic they had stripped from Joseph, dip it in goat's blood (cf. 27:9ff., where Jacob uses a goat to deceive his own father), and present it to Jacob as evidence that a wild animal has killed Joseph. Jacob buys the story and vows to mourn Joseph until his dying day. The chapter ends noting the further sale of Joseph in Egypt — a sale that lands him in the high-ranking company of none other than the captain of Pharaoh's bodyguard and foreshadows the fulfillment of the prophetic dreams that helped get Joseph into trouble in the first place.

38 Judah and Tamar

This sidelight on the shortcomings of Judah and his sons illuminates the ancient Near Eastern obligation of levirate (from Heb. *levir,* "brother-in-law") marriage (Deut. 25:5-10), wherein the brother of a deceased man must marry his brother's childless widow and produce children who will continue his brother's name and thus the family line. Judah's intermarriage with the Canaanites causes heartache and problems from the start. His firstborn son, Er, becomes so wicked that God takes his life, thereby leaving childless Er's widow,

Tamar. Judah's second son, Onan, sabotages his own performance of his duty on behalf of his deceased brother because he wants Judah's inheritance to fall to him (not to any son he might produce for his brother through Tamar), so God takes Onan's life also. Fearing for the life of his third son, Shelah, Judah puts off marrying him to Tamar, apparently with no intention of fulfilling his patriarchal duty to her (v. 11; cf. v. 14).

Judah's neglect of this responsibility leads Tamar to take matters into her own hands. She disguises herself as a veiled and therefore married temple-prostitute and sets out for the sheep-shearing festivities at Timnah with the intention of encountering her father-in-law. Undoubtedly well acquainted with Canaanite fertility rites practiced at such festivals, Judah hires Tamar at the city gate (where legal transactions often take place) and has intercourse with her without recognizing her true identity. But Tamar exacts a pledge of payment — Judah's seal-necklace and staff, her possession of which saves her in the end.

Although Shelah and Tamar had not married, Judah probably considered them betrothed. But Judah's intent to kill Tamar by burning her when he discovers her "adultery" once again goes beyond the normal punishment for the crime (although an adulteress could receive the death penalty, death by burning applied only to more serious offenses; Deut. 22:21; Lev. 21:9). The evidence Tamar presents in her defense demonstrates Judah's own guilt, not only as co-adulterer but also as neglecter of his duty to her; to his credit, Judah admits her moral and legal superiority over him. The birth of Perez and Zerah, Tamar's twin sons, once again pictures the younger (Perez) prevailing over the elder. This story's appearance here emphasizes the continuing sins of Judah (cf. 37:26) and contrasts Judah's immoral behavior with Joseph's righteous refusal of the sexual advances of his Egyptian master's wife in chapter 39.

39-40 Joseph, Potiphar, and Prison

Chapters 39–50 picture life in Egypt as typical under the Semitic Hyksos pharaohs, who ruled 1710-1570 B.C. from their capital of Avaris (in

Caravan of West Semitic ("Asiatic") merchants en route to Egypt; painting from the tomb of Khnumhotep II (ca. 1890 B.C.). *(Erich Lessing / Art Resource, NY)*

the eastern part of the Nile Delta, in the same region as the land of Goshen [45:10]).

At the outset of Joseph's sojourn in Egypt, the biblical account confirms God's presence with this favored son turned foreign slave by pointing out that Joseph's master, Potiphar, receives God's blessing through him in fulfillment of God's promise to Abram (12:2-3) and by emphasizing the high position to which Joseph rose in Potiphar's house. But Joseph's success and handsome appearance lead to his downfall as well — not through any fault of his own, for Joseph remains supremely faithful both to God and to Potiphar, but through the revenge Potiphar's wife exacts on Joseph for rejecting her sexual advances. (The beginning of this story resembles the Egyptian *Tale of Two Brothers* in the basic plot of seduction, rejection, and false accusation.)

Taking the word of his wife that Joseph attempted to rape her, Potiphar unjustly sends Joseph to prison, but God remains with Joseph and elevates him to a position of significant responsibility even in this humble circumstance. Joseph's ability to interpret the dreams of two of his fellow prisoners — Pharaoh's chief cupbearer and chief baker — further demonstrates God's continued presence with Joseph (40:8).

41:1-52 Joseph's Rise to Power

Although not immediately (40:14, 23; 41:1), God again reverses an injustice done to Joseph, this time by working through the relationships Joseph develops in prison to bring him eventually into the service of Pharaoh himself. One night, Pharaoh dreams two perplexing dreams. (Dual dreams indicate the surety of their fulfillment; cf. Joseph's two dreams in ch. 37 and the one dream each of the cupbearer and baker in ch. 40.) But even with extensive training in dream interpretation and a library of reference works available to Egyptian "magicians," none of Pharaoh's wise men can interpret his dreams.

Then the chief cupbearer finally remembers Joseph to Pharaoh. Taken hurriedly out of prison and prepared for a court appearance according to Egyptian custom, Joseph finds himself face to face with Pharaoh and agrees to let God speak through him concerning the dreams (41:16; God communicates with Joseph via dreams, rather than appearing and speaking to him directly as with Abraham, Isaac, and Jacob). Pharaoh recognizes Joseph's wisdom and the divine presence with him, and so, at age 30 and after 13 years of slavery and imprisonment, Joseph rises to the high position of Pharaoh's second in command (vv. 40-45). Here he assumes the task of implementing his own strategy (vv. 34-35) for saving Egypt from starvation during the seven-year famine to come.

During this time, Joseph marries Asenath from On (or Heliopolis, the Egyptian center of sun worship, 10 miles north of Cairo) and fathers two sons, to whom he gives Hebrew names (Manasseh and Ephraim) with meanings that recognize God for delivering and prospering him.

41:53–45:24 Joseph's Dreams Fulfilled

The years of plenty pass quickly, and famine sets in, not only throughout Egypt but also in Canaan. Knowing of Egypt's stores of food, Jacob sends 10 of his sons (all save Benjamin, Joseph's only full brother and the one remaining son of Jacob's favorite wife, Rachel) south to buy grain. Joseph recognizes his brothers, and their bowing down to him triggers his recollection of his dreams of 20 years prior. Keeping to himself his identity as their long-lost brother, Joseph accuses them of spying, imprisons them, and then keeps Simeon (who had shared in murdering the Shechemites) hostage before giving them grain and sending them home with a charge to bring Benjamin to Egypt to prove their innocence and secure Simeon's release. Reuben recognizes the demand as divine justice for the brothers' past treatment of Joseph (42:22).

The brothers' discovery of their returned payment for the grain, the absence of Simeon from the returning party, and the demand that Benjamin journey to Egypt distress Jacob greatly, and he refuses to let Benjamin go despite Reuben's promise to guard him personally. But when their food runs out, Jacob once again sends his sons to Egypt, this time accepting Judah's pledge of responsibility for Benjamin and also sending gifts and extra money in hopes of placating any anger against his sons held by Pharaoh's household.

The brothers meet with a far different welcome on their second trip to Egypt — the formerly harsh Joseph plans to host them at a special meal in his own house! But the brothers' guilty consciences prevent them from enjoying the prospect, and now they fear a fate like that into which they had sold Joseph (43:18)! True to his word, Joseph releases Simeon, and the banquet proceeds.

But the meal serves as a foil for Joseph's subsequent plans to instill fear in his brothers. He sends the 11 toward home loaded with grain, again secretly returns their money to their sacks, and this time frames Benjamin with the more serious offense of stealing the silver divination cup Joseph apparently used in interpreting events (by analyzing the movement of oil drops in water).

Their unwitting theft exposed by Joseph's steward, the brothers return to the city wondering how to clear Benjamin. Judah now takes the lead in guarding Benjamin's fate even to the point of offering himself as Joseph's slave in Benjamin's place.

The brothers wish death upon the one who had stolen Joseph's cup and offer that the

With the increase of urbanization during the Middle Bronze Age, the patriarchs maintained a seminomadic lifestyle. *(Phoenix Data Systems, Neal and Joel Bierling)*

The Patriarchs and Their Neighbors

The book of Genesis contains references to other peoples who lived in Mesopotamia, Egypt, and Syria-Palestine in ancient times; but the chronology of the ancestral narratives is not precise, making it impossible to know exactly when Abraham, Isaac, and Jacob lived. A majority of scholars place them in the Middle Bronze Age (2000-1550 B.C.), a view based on archaeology and cultural comparisons with the ancient Near East. This period of ancient history is marked by the movement of ethnic groups and the emergence of new empires replacing the older powers of the Early Bronze Age.

Israel's ancestors were not aborigines who appeared at the dawn of human history, but instead the beneficiaries of a rich cultural heritage. By the time Abraham was born, the world had witnessed the rise and fall of two of the world's great civilizations. Egypt's Old Kingdom period, with its great pyramids and sovereign pharaohs, occurred during the Early Bronze Age (3300-2000). This was Egypt's classical period, in which all of its significant cultural features flowered and became normative for the rest of ancient history. In Mesopotamia, the Sumerians had given human civilization its initial form and shape, then gradually gave way to the first true empire in world history, the Semitic empire of the Akkadians. At the turn of the 2nd millennium, large groups of Northwest Semitic peoples began migrating to all parts of the Fertile Crescent, bringing the Early Bronze Age to a close amid destruction across the Near East. These newcomers were called Amorites ("Westerners"), who many scholars believe were the ancient ancestors of the Hebrews and Arameans of the biblical period.

Near the beginning of the Middle Bronze Age, the Amorites arrived in Mesopotamia in such large numbers that they dominated the next millennium of Mesopotamian history. They established major power centers at Babylon on the Euphrates and at Assur and Nineveh farther north along the Tigris. This was the period in which Hammurabi unified the region and issued his famous law code, which preserved legal traditions reaching back into the 3rd millennium. Many scholars believe that Abraham was an Amorite from Mesopotamia.

The Middle Bronze Age ushered in perhaps the most prosperous period of Egypt's history. During the so-called Middle Kingdom empire, royal power became gradually centered in the pharaonic crown of the 11th, 12th, and 13th Dynasties (ca. 2000-1700). International trade conducted across the Sinai Peninsula and the Mediterranean Sea with the various powers of Syria-Palestine resulted in unprecedented wealth and contributed to a flourishing of the arts in the golden age of Egyptian culture. Toward the close of the Middle Bronze Age, Semitic peoples from Asia filtered into the Nile Delta, which slipped from the pharaoh's grasp. Eventually the foreigners, known as "Hyksos" (an Egyptian term for the Asiatic princes), conquered all of Egypt, which they ruled for the last century of the Middle Bronze Age. Many scholars assume the Hyksos period of Egyptian history to be the most likely time when Joseph and the ancestors of Israel entered Egypt and settled in Goshen in the Nile Delta. This would locate the Joseph narrative between the Egyptian Middle Kingdom and New Kingdom periods (ca. 1700-1550).

Syria-Palestine during the age of Israel's ancestors experienced urbanization and resettlement of outsiders, especially in the central and southern highlands. The region's gradual recovery from the upheavals at the end of the 3rd millennium was probably due to the settlement of Amorite seminomads there, a phenomenon evident across the biblical world. The migration of Israel's ancestors may well have been part of this movement toward the beginning of the Middle Bronze Age (ca. 2000). Syria-Palestine was also influenced by Hurrian (biblical "Horites") and other Indo-European groups. Various of these groups achieved unification in Asia Minor, and the Hittite Old Kingdom would emerge there toward the end of the Middle Bronze Age. The ancestral narratives of Genesis mention the presence of these groups in

Syria-Palestine, and the most likely time for these events was during the Middle Bronze Age.

According to Genesis, the central features of ancestral religion were the covenant and its promises: land, descendants, and the promise to become a blessing to the nations (Gen. 12:1-3, and frequently throughout). In a fashion quite different from later Mosaic religion, Israel's ancestors worshipped God without priests or prophets, and often received revelations through visions and dreams. The religious practices and expressions described in Genesis 12–50 fit well in the Middle Bronze Age and are what we might expect from transitory, migrant Amorites looking for land to settle and clans to leave behind.

For Further Reading

Hoerth, Alfred J., Gerald L. Mattingly, and Edwin M. Yamauchi, eds. *Peoples of the Old Testament World*. Grand Rapids: Baker, 1994.

BILL T. ARNOLD

---

rest submit to slavery (44:9). Yet apparently at Joseph's instruction (cf. 44:17), the steward rejects the suggestions as too severe and lessens the proposed punishment (v. 10).

Judah's admission of the brothers' shared guilt and his eloquent plea on Benjamin's behalf cause Joseph to break a third time, and he finally identifies himself to his brothers. Joseph comforts them, explaining that everything had happened according not to their plan but to God's, in order that Joseph might ultimately save their lives.

Joseph's charge that his brothers bring their father and his entire household (including the families of his brothers) to Egypt to live in the choicest of pasturelands there, the favor the brothers find in Pharaoh's sight, and the material wealth they gain again fulfills God's promise that his chosen line will serve as a blessing to others (12:2-3).

45:25–47:26 Jacob's Move to Egypt

Jacob can scarcely believe his ears when he learns of Joseph's fortune. As he journeys to Egypt accompanied by the members of his household (70, a multiple of the sacred number seven), God pledges in a vision that he will make Jacob "a great nation" in Egypt and then bring him back to Canaan.

Eager to see his father, Joseph travels to Goshen to meet Jacob. Their tearful but happy reunion also provides an occasion for Joseph to coach his brothers on how to approach Pharaoh concerning their need for pastureland. Already well disposed toward Joseph's family, yet "loathsome" of their occupation as shepherds, Pharaoh readily agrees to allow Jacob and his retinue to settle off to themselves in Goshen. (Not only does this meet their immediate needs for food for their flocks, but it also lessens the possibility of their intermarrying with Egyptians and thereby losing their group identity.) Pharaoh shows even further generosity in offering Joseph's relatives jobs as royal herdsmen — employment that perhaps prospers them even more when Joseph buys the Egyptians' livestock for Pharaoh in exchange for food (47:16-17). In both this act and his later buying of the Egyptians' land in exchange for food, which makes them tenant farmers (here "slaves"), Joseph shows benevolence and mercy, not cruelty, for by this means he preserved their lives (47:25).

47:27–50:14 Jacob's Death and Burial

Jacob's family prospers in Egypt for 17 years before the time comes for him to die. Jacob indeed views Joseph as his heir and makes Joseph promise to bury him in the family tomb (at Machpelah; 23:20). Jacob also pronounces a dying blessing on Joseph's sons, whom he adopts as his own, and again the younger (Ephraim) is elevated above the older (Manasseh). Perhaps this caused Joseph to realize for the first time how his own older brothers felt about Jacob's preferring him over them (48:17-19). Jacob then seals the choice of Joseph as his heir both by passing on to him the promise of God's presence (48:21) and bequeathing him an extra amount of his inheritance (v. 22). Then, in one of the oldest poems in the Old Testament, Jacob pronounces blessings on his sons that preview the fulfillment of God's covenantal promises: as a group, they will prosper in every way and occupy all regions of the promised land (but contrast the judgments in 49:3-7 with vv. 8-27).

Joseph treats his father with great respect in death, as he had in life — he has Jacob's body embalmed, and the Egyptians mourn him just two days short of the time they mourned their Pharaohs. Joseph obtains permission from Pharaoh to take Jacob's body to Canaan for burial, and once more the brothers unite to bury their father (cf. 25:9; 35:29). On their journey to Canaan, the entourage takes an indirect route that may be similar to the one the Israelites later followed during the exodus.

50:15-26 Joseph's Death

Upon their return to Egypt, Joseph's brothers fear that, with Jacob gone, Joseph might now treat them harshly. But Joseph calms their fears and promises to provide for them and their families. Then, before he dies (at age 110 — the age Egyptians considered ideal), Joseph "bequeaths" the covenantal promise of land to his brothers (v. 24), now the patriarchs of the fledgling nation of Israel (12:2), and exacts from them a pledge to return his remains to Canaan.

Exodus

"Exodus" (Greek for "a going out, exit") takes its name from the event through which God begins to fulfill his promise to the patriarchs of a land of their own — a promise he made in Genesis. Through the central figure of Exodus, Moses, God makes himself known to his people by name. Using Moses as leader of the emerging nation, God delivers the "sons of Israel" from 400 years of slavery in Egypt. With Moses as mediator, God enters a new covenant with the descendants of Abraham through Isaac and Jacob. And at Moses' appeal, God agrees to live among the Israelites in a special tent built according to his instructions. In these ways, God establishes an intimate relationship with his people.

The chosen people come to know their God in Exodus: he is caring, compassionate, and forgiving, yet he is also holy, just, and jealous. God's presence among the Israelites set them apart as God's holy nation, and the laws in the Decalogue (20:2-17) and the Book of the Covenant (20:22–23:33) were intended to enable the Israelites to remain in God's presence. But throughout Exodus, the Israelites' lack of faith in God and their disobedience to his commands stand in sharp contrast to God's consistent faithfulness to his people. The Israelites learn the hard way that God requires their obedience and their loyalty to him alone, and Exodus clearly illustrates that it is God who takes the initiative in redeeming sinful humanity.

Background

Although the primary interest of Exodus consists in theology, not history (in the modern sense), scholars have proposed two main theories regarding the date of the Israelite exodus from Egypt narrated here. The "early date" receives support from a literal reading of the text, in that 1 Kgs. 6:1 says Solomon began building the first temple in the fourth year of his reign (ca. 966 B.C.) and 480 years after the Israelites left Egypt. Adding 480 years to 966 puts the exodus at ca. 1446. Most of the archaeological evidence for the Israelites' entry into Canaan, however, supports a "late" 13th-century date for the exodus — a date which a more figurative interpretation of "480 years" could achieve by considering the number to represent 12 generations of 25 (rather than of 40) years. No extrabiblical texts discovered to date mention the exodus, and the book itself gives few historical clues that could help pinpoint more specifically the timing of the event described. (See "The Exodus" [110-11].)

Authorship

As with Genesis, Exodus does not give direct information concerning its author or date of writing. Tradition assigns its authorship to Moses; the Documentary Hypothesis considers it a compilation of material by several editors.

1 From Favored Friends to Oppressed People

Verses 1-7 recap the migration of Jacob's household to Egypt, detailed in Genesis, and then move quickly to the current situation (mid to latter 2nd millennium B.C.) several centuries after the death of Joseph. The generation of Jacob's sons has passed, but their descendants have become numerous and mighty. (The biblical "sons of Israel" [our "Israelites"] now refers to all Jacob's descendants, not just his 12 immediate sons.)

But this great blessing (which fulfills God's promise to make the patriarchs "a great nation" [Gen. 12:2]) does not come without difficulties. A new (unnamed) "Pharaoh" — one unfamiliar with Joseph and his service to Egypt — grows fearful of the now powerful Israelites. Rather than viewing their prosperity as a blessing to his own kingdom (contrast Gen. 26:28; 30:27), Pharaoh perceives them as a threat; therefore, he drafts them into forced labor to build two store cities (Pithom and Rameses; some associate the latter with Pharaoh Ramesses II [1290-1224 B.C.]) and also attempts to halt their population growth. But Pharaoh's efforts to dominate the Israelites produce an undesired result: the foreign sojourners multiply even more and occupy even greater territory. Getting no cooperation from the Hebrew midwives, who show reverence for God rather than obeying Pharaoh's command to kill all newborn Hebrew boys, Pharaoh instructs the Egyptians to put infant Hebrew males to death by throwing them into the Nile.

2 Hope for Deliverance

If chapter 1 reveals the plight of the Israelites in Egypt, chapter 2 sets the stage for their deliverance. From his birth, the Hebrew Moses maintains close associations with Pharaoh's house and repeatedly escapes death at Pharaoh's hand. One of Pharaoh's own daughters rescues Moses from death by drowning and adopts him as her own. (The same Hebrew word is used for Moses' floating basket-cradle and Noah's ark. God delivers both Noah and Moses from a watery grave and uses each to provide deliverance and a new beginning — Noah for all humanity and Moses for the Hebrew people.) But later, as a 40-year-old adult (cf. Acts 7:23) fully aware of his ancestry — and therefore of the oppression of his people by the very household that has nurtured him as an Egyptian prince — Moses kills an Egyptian taskmaster in defense of a fellow Hebrew. As a result, he flees from Pharaoh's murderous hand once again.

Settling in Midian (east of Sinai around the Gulf of Aqabah) among the descendants of Abraham and Keturah, Moses marries the daughter of a priest and becomes a shepherd (3:1). His new lifestyle must have differed dramatically from the life he led in the Egyptian royal court, where undoubtedly he learned to read and write Egyptian hieroglyphics and cursive scripts, studied Egyptian law, and acquired additional skills alongside other foreigners

receiving training for official service to Egypt. Yet this nomadic life in the desert must have prepared Moses well for his role in delivering his people out of Egypt and leading them to Canaan.

Chapter 2 closes noting God's awareness of the Israelites' oppression in Egypt and his remembrance of his covenantal promises (cf. Gen. 15:13-21). The mention of both foreshadows God's impending action on his people's behalf.

3:1–4:17 God's Charge to Moses

As he did with Abraham, Isaac, and Jacob, God speaks to Moses directly, yet here God appears not as a man but in flames of fire. (Throughout Exodus, fire and smoke symbolize God's presence; esp. 19:18.) The sight of a burning but unconsumed bush at Horeb (traditionally identified with Jebel Musa in the southern Sinai Peninsula; Moses later receives the Ten Commandments at Horeb [= Mount Sinai of ch. 19]) captures Moses' attention, and he responds to God's call from the midst of the bush with reverent obedience. When God identifies himself as the God of the patriarchs, Moses hides his face out of fear that looking at God will cause him to die.

God then reveals to Moses his compassion for the enslaved Israelites as well as his plan to deliver them — through Moses! Moses immediately makes excuses as to why he cannot return to the Egyptian court where he grew up or to the people in whose defense he had acted previously. First he questions his worthiness for the task, and God responds by pledging his presence with Moses. Then Moses questions whether the Israelites will believe him or trust his sender and therefore his mission. God responds by identifying himself further: not only is he the God of the Hebrew patriarchs of the past, but he is also the God of the present (I AM WHO I AM [= perhaps a pun on Yahweh, God's personal name, translated and written "LORD" and sometimes read as "Jehovah"]), and also the God of the future (3:15) — the God who will fulfill his covenantal promise of a land for his chosen people (3:17).

Despite God's assurance to Moses that the Israelites will listen to him, Moses further doubts they will believe him. God then gives Moses three signs (similar to the magic of Egyptian religion and therefore familiar to the Israelites; cf. 7:12, 22) that show God's power over the natural order. Two of the signs God demonstrates immediately: Moses' staff turns into a serpent and then back into a staff; next, Moses' hand becomes leprous and then well again. The third sign — that water from the Nile poured on the ground by Moses will turn to blood — God will display only in Egypt. But Moses further resists his assignment by appealing to his lack of eloquence. God answers that he, the creator of the mouth, will "teach" Moses what to say. God's responses to all Moses' excuses underscore that God himself will accomplish the deliverance of his people; Moses will serve merely as God's human instrument.

Having run out of excuses, Moses pleads that God send someone else. Although Moses' request makes God angry, God provides him with tangible support: Moses' older brother Aaron will speak for him (7:7), and Moses' staff will help him perform the "signs."

4:18–5:23 Moses Returns to Egypt

Moses can resist God's command no longer and sets out for Egypt with his family and his staff (a sign of divine authority). God repeats the warning that Pharaoh will not listen to Moses (cf. 3:19) because God himself will harden Pharaoh's heart in order to show his power to the Egyptians and establish himself as God supreme over them (7:3, 5; cf. 8:15, 32, where Pharaoh hardens his own heart).

In a mysterious encounter on the way to Egypt, God seeks to kill Moses. Moses has failed to administer to his son Gershom the sign of the covenant (given to Abraham in Gen. 17:10-14), but Zipporah circumcises the boy in time to spare Moses.

As promised in 4:14, Aaron meets Moses in the wilderness, and Moses reports God's plans to deliver the Israelites from their Egyptian oppressors. Although God charges Moses only with performing the "signs" before Pharaoh, Moses does so for the Hebrew elders first, and they believe; when he later performs the same signs for the Egyptians, they do not believe, so

further signs will be required (7:3-4). Moses and Aaron then approach the pharaoh (one unknown to Moses; 2:23; 4:19) and request that he allow the Israelites to go into the wilderness to worship God. The number and might of the Israelites during Moses' earlier years in Egypt had led the former pharaoh to seek their domination. That development led to the Israelites' becoming the core of the Egyptian workforce, and the new pharaoh, who does not recognize God in any way (5:2), will not spare this valuable resource even for a few days. Not only does he refuse, but he also imposes even harder labor — so much harder that the Israelites turn against Moses (5:21), and Moses regrets his decision to obey God (vv. 22-23).

Bricks of mud mixed with straw, with a mud and dry-grass mortar, one of the most common building materials in Egypt and Palestine from prehistoric to Roman times. *(Wikimedia Commons)*

6:1-13 God Claims the Israelites as His Own

The time has come for God to act. He identifies himself again, but now in a way that emphasizes his personal relationship with his chosen people: they know him by name, and he here affirms his power and authority by pledging to deliver them to their own land. God also

The Exodus

Exodus is the Greek word for "going out," the name of the book in the Greek version of the Hebrew Bible (OT). It refers to the Israelites' going out of Egypt and beginning their return to the promised land. This migration of people took place because God brought the people out of Egypt by means of miracles carried out in part by his chosen agent, Moses. The story of this event is found in Exodus 1–15 and referred to throughout the Bible. It is remembered and celebrated as the first of a series of God's actions of salvation in behalf of his people. The exodus event is foundational for the Israelites' faith and practice.

While Egypt had been a place of refuge for Jacob and his sons during a famine (Genesis 42–49), it later became a place of bondage. The family had grown so large that the king of Egypt tried to reduce their numbers by oppressing them with hard labor and tried to control their population growth by having new baby boys killed at birth. One young boy, Moses, is miraculously spared from this disaster and raised by Pharaoh's daughter. When he witnesses an Egyptian beating a Hebrew man, Moses kills the Egyptian and then flees to the land of Midian. The people cry out to God because of the oppression, and God hears their prayers. Moses, who is shepherding for his father-in-law Jethro, is called by God to lead his people out of Egypt. Moses is very reluctant about this, and God must convince him and equip him to return to Egypt.

Moses intercedes for his people, but Pharaoh does not want to let them go. He makes life even more miserable for the Israelites. God sends a series of 10 plagues that show God's power over Pharaoh and the Egyptian gods. Only after the death of the firstborn of Egypt are the Israelites finally allowed to leave. When after a change of heart Pharaoh orders his army to pursue the Israelites, the Red Sea parts miraculously, the Israelites rush through, and the Egyptian soldiers following them are drowned when the waters return.

The exodus is viewed as a historical event that brings about physical deliverance for the people. But it is not the historical details that are of primary importance. Instead of noting natural causes for events, biblical authors confess that God has been active in history working through people such as the midwives and Moses and controlling nature such as the plagues and the waters of the Red Sea. The story is meant to help future generations celebrate the wondrous events, and the account even contains instructions for liturgical celebration of the event.

The report lacks the details necessary to situate this story within the sequence of events known in Egyptian history with any degree of certainty. For instance, the name of the specific pharaoh is not mentioned. There are no reports of this event in sources outside the Bible. Some particular details in the biblical texts are problematic. 1 Kings 6:1 notes that the exodus took place 480 years before the fourth year of Solomon (ca. 966 B.C.), which would suggest ca. 1446 for the exodus, but it is argued that the reign of Ramesses II (1279-1213) fits the time when cities were built as suggested in Exod. 1:11. According to Exod. 12:37, some 600 thousand men went out of Egypt. If one adds women and children, this means that well over 2 million people came out of Egypt, yet Pharaoh sent only some 600 chariots in pursuit of them (Exod. 14:7). The locations of cities in Egypt and the exodus route are not known for certain. Various scholarly proposals have been made to provide a historical framework for the story. Some scholars try to draw upon general information known about the history and geography of the time and propose the most plausible details that fit with the biblical story. The Merneptah Stela, celebrating the military victories of Ramesses II's successor ca. 1220, is the first written external account that mentions Israel as a people living in Canaan and supports the exodus as taking place shortly before this time.

The exodus event means that God has shown love and care to his people. He has sided with the oppressed against the oppressors. This involves physical deliverance from physical slavery. The Israelite people celebrated the exodus with singing and rejoicing. One finds words of this celebration in the Song of Moses (Exod. 15:1-18) and the Song of Miriam (Exod. 15:20-21). The event is a common theme of thanksgiving psalms or a motif of such psalms (Psalm 114). Even before the crossing of the Red Sea takes place, liturgical instructions concerning the Passover, the Feast of Unleavened Bread, and the redemption of the firstborn interrupt the flow of the story of the deliverance in Exodus 12–13. These practices are all related to key exodus events.

Not only do people respond with gratitude when they remember the exodus, but they are also motivated to live their lives differently in response to God's action in their behalf. Now that they have experienced God's deliverance and grace, they are called upon to enter into a covenant with God, which means that they must follow God's instructions (Exodus 19). These instructions are revealed to the people through Moses beginning with the Ten Commandments and including several collections of laws found in Exodus 20–Numbers 10. The exodus provides the motivation for particular laws. Of special importance is the concern not to oppress others and to be compassionate to those who are in trouble, such as the poor and the sojourners (Lev. 19:33-34; 25:35-37). Here they are to imitate God, who has delivered them from slavery; they should not enslave others but be compassionate. Since the Israelites have been slaves themselves, they should have empathy with others similarly oppressed (Exod. 23:9; Deut. 15:15).

While the exodus event is unique, it is also viewed as a paradigm for God's continued activity in our world. The pattern of events associated with the exodus, including oppression of a group of people, crying out to God for help, God's deliverance of the people, and their celebration of that deliverance, is central throughout the Bible. Complaint psalms reflect this basic pattern for individuals as well as groups. Even the central New Testament event of Jesus' death and resurrection fits this pattern. Throughout history individuals and groups of people experiencing all kinds of oppression have sought help and deliverance from the same God who delivered the Israelites from Egyptian bondage.

For Further Reading

Fretheim, Terence E. *Exodus*. Interpretation. Louisville: Westminster John Knox, 1991.

Kitchen, K. A. "The Exodus." *ABD* 2:700-708.

Larsson, Göran. *Bound for Freedom: The Book of Exodus in Jewish and Christian Traditions*. Peabody: Hendrickson, 1999.

Walzer, Michael. *Exodus and Revolution*. New York: Basic, 1985.

STEPHEN A. REED

reaffirms that the covenant now extends not just to one individual but instead to all the Israelites in bondage in Egypt. But by the time God determines to act, the Israelites have already lost hope, and Moses, too, loses confidence. If his own people will not listen to him, how will Pharaoh? Here again, Moses' and the Israelites' lack of faith highlights God's role as sole deliverer of his people.

6:14-27 The Genealogy of Moses and Aaron

The genealogy here appears intent on establishing Moses and Aaron as descendants of Jacob's son Levi (esp. vv. 26-27), whose descendants became Israel's priests (Num. 26:57-65).

6:28–11:10 Signs and Wonders

God bolsters Moses' courage to approach Pharaoh once again. This Moses does, accompanied by Aaron, and the two perform "signs," or "wonders," designed to instill respect for God. The account of the signs shows a progression in Pharaoh's knowledge of God (compare 5:2 with 8:28; 9:27; 12:32), but it also demonstrates that mere knowledge does not necessarily result in sincere repentance or true humility before God. Pharaoh first asks for a sign to prove God's power; through Moses and Aaron, God produces 11 wonders. Yet even after receiving the proof he asks for, Pharaoh's knowledge leaves him faithless.

Pharaoh's magicians duplicate the first sign, in which Moses' staff turns into a serpent (7:10-12; cf. 4:3). Although Moses' serpent swallows up the magicians' serpents, Pharaoh remains unimpressed.

Beginning with the second sign (which becomes the first plague), God uses Moses and Aaron to issue specific warnings concerning most of the punishments that await the

Egyptians if Pharaoh refuses to allow the Israelites to worship God in the wilderness. By sending the very punishments he has warned about, God displays the ability to do what he says he will do. In addition, God starts and stops the punishments at will and, beginning with the fourth sign, limits their geographical extent to protect his people. God gives Pharaoh every opportunity to recognize God's supreme power and to humble himself before God (cf. 9:16-17), yet Pharaoh's heart remains hardened.

Pharaoh's magicians also duplicate the second sign — turning the water of the Nile into undrinkable "blood" (7:20; cf. 4:9). Perhaps unusually high flooding of the Nile (flooding occurred annually between June and October prior to the building of the Aswan dam) washed red clay soil from Ethiopia into this part of the Nile, or perhaps God caused red algae to pollute the water. But these explanations do not account for Moses' prior performance of the sign before the Israelites (4:30), the magicians' duplication of the wonder (7:22), or the transformation of the water contained in vessels throughout Egypt (7:19). Whether God worked through or overruled the natural order to accomplish this sign, the shortsighted pharaoh shows no concern about the occurrence (7:23).

After one week, God causes frogs escaping the putrid river waters to infiltrate the Egyptians' homes. Again Pharaoh's magicians mimic the sign, but the situation has become a nuisance, and so, recognizing God's power, Pharaoh agrees to let the Israelites worship God if Moses and Aaron will persuade God to stop the plague (8:8). But acknowledging the power of God does not produce humility in Pharaoh, and he goes back on his promise once he gets what he wants, relief from the frogs (8:15).

God gives Pharaoh no warning concerning the next plague — gnats (8:17), undoubtedly attracted by the piles of rotting frogs heaped up throughout Egypt. This sign Pharaoh's magicians cannot reproduce, and even they recognize the plague as coming from the "finger of God." But Pharaoh remains defiant.

God does issue a warning concerning the next plague — insects — and this time he gives Pharaoh even greater reason to acknowledge his supremacy. In this plague God will distinguish between the Egyptians and the Israelites by preventing the insects from affecting the land of Goshen, where his people dwell. From this point on, the punishments do not affect the Israelites. God also shows his power over time by informing Pharaoh when the plague will strike (8:23). The destruction brought by the insects initially causes Pharaoh to grant the Israelites permission to make sacrifices to God "within the land." But Moses insists they must worship God in the wilderness so as not to offend the Egyptians with their sacrificial practices. Not only does Pharaoh agree to the proposal; he also charges Moses to pray for him personally (8:28). Remembering Pharaoh's earlier broken promise, Moses departs warning Pharaoh not to "deal deceitfully again."

Pharaoh does go back on his word, and now God determines to cause the Egyptians' livestock to die (perhaps of diseases carried by the insects). Again God tells Pharaoh when the plague will begin, and again he informs him that it will not affect the Israelites. Even after confirming that none of the Israelites' livestock have died (9:6), however, Pharaoh remains unmoved.

Although Pharaoh's magicians had demonstrated their power to duplicate earlier signs, they now prove powerless even to protect themselves from the next plague — boils (9:11). Indeed, they become too sick even to stand before Pharaoh.

Some of Pharaoh's servants believe Moses and heed his warning about the punishment of hail, but still some do not (9:20-21). Again God protects his people in Goshen (9:26). With the ruin of Egypt's crops of barley and flax (used in the country's important linen industry), Pharaoh finally appears to acknowledge his sin and God's righteousness; and he again promises to allow the Israelites to go. But Moses lets Pharaoh know that he detects the king's insincerity. Still Moses prays to God to stop the hail, and predictably Pharaoh cancels his permission a third time.

Convinced of God's power to bring on the threatened plague of locusts (which would obliterate any crops and other vegetation not ruined by the hail; cf. 9:32) and with the entire country already "destroyed," Pharaoh's servants persuade him to grant the Israelites their request. But when Pharaoh learns that even the women, children, and flocks will go, he suspects his labor force will never return, and he gives only the men permission to leave. So the locust plague proceeds. Pharaoh repents insincerely again and God stops the plague, but Pharaoh still will not let the people go.

Pharaoh receives no warning about the sign of darkness, and it results again in Pharaoh's giving at least some ground. He agrees that all the people may go, but not the animals. Moses' standing firm makes Pharaoh angry and causes him to send Moses away for the last time with a warning never to approach him again. Moses leaves defiantly, confirming that indeed he will never see Pharaoh's face again. Here Moses displays a complete transformation from the wilting figure at the burning bush to the confident spokesman in Pharaoh's court. If the signs and wonders did not produce a heartfelt change in Pharaoh, they surely did in Moses.

By now Moses has gained the respect of Pharaoh's servants and the Egyptians at large (11:3), even if not of Pharaoh himself. Now God announces the final blow: the death of every firstborn Egyptian, both human and beast. Not only will this judgment gain God's people permission to leave Egypt, but Pharaoh will actually drive them out. The Israelites will emerge a free people made wealthy by the Egyptians themselves (cf. 3:21-22; 11:2-3; 12:35-36).

12:1-36 The Passover and the Final Sign

Up to this point, God takes complete initiative in protecting the Israelites from the punishments he inflicts on Egypt. But now he will require them to do their part in claiming divine protection. To prevent the deaths of their firstborn sons and animals, the Israelites must mark the lintels of their doors with the blood from an animal sacrifice (a lamb or a goat), and then they must eat the meat of the sacrificed animal. (Cf. the consecration rituals in Exodus 29; Leviticus 8. The participation of every Hebrew atoned for each individual's sins and set the nation apart as holy before God.)

God gives specific instructions regarding the nature of the sacrifice and also the timing

of an annual, weeklong Feast of Unleavened Bread they must hold to commemorate the divine judgment's "passing over" their first-born. (Passover marks the first day of the feast; the celebration begins at twilight on the night of a full moon in March/April, which would have provided light for the Israelites on their midnight departure from Egypt.) The regulations specify the types of foods the Israelites must eat (the bitter herbs recall their suffering in Egypt), how they must prepare the foods, how and where they must eat the meal, and the clothes they must wear. The prohibition of eating anything with leaven figures as especially important (the Israelites' quick departure from Egypt did not allow them enough time for their dough to rise); disobeying this command would result in the offender's being "cut off from Israel." Interpretations of this phrase range from premature death to excommunication from the Israelite community, loss of inheritance rights, dishonor in death through burial outside the family tomb, and alienation from one's ancestors in the afterlife (cf. Gen. 17:14; Lev. 7:21; Num. 9:13; Judg. 21:1-7). The annual celebration of the Feast of Unleavened Bread instituted here and first carried out one year later (Num. 9:1-14) becomes another sign of God's everlasting covenant with his people (cf. Gen. 17:13).

The New Testament portrays Jesus as the ultimate Passover sacrifice (see 1 Cor. 5:7), whose bones remain unbroken on the cross (John 19:36; cf. Exod. 12:46). The Last Supper, most likely a Passover meal (Matt. 26:17), becomes the commemorative Lord's Supper (1 Cor. 11:23-33).

The death of all the Egyptian firstborn (males?) parallels and perhaps repays the murder of the Hebrew boys during Moses' infancy. The text does not indicate how God carried out this final judgment, but the anguish that ensues produces the effect God promised: Pharaoh and the Egyptians willingly give the Israelites anything they ask for just to make them leave.

12:37–13:16 Further Instructions Regarding the Passover

The Israelites' initial journey from Rameses to Succoth took them 25 miles southwest. Their number, given as 600 thousand men, seems elevated (cf. Num. 1:46; 11:21; 26:51; estimates for the total population, including women and children, based on this number range from 2 to 3 million). A technical meaning for the Hebrew word "thousand" (such as "clan") or later census data inserted here may account for this seeming exaggeration. In any case, the fact that God later must provide them with food miraculously, since the wilderness cannot support their numbers (16:15), indicates that they comprise a very large group. The theological point is that God has made good on his covenantal promise of blessing by greatly increasing the number of Abraham's ancestors from the 70 (men) who migrated to Egypt in Joseph's day to the "great nation" that now exists. Verses 41-42 emphasize the fulfillment of God's indication that his people would spend four centuries as slaves in a foreign land before he delivered them in the fourth generation from their oppression (cf. Gen. 15:13, 16).

God's requirement that his people dedicate to him every firstborn male further commemorates the Israelites' deliverance from Egypt. They must sacrifice firstborn male beasts (or "redeem" them by sacrificing another beast instead), but they must redeem firstborn male sons (a command that confirms God's rejection of human sacrifice).

13:17-22 The Journey Out of Egypt

The account now begins to focus more specifically on the Israelites' exit from Egypt — the exodus. To avoid a military confrontation with the Philistines along the Mediterranean coast, God leads his people on a longer, more southerly route toward Canaan by way of the wilderness and the Red Sea (Heb. literally "Sea of Reeds"; see "Route of the Exodus" [116]). Although Moses had never met Joseph, he takes Joseph's remains out of Egypt in fulfillment of the Israelites' earlier promise (Gen. 50:24-25).

The account indicates that God maintained his presence with the Israelites in a pillar of cloud during the day and a pillar of fire during the night. Whether the pillars represent natural or supernatural phenomena here, the Bible often uses clouds and fire to represent God's

presence elsewhere (the burning bush, 3:2; the cloud covering Mount Sinai, 24:15-16).

14 Egypt's Final Judgment

Not even the death of Pharaoh's own firstborn causes him to fear God permanently. And not even the protection of their own firstborn from death at the Passover causes the Israelites to trust God completely. With Pharaoh having changed his mind one last time and the Egyptian army hot on their heels, the panicky Israelites blame Moses for putting them in a fearful predicament. But God delivers his people from Pharaoh's clutches, first by protecting them from behind (14:19) and then by creating an escape through the waters of the Red Sea — the same waters that swallow up the pursuing Egyptian army. (The Bible often associates water with death [Ps. 69:1-2; Jonah 2:2-6; Matt. 18:6; Rev. 18:21], so the Israelites' deliverance through the midst of water emphasizes God's divine protection of his chosen people amid otherwise certain doom.) God accomplishes this miraculous deliverance to demonstrate to the Egyptians his sovereignty (14:17-18), but his action also produces a reverence for God and a belief both in God and in Moses on the part of the Israelites that not even the previous signs taken together could produce (14:31).

15:1-21 The Israelites' Song of Victory

The Israelites praise God for his defeat of the Egyptians with a victory song that retells the story of chapter 14 in poetic form and with music and dancing led by Moses' and Aaron's sister, the prophetess Miriam (cf. Num. 12:2-15). The archaic poem in vv. 1-18 may represent the oldest writing in the Bible.

15:22–17:7 The Grumbling Resumes

The memory of God's mighty deeds of deliverance fades relatively quickly in the Israelites' minds and, faced with the lack of drinkable water in the wilderness at Marah, they grumble at Moses, through whom God performs another miracle to provide for their needs (cf. 17:1-7, where God also provides them with water at Rephidim). Here God tests his people by making clear that they must obey him in order to avoid the diseases he inflicted on the Egyptians. In other words, the Israelites must keep their end of the bargain to realize the blessings of their covenant with God.

As the Israelites move on, their grumbling continues, now over lack of food. Their memories of life in Egypt grow rosy as they compare the barrenness of the wilderness with the plenty they knew formerly. Once again, God responds: in the morning he sends a staple food (the breadlike "manna," which they would eat for 40 years until they entered Canaan; cf. Num. 11:7-9) and at night, meat (quail). But God's testing of the Israelites continues. He gives specific instructions concerning the gathering of the manna (an "omer" equals about two quarts) and twice finds at least some of the people disobedient to his commands (16:20, 27). Here God also requires them to observe a day of rest — the Sabbath (16:29-30; cf. Gen. 2:3).

17:8-16 Victory over the Amalekites

In the battle initiated by the Amalekites (nomadic descendants of Esau) at Rephidim, Joshua emerges as the Israelites' prime military commander (who will later succeed Moses). Joshua and his handpicked fighting force defeat their attackers, but the victory belongs to God, whose covenantal curses fall on the Amalekites from this point on.

18 Jethro's Visit

In contrast to the Amalekites, Moses' Midianite father-in-law Jethro welcomes the Israelites. Jethro returns his daughter and grandsons to Moses (the text does not indicate when Zipporah and Moses parted) and rejoices in God's actions on behalf of the Israelites. Further, he shows concern for Moses' welfare and advises him to delegate responsibilities in the administration of judgments between disputing parties. Moses appoints "able men" as leaders over various-sized groups of Israelites, but Moses continues to judge their major disputes.

The barren Sinai wilderness, through which the Hebrew people would wander for 40 years. *(Richard Cleave, Pictorial Archive)*

19 Return to Mount Sinai

As God promised Moses in 3:12, the Israelites journey to Mount Sinai (= Horeb, 3:1), where God appeared to Moses in the burning bush. God again speaks directly to Moses and instructs him in preparing the Israelites to meet their God.

Verses 5-6 set the stage for the establishment of a new covenant between God and his people, whom God will make "a kingdom of priests and a holy nation." Moses instructs the people not to touch the mountain (cf. the "holy ground" around the burning bush, 3:5), on which God descends in a fearful mix of clouds, smoke, and fire (cf. the protective pillars of cloud and fire during the Israelites' departure from Egypt; 13:21-22), accompanied by thunder, lightning, and the quaking of the earth, in order to create a lasting impression of his power and holiness (cf. 20:20). Not even the priests (established as an order only after Sinai) may accompany Moses and Aaron up the mountain to meet with God.

20:1-17 The Ten Commandments

God addresses the Israelites directly by issuing the Ten Commandments (Decalogue) as the basis of his covenant with them. The account

Route of the Exodus

Despite the importance of the exodus in forming and binding Israel as a nation and the people of God and as a central theme in Hebrew thought, no direct material evidence of the event has yet been discovered, and the biblical account remains the only written record.

The exodus begins at Rameses (Egyptian *Pi-Ramesse,* modern Qantir), one of the store-cities in the territory of Goshen in the north-eastern Nile Delta where the Hebrews were enslaved to make mud bricks. Warned by God to avoid the northern "Way of the Land of the Philistines" (Exod. 13:17; also called the Way of Horus), the normal route between Egypt and Canaan heavily fortified by Egyptian troops, the Hebrews headed southeast to Suc-coth (Tell el-Maskhuta) and Etham (near modern Ismailia). Apparently unable to penetrate the "Wall of Shur," a line of fortresses along an ancient canal connecting the Nile River and the Mediterranean Sea, the Hebrews were forced to turn back northwest, camping on the edge of the wilderness before crossing the "Sea of Reeds" (Heb. *yam suph,* traditionally translated "Red Sea"), somewhere in the chain of lakes including Lake Menzaleh, Lake Sirbonis, and the Bitter Lakes.

Numerous difficulties hinder identification of the exact route taken after leaving the delta region. Although archaeological exploration has confirmed some of the sites mentioned, the lack of permanent settlement in the Sinai Peninsula has not favored historical conti-nuity in the naming of places or geographical features. As a result, various routes have been proposed.

The prevailing view is that the Israelites proceeded south on the Way of the Wilderness along the eastern coast of the Gulf of Suez. Tentative identification of such sites as Marah and Elim in the early stages of the exodus favor this route. The obscurity of later sta-tions suggests the rugged southern terrain, where ancient Egyptian copper and turquoise mines were located. Most important to this the-ory is the traditional identification of Mount Sinai (Horeb) with Jebel Musa. From here the group headed northeast toward Kadesh-barnea.

The Route of the Exodus

For Further Reading

Bimson, John J. *Redating the Exodus and the Conquest.* 2nd ed. JSOT Supplement 5. Sheffield: Almond, 1981.

Hoffmeier, James K. *Israel in Egypt.* New York: Oxford University Press, 1997.

Kitchen, K. A. *On the Reliability of the Old Testament.* Grand Rapids: Wm. B. Eerdmans, 2003.

contains elements of the treaty pattern typical in the ancient Near East (see "Covenants" [141-44]): God identifies himself, describes his past relationship with the Israelites, outlines their obligations to him, and states consequences for obeying or disobeying. Yet the 10 "words" speak most directly to issues of the heart, rather than detailing legal regulations.

The first four commandments define the Israelites' relationship to God and distinguish them from other ancient peoples: they must serve the one God only, without making images (idols) that might tempt them to false worship (cf. the golden calf, ch. 32), and they must honor God's nature (represented by his name) and emulate him in their work and rest (cf. 16:29-30). The last six commandments flow naturally from observing the first four — they establish social boundaries among the Israelites themselves. Honoring others at every level and in every relationship lies at the heart of these commands (cf. Matt. 22:37-40). The encounter with God instills such fear in the Israelites that they request that all further communication with God come through Moses.

20:22–23:33 The Book of the Covenant

This next narrative of the events at Mount Sinai contains our oldest record of Jewish law, the Book of the Covenant, which comprises judgments (case laws) and statutes (specific commands) that define religious and civil rules and specify punishments for breaking them. This law code restates and expands the preceding Ten Commandments. The Book of the Covenant departs from other ancient Near Eastern law codes in several respects: its appeal to divine authority; inclusion of both sacred and secular laws; applicability to all strata of society (even slaves have rights; 21:1-11, 26-27); the high value placed on human life (over against material possessions); and limited judgments that prevent overly severe punishment and ongoing feuds but at the same time take offenses seriously enough (the *lex talionis,* 21:23-25). See "Law in Israel and in Judaism"(153-55).

The laws show God's special concern for society's weaker members (widows, orphans, slaves, foreigners, and the injured; the prohibition against releasing a female slave in 21:7 protects rather than punishes her by demanding her master's continuing responsibility for her). That guilty parties must make restitution to those they have hurt emphasizes God's concern for justice beyond mere punishment (21:34-36). The death penalty prescribed for certain transgressions distinguishes just killing from murder (prohibited in 20:13) and emphasizes the seriousness with which the Israelites viewed

Jebel Musa, traditionally identified with Mount Sinai (Horeb). *(Richard Cleave, Pictorial Archive)*

crimes such as dishonoring one's father or mother (21:15, 17), witchcraft (22:18), and bestiality (common in Canaanite religion; 22:19).

The laws concerning the observance of religious feasts in 23:10-19 anticipate the Israelites' settled agricultural life in Canaan. The Feast of Unleavened Bread commemorates the Passover (cf. 12:14-20); the New Testament refers to the Feast of Harvest (= Feast of Weeks) as Pentecost because of its observation 50 days after Passover; and the Bible also refers to the Feast of Ingathering as the Feast of Tabernacles or Booths. Exodus 23:19 provides the basis for Jewish kosher laws prohibiting eating meat and dairy products together.

The Book of the Covenant concludes with an outline of the blessings the Israelites will realize for obeying God's laws: God's protection and the fulfillment of the promise of land he gave originally to Abraham (23:20-33; under David and Solomon the Israelites controlled Canaan within the boundaries God sets in 23:31). These verses also warn against the inhabitants of Canaan, who worship other gods: the Israelites must overthrow them and drive them out, with God's help, in order to avoid the temptation to worship other gods (23:33).

24:1-11 The Ratification of the Covenant

After Moses writes down the laws God has given to the Israelites, he enlists help in ratifying the covenant through a ritual involving animal sacrifices and the sprinkling of blood on the people (reminiscent of the consecration by blood at the Passover; 12:21-23), the reading of the laws aloud, and Moses' ascent up Mount Sinai with Aaron, Aaron's sons Nadab and Abihu, and other Israelite leaders. The group survives their vision of God (cf. Gen. 32:30), and they seal the covenant by eating a meal together. Whereas earlier God established covenants with individuals (Noah and Abraham), this "Mosaic Covenant" involves the nation of Israel as a whole.

24:12–27:21 Instructions for the Tabernacle

Moses and Joshua ascend Mount Sinai to receive the stone tablets inscribed with the Ten Commandments, which Moses finally receives

in 31:18. Before he departs, Moses instructs the people to leave legal decisions to Aaron and Hur (paired earlier in supporting Moses' raised arms during the Israelites' battle with the Amalekites; 17:12). Moses will spend 40 days on top of Mount Sinai. The Bible associates the number 40 with significant transitions in salvation history: the flood lasted 40 days; the Israelite spies spent 40 days in Canaan; Elijah's journey to Horeb took 40 days; Jesus spent 40 days in the wilderness at his temptation; and 40 days passed between Jesus' resurrection and his ascension.

Exodus 25 records God's detailed, though still incomplete, instructions to the Israelites for building and furnishing a sanctuary as God's residence. The Israelites were undoubtedly familiar with portable tent-shrines used in Egyptian religion from their long history in Egypt (see "The Tabernacle" [135-36]). In this way, God makes clear that he will not remain on the mountain but instead will come down to live among his people (29:45-46; cf. John 1:14; 6:38).

God requires his people to donate the best of materials for his house — gold, silver, fine linen, wood from the acacia tree (one of the only trees that grows in the desert) — but he wants only contributions that come from sincere intentions to honor him (25:2). Since God caused his former slave-people to become rich through goods given to them by the Egyptians (12:35-36), the Israelites' contributions for the tabernacle represent a return to God of blessings he first bestowed on them.

The tabernacle's furnishings include the ark of the covenant (cf. Deut. 10:8), a wooden chest overlaid with pure gold that will contain the stone tablets inscribed with the Ten Commandments (= the "testimony"). The ark's lid later figures in the annual ritual of atonement for Israel's sins (Lev. 16:15-16); it serves as a "mercy seat" protected by cherubim, ancient Near Eastern guardians of holy places. (Cherubim also guard the tabernacle as a whole at its outer curtain-walls, and they guard the inner holy of holies from the larger holy place; 26:1, 31.) Poles passed through golden rings attached to the ark will enable the Israelites to transport the chest without actually touching this holy throne of God. In addition to a seat for God, the tabernacle must house a table with bread placed on it and a lampstand for light — the basic household necessities, which symbolize God's immediate presence. The lampstand, which provides the only light in the tabernacle, appears treelike, with flower-cups for lamp oil fixed on its seven branches. God charges the Israelites to provide olive oil to keep the lamps burning continually (27:20) — a task assigned to Aaron and his sons in 27:21.

Curtains will form the walls of the tabernacle itself, and various layers made from goats' hair cloth, dyed rams' skin, and fine hide will overhang the curtains and protect the rectangular tent against the weather. An inner curtain will separate the holy of holies, which will contain the ark where God in Spirit will "sit," from the holy place, which will house the table and lampstand. The inner curtain thus represents the moral barrier between sinful humans and a holy God.

A curtain-fenced courtyard will surround the tabernacle. An altar opposite the entrance to this buffer zone between the Israelites' camp and God's house will stand in front of the entrance to the tabernacle itself. Because the priests will make atonement for Israel's sins at the altar, this consecrated location will become the place where God meets with the "sons of Israel" and speaks to them (29:42-43).

Not only will the Israelites give their goods — jewelry, perfume, animals — but they will also donate their labor in constructing and furnishing God's tent. The many skills the project will require include weaving and spinning, dyeing (using the murex shell for the royal color purple and the cochineal insect for scarlet), embroidery, metalworking and engraving, cutting and polishing of gemstones, tanning, and construction. Although twice the size of the Israelites' portable tent-shrine, the temples built by Solomon and later by the returned exiles follow the tabernacle's basic plan.

28 Instructions for the Priestly Clothing

God sets apart Aaron and his four sons to serve in the tabernacle as priests. As high priest, Aaron must wear garments that reflect the same glory and beauty as God's house, and so many of the same materials used in the tabernacle will go into them: purple and scarlet fabric, fine linen, gold, precious stones. Both the high priest's breastplate and ephod (probably a kind of waistcoat worn over other clothes) will contain the names of the 12 "sons of Israel" and thereby identify Aaron as representative of all the Israelites in his priestly duty of making atonement for sins. The pouch of the breastplate will also contain the Urim and Thummim ("the Lights and the Perfections"), elements of uncertain form used in determining God's will. The tinkling of the bells attached to the hem of Aaron's blue robe will identify Aaron audibly, and the golden plate engraved with "Holy to the Lord" will identify him visibly as God's appointed mediator on behalf of the Israelites when he enters God's presence in the holy of holies. That both Aaron and his sons must wear undergarments will guard against inappropriate exposure (cf. 20:26) and unseemly behavior (cf. Gen. 9:21-23) in God's house.

29 The Consecration of Priests

While God determines to dwell among his people, their sin prevents them from approaching him directly and freely. Even the priests, whom God sets apart to represent the Israelites, must undergo a ritual of consecration to atone for their sins and make them acceptable in the presence of a holy God. This rite involves bathing, clothing, anointing, and sacrificing.

The priests' act of placing their hands on the heads of the bull and the rams symbolizes the transfer of their guilt to the sacrifice. The blood dabbed on the "horns" of the altar purifies it too from contact with ritually unclean individuals. (As vertical projections from tops of the altar's four corners, the horns prevented the wood and sacrifices from falling off; a person fleeing for his life could claim asylum by grabbing onto the altar's horns — the specially consecrated parts of the altar; cf. 1 Kgs. 1:50-51; 2:28.) Whereas in the previous chapter elements of Aaron's clothing appeal to God's hearing and sight, now the priests' burnt offerings will provide a "pleasing (= fragrant) aroma" to God's sense of smell (v. 18; the text anthropomorphizes God).

The sacrificial blood placed on the priests' right ears, thumbs, and big toes symbolizes their consecration to hear and obey God's commands. God provides sustenance for Aaron and his sons by reserving a portion of the sacrifice for their consumption (vv. 31-35). See "Sacrifices and Offerings" (124-25)and "Holy, Clean, and Unclean" (127-28).

30 Further Instructions for Service in the Tabernacle

At the tabernacle's entrance, a burnt offering would serve as a pleasing aroma to God; inside the tent, incense made according to a special recipe and burned on a special altar would provide a fragrant scent. As with the ark of the covenant, gold would overlay the incense altar made of acacia wood, consecrated by the high priest once a year (probably on the Day of Atonement). The Israelites receive strict instructions not to duplicate the particular mix of spices used in the incense for the tabernacle; neither may they copy the recipe for the anointing oil used to consecrate the tent, its furnishings, and the priests. One additional furnishing — a bronze washbasin — would hold water for Aaron and his sons to cleanse themselves for priestly service (cf. 29:4). God would require each Israelite of at least 20 years of age to make a monetary contribution as "atonement money" to cover the costs of the tabernacle service. Rich and poor must pay the same amount, since each individual stands equally guilty before God.

31 Moses Receives the Stone Tablets

Moses' meeting with God on Mount Sinai ends with an affirmation that God, through his spirit, has already equipped craftsmen among the Israelites with the skills necessary to carry out his commands. God reminds the Israelites that they must pay special heed to their covenant with him through observance of the Sabbath (cf. 20:8-11), whereby they mirror his image and activity most closely (cf. Gen.

2:2-3). Finally, Moses receives two stone tablets inscribed "by the finger of God" with the "testimony" (the commandments contained in 20:2-17).

32 The Golden Calf

It does not take long for the Israelites to lose faith during Moses' 40-day absence from them. The people think not of God but of Moses as their deliverer, and their need for a visual symbol of the divine presence prompts them to ask Aaron to make gods for them (v. 1). Either fearing the crowd or having himself lost faith, Aaron complies by fashioning a young bull from the Israelites' golden jewelry and identifying it as the God who brought them out of Egypt — exactly what God prohibited in the Ten Commandments (20:4). (The bull-calf represented Baal, the storm-god and god of fertility in Canaanite religion.) The forgetful Israelites celebrate by feasting and worshipping the idol with offerings.

God sees how little time it has taken the Israelites to forsake him; he determines to annihilate the descendants of the patriarchs and make a great nation of Moses instead. Unselfishly, Moses ignores the offer and intercedes for the Israelites. Moses first points out the negative testimony God's destruction of his people would produce among the Egyptians. He also reminds God of his promises to Abraham, Isaac, and Jacob. God changes his mind and spares the Israelites from total destruction; however, God will indeed punish them for this sin in the days to come (v. 34).

Moses carries the stone tablets as he and Joshua descend from the mountain. When Moses sees the disorderly way in which the Israelites are carrying on, he becomes so angry that he dashes the tablets to the ground — an act that symbolizes the Israelites' breaking of their covenant with God. Moses grinds the golden calf into powder and scatters the powder over the water, which he then forces the Israelites to drink. He holds Aaron accountable for the people's sin, but Aaron tries to deflect responsibility much as Adam and Eve did for their sin (Gen. 3:12-13).

To restore order, Moses then takes punitive

action against the people. The Levites (Moses' own tribe, but Aaron's too) rally with Moses to the Lord's side and kill 3000 Israelites — presumably those found worshipping the golden bull-calf. But the next day, Moses shows solidarity with those still living by asking God to include him among the Israelites whom God will blot out of his book if God will not forgive them (cf. God's "book of life" in Rev. 3:5; 13:8; 21:27). God refuses; for the present, he holds each individual accountable for his or her sin by "smiting" (perhaps with a plague) those who broke the covenant. Yet God also charges Moses to continue his mission of leading the Israelites to the promised land.

33 Moses Seeks God's Will

God's holy nature requires that he punish sin. In an act of grace toward the deliberately sinful Israelites, God announces that he will not live in their midst after all, lest he destroy them. God commands the people not to wear their remaining "ornaments," or jewelry, with which he had blessed them through the Egyptians but which they have used in breaking the covenant. But God reaffirms to Moses that despite their obstinacy the patriarchs' descendants will inherit the land "flowing with milk and honey" — the land of God's promise — with the help of one of his angels.

Verses 7ff. describe how Moses used to meet with God personally in a tent pitched outside the Israelites' camp. (This "tent of meeting" preceded the tabernacle, also called by that name.) Once again, Moses entreats God to change his mind and accompany the Israelites on their journey (cf. 32:11-13). He also seeks the ability to discern God's will, and God rewards Moses' earnestness by granting his request: God will indeed go with his people and even allows Moses to see him, but only from the back, lest Moses die by looking at God's face (cf. 3:6). No matter how much Moses pleases God, he still carries with him the taint of human sin.

34 The Covenant Renewed

In God's infinite mercy and patience, he accepts Moses' repentance on behalf of the Israelites and renews his covenant with them. But God also stresses that his forgiveness will not prevent the guilty from escaping the consequences of their sin. Moses again spends 40 days and nights meeting with God on Mount Sinai, where God repeats the terms of the covenant. God places special emphasis on his command that the Israelites destroy the trappings of Canaanite religion and form no alliances with pagan peoples when they arrive in Canaan, lest they follow other gods. God will not tolerate any rivals for his people's worship.

Moses descends the mountain equipped with a second set of stone tablets inscribed with the Ten Commandments. His face appears illuminated from his audience with God, and he dons a veil in an attempt to prevent the reflection of God's glory from fading (cf. 2 Cor. 3:12-18), perhaps so the Israelites will remain convinced of the divine origin and authority of his words.

35–40 Moses Sets Up the Tabernacle

Moses and the Israelites follow to the letter the instructions God gave for making, furnishing, and serving in his house (chs. 25–31). But before the Israelites begin work on the tabernacle, Moses reemphasizes God's command that they observe the Sabbath. The Israelites must observe a day of rest even while undertaking the important task of building a house for God.

The Israelites contribute generously of their labor and their material possessions for the project. Their freewill donations amount to so much, in fact, that Moses must call a halt to all offerings. Bezalel, of the tribe of Judah, supervises the project with the assistance of Oholiab, of the tribe of Dan (31:2, 6); the two train others in the skills needed to complete the task, and together the Israelites make everything according to God's instructions. The account here includes details such as the specific types of precious and semiprecious stones used for the priestly vestments and the amounts of gold, silver, and bronze donated for the project. After Moses inspects and approves all the work, he blesses the people and then receives instructions from God to set up and consecrate the tabernacle and to clothe, anoint, and consecrate the priests. This must occur on the first day of the first month, the first anniversary of the Israelites' deliverance from Egypt.

After Moses prepares the tabernacle for use and the priests for service, God descends on his house in a cloud and occupies it. He now lives among his people, his presence visible in the cloud over the tent by day and in its firelike appearance by night (cf. Num. 9:15). As long as the cloud remains over the tent, the Israelites remain encamped. When the cloud lifts, they move on toward the promised land. The tabernacle will serve as God's house and as the focal point of Israelite worship for the next 300 years, until Solomon builds the first temple. (The 480 years indicated in 1 Kgs. 6:1 are thought to be an ideal number suggesting construction of the temple at the midpoint between the exodus and the return from exile or perhaps representing one generation [40 years] for each of the 12 tribes.)

Leviticus

Leviticus — named after the tribe of Levi, which inherited the Israelite priesthood — restates and expands the Law given to Moses on Mount Sinai as recorded in Exodus 20–23. But not all Levites became priests (only Aaron and his descendants), and not all of Leviticus focuses solely on the rituals of the ancient Israelite priesthood. While chapters 6–17 provide instruction for the priests in conducting worship, chapters 1-5 and 18–27 focus mainly on guiding the Israelite community in matters of practical holiness. Chapters 17–26 are often identified as the "Holiness Code."

Holiness evidenced by ritual purity and personal morality represented a new development in religion in the Near East of the 2nd millennium B.C. and signaled Israel's distinctiveness from other nations. More importantly, holiness made possible the Israelites' appropriation of God's grace and forgiveness evidenced by his continuing to dwell in their midst (cf. Exodus 33).

Content

The account in Leviticus flows logically from the setting presented at the end of Exodus, with the Israelites poised to celebrate God's dwelling among them by beginning the service of the newly erected tabernacle. By giving detailed instructions concerning ritual purity and the sacrificial system, Leviticus emerges as a rulebook for the priests in exercising their duties in the tabernacle and a handbook for their teaching of the laity, particularly regarding the maintenance of ritual cleanness. See "Holy, Clean, and Unclean" (127-28).

In the latter half of the book, instructions for the nation as a whole address all areas of life — worship (through celebration as well as sacrifice), personal morality, family and community relationships, the treatment of resident aliens, and economic dealings (especially regarding land and property). Many of these laws provide the roots for Christian principles mandated in the New Testament, such as loving one's neighbor, caring for society's weak and oppressed, resisting conformity to the world, and carrying out not only the letter but also the spirit of the Law (esp. ch. 19).

Authorship

Although Leviticus does not identify its author directly, the writer presents God as communicating his laws to Moses, to whom traditionalists ascribe the authorship of the book. The Documentary Hypothesis attributes the present form of Leviticus to the priestly line of the exilic period and dates the material to the late 6th century B.C., although it recognizes that much of the book's content predates the exile by many years. Another view posits that preexilic editors closer to Moses' time compiled Leviticus.

1–7 Sacrifices

God commands the Israelites to offer five kinds of sacrifices — three voluntary, and two compulsory. Unlike the sacrifices in other ancient Near Eastern religions, these offerings were not attempts to manipulate God for personal gain; rather, they represented thankful responses for God's blessings, effected forgiveness of sins, and restored fellowship with God and neighbor. Both the poor and the wealthy received complete forgiveness by means of their obedient observance of the sacrificial rites regardless of the monetary value of their offerings. Although God's instructions require the Israelites to give of their best to God, the sacrificial system does not impoverish them, for God's primary interest is the contrite hearts evidenced by the offerings, not the material value of the sacrifices themselves (cf. 1 Sam. 15:22; Mark 12:33).

Sacrifices and Offerings

According to the biblical witness, the offering of sacrifices is as old as the relationship between God and Israel. The people as a community of faith join themselves with Yahweh, the god they will serve, in the ritual of a sacrificial meal. Both the account in Exod. 18:12, where Moses, Aaron, and the elders of Israel encounter Yahweh in the wilderness, and the binding of the people in covenant at Sinai through the offering of sacrifices followed by eating and drinking attest to the significance of sacrifice for the Yahweh-Israel relationship (Exod. 24:1-11).

The language of sacrifice and offering found in the biblical text shares common features with other societies of the ancient Near East. The offering of food to the gods was an important aspect of the religious expression of surrounding cultures. Whether or not the people of Israel understood their sacrifices along similar lines (cf. Lev. 1:9, 13, 17), it is important to understand how the sacrifices offered to God define and reflect both the character of God and the nature of the covenantal relationship that binds God and people together.

The place of sacrifice and offering is woven throughout the biblical story. From initial spontaneous acts of gratitude in which one's best produce is dedicated to God, whether animal or vegetable, to a systematic fulfillment of a regimented sacrificial system that develops later in Israel's history, sacrifice and offering work to affirm, enhance, repair, and sometimes restore the relationship between worshipper and God. When the Philistines threaten Israel, Samuel intercedes on their behalf by sacrificing to the Lord (1 Sam. 7:7-10). Saul (who was not a priest) receives condemnation for a similar act (1 Sam. 13:8-13). On the occasion of bringing the ark into Jerusalem, David offers "burnt offerings and offerings of well-being before the Lord" (2 Sam. 6:17-18), and Solomon offers regular sacrifices and offerings in the temple (1 Kgs. 9:25).

Israel's early history allowed for sacrifices to be offered on family altars, at local shrines, and at high places. Such acts gave way to the demand that legitimate sacrifices be offered only at the temple (Deut. 12:13-14), with strict condemnation of the high places as Israel's cult became centralized in Jerusalem.

"Offering" is a broader term than "sacrifice." Any sacred gift or donation given to the deity or to the deity's cultic personnel at an altar or cult place is an "offering." A "sacrifice" is a gift that is burned totally or partially as a part of the offering ritual. A variety of sacrificial terms are used in describing the manner or substance of the offering, the place or timing, and the purpose or motive.

A "burnt offering" (Heb. 'olah) refers to an offering that is wholly burned on the altar. An unblemished male animal, ranging from a bird to a bull, was brought by the presenter to the altar. The presenter identified the offering as his, for his need or benefit, by placing his hand over the animal. Either the presenter or priest would slaughter the animal, splash or pour out its blood against the altar, and burn the animal for the purpose of allowing its smoke or odor "to go up" or "ascend" ('alah) pleasantly to the deity. Biblical examples suggest that the burnt offering was at times used to gain the attention of the deity in order that the worshipper might then present his primary concerns (cf. Num. 23:1-6; 1 Kings 18) and at other times for expiation or atonement (Lev. 1:4; Job 42:8), as well as to fulfill of a vow or as a freewill offering (Lev. 22:17-19; Num. 15:3).

Grain or cereal offerings (minhah) are closely associated with the burnt offering. Whether as grain, flour, or bread; mixed with oil, frankincense, and salt; presented raw or formed into cakes and cooked, the grain offering moved from being burned in its entirety to a time when only a part was burned and the remainder consumed by the priests (Lev. 2:1-16, esp. vv. 8-10). Not only were cultic personnel provided for by such offerings, but the poor were likewise included in a sacrificial system that might otherwise exclude them. Over time, offerings of incense became daily fare (Exod. 30:1-8).

Sometimes translated as "peace offering" or "communion offering," the sacrifice of well-being (zebah shelamim) establishes or maintains communion with the deity. The emphasis is on a right relationship between the worshipper and God. Similar in procedure to the burnt offering, the sacrifice of well-being differs in that all participants share in the distribution of the meat. Blood and fat, considered as life-giving, belong to God. The priest receives the breast and right leg, and the person bringing the

Sacrificial altar in the 10th/9th-century Israelite temple at Arad; made of unhewn field stones, 5 × 5 cubits (2.5 × 2.5 m.). *(Phoenix Data Systems, Neal and Joel Bierling)*

sacrifice keeps the remainder (Lev. 7:28-34; 10:14-15). This sacrifice follows the burnt and grain offerings in passages that present them in 1-2-3 order (Leviticus 1–7; Josh. 22:23, 29; 1 Kgs. 8:64; Jer. 33:18; Amos 5:22). Particular usages of the sacrifice of well-being occur in celebratory moments, both public and private. The thanksgiving offering expresses gratitude for God's deliverance (Lev. 7:12-15), the votive offering seeks to secure the aid of the deity through payment of a vow (Lev. 7:13), and the freewill offering celebrates life's goodness. Each is found within official religious expression as well as in family religious practices.

Two sacrifices serve to bring about atonement: the purification offering *(hatta't)* and the reparation offering *('asham)*. The first is often called a "sin offering" and is designed to purify the altar or sanctuary. Should other sacrifices be offered, they must come first with the blood of the sacrifice serving a purifying role. The benefit to the worshipper was the removal of his guilt, with all the meat being given to the priests. Should the offering be for the benefit of the high priest or community, the entire offering was burned outside the camp and no one could eat of it (Lev. 4:1–5:13; 9:7-21; 14:19). The reparation offering, likewise called a "guilt offering," occurs often with the purification offering and is in many cases difficult to distinguish from the sin offering (Lev. 5:14–6:7; 7:1-7). Numbers 5:5-8 has restitution being made to the wronged person as well as a fine of 20 percent accompanying the reparation offering.

Over time a set pattern developed of daily sacrificial ritual at the temple that would be supplemented on occasion by particular sacrifices of individual worshippers. Special festivals or days of worship would occasion other sacrifices, such as the Passover lamb (Exodus 12) and the Day of Atonement's scapegoat (Leviticus 16).

The ritual practices of sacrifice and offering served to maintain an order of holiness and purity, provide the means for consuming the flesh and meat, and bind people and God in community. Additionally, the presentation of the tithe and firstfruits (Deut. 12:6) became a celebratory means by which God was thanked (Deut. 14:22-26) and two categories of people were cared for — the priests and those in priestly service (Deut. 14:27-28; 26:12; Num. 18:21-32; Neh. 10:37-38; 13:10-12) and those without regular means of support from the land — resident aliens, orphans, and widows (Deut. 14:28).

When the true meaning of sacrifice becomes lost in ritual, prophetic critique is harsh (Amos 5:21-27; Isa. 1:11-17; Mal. 1:6-14). Yahweh is not a god who needs to be fed (Ps. 50:13) but rather a god who demands obedience and justice (Amos 5:24), a god who delights in legitimate sacrifices (Ps. 51:19).

For Further Reading

Anderson, Gary A. "Sacrifice and Sacrificial Offerings (OT)." *ABD* 5:870-86.

Brueggemann, Walter. *Reverberations of Faith: A Theological Handbook of Old Testament Themes.* Louisville: Westminster John Knox, 2002.

Miller, Patrick D. "Sacrifice and Offering in Ancient Israel." *The Religion of Ancient Israel.* Louisville: Westminster John Knox, 2000, 106-30.

KANDY QUEEN-SUTHERLAND

Voluntary sacrifices include the burnt offering (ch. 1; 6:8-13), which functions mainly to atone for sins, but which also expresses thanksgiving or announces a vow of obedience. Although all the sacrifices involve burning a portion of the offering, the burnt offering is the only sacrifice completely consumed by fire (with the exception of the hide). As with the other animal sacrifices, the burnt offering must come from the offerer's own herd or flock (not from the wild) to ensure that the sacrifice costs the offerer something. This requirement also ties the offerer to the animal in the transfer of guilt by the offerer's laying a hand on the animal's head. Further, as God required the best of materials for the construction and furnishing of the tabernacle, he also requires the best of animals — unblemished ones — as sacrifices.

The second voluntary sacrifice, the grain or cereal offering (ch. 2; 6:14-18), often accompanied other sacrifices (cf. Num. 15:1-16). The poor could give a grain offering by itself in place of an animal. Oil and frankincense mixed with finely ground flour add value and express joy in this offering. (The offering of firstfruits requires only whole grains.) The grain offering cannot include leaven or honey (perhaps because these ingredients cause fermentation and therefore symbolize corruption), but it must include salt (perhaps as a preservative symbolizing the offering's perpetual effectiveness). The priests are to burn only a small portion of the grain offering on the altar and eat the remainder. In this way, God provides sustenance from grain for the landless priestly tribe.

The voluntary peace, or fellowship, offering (ch. 3; 7:11-36) restores relationships, both between God and his people and between individuals and their neighbors. It serves both personal and communal functions and provides an occasion for a shared meal between family and friends. This offering could signify personal thanksgiving or the fulfillment of a vow and later accompanied the dedication of the first temple (1 Kgs. 8:63-66) and Saul's appointment as king (1 Sam. 11:15). No one may eat the sacrificed animal's fat (considered the best and richest part and therefore God's portion) or the blood (which symbolizes life). As

with the other animal sacrifices except those offered as burnt offerings, the priests take their prescribed portion of meat as God's provision for their sustenance.

The offering for unintentional sin (4:1–5:13; 6:24-30), required when an individual realizes his or her transgression, does not so much achieve atonement as cleanse from sin — which breaks a person's relationship with God and endangers the welfare of the entire community. Because it applies to inadvertent offenses, not to deliberate wrongdoing, it also purifies the ritually unclean (e.g., a woman after giving birth, or an individual with a skin disease). A gradation exists in the sacrifice required that reflects the degree to which the offense of one individual affects the congregation of Israel as a whole. While the high priest, God's special representative of all the people, must sacrifice the most costly of animals — a bull — the common poor person may offer a bird or some grain.

The guilt offering (5:14–6:7; 7:1-10) makes right a wrong by requiring not only sacrifice but also compensation. Again, the kinds of sacrifices offered may vary depending on the economic status of the offerer, but all offenders must make restitution of 120 percent for their misdeed. Leviticus 5:17 allows no escape from the guilt of sin: even the person unaware of his offense will "bear his punishment" and must offer an atoning sacrifice.

In all these cases, the offerer prepares the sacrifice either by grinding and mixing the grain, oil, and incense, or by slaughtering, skinning, cleaning, and cutting up the animal. The priest sprinkles the blood on the altar and/or arranges the offering on it. In 6:9–7:36, God gives additional instructions to the priests concerning their specific duties and entitlements regarding each kind of sacrifice. The "wave [or 'elevation'] offering" (7:30) probably involves the offerer's raising his sacrifice as he hands it over to the priest in a symbolic gesture of transferring its ownership from the human realm to that of the divine. The "pleasing aroma" the offerings provide for God symbolizes God's pleasure with his people for their obedience (and perhaps makes possible his continued dwelling among them).

Holy, Clean, and Unclean

Modern readers may be puzzled that in the Bible there is a connection between the ideas of holy and clean/unclean. Leviticus 10:10 assumes their association: "You must distinguish between the holy [Heb. *qodesh*] and the profane [or 'common'; *hol*], between the unclean *[tame']* and the clean *[tahor]*" (NIV). To understand these concepts and their relationship, let us examine the concept of holy, show its connection with clean/unclean by a specific example in the life of David, and then discuss the interpretation of these concepts in the New Testament.

When David fled King Saul, he came to the sanctuary at Nob and requested food for himself and his men from Ahimelech the priest. The priest replied to David, "I don't have any ordinary *[hol]* bread on hand; however, there is some consecrated *[qodesh]* bread here — provided the men have kept themselves from women" (1 Sam. 21:4 NIV). The consecrated bread was the 12 loaves in the sanctuary, known as the "bread of the Presence" (KJV "shewbread"), which after their weekly removal could be eaten by the Aaronic priests (1 Sam. 21:6; Lev. 24:5-9). The rationale behind the consecrated bread versus the ordinary bread was its status in relation to God. Only God is by nature holy (Isa. 6:3-5), meaning that he is morally perfect in his character and in his acts. All persons, creatures, and things are dependent on God's holiness, becoming holy when they move from the common sphere to the holy sphere (e.g., priests, Lev. 8:30). Because of the presence of God among his people (Exod. 25:8), any person or thing related to him was holy. This was especially but not exclusively true of Israel's worship, such as places (tabernacle/temple), persons (priests), things (altar), rituals (sacrifices), and time (Sabbath). The important ideas of holy are divine presence and relationship to the Holy One.

In our Samuel passage, Ahimelech provided the sacred bread on the condition that neither David nor his men had engaged in sexual relations. This requirement reflects the purity laws concerning clean and unclean. Leviticus 15:18 instructs persons who have had sexual intercourse to wash themselves, indicating that they were in the condition of ritual uncleanness until evening (cf. Exod. 19:15). Anyone who was ritually "unclean" could defile the holy by contact. Thus the spheres of holy and clean/unclean can overlap, creating the very complex regulations practiced by the Israelites. The world of the clean/unclean pertained to the physical existence of the people, especially foods (Leviticus 11; Deuteronomy 14) and persons (Leviticus 12-15; Num. 5:2-4). The rationale behind Ahimelech's objection explains the relationship of holy and clean/unclean. David's men had been consecrated to the Lord; if they became unclean through sexual intercourse, by eating the holy bread they would defile the sanctuary and the Lord (Lev. 15:31). Ritual purity was necessary for any person or thing that approached or pertained to the holy, requiring regular purification of the sanctuary from sin and uncleanness. Purity laws also applied to other areas of life (e.g., skin disease, Leviticus 13-14). The primary purpose for these laws was to acknowledge the presence of God in Israel's midst, distinguishing the people of God thereby from the nations (Lev. 20:25-26). The holy character and actions of the Lord and the demands made on his people to imitate his holiness (Lev. 19:2; 20:7; Deut. 23:14) necessitated redemption and sanctification (Exod. 19:6), for the people were both sinful and impure.

The Hebrew psalmists and prophets especially employed the language of holy — clean/unclean to describe sinful moral and ethical behavior (Isa. 6:5; Ps. 51:7). Jesus and the church also emphasized this ethical or spiritual significance (Mark 7:18-23; Heb. 1:3). The popular Greek terms in the Septuagint and New Testament for "holy" *(hagios)* and "sanctify" *(hagiazo)* translate the Hebrew word group for "holy" *(qadosh)*. The New Testament writers affirmed the Old Testament understanding of God as holy (John 17:11) and the people of God (church) as sanctified (1 Pet. 2:9). In particular, the New Testament shows that the redemptive sacrifice of Jesus Christ by his

---

Food Laws

Clean Animals
Quadrupeds that chew the cud and have cloven hooves
Ox, sheep, goat, deer, gazelle, roebuck, wild goat, ibex, antelope, mountain sheep
Fish with scales and fins
Other birds
Leaping insects
Locusts, cricket, grasshopper

Unclean Animals
Those that do not
Camel, rock badger, hare, pig
Quadrupeds with flat paws
Dogs, cats
Fish without scales and fins
Lobsters, crabs, shrimp, shellfish
Carnivorous or swamp-dwelling birds
Eagle, vulture, osprey, buzzard, kite, raven, ostrich, nighthawk, sea gull, hawk, owl, cormorant, water hen, pelican, stork, heron, hoopoe, bat
Winged insects
Swarming creatures
Weasel, mouse, lizard, gecko, crocodile, chameleon

---

death and resurrection sanctifies those who believe, fulfilling the demands that God's presence places on his people (John 17:17-19; 1 Cor. 1:30). By drawing on the imagery of Old Testament cult and covenant, the writer to the Hebrews declares that Christ is both perfect high priest, tabernacle, and atoning sacrifice, whose shed blood sanctifies believers once and for all, requiring no further offering (Heb. 9:11-14: 10:1-18). Through the gift of the indwelling Holy Spirit (Rom. 15:16; 1 Cor. 6:11), the individual (6:19) and the church (3:16-17) are holy vessels who must cast off sinful living. The sanctifying presence of the Spirit (1 Pet. 1:2) requires Christians to seek a lifestyle of love and blameless conduct (Rom. 12:1; 1 Thess. 3:12-13; Heb. 12:10; 1 Pet. 1:14-16; 2:5). Sanctification also has an eschatological dimension, when at the coming of Christ the church will be presented and dwell with God in all eternity (1 Thess. 3:13; 5:23; Rev. 20:6; 21:2-3). The New Testament authors viewed the holiness of God's people primarily as one's right relationship with God through the sanctifying work of Christ, not cultic purity through ritual observance. The Apostle Paul often referred to Christians and to his readers as "the holy ones/saints" (Rom. 1:7; 15:31), indicating their redemption and sanctification in Christ (Rom. 1:4; 1 Cor. 1:2; Col. 1:12).

For Further Reading

Lenchak, Timothy A. "Clean and Unclean." *Eerdmans Dictionary of the Bible,* ed. David Noel Freedman. Grand Rapids: Eerdmans, 2000, 262-63.
Peterson, David G. "Holiness." *The New Dictionary of Biblical Theology,* ed. T. Desmond Alexander and Brian S. Rosner. Downers Grove: InterVarsity, 2000, 544-50.

KENNETH A. MATHEWS

Although foreign and seemingly gory to modern Westerners, the ancient Israelite sacrificial system represented a much more humane, orderly, and reverent means of worship than that of other ancient Near Eastern religions, which included rituals of divination using animals' entrails, sexual and fertility rites, occult practices, the shedding of blood through self-mutilation, and human sacrifice. Christ's death on the cross made the sacrificial system unnecessary by achieving atonement for sin, cleansing from unrighteousness, payment of the debt of sin, and restored fellowship with God (cf. Eph. 1:7; Col. 1:20; 1 John 1:7).

8–10 Institution of the Priesthood

Now that the priests and people know how and what to sacrifice to God, the ceremony to consecrate the priests outlined in Exodus 28–29 proceeds. In front of the congregation gathered at the entrance to the tabernacle, Moses conducts the elaborate, seven-day ritual, which involves clothing Aaron with the priestly vestments; anointing him, his sons, and the objects set apart for worshipping God; and offering sacrifices on behalf of the newly ordained priests. The sin offering cleanses Aaron and his sons ritually, the burnt offering achieves their spiritual cleansing through atonement, and the peace offering establishes their fellowship with God.

Yet these outward signs of dedication to God and adherence to his commands do not reach the hearts of Aaron's sons Nadab and Abihu, who begin their priestly duties by offering "strange fire before the Lord." Whatever the nature of this action, it clearly represents a disregard for God's commands regarding priestly service. Lest anyone believe from the outset that the Lord tolerates priestly disregard for his holiness and his commands, God strikes Nadab and Abihu dead. Then God commands Aaron that Israel's priests refrain from drinking alcohol before attending to their duties — a departure from Canaanite religious practice. The entire incident surrounding Nadab's and Abihu's death emphasizes the higher standard to which God holds those he places in positions of spiritual leadership and evidences the greater judgment those leaders incur for causing others to stray (cf. Jas. 3:1).

Yet neither do Eleazar and Ithamar, Aaron's surviving sons, follow God's instructions. Instead of eating the meat of a sin offering to achieve atonement for the Israelite congregation, they let it burn up (10:16-18). Aaron intercedes with Moses on their behalf, apparently attributing their breach to the recent death of their brothers, and Moses accepts Aaron's explanation.

11 Laws regarding Food

God wants the Israelites to stand out from other peoples not only in their religious beliefs and practices ("holiness"), but also in practical ("common") matters, including eating habits. Here God prohibits his people from eating specific animals, fish, birds, and insects — in many cases, creatures that today are identified as particularly likely to carry and spread disease easily in hot climates.

Foods forbidden for consumption consist of flesh-eating animals, birds of prey or carrion, pigs, vermin, and shellfish. Permitted foods include animals with cloven hoofs that also "chew the cud" (primarily domesticated animals), sea creatures that have both fins and scales, birds not listed as forbidden, and four kinds of locusts.

Chapter 11 also outlines procedures for ensuring that the Israelites do not consume contaminated food or water, as well as rules for purifying anything that has become defiled through contact with dead creatures' carcasses. Note that physical contact with live animals declared as unclean for consumption does not result in ritual contamination.

12 Ritual Cleansing after Childbirth

Sexual intercourse, conception, pregnancy, and childbirth do not constitute sins for which an Israelite wife needs atonement. Humans are to "be fruitful and multiply" (Gen. 1:28); motherhood is a woman's social crown, and children are a blessing from God (Gen. 30:1-24). Rather, the woman's issue of blood for several weeks following delivery makes her ritually unclean (as does monthly menstruation); since blood represents life, the mother's continued loss of blood signifies an unnatural and therefore "unclean" state of losing life.

To allow time for the blood loss to stop, the woman must remain confined for several weeks after giving birth — twice the amount of time for bearing a girl as for a boy (perhaps in anticipation of the girl's one day giving birth herself). Following the mother's period of confinement, she must offer a burnt offering (perhaps partly to express thanksgiving for her child) and a sin offering (cf. Luke 2:21-24). These sacrifices achieve her atonement and cleansing.

13-14 Treating and Cleansing from Skin Diseases and Fungi

Priests must also diagnose, treat, and ritually cleanse people, fabrics, and houses affected by various skin diseases and fungi all classed under the general category of "leprosy" (not modern Hansen's disease). The instructions here provide basic guidelines for distinguishing temporary conditions from chronic ailments, for pronouncing people and items with "leprous" spots ritually clean (in cases of stable or healing states) or ritually unclean (in cases of infectious and spreading states), and for preventing defilement of the holy (normally by isolating the infected person or item).

As with mourners, individuals declared unclean must tear their clothes, sport messy hair, and cover their faces. They must verbally warn others of their diseased state (13:45) and live outside the Israelite camp to avoid physical contact with others. Neither may they enter the tabernacle court to worship and offer sacrifices. Again, however, moral wrongdoing does not figure in "uncleanness" (cf. ch. 12), and chapter 14 describes the process of ritually cleansing a person whose skin disease has healed. The lengthy ceremony publicly reverses the social isolation made necessary by the disease and welcomes the healed individual's return to worship through sacrifice.

Priests must treat houses "infected" with fungi, mildew, dry rot, and the like in a similar manner. After quarantining the house and ordering the replacement of necessary parts, the priest must anoint the "healed" house by using cedar wood, hyssop, and blood from a bird (to symbolize renewed life; cf. the ritual for humans healed of skin diseases, 14:1-32). But a house in which the problem persists must be torn down.

15 Cleansing from Bodily Discharges

Both natural and abnormal bodily discharges from male and female reproductive organs render an ancient Israelite unclean and require washing and waiting before the resumption of worship at the tabernacle (cf. Mark 5:24-34). That men and women become ritually unclean from sexual intercourse does not suggest the sinfulness of sexual activity. Rather, the declaration of a person's ritual uncleanness after sex makes it clear that God rejects sexual and fertility rites as part of Israel's worship.

16 The Day of Atonement

Yom Kippur, the solemn Day of Atonement (23:27-28), represents Israel's cleansing from sin so God may continue to dwell in their midst. Six months after Passover, the Day of Atonement continues to represent the highest holy day in the Jewish religious calendar.

God's instructions here dictate that Aaron (and subsequent high priests) enter the tabernacle's holy of holies only on this one day of the year. Clad in simple clothing (in contrast to the elaborate priestly vestments worn on other days), Aaron must atone for the sins of all the priests, including his own, through the sacrifice of a bull, whose blood he must sprinkle on and in front of the lid of the ark of the covenant. He must also make atonement for the people by sprinkling a goat's blood before the ark and then purify the altar outside the tabernacle with the blood of the bull and goat.

The ceremony reached its climax when Aaron symbolically transferred the Israelites' guilt to a second, live goat by laying his hands on the goat's head and confessing all Israel's sins, after which he would drive the scapegoat away into the wilderness to represent the removal of the people's iniquities both from sight and from memory. Scholars dispute the meaning of Azazel ("scapegoat," "goat of removal"), but the term certainly does not represent an offering to a demon (cf. 17:7). Burnt offerings and cleansing rituals conclude the atonement ceremony. The institution of this observance as a permanent statute ensures that the Israelites continue to confess their sinfulness before a holy God and celebrate his forgiveness and mercy.

The author of Hebrews connects the significance of Jesus' death on the cross with the purposes of the Day of Atonement (Heb. 9:1–10:22) and adds that Christ's sacrificial blood achieved eternal atonement and free access to God once and for all (esp. 9:12; cf. 2 Cor. 5:21; 1 Pet. 2:24).

17 Additional Food Laws

Chapter 17 further addresses the regulations regarding the sacrifice of animals and the eating of meat. The Israelites viewed the killing of domestic animals as sacrifice; therefore, God requires his people to sacrifice any domestic animal killed for its meat as a fellowship offering to him at the tabernacle (cf. Deut. 12:13-18). This ensures the Israelites' faithfulness to God alone by guarding against their ritual recognition of spirits of nature, such as the "goat demons" worshipped by the Egyptians (v. 7). The prohibition against eating blood appears again; here blood commands special respect, because blood represents life, and the sacrificed life effects atonement (vv. 10-14). The restrictions apply not only to the Israelites but also to outsiders living with them in order to prevent both idolatry and the introduction of foreign religious practices into Israel's worship.

18 Sexual Purity

Israel's distinctiveness from its neighbors must extend beyond purely religious rituals and into many practical areas of life, including sexual relationships. The sexual taboos given here ensure healthy social relationships within the Israelite community by guarding against jealousy and rivalry and also honor God by preserving the sexual relationships implied and established at creation.

The Israelites must honor their own marriage bonds but resist the practices of their neighbors. They must avoid incest by refraining from sexual relations with persons related through blood and birth as well as those related through marriage. Whereas the Egyptians and Canaanites incorporated all manner of perversions into their religious practices, the Israelites must not "defile" themselves by engaging in "abominations," such as adultery, child-sacrifice, same-sex intercourse, or bestiality, lest God judge them in the same manner as the Canaanites (by causing the land to spew them out).

19 Practical Holiness

If the first chapters of Leviticus primarily legislate *ritual* holiness, chapter 19 makes clear that God also requires of his people a *practical* holiness in both public and private life that results from fearing God (emphasized by the repeated phrase, "I am the Lord") and that results in loving others in both word and deed (vv. 18, 34). Each of the Ten Commandments appears in some form here, with added directives that emphasize the importance of carrying out not only the letter but also the spirit of the laws. Not only must an Israelite refrain from robbery — he must not even delay paying a worker promptly (v. 13); an Israelite may express anger toward another, but he must not allow his anger to turn into heartfelt hatred (v. 17); and not only must a person restrain himself from taking vengeance on another — he must not even bear a grudge (v. 18). The Israelites' oppression as slaves in Egypt gives birth to admonishments to love the needy and the resident alien through practical acts of concern (vv. 10, 33-34). Care must extend beyond one's neighbor to include the rest of God's creation — both land and animals (vv. 19, 23-25; cf. 25:1-7). So holiness must manifest itself not only in rejection of pagan practices (vv. 26b-30), but also in the performance of just and merciful acts — in right behavior.

20 Penalties for Covenantal Offenses

For the Israelites, breaking God's covenantal laws demands serious punishment. Offenses against God and neighbor measured by the Ten Commandments and prohibited in chapters 18 and 19 incur penalties ranging from capital punishment (administered by the Israelites themselves) to the "cutting off" of a person from the Israelite community and to childlessness (both administered by God). The severity of the punishments guards Israel's distinctiveness from other nations and, more importantly, preserves the holy status conferred on them by God.

21–22 Priestly Holiness

Israel's priests must conform to a higher standard of behavior than the common Israelite, and the high priest must adhere to the highest standard of all. This hierarchy of holiness applied to Israel's priests provides an internal model of the Israelite nation's distinctiveness from her neighbors through her commitment to holiness and godly behavior. Special restric-

The Calendar of Israel's Worship

When God miraculously rescued the descendants of Abraham, Isaac, and Jacob from the tyranny of their enforced enslavement in Egypt, he set in motion a process designed to create a nation that would be radically different from all others. Based on the covenant made at Mount Sinai, the newly formed theocracy was meant to be "a kingdom of priests," mediating between God and the nations, and "a holy nation," mirroring God's moral perfection in their daily lives (Exod. 19:6). To support these objectives, various institutions (the tabernacle, the Aaronic priesthood) and practices (the Levitical sacrificial system, the distinction between clean and unclean foods) were set in place during Israel's temporary sojourn at Mount Sinai. As part of these new arrangements a calendar of special days and times was also inaugurated.

Alongside the weekly Sabbath and monthly new moon celebration, arrangements were put in place for the three annual pilgrimage feasts of Unleavened Bread (incorporating Passover), Weeks, and Tabernacles. In addition, the seventh month of the year (Tishri) started with the Feast of Trumpets, to be followed on the 10th day of the month by the Day of Atonement. (For a detailed list, see Leviticus 23; Numbers 28–29 catalogues the special offerings associated with each of these occasions.) Beyond these weekly, monthly, and annual occasions, the Israelites were also expected to observe as special times every seventh year and every 49th (or

Feasts and Festivals

March			**September**	
Month 1			Month 7	
Nisan (Abib)	14 Passover		Tishri (Ethanim)	1 Trumpets/New Year
	15-21 Unleavened Bread			10 Day of Atonement
				15-21 Tabernacles/Booths/Ingathering
April				
Month 2			**October**	
Iyyar (Ziv)			Month 8	
			Marchesvan (Bul)	
May				
Month 3			**November**	
Sivan	6 Weeks/Harvest		Month 9	
			Kislev	25-Tebet 2 Lights/Dedication
June				
Month 4			**December**	
Tammuz			Month 10	
			Tebet	
July				
Month 5			**January**	
Ab			Month 11	
			Shebat	
August				
Month 6			**February**	
Elul			Month 12	
			Adar	14 Purim

possibly 50th, depending upon how the biblical evidence is interpreted) year — the Year of Jubilee. (Much later in Israel's history, the Feast of Purim was introduced [see Esther] and the festival of Lights [or Hanukkah], celebrating the cleansing of the temple by Judas Maccabeus in 164 B.C.)

Although it was the most common of all the special days, the weekly Sabbath, along with the Day of Atonement, was the most sacred. On these days all work was prohibited (Lev. 23:3, 28). In contrast, the pilgrimage festivals of Unleavened Bread, Weeks, and Tabernacles and certain other days were considered less holy and required only refraining from regular work (Lev. 23:7, 21, 25, 35). Likewise, while the Israelites were expected to make particular offerings on the first day of each month at the new moon, they were permitted to work on these days, indicating that these were the least holy of all special days.

The importance of the Sabbath is evident from the prominence given it in connection with the making of the covenant at Sinai. Just as the rainbow and circumcision function as signs for the covenants with Noah and Abraham respectively, the Sabbath is the sign of the Sinai covenant (Exod. 31:12-18). The Lord's instructions to the Israelites underline its significance: "Above all you shall keep my Sabbaths, for this is a sign between me and you throughout your generations, given in order that you may know that I, the Lord, sanctify you" (Exod. 31:13). Not only do God's comments explain why the Sabbath receives special mention in the Ten Commandments (Exod. 20:8-10), but they also show the importance

of the link between the idea of holiness and the Sabbath. By setting one day in seven apart, God intended the Sabbath to be a regular reminder to the people that they were to be a holy nation. Moreover, since it was the sign of the covenant between God and the Israelites, anyone who deliberately profaned the Sabbath was viewed as defiantly rejecting God's rule; by failing to maintain the sanctity of the Sabbath an individual put at jeopardy his or her right to be part of God's people (Num. 15:32-36).

For the Israelites, holiness as it applied to time was graded on the basis of how much or how little work could be undertaken. As Exod. 20:11 reveals, this outlook is reflected in Gen. 2:3, where the divine sanctification of the seventh day is linked directly to God's resting from his work. Underlying this is the idea that resting either sanctifies the day in some manner or maintains the sanctity already imparted to the day. Consequently, to maintain the holiness of the Sabbath, the Israelites, including their servants and animals, were divinely instructed to refrain from all labor.

While the Sabbath was a weekly reminder to the Israelites of their unique status as a holy nation, the pilgrimage feasts of Unleavened Bread, Weeks, and Tabernacles were annual reminders of how God had delivered the people from the oppressive rule of the Egyptian pharaoh. The idea of recalling God's past actions is particularly obvious in the Passover meal, which reenacted the events of the 14th day of the month of Abib, when God slew the firstborn of the Egyptians, passing over the houses of the Israelites because of the blood sprinkled on their door

frames (Exod. 12:1-51). Although the Passover meal bore witness to the events in Egypt, a full week was dedicated to celebrating the divine deliverance of the Israelites. The eating of unleavened bread became a hallmark of this particular week (Exod. 12:14-20; 13:3-10). Similarly, the Feast of Tabernacles (or Booths), with its focus on the Israelites' living in temporary structures for a week, was designed to recall the wilderness experience of the Israelites, when they lived in tents during their journey from Egypt to the land of Canaan, and to allow later generations to experience it for themselves and thus connect with that event.

Aside from remembering the past, the pilgrimage feasts also celebrated God's goodness toward the Israelites through the provision of bountiful harvests in the land of Canaan. For this reason, Unleavened Bread is associated with the firstfruits of the barley harvest, Weeks (also called the Feast of Harvest in Exod. 23:16; cf. 34:22) is linked to the firstfruits of the wheat harvest, and Tabernacles (called the Feast of Ingathering in Exod. 23:16; 34:22) coincides with the end of Israel's agricultural cycle after the grapes were harvested. Out of gratitude the Israelites were expected to bring the best of their firstfruits to the Lord. In this way they recalled that the exodus was not only about deliverance from bondage but also about enjoying a new life of bounty under the security of God's reign.

The pilgrimage feasts were predominantly joyful celebrations (even though the necessary offering of sacrifices would have been a vivid reminder of human failure and the need to repent), but the Day of Atonement was an exceptionally solemn occasion with particular attention being given to the process by which the high priest atoned for the sins of the nation. On this day the people fasted, acknowledged their sins, and looked to God for forgiveness.

Although Israel's sacred calendar was intended by God to help establish and maintain the holy status of the newly formed nation of Israel and to provide testimony to that status, the limited evidence available suggests that the people became exceptionally lax about celebrating these occasions or did so in a way that invited God's condemnation of their hypocrisy (e.g., Isa. 1:11-14). Later, in the postexilic period greater attention appears to have been given to observing Sabbaths and festivals. The four Gospels bear witness to the importance of these occasions in the time of Jesus, although there were differing attitudes toward how the Sabbath in particular should be kept. Significantly, the crucifixion of Jesus takes place at Passover, providing justification for the idea that through his sacrificial death a new exodus is inaugurated (cf. 1 Cor. 5:7).

T. DESMOND ALEXANDER

tions apply to the priests regarding mourning and marriage. Just as physically defective animals may not serve as acceptable sacrifices, so men from the priestly line with physical defects, abnormalities, diseases, and ritual uncleanness may not fulfill priestly duties (cf. 1 Tim. 3:1-13; Tit. 1:5-9).

23 Feasts and Festivals

The covenantal law builds the celebration of God's goodness into the life of the Israelites throughout the year. The appointed festivals mark agricultural seasons, incorporate sabbatical principles, and remind Israel of her history of redemption. Passover, followed immediately by the Feast of Unleavened Bread, occurs in the spring (March/April), and both celebrate Israel's exodus from Egypt. The offering of firstfruits at the end of the Feast of Unleavened Bread (April) anticipates the Feast of Weeks (or Pentecost), which occurs 50 days later (June) and concludes the grain harvest. See "The Calendar of Israel's Worship" (132-34).

A group of three religious observances also occurs in the fall (September/October) at the end of the agricultural calendar. A festival announced by trumpets heralds the new year; the Day of Atonement fosters a spirit of repentance and establishes a spiritual "clean slate" for the year to come (ch. 16); and the Feast of Tabernacles (or Booths), at the end of the olive and grape harvests, celebrates the completion of the ingathering of the year's crops and preserves the memory of Israel's tent-dwelling days in the wilderness. As the festival year begins with a

Clay incense burner, ca. 3500 B.C. *(Richard Cleave, Pictorial Archive)*

reminder of God's delivering Israel from slavery in Egypt, so does it end.

24:1-9 Provisions inside the Tabernacle

Expanded instructions for activities inside the tabernacle's holy place include the provision for continual light from the lampstand and the placing of 12 loaves of fresh bread (one to

The Tabernacle

Within the account of the divine deliverance of the Israelites from bondage in Egypt and the journey to the promised land of Canaan that followed, the construction of the tabernacle occupies a major place. Modern readers may find the detailed reporting of the Lord's commissioning speech in Exod. 25:1–31:11 and the almost identical compliance account in 35:1–40:33 uninspiring unless they learn to appreciate fully the significance of what happens here. At the very heart of these events is the transformation of the Israelites into a holy nation as the Lord, the incomparable king of all creation, comes to dwell among his chosen people. What begins as a dramatic, but temporary, theophany in Exodus 19, when God reveals something of his majestic power on Mount Sinai, ends with a cloud covering the newly constructed tent and "the glory of the Lord" filling the tabernacle (Exod. 40:34-35).

Resembling tentlike structures from the Bronze Age period of the ancient Near East, the tabernacle and its furnishings were made from approximately 1 ton of gold, 4 tons of silver, and 2.5 tons of bronze. The lavishly decorated structure (see diagram) consisted of an outer courtyard, approximately 50 m. by 25 m., surrounded by a curtain about 2.5 m. high, within which was placed a tent about 5 m. wide and 15 m. long. The tent itself was divided into two parts, the holy of holies (5 m. × 5 m.) and the holy place (5 m. ×

10 m.). Placed at the center of the Israelite camp, the tent and surrounding courtyard were a powerful witness to the reality of God's presence among the people.

In Exodus three different expressions are used for the tent. "Sanctuary" (Heb. *haqqodesh*) reflects the holy or sacred nature of the structure. While God's presence makes the entire area holy, differing degrees of holiness exist within the tent and courtyard. At the heart of the tabernacle was the holy of holies, which housed the ark of the covenant — a gold-plated chest that functioned, in part at least, as a divine throne. The holy of holies was considered to be so holy that only the high priest could enter it. A veil embroidered with cherubim separated the holy of holies from the holy place; the cherubim were a reminder that the way into God's immediate presence was barred to sinful

human beings (cf. Gen. 3:24). The holy place, which ordinary priests could enter, held the menorah or seven-branched lampstand, symbolizing the tree of life; the table of the presence, on which 12 loaves of bread were placed; and the gold-plated incense altar. Moving outside the tent itself, the courtyard was considered to be less holy; ordinary Israelites were granted limited access to it, but not to the tent itself. Here stood the laver or basin for washing and the large altar where sacrifices were made; both objects were made of bronze, reflecting the lesser holiness of this area. The location of the laver and altar between the entrance to the courtyard and the tent reinforced the idea that anyone who wished to approach God must first atone for sin and be cleansed.

The divine tent is also frequently called the "tabernacle"

Model of the tabernacle at Timna Park, Israel. *(Wikimedia Commons)*

(hammishkan), underscoring the concept of "dwelling." Like the Israelites themselves, God would dwell in a tent during the journey to the promised land. The tent indicated God's commitment to be continually present among his people, a presence symbolized through the burning of the lamps and the placing of bread on the table within the holy place.

The third term, "tent of meeting," highlights its role as the interface between God and humanity. Here God addressed the people through Moses and the priesthood. Before the completion of the tabernacle, a temporary "tent of meeting" was created outside the Israelite camp, where God spoke on a regular basis with Moses (Exod. 33:7-11). This temporary arrangement ceased when the tabernacle was built.

The theological significance of God's presence among the Israelites cannot be overstated. In this event we witness a remarkable advance following Adam and Eve's expulsion from the garden of Eden. Where previously God had exiled humanity from his presence, he now deigns to live in their midst.

To highlight this point, subtle links are made between the garden of Eden and the tabernacle; for example, the menorah has features reminiscent of the tree of life.

Yet, while the significance of God's presence among the Israelites should not be underestimated, this was no complete return to the conditions that existed at the dawn of creation. God was living closer to the people, but access into his immediate presence was still severely restricted; no one but the high priest was permitted to enter the holy of holies, and even this was limited to once per year, on the Day of Atonement.

While the construction of the tabernacle enabled God's redemptive plan to take an important step forward, this was not the goal in itself. Later, when the land of Canaan was secured under the reigns of David and Solomon, the tabernacle was replaced by the Jerusalem temple. Although both tabernacle and temple formed an important bridge between God and the people of Israel, with the coming of Jesus Christ the physical temple gave way to a spiritual temple. Significantly, Jesus Christ

himself prepared for this development, for "the Word became flesh and dwelt [lit. 'tabernacled'] among us, and we have seen his glory, glory as of the only Son from the Father, full of grace and truth" (John 1:14). With good reason Jesus saw his body as a new temple; when people encountered Jesus, they encountered God.

Following Christ's ascension and the coming of the Holy Spirit upon believers, the church became the dwelling place or temple of God (Eph. 2:19-22). Drawing on imagery associated with the construction of the tabernacle, Paul describes how, like Bezalel and Oholiab, he was gifted by God to be a "skilled master builder," laying a foundation upon which others were to build (1 Cor. 3:10). Christians continue to be gifted by God for the task of building his temple. While the church, like the tabernacle, is to be filled with God's glory in this age, Revelation 21–22 anticipates a future age when God and humanity will live together in harmony on a re-created earth without a temple.

T. DESMOND ALEXANDER

represent each tribe) on the table each Sabbath. The loaves, sometimes called the bread of the Presence, provide sustenance for the priests (cf. 1 Sam. 21:1-6; Matt. 12:3-4).

24:10-23 Penalties Restated

For the ancient Israelites, blasphemy — a breach of the third commandment (Exod. 20:7) — represents an utter rejection of the God who redeemed them. To drive home the seriousness of this offense and to purge the nation of those who threaten to corrupt its devotion to God (whether Israelite or resident alien), the congregation as a whole must take responsibility in administering the death penalty by stoning the blasphemer.

The instructions concerning the specific incident of blasphemy addressed here provide an occasion to restate penalties for several other offenses. The principle for administering justice consists in the *lex talionis,* which curbs individual revenge and ongoing feuding by insisting on punishments that take offenses seriously enough but also limit the extent of retribution and prohibit overpunishment (in contrast to other ancient Near Eastern law codes). The *lex talionis* represented a great advance in legal history by taking vengeance out of the hands of private individuals and fixing sentences in a judicial system. In certain instances the Israelites may have substituted monetary fines for prescribed punishments-in-kind (cf. Exod. 21:18-19; Num. 35:31ff.).

25 Sabbatical and Jubilee Years

Chapter 25 anticipates Israel's future occupation of Canaan. God's command to allow the land a sabbatical every seventh year expands the instruction in Exod. 23:10-11 to sow for six years and let the land lie fallow during the seventh. The Israelites must afford the land an additional sabbatical every 50th year — the Year of Jubilee, during which property sold over the previous five decades reverts back to its original owner. The Year of Jubilee, which begins on the Day of Atonement, also occasions the forgiving of unpaid debts and the freeing of impoverished Israelites forced to sell themselves into bondage. Thus restoration and regained liberty emerge as the central themes of the Sabbatical and Jubilee years.

The rules governing the Year of Jubilee keep community relationships in check by making overlending unwise, by preventing an unlimited increase in the gap between rich and poor, by preserving the equitable distribution of land among the tribes, by protecting families and clans from geographic poverty and alienation, and by reminding the Israelites that they "possess" the land only to the degree that God, the true owner, "loans" it to them. Neither do the Israelites own their countrymen who sell themselves as workers; the Israelites must treat the unfortunate not as slaves but as hired hands, for they also belong to God (vv. 39-43). But because God is the true owner both of the land and of his people (cf. Ps. 24:1), the Israelites — both rich and poor to an equal degree — can expect God's blessing, protection, and provision as long as they fulfill their covenantal responsibilities (vv. 18-22; cf. 26:3-12).

26 Blessings, Curses, and Repentance

Faithfulness to the covenant carries for the Israelites the blessings of agricultural prosperity, peace, population growth, and God's presence — a symbolic return to Eden, where God walks among his creation (26:12; cf. Gen. 3:8). The consequences of breaking the covenant reverse those blessings by bringing fear, disease, famine, violence, death, oppression by enemies, and exile. Although God pledges to inflict severe punishment on the Israelites if they disobey his commands, he also promises to restore the covenantal blessings in response to their true repentance.

27 Vows and Dedications

Mosaic law mandates giving to God the regular tithe, the firstfruits from the field, the firstborn of domestic animals, and the consecration of firstborn sons. At times, individuals might also make voluntary vows or dedicate additional items or persons to God to reflect special thankfulness or specific commitments.

To dedicate someone or something to God means to give it over to the service of the priests and the tabernacle. A person dedicated to God might assist the priests in ritually permissible ways (cf. 1 Samuel 1–2). Crops gleaned from a dedicated field might provide food for the priests. Money acquired through the sale of a dedicated house might serve as income for the priests or otherwise fund necessary expenditures for the service of the tabernacle.

An individual may take back a vow by "redeeming" the item or the individual through a payment of money, sometimes at a price exceeding the original value of the goods or services. But emphasis falls on the need to honor God fully by taking vows seriously and by fulfilling them with honesty and integrity.

Numbers

The fourth book of the Pentateuch takes its name from the recording of two censuses of Israel's population: one in the second year after the exodus, before the Israelites broke camp at Mount Sinai (chs. 1–4), and one just prior to their entering the promised land 38 years later (ch. 26). The Hebrew title relates to the book's setting: "In the desert."

Content

The events at the beginning of Numbers overlap with those at the end of Exodus. Although Numbers does not proceed in strict chronological order, three main sections chart Israel's progress toward claiming God's covenantal promise of land. In the first section (chs. 1–10) God, through Moses, prepares the Israelites for departure for a life with him in Canaan. Social organization and the establishment of centralized worship characterize this section, and the demand for strict adherence to God's commands emerges as a basic theme.

In chapters 11–25 the Israelites rebel. The congregation's complaints against God reach their climax when the Israelites fail the test of faith by refusing to enter the land God has promised for fear of Canaan's strong cities and mighty inhabitants (chs. 13–14). Their refusal dooms them to 38 more years of homelessness as desert nomads and robs the current adult generation of their covenantal blessing of land. Then the Levites rebel by grasping for greater position and power (chs. 16–17). Finally, even Israel's top leaders, Moses and Aaron, forfeit the privilege of entering Canaan by failing to honor God at Meribah (20:12), and they receive the same sentence as the rest of the rebellious generation: death in the desert. Only Caleb and Joshua, who remain fixed in their faith in God, prove worthy to accompany the next generation of Israelites into the promised land.

In the final section (chs. 26–36) the Israelites who refused to claim Canaan have died, and the nation sits on the plains of Moab poised to cross the Jordan. The Israelites have already subdued the peoples east of Canaan in Transjordan and have captured their land. Now God prepares the new generation practically and spiritually to possess and divide their inheritance in Canaan proper.

The alternating accounts in Numbers set the Israelites' tendency toward discontent, disobedience, and lack of faith over against God's longsuffering, forgiveness, and covenantal faithfulness. In also upholding God's uncompromising holiness, Numbers highlights the consistent and determined initiative God takes in redeeming sinful humanity — a theme prominent in the book of Exodus as well.

Composition

While the Pentateuch refers to Moses' writing down of certain laws, songs, and other accounts (33:2; Exod. 17:14; Deut. 31:9), evidence suggests that later editors drew his writings together and incorporated additional information to produce the "Five Books of Moses." In Numbers this includes the repeated phrase, "The Lord spoke to Moses," as though a third party is recording the events. Yet although Numbers weaves together a mix of literary types — including legal passages, narrative accounts, speeches, and administrative material — the book displays a considerable degree of unity.

1 Israel's First Census

In preparation for leaving Sinai in order to possess the promised land, God commands Moses and Aaron to enlist the help of tribal leaders in taking a head count of all Israel's adult males able to fight in war. The census proceeds according to the clans and families descended from Jacob's sons, but it excludes the Levites, whose sole responsibility is to maintain and guard the tabernacle. Dividing Joseph's line according to his sons Ephraim and Manasseh restores the total of tribes numbered to 12.

Judah emerges as the largest tribe and remains so throughout Israel's history. The total number of males at least 20 years old amounts to more than 600 thousand. This parallels the figure for those who left Egypt under Moses' leadership one year earlier (Exod. 12:37), as well as the number in the second census taken 38 years later (Num. 26:5-51). These figures imply a total population of 2 to 3 million — a very large number for a desert to support, and comparable to the population of Canaan in the latter half of the 2nd millennium B.C. (cf. Exod. 12:37). As elsewhere, "thousand" here probably means "clan" or "military unit" rather than the number 1000.

2 The Arrangement of Israel's Camp

Four groups of three tribes position themselves on the east, south, west, and north sides of the tabernacle, which sits at the camp's center. The Levites' camp provides a buffer zone on all sides of the tabernacle to shield God's dwelling place from the non-Levitic Israelite population. Although in the census Reuben appears first (1:5), Judah receives the place of honor in the Israelite camp: the east side facing the entrance to the tabernacle. The Israelites' march through the desert toward Canaan proceeds according to the order established for the camp, with Judah taking the lead.

3 The Levites Redeem Israel's Firstborn

At the Passover in Egypt (Exod. 13:1-16), God claimed Israel's firstborn as specially dedicated to him, and the elders of the individual households acted as priests in carrying out God's instructions for family worship (Exodus 12). With the establishment of a central sanctuary in which to conduct worship in accordance with a national covenant, God declares Israel's firstborn as "redeemed" by accepting the Levites in their stead for service to him. Since the rest of the nation's firstborn males outnumber the male Levites, Moses collects a sum of money equal to about six months of a laborer's wages for each unredeemed layman and gives it to the priests.

Three clans form the tribe of Levi: Kohath (directed by Aaron's son Eleazar, who later inherits the high priesthood), Gershon, and Merari (both directed by Aaron's other surviving son, Ithamar). The Kohathites receive the most sacred duties, including care for the ark of the covenant and the other furnishings inside the tabernacle. The priests (Aaron's family) play an even more exclusive role by carrying out the tabernacle's service.

As God assigns specific camp locations to each of Israel's tribes, so he designates certain living areas around the tabernacle to the individual Levitical clans. Moses and the priests camp on the east side, opposite the tabernacle's entrance (cf. Judah's place of honor in 2:3).

4 Instructions for Moving the Tabernacle

A second census of the Levites numbers males between ages 30 and 50, who will assist the priests in disassembling the tabernacle, transporting it, and re-erecting it when the Israelite camp changes locations. Counted according to clan, these men total 8580.

God's instructions for moving direct the priests to cover the tabernacle furnishings with blue cloths, which distinguish these most sacred items from the scarlet and purple curtains hung as the walls of the tent and which serve as a visual warning — on pain of death for dishonoring God — not to touch the objects or look beneath the curtains that cover them. The Kohathites will transport the furnishings from camp to camp. The Gershonites will carry the tabernacle's curtains and coverings, and the Merarites will use wagons pulled by oxen to move the tent's framework.

5 Purifying the Camp

For God's chosen nation, order and purity must go hand in hand. With the Israelite camp's logistical arrangements established, the purifying of its members must now take place. The ritually unclean must move out of the camp proper (cf. Leviticus 11–15), community members must restore right relationships with each other (cf. Lev. 6:1-7), and husbands must ensure the purity of their marriage relationships. Jealous husbands must submit wives suspected of adultery to a trial by ordeal administered by God's appointed priest, with God as judge. A husband's authority over his wife is thereby limited, leaving any punishment to God.

6:1-21 The Nazirite Vow

An Israelite layperson who wishes to set himself apart for God in a special way, usually for a limited period of time, may make a Nazirite vow (from Hebrew "vow"; it does not identify a "Nazarene," from Nazareth; cf. Leviticus 27). While God requires priests to abstain from drinking wine before performing their priestly duties (Lev. 10:9), a Nazirite must refrain from eating all grape products, fermented or not, for the entire period of the vow. Like the priests, the Nazirite must take special care to avoid ritual defilement through contact with a corpse. The visual sign of a Nazirite consists in his allowing his hair to grow while fulfilling the vow (cf. Judg. 13:5; 16:19-31; Acts 18:18; 21:20-26).

6:22-27 The Priestly Blessing

This very ancient Israelite poem sums up the covenantal blessings by invoking on the congregation God's protection, presence, pleasure, grace (ill-deserved favor), attentiveness, and peace (well-being in all areas of life).

7 Gifts for the Tabernacle Service

Here Numbers flashes back one month and describes the gifts and offerings Israel's 12 tribal leaders presented for the consecration of the tabernacle, the altar, and the priests. The Gershonites and Merarites receive carts and oxen to carry out their assignments as Levites. Then one tribe per day gives an equal amount for the 12-day consecration ceremony, beginning again with the honored Judah. With the ceremony completed, Moses enters the tabernacle, and God speaks to him from the mercy seat on the ark of the covenant.

8 Preparation of the Levites

After Aaron lights the tabernacle's lamps, the Levites receive their commission to the tabernacle service. Their preparation includes shaving and washing as part of their ritual cleansing. God instructs the congregation to lay their hands on the Levites, apparently to represent the Levites' taking the place of Israel's firstborn as dedicated to God. After Aaron presents the Levites as a wave offering to the Lord, they receive atonement by laying their hands on the heads of two bulls, one sacrificed as a sin offering and the other as a burnt offering. While the second census of male Levites numbered men between ages 30 and 50 able to work at the tabernacle (ch. 4), the instructions here are to begin counting at 25 years old.

9:1-14 Passover Observed

This second Passover occurs one month prior to the census recorded in chapter 1 and just before the Israelites embark on their journey toward Canaan. Here a case study occasions the establishment of guidelines for the ritually unclean and those away from home to observe the Passover: they may celebrate it one month late. Lest any Israelite think this exception lessens the obligation of those able to observe the occasion at the proper time, God makes clear that neglect of one's duty in this regard will result in being "cut off" from the Israelite community (v. 13).

9:15-23 God Leads in a Cloud

The Israelites have spent almost 14 months encamped at Sinai, and they observe God's presence with them in the cloud that rests over the tabernacle. The pillars of cloud and fire protected the Israelites on their exodus from Egypt; now the cloud, which appears firelike at night, directs their movements as they proceed toward Canaan (cf. Exod. 14:19-24).

10 The Israelites Set Out for Canaan

Silver trumpets provide a mass communication system for the large Israelite population. Aaron's sons will sound different trumpet blasts to signal

Covenants

A covenant is an agreement between two parties in which one or both promise under oath to perform or refrain from certain actions. The concept of covenant (Heb. *berit;* Gk. *diatheke*) has long been recognized as an important framework for interpretion within the Bible. The Bible itself comes to us as the "Old" and "New" Testaments (= "covenants"). Within these Testaments, both the theology and the chronology of the biblical story are structured around six covenantal interactions — with Adam, Noah, Abraham, Moses, David, and the church.

In the 20th century new discoveries demonstrated that this *biblical* concept of covenant relates to a *secular* concept borrowed from the larger ancient Near East and maintained by later biblical writers because of its seminal role in the self-revelation of Yahweh to his people. In 1931 Viktor Korošec published a study of treaty documents from the ancient Hittite Empire in Anatolia (ca. 1400–1180 B.C.). In 1954 biblical scholar George E. Mendenhall recognized that the literary form of these secular diplomatic texts could be correlated to the covenant of Israelite and later Christian tradition. Specifically, he argued that the form of the Decalogue in the Book of the Covenant (Exodus 20–23) and the form of the book of Deuteronomy resembled what Korošec had named the Hittite "suzerainty treaty." In 1970 Moshe Weinfeld argued for similar parallels between "the covenant of grant" from Assyrian tradition and the divine covenants with Abraham and David. As numerous publications and epigraphic discoveries have since illustrated, the concept of covenant, in all of its various forms and functions, was widespread throughout the ancient Near East, and the matrix of ideas expressed by this secular concept clearly stands behind the biblical tradition.

Recent sociological studies demonstrate that the ideological foundation of covenant-making was "fictive kinship." In the tribal cultures of the ancient Near East, all societal privileges and responsibilities derived from a person's familial relationships. The more closely related two individuals were, the greater their responsibility to one another; the more distantly related, the lesser their responsibility. If one needed to create a relationship of privilege and responsibility with non-kin, a *fictive* kinship bond could be established by which both parties agreed to *act* like family. This ideological framework has profound implications for the old covenant's identification of Israel as God's "son," and the new covenant language of "adoption" and "marriage" as regards the church. Fictive kinship could function on the individual, tribal, or national level. Covenant could operate on all of these levels as well. At least two secular covenantal forms were incorporated into the heart of Israelite and, thereby, Christian theology: the suzerain/vassal treaty of the 2nd-millennium Hittite world and the covenant of grant.

The Suzerain/Vassal Covenant

In the ancient world the suzerain/vassal treaty was used to govern international relations by defining a relationship between two nations of unequal size and strength. The treaty granted the suzerain (the "big" king) authority over the land and people of the vassal nation (the "little" king). Legally, the suzerain owned all the vassal's land and produce. Although the suzerain typically allowed the vassal to continue to rule his own people, and thereby to maintain his own government and traditions, the vassal was expected to pay regular tribute as well as to provide military assistance whenever required. In return, the vassal received domestic and international protection by his suzerain's superior military forces. Frequently, the vassal also received a land grant. All considered, the most important stipulation in any suzerain/vassal treaty was "loyalty" (Heb. *hesed*), a term often translated in English Bibles as "loving-kindness, (steadfast) love, mercy." *Hesed* (in this context it literally means "covenantal faithfulness") communicates the type of loyal behavior that comes from blood: what a patriarch shows to his family, what a firstborn owes to his father. If a vassal dared to make a covenant with another suzerain — an unthinkable situation within the family metaphor — he had committed high treason and would be severely punished. In many ways this somewhat technical term captures the very heart of the redemption story. Throughout history Yahweh has offered both his extravagant covenantal blessings and his unwavering *hesed* to his people (cf. Psalm 136); he has asked only for their *hesed* in return.

The format of the suzerain/vassal treaty is clearly reflected in the covenant made between Yahweh and Israel on Mount Sinai. Having triumphantly led his people out of the land of their now-defeated oppressors, and having brought these offspring of Abraham to himself at Sinai, the great king, Yahweh, extends to the tribes of Israel a suzerain/vassal treaty by which this rabble of slaves will be transformed into a nation (Exod. 19:5-6). Although the people of Israel "were once not a people," by means of his treaty with them at Sinai Yahweh makes them "the people of God" (cf. 1 Pet. 2:9-10). In exchange, Yahweh requires of Israel the typical duties of a vassal: absolute loyalty, regular tribute (a schedule of required offerings), and military availability (the "holy war" of Israelite tradition). If Israel will be loyal to the covenant, the nation will obtain the privileges of loyal vassalage: a secure international and domestic position in the promised land. A comparison between the six-part, 2nd-millennium Hittite treaties and the Mosaic covenant as recorded in the Book of the Covenant and the book of Deuteronomy yields the following results.

The Covenant of Grant

Just as the suzerain/vassal treaty was well known in the ancient Near East, so was the covenant of (royal) grant. The grant was a gift bestowed by a higher-ranking official upon an individual who had distinguished himself by loyal service. Quite common between kings and their various officials or wealthy masters and their servants, the gift given was typically a land grant or an enduring office. These secular grants have been compared to the Abrahamic and Davidic covenants. By means of his covenant with Abraham, Yahweh promises to his people the land of Canaan (Gen. 12:1; 15:7-21; 17:8); by means of his covenant with David, Yahweh promises to his people an ongoing dynasty and the domestic security that such a dynasty would bring (2 Sam. 7:10-17; Psalms 89, 132). The offer of both of these covenants was based on past obedience and continuing loyalty. (Although many have characterized these grants as "promissory," as distinguished from the "obligatory" covenant at Sinai, recent scholarship has shown that these ancient grants, like the suzerain/vassal treaty, retained a number of conditional elements.) In the biblical scheme, the Abrahamic covenant may be understood as a precursor to the Mosaic covenant, and the Davidic covenant as a subcategory of the Mosaic.

The Biblical Theology of the "Old" and "New" Covenants

The comparison of the ancient treaties and the biblical covenants raises several critical theological points. The first is the theol-ogy of the *historical prologue* of the suzerain/vassal treaty. In the secular treaty the historical prologue provided the reason the vassal should participate in the covenant and accept the suzerainty of the great king. At present, the evidence indicates that this feature disappeared after the 2nd-millennium Hittite treaties. It is noticeably absent from the 1st-millennium Assyrian treaties. This shift in structure reflects a shift in ideology: whereas the motivational scheme of the Hittite treaties was, at least theoretically, built upon gratitude for past acts of grace, the Assyrian treaties were founded upon fear of future reprisal. This distinction between 2nd- and 1st-millennium treaties is not only important to dating the Sinaitic covenant (it places the ideology of the Sinaitic covenant squarely in the 2nd millennium), but it is also critical to our understanding of who Yahweh is. In Israel's case, the formulaic summary of its historical prologue with Yahweh may be found restated throughout the Hebrew Bible: "I am Yahweh your God, who brought you out of the land of Egypt, out of the house of slavery; *therefore,* you will. . . ." This is significant because the Israelites were not being asked to obey Yahweh's stipulations in order to *win* his grace; they were being asked to obey Yahweh's stipulations *because* the faithful suzerain already had shown his grace. Hence the stipulations of both old and new covenants *follow* God's gracious acts of redemption, regardless of whether that act is deliverance from slavery to Egypt or deliverance from slavery to sin (Col. 1:13; cf. Rom. 5:1-11; 1 Cor. 6:20).

A second ideological aspect of

I. Preamble/Title: Gives the title(s) of the superior party	"I am the Lord your God . . ." (Exod. 20:2a; Deut. 5:6a)
II. Historical prologue: Furnishes the basis of the vassal's obligation and motive for accepting the stipulations as binding	"who brought you out of the land of Egypt, out of the house of slavery" (Exod. 20:2b; Deut. 5:6b)
III. Stipulations/obligations of the treaty	"You shall have no other gods before me . . . you shall not make wrongful use of the name of the Lord your God . . . remember the Sabbath day . . . you shall not murder . . ." (Exod. 20:3-17; Deut. 5:7-21; cf. Deut. 6:1-27:26)
***Oath**	"Moses came and told the people all the words of the Lord and all the ordinances; and all the people answered with one voice, and said, 'All the words that the Lord has spoken we will do.'" (Exod. 24:3; cf. Josh. 24:24)
***Ratification ceremony/sacrifice**	(Exod. 24:4-8)
IV. Deposition of the document in the temples of both parties and provision for periodic reading of the treaty before the people of the vassal nation	"Then Moses turned and went down from the mountain, carrying the two tablets of the covenantal [one for each covenant partner] in his hands . . ." (Exod. 32:15-16; Deut. 10:3-5; 31:24-26; cf. Exod. 25:21; 40:20)
	"you shall read this law before all Israel in their hearing. Assemble the people — men, women, and children, as well as the aliens residing in your towns — so that they may hear and learn to fear the Lord your God and to observe diligently all the words of this law." (Deut. 31:11-12; Exod. 24:7; Deut. 27:2-8; cf. Josh. 8:30-35)
V. List of witnesses: Typically the respective deities of the oath-taking parties	"I call heaven and earth to witness against you today" (Deut. 4:26; 30:19–20; 31:28)
VI. Curses and Blessings: A description of what the suzerain would do to/for the vassal if he failed to keep/kept the covenant	(Curses: Deut. 27:1-26; 28:15-68; blessings: Deut. 28:1-14)

the ancient treaties borrowed into the old and new covenants is *exclusive* loyalty. Yahweh expresses his demand for exclusive loyalty in this manner: "You shall have no other gods before me" (Exod.20:3).

Whereas monotheism was a new, radical (and difficult) idea in Israel's polytheistic world, by putting this new idea in *political* terms Yahweh bridges the gap in understanding. The message here

is, "Just as you would never bind yourself to more than one suzerain, you will not bind yourself to more than one deity." This is why the stipulations of the Decalogue begin with a detailed discussion of what exclusive loyalty (monotheism) will look like in Israel's worship. This requirement of exclusive loyalty is also why the 1st-century confessions of Christian faith all included the affirmation that Jesus Christ (not Caesar or any other deity) is Lord (Rom. 10:9; cf. Phil. 2:9-11; Col. 1:13-14). The new covenant adds to the ancient idea by means of the Incarnation: Jesus is both the divine suzerain to whom exclusive allegiance is due and the human mediator whose task it is to lead the nation in obedient vassalage.

As was typical of any secular treaty, after Israel swears fidelity to Yahweh's *berit,* the oath is sealed by a sacrificial ceremony and fellowship meal (Exod. 24:8). In this moment, the children of Abraham become the nation of Israel by oath. By oath the God of the cosmos becomes their sovereign lord. Turning to the new covenant, a similar interaction marks the first communion meal recorded in Matt. 26:26-28. On that Passover night, Jesus transformed a new rabble of slaves into his covenantal people, when the *church* was set apart by means of sacrifice and blood. Note the intentional echo:

Moses: "This is *the* blood of the covenant";

Jesus: "This is *my* blood of the covenant."

This parallel is not coincidental. As Moses sprinkled the blood of bulls upon the people of Israel in order to ratify the "old" covenant at Sinai, so Jesus, the second Moses, distributed *his own* blood to the people in order to ratify the new covenant (cf. Heb. 9:11-15). In the sacrifice of Christ, as commemorated in the communion meal, the new covenant was ratified, and this time the oaths were sealed with the blood of God the Son.

How does this covenantal heritage inform redemption history? By the 1st century, it had become painfully apparent that Israel had failed as Yahweh's covenantal partner. The children of Abraham had not kept *hesed* and, therefore, their land grant was in jeopardy. Moreover, the sons of David had failed to keep covenant, and their enduring office also had been suspended. But the hope remained that the promise of Jer. 31:31-34 might yet come to pass — a *new* covenant. This hope was fulfilled when a son of David appeared declaring that he had come to bring that new covenant, offering vassalage to a *new* Israel (= converts from all the nations), and even offering to transform the hearts of his subjects such that they would be *able* to keep *hesed.* It is the explanation of the character of this new covenant that occupies the bulk of the New Testament.

For Further Reading

Dumbrell, William J. *Covenant and Creation: a Theology of Old Testament Covenants.* Carlisle: Paternoster, 1997.

Hillers, Delbert R. *Covenant: The History of a Biblical Idea.* Baltimore: Johns Hopkins University Press, 1969.

McCarthy, Dennis J. *Treaty and Covenant.* Rev. ed. Analecta Biblica 21A. Rome: Pontifical Biblical Institute, 1978.

Mendenhall, George E. *Law and Covenant in Israel and the Ancient Near East.* Pittsburgh: Biblical Colloquium, 1955.

Weinfeld, Moshe. "bᵉrîth." *Theological Dictionary of the Old Testament* 2:253-79.

SANDRA RICHTER

---

the summoning of Israel's leaders or the entire congregation, the impending movement of the camp, alarms in war, and the celebration of feasts.

Having made this last provision for the journey toward Canaan, the Israelites follow God's cloud on a three-day journey from the Sinai wilderness to the wilderness of Paran. Now the tabernacle follows the first cohort of tribes so the Gershonites and Merarites can set it up before the Kohathites arrive with the sacred tabernacle furnishings. The ark of the covenant heads the procession. Moses persuades his brother-in-law Hobab to remain as a guide through the wilderness rather than returning to his home in Midian.

Moses' words at the beginning of each stage of the journey are both a blessing of God and an invocation of God's protection of the Israelites for the sake of his own glory, for he dwells among them. At the end of each day of traveling, Moses beckons the Lord to remain with his people.

11 The Complaining Begins Again

Even after God miraculously delivers the Israelites from slavery, rains down manna in the desert for them, and agrees to live in their midst, the Israelites find food for complaint. Not even God's display of his displeasure at the Israelites' ingratitude prevents them from allowing the greedy resident aliens among them to infect their attitude. The Israelites remember their life in Egypt through rose-colored glasses and hunger for the variety of food available there.

Moses becomes so frustrated with the Israelites' weeping over their lack of meat and his own inability to satisfy their desire that he asks God to relieve him of his responsibilities by killing him. God does not grant Moses' death wish; instead, God empowers 70 Israelite elders who will share the burden of leadership with Moses. The elders demonstrate their receipt of God's spirit by prophesying, and Moses shows his relief at the spreading of the leadership burden by expressing his wish that God would send his spirit on all the Israelites (v. 29).

God's answer to the Israelites' ungrateful cry for meat becomes part of their punishment as well (vv. 19-20). He satisfies their craving by causing a three-foot-deep layer of quail to fall a day's journey on all sides of the camp, and even those Israelites who gather the least come away with 11 bushels' worth of fowl. But God soon punishes them for their complaining spirit by striking them with a "very severe plague," which causes the greedy to die.

12　Aaron and Miriam Challenge Moses' Authority

Aaron and Miriam use their brother's marriage to a foreigner as an excuse to challenge his authority. Their grasping for power and position contrasts with Moses' humility and steadfast obedience to God. Because Moses displays these qualities, God exalts him before Aaron and Miriam. Moreover, God punishes Miriam with "leprosy" (cf. Leviticus 13), so, rather than gaining the power she seeks, she loses even basic community with her people (v. 14; cf. Lev. 13:46). Aaron repents of his and Miriam's sin, and perhaps Aaron's contrite heart deters God from punishing him. Moses might have rejoiced at being cleared by God, but instead he intercedes on Miriam's behalf. God agrees to

Wilderness of Paran, where the Israelites camped after leaving Sinai. *(Richard Cleave, Pictorial Archive)*

heal Miriam, but only after she bears the shame of her sin for a full week. When Miriam returns to the camp proper, the Israelites move on.

13–14　Possession of Canaan Postponed

With the Israelites at Kadesh-barnea, near the southern border of the promised land, Moses commissions an advance team to gather information about Canaan, apparently at the prompting of the Israelites themselves (cf. Deut. 1:22). The group of spies includes one leader from each tribe along with Moses' servant Hoshea, who later assumes Moses' leadership position. Moses changes Hoshea's name ("to save") to Joshua (= "Jesus" in Greek), "The Lord saves," in anticipation of God's future deliverance of the Israelites from their enemies in Canaan.

The spies travel 250 miles north and spend 40 days during late summer (when the grapes ripen) assessing the number and strength of Canaan's inhabitants, whether their cities are open or walled, the lay of the land, and its vegetation and fruit. Their mission takes them from the wilderness of Zin in the south to Rehob in the northern hill country and includes a visit to Hebron, home of the patriarchs' family tomb.

The spies return with grapes, pomegranates, and figs as evidence that indeed the land does flow "with milk and honey" (cf. Exod. 33:3). But countering their good report about the land itself, 10 of the spies discourage any attempt to take possession of Canaan because of the strength of its inhabitants and because of its large, fortified cities (13:28, 32-33).

The majority report so discourages the Israelites that they conspire a mutinous plan to return to Egypt. Moses and Aaron plead for God's mercy on the rebellious people, and Joshua lends his support to the Israelite leadership by joining the primary dissenter, Caleb, in tearing his clothes as though mourning for God's unavoidable judgment on the Israelites' faithlessness. Joshua's and Caleb's attempts to dissuade the masses from disobeying God meet with the people's call to stone them.

Refusing to tolerate his people's faithlessness, which amounts to outright rejection of the covenant he has established with them, God again determines to dispossess Abraham's descendants and create an even greater nation through Moses. But just as he had done previously in the incident of the golden calf (Exodus 32), Moses refuses God's determination to exalt him in favor of upholding God's own reputation among the Egyptians and Canaanites. Moses intercedes on the Israelites' behalf, and God pardons them.

Figs, among the lush produce gathered by the spies sent into Canaan (Numbers 13). *(Richard Cleave, Pictorial Archive)*

Their sin will bear a consequence, however: the Israelites will spend one year wandering in the wilderness for each day the spies spent in Canaan (14:25, 34). In this way, God will grant the faithless generation's careless wish to die in the desert (14:2). Not only will Joshua and Caleb escape punishment, but Caleb will also realize God's blessing for his obedient spirit (14:24).

Judgment for the 10 faithless spies comes

quickly — they die from a plague sent by God. The Israelites then experience a change of heart, but too late. They acknowledge their sin but follow up their repentance with further disobedience by trying to forgo God's punishment and enter Canaan against his will. (Moses does not participate.) Because God does not go with the Israelites, the Amalekites and Canaanites can and do drive them south out of the hill country.

15 The Promise Reaffirmed and Obedience Emphasized

God has merely postponed, not nullified, the fulfillment of his promise of land to Abraham's descendants. God instructs the Israelites to offer sacrifices when they finally do enter the land. The required offerings include products from the land itself: grain, oil, and wine as a libation (liquid offering). In this way, the Israelites will offer back to God a portion of what he has given to them.

The instructions also provide for resident aliens to participate in Israel's worship and thereby to benefit from the blessings of the covenant — but only if they obey the same laws God mandates for the Israelites (cf. Lev. 17:10, 13; 18:26).

Offerings will bring atonement only for those who sin unintentionally. In cases of intentional disobedience of God's laws, the transgressor's only recourse is to cast himself on God's sheer mercy. As a constant reminder of the seriousness with which the Israelites must take these laws, they must now wear blue tassels on the corners of their garments.

16 Korah's Rebellion Quelled

Just as Miriam and Aaron had earlier failed to understand that Moses' "power" lay only in his obedience to God's commands, so now a group of Levites and Israel's leaders seek to seize the power they mistakenly believe belongs to Moses and Aaron, rather than recognizing that these men hold their positions only at God's appointment (cf. ch. 12). Korah, a Kohathite Levite, joins forces with several Reubenites in rallying 250 of Israel's leaders to challenge Moses' and Aaron's authority. Ignoring the faithlessness the

Israelites displayed when presented with the opportunity to enter Canaan and instead professing the people's holiness (v. 3), these instigators blame the brothers for failing to fulfill a promise that is God's to keep (vv. 13-14).

Moses recognizes their thirst for greater power through elevation to priestly status (vv. 9-10). He also deflects blame from Aaron, but the further charge of the Reubenites Dathan and Abiram that Moses has tried to deceive the people by bringing them *out* of a land flowing with milk and honey (Egypt) rather than *into* one so angers Moses that he challenges them to a trial by ordeal so that God might demonstrate his choice of leaders and priests. Korah and his band cooperate, only to have God annihilate them all for challenging his authority and spurning his will (vv. 31-33).

God reaffirms Aaron's and his family's sole appointment to the priesthood (vv. 39-40), but the Israelites fail to recognize that it was God who punished their defiant leaders and instead accuse Moses and Aaron. Poised to consume the entire assembly once more, God ominously descends on the tabernacle (v. 45; cf. v. 21). But this time, Moses' and Aaron's intercession alone is not enough: Aaron must run through the crowd making atonement for the congregation with a smoking censer. While the rebels' incense ignited the fire of God's wrath to consume them, Aaron's offering of the "pleasing aroma" checks the plague God has already begun to inflict.

17:1-11 Aaron's Position Reaffirmed

God provides the Israelites with a sign that indeed he has chosen only Aaron's line to serve as his priests. The rod of Aaron — the only one that sprouts and produces fruit overnight — will serve as a perpetual, visual reminder of God's reaffirmation of his will for the Israelite priesthood.

17:12–18:32 The Levites' Rights and Responsibilities

Finally the Israelites recognize that God will indeed enforce his lordship. But this realization produces fear, for they had allied themselves at least in spirit with Korah and his cohort; and now they fear that approaching the tabernacle will result in their deaths, too. God therefore declares that the entire tribe of Levi will share and bear the guilt of the people's offenses against proper worship. The Levites will also forfeit their inheritance of land in Canaan. Instead, their inheritance will be lives of full-time service to God.

But God will provide for the landless Levites, who are free from the normal responsibilities for food and survival: the leftovers of the Israelites' sacrifices will be food for the Levites — sacrifices that represent both the choicest of animals and the best of the land's produce, as well as its firstfruits. In addition, God gives to the Levites the tithe he requires of the Israelites, but the Levites must in turn tithe in support of the priests one tenth of the best that they receive.

19 The Ritual of the Red Heifer

God had commanded that the ritually unclean move outside the camp proper before the Israelites left Sinai (5:1-4). Now he prescribes a ritual to purify any camp residents who become unclean through contact with a human corpse. The procedure guards against defilement of the tabernacle.

That the slaughter of the red heifer takes place outside the camp, and not at the altar inside the tabernacle court, indicates that the animal does not represent a sacrifice to God (contrast Lev. 17:3-5). The mixture of water and its ashes after burning restores cultic purity by absorbing the impurities that have contaminated the physical body.

20 Miriam and Aaron Die and Moses Disobeys

The beginning of the 40th year after the exodus finds the Israelites back at Kadesh-barnea, where their faithlessness had earlier resulted in postponement of their entrance into the promised land (chs. 13–14). Chapter 20 first makes passing note of Miriam's death at Kadesh before going on to relate how Moses and Aaron fail to honor God. The Israelites have not changed their ways after four decades: once again, they grumble about the lack of water in the wilderness, and once again God provides for their needs. But this time Moses' frustration with the people leads to his carelessness in following God's instructions, and Aaron participates in the folly.

The brothers' sin occurs at three levels: failure to credit God for the provision of water (v. 10); striking the rock, rather than speaking to it (compare v. 8 with v. 11; cf. Exod. 17:6); and dishonoring God publicly (v. 12). Not only will God strip Aaron of his position as high priest, neither will God allow him to enter the promised land. Aaron is defrocked and dies on Mount Hor, on the border with Edom, and Eleazar assumes his father's position as high priest.

God's punishment of Moses by also disallowing him to enter Canaan seems harsher in view of Moses' steadfast faithfulness over the years. But Moses' inclusion in God's judgment emphatically underscores the peculiar care required of religious leaders in exercising their responsibilities (cf. Leviticus 21–22).

Nevertheless, Moses continues to pursue his mission by attempting to lead the Israelites to Canaan by way of Edomite territory. In requesting the Edomites' permission to travel up the King's Highway, he appeals to the Israelites' blood relationship to the Edomites (v. 14). But the king's refusal of passage forces the Israelites to take a long detour south and west.

21 Progress toward Canaan

Not only do the Israelites' own relatives hinder their progress toward Canaan, so do other neighboring peoples. The Canaanites of Arad (Hormah), west of Edom, attack but are defeated when the Israelites vow to exercise their faith in God's covenantal promises by destroying the Canaanites and their cities if God will grant them victory. Soon afterward, however, the Israelites once again complain about their "miserable food" and lack of water, and God punishes them with a plague of "fiery serpents." The people repent, and God provides a means of healing for anyone bitten by the venomous snakes: the victim must look upon a bronze serpent made by Moses and raised on a standard

in the wilderness (cf. 2 Kgs. 18:4; John 3:14-15). Today the serpent remains a symbol of modern medical practice.

From this point on, the Israelites make rapid progress toward the promised land and realize great success in defeating those who oppose them. They defeat and occupy all the cities of the Amorites, whose territory stretches from the Arnon River in Moab up to the Jabbok River in Gilead. The Israelites also gain control of Bashan, northeast of the Sea of Galilee.

22–24 Balaam Blesses Israel

Having taken most of the Transjordanian territory north of Edom, the Israelites return south to Moab opposite Jericho. Well aware of the Israelites' successes and fearing his own impending downfall, King Balak of Moab enlists the help of the Midianites in sending for supernatural help from Balaam, a renowned diviner who lives a good distance north near the Euphrates River. Midian lies well to the south of Moab and just east of the Sinai Peninsula, but the account indicates that some Midianite tribes lived in Moab at this time. Before accepting the invitation to come and utter a curse against the Israelites, however, Balaam seeks the will of God. God warns Balaam not to fulfill the request, and Balak's envoys return to Moab alone.

Balak tries again by sending a larger contingent of higher-ranking leaders, who offer Balaam great wealth in exchange for his services. Balaam again makes clear that he can do nothing outside God's will; this time God allows Balaam to go to Moab with the understanding that he will speak only as God instructs him. On the journey, the angel of the Lord opposes Balaam by intimidating the donkey on which Balaam is riding. Because Balaam cannot see the angel, he urges his beast on with a whip. Miraculously, the donkey speaks in protest. Then the angel appears to Balaam, and Balaam confesses his unwitting sin of opposing the Lord. God uses the episode to impress upon Balaam the importance of obeying God with his tongue when he arrives in Moab.

Three times Balak offers sacrifices to Baal, the Canaanite god of war and fertility, in preparation for Balaam's curse on the Israelites; three times Balaam cannot help but bless God's people instead. Then, in a fourth and final oracle, Balaam anticipates a future king who will defeat Israel's enemies completely (24:17).

Couched in poetic verse, Balaam's blessings recall God's promises to the patriarchs: Jacob's descendants appear innumerable (23:10; cf. Gen. 28:14); God goes with the Israelites (23:21; cf. Gen. 28:15); he has brought them out of Egypt (23:22; 24:8; cf. Gen. 15:13-14) and will vanquish their enemies (24:8; cf. Gen. 15:18-21; 22:17); and those who bless Israel will receive blessing, but those who curse God's people will bring curses upon themselves (24:9; cf. Gen. 12:3). This final pronouncement prompts the frustrated and furious Balak to send Balaam packing without the promised remuneration, but Balaam utters a parting oracle that both recognizes that the covenantal curses on Israel's opponents have begun and confirms that they will continue.

Though Balaam appears God-fearing here (esp. 22:18), the Israelites later find him in the company of their Midianite foes when they slay the lot (31:8). The New Testament, perhaps keying on 31:16, regards Balaam as a wayward and wicked prophet motivated by personal gain (2 Pet. 2:14-16; Jude 11; Rev. 2:14).

25 The Israelites Worship Baal

Four decades of isolation in the desert have not solidified the Israelites' devotion to God alone. In succumbing to the sexual temptations of the Moabite and Midianite women living near them, the Israelites also participate in Canaanite religious rituals, even bowing down to worship the fertility-god Baal. The Lord orders the execution of the idolaters and sends a devastating plague that claims the lives of 24 thousand Israelites. Phinehas, grandson of the late high priest Aaron, checks the plague by diverting God's wrath: in righteous indignation, Phinehas slays an Israelite man and a Midianite woman after the two enter his tent (presumably to engage in sexual relations) in plain sight of Moses and the Israelites weeping over their sin at the tabernacle. God rewards Phinehas by extending to him a covenant of perpetual

priesthood before ordering revenge on those Midianites living in Moab.

Israel's sin in these instances consists primarily in mixing with foreign peoples and thereby endangering the integrity of their holy community. The social and religious interplay between the Israelites and inhabitants of Canaan continued to threaten the chosen people's covenantal relationship with God throughout their history in the promised land and ultimately resulted in the downfall first of Samaria to the Assyrians in 722 and then of Judah to the Babylonians in 587/6.

26:1–27:11 The Second Census and Allotment of Land

The 40 years of wilderness wandering over, Israel stands on the brink of entering Canaan. Having defeated the promised land's Transjordanian neighbors, the new generation of Israelites must now organize themselves to take possession of their covenantal inheritance. A second census reveals only a slight decrease in the number of their fighting force, despite the thousands struck down by God for disobedience in the previous four decades (compare 1:46 with 26:51). Instructions for dividing up the land according to the size of each tribe ensures an even distribution of people throughout Canaan — an important measure for sustaining a society based on farming. From the previous generation of Israelites, only Caleb and Joshua remain to claim the covenantal promise of land (cf. 14:30).

That Zelophehad, a descendant of Joseph through Manasseh, left no sons to inherit land (26:33) gives rise to the appeal of his five unmarried daughters that they receive their father's portion. Through Moses, God grants their request and establishes a law concerning landed inheritance that protects as members of society single, brotherless women otherwise dependent on male family members (27:1-11). The law specifies alternative lines of inheritance that keep land allotments within the tribe to which they originally belonged. (See the restrictions concerning the marriage of Zelophehad's daughters in ch. 36.)

27:12-23 The Commissioning of Joshua

Though Moses will not enter the promised land because of his sin at Meribah (20:12), God will allow him to survey Canaan from the top of the Abarim mountain range (Mount Nebo) before he dies. Putting his own interests aside once again, Moses appeals to God not on his own behalf but for the Israelites, who will need a leader to replace him. God instructs Moses to commission Joshua, his faithful servant and proven leader, as his successor (cf. 14:6-9; Exod. 33:11). Moses symbolically transfers his authority to Joshua by laying his hands on him in front of the high priest Eleazar and the entire Israelite congregation. In this way, God makes continued provision for a shepherd of his sheep as he prepares the Israelites to enter Canaan.

28-30 Offerings and Vows

Through Moses and Eleazar, God has prepared this new generation of Israelites militarily and logistically to enter the promised land; now he must prepare them spiritually by communicating his instructions concerning sacrifices and vows. Moses had given these commands to the previous generation, but through their faithlessness they forfeited this honor. Now their offspring's opportunity has come, and God prepares them in the same way.

Instructions for daily, Sabbath, and monthly offerings precede those for festival and freewill offerings (chs. 28–29). Repeating the unconditional obligation of men to keep their vows (30:2), Moses adds regulations concerning vows made by women — vows that may involve sacrifices or tithes. Husbands and fathers may confirm or annul the vows they overhear their wives and unmarried daughters make. God will not hold guilty a woman who fails to keep a vow annulled by a man in authority over her. This provision lends both spiritual protection to Israelite women, who live in a patriarchal system that does not generally recognize them as independent of male authority, as well as economic protection to men, who must provide for their wives and daughters.

31 Vengeance against the Midianites

God now orders the Israelites to take vengeance on the Midianites for leading his people astray. God has already held the Israelites responsible for breaking the covenant by worshipping the Baal of Peor (25:8-9); now he will use Israel to punish the perpetrators of his people's sin in that incident.

Each Israelite tribe contributed an equal amount in the consecration of the tabernacle, so now each must send an equal number of men to war. Under Phinehas's priestly leadership, 12 thousand Israelites slay all the Midianite men, including their five tribal kings and the diviner Balaam, who masterminded the plan to tempt Israel to sin (v. 16). Though God's purpose here does not include the total annihilation of the Midianites but only righteous vengeance for their subversive acts in diverting the Israelites' true worship of God, Moses scolds the army for sparing the Midianite women, for women carried out Balaam's plan. Moses orders the execution of all but the virgins, as well as any remaining Midianite boys, since both pose a continuing threat to Israel's fidelity to God's covenant. The command shows that the requirements of God's holiness surpass the value of human life.

In keeping with the laws concerning contact with a corpse, the warriors must remain outside the Israelite camp for one week and observe the appropriate rites of purification (cf. 19:11-13). They must also purify the booty they have taken in battle and then divide it in an orderly fashion that benefits the entire Israelite community. Those who fought receive the most per person: half of the live spoils go to the 12 thousand warriors, who must contribute one five-hundredth of their portion to the high priest. The rest of the Israelites receive the other half, from which they must give one-fiftieth to the Levites. The warriors make a freewill atonement offering of all the gold they captured in battle to thank God for sparing every Israelite soldier.

32 The Transjordanian Tribes

The fertile pastureland east of the Jordan River looks appealing to the Reubenites and Gadites, who have numerous flocks and herds, and they would rather possess the land they see than take a chance on what lies ahead. Moses appeals to the previous generation's mistake in warning that settling for land outside Canaan might discourage their countrymen from taking possession of the land of God's promise. The petitioners offer a practical plan that will satisfy both their desire and God's will: they will leave their flocks and families in Jazer and Gilead while their fighting men accompany the rest of the Israelites into Canaan and help them claim their covenantal inheritance. Moses accepts the plan but impresses on the Reubenites and Gadites their obligation to fulfill their promise (v. 23). After displacing the Amorites in Gilead, half the tribe of Joseph's son Manasseh also opts to settle east of Jordan.

33:1-49 A Summary of the 40-Years' Journey

After setting out from Rameses in Egypt, the Israelites pitched their tents at 40 campsites during their four decades of wilderness wanderings. Most of these sites' geographical locations are difficult to pinpoint today. Aaron dies during the 40th year at age 123 (vv. 38-39). The section closes with the Israelites encamped across a several-mile stretch on the plains of Moab opposite Jericho.

33:50–34:29 Claiming and Apportioning the Land

God instructs the Israelites to "drive out" all Canaan's inhabitants and destroy the trappings of their religion completely. If the Israelites fail in this mission, they will seal their own fate, for the foreigners will thwart Israel's obedience to God, and God will punish his people in the same way that he plans to punish the heathen. To give the Israelites a clear understanding of the scope of their task, God sets forth the borders of the promised land (cf. Joshua 13–19) that the remaining nine and a half tribes are to inherit (ch. 32). The high priest Eleazar and Moses' successor, Joshua, will preside over the distribution of the land by lot (cf. 26:53-56), and one leader from each tribe that inherits land in Canaan will help with this task.

Not until the reigns of David and Solomon in the early 1st millennium did Israel's territory reach the prescribed borders, from Dan in the north to Beer-sheba in the south (1 Kgs. 4:24-25).

35 Cities for the Levites

Israel's tribes must designate 48 cities as homes for the landless Levites, as well as pastureland around the cities for the Levites' flocks and herds. Six of these cities (three in Transjordan and three in Canaan) will serve as cities of refuge (Joshua 20–21). Any manslayer — Israelite or foreigner — may flee to one of these cities and claim asylum from those seeking blood revenge until a fair trial occurs. If found innocent of intentional murder, the fugitive gains protection from his would-be assailants by remaining inside the city to which he fled. Only the death of the high priest living at the time the accident occurred frees him from this restriction. If, however, more than one witness gives evidence that the culprit committed intentional murder, he must receive the death penalty (cf. 15:30-31). Ransom money may neither restore an unintentional killer to his home prior to the death of the high priest nor redeem the life of a murderer (contrast 3:45-51; 15:22-29).

While the rules concerning manslaughter and murder make justice a priority, their main function is to maintain the ritual purity of the land in which God dwells with his people (vv. 33-34). The Levites' physical presence throughout Canaan will serve as a constant reminder to the Israelites of their covenant with God.

36 Clarifying the Rules of Inheritance

The final chapter clarifies the rules concerning the inheritance of land — rules established in response to the granting of land to Zelophehad's unmarried daughters (27:1-11). Land must remain within the tribe that originally received it by lot; therefore, single women who inherit land must marry within their tribe, since their children — the heirs to the land — will belong to her husband's tribe.

Deuteronomy

Deuteronomy does not contain a "second law," as its Greek name would imply, but a second giving of the Mosaic law, which the Israelites received at Sinai. Deuteronomy both restates and explains the Law outlined in Exod. 20:22–23:19 for the historical situation immediately before to the Israelites' entry into Canaan. This fifth and final book of the Pentateuch is also the first book of what scholars call the Deuteronomistic History, which focuses on Israel's life in Canaan up to the Babylonian exile and which includes Joshua, Judges, 1-2 Samuel, and 1-2 Kings.

Authorship and Audience

Scholars take different positions regarding the authorship and original audience of Deuteronomy. Traditionalists maintain that the book preserves a faithful record of the words of Moses, though few would regard Moses as its final author, since at a number of points Deuteronomy refers to Moses in the third person and since the book's final chapter records Moses' death (cf. ch. 34). In this view, the original audience is the new generation of Israelites that has "grown up" during the 40 years of wilderness wandering and replaced its faithless fathers, who refused to enter the land of God's promise after leaving Sinai in the mid-to-late 2nd millennium B.C.

Others view the book as directed toward a much later, 7th-century group, probably settled in the southern kingdom of Judah during the divided monarchy. This position sees Deuteronomy functioning as reform law in addressing the religious, economic, social, and political concerns of the day, with an editor using Moses' name to lend authority to the book's content.

Deuteronomy aided the religious reforms of Judah's King Josiah in the late 7th century (2 Kings 22–23), but the book seeks to bring not only external change but also sincere, internal devotion to God (6:4-9; 10:12-13). That the New Testament authors quote Deuteronomy more than 80 times reveals this book's importance in the development of Christianity from its beginnings.

Structure

The overall structure of Deuteronomy includes the various elements of an ancient Near Eastern treaty, with God as the "overlord" and the Israelites as his "vassals" (see "Covenants" [141-44]). Two introductory speeches by Moses begin the book (1:1–4:43; 4:44–11:32). These addresses remind the Israelites of their history with a loving and faithful God and call them to covenantal obedience. This new generation must regard the covenant as their own and not simply as binding on their ancestors. The repetition of the Ten Commandments in 5:6-21 provides the basis for the laws expounded in the legal core of Deuteronomy (chs. 12–26). Moses' lengthy concluding remarks (chs. 27–33) look forward to Israel's life in Canaan and put forth a choice: covenantal obedience, which will lead to life, or disobedience, which will lead to death (30:15-20). God himself anticipates Israel's faithlessness but also pledges his redemption and blessing (31:16-21). Moses' death occasions the transfer of leadership to Joshua (ch. 34).

1–3 A Review of Israel's Journey

1 In Deuteronomy 1–4, Moses recites to the Israelites a condensed account of their journey from Mount Sinai (always called "Horeb" in Deuteronomy) to the plains of Moab. The account begins at the end of the 40th year since the exodus from Egypt, and the address takes place with the nation encamped on the eastern side of the Jordan River in Moab. In his first speech, Moses highlights God's command that

Law in Israel and in Judaism

The psalmist's cry "Oh, how I love your law!" (Ps. 119:97) highly commends one of Israel's lasting legacies. Joyous feasting and generous giving, not mourning, marked the day of its reading (Neh. 8:9-10). Israelite law drew on the rich legal culture of Mesopotamia — law codes such as the Laws of Ur-Nammu (ca. 21st century B.C.) and Hammurabi's Code (ca. 18th century). It inherited its casuistic ("If . . . then") and *lex talionis* ("eye for an eye") legal formulas from ancient law (Exod. 21:26; Deut. 19:21). But for Israel, "law" (Heb. *torah*) meant not simply "legal code" but "teaching" or "instruction." That is why the first section of the Hebrew canon — comprising both narratives and laws — bears the name Torah. The Pentateuch gives Israel "instruction" through both lives and law, instruction so treasured as to evoke love.

Law and Laws in Israel

Biblical tradition roots law in God's revelation to Moses at Mount Sinai (Josh. 8:31; 2 Chr. 33:8; Neh. 10:29). Moses received the law at Sinai (Exodus 20–Numbers 10), later proclaimed new laws (e.g., Num. 27:1-11), and preached the expanded Sinai legislation beside the Jordan (Deuteronomy 12–26). Moses wrote the law — probably the core of Deuteronomy (Deut. 31:24; 2 Kgs. 14:6) — into a "book," which survived (Josh. 23:6; 2 Chr. 25:4) and was later rediscovered

(2 Kings 22). But biblical laws show evidence of a process of growth and adaptation long past Moses' time. For example, Exod. 20:24 permits Israel to build an earthen altar to honor God anywhere, but Deuteronomy insists that Israel perform all worship at the single place chosen by God himself (Deut. 12:5; 16:2, 16). Most scholars believe the reference is to the temple in Jerusalem and associate Deuteronomy's policy of a central sanctuary with the religious reform of King Josiah (ca. 620 B.C.; 2 Kings 23). Thus the term "law of Moses" affirms him not as its writer, but as its founder — the giver of Israel's first laws and the legal authority whose work later Israelite scholars would extend.

That extension incorporates four legal collections into the Torah. The language and simplicity of the Book of the Covenant (Exod. 20:22–23:33) mark it as the earliest (ca. 1100; cf. Exod. 24:4). Included are two types of legal material: judgments (case laws) and statutes (specific commands) that define religious and civil rules and specify punishments for breaking them. The Bible's best-known collection, the Decalogue (Exod. 20:1-17; Deut. 5:6-21), forms its table of contents. It offers a Sinai covenant in miniature — a brief historical prologue with 10 instructions. The Holiness Code (Leviticus 17-26), probably a compilation by priests (perhaps ca. 700 or 500), aims to promote holiness in the community (Lev. 19:2).

The date of the Deuteronomic Code (Deuteronomy 12–26) is uncertain, but many of its laws are thought to be ancient, perhaps even Mosaic (cf. Deut. 31:24), and a preliminary collection probably compiled in the northern kingdom before it fell (722). Most scholars consider it to be the "book of the law" found in 621 (2 Kgs. 22:8). (See the introduction to the Historical Books. [165-69].)

Israelite laws articulate Israel's community vision and values. Unlike other ancient codes, Israelite law requires equal treatment for all citizens, carefully limiting royal power (Deut. 17:14-20) and sternly outlawing favoritism (Lev. 19:15; Deut. 16:19; cf. Jas. 2:9). The *lex talionis* formula ("eye for an eye") curbs excessive revenge by requiring equivalent compensation for injury or loss (Lev. 24:20). The law's concern to preserve national purity also closes the loopholes of some Mesopotamian laws, which permit the substitution of fines or compensation for execution in capital crimes (Exod. 21:12, 17; Lev. 20:9; Deut. 13:5). But refreshingly humane laws, for example, protect a female slave from abuse (Exod. 21:7-11) and permit mercy toward an irresponsible ox owner (21:28-30). Ultimately, Israelite law promotes loyalty to Israel's covenant with Yahweh. It regulates which prophets Israel should obey and which they should stone for promoting idolatry (Deut. 13:1-5; 18:9-22).

Local judges or elders adjudicated criminal and civil cases at the city gate (Exod. 18:21-22; Deut. 16:18; Ruth 4:1-10). Priests and Levites at sanctuaries answered "Yes/No" questions by casting lots (Urim and Thummim; Exod. 28:30), visually inspected for ritual uncleanness (Leviticus 13–14; cf. Num. 5:11-31), and decided difficult cases referred to them (Deut. 17:8-13). The king himself was the highest court-of-appeals for aggrieved citizens (2 Sam. 15:2; 2 Kgs. 6:26-29; 8:5-6).

The Law in Judaism

In Judaism — the form of Israel's religion after the exile — Torah refers both to divine revelation as a whole and to its specific statements (commandments, proverbs, stories). Obedience of Torah is the heart of Judaism, but not in a rigid, legalistic sense. Law represents Israel's practical response to God's gracious acts — his election of Israel, rescue from slavery, and covenantal relationship. As Ben Sira wrote (ca. 180 B.C.), "Those who fear the Lord seek to please him, and those who love him are filled with his law" (Sir. 2:16). But the law omits many matters or seems contradictory, so Judaism offers interpretation of biblical laws and the guidance of interpretive authorities (priests, scribes, lay teachers). The Pharisees of Jesus' day were prominent lay teachers praised for their precise interpretation of Mosaic law (Acts 22:3; 26:5). They also obeyed their own special rules — "traditions" received from the sect's ancestors. They washed their hands before eating (Matt. 15:2; Mark 7:3; Luke 11:38) and practiced ʿerub — the linking of adjacent houses as a single house by cross-beams to avoid violating the Sabbath, still a common practice in Hasidic neighborhoods. But recent studies cast doubt on the common impression that Judaism recognizes a Mosaic oral law parallel to the written law. The Pharisees apparently taught that, while a good Pharisee obeyed both the "traditions" and Mosaic law, a good Jew need only fulfill the latter.

The center of Judaism is the local synagogue, an innovation first attested in Egypt (mid-3rd century B.C.). Considered customary, the weekly Sabbath service featured teaching and Scripture readings (Acts 13:15 mentions "the law and the prophets"; cf. Luke 4:17). Modern synagogues architecturally feature the ark, which stores the Torah scroll, and their Torah readings on Sabbaths and during annual festivals complete all of its 54 sections each year. Ancient Greco-Roman writers confirm Jewish observance of the Mosaic law on monotheism, circumcision, Sabbath, and food laws. Jews throughout the Roman world also continued to pay the half-shekel temple tax, to fast on the Day of Atonement, to send firstfruits and free-will offerings to Jerusalem, and to attend annual feasts of pilgrimage there (Passover, Booths, and Weeks). Loyalty to Moses underlies Jewish criticism of early Christian beliefs and practices as violations of Mosaic law (John 19:7; Acts 6:13; 18:13; 21:28), criticism that Paul denies (Acts 24:14; cf. 28:17).

The Jewish historian Josephus called the laws "simple and familiar" — far fewer and easier to grasp than modern tax laws! — and many laws find consistent observance in a daily routine.

Ancient Jews sought to obey the Shema (Deut. 6:4-9) by fixing it on doorposts or wearing select parts of the Law, and "zeal for the law" (1 Macc. 2:58; cf. Acts 21:20) led many to die rather than violate the Law or permit the defilement of Jerusalem or the temple. Judaism features epitomes of the law — short statements that

Stela of Hammurabi receiving symbols of authority from the seated sun-god Shamash. Below are listed 282 laws. *(Louvre; photo by Mitchell G. Reddish)*

voice its basic thrust (e.g., Rabbi Hillel's comment, "What is hateful to you, do not to your neighbor: that is the whole Torah, while the rest is commentary . . ."; cf. the "Golden Rule," Matt. 7:12). Jesus' pronouncement on the "great- est commandment" reflects this practice (Mark 12:28-31; cf. Deut. 6:4-9; Lev. 19:18, 34), as do some of Paul's comments (Rom. 13:10; Gal. 5:14). Affirming Israel as the people through whom "the im- perishable light of the law was to be given to the world" (Wis. 18:4), rabbis often compiled lists of seven laws for interested Gentiles to observe.

ROBERT L. HUBBARD, JR.

the Israelites take possession of the land he promised to the patriarchs (Gen. 15:18-21) and God's fulfillment of his promise to multiply Abraham's descendants (Gen. 15:5). Moses then cites his appointment of tribal leaders to help with administrative tasks (Exod. 18:13-26; Num. 11:14-17); the report of the spies sent to scope out Canaan and the Israelites' faithless response (Num. 13:1–14:25); God's disallowing the current generation to enter the promised land as punishment for their rebelliousness (Num. 14:26-38); and Moses' similar sentence for failing to honor God (Num. 20:7-12). The chapter ends by noting the Israelites' failed attempt to enter Canaan against God's will (Num. 14:39-45).

2 Deuteronomy 2 fills in a few details about the wasted years of wilderness wandering — years passed over quickly in Numbers. The first half of thc chapter mentions the Israelites' journey from Kadesh-barnea, near the southern border of Canaan, to Mount Seir, south and east of the Dead Sea. It goes on to recount Moses' attempt to lead the Israelites through Edomite territory (Num. 20:14-21) and the nation's detour through the wilderness of Moab. The account stresses that God will not give the Edomites', Moabites', or Ammonites' land to Israel inasmuch as he gave it as an inheritance to Esau and to Lot's sons. Here at least the Edomites appear to have treated their Israelite kin in a friendlier manner than Numbers portrays (vv. 28-29).

The generation of Israelites that refused to enter Canaan 38 years earlier has died (cf. Num. 14:29-32). The death of these rebels occasioned the new generation's opportunity to move to- ward staking their claim in the promised land. The Israelites' defeat of the Amorites at Hesh- bon signals the beginning of God's judgment on the sinful inhabitants of Canaan foreshadowed in Gen. 15:16.

3 The recounting of the journey continues with the Israelites' defeat of Og, Amorite king of Bashan and leader of the mighty Rephaim (cf. Num. 21:33). The emphasis on this people's number and might, their heavily fortified cit- ies, and the large size of their king's iron bed emphasize God's power to bring the Israelites success in the face of seemingly overwhelming odds (v. 11). Thus the Israelites' victory serves as a foil to the previous generation's lack of faith (Num. 13:28-33).

When the tribes of Reuben, Gad, and half- Manasseh claimed their landed inheritance east of the Jordan (cf. Numbers 32), they displaced not their distant cousins in Edom, Moab, and Ammon, but the Amorites and Canaanite peo- ples living in Bashan and Gilead, north of Am- monite territory. After briefly acknowledging Joshua as Moses' successor (v. 21), the text tells of Moses' glimpse of the promised land from the Pisgah ridge, ca. 9 miles northeast of the Dead Sea, while the Israelites remain camped on the plains of Moab (cf. 34:1, "Mount Nebo").

4:1-43 Exhortations to Covenantal Faithfulness

The retelling of Israel's journey with God provides the basis for Moses' appeals to the congregation, which end this first introduction to the Deuteronomic law. He reminds them that they know what to do to keep God's laws, have experienced the punishment for disobedience, and should now recognize the honor God has extended to them by establishing his covenant with them and should pursue lives of faithful- ness to God. Moses urges not routine legalism but spiritual discipline and heartfelt obedience, which will result in the good life that God intends for his people.

By recalling the manner in which God communicated his covenant with the Israelites at Sinai, Moses reminds them to honor God's distinctively spiritual nature by refraining from fashioning images to represent him (vv. 15-18). He also warns them against worshiping his creations in nature (v. 19). Because Moses knows he will not accompany the Israelites into Canaan, he fears their spiritual waywardness in his absence, warns them of the consequences of covenantal disobedience, which include exile, and even calls down this curse should they disregard God's commands (vv. 26-28). But God is compassionate and gracious, as well as jealous (v. 24), and will not reject his repentant people (v. 31). Indeed, God has already acted on Israel's behalf in ways unique among the nations. He has shown himself supremely willing and able to care for his people's every need, and he will continue to do so if only they obey him.

Finally, Moses names one city of refuge in each Transjordanian tribe's territory (cf. Num. 35:11-14).

4:44–11:32 The Ten Commandments as the Basis for Obedience

4:44–5:33 Moses' second speech recalls Israel's history and looks forward to the nation's life in the promised land as it focuses on the Law given at Sinai. He exhorts the new generation of Israelites to regard the Law as their own covenant with God (5:3) and restates the Ten Commandments (5:7-21). Remembering the Law, following it, and teaching it to one's children emerge as central themes throughout these chapters. By repeating the Law and drawing lessons from the previous generation's disobedience of it, the speech stresses that the fear of God, personal humility, and remembrance of covenantal history (both of God's faithfulness and the Israelites' unfaithfulness) will keep this new generation on the path of obedience and prevent the blessings of material prosperity in the promised land from lulling them into laxness in their devotion to God.

Deuteronomy demonstrates concern for the weaker members of society in 5:14-15, where the purpose of Sabbath observance is to offer rest to servants and for the Israelites to remember their deliverance by God from slavery in Egypt. (Contrast Exod. 20:10-11, which grounds the practice in God's having rested on the seventh day of creation.)

6 In 6:10–9:6 Moses delivers eight sermons that call the Israelites to remember their past and teach their children in the ways of God. Each sermon describes a particular situation — either from the past or in anticipation of the future in Canaan — and draws conclusions that lead to practical applications for life under the covenant. The units are 6:10-15, 16-19, 20-25; 7:1-16, 17-26; 8:1-6; 7-20; and 9:1-6.

Judaism's central prayer, the Shema ("Hear"; 6:4-9), communicates the essence of Israelite religion: Israel recognizes only one God, whom they must love with every fiber of their being. Furthermore, God's Law must permeate the entirety of an Israelite's life (vv. 20-25). Orthodox Jews continue to obey the command to bind the Law to their bodies by fastening small boxes containing miniature copies of the Law (phylacteries) to their foreheads and right arms (v. 8). Many Jews also attach cylinders containing copies of the Law *(mezuzoth)* to their doorposts (v. 9).

7 Through the Israelites, God will now bring judgment on the "many nations" that inhabit Canaan, including the accursed descendants of Noah's errant son Ham (Gen. 9:20-25). Earlier, God saved a remnant of humanity from the judgment he brought about by the flood as part of his plan to redeem his creation; now the Israelites represent that remnant, and God commands them to purge the promised land of all forms of wickedness — including humans — in order to further his redemptive purposes through them. Their obedience to this command, which includes eradicating the worship of the Canaanite fertility-god Baal, will bring great blessing from the only true God in the very realm of Baal's supposed power (vv. 13-14). The Lord himself will accomplish the task through them (vv. 17-24).

8 Chapter 8 remembers the Israelites' days in

the desert as an opportunity for growth in faith. In the wilderness, God both humbled his people and faithfully provided for them to teach them that life in its fullest sense comes not from mere food but from obedience to God's will (v. 3). After detailing the bounty of the land the Israelites will soon inherit (vv. 7-10), Moses warns against developing the pride and self-reliance that material blessing can induce. These traits would signal that the Israelites had forgotten the lessons of their past, as well as the Giver who grants the blessings. Forgetfulness can easily lead to idolatry, and idolatry for the Israelites will lead to inevitable judgment (vv. 19-20).

9 The Israelites must not view their defeat of the Canaanites as resulting from their own power or as a reward for their worthiness to possess the land, but as the work of a mighty God, who precedes them in battle and who uses them to mete out just judgment on the wicked. Moses reminds the Israelites of their waywardness in worshipping the golden calf at Sinai as a way to dispel any illusions of self-righteousness.

10 Verses 6-9 interrupt Moses' speech, which now centers on his second reception of the stone tablets, to detail the Israelites' itinerary in the wilderness and report the commissioning of the Levites. In vv. 12-13, Moses summarizes God's requirements of the Israelites: fear (respect, as shown by right worship of him alone), total obedience, and love for him (cf. 6:5). Moses' exhortation that the Israelites "circumcise" their hearts encourages a covenantal obedience that stems from sincere and internalized devotion to God (cf. Jer. 4:4). Deuteronomy's emphasis on God's impartiality and his concern for the weak in society is again clear in vv. 17-19. The 70 ancestors of the Israelites mentioned in v. 22 include only the males of the patriarch Jacob's household (cf. Gen. 46:26-27).

11 Chapter 11 contrasts the potential blessings and curses that lie before the Israelites in Canaan. God himself tends Canaan's fields and makes the land fruitful, unlike in Egypt, where only the laborious work of sowing and irrigation produced crops (vv. 10-12; contrast Num. 16:12-14). Yet God controls Canaan's yield and

the Israelites' future in the promised land, and only by their obedience will they realize God's good promises (vv. 13-17). Verse 29 alludes to the ceremony on Mounts Ebal and Gerizim, near the centrally located city of Shechem, that will celebrate the Israelites' anticipated future conquest of Canaan in its entirety (cf. chs. 27–28; Josh. 8:30-35).

12–26 Specific Instructions for Life in Canaan

Many scholars regard chapters 5–30 as the oldest part of the book, whose discovery in the temple aided King Josiah's reforms in the late 7th century (cf. 2 Kings 22–23). Chapters 12–26 form the legal core of these chapters by detailing specific laws the Israelites must follow in Canaan. These regulations find their basis in the Book of the Covenant (Exod. 20:22–23:33) and include, among other materials, both apodictic laws (straight commands and prohibitions) and casuistic laws (case laws that prescribe specific penalties; see "Law in Israel and Judaism" [153-55]).

12:1-28 From the outset of the Israelites' entry into the promised land, they must destroy all trappings of Canaanite religion — from altars to idols. The purpose of this command is to obliterate the names of the idolaters' gods, for according to ancient Semitic thought the essence and power of any being lay in its name (cf. 7:5, 25). The Israelites must establish an entirely new place of regular worship in a location chosen by God where they would remember his name alone (v. 5). This place became Shiloh, where the high priest Eli and his protégé Samuel served (cf. Jer. 7:12). Jerusalem replaced Shiloh under David and Solomon, the latter of whom built the first temple. After the kingdom of Israel divided following Solomon's death, the northern tribes established two unauthorized rival shrines — in Bethel and Dan.

The regulations here allow for some slaughtering and eating of meat, including animals that do not qualify for sacrifice, within the gates of the Israelite settlements in Canaan. This allowance grows out of a recognition that most Israelites would find it difficult to travel to a single, central shrine from geographically widespread tribal territories (vv. 15-28; contrast Lev.

Canaanite altar at Megiddo, focus of the largest extant Early Bronze I temple in the Levant.
(www.HolylandPhotos.org)

17:1-7). The present commands, however, clearly uphold both the prohibition of the consumption of blood (Lev. 17:10ff.) and the directive to offer official sacrifices only at God's altar (vv. 17-18, 26-27).

12:29–13:18 The Israelites must neither imitate the worship practices of the Canaanites (12:30-31) nor succumb to the temptations to worship other gods held out by false prophets, cherished relatives and friends, or entire communities of wayward countrymen. On the contrary, they must put to death any who seek to seduce them away from the worship of God alone (ch. 13). The books of Kings illustrate both the Israelites' failure to honor this ban on Canaanite religion and the tragic consequences.

14 The laws in vv. 1-21 set the Israelites apart as a holy nation (see "Holy, Clean, and Unclean" [127-28]) by prohibiting Canaanite mourning practices and detailing observance of food laws (cf. Leviticus 11). Because animals that had died on their own would not have had their blood drained out, the Israelites must not eat them. Boiling a kid in its mother's milk may reflect a Canaanite practice.

The latter half of chapter 14 echoes laws regarding tithing given in Leviticus 27 and Numbers 18. Tithing (the giving of one-tenth) accomplishes several purposes: it reminds the Israelites that their possessions (animals, produce, etc.) comprise gifts from a gracious God; supply sustenance for the Levites, who lack a tangible inheritance in the promised land; and provide occasions for family and community fellowship centered around the worship of God. Verses 24-26 allow the offerer who lives a distance from the central shrine to exchange his tithe for money, which he can easily carry on his journey to the sanctuary and then use to purchase food and/or drink to present once he arrives.

15 Chapter 15 requires generosity among the Israelites by restating laws concerning the forgiveness of debts in the Sabbatical Year (cf. Leviticus 25). Masters of slaves released during the seventh year must supply the necessary goods to ensure their successful and lasting independence. These laws transform the motivation for lending from one of economic gain (through accumulation of interest and labor; 23:19-20) to simple, heartfelt benevolence toward needy countrymen. The prescriptions also aim to check poverty and the escalation of class distinctions based on material wealth.

16:1-17 Deuteronomy 16 shows less interest in the specific details of Israel's three great festivals than in their functioning to bring the entire Israelite community together at the central place of worship to remember their history as slaves in Egypt, celebrate their deliverance by God, and rejoice in God's blessings through the fruitfulness of the land (esp. vv. 11, 16). Leviticus 23 gives more detailed information regarding Israel's religious festivals.

16:18–17:20 This section addresses issues regarding Israel's judicial, political, and social structures and intersperses laws to prevent religious unfaithfulness (e.g., Canaanite cultic practices, 16:21-22; and the offering of defective animals as sacrifices, 17:1).

Israel's theocracy does not separate societal justice from religious purity. It requires judges to decide fairly and impartially. If a local judge finds a particular case too ambiguous to discern, he must refer it to a higher tribunal and allow the Levitical priests to render a verdict. The punishment for failing to honor the priests' judgment is death. Israel's justice system requires more than one witness to condemn a backslider or murderer to death.

The instructions in vv. 14-20 regarding a king for Israel recognize the nation's comparison of itself to its neighbors. While God does not prohibit the appointment of a human king, God stipulates that he himself will select the monarch from among the Israelites. The human king must devote himself to studying God's law rather than to amassing war machinery, wealth, and wives. In this way, he will remain humble toward God and countrymen in his heart. Nevertheless, many of Israel's kings did marry foreign wives, whose introduction of foreign gods greatly contributed to the nation's religious — and therefore divinely orchestrated political — downfall. Solomon figures as the prime example (1 Kgs. 10:26–11:8).

18 Verses 1-8 encapsulate the rights of the Levites as a tribe to receive from their fellow Israelites support for livelihood, since their inheritance consists not in land but in sharing the offerings made to God in exchange for full-time religious service (cf. Numbers 18).

The remainder of the chapter prohibits the Israelites' adoption of the pagan religious practices of child sacrifice and manipulation of the spiritual world through witchcraft, divination, and the like (cf. Lev. 20:1-6). Rather than relying on pagan mediums and spiritualists to determine God's will in specific circumstances, the Israelites must heed the words of a divinely appointed prophet, whom God will raise from their midst to replace Moses and whose fulfilled prophecies will confirm his authenticity.

19 This chapter repeats the command that the Israelites establish geographically dispersed cities of refuge to which unintentional manslayers may flee for asylum from blood avengers (cf. 4:41-43). These provisions serve to curb undeserved punishment in a social system that begins by assuming guilt and requires proof of innocence. But one found guilty of intentional murder loses the right to asylum in the cities of refuge and becomes subject to the death penalty. A witness who falsely accuses another person becomes subject to the punishment he seeks for the accused, up to and including death. This potentiality, combined with the requirement of at least two witnesses to establish the guilt of an accused person, serves to deter the bearing of false witness. Verse 21 repeats the *lex talionis* in confirmation of these guidelines (cf. Exod. 21:23-25; Lev. 24:17-20).

Verse 14 sets forth a principle of great importance for a nation that derives its livelihood from the land: neighbors must honor each other's territorial boundaries and refrain from usurping another's ancestral inheritance.

20 Israel's priests must inspire the nation's citizens as they prepare for divinely instituted war in Canaan. To prevent another man's staking claim to one's property or wife, valid excuses for nonparticipation in battle include ownership of a newly built home or recently sown field and engagement for marriage. The fainthearted must also remain at home so their fear does not spread among the troops.

The Israelites must offer terms of peace to cities outside Canaan. The inhabitants of those cities that surrender without a fight shall become subordinate to Israel. In those cities that resist, the Israelites must kill all the men but may take everything else for themselves as booty. By contrast, the Israelites must kill "anything that breathes" in cities within Canaan, leaving no one to lead them astray from the true worship of God (cf. 7:1-5). Israel may use only nonfruit-bearing trees in making siegeworks for war; in other words, the Israelites must not destroy the bounty of the land, which God intends as a component of his gift to them.

21 Lacking a known culprit, the elders of the city nearest a murder victim found lying in open country must assume responsibility for obtaining God's forgiveness for the crime and for reestablishing the nation's purity before him. The atonement ritual prescribed involves the elders' washing their hands over the body of a slain heifer to substitute for executing the unknown murderer.

God allows Israelite men to marry foreign women from defeated cities outside Canaan. The women's status as foreign captives is not a valid reason for their Israelite husbands to mistreat them, however. A husband who no longer wants his foreign wife may not sell her, but instead must grant her freedom. This law serves as a check against any tendency toward marrying foreign wives purely for economic gain. It also protects the dignity of women made particularly vulnerable in a patriarchal society during wartime.

Verses 15-17 prohibit a patriarch's playing favorites by insisting that a man's firstborn son receive his rightful inheritance even if born of an unloved wife (cf. Jacob's preference of Rachel's son Joseph above the older sons of Leah; Genesis 29–30, 37). That disobedient Israelite sons may receive the death penalty for persistent obstinacy toward their parents demonstrates the seriousness of God's command that children honor their fathers and mothers and thereby preserve the stability of the family as the foundation of Israelite society. The hanging of a body on a tree (vv. 22-23) refers to further shaming an executed individual through exposure of his corpse.

22 These laws flesh out some of the practical implications of loving one's neighbor as oneself (cf. Lev. 19:18). The laws include caring for a countryman's lost property and restoring it to him as well as maintaining one's own property so as to ensure the safety of other people. God's concern with the order he established at creation emerges in laws that respect the distinctiveness of the sexes (v. 5), products of the land (vv. 9, 11), and animal species (v. 10). Tassels on garments (v. 12) serve as constant reminders to follow God's commands (cf. Num. 15:37-40).

The laws in vv. 13-30 address sexual purity, not as a private matter but as a community concern. They protect women from sexual slander by disgruntled husbands and in cases of rape clear them from the social and punitive consequences of adultery. A bloodstained sheet could prove a woman's virginity on her wedding night or her menstrual and therefore nonpregnant state. Both instances protect her eligibility for marriage. But the laws' purpose is to preserve the honor of the patrimony more than to guard the rights of women. For the sake of the Israelite community as a whole, the laws require responsible sexual behavior by prescribing serious punishments, including the death penalty, for adultery and sexual activity outside marriage.

23 Laws concerning the right to participate in community worship at the central sanctuary ensure the congregation's ritual purity and strengthen the Israelites' national distinctiveness. The prohibitions in vv. 1-2 may constitute rejection of pagan religious practices involving castration and cult prostitution resulting in pregnancy. Although, for historical reasons, no Ammonite or Moabite may worship in the Israelite assembly, descendants of the Edomites and Egyptians may participate by virtue of their blood relationship to Israel through Jacob and their initial hospitality to God's people through Joseph.

Verses 9-25 address a range of issues, including the cleanness of the Israelite army camp, asylum for foreign slaves, cult prostitution, interest on loans, vows to the Lord, and the rights and restrictions involved in taking sustenance from a countryman's vineyard or field. Regarding asylum, contrast the Old Babylonian Code of Hammurabi, which prescribes the death penalty for harboring runaway slaves.

24 Verses 1-4 do not institute or sanction divorce; rather, they regulate the divorce that the ancient Israelites already practiced. The laws here protect women by requiring of a husband serious reflection and legitimate, written grounds for divorcing his wife — he may not remarry her if she marries another man and is divorced a second time. Also, the writ of divorce enabled the woman to refute a former husband's false charge of desertion.

The Israelites' knowledge of their history as slaves in Egypt must temper their exercising of individual rights so as to show mercy to the weaker members of society. A millstone taken as a pledge would deprive the owner of his means to make food; a cloak kept overnight as a pledge would deprive the owner of his protection from the night air; wages withheld from a servant would deprive him of his daily needs. Farmers and vinedressers must leave the leftovers from their fields and fruit trees for those without other means of support (cf. Ruth 2:15-16).

While people must act in the interest of society as a whole, they must suffer the consequences of their sins as individuals. Not even children and parents may substitute for each other for transgressions deserving the death penalty (v. 16).

25 By setting an upper limit on the number of lashes administered, verses 1-3 prohibit excessive and degrading punishment of an Israelite found guilty by the court. Later practice reduced the maximum 40 "stripes" to 39 to prevent the unintentional transgression of this law through miscounting (cf. 2 Cor. 11:24).

The law regarding levirate marriage outlined in vv. 5-10 finds expression in Ruth 4. The unusual and severe punishment for a woman's potentially damaging a man's genitals during a fight (vv. 11-12) likely reflects the social importance of the man's ability to father children. Verses 13-16 echo the call for just weights in Lev. 19:36 (cf. Prov. 20:10, 23).

26 This chapter anticipates the Israelites' settled life in Canaan and elaborates the required ceremonies involving presentation of firstfruits to God and giving the third year's tithe in support of Levites, resident aliens, orphans, and widows as instructed in 14:28-29. The first ceremonial prayer remembers God's gracious deliverance of Israel from Egypt and recognizes his gift of a bountiful land. "My father was a wandering Aramean" (v. 5) is a statement of faith, or "credo," referring to Abraham, who stayed at Haran in the region of Aram-naharaim before continuing on to Canaan. The second prayer declares the offerer's obedience and ritual purity and invokes God's blessing.

The last four verses conclude this legal core of Deuteronomy by reaffirming Israel's covenantal relationship with God as stipulated in these 15 chapters. Verse 16 charges the Israelites to obey with care and sincerity the commandments recorded in chapters 12–26; verse 17 reminds them of their promise to do so; verse 18 affirms God's commitment to his people; and verse 19 states the lofty rewards of obedience, whose purpose ultimately consists in honoring God.

27 A Ceremony to Ratify the Covenant in Canaan

Moses, Israel's elders, and the Levitical priests instruct the people to ratify their covenant with God soon after they enter Canaan in a ceremony similar to the sealing of secular treaties in the ancient Near East (see "Covenants" [141-44]). First, they must record the law (the commandments in chs. 12–26) on lime-plastered stones and display them on Mount Ebal, near the centrally located city of Shechem. Next, they must make peace offerings to God on an altar built not according to Canaanite custom but according to divine instruction (cf. Exod. 20:25-26). Finally, six tribes stationed on Mount Gerizim shall pronounce blessings on the nation, and the other six, on Mount Ebal, shall

Mounts Gerizim and Ebal, from which the Israelite tribes pronounced the blessings and curses in the covenant ratification ceremony at Shechem. *(www.HolylandPhotos.org)*

pronounce the covenantal curses (cf. 11:26-29; Josh. 8:30-35).

The text records only the 12 curses to be uttered and to which the people must consent with an acknowledging "amen" ("let it be so"). The curses single out transgressions of the second, fifth, sixth, and possibly eighth of the Ten Commandments, which prohibit making idols, dishonoring parents, murder, and theft. The curses also take up the themes of caring for society's weak and of sexual purity, particularly regarding familial relationships. Verse 26 covers the remainder of the Deuteronomic commandments under the general designation of "law."

28 Blessings and Curses

By spelling out the covenantal sanctions, chapter 28 rounds out the ancient Near Eastern treaty structure of Deuteronomy. This section devotes the majority of space to the curses, which speak in both personal and communal terms in detailing the ways in which disobedience to the covenant will result in conditions exactly opposite to the blessings promised for faithfulness.

Verses 1-14 focus on the abundant fertility of land, animals, and the people themselves in outlining the prosperity that covenantal obedience will produce at all times and in all ways. This emphasis elevates God's power over the Canaanite deity Baal's supposed realm of rule. In addition to the blessings of land and progeny (vv. 8, 11), the promises of protection from enemies and blessing on other nations (vv. 7, 12) hark back to God's promise to Abram (Gen. 12:1-3). These blessings, which bring life in its fullest sense, embody what it means for God to claim the Israelites as his own people (v. 9).

The next 54 verses detail the deathly consequences of covenantal disobedience. The curses in verses 15-19 parallel the general blessings in verses 2-6. The curses also warn of divinely sent illnesses and plagues that recall the punishments God poured out on the Egyptians prior to the exodus (vv. 21-22, 58-61). Confusion, vulnerability, heartache, and fear will add to life's miseries (vv. 28-34, 65-67). Exile will reduce the Israelites to their preelected state: vassals to a foreign power and subject to powerless idols (v. 36, 49-52, 64). God will render the Israelites' labors and possessions useless in his quest to destroy the nation (vv. 38-48).

Israel's besiegement by a foreign power will produce famine, which will cause the abominable behavior of parents' killing and eating their own children (vv. 53-55; cf. Jer. 19:9). Family discord will become the norm in previously harmonious households (vv. 54-57). The nation will be reduced in number, and those who remain will not even be able to sell themselves as slaves in a foreign country (v. 68). God will take as much delight in destroying his disobedient people as he does in prospering an obedient nation (v. 63).

29–30 Moses Presents a Choice

Moses' third speech resumes several themes from his discourses in chapters 1–11. Here he appeals to Israel's history in reminding them not only of the wonders God has worked on their behalf but also of God's power to bring about both the blessings and curses of the covenant. Moses' words confirm that the Law applies to the present generation as well as to coming generations (29:10-15; cf. 5:3). He summarizes the devastating consequences of unfaithfulness (29:18-28) yet inspires hope for restored blessings to a repentant Israel, even in the event that God must punish them for disobedience to the full extent warned in the covenantal curses (30:1-10).

Moses points out the clarity and accessibility of the Law, thereby placing direct responsibility on the Israelites for their actions regarding the covenant (30:11-14). Though God's plans for the future remain hidden, the Israelites know and understand what God expects of them now (29:29), and God himself will enable the Israelites to honor him through covenantal faithfulness (30:6; cf. 10:12, 16); therefore, disobedience will prove nothing but deliberate. Moses sets before the Israelites the choice between life and death and concludes with a hopeful reminder of God's covenantal promises to Israel's ancestors, the patriarchs (30:15-20).

31 Moses' Final Acts

Moses announces his impending death and endorses Joshua as the Israelites' military leader in taking possession of Canaan. In his charge to the nation as a whole and to Joshua individually, Moses inspires courage and trust in God's promises based on God's past faithfulness to his people.

Moses entrusts the written law to the priests and Israel's elders. To ensure the education of future generations in the covenantal provisions and requirements, he commands the reading of the Law to the Israelite assembly every Sabbatical Year at the Feast of Booths.

God meets Moses and Joshua at the tabernacle and foretells Israel's future unfaithfulness through worship of other gods. Despite knowing what lies ahead, God gives Joshua marching orders to lead the Israelites in possessing the promised land and pledges his presence with him.

Moses places the book of the Law beside the ark of the covenant as a witness against the Israelites' future disobedience and prepares to teach the assembly a divinely inspired song that will serve the same purpose.

32:1-47 The Song of Moses

The poetic form of Moses' song enables its memorization by the Israelites, who like their contemporaries passed on much of their historical traditions orally. Following the format of an ancient Near Eastern covenantal lawsuit, the Song begins with the invocation of witnesses to the proceedings (heaven and earth, v. 1). Verses 4-6 summarize the reason for the lawsuit — Israel's disobedience. Verses 7-14 detail God's election of Israel and his loving care for them. The indictment of Jeshurun (a poetic name of Israel) for her irrational and unnatural idolatry appears in vv. 15-18, and vv. 19-25 hand down the guilty verdict and a bitter sentence that recalls the covenantal curses detailed in 28:15-68.

The remainder of the Song departs from the lawsuit format by adding a final section that rules out the Israelites' complete destruction. Though God will use Israel's enemies to punish his people, he will curb their penalty (vv. 26-27). When Israel sinks to the bottom, when the false gods they have foolishly pursued fail them, God

Jordan Valley as seen from Moses' vantage point on Mount Nebo. *(Richard Cleave, Pictorial Archive)*

will rise up to avenge his people against their spiritually ignorant enemies and vindicate his name (vv. 28-43). The punishment and restoration foretold here point to the 70-year Babylonian exile and return of Israel to Canaan in 538.

32:48-52 God's Final Instructions to Moses

God instructs Moses to climb Mount Nebo to catch a glimpse of Canaan before he dies on that mountain, as Aaron did on Mount Hor. The brothers' punishment for failing to honor God at Meribah barred them from entering the promised land (Num. 20:1-13).

33 The Blessing of Moses

Moses assumes the role of "father" to the nation of Israel as he blesses each of the 12 tribes before he dies (cf. Genesis 49). The hopes and prayers that the blessings convey presuppose Israel's covenantal obedience and anticipate the fulfillment of God's promises of possessing Canaan and prospering in it. Reference to Moses in the third person (v. 4) may signal that verses 4-5 represent a response by the assembly to Moses' opening words.

Reuben's short blessing reflects Jacob's dying sentence on him (Gen. 49:3-4) and may be viewed against the backdrop of Korah's rebellion, in which the Reubenites Dathan and Abiram participated (Numbers 16).

The absence of Simeon from the list probably

reflects that tribe's absorption into the tribe of Judah near the beginning of Israel's settled life in Canaan. In this case, Judah's blessing would include Simeon as well (v. 7). The phrase, "bring him to his people," may be a prayer for a reunited kingdom. (The northern tribes split off from Judah and Simeon following Solomon's death in the late 10th century and formed the kingdom of Israel as distinct from the southern kingdom of Judah.)

The blessing of Benjamin appears to hint at God's choice of Jerusalem as the location for the tabernacle (and later the temple). God's dwelling "between his shoulders" seems to picture the mountain ridges of this hill-country site in Benjamite territory.

Joseph's blessing acknowledges that he ranks first among his brothers (v. 16) and wishes the abundance of nature, military success, and numerical increase on his tribe, which inherited the names of his sons, Ephraim and Manasseh. Part of Manasseh settled east of the Jordan River, as did Gad, whose blessing praises this tribe for their brotherly aid in conquering the promised land proper (cf. Numbers 32).

34 The Death of Moses

After ascending Mount Nebo and viewing the expanse of land God promised to the patri-archs, the central figure in the books of Exodus through Deuteronomy dies east of the Jordan in Moab. This chapter refers to Moses in the third person and praises him for his exceptional prophetic role, arguing against its authorship by Moses.

Moses had known of his fate for some time (Num. 20:12; 27:12-14). While the great prophet ultimately would not escape punishment for his sin at Meribah, God continued to bless him with good health in old age and honors him in death with a divine burial (vv. 6-7). The Israelites mourn him for 30 days and then embrace the leadership of his successor, Joshua, who inherits Moses' spirit of wisdom (v. 9). Moses' epitaph singles him out as a unique figure in Israel's history (vv. 10-12).

Deuteronomy closes with a new generation of Israelites prepared to take possession of Canaan under a new leader chosen by God to further his work of redeeming sinful humanity. The record of this redemptive history begins in Genesis immediately after the fall. Thus the Pentateuch as a whole provides hope for the restoration of humankind's intimate relationship with the God who lives in their midst — a relationship lost through sin in Eden and made possible by Israel's covenantal obedience in a new garden — the promised land flowing with milk and honey.

The Historical Books

Nine Old Testament historical books come between the Law (Genesis–Deuteronomy) and the poetry (Job–Songs) and narrate 700 years of Israelite history from the death of Moses (Josh. 1:1) to the lives of Esther and Mordecai in Persia (Esther 1-10). Their order mirrors the order of books in the Septuagint, the Greek translation of the Hebrew Bible, in which Ruth bridges Judges and 1-2 Samuel, while the postexilic books (1-2 Chronicles, Ezra–Nehemiah, Esther) follow up 1-2 Kings. (See "Why Are These Books in the Bible?" [18-24]) The historical books derive from an earlier historical work that scholars call "the Deuteronomistic History." Deuteronomy formed the preface, and its view of history shaped the history proper (Joshua–2 Kings). The first edition of this history probably ended with the reign of King Josiah (ca. 620 B.C.; 2 Kings 23), but a second edition (ca. 550) extended the history to its present form (2 Kings 24–25). Its compilers drew on ancient written sources — lists of cities and boundaries (Joshua 14–19), the "Ark Narrative" (1 Samuel 4–6 + 2 Samuel 6), the "Court History of David" (2 Samuel 7–1 Kings 1), royal annals of the northern and southern kingdoms, and the lives of Elijah and Elisha (1 Kings 17–2 Kings 13). Completed in exile in Babylon, this history assessed Israel's past to prepare Israel for its future after restoration from exile in Babylon.

From Joshua to Jehoiachin: Preexilic and Exilic History

Five books narrate the story of Israel from its entrance into Canaan (ca. 1200) to its exile in Babylon (560). Named for its hero, the book of **Joshua** details how Yahweh conquered Canaan for Israel (Joshua 1–12) and how Israel settled there (chs. 13–24). Two important speeches — Yahweh's to Joshua (1:1-9) and Joshua's farewell to Israel (ch. 23) — bracket it. They sound its main themes: the land as Yahweh's gracious gift to Israel and Israel's need to remain loyal to him despite Canaanite influences. Two solemn religious ceremonies — the crossing of the Jordan (chs. 3–4) and conquest of Jericho (ch. 6) — feature the ark of the covenant, symbol of another theme — that Yahweh, not Israel, wins the victories (e.g., 10:42). To the Great Warrior alone fall Ai (chs. 7–8) and the allied armies of southern (chs. 9–10) and northern Canaanite cities (ch. 11). The book also stresses how Joshua faithfully carries out Moses' instructions (8:30-35; 11:15; chs. 14,

Ruins of Shiloh, the center of Israelite tribal administration and worship following the conquest and settlement in Canaan. *(Richard Cleave, Pictorial Archive)*

20–21), distributes the land among the tribes (chs. 14–19), and leads Israel in a solemn covenant-renewal ceremony (ch. 24).

The book of **Judges** details Israel's settled life under the "judges," who led Israel for 200 years after Joshua's death. Some judges settled legal matters (see, e.g., Judg. 12:8-15; cf. 4:4-5), but most were spirit-empowered military heroes who delivered Israel from local or regional oppressors — e.g., Deborah and Gideon in the north (4:5, 6; 6:35), and Samson in the west (14:19; 16:1). The book has two parts — reports of the judges' exploits (chs. 1–16) and an appendix of other events (chs. 17–21). It portrays the period as a sad, repeated cycle of Israelite disobedience, slavery to invading nations, divine rescue through judges, and peace (chs. 2–10). Jephthah's sacrifice of his daughter to keep a vow (ch. 11) troubles readers, but the book probably aims starkly to contrast their devotion to Yahweh against Israel's fickle behavior. The Samson story (chs. 13–16) marks God's own unsought response to the gravest threat, the Philistines (who caused the Danites to move far north, ch. 18), a rescue finished by David (2 Sam. 8:1). The appendix treats two other ominous threats, an idolatrous shrine to Yahweh at Dan (chs. 17–18) and civil war among the tribes (chs. 19–21). The book's varied contents sound its main theme: Israel's need for central leadership by a king (17:6; 18:1; 19:1; 21:25).

The book of **Ruth** reports a peaceful interlude amid the larger chaos. Most scholars date this lovely short story about a family from Bethlehem to either the late monarchy (ca. 700) or postexilic period (ca. 450). The book has two parts — the story of David's ancestors (1:1–4:17) and the king's genealogy (4:18-22). Central to the story is Ruth's remarkable devotion to Naomi (Heb. *hesed*) — her stunning statement (1:16-17), risky gleaning of food (ch. 2), and bold marriage proposal to Boaz (ch. 3). Central also are Boaz's generosity with food (ch. 2) and his clever initiative as "kinsman-redeemer" — the duty whereby, as close relative, he "redeems" Elimelech's childless family by marrying Ruth, providing an heir (Obed), and caring for Naomi's property (chs. 3–4; cf. Deut. 25:5-10). Obed symbolizes the reversal of Naomi's tragic fate and the reward of Ruth's faithfulness (2:12); and, surprisingly, the newborn turns out to be King David's grandfather (4:17b). The story celebrates the work of divine providence hidden behind the efforts of Ruth and Boaz — a centuries-long process according to the genealogy (4:18-22) — that brought David to power.

1-2 Samuel trace the complex saga of David's rise and lengthy rule. Two poetic pieces — the Song of Hannah (1 Sam. 2:1-10) and the Last Words of David (2 Sam. 23:1-7) — bracket the books around their main theme, God's sovereign appointment of righteous leaders and judgment on wicked ones. Samuel, son of the devout Hannah, exemplifies the righteous leader. He announces the end of Eli's corrupt priestly family (1 Samuel 3), reluctantly anoints Saul (chs. 8–10), and warns Israel to stick with Yahweh (ch. 12). Interestingly, 1 Samuel incorporates narratives both for and against the new royal institution, an indication of how controversial it was at first. Despite early promise (chs. 11, 14), Saul's disobedience (chs. 13, 15) shows him to be a wicked leader, and Yahweh sends an "evil spirit" (the Hebrew probably means a "bad depression") to symbolize his rejection as king. Tragically, after failing to find and kill David (chs. 18–30), Saul dies by his own hand rather than face the Philistine victors (ch. 31). David models the righteous leader par excellence. Anointed king-designate by Samuel (ch. 16), David passes up two chances to kill Saul (chs. 24, 26) — he accepts God's timing over a human coup. Victories by his guerrilla band rout Judah's enemies and win him popularity (chs. 23, 27, 30).

David first becomes king of Judah and then becomes king of the northern tribes, too (2 Samuel 2–5). He captures his new capital, Jerusalem, brings the ark of the covenant there (chs. 5–6), and receives God's promise that his family will always rule Israel (ch. 7) — a truly new leadership innovation for Israel. Unlike Saul, David repents of his sins in the Bathsheba incident (chs. 11–12), but 2 Samuel details the resulting divine punishment — two bloody coups against him (chs. 13–20). An appendix rounds out the report of his reign (chs. 21–24), including his defeat of the Philistines (ch. 21), his poetic praise of Yahweh (chs. 22, 23), and his experience of God's mercy after his sinful census (ch. 24). The latter led him to purchase the site where the temple would later sit.

Life under the monarchy is the focus of **1-2 Kings.** The first chapters portray Solomon as a wise king who built an empire, brought Israel great prosperity, and left the temple as his lasting legacy (1 Kings 3–10). But 1 Kings also regards his worship of foreign gods as the root of the nation's doom (ch. 11). His punishment inaugurates the second focus of the books — the divided kingdom (1 Kings 12–2 Kings 17), with the Davidic dynasty ruling "Judah" (Judah and Benjamin) and another king ruling "Israel" (the northern tribes; ch. 12). Sadly, Israel's first king makes a fatal misstep — the "sin of Jeroboam," a new, idolatrous religion (1 Kgs. 13:26-33) that later kings fail to uproot. But the books' true villains are King Ahab and Queen Jezebel, whose state-sponsored idolatry the prophets Elijah and Elisha battle (1 Kings 17–2 Kings 9). The books cast Elijah as a new Moses who shows that Yahweh, not Baal, controls the rain (1 Kings 17–19) and who condemns Ahab's dynasty (1 Kings 20–2 Kings 1). His successor, Elisha, continues the battle with a series of miracles (2 Kings 2–8; cf. 13:14-21) and anoints Ahab's successor, the dynasty of Jehu (chs. 9–10). But coups and countercoups weaken Israel (chs. 11 15) until it falls to Assyria (722 B.C.), as punishment, 2 Kings stresses, for its idolatry (ch. 17). The books' final chapters follow the kingdom of Judah alone (2 Kings 18–25). Sadly, religious reforms by Hezekiah (chs. 18–20) and Josiah (chs. 22–23) cannot offset the idolatry of Judah's counterpart to Israel's Ahab — King Manasseh (ch. 21). Judah limps through two decades of puppet-kings and falls to the Babylonians, who destroy Jerusalem and the temple and carry thousands into exile (chs. 24–25). Samuel's early warning about idolatry proves true (1 Sam. 12:25), but Nebuchadnezzar's release of Jehoiachin from prison ends 1-2 Kings on a hopeful note (2 Kgs. 25:27-30).

Postexilic Historical Books

The remaining historical books originated as the community rebuilt its ruined land following the exile in Babylon and reckoned with its tragic past. **Chronicles** has two parts — the genealogies (1 Chronicles 1–9) and the history of the monarchy (1 Chronicles 10–2 Chronicles 36) — and draws (often word-for-word) on other biblical books (Genesis, 1-2 Samuel, 1-2 Kings, Psalms) and extrabiblical sources (see 1 Chr. 29:29; 2 Chr. 9:29; 20:34). Its ending with Cyrus's decree (538) and its dependence on other books imply a compilation date after ca. 350 but before the books' translation into Greek (ca. 200). Some scholars credit Chronicles, Ezra, and Nehemiah to the same author ("the Chronicler"), either as a single work or as two separate books (Chronicles, Ezra–Nehemiah), but others consider them as three independent works. The opening genealogies and list of returnees (1 Chronicles 1–9) sound two key themes — the indivisibility of Israel and the community's continuity with Israel's storied past. Chronicles affirms God's continuing commitment to Israel but gives special prominence to Judah, Levi, and Benjamin. It barely mentions the northern kingdom, spotlighting the Davidic dynasty as central to Israel's national life. It credits David with the temple's construction plans, organization, and worship personnel (1 Chronicles 22–26) and adds material to highlight the religious reforms of Jehoshaphat (2 Chronicles 17, 19), Hezekiah (2 Chronicles 29–31), and Josiah (2 Chronicles 34–35). Its message seems to be that temple worship under the Levites and covenantal obedience, rather than a ruling king, fulfill the Davidic covenant (2 Samuel 7).

Ezra and **Nehemiah** offer the only record of Cyrus's decree and of events in postexilic Judah. The books probably originated in Judah, if not Jerusalem, ca. 400 as a single work (Ezra–Nehemiah), since that is how they appear in the earliest manuscripts. They are composed of three parts: reports on the decree's implementation (Ezra 1–Nehemiah 7); Judah's celebration of resumed community life under Torah (Neh. 8–13:3); and Nehemiah's report of his reforms (Neh. 13:4-31). The books highlight three rebuildings — the temple by Zerubbabel and the high priest Joshua (538-515), the Jewish community by the priest Ezra (458-457), and Jerusalem's walls by Nehemiah (445-444). They also report official letters with the Persian court in Aramaic, incorporate extensive lists from archives, and include first-person reports probably drawn from the written "memoirs" of Ezra and Nehemiah. Archaeological evidence and extrabiblical sources generally fit well with the reports of Ezra–Nehemiah. The books stress the importance of the whole Jewish community, the crucial role of written documents (especially the Torah), and the holiness of both the temple and the whole city of Jerusalem.

Esther reports how a remarkable escape from annihilation (mid-5th century) led Jews to celebrate a new festival, Purim. The book's familiarity with Persia, its court and customs, and its lack of Greek influences suggests a Jewish author in the 4th-3rd centuries. Set in Susa, the story of rescue (chs. 1–8) details the cleverness and courage of beautiful Queen Esther and a remarkable series of coincidences, which enable her to expose Haman's secret plot and the Jews to defend themselves against their enemies. She and her uncle, Mordecai — by then imperial vizier under the king (cf. ch. 10) — institute Purim empire-wide to celebrate the escape (ch. 9). A major theme of the book is role reversal — from domination to downfall (Vashti, Haman, the Jews' enemies) and from certain doom to victory (Esther, Mordecai, the Jews). The vengeance of Jews against their enemies may trouble some readers, but one must take seriously the deathly danger that necessitated the Jews' preemptive strike against their enemies. Though the book never mentions God, the coincidences imply the hidden hand of divine providence at work.

Robert L. Hubbard Jr.

Joshua

Joshua picks up where Deuteronomy left off, after Moses' death. Titled after Israel's Egyptian-born military leader during the so-called conquest of Canaan, Joshua represents the second book of the Deuteronomistic History, which gives an account of Israel's life in Canaan. Tradition refers to Joshua, Judges, and the books of Samuel and Kings as the Former Prophets. Joshua presumes its readers' knowledge of the preceding books (compare 24:32 with Gen. 50:25; Exod. 13:19; 14:6-15 with Num. 14:24, 30), and the book draws many parallels between Joshua and his predecessor and former master, Moses. (On their relationship and the transfer of leadership, see Exod. 24:13; Num. 13:1-16; Deuteronomy 31, 34.)

Content

Joshua's theological focus consists in God's fulfillment of his covenantal promise of land — a promise first made to Abraham (Gen. 12:1). With God fighting for the Israelite army, Joshua leads his troops in claiming Canaan by dispossessing its pagan inhabitants; at the entrance to God's tent, Joshua and the high priest Eleazar oversee the division of the land among the Israelite tribes. But peppering the narrative are frequent reminders that the Israelites must be faithful to the covenant if they are to retain and realize further their divinely favored status.

Background

The date and manner of the conquest of Canaan under Joshua remains unresolved. Taken at face value, internal evidence from the Old Testament itself seems to favor an early date, ca. 1400 B.C. (cf. 1 Kgs. 6:1; Judg. 11:26), as does archaeological evidence from two cities that figure prominently in Joshua's account of the conquest: Jericho and Hazor. The numbers given in the texts cited, however, may convey a symbolic message, not a literal accounting, and the majority of archaeological evidence both within and outside Canaan favors a later date, ca. 1240, for Israel's initial military activity and settlement in and around the promised land. While overall Joshua conveys the sense that the Israelites accomplished the conquest quickly and completely, the book of Judges pictures the process of possessing Canaan both as prolonged and partial. See "Entering the Land" (172-73).

Authorship

The author of Joshua remains unnamed. Some scholars see in the book editorial strands of material they identify in the Pentateuch (E and P; see "Authorship" [177] in the commentary on Genesis). Internal, textual evidence suggests that the oral traditions that preserved the memory of events recorded in Joshua found their way into written form around the time of Samuel and before David conquered Jerusalem (compare 15:63 with 2 Sam. 5:6-10). The repeated statement that certain monuments and traditions endured "to this day" (4:9; 13:13) probably indicates that an editor compiled the book some time after the events it records.

1 Preparing to Enter Canaan

The reminder of Moses' death and the reference to him as the "servant of the Lord" link Joshua and Deuteronomy literarily (1:1-2; cf. Deut. 34:5). Chapter 1 confirms God's determination to fulfill his one remaining covenantal promise to his people by relating his charge to Joshua to lead the Israelites across the Jordan to possess Canaan. God's presence with Moses' successor and former servant (cf. Numbers 13) provides the foundation for the courage Joshua must display in undertaking his military task (vv. 5-6; cf.

Gen. 26:24; 28:15; 39:2; Exod. 3:12). The exhortation to "be strong and courageous" emerges as the clarion call (vv. 6-7, 9, 18), one bolstered by God's promise to do for Joshua what he promised to Moses (vv. 3-5; cf. Deut. 11:24-25). Since Joshua's covenantal obedience will guarantee his success in the land, he must devote his thoughts to the "book of the law" (cf. Deut. 31:24-26) and take care to obey it completely (cf. Deut. 17:18-20 for similar instructions for a hypothetical human king of Israel).

In obedience to God, Joshua orders that the Israelites prepare to enter the promised land within days. He also reminds the Transjordanian tribes — Reuben, Gad, and half-Manasseh — of their responsibility to help their countrymen claim the covenantal inheritance in Canaan, and these tribes pledge their allegiance to Joshua's leadership (cf. Num. 32; Deut. 3:12-20). Indeed, they form the vanguard that leads the invasion force across the Jordan.

2 Rahab and the Spies

As Moses had done with Joshua and 11 other Israelite men 40 years earlier, so now Joshua sends spies into Canaan in preparation for taking possession of the promised land (cf. Numbers 13). This time, however, the reconnaissance mission reveals the Canaanites' fear of the Israelites rather than producing in the Israelites a stifling fear of Canaan's inhabitants (contrast Numbers 14).

At Joshua's direction, the two spies concentrate on Jericho, where they find discreet lodging with a local harlot named Rahab. Along with others throughout Canaan, Rahab has heard of God's activities on the Israelites' behalf (v. 10). Because Rahab believes God will also grant the Israelites victory when they invade Canaan, she forms an alliance with the spies by supplying valuable information and then hiding them from the city officials, who at the advice of the king's informants come knocking in an attempt to capture the Israelite spies (v. 11; cf. Heb. 11:31). Rahab sends the officials out the city gate in pursuit of the spies along the roads; meanwhile, she lowers the spies from her window in the city wall and directs them into the hills until the Jericho

posse gives up the search and the spies can return safely to their camp in Transjordan. In exchange for her help, Rahab receives the spies' promise of deliverance from doom for herself and her family through the sign of the scarlet cord she leaves hanging in her window (cf. 6:22-25). The spies' faith-filled report to Joshua concerning the Israelites' imminent mission of conquest contrasts sharply with the fear-inspiring warnings of the earlier spies, save Joshua and Caleb (v. 24; contrast Num. 13:28-33).

Jericho marked the land's midpoint between north and south, and the city sat west across the Jordan River opposite Shittim ("acacias"), where the Israelites camped. As in many other 2nd-millennium cities, casemate walls may have surrounded Jericho. Casemates consisted of two parallel walls that encircled a city, with ample space between them for rooms separated by crosswalls. Rahab's house may have sat between the two walls of such a fortification or simply up against a single wall; in either case, her window cut the city's perimeter defense. A flat roof covering Rahab's house provided space for drying flax, which she probably used to spin linen thread and under which she hid the spies.

Rahab figures prominently in this story despite her unholy profession. Later, she becomes a naturalized Israelite through marriage to Salmon. The Bible later traces Rahab's line, from her son Boaz, to his descendant King David, to Jesus himself (cf. Matt. 1:5-6, 16).

3 The Israelites Cross the Jordan

Just as God delivered the Israelites from Pharaoh's clutches by miraculously providing passage through the Red Sea, God now brings his people into the promised land by temporarily stopping up the normally tame and narrow Jordan River, swollen in springtime from the melting snows of Mount Hermon, until the nation has crossed into Canaan. That the ark of the covenant, not Joshua, enables the miracle, reveals the lesser position Joshua assumes, as compared to Moses, in communicating God's will, and previews the prominent position the ark will assume in representing God's presence and protection throughout the book. Yet God

Entering the Land

Throughout their long wanderings following their escape from Egypt, Israel cherished the promise of land given to Abraham (Gen. 12:7; Exod. 3:8). To enjoy that promise, Moses' mandate was that Israel annihilate the land's Canaanite inhabitants, destroy their idols, and settle down (Deut. 7:1-5; 20:16-18). But biblical reports offer differing pictures of events — pictures of both complete (Joshua 1–12) and incomplete conquest (Joshua 13; Judges 1). Some scholars view the latter accounts as the more accurate, but others suggest that, taken together and illumined by archaeology, both offer a general though not always completely clear picture of Israel's entrance into Canaan.

Egypt still exercised its historic control over Canaan when Israel arrived (mid-13th century B.C.). The pharaoh had governors and officials in major cities (e.g., Gaza, Megiddo) and garrison towns in others. Most of the local population lived along the coast and in the Jezreel and Jordan valleys, and petty city-states dominated daily political and economic life. Egyptian records prominently mention Ashkelon, Gezer, Megiddo, Beth-shean, Hazor, and Jerusalem. They also report major military campaigns to suppress rebellions in Canaan by Pharaohs Seti I (ca. 1290), Ramesses II (ca. 1275), and Merneptah (ca. 1220). In the early 12th century, both Merneptah and Ramesses III defeated the "Sea Peoples," sea-borne invaders of Canaan from the Aegean. Among them were the Philistines who seized and settled in Ashdod, Ashkelon, Ekron, Gath, and Gaza. Archaeological remains of this chaotic period confirm the destruction and pillage of many Canaanite towns (e.g., Bethel, Beth-shemesh, Hazor) and suggest a declining standard of living for their residents. But the evidence prevents our distinguishing destruction made by Egypt and the Sea Peoples from that by Israel or other invaders. Besides, the Bible claims that Israel "attacked" many cities but "burned" only Jericho, Ai, and Hazor — apparently excep-

Detail of the Merneptah Stela (ca. 1210-1207 B.C.) containing the earliest known reference to Israel outside the Bible. *(Cairo Museum)*

tions to the rule since Moses had promised to Israel cities in Canaan (Deut. 6:10).

Exodus 23:28-29 anticipated a long, gradual conquest and settlement because of Israel's small population (cf. Deut. 7:7). Semino-madic little Israel would need time to attain numbers large enough to control Canaan. Joshua and Judges yield glimpses of that extended process. Granted, Joshua 1–12 portrays it as a Blitzkrieg-type conquest of Jericho and Ai (chs. 2, 6–8) followed by victorious southern and northern campaigns (chs. 9–11) — and 11:23 reveals that "Joshua took the whole land. . . ." But 13:1-6 lists vast areas still unconquered, and early settlement reports acknowledge surviving cities and peoples, some of whom Israel enslaves rather than annihilates (15:63; 16:10; 17:12-13, 16; Judg. 1:18-36). Inexplicably, seven tribes had to find their own land for Joshua to allot (Josh. 18–19) — undoubtedly a lengthy procedure. One telling comment (Judg. 1:28) suggests a long struggle, with land and cities possibly changing hands several times. In retrospect, Joshua 12 could rightly celebrate Yahweh's stunning conquest of 31 kings, but at the time the process of possessing the land was probably slow-going and involved both advances and setbacks. Apparently, the most resistant strongholds lay along the coastal plain, on the southern ridge of the Jezreel Valley, and in Jerusalem.

Archaeological evidence for the period illumines our understanding, but only somewhat. Neither Jericho nor Ai shows traces of significant occupation or destruction at the time. Some scholars believe that centuries of erosion may have washed away relevant mudbrick ruins at Jericho, but one scholar recently claimed to find overlooked evidence for its destruction in older excavation reports. Ai means "ruins," a name perhaps earned by centuries as a ghost town (ca. 2500-1200), and some scholars view Joshua 8 as simply an explanation of the city's stunning ruins. But Ai had few residents (7:3), and forces from nearby Bethel joined those of Ai in chasing Israel (v. 17). This suggests that the "ruins" may have been a lightly manned defensive outpost for Bethel and unlikely to leave behind traces of occupation.

Some evidence points positively toward Israel's presence in Canaan. The victory stela of Pharaoh Merneptah lists an "Israel" among Egypt's conquests in Canaan (ca. 1220) — the first nonbiblical reference to it. Interestingly, it classifies Israel not as a nation or city but as a people living in open country. Archaeological remains also attest a significantly increased population in the central highlands and an explosion of new settlements between ruined cities. They also show the sudden appearance of a non-Canaanite pottery style and of a new kind of dwelling, the "four-room house." No inscriptions connect these new developments with "Israel," but the convergence of biblical and archaeological data point in that direction. One surprising discovery — the virtual absence of pig bones in these areas — strongly suggests that these new settlers were Israelites (Lev. 11:7-8). If so, initially Israel settled in towns or villages in the central highlands rather than in cities — in other words, *not* in areas the Bible lists as unconquered.

Scholars have recently proposed several theories to explain the conquest of Canaan. The "peaceful infiltration theory" claims to find the "real history" behind the Bible's idealized picture — a gradual movement into Canaan's vacant central mountains by six tribes, who grew large enough to take over the whole land peacefully. The "peasant's revolt theory" argues that some Israelite tribes settled peacefully in Canaan, that others arrived later after experiencing the "exodus," and that the united tribes overthrew their Canaanite oppressors. But the archaeological evidence of destruction undermines the former theory, while the latter lacks persuasive evidence of pre-infiltration Israelites. The "minimalist theory" proposes that Israel did not enter Canaan from outside but sprang up inside as a branch of the Canaanites that became "Israel" centuries later. But besides its excessive skepticism of biblical evidence, this theory founders on the archaeological evidence reviewed above.

The details concerning Israel's entrance into Canaan remain a matter of dispute. The Bible itself shows awareness of their complexity, and its different pictures in part derive from the genres of the reports. Joshua 1–12 offers a theological, celebratory "big picture" from a retrospective distance, Judges 1 a more realistic report "on the ground" probably closer to events. The fullest understanding of Israel's entry into Canaan emerges from careful consideration of both.

ROBERT L. HUBBARD JR.

accomplishes the feat to inspire the Israelites' confidence in their new leader (v. 7).

God's people must purify themselves ritually in preparation for the start of their divinely sanctioned holy war (v. 5). They must demonstrate their reverence for God by maintaining a respectful distance (a little more than half a mile) between themselves and God's "throne," the ark (v. 4).

The crossing proceeds according to God's directions, with the Jordan ceasing to flow as soon as the priests carrying the ark dip their feet in the water. Landslides in A.D. 1267 and 1906 dammed the Jordan, and a collapse of the clayey riverbank soil caused by an earthquake in 1927 blocked up the river's waters for 21½ hours at the same place cited by the present text: Adam (modern Tell ed-Damiye), ca. 18 miles north of Jericho.

4 Memorials Commemorate the Crossing

Joshua and one representative from each of the tribes erect two piles of 12 stones each to memorialize their crossing of the Jordan "on dry ground." One cairn stood at the Israelites' first campsite in Canaan (Gilgal, "circle"; v. 19), and the other rested in the middle of the Jordan where the priests stood with the ark to hold back the waters. John the Baptist conducted his ministry and baptized Jesus in this same part of the Jordan.

Chapter 4 takes pains to note the careful obedience of Joshua to God and of the Israelites to Joshua. Verse 12 mentions in particular the faithfulness of the Transjordanian tribes (Reuben, Gad, and half-Manasseh) to their communal commitment — they even cross before their countrymen (cf. 1:12-15). As God promised in 3:7, Joshua's leadership in crossing the Jordan gains the Israelites' reverence for him, much as they had earlier respected Moses.

5 Ritual Preparations for Holy War

Chapter 5 presents still more parallels with the account of Moses and the previous generation of Israelites. All males must undergo circumcision — a practice not applied to males born during the 40 years of wilderness wandering. God's command of a "second" circumcision applies to males over 40, whose initial, partial circumcision took place in Egypt. The abundance of flint in Canaan provided a ready tool for the task. The nation's vulnerability, caused by its fighting force's temporary disablement, does not prove a cause for concern, because the Israelites' miraculous crossing of the Jordan has struck fear of them in the hearts of Canaan's inhabitants (v. 1). The circumcision of Israel's males serves to mark the nation as a whole with the sign of the covenant (v. 8; cf. Gen. 17:10-11).

The day after celebrating the Passover, the Israelites eat some of the Canaan's crops. Beginning the next day, God's provision of manna ceases, for now his people can find food from the land "flowing with milk and honey."

The appearance of the "captain of the Lord's host" to Joshua at Jericho signals the divine aid available for the mission of conquest and fore-shadows Jericho's impending downfall. Yet the angelic commander makes clear that he fights not for humans but for God, and therefore Joshua's and the Israelites' obedience to God's covenant will determine the extent of divine aid they receive. Disobedience may occasion divine opposition. Joshua removes his sandals in recognition of the holy ground on which he stands in the presence of God's heavenly representative (cf. Moses at the burning bush, Exod. 3:5).

6 The Fall of Jericho

While Abraham acquired water rights and purchased a plot of land for a family grave in Canaan centuries earlier (Gen. 21:22-34; 23), the account of the conquest of Jericho signals the first major step in Israel's claiming her covenantal inheritance in the promised land. An important oasis guarding the main routes into the heart of Canaan, Jericho ("moon city," probably dedicated to the Canaanite moon-god) was the first pagan enclave put under the "ban." The ban dictated that the Israelites kill all people and animals in the Canaanite cities they conquered and also prohibited them from taking precious metals as personal booty. Instead, these spoils were to go into the treasury for the Lord's house. From the beginning, then, the Israelites violate the rules of holy war by sparing Rahab and her family, though God redeems the Israelites' gracious action in his plan of salvation not only for Rahab but also for the rest of humanity throughout the ages.

The Israelites take Jericho in a ritualistic manner that both announces the commencement of the holy war and wreaks psychological havoc on the city's inhabitants. On each day of their six-day siege, the Israelite warriors conduct about a half-mile march around the city, bearing the ark of the covenant and with seven priests blowing rams' horns sandwiched between the forward and rear contingents. As in the account of creation, the seventh day marks the day of completion and perfection. On this day, the Israelite soldiers march around the city seven times before joining their voices with the trumpet blasts in a thunderous shout, at which time the walls of Jericho fall and give the invaders free access to the city. After de-

The Divine Warrior

After God rescues Israel from an angry pharaoh at the Red Sea, Moses leads the people in a song that proclaims:

> The LORD is a warrior;
>   the LORD is his name.

(Exod. 15:3)

This verse is the first explicit reference to God as a warrior, but it is far from the last. Throughout the Bible, God's people recognized that the Lord was in the midst of their struggles, fighting on their behalf.

In the Old Testament God's warfare took the form of conflict against Israel's flesh-and-blood enemies. The examples are too numerous to mention with any degree of completeness. A prime example, however, is the battle of Jericho. Before the battle, Joshua encountered a mysterious figure outfitted like a warrior (Josh. 5:13-15). As the story unfolds, it becomes clear that this is an appearance of God as warrior, who then gives Joshua strategy for the upcoming battle. The strategy itself demonstrates the heart of the theology of divine warfare. Victory is not the result of human ability or resources, but rather is the result of God's will. Thus Israel's role is simply to march around the city once a day for six days, and then seven times on the climactic seventh day. At their lead was the ark of the covenant, the most potent symbol of God's presence. On the last day, after the seventh circuit, the priests sounded the horn with a loud blast while the people shouted. Without lifting a weapon, then, the venerable walls of that ancient city crumbled, and Jericho was theirs (Joshua 6).

Throughout the period of the conquest, the judges, and the monarchy, God appeared to his people as a warrior. The prophet Nahum, for instance, provides an example of a relatively late instance of the divine warrior's action on behalf of Israel. As Nahum looked forward to the destruction of the oppressive city of Nineveh, he saw as its cause the appearance of the divine warrior, who is:

> A jealous and avenging God;
>   the LORD takes vengeance
>   and is filled with wrath.
> The LORD takes vengeance on
>   his foes
> and maintains his wrath
>   against his enemies.

(Nah. 1:2 NIV)

When Nineveh fell in 612 B.C., the human eye saw the destroying force as Babylonians and Medes, but the reality was that God caused the destruction of Nineveh.

Unfortunately for Israel, however, God was not always on their side. Indeed, Israel's covenant with God made it clear that God would fight for them when they were obedient, but he would judge them and defeat them when they were disobedient (Deut. 28:7, 64-68). Lamentations illustrates this sad truth. Because of Israel's persistent rebellion, God ultimately brought the Babylonians against Jerusalem, destroying the city and leveling the temple. The author of Lamentations knows full well who was behind this tragedy:

> The Lord is like an enemy;
>   he has swallowed up Israel

(Lam. 2:5 NIV)

Even so, this is not the last word on the subject in the Old Testament. During the exile and after, God raised up prophets who looked into the future and saw redemption in the form of the coming warrior. Daniel 7 announces that God will send a cloud rider, "one like a son of man," to destroy the forces of evil, represented in the chapter as a series of hybrid monsters coming out of a chaotic sea. It is with this note of hope that the Old Testament ends.

The New Testament completes the picture in a surprising fashion. While many, including John the Baptist himself (Matt. 3:7-12), expected a violent Messiah, Jesus died on the cross rather than leading a successful battle against the Romans. Paul understood, however, that Jesus' death was a great victory over Satan and the spiritual powers and authorities (Col. 2:13-15). Jesus is the divine warrior, and his death informs his followers that their struggles are spiritual and must be waged with spiritual and not physical weapons (Eph. 6:10-20). Moreover, the New Testament tells us that, though the victory has been secured, the war is not yet completed. The book of Revelation and other apocalyptic passages announce that at the end of time Jesus will appear again and bring the battle to a final conclusion (cf. Rev. 19:11-16).

TREMPER LONGMAN III

stroying Jericho completely, the Israelites place Rahab and her family outside the Israelite camp until the foreigners observe the necessary requirements for ritual purification and incorporation into the Israelite community. Jericho, whose history dates back to 7000 B.C., lay dormant for four centuries, until the curse announced in v. 26 was realized during the reign of the faithless Israelite king Ahab (see 1 Kgs. 16:33-34).

7 Achan Disregards the Ban

Israel's military disgrace at Ai ("the ruin"; traditionally identified as et-Tell but not confirmed archaeologically) contrasts sharply with the nation's devastating victory over Jericho. Evidently, the captain of the Lord's host fought for the Israelites at Jericho but abandons, if not fights against, them at Ai (cf. 5:13-14), for in secretly defying the ban on taking booty from Jericho the Judahite Achan ignites God's anger against the nation as a whole. Ignorant of Achan's disobedience, Joshua orders an assault on Ai, but the attack fails miserably. In petitioning the Lord, Joshua learns the reason for his army's defeat. A series of lot-castings singles out the culprit, Achan, whose confession nevertheless does not save him or his presumably co-conspiring family from the death penalty (vv. 20-21; cf. the fate of Korah, Dathan, and Abiram and their families in Num. 16:25-33). As the entire nation suffered because of Achan's sin, so it must participate in meting out his fatal punishment by stoning and burning (cf. Lev. 24:10-23). This action completes the congregation's consecration and purification from sin (v. 13; cf. 3:5). Achan's family cairn in the Valley of Achor ("trouble") stands as a reminder of each individual Israelite's responsibility to obey God's commands in order for the nation as a whole to realize the covenantal blessings.

8 The Defeat of Ai

In his second assault on Ai, Joshua takes his orders from God rather than relying on the advice of the Israelite spies. With God's promise of victory, Joshua musters the entire fighting force but positions a relatively small contingent behind the city between Bethel (now diminished, but several centuries earlier a prosperous and well-fortified city) and Ai. The majority of Israelite soldiers lure the men of Ai to chase them as Joshua's men this time fake a retreat. The Israelite ambushing force storms the now undefended city and sets it on fire. With the smoke from Ai rising in the distance, the Israelite army turns on its homeless pursuers and slays all of them as well as the city's inhabitants fleeing from the destruction. The Israelites take the king of Ai captive but subject him to the dishonorable death of hanging on a tree (perhaps impalement on a pole; cf. Deut. 21:22-23). This time, the Israelites take cattle and spoils from Ai with God's express permission (vv. 2, 27).

Verses 30-35 record Joshua's fulfillment of God's command that the Israelites conduct a ceremony to ratify the covenant in the promised land (cf. Deuteronomy 27). This takes place near Shechem (ca. 20 mi. north of Bethel and Ai) on Mounts Ebal and Gerizim and involves the offering of sacrifices and recitation of the Mosaic law. (The patriarch Jacob had earlier purchased land at Shechem; Gen. 33:18-19.)

9 A Treaty with the Hivites of Gibeon

Aware of the Israelites' military successes since entering the promised land, the Canaanite kings form an alliance against Israel. But the Hivites (Hurrians) of Gibeon (probably el-Jib) develop another plan. Rather than taking their chances with the alliance, they scheme to

Hazor, a strategically important city controlling northern Canaan, "utterly destroyed" by Joshua and the Israelites. *(Richard Cleave, Pictorial Archive)*

trick the Israelites into making a peace treaty with them. Bedraggled envoys from Gibeon convince Joshua that they have come from a far-off country to become servants of the people for whom God has accomplished the mighty works that have gained international renown. Ignoring the lesson from Ai about taking action without consulting God (7:2-5), Joshua enters into a treaty with the disguised Gibeonites (note the covenantal meal in v. 14; cf. Exod. 24:3-11), only to learn later their true identity as inhabitants of Canaan, with whom God has forbidden the Israelites to make covenants (Exod. 23:32). But Joshua cannot cancel the agreement, and much to his chagrin the Hivites' four cities come under the protection of the treaty (vv. 16-18). Though the covenant reduces the Gibeonites to slavery, at least they secure for themselves protection from annihilation by the Israelites. Later they serve the Israelites in Jerusalem, the place of God's choice (v. 27). That God punishes Israel for Saul's slaying of the Gibeonites some 200 years later, and that David allows the Gibeonites to take revenge against Saul's house for the killing, testify to the enduring and binding nature of covenantal agreements in the ancient Near East (2 Samuel 21).

10 Five Kings Attack Gibeon

Alarmed by the nearby Gibeonites' defection, Jerusalem's king Adoni-zedek ("my Lord is righteous") rallies four other Canaanite kings to march against this major stronghold. In response, Gibeon calls on Joshua's army to fulfill its treaty obligation of helping defend the city. Joshua and his troops take all night to complete the 22-mile, uphill march from their camp at Gilgal. They soundly rout Gibeon's attackers, whom God pelts with fatal hailstones that kill more Canaanites than Joshua's army does. Verses 12-14 acknowledge God's hand in the Israelites' amazing victory, whether the text relates a miraculous extension of daylight, an unusual refraction or diffusion of light, a divine prolonging of the dawn darkness, an astrological omen — the sun and moon in the same sky — or a poetic metaphor emphasizing God's power over nature. Because of the Aijalon Valley's location along a major east-west roadway (v. 12), this setting has played host to numerous battles throughout the centuries.

Despite the Israelites' decisive victory, the allied kings escape to the cave of Makkedah, in which Joshua's men close them up. When Joshua arrives, he initiates a symbolic ritual wherein the Israelites place their feet on the necks of the captive kings to signify their total subjugation (cf. 1 Kgs. 5:3; Ps. 110:1; 1 Cor. 15:25-28) before killing them and humiliating them further by exposing their dead bodies (cf. 8:29).

Verses 28-43 relate Joshua's initial, though apparently short-lived, conquest of the major regions of Canaan as far south as Kadesh-barnea, as far west as Gaza, and as far north as Gibeon — the Negev, Shephelah (lowland), and hill country (cf. ch. 13 for a different picture). Canaanite survivors of the battle at Gibeon who managed to flee home for refuge meet their death in Joshua's subsequent southern campaign, wherein he completely destroys the cities of the kings allied with Adoni-zedek, as well as Makkedah, Libnah, and Gezer — the strategic cities of the south. Jerusalem avoids annihilation, but the territorial conquest and the obliteration of the Canaanite population in these regions appear otherwise complete, thanks to God's fighting on Israel's behalf (v. 42; contrast the picture of the conquest painted by ch. 13 and the book of Judges; see "Entering the Land" [172-73]).

11 Joshua Defeats the Northern Alliance

On hearing of Joshua's military exploits in the south, the king of Hazor, who heads Canaan's northern territories (v. 10), forms a second, more formidable alliance against the Israelites. Located 10 miles north of the Sea of Galilee along the trade route between Egypt and Mesopotamia, Hazor's 200-acre metropolis housed 40 thousand inhabitants during this period — four times as many as King David's Jerusalem. The Canaanite force assembles with horses and chariots at the waters of Merom, which drain southeast into the Sea of Galilee. The victory of Joshua's army once again appears decisive and complete as the Israelite fighting force follows God's battle instructions to the letter. Joshua even pushes the enemy 40 miles north to Sidon, on the coast of Lebanon (v. 8). As before, Joshua follows his victory on the battlefield with the capture and destruction of the allies' cities and their inhabitants (though he sets fire only to Hazor) to complete the conquest of the north. (Again, contrast ch. 13 and Judges.)

Verses 12, 15, 20, and 23 remember Moses as the one to whom God originally gave his commands regarding possessing the promised land. Joshua appears utterly faithful to the divine instructions communicated through his predecessor (esp. v. 15). If 10:1–11:15 give the impression that Joshua completed these victories within a relatively short period, v. 18 dispels that notion. Judging from Caleb's stated age at the beginning and end of this phase of the conquest, the triumphs thus far spanned seven years (cf. 14:7; Deut 2:14). Verse 20 recalls God's hardening of Pharaoh's heart and Sihon of Heshbon's spirit (Exod. 4:21; Deut. 2:30). That the Israelite army even defeats the mighty Anakim living in Canaan's hill country testifies to the unfounded faithlessness of the previous generation of Israelites, who refused to enter the promised land in part for fear of these giant warriors (but cf. 14:12; on the Anakim, see Num. 13:25–14:4). Some Anakim remain in three of the five Philistine strongholds: Gaza, Gath, and Ashdod. Verse 23 makes brief men-

tion of Joshua's parceling out the conquered land to the Israelite tribes.

12 A Summary of Successes

Verses 1-6 summarize Israel's military successes in Transjordan and state the boundaries of their territorial claims in the east as far north as Mount Hermon, on the Israel/Lebanon border, and as far south as the Pisgah ridge (home to Mount Nebo), at the northern end of the Dead Sea. The defeated kings Sihon and Og controlled large territories east of the Dead Sea ("Salt Sea," "sea of the Arabah") and Sea of Galilee ("Sea of Chinneroth"), respectively (cf. Num. 21:21-35; Deut. 2:24–3:11). The Arabah refers to the wide Jordan Rift Valley between the two seas. The 31 defeated Canaanite kings listed in vv. 9-24 mostly represent city-states in each major region of Canaan, as well as individual ethnic groups whose land God promised to give to Abraham's descendants (v. 8; cf. Gen. 15:18-21).

13–21 Apportioning the Land

13 The distribution of Israel's inheritance in Canaan begins before the completion of the conquest. Philistine city-states on and near Canaan's southern Mediterranean coast remain untaken, along with large areas to the north on the plain of Phoenicia and in Lebanon (cf. Judg. 3:1-5). Not until David at least two centuries hence will Israel defeat the Philistines and subdue the Syrians in the north, but even David cannot lay claim to Phoenicia, and the additional territories he does control slip away after his son Solomon's reign. Neither do the Israelites completely dispossess all the Canaanites living in the areas they manage to dominate (v. 13; 15:63; 16:10).

The remainder of chapter 13 rehearses Moses' allotment of lands east of the Jordan to the tribes of Reuben, Gad, and half-Manasseh (cf. Numbers 32; Deut. 3:12-17). The text again reports that Levi has already "received God" (the service of the tabernacle and later the temple) as its inheritance, rather than land (vv. 14, 33; cf. Deut. 18:1-2). Verse 22 mentions Balaam, the professional diviner who figures prominently in Numbers 24.

14 Joshua, the high priest Eleazar, and heads of households from the remaining nine and one-half tribes participate in the division of territory west of the Jordan. Eleazar may have used the Urim and Thummim in casting lots to assign land to the various tribes (cf. Exod. 28:30). The distribution includes setting aside Levitical cities according to God's instructions in Num. 35:1-8. In making a special request for his own landed inheritance in the hill country south of Jerusalem, Caleb appeals to Moses' promise of a reward for the faith Caleb showed as a spy (v. 9; cf. Num. 14:24) — a faith undiminished and undaunted by the prospect of battle with the remaining Anakim (cf. 11:21-22). Caleb receives Hebron, which later becomes a city of refuge but whose surrounding fields and villages Caleb retains as his possession (cf. 15:13-14; 21:11-13).

15 Judah receives a large parcel of land covering southern Canaan that cuts due west of the Dead Sea from its northern and southern extents. Judah's territory includes land in the hill country, Shephelah (lowland), coastal plain, Negev (south), and wilderness and incorporates Caleb's territory (vv. 13-19), the cities of the Philistines, and Samson's hometown of Timnah (v. 57). At least part of Jerusalem, which remains under Jebusite control until David's reign (2 Sam. 5:6-10), falls within Judahite territory (compare vv. 8, 63; Judg. 1:8 with 18:16; Judg. 1:21).

16–17 The tribes named after Joseph's sons, Ephraim and Manasseh, inherit large parcels of land north of Judah that extend from the Jordan Valley west through the central hill country and the coastal plain to the Mediterranean. Though the southernmost Ephraimites fail to drive out the Canaanites in Gezer, the tribe does reduce them to servanthood (16:10). Much later, Solomon gains control of Gezer (1 Kgs. 9:16-17). The daughters of Manasseh's sonless descendant Zelophehad receive land in Canaan in accordance with God's ruling in Num. 27:7 (17:4).

Manasseh already possesses additional territory east of the Jordan (17:1; cf. Numbers 32; Deut. 3:12-20), but Ephraim and Manasseh complain that they have not received enough land to support their numbers. They blame this on their drawing only one lot between them, despite the fact that they both receive separate and comparatively large territorial allotments in Canaan (v. 14). Joshua wisely identifies the real problems: despite the fact that their very numbers give them strength, Joseph's descendants lack the faith and nerve to drive the Canaanite charioteers out of the plains, and they lack the industriousness to clear the forested hill country for habitation. Their great size itself holds the key to solving their perceived problem, and Joshua leaves his response at that.

18 Though 14:1-5 indicates that all the western tribes received their assignments of inherited land at Gilgal, 18:2 reveals that seven tribes put off taking possession of their territories. With Israel's base camp, including the tabernacle, now repositioned at Shiloh, Joshua challenges the procrastinating tribes to claim their inheritance by sending representatives to survey the remaining land before he and Eleazar cast lots to determine the distribution of territory (cf. 19:51; for the territorial assignments outlined in chs. 18–19, cf. the list of tribal cities in 15:20-62). Following the surveyors' report, Benjamin's lot sandwiches this tribe between Judah on the south and Ephraim on the north, and the assignment includes at least part of Jerusalem (compare 15:8 with 18:16; also 15:63; Judg. 1:8 with Judg. 1:21).

19 Simeon's lot follows Benjamin's. Because Judah received more land than it could manage, Simeon inherits territory within Judah's allotment — including the Negev city of Beer-sheba, where Abraham first gained a small but significant claim to land in Canaan by legally acquiring water rights (Gen. 21:22-34). Eventually, Simeon was absorbed into the tribe of Judah.

Zebulun's inheritance falls in the central landscape north of Manasseh. The Bethlehem of v. 15 refers to a northern town that bears the same name as the city of Jesus' birth that lies south of Jerusalem.

Issachar's lot sits southeast of Zebulun's and includes the fertile Jezreel Valley. Mount Tabor marks Zebulun's western border, and the Jordan River south of the Sea of Galilee defines the tribe's eastern extent.

Asher receives land along Canaan's northern

coast (mostly north, but also a bit south, of modern Haifa). Prominent cities, such as Rehob and Aphek and the ports of Tyre and Achzib, fall to Asher.

Naphtali's allotment arcs around the western side of the Sea of Galilee but remains east of Zebulun. Naphtali extends northwest of the Huleh basin (north of the Sea of Galilee) and borders Asher on its west. This tribe's territory includes the main trade route running from Jezreel to areas north of Canaan.

Dan's portion lies primarily in the lowland west of Jerusalem in an area inhabited by Amorites and Philistines (cf. Judg. 1:34 and the stories of the Danite Samson in Judges 13–16). The Danites fail to defeat their southern foes, and this tribe eventually migrates to the far north above Naphtali, where their military efforts find success (cf. Judges 18).

Finally, the Israelites present Joshua with an inheritance of his own (vv. 49-50; cf. Judg. 2:9), as Joshua had done with his faithful comrade spy, Caleb (14:13-14). Verse 51 indicates that the lot-casting took place "before the Lord, at the doorway" of the tabernacle to convey God's control over the apportioning process and his sanctioning of it.

20 The Israelites set apart the six Levitical cities of refuge provided for in Num. 35:6; Deut. 19:1-10. Deuteronomy 4:41-43 has already recorded the designation of three of these cities among the Transjordanian tribes. The unintentional manslayer who flees to one of these cities receives a pretrial by the elders, who exercise their legal authority at the city gate, before he undergoes a public trial by the congregation (vv. 4, 6). The cities of refuge provide the manslayer with asylum from his accidental victim's blood avengers.

21 Aside from the six cities of refuge, the Levites receive 42 additional cities (and their surrounding pasturelands) spread throughout the tribal territories, not as an inheritance (cf. 18:7) but simply as designated dwelling places for the Levites in accordance with God's provision in Num. 35:6-8. Aaron and his priestly Kohathite descendants receive cities in the southern tribes of Judah, Simeon, and Benjamin, territory that includes Jerusalem, which became home to the tabernacle

in David's time and the temple during Solomon's reign. Caleb retained the pasturelands surrounding his individual inheritance at Judahite Hebron, where he defeated the descendants of Anak (v. 11) — renowned warriors related to the mighty Nephilim (cf. Num. 13:33; Deut. 9:2).

The cities allotted to the rest of the Kohathites lie in the next ring out from Jerusalem: in Ephraim, Dan (prior to this tribe's migration north; ch. 19; cf. Judges 18), and half-Manasseh west of the Jordan. The Gershonites' cities lie far north in Issachar, Asher, Naphtali, and half-Manasseh in Transjordan. The Merarites also receive allotments on both sides of the Jordan: in Zebulun on the west and in Reuben and Gad on the east. On the Levitical responsibilities of the Kohathites, Gershonites, and Merarites, cf. Numbers 3.

Verses 43-45 emphasize the fulfillment of God's one heretofore outstanding promise to Abraham: that of land (Gen. 12:1-3). God's promises to Joshua in 1:5-6 regarding the Israelites' conquest of Canaan find theological completion in vv. 43-44. But Judges 1 will soon make clear that, from a practical standpoint, prolonged struggles to possess and retain the promised inheritance lie ahead.

22 The Transjordanian Tribes Return Home

With Canaan subdued and divided between the nine and one-half western tribes (contrast Judges 1), Joshua dismisses the supporting soldiers of Reuben, Gad, and half-Manasseh to return to their families and territorial holdings in Transjordan (For their obligation to help conquer Canaan, cf. 1:14-15; Numbers 32; Deut. 3:12-20.) These tribes' action of building an altar on the eastern fringe of Canaan as they exit the promised land looks like disobedience to the western tribes, however, since legitimate sacrifice has, up to this point, centered around the tabernacle (now at Shiloh) in accordance with God's command in Deut. 12:13-14. Recalling God's previous judgment on the entire nation for the sins of individual Israelites and fearing similar corporate punishment for their kinsmen's transgression, the western tribes begin preparing for holy war against their Transjordanian countrymen (on Peor [v. 17] see Num. 25:1-9; on Achan [v. 20] see 7:1-26). Before

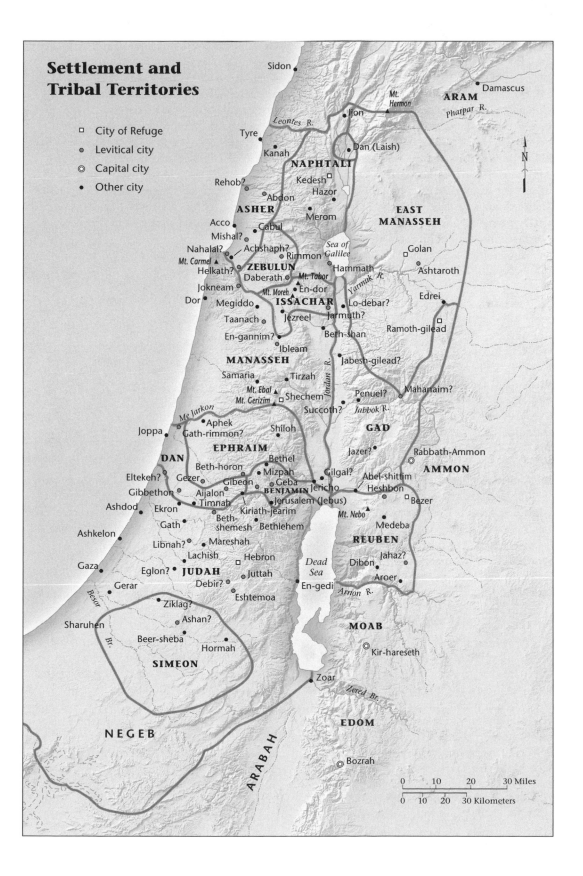

Settlement and Tribal Territories

□ City of Refuge
● Levitical city
◎ Capital city
• Other city

Sidon

Mt. Hermon

ARAM

Damascus

Ijon

Leontes R.

Pharpar R.

Tyre

Dan (Laish)

Kanah

NAPHTALI

Kedesh □

Rehob?

Hazor

Abdon

Merom

ASHER

EAST
MANASSEE

Acco

Cabul

Mishal?

Achshaph?

Golan □

Nahalal?

Rimmon

Sea of
Galilee

Mt. Carmel ▲

Hammath

Ashtaroth

Helkath?

ZEBULUN

Daberath

Mt. Tabor ▲

En-dor

Yarmuk R.

Edrei

Jokneam

Mt. Moreh ▲

ISSACHAR

Lo-debar?

Dor •

Megiddo

Jezreel

Jarmuth?

Ramoth-gilead □

Taanach

Beth-shan

En-gannim?

Ibleam

Jabesh-gilead?

MANASSEH

Samaria

Tirzah

Mt. Ebal ▲

Penuel?

Mahanaim?

Mt. Gerizim ▲

Shechem

Succoth?

Jabbok R.

Me Jarkon

GAD

Aphek

Shiloh

Joppa

Gath-rimmon?

Jazer?

Rabbath-Ammon ◎

EPHRAIM

Bethel

DAN

Beth-horon

Mizpah

Gilgal?

AMMON

Eltekeh?

Gezer

Geba

Jericho

Abel-shittim

Gibbethon

Aijalon

Gibeon

BENJAMIN

Heshbon

Timnah

Jerusalem (Jebus)

Bezer □

Ashdod

Ekron

Kiriath-jearim

Mt. Nebo ▲

Gath

Beth-
shemesh

Bethlehem

Medeba

Libnah?

Mareshah

REUBEN

Lachish

Hebron

Dibon

Jahaz?

Eglon?

JUDAH

Juttah

Aroer

Gaza

Gerar

Debir?

En-gedi

Arnon R.

Eshtemoa

Ziklag?

Dead
Sea

Sharuhen

Ashan?

MOAB

Besor Br.

Beer-sheba

Hormah

SIMEON

Kir-hareseth ◎

Zoar

Zered Br.

NEGEB

ARABAH

EDOM

Bozrah ◎

| 0 | 10 | 20 | 30 Miles |

| 0 | 10 | 20 | 30 Kilometers |

Ashkelon

Jordan R.

N

the nine and one-half tribes initiate a fight, however, Eleazar's son Phinehas, who earlier defended the right worship of God over Baal (Numbers 25), and 10 Israelite tribal chiefs confront their kinsmen with the perceived problem. Alarmed at their brothers' interpretation of their actions in building the altar, the Reubenites, Gadites, and Manassehites insist that their intentions consisted not in rejecting God but, rather, in ensuring the preservation of their "portion in the Lord." Their acknowledgment of Israel's God in v. 22 testifies to their sincerity, and their explanation satisfies Phinehas and his companions. With civil war staved off, the altar remains as a monument to the 12 tribes' religious solidarity.

23 Joshua's Parting Address

Joshua's admonition to the Israelites at the end of his life includes reminders made familiar by Moses in his speeches in Deuteronomy 1–11; 28:1–31:13. The Israelites must remain faithful to God and his covenant with them (vv. 6-8); they must use their experience of the covenantal blessings realized thus far as inspiration for their continued love of their Lord and as the basis of their hope for the future (vv. 9-11); they must remember that the curses of the covenant, which include God's destruction of his chosen nation, will surely materialize if Israel persists in breaking the covenant (vv. 12-16).

The Great Sea of v. 4 refers to the Mediterranean. Verses 5 and 13 preview the picture in Judges 1 of the conquests that remain at the end of Joshua's life.

24 The Covenant Confirmed Again at Shechem

Joshua 24 portrays a second confirmation of the covenant at Shechem (cf. 8:30-34). The format follows that of a 2nd-millennium overlord-vassal treaty (see "Covenants" [121-24]) and begins in typical fashion by identifying the initiator of the covenant (here, God; v. 2). Verses 2-13 begin with Abraham in recounting the history of God's relationship with his people. This section mentions God's intervention in the Balak/Balaam incident (vv. 9-10; Numbers 22–24) and uses the image of the hornet probably to illustrate the panic God struck in Israel's Amorite enemies Sihon and

Og and their subjects (cf. Num. 21:21-35). The chapter then lays out the covenantal stipulations, which stress loyalty to God alone (vv. 14-18). As Moses forwarded a choice between life-giving covenantal obedience and death-producing transgression (Deut. 30:15-20), so now Joshua challenges the Israelites to "choose whom you will serve" (v. 15). By declaring his own determination to follow God, Joshua sets an example that the congregation follows with enthusiasm. A summary of the covenantal curses (vv. 19-20) appears before the conclusion to the ceremony:

Late Bronze fortress temple at Shechem featuring a great standing-stone *(masseba)* **in the forecourt. Here the twelve tribes confirmed the covenant entered at Sinai.** *(Phoenix Data Systems, Neal and Joel Bierling)*

Israel's erection of a memorial stone as a witness to the covenant (v. 27).

Another era in Israel's history passes with the death of Moses' and Aaron's successors, Joshua and Eleazar (vv. 29, 33), but v. 31 emphasizes Joshua's continued positive influence on the Israelites even after his passing. The reckoning of Joshua's age at death (110, v. 29) parallels that of Joseph and may symbolize an age considered ideal in the ancient world (cf. Gen. 50:22). The Israelites fulfill their ancestors' promise to Joseph on his Egyptian deathbed (Gen. 50:24-25; Exod. 13:19) by burying Joseph's remains in the promised land at Shechem, where his father Jacob had purchased the second parcel of land in Canaan owned by the patriarchs (Gen 33:18-19) and where the Israelites have reconfirmed their covenantal fidelity.

Judges

The second book of the Former Prophets and third in the Deuteronomistic History, Judges centers on Israel's life in Canaan after the death of Joshua and before the rise of Samuel, who anoints Saul ca. 1020 B.C. as a first step toward establishing the Israelite monarchy. In the absence of a single, central leader for Israel during the bulk of these last two centuries of the 2nd millennium, God raises up "judges" who exercise judicial authority and/or provide military leadership to rid Israel of foreign oppression. The book's repeated phrase, "there was no king in Israel; everyone did what was right in his own eyes," attests to the political and religious diversity that characterized this time in Israel's history.

Content

A two-part introduction and two-part epilogue frame the book's main body (3:7–16:31), which demonstrates the fulfillment of Joshua's prophecy that the Israelites would not be able to resist the temptation to worship foreign deities instead of serving God alone (Josh. 24:19-27; cf. God's own foretelling in Deut. 31:16-18). The cycle of Israel's losing faith, divinely sanctioned foreign oppression (= the covenantal curse), the nation's cry for help, God's deliverance, and "rest" for the land repeats itself, with some variation, in a manner that recalls Israel's recurring grumbling and disobedience answered by God's faithfulness and grace during the period of the wilderness wanderings. Israel's failure to keep God's covenant gives the reason for their failure to conquer the promised land in the kind of comprehensive way that accords with the promises given to the patriarchs and with the overall picture of the conquest portrayed in Joshua (Josh. 23:1-5; cf. Gen. 15:18-21; 28:10-15). Yet Judges picks up the Bible's overarching theme of God's continued initiative in redeeming sinful humanity.

Background

Twelve judges appear in this book, most hailing from Canaan's central hill country. Deborah's military colleague Barak, the Kenite heroine Jael, and Gideon's son Abimelech also figure prominently, but they do not serve as judges. Five "minor" judges receive only brief biographical information. The careers of the remaining seven "major" judges appear varied in character. Deborah renders judicial decisions, Jephthah leads a tribal military coalition, and Samson carries out personal vendettas. Most of the major judges display serious moral flaws evidenced in behavior such as sexual promiscuity (Samson) and idolatry (Gideon). The shortcomings of these divinely appointed leaders highlight more intensely God's work of pure grace and mercy in delivering the entire nation of undeserving Israelites from the curses they have called on themselves as a result of their covenantal disobedience. Indeed, only once in Judges do we see the Israelites repent of their sins (10:10-16). Hebrews 11:32 singles out Gideon, Barak, Samson, and Jephthah for their commendable faith regardless of their moral imperfections.

Though the book portrays the judges as arising in sequence over some 400 years, their careers probably overlapped, and the time designations for the periods of "rest" between their tenures most likely represent numbers of generations (one generation = "40 years") rather than precise numbers of years.

Authorship

Jewish tradition views Samuel as the author of Judges, but most modern scholars see the present form of the book as an editorial compilation of material from a variety of sources (possibly including Samuel) from a wide range of periods. Sections probably composed closest to the actual time of the events include the opening chapter, the Song of Deborah (ch. 5), and the concluding stories spanning chs. 17–21. Most scholars believe that the Deuteronomistic Historian who edited Judges did his work either in the 7th century during the reign of Judah's king Josiah or in the 6th century during the Babylonian exile.

1 The State of the Conquest

From the very start, Judges paints a less complete picture of the Israelites' initial possession of Canaan than does Joshua (Josh. 23:1-13). Judges 1:1 reveals that the previous allotment of the land merely represented a preliminary step in the tribes' taking possession of their assigned territories, for many non-Israelite ethnic groups living in Canaan (Canaanites, Amorites, and Perizzites) remain unconquered after Joshua's death.

God chooses Judah, from whose line David and eventually Jesus would come, to take the initiative in continuing the effort. Judah enlists the aid of Simeon, and the two tribes realize great success in capturing their allotted territories in the southern hill country. They render the king of Bezek useless in battle by cutting off his thumbs and big toes to prevent him from grasping a sword and moving agilely (v. 6). Verse 8 even asserts that Judah captured Jerusalem, on Judah's northern border with Benjamin (but contrast Josh. 15:63 and the Benjamites' failure in Jerusalem, v. 21). In fact, Israel did not take decided control of Jerusalem until the time of David (2 Sam. 5:1-10). Neither could the Judahites conquer their inheritance in the southwestern plains, supposedly because of the Canaanites' superior military machinery (iron chariots, v. 19; but see the theological reason given in 2:20–3:4). The assertion in v. 18 that Judah conquered Gaza, Ashkelon, and Ekron — three of the five cities of the Philistine pentapolis located in Canaan's southwestern plains — seems unlikely in view of v. 19, for the Philistines exercised exclusive control over the iron industry in Canaan at the beginning of the Iron Age (cf. 3:1-3). (The Greek Septuagint reads "not" in v. 18 and

reverses the result of Judah's efforts against the three cities.)

Verse 10 records the Judahites' attack against Hebron, but both verse 20 and Joshua credit the city's actual capture to Caleb (Josh. 15:14), to whom Joshua awarded the city as an inheritance (Josh. 14:6-15). Caleb's shrewd daughter, whom he obligates by a wedding gift of land to live in the dry, infertile Negev ("south"), wisely secures water rights from her father (vv. 12-15). The descendants of Moses' father-in-law Hobab leave the oasis of Jericho ("the city of palms") for an undoubtedly nomadic life in the barren Judean wilderness (v. 16).

After mentioning the Benjamites' failure at Jerusalem (v. 21), the text continues its northbound progression on the map of allotted tribal

Judges of Israel	
Othniel	Jair
Ehud	Jephthah
Shamgar	Ibzan
Deborah	Elon
Gideon	Abdon
Tola	Samson

territories by touching on the success of the "house of Joseph" (Ephraim and Manasseh) in the Ephraimite hill country at Bethel ("house of God," vv. 22-25). The Hittites in v. 26 are one of the peoples that make up the Canaanites. Past this verse, ch. 1 records only the northern tribes' failure to drive out specific cities' Canaanite inhabitants, though several tribes gain enough power to reduce these peoples to vassalage (Zebulun, Naphtali, and Ephraim ["the house of Joseph," v. 35]). Dan (v. 34) originally settled in the southern hill country but later migrated to Canaan's northern extreme, for which reason the text mentions this tribe last in its geographical journey from south to north (cf. ch. 18).

2:1-19 The Reason for Israel's Military Failures

God's angel ("messenger") travels from Gilgal, site of Israel's first camp in Canaan, to Bochim (undetermined location) to announce why the

Israelites have failed to conquer the promised land: they have transgressed the covenant and have thereby invoked the covenantal curses (v. 2; cf. Joshua 9). The Israelites try to make amends by expressing sorrow and offering sacrifices. Verses 1-5 thus set the stage for the judges' activities of deliverance throughout the rest of the book.

Verses 6-9 recap the Israelites' religious posture at the end of Joshua (Josh. 24:28-31), and v. 10 begins to explain the spiritual regression of the nation after the death of Joshua and his righteous contemporaries. Evidently, the early Israelites did not adequately teach their children the Law (cf. Deut. 6:7, 20-25) — for at the heart of this generation's sin lies their forsaking the worship of Israel's God for service to Canaan's fertility gods Baal and Astarte. The nation's punishment consists not only in God's withholding his blessing but also in his actively distressing the Israelites (vv. 14-15).

Verses 16-19 preview the cycle of Israel's deliverance from her divinely appointed oppressors as an act of God's mercy, followed eventually by the nation's further spiritual decline and resulting divinely ordained oppression — a cycle that will characterize the stories surrounding the 12 judges.

2:20–3:7 God Tests His People

God's purpose in allowing Canaanite peoples to remain in the promised land now becomes to test the transgression-prone Israelites' devotion to him and to teach coming generations how to conquer and defend their land (2:20–3:4). But the Israelites set themselves up for failure: living among the inhabitants of Canaan leads to intermarriage (forbidden in Deut. 7:3), which in turn leads to spiritual decay (vv. 5-7).

3:8-11 Othniel's Victory

These verses record the first specific punishment God inflicts on his disobedient people — subjection to Mesopotamia (the land between the Tigris and Euphrates Rivers; some scholars emend the text to refer to Edom, east of the Dead Sea, since a southern military confrontation with far-flung Mesopotamia seems

unlikely). In time, God delivers the Israelites from their affliction through the judge Othniel — a Judahite relative of Caleb who proved his military prowess in 1:12-13. As with the coming champions Gideon, Jephthah, and Samson, God's spirit specially equips Othniel for the job (v. 10). This judge's victory over his nation's oppressors brings a generation of relief for Israel ("40 years," often a symbolic number in the Old Testament).

3:12-30 Ehud vs. Eglon

The Israelites slide back into faithlessness after Othniel's death, and now the Transjordanian king Eglon of Moab and his coalition of Ammonites (to his north) and Amalekites (from the desert) subdue the chosen people. They even capture Jericho ("the city of palms," v. 13), where Israel had realized its first victory in Canaan (Joshua 6). Israel's cries to the Lord result in God's raising up a second deliverer — the lefthanded Benjamite Ehud, who clouds his purpose to assassinate Eglon under the guise of offering tribute and, upon returning to the king alone, employs the element of surprise by strapping a concealed weapon on his unsuspected right thigh (on the lefthanded Benjamite sureshots, see 20:16). Having accomplished his deadly deed in a private encounter with the indisposed Eglon, Ehud escapes the scene of the crime to lead his countrymen in defeating the kingless Moabites (descendants of Abraham's nephew Lot) at the fords of the Jordan. The victory initiates an 80-year (two generation) period of national rest from foreign oppression.

3:31 Shamgar vs. the Philistines

Though Shamgar's saving of Israel by slaying 600 Philistines (probably an organized fighting force) receives only brief notice (v. 31), this judge's reputation must have endured, for his name appears again in 5:6. Shamgar's make-do fighting method of using a long, metal-tipped pole (an ox goad) as a weapon brings to mind Samson's use of a donkey jawbone to kill nearly twice as many Philistines (15:15). Shamgar's identification as "the son of Anath" may reflect

Weapons and Warfare

In biblical times hunting and warfare were significant parts of life. An individual hunter or soldier had numerous weapons that could be used offensively or defensively. Offensive weapons can be divided into short-range, medium-range, and long-range weapons. Short-range weapons were used in hand-to-hand combat. The most common short-range weapon was the sword of various lengths and shapes. It was carried in a sheath or scabbard. One of the most unusual swords was a sickle sword, shaped like a sickle and used for slashing instead of stabbing (Judg. 21:10). Swords were made of copper or bronze in the earliest periods, but by the monarchy period those metals were replaced by carburized iron, which was much harder and more valuable. Other short-range weapons included the club (Prov. 25:18) or the mace with either a stone or metal head. The spear was a long stick with a sharp blade attached to the end and used for stabbing or thrusting (John 19:34).

The most common medium-range weapon was the javelin, which was generally smaller than the spear (1 Sam. 17:6-7). It was essentially a long arrow with a string looped around the shaft. The spin caused by the string's unwinding increased the throwing distance and accuracy. Another medium-range weapon was a type of spear that was light enough to be thrown.

The two long-range weapons were the sling and stone (Judg. 20:16) and the bow and arrow (Jer. 50:14). The latter had the longest range and could be effective up to 175-200 yards, while the composite bow could reach up to 500 yards in exceptional cases. The sling included a small pouch for the stone with a long string attached on both sides. The slinger then circled the sling over his head several times before one string was released. The stone flew out of the pouch at speeds up to 100 mph, with a maximum distance of 200 yards. David's long-range sling and stones put Goliath in range; Goliath had only medium-range and short-range weapons (1 Sam. 17:5-7) and tried to move closer to David (vv. 41, 48) to get within range of him.

Horses provided soldiers with mobility and speed, and the iron chariot pulled by two horses provided a mobile platform for two or

Four-chamber city gate at Tel Dan; Iron II (mid-9th century B.C.). (*www.HolyLandPhotos.org*)

three soldiers. But the iron chariot was valuable only in flat and open land, not in wooded areas or hilly terrain. Ancient Israel probably did not use chariots and horses until the time of Solomon, and that is why they had to settle in the hill country and could not drive out the people of the coastal plain (Judg. 1:19).

Defense against offensive weapons included the shield made from leather, wood, or metal in all shapes and sizes. The larger shield often required a shield-bearer to hold it in front of the warrior (1 Sam. 17:41). Armor was worn to protect the body and free the hands for fighting. Helmets of metal or leather came in a variety of shapes and with decorations to distinguish enemy from comrade. The coat of mail protected against the arrow, but it was heavy and expensive. It was made of 700-1000 small metal plates tied or sewn together in fishlike scales. The metal breastplate covered the neck and torso, with a second piece protecting the back (Eph. 6:14).

Leg armor or greaves covered the shins (1 Sam. 17:6).

In the Old Testament period towns, except for the smallest, had to be protected by encircling walls. Since the building of such walls was expensive, they covered only a small area of the town housing the most important buildings. Most of the people lived and farmed outside the city walls but ran inside the walls in time of attack. The complex gate system with large doors, posts, and bars was designed to make enemy access extremely difficult. The enemy brought the city under siege when it attacked, allowing no one to go into or out of the city (Josh. 6:1). The goal was to enter the city by tunnelling under the wall, scaling the wall, or weakening the wall and breaking through it or through the gate. Battering rams with wheels, to make them mobile, and a long beam with a metal tip were used to dislodge the stones and weaken the wall. Entry through a water system (if found) could also be used to enter the town. Inside the

walls extensive storage of food and water was necessary to survive the siege as long as possible (Samaria, 2 Kgs. 17:5-6; Jerusalem, 25:1-2). In the New Testament period great empires engaged in war, but individual Jews were infrequently involved in standing armies.

Symbolic references to weapons and warfare are frequent in the Bible. God is a "man of war" (Exod. 15:3), and his power and might are often depicted in shattering the weapons of war (Ps. 76:3). Victory in battle was described as a blessing from God (Psalm 18). God's protection is symbolized by the shield (Gen. 15:1; Prov. 30:5), but he also breaks the bow and thereby defeats the nation (Jer. 49:35). Taking his cue from the Roman soldier, the author depicts the Christian as one who suffers as a good soldier (2 Tim. 2:3) and one who should put on the whole armor of God in order to stand against the Devil (Eph. 6:10-17).

JAMES C. MOYER

a military title rather than a genealogical note, since Anath is the Canaanite goddess of war.

4–5 Deborah and Barak vs. Jabin and Sisera

The account of the Israelites' fourth deliverance departs from the previous three in several respects: it occurs in central and north Canaan; its heroes are women; its prophetess/judge, Deborah, already sits in office when the crisis comes to a head; and Deborah exercises her judgeship in the legal/administrative realm.

As a prophetess, Deborah brings a message from God for Barak to lead the two northernmost tribes against Israel's current oppressor, King Jabin of Hazor, and his army commander Sisera. Since Josh. 11:1-11 records the defeat of Jabin about 200 years earlier, some scholars

have suggested that "Jabin" is a kingly title rather than a personal name. Others take the Judges account to refer to a different king named Jabin. In any event, Barak is reluctant to take on the assignment and accepts it only on condition that Deborah accompanies him. Deborah agrees but advises Barak that the honor for their divinely ensured victory will go to a woman. The Israelite troops muster near some of Moses' relatives by marriage (compare 4:11 with 1:16) and take their position on Mount Tabor, a prominent mound whose slopes rise steeply from the surrounding Jezreel Valley. Despite possessing the military advantage, Sisera's 900-chariot-strong army meets with total defeat, and Sisera escapes on foot.

The exhausted commander finds feigned hospitality in the nearby tent of Israel's kinswoman by law, the Kenite Jael, whose household lives in peace with Sisera's king (cf. 4:17 and 11). Jael demonstrates her family loyalty over treaty ties by applying a hammer and tent peg to Sisera's temple to give him permanent rest. Jael thus emerges as the heroine of whom Deborah spoke in v. 9, but v. 23 quickly ascribes the victory to God.

Chapter 5 relates this same story of deliverance in the form of a victory song, some of oldest Hebrew poetry in the Old Testament. The poem gives a more dramatic presentation of the events than the prose account in ch. 4. Judges 5:19 mentions Taanach and Megiddo, important cities that guarded trade routes through the strategic Jezreel Valley. Verses 24-27 praise Jael for her cunning and courage. The record of Israel's deliverance from Jabin ends with the notation in v. 31 that peace ensued for another generation ("40 years").

6–8 Gideon vs. the Midianites and Amalekites

Because Israel again abandons the faith, God allows raiders from the east to threaten the people's livelihood (6:4-5). Verse 11 pictures Gideon as "beating out" his grain in a winepress, instead of threshing it in the open, to hide his activity from the Midianites (descendants of Abraham by Keturah; Gen. 25:1-4).

The announcement of Israel's covenantal transgression by an unidentified prophet underscores the undeserved graciousness God will soon show in delivering Israel from this oppression (6:8-10). The appearance of the angel of the Lord (here God himself; 6:14, 16, 22-23) provides an early clue to the theological significance of this account and begins a series of parallels with the call of Moses in Exodus 3. (Both men are hiding from enemies when they receive their call, both protest and are reluctant to accept the task, and both receive a divine promise and miraculous signs.) The angel sits under an oak tree to commission Gideon as the nation's next deliverer (6:11-14; cf. Deborah's judgment seat, 4:5).

Gideon cites his humble status as the youngest son of his tribe's most humble family in expressing his reluctance for the task (6:15). God's choice of the least socially powerful in-

dividual to accomplish his purpose contributes to the account's focus on God's power rather than Israel's. The "youngest son" theme recalls the narratives concerning Abel (Genesis 4), Jacob (Genesis 25–35), Joseph (Genesis 37–50), and later David (1 Samuel 16–1 Kings 2).

As with the patriarchs and Moses, God promises to "be with" Gideon (God himself will bring about deliverance) and validates that assurance with three signs. The first sign — the spontaneous consumption of Gideon's offering — firmly establishes God's identity (6:21). With Gideon's fear upon realizing he has seen God face to face (6:22-23), compare Jacob's response in Gen. 32:30 and Moses' reaction in Exod. 3:6.

As Gideon tested God regarding his identity (6:17), so now God tests Gideon regarding obedience. Gideon carries out God's command that he destroy his father's altar to the Canaanite fertility-god Baal, as well as the wooden idol of Baal's wife Asherah. But he uses the cover of darkness to cloak his timidity in asserting his divinely-sanctioned leadership. Nevertheless, Gideon passes the test and gains a new name, Jerubbaal — one that thumbs the nose at Baal and implies the false god's powerlessness (6:31-32).

The eastern raiders' muster in the Jezreel Valley (where the confrontation between Deborah/Barak and Jabin/Sisera took place, chs. 4–5) provides a further test of Gideon's ability. The spirit-empowered deliverer (6:34) summons troops from four northern tribes, but before initiating a military confrontation he seeks a double confirmation of God's promise of victory, and God provides two additional signs of assurance. Gideon's use of a fleece in establishing God's will gives rise to the expression "lay out a fleece" for determining what course of action one should pursue (6:33-40).

Through God's instruction, Gideon reduces the size of his army to a mere 300 men (7:5-7), for God wants to establish that he, not the Israelite warriors, will win the victory. Obviously this group consists of those with the greatest faith in God's power to prevail over a virtual swarm of enemies with so few men (7:3; cf. 6:5).

God uses the Midianites themselves to steel Gideon for his task by providing Gideon opportunity to overhear a prophetic dream related in the Midianite camp — a dream that predicts Israel's impending victory over the raiders (7:10-15). Gideon worships God before initiating his battle plan, which uses the element of surprise coupled with noise, fire, and cover of darkness to confuse the Midianites so they turn their swords against each other (7:15-22).

Gideon's plan works — apparently without engaging his seemingly unarmed troops in any fighting — but the Midianite survivors flee. With the Israelite army in hot pursuit, the centrally located tribe of Ephraim now becomes involved and captures and kills two Midianite leaders — a privileged act that Gideon points to in defusing the Ephraimites' offense at not having been summoned to join the initial confrontation (7:24–8:3).

Still in pursuit of two other Midianite kings, Gideon requests refreshment for his troops from two Transjordanian towns in Manasseh's territory — Succoth and Penuel. By refusing Gideon's request, both towns show lack of faith in God's ability to bring about the kings' capture. After Gideon completes his mission successfully, he punishes them soundly (8:4-17), then kills the Midianite kings to avenge his brothers' blood (vv. 18-21).

Gideon appears more vulnerable to the temptations of possessions than of power. He refuses his countrymen's request that he begin a dynasty to rule over them and instead declares God as their leader (contrast his son Abimelech's response in ch. 9). But Gideon's desire for material wealth, demonstrated by his taking valuables from the Midianite kings he slays (8:21, 26) and his amassing of gold, leads to his fashioning an ephod (perhaps a priestly vestment [Exod. 28:28-30] or an image of God, which the Second Commandment [Exod. 20:4] forbids), and he and his countrymen worship the idol (= "play the harlot," 8:27). Through these acts, Gideon nullifies the good he had done earlier in tearing down the sanctuary of Baal and Asherah (6:25-27). Nevertheless, the text remembers Gideon as a man of God blessed with an abundance of sons and a long life, one whose memory the Israelites should have honored but did not (8:30-32, 35; 9:16-20). Gideon's military leadership results in another

Mount Tabor and the Jezreel Valley, where Barak defeated the army of Hazor. *(BiblePlaces.com)*

generation of peace for Israel (8:28), but after his death the Israelites once again revert to Baal-worship (Baal-berith, "Baal of the covenant").

9 Abimelech's Rise and Fall

This extended aside from the stories of deliverance through the judges demonstrates divine retribution — here, for mass murder (not for Abimelech's grasping after political power; v. 56). Gideon's son by a Shechemite concubine convinces his hometown blood relatives to make him their leader. To accomplish this task, Abimelech and his band of hired ruffians publicly execute Abimelech's half brothers, who ruled over the mixed Canaanite-Israelite population of Shechem, and Abimelech becomes the city-state's king. Beth-millo ("house of the filling," v. 6) probably represents a fortress on an artificial mound near Shechem. The pillar, or standing stone, mentioned here likely figured in pagan religious practices.

But one brother, Jotham, escapes the bloodbath and flees to Mount Gerizim, which, along with Mount Ebal, overlooks Shechem (cf. Josh. 8:30-35 for the ratification of the covenant here after Israel's defeat of Jericho and Ai). There Jotham relates a parable denouncing the violence and calls for the destruction of Abimelech and the Shechemites.

Three years later, God exercises his power over an evil spirit to cause strife between

Abimelech and the Shechemites. An outsider, Gaal the son of Ebed ("servant"), fans the flames of rebellion, and a showdown between Abimelech and the Shechemites ensues. Abimelech destroys Shechem, sows it with salt to signify the irreversibility of the city's downfall, and burns to death those who have taken refuge in the city fortress's temple of El-berith ("God of the covenant"; contrast "Baal-berith," 8:33; 9:4).

Abimelech does not enjoy his victory for long, however. In his effort to take Thebez (modern Tubas, north of Nablus), a woman on top of the city wall drops on his head a skull-crushing, wheel-like millstone used for grinding grain, and he commands his armor-bearer to finish him off with a sword to avoid the disgrace of death by a female (cf. 2 Sam. 11:21, which remembers him in exactly this way). Divine retribution thus comes full circle in the fulfillment of Jotham's curse (vv. 56-57; cf. v. 20). For the second time in Judges a woman has felled a man (cf. chs. 4–5).

10:1-5 Tola and Jair

The text does not tell enough about these "minor" judges to determine whether their roles consisted mainly in administering judgments or in delivering Israel from oppressors — or both. Verse 1 does indicate that Tola "save[d]" Israel. Other minor judges appear in chapter 12.

10:6–12:7 Jephthah vs. the Ammonites

The picture of Israel's apostasy (abandoning the faith) now intensifies as the nation serves not only Canaanite and Philistine gods but also those of the lands to their north (Syria and Sidon) and west (Moab and Ammon). Their transgressions result in divinely caused oppression by the Philistines and Ammonites; thus Judges' focus returns to the southern tribes and turns east to the Transjordanian Gileadites. For the first time in the book, Israel repents from her sin, but God's heart does not soften immediately.

The Israelites find their own deliverer in the Gileadite Jephthah, an exiled son of a harlot eager to regain social position and achieve tribal power. Only later does God confirm this choice

(11:29). Jephthah first makes a rough attempt at diplomacy to stave off a military confrontation with the advancing Ammonites, but they respond by telling the Gileadites to give back their land — peaceably. Jephthah counters that God delivered the land to the Israelites, and his invocation of the Lord's immediate judgment between Israel and Ammon makes battle inevitable (11:27).

Before the engagement, however, Jephthah makes a conditional vow that, if God grants him victory, he will offer as a burnt offering whatever comes out of his house first upon his return home. Jephthah may likely have expected an animal to wander out, since animals lived on the ground floor of ancient Near Eastern houses, but instead his only child, a virgin daughter, appears. With her surprising cooperation, the devastated Jephthah makes good on his heartbreaking but binding vow (cf. Num. 30:2), although his following this Ammonite religious practice surely offended rather than pleased God (contrast Abraham's divinely aborted sacrifice of Isaac in Genesis 22, which constituted a divine test of faith).

Jephthah's troubles do not end with his daughter's death, for Ephraim takes offense that he excluded them from the battle against the Ammonites (cf. 8:1-3). Jephthah's accusatory explanation triggers tribal feuding, and his forces gain the upper hand. Their imposition of a pronunciation test on anyone seeking to cross the Jordan from Gilead into Ephraim routs out retreating Ephraimites and sheds light on the differences in dialect between the two tribes (and presumably between others as well). In modern usage, the text's password, "shibboleth," indicates a "litmus test" for authenticity. The 42 thousand Ephraimites killed may represent an exaggeration resulting from difficulty in interpreting the Hebrew word for "thousand" (cf. Exod. 12:37–13:16).

12:8-15 Ibzan, Elon, and Abdon

These three minor judges return us to Canaan proper. As with the others (cf. 10:1-5), only scant biographical information appears here. The note concerning Ibzan's children marrying "outsiders" may refer to Israelites outside Ibzan's lineage or to non-Israelites. The donkey-riding descendants of Abdon recall the judge Jair's mounted sons (10:4).

13–16 Samson vs. the Philistines

13 Israel's Philistine oppressors, who maintained strongholds in five southern cities on and near the Mediterranean coast, succeeded in preventing the Danites from possessing their landed inheritance on Canaan's coastal plain (Josh. 19:40-48). But before all the Danites migrated to the far north (ch. 18), their champion Samson gave the Philistines plenty of trouble.

The account of Samson's conception by a previously infertile woman recalls the reversal of the barrenness of Sarah, Rachel, and Rebekah (cf. Elizabeth; Luke 1:7, 13). The angel of the Lord's appearance to Manoah's wife to announce her impending pregnancy parallels Gabriel's meeting with Mary (Luke 1:26-38). Manoah's fear upon realizing that he has seen God contrasts with his wife's insights into their encounter with the divine (contrast vv. 16-18 with v. 6; v. 22 with v. 23).

The restrictions on Samson as a lifelong Nazirite (one specially consecrated by a vow) begin in the womb; Samson's mother must therefore refrain from consuming any products of the vine as well as ritually unclean foods (Num. 6:1-21). Verse 25 foreshadows God's impending work through Samson despite the absence of a reported cry by the Israelites for deliverance from Philistine rule. Indeed, Judah even protests Samson's militant acts against these uncircumcised oppressors (15:11; cf. 14:3; of all Israel's neighbors, only the Philistines did not practice circumcision).

14–15 If Samson's dedication as a Nazirite suggested that he would grow into a pious, peace-loving adult, chs. 14 and 15 quickly dispel that notion. But God's plan for Samson uses his he-man tendencies to bring judgment on the Philistines, though their punishment falls short of bringing deliverance to the oppressed Israelites.

Samson's insistence on marrying a Philistine woman violates God's command prohibit-

Abimelech's victory at Thebez was eclipsed when he was crushed by a millstone (Judges 9). Shown here a collection of ancient basalt grinders.
(www.HolyLandPhotos.org)

ing intermarriage with pagan peoples (Deut. 7:3). His repeated handling of the carcass of a lion he has killed transgresses the prohibition against a Nazirite's coming into contact with dead bodies (Num. 6:6), and his eating honey from a hive inside the carcass represents a breach of Israelite food laws (Lev. 11:32-40).

That Samson's wife betrays the answer to his wedding party riddle enrages the bridegroom. He takes vengeance on 30 unfortunate (and unwitting) Philistines of Ashkelon (23 mi. southwest) in order to make good on his wager to provide high quality, linen outfits for his cunning guests, and then he shames his bride and in-laws by returning to his father's house before consummating the marriage. The woman's father interprets Samson's actions as calling off the marriage and he hastily weds his daughter to Samson's best man to minimize the disgrace Samson has caused the entire family.

Just when Samson's anger cools enough for him to make up with his wife, who continues to live in her father's house according to Philistine custom, he discovers his loss of her to his former friend, and his rage ignites with even greater intensity. The Philistines answer Samson's revenge of burning their crops by burning to death his would-be wife and father-in-law, who, ironically, suffer the same fate previously threatened by the stymied wedding guests (14:15). Samson responds with even more violence before he holes up in a cave in Judah.

The Philistines gain Judah's cooperation in their pursuit of Samson, and the intimidated Judahites bind and hand their captured countryman over to the enemy. But the spirit-empowered strong man bursts his bonds and lays 1000 of his Philistine assailants flat using the jawbone of a donkey. God demonstrates his approval of Samson's judgment on the Philistines by miraculously providing him with water in answer to his prayer (15:18-19). It was just the sort of back-and-forth vengeance these chapters outline between Samson and the Philistines that Israel's *lex talionis* sought to curb (cf. Exod. 21:23-25).

16 Samson's weakness for women continues to get him into trouble, now with the deceitful, probably Philistine Delilah. Swayed by her wiles and at least temporarily overconfident of his physical strength apart from God (v. 20), he is captured by the Philistines. The account of Delilah's betrayal continues to portray Samson as a powerful, one-man militia, whose subjection the Philistines relish (vv. 23-25), rather than as leader of a pan-Israel fighting force.

Despite his past moral shortcomings, the blinded but reinvigorated slave Samson accomplishes God's purpose to judge the Philistines even more harshly at his death than throughout his life (compare 14:4 with 16:30). In doing so, Samson demonstrates God's power over the Philistine grain-god Dagon, whose party Samson quite literally crashes. Judges represents Samson as the last of Israel's judges and the only one to die in the line of divinely assigned duty. His judgeship lasted two decades, but not until David would the Israelites gain rest from the Philistine oppressors God used Samson to afflict.

17–18 Micah, Dan, and the Whimsical Levite

These chapters flesh out examples of the Israelites' covenantal disobedience referred to throughout earlier chapters in Judges. That wayward Levites figure in this account and in

the book's concluding section (chs. 19–21) demonstrates the moral decline of Israel's religious leadership in addition to that of the nation at large.

While the Mosaic Law expressly prohibited divination and the making of graven images (Deut. 18:10; Exod. 20:4), the self-confessed Ephraimite thief Micah engages in just such activities — with the blessing of his unreproaching mother — and does so in the name of the Lord (17:5, 13; on Micah's ephod, see 8:27). Micah even assumes divine authority in setting up his own shrine. In consecrating a private, non-Aaronic priest (cf. Num. 8:5-26), who himself ignores God's provision for his dwelling-place in one of Israel's 48 Levitical cities (Joshua 21), Micah disregards the Law God ordained him to teach and enforce. In addition, he accepts wages for his services rather than relying on tithes as a means of support (17:10; cf. Numbers 18; Leviticus 27). Micah's skewed understanding of how to please God seems to have pervaded the nation's religious thought during this premonarchical, judicially decentralized period in Israel's history (17:6).

The Danites' migration from their landed inheritance near Jerusalem, which later became Israel's religious center, to Canaan's northern extremity (25 mi. north of the Sea of Galilee) symbolizes the extent to which they stray from religious orthodoxy. Not only do they abandon their divinely allotted territory after failing to wrest it from the Philistines (cf. 1:34), they also appropriate Micah's unorthodox, whimsical priest and forbidden ritual objects and employ them in the unacceptable religious shrine they establish as a rival to the sanctuary at Shiloh (ch. 18). King Jeroboam I will later choose this Danite center of idolatry as one of two northern shrines to rival orthodox worship in Jerusalem (1 Kgs. 12:25-30). Judges 18:30 foreshadows the ultimate result of Israel's disobedience: the "captivity of the land," which came in the form of Assyrian subjection of the northern kingdom in the late 8th century.

19–21 Outrage and Response

Unlike the relatively innocuous Levite of chs. 17–18, the one who figures prominently in

Judges' final episode appears insincere, hard-hearted, and ruthless. Unfortunately, it is just such a character that the entire nation — from Dan in the far north to Beer-sheba in the far south — is willing to rally around in the kind of unity that not even the most influential of the judges appears to have engendered among them (20:1).

Though at first the Levite appears victimized by his unfaithful Judahite concubine (a lower-ranking wife recognized by Israelite law), whom he determines to woo back tenderly, the account turns this picture upside down by the end of ch. 19.

In the meantime, the overly generous hospitality of the Levite's father-in-law in Bethlehem sets up a foil for the near total lack of hospitality shown to him by his Benjamite countrymen in Gibeah on his journey back to Ephraim — hospitality he so took for granted that he passed up the earlier opportunity to lodge in Jebus.

Rabble-rousers in Gibeah approach the Levite's elderly host with the same request that the men of Sodom made to Lot (19:22; Gen. 19:5), and they receive a similar response — one that honors the current code of hospitality: sexually abuse these women, but leave my male guest alone. That later in the account the entire Benjamite tribe demonstrates solidarity with Gibeah's "worthless fellows" who rape the Levite's concubine strengthens the tie with the Genesis event, wherein all the men of Sodom join in the atrocious demand to engage in sexually abusive behavior (20:13-14).

The Levite's concubine becomes the only victim, and she pays for her husband's callousness with her life, whether the all-night abuse caused her death or the Levite himself dealt the final blow on their return home (19:29). The Levite's self-interest over his now obviously feigned affection for his wife (cf. 19:3) comes to the fore in several ways. First, 19:25 suggests that the Levite himself may have handed over his wife to her abusers to avoid personal harm. Second, the text records no attempt by the Levite to rescue his wife from her night-long ordeal. Neither does he show an ounce of concern for her well-being when in the morning he discovers her prostrate body lying at their host's doorway (19:27-28). Finally, rather than grieving over his wife's

brutalization, the Levite further debases her by chopping up her body, the severed members of which serve as a summons to the tribes to find an appropriate means to retaliate against the Benjamites — ostensibly for their murder of the concubine but more likely in the Levite's mind for disgracing him by abusing his wife (cf. Saul's summoning Israel's troops in 1 Sam. 11:6-7).

Except for Benjamin, in whose territory Gibeah lies, the tribes unite in their determination to punish the inhabitants of Gibeah, and each tribe commits 10 percent of its men to the task (20:10). The Israelite forces plan their battle strategy by consulting God at Bethel, sister shrine to the Danites' sanctuary and current home of the ark of the covenant (20:27). But though they rally to mete out punishment as a group, they also suffer a limited amount of divinely allowed corporate punishment for the sins of their Benjamite countrymen and do so at the Benjamites' own hands (20:21-25; cf. the punitive results of Achan's sin in Joshua 7).

The portrayal of the battle against Gibeah appears similar to Joshua's military victory against Ai. Gibeah's warriors pursue their assailants outside the city because of their false confidence in the inevitability of another victory. Thus they leave Gibeah vulnerable to Israelite ambushers, and the coalition slays the Benjamites on the open battlefield (20:36ff.; cf. Joshua 8). Benjamin's siding with its wayward tribesmen ultimately results in the near extinction of the entire tribe when its punishers enforce the ban (cf. Joshua 6) and pledge not to intermarry with the defiant tribe (21:1-3).

But in contrast to their behavior in the civil war between Gilead and Ephraim under Jephthah (12:1-6), the aggressors here lament their victims' fate, and they go to morally objectionable lengths to reverse the consequences of the punishment. Not only do the Israelites shed more of their brothers' blood to provide virgin brides for 400 of the surviving Benjamite bachelors (21:10-12; cf. Num. 31:17-18), they also approve the Benjamites' kidnapping of Israelite women at Shiloh to make up the difference (21:19-21). By creating a legal loophole through the kidnapping provision (21:22), the Israelites turn a blind eye to their purposeful disobedience of their own vow and display complete disregard for the spirit in which they uttered it. The episode spanning chs. 19–21 pictures a morally clueless Israel attempting to enact covenantal law — an attempt doomed to go awry for lack of spiritual leadership and the resulting individualism created by this vacuum (21:25). The book may imply that crowning a king might not be such a bad idea (cf. Deut. 17:14-20).

Ruth

The events recorded in Ruth occur during the period of the judges (late 2nd millennium B.C.). In focusing on the ordinary life of a particular Judahite clan rather than on the nation of Israel in relation to her Canaanite neighbors, this book paints a far more serene picture of Israel's community life in the promised land than Judges does. Ruth emphasizes faithfulness even to the spirit of the Law in daily life and personal relationships, and in this way contrasts with the portrayal of Israel's deliberate and at times hypocritical religious disobedience throughout Judges. Ruth herself emerges as a model convert to Judaism (cf. Lev. 19:33-34; Josh. 6:22-26). Beyond developing the theme of faithfulness, Ruth establishes another link in the genealogical chain leading to Israel's royal line, which begins with David and culminates in Jesus (Matt. 1:1-17, esp. v. 5).

Background

Scholars often point to the account of Ruth's "redemption" by Boaz as a classic example of the levirate marriage obligation spelled out in Deut. 25:5-10. But that passage places the responsibility of fathering a child for an Israelite man who dies sonless only on his brother(s) in order to carry on the "name" of the deceased. The importance of producing a son probably consisted not so much in elevating his social status (as childbearing did for women; cf. Gen. 16:1-5; 1 Sam. 1:1-7) or in enjoying family life, though indeed offspring did signify God's blessing (4:11; cf. Gen. 15:5). Rather, a man needed an heir, for possession of land in Canaan by his genealogical line preserved his family's continued participation in the covenantal promise (Gen. 15:18-21; Num. 36:7-9). According to Mosaic law, daughters could inherit their father's property, but only in the absence of sons to maintain the family estate (Num. 27:1-11; 36).

The book of Ruth weaves together the regulations regarding landed inheritance and levirate marriage (esp. Num. 27:11; Deut. 25:5-6); Ruth substitutes for Naomi, Elimelech's wife, who according to 1:11 has passed childbearing age. Boaz's action in marrying his close relative's widowed Moabite daughter-in-law is motivated by his assuming responsibility to father an heir for Elimelech to maintain his family's separate, landed inheritance. In going beyond the letter of the Law, Boaz's behavior parallels Ruth's own voluntary, sacrificial fidelity to her widowed Israelite mother-in-law, who had no legal means of support.

The names of those who figure in the story of Ruth enhance the message of the book's eloquent narrative. Elimelech's name ("my God is king") acknowledges from the start divine supremacy in orchestrating what promises to be a devastating future for his family. After losing her husband, sons, and consequently her social status, Naomi ("pleasantness") rejects her name in favor of Mara ("bitter"), but her life becomes "pleasant" again by the end of the book. The names of Elimelech's and Naomi's sons, Mahlon ("weakness, sickness") and Chilion ("annihilation, consumption"), suggest these men's ultimate fate. The name Ruth probably goes back to the word for "friend, companion" — a role Ruth fulfills above and beyond the call of duty in relation to Naomi. The name of Ruth's Moabite sister-in-law Orpah means "back of the neck," which Orpah turns to Naomi upon departing for her "mother's house" in Moab. The meaning of Boaz is less certain, but some have translated it "In him there is strength."

Composition

Suggestions for the date of the book range from 950 to the 5th century, though the events recorded occurred before the time of David, who became king of Israel ca. 1000. The book claims no particular author, and the original manuscript may have undergone later editorial changes before reaching its current form. Jewish congregations read Ruth publicly during the Festival of Weeks, which follows Passover.

1 Naomi's Bitter Plight

Famine in Canaan prompts a Judahite family to move some 50 miles from their home in Bethlehem ("house of bread") to Moab, the territory on the southeastern side of the Dead Sea in which Lot settled. The death there of Elimelech, the husband, and the eventual deaths of his two married sons leave the family matriarch, Naomi, destitute.

While her childless, widowed daughters-in-law may regain economic support by returning to their "mothers' houses" in Moab and may even find second husbands through whom they can bear children, the aging Naomi's fortunes look hopeless. As a single female in a patriarchal society, she lacks a means of economic support; as a childless widow, she lacks inheritance rights of her own; and as an older woman, she can no longer bear sons through whom she might claim her dead husband's landholdings back in Bethlehem. Unwilling to subject her daughters-in-law to a fate bound up in her own, Naomi releases them from any obligation to follow her on her journey back to Canaan, where by now the famine has ended. But one daughter-in-law, Ruth, does the unexpected by refusing to desert the protesting Naomi, and the arrival of the two widows in Bethlehem at the beginning of the barley harvest stirs up the town. Ruth's lifelong pledge of faithfulness to Naomi's people and to her God contrasts sharply with the idolatrous behavior of the Moabite women in Numbers 25.

2 The Widows' Fortunes Begin to Change

Verse 1 allows the reader to understand the significance of the events that unfold in this chapter before the story's own subjects do. The poverty-stricken women agree that Ruth should glean in the fields in keeping with the Law's provision for the "needy and the alien" (Lev. 19:9-10; 23:22), but Ruth knows nothing of Boaz or his relationship to Naomi when she begins her day's work. Neither does Naomi know that Ruth will be gleaning in Boaz's field.

Boaz, however, immediately learns Ruth's identity as daughter-in-law to his kinswoman by marriage, Naomi. Recognizing his responsibility as a "redeemer" to his deceased clansman Elimelech's family — and honoring Ruth for her self-sacrificial faithfulness to Naomi — Boaz surprises Ruth with generosity beyond what the Law requires (the ephah container in v. 17 held about 5 gal.). Perhaps Boaz's unusually kind care for this non-Israelite woman stemmed from feeling a bond with her, for his own mother, Rahab (the harlot from Jericho), was also a foreigner grafted into Israel's community after taking great personal risk in harboring Israelite spies at the outset of the conquest (Joshua 2; cf. Matt. 1:5). Both Ruth and Naomi come to realize how God has directed the day's course of events, and Ruth continues to support her mother-in-law by gleaning in Boaz's field through the barley and wheat harvests.

3 Ruth and Boaz at the Threshing Floor

With the grain harvest over and Ruth now an accepted member of the Bethlehemite community, Naomi devises a plan to provide security for her daughter-in-law. But the plan requires boldness on the part of the heretofore humble Moabitess (cf. 2:10), for it essentially requires her to propose marriage to her voluntary master (v. 9; cf. Ezek. 16:8). Unwavering in her obedience to Naomi, Ruth now surprises Boaz by putting him in a potentially compromising situation during the night at the local threshing floor, where he guards his grain pile in slumber. Upon awaking in the dark, the startled Boaz handles the situation honorably and pledges to see that Ruth is "redeemed" either by her closest kinsman or by Boaz himself. In making this promise, Boaz realizes the potential for his role as redeemer to intensify from merely providing protection and support to producing descendants who will not be considered his own but his relative Elimelech's.

Women in the Old Testament

Primarily portrayed as wives and mothers, women in the Old Testament represent a host of roles spanning millennia. The biblical text includes named and unnamed women appearing as queens and commoners, prophetesses and diviners, heroines and villainesses. The text contains portraits of women in various life stages as child, virgin, wife, mother, and widow. In addition, women emerge in stylized, allegorical form in Proverbs as Dame Folly (portrayed as an adulteress) and Dame Wisdom, two voices competing publicly in the marketplace (Proverbs 7–9). The Song of Songs extols a woman's beauty in a collection of love songs that also vividly depict the open, free, sexual enjoyment of a handsome man and beautiful woman.

Because men predominate the Old Testament accounts, women seem at first reading to be not of central importance. Men assume the dominant positions in the family as fathers and husbands and in society as kings, priests, military leaders, and judges. But a closer reading shows women's importance. Because of the relative brevity of space women receive, each appearance of a woman may be seen as heralding a major textual event. Furthermore, the absence of textual space about women does not mean that women played a small role in Israelite society. Quite the contrary. Those accounts devoted to law and narration support the significant contribution of women throughout the ages to Israel's religious and cultural development.

The biblical text sheds light on women in creation, family and society, and religious matters, as well as by allegory and through specific examples. Even anonymous and silent women receive significant textual treatment.

Creation

The creation story shows that together male and female reflect the image of God (Gen. 1:27). Both sexes share equally in dignity before God, ability to sin, responsibility for sin, and capacity for good or evil. This joint reflection continues in the Bible's portrayal of God as having both traditionally male and female characteristics. God is both mighty warrior (Exod. 15:3) and one who is like a midwife, seamstress, mother, nurse, and hen (Pss. 22:9-10; 71:6; 91:4; 139:13; Isa. 49:15; 66:9, 13). Unlike other ancient Near Eastern religions, which show the gods marrying and having children, the Bible never portrays God with a consort.

Genesis 1 and 2 exemplify the view that man and woman complement each other and stand incomplete when alone (Gen. 2:18). The woman, created to share the man's workload as his companion, nonetheless has a free will and stands accountable individually before God. The first woman, named Eve by her husband Adam after the fall (Gen. 3:20), presents a complex picture. Because the serpent addressed her and not the man, scholars speculate she was the more creative, vulnerable, or spiritually attuned partner — or maybe just the one available at that moment! Her punishment because of her sin of disobedience involved hatred between her offspring and the serpent's, increased pain in childbearing, and a change in status from being an equal partner with her husband to having him rule over her (Gen. 3:15-16). Scholars puzzle over the derivation of the Hebrew word for "woman," 'isha; perhaps it comes from 'ish, "man," or from the root '-n-š, meaning "soft and delicate."

Family and Society

Women remained under the protection of their fathers and then their husbands throughout their lives; as Israel grew and divided into tribes, women married within their tribe or clan. While these restrictions may seem confining, they also gave women a measure of security and status. As with a man, the biblical text most frequently defines a woman in terms of function and family relationships. She is wife, mother, daughter, widow, servant, or slave. The law required virginity upon marriage only of the woman (Deut. 22:13-21).

Women did not share the same societal rights as men, for sons as heirs received property. But if a father died without sons and close male relatives, as in the case of the daughters of Zelophehad, daughters did inherit, but with the stipulation that they could choose whom they married within their father's tribal clan (Num. 27:1-11; 36). Similarly, the law specified that a husband could initiate a divorce proceeding, not a wife. A man might marry more than one wife, but the law forbade him from abusing his first wife by depriving her of food, clothing, and marital rights (Exod. 21:10).

Unlike in neighboring societies, an Israelite woman was not considered a man's property. A young girl and an unmarried young woman — both states synonymous with virginity — were vulnerable in Israel; consequently, the Law protected them against rape but not against being sold into slavery. Young women had a say in choosing their life partners (Gen. 24:58; Ruth 3:9), but their parents, while taking their feelings to heart, more consistently chose for them. Scholars argue that texts showing the degradation, sacrifice, murder, mutilation, and abuse of women (e.g., Gen. 19:8; Judg. 11:30-40; 19; 21) reflect not a biblical view but rather the prevailing lawless and violent conditions of Israel's neighbors.

Genealogies mention women, although less frequently than men. Serah, a daughter of Asher, appears three times in genealogies (Gen. 46:17; Num. 26:46; 1 Chr. 7:30), a fact attesting to her significance, but the narrative excludes further explanation about her. Rabbinic tradition, however, fills in with many stories about Serah; one claims that she grew up in Jacob's household in Canaan and at the request of Joseph's brothers conveyed through her music the news that Joseph was alive in Egypt.

The biblical text presents a healthy view of sexual love, one that includes pleasure of one's spouse up through old age (Gen. 18:12). The Song of Songs forthrightly presents the woman as an equal participant in romantic love; the woman both openly loves a man and openly returns his admiration. The text sees sexuality and sexual love as a good gift from God (Gen. 2:23). Psalm 45:11 speaks of a bride as desired and admired. The text mentions the beauty of Sarah, Rachel, Rebekah, Abigail, Bathsheba, and Esther. The text frequently displays God's all-encompassing love for his covenantal people in sexual terms. The verb "to know" represents the intimate, sexual

Baking flat bread-cakes in a clay oven, among the household tasks of women in ancient Israel. *(Phoenix Data Systems, Neal and Joel Bierling)*

knowledge of a man and a woman; God often uses this verb to signify how his people have forsaken him (Jer. 4:22).

A woman's status depended in part on whom she married and on his extended family connections. Women saw childbearing as a means to status and security (1 Sam. 1:6). Barrenness represented a curse (cf. Sarai, Gen. 11:30). Once widowed and without children, a woman's plight was serious, for no one necessarily as-

sumed legal responsibility for her care. The text presents the plight of some childless women, however, as divinely ordained. Specific children — such as Isaac, Joseph, Samuel, and Samson — born to Sarah, Rachel, Hannah, and the wife of Manoah late in life or after an angelic announcement were divinely favored and often marked as community deliverers. A newly married man received exemption from military service and other duties for a year in order to "bring happiness to the wife he has married" (Deut. 24:5); obviously, it was hoped that within that year she would become pregnant.

The Bible strongly condemns adultery as leading to death for both the man and woman (Prov. 5:15-23; Deut. 22:22). Hosea's wife Gomer abandons her husband for multiple lovers, yet her husband, on God's command, buys her back (Hosea 3); this marital example illustrates God's redemptive love for adulterous Israel. The Law gives the husband and not the wife the right to initiate divorce (Deut. 24:1), but the biblical corpus throughout takes care to minimize opportunities for divorce. Malachi 2:15-16 states God abhors three things: a man's discarding the wife of his youth, divorce, and marital violence. The Bible treats prostitution, however, somewhat ambiguously as defiling the land (Lev. 19:29), as a social status (1 Kgs. 3:16), and as a metaphor for spiritual unfaithfulness (Isa. 1:21).

A widow came under the protection and supervision of a near kinsman; if she were childless and of childbearing age, the kinsman's duty included raising up children to carry the dead man's name. Tamar forced Judah to recognize her legal rights to progeny (Genesis 38), and Boaz took seriously his responsibility to raise up offspring for Mahlon (Ruth 4:10).

Proverbs reinforces the sixth commandment, to honor one's father and mother, by stressing that men and women share equally regarding the joys, sorrows, and responsibilities of parenthood. A mother must be obeyed and, even when elderly, deserves respect (Prov. 1:8; 23:22).

Religious Practice

The Law declared a woman unclean during menstruation and prohibited sexual intercourse during her monthly cycle (Lev. 18:19). While the Law reserved the priesthood for men and passed it on from father to son, both a woman and a man could become Nazirites (Num. 6:2). Women participated as singers in temple worship after the exile (Ezra 2:65; Neh. 7:67).

Allegory

Women frequently appear in the text as allegorical figures. The women in Proverbs present interesting studies. Some are stock characters — the prostitute, adulteress, nagging wife, gossip, busybody, and mother. Others, notably Dame Folly and Dame Wisdom, illustrate for impressionable young men the paths to failure or success in life. Proverbs ends on a high note by extolling the qualities of an exemplary wife (31:10-31). This energetic woman, an organizational genius, engages in real estate, selects fine material, makes garments from linen, works far into the night for her household's good, and gives generously to the poor. Led by her husband and children, all who know her praise her.

In contrast, Ezekiel 16 portrays Jerusalem as a baby, a girl, and a desirable woman of marriageable age who forsakes her husband (God), practices infidelity with her lovers, and sacrifices her sons and daughters as food for idols. Ezekiel 23 likens both Israel and Judah to two sisters, Oholah and Oholibah, who became prostitutes in Egypt and made political alliances with foreign powers against the Lord's will.

Significant Named Women

The consorts of the three patriarchs — Abraham, Isaac, and Jacob — were the matriarchs Sarah, Rebekah, and Leah, Rachel, Bilhah and Zilpah, respectively. Hagar, the concubine of Abram, slave of Sarai, and mother of Ishmael, is the only person in the Bible to give a name to God, calling him "The God who sees" (Gen. 16:13). Important converts include Rahab, the prostitute and innkeeper at Jericho (Joshua 2), and Ruth, the Moabitess, the great-great-grandmother of David. Two books bear women's names: Ruth and Esther. The text lists four prophetesses: Miriam (Exod. 15:20), Deborah (Judg. 4:4), Huldah (2 Kgs. 22:14), and Noadiah, a false prophetess (Neh. 6:14). Esther, as queen of Persia, saved her people from destruction. The text condemns Jezebel and Athaliah, foreign queens of Israel and Judah, for bringing in the worship of alien gods.

Anonymous and Silent Women

The biblical text presents an array of anonymous men and women such as servants, soldiers, and townspeople, characters whose textual usefulness comes by way of their function. For example, Saul seeks the spiritual help of the witch or medium of Endor (1 Samuel 28). The wife of Jeroboam, a character both muzzled by the narrator and anonymous, nonetheless receives tremendous biblical importance: to her comes the first prophetic word not only of the upcoming annihilation of Jeroboam's household, but also of God's intention to uproot and scatter Israel (1 Kings 14). Rizpah, Saul's concubine, figures twice in the biblical text but never speaks. In 2 Samuel 3, involvement with her as one of the royal harem shifts sovereignty over Israel from Ishbosheth to David, and in 2 Samuel 21 her courage in defying David brings about a proper burial for Saul and Jonathan. The text confirms Elijah's status as a prophet through the words of the widow of Zarephath (1 Kgs. 17:24).

For Further Reading

Meyers, Carol, ed. *Women in Scripture*. Grand Rapids: Eerdmans, 2001.

ROBIN GALLAHER BRANCH

4 Boaz Marries Ruth

True to his word and to Naomi's prediction (3:18), Boaz does not delay in assembling a quorum of elders at the city gate, where official business took place, to settle the issue of Ruth's redemption. Elimelech's closest relative changes his mind about taking the opportunity to buy Elimelech's land when he discovers that Ruth comes with the package, for at this point he real-izes that the inheritance will not simply be added to his own territorial claim but will instead revert to Ruth's sons (through him!) in order to maintain Elimelech's inheritance separately. In addition, Ruth and her children will add to the relative's expenses by becoming his dependents.

Harvesting winter vegetables. *(Phoenix Data Systems, Neal and Joel Bierling)*

As next in line, Boaz assumes the levirate responsibilities and accepts the relative's sandal to seal symbolically the legal transfer of rights. The crowd's blessing on Boaz's and Ruth's union cites Rachel and Leah, who with their hand-maids bore the ancestors of Israel's 12 tribes (= "built the house of Israel"; Genesis 29–30; 35:16-18), and also mentions Tamar, mother of Boaz's ancestor Perez, through whose line David (and eventually Jesus) would come (Genesis 38; Matthew 1).

The birth of Ruth and Boaz's son Obed completes the reversal of Naomi's fortunes and represents another link in the chain of Israel's royal, Judahite line. The Bethlehemite women indirectly glorify Ruth by asserting that her loving treatment of Naomi exceeds that of the perfect number of sons (seven, v. 15). The concluding genealogy tracks 10 generations of David's ancestors.

1 and 2 Samuel

1 and 2 Samuel take their name from the eminent prophet, not because he authored them but because he represents the first of the books' three main characters to appear. Indeed, the figure of Samuel dominates the first dozen chapters of this originally one-volume work. The Septuagint (the ancient Greek translation of the Hebrew Bible) first separated Samuel and Kings into two books each and called the resulting four volumes the "Books of the Kingdoms."

1 and 2 Samuel are considered part of the Deuteronomistic History, which extends through 1 and 2 Kings. The books of Chronicles offer another version of the history recounted in Samuel and Kings (see "The Two Histories" [229-30]).

1 Samuel

The events of 1 Samuel take place from about midway through the 11th century to 1000 B.C. The book includes the familiar accounts that describe Hannah's impassioned prayer for a son; Eli's recognition of God's nighttime call to the boy Samuel; David's slaying of Goliath; the friendship between David and Jonathan; Saul's hostility toward his rival, David; and Saul's tragic suicide on Mount Gilboa. Beginning with Samuel's anointing of Saul as king and then of David, 1 Samuel traces the early years of monarchy in Israel.

Chapters 1–12 develop Samuel's rise to national, spiritual leadership to replace the wayward priests of Eli's household. Chapters 13–31 center on Saul's rise and fall while weaving in accounts of David's military skill and its psychological effect on the king. Saul's disobedience in ch. 15 results in his ultimate inability to do any right in God's eyes, while David can do no wrong. The overarching theological theme of the book thus contrasts the results of disobedience, which leads to disaster, and obedience, which leads to blessing.

2 Samuel

2 Samuel focuses on the career of David, the "man after God's own heart" (cf. 1 Chronicles 11–29). The book takes the shepherd-champion from self-imposed exile among the Philistines to kingship, first over Judah and then over all the tribes at the beginning of the 10th century. It shows how David centralizes Israel's government and religion in the strategically located city of Jerusalem, but it also details Absalom's rebellion, which temporarily forces the king out of the capital.

During David's reign, a united kingdom of Israel pushes its boundaries to their farthest extent in the nation's history. God's covenant with the king includes the promise of a Davidic dynasty, which gives birth to prophecies concerning the Messiah and which finds its ultimate fulfillment in Jesus. 2 Samuel also shows David's sinful side, most notably in his adultery and treachery involving Bathsheba and her husband Uriah. Yet this king's humble, contrite heart and his willingness to accept God's punishment both distinguish him from his predecessor, Saul, and preserve his favored status in God's eyes.

The final chapters include two of David's psalms. Chapter 24 recounts David's purchase of land that will later become the site for Solomon's temple.

Authorship

While the author-editor of the books remains anonymous, he may have incorporated some of Samuel's own writings (1 Sam. 10:25) along with material from other prophetic sources (2 Sam. 1:18; 1 Chr. 29:29), as well as the poems David quotes in 2 Sam. 1:19-27; 22:2-51; 23:2-7. 1 Samuel 27:6 suggests that the work was composed after the monarchy had divided (after 900). Although some scholars argue for a late, 6th-century date, a consensus suggests two or more stages of editing, with completion likely in King Josiah's day (late 7th century). Further additions may have come during the Babylonian exile.

Text

Difficulties exist in establishing the original Hebrew text of certain passages. Differences between the Hebrew (Masoretic) text and the Septuagint contribute to the problem, and the Greek sometimes agrees with the text of a much older (and therefore presumably more original) Hebrew manuscript of portions of 1 Samuel found among the Dead Sea Scrolls (1000 years earlier than the Masoretic Text). Nevertheless, many of the differences are minor. Despite the textual questions, the message of 1 and 2 Samuel — God's activity in accomplishing the ultimate purposes of his kingdom, despite Israel's desire for a monarchy "like the nations" — remains clear and intact.

1 Samuel

1 Hannah Prays for a Son

In her childlessness, Hannah keeps company with women who figure prominently for eventually bearing sons who fulfill important roles in Israel's covenantal history. Sarah, Rebekah, and Rachel — the mothers of Isaac, Jacob, and Joseph — all wanted God to reverse their barrenness to remove the social stigma attached to childless wives. Like Sarah, who became the object of Hagar's contempt (Gen. 16:5), Hannah must endure the taunts of her husband's other wife, Peninnah, who, though apparently less loved than Hannah, nevertheless has achieved respectability through bearing children (cf. Leah, Gen. 29:30-35). But Hannah's willingness to commit her son to lifelong service of God in a location that affords her only annual contact with him shows that her desire for a son is far greater.

Hannah utters her petition and vow silently at God's tent shrine in Shiloh, unaccompanied by her husband Elkanah but within earshot of the high priest Eli. Because Israelite worshippers normally prayed out loud, and because Eli sees Hannah's lips moving but hears no sound, he mistakes her prayerful abandon for drunken stupor. In explaining her purpose to Eli, however, Hannah does not reveal the substance of her petition, and only she knows about her promise.

God honors Hannah's prayer for a son; and, after nursing him for three years, she honors her vow to dedicate the boy, Samuel, to God's service by leaving him in Eli's care at the Shiloh sanctuary. Elkanah demonstrates both his love for Hannah and his own personal piety by supporting his wife in her resolve to fulfill the vow (v. 23). From the time he first learns of Hannah's pledge, Elkanah recognizes that God's claim on Samuel is greater than his own.

2:1-10 Hannah's Song of Praise

Before leaving for home without her young son, Hannah acknowledges God's goodness to her. Behind Hannah's poetic expression lies her struggle with Peninnah (esp. v. 5; on the blessing of "seven" children, cf. Ruth 4:15), yet Hannah's thoughts extend far beyond her own circumstances to praise God for his holiness and stability (v. 2), knowledge (v. 3), power (vv. 9-10), and his reversal of the fortunes of the weak and the poor (vv. 4, 7-8). The reference to "his king" in v. 10 probably reflects a later editorial hand.

2:11-36 The Fate of Eli's House

The opening verses set the ministerial activities of "the boy" Samuel in stark contrast to Eli's corrupt and spiritually ignorant "sons of Belial" (= "worthless men"). Hophni and Phinehas make a mockery of the priesthood and the sacrificial system by disregarding the laws that regulate their right to a share of the offerings made to God (Num. 18:8-20; Deut. 18:1-5) and by using their position and power to satisfy their own selfish desires (esp. vv. 16, 22). Their ritual transgressions go far beyond those of Aaron's sons, and God will punish them in the same way (cf. Lev. 10:1-2).

Hannah and Elkanah remain involved in the life of their son Samuel (vv. 18-21), who performs his ministerial duties properly (v. 26). This account contrasts their influence on Samuel and the lack of authority Eli wielded over his sons. Verse 25 attributes Hophni's and Phinehas's ignoring their father's reproach to God's determination to do away with them for their continued sin (cf. God's hardening of Pharaoh's heart; Exod. 4:21; 7:3).

An unnamed prophet ("man of God," v. 27) reveals to Eli that God will hold him responsible for the midsirected priesthood of his sons. In foretelling the massacre at Nob (ch. 22), v. 31 harks back to the theme of the divine reversal of people's fortunes displayed in Hannah's song. While v. 35 appears to refer to Samuel as the "faithful priest" whose "house" God will establish to replace Eli's line, it is actually the high priest Zadok who embodies the fulfillment of this prophecy during David's reign (2 Sam. 8:17). "My anointed" (v. 35) refers to the Davidic line of kings.

3 Samuel Becomes God's Prophet

At this time in Israel's history God rarely communicated directly with his people, so neither Samuel nor Eli immediately understands when God summons Samuel's attention. The young boy's call to prophetic office occurs just before dawn while he dutifully attends his watch over the sanctuary lamp, which will soon need refilling after burning all night (Lev. 24:1-4). God informs Samuel of his plans for Eli's uncontrolled priestly house, and when the boy relays God's words the aged priest resigns himself to God's promised judgment (v. 18; cf. 1:23). Remarkably, Eli neither attempts to change God's mind by forcing change on his sons nor apologizes for his own failure. Though the priestly power remains for a time with Eli and his sons, Samuel's reputation as a prophet of the Lord spreads throughout Canaan. Samuel's prophecies reach fulfillment because of God's presence with him (v. 19).

4 The Philistines Capture the Ark

The powerful Philistines, who controlled Canaan's southern coast and monopolized the iron industry, engage the Israelites in battle in the territory of Ephraim (cf. Judges 1). The Philistines' decided victory puzzles the Israelite leadership and prompts them to send for the ark of the covenant, God's symbolic throne normally housed in the tabernacle, for they believe God's presence in their camp will ensure victory in a coming confrontation with the Philistines (cf. the ark's presence at the battle of Jericho; Joshua 6).

That Eli's evil sons accompany the ark on the 20-mile journey from Shiloh to the Israelites' war camp is an omen of disaster. Not only do the Philistines again emerge victorious, they also capture the ark. The accompanying deaths of Hophni and Phinehas fulfill God's foretelling in 2:34, and Eli's fatal fall from Shiloh's city gate upon hearing of the ark's capture completes the fulfillment of God's judgment on this family. Verse 18 places Eli in the line of judges who ruled Israel.

Phinehas's widow becomes an indirect casualty of the curse on Eli's house, for she dies in childbirth brought on by the devastating news about her family and the ark. Her parting words lay greater emphasis on her grief over the removal of God's presence from Israel than on the death of her husband, and she does not even find comfort in the birth of her son, whom she names to commemorate the disastrous day (Ichabod, "Where is the glory?"). Her recognition of God's "departure" contrasts with the Israelites' assumption that God would fight for his people regardless of their faithlessness.

5 God Among the Philistines

Lest the the Philistines' capture of the ark be seen as a sign of God's weakened power, ch. 5 reveals the opposite. The Philistines' initial fears about the might of Israel's God are realized in the form of sickness and death similar to the plagues God inflicted on the Egyptians (cf. the golden mice in 6:4, which suggest bubonic plague). Their powerless idol, Dagon, whom they undoubtedly credited for their victory over the Israelites, cannot even stand in God's presence (vv. 3-4). Offering the ark in worship at Dagon's feet results first in the statue's falling prostrate before God's throne and then in the "mutilation" of Dagon in a manner similar to the fate of a captured king (cf. Judg. 1:6-7). Thus the Philistines' apparent victory in capturing the ark turns into a curse and creates in them great fear and dread.

6:1–7:2 The Ark Returns to Israel

The Philistines take seven months to circulate the ark between their five cities before they decide to send it back to the Israelites. Still wondering whether the disasters outlined in ch. 5 represent coincidences or judgments by Israel's God, the Philistines devise a plan to determine the answer. Their religion allows them to recognize gods other than their own, so their leaders advise offering before the ark golden representations of the plagues the Philistines have suffered since the ark's arrival among them. The offering both acknowledges to God the Philistines' guilt in dishonoring him and pays him valuable tribute. So the Philistines send God away with riches in an attempt to escape further punishment (cf. Exod. 12:35-36).

The Philistines hoist the ark onto a cart hitched to two cows that have never been yoked. The direction the cows take while listening to the cries of their new calves will resolve the Philistines' question concerning the cause of their affliction. God's overruling the cows' natural instinct to return to their young by instead returning his throne to the Israelites would prove his hand in the recent catastrophes. The removal of the golden objects that represent the Philistines' suffering would

end the plagues through a form of sympathetic magic.

The ark's unguided arrival in Israel's Levitical town of Beth-shemesh confirms for the Philistines that indeed God had caused the disastrous events of the previous seven months. The people of Beth-shemesh welcome the ark's return and sacrifice to God the cows that brought it. But some curious Beth-shemites peek into the sacred covenant box and pay with their lives. God will tolerate neither the paganism of the Philistines nor the covenantal transgressions of his own chosen people. Fearing further divine judgment, the Beth-shemites pass the ark off to a sister town, Kiriath-jearim, a few miles north. The ark remains in Kiriath-jearim and never returns to Shiloh.

7:3-17 Samuel's Leadership Effects National Change

Eli's death left a 20-year leadership vacuum in Israel and cleared the way for Samuel's emergence as the nation's new spiritual shepherd and her last judge (vv. 6, 15-17). Samuel does not hesitate to call the Israelites to repentance and fidelity to God alone, and the people respond by deserting their adopted foreign gods on the promise of deliverance from Philistine oppression. Samuel's prophetic words receive fulfillment in the Philistines' military challenge of Israel at Mizpah, when God again acts on his people's behalf, even without the ark. Samuel sets the Israelites' current conquest at Mizpah over against their past defeat by naming a commemorative victory monument after the site of their previous slaughter by the Philistines (Ebenezer, "stone of help"). Israel benefits from God's covenantal faithfulness throughout Samuel's life (which includes most of Saul's reign), presumably because he continues to keep them on the path of obedience to God. Israel regains possession of its border towns between the two inland Philistine cities of Ekron and Gath, and Samuel exercises regular, judicial authority on his annual circuit of Israel's four sanctuary towns, which include Samuel's ancestral home of Ramah.

Judges and Kings of Israel and Judah

Leadership in Israel was exercised by different people in different offices performing different functions. The major leadership positions were those of prophet, priest, king, and judge. Prophets were mouthpieces for God, speaking directly for him about conditions in the present and in the future. Priests were spiritual intermediaries between God and the people, offering sacrifices on their behalf and providing spiritual leadership and direction.

Moses was the first judge recorded in the Scriptures (Exodus 18). He helped to resolve all the people's disputes, providing judicial opinions based on God's laws, but this was an inefficient model, as his father-in-law Jethro pointed out to him. He urged Moses to set up representative judges who would handle most cases. Moses instructed them in God's laws, and he decided the most difficult cases himself.

Later, judges were primarily military-style leaders raised up on an "as-needed" basis during the centuries immediately following Israel's entry into the land of Canaan under Joshua. Most did not normally hold court, listen to complaints, or make legal decisions in the manner of Moses or modern-day jurists. The typical judge was primarily a leader who delivered the nation from foreign threats or oppression. God raised up successive judges in response to the people's distressed cries for help. Judges 2:16 provides a key

to understanding who they were: "And the Lord raised up judges, who delivered them from the hand of those who plundered them." Deborah was a significant exception to this, because, in addition to the military role she played (Judges 4), she did render judicial verdicts under the "palm of Deborah" (Judg. 4:4-5). Samuel was the last of the judges, and he also performed both roles (1 Samuel 7).

Many scholars have seen a distinction in the roles or offices of judge. The "major" judges are seen as charismatic, military leaders, whose primary function was to deliver Israel (Othniel, Ehud, Shamgar, Deborah, Gideon, Jephthah, Samson), and the "minor" judges (Tola, Jair, Ibzan, Elon, Abdon) are seen mainly as juridical leaders, whose major function was to dispense justice.

The case is not as clear as many would have it, however. The Scriptures themselves do not mention such a distinction. Also, the account of Jephthah occurs in the midst of those of the so-called "minor" judges, carrying many features of these short reports, and yet he is clearly a "major" judge by virtue of his activity. Also, both Othniel (Judg. 3:9-10) and Tola (10:1-2) not only "judged" but also "delivered" Israel, as did Deborah and Samuel. The terms "major" and "minor" are useful primarily in describing the length and style of the narratives that inform us about each judge, not in distinguishing between functions they performed.

Israel's kings came after the judges. God had promised the patriarchs that kings would be part of their heritage (Gen. 17:6, 16; 35:11; 49:10), but the first kings did not appear until centuries later. They were to be models of spiritual devotion as they led the nation. Gideon's son Abimelech set himself up as "king" by killing 70 of his brothers in an abortive grab for power (Judges 9), but the first recognized king in Israel was Saul. He disqualified himself by his actions (1 Sam. 13:13-14; 15:26-29), leading to the anointing of David. God promised David that a descendant of his would always remain on the throne (2 Samuel 7).

The model for royal leadership is found in Deut. 17:14-20. Here God instructed Israel to appoint as king someone whom he would choose, who was an Israelite (not a foreigner). The king was not to accumulate horses (i.e., military power) for himself, wealth, or many wives, in order that his heart should be properly oriented to God rather than to these things. The key to success for the king was that he should write for himself a copy of the Law and obey it himself. In this way, the king would model for the people how to live.

When Israel did ask for a king, the great irony is that it was for a king to "judge" them (1 Sam. 8:5). In other words, they were asking for a king to do for them what the judges did: deliver them militarily. This is confirmed by their words later, when they repeated their request for a king "to judge us and to go out before us and fight our battles" (1 Sam. 8:20). Of course, the people had already known military deliverance under the judges. But the judges were raised up by God to fight on an as-needed basis, while in asking for a king the people were requesting a standing army ("like the nations") and a large bureaucracy, as Samuel warned them (1 Sam. 8:11-18). This would prove to be a heavy burden and tempt the people to trust in the king, rather than in God. Up to this point, God's people had been regularly delivered by the leaders whom he chose, whether they were the judges or individuals such as Moses or Joshua. Now, however, they desired to look to the kings for their deliverance.

The kings certainly were to have military responsibilities, as seen, for example, in the successes of such good kings as David (e.g., 1 Sam. 18:14; 30:6; 2 Sam. 5:19, 25; 8:6, 14) and Hezekiah (2 Kgs. 18:7-8), but their military successes ultimately came from the hand of God. When the Israelites asked for a military-style king, they were "deposing" God as their king and warrior. The *institution* of kingship was something that God certainly favored, in the right time, but the *type* of king that Israel asked for — one that flew directly in the face of the instructions given in Deuteronomy — made their request wrong and constituted a rejection of God himself (1 Sam. 8:7).

The united kingdom established under Saul was relatively short-lived: it lasted only 120 years and then was divided into two because of Solomon's disobedience (1 Kings 11–14). The northern kingdom, Israel, had 19 kings, all of whom were wicked, and God eventually allowed this kingdom to perish (2 Kings 17). The southern kingdom, Judah, lasted longer, was more stable politically, and consisted entirely of descendants of David. It had 20 kings, 12 of whom were wicked, eight of whom were good.

Judah survived many political ups and downs, and even exile, because of God's promises to David, typified by this one: "Nevertheless, for the sake of his servant David, the Lord was not willing to destroy Judah. He had promised to maintain a lamp for David and his descendants forever" (2 Kgs. 8:19 NIV). After the exile, there were no more kings sitting on a political throne in Jerusalem, but the line of David was still alive, in the person of Zerubbabel (Ezra 3:2; Matt. 1:12). The hope of the restoration of the Davidic house is a theme found in the Old Testament prophetic books as well (e.g., Amos 9:11-15; Isa. 11:1), and it is brought to fruition with the coming of the ultimate Davidic king, "Jesus Christ, the son of David, the son of Abraham" (Matt. 1:1). The royal promises first given to the patriarchs were now completed.

DAVID M. HOWARD, JR.

8 The People Demand a King

The text now skips to the latter years of Samuel's life. Samuel's sons have perverted the judicial system as Eli's sons did the priesthood, and the people use the current corruption in Beer-sheba as an excuse to demand a human king. Behind their demand lay the continued Philistine threat, and their rejection of God's kingship demonstrates an unwarranted lack of faith in God's ability to prosper or even sustain them as a nation.

God sees his people's rejection for what it is, but he resigns himself to giving them what they think they want. Before appointing a king, however, God through Samuel gives Israel a chance to change its national mind-set by spelling out the consequences of a centralized government for the individual Israelite: military draft, forced labor, taxation, and tyranny (all of which conse-quences came about under Solomon). In effect, the Israelites' own human king will become their oppressor.

Despite the warning, the people insist on a king, and now they express the real reason behind their demand: they want to "be like all the nations." The Israelites' idea of a human king as judge and military leader contrasts sharply with the ideal God emphasizes in Deut. 17:14-20, yet he decides to grant their wish. The people still recognize God's authority enough to demand that his prophet Samuel appoint a king over them rather than acting completely independently of God's direction.

9:1–10:16 Samuel Anoints Saul Privately

The account of Saul's appointment as Israel's first king demonstrates that God remains in control of his people's affairs and that, in answering their demands, he does things his way. God chooses as king a man who will embody his people's ideal for a leader, yet whose ancestry and personality make him a surprising choice. Saul appears ignorant of his countrymen's demand for a king and of Samuel's identity (9:18-19). When the prophet ("seer"; 9:11) hints at Saul's political future, Saul reacts with surprise by acknowledging his humble position not only in relation to the Israelite nation but even within his own tribe (9:20-21).

Saul's seemingly childlike innocence highlights the dramatic change that comes over him when Samuel's prediction of Saul's prophetic, spirit-filled experience comes true in the king-designate's hometown of Gibeah (10:5-11). Saul's fellow townspeople notice the surprising transformation and find it so hard to believe that they crack sarcastic jokes about him (10:11-12).

All the while, God is working behind the scenes. He directs events to ensure that Saul and Samuel will meet. Samuel's typical Near Eastern hospitality includes boarding Saul in his spare room — the flat roof of his house (9:25-26). Through Samuel, God gradually reveals his plans for Saul's future. Finally, God confirms the legitimacy of Samuel's private anointing of Saul as ruler over "his [God's] inheritance" (10:1) by bringing to pass Samuel's predictions concerning Saul's future (10:9). The account reveals that Samuel's leadership includes priestly activities, which he performs at "the high place," one of the open-air shrines that preceded the temple (9:12; 10:13).

Saul's private anointing complete and confirmed, his public anointing remains, and this will signal the formal beginning of his duties in delivering Israel from Philistine oppression and in governing God's people (9:16-17; cf. David's public and private anointings, 16:1-13; 2 Sam. 2:4). For now, Saul keeps his political future to himself (10:16).

10:17-27 Saul's Public Appointment as King

Samuel indicts the Israelites for rejecting God's direct rule and announces the imminent fulfillment of their demand for a human king. Lots are cast, and Saul is publicly appointed ruler over Israel. Saul's physical stature, commonly viewed as a qualification for leadership, outweighs his timidity, evident by his hiding among the military baggage to avoid detection. By choosing Saul, God appears to be mocking his people for their foolishness in choosing human frailty and foibles over divine power and faithfulness. Yet God has already begun to engender the Israelites' sincere and active loyalty to Saul (vv. 24, 26). Samuel's briefing in v. 25 initiates the Israelites into their contractual relationship with the man who will rule them as king.

11 Saul's First Military Test

The first test of Saul's leadership comes in an Ammonite military threat against Jabesh-gilead in the Transjordanian territory of Manasseh. Deflated from fear, the Jabesh-gileadites offer to break their covenant with God by making a treaty with the Ammonites. But the Ammonites' terms involve mutilation, and their potential victims are reluctant to comply. Foolishly the overconfident Ammonites allow passage through their lines to the besieged city's messengers, who cross the Jordan to seek military backup from their kin.

The messengers find their Saul doing manual labor, but God's spirit again transforms the timid, gentle giant, this time into a fiery general. Saul summons a pan-Israel fighting force by distributing the cut-up bodies of two oxen (cf. Judges 19). On the surprisingly large number of troops that Saul musters, cf. Exod. 12:37–13:16.

Saul and his men realize success in delivering the Jabesh-gileadites, in part because the latter lead the Ammonites to believe they are about to surrender (v. 10). The victory confirms in the Israelites' minds Saul's fitness to serve as king, and Saul justifies his generosity toward those who doubted him earlier by attributing the military accomplishment to God. The Jabesh-gileadites later demonstrate their undying gratitude by honoring Saul's dead body (31:11-13).

Gilgal, site of Israel's first camp after crossing into the promised land and a town on Samuel's annual judicial circuit, provides the setting for Saul's public inauguration. Yet the entire episode portrays Saul more as a judge than a king.

12 Samuel's Final Address

Samuel's stern speech marks his final public appearance in the narrative, which will afterward focus on Saul's activities as king. Samuel speaks against kingship, not against Saul, and the foundation for his criticism of the Israelites' demand for a monarch rests in their rejection of God as their king (v. 12).

Samuel first establishes his own upright behavior with respect to his leadership of Israel (vv. 3-5; contrast 8:11-18). He then emphasizes God's past provision of leaders to deliver Israel from oppression: Jerubbaal (= Gideon), Barak, Jephthah, and Samson.

Israel's disobedience in serving the Canaanite fertility gods (v. 10) is the reason God has sold them into oppression by foreigners. Samuel warns that having a king will not save them from future subjection if they continue their sinful, idolatrous ways. The Israelites may have a monarch, but God retains absolute control over their destiny.

Samuel's message receives dramatic confirmation through an unseasonable thunderstorm, which he calls on God to produce as a sign of the validity of his prophetic words (cf. v. 17). The downpour convinces the Israelites to repent of their request for a human king, but their change of heart will not reverse the political course on which they have already embarked. Samuel pledges his continued intercession for the Israelites and reassures them of God's abiding faithfulness, but he ends by repeating the devastating consequences of faithlessness (vv. 22-25). Verse 20 echoes the encouragement to heartfelt service of God prevalent throughout Deuteronomy (e.g., Deut. 10:12).

13:1-14 Saul Oversteps his Bounds

Chapter 13 pictures a permanently changed Saul. Instead of pursuing pastoral chores, he now spends his time battling the Philistines with the help of his officer-son, Jonathan. After an initial defeat, the Philistines muster a substantial and well-equipped fighting force ("thousand" may indicate a military unit, rather than a number), and the Israelites begin to wilt. Behind the scenes, Samuel still appears to aid God's direct-

Gibeah, Saul's hometown and the headquarters of his monarchy. *(Richard Cleave, Pictorial Archive)*

ing of Saul's military engagements. But Samuel's tardiness in bringing God's counsel regarding Saul's current efforts against the Philistines prompts the desperate king to substitute for the prophet by offering sacrifices in an attempt to bolster the courage of his dwindling forces, who flee to hiding places. Saul's presumptuous ritual act betrays a disregard for Samuel's divinely-bestowed authority over him and dooms any dynastic dreams Saul might have entertained. David will be the "man after [God's] own heart" alluded to in v. 14 (cf. Acts 13:22).

These events take place in the hill country of Benjamin presumably toward the beginning of Saul's kingship. Control of Gibeah and the strategic Michmash pass meant control of the entire Aijalon Valley to the west via the trade routes. The Hebrew text of verse 1 is incomplete regarding Saul's age and the years he reigned as king.

13:15–14:52 Jonathan's Victory at Michmash

Saul neither repents nor retreats for overstepping the bounds of his authority, and he continues to prepare for war with the Philistines.

The Philistines' monopoly on iron-working supplies them with superior weaponry and puts the Israelites at a military disadvantage (cf. Judg. 1:19), but Saul unites his fighting contingent with Jonathan's at Gibeah to generate strength in numbers. Unbeknownst to Saul, Jonathan and his armor-bearer sneak out of camp to confront the Philistines at the Michmash pass. Jonathan anticipates victory over their "uncircumcised" enemies (14:6). His great faith in God despite being outnumbered 10 to 1 (14:14) and the test he applies to discern God's will (14:8-13) recall Gideon's exploits against the Midianites and Amalekites (Judg. 6:36–7:23).

Puzzled by the confusion and havoc his watchmen observe in the Philistine camp, Saul discovers Jonathan's absence and summons Ahijah to help discern the meaning of the situation by using the priestly "ephod" that contained the Urim and Thummim for casting lots (following the Greek text; cf. 14:3). But Saul stops Ahijah short and sends his troops in pursuit of the fleeing Philistines.

The troops eagerly eat the meat of their spoils without draining the blood, thus violating the commandment in Lev. 17:10-14. Yet it is Jonathan's unwitting sin of eating before evening that transgresses the oath under which Saul had earlier in the day put his troops and prevents God's communication with Saul when the king finally gets around to discerning the Lord's will (14:24, 27, 37-38). The casting of lots determines Jonathan as the sinner, and the Israelites must intervene to save their human deliverer-of-the-day from his own father's determination to put him to death for violating the oath, albeit involuntarily. The troops' hailing of Jonathan's heroism over his father's military accomplishments and Saul's resolve to kill his son foreshadow the tense relationship that will develop between Saul and David. The parallel that develops between Saul's heir, Jonathan, and Jonathan's replacement, David, underscores God's denial of dynastic succession for Saul as punishment for his disobedience in 13:8-14 (cf. 18:6-9; 19:1).

Chapter 14 ends by summing up Saul's military exploits over Israel's neighbors in Transjordan (Moab, Ammon, and Edom) as well as the Philistines in Canaan and the desert-dwelling Amalekites. A brief genealogy names the members of Saul's nuclear family, including his son Ishvi (short for Ishbosheth), whom Saul's army captain, Abner, later sets up as king to rival David (2 Sam. 2:8-10); and Saul's daughter Michal, whom he gives in marriage to David (18:20-29).

15 God Rejects Saul as King

By disregarding the ban (cf. Joshua 6) applied to the battle with the menacing Amalekites (v. 3), Saul loses God's confirmation as Israel's king. God announces his rejection of Saul to Samuel, who grieves over the reversal of Saul's fortunes and whose duty it becomes to confront Saul with the news. Saul protests his own compliance with God's command regarding the ban (vv. 13, 20) and deflects responsibility for sparing the best of the spoils on his troops, to whom he attributes righteous motives for doing so (vv. 15, 21). Only after Samuel challenges Saul with God's preference of obedience over sacrifice does Saul confess his sin, brought on by his weakness under pressure from "the people" (v. 24).

But Saul's admission offers too little too late, and his reluctance to repent from willful disobedience to God's clear command stands in sharp contrast to Jonathan's ready acceptance of responsibility for unknowingly violating an unreasonable oath imposed in his absence by his father (14:24-30, 43). With divine approval withdrawn, Saul seeks honor from his fellow humans (v. 30). Samuel symbolically completes the ban by "hewing to pieces" the spared Amalekite king Agag before the prophet and the alienated king return to their respective homes, never to meet again in public.

16:1-13 Samuel Anoints David

With Saul still functioning as king, God selects a successor to please not the people but himself. The text reveals a number of parallels between Saul and David: both lack social power; both are found tending their fathers' animals; both appear handsome; both are initially anointed in private; both are empowered by the spirit of the Lord following their anointing (cf. 9:1–10:16; Judg. 3:10). But God's choice of David ignores both his outward advantages and disadvantages and instead considers the state of David's heart, which parallels God's own (v. 7; cf. 13:14; Deut. 10:12-16). This initial ritual of setting David apart signals the beginning of his divine preparation for national leadership. Once again, a youngest son is elevated to a divinely-favored position (cf. Abel, Jacob, and Joseph).

16:14-23 David Enters Saul's Court

When the spirit of the Lord empowers David, that same spirit departs from Saul, and God causes an evil, terrorizing spirit to take its place. The switch occasions the beginning of a personal relationship between Saul and David in which David endears himself to Saul through his calming music, played on the harp. Verse 18 also extols David's valor as a warrior, undoubtedly as part of Israelite efforts against the Philistines (ch. 17), and foreshadows his future military successes, which far exceed Saul's own and which unintentionally undermine his relationship with the current king (18:7).

17 David Defeats Goliath

The well-known account of David's confrontation with Goliath pictures David as the classic embodiment of faith in God and zeal for

Relief from the main temple of Ramses III at Thebes showing a captured Philistine warrior. *(Erich Lessing / Art Resource, NY)*

his honor. David's past exercise of superior strength in defending his father's sheep (vv. 34-36) undergirds his confidence that God will empower him to defend the name of "the living God" by doing to Goliath what the insulting giant vows to do to him (vv. 44 and 46). David's faith contrasts sharply with the nation's general forgetfulness of God's mighty acts on their behalf, and his faithfulness prompts God to trust him for the task.

Sent by his father to deliver lunch to his three eldest brothers, the youthful David publicly expresses his disgust at Goliath's taunts and so earns the rebuke of his siblings. Against all human odds and to the dismay of the trembling Israelite king and army, the comparatively unarmed David approaches the metal-clad giant and announces his impending doom. David's opening proclamation of faith underscores that his seemingly impossible victory belongs to God.

Saul's query regarding David's family heritage seems odd here in light of 16:18-19 and in view of David's already established role as Saul's personal musician and armor-bearer. Suggested solutions consider the possible use of different sources for chapters 16 and 17 and the likelihood that Saul wanted to confirm his intended son-in-law's support.

18 David's Success Breeds Saul's Jealousy

Jonathan fosters with David a friendship so deep that he, in effect, voluntarily hands over to David his place as crown prince in the symbolic act of giving David his robe, armor, and weapons. Recent attempts to see David's and Jonathan's intimate friendship as a homosexual relationship lack an accurate cultural understanding of male-to-male relationships in the ancient or modern Near East.

David's military success, with the accompanying acclaim of the people, breeds the opposite reaction in Saul, and the divinely rejected king becomes uncontrollably jealous. Saul's attempts to spear David fail completely, and the king's further plots to ensure David's death in battle against the Philistines only further strengthen David's military position and public popularity. Saul even offers his daughters in marriage to David as a means to ensure David's eventual death in military service against the Philistines. Not only does David realize twice the success required by Saul to win Michal's hand, he also enjoys Michal's love (vv. 25-28). Added to Jonathan's affection for David, Michal's love for him further fuels Saul's intensifying jealousy, and Saul finally recognizes God's presence with his eventual replacement (v. 28).

That Saul can only fear David for his success (esp. vv. 8-9), rather than embrace him for it as the people and Saul's family do, shows the king's attempt to deny God's rejection of him (13:13-14; 15:26-29). Saul's continued, desperate grasping for power cannot thwart God's continued tearing of the kingdom from him — a certain eventuality symbolized in Saul's own tearing of Samuel's robe (15:27).

19–20 David and Jonathan Part

Both Jonathan and Michal show their devotion to David in acts that protect him from their murder-bent father. Jonathan twice tries to reason with the king. His initial success in convincing Saul not only of David's innocence but also of his faithful service turns sour when Saul's black mood returns and causes him to make another attempt on David's life (19:1-10). Using the household idol as David's bedridden double, Michal helps her husband escape through a window. David finds temporary refuge in Ramah in the company of Samuel and his school of prophets, whose infectious prophesying foils the mission of three sets of Saul's henchmen before the pursuing king himself falls into ecstatic frenzy (19:18-24; cf. 10:11).

David secretly seeks from Jonathan a reason for Saul's rage (20:1). The friends agree on a means to confirm Saul's posture toward David: Saul's reaction to David's absence from the dinner table for the feast day that marked the beginning of the new month (20:5) would reveal the king's true intentions. Jonathan also devises an archery signal to communicate the answer to David (20:18-22), and the two make a solemn covenant that honors their binding friendship by keeping both their "houses" from using political power and military might against each other (20:16-17; cf. 18:3).

Saul rejects Jonathan's explanation for

David's empty seat and immediately suspects his son of foolishly forsaking him for the fugitive (20:27-30). In his rage, Saul turns his spear on his own son. Jonathan communicates the bad news to David by the previously agreed-upon sign, and the fast friends grieve their good-byes (20:35-42). Ironically, Saul's desperate efforts to strengthen royal power and preserve public popularity secure only increasing alienation from his closest family members, his most faithful supporter, the prophet who first anointed him, and ultimately God himself (esp. 22:6-19).

21:1–22:5 David on the Run

David loses no time in fleeing from Saul. The defenseless fugitive heads for Nob, probable successor to Shiloh as the site of Israel's central sanctuary. Ahimelech, chief priest at Nob, accepts David's story about Saul's having hastily sent him and his companions on a secret mission (21:2, 8). In good faith, Ahimelech supplies the needy band with food from the sanctuary normally only allowed to the priests (Lev. 24:5-9), assuming that David and his men have kept themselves ritually pure for holy war by abstaining from sexual intercourse. Ahimelech also gives David a weapon that the renowned warrior has used before — the sword of Goliath (17:51). But Doeg, a servant of Saul, overhears and will later make Ahimelech pay for his unintended treason against the king (21:7; cf. 22:18-19).

The southern coast of Canaan, controlled by the Philistines in the 12th–13th centuries B.C. *(Richard Cleave, Pictorial Archive)*

David hastens west out of Israelite territory in hopes of avoiding recognition among the Philistines of Gath. But David's high military profile has gained him the reputation of "king of the land" (21:11), and only his feigned insanity leads the local king, Achish, to discount the apparent madman's potential threat (cf. the Hebrew title of Psalm 34).

Heading east once again, David enters his native Judahite territory. There he gathers his father's household and a sizeable group of sympathizers before proceeding across the Jordan into Moab (home of his ancestress, Ruth; Ruth 4:13-17; Matt. 1:5-6) to deposit his parents in relative safety beyond Saul's reach. At the prophet Gad's prompting, David returns to Canaan, where the obsessed Saul continues his relentless pursuit.

22:6-23 Saul's "Ban" against Nob

Saul's personal insecurity turns into full-blown paranoia, and his fears of isolation become self-fulfilling prophecies as he becomes increasingly blind to reality. The king imagines David lying in ambush and suspects his servants and son of conspiracy (vv. 8, 13). Doeg resurfaces by tattling on the priest Ahimelech (21:7; cf. the heading of Psalm 52), whose protestations of innocence fail to save him or his fellow priests from the sword. In contrast to Saul's disobeying God's earlier command to destroy the Amalekites totally (15:3, 24), the king here orders his own "ban" against the priests and inhabitants of Nob and thereby fulfills the prophecy against Eli's house foretold in 2:27-36. By carrying out the slaughter of priests through Doeg, Saul has now cut himself off from God's counsel and has provided David with a personal line of communication to God in the form of Ahimelech's son Abiathar, the sole surviving escapee, who seeks refuge with the guilt-ridden David.

23 David Keeps Moving

Saul's attack on Nob, a city that he is duty-bound to protect, contrasts with David's assuming the royal task of delivering the Keilahites from the Philistines. But David does not take this initiative without first seeking God's advice, presumably through Abiathar and the ephod (vv. 9-12). Though the Keilahites surely felt grateful to David, their fear of Saul's wrath would have sidelined their gratitude when Saul's army arrived at the city to capture their deliverer (v. 12). Kept on the move, David and his growing band of mercenaries (v. 13; cf. 22:2) seek safe haven in the southern wilderness of Judah, where Jonathan has no trouble finding his fugitive friend, in contrast to the futile efforts of his father. Jonathan's encouragement reveals his conviction that David's destiny consists in succeeding Saul as king. That Saul also shares this knowledge makes his pursuit of God's chosen heir to the throne all the more desperate and vain (v. 17).

Perhaps to protect their scarce sources of food and water in the wilderness, the Ziphites pledge to hand over David and his 600-strong militia to Saul, who sits in state at Gibeah. But again God thwarts Saul's efforts to capture his prey, this time by diverting the king's military attention to a timely Philistine raid (vv. 26-27).

24 David Spares Saul's Life

The mountainous region of En-gedi, which rises steeply from the western shores of the Dead Sea at its north-south midpoint, provided ample hiding space for David and his band. Seemingly by coincidence, Saul stops in the exact cave where his intended targets have holed up (v. 3). Resisting the urging of his men to take revenge on the king, David discreetly cuts off a corner of the unsuspecting Saul's robe as the king relieves himself in the darkness (v. 4). Even this minor act against "God's anointed" disturbs David's conscience, however, and he feels compelled to reveal himself to Saul after the king's departure from the cave puts some distance between them (vv. 5-8).

David's words and actions acknowledge Saul's authority. He calls Saul "my lord," "the king," "the Lord's anointed," and "my father," and falls facedown on the ground in total submission (vv. 8-11). By revealing his exact whereabouts, David also makes himself completely vulnerable to potential attack by Saul's army. But David also holds up the severed corner of the robe as evidence of his righteous intentions toward Saul (v. 11), and, for the moment, David's words convince the king both of David's innocence and of his morally superior right to the throne (vv. 17-20). Deeply moved, Saul abandons his current pursuit of David, whom he even calls "my son" (v. 16), but not before exacting a pledge to preserve the lives of Saul's descendants (vv. 21-22), who will carry on the family name.

25 Abigail Intervenes

The tension between David and Saul at least temporarily relieved, the text makes a surprisingly brief mention of Samuel's death (v. 1) and quickly moves on to picture David's continued independence from Saul even in the absence of support from the high-profile prophet. David's men have voluntarily guarded the shepherds and flocks of the wealthy Calebite Nabal, the apt meaning of whose name ("fool") soon becomes evident. Since the sheep-shearing season has arrived, Nabal's stocks are up, and David requests from Nabal payment in goods (food) for protective services rendered. Though Nabal spurns David's request, the "worthless man['s]" (vv. 17, 25) wife Abigail recognizes David's destiny (v. 28) and secretly sends a generous repast. By dismissing Nabal as an insignificant fool and assuming the blame for the ingrate's stingy behavior, Abigail affords David opportunity to save face for failing to punish her husband by generously bestowing on her his forgiveness of Nabal's house (v. 35). Abigail's gift, humility, and words of blessing defuse David's hostile intentions so completely that he eagerly marries Abigail after God himself takes vengeance on Nabal by punishing him with untimely death (v. 39).

Abigail's intelligent intervention prevents David from initiating a blood feud with his fellow countrymen (vv. 26, 31) and so ruling out important alliances with Judahite clans that could provide David with military and political support. Instead, by taking Abigail and Ahinoam in marriage, David seals such alliances with his tribesmen — alliances made all the more essential by Saul's dissolving the marriage between David and the royal daughter Michal, presumably to remove any trace of

his rival's rightful inheritance of Saul's throne (v. 44).

26 David Spares Saul Again

For a second time, the Ziphites betray David's whereabouts to Saul, whose renewed jealousy sparks another hunt for the renegade band in the Judean wilderness (cf. 23:19-20; heading of Psalm 54). David sneaks into the camp of Saul and his army, who slumber in a "deep sleep from the Lord" (vv. 7, 12), accompanied by Abishai, son of David's stepsister Zeruiah.

In resisting Abishai's urging to slay "the Lord's anointed" (v. 9; cf. 24:6), David reserves for God any righteous vengeance on Saul (v. 10). But again David takes evidence of his opportunity to do Saul in (vv. 12, 15-16). Again he reveals his position in confronting Saul with his innocence (vv. 17-20). Again he acknowledges Saul's authority by addressing him as "my lord," "the king," and "the Lord's anointed" (vv. 17, 20, 23). Again Saul repents of his evil intentions toward his "son" (vv. 17, 21, 25), whom he blesses and whose ultimate success he predicts (v. 25). Saul even calls himself a "fool" (v. 21), possibly foreseeing a fate like that of Nabal (ch. 25).

27:1–28:2 David Returns to Gath

David accuses Saul of driving him out from Israel's landed inheritance (26:19). He acts on this conviction by departing for Philistine territory, where he, his men, and their families receive the welcome of none other than Achish of Gath (27:1-2), who once before underestimated David (21:10-15). Achish must know that Saul considers David his enemy, so David again easily dupes the Philistine king by pretending to be a traitor to Israel, whose king has sought to kill him. From Ziklag, just west of the southern Judahite frontier and bordering on its south enemies of both Israel and the Philistines, David destroys cities and tribes that threaten the Judahites. But he convinces the gullible Achish that he is raiding his own native nation and her allies. David continues to indebt himself to his Judahite countrymen by carrying out bans that even Saul has failed to enforce (27:9).

28:3-25 Saul Consults a Medium

Having given up his hunt for David, Saul leads his army to the northernmost end of the hill country, opposite which the Philistines have gathered to prepare for battle on the Jezreel plain, where their chariots would give them a military advantage (v. 4). God's final rejection of Saul as king becomes evident in his complete silence toward Saul's inquiries concerning the impending confrontation. In desperation, Saul ventures *incognito* perilously close to the Philistine camp to consult a medium (vv. 7-8), whose reluctance to grant her unrecognized king's request stems from his earlier having outlawed such practices (v. 9). But conjure she does, and the apparition of Samuel betrays Saul's identity to the astonished medium (v. 12). Perturbed at the disturbance of his afterlife, Samuel chastises Saul (vv. 16-18) before prophesying Saul's death and the Israelites' defeat the next morning (v. 19). The medium kills her fatted calf and forces a symbolic last meal on the totally deflated king before he departs to face his own slaughter (vv. 23-25).

29 David Relieved from Duty

The note that the Philistines muster at Aphek, in the Ephraimite lowlands well south of the Philistine army's current objective at Shunem, just north of Jezreel, indicates that the events of this chapter occurred prior to those in chapter 28. Because the Philistine king Achish trusts David so completely, he includes the presumed defector and his men in the military contingent he contributes to the impending battle against Saul. But the other Philistine commanders display more justified suspicion regarding David's potential to turn against them in the fray, and they pressure Achish into sending David back home to Ziklag before continuing their northbound march (v. 4; cf. 27:6). In this way, David avoids even the slightest hint of responsibility for Saul's death in the coming battle. He can also keep up his pretense with Achish without having to oppose his own countrymen militarily.

30 David Raids the Raiders

David returns to Ziklag to find it plundered and burned by the Amalekites. At God's word and with the help of an abandoned Egyptian slave, whom the Amalekites left to die, David and his men catch the celebrating raiders off guard, slaughter the lot, and repossess their stolen families, flocks, and goods. David gives some of the livestock captured as battle spoils to his increasingly indebted Judean countrymen, who also suffered in the Amalekites' raid (v. 26; cf. 1, 14). The Amalekites, who became a stumbling block for Saul (28:18), serve as David's alibi in denying potential accusations of his involvement in the death of Israel's king during the simultaneous battle between Saul and the Philistines (ch. 31).

31 Saul's Suicide on Mount Gilboa

Cf. 1 Chronicles 10.

Despite the serious character flaws that Saul increasingly displays, the king's heart never appears despicably wicked to the core; therefore, his defeat (v. 1), suicide (v. 4), and the humiliating treatment by the Philistines of his decapitated body (vv. 9-10) seem all the more tragic. Saul's sole honor in death comes at the hands of the Jabesh-gileadites, who bravely demonstrate their gratitude for Saul's first act of deliverance as God's anointed king (ch. 11). Though David had promised not to wipe out Saul's house (24:21-22), the Philistines jeopardize the preservation of Saul's name by slaying three of his sons, including the brave and faithful Jonathan (v. 2).

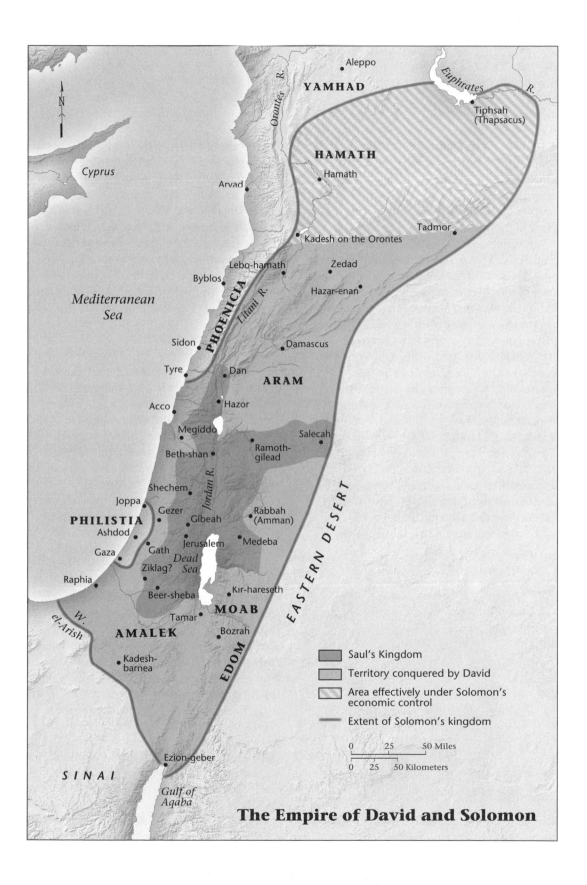

Aleppo

YAMHAD

Euphrates

R.

Tiphsah
(Thapsacus)

Cyprus

HAMATH

Hamath

Arvad

Tadmor

Kadesh on the Orontes

Lebo-hamath

Zedad

Byblos

Hazar-enan

Mediterranean
Sea

Sidon

Damascus

Tyre

Dan

ARAM

Acco

Hazor

Megiddo

Salecah

Beth-shan

Ramoth-
gilead

Shechem

EASTERN DESERT

Joppa

Gezer

PHILISTIA

Gibeah

Rabbah
(Amman)

Ashdod

Jerusalem

Medeba

Gaza

Gath

Dead
Sea

Ziklag?

Raphia

Beer-sheba

Kir-hareseth

W.

Tamar

MOAB

el-Arish

AMALEK

Bozrah

Kadesh-
barnea

EDOM

Saul's Kingdom

Territory conquered by David

Area effectively under Solomon's
economic control

Extent of Solomon's kingdom

0   25   50 Miles

0   25   50 Kilometers

Ezion-geber

SINAI

Gulf of
Aqaba

The Empire of David and Solomon

2 Samuel

1 David Laments Saul and Jonathan

The focus now turns back to David, who has returned to Ziklag after destroying his Amalekite enemies while the Israelite-Philistine battle takes place in the north. In 1 Samuel Saul's and David's treatment of the Amalekites contrasts the two leaders (compare 1 Samuel 15 with 30), but here an Amalekite ties the men together by making the 100-mile journey from Mount Gilboa to Ziklag to bring news of Saul's death to his successor. Apparently a resident alien in Israel (v. 13), this foreign messenger claims ultimate responsibility for Saul's death as an act of mercy (vv. 9-10; contrast 1 Sam. 31:4-5). Perhaps his less-than-honest story represented an attempt to endear himself to the expected successor to the throne by demonstrating loyalty to David over his former oppressor, Saul. Whatever the Amalekite's reason, David's grief over the loss turns to anger at the man's claimed presumption to destroy "the Lord's anointed" (vv. 11-14; contrast 1 Sam. 24:6; 26:11), and, already assuming a kingly posture, David orders the Amalekite's execution (v. 15).

The national lament that David chants

The pool of Gibeon, focal point of the civil war following the death of Saul. (www.HolyLandPhotos.com)

mourns the divinely rejected King Saul. It seeks to preserve respect for Saul by keeping from his Philistine enemies the news of his death in battle (v. 20). The song curses Canaan's Mount Gilboa, where Saul died and where his leather shield was not even "anointed" with oil to keep it from drying out and cracking (v. 21). It also remembers the intimate, brotherly relationship between David and Jonathan (v. 26; cf. 18:1ff.). The poem was included in the book of Jashar, a lost collection of songs honoring Israel's war heroes (cf. Josh. 10:13).

2 The Beginning of Civil War

With Ziklag destroyed and Saul dead, David sees his opportunity to return to his native Judah, but he does so only at God's direction (v. 1; cf. 1 Sam. 23:9-12). David's careful cultivation of his tribe's support even during his self-imposed exile (1 Sam. 30:26-31) now pays off as Judah (which by now probably incorporated Simeon) immediately makes David its king (v. 4; cf. Samuel's private anointing in 1 Sam. 16:13). David's official expression of gratitude to the Transjordanian Jabesh-gileadites for their rescue and burial of Saul's body shows that David believes himself the rightful heir to the throne over all the tribes (vv. 5-7).

But probably in an attempt to retain his military power, Saul's army commander, Abner, whisks off Saul's surviving son, Ishbosheth (substituted for his actual name, Ishbaal, "man of Baal") to the Transjordanian city of Mahanaim and sets him up as an easily manipulated pawn-king over the northern and Transjordanian tribes (vv. 8-9; cf. 3:6-11). (Because "baal" refers to the Canaanite fertility-god, later scribes substituted "bosheth," "shame"; cf. Eshbaal/Ishbosheth, Meribbaal/Mephibosheth.) The inevitable struggle for total control of the country begins in Gibeon near the Benjamite-Judahite border by agreement between Ishbosheth's and David's power-brokering army commanders. Twelve each of Abner's and Joab's soldiers face off at the "pool of Gibeon" (a 37 ft. wide, 35 ft.

Painted jug with characteristic Philistine artistic motifs; from a tomb at Tell el-Fâr'ah (Sharuhen), 12th century B.C. *(Israel Antiquities Authority)*

deep cistern, attested archaeologically) to engage in representative, hand-to-hand combat to determine the undisputed king. But because all 24 combatants kill each other, the conflict fails to decide the winner. Joab's men gain the upper hand in the fighting that follows (vv. 12-17).

Forced to flee, Abner pleads with Asahel, Joab's brother and David's nephew, to cease his personal pursuit (vv. 21-22). The request reflects Abner's desire to avoid initiating a blood feud with his countryman and military counterpart Joab, as does Abner's later encouragement of Joab to restrain his army from further fighting (v. 26). Asahel's refusal to let up leads to Abner's unintended killing (suggested by his use of the butt end rather than pointed end of his spear; v. 23) of the son of David's stepsister Zeruiah.

With Asahel slain, the fight becomes personal, and the third brother, Abishai, joins Joab in pursuing Abner. The uniting of the Benjamites with Abner's retreating but now well-positioned army produces a formidable fighting force, and Joab ultimately agrees to

quit the present conflict while he is ahead (vv. 25-28, 30-31). He will soon seize another opportunity to avenge his brother's death (3:20-27). While Joab and his forces return to David at his first capital in Hebron, one of the cities of refuge, Abner and his men march through the Jordan Valley (the "Arabah" here) and back to Ishbosheth, but a two-year civil war will follow (vv. 29, 32).

3 Abner's Defection and Murder

Abner surely senses his waning power against Judah (v. 1), and Ishbosheth's challenge concerning Abner's alleged claim on a concubine the puppet-king inherited as part of his father's harem (v. 7) pushes the army commander over the emotional edge. Abner may have orchestrated this opportunity to pick a fight with the weaker Ishbosheth (cf. v. 11) and provide an excuse to defect to David ("a dog's head for Judah" in v. 8 means "a contemptible supporter of David"). Abner vows to deliver the non-Judahite tribes to the southern king. David's only possibility for making a covenant with Abner is to regain Saul's remarried daughter, Michal, as his wife (cf. vv. 2-5; 1 Sam. 18:20-29; 25:44). Marriage to Michal will have politically symbolic value in validating David's kingship over the northern tribes. David and Abner seal their agreement by sharing a covenantal meal in Hebron (v. 20).

When Joab learns of the occasion, he accuses Abner of spying. Joab orders the surrendering soldier brought back and then kills him to avenge Asahel's blood (vv. 26-27, 30). Unaware of the plot until Joab had carried out his murderous plan, David again avoids responsibility for spilling the blood of a countryman (v. 28; cf. 1 Sam. 25:26ff.). His sincere words and deeds counter any possible rumors that he had ordered his commander to carry out the vicious crime.

David's curse on the house of Joab includes conditions that rendered a person ritually unclean (discharges and skin diseases) and the charge of "women's work" (= "holds a spindle"; v. 29). He requires Joab and his contingent to join him in mourning Abner and in giving the fallen commander a proper burial. The Judahite king's honoring of his former opponent wins the respect of the northern and Transjordanian tribes (vv. 36-37). David leaves the punishment of his nephew Joab to God (v. 39), but he resents Joab's actions for years to come (cf. 1 Kgs. 2:5).

4 Ishbosheth's Assassination

Abner's death initiates a ripple effect that first causes Ishbosheth to lose his nerve and then grows into national dismay (v. 1). Two unit commanders seize the chance to assassinate the pitiful northern king with the expectation that their revenge on the house of Saul will gain reward from David, the obvious successor to the northern throne (v. 8). David despises their deed, however, and "rewards" them with execution (vv. 9-12). He honors his "righteous" rival Ishbosheth by burying his severed head in the still fresh grave of the late king's murdered commander, Abner (cf. 3:27, 32).

5 David Unites His Nation

Cf. 1 Chr. 11:1-9, 14.

The northern tribes voluntarily unite with Judah under David (vv. 1-3). Five years after Ishbosheth's death, David moves his capital to a more central location between the northern and southern tribes by defeating the Jebusites of Jerusalem's seemingly invincible stronghold. They taunt that even their blind and lame could successfully defend it (vv. 6-9; Millo, "filling," is the steeply sloped area that the Jebusites terraced to build their city). Jerusalem ("Zion," v. 7; the "City of David," v. 9) lay on the border of Judah and Benjamin, and this Canaanite prize remained under Judah's control for the next four centuries. Verse 8 suggests that David's soldiers mounted a surprise attack by sneaking into the city through a shaft that extended from Jerusalem's water source, which lay outside its fortifications, to a pool within the city walls.

The Phoenician king Hiram, who reigned 979-945 B.C. from his seaport capital Tyre, formally recognizes Israel as a new regional superpower (v. 11; cf. ch. 8). He will later contribute valuable goods and services to help build Solomon's temple (1 Kings 5–7). The Phi-

listines, however, remain determined to defeat their formerly presumed ally. David continues to acknowledge God as the source of his success (v. 12; cf. v. 10) and to seek divine direction in his confrontations with his most pressing enemies (vv. 19, 23; cf. 2:1; 1 Sam. 23:9-12). He further strengthens his kingdom by sealing additional alliances through marriage to Jerusalemite women (v. 13), though the rivalry that develops between his sons by multiple mothers will cause him constant grief (cf. ch. 13).

6 Jerusalem Becomes Israel's Religious Center

Cf. 1 Chronicles 13, 15–16.

Having established Jerusalem as his nation's political capital, David now moves to make the city Israel's religious center as well. He first moves to the new capital the ark of the covenant, which remained in Kiriath-jearim (called Baale-judah in v. 2; cf. Josh. 15:9) after its brief sojourn among the Philistines (1 Sam. 4:1–7:1). In fear and anger, however, David temporarily abandons his plan when God strikes dead one of the guardians of the ark (v. 3) for touching the sacred box in an attempt to protect it (vv. 6-9). Significantly, David does not appear to consult God about the move, and the resulting death of Uzzah shows that God will not blindly bless David's every action.

Eventually, David brings the ark to Jerusalem amid much fanfare and celebration. In his wife Michal's eyes, the scantily clad king humiliates himself in his public display of joyful abandon (v. 20). That both God and David reject her rebuke becomes evident in her lifelong barrenness (v. 23), which keeps her from providing a Saulide heir to the Davidic throne and thus feeds the future rivalry between David's sons by his other wives.

David's centralizing of Israel's government and religion distinguish him as a king in the true, ancient Near Eastern sense. Saul, though called a king, functioned more as an Israelite judge. Solomon, who fails to inherit his father's ability to compromise for the sake of his nation, will emerge as more of a tyrant.

7 The Davidic Covenant

Cf. 1 Chronicles 17.

Having spent many years freeing his country from outside military threats, David now finds time to ponder domestic issues. Through the prophet Nathan, God cancels David's plan to replace the mere tent that houses God's throne with what David considers a proper home. David's dream house for the divine appears unimportant to God (v. 7), but he rewards David's sincere and honorable intentions by establishing a covenant with the well-meaning king. This covenant builds up *David's* "house" by ensuring the preservation of a Davidic dynasty (esp. vv. 12 and 16; see "Covenants" [141-44]).

David responds in humility (esp. v. 18) with an outpouring of praise on behalf of the nation (vv. 23-24) and full acceptance of God's plan, which indicates that a descendant of David (one who is not a warrior but a man of peace; 1 Chr. 22:7) will build the house the king has envisioned (v. 13). David does not abandon his dream, however, and he later lays the groundwork for the project by providing his successor with materials, architectural plans, and instructions for coordinating temple services, such as music and worship (1 Chr. 22:2ff.; 28:11ff.).

God's promise to establish the Davidic dynasty forever does not die with the Babylonian king Nebuchadnezzar's conquest of Judah in 587/86, for this covenant gives birth to Israel's hope for the Messiah and finds its ultimate fulfillment in Jesus, born in David's hometown of Bethlehem and "of the house and lineage of David" (Luke 2:4).

8 A Summary of David's Victories

Cf. 1 Chronicles 18.

Recorded here are David's victories in securing peaceful borders for Israel (cf. 7:1). The placement of this chapter immediately after God's establishment of the Davidic covenant demonstrates that God had already been fulfilling those promises (esp. vv. 9-11).

David's harsh treatment of the Moabites in Transjordan (v. 2) seems odd since he had entrusted them with the safety of his parents when Saul was seeking his life (1 Sam. 22:3-4).

Verses 3-10 mention kingdoms north of Israel as far as the Euphrates River. David recognizes the divine origin of his victories (v. 6; cf. v. 14) by dedicating the valuable war spoils and tribute to the Lord (vv. 11-12). Verse 12 summarizes the king's victories geographically before vv. 13-14 return south to Edom and the Valley of Salt (probably the area south of the Dead Sea).

Verses 15-18 list David's military and religious officials (cf. 20:23-26). Ahimelech, son of Abiathar, the lone priest of Nob to escape Saul's slaughter, has inherited his father's priestly position and shares the office with Aaron's descendant, Zadok (v. 17). By appointing both a northern descendant of Moses and a southern Aaronide as chief priests, David wisely unites the nation religiously as well as politically. The Cherethites and Pelethites (v. 18) are Philistine mercenaries. Though David's sons may have performed some priestly functions, the parallel verse in 1 Chr. 18:17 focuses on their political role as "chiefs" or "heads."

9 David Restores Mephibosheth

Seeking a way to honor his close friend Jonathan in death, David summons Jonathan's lame son Mephibosheth (Merib-baal), whose nurse had saved him from those who killed his uncle, King Ishbosheth (4:4). David goes beyond his promise not to wipe out Saul's descendants and name (1 Sam. 24:21-22) by restoring the late king's family property (in Benjamin) to this sole-surviving male descendant, thus ensuring the unbroken participation of the "house" of Saul in the promised covenantal inheritance. David essentially adopts Mephibosheth by providing for him a permanent place at the palace table.

David may have brought Mephibosheth to Jerusalem to keep a watchful eye on this potential heir to the kingship. The emphasis here, however, is David's generosity toward the late Jonathan. Mephibosheth's physical limitation makes him a highly unlikely rival to the throne.

10 Israel Defeats the Ammonite/Syrian Alliance

Cf. 1 Chronicles 19.

Misunderstanding of David's offer of support for the new Ammonite king Hanun results in full-scale war against an Ammonite-Syrian alliance. Joab and his brother Abishai successfully rout both foreign armies, but the Syrians regroup for another battle. Defeated again, the Syrians make peace with Israel and resist future Ammonite calls for military aid. This second battle may represent the conflict in 8:3-5.

Whether David had other motives in sending his ambassadors to Hanun (maintaining a peace treaty with the Ammonites or spying, as Hanun's advisers suspect), the text portrays David as the offended party whom God ultimately avenges against his enemies. This chapter provides the background for David's adultery with Bathsheba.

11 David's Sin against Uriah

While his army was battling the Ammonites, David was resting in Jerusalem (vv. 1-2). From his perch on the palace roof, David spies the temptingly beautiful Bathsheba as she bathes in her walled but unroofed courtyard. The king's visual lust finds physical opportunity afforded by the absence of her husband Uriah, one of David's elite military guard, and a one-night palace affair ordered by the most powerful man in the land follows (v. 4; on Bathsheba's need for ritual purification after menstruation, cf. Lev. 15:19-24). Bathsheba becomes pregnant (v. 5).

David tries to cover up the moral breach by summoning the unwitting husband from the battlefield and encouraging him to visit his wife's bed ("wash your feet," an expression for sexual intercourse; v. 8). David's goal is to make Uriah appear to be the father of Bathsheba's baby (vv. 6-10). In his sexual restraint even while forcibly intoxicated, however, Uriah conducts himself more honorably than the king (v. 13; the laws of holy war prohibited active soldiers from engaging in sex; 1 Sam. 21:4-5). David must find another plan.

By Uriah's own hand, David sends word to Joab instructing the commander to leave Uriah without backup on the most precarious frontline position possible. There the honorable Hittite meets his death along with several other innocent bystanders to the potential royal scandal (vv. 14-17), and David becomes responsible for the death of his countrymen even though he did not shoot the arrows that slew them. Joab's battle report to David (vv. 18-21) refers to the death of Abimelech, the judge Gideon's son (Judg. 9:50-57).

To all appearances, David's marriage to the widowed Bathsheba seems legitimate, but God knows what the people do not (v. 27; contrast v. 25). Thus David, at the height of his political career, takes a moral nosedive — one that produces bittersweet fruit (ch. 12) and charts a course for future heartache.

12:1-25 The Consequences of David's Sin

After hearing the prophet Nathan's cleverly veiled rebuke, David pronounces judgment on himself. God's anger against David seems to center less on his illicit sex with Bathsheba than on the wealthy and successful king's having robbed a commoner of what little he had and then killed him (v. 9). Yet while David unwittingly condemned himself to death — the prescribed punishment for adultery (Deut. 22:22) — God will spare his life (vv. 5, 13). The consequences of the king's sin, however, will break his heart, beginning with the death of his firstborn son by Bathsheba (vv. 14, 18) and extending to fatal strife among his other sons (v. 11). God also vows that the punishment for David's secret sin will include the king's public humiliation (v. 11; cf. 16:21-22). There is no one left whom David can compensate for his sin against Uriah (v. 6) and therefore no way to soothe his guilty conscience.

To David's credit, he does not hesitate in confessing his sin (v. 13). As he must, David relies solely on God's mercy and forgiveness. He does not abandon petitioning God to defray his punishment (vv. 16-17, 22), but he accepts the consequences of his sin when they come, and he worships rather than rejects the righteous God who punishes him (v. 20).

When Solomon is born to David and Bathsheba, Nathan gives the future king a second name, Jedidiah, whose meaning, "Beloved of the Lord," reassures the parents that their child will live (vv. 24-25). That David's initial lust for Bathsheba turns to love appears evident in his comforting her after the death of their firstborn son and in his continued intimacy with his newest wife (v. 24).

12:26-31 Victory at Rabbah

Cf. 1 Chr. 20:1-3.

Chapter 12 flashes forward to the battle at the Ammonite capital, Rabbah (modern Amman), where the loyal Joab has reserved the final victory for his uncle, the king. David's defeat of the royal city dramatically demonstrates God's forgiveness of the flawed monarch and signals his continued presence with David. David takes as a prize the 75-pound crown from the statue of the Ammonite god Milcom.

13 Amnon Rapes His Sister

Sexual lust triggers another murderous plot that produces heartache for David. David's firstborn son, Amnon, commits both rape and incest with his virgin half-sister Tamar (vv. 11-14). Tamar's pre-rape plea that Amnon appeal to the king to support a marriage between the half-siblings (v. 13) may represent an attempt to buy time so David could halt her otherwise certain disgrace. David probably would have denied the marriage request, for though Israelite law permitted the wedding of cousins, it prohibited brother-sister sexual relations (Lev. 18:9, 11).

Amnon's frustration over the difficulty of "doing anything" to Tamar (v. 2; overseers strictly guarded virgins and therefore marriageable daughters) foreshadows his selfish purpose early in the account. That Amnon simply desires Tamar, but does not truly love her as he protests (v. 4), becomes evident in his casting her off in disgust immediately after having satisfied his sexual urge (vv. 15, 17). Tamar mourns her disgrace by heaping ashes (or dust) on her head and tearing her clothes (v. 19).

At home Tamar finds a sympathetic but calculating defender of her honor in her full brother Absalom (vv. 20-22, 32). David's inaction after learning of the incident, which angers him greatly, fails to resolve the domestic discord, inspire paternal trust and respect on Absalom's part, or at least curb the lurking violence and rebellion (v. 21). Perhaps David believes his own sexual indiscretion with Bathsheba has weakened his moral voice in such matters. Or perhaps his bravery on the battlefield simply gives way to meekness on the home front (cf. 1 Kgs. 1:6).

Absalom's hatred for Amnon brews for two years before he avenges his sister by murder, carried out by Absalom's servants at his express order (vv. 23, 28-29). No doubt caught off guard after the long interval between the nearly forgotten crime and the surprise punishment, Amnon has no chance.

The consequences for Absalom include a self-imposed, three-year exile in his maternal grandfather's kingdom to escape capital punishment for murder. The results of Absalom's actions also adversely affect others, not the least David (vv. 37, 39).

14 Absalom's Return
to Jerusalem

David's softening toward Absalom suggests to Joab that the king might allow Absalom as crown prince to return to Jerusalem (v. 1). The message that Joab places in the "wise woman's" mouth reveals the army commander's interest in a smooth transition of royal power after David's death, for through her words he couches Absalom's return in terms that place the welfare of the nation over the punishment of a single individual (vv. 13-14).

As with Nathan's parable (12:1-4), the current story summons David's self-judgment. As king, David overrules the law that prescribes the death penalty for his murdering son, but as a father he withholds full forgiveness. Absalom returns from exile but remains banished from the royal court (vv. 23-24). After two years, Absalom will no longer tolerate this humiliation (v. 32), which contrasts with the praise afforded him by nearly everyone else (vv. 25-27).

It takes another destructive act to get Joab's attention and an audience with the king (vv. 30-31). But David's fatherly affection will prove too little too late (v. 33).

15 David's Flight from Absalom

For a second time, Absalom successfully deceives his father to gain permission for an evil-bent trip (vv. 7-9; cf. 13:23-27), but now David himself is his son's target. As David fled from his predecessor at the beginning of his public career, he now finds himself fleeing his would-be successor. The king's Transjordanian flight from Jerusalem when Absalom bids for the throne — launched from David's first capital of Hebron (v. 10) — again contrasts David's and Saul's approaches to divine intervention. While Saul attempted to retain power through aggression against his perceived enemy, David steps aside and awaits a further sign from God (vv. 25-26).

The king has good reason to flee Jerusalem, for Absalom's personal cultivation of popular affection and his shrewd undermining of support for David, coupled with his gathering necessary military personnel and machinery, positioned him well for takeover (vv. 1-6). David's reaction, however, shows his humble acceptance of the promised punishment for his sin involving Uriah and Bathsheba (cf. 12:10-11). He even calls Absalom the "king" when urging his loyal military commander Ittai to defect (v. 19). David's decision to vacate the capital saves it from large-scale destruction in an inevitable siege by Absalom.

Still, the king remains hopeful and does not slink passively out of the picture. His 600-strong force of Philistine mercenaries (v. 18; cf. 1 Sam. 23:13) accompany him in his retreat. David also commissions trusted loyalists to remain in Jerusalem as informants, including his respected "friend" (an official title for a counselor) Hushai, as well as the chief priests Zadok and Abiathar, whose sons will act as secret couriers between the royal court and the king. Hushai is also to serve as a double agent by thwarting the advice that Ahithophel, David's adviser-turned-traitor (cf. 16:23) and Bathsheba's grandfather, gives Absalom. Hushai

accomplishes his goal and so answers David's current prayer (v. 31; cf. 17:1-14).

16 Absalom Claims Jerusalem

As David leaves Jerusalem, he encounters opposite reactions from two former supporters of Saul. Ziba, whom David previously appointed to work the land he restored to Saul's lame grandson, Mephibosheth (9:9-13), provides the king with transportation and refreshing sustenance. Ziba convinces David that Mephibosheth has remained in the capital in hopes of taking David's place (v. 3). David then encounters a relative of Saul who, recognizing the king's politically weakening state, hurls verbal and physical abuse, thus enraging the loyal Abishai (v. 9); but David's restraint defers the revenge (vv. 10-12).

Meanwhile, Absalom claims the throne in Jerusalem. As instructed by David, Hushai feigns defection to Absalom by declaring steadfast loyalty to the people's choice for king. Convinced by Hushai's pledge of support, Absalom takes Ahithophel's advice that he publicly display his takeover of David's abandoned concubines, a sign of claiming the throne, thereby proclaiming his permanent break from his father and fulfilling the forewarned consequences of David's sin against the house of Uriah (12:11). By eliminating any possibility of father-son reconciliation, the act frees Absalom's supporters to cast their lot openly with the rebel.

17 Absalom's Fateful Choice

Ahithophel proposes swift action that will protect the challenger to the throne, ensure his succession, and avoid civil war. Ahithophel wants to pursue the king quickly and kill only him, while putting David's mercenaries in Absalom's service (vv. 1-4). Hushai cleverly counsels a delay, which will allow David time to escape. Because Hushai appeals to Absalom's pride in advising him personally to lead a united Israelite force to pursue David, his counsel ultimately wins out — evidence that God remains on David's side (vv. 5-14). After near discovery by Absalom's servants, the priests' sons Ahimaaz and Jonathan bring word to David to stay one step ahead of Absalom by quickly crossing into Transjordan (vv. 15-21). While David and his men receive aid in the late Ishbosheth's fortified capital of Mahanaim, Absalom pursues them across the Jordan, with Amasa filling his cousin Joab's role as the rebel's army commander (vv. 24-29). Ahithophel realizes the inevitably devastating consequences for Absalom of following Hushai's advice, and he commits suicide (v. 23).

18:1–19:8 The Death of Absalom

David organizes his troops to win, but he publicly charges his three commanders to "deal gently" with Absalom. The troops insist that David remain in the city rather than accompany them into battle (18:1-5). The rebel force proves no match for David's veteran army, and the forest setting of the battle causes further difficulties for the contenders (18:6-8). Absalom's mount leaves him dangling from a tree branch, perhaps by his previously enviable hair (cf. 14:26), and Joab, knowing that only the death of either David or Absalom can resolve the current unrest, disregards David's compassionate orders by seizing the opportunity to spear the now vulnerable threat to the throne (18:9-15).

Knowing that the sight of the priest's son, Ahimaaz, will cause David to expect good news, Joab sends a Cushite (Ethiopian/Nubian) slave to deliver the bittersweet battle report (18:19-21). Ahimaaz takes the longer but easier Jordan Valley route to Mahanaim and arrives first, but he holds his tongue concerning Absalom (18:22-30). David's hopeful anticipation turns to bitterest grief when he learns of his son's death (18:31-33).

The king is paralyzed by Absalom's death, thus demoralizing David's faithful troops, who have just won a most important battle in restoring him to the throne (19:3). Only the coldly rational Joab can compose the king so he does not lose the political ground his army has just regained for him on the battlefield (19:5-8).

19:9–39 David Returns to Judah

David wins back his tribesmen's loyalty by replacing his own commander, Joab, with Ab-

salom's officer, Amasa, in effect punishing Joab for his faithfulness and foresight and rewarding Amasa for his treason (vv. 11-14).

On the less-than-triumphal return, previously questionable characters scramble to explain themselves to the restored monarch. Shimei, the Benjamite who cursed David on his retreat from Jerusalem (16:5-8, 13), begs for forgiveness. Though David pledges not to kill him (again, against the wishes of Abishai), the king's last words to Solomon order Shimei's death (cf. 1 Kgs. 2:8-9). Mephibosheth's explanation for remaining in Jerusalem during the revolt seems plausible, if not likely, in view of his lameness, but his servant Ziba is rewarded for his supposed loyalty (vv. 24-30). Preferring his independence, Barzillai respectfully declines his royal reward (vv. 33-38).

19:40–20:26 Sheba's Revolt

The quelling of Absalom's rebellion did not restore complete tribal harmony. Though the Judah-based revolt failed, it nevertheless watered the seeds of national division, which eventually sprouted into the split of the kingdom after Solomon's death. The northern and Transjordanian tribes may have expected David to reward them for their support by transferring his capital to their territory, and they blame the Judahites for stealing back the king (19:41-43).

In response to David's move home, another Benjamite, Sheba, stirs up rebellion against David (20:1-2). Amasa delays in carrying out David's command to muster a posse, and the king falls back on Abishai to stamp out this new revolt before it gets out of hand (20:4-6). Joab again seizes the opportunity to strike down a challenger — his rival, Amasa (cf. Joab's murder of Abner; 3:26-27).

Having forcibly reclaimed his position as military commander, Joab takes over the lead in tracking down Sheba, whom he finds in the far north near Dan. The pursuers build an earthen ramp up the hill where lies the walled city harboring Sheba (20:14-15). When the city's inhabitants see Joab's powerful army, they toss Sheba's severed head over the wall to Joab to stop the siege (20:16-22). Again Joab has defended David's political career, but David never forgives his commander for his brutal methods (cf. 1 Kgs. 2:5-6).

The list of David's cabinet includes a director of forced labor (= Adoram, vv. 23-26). This issue will eventually break up the united kingdom, and Adoram will pay with his life for the people's anger over this heavy burden (1 Kgs. 12:18).

21–23 Reviewing David's Career

These chapters represent a break in the generally chronological record of David's reign. Most of the accounts flash back to events recorded before ch. 20.

21:1-14 Blood Revenge for Gibeon This is the first mention of Saul's attempt to wipe out the Gibeonites, Canaanites with whom Israel had earlier made a covenant (Joshua 9). The text explains a three-year famine as God's punishment for Saul's breaking the pact (v. 1). The Gibeonites require blood revenge on Saul's house, and David hands over two sons of Saul's concubine Rizpah and five sons of Saul's daughter Merab (cf. 1 Sam. 18:17-19). The Gibeonites kill the men, but their main interest is to display their dead bodies instead of burying them, thus adding insult to injury.

Rizpah lessens the humiliation by covering the victims' corpses and for six months protects them from consumption by wild animals. Her action shames David into gathering the remains of Saul and his dead descendants and burying them in the family tomb. That the Gibeonites' revenge does indeed "bless the heritage of the Lord" (v. 3) becomes evident in the eventual return of rain, which will end the famine (v. 10).

21:15-22 Past Triumphs These verses recap some of David's past victories over the Philistines. Verses 16-17 provide background for the Israelites' objection to David's going into battle in 18:2-4.

Verse 19 appears to contradict the account of David's slaying of Goliath (1 Sam. 17:31-52). Some scholars take 1 Chr. 20:5 as indicating that Elhanan killed not Goliath but his brother Lah-

mi. Others suggest that "Elhanan" represents David's personal name, whereas "David" was his throne name.

22 David's Song of Praise Psalm 18 repeats this poem with only minor variations. Both passages introduce imagery that likens God to a rock (vv. 2-3, 32) and picture his deliverance as a mighty act of nature (vv. 8-17). David's declaration of his own righteousness reflects the king as portrayed before the Uriah-Bathsheba episode (vv. 21-25). Within the structure of 1-2 Samuel, this psalm parallels Hannah's song of praise in 1 Samuel 2.

23:1-7 David's "Last Words" The heading "last words" (v. 1) likely identifies this poem as the last psalm David penned. (His final instructions to Solomon appear in 1 Kgs. 2:1-12.) At first, this song may appear self-exalting, but David's purpose is to emphasize the abundant blessings of the covenant God made with "his anointed." David professes that he has ruled over Israel "in the fear of God." The king, therefore, confidently anticipates God's continued fulfillment of his covenant by establishing the promised Davidic dynasty (v. 5).

23:8-39 David's Mighty Men David's elite guard receives special mention, for they helped David win the victories that catapulted him to the throne and kept him there. "The Three" (vv. 8-12) were David's most distinguished warriors. The mention of David's craving for a drink from the well at his hometown Bethlehem relates to the Philistine campaign in 5:17-25. "The thirty chiefs" refers to the group listed in vv. 24-39. Abishai was the best of this corps and therefore its commander. Benaiah's exploits earn him command of David's Philistine mercenaries. The individual listing of "the thirty" actually includes 37 names. Undoubtedly, David replaced those who died in the line of duty, including Joab's and Abishai's brother Asahel (cf. 2:18-23) and Uriah the Hittite, whose name appears last.

24 The Census and the Plague

Cf. 1 Chronicles 21.

The text does not explain God's anger

against his people, nor is it clear that David's census-taking was sinful — merely that David thinks it was (v. 10) and that God allows him to believe so by offering him a choice of punishments through the prophet Gad (vv. 12-13; compare the census totals in v. 9 with Numbers 1). The choices make clear that the punishment will befall the nation as a whole, not the king in particular. David relies on divine mercy in leaving the decision to God, and a plague claims the lives of 70 thousand Israelites (vv. 14-15).

David persists in assuming the blame (v. 17), and he buys the threshing floor of Araunah on which to make sacrifices so God will stop the plague (v. 21). The conscience-stricken king insists that the act should cost him something (v. 24), and he proceeds with the offering without seeming to know that God has already ordered the end of the plague (v. 16). The site of David's offering lay close to the place of Abraham's near sacrifice of Isaac and would later become the foundation for the first temple, built by Solomon (Gen. 22:2; 2 Chr. 3:1).

1 and 2 Kings

The books of Kings complete the history of Israel's monarchy begun in 1 and 2 Samuel by extending the account from the death of David and the accession of Solomon (970 B.C.), under whose rule the united kingdom reached its political and economic apex, to the freeing of King Jehoiachin by the Babylonians (561/60), when the first divided and then conquered and exiled nation existed only as the Diaspora.

The Greek translation of the Old Testament (Septuagint) first separated Samuel and Kings into two volumes each and called the resulting set the "Books of the Kingdoms." 1 and 2 Kings also bring to an end the Deuteronomistic History (Joshua through Kings). Chronicles offers another version of the history recounted in Samuel and Kings (see "The Two Histories" [229-30]).

1 Kings

1 Kings begins with the transfer of power from David to Solomon. Solomon's building enterprises, including erection of a lavish temple and an elaborate palace complex, evidence the unprecedented success of his kingdom. The intensification of the king's forced labor policy for such projects, however, spawns a popular rebellion after his death (ca. 930), and the kingdom splits between Judah (including subsumed Simeon) in the south and the remaining 10 tribes ("Israel") in the north. The Davidic dynasty continues in Judah, but a series of often rapid and always bloody dynastic changes characterizes the northern monarchy.

The book demonstrates that the monarchy failed to ensure the covenantal requirement of national, sacrificial worship of God alone at one central sanctuary — despite the presence of Solomon's temple! Even Solomon worships pagan gods. When Jeroboam ascends the northern throne after Solomon's death, he sets up sanctuaries to rival the Jerusalem temple and sets in motion a pattern of religious failure that will reach new lows with Ahab, whose death marks the end of 1 Kings. Even Elijah's dramatic demonstrations of God's power in challenging the prophets of Baal, introduced by Queen Jezebel, fail to bring lasting repentance by this wicked king.

2 Kings

2 Kings opens with the last acts of Elijah, his ascension to heaven in a whirlwind accompanied by a fiery, horse-drawn chariot, and the succession of Elisha to Elijah as prophet. Accounts of miracles performed by Elisha — several of which parallel miracles performed by Elijah — establish the former apprentice's authenticity and authority.

During Elisha's prophetic tenure, the northern kingdom begins to reap the punishment for its covenantal disobedience. Israel's trouble starts with the Syrians, who attempt an unsuccessful siege of the capital, Samaria. "Jehu's purge," which leads to the fall of the Omride dynasty and for the time rids Israel of Baal worship, fails to bring lasting covenantal obedience, and Samaria's fall to the Assyrians in 722/21 marks the end of the northern kingdom.

The Davidic dynasty of Judah includes a number of "good" kings — most notably Hezekiah, who at the advice of the prophet Isaiah withstands an Assyrian siege of Jerusalem, and Josiah, whose thorough religious reforms based on the "book of the law" (probably Deuteronomy) discovered in the temple represent Judah's last resurgence of covenantal fidelity. Even these kings' sincere attempts to reestablish right worship of God alone cannot reverse the Lord's determination to punish the southern kingdom, however, and Jerusalem's destruction by the Babylonians under Nebuchadnezzar in 587/86 sounds the final death knell for Judah — as the prophet Jeremiah had repeatedly warned.

Kings blames both Israel's and Judah's unfaithful rulers for the eventual fall of their kingdoms and demonstrates the failure of human kingship to secure the people's desired position among the nations. God's ultimate rule throughout the history of the monarchy shows him both as longsuffering by delaying punishment and also demanding justice by staying his punitive course even through periods in which obedience prevails.

Composition

Most scholars believe that the books of Kings originated in the late 7th century, the time of Judah's reformer, Josiah, and were revised in the mid-6th century during the Babylonian exile. Much of the source material used in their composition, however, dates closer to the events recorded. The books themselves mention three works: the Book of the Acts of Solomon, the Book of the Chronicles of the Kings of Israel, and the Book of the Chronicles of the Kings of Judah. Another literary tradition reflected in the text contains the books' prophetic material — especially that concerning Elijah and Elisha.

1 Kings

1 Solomon's Inauguration

With David's health waning, his eldest surviving son and natural successor, Adonijah (2 Sam. 3:4), tries to enlist the support of David's army commander, Joab, and one of the chief priests, Abiathar, for a sacrificial ceremony to establish his claim to kingship. Adonijah invites all of his brothers, save Solomon, plus local Judeans, but he keeps his plans secret from the dying David. Nor does David's special guard of "mighty men" attend the occasion held on the Judah-Benjamin border at En-rogel.

The prophet Nathan learns of the surreptitious celebration, however, and he plots with Bathsheba to have the king name Solomon as successor. That nowhere else does the text mention an earlier promise suggests that Nathan is manipulating the now senile David. At David's instructions and with the king's Philistine mercenaries on hand, Nathan, the other chief priest Zadok, and Benaiah, who commands the mercenaries, quickly conduct a rival ceremony in which Zadok anoints Solomon as king. Solo-

mon then sits on his father's throne as co-regent with David.

On hearing this news, the shocked Adonijah immediately relents, and his supporters swiftly disperse. Fearing for his life, he clings to the horns of the altar until Solomon vows not to slay him. Though in his preparations for a takeover Adonijah follows in Absalom's footsteps, he nevertheless lacks his older brother's boldness to finish what he has begun (v. 5; cf. 2 Sam. 15:1). Though the youngest of David's sons, Solomon nevertheless knows enough to watch out for further mischief by his rival elder brother (vv. 51-53).

2:1-12 David's Death

David's parting words to Solomon urge the new king to honor the Mosaic law and so ensure that he succeed and the Davidic dynasty continue. Fulfillment of the Davidic covenant depends on the royal descendants' sincere devotion to God (cf. Deut. 10:12). Solomon need not uphold his father's vows of nonviolence toward Joab and

Shimei. In fact, David appears bent on their eventual execution. By contrast, the king never forgot Barzillai's friendship in his time of great need (cf. 2 Sam. 17:27-29; 19:31-39).

2:13-46 Solomon Punishes the Opposition

Accepting Solomon's ascension to the throne, Adonijah convinces the queen mother, Bathsheba, to request that David's deathbed nurse become Adonijah's wife. But seeing this as a claim on David's harem and so another bid for the throne, Solomon wastes no time in doing away with his last rival (cf. 2 Sam. 3:6-11; 16:20-23).

Solomon then dismisses Abiathar from the priesthood for having supported Adonijah in his previous bid for kingship (cf. 1 Sam. 2:27-36 for the curse on Eli's house).

On hearing the news concerning Adonijah and Abiathar, Joab claims asylum by fleeing to the sanctuary and grasping the horns of the altar. Solomon, however, orders Joab slain on the spot, not because of his support for Adonijah but in response to David's deathbed charge (vv. 32-33). Benaiah, Joab's reluctant executioner, replaces his victim as army commander.

For three years, Shimei fares well under house arrest in Jerusalem, which limits contact with any possible opponents among Saul's remaining relatives. Shimei's innocent journey to retrieve his servants from Philistine territory violates Solomon's restrictions, and again Benaiah wields the fatal sword.

3 Solomon Asks for Wisdom

Cf. 2 Chr. 1:3-12.

His reign secured, Solomon begins creating foreign alliances (here with weakened, 21st-Dynasty Egypt) and strengthens Jerusalem's fortifications. He also shows concern to honor God. The Lord rewards Solomon's abundant sacrifices at the nation's main shrine in Gibeon by offering to grant any royal request. Solomon's utmost desire for personal wisdom to govern God's people justly pleases the Lord and prompts him to grant unmatched material wealth and respect, as well as long life, if the king remains faithful. Solomon's shrewd means of judging between two prostitute mothers who

claim the same infant provides immediate proof of God's gift.

Israelite rituals, conducted at shrines, or "high places" such as at Gibeon, often incorporated pagan rites. This made the need for centralizing worship urgent. Later prophets condemn the high places (cf. v. 3), though Mosaic law provided for limited use of local shrines (cf. Deut. 12:15-28). In verse 15, Solomon gives additional offerings at the tent shrine in Jerusalem.

Kings of Judah and Israel

United Monarchy
Saul (1030-1010)
David (1010-970)
Solomon (970-931)

Divided Monarchy

Judah	*Israel*
Rehoboam I (931-915)	Jeroboam I (931-910)
Abijam (915-914)	
Asa (914-874)	
Nadab (910-909)	
Baasha (909-886)	
Elah (886-885)	
Zimri (7 days 885)	
Jehoshaphat (874-850)	Omri (885-873)
Joram (850-843)	Ahab (873-851)
Ahaziah (843)	Ahaziah (851-849)
Athaliah (842-837)	Jehoram (849-843)
Joash (837-800)	Jehu (843-816)
Amaziah (800-783)	Jehoahaz (816-800)
Uzziah (783-?)	Jehoash (800-785)
Jeroboam II (785-745)	
Zechariah (6 mo. 745)	
Jotham (?-742)	Shallum (1 mo. 745)
Ahaz (742-727)	Menahem (745-736)
Hezekiah (727-698)	Pekahiah (736-735)
Manasseh (697-642)	Pekah (735-732)
Amon (642-640)	Hoshea (732-722)
Josiah (640-609)	
Jehoahaz (3 mo. 609)	
Jehoiakim (609-598)	
Jehoiachin (3 mo. 598-597)	
Zedekiah (597-587/86)	

The Two Histories

The Old Testament preserves two parallel histories of Israel and Judah, the first found in the books of Joshua–2 Kings and the second in 1-2 Chronicles. They were written at different times and for different purposes.

The first history chronicles the entry of Israel into the long-promised land of Canaan (Joshua), life in the land during a decentralized, chaotic period (Judges), and the establishment of the monarchy in fulfillment of God's promises to the patriarchs (Gen. 17:6, 16; 35:11; 49:10; cf. Deut. 17:14-20). It details the life of Israel's greatest king, David (1-2 Samuel), and then chronicles the ebb and flow in fortunes of the divided kingdoms of Israel and Judah, ending with

High place at Dan where Jeroboam I installed a golden calf intending to rival the Jerusalem sanctuary; Iron II, 10th century B.C. *(Phoenix Data Systems, Neal and Joel Bierling)*

Israel extinct and Judah in exile (1-2 Kings). It echoes many of the themes in Deuteronomy, leading many scholars to propose a

Sources for the Historical Books

Book of Jashar	Josh. 10:13; 2 Sam. 1:18
Book of the Acts of Solomon	1 Kgs. 11:41
Book of the Chronicles of the Kings of Israel	1 Kgs. 14:19; 15:31; 2 Kgs. 10:34
Book of the Chronicles of the Kings of Judah	1 Kgs. 14:29; 15:7; 2 Kgs. 8:23
Book of the Kings of Israel	1 Chr. 9:1; 2 Chr. 20:34
Book of the Kings of Israel and Judah	2 Chr. 27:7; 35:27
Book of the Kings of Judah and Israel	2 Chr. 16:11; 25:26
Book of the Chronicles	Neh. 12:23
Records of the seer Samuel	1 Chr. 29:29
Records of the prophet Nathan	1 Chr. 29:29
History of the prophet Nathan	2 Chr. 9:29
Records of the seer Gad	1 Chr. 29:29
Prophecy of Ahijah the Shilonite	2 Chr. 9:29
Visions of the seer Iddo	2 Chr. 9:29
Annals of Jehu son of Hanani	2 Chr. 20:34
Book of the Kings of Israel	2 Chr. 20:34

hypothetical "Deuteronomistic History" that included Deuteronomy as well, although this involves discounting many significant connections between Moses and Deuteronomy.

This history was completed during the exile of Judah, and it shows why God's people had suffered this fate: it was because of their sins (2 Kgs. 17:7-23; 24:3-4). But it was also intended to give them hope for the future, if only they would listen to God's spokespersons, the prophets, and repent. It shows that God was a gracious God, after all. It ends on a forward-looking note, keeping alive the promises that God had made to David (2 Kgs. 25:27-30; cf. 2 Samuel 7).

The history in 1-2 Chronicles was written at a later time, and it is at once more ambitious and more limited in scope. Starting with Adam, its focus is a grand, messianic one, showing how God worked in spite of his people's waywardness and pointing to his constancy in history from the very beginning. This history focuses only on the kingdom of Judah (not Israel), and on God's promises to David and his descendants. It has its own story to tell, paralleling the earlier history in many spots, but leaving out much material and also adding much not found in the earlier history. Its vision is one of a God who rewarded faithfulness and punished rebellion, who especially blessed the Davidic line, and who valued worship properly expressed in the temple through prayer and proper sacrifices.

DAVID M. HOWARD, JR

4 Solomon's Divinely Granted Success

Solomon greatly expanded Israel's government, as evident from the list of his cabinet and administrators (contrast David's staff, 2 Sam. 8:16-18; 20:23-26). God indeed fulfilled his promise of wealth and fame, as seen in the list of Solomon's tributary and territorial holdings (vv. 21, 24); resources for daily provisions to support the royal family (11:3) and his bureaucracy (vv. 1-6; cf. vv. 22-23, 27-28); numerous military reserves (v. 26); and international reputation for knowledge and wisdom surpassing that of his contemporaries (vv. 29-34).

Solomon's accumulation of a vast harem and thousands of war horses (v. 26; probably 4000; cf. 2 Chr. 9:25) directly violates God's restrictions on a monarch (Deut. 17:14-20), as does the amassing of "silver and gold." Solomon's wives and the material requirements of his bureaucracy eventually lead to the religious and political split of the kingdom after his death. The burden for supporting the government falls entirely on the non-Judahite tribes, whose territories Solomon evidently redistricted for purposes of taxation. David's census in 2 Samuel 24 may have provided the basis for the redistricting.

During Solomon's reign, nevertheless, Israel enjoyed abundant prosperity and uninterrupted peace with lands as far-flung as northwestern Mesopotamia and Egypt (vv. 20-21, 25). Biblical history would remember Solomon as the source of many enlightened proverbs, songs, and sayings (e.g., Psalms 72, 127; Prov. 10:1–22:16) and the inspiration for Ecclesiastes and the Song of Solomon.

5 Temple Preparations

Cf. 2 Chronicles 2.

As a result of David's conquests, Solomon's kingdom enjoyed "rest on every side" (v. 4; cf. Deut. 12:9-10). With the ark of the covenant already in Jerusalem, the task now falls to Solomon to build the temple his father envisioned (v. 5; cf. 2 Samuel 7). David's good relationship with the Phoenician king Hiram has enabled Solomon to exchange annual supplies of grain and olive oil for cedarwood from the mountains of Lebanon (cf. 2 Sam. 5:11).

The treaty arrangements for this exchange of goods and services further cements relations between the two kingdoms, but Solomon's conscription of thousands of forced laborers plants seeds of discontent in his own nation that will lead to crisis for his successor, Rehoboam (ch. 12; cf. God's warning in 1 Sam. 8:10-18). Hiram also supplied laborers and skilled craftsmen for the project from the Phoenician seaports of Sidon and Gebal (= Byblos).

The Temple

Physical Design

Although the temple of Yahweh in Jerusalem was built as a permanent structure, ironically we actually know less about it than we do about the tabernacle, which by design was a temporary structure. Many of the temple's features mirrored those of the tabernacle, though on a much grander scale. The differences were determined largely by the fact that the tabernacle was a portable residence, while the latter served as Yahweh's permanent dwelling place on Zion. The temple compound seems to have consisted of three courtyards: a "great court" to the south of and below the Temple Mount, encompassing the royal buildings (1 Kgs. 7:12); a "middle court," which included Solomon's palace south of the Temple Mount (2 Kgs. 20:4); and a paved "inner court" surrounding the temple itself (1 Kgs. 6:36; 2 Kgs. 16:17; 2 Chr. 7:3). Unlike the later temple built by Herod, the original temple did not restrict Gentiles or women to separate courts.

The temple resembled the tabernacle in its orientation on an east-west axis, with the entrance to the east side and the holy of holies to the west, its proportioned rectangular shape, and its two-room design. But its signature feature involved two apparently free-standing columns at the front, each 18 cubits high and identified by name as Jachin and Boaz (1 Kgs. 7:15-21). These seem either to have represented the pillars upon which the world was thought to rest or served as alternatives to the fearsome bovine or leonide figures often stationed at the entrance of ancient temples to ward off hostile forces. One entered the temple through a rectangular vestibule ('ulam), 20 cubits wide by 10 cubits deep. Beyond this was the great hall ("holy place"), measuring 20 cubits wide by 40 cubits deep. At the very back was the inner sanctum (debir, "holy of holies"). Although the building itself was 30 cubits high (1 Kgs. 6:2), the inner sanctum was a perfect cube, 20 cubits wide by 20 cubits deep by 20 cubits high (v. 20). The differential in height suggests either that the holy of holies was a self-contained box within the temple structure or that it was raised 10 cubits off the ground. In the center of the room stood the ark of the covenant, housing the original written copies of the Decalogue; but two gigantic cherubim, 10 cubits high and having wingspans of 10 cubits, dominated this room. They were made of olive wood and plated with gold (1 Kgs. 6:23-28). The south, west, and north walls of the main structure were buttressed on the outside by three-story structures, apparently designed to house temple personnel and to store temple furniture and utensils (1 Kgs. 6:5-10).

Construction

Although the temple in Jerusalem is commonly referred to as Solomon's temple, this designation is misleading, if not false, because it overlooks the roles of both Yahweh and David in its construction.

The Role of God Just as human kings determine the locations and designs of their palaces, so in the ancient world temples were built according to the will of the deity. Accordingly, the book of Exodus presents the tabernacle entirely as a divine product: Yahweh designed it, prescribed the materials, inspired those who contributed materials, chose the persons who should build it, endowed craftsmen with special gifts to create it, determined the date of its erection, and with the entrance of his glory put his imprimatur on the result (Exodus 25–31, 35–40). The same can be said of the temple on Zion. (1) Yahweh chose the place where (Deut. 12:5, etc.; cf. Pss. 78:68-69; 132:13-18) and the time when it would be built (Deut. 12:10; cf. 2 Sam. 7:1, 13). (2) Yahweh determined its functions: to be a place where one could seek him (Deut. 12:5), see his face (31:11; cf. 16:16), rejoice before him (12:12, 18; 14:26; 16:11-12, 14; 26:11), hear the Torah read publicly (31:11), learn to fear him (14:23; 31:9-13), eat before him (12:7, 18; 14:23, 26, 29; 15:20; 18:6-8), present sacrifices and offerings to him (12:11, 26-27; 14:22-27), celebrate the annual pilgrimage festivals, Passover, Weeks, Booths (16:1-17; 31:9-13), recall his saving grace (26:1-11), and settle legal disputes before his representatives, the Levitical priest or the judge (17:8-13). (3) Yahweh determined the personnel, authorizing Levites to serve in his name (18:6-8). (4) Yahweh designed it and its furnishings, revealing the details to David in the form of a written blueprint directly from his hand (1 Chr. 28:9-19). (5) Yahweh created the conditions for its construction (2 Sam. 7:1; 1 Kgs. 5:3). (6) Yahweh chose the one who should actually build it (2 Sam. 7:13; 1 Kgs. 5:5). (7) Yahweh endowed the builder with special wisdom (1 Kgs. 5:12). (8) Yahweh gave his stamp of approval to the building when it was completed (1 Kgs. 8:9-11; cf. Exod. 40:33-38). (9) Yahweh claimed it as his own temple/ house (e.g., Isa. 56:7; Jer. 12:7; Ezek. 23:39; Hag. 1:9; Zech. 9:8), and others recognized it as "the house of Yahweh" *(bet YHWH)*. In short, it was the place where he established his name (1 Kgs. 5:5; 8:16-19, 29; 9:3, 7; 11:36; Jer. 7:10-14; 32:34; 34:15).

The Role of David If any credit for the construction of the temple is given to a human being, it must go to David, for several reasons: (1) David brought the ark of the covenant, perceived as the throne of Yahweh and called by "the Name," to Jerusalem (2 Sam. 6:1-23), the place chosen by Yahweh for his eternal dwelling place (cf. 1 Chr. 21:18–22:1; Pss. 48; 78:67-72; 87:1-3; 132:13-18). (2) Through David Yahweh gave Israel rest from all her enemies (2 Sam.

7:1), in fulfillment of the requirement declared by Moses in Deut. 12:10. (3) As the divinely chosen king of Israel, David recognized his obligation as patron of the cult and proposed to Nathan that he build a temple for Yahweh in Jerusalem (2 Sam. 7:2-6). (4) As the initiator of the project, David charged Solomon to build the temple, declaring explicitly that he was Yahweh's chosen instrument for the project (1 Chr. 22:6-13). (5) David gathered a major portion of the resources needed to build the temple (1 Chr. 22:14). (6) David assembled the craftsmen to do the work, commissioned them, and blessed them (1 Chr. 22:15-16) and charged all the leaders of Israel to support Solomon in the project (vv. 17-19). (7) David organized the temple personnel, including the supervisors, gatekeepers, musicians, the priesthood, and the temple treasurers (2 Chronicles 23–26). (8) In anticipation of the constructed temple, David dedicated the temple furniture and vessels to Yahweh (1 Kgs. 7:51). (9) David received the written blueprint of the temple directly from

the hand of God (1 Chr. 28:9-19). In short, David's role in relation to the building of the temple parallels that of Moses in connection with the tabernacle.

The Role of Solomon If David was to the temple what Moses was to the tabernacle, then Solomon, his son, fulfilled the role of Bezalel. Like Bezalel (Exod. 31:1-6; 35:30-35) he was specifically chosen by Yahweh to execute the plan revealed to David (2 Sam. 7:13 = 1 Chr. 17:12; 28:5-10) and was specially gifted with wisdom for the task (1 Kgs. 5:12). For the project Solomon received great assistance from Hiram, king of Tyre (1 Kgs. 5:1-12), and a master craftsman also named Hiram, whose father was Tyrian but whose mother was an Israelite from the tribe of Naphtali (1 Kgs. 7:13-50). He also involved thousands of others, including conscripts from within Israel (1 Kgs. 5:13-18);

A depiction of Solomon's Temple; engraving by Jacob Judah Leon, 1665 *(Wikimedia Commons)*

whether these were Israelites or Canaanites living in Israel is not clear (cf. 1 Kgs. 9:15-23). When it was completed, Yahweh confirmed the work of Solomon and his aids by taking up residence in the temple. Solomon's prayer of dedication in 1 Kings 8 is one of the most important passages for determining the significance of the temple.

Significance Like all ancient Near Eastern temples, the temple on Zion served first and foremost as Yahweh's residence. As such it was the object of his special affection (Ps. 132:13-18) and the reflection of his transcendent glory (1 Kgs. 8:12-13). Solomon rightly recognized that in a literal sense the earth itself is inadequate to house God (1 Kgs. 8:27), but this place functioned as a glorious symbol of his presence on earth. From his temple on Zion Yahweh would administer justice not only in Israel but also to all the earth (Isa. 2:3-4; Mic. 4:2-5). To Zion his people would come to present their petitions and seek his aid,

with the assurance that when they sought him with undivided heart he would hear them, even if they prayed from distant lands (1 Kgs. 8:28-30).

In its design and function the temple represented an earthly microcosm of the heavenly residence of Yahweh. This cosmic significance is suggested by several features. (1) It took seven years to build (1 Kgs. 6:37-38), corresponding to the seven days of creation. (2) The pillars Jachin and Boaz seemed to symbolize the pillars on which the earth was founded (Job 26:5-14; Ps. 75:3). (3) The decorative carvings of cherubim, palm trees, and open flowers recalled the garden of Eden (1 Kgs. 6:29, 32, 35). (4) The 10 massive lavers each holding more than 240 gallons and set on elaborate stands (1 Kgs. 7:27-39) may have represented the primordial waters of *tehom*, "the great deep."

In practical terms, however, for the Israelites the temple was a place of revelation, where Yahweh would speak to his people and reveal glory and grace. At God's gracious initiative it provided a place and a means of maintaining open communication with their God. Through the sacrifices and the intermediary work of the priests, their sins could be removed; and through their festivals they could express their gratitude in praise to God. According to the book of Hebrews, as the successor to the tabernacle the temple expressed in replica form the heavenly residence of God, where Jesus, the messianic son of David, offered himself and once for all for the sins of his people, and where he intercedes perpetually as the Davidic high priest on their behalf before God the Father.

DANIEL I. BLOCK

6 Solomon Builds the Temple

Cf. 2 Chronicles 3.

Solomon begins building the temple in 966, four years after ascending the throne. Verse 1 designates this year as the 480th following the exodus, thus prompting some scholars to establish an "early date" of 1446 for that event. Others view the 480 years as a generalized designation representing 12 generations (for Israel's 12 tribes) of 40 years, rather than a precise number. Archaeological evidence supports a "conquest" date in the mid-to-late 13th century and so a later date for the exodus than a literal interpretation of this verse would imply.

Over the course of the seven-year project, workers complete an elaborately decorated, two-section building and a large outdoor porch similar to the basic floor plan of the tabernacle, though not its extravagance. The temple itself measures 90 × 30 × 45 feet — sufficient for the

required priestly service but not to accommodate large gatherings of worshippers. The porch measures 15 × 30 feet and is flanked by storerooms. As in other ancient Near Eastern records, the king receives personal credit for erecting the edifice and for fashioning the elaborately carved decorations and gleaming, gold-overlayed furnishings.

During the exodus and wilderness wanderings, the Israelites needed a portable shrine in which God could dwell among them. Now that God has firmly established them in the promised land, he intends to establish a permanent home in their midst. His personal presence among his chosen people requires covenantal obedience (vv. 12-13).

7:1-12 The Palace Complex

Collectively known as "his house" and "the House of the Forest of Lebanon," the costly buildings that made up Solomon's palace complex included royal residential buildings, the Hall of Pillars, and the Hall of the Throne (where Solomon rendered judicial decisions). The complex dwarfed the temple in size (cf. 6:2) and took almost twice as long to complete.

7:13-51 Hiram's Bronze Work

Solomon appears to exercise free rein in organizing this massive project. He brings a second Hiram from Tyre — not the king of ch. 5 but a skilled craftsman and son of a Naphtalite woman from Israel's far north — to oversee the casting of bronze objects for the temple. Hiram's principal contributions include two freestanding, highly decorated pillars placed outside the temple entrance (vv. 15-22; cf. 2 Chr. 3:15-17); an enormous bowl, "the sea," capable of containing almost 10 thousand gallons of water for ritual cleansing (vv. 23-26; cf. 2 Chr. 4:2-6); and 10 large water basins with wheeled stands (vv. 27-39). The combined weight of these items is so great that it cannot be measured (vv. 40-47; cf. 2 Chr. 4:11-18).

8 Solomon Dedicates the Temple

Cf. 2 Chr. 5:2–7:10.

The dedication of the temple represents a significant landmark in Israel's history. The temple makes possible the centrally regulated worship that Israel so urgently needs to maintain religious fidelity. It also provides a dwelling place for God's "name," rather than a material representation of him, as would contemporary pagan shrines.

The dedication ceremony shows significant parallels to the consecration of the priesthood and the tabernacle. Myriad sacrifices contribute to the sanctification of the temple precinct (v. 5). God demonstrates his approval by indwelling the temple in a thick cloud after Solomon installs the ark of the covenant in the holy of holies (vv. 10-11; cf. Exod. 40:34-38). Solomon's speech incorporates many of the themes in Moses' final public address, including a reminder of God's past faithfulness (v. 56) and the threat of banishment from the promised land for covenantal disobedience (vv. 46-53; cf. Deuteronomy 29–30). A weeklong feast possibly followed by the Feast

of Tabernacles concludes the ceremony (vv. 65-66; cf. 2 Chr. 7:8-10).

Solomon also introduces new themes to reflect new times. The king calls on God to honor his promise of an everlasting Davidic dynasty (vv. 25-26; cf. 2 Sam. 7:12-13). He recognizes that neither earth nor the temple can confine God's presence (v. 27). Yet he invokes God's focus on the temple as the central sanctuary where God's people will direct their prayers in worship (vv. 28-53).

9:1-9 A Warning Repeated

Cf. 2 Chr. 7:11-22.

In a second vision (cf. 3:5-14), God confirms that he has granted Solomon's plea to focus on the temple (v. 3). Then, at the peak of Solomon's reign and the nation's outward success, God reminds the king that covenantal disobedience will completely reverse Israel's fortunes, including exile and destruction of the temple. Though Solomon abandons the faith (cf. 11:1-3), God remains true to his promise of a Davidic dynasty.

9:10-14 Solomon Mortgages Property

Solomon gives the king of Tyre 20 cities on the northern border of Israel and Phoenicia as security against a loan, suggesting he could no longer fund his extensive building projects solely through taxation (but cf. 2 Chr. 8:1-2). Hiram recognizes that his newly acquired property is no prize (Cabul, "good for nothing"; v. 13).

9:15-28 Other Activities

Cf. 2 Chronicles 8.

In addition to strengthening Jerusalem's defenses and the steeply sloped, terraced area of the City of David (= "Millo," v. 15), Solomon fortifies Hazor in the far north, Megiddo west of the Jezreel Valley, and Gezer, the northernmost Philistine city. All three cities guarded important north-south, international trade routes that connected Egypt and Syria-Mesopotamia through Canaan. The labor for Solomon's ambitious projects comes from native Canaanites, now Israelite slaves, and Israelite conscripts to forced labor.

The king also creates a merchant navy and joins the seafaring Phoenicians in conducting trade to the south via the Red Sea. Ophir (v. 28) probably lay in South Arabia or East Africa.

According to verse 25, Solomon performed priestly duties for the Feast of Unleavened Bread at Passover, the Feast of Weeks at the harvest of firstfruits, and the Feast of Tabernacles at the end of the harvest season (cf. 2 Chr. 8:13).

10 Fame and Wealth

Cf. 2 Chronicles 9.

Chapter 10 underscores God's fulfilling the promises of wisdom, fame, and wealth made to Solomon in 3:12-13. Having heard of the king's reputation in far-off Saba (modern Yemen, the southwestern Arabian peninsula), the Queen of Sheba travels to confirm the reports in person. After testing Solomon's wisdom and enjoying his lavish hospitality, she comes away with an even greater opinion of him than she expected.

Canaan's strategic geographical location positioned Solomon to take advantage of trade (vv. 15, 22, 28-29). Major north-south trade routes along the Mediterranean coast, through the hill country, and along the Transjordanian plateau — all west of the formidable Arabian Desert — were the most viable land connection between Arabia/Egypt/Africa and Mesopotamia/Asia. Solomon's navy probably gained access to Asia Minor via the Mediterranean Sea and the Asian continent via the Red Sea and Arabian Sea. Peaceful borders allowed flourishing trade and tourism to boost Israel's economy to an unprecedented level (cf. v. 27).

Solomon's military might also prospered from the economic boom, and he stationed war horses, chariots, and horsemen in Jerusalem, as well as in the fortified cities of Gezer, Megiddo, and Hazor (v. 26; cf. 4:26). Yet his import of horses from Egypt (vv. 28-29) directly violates God's prohibition in Deut. 17:16.

11 Solomon's Spiritual Downfall

So far, 1 Kings presents Solomon as a tremendous success story. Yet several cracks in the foundation of that success have already begun

to appear (cf. Deut. 17:14-20). Solomon's wealth leads to excess, and his amassing of war horses is an abuse of power. Now intermarriage with foreign wives irreparably widens the breach. By cementing his nation's political security through numerous marriage alliances, Solomon opens the door to his wives' foreign gods and ultimately falls prey to spiritual decay. Through infidelity to God's covenant with David, Solomon jeopardizes not only the promised dynasty but also his people's place in the promised land itself (v. 33; cf. 9:4-9).

Though David displayed obvious moral faults, he never forsook God for foreign deities. By contrast, Solomon pursues foreign gods (vv. 5-7), worship of which included child sacrifice (cf. 2 Kgs. 23:10), cult prostitution, and other covenantally forbidden fertility rites. The king who built the temple of the one true God now builds shrines for pagan pretenders. Because of Solomon's spiritual straying, God plans to hand the northern tribes over to a lesser figure ("servant"; cf. v. 26). For David's sake, however, God will exact the punishment not on Solomon but on his successor, Jeroboam.

Toward this end, God raises up adversaries to Solomon — Hadad in southern Transjordan, whose close friendship with the Egyptian pharaoh sounds an ominous alarm; Rezon to the northwest in Syria, whose grassroots military activities parallel David's early career; and Jeroboam. The king had made Jeroboam

City of David, with houses and the Millo terrace.
(Phoenix Data Systems, Neal and Joel Bierling)

overseer of forced labor drafted from the "house of Joseph" (his native tribe of Ephraim plus Manasseh). Now, however, Solomon copies Saul by seeking to put to death his prophetically appointed rival. Ahijah assumes a role similar to Samuel's in designating a new king for Israel (vv. 29-38; cf. 1 Samuel 9–10, 15–16). The prophet's words in verse 38 recall the dynastic language and covenantal conditions God uses with David and Solomon in 2:3-4; 9:4-5.

Jeroboam escapes to Egypt for the duration of Solomon's reign. His host, Pharaoh Shishak (v. 40), founder of Egypt's 22nd Dynasty, later sends troops against Jerusalem (14:25-26). 2 Chronicles 9:29-31 parallels vv. 41-43 here. The otherwise unknown Book of the Acts of Solomon (v. 41) may have contained Solomon's court records.

12 The Kingdom Splits

Cf. 2 Chr. 10:1–11:4.

Rehoboam's succession to kingship in Judah meets with no apparent challenge from his undoubtedly numerous brothers (cf. Solomon's 1000 wives, 11:3). Rehoboam's northern subjects, however, waste no time in dispatching Jeroboam — a former overseer of forced labor (11:28) — to champion their cause of reduced government service as a condition for their allegiance. God causes Rehoboam to reject the wise counsel of his seasoned elders to honor the people's request, and the king vows instead to make his countrymen's lives harder (v. 11; cf. Exod. 5:7-14).

In their determined refusal to acknowledge Rehoboam as king, the northern tribes echo the defiant words of the Benjamite rebel Sheba to David (v. 16; cf. 2 Sam. 20:1). They add an exclamation point to their declaration of open rebellion by stoning to death the forced labor bureau chief, Adoram (= Adoniram, 4:6; 5:14). A prophetic oracle stops Rehoboam from initiating a civil war, and in accord with God's plan Jeroboam begins his reign from Shechem while Rehoboam rules Judah from Jerusalem.

As did David, Jeroboam recognizes the importance of religion to consolidating his nation. To discourage his subjects from making

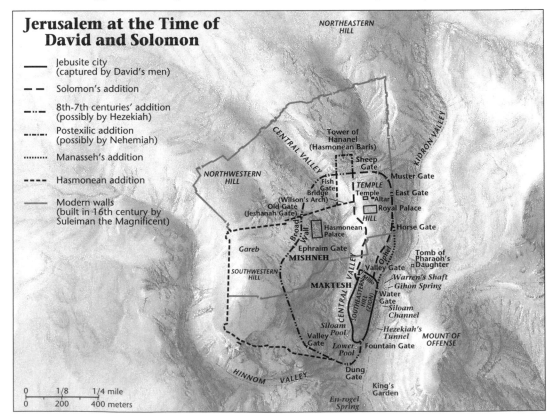

Jerusalem at the Time of David and Solomon

— Jebusite city (captured by David's men)
– – Solomon's addition
–··– 8th-7th centuries' addition (possibly by Hezekiah)
–·–· Postexilic addition (possibly by Nehemiah)
········· Manasseh's addition
- - - - Hasmonean addition
— Modern walls (built in 16th century by Suleiman the Magnificent)

NORTHEASTERN HILL
CENTRAL VALLEY
KIDRON VALLEY
Tower of Hananel (Hasmonean Baris)
Sheep Gate
Fish Gate
Bridge (Wilson's Arch)
Old Gate (Jeshanah Gate)
TEMPLE
Temple
Altar
TEMPLE HILL
Muster Gate
East Gate
Royal Palace
Horse Gate
NORTHWESTERN HILL
Broad Wall
Hasmonean Palace
Ephraim Gate
MISHNEH
Gareb
SOUTHWESTERN HILL
MAKTESH
Valley Gate
Ophel
Tomb of Pharaoh's Daughter
Warren's Shaft
Gihon Spring
Water Gate
Siloam Channel
CENTRAL VALLEY
SOUTHEASTERN HILL (ZION)
Siloam Pool
Valley Gate
Lower Pool
Fountain Gate
Hezekiah's Tunnel
MOUNT OF OFFENSE
HINNOM VALLEY
Dung Gate
King's Garden
En-rogel Spring

0   1/8   1/4 mile
0   200   400 meters

pilgrimages to the temple in the rival capital, Jeroboam fashions golden calves reminiscent of Aaron's idol and declares them Israel's god(s). He sets them up at Bethel in the south and Dan in the north and elsewhere establishes additional, lesser shrines (= "high places"). He inaugurates a feast day (probably to rival the Feast of Tabernacles; vv. 32-33; Lev. 23:34-43), and appoints non-Levitical priests. In trying to tighten his grip on political power, however, Jeroboam seals his own doom, for he forgets the conditions of his appointment to kingship, namely, covenantal fidelity (cf. 11:38). Israelite history would ultimately point to Jeroboam as the model of the unfaithful king by measuring later rulers against the standard of "the sins of Jeroboam" (14:9-10).

13 Jeroboam Warned

A Judahite prophet confronts Jeroboam with the announcement of a future Davidic king who would defile the unlawful Bethelite altar. Josiah, who instituted the nation's most thoroughgoing religious reforms (2 Kings 23), would not appear for over 300 years, but two signs immediately confirm the authenticity of the prophecy: the altar splits apart on the spot, and the incensed Jeroboam's hand withers instantly when the king gives orders against the "man of God."

Through trickery, a second, northern prophet undermines the first prophet's initial steadfast obedience to God's directives. The Judahite prophet's giving in to seemingly harmless temptation ensures his own imminent death at the jaws of a lion (ironically, the symbol of Judah's tribal strength).

The incident demonstrates the consequence Jeroboam can expect for covenantal disobedience. Though initially awakened to the now perilous future of his political position, Jeroboam nonetheless persists in rejecting the faith and boldly defying the Law, most notably by canceling all requirements for ordination to his already illegitimate priesthood and himself acting as priest.

14:1-20 Ahijah's Prophetic Condemnation

Jeroboam's desperate scheme to gain information from the prophet who announced his

kingship demonstrates the depth of his delusion concerning the power of God. The essentially blind Ahijah minces no words in informing Jeroboam's disguised wife that the king's own sinfulness has guaranteed the death of their ailing son Abijah, the eventual death and humiliating exposure of the rest of his doomed male relatives, and the ultimate collapse of his promised dynasty. The only mercy God will show Jeroboam's house is his son's honorable burial (v. 13). Furthermore, the northern kingdom will suffer exile in Mesopotamia because of the Israelites' following in Jeroboam's footsteps (vv. 15-16).

The immediate death of Abijah on the queen's return home to Tirzah and the national mourning of the deceased prince as foretold by the prophet confirm the future fulfillment of the rest of his words. Baasha will soon slay Jeroboam's entire household (15:25-29), and the Assyrians will eventually conquer Israel and deport its population.

The summary notes on Jeroboam's reign and death follow the typically brief format begun with Solomon in 11:41-43 and continued throughout the books of Kings. The lost Book of the Chronicles of the Kings of Israel (v. 19) likely preserved a more complete account of Israel's history than the theologically oriented 1 and 2 Chronicles.

14:21–15:24 Rehoboam, Abijam, and Asa of Judah

Cf. 2 Chr. 11:5–16:14.

From this point on, Kings presents chronologically parallel information about the northern and southern rulers. Judah's kings Rehoboam, Abijam (Abijah in Chronicles), and Asa ruled during the 22 years of Jeroboam's reign in the north, and accounts of their activities appear next in the text. (Asa's rule continued after Jeroboam's death.)

Marked by high places, Asherim, and cult prostitution, Judah's religious pursuits during Rehoboam's reign appear just as wayward as her sister kingdom's to the north. Jeroboam's former Egyptian host, Shishak, plunders the Jerusalem palace and temple but does not conquer the city. That Rehoboam could replace the stolen golden shields only with bronze copies testifies to Judah's economic recession following Solomon's reign (cf. 10:16-17). A persistent state of civil war between Judah and Israel compounds the threats to the southern kingdom.

As with the other Judahite and Israelite kings, the text measures Abijam against the spiritual standard set by David, whose devotion offset his flawed personal behavior. Abijam comes up short, but his son Asa (the "lamp," 15:4) will reform religious matters.

Asa does away with male cult prostitution and idols and even deposes his idolatrous mother (or possibly grandmother), Maacah, though he fails to eliminate Judah's high places. Baasha ascended the northern throne just two years after Asa's succession in Judah, and the conflict between the kingdoms continued during their reigns. When Baasha attempts to isolate Judah from the north, Asa offers a bribe of the royal and temple treasuries to steal from his rival king an alliance with Syria's Ben-hadad. Baasha withdraws to stave off Syrian incursions on Israel's northern border, and Asa regains unhindered passage to and from the capital. He dismantles Baasha's abandoned fortifications at Ramah (a few miles north of Jerusalem) and uses the materials to strengthen defenses in the neighboring Benjamite cities of Geba and Mizpah to guard against a repeated blockade. That the elderly Asa has "diseased feet" (v. 23) probably means he has venereal disease.

15:25–16:14 Nadab, Baasha, Elah, and Zimri of Israel

The account turns to Asa's contemporaries in Israel. The brief reign of Nadab, who succeeds his father, Jeroboam, is characterized with a similarly brief evaluation: like father, like son. Nadab's siege of Gibbethon reveals that Israel has lost political ground to the Philistines, whom David had silenced. Ahijah's prophecy of doom for Jeroboam's dynasty (14:14) falls on Nadab through Baasha, whose conflicts with Asa are recorded earlier in ch. 15. Baasha in turn furthers the "sin of Jeroboam" during his 24-year reign, and the account continues to paint the following northern kings in this same negative light.

The pattern of succession, covenantal disobe-dience, assassination, and usurpation continues with Baasha's drunken son Elah, whose chariot commander Zimri murders him and seizes the throne.

16:15-34 Omri's Dynasty Begins in Israel

Zimri lasts a week on the throne at Tirzah. When challenged militarily by Elah's popularly acclaimed commander, Omri, he commits suicide. Omri must defeat a rival for the kingship before assuming full power. After six years, he moves the northern capital from Tirzah to the "hill of Samaria," where he builds the city that will remain Israel's capital until the fall of the northern kingdom to Assyria (722/21). During that whole period (ca. 150 years), Assyrian records refer to Israel as "the land of Omri" and thus testify to this king's political power and international reputation despite his relatively unremarkable mention in the biblical text. An inscription of Moab's contemporary King Mesha remembers Omri as having conquered central Transjordan's Medeba plateau (cf. 2 Kgs. 3:4-5)

Omri's accession spawns a stable but religiously despicable dynasty, whose degenerate character intensifies with his son and successor, Ahab. Ahab's politically and economically advantageous marriage to the Baal-worshipping, Phoenician princess Jezebel leads to the official introduction in Samaria of Baal cult practices, in which Ahab participates (v. 31; "Baal" here is the Phoenician storm- and fertility-god, Melqart).

The tragedies that befall Hiel when he rebuilds Jericho (v. 34) fulfill the prophecy in Josh. 6:26.

17 Elijah Appears

Ahab's blatant paganism sets the stage for a prophetic conflict. After a brief mention of Elijah's ("my God is Yahweh") prophecy concerning an extended drought that pits Yahweh's power over nature against Baal's, the text leaves Ahab behind to concentrate on establishing Elijah's authenticity as a prophet of God.

God works through nature to provide food for Elijah. Elijah's prediction of drought comes true and forces him at God's directive to travel northwest from his native territory in Transjordan (Gilead) in search of greener pastures on the Phoenician coast. A second prophecy is fulfilled when his Sidonian hostess's meager remains of flour and oil miraculously replenish themselves and supply enough bread to feed her family and guest "for many days." The deathly illness of the widow's son occasions an opportunity for Elijah to petition God to revitalize the boy. The divine granting of Elijah's request turns the mother's bitterness to belief, as evidenced in her confession of Elijah's prophetic authenticity (v. 24; cf. 2 Kgs. 4:18-37).

Elijah appears the model of obedience to God's commands and thus contrasts with the devious and deceived prophets of ch. 13.

18 The Contest at Carmel

The contest between Elijah and the prophets of Baal showcases God's absolute power in the face of the pagan deity's utter impotence. The setting is the Carmel mountain range, which extends southeast from the modern coastal city of Haifa. After three years of drought, Elijah returns to a naturally devastated and spiritually deprived northern kingdom. Only 100 true prophets of God survive Jezebel's purge (v. 4), but they remain in hiding. Ahab's godly servant Obadiah secretly provides for them at his own personal risk.

Elijah turns Ahab's accusation, "troubler of Israel," back on the king (vv. 17-18), recalling Deut. 11:17, where the promised curse for serving other gods, as Ahab has done, is drought and infertility of the land. He chides the Israelites for waffling between "two different opinions," trying to serve both God and Baal.

Displaying unflinching faith in God, Elijah suggests a contest that puts him at a great human disadvantage but the outcome of which will establish once and for all the one, true God. By himself, Elijah takes on 450 prophets of Baal at Carmel, thought to be a traditional site for Baal worship. Elijah allows his opponents the entire day to call down fire from heaven to consume their sacrifice. Despite the prophets' ritual leaping, crying out, and self-mutilation, however, the sacrifice lies rotting on the pagan altar. Elijah mocks their carrying on, suggesting that Baal's failure to respond might be the result of his need

for private time to answer nature's call (= "gone aside," v. 27).

When Elijah's turn comes, he builds a proper Hebrew altar with 12 stones to represent the 12 tribes. He puts himself at further disadvantage by drenching his sacrifice and everything around it with 12 pitchers' worth of scarce and precious water. A simple prayer for God to perform a sign that will display his glory results in the spontaneous and complete consumption by fire of everything Elijah has prepared, and the people can do nothing but acknowledge God's lordship (cf. 2 Kgs. 1:12).

Elijah counters Jezebel's attempted extermination of God's prophets by ordering the slaughter of the prophets of Baal. God's "word" brings about the end of the drought through a heavy rainstorm (cf. 17:1; 18:1, 41), and the "hand" of the Lord empowers Elijah to outrun Ahab's chariot over the 17-mile stretch to the king's summer palace at Jezreel.

19 Elijah Flees to Horeb

Jezebel's murderous threat to Elijah on discovering the fate of her prophets causes him to flee deep into Judahite territory. Aided by God's angel, the prophet finds strength to travel further to Mount Horeb, site of Moses' encounters with God (cf. Exod. 3:1-2; 19:16-24). Elijah's 40-day fast and journey into the wilderness recall Israel's wilderness wanderings and Moses' fasting at Sinai. Indeed, Kings portrays the prophet as the "new Moses" (compare v. 8 with Exod. 24:18; vv. 9-11 with Exod. 33:17-23; v. 21b with Exod. 24:13; also 18:31-32 with Exod. 24:4; 2 Kgs. 2:8 with Exod. 14:21-22; cf. also Matt. 17:3).

In a "sound of sheer silence" totally opposite his dramatic, mountaintop utterance at Carmel, God challenges Elijah's flight from Jezebel and instructs him to return to enemy territory. The next prophetic tasks will be anointing new kings over Syria and Israel in addition to a successor for Elijah. The three leaders will accomplish a divinely orchestrated purge of Israel's idolaters. The number given for the God-fearing Israelites who will survive (7000) is symbolic, based on seven ("perfection").

Elijah "anoints" Elisha ("God is salvation")

Mount Carmel, where Elijah challenged the 450 prophets of Baal (1 Kings 18). *(Richard Cleave, Pictorial Archive)*

by throwing his cloak over the industrious field laborer (cf. 2 Kgs. 2:8, 13-14) and then grants Elisha's request to bid his family farewell. The anointing of the new kings will fall to the new prophet (2 Kings 8–9).

20 The Syrians Besiege Samaria

Elijah disappears as quickly as he appeared in ch. 17. Ahab seems more open to God's leading through the prophets in this account of Syria's siege of Samaria. While at first willing to hand over his family and wealth to the 33-king alliance headed by Ben-hadad, Ahab balks when the enemies' terms of surrender go too far. A prophet of God appears to Ahab and lays out the divine strategy for a preemptive strike against the enemy coalition. The troops Ahab musters from outlying provinces soundly rout the Syrians, but the anonymous prophet predicts a second attempt.

Surmising that Israel's God must rule over the mountains, the Syrians draw out to the plains the comparatively tiny army of Israel. Determined to defend his reputation in the face of the Syrians' denial of his omnipotence (v. 28), God delivers the adversaries into the Israelites' hands. This second battle turns the tables on Ben-hadad, who must now surrender to Ahab and beg for his life. But Ahab fails to carry out God's directive to destroy even the Syrian king, and another prophet foretells Ahab's death as punishment for sparing Ben-hadad's life (v. 36; cf. 13:11-32).

Rather than repent, Ahab simply goes home and sulks. Assyrian records reveal that Ahab joined forces with Damascus in battling Shalmaneser III at Qarqar in northern Syria (853).

In portraying God as fighting for the northern kingdom, which Kings generally characterizes as thoroughly wicked, this chapter demonstrates God's continued care for his chosen, though mostly unfaithful, people. The Greek Septuagint places ch. 20 after the Hebrew Bible's ch. 21 and thus reverses the order of events.

21 Judgment on Ahab and Jezebel

Ahab's coveting a subject's vineyard violates the Tenth Commandment (Exod. 20:17). Even worse, Hebrew law forbade the permanent sale of property outside one's family and tribe, and Ahab surely knew this (cf. Lev. 25:25-28; Num. 36:7). His father Omri had managed to purchase land, however, and thus set the precedent for Ahab's effort here (cf. 16:24).

Jezebel thinks it ridiculous that the Israelite monarch should be denied what he wants, and the pouting Ahab turns a blind eye to his wife's murderous scheme that targets the landowner, Naboth. The Phoenician princess shows good knowledge of Israelite law in rounding up the required minimum of two witnesses to deliver against Naboth trumped-up charges of blasphemy, a violation punishable by death (cf. Lev. 24:10-16, 23). She uses Israelite law to commit an illegal transaction.

Ahab shows no remorse when he learns of Naboth's stoning. Instead, he proceeds to take possession of the coveted vineyard — an act that constitutes stealing from Naboth's rightful heirs (cf. God's warning in 1 Sam. 8:11-17). Elijah reenters the narrative to pronounce divine judgment first on Ahab, whom God holds ultimately responsible for Naboth's murder, and then on the wicked queen, whom the account blames for inciting her husband to evil (v. 25). Their mutual responsibility for each other's wicked actions ushers in their individual death sentences (intensified for Ahab from 20:42) as well as the promised end of Ahab's dynasty (vv. 21-24; cf. 14:10-11).

Ahab's contrition wins him a stay of punishment, but his sin of "selling himself" to the

The Divided Monarchy —
Israel and Judah

N

Mediterranean
Sea

PHOENICIA

ARAM

Beirut

Sidon

Damascus

Litani R.

Mt. Hermon

Pharpar R.

Tyre

Dan

Kedesh

Hazor

Acco

J. Jarmuk

Mt. Carmel

Sea of
Galilee

Ashtaroth

Mt.
Tabor

Kishon

Mt. Moreh

Yarmuk R.

Edrei

Megiddo

Beth-shan

Ramoth-gilead

Taanach

R.

Ibleam

Mt.
Gilboa

Jabesh-gilead?

Jordan R.

Samaria

Tirzah

Mt. Ebal

Succoth?

Penuel?

Mahanaim?

Yarkon R.

Mt. Gerizim

Shechem

Jabbok R.

Joppa

Aphek

Shiloh

ISRAEL

Rabbah (Amman)

Bethel

Gezer

Jericho

AMMON

Aijalon

Jerusalem

Mt. Nebo

Heshbon

Ashdod

Gath

Bethlehem

Medeba

Ashkelon

Mareshah

Gaza

Hebron

Dibon

Gerar

Besor Br.

Dead
Sea

Amon R.

Raphia

JUDAH

MOAB

Beer-sheba

Kir-hareseth

PHILISTIA

Zered Br.

WILDERNESS

W. el-Arish

Region
periodically
contested
by Judah
and Edom

Bozrah

Kadesh-
barnea

EDOM

WILDERNESS

| 0 | 10 | 20 | 30 Miles |

| 0 | 10 | 20 | 30 Kilometers |

pursuit of Canaanite gods tips the scales against his dynasty's future (vv. 25-29; cf. 2 Sam. 12:1-13).

22:1-40 Ahab Meets His Death

Cf. 2 Chronicles 18.

Asa's son Jehoshaphat, king of Judah (15:24), makes peace with the northern kingdom (v. 44; contrast 15:16). 2 Kings 8:18, 26 reveals that a marriage alliance between Jehoshaphat's son Joram and Ahab's daughter Athaliah sealed this peace, but it also occasioned the opportunity for Ahab to break his treaty with Ben-hadad (cf. 20:34). The southern king's going "down" to the northern king means that he descended from Jerusalem, Judah's mountaintop capital in the hill country (v. 2).

Ahab, who remains unnamed until verse 20, convinces Jehoshaphat to help retake the important Transjordanian outpost of Ramoth-gilead from the Syrians (cf. 4:13). The king of Judah, however, wants divine approval of the plan. Four hundred prophets tell Ahab what he wants to hear, but Jehoshaphat appears suspicious of the origin of their prophecies. Under pressure, Ahab summons Micaiah, whom he hates because of the prophet's consistently negative words against him. Admonished to be straightforward, Micaiah reveals that a divine ruse has been in play, and he predicts disaster on Ahab in the battle. The circumstances of Micaiah's vision verify the authenticity of his prophecy (vv. 19-23; cf. Jer. 23:16-17).

Micaiah's words are lost on Ahab, however, and he casts his lot with the prophet Zedekiah and company. With Micaiah imprisoned in Samaria, Jehoshaphat dressed as a decoy, and Ahab traveling under cover as though he

could restrict God's power or thwart his plans, the kings challenge Ramoth-gilead. That the godly Jehoshaphat participates despite the doom-saying oracle, which Ahab obtained only at Jehoshaphat's insistence, seems surprising.

The Syrians of Ramoth-gilead abandon their targeted engagement with Jehoshaphat when they discover his true identity, while a randomly shot arrow finds its mark in a chink in the disguised Ahab's armor. Micaiah's prophecy comes true when the Hebrews abandon the battle and Ahab bleeds to death from his wound. Elijah's words are fulfilled when the dogs of Samaria lick the king's blood from the pool used in washing off his chariot (v. 38; cf. 21:19).

The archaeological discovery of the elaborately carved Samaria ivories sheds light on the reference to Ahab's "ivory house" (v. 39).

22:41–2 Kgs. 1:1 Jehoshaphat of Judah

Cf. 2 Chronicles 17-20.

Jehoshaphat emulates his father, the "good" king Asa. Though he also fails to dismantle the "high places," he continues to expel male cult prostitutes from Judah. Jehoshaphat attempts to revive Solomon's international trade ventures via the Red Sea — and Ahab's son and successor, Ahaziah, even tries unsuccessfully to become involved — but the effort fails due to a wounded fleet. Jehoram (Joram) succeeds Jehoshaphat on the Davidic throne.

Israel's Ahaziah also follows in his father's footsteps, but for evil, not good. During Ahaziah's brief reign, Moab gains independence from Israelite control.

2 Kings

1:2-18 Ahaziah of Israel

Ahaziah's attempt to learn his fate from the storm-god Baal displays the influence of Canaanite deities introduced by his father Ahab and brings a divine death sentence foretold by Elijah. Baal-zebub ("lord of the flies") is probably a derogatory twist on the Canaanite "Baal-zebul" ("Prince Baal").

In a repeat of his role in summoning God's power on Mount Carmel, Elijah twice calls down fire from heaven to consume the messengers from the king. Not until the commander of the third company of soldiers shows respect for God does the "man of God" agree to accompany them. Once in Samaria, Elijah delivers the prophetic threat to Ahaziah personally. The death of the sonless Ahaziah does not bring about the anticipated end of the Omride dynasty (prophesied in 1 Kgs. 21:29) but instead occasions the accession of Jehoram/Joram (Ahaziah's brother or son, not the contemporary Judahite king Jehoram; cf. 3:1) to the northern throne. To distinguish the northern and southern kings here, we refer to the northern king as "Joram" and the southern as "Jehoram."

2 Elisha Succeeds Elijah

Elisha refuses to allow Elijah to face his final time on earth alone. The two descend from the hill country into the Jordan Valley, where Elijah uses his mantle (also used in "anointing" Elisha) to part the waters of the Jordan River in an act that recalls Moses' parting of the Red Sea. Once in Transjordan near the site of Moses' death, Elisha asks to become Elijah's prophetic heir by receiving a spiritual inheritance equal to that of an eldest son, a "double portion."

That Elisha sees his master taken up to heaven in a whirlwind indicates that God has granted his request. The fiery horses and chariot signify God's presence at Elijah's assumption (cf. Exod. 3:2; 13:21).

The remainder of the chapter offers public confirmation of Elisha's succession to Elijah's prophetic office. He uses Elijah's mantle to re-part the Jordan (and he crosses back to Canaan proper, as did Moses' successor, Joshua; Josh. 3:14-17). His implication that Elijah has permanently departed reaches the prophets of Jericho, who witness the Transjordanian events. Using salt symbolically, he miraculously purifies Jericho's waters. Skeptical lads at Bethel demanding proofs of Elisha's authenticity meet their doom as a result of his curse on them.

Elijah ascends to heaven in a fiery chariot as Elisha receives his mantle; Stella Maris monastery, Mount Carmel. *(Erich Lessing / Art Resource, NY)*

3 Joram's Moabite Campaign

Verse 1 conflicts with 1:17 on the year of Joram's accession (cf. 1:17). The text is comparatively kind to this northern king by likening his reign to those of the "merely" degenerate Jeroboam (1 Kings 12–14), not the thoroughly faithless Ahab (1 Kgs. 16:29-33; 18–22).

According to the Moabite Stone (or Mesha Stela; late 9th century b.c.), Moab had become Israel's vassal during the reign of Omri. The region rebelled during Ahaziah's brief reign (1:1), and now Joram follows Ahab's strategy in teaming up with Jehoshaphat, king of Judah, in an attempt to regain control of this Transjordanian territory east of the Dead Sea (cf. 1 Kings 22). That Jehoshaphat appears to have appointed a non-native deputy to rule in Edom explains that region's willing participation in the coalition (cf. 1 Kgs. 22:47).

The allied army's march through the arid south leaves them short of water and makes Joram think his mission might be ill fated. Jehoshaphat again insists on seeking divine confirmation and this time finds Elisha, who had served as Elijah's assistant or apprentice (v. 11; cf. 1 Kgs. 22:7). Elisha's sarcastic greeting of Joram recalls Ahaziah's bypassing God (through Elijah) in seeking counsel from the Canaanite god Baal-zebub (1:2-3). Only the favored southern King Jehoshaphat's presence persuades Elisha to cooperate.

Like the ecstatic prophets, Elisha summons music to prepare him for communicating God's prophetic word (cf. 1 Sam. 10:5). As with Elijah on his footrace to Jezreel (1 Kgs. 18:46), the "hand of the Lord" empowers Elisha for the task. After foretelling God's miraculous provision of abundant water and victory over the Moabites, Elisha disappears from the account. Notably, Elisha's prophecy commands an attack against Moab's cities, its land, and even its trees, but it does not require the obliteration of its human population, for Moab lay not in Canaan proper but in Transjordan (vv. 16-18; cf. Deut. 20:10-15).

The water both sustains the coalition forces and confuses the enemy. The Moabites lose the battle, but Mesha's public sacrifice of his crown prince on top of the city wall so bolsters the remaining Moabites and so repulses the Israelites that they fail to finish the job by taking the capital itself. Their return home leaves the ultimate results of the campaign in limbo. While the Moabite Stone claims a successful rebellion against Israel, it does not specifically address Joram's effort to reclaim the region.

4 Elisha Performs More Miracles

In relating four more of Elisha's miracles, this chapter interrupts the account of Israel's and Judah's kings. It remains unclear where the episodes fit chronologically. Elisha's works on behalf of common Israelites flesh out the Deuteronomic concern for society's least powerful individuals (cf. Deut. 24:10-22).

The first miracle parallels Elijah's increasing the widow of Zarephath's flour and oil (1 Kgs. 17:13-16). Here the widow of a member of the prophetic community faces the subjection of her two sons to slavery to work off the family debt (cf. Lev. 25:39-41). Elisha's miracle supplies her with a marketable commodity to use in paying off her debt, leaves enough to support her family, and enables her sons to remain with her to work the land.

The account of the Shunammite woman and her son also parallels Elijah's dealings with the widow of Zarephath. Here practical kindness of a sonless Shunammite woman toward Elisha issues in his promising her a baby boy. Elisha's offer to speak to the king on her behalf suggests that he exercised influence in the Israelite royal court, in contrast to Elijah's tense relationship with Ahab. The advanced age of the woman's husband and her own unbelieving response to Elisha's prophecy recall the situation with Abraham and Sarah (Gen. 18:10-12).

The woman does bear a son, but as a young boy he apparently suffers sunstroke and dies. Determined to reach Elisha at Mount Carmel, the desperate mother brushes aside her husband's protests that the day is neither a Sabbath nor a new moon, favorable days for consulting a prophet. On encountering Elisha, the woman regrets his blessing-turned-curse and uses Elisha's own words to Elijah in vowing not to leave him (v. 30; cf. 2:2, 4, 6). Elisha travels home with her and employs Elijah's methods in enlivening

Society and Daily Life in the Old Testament

In the world of the ancient Near East, the central issue facing every person was coping with environmental conditions. In Egypt and Mesopotamia, this meant adapting to the limits posed by the predictable yearly inundations of the Nile River in Egypt and the unpredictable flooding of the Tigris and Euphrates Rivers in Mesopotamia. The land bridge of Syria-Palestine also had to cope with water problems, but these were based more on average annual rainfall amounts than on irrigation. Necessarily, the civilizations that developed in these lands based their calendar, their workday, their religious festivals and theology, and even their warring on the manifestations of the weather, the change of seasons, and the topography of their lands.

The panhandle of Syria-Palestine makes up less than 60 miles of landmass, west to east, between the 34th and 36th meridians of longitude and 350 miles, north to south, between the 31st and 33rd meridians of latitude. Nonetheless, there are four clearly defined geographical and climatic zones. Moving from west to east, the first zone is a coastal plain along the shore of the Mediterranean Sea. The plains are separated by foothills (Shephelah) from the hills west of the Jordan River, making up the second zone in which the Israelites settled. The third zone is the valley created by the Jordan River and the Dead Sea (Arabah), and the fourth is the hills or plateaus east of the Jordan River. To the south, this panhandle is separated from the Sinai desert by the Negev, which provides perennial springs or wells large enough to support a few permanent settlements.

The region enjoys only two seasons, wet and dry, although snow does occur in the hill country near Jerusalem and in the Mount Hermon range north of the Galilee. Moist winds blowing west to east create the wet season, hot dry winds blowing from east to west create the dry. The plains cause temperature changes in the winds blowing off the Mediterranean Sea, thus creating the rain.

With the withdrawal of the Egyptians and the Hittites from Syria-Palestine, its population dropped dramatically at the end of the Late Bronze Age. Cities and towns collapsed. By 1250 B.C. perhaps as much as 60 percent of the population had died from starvation due to crop failures that followed subtle changes in climate, regional wars, and the exhaustion of natural resources. These disasters were not isolated, but ongoing. Such tragedies and hardships afflicting the slave or surplus economies of Mesopotamia, Egypt, and Syria-Palestine gave rise to free peasant or subsistence economies such as that in early Israel.

Some of Egypt's and Hatti's former villagers and slaves in Syria-Palestine took advantage of their

Drawing water at the well, an essential factor in the establishment and survival of settlements and a focal point of community life. *(Richard Cleave, Pictorial Archive)*

245

newfound freedom and tried to ensure their households against an uncertain future by migrating into the hills, where they re-established abandoned villages or founded new ones of their own. The writing, language, material culture, and religious traditions of the Israelite tribes who resettled or founded these villages link them to the Canaanite culture found throughout Syria-Palestine. More than likely, these early villagers were social survivors who fled the famine, plague, and war that brought the Late Bronze Age to an end.

The economy in these Hebrew villages was a subsistence economy, not a surplus or slave

Almanac from Gezer, an agricultural calendar or manual outlining the planting, harvesting, and care of crops; 10th century B.C. *(www. HolyLandPhotos.org)*

economy like that common throughout the city-states of Syria-Palestine. In this subsistence economy, there was no monarch; therefore, there were no taxes and no army, and there were no slaves. The challenge facing early Israel was not so much a military

conquest, as portrayed in Joshua and Judges, but rather farming a difficult and demanding land. The late 10th-century Gezer Almanac shows that planting and harvesting governed their lives.

A standard harvest in these hills produced 10 to 15 percent more grain than was needed to plant it. While positive changes in the quality of the land, the number of farmers available, and the way in which they worked could increase the standard harvest, there was always the greater risk of negative changes that could destroy the economy of the village and its households altogether. Fields that produced as little as a 10 to 15 percent harvest in good years failed altogether in three years out of ten.

To get the most from the human labor available in the village, farmers used a variety of techniques. They managed their time, pooled their labor, with both men and women working the fields, and had as many children as possible. Farmers in early Israel staggered sowing by planting a single crop in several stages over a period of time. Although it would be impossible to care for a single large crop at one time, the number of farmers available could handle the same-sized crop one section at a time. Farmers also planted a variety of vine, tree, and field crops, mixing a variety of cereals with fruit and nut crops.

By living together in pillared, low-roofed houses, farmers pooled their labor. Together, farmers cleared land, terraced fields, planted, cultivated, and harvested crops. The basic plan of the pillared house was a simple rectangle divided into three areas by a row of four roof-supporting

pillars and a solid inside wall. Some houses had an additional room across the back of the basic rectangle entered through a door off the main section of the house.

The inhabitants wore a loin-cloth and a tunic. Everyone had a cloak that doubled as a blanket. In areas where water was precious, few bathed or regularly washed their clothes (Gen. 27:27). Health care was based on herbal remedies (Gen. 30:14), basic first aid for cuts and fractures, and rituals and prayers (Ps. 38:1-5).

There was no furniture in their homes. People sat cross-legged on the packed clay and stone floor or on a stone ledge along the base of the inside wall of the house. Flat stones were used for stools. Everyone slept on the floor. Several households shared a common outdoor courtyard kitchen. Bread was baked on a pottery bowl inverted over the coals (Hos. 7:8) or in a domed mud and plaster oven.

Most village farmers also maintained at least a small herd of sheep and goats as an economic hedge against famine. Herding was often carried out by youngsters and therefore did not deprive the village of needed field labor (1 Samuel 16). The villagers also raided passing caravans transporting goods between Syria and Egypt, or occasionally served as transit agents, taxing goods that passed through their territory. In some cases, farmers served as trading partners, especially in metals that were acquired as imports and shaped into tools. By combining farming with herding, raiding, trading, and manufacturing, they distributed their labor more evenly throughout the season and ensured themselves against facing the dry season without having produced any food at all.

Eventually, in their attempt to compete with other Canaanite and Philistine cultures, the early Israelite villages had to transform their strictly rural culture into a society centered on an urban-based monarchy. This required new social accommodations and meant the establishment of social boundaries and the recognition of power groups outside normal kinship relationships. At this point, more than in the village culture, social stratification determined task differentiation, leadership responsibilities, and relative levels of power. The new social landscape was defined by domination of others and accomplished by various means — including physical force, social or psychological control, and economic coercion.

In ancient Israel there existed a patrilineal, segmentary lineage system in which each of its households *(bet 'abot)* belonged to a lineage *(mishpaha)*. These lineages, in which membership and inheritance were based on the father, made up a clan. The clans formed several larger units called phratries, and the phratries comprised the tribe. Its lineages were also, once the Israelites entered Canaan, described as localized, having their own designated territories (Joshua 13–19). These social groupings are not necessarily evolutionary. They all continued to exist and served as the basis of personal identity, even after the monarchy was established, and there was no linear progression that required each to exist in turn for the monarchy to be established.

Social Custom and Law

Social custom and law, as it developed in the village and was transmitted and transformed in the urban setting, was defined by the people's sense of honor and shame. These two concepts revolve around both a sense of self and recognition of behavior by others, and they provide the basis for social reward and social control. Those who obeyed the covenant with Yahweh, upheld the rights and obligations of their households, and set an example of hard work and devotion to family were designated as honorable and looked to for advice. Shame resulted from antisocial behavior, violations of the religious code, and physical deformity or illness. The gate court and later the royal court system provided the legal basis for dealing with shameful and antisocial behavior.

Marriage Marriage customs fit under the category of "honor and shame" since they also involve "proper" behavior. In ancient Syria-Palestine, as in the modern Mediterranean region, they encompass an emphasis on female chastity and the desirability of premarital virginity.

Within the ancestral narrative, the one criterion that surfaces most often is endogamy, marriage within a specific group. Authority for this position, which establishes a preferential pool of eligible marriage partners, is presented in the ancestral narratives, where solemn oaths are taken to insure this practice (Gen. 24:2-6; Abraham and his servant). Family tensions are created when the principle is violated (Gen. 26:34-35; Esau's wives).

These episodes may reflect attitudes or customs that actually date to the postexilic period's emphasis on "in-marrying," which formed a part of the Jewish Identity Movement of that era (cf. Ezra 9–10; Neh. 13:23-27). They may even be based on a postexilic interpretation of the Deuteronomist's accusations regarding Solomon's marriages (1 Kings 11; Neh. 13:26) and the need to insure a pattern of "correct" marriages in the genealogical narratives that form the roots of the nation.

No such restrictions are evident when one examines the marriage practices of the royal family in general, however. It is possible that the higher levels of society may have felt that they were, or may actually have been, above the restrictive traditions adhered to by the peasant and/or middle classes, or they may have had a different set of restrictions placed on them all together. The political realities of a king's position that required a show of "dominance" through political marriage alliance may have also mitigated adherence to previous custom.

Marriage is often thought of as an event, while in some societies it is a long-drawn-out process, with several stages. In the biblical text, certain procedures were to be followed that would establish the alliance between families and spell out the contract in exact terms. Contained within the legal action of betrothal was the final choice of partners, usually made by the male heads of household of the two families, and the agreement on bride-price and dowry (Gen. 24:52-54). There are some exceptions to this rule, in which a socially unattached male arranges his own marriage with the bride's family (see Jacob in Genesis 29), but these are rare.

Considerations regarding a prospective marriage alliance had

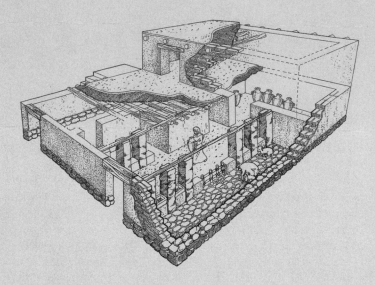

Artist's reconstruction of the Israelite "four-room house." *(Giselle S. Hasel)*

their economic side, of course, and many times a marriage was made on strictly economic grounds, with the intent of further enriching both families or strengthening the manpower of the group (Gen. 34:21; Exod. 2:21). Other considerations included kinship obligations (Gen. 24:3-4), political advancement (David's marriages to Michal in 1 Sam. 18:17-28 and Ahinoam in 1 Sam. 25:43), and, occasionally, personal desire (Judg. 14:3; 2 Sam. 11:27).

The concept of inheritance is also an integral part of the system of marriage customs, especially with regard to the ability of the male to transmit his goods and property to a son and the ability of the female to produce an heir for her husband. This sometimes required legal side steps: adoption (Gen. 15:2), the law of levirate obligation (Deut. 25:5-10), or the compromise involving the daughters of Zelophehad (Num. 36:2-12; Josh. 17:3-6). The precedent for inheritance rights is set in the ancestral narratives with the promise made to Abraham that he and his descendants would receive

Canaan as their special domain. Since there eventually developed several collateral lineages claiming Abraham as their common ancestor, some distinction had to be developed that would designate those who had the right to live in and exploit the promised land. Two basic criteria emerged: the blessing associated with the covenant and physical presence within Canaan.

Hospitality Another social custom that demonstrates "right behavior" in ancient Syria-Palestine is hospitality. The following protocol emerges from the biblical narrative.

(1) There is a sphere of hospitality that comprises a zone of obligation, for both the individual and the village or town, within which they have the responsibility to offer hospitality to strangers. The size of the zone is of course smaller for the individual than for the urban center. The basis for this obligation is reciprocity. In the ancient Near East reciprocal gifting of water, food, and shelter meant

the traveler had a greater chance of survival on the road. It also lessened the instances of theft, raiding, and murder that might have occurred in an inhospitable land where every person's hand was turned against another.

Thus it becomes the responsibility of each person to offer hospitality to strangers, defined as persons not of their kinship or communal group, who enter the sphere he owns or controls. This is to be done: (a) to give back to God a portion of what has been given to them (Deut. 16:17); (b) to set up attendant obligations on others that they be properly treated should they ever play the role of guest themselves (Deut. 23:24-25), and to protect the reputation of the host or the village as a place where hospitality is freely given; and (c) to protect themselves from possible violence and the threat of loss of property by transforming the stranger into a guest.

(2) The stranger must be transformed from potential threat to an ally by the offer of hospitality. No society can tolerate a hostile presence within it for long. When a stranger approaches a village or dwelling place, by definition this person is a threat to inhabitants of that place. One reason for this is that a stranger has no status; there are no rules that apply to him since he is a person without a place in society. To avert hostility, the stranger must be neutralized by temporary adoption into the community.

(3) Only the male head of household or a male citizen of a town or village can make the offer of hospitality. Within this male-dominated legal framework it is his right and responsibility, therefore, to serve as host. His wife and

daughter(s) may serve the guest as well, but only at the behest of their husband or father (Gen. 18:6). Independent action on their part, such as Sarah's questioning of the guests' statement, would be a breach of custom (v. 13).

(4) The invitation can include a statement of the time span for the period of hospitality, but this can then be extended, if agreeable to both parties, on the renewed invitation of the host.

(5) The stranger has the right of refusal, but this could be considered an affront to the honor of the host and could be a cause for immediate hostilities or conflict if proper respect is not shown to the host. While the stranger is generally at the mercy of his host or host city, the visitor may refuse hospitality, based perhaps on a desire to continue one's journey (Judg. 19:9-10) or, as in the case of the angels' visit to Sodom (Gen. 19:2), on the legal inappropriateness of the one making the invitation.

(6) Once the invitation is accepted, the roles of the host and the guest are set by the rules of custom. The guest must not ask for anything, but it is his/her obligation to accept what is offered. It is typical for the host to make a modest offer to the guest (usually water, food, shelter, and a foot washing). This does not rule out more being given to the guest, but it does protect the host who

may find himself in the dishonored position of offering more than he can deliver. The guest is expected to reciprocate with news, predictions of good fortune, or gracious responses based on what he has been given. Just as it is inappropriate for the guest to ask for something from the host, it is totally inappropriate for the potential or actual host to ask questions of his guest. The guest can only volunteer these matters.

(7) The guest remains under the protection of the host until he/she has left the zone of obligation of the host. The sphere or zone of obligation that the guest enters and leaves has its limits. There will be spaces between these zones that were uninhabited in the sparsely populated area of ancient Palestine. In those areas travelers were truly on their own and were subject to the dangers of the road — brigands, wild animals, hostile climate, and uncertain terrain. This then magnifies the importance of the hospitality ritual when a traveler enters the zone of obligation of an individual household or population center.

In summary, the village-based culture of ancient Israel required strict attention to the land and to the social obligations inherent to small, relatively isolated populations. The intensive labor necessary to maintain the food supply and, when possible, to produce a

surplus blurred the work roles of the sexes, although females were still strictly monitored with marriage and sexual taboos dominating their social choices. Inheritance patterns also contributed to the development and the rigidity of the social order, though the growth of urban centers did modify these customs somewhat. Finally, the concept of reciprocity, found in the hospitality code as well as in much of the legal formulations, further defined "insider"/"outsider" roles and established a sense of honor and shame that dominated most social actions and reactions.

For Further Reading

Borowski, Oded. *Agriculture in Iron Age Israel.* Winona Lake: Eisenbrauns, 1987.

Callaway, Joseph A. "A Visit with Ahilud: A Revealing Look at Village Life When Israel First Settled the Promised Land." *BAR* 9/5 (1983): 42-53.

Hopkins, David C. *The Highlands of Canaan.* Sheffield: Almond, 1985.

Matthews, Victor H. *Manners and Customs in the Bible.* Peabody: Hendrickson, 1988.

———, and Don C. Benjamin. *Social World of Ancient Israel, 1250-587 B.C.E.* Peabody: Hendrickson, 1993.

Stager, Lawrence E. "The Archaeology of the Family in Ancient Israel." *BASOR* 260 (1985): 1-35.

VICTOR H. MATTHEWS

the boy, whose corpse lies stretched out on his own bed (vv. 21, 34-35; cf. 1 Kgs. 17:19, 21). Elisha's dealings with the woman continue in ch. 8.

The next two miracles involve Elisha's provision of food for the hungry. The famine of verse 38 may represent that in 8:1. Elisha uses flour symbolically when he purifies a stew unknowingly made from poisonous gourds for the prophetic community (cf. his similar use of salt to purify the waters of Jericho in 2:19-22). Then at least 100 men (the same community of prophets?) get their fill of flat bread and corn from a modest offering of firstfruits to Elisha.

5 Elisha Cures a Syrian General

Although Israel and Syria (= Aram) often engaged in military confrontations (cf. 6:8, 24; 10:32-33; 1 Kings 20), two kingdoms are on friendly enough terms for the Syrian king to send his chief military officer, Naaman, to the Israelite king to seek healing from a serious skin disease (probably not the leprosy of modern Hansen's disease; cf. Leviticus 13–14). The panicked Israelite king mistakenly interprets the impossible request as Syria's move to pick another fight, but Elisha comes to his king's rescue.

Naaman takes offense at Elisha's impersonal communication of a too-simple prescription that he wash himself seven times in the Jordan River. Naaman's servants convince their master to try the potential cure, however, and the successful results lead to Naaman's religious conversion. He requests enough Israelite dirt to accommodate an altar to God back in Syria so he can worship Yahweh on "holy ground," perhaps believing he could worship God only on Israelite soil (cf. Psalm 137). Elisha refuses any payment-in-kind for his role in the miracle, but his servant Gehazi pursues the departing Naaman determined to take some of the reward meant for his master. Gehazi's deceptive tactics work with Naaman but not with the prophet, and as punishment for his greed the servant contracts the same skin ailment as Naaman.

While the account shows God's unbounded mercy toward a non-Israelite (and his punishment of one of his chosen people), the primary purpose of the episode is to demonstrate God's

unique and cosmic sovereignty (cf. v. 15). Indeed, the miracle has a profound effect on Naaman, who takes his newfound dedication to God to his homeland, but there the pressure to continue worshipping his native national god will require him to act out old religious practices (v. 18).

6:1-7 Elisha Heads the Prophets

Under Elisha's leadership the prophetic community outgrows its living space. He joins them as they move to the Jordan Valley, where abundant trees provide building materials for new accommodations. The Israelites had edged in on the Philistines' iron-working monopoly, as evident from the sunken iron ax head. Elisha helps a prophetic underling by causing the borrowed implement to float, thereby allowing its recovery.

6:8-23 Elisha Deflects a Syrian Raid

Elisha ruins the Syrians' attempt to mount a surprise attack when he advises the king of Israel (presumably Joram) on the enemy's position. The Syrian king suspects one of his own men of betrayal, but his servant blames Elisha, whom the king determines to capture to prevent future interference with his plans.

Elisha remains calm when the Syrian army surrounds his refuge in Dothan, which guarded access to the hill country 10 miles north of Samaria. God's protective "horses and chariots of fire" (v. 17) recall Elijah's assumption into heaven (cf. 2:11). Elisha's prayer that God "blind" the enemy petitions their lack of insight — a quality the "man of God" possesses in abundance. Elisha leads his would-be captors into their own potential captivity at the Israelite capital, where God finally lifts their confusion. The king of Israel follows Elisha's instruction not only to show mercy by sparing their lives but further to treat them hospitably. The disarming goodwill staves off the Syrian raid, at least for the time.

6:24–7:20 Samaria under Siege

The Syrians' siege of Samaria leaves the Israelite king at a loss to help his starving people, and the resulting famine reduces mothers to cannibalize their own children (cf. Lam. 4:10 concerning Jerusalem). Even a relatively meatless head of an unclean animal and one half cup (= one-fourth kab) of similarly worthless commodity sell for exorbitant prices. The mothers' shocking atrocity jolts the already grieving king into rebellion against Elisha's counsel to hold out against the attacking army (6:33). The royal officer vainly sent to behead the prophet (who in these dire straits has attracted the company of the city's elders) meets instead with Elisha's prediction of the coming reversal of Samaria's fortunes, but his disbelief at the prospect earns him a prophetic curse. That the king "leaned" on the officer's "hand" means that the military man was his chief adviser (7:2). The "windows in heaven" refer to rain (7:2, 19).

Meanwhile, four "lepers" plot to seek asylum at the Syrian camp, only to discover it abandoned and so plunder the tents. Their consciences stirred, they report the news to the Israelite king, who immediately suspects Syrian trickery. Nevertheless, the lepers' story checks out. In the Syrians' panicked flight from an imagined mighty force of Israelite allies, they leave a trail of hastily shed equipment all the way to the Jordan River. Elisha's prophecy concerning Samaria's restored economy comes true, thanks largely to the spoils the Syrians left behind, and his would-be assassin dies as predicted in the mass Samarian charge to possess the treasures.

8:1-6 The Shunammite Woman Rewarded

Elisha further rewards the Shunammite woman who provided him with regular hospitality (4:8-41) by warning her of a coming seven-year famine. When she returns home after spending years in apparently unaffected Philistine territory, Elisha's servant Gehazi introduces her to the Israelite king, who restores all of her land and its fruits.

8:7-15 Hazael Becomes King of Syria

Elisha journeys to Damascus, where he fulfills God's charge to his prophetic predecessor to anoint Hazael king over Syria (1 Kgs. 19:15).

The reigning Syrian king's question to Elisha parallels Ahaziah's query concerning the future of his health (1:2), but ironically, while the Israelite king sought counsel from a pagan god, here the pagan king seeks an oracle from the prophet of Yahweh.

Elisha knows that Ben-hadad's illness will not kill him, and therefore the prophet tells Hazael to deliver a hopeful message of recovery. Elisha also knows that Hazael will murder his master, so in the next breath he foretells Ben-hadad's death. Back at the palace Hazael turns Elisha's announcement of his future kingship into a self-anointing by force.

8:16-27 Jehoram and Ahaziah of Judah

After an extended interruption by the Elisha accounts, the narrative returns the focus to Israel and Judah's kings. A southern Jehoram first reigns with and then succeeds his father, Jehoshaphat, on the Judahite throne (v. 16). Jehoram's marriage to the northern King Ahab's daughter Athaliah (cf. ch. 11) leads him astray in religious matters (vv. 25-26). Edom, a region across the Jordan to the southeast, and Libnah, a city on Judah's southwest border with the Philistines, mount successful revolts during Jehoram's reign. Jehoram's and Athaliah's son, Ahaziah, next ascends Judah's throne.

8:28-9:37 The Omride Dynasty Ends

Cf. 2 Chronicles 22.

As had his grandfather Jehoshaphat, Ahaziah joins his northern royal counterpart in a military confrontation against the Syrians at Ramoth-gilead, this time to defend it (cf. 1 Kings 22). Hazael surfaces as the Syrian king trying to reconquer the trade outpost (cf. 8:15). That both Israel's King Joram and Judah's King Ahaziah have withdrawn 40 miles from the battle scene at Jezreel, where Joram is recovering from a wound, sets the stage for the inauguration of Jehu, whom God will use to fulfill Elijah's prophecy against the wicked house of Ahab (1 Kgs. 21:17-24).

Elisha sends a young prophet to Ramoth-gilead to anoint the military captain Jehu as king over Israel in fulfillment of God's final

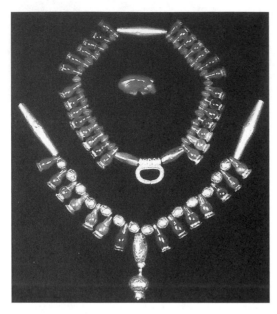

Royal seal and jewelry attributed to Queen Jezebel of Israel. *(Richard Cleave, Pictorial Archive)*

commission to Elijah (1 Kgs. 19:16). Joram's servants enthusiastically embrace the idea of a coup. The prophet's accompanying message that commissions Jehu to "avenge the blood of all the servants of the Lord" emboldens the military man to embark on a furious ride to Jezreel. Met by Ahaziah and the apparently recovered Joram in the vineyard of Naboth (cf. 1 Kgs. 21:1-16), Jehu's fatal arrow slays the northern king, and the dynasty of Omri comes to an end

as prophesied (9:26; 1 Kgs. 21:19). That Jehu's servants also shoot the fleeing allied southern monarch, Ahaziah, may find reason in his blood link to the Omride dynasty through his mother Athaliah, Omri's granddaughter (8:26).

Meanwhile, Jehu continues toward the northern capital. Jezebel greets Jehu with knowing sarcasm by calling him Zimri, the name of the usurping servant of Israel's King Elah (1 Kgs. 16:8-10). Jezebel has adorned herself for a royal audience (9:30). Jehu has no trouble inspiring several officials to throw the wicked queen mother out the window, and his chariot team tramples her body. Jehu then feasts in celebration while wild dogs devour her corpse — again in fulfillment of Elijah's prophecy (1 Kgs. 21:23).

10 Jehu's Purge

Back in Jezreel, Jehu develops strategies to eliminate the rest of Ahab's descendants and supporters. He manipulates the intimidated overseers of the royal children into slaying them all ("70 sons" may represent the entire family). His political pathway cleared, Jehu proceeds toward Samaria to pursue a religious purge. On the way, he chances upon a sizeable company of the slain southern King Ahaziah's relatives and orders them killed as well.

Jehu then encounters one sympathetic to the coming religious purge — a Rechabite, a member of an austere Yahwistic sect (cf. Jeremiah

Panel of Shalmaneser III's Black Obelisk depicting Israel's King Jehu offering tribute to the Assyrian monarch; Nimrud, 841 B.C. *(British Museum)*

35). Once in Samaria, Jehu pretends intense devotion to Baal and summons all Israel's Baal-worshippers for a great sacrificial ceremony. After packing the unsuspecting victims into the pagan shrine, he looses his military on the lot and thus completes the bloodbath. The destruction and desecration of the shrine pave the way for religious reform in Israel.

Unfortunately, Jehu's zeal for the Lord does not extend beyond purging his kingdom of baalism. He pursues the "sins of Jeroboam" by allowing worship at Jeroboam's sanctuaries in Bethel and Dan (cf. 1 Kgs. 12:25-33). Jehu's faithful execution of his commission to wipe out Ahab's household earns the new king a divine promise of a dynasty, but his overzealous violence in accomplishing the task limits it to four generations.

The political fallout of Jehu's religious shortcomings is Israel's loss of Transjordanian territory to Syria's King Hazael (cf. 8:12). The Black Obelisk records the Assyrian king Shalmanezer III's 841 defeat of Hazael and the collection of tribute from Jehu. Thus Jehu's 28-year reign receives mixed reviews, and his son Jehoahaz succeeds him.

11 Athaliah of Judah

Cf. 2 Chr. 22:10–23:15.

Back in Judah, Queen Mother Athaliah (Omri's granddaughter through Ahab and Jezebel) sees her son Ahaziah's death as an opportunity to seize power. She orders all the rival royal sons slain and thus jeopardizes continuation of the promised Davidic dynasty. But the princess Jehosheba rescues the baby Jehoash/Joash from the slaughter, and he lives in the temple undetected by the queen and protected by Jehosheba's husband, the priest Jehoiada (2 Chr. 22:11). To distinguish the southern Jehoash from the northern king of the same name, we refer to the Judahite by the shortened form of the name, "Joash." After six years, Jehoiada brings the young Davidic heir before the royal guard and Carite mercenaries, and gains their support for a military coup. Overhearing the celebration at the anointing of the seven-year-old Joash, Athaliah rushes to the temple shouting, "Treason." The illegitimate queen's swift execution

(outside the temple, to preserve its sanctity) brings joyful relief to Judah, and Jehoiada leads the people in confirming their covenant with God, thus formalizing the relationship between the people and their new king, and destroying the temple of Baal, apparently introduced by Athaliah, Jezebel's daughter.

12 Joash Repairs the Temple

Cf. 2 Chronicles 24.

Kings remembers Joash as one of Judah's most faithful rulers (but cf. 2 Chr. 24:17-22). During his earlier years, Joash orders repairs to the temple — presumably the precincts "broken into" and taken over for Baal worship during his grandmother Athaliah's reign (cf. 2 Chr. 24:7).

The priests, delegated to carry out the temple renovation, pocket the money designated for the project and do nothing to further the work (vv. 7-8). As a consequence, Jehoiada creates a lockbox for collecting freewill offerings, and project administrators pay a variety of craftsmen to execute the extensive repairs. Dedicated offerings continue to support the priests (v. 16).

The economic decline in Judah suggested by Joash's fund-raising challenges also produces a decrease in military strength. Joash has to assume the posture of a vassal by buying off Syria's King Hazael (with tribute taken from the temple treasury) rather than fighting to defend Jerusalem. That Hazael's army could penetrate as far south as Jerusalem shows the even greater weakness of the northern kingdom, which Jehu's son Jehoahaz now rules (13:1-7).

Though the author does not comment on the motive for Joash's assassination by his servants, it may be their discontent with the slumping fortunes of the kingdom. 2 Chronicles 24:17-22 reports it as retribution for the king's murder of Jehoiada's son.

13:1-9 Jehoahaz of Israel

Finding his kingdom under constant oppression by Hazael and his successor (a different Ben-hadad from the one Ahab defeated in 1 Kings 20) as divine punishment for Israel's covenantal unfaithfulness, Jehu's sinful son and successor Jehoahaz calls on God for help in troubled times. Though God grants the northern kingdom relief through an unidentified deliverer, his mercy does not bring spiritual change. The "Asherah" (v. 6) were carved, wooden poles representing the Canaanite fertility-goddess. The meager military force left to Jehoahaz contrasts sharply with Ahab's ability to field 2000 chariots alone at the battle of Qarqar.

13:10-25 Jehoash of Israel

These verses alternately refer to the Israelite king Jehoahaz's successor as Jehoash and Joash.

After a brief summary of Jehoash's typically sinful reign, the text records Elisha's last, deathbed prophecy: Israel's success in regaining territory lost to the Syrians under Jehoahaz. Even the prophet's remains retain the power to restore life (cf. ch. 4).

14:1-22 Amaziah of Judah

Cf. 2 Chronicles 25.

When Amaziah secures his succession to the Judahite throne, his first act is to slay his father Joash's assassins. Citing Deut. 24:16, he spares the murderers' sons (v. 6).

Amaziah's victory over Edom in an area south of the Dead Sea goes to his head, and he challenges his northern counterpart, Jehoash, to a military face-off. Amaziah's persistence forces Jehoash's hand, and Judah suffers a decided defeat: Jehoash captures Amaziah, and the Israelite army proceeds to Jerusalem, where they badly damage the city's northwestern walls before raiding what was left of the temple and palace treasuries (cf. 12:18) and taking hostages back home to Samaria.

Amaziah's foolhardiness catches up with him 15 years later, when he meets a fate similar to his father's: murder at the hands of his fellow Judahites. His teenaged son, Azariah (also called Uzziah; ch. 15), succeeds him, while a second Jeroboam rules in Israel. Elath, whose recovery from the Edomites and rebuilding by Azariah was undoubtedly aided by Amaziah's victory in Edom, lay near Solomon's naval base, Ezion-geber, at the northern end of the Gulf of Aqaba (1 Kgs. 9:26).

14:23-29 A Second Jeroboam of Israel

Jeroboam II builds on his father Jehoash's renewed success over the Syrians (13:25) by reclaiming territory from southern Syria (the northern extent of Solomon's kingdom) to the Dead Sea (= Sea of the Arabah). The wording of verse 28 regarding the recovery of Damascus and Hamath remains difficult to interpret. Verse 25 contains the sole Old Testament reference to the prophet Jonah outside the book that bears his name. Amos and Hosea speak to the social corruption and religious decay of Israel's 41-year resurgence on the international political scene under Jeroboam II. These omens bode disaster for the northern kingdom on the not-too-distant horizon.

15:1-7 Azariah/Uzziah of Judah

Cf. 2 Chronicles 26.

The account of Azariah's 52-year reign receives expanded attention in Chronicles, which relates his victories over the Philistines and Arabs, his reduction of Transjordanian Ammon to vassalage, and his prideful presumption in performing priestly duties — an act that results in God's permanently punishing him with a skin disease, which made him ritually impure for worship at the temple. The ailment forces Azariah to live in isolation while his son Jotham carries out the duties of king. Uzziah/Uzziahu (vv. 13, 30, 32, 34) and Uzza (21:18) refer to Azariah, the year of whose death marks the divine call of the prophet Isaiah (Isaiah 6).

15:8-31 Israel's Mid-Eighth Century Kings in Bloody Succession

Zechariah represents the promised fourth generation of successors to Jehu's dynasty (10:30). After six months, Shallum assassinates and replaces him. Shallum lasts only one month before he is killed and replaced by Menahem (from Tirzah, former capital of the northern kingdom). The horrendous fate of Tiphsah/ Tappuah, a town of uncertain location, served as a warning to any others that might refuse to acknowledge Menahem as king.

Menahem establishes a 12-year, two-generation dynasty but reduces Israel to vassalage under the powerful Assyrian kingdom, ruled by Tiglath-pileser III (= Pul, v. 19). Menahem's son Pekahiah rules for only two years before his military captain Pekah's murderous takeover, aided by the Gileadites, who formerly supported Saul.

During Pekah's 20-year reign, Assyria conquers significant territory in northern Israel and pursues its policy of population deportation, probably as a response to Pekah's attempts to cast off Assyrian domination. Pekah's failures end in Hoshea's taking his turn at royal assassination and seizing the throne.

15:32-38 Jotham of Judah

Cf. 2 Chronicles 27.

Azariah/Uzziah's son Jotham makes the religious sphere a significant priority by rebuilding the "upper gate" of the temple, but his reign sees the beginnings of prolonged military struggles against his fellow Hebrews in Israel and the Syrian king Rezin. God's determination to punish not only the openly wicked northern kingdom but also the generally righteous southern kingdom begins to become apparent.

16 Ahaz of Judah

Cf. 2 Chronicles 28 and Isaiah 7.

One of the few kings of Judah condemned by the author, Ahaz makes human sacrifices of his own sons (v. 3; cf. 17:31; Lev. 18:21). During his reign, Judah loses control of Elath, and the Edomites and Philistines plague his kingdom (2 Chr. 28:17-18).

Military pressure from the allied kings Pekah of Israel and Rezin of Damascus — probably intended to force Ahaz to join their anti-Assyrian league in resisting the rapidly rising Mesopotamian superpower — eventually prompts Ahaz to do the opposite — appeal to Assyria for help. In doing so, Ahaz rejects the counsel of the prophet Isaiah (Isaiah 7). The Assyrian king Tiglath-pileser III responds by conquering Damascus and executing Rezin (732), but Judah has paid heavy tribute for the favor and also lost a good measure of independence. After meeting Tiglath-pileser in Damascus, Ahaz installs a foreign-style altar in the Jerusalem temple and eventually turns to worshipping Syrian gods (cf. 2 Chr. 28:23).

17 Hoshea and the Fall of Israel

Assyrian records reveal that Tiglath-pileser III appointed (or confirmed) Hoshea to the Israelite throne. Hoshea makes a catastrophic mistake in trying to defy the new Assyrian king, Tiglath-pileser's son Shalmaneser V, by withholding the annual tribute and appealing to the now relatively powerless Egypt for help in freeing his kingdom from Assyrian domination. Israel pays dearly. Under Shalmaneser and his successor, his brother Sargon II, the Assyrians invade the entire northern kingdom, conquer its capital after a three-year siege (722), depose and imprison Hoshea, deport a large part of Israel's population to far-off northern and eastern parts of the Assyrian empire, and repopulate Samaria and significant areas of the new Assyrian district with conquered foreigners from Mesopotamia. By creating dependency on Assyria, this consistent wartime strategy of population reorganization reduced the likelihood of revolt.

The text makes clear that Israel itself bears the responsibility for its misfortune. As a nation, the northern kingdom has repeatedly and flagrantly disobeyed the covenant with Yahweh, consistently disregarded God's warnings through his prophets, and forsaken its mighty deliverer from Egypt for all manner of foreign gods (cf. Lev. 18:3, 24-28, which forewarn exile). The high places, made illegitimate by the Jerusalem temple, have continued in use, and the worship of the Canaanite fertility gods Baal and Asherah has flourished. The Israelites have even practiced child sacrifice (v. 17; cf. v. 31).

Verses 21-22 blame the first northern king, Jeroboam, for starting Israel down the path of disobedience (cf. 1 Kings 12–14, esp. 14:15-16). Significantly, however, God does not destroy his people but instead merely "remove[s] them out of his sight" (v. 18) and denies them participation in the landed inheritance promised to Abraham and his descendants. That Judah has followed in Israel's footsteps serves as an omen of disaster to come for the remaining southern kingdom (v. 19).

God sends lions to attack Israel's new inhabitants, thus prompting the Assyrian king to bring back one Israelite priest to instruct the people in proper worship. Still, God becomes just one of many gods served by Judah's new neighbors (vv. 35-39).

18 Hezekiah Faces Assyrian Invasion

Cf. 2 Chronicles 29–32; Isaiah 36; Mic. 1:10-16.

Hezekiah restores pure Yahwistic worship and in so doing at least partially and temporarily reverses Judah's political fortunes. Thus far the only king who measures up to David's standards, Hezekiah rids Judah of Canaanite worship, destroys Moses' bronze serpent that had come to be revered as an idol (cf. Num. 21:8-9), regains Philistine territory conquered by the Assyrians, and otherwise defies Assyria. (Verses 9-12 summarize Israel's fate for the same failed attempt; contrast Ahaz's actions in ch. 16.)

Hezekiah's rebellion brings an unwanted but probably not unexpected contest with Sennacherib, successor to Sargon II, who finished off the northern kingdom. When in 701 the new Assyrian king captures Judah's outlying fortified cities, Hezekiah loses his nerve. (Stone-carved reliefs, found in the ruins of Sennacherib's palace at Nineveh, depict the siege and conquest of Lachish, 30 mi. southwest of Jerusalem.) The Judean king hopes to divert the Assyrian army away from Jerusalem by stripping the temple and palace of their gold and silver as an offering of tribute to Sennacherib, but this strategy fails. Sennacherib sends his three top army officials to intimidate the king and inhabitants.

The chief Assyrian field commander, Rabshakeh (a military title), uses the common Hebrew dialect, rather than the international diplomatic language of Aramaic, to make sarcastic fun of Judah's own military (v. 23). He belittles her only hope for an ally (Egypt; cf. Isa. 30:1-5; 31:1-3); asserts Assyria's divine warrant to conquer the southern kingdom (v. 25); warns of the starvation that will result from a siege of Jerusalem (v. 27); seeks to undermine Hezekiah's reliability (vv. 29-32); promises the good life in exchange for surrender (v. 32); and boasts of Assyria's past

military success (vv. 33-35). The Rabshakeh's discrediting of Judean hope for help from God, however, goes too far, and the Assyrian army will pay for overstepping divine bounds.

Some scholars believe that vv. 13-16 deal with Sennacherib's 701 Judean campaign, while the confrontation at Jerusalem refers to a later military effort. The Assyrian Taylor Prism records Sennacherib's boast that he shut up Hezekiah in Jerusalem "like a bird in a cage," but it makes no mention of the Assyrian disaster recorded at the end of ch. 19.

19 Disaster for the Assyrians

Cf. 2 Chr. 32:9-23; Isaiah 36–39.

Hezekiah reacts to the report of the Rabshakeh's message in the same way as his representatives — in an outward display of mourning. The prophet Isaiah now appears. (Isaiah 1:1 indicates that he had been a prophet since the reign of Azariah/Uzziah.) He delivers a message of hope for deliverance without military engagement.

God causes the blasphemous Sennacherib, now attacking Libnah 10 miles north of Lachish, to respond to reports of a pressing military threat by the Nubian Tirhakah (later pharaoh of Egypt; cf. v. 9). Before departing from Judah, Sennacherib warns that he will return, but Isaiah prophesies the king's violent death in his own land.

Hezekiah's prayer concerning Sennacherib's threat wins for Judah a divine promise of deliverance. The Judahite king acknowledges God's enthronement above the cherubim, guardians of holy places whose wings overstretched the mercy seat on the ark of the covenant (v. 15; cf. Exod. 25:17-22). Verse 28 pictures God humiliating the prideful Assyrians as they themselves did conquered kings, that is, by treating them as beasts through whose noses they would drive a ring as a lead. God determines to accomplish the victory for the sake of his own reputation and for the righteous King David, to whom he promised an enduring dynasty (v. 34).

The angel of the Lord miraculously causes the Assyrian army to die off overnight (cf. Exod. 12:29; 2 Sam. 24:15-17). Sennacherib returns home in disgrace and meets with death by the sword (2 Chr. 32:21; Isa. 37:36-38). Two of his own children figure as the assassins, and they escape to Ararat (modern Armenia).

20:1-11 Hezekiah Wards Off Death

Cf. Isaiah 38.

God's promise to deliver Judah from Assyria (v. 6) indicates that Hezekiah's fatal ailment occurs at least before the events at the end of chapter 19. Through earnest prayer, Hezekiah wins divine healing through a fig poultice — the standard ancient folk treatment for skin ulcers — that Isaiah applies to Hezekiah's infected boil. The miraculous directional reverse of a shadow cast on a stairway offers the sign of Hezekiah's restored ritual cleanliness so that he may resume worship in the temple.

20:12-21 Hezekiah Entertains Babylonian Well-Wishers

Cf. Isaiah 39.

No doubt in hopes of gaining an ally in Judah, the king of Babylon sends his envoys to the ailing Hezekiah from his fledgling kingdom south of Assyria. That Merodach-baladan ruled in Babylon prior to Sennacherib's assault on Jerusalem also places this account before events recorded at the end of chapter 19. Isaiah's anxiety over how much of Jerusalem's treasures Hezekiah has shown to his Babylonian guests suggests that the extent of their viewing will affect the degree to which Babylon will eventually conquer the southern kingdom. The guests have seen it all, and the disapproving Isaiah thus prophesies Judah's complete conquest by the rising Mesopotamian power. Hezekiah responds that at least his hospitality will bring peace with Babylon during his own reign. The prospect of his own sons' deportation and the end of the Davidic dynasty seems not to bother him.

Verse 20 refers to Hezekiah's (Siloam) tunnel, an underground conduit that supplied ancient Jerusalem with water (cf. 2 Chr. 32:30).

21 Manasseh and Amon of Judah

Cf. 2 Chronicles 33.

If Hezekiah's reign represented Judah's next

to last gasp of national righteousness, his long-reigning son Manasseh revives and intensifies Judean disobedience. Later chapters will focus the blame for the Babylonian exile on this king (23:26-27; 24:3).

Manasseh — likened to the wicked Israelite king Ahab in contrast to Hezekiah, who measured favorably against the standard of David — embodies the sum of all the individual evils attributed to Judah's kings. He rebuilds forbidden sacrificial sites in the countryside; reestablishes Baal worship; sets up an idol of Baal's wife, Asherah, in the temple; erects altars to a host of foreign gods in the temple courts; practices child sacrifice, witchcraft, and divination; and pursues unwarranted, widespread violence (v. 16). Manasseh's subjects follow his religious example and so become more wicked than the Amorites (= Canaanites), whom God helped them displace.

This renewed disobedience ensures the southern kingdom's eventual realization of the covenantal curses, despite Manasseh's belated change of heart recorded in 2 Chr. 33:10-17. Verse 13 uses architectural imagery in comparing Judah's apostasy to the standard of wickedness set by the already punished northern kingdom.

Manasseh's son Amon follows in his father's footsteps. His servants assassinate him after he reigns only two years, but those Judeans dedicated to preserving the Davidic dynasty avenge his death and place his eight-year-old son Josiah on the throne. Both Manasseh and Amon are buried in the "garden of Uzza" (vv. 18, 26), probably an extension of Azariah/Uzziah's royal burial ground.

22 Josiah Discovers the Law

Cf. 2 Chronicles 34.

Josiah figures as the second of Judah's kings to rise to David's standard of covenant obedience. His order that the high priest Hilkiah use the money from the temple collection box to pay workers to repair the Lord's house (perhaps from damage done by Manasseh and Amon; cf. ch. 21) leads to the discovery of the "book of the law" (probably Deuteronomy). Josiah seems unaware of the religious regulations spelled out in the document and shows genuine remorse for Judah's departure from the covenant.

The prophetess Huldah confirms the inevitability of the covenantal curses. Her home in Jerusalem's "Second Quarter" probably lay north of the old City of David near the temple and palace complex. The Lord rewards Josiah's sincere contrition with a promise not to carry out the ultimate punishment on Judah during his reign.

23:1-30 Josiah's Reforms

Cf. 2 Chronicles 34–35.

Knowing God's determination to punish Judah does not stop Josiah from pursuing thoroughgoing religious reforms. The public reading of the book of the law fulfills the command in Deut. 31:10-13 and spawns a renewal of the Mosaic covenant that, at least for Josiah, accords with the heartfelt sincerity required by God. Josiah stands in the traditional location for the anointing of kings ("by the pillar," v. 3) to lead his people in the ceremony.

On orders from Josiah, Hilkiah coordinates the cleansing of the temple from the trappings of Baal/Asherah-worship. The king also does away with worship of the sun and moon; pagan priests (even those left in Samaria; v. 20); cult prostitution; and child sacrifice to the Ammonite god Molech. The "place of burning," or "Topheth" shrine of verse 10, lay in the Hinnom Valley on Jerusalem's south side. Josiah defiles the high places, including those Solomon built under the influence of his foreign wives (v. 13; cf. 1 Kgs. 11:1-8), and altars both within Jerusalem and outside Judah as far away as Samaria, capital of the fallen northern kingdom. That 2 Chr. 34:6 extends Josiah's reforms even farther north into the former territory of Naphtali reveals the declining strength of Assyria. Josiah's desecration and destruction of the altar at Bethel fulfill the prophecy during the reign of the first northern king, Jeroboam (vv. 17-18; 1 Kgs. 13:2).

As the climax to his reforms, Josiah commands a kingdom-wide celebration of the Passover on a scale unparalleled since the days of the judges some 450 years earlier. In 609 this uniquely righteous king meets his death at the hands of the Egyptian pharaoh Neco, while en route to reinforce the Assyrian army, which had lost its capital of Nineveh to the rising Babylonian power (cf. 2 Chr. 35:20).

23:31-34 Jehoahaz/Joahaz of Judah

Cf. 2 Chr. 36:1-4.

Josiah's attempt to stop the Egyptians from aiding a resurgence of Assyrian power may have bought Babylon the time it needed to deliver the final blow to Assyria at Haran. Abandoning his now obsolete mission to the north, Neco follows up his killing of Josiah by taking prisoner the Judahite king's successor, Jehoahaz, who lasts only three months on the throne. That Neco imposes a fine on Judah, appoints the region's new king, and takes the liberty of changing the king's name all signify that Judah has become an Egyptian vassal. After initially imprisoning Jehoahaz in southern Syria, Neco removes him to Egypt. 2 Kings characterizes Jehoahaz and all succeeding Judean rulers as religiously unfaithful.

23:35–24:7 Eliakim/Jehoiakim of Judah

Cf. 2 Chr. 36:5-8.

Jehoiakim dutifully pays Judah's tribute to Pharaoh Neco but eventually finds his kingdom subservient to the current superpower, Babylon, which has conquered all Egyptian territorial holdings from southern Canaan (including Transjordan) north and east around the Fertile Crescent. The deciding battle took place in 605 at the northern Syrian city of Carchemish, where the Egyptians established an outpost in 609. After three years of Babylonian (= Chaldean) domination under Nebuchadnezzar, Jehoiakim attempts to defect back to Egypt despite the prophet Jeremiah's warnings of the futility of such an effort (Jer. 22:13-19).

24:8-17 Jehoiachin of Judah

During the reign of the next Judahite king, Jehoiachin, the Babylonian army responds to the rebellion by besieging Jerusalem. Jeremiah pronounces divine judgment on Jehoiachin (Jer. 22:24-27), and the king surrenders (in

597, according to the Babylonian Chronicle). The resulting deportation of all but the poorest Judahites to Babylon, the land of Abraham's ancestors, brings history full circle for all but a remnant of God's chosen people.

24:18-20 Mattaniah/Zedekiah of Judah

Though depleted of its treasures, Jerusalem continues to serve the Babylonian empire under the puppet-king Mattaniah (Jehoiachin's uncle and the former king Jehoahaz's brother), whom Nebuchadnezzar renames Zedekiah to signify his subjection to Babylon. Zedekiah's persistence in evil ensures the fulfillment of the covenantal curses earned by Judah over the previous four centuries (vv. 19-20). Disaster will result from Zedekiah's anti-Babylonian rebellion, also instigated by Edom, Moab, Ammon, Tyre, and Sidon and warned against by the prophet Jeremiah (Jer. 27:1-15).

25 The Babylonians Destroy Jerusalem

Cf. 2 Chr. 36:11-21; Jeremiah 37–39.

Again Nebuchadnezzar responds to Judahite rebellion by besieging Jerusalem (589/88). Severe famine sets in after four months of the 18-month siege. When the Babylonian army succeeds in breaking into the city, the Judahite king and soldiers flee out of the back gate and take the road to Jericho, probably hoping to find refuge among fellow Transjordanian rebels. Captured and deserted by his army before reaching the Jordan River, Zedekiah receives a typically harsh sentence from Nebuchadnezzar at Babylonian headquarters in Riblah, Assyria's former southern Syrian base on the Orontes River. Zedekiah must watch the slaughter of his sons before being blinded, bound in chains, and deported to Babylon.

A second deportation follows the destruction of Jerusalem by fire and the breaking down of its fortification walls (587/86). The poorest of the poor are left to work the land and supply the Babylonian king with its surplus of fruits and crops. Nebuchadnezzar's army carries away to Babylon all remaining temple treasures. Nebuchadnezzar makes an example of a dozen political and religious leaders and 60 Judahite citizens by executing them at Riblah.

The Babylonian king appoints Gedaliah — probably a member of the Jerusalem establishment whom Babylon could trust — to oversee Judah from Mizpah. Judah's surviving military leaders meet with Gedaliah, who counsels their peaceful subjection to Babylon (cf. Jer. 27:12). Within seven months, however, Gedaliah meets his end at the hands of a Davidic relative in a plot hatched by the king of Ammon (cf. Jer. 40:14). The assassination prompts the surviving Hebrew remnant (including Jeremiah; Jeremiah 43) to flee to Egypt for fear of Babylonian retaliation. The statement in verse 21 summarizing Judah's exile echoes the language concerning Israel's deportation in 17:23.

As for Jehoiachin, he regains not only relative freedom but also a good measure of honor by decree of Nebuchadnezzar's successor, Evil-merodach (Amel-Marduk). After a 37-year imprisonment, the Davidic descendant finds himself enthroned as a symbolic king in Babylon — a turn of events that may foreshadow the restoration.

Judah after the
Fall of Israel

- Independent kingdom
- Semi-independent kingdoms
- Assyrian provinces
- Province boundary

N

Sidon
SIDON
MANSUATE
Damascus
Mt. Hermon
Leontes R.
Ijon
Pharpar R.
Tyre
TYRE
Abel-beth-maachah
Dan
DAMASCUS
Kedesh
Hazor
KARNAIM
Acco
Chinnereth
Jotbah
Karnaim
Mt. Carmel
MEGIDDO
Sea of Galilee
Aphek
Mt. Tabor
Yarmuk R.
Dor
Shunem
Jezreel
Megiddo
Ramoth-gilead
Taanach
Beth-shan
GILEAD
HAURAN
Mediterranean
Sea
Ibleam
Dothan
Jordan R.
Jabesh-gilead?
DOR
Samaria
Shechem
Succoth
Penuel
Mahanaim
Mt. Gerizim
Jabbok R.
SAMARIA
Akrabatta
Me Jarkon
Shiloh
AMMON
Joppa
Aphek
Bene-berak
Jazer
Beth-dagon
Lod
Bethel
Ai
Ramah
Beth-gilgal
Rabbah
Jabneel
Mizpah
Geba
Jericho
Shittim?
Heshbon
Gibbethon
Aijalon
Gibeon
Anathoth
Mt. Nebo
Sibmah
Ashdod
Ekron
Timnah
Beth-shemesh
Jerusalem
Medeba
Jahaz
Gath?
Azekah
Bethlehem
Ashkelon
Moresheth-gath
Adullam
Gath?
Ataroth
PHILISTIA
Mareshah
Beth-zur
Dead Sea
Dibon
Gaza
Lachish
Adoraim
Hebron
Aroer
Bethel-ezel
Ziph
En-gedi
Arnon R.
Gerar
Besor Br.
Ziklag?
Debir?
MOAB
Sharuhen
JUDAH
Ar?
Raphia
Beer-sheba

| 0 | 10 | 20 | 30 Miles |
| 0 | 10 | 20 | 30 Kilometers |

Zoar
Kir-hareseth
(Kir, Kir-heres)
Zered Br.
Tamar
EDOM

1 and 2 Chronicles

In recounting sacred history, 1 and 2 Chronicles cover the period of Israel's monarchy (ca. 1000-587 B.C.). Originally one book, they also include material and language from the Pentateuch (Genesis–Deuteronomy), the Deuteronomistic History (Deuteronomy–2 Kings, excluding Ruth), and Psalms. Writing for Jews who returned to Jerusalem following exile, the Chronicler presents the motivation for their rebuilding a life centered around a central sanctuary by focusing on the history surrounding Solomon's temple recorded in Samuel and Kings. Some scholars view Chronicles as related to Ezra and Nehemiah, which focus on the Jews' life and worship immediately following their return to Canaan.

Though the northern and southern kingdoms went into exile separately, the Chronicler views the Hebrews as a unified people and generally uses "Israel" to refer to the entire nation. The book shows an interest in the former northern kingdom only to the extent that it affected Judah, seat of the only legitimate monarchy — that of David — and home of the only legitimate central sanctuary — the temple. The Chronicler assumes readers' knowledge of the history in Samuel and Kings and therefore feels free to expand certain themes there while omitting sections that detract from his theological purpose. Numbers (of people, amounts, etc.) often differ significantly between parallel accounts in Chronicles and Samuel/Kings.

1 Chronicles

The first nine chapters of 1 Chronicles provide a summary of Israel's history from the beginning of time to the return of the Babylonian exiles to Jerusalem. From chapter 11 forward, the book concentrates on the reign of David, and much of the material parallels passages in 2 Samuel. The Chronicler omits episodes that portray David in a bad light (e.g., his adultery with Bathsheba and arrangement of her husband Uriah's death), and expands David's plans and preparations for the temple. By the end of the book, Solomon reigns securely over a well-established kingdom built by David and is poised to build a magnificent house for God.

2 Chronicles

Much of 2 Chronicles finds parallels throughout 1-2 Kings. In chapters 1–9, the Chronicler treats Solomon's reign from the perspective of his activities in building the temple and instituting its services. The remainder of the book traces the reigns of Judah's good and bad kings and establishes the basis for God's judgment of the southern kingdom by exile in Babylon — Judah's religious adultery in pursuing foreign gods. References to the prophets Isaiah, Jeremiah, and other "messengers" testify to God's compassionate nature in giving Judah every opportunity to repent.

During the period in which the events of 2 Chronicles take place, Assyria conquers the northern kingdom of Israel (alluded to but not recorded in 2 Chronicles), then Babylon overpowers Assyria, and finally Persia replaces Babylon as the region's superpower. In accordance with the Chronicler's interest in the temple, the book closes with the Persian king Cyrus's edict charging Jews to return to Jerusalem to rebuild God's house (538).

Authorship

Many scholars view Chronicles as literarily related to Ezra and Nehemiah and believe that Ezra himself wrote all three books. Ezra lived in the late 5th century, nearly 100 years following the initial wave of Jewish returnees to Jerusalem under Sheshbazzar. In a number of passages Chronicles takes the return of the Babylonian exiles for granted, thereby suggesting that the earliest possible date for the work's composition could not precede 539, when the

Persian king Cyrus issued his edict allowing the return (see "Exile and Return" [281-83]). If Ezra did not write Chronicles, its author remains unknown.

1 Chronicles

1-9 Historical Connections

Before starting his narrative proper, the Chronicler uses selective genealogical outlines and other lists to connect his audience of repatriated Jews to their theological history. He increasingly narrows the focus to the royal line of Judah, for the activities of David's descendants will form the basis for the Chronicler's discussion of his primary interest — the second temple as the center of Jewish worship.

Since the Jews would have been quite familiar with both the literary genre here employed and the fuller history on which these chapters draw, the author truncates his lists and assumes an amount of historical knowledge necessary for his readers' understanding of his meaning and purpose. That in biblical genealogies "father" may refer to any male ancestor and "son" to any male descendant helps explain the unusually long periods of time spanned by the relatively few individuals listed. For example, 900 years separate Issachar and David (7:1-2), but these two verses mention the "sons" of only two generations between the men.

1:1-2:2 From the Beginning of Time to the Beginnings of a Nation 1 Chronicles 1:1-27 rehearses genealogical history from Genesis 1–12 beginning with Adam, through the descendants of Noah's sons, and ending with Abraham. Verses 28-42 trace Abraham's descendants through Ishmael and Isaac and

Isaac's descendants through Esau and Jacob, renamed Israel.

The kings of Edom outlined in 1:43-54 represent the descendants of Esau, who settled in the northern Edomite region of Seir (Gen. 32:1–33:20). The list of Jacob's sons — ancestors of Israel's 12 tribes — lays the groundwork for the development of Judah's royal line.

2:3-55 From the Beginnings of a Nation to the Birth of a Monarchy In keeping with his primary interests, the Chronicler devotes the bulk of chapter 2 to detailing King David's ancestors, the descendants of Judah. He makes no mention of Saul, Israel's first "king" (cf. 2 Samuel 6).

Chelubai in 2:9 is another form of "Caleb," but scholars disagree on whether the name refers to Joshua's co-spy (Numbers 13–14). 1 Samuel 16–17 refer to Jesse's "eight" sons and name the oldest three plus the youngest, David; in 2:13-15 David is the last of seven. Ziph, Hebron, Kiriath-jearim, and Bethlehem (vv. 42, 50, 51) refer to towns; "father" here indicates the towns' founders.

3:1-4:23 From the Birth of a Monarchy to the Fall of a Dynasty Chapter 3 traces David's royal descendants. The list of sons born to him in Hebron repeats that in 2 Sam. 3:2-5 (Daniel here = Chileab in 2 Sam. 3:3). Verse 10 follows the dynastic line through David's and Bathsheba's son Solomon, builder of the first temple, and his son Rehoboam, whose refusal to lighten his people's workload led to the withdrawal of

the 10 northern tribes from the kingdom. The Chronicler then names the rest of the kings of Judah in succession but makes no mention of Queen Athaliah, daughter of Ahab and Jezebel (2 Kings 11).

The book later acclaims Hezekiah and Josiah (3:13-15) as Judah's religiously reforming kings, while it focuses the blame for the ultimate fall of Judah on the thoroughly wicked Manasseh (3:13).

The individuals listed in 3:24 represent Davidic descendants contemporary with the Chronicler himself. The first half of chapter 4 offers a selectively annotated list of Judah's descendants that includes geographical, vocational, and personal information about specific individuals and groups.

4:24-43 Descendants of Simeon Simeon originally inherited territory in the midst of southern Judah (Josh. 19:1-9). The larger tribe had absorbed Simeon by the beginning of David's military career. Evidently at some point, the Philistines conquered the Simeonite city of Ziklag; 1 Samuel 27 relates that the Philistine king Achish of Gath gave Ziklag to David in exchange for his supposed raids on his fellow Hebrews. Around the time of Hezekiah (late 8th to early 7th centuries) a remnant of the Simeonites moved east of the Jordan to the mountainous region of Seir in northern Edomite territory (vv. 41-42).

5 Transjordanian Tribes Verse 1 remembers Jacob/Israel's firstborn son Reuben for his sexual transgression with his father's concubine (Gen. 35:22) and thereby justifies Judah's rise as father of the Hebrew royal line. Preferring Gilead's good grazing land east of the Jordan, the Reubenites and Gadites waived their land rights in Canaan proper, and half the tribe of Manasseh (descendants of Joseph's eldest son) joined them (Numbers 32). Reuben settled farthest south, Manasseh farthest north, and Gad between them.

The mention of several kings punctuates this genealogy with time markers: Tilgath-pilneser (Tiglath-pileser, vv. 6, 26) ruled Assyria in the mid to late 8th century; Saul (v. 10) ruled Judah in the late 11th century; Jotham of Judah and Jeroboam II of Israel ruled during the 8th

century (v. 17; cf. 2 Kings 14-15). Verses 25-26 agree with the theology of 2 Kings that the Transjordanian tribes' covenantal infidelity gave the reason for their conquest and exile by the Assyrians (ca. 733).

6 The Priestly Levites The sheer length of this chapter testifies to the Chronicler's primary interest in Israel's central sanctuary and worship. Only the verses that develop Judah's royal line take up more space in these opening chapters.

The Chronicler traces the priestly line from Levi (early 2nd millennium) to the Babylonian exile (early 6th century). He begins with Israel's high priests, descendants of Levi's son Kohath (vv. 1-15). The Kohathites performed the most sacred duties in caring for the tabernacle under their clansman Aaron, the Hebrews' first high priest. Aaron's siblings, Moses and Miriam, receive only passing mention in verse 3. The high priesthood continues through the descendants of Aaron's third son and successor Eleazar, not through Aaron's elder but errant sons Nadab and Abihu, whom God struck dead for their priestly trifling with "strange fire" (Leviticus 10). Jerusalem's last preexilic high priest, Jehozadak, completes the list (v. 15).

The families of all three of Levi's sons appear in the next 15 verses. Special mention is made of the prophet Samuel (v. 28), who performed priestly functions (cf. 1 Sam. 2:11, 18) and whose appearance in this Levitical genealogy establishes the legitimacy of those activities.

A roster of families of singers appointed by David who ministered first in the tabernacle and then in the temple appears next (vv. 31-48), followed by Aaron's descendants (vv. 49-53). Zadok (v. 53) served as high priest with the northerner Ahimelech during David's reign (2 Sam. 8:17).

Joshua 21:1-42 forms the basis for the list of cities allotted from all the tribes of Israel to the otherwise landless Levites, and Josh. 20:1-9 provides the source for the Levitical cities of refuge. Hebron, originally given by Joshua to his comrade spy Caleb (Numbers 13-14; Joshua 14), reverts to the Levites, but the Calebites retain the city's surrounding pasturelands in

Priests and Levites

In the Old Testament as it has come down to us, the tribe of Levi was specially set apart by God for service at the sanctuary. While the descendants of Aaron functioned as priests, with particular responsibility for the offering or sacrifice, the rest of the tribe, "the Levites," assisted them in a variety of ways. This might include menial tasks associated with the care of any large institution, but also more specialized functions, such as leading music in worship.

These roles face in two directions. On the one hand, they look toward God. Priests, and to a lesser extent Levites, are frequently said to stand in God's presence and to serve him. Such language draws on the picture of the sanctuary as God's royal court, where his ministers and servants have privileged access in order to serve the king's needs and carry out administrative tasks. On the other hand, the priests and Levites relate to the people as a whole, undertaking sacral duties on their behalf in a sphere to which the laity did not have access.

It is thus clear that the priests and Levites had an important task as mediators between God and his people, and we should keep this capacity in mind when encountering the less frequently mentioned tasks of teaching and instruction in Torah — God's revealed way of life for his people — as well as judicial arbitration in a wide variety of contexts. Prophets and kings were other important mediators in the Old Testament period, but institutionally the priests and Levites outlasted these others by far.

Because of its importance and specialized work for Israel, the tribe of Levi as a whole did not receive any landed inheritance instead but lived dispersed throughout the country in specially designated towns. It was to be supported financially by the tithes of the people and by a share in the sacrifices that were offered at the sanctuary. Since this was frequently neglected, however, Deuteronomy in particular recognizes that the Levites were often among the poorest of the people, and it commends them, along with other disadvantaged groups, to the charitable support of the majority.

The Old Testament itself recognizes that the roles of the Levites developed with changing circumstances through time. Once the ark of the covenant had come to rest in the temple, time formerly given to attendance upon it was released for new duties. Similarly, the needs of the new temple in Jerusalem involved many new tasks. The experience of the exile (and involvement in the circumstances that led up to it) is also said to have resulted in a redistribution of duties. The division of priests and Levites into a rotation of 24 "courses" for fortnightly service at the temple throughout the year, as known from the New Testament, the Dead Sea Scrolls, and later Jewish writings, seems to have developed at the very end of the Old Testament period at the earliest.

In a history of a thousand years or more, this is scarcely surprising, but scholars have differed widely in their chronological plotting of this process. Many have argued that the developed pattern sketched above was only its culmination, reflected historically in such late books as Chronicles, Ezra, and Nehemiah. But, because it is also attested in the "Priestly" portions of the Pentateuch (especially Leviticus, but also the closing chapters of Exodus and significant parts of Numbers), they have concluded that these, too, must reflect the end of the process and so be dated to the exile or after, not to the time of Moses and the early history of Israel. Others observe in response that our sources are selective and partial, so that it would be hazardous to detail the history of an institution that in fundamentals was certainly very ancient.

Either way, it was the developed view that became normative and that persisted with only minor changes down to New Testament times. Only with the destruction of the temple in A.D. 70 did the role of priests and Levites within Judaism undergo fundamental change.

H. G. M. WILLIAMSON

fulfillment of Moses' original promise (vv. 55-56; cf. Deut 1:36).

7 Tribes West of the Jordan Despite the Chronicler's omission of the non-Davidic and therefore, for him, dynastically illegitimate northern kings, he does not leave out the genealogies of the northern tribes, for he views Israel as a united kingdom, as in David's day. In comparison to the attention given the royal Judahite line, however, the genealogies here appear quite brief. Nevertheless, they do introduce a new detail — that of past tribal military strength.

Some scholars suggest that verses 6-11 rehearse not the genealogy of Benjamin but that of Zebulun, since a separate list of Benjamin's descendants appears in the next chapter, the sons of Benjamin in verse 7 do not harmonize with any other Old Testament genealogy of Benjamin, and the present chapter makes no specific mention of Zebulun or Dan. Further, they view verse 12 as representing the end of a lost genealogy of Dan. Others believe that the Chronicler purposely omitted these tribes.

The daughters of Zelophehad (v. 15) figure prominently in Numbers 27; Joshua 17. Their request of Moses that, since their father died without sons, they receive his share of land in Canaan led to the establishment of inheritance rights for unmarried women (cf. Numbers 36).

8 Benjamites and Saul The Chronicler gives the Benjamites special attention as the tribe that produced Saul, Israel's king who bridged the period of the judges and the rise of monarchy proper under David. Verses 1-28 list the families of the tribe of Benjamin, and the remainder of the chapter traces the specific line of Saul. 1 Chronicles 9:35-44 repeats Saul's genealogy as a preface to chapter 10, which relates the account of Saul's death.

9 Postexilic Resettlement of Jerusalem By skipping forward in time to describe the resettlement of Jerusalem by representatives from both northern and southern tribes following the Babylonian exile (late 6th century; v. 3), the Chronicler helps his original audience

relate more personally to his account. The text continues to center on the Jerusalem sanctuary by focusing on the return and service of the priests (vv. 10-13; cf. Neh. 11:10-14), Levites (vv. 14-16; cf. Neh. 11:15-18), gatekeepers/guards (vv. 17-27; cf. Neh. 11:19), "domestic" caretakers (vv. 28-32), and musicians (v. 33; cf. 6:31-47).

10 Saul's Death as a Preface to David's Reign

Cf. 1 Samuel 31; 2 Sam. 1:1-11.

Chapter 10 recounts Saul's death in battle on Mount Gilboa, his disgrace at the hands of the Philistines, and the honor shown his corpse by the Jabesh-gileadites as a preface to the Davidic monarchy. Because the Chronicler wants to emphasize the annihilation of a Saulide dynasty, he claims that all heirs to Saul's throne "died together" (v. 6; cf. 1 Sam. 31:6). In fact, Saul's general, Abner, carried off to Transjordan Saul's son Ishbosheth, who "ruled" for two years as Abner's puppet-king while David led the nation from Hebron (2 Sam. 2:8-11). Saul's grandson Mephibosheth also survived him (2 Sam. 4:4).

Saul's disobedience to God (in improperly assuming the duties of a priest and in sparing the life of the Amalekite king; 1 Samuel 13; 15) and his turning to a medium (to consult the spirit of the deceased prophet Samuel; 1 Sam. 28:3-25) emerge as the reasons for his death. The statement that God himself killed Saul clearly communicates the Old Testament view of divine control over the course of human events (v. 14).

The Chronicler passes over Saul's doomed career as king much as he makes mere mention of the Babylonian exile (9:1). It is David's covenantally faithful and therefore divinely blessed reign that will provide inspiration and hope for the restored community in Jerusalem.

11–12 David Becomes King

Cf. 2 Sam. 5:1-10; 23:8-39.

Aiming to present Israel as a unified nation, the Chronicler bypasses David's initial acclamation as king over Judah alone and instead begins the history of David's reign with his public anointing at Hebron by the elders of "Israel" (for the Chronicler, Israel and Judah together). The account skips forward to relate David's capture of Jerusalem, and 11:6 reports how the king's cousin Joab earned his position as chief military commander. "Millo" (11:8) refers to the steeply sloped, terraced area of the City of David.

1 Chronicles 11:41-47 expands by 17 names 2 Samuel's list of David's elite military guard. The Chronicler's placement of this list at the beginning of the account demonstrates the strong support Israel afforded this "right kind" of king.

Chapter 12 emphasizes the defection to David of skilled Benjamite warriors — Saul's own kinsmen (esp. 12:2, 29) — in addition to trained military men from each of the remaining tribes both west and east of the Jordan. The Chronicler praises each group of tribal representatives and singles out their particular areas of expertise, both military and intellectual (e.g., 12:2, 32). Coupled with the massive size of the army gathered for David's anointing at Hebron (340 thousand — the largest muster in the Old Testament), this tack bolsters the Chronicler's characterization of David's army "like the army of God" (12:22).

Amasai's inspired speech confirming the good intentions of the joint Benjamite-Judahite contingent lends prophetic legitimacy to David's rise to the kingship (12:18).

1 Chronicles 12:19 defends David's loyalty to his fellow Hebrews during his premonarchic sojourn among the Philistines, when his army of Saulide defectors was gathering to him at Ziklag (cf. 1 Sam. 27:5-7; 29:2-9). In 12:21, the Chronicler alludes to the Amalekite raid in 1 Samuel 30.

Not only does David's army bring military skills to the battlefield, but it also embraces David as king with heartfelt sincerity and unified purpose. The group contributes generously to the festivities celebrating David's unanimous anointing (12:38-40).

13 David's Attempted Transfer of the Ark of the Covenant

Cf. 2 Samuel 6.

In bypassing for the moment the expansion of David's family and his further defeat of the Philistines (2 Sam. 5:11-25), the Chronicler reveals his eagerness to emphasize David's establishment of Jerusalem as Israel's central worship site. He contrasts David's determination to seek God's will with the religious neglect that characterized Saul's reign (v. 3). Verse 5 emphasizes the "all Israel" theme by detailing national south-north borders unsurpassed anywhere else in the Old Testament (beyond the usual designation "Beer-sheba to Dan"; cf. 21:2).

14 David Gains International Respect

Cf. 2 Sam. 5:11-25.

David's family grows, as does his international reputation. Verses 5-6 contribute two additional names to 2 Samuel's list of David's children — Elpelet and Nogah. The Chronicler credits David with burning rather than collecting the Philistines' idols after he defeated their army at Baal-perazim (cf. 2 Sam. 5:21), and the divinely aided military exploits that result from David's obedience to God issue in divinely inspired international respect for the Israelite king (contrast Saul's religious and military failures in ch. 10).

Ruins of the Omride royal residence at Samaria; 9th century B.C. *(Phoenix Data Systems, Neal and Joel Bierling)*

15:1–16:3 The Ark's Successful Transfer to Jerusalem

Cf. 2 Sam. 6:12-23.

David acknowledges his failure to follow Mosaic law in his first attempt to transfer the ark and now prepares to move it according to proper procedure (cf. Exod. 25:14-15). The king calls on his southern and northern high priests, Zadok and Abiathar, and the Levites to help in the effort. The Chronicler details extensively the organized fanfare that attends the procession, with special attention to the role of music. Conscious to portray David only in a good light, he dresses the king in dignified attire and abbreviates Michal's criticism of her husband for his celebrative abandon (vv. 27, 29; contrast 2 Sam. 6:16, 20). The ark comes to rest in a new tent prepared by David, while the tabernacle remains at Gibeon (16:37-42; 21:29).

16:4-43 Instruction in Praise

With the ark now in Jerusalem and the tabernacle and altar still at Gibeon, David organizes the Levites into two groups to ensure proper worship at both places. The Asaphites remain in the capital (presumably with the co-high priest Abiathar), and the families of Heman and Jeduthun accompany the Judahite high priest Zadok at Gibeon.

The poetic words of praise David assigns the Asaphites to sing before the ark recall three Psalms (compare vv. 8-22 with Ps. 105:1-15; vv. 23-33 with Psalm 96; vv. 34-36 with Ps. 106:1, 47-48). Verses 8-22 define praise and set forth God's covenant as the reason for Israel's praising him. Verses 23-34 assert God's sovereignty over all the nations of the world and, by inference, all other gods. Verses 35-36 charge the congregation to join in the offering of praise. See "The Psalms in Worship" (348).

17 The Davidic Covenant Reaffirmed

Cf. 2 Samuel 7.

Four hundred years before the Babylonian exile, God promised David an everlasting dynasty. Because God's punishment of Judah at the hands of Babylon brought an apparent end to that dynasty, it may seem odd that the Chronicler emphasizes the Davidic covenant to his audience of postexilic Israelites, who have returned to a Jerusalem ruled by the Persian Empire. The exiles, however, understood that it was their own national disobedience that led God to invoke the covenantal curses; so rather than producing a lack of faith in God's promises, their punishment gave birth to the hope for a Davidic Messiah. By reminding the Jerusalem community of God's promise to David, then, the Chronicler encourages the returnees to renewed obedience, which will result in a renewal of the covenantal blessings.

18–20 A Summary of David's Victories

Cf. 2 Samuel 8; 10; 12:26-31; 21:18-22.

By concentrating on the divinely orchestrated military successes David realized against the Philistines (to his west), the Syrians (to his north), and the Ammonites (to his east in Transjordan), the Chronicler sets the stage for the period of national rest that will follow during Solomon's rule — a period characterized by a peacefulness appropriate for the building of the temple. The accounts of David's wars in these three chapters span 14 chapters in 2 Samuel (chs. 8–21) but leave out details concerning Saul's grandson

Icon depicting the ark of the covenant, brought by David to his new capital at Jerusalem. *(Richard Cleave, Pictorial Archive)*

Mephibosheth, David's adultery with Bathsheba and his arrangement to have Uriah killed (cf. 2 Samuel 11–12), and the evil and distress in David's household afterward (most of 2 Samuel 13–21).

The seemingly exaggerated numbers of soldiers and chariots involved in David's battles is neither unique to the Old Testament nor to other ancient Near Eastern military accounts.

2 Samuel 8:18 indicates that David's sons served as "priests," while the Chronicler emphasizes their political role (18:17; cf. 2 Samuel 8). In 20:5, the Chronicler preserves David's reputation as slayer of the giant Philistine Goliath (1 Sam. 17:50-51; cf. 2 Samuel 21).

21:1–22:1 God's Redemption of David's Sin

Cf. 2 Samuel 24.

It now becomes clear that the Chronicler's interest in the temple overshadows his interest in presenting David as beyond reproach. He even heightens the intensity of the king's guilt in giving in to temptation by multiplying the objections of his army-commander cousin, Joab, to taking the census, which apparently violates the covenant. Joab refrains from numbering the custodial tribes of the tabernacle, Levi and Benjamin (where the tabernacle's home at Gibeon lay).

David's repentance leads to his purchase of a threshing floor from Ornan (= Araunah in 2 Samuel), a native Canaanite inhabitant of Jerusalem. The king converts into a sacrificial site this flat, open space used for threshing and winnowing grain. By greatly increasing the price David pays (or perhaps by stating the cost of the entire area at 600 shekels of gold, rather than that of the threshing floor alone at 50 shekels of silver), the Chronicler elevates the value of this future site of the temple (22:1). The "fire from heaven" that consumes David's offering demonstrates divine approval of his action (cf. Lev. 9:24).

22:2–23:1 David Charges Solomon to Build the Temple

The Chronicler adds to the record in 1 Kings David's charge to Solomon to build the temple,

for which David has made elaborate and abundant preparations. This account ignores the shaky transfer of political power to Solomon recorded in 1 Kings 1, as well as David's dying charge that Solomon fulfill the king's last, vengeful wishes (cf. 1 Kgs. 2:5-9). Rather, the Chronicler takes Solomon's succession to the throne as accomplished fact and optimistically stresses the state of readiness for the temple project. Only David's charge that Solomon remain faithful to covenantal law to ensure his prosperity appears in both passages (22:12-13; cf. 1 Kgs. 2:3).

Not only did David wage the divinely sanctioned wars that allowed him to pass on a kingdom at peace, but he also gathered the personnel and materials necessary for his youthful successor's building of an "exceedingly magnificent," internationally "famous and glorified" house for the Lord (22:5). David drafted non-Israelites to hew out stone (22:2), imported large quantities of the highest quality timber (v. 4), amassed a limitless amount of valuable metals (vv. 14, 16), and organized a skilled construction crew (v. 15) — all in addition to his legal purchase of the building site (21:18-25), where the Islamic shrine the Dome of the Rock sits today. Islamic tradition holds that Muhammad ascended to heaven from here, and Jewish tradition assigns Abraham's near sacrifice of Isaac to this spot ("Mount Moriah," Gen. 22:2).

23:2-32 The Levites Reorganized

David's plan to centralize Israel's worship at the temple affected the Levites, whose duties throughout the nation's history had focused on care for the portable tabernacle, now pitched permanently at Gibeon (21:29). A census of the Levites provides a basis for reorganizing their religious service. On the original duties of the descendants of Levi's sons, Gershon, Kohath, and Merari, see Num. 3:14-37.

That some verses put the beginning of a Levite's service at age 30 and others at age 20 indicates the Chronicler's drawing on traditions from different periods in Israel's history (cf. vv. 3, 24, 27; Num. 4:3). The services performed by Levites at the temple include building maintenance, administration, security, musical praise, and assistance of the special class of Levites — those priestly descendants of Aaron whose responsibilities verses 28-31 summarize. The numbers of Levites assigned to the duties outlined seem strikingly large.

24 Priestly and Levitical Divisions

The casting of lots preserves God's decision-making power in dividing the priests and Levites into shifts to perform the temple service. Descendants of Aaron's sons Eleazar and Ithamar make up the 24 divisions of priests.

The list of Levitical families in verses 20-30 takes the corresponding account in 23:12-23 one generation further.

25 Prophetic Musicians

Twenty-four groups of 12 musicians each served the temple in family rotations arranged according to lot without regard to members' status or seniority. The musicians' prophetic role recalls the band of prophets Saul encounters following his private anointing by Samuel (1 Sam. 10:5, 10) and Elisha's summoning of minstrels to aid his prophesying in 2 Kgs. 3:15. The Psalms mention all three heads of these musical families — Asaph, Heman, and Jeduthun. On the singers, see chapters 6, 15–16.

26 Guardians of the Temple and Its Treasures

Lots determine the assignments of Levites from the families of Kohath, Merari, and Obed-edom to guardianship of the temple at its gates and in its surrounding precincts. The Levites must also manage the temple's store of "dedicated gifts" (including taxes-in-kind, war spoils, and freewill offerings) dating back to the time of Samuel. Two Kohathite families receive secular and religious duties in the country at large — the Izharites, assigned to official and judicial capacities, and the Hebronites, charged with overseeing the affairs of God and king both west and east of the Jordan.

27 David's Army and Civil Servants

David chooses commanders for each of his 12 army divisions from among his special guard, the mighty men named in 11:11-47 (cf. 2 Sam. 23:8-39). These troops served in shifts, as did the Levites.

The list of tribal "princes" (v. 22) leaves out Gad and Asher but includes two chiefs for Manasseh, who holds territory both east and west of the Jordan (vv. 20-21), and inserts Aaron separately from Levi (v. 17). There follows a note concerning the census ordered by David and opposed (though carried out) by Joab (ch. 21). To ensure fulfillment of God's promise of an innumerable nation, Israelite males under the age of 20 were ineligible for military service and therefore did not figure in the census of fighting men (v. 23).

The naming of David's 12 senior civil servants in charge of storehouses, agriculture, and livestock and a list of his personal advisors rounds out this chapter and also the entire outline of David's religious and royal administration that began in chapter 23. The "king's friend" (v. 33) is an official title for David's trusted advisor, Hushai (cf. 2 Sam. 15:37). "Shephelah" (v. 28) is Israel's lowland region between the Mediterranean coast and the hill country of Judah.

28–29 David Passes the Baton to Solomon

These last two chapters resume the account of kingly succession briefly introduced in 23:1. David formally and publicly charges Solomon with building the temple according to the plans David has received from God, which parallel those for the tabernacle (28:11-19; cf. Exodus 25–27), and using the materials David has gathered for the project (29:2-9). David emphasizes *God's* choice of Solomon as successor to the throne and builder of the temple (28:5-6).

The king also charges his son to sincere covenantal faithfulness and warns that disobedience will lead to divine rejection — a point surely not lost on the Chronicler's audience of returned exiles. This is the first clear appearance of the reward-punishment theme emphasized in 2 Chronicles 10–36 (28:9; contrast the language of Deut. 10:12). David's warning that Solomon act courageously and without fear recalls Moses' speech to his successor, Joshua (28:20; cf. Deut. 31:7). That Solomon can expect to enjoy the backing of both David's officials and the nation's population at large with regard to the temple project should bolster his confidence despite his youth and inexperience (28:21–29:1).

David sets an example of generous giving to God by donating vast stores of his personal wealth toward constructing and furnishing the temple. His officers and administration follow suit, and the Chronicler stresses their whole-hearted willingness in doing so. The land of Ophir (29:4), source of David's gold, probably lay in South Arabia or East Africa. Unlike the talent, a measurement of weight, the daric (29:7) was a gold coin of the Persian Empire, which rose some 400 years after David's and Solomon's day. The daric's mention here provides evidence for dating the Chronicler's account.

David's deeply moving prayer of response at the people's generosity weaves together characteristics of three major types of psalms — hymns, psalms of thanksgiving, and petitions.

The prayer acknowledges God as supreme and the sole source of earthly wealth and honor (29:10-19). It contrasts human unworthiness to receive God's good gifts (29:14-15). The king's closing petition that God grant his son a "perfect heart" to remain obedient to God's laws precedes Solomon's official anointing as king and the accompanying two-day festival of celebration.

The Chronicler presents David, Israel's ideal king, as voluntarily handing over the kingdom from a position of personal physical strength (contrast 1 Kgs. 1:1, 15, 47-48). The ease of Solomon's succession also contrasts with the account in 1 Kings, which details his older brother Adonijah's effort to take the throne (contrast 29:24 with 1 Kings 1). The passing reference to Solomon's "second" coronation alludes to Solomon's hasty first anointing in response to Adonijah's surprise bid for the kingship (29:22).

A note concerning Solomon's prosperity and his unopposed rule precedes a final summary of David's reign and death.

2 Chronicles

1 Solomon Blessed with Wisdom, Wealth, and Honor

Cf. 1 Kings 3; 10:26-29.

The Chronicler portrays Solomon as the religiously righteous image of his father, David. While David built the kingdom, Solomon will build the temple and thus emerge as David's perfect kingly complement. Taken together, the reigns of father and son produce Israel's "golden age" geographically, economically, socially, and — most important for the Chronicler — religiously.

The Chronicler omits any negative commentary concerning Solomon's frequenting the "high places" (cf. 1 Kgs. 3:3) and takes care to legitimize the king's offering at Gibeon by emphasizing his use of the altar made in Moses' day by God's appointed craftsman, Bezalel (v. 5). Solomon's humble request for wisdom and knowledge from God earns the additional blessings of unequalled wealth and honor.

2 Solomon Solicits Hiram's Help

Cf. 1 Kings 5; 2 Sam. 5:11-12.

By adding verses 4-6 to the account in 1 Kings 5, the Chronicler underscores Solomon's piety and humility before God. "Huram" is a variant form of "Hiram," used in Kings. Chronicles distinguishes between the two Tyrian Hirams — the king and the craftsman (vv. 3, 13). The long form of the craftsman's name, Huramabi, means "Hiram is my father."

3:1–5:1 Building and Furnishing the Temple

Cf. 1 Kings 6–7.

The Chronicler offers only a summary account of the building and furnishing of Solomon's temple. That he omits any mention of the palace complex reveals his singular interest in the religious sphere represented by this central sanctuary.

2 Chronicles 3:1 links Mount Moriah, the site of Isaac's near sacrifice, with the threshing floor David bought as a place of sacrifice (1 Chr. 21:18-26). A cloth veil reminiscent of that in the tabernacle separates the temple's holy and most holy places (v. 14; cf. Exod. 26:31; cf. 1 Kgs. 6:31-32: wooden doors).

Solomon's "molten sea" (4:2) holds some 14,500 gallons of water necessary for ritual washing by the temple priests (cf. 1 Kgs. 7:26). Solomon and the Tyrian craftsman Hiram collaborate on the temple project much as Moses and Bezalel did regarding the tabernacle (cf. Exod 38:21-22).

5:2-14 Solomon Installs the Ark in the Temple

Cf. 1 Kgs. 8:1-11.

The temple complete, Israel's elite gather to celebrate the installation of the ark of the covenant in its new house. The ceremony occurs in the "seventh month," around the time of the Feast of Tabernacles. The Levites transport the ark from its shelter south of the Temple Mount, and bring the portable tabernacle (= "tent of meeting," v. 5) from Gibeon (1:3) for permanent storage in the new sanctuary. Verses 11-13 correlate Solomon's installation of the ark in the temple with David's transport of the ark to Jerusalem (1 Chronicles 15–16). God signifies his acceptance of the new dwelling place for his name (6:6) by filling it with the cloud of his glory (v. 14; cf. Exod. 40:34-35).

6 Solomon's Prayer

Cf. 1 Kgs. 8:12-53.

Solomon's prayer for his people recognizes the absolute faithfulness of God in keeping his covenantal promises. The king recognizes God's standard of righteousness by publicly kneeling to ask for the forgiveness of covenantal transgressors who repent sincerely. The reference to Israelite captivity in exile (vv. 36-39) surely held special meaning for the postexilic returnees to Jerusalem, along with Solomon's particular call on God to continue fulfilling his promise of a Davidic dynasty in their now Persian-ruled kingdom (vv. 16, 42). Verse 5 contains a rare mention of the Exodus by the Chronicler. Verses 41-42 quote Psalm 132:8-10.

7 God Answers

Cf. 1 Kgs. 8:54–9:9.

God answers Solomon's prayer in a dramatic, publicly observable act followed by a personal word to the king. He demonstrates his acceptance of the people's worship by sending fire from heaven to consume the burnt offering and sacrifices (cf. 1 Chr. 21:26; Lev. 9:24). After their

Dome of the Rock on the site of Solomon's temple, with the surviving Western Wall in foreground.
(Richard Cleave, Pictorial Archive)

seven-day celebration, God confirms to Solomon privately his commitment to the forgiveness and restoration of his people, as well as to a permanent Davidic dynasty. Two requirements applied, however: God's errant people must repent, and the king must keep the covenant, particularly by worshipping only God. Otherwise, the temple would serve only as a public testimony to Israel's foolish unfaithfulness. The lesson was surely not lost on the Chronicler's postexilic audience, for whom the site of the destroyed temple presented a visual reminder of God's commitment to fulfilling the covenantal curses, but for whom the realized restoration to the promised land provided an immediate reason to trust in God's faithfulness to the promised blessings.

8:1-16 Solomon's Building Activities

Cf. 1 Kgs. 9:10-25.

King Hiram (= Huram) of Tyre apparently returns to Solomon the shabby Galilean cities the Israelite king gave him as security against a loan for his material contributions to the temple and palace complex (cf. 9:13-14). The Chronicler's account contradicts 1 Kings 9:11, perhaps to avoid portraying Solomon as giving away parts of Israel's covenantally promised inheritance.

In order to preserve the ark's sanctity, Solomon moves his Egyptian wife out of the City of David, which lay next to the Temple Mount at its southern end (v. 11). Other than the apparent pagan influence of the Pharaoh's daughter, the Chronicler makes no mention of Solomon's foreign wives (contrast 1 Kgs. 11:1-13). Solomon carefully follows the requirements of Moses and David. His own orders are carried out concern-

City gate at Megiddo, part of Solomon's extensive building projects. *(www.HolyLandPhotos.org)*

ing the building of the temple, and thus he emerges as the third in a succession of three great leaders of Israel (vv. 13-16).

8:17–9:31 Solomon's International Activities and Fame

Cf. 1 Kgs. 9:26–10:26; 11:41-43.

The Chronicler reports that Solomon's kingdom extends from the "Euphrates River to the . . . border of Egypt" (9:26; cf. 1 Kgs. 4:21), the northern and southern boundaries of the land God promised to Abraham (Gen. 15:18). This addition to the Kings account elevates Solomon as the king worthy to enjoy the fulfillment of this divine promise.

The Queen of Sheba provides impartial testimony to the grandeur of Solomon's kingdom and the limitlessness of his wisdom, both of which exemplify the unbridled blessing God bestows on the covenantally faithful. Whether Solomon's Tyrian-staffed ships actually sailed as far as Tarshish in Spain remains unclear (v. 21). "Ships of Tarshish" may identify them simply as oceangoing vessels (cf. 1 Kgs. 10:22).

To preserve Solomon's righteous image as the builder of the temple, the Chronicler omits negative evaluations of the king, including accounts of his religious waywardness, God's determination to punish him by wresting all but one tribe from his Davidic successors, and the external and internal opposition God raises to split the kingdom (1 Kgs. 11:1-40; cf. 1 Chronicles' similar omission of David's misdeeds and family problems). Thus in Chronicles Solomon dies a covenantally obedient and therefore divinely blessed monarch.

10:1–11:4 The Kingdom Divides

Cf. 1 Kgs. 12:1-24.

Since the Chronicler has omitted material that taints Solomon's image as a righteous king, he has not yet had reason to introduce Jeroboam or his coming role in God's punishment (cf. 9:29; 1 Kgs. 11:26-40). Now that the kingdom is about to split, Jeroboam enters unannounced as the popularly acclaimed spokesman for the drafted Israelite laborers.

Rehoboam's rejection of the wise counsel of

his father's elders represents an example of God's working behind the scenes to accomplish his purposes for deliverance and for punishment (v. 15). Through the prophet Shemaiah God confirms his orchestration of the national split and so avoids civil war (11:4). Ahijah's prophecy concerning Jeroboam (v. 15) appears in 1 Kgs. 11:30-39.

In this section, the Chronicler uses "Israel" to refer to the northern tribes apart from Judah. Normally, he uses the term to encompass the entire Hebrew nation.

11:5–12:16 Rehoboam's Successes and Failures

Cf. 1 Kgs. 14:21-31.

Free from the responsibility of reuniting the nation, Rehoboam focuses on fortifying Judah by building up a number of cities surrounding the capital, Jerusalem. Of all the sites listed, only Aijalon lies north of Jerusalem, well into Benjamite territory, with Zorah lying almost due west of the capital and the rest scattered around the southern hill country and lowland region. Rehoboam appears to be watching for attacks by his southern neighbor Egypt, not his northern sister Israel (but cf. 12:15).

The Chronicler pictures the northern priests and Levites flocking to Judah because Jeroboam has replaced them with illegitimate priests who would serve the high places — rivals to the only legitimate sanctuary, the temple. On Jeroboam's "calves," see 1 Kgs. 12:28-32.

For the first three years of his reign Rehoboam "walked in the way of David and Solomon" (11:17) — which for the Chronicler means covenantal faithfulness. As a result, God blesses both his kingdom and his family, as evidenced by Rehoboam's fathering many children. Rehoboam passes over his firstborn son in favor of Abijah (= Abijam in Kings), the eldest of his favorite wife, as successor to the throne (13:1). For now, Rehoboam appears to have inherited some of his father's capacity for wisdom (11:23).

After a productive three-year reign, Rehoboam and his strengthened southern kingdom become overconfident, and they forsake the covenant. As punishment, God sends Pharaoh Shishak, who reunited Egypt and founded her 22nd Dynasty, on a successful invasion of Judah.

Ezion-geber at the northern end of the Gulf of Aqabah, where Solomon maintained a fleet of ships for his far-reaching commerce. (Richard Cleave, Pictorial Archive)

Shishak's own records list upwards of 150 towns captured. Shemaiah's prophecy brings a national repentance not mentioned in Kings. The people's contrition curbs God's wrath, and rather than conquering the capital Shishak merely plunders it (12:9). The invasion's aftereffects will include Egyptian domination of Judah for many years.

In these two chapters, the Chronicler provides a concise case study in how the covenant works. Obedience results in blessing; disobedience leads to punishment; repentance brings restoration. The pattern repeats itself throughout the rest of 2 Chronicles.

13 Abijah Battles Jeroboam

Cf. 1 Kgs. 15:1-8.

While Kings paints Abijah in a totally negative light, Chronicles pictures him as waging a holy war with the just goal of reestablishing Davidic rule over a united Hebrew kingdom. Abijah blames Rehoboam's failure to enforce the perpetual "covenant of salt" on the former king's youth and timidity (but see 11:1-4). The ancients used the preservative to symbolize the eternal nature of a covenant in treaty ratification ceremonies.

Here Abijah defends Judah's proper worship of God (contrast the kingdom's lapse in his father's reign, ch. 12), and he criticizes Jeroboam's continued disobedience (vv. 8-9; cf. 1 Kgs. 12:25-

33). The Davidic king portrays the northern tribes' military resistance as a fight not against humans but against God, and he predicts their inevitable defeat (v. 12). Even Jeroboam's larger army and superior military strategy cannot produce a victory over the army of the faithful, on whose side God fights (vv. 13-15). Though Abijah wins the battle decidedly, the kingdom remains split.

Jeroboam's permanently weakened kingdom and divinely effected death contrast with the righteous Abijah's growth in power and offspring.

14 Asa's Righteous Reign

Cf. 1 Kgs. 15:9-24.

That Abijah's successor, Asa, must purge Judah of Canaanite religious trappings paints a far different picture of Abijah's reign than does chapter 13. The initial decade of peace God grants Asa's kingdom constitutes God's blessing for the king's righteous actions (vv. 1, 6). In contrast to Kings, however, Chronicles will also criticize Asa for his later lack of faith (16:7-10).

Like his father, Asa emerges as a military underdog whose outnumbered army faces an intimidating fighting force, this time from the south. Again, God produces overwhelming victory for the faith-filled Judahites and irrecoverable defeat for the opponent, Zerah of Ethiopia, probably an Egyptian or Arabian chieftain.

15 Asa's Further Reforms

Inspired and emboldened by the prophet Azariah, Asa pursues further religious reforms. Azariah's description of an unspecified period in Israel's history may recall the time of the judges (vv. 3-4).

Asa follows up his destruction of Judah's high places and foreign altars with the removal of "abominable idols" and the restoration of the proper temple altar. His reforms extend into Ephraimite cities over which he has gained control. Northern defectors from Ephraim and Manasseh recognize God's presence with Asa and cast their lot with the southern king. Long before Asa's time, Judah absorbed Simeon, whose territorial inheritance lay in the midst of the larger tribe's (Joshua 19).

Around the time of the Feast of Weeks, the faithful rededicate themselves to pursuing the Lord wholeheartedly (vv. 12-13; cf. Deut 4:29). They resolve to impose the death penalty on any fellow Hebrews who refuse to seek God.

Regarding Maacah's deposition (v. 16), see 1 Kgs. 15:13. Verse 17 clarifies that Asa's dismantling of the high places in 14:3-5 did not extend to the northern kingdom.

16 Asa Seeks Human Help

Cf. 1 Kgs. 15:17-24.

While Kings simply reports the events surrounding Asa's appeal for Syrian help in defending Judah from the invading northern kingdom, Chronicles uses the episode to pronounce judgment on Asa for seeking human help rather than divine intervention late in his reign. Not only does the prophet Hanani's message fail to humble the king, but it also triggers Asa's persecution of the prophet and his oppression of innocent bystanders (v. 10). The Chronicler further criticizes Asa for seeking medical treatment rather than divine healing for a severe ailment, probably venereal disease ("diseased feet"; v. 12).

17 Jehoshaphat Blessed for Obedience

Asa's successor, Jehoshaphat, maintains the military strength of the southern kingdom. More importantly for the Chronicler, this king continues religious reforms in Judah and expands them to include door-to-door Levitical instruction in Mosaic law. The "book of the law of the Lord" (v. 9) probably refers to the Pentateuch (Genesis–Deuteronomy) or parts of it.

In the Chronicler's scheme, Jehoshaphat's international respect constitutes divine blessing for the king's covenantal obedience. Chapters 17, 19, and 20 contain mostly new material about Jehoshaphat not in Kings.

18 Jehoshaphat's Alliance with Ahab

Cf. 1 Kings 22.

Chapter 18 repeats almost verbatim the account in 1 Kings 22, but the Chronicler's introductory commentary in verses 1-2 highlights Jehoshaphat as the account's central figure rather than Ahab. The northern and southern kings sealed an alliance (v. 1) through the marriage of Jehoshaphat's son Jehoram to Athaliah, the daughter of Ahab and Jezebel who later seizes the throne and executes all but one rescued heir to the Davidic dynasty (21:6; 22:10-12).

19 Jehoshaphat Concentrates on Domestic Matters

Jehoshaphat's safe return to Jerusalem contrasts with Ahab's slow death beside the battlefield (18:34). After Jehoshaphat has unadvisedly participated in the alliance with the faithless northern king, a second prophet, Jehu, appears to scold him (v. 2). Jehu's father Hanani prophesied against Jehoshaphat's father Asa in 16:7; it was probably his grandfather Jehu who prophesied against Israel's king Baasha in 1 Kgs. 16:1-7. Neither Jehu represents the northern king of that name.

The prophet also commends the king for what he has done right, namely, seeking God, and Jehoshaphat responds by personally engaging in missionary efforts throughout his territory (contrast Asa in 16:10). He also appoints lay judges to settle civil disputes (v. 11) both in Jerusalem and outlying areas, and he assigns judicial duties to Levites, priests, and tribal heads in Jerusalem to hear cases addressed by Mosaic law (vv. 8, 11). The chief priest and leader of the Judahite tribe preside over Jerusalem's dual religious and civil supreme court (cf. Deut. 17:8-13).

20 God Fights for Judah

Facing invasion from almost all of Transjordan, Jehoshaphat turns to God, and his people follow suit. The Meunites hail from Edom, near Mount Seir, south and east of the Dead Sea (v. 1; cf. Deut. 2:1). In verse 2, some ancient manuscripts read "Syria" as the origin of the invaders from "beyond the sea," while others read "Edom." The attackers' current position at En-gedi, halfway up the western side of the Dead Sea, makes the best sense with a southern, or Edomite, invader in view.

The king's prayer at the temple reminds the all-powerful God of his work in clearing the way for the chosen people to settle in the promised

land before asking that God protect the covenantal inheritance he has granted his people, who stand powerless apart from him (v. 12; cf. Deut. 20:2-4). An oracle from one of Israel's Asaphite singers promises God's deliverance of Judah without her army's even needing to fight. The Judahites gather some 10 miles south of Jerusalem near Tekoa, home of the shepherd-prophet Amos, where Jehoshaphat urges his people to trust the Lord for success. It takes the Judahites three days to collect all the spoils from their dead enemies, and the deliverance discourages other nations from attacking Judah for fear of her invincible God.

Verse 33 contradicts the claim in 17:6 that Jehoshaphat tore down the Judahite "high places," local shrines where Canaanite practices often entered into Israelite worship. Jehoshaphat may well have tried his best to remove them, but his subjects evidently persisted in using them (cf. 1 Kgs. 22:43).

The negative lesson of Asa's failed attempt at alliance with Ahab (ch. 16) and Jehoshaphat's positive lesson of God's accomplishing for Judah a victory without military engagement do not prevent the king from later allying himself with Israel's King Ahaziah. The wickedness of this act is the lack of faith in God that it demonstrates. Chronicles thus regards as punishment the failure of the kings' joint effort to revive seafaring trade, initiated by Solomon (v. 37).

21 Jehoram of Judah

Cf. 2 Kgs. 8:16-24.

Here for the first time Chronicles portrays a Judahite king as thoroughly evil. Jehoram's wife Athaliah, the daughter of Ahab and Jezebel, is blamed for her husband's wickedness. Only God's faithfulness to his covenant with David protects this religiously weak link in the dynastic chain.

By listing Jehoram's younger brothers and mentioning their father Jehoshaphat's generosity toward them, the Chronicler suggests that Jehoshaphat may have appointed Jehoram to the throne only because he was the eldest (vv. 2-3). Previous kings had chosen successors other than their firstborn (David chose Solomon, Rehoboam chose Abijah). Jehoram's brothers soon become casualties of their father's unwise decision, for the new king slays all potential rivals to the throne — a bad omen for what lies ahead. The revolts of the Edomites, Libnites, Philistines, and Arabs all represent divine punishment for Jehoram's leading Judah away from God.

The credit to Elijah of a prophetic letter to Jehoram seems somewhat curious, for 2 Kgs. 3:11 indicates that Elisha has already replaced Elijah during the reign of Jehoram's father Jehoshaphat. Also, Elijah's career focused on the northern kingdom, not Judah. Some scholars suggest that the Chronicler penned the prophecy in Elijah's name to create a parallel between the great prophet's railings against Israelite disobedience, epitomized by Ahab, and the divine judgments against Judah for adopting a distinctively northern brand of apostasy, perpetrated by Ahab's daughter Athaliah.

God's punishment of Jehoram leaves the king with only one son to inherit the Davidic throne. Deprived of almost all of his family, the unfaithful Jehoram dies a lonely, painful, humiliating death. Consistently with the Chronicler's interpretation, the king's punishment continues through his dead body's banishment from the royal tombs. The people of Judah neither honor Jehoram formally with a funerary fire (cf. 16:14; Jer 34:5) nor show regret for his demise (v. 20). The Chronicler provides no further sources for information about this wicked king (contrast 13:22; 16:11; 20:34).

22:1-9　Friendship with Israel Earns Ahaziah the Death Sentence

Cf. 2 Kgs. 8:25-29.

Under the influence of his northern-born mother, Athaliah, Ahaziah performs just as wickedly as his father, Judah's Jehoram (not the northern King Jehoram/Joram of v. 5). The Chronicler's likening of Ahaziah's behavior to the wicked, northern house of Ahab's conduct intensifies the portrayal of Ahaziah's disobedience.

Verses 7-9 summarize the events surrounding "Jehu's purge" in 2 Kgs. 9:14-28. That Ahaziah's divinely ordained death coincides with God's destruction of the northern "house of Omri" puts

the extent of Judah's wickedness during this time on par with Israel's.

22:10–23:21　Athaliah's Rise and Fall

Cf. 2 Kings 11.

The Chronicler adds several details and his own emphasis to the account in Kings. He makes explicit the marriage of Jehoshabeath (= Josheba in Kings) to the priest Jehoiada, who leads the conspiracy against Athaliah (22:11). The Chronicler dismisses the illegitimate queen's six-year reign in one phrase (22:12b) and devotes all of chapter 23 to the day of her death. He emphasizes the role of the priests and Levites in restoring the Davidic descendant, Joash, to Judah's throne and in reestablishing proper Levitical supervision of the temple activities (23:4-8, 18). As elsewhere, the Chronicler highlights the role of musicians, here in Joash's acclamation ceremony and in the temple service (23:13, 18).

While Kings mentions religious and civil covenants made at Joash's ascension to the throne, Chronicles focuses on the religious covenant only (23:16; cf. 2 Kgs. 11:17). Through Jehoiada, the military and civil leadership has already promised support for the new king and has garnered it kingdomwide (23:1, 3, 8).

24　The Easily Influenced Joash

Cf. 2 Kgs. 11:21–12:21.

The Chronicler presents Joash's reign in two phases. During the life of the priest Jehoiada, Joash's spiritual and adoptive father (22:11-12), the king displays religiously admirable behavior, such as repairing the temple. The tax in verses 6 and 9 harks back to Exod. 30:12-16. The mention of Joash's growing family (v. 3) demonstrates God's blessing on the righteous king, and it relieves the tension over the threatened Davidic dynasty — a tension created by Athaliah's murder of all potential heirs to Judah's throne save the infant Joash. The Chronicler emphasizes Jehoiada's blessedness and importance by highlighting the priest's advanced age at death (130) and his burial "among the kings" (vv. 15-16).

Judah's religiously wayward officials gain influence after the priest's demise, however, and Joash bends to their mold. Jehoiada's son Zechariah becomes a martyr for his prophetic warning against Judah's disobedience. God punishes Judah through the Syrians, who despite their inferior numbers realize a decided victory over Joash's army. Joash dies as a result of a conspiracy against him for his own successful conspiracy to kill Zechariah. The king's blessed beginning contrasts with his dishonorable exclusion from burial in the "tombs of the kings" (v. 25).

25 Amaziah's Foreign Victory and Domestic Defeat

Cf. 2 Kings 14.

Verses 5-13 contain material not present in the Kings account. They describe Amaziah's hiring of warriors from the northern kingdom to participate in Judah's invasion of Edom, an unnamed prophet's convincing of Amaziah to dismiss them, and Amaziah's subsequent victory over the Edomites while the discharged northern troops, probably angered by their lost opportunity to snatch up spoils in Edom, seize their opportunity for revenge by looting Judahite cities.

Despite Amaziah's reluctant obedience in dismissing the northern troops, the lack of faith he displayed by hiring the mercenaries in the first place indirectly occasions his defeat back home. After Amaziah's Edomite victory, the king adopts Edomite gods and thereby seals his doom, which God brings about through Amaziah's overconfident picking of a fight with the Israelite king Joash (Jehoash), presumably in retaliation for the miffed northerners' raid on Judah. Amaziah dies the victim of an internal conspiracy spawned at the outset of his flirting with the gods of Edom.

26 The Pride and Fall of Uzziah

Cf. 2 Kgs. 15:1-7.

Yet another of Judah's kings falls prey to the pride that precedes a fall. Uzziah's initial attention to the spiritual guidance of Zechariah (probably a priest, not the writing prophet by that name) results in the king's political success. Uzziah (also spelled "Azariah") reestablishes Judahite control of Solomon's former Red Sea port at Elath; realizes military victories over

neighboring peoples, some of whom pay him tribute; strengthens his kingdom's defenses; boosts Judah's economy through agriculture; and develops a strong, well-prepared army.

Uzziah's pride in his great political power leads him to perform religious duties reserved for the priests, and God's punishing the king with an enduring skin disease leaves him ritually unfit for the rest of his life even to set foot in the temple. It also rules out his direct governance of Judah and necessitates his burial in a royal graveyard rather than the City of David's tombs of the kings (v. 23). The year of Uzziah's death coincided with the timing of Isaiah's call as a prophet (Isaiah 6).

27 Jotham Extends Uzziah's Political Control

Cf. 2 Kgs. 15:32-38.

Jotham's reward for his personal righteousness comes in the form of intensified political control over the Ammonites and the increased security and wealth of his kingdom. Nevertheless, Jotham's subjects did not follow his good example (v. 2), and the account in Kings notes the beginnings of divinely sent punishment from the north (2 Kgs. 15:37).

28 Ahaz Shuts the Temple Doors

Cf. 2 Kings 16; Isaiah 7.

If the Chronicler could find no *fault* in Jotham, he can find no *good* in Jotham's successor-son Ahaz. Judah's defeat by Syria (under King Rezin; 2 Kgs. 16:5) and Israel directly results from the king's open disobedience (vv. 5-6), which includes child sacrifice in Jerusalem's Hinnom Valley (v. 3).

The presence of a true prophet of God in the north (Oded, v. 9) and, even more surprisingly, the Israelites' heeding of his warning against enslaving their Judahite kinsmen present a striking reversal of the usual role played by the generally wayward northerners. After treating their captives as honored guests, the Israelites usher them to Jericho, just short of Jerusalem by a 20-mile, brutal climb. (Jericho lies ca. 1000 ft. below sea level, Jerusalem ca. 2300 ft. above sea level.)

Ahaz loses much of the ground gained for Judah by his grandfather Uzziah (vv. 17-18;

cf. 26:6-7). In response to Ahaz's appeal to the Assyrians for help in defending his kingdom, Tilgath-pilneser (= Tiglath-pileser III) instead levies a heavy tribute on Judah (vv. 20-21). By this time, the northern kingdom has fallen to Assyria (30:6; 2 Kings 17), but despite the foreboding omen, Ahaz does not repent. Instead, he intensifies his worship of foreign gods and even takes steps to prevent proper worship of the Lord at the temple (v. 24).

29 Hezekiah Reinstates the Temple Service

Religiously speaking, Hezekiah embodies the complete opposite of his father Ahaz, shown clearly in the new king's speedy reopening of the temple. The Chronicler devotes three chapters to Hezekiah's religious reforms, which Kings summarizes in a mere four verses (2 Kgs. 18:3-6). As in discussing David's and Solomon's reigns (1 Chronicles 11–29; 2 Chronicles 1–9), he bypasses politics and proceeds immediately to temple matters.

Hezekiah charges the priests and Levites with consecrating themselves for resuming proper worship at the temple. The Levites take 16 days to sanctify themselves and the temple and accoutrements of Yahwistic worship, which Ahaz defiled (28:24), and they finish the job two days past the date prescribed for the Passover (v. 17; cf. Num. 9:1-5). Sacrifices follow to consecrate the temple for immediate and future use and to make atonement for the people's sin. Various kinds of voluntary offerings round out the temple's rededication, including burnt offerings too numerous for the priests to handle without help from the Levites.

30 The Passover Celebration Renewed

Numbers 9:6-11 allows observation of the Passover one month late, under certain circumstances. Hezekiah takes advantage of this law to initate his program of religious reforms with a Passover celebration unparalleled since Solomon's day. Royal messengers sent not only throughout Judah but also to the far reaches of the now-defunct northern kingdom (= "Beersheba to Dan," v. 5) summon the people to Jerusalem's temple to recommit themselves to serving God. Though some of the Israelites who escaped deportation by the Assyrians only laugh at the prospect, others heed Hezekiah's call.

The pilgrims gathered in Jerusalem take it upon themselves to toss the city's pagan altars (28:4, 25) into the Kidron Brook, located in the valley between Jerusalem and the Mount of Olives. Shamed by their lay countrymen's outdoing them in zeal for the restoration of pure Yahwistic worship, the priests and Levites who lagged behind finally join in by bringing sacrifices (v. 15).

Sincerity of heart trumps ritual purity as a requirement for participation in the community observance (vv. 18-19). The weeklong Feast of Unleavened Bread follows immediately, and the joyful atmosphere inspires mutual agreement to extend the celebration for an extra week (v. 23).

31 Hezekiah's Reforms Take Root

Hezekiah's royally initiated religious reforms continue to see fulfillment by the grassroots populace, who enthusiastically pursue the king's policy even in parts of the old northern kingdom. The surprising generosity of the people in tithing throughout the harvest season (May/June–September/October) to support the priests and Levites reengaged in temple duties produces a budget surplus. Hezekiah establishes a task force to ensure the equitable distribution of the extra provisions among the members of the territoriless tribe of Levi living in and outside Jerusalem. The Chronicler's commendation of Hezekiah in verses 20-21 makes clear the author's regard for him as the nation's greatest king.

32:1-23 Assyria Threatens Judah

Cf. 2 Kings 18–19; Isaiah 36–37.

In the face of military threat by the Assyrian conquerors of the northern kingdom, Hezekiah fortifies Jerusalem and forestalls any besieging army's access to natural water supplies outside the city walls. The opening words of this chapter portend the doom of Sennacherib's effort in view of the Chronicler's theology that obedience leads to divine reward. The Chronicler's omission of any reference to Hezekiah's initial but withdrawn surrender to Sennacherib preserves the untarnished image of the Judahite king that Chronicles has presented thus far (cf. 2 Kgs. 18:14-16). Judah's miraculous deliverance is the reward for Hezekiah's faith. Sennacherib's humiliating defeat and eventual assassination are his punishment for belittling Judah's God.

32:24-33 Hezekiah's Repentance and Death

Cf. 2 Kings 20; Isaiah 38–39.

Hezekiah's mortal illness and haughty ungratefulness for God's "sign" that he will recover (2 Kgs. 20:8-11) come as a surprise in the Chronicler's account. Even this heretofore exemplary king falls to the sin of pride, as have his religiously wayward predecessors (Joash, Amaziah, and Uzziah; chs. 24–26). Nevertheless, the Chronicler does greatly abbreviate his account and ends it on the high note of Hezekiah's repentance and the diverting of God's wrath. Verses 27-30 further evidence Hezekiah's divine blessedness and emphasize his accomplishments.

Verse 31 briefly notes the visit of well-wishers from the rising power Babylon (cf. Isaiah's devastating prophecy against Judah based on Hezekiah's hospitality toward these foreign guests; 2 Kgs. 20:16-18).

Overall in Chronicles, Hezekiah's reign represents a resurgence of Solomonic rule. He rededicates the temple, reestablishes its prescribed services, restores the people's religious allegiance to a central sanctuary, and reunites the northern and southern tribes around the worship of Yahweh.

33 Religious Decline under Manasseh and Amon

Cf. 2 Kings 21.

Manasseh converts the temple into a pagan shrine, revives child sacrifice in the Hinnom Valley, and takes up forbidden occult practices (v. 6; cf. Deut. 18:10-11). The king and people refuse to heed divine warnings, so God sends the Assyrians to conquer them.

While Assyrian records name Manasseh as a vassal, the Judahite king's exile in Babylon and his humble repentance as a prisoner there go unmentioned in the thoroughly negative account in Kings. According to the Chronicler,

Manasseh's repentance wins him restoration to Judah's throne, after which he rids Jerusalem and the temple of pagan paraphernalia and orders kingdom-wide fidelity to God.

Manasseh's successor, his son Amon, reinstitutes paganism and fails ever to repent. He becomes the murder victim of an internal conspiracy. That the general populace then kills the conspirators evidences Judah's intense allegiance to religious disobedience as embodied by the wicked king.

34:1–35:19 The Reforming King Josiah

Cf. 2 Kgs. 22:1–23:27.

The religious see-sawing of Judah's kings continues with Josiah, whose covenantal obedience thoroughly contrasts with that of his predecessor, Amon. The accounts of Josiah in Chronicles and Kings overlap significantly, though the order of events does not always coincide. Both books pay similar attention to Josiah's repair of the temple, his discovery of the "book of the law" (probably Deuteronomy), his consulting Huldah the prophetess, and the resulting community renewal of the covenant.

In general, the Chronicler elevates Hezekiah as the greatest of the Hebrew kings since David, while Kings gives Josiah that prominence. Kings and Chronicles emphasize different aspects of Josiah's religious activities. 2 Kings gives detailed information about the specific ways in which Josiah purged the kingdom of paganism (2 Kgs. 23:4-20), while 2 Chronicles summarizes these acts (34:3-7, 33). 2 Kings summarizes Josiah's Passover celebration (2 Kgs. 23:21-23), while 2 Chronicles carefully details this elaborate event (35:1-19). While in 2 Chronicles Hezekiah celebrates Passover as the beginning of his reforms, for Josiah the commemorative event and immediately following Feast of Unleavened Bread represent the culmination of his reforming activities. The Chronicler's mention of the prophet Samuel (35:18), whose activity bridges the gap between the period of the judges and the institution of Israel's monarchy, makes more specific 2 Kings' general reference to the judges when praising the revived magnificence of Josiah's Passover celebration (2 Kgs. 23:22).

35:20-27 Josiah's Death

Cf. 2 Kgs. 23:28-30.

Egypt's Pharaoh Neco, traveling north through Canaan on his way to help Assyria fight Babylon at the battle of Carchemish, warns Josiah not to try to stop him. The Chronicler confirms Neco's claim of divine sanction for his mission, and thus Josiah's mortal wound is attributed to his disobeying God.

Jeremiah in verse 25 is the biblical prophet, but the "lament" here is not the book of Lamentations.

36:1-4 Jehoahaz/Joahaz

Cf. 2 Kgs. 23:31-34.

Pharaoh Neco swiftly deposes Josiah's successor, Jehoahaz, after defeating the Judahite army, which Josiah commissioned to oppose the Egyptian march north.

36:5-8 Eliakim/Jehoiakim

Cf. 2 Kgs. 23:35–24:7.

Jehoiakim rules for 11 years as an Egyptian vassal before Babylon conquers the region and assumes the role of Judah's overlord. The account in Kings notes that Jehoiakim rebelled against Babylon but omits any mention that Nebuchadnezzar deported him.

36:9-10 Jehoiachin

Cf. 2 Kgs. 24:8-17.

The Chronicler does not relate Jehoiachin's surrender to Nebuchadnezzar's besieging army or the exile of Jerusalemites, both of which events Kings details, but both accounts record Jehoiachin's deportation to Babylon along with the temple treasures.

36:11-21 Zedekiah and the Fall of Judah

Cf. 2 Kgs. 24:18–25:30.

Rather than buckle under Babylonian pressure, as did his immediate predecessor Jehoiachin, Zedekiah invites further confrontation by resuming the rebellion begun by Jehoiakim. Zedekiah's obstinacy also extends to the religious sphere, and he refuses to humble himself in response to God's communications through the prophet Jeremiah (v. 12). Neither do Judah's leaders heed the calls to repentance that God in mercy repeatedly delivers by divine messengers (v. 16; cf. the northern remnant in 30:6-10). Thus both king and kingdom reach the point of no return. Their iniquity becomes complete, as it did for the Canaanites who preceded them in the promised land, and God will punish them similarly — by driving them out.

While the Kings account leaves the poorest of Judah's poor in the land following the Chaldean (= Babylonian) destruction of Jerusalem and the deportation that followed, Chronicles pictures Jerusalem as a virtual ghost town and the land as enjoying a 70-year rest, apparently in some measure to make up for the Hebrews' failure to observe the Sabbath Years for much of their history (v. 21; cf. Jer. 25:11-13; 29:10-14; Lev. 26:34-39).

36:22-23 Cyrus Sets the Stage for Return

That the last two verses of 2 Chronicles represent almost a carbon copy of Ezra 1:1-3 suggests that at some point an editor added them to link the two books. Some scholars believe the addition occurred as a result of separating Chronicles from Ezra.

In Cyrus's edict allowing the Hebrews to return to Jerusalem (538), the Persian king surprisingly claims a command from God to rebuild the temple. This mandate becomes the reason for the return of God's chosen people to the city designated as the dwelling place for his name — Jerusalem (Deut. 12:5). Thus begins the fulfillment of Jeremiah's prophecy of hope for restoration (cf. Jer. 24:4-7).

Exile and Return

Toward the end of the divided monarchy, Israel and Judah came under the domination first of the Assyrians, then the Babylonians, then the Persians. The era of kings in Israel and Judah came to an end in two stages. In the northern kingdom of Israel, King Hoshea (732-724 B.C.) tried to make some political gain by switching his allegiance to Egypt. This provoked the Assyrians to invade, led first by Shalmaneser V (d. 722) and then by his successor, Sargon II. Samaria, the capital, fell in 721 after a three-year siege. More than 27 thousand Israelites were taken into exile, according to Sargon's records. The apocryphal book of Tobit claims to be about an exiled northerner at this time. According to 2 Kings 17, the land was repopulated with non-Israelites. There was never formally a return to Samaria.

2 Kings 17 provides the fullest theological explanation for the exiles from both north and south: idolatry, borrowing of foreign religious practices, and the failure to keep the statutes of the Law are highlighted, but no doubt there were political and economic reasons as well, since both kingdoms found themselves as pawns in the rivalries between the great empires to the northeast and Egypt to the south. Because the traditions of Israel and Judah were both collected and spread chiefly from Jerusalem from the end of the 6th century onward, the exile of the leadership and army (8-10 thousand in 597 according to

Deportees from Ekron with Assyrian escort; 7th-century-B.C. relief from Nineveh. *(Erich Lessing / Art Resource, NY)*

2 Kgs. 24:14-16; 3000 according to Jer. 52:28) from Judah in the south appears to have been more significant than that from the north. The southern exile took place in two stages, first after the surrender of Jehoiachin to the Babylonians in 597, second after the defeat of the rebellious Zedekiah in 587/586. Not everyone was taken into exile; for many people much of daily life would have continued as before, though probably with a different system of taxation.

Not everyone who was in exile returned when Cyrus apparently

encouraged them to do so with Zerubbabel in 539/538 after the Persian defeat of Babylon. We cannot be certain why some Jews remained in Babylon, but it is likely that there was little economic advantage to life in Judah. Throughout the Persian period the way of life was predominantly subsistence agriculture and the returns from the land in Judah probably meager. The rebuilt Jerusalem was the only significant urban settlement in Judah until the Greek period, and that quite possibly only from the time of Nehemiah (445). For those who did return there was a period of social restructuring and regrouping. Those who had not gone into exile may have had lands confiscated from them by the returnees. No longer was there a court. The responses to the exile were many and various, and thus the religious expression of the early postexilic period is characterized by several different emphases.

The textual sources for the early postexilic period are very rich, but the writing of precise history from the books of Ezra-Nehemiah in particular, and from nonbiblical sources, is extremely problematic, not least because there are enormous gaps in data. Most scholars are of the opinion that much that is now found in the Old Testament was edited in its final form in the late 6th or 5th centuries. Although there are traces of royal ideology in some of these texts, the strength of Israelite identity is based on the twin foundations of the Law and the cult: those reflect the creation of a self-conscious theocracy. The temple was rebuilt by 515 (Ezra 6:15), but in quite what way is unclear (cf. Hag. 2:3-9; Ezra 3). As Israel's institutions were reformed and re-established, there was probably considerable tension between the representatives of these two pillars, the predominantly lay lawgivers and the priests. They seem to have recognized that they needed each other, however. There were other responses as well, some of which overlapped to some extent with those of the lawgivers and priests.

The Law

The place of the Law is dominant in two sets of writings. The completion of the Deuteronomistic History at the end of the 6th century was a significant achievement. It provided what amounted to a contemporary political commentary. Earlier Israelite traditions were crafted into a chronological narrative from the time of the entry into the land under Joshua. Armed with this history, the leaders of Judah as they themselves entered the land after the return from the exile were equipped to avoid repeating the mistakes of the past. Events from Joshua to the exile were measured against the standards set in Deuteronomy, especially the statutes and ordinances of Deuteronomy 12–26. It could readily be seen that few past leaders had done what was right in the eyes of the Lord. In particular, it seemed to be recognized that there was no place in the restored community for a king; in fact, any reader of the history books would be encouraged to think that the prophets, such as Samuel and Elijah, were of more significance than most of the kings.

The Law itself was also edited into its final shape. The five books together provided a kind of constitution. From creation to the entry into the land, the Pentateuch described the restored community's special place in God's universal plan. Through the promises to Noah, the restored community could believe itself to be symbolic of humanity's fresh start; through the divine commitment made to Abraham the people could reclaim the land as their rightful inheritance; and through the revelation to Moses they had the basis for a distinctive but civilizing social ethic. As Ezra proclaimed the Law afresh (sometime during the reign of Artaxerxes I [465-424]), it could be seen as replacing the prophets of earlier times. No longer would the word of God come through spirit-filled individuals who would act as the people's conscience; rather, it was available for all to hear, study, and apply. Moses was identified as the prophet above all others, and every member of the community was offered renewed individual responsibility.

The Temple

The rebuilding of Jerusalem was portrayed in some writings of the restoration period as primarily about the reconstruction of the temple (Haggai 1–2). Virtually no archaeological remains of the second temple survive (other than Herod the Great's 1st-century rebuilding work), but many consider that it was not such an elaborate edifice as that constructed by Solomon. The books of Chronicles, compiled at the end of the 5th century, represent some of the views of the priestly leaders of the restored community. Chronicles reworks the history of Israel and Judah with a nostalgic appeal to the times of David and Solomon; there is much in genealogies and descriptions of sacred space that asserts preeminence for the priests.

The books of Psalms continued to develop. Perhaps not many new Psalms were written, but there seems to have been a political interest in collecting together those that stressed the kingship of God (Psalms 93, 95–99). As the Dead Sea Scrolls have shown, the Psalter took various forms in the Second Temple period, but one of the forms put the Psalms together in five books as a spiritual collection to match the Law and maybe even to reclaim it for the priesthood from the lay community.

Prophecy

Although the era of the great prophetic figures of the 8th and 7th centuries was never to return, prophetic activity continued in refashioned forms in the period after the return. This refashioning can be summed up as having to do with future aspirations more than with contemporary social justice. The book of Isaiah was completed during the exile or shortly thereafter with passages that look to the glory of a restored Jerusalem beyond any that might be built by Zerubbabel or even Nehemiah. The book of Jeremiah is adjusted to fit the changed situation and published in at least two forms. (The longer one eventually made it into the Jewish canon.) Some of those whose work was eventually included among the 12 Minor Prophets were active in the early Second Temple period and concerned to speak out about the rightful place of the temple in Jewish life (Haggai, Zechariah, Malachi).

Wisdom

There was an ongoing tendency in the postexilic period to redefine the community in ways that made it inward-looking and very distinctive from the surrounding peoples. For example, Nehemiah spoke against all forms of intermarriage. Nevertheless, there was also a continuing trend among some of the educated elite of the community to interact with all that was best of neighboring cultures. This is most clearly visible in the emerging collections of wisdom writings that contain proverbial reflection on the universals of the human condition, on wealth and poverty, on social relations, and on undeserved suffering.

Apocalyptic

Apocalyptic writing emerged during the exilic and postexilic periods as a development within prophecy. From Isaiah 24–27 (early postexilic) to Zechariah 9–14 (late 4th century), visionary material is preserved that suggests that a few influential members of the community were not satisfied with the way things had developed under the Persians. These were perhaps inspired by Persian writings they looked to for divine intervention or some form of compensation for their present circumstances.

Popular Religion

All the descriptions in this brief survey depend upon the written records that survive, mostly in the Old Testament. The beliefs and practices of those Jews in Judah who did not hold power in the two centuries of Persian dominance have not survived. Also, there is little distinctive archaeological evidence for the period, so it is difficult to gauge precisely what forms popular Jewish religious practice took.

All through the periods of exile and return, Israel is under foreign domination. Sometimes this is close at hand and domineering, but more often it seems to have been largely distant and benevolent. The various expressions of religion in Judah during the postexilic period reflect this wider political and economic situation. A sense of realism generally prevailed, and what nationalism there was did not result in attempts to launch military campaigns to reestablish political independence until the Maccabean Revolt (167-164).

As noted, not everybody returned to Judah after the exile was officially declared over. Throughout the postexilic period, Jewish communities in the dispersion in Asia Minor, Egypt, and Babylon seem to have flourished. Sometimes local populations reacted negatively against the economic success and influence of their local Jewish communities. Nothing has survived of Jewish life in Asia Minor during this period; however, the book of Esther and parts of Daniel as well as several noncanonical writings illustrate aspects of life in the Persian Empire. The translation of first the Pentateuch and then the rest of the Scriptures into Greek from the 3rd century onward demonstrates the strength of the Jewish communities in Egypt, as do also the Elephantine papyri and other noncanonical writings usually associated with the communities there.

For Further Reading

Grabbe, Lester L. *Judaism from Cyrus to Hadrian.* 1: *The Persian and Greek Periods.* Minneapolis: Fortress, 1992.

——. *Judaic Religion in the Second Temple Period: Belief and Practice from the Exile to Yavneh.* London: Routledge, 2000.

Sacchi, Paolo. *The History of the Second Temple Period.* JSOT Supplement 285. Sheffield: Sheffield Academic, 2000.

GEORGE J. BROOKE

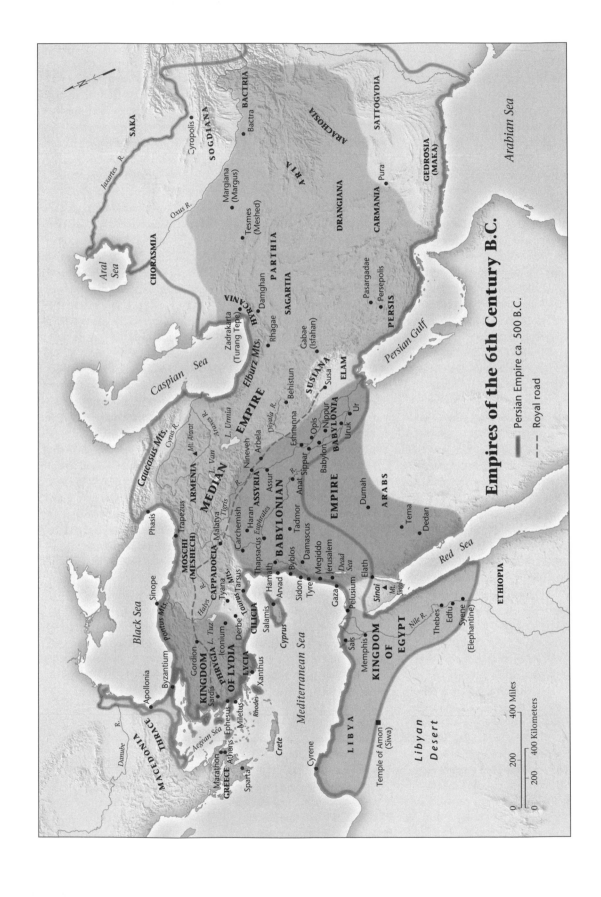

Empires of the 6th Century B.C.

—— Persian Empire ca. 500 B.C.

- - - Royal road

Arabian Sea

SAKA

Cyropolis

SOGDIANA

BACTRIA

Bactra

ARACHOSIA

SATTOGYDIA

Iaxartes R.

Oxus R.

Margiana
(Margus)

ARIA

GEDROSIA
(MAKA)

Pura

CARMANIA

DRANGIANA

CHORASMIA

Aral
Sea

Tesmes
(Meshed)

PARTHIA

Damghan

Rhagae

SAGARTIA

Pasargadae

Persepolis

PERSIS

Caspian
Sea

Elburz Mts.

HYRCANIA

Zadrakarta
(Turang Tepe)

Gabae
(Isfahan)

Persian Gulf

EMPIRE

Mt. Ararat

L. Van

L. Urmia

MEDIAN

Behistun

SUSIANA

Susa

ELAM

Caucasus Mts.

Cyrus R.

Araxes R.

ARMENIA

Nineveh

Arbela

Diyala R.

Eshnunna

Opis

Ur

Uruk

Nippur

BABYLONIA

Babylon

Sippar

Phasis

Trapezus

MOSCHI
(MESHECH)

CAPPADOCIA

Malatya

Tyana

Tarsus

Taurus Mts.

ASSYRIA

Haran

Assur

Anat

Carchemish

Euphrates R.

Tigris R.

EMPIRE

Dumah

ARABS

Tema

Dedan

Sinope

Pontus Mts.

Gordion

KINGDOM

Iconium

L. Tuz

PHRYGIA

OF LYDIA

Derbe

CILICIA

LYCIA

Salamis

Cyprus

Thapsacus

BABYLONIAN

Hamath

Arvad

Sidon

Tyre

Damascus

Tadmor

Megiddo

Jerusalem

Dead
Sea

Elath

Byzantium

Apollonia

Sardis

Ephesus

Miletus

Rhodes

Xanthus

Black Sea

Mediterranean Sea

Crete

Gaza

Pelusium

Sinai

Mt.
Sinai

Red Sea

ETHIOPIA

THRACE

MACEDONIA

Danube R.

Marathon

Athens

Sparta

GREECE

Aegean Sea

Sais

Memphis

KINGDOM
OF
EGYPT

Nile R.

Thebes

Edfu

Syene
(Elephantine)

Cyrene

LIBYA

Temple of Amon
(Siwa)

Libyan
Desert

0   200   400 Miles

0   200   400 Kilometers

Ezra

Together, the books of Ezra and Nehemiah originally formed a single work named for Ezra, the priestly scribe who helped establish in Judah a religiously purified community of returned exiles. The Christian Old Testament's 10-chapter book of Ezra represents a selective historical narrative that relates the Jewish remnant's return to the promised land and the events of major theological significance during their first century or so back home (ca. 538-457 B.C.).

Both Ezra and the immediately preceding 2 Chronicles remain silent about the years of the Babylonian exile and the Persian conquest of Babylon (539; see "Exile and Return" [281-83]). Instead, the books move directly to Persian king Cyrus's edict charging the Jews to rebuild the temple in Jerusalem, in accord with the Persian policy of returning exiled subjects and encouraging them to pursue their national religions. Though only about 50 thousand Jews resettle in Judah — a mere handful compared to the number that populated Canaan after the exodus (cf. Num. 1:20-47) — God's involvement with this remnant demonstrates his continued initiative in redeeming sinful humanity.

Persian Kings
Cyrus II (559-530)
Cambyses II (530-522)
Darius I (522-486)
Xerxes I (486-465)
Artaxerxes I (465-424)
Darius II (424-404)
Artaxerxes II (404-359)
Artaxerxes III (359-336)
Darius III (336-330)

7:1ff. as leader of a second group of returnees to Judah. This journey probably took place in 458, during the reign of Artaxerxes I. The concrete establishment of an accurate chronology of the events recorded in Ezra and Nehemiah eludes us, however, and some scholars believe that Nehemiah returned *before* Ezra, with Nehemiah arriving in 445 and Ezra in 398 (during the reign of Artaxerxes II). But this view requires a significant rearrangement of the current text in both books.

Content

Chapters 1–6 deal with the initial return from Babylon and the rebuilding of the temple under the leadership of the Persian-appointed Jewish governor Zerubbabel and the priest Jeshua (from 538-516). The writing prophets Zechariah and Haggai give the Jews courage to complete the project. These chapters seem concerned to establish the rebuilt temple and its service as the sole legitimate successor to the religious institutions of preexilic Jerusalem, perhaps to combat the rival sect later known as the Samaritans.

The final four chapters (plus Nehemiah 8) center on the activities of Ezra, introduced in

Composition

The questions concerning the dating of Ezra's activities in Judah/Jerusalem make it difficult to determine when the author of Ezra-Nehemiah composed the work and for what original audience and purpose. Some portions of Ezra are written in the first person and represent Ezra's personal memoirs. Other parts use the third person. Ezra 4:8–6:18 (mostly correspondence with the Persian royal court) is written in Aramaic. Other sections appear in Hebrew.

Ezra himself may have authored or compiled this material, or an editor (perhaps the Chronicler or a member of his writing circle)

may have drawn on various sources (including Nehemiah's memoirs) to produce our current text of both books. Scholars who hold the latter view often propose an editorial combining of Ezra's and Nehemiah's memoirs ca. 400, with Ezra 1–6 representing the editor's own composition.

1 Cyrus Allows the Return

Ezra restates Cyrus's edict allowing exiled Jews in Babylon to return to Judah and charging them to rebuild the temple (cf. 2 Chr. 36:22-23; also 6:3-5). The biblical writer attributes Cyrus's directive, issued in 538, to the divine fulfillment of Jeremiah's prophecy (Jer. 24:4-7; 29:10). In order to cultivate loyalty to the empire, Persian policy offered return and renewed worship of national gods to all the exiled subjects that the new regional power inherited through its conquest of Babylon. In the case of the Jews and Judah, this policy would afford the empire a local base of support for its efforts to expand into neighboring Egypt.

Not only does Cyrus allow the Jews to return to Canaan, he also provides the means for their mission by instructing Babylonian locals and Jews who choose not to go to donate goods and valuables. Cyrus entrusts the transport of the temple treasuries to Sheshbazzar, who becomes the first governor of the Persian province of Judah (5:14). Sheshbazzar bears a Babylonian name, but his title "prince of Judah" identifies him as a Hebrew.

2 Listing the Returnees

The list of returnees cements the connection between the postexilic community and its predecessors in the promised land (cf. Nehemiah 7). The Davidic descendant Zerubbabel heads the group (on his lineage, see 1 Chronicles 3) and succeeds Sheshbazzar as civil governor.

A list of lay families, priests, Levites, and other religious personnel precedes a note about returning hopefuls who could not prove their Hebrew ancestry. These suffer at least initial exclusion from the priesthood to protect the purity of that office, but they appear to remain in the community of returnees. The priests would later use the Urim and Thummim to determine the qualification of those of questionable descent (v. 63; cf. Exod. 28:30).

That the exiles not just return to Jerusalem but resettle in their home cities strengthens the parallel between the pre- and postexilic Jewish communities. The number of the entire assembly of returnees (v. 64), plus servants and singers (v. 65), exceeds the sum of the numbers given in verses 3-60 and may include women (and perhaps children). The accounting of 7337 servants suggests that the returnees enjoyed a higher standard of living than generally assumed.

Cyrus cylinder (536 B.C.) permitting release of captives back to their own lands and aiding the restoration of their temples. *(British Museum)*

3 Laying the Foundation for the Temple

At the beginning of the Jewish religious year (September/October) the leading priest Jeshua and Governor Zerubbabel rebuild the central altar on its original site. They immediately initiate regular sacrifice and worship practices that strictly follow Mosaic law (Leviticus 1–7) and Davidic instruction (1 Chronicles 15–16; 23–26). The presence of hostile neighbors may fire the returnees' enthusiasm as they seek to ensure God's protection from external threats.

Preparations for rebuilding the temple include importing timber from the Phoenician coastal cities of Tyre and Sidon, as Solomon did for the first temple (2 Chronicles 2). After two years, construction begins with the laying of the foundation. The limited number of returned Levites may have necessitated lowering the age limit for foremen to 20 (v. 8; cf. Num. 4:23, 30; 8:24). The exuberant ceremony celebrating the completion of the foundation recalls Solomon's dedication of the first temple (vv. 10-11; cf. 1 Kings 8; 2 Chronicles 5–7). The older returnees who remember that glorious sanctuary weep openly, perhaps for joy over the beginnings of the new temple and sorrow for the loss of first, whose grandeur would go unparalleled.

By demonstrating the second temple's structural continuity with Solomon's sanctuary and by stressing the priestly resumption of divinely-ordained religious practices, the writer continues to build a strong case for the legitimacy of worship at the new temple.

4 Local Opposition Halts Work

The returned exiles refuse an offer of help from non-Jewish neighbors, whose ancestors the Assyrian emperor Esarhaddon deported to Canaan in the early 7th century to replace the exiled Israelite population. At first friendly, the neighbors claim to honor Yahweh, whom they apparently regard as a national god of Canaan, but they also continue to worship idols (cf. 2 Kgs. 17:41). The Jews realize that these neighbors' incorporation into the community and their participation in the temple project would jeopardize the purity of postexilic Yahwism. The rejected would-be friends turn against the Jews

and make so much trouble that work on the temple ceases for the rest of Cyrus's reign (to 530) until the second year of Darius's rule (520).

Similar opposition occurred later during the reigns of the Persians Ahasuerus (= Xerxes, 486-465) and Artaxerxes I (465-424; vv. 6-23). The enemies' second letter (to Artaxerxes) comes from the officials of Samaria, which the Assyrian Osnappar (Aramaic for "Ashurbanipal," 669-627) repopulated with foreigners. The region "Beyond the River" (v. 10) refers to the Persians' fifth satrapy, the province west of the Euphrates stretching to the Mediterranean Sea and including Syria and Palestine. The officials compose their letter in Aramaic, the official Persian diplomatic language, which the text of Ezra preserves.

The letter speaks of the Jews' efforts to rebuild the walls and foundations of Jerusalem, a task taken up by Nehemiah well after the completion of the temple (Neh. 2:1-8). The officials instill in Artaxerxes mistrust of Jewish loyalty to Persia by bringing up Jerusalem's history of rebellion against foreign overlords. Artaxerxes confirms the report by checking historical records, suspects future revolt, and orders an immediate and forcible halt to the repairs.

Though it relates to a later period, this section contrasts with verses 1-5 and 24, thus demonstrating the renewed hostility between the old northern Israelite territory, now populated with Samarians, and Judah, whose returned inhabitants closely guard their religious purity. Thus the episode further reinforces the legitimacy of worship at the second temple.

5–6 The Temple Rebuilt

Encouraged by the prophets Haggai and Zechariah, the Jews resume rebuilding the temple during the last two years of Persia's King Cambyses, unnamed in the text. The Persian provincial governor challenges the Jews' authority to pursue the project but does not hinder their progress while investigating the matter with the Persian royal court. The governor's letter to King Darius includes a report of the Jews' explanation for Jerusalem's destruction by the Babylonians: God's punishment for Judah's religious waywardness. The explanation diverts attention away from Jerusalem's former rebelliousness against foreign overlords and demonstrates God's sovereign power. According to the letter, the Jews credit Sheshbazzar, Jerusalem's first Persian-appointed Jewish governor, with laying the temple's foundations. (Ch. 3 attributes this work to Sheshbazzar's successor, Zerubbabel, and the priest Jeshua.)

Perhaps at least partly fearful of a God who powerfully punishes his own people, Darius confirms Cyrus's original edict, which he finds in the royal summer residence of Ecbatana and which charges the Jews with rebuilding the temple. Darius's request for prayer to Yahweh on his behalf recalls the Egyptian pharaoh's similar charge to the Hebrews following the plague of insects prior to the exodus (Exod. 8:28). Darius orders that the taxes from the royal treasury fund the Jews' project, that the Persian governor provide all the required elements of the temple's service, and that violators of the edict meet with death by impalement on a beam from their own ruined houses.

Builders complete the temple in the next four years. Artaxerxes, who ruled well after the temple's completion and dedication, may receive mention in verse 14 because of his provisions for the temple in Ezra's day (ch. 7). After the dedication ceremony, the priests and Levites assume duties here said to follow Mosaic law (6:18) but in 1 Chronicles 23–26 attributed to David's organizational pattern. The spring Passover celebration and observance of the Feast of Unleavened Bread follow. Non-Hebrews who have dedicated themselves to the worship of God alone join the community of Jews in these events. The references to Darius as "king of Assyria" (6:22) and Cyrus as "king of Babylon" (5:13) identify the Persian monarchs as rulers over the conquered territories of these bygone empires.

7 Ezra Leads a Second Return

Chapter 7 skips forward some 80 years to relate the next major religious development for the postexilic Jewish community: the leadership of Ezra, often viewed as a second Moses.

Artaxerxes I has assumed the Persian throne (from 464). The priestly scribe Ezra, who traces his lineage to the father of the priesthood, Aaron, leads a second return to Judah with royal sanction. The 900-mile journey takes the group of clergy, laypeople, and religious personnel 14 weeks (ch. 8).

Artaxerxes's decree, preserved in Aramaic (vv. 12-26), charges Ezra with delivering gifts and grants for the beautification of the temple; ensuring the proper use of donations; appointing magistrates to render judgments according to Mosaic law; and coordinating the teaching of that law throughout the Persian province to which Judah belonged. During the exilic and postexilic periods, the Hebrew Scriptures increasingly became fixed as the primary sources of religious authority. This led to the elevation of the teaching role of priestly scribes such as Ezra. Artaxerxes's edict also grants tax-exempt status to those involved in Jewish religious service, and it sanctions various forms of punishment for transgressors of Jewish religious law, which the king puts on par with his own civil decrees (v. 26).

Ezra's personal note of thanks to God for inspiring Artaxerxes to "glorify the house of the Lord" (v. 27) continues the Old Testament theme of God's sovereign use of foreign nations to accomplish his purposes for his people, for both punishment and blessing. The remaining chapters include additional sections that reflect Ezra's memoirs.

8 The Returnees and Their Journey

Several thousand priests and laypeople (some 1500 men plus their families) join Ezra at a place called Ahava to form the second wave of returnees. This time no Levites volunteer to go, perhaps because they know they will serve in subordinate roles to the priests in Jerusalem; so Ezra summons Levites from the temple at Casiphia to join the group.

Ezra's public statement of confidence in God's protection prevents his requesting a Persian military escort (cf. Neh. 2:9). Instead, the entire assembly fasts and prayerfully petitions God for traveling mercies.

Nehemiah entrusts to the priests and Levites the transport to Jerusalem of some 19 tons of silver and 3 tons of gold. Though Persian dona-

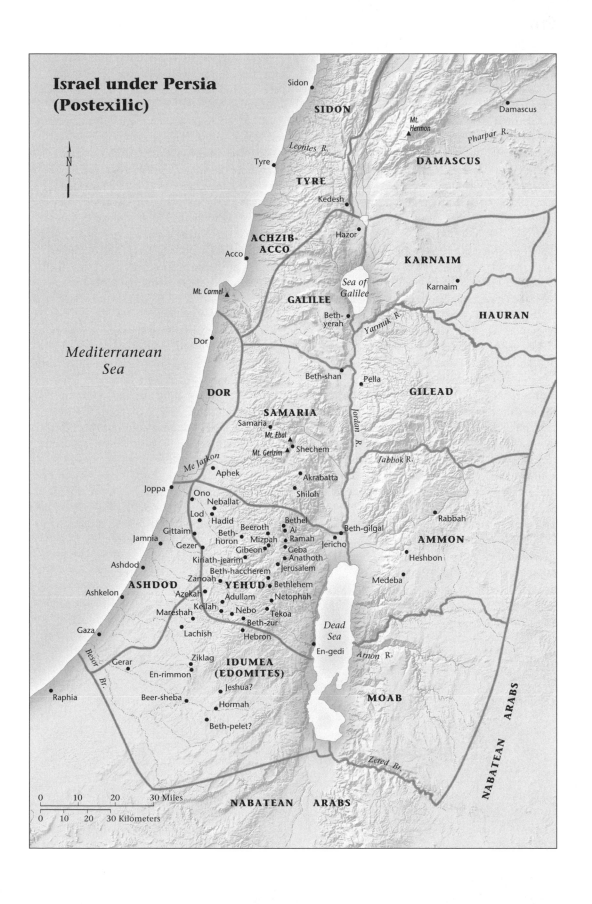

Israel under Persia
(Postexilic)

N

**Mediterranean
Sea**

Sidon

SIDON

Damascus

Mt.
Hermon

Pharpar R.

Leontes R.

DAMASCUS

Tyre

TYRE

Kedesh

Hazor

ACHZIB-
ACCO

Acco

KARNAIM

Karnaim

Mt. Carmel

*Sea of
Galilee*

GALILEE

Beth-
yerah

Yarmuk R.

HAURAN

Dor

DOR

Jordan R.

Beth-shan

Pella

GILEAD

SAMARIA

Samaria

Mt. Ebal

Shechem

Mt. Gerizim

Jabbok R.

Me Jarkon

Aphek

Akrabatta

Shiloh

Joppa

Ono

Neballat

Bethel

Lod

Hadid

Beeroth

Ai

Beth-gilgal

Rabbah

AMMON

Gittaim

Beth-
horon

Mizpah

Ramah

Jericho

Jamnia

Gezer

Gibeon

Geba

Anathoth

Heshbon

Kiriath-jearim

Jerusalem

Ashdod

Beth-haccherem

Zanoah

YEHUD

Bethlehem

Medeba

ASHDOD

Azekah

Adullam

Netophah

Ashkelon

Keilah

Nebo

Tekoa

Mareshah

Beth-zur

Gaza

Lachish

Hebron

*Dead
Sea*

*Besor
Br.*

Gerar

Ziklag

En-gedi

Arnon R.

En-rimmon

IDUMEA
(EDOMITES)

Jeshua?

NABATEAN ARABS

Raphia

Beer-sheba

Hormah

MOAB

Beth-pelet?

Zered Br.

| 0 | 10 | 20 | 30 Miles |

| 0 | 10 | 20 | 30 Kilometers |

NABATEAN   ARABS

tions to the temple were undoubtedly generous, the amounts in verses 26-27 seem exaggerated.

God protects the Jews on their journey to Jerusalem, where, after several days of rest, they hand over the Persian gifts to four temple priests and Levites, who meticulously record their receipt. The returnees offer sacrifices and then deliver copies of Artaxerxes's edict to the appropriate provincial officials. A single "satrap" governed each province and supervised several subordinate "governors" (v. 36).

9–10 Reversing the Flow of Apostasy

Concerned Jewish leaders inform Ezra that the returnees have already begun to violate religious law by, and as a result of, intermarrying with foreigners, who presumably worshipped foreign gods. Priests and Levites are pursuing the practice, and community leaders too are setting the bad example. The lesson of the Hebrew kings in this regard stood in jeopardy of being lost on the Jewish remnant (cf. 1 Kgs. 11:1-11).

For the most part, the peoples named in the standard list of pre-Israelite inhabitants of Canaan (9:1) did not exist in Ezra's day. But Ezra applies Mosaic law to contemporary times by interpreting the prohibition against intermarriage to extend to any foreigners who, presumably, worshipped gods other than Yahweh (cf. Exod. 34:11-16; Deut. 7:1-5). The spirit of the law sought to preserve the purity not of the Hebrew race but of Hebrew religion (cf. the inclusion of non-Jewish adherents to Mosaic law in 6:21).

Ezra responds to the news as though in mourning (9:3). His confessional prayer on behalf of his people lacks any request for favors — even for forgiveness. Ezra recognizes the Jews' corporate responsibility for the actions of individual community members by acknowledging that God would be justified in destroying the remnant he allowed to escape Judah's previous punishment by the Babylonians.

Ezra's public mourning at the temple draws a crowd of sympathizers, one of whom proposes a covenant requiring divorce from all foreign wives. Ezra summons to Jerusalem all Judah and Benjamin and announces the plan, which, apart from a mere handful, the assembly embraces. A special commission takes two months to dissolve the marriages.

Divorce in this context represented the righting of a moral wrong. As history had shown and current circumstances were demonstrating, religiously mixed marriages inevitably led to Hebrew religious failure, which would ultimately result in the loss of the Jewish remnant's identity as the distinctive community of God's chosen people. Reversing the flow necessitated divorce (but cf. Mal. 2:14-16; 1 Cor. 7:10-16).

Guilty priests, who should have set a faithful example, head the list of transgressors. 1 Esdras 9:36 sheds light on the last half of verse 44 by noting the dismissal of the foreign wives and their children. Thus, within one year after his arrival in Judah, Ezra had made possible a religiously purified community of returned exiles.

Nehemiah

The book of Nehemiah (part of the originally unified Ezra-Nehemiah) draws on the personal memoirs of the royal Persian cupbearer-turned-Jewish-governor and other sources to describe a third return to Jerusalem of Babylonian exiles. The journey occurs in 445 B.C., during the reign of the Persian king Artaxerxes I. The Jerusalem community's principal achievement during Nehemiah's tenure was its rebuilding of the city's walls, despite relentless opposition by the governor of the former Israelite capital of Samaria (Sanballat) and his allies. Nehemiah's personal account of these events appears in chapters 1–7.

The priestly scribe Ezra resurfaces in Nehemiah 8 to deliver a public reading of the Mosaic law. Many scholars believe this chapter originally belonged between chapters 8 and 9 of Ezra, with an earlier version of Neh. 9:1-5 appearing in Ezra 10. Some also believe that Ezra and Nehemiah conducted their work in Jerusalem not as contemporaries but in tandem, with Nehemiah's return and activities actually preceding Ezra's by nearly 50 years. This view has lost support in recent years.

Community confession and recommitment to the Mosaic covenant characterize chapters 9–10. Chapters 11–13 relate the activities that followed, including Nehemiah's institution of reforms, and bring to a close the Old Testament historical narrative.

Authorship

Most of Nehemiah is written from a first-person perspective as Nehemiah's own memoirs. Chapters 8–11 report exclusively in the third person (esp. 8:9). That 13:26 cites Solomon's marriages to foreign women as the cause of his religious failure argues against the Chronicler's authoring Ezra-Nehemiah, for Chronicles omits all mention of these marriages in an effort to portray the Davidic builder of the first temple in a good light.

1 Nehemiah's Response to Jerusalem's Plight

Verse 1 dates the initial events of Nehemiah to November/December 446 (= the month of "Chislev" in "the twentieth year" of Artaxerxes I). Nehemiah, identified in verse 11 as the king's cupbearer, is living in the Persian winter palace at Susa, where his responsibilities include tasting Artaxerxes's wine as the last line of defense against poisoning the king, and guarding the imperial living quarters.

A visit from this royal butler's brother and

Hasmonean tower built on a portion of the wall of Nehemiah; surviving traces can be seen in the lower courses of the tower and in other portions of the wall behind and beside the tower. *(William S. LaSor)*

his Judahite traveling companions occasions Nehemiah's inquiry after Jerusalem and its community of Jews returned from exile in Babylon. Likely, the historical circumstances described in Ezra 4, which records Artaxerxes' order that building in Jerusalem cease (Ezra 4:21), lie behind the disheartening response Nehemiah receives. Jerusalem's reportedly dilapidated condition sends him into a four-month period of mourning (cf. 2:1; Nisan is the first month of the Hebrew year, March/April).

Nehemiah's confession of personal and national sin responds to the echo of Deuteronomistic theology, which views Hebrew misfortune as punishment for covenantal disobedience (cf. Deut. 28:15-68). Nehemiah also prays that God remember his promises of restoration to the faithful (cf. Deut. 30:1-5). The cupbearer's request that God grant him success and "mercy in the sight of this man" (Artaxerxes) leaves one wondering just what Nehemiah has in mind.

2 Nehemiah Begins Work in Jerusalem

Artaxerxes notices Nehemiah's unusually mournful behavior. The king's inquiry as to the source of his butler's remorse instills fear in Nehemiah, perhaps because he knows that a truthful response could be viewed as disloyalty, since Artaxerxes' own orders prevented the Jews from improving Jerusalem's physical condition (Ezra 4:17-24). Nehemiah may be risking his life by expressing grief over Jerusalem's sad state, but Artaxerxes responds favorably by granting a leave of absence and permission to begin rebuilding. He even provides a military escort for the 1100-mile journey and timber from the royal forest.

Along the way, Nehemiah delivers to the governors of the province in which Judah lies written proof of royal authority to pursue his mission, but the news ruffles the feathers of Samaria's governor (Sanballat), a powerful Transjordanian Ammonite official (Tobiah), and later a north Arabian tribal chief (Geshem, of Kedar). Once in Jerusalem, Nehemiah takes a secret nighttime tour to inspect the remains of some of its southern walls and gates. Not until Nehemiah determines for himself the extent of his task does he reveal his plan to Jerusalem's

Jewish inhabitants. Their immediate support in renewing the building emboldens Nehemiah to defy the regional opponents, who continue making trouble throughout the project (chs. 4; 6).

3 The Community Work Crew

No doubt the rebuilding of Jerusalem's 10 gates and 1.5 miles of walls proceeds according to a master plan. Nehemiah organizes families to work on sections of the fortifications closest to their homes, community groups to rebuild portions in their districts, and professionals to repair segments that protect areas important to their vocations. Natural competition and each group's particular stake in the outcome likely contribute to its swift completion in just 52 days, despite the persistent opposition of Sanballat and allies (6:15). The community construction project includes women and incorporates men from a wide variety of occupations — priests, perfumers, politicians, temple servants, merchants, and goldsmiths. Though some refuse to participate, others take on extra assignments (cf. vv. 5, 27).

The description of the work progresses counterclockwise from the easternmost gate on the city's north side (the Sheep Gate). Many of the physical features and locations named remain unknown. With the exception of the 9-ft.-thick section of wall built higher up the steep slope ascending from the Kidron Valley on the City of David's southeastern flank, the rebuilt walls follow the contours of the fortifications destroyed by the Babylonians 150 years earlier.

4 Warding Off Opposition

Sanballat's extreme anger over the rebuilding program suggests that the Samarian governor assumed a degree of jurisdiction over Jerusalem — jurisdiction increasingly threatened with each course of stones the Jews add to the fortifications. That the belittling allied opposition actually takes the project quite seriously becomes clear in their conspiracy to attack from all directions. The inhabitants of formerly Philistine Ashdod represent the western flank, with Sanballat of Samaria to the north, the Ammonites to the east, and the Arabs to the south. Thanks to Jewish informants who spoil the element of surprise and allow Nehemiah to implement a strategic defense plan, Sanballat and company abandon their plot, and the Jews resume work but remain on high alert.

Nehemiah's habit of coupling petitionary prayer with practical action becomes increasingly evident as this account of his bold activities unfolds (v. 9; cf. 2:4; 6:9, 14).

5 Averting Socio-Economic Crisis

External opposition is not the only threat to the success of Nehemiah's task. Tensions between Jews also jeopardize the unity necessary to complete the project. Famine has produced a crisis by forcing poor Jews to give their children as slave-pledges against debt and by requiring landowners to mortgage their property to get food. As the poor become poorer, they must borrow to pay their taxes to the Persian government. Worst of all, the creditors are Jews themselves.

Though Mosaic law permitted short-term debt-slavery (more properly, servanthood; Lev. 25:39ff.) and the temporary sale of property to fellow countrymen as payment for debt, the Law also provided for the redemption of slaves (v. 8) and set forth regular times of release and the return of property (cf. Exod. 21:2-11; Leviticus 25; Deut. 15:1-18). Publicly, Nehemiah now calls on the more economically fortunate among the postexilic community to follow the spirit of the Law by forgiving all debts, returning all property to its original owner, and freeing all slaves. The creditors consent, and Nehemiah puts the priests under a representative oath to bind the agreement.

Verses 14-19 comprise the first of Nehemiah's "Remember me" prayers (cf. 6:14; 13:14, 22, 29, 31). The verses outline the good example set by Nehemiah regarding sacrificial generosity toward the Jewish community — a policy he follows during his entire 12-year tenure as governor of Judah (v. 14). Not only does Nehemiah refuse the locally tax-funded food allowance to which he is entitled as an official of the Persian government (40 shekels — about 1 pound — of silver per day), but he also shares his daily dinner with a small army of friends and countrymen. He shows leadership in the trenches to boot by getting his hands dirty with the work (v. 16).

6 Dismissing Threats and Completing the Walls

Having abandoned their plan to stop the Jews' rebuilding efforts by an assault on Jerusalem (ch. 4), Sanballat and company try to lure Nehemiah into a trap some 24 miles northwest of the city. Frustrated by his first four refusals of diplomatic talks, the enemy leaders tell Nehemiah of a rumor that he intends to revolt against Persia and have himself declared a king, the report of which would invite royal retribution on the governor and his city. Seeing through the scheme, Nehemiah lets the bait lie.

Neither does the suggestion of an assassination attempt persuade Nehemiah to seek refuge in the temple, which only priests could enter.

Bolstered by unwavering faith in God and inspired by the conviction that God ordained his mission, Nehemiah remains concentrated on the task at hand. In less than two months, Jerusalem's 1.5-mile perimeter wall stands tall again, and the surrounding nations shudder in recognition of the power of God, who enabled the accomplishment.

7 Preparing to Repopulate Jerusalem

Nehemiah's vision for Jerusalem and the Jews extends beyond mere completion of the city's fortifications to its continued security. After appointing civil guards, assigning personnel for temple service, and naming his godly brother governor, Nehemiah prepares to inventory Judah's Jewish population with an eye toward relocating residents of outlying areas to the now-underpopulated, underguarded Jerusalem, which mostly still lies in ruins. Nehemiah's discovery of the list of initial returnees who accompanied Zerubbabel in 538 will provide the basis for the population redistribution (cf. 11:1ff.). Verses 6-73 repeat almost verbatim the list in Ezra 2.

8 Ezra's Public Reading of the Law

Chapter 8 disrupts Nehemiah's memoirs, which resume in 12:31. This disruption, coupled with the sudden introduction of Ezra in 8:1, leads scholars to suggest that this chapter originally belonged between chapters 8 and 9 of Ezra and that the compiling editor of Ezra and Nehemiah repositioned the chapter to highlight the converging influence of the two men's careers, Ezra's primarily in the religious sphere, and Nehemiah's mainly in the civil realm.

Whatever the original chronological setting of the events described here, they occur on the date later celebrated as the Jewish New Year (v. 2), and their theological significance rings true for the community of returnees. The people take the initiative in inviting Ezra to read to them the Law (portions of Genesis–Deuteronomy). Ezra symbolically conveys the accessibility of the Law to nonpriests by choosing 13 lay leaders to stand with him while he reads. Verses 8-9 demonstrate the teaching role of the Levites, who help the people understand what they hear. The congregation's deeply emotional response suggests that they realize their religious failings, and it evidences their ready willingness to renew their covenantal relationship with God. The Levites admonish the people to observe the occasion not with mourning but with joyful celebration.

On the next day, family heads, priests, and Levites gather to Ezra for further instruction in the law and realize that it is time for the Feast of Tabernacles (or "Booths") commemorating the exodus from Egypt. The entire Judahite community of returnees observes the weeklong celebration, which the Hebrew people have neglected since the days of Joshua, who led the chosen people into the promised land some eight to 10 centuries earlier.

9 A Corporate Prayer of Confession

The present structure of Nehemiah 8–10 portrays the unusual order of community celebration followed by corporate mourning, characterized by the people's fasting, wearing of sackcloth, and covering themselves with dirt. Grief over their sin and that of their ancestors occasions their communal confession in a prayer led by the Levites.

The prayer begins with praise to God and acknowledgment of his sovereignty evidenced in creation. It quickly moves to a rehearsal of God's work on behalf of the Hebrews, beginning with his decision to bless Abram and his descendants (Gen. 12:1-3; 15:18-21). The prayer remembers great events in Israel's history, acknowledges God's longsuffering in continuing to fulfill the Abrahamic covenant even in the face of the people's disobedience, and acknowledges God's justice in finally judging his defiant people through foreign conquerors (Assyria and Babylon). At the same time, they take courage that God has not abandoned them in their punishment, and they find hope in God's promise of restoration for a repentant people (cf. Deut. 30:1-10) — a promise not yet fully realized by the returnees, who remain subject to a foreign power in the promised land.

10 Signing the Covenant

The prayer of confession in chapter 9 becomes the basis for renewing the covenant. By signing the agreement, Nehemiah and leaders in the religious and civil spheres acknowledge on behalf of the people the curses that befall those who disobey.

Verses 28-39 outline specific laws on which Nehemiah bases his reforms recorded in chapter 13. The verses recall laws that prohibit intermarriage with foreign peoples (cf. Exod. 34:16; Deut. 7:1-4); require observance of sabbatical years (cf. Exod. 23:10-11; Lev. 25:2-7); and require communal support of the temple and priestly tribe (cf. Num. 18:8-32). The "appointed times" (v. 33) refer to the feasts and festivals described in Leviticus 23.

11:1–12:26 A Human Inventory

Chapter 11 resumes the concern for increasing Jerusalem's population (ch. 7), though the perspective here does not appear to reflect Nehemiah's personal memoirs. Lot-casting to determine God's will designates one-tenth of Judah's Jewish population as a human tithe assigned to relocate from the country to the sparsely inhabited former capital. Verses 6, 9, and 14 suggest Jerusalem's defense as at least one motive for this move.

1 Chronicles 9:2-17 largely parallels the list of Jerusalem's inhabitants in verses 3-19. The list includes men of Judah and Benjamin, secular leaders, priests, Levites, and gatekeepers. 1 Chronicles 25 details the regulations David established concerning the temple singers' service (vv. 22-23).

Additional lists unrelated to repopulating Jerusalem are preserved in 11:25–12:26. These inventories provided a framework for the returned community's reorganization. The broad geographical distribution suggested by the list of postexilic Judahite settlements (11:27-36) does not so much reflect the historical realities of the day as recall the Hebrews' ideal territorial possessions in the promised land (cf. Joshua 15) and establish renewed hope for the Jews' future there.

Nehemiah 12:1-26 positions the priests and Levites of the initial return under Zerubbabel (538) alongside those present in Nehemiah's time. The list of Levites again highlights the singers, here pictured as carrying out their musical service antiphonally (12:8-9). "Darius the Persian" (12:22) probably refers to Darius I and distinguishes him from the earlier "Darius the Mede." During the reign of Darius I, the Jews rebuilt the temple (completed in 515).

12:27-47 The Dedication of Jerusalem's Rebuilt Walls

The account resumes Nehemiah's personal perspective in verse 31, as the governor's career reaches its climax with the dedication of Jerusalem's rebuilt walls. Two groups, each composed of priests and Levites, begin the ceremonial procession at the westerly-positioned Valley Gate. Accompanied by Ezra — religious counterpart to the leading civil servant, Nehemiah — one group ascends to the top of the thick wall, presumably by stairs on its inner side. This contingent walks in a counterclockwise direction, while the second group, accompanied by Nehemiah, follows them up but proceeds the opposite way. The two groups meet at the temple, halfway from their starting point, where

they conduct a joyous celebration filled with singing, sacrifice, and attention to practical matters David prescribed for the temple service (1 Chronicles 25–26) and Solomon carried out (2 Chr. 5:11-14). On the ritual purification of people as well as objects (v. 30), cf. Exodus 35–40 (priests and tabernacle); Leviticus 8–10 (priests), 13–14 (people, houses, fabrics), 16 (the altar).

13 Nehemiah's Reforms

After serving as governor of Judah for 12 years, Nehemiah returned for a time to his position as royal cupbearer in Artaxerxes' court (433). Nehemiah's memoirs now resume with an account of his second term as governor in Jerusalem.

During the unspecified time of Nehemiah's absence from the refortified Jerusalem, the Jews have abandoned their covenantal promises, which they earlier ratified (ch. 10). The high priest Eliashib has even housed Nehemiah's earlier Ammonite opponent, Tobiah, in one of the temple's storerooms, and Eliashib's grandson has violated covenantal law for priests by marrying a Gentile wife (v. 28; cf. Lev. 21:14; Ezek. 44:22) — a daughter of Nehemiah's former Samarian archenemy, Sanballat.

The Jews have so neglected the required support for the Levites that these impoverished temple servants have abandoned their work in Jerusalem and returned to farming in the Judahite countryside. The Jerusalemites show complete disregard for the Sabbath by conducting work and commerce on this holy day. Also, intermarriage with foreigners has even produced children who cannot communicate with their Jewish relatives.

Knowing that the eventual outcome will be the disappearance of the Jewish community as a unique society, Nehemiah chastises individual transgressors by delivering physical blows as well as verbal lashings (v. 25). He purifies and reorders the Jewish community anew to safeguard its distinctiveness as the remnant of God's chosen people (cf. Ezra 10). But the Jews' recent communal disobedience in the absence of a central, covenantally minded leader suggests that they will continue to repeat the history of religious infidelity perpetuated by their ancestors.

Esther

In Protestant Bibles, Esther appears at the end of the Historical Books, whereas Jewish Bibles group it with the Writings (Job–Song of Songs). The Greek translation (Septuagint) and Roman Catholic Bible incorporate more than 100 extra verses, the Apocrypha's Additions to Esther, into a 16-chapter version. This longer Esther displays a greater emphasis on religion than the shorter book.

The events described in Esther occur during the height of Persia's political dominance in the early to mid-5th century B.C. The first return of the Jews to Judah (538) takes place 55 years before the account in Esther begins (483). Many Jews remain in Persia, and Esther concentrates on the fortunes of this Jewish dispersion, in contrast to Ezra and Nehemiah, which focus on the Jewish community back in Judah during roughly the same period.

Content

According to Esther, the Persian king Xerxes (Heb. "Ahasuerus," 486-465) replaces his insubordinate queen with a young Jewish woman, Esther, in 479. That she is a Jew remains hidden at first. After Esther becomes queen, Xerxes' recently promoted second in command, Haman, plots to kill all the Jewish people as punishment for the refusal of one Jew — Esther's cousin Mordecai — to pay him homage. As the plot unfolds, the brave Esther becomes the key figure in reversing the fortunes of her people. The survival of the Jews through this most serious of ancient threats to their survival provides the basis for the Jewish festival of Purim.

Surprisingly, the book of Esther contains no mention of God, nor does it anywhere refer to prayer. It implies God's work on behalf of his people rather than asserting divine providence outright. In this way, Esther conveys the responsibility of humans to take practical, righteous action in accomplishing God's divinely orchestrated plan of salvation.

Background

Scholars recognize the accuracy of the many historical details in Esther — the extent of the Persian Empire from India to Ethiopia (1:1); the Persian postal system; the practice in Persia of lot-casting, confirmed archaeologically by the word "puru" (= "lot") inscribed on an ancient die; and the execution by hanging or impalement of the condemned. Nevertheless, some consider the events too improbable and coincidental and thus view the book as a historical novel valued primarily for its theological message concerning God's continued care for his people. But the very existence of the Feast of Purim argues for the historical nature of the Esther account.

Authorship and Date

The unnamed author exhibits a pro-Jewish outlook and good knowledge of Persian royal court customs. These factors may argue for a Hebrew writer employed by the central Persian government. The notation that many Gentiles converted to Judaism as a result of Haman's downfall and Mordecai's promotion (8:17) allows the possibility that a Persian convert authored the book.

No known literary sources refer to the book of Esther, and therefore estimates as to its time of authorship rest solely on internal evidence gleaned from the account. The book views the reign of Xerxes as a past event. Although some scholars suggest that the author wrote Esther during the reign of Artaxerxes I (465-424), others date it as late as the 4th or 3rd century.

1 Xerxes Deposes Queen Vashti

Three years have passed since the vastly wealthy and powerful Darius I, during whose reign Ezra and the postexilic Jewish community finished rebuilding the Jerusalem temple, passed the Persian throne to his son Xerxes I (Heb. "Ahasuerus," Ezra 4:6). Having quelled early opposition to his succession, Xerxes now securely rules a far-reaching empire that stretches from the Indus River (located in modern Pakistan some 1800 mi. east of Babylon) westward around the Fertile Crescent and south through Palestine and Egypt to the Upper Nile in northern Sudan. At the beginning of the account in Esther (483), Xerxes has just spent six months publicly showing off his wealth in his winter capital of Susa.

Described by the Greek historian Herodotus as unpredictable, sensual, and cruel, Xerxes caps off his exhibition with a weeklong stag party (vv. 5-8). On the last day of the celebration, the drunken king decides to show off his beautiful (chief?) wife Vashti ("best" or "beloved"). But the queen refuses to be put on display.

Taking his advisers' counsel, Xerxes punishes Vashti by deposing her for defying his summons, lest wives throughout the empire follow the queen's supreme example of spousal disobedience. Copies of the king's edict declaring Persian husbands' ultimate familial authority (v. 22) circulate by the efficient courier system established earlier by Cyrus. Yet the circumstances that provoke the decree highlight the irony that the unapproachably powerful Xerxes rules over 127 provinces spanning nearly 4000 miles (v. 1), yet he sees his personal authority publicly defied under his own roof.

2:1-18 Esther Becomes Queen

After four years and two disastrous battles against the Greeks (at Thermopylae and Salamis), Xerxes finally replaces Vashti (v. 16). Apparently, none of his current concubines will do. In typically extravagant style, he follows the advice of his underlings in summoning to his harem "all the beautiful young virgins" from throughout the empire for a year's worth of beauty treatments in preparation for their

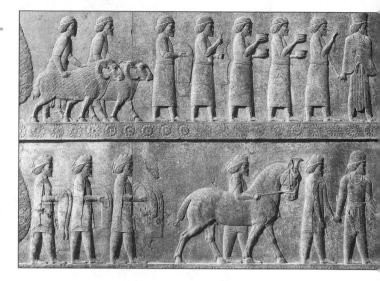

Reliefs depicting tribute-bearing delegates, on the eastern stairway of the audience hall (apadana) of Darius I at Persepolis. *(Oriental Institute, University of Chicago)*

tryout with the king. From among them Xerxes will choose his queen.

Enter Mordecai, guardian of his beautiful orphaned cousin Esther — both Jews descended from important Hebrew families taken captive by the Babylonian king Nebuchadnezzar more than a century earlier. The names in Mordecai's Benjamite family line recall King Saul's father Kish and Saul's fiercely supportive relative Shimei (v. 5). Esther's Hebrew name, Hadassah, means "myrtle." Once settled in the palace precincts, Esther quickly becomes the favorite of the harem manager, Hegai. Esther maintains her respect for Mordecai by following his instructions not to reveal her Jewish identity.

Esther's willingness to follow the advice not only of Mordecai but also of Hegai serves her well when her time comes to spend the night with the king in December/January 479. She becomes Xerxes' favorite too, and he crowns her queen, still unaware of her ancestry.

2:19-23 Mordecai Exposes a Conspiracy

While sitting at the king's gate, where officials conduct the business of the court, Mordecai — himself possibly now an official (cf. 3:2) — overhears two palace guards plotting against

Xerxes' life. He reveals the conspiracy to his cousin the queen, who passes the word on to her husband and credits Mordecai for thwarting the assassination. The conspirators hang and the incident is recorded in the royal annals (v. 23), but Mordecai goes unrewarded for his loyalty to the king.

3 Haman Plots to Kill the Jews

Chapter 3 introduces the villain — Haman, a descendant of King Agag who ruled Israel's natural enemies, the Amalekites, and whose sparing cost Saul his kingship (Exod. 17:8-16; Deut. 25:17-19; 1 Samuel 15). Xerxes has recently appointed the non-Persian Haman as his right-hand man and has ordered Persian subjects to bow in his presence. The account thus pits Haman, a descendant of Saul's enemy, against Mordecai, a descendant in Saul's Benjamite line.

Mordecai's revelation of his Jewish roots in association with his refusal to bow before Haman gets more than just Mordecai into trouble. Xerxes' supremely offended prime minister resolves not only to execute Mordecai but also to exterminate all Jews throughout the empire.

Initially, Haman shows patient restraint by postponing the slaughter nearly one year, in accordance with the determination by lot-casting (= "Pur," v. 7) of a lucky day for the slaughter (contrast 5:9-14). Ironically, the lot falls on the 13th of a month, a number considered unlucky by the Persians. Haman easily obtains Xerxes' approval of the murderous plan by accusing "a certain people" (the Jews, whom he never names to the king) of a bent toward civil disobedience and by arguing that the diverse geographical distribution throughout the empire of this supposedly subversive people poses a threat to the Persian government. In reality, Haman's concern lies less with Jewish conformity to Persian law than with Mordecai's perceived personal insult.

Haman's bribe, in which he promises to donate to the royal treasury a hefty weight of silver (two-thirds of the government's annual budget), tips the scales in his favor, and the king hands over his signet ring to sign the proposal into law. The Persian postal service quickly delivers the order to wipe out the Jewish race and to plunder their possessions on the 13th of Adar (February/March; cf. v. 7). The edict throws the city of Susa into disarray, while Haman and the king relax with a drink.

4 Mordecai's Challenge to Esther

Mordecai and all Jews throughout the empire respond to the news of their impending doom with intense mourning. Mordecai adds public protest to his display of grief by wailing his way through Susa till he reaches the palace gate. His mourning attire bars him from entering the palace precincts and therefore from making direct contact with Esther. But Esther also learns of the plot against her people and of Mordecai's state. Her gift of clothes to her former guardian may signal a desire to see him personally, but by rejecting the gift Mordecai also rejects any invitation it might represent.

By courier Mordecai relays the details of the plot and orders Esther to intervene with the king. By now, some five years have passed since she became queen, and Esther no longer accepts Mordecai's direction without analyzing its personal consequences. Her objection to his appeal rests in the risk that her unbidden approach of the king would pose to her own life. Mordecai replies that Esther's own last chance lies in pleading with the king, for the law requires her execution too, despite her position as queen.

Mordecai reveals his conviction that deliverance for the Jews will arise from elsewhere even if Esther remains silent. Then he suggests that perhaps her destiny as an (unlikely) ascendant to Persian royalty lies in playing a role in that deliverance.

Persuaded by Mordecai's reasoning, Esther accepts his challenge. But she requires Susa's Jews to join her in a three-day fast to bolster her courage and prepare her spiritually for this risky encounter with the king.

5 Dinner for Three

The sight of Esther breaks Xerxes' monthlong neglect of his queen. He knows the risk Esther takes in approaching him unsummoned and suspects something serious must be troubling her. Rather than taking immediate advantage of Xerxes' offer to solve her problem, Esther extends a dinner invitation to the king and his second in command — her own enemy, Haman.

Sated with food and wine, Xerxes again invites Esther to express her request, but again she sidesteps the matter and delicately maneuvers the king's *offer* of help toward a royal *commitment* to grant her request. The wording of Esther's response ensures that, by accepting another invitation to dinner the next day, Xerxes is promising to do what she asks, even though he has no clue as to what's coming (v. 8).

The account leaves us in suspense by omitting the king's reply to Esther's second invitation. Instead, the self-important Haman, after leaving the first evening's banquet, curbs his disdain for the unsubjecting and unflappable Mordecai by boasting to family and friends. The prime minister emerges as a mini-Xerxes, whose great ego requires constant stroking and who cannot tolerate personal opposition.

Haman's friends offer a solution to his distress over Mordecai: execute him publicly (even before the legislated Jewish doomsday) on a 75-ft.-high gallows and then celebrate! Completely unaware of Mordecai's relationship to the queen and of Esther's Jewish ancestry, to say nothing of Mordecai's key role in thwarting the king's assassination (2:21-23), Haman orders the construction of the gallows in blissful ignorance of his own impending fate.

6 The Tables Start to Turn

As Haman prepares Mordecai's execution, Xerxes plans to honor the loyal Jew. Midnight readings on the king's sleepless night between Esther's banquets remind him of Mordecai's part in saving his life. Fully aware that Mordecai is a Jew but oblivious of the approaching slaughter (3:8-15), Xerxes determines to grant Mordecai a long-overdue reward.

When Haman arrives in the morning, ready to present his charge against Mordecai, Xerxes solicits the prime minister's ideas on celebrating an as-yet-undisclosed honoree. Believing the king has him in mind, Haman suggests dressing the honoree in the king's clothes, mounting him on the king's horse, and having a royal dignitary parade him through the city square while proclaiming his greatness.

Mordecai apparently accepts the king's honor, perhaps finding irresistible the irony of Haman's visible, public role in rewarding the one who refuses to honor Haman. In any case, the mortified but duty-bound prime minister ends up humiliating himself by advertising his intended victim's royal recognition under the prominent shadow of the gallows he built for Mordecai's execution. Haman's family and friends see the handwriting on the wall for him.

7 Haman's Last Meal

The (presumably providential) coincidences of the previous chapters now reach a tragic climax for Haman. During the second banquet with Xerxes and his right-hand man, Esther reveals her request to the king — the sparing of her life and those of her people. Again, Xerxes does not realize that Mordecai shares the Jews' death sentence. Neither does Xerxes know about Haman's evil plans for Mordecai, or of his queen's blood relationship to her doubly doomed cousin — a relationship about which Haman presumably is also unaware.

When Esther identifies Haman as mastermind of the murderous plan that orders her own execution, Xerxes reins in his rage. Unwittingly, Haman has tricked the king into signing his queen's death warrant. To reason out the situation for himself, Xerxes steps out to get some air. Now it is the entrapped and terrified Haman who must beg for his life, and he must do so before a Jewish woman. Again, timing works against Haman, for as the king reenters the banquet hall he observes his pleading prime minister falling all over the queen, who lies prostrate on her couch. At best, the scene looks to Xerxes like an assault. This additional, personal offense seals Haman's doom. The covering of Haman's face (v. 8) presages his execution, which follows swiftly on the gallows now identified to Xerxes as Haman's intended instrument of death for the faithful Mordecai.

8 Mordecai Replaces Haman and Issues a New Edict

Only after Haman's execution does Xerxes become aware of Esther's relationship to Mordecai and of the queen's identity as a Jew. Esther inherits Haman's household — thanks to ancient Near Eastern law, which dictated that the property of condemned criminals revert to the crown. Her cousin receives Haman's authority, represented by the king's giving of his signet ring to Mordecai (v. 2). Nevertheless, the decree ordering the annihilation of the Jewish race cannot be cancelled according to Persian law, intended to save face for the king. But Xerxes can and does answer Esther's impassioned plea for her people by suggesting the proclamation of a new, unalterable edict, the contents of which he leaves up to his Jewish queen and prime minister.

By declaring the Jews' right to organize and defend themselves — even to destroy and plunder their would-be murderers (cf. 3:13) — on the day of their intended doom, Mordecai words the decree in a way that effectively annuls Haman's edict. The new proclamation results in the conversion to Judaism of many fearful Persians.

9 The Jews Celebrate

Nine months later, on Haman's intended doomsday for Mordecai's people, Jews attack their would-be assassins throughout Persia and prevail completely. The reported number of slain enemies, though suspiciously high, is still far lower than a slaughter of all Jews living in Persia would have been (vv. 6, 15-16). The Jews follow their forefather Abraham's example in forgoing the right to plunder their defeated enemies' property (8:11; cf. Gen. 14:21-24).

Haman's 10 sons (vv. 7-9) die during the fight in Susa. Esther accepts Xerxes' offer of an additional request by asking for a one-day extension of the Jews' permission to pursue their enemies in Susa and by petitioning for the hanging (perhaps impalement) of Haman's dead sons, presumably as public humiliation. Through his generous behavior toward Esther, Xerxes displays a degree of respect for the queen that his earlier treatment of Vashti sorely lacked (1:10ff.).

Jews throughout the provinces celebrate their reversal of fortunes with feasting. Mordecai writes legal orders that all future generations of Jews commemorate their survival by celebrating on the anniversary of the two days when first the provincial Jews and then their Susan relatives rejoiced. A summary of the events leading to the formal establishment of this festival, called Purim, explains its basis (vv. 24-28). Empire-wide, Esther sends royal written confirmation of the new "appointed seasons."

Haman's failed genocidal plot thus solidified the Jewish community rather than eradicating it. Modern observance of Purim includes fasting on the 13th of Adar (February/March) followed by feasting, gift-giving, charity, and reading aloud the book of Esther on the following two days.

10 An Addendum

This postscript diverts attention away from Esther and onto Mordecai. By emphasizing the far-reaching geographical extent of Xerxes' authority coupled with the great influence and widespread popularity that his Jewish right-hand man firmly commands, the addendum conveys the security the Jews now enjoy as subjects of the Persian crown.

Poetry and Wisdom Literature

Poetry

Poetry is hard to define, but its most recurrent characteristic is its use of compressed language. Poetry says a lot, using relatively few words. Poetry's terseness indicates that it is highly structured, self-conscious writing. Not only is the poet concerned to communicate a message, he or she also desires to express it in a memorable way. With poetry, how something is written is as important as what is written.

Hebrew poetry creates the **compression of language** in a variety of ways. The poet may omit many indicators of syntax such as conjunctions ("and," "but," "therefore") or direct object markers. These words are small, but they indicate how words and clauses relate to one another. Their less frequent use (compared with prose) raises the level of ambiguity of communication and requires the reader to work harder at understanding. Ellipsis also accounts for the brevity of the poetic line. Ellipsis describes the poet's tendency to omit a word or phrase from the second part of a parallel line (see below). Often it is the verb that is omitted, as in this example from Ps. 88:6:

> You have put me in the lowest pit,
>> in the darkest depths.

These omissions explain why poetry is terse and intentionally ambiguous. Hebrew poetry communicates adequately — it is not totally ambiguous — but without the high level of precision typical of prose.

Why did the biblical writers use so much poetry as a vehicle of God's Word to humanity? The Old Testament in particular is filled with poetry. Genesis contains both shorter and longer poems (cf. Gen. 1:27 and ch. 49), as do the other books of the Pentateuch (most notably Exodus 15 and Deuteronomy 33). The historical books present powerful poems, for instance Judges 5, Deborah's celebration of victory over the Canaanites. Many of the prophets also delivered their divinely inspired oracles in poetic form. Some scholars consider the poetry of Isaiah, Micah, and Nahum among the best, and most prophets have long sections of poetry.

The term "poetical books," however, is most closely associated with four of the five books in the following section of this *Companion*. The first three books were noted as poetic by the earliest scribes, since they used a special system to accent them in Hebrew. Most notable is the massive book of **Psalms,** the hymnbook of the Old Testament, containing not only hymns but also laments, thanksgivings, and songs of confidence and remembrance and wisdom. **Job,** too, is poetry except for the prose frame, which narrates the opening and closing of the plot. The poetry carries the dialogue, which signals that Job is a story with universal implications. **Proverbs** has a clear, poetic format, with the first nine chapters composed of extended discourses, while the remainder of the book is a collage of two-line statements (called bicola) with only an occasional more extended poetic structure (as in Prov. 31:10-31). Surprisingly, the clearly poetic **Song of Songs** was not accented in Hebrew as poetry but no doubt fits the modern recognition of the book as poetic.

But again, Why so much poetry in the Old Testament? We are led to speculate based on the nature of poetry itself. Besides poetry's lack of concern with precision of communication, in general it appeals to the whole person more than prose. Poetry does indeed inform the intellect, but it also arouses our emotions, stimulates our imagination, and appeals to our will. The presence of poetry in the Bible reminds us that God is interested in more than our minds; God is concerned to speak to us as whole people.

This point is underlined by consideration of another characteristic of Hebrew poetry — its use of **imagery.** To be sure, figures of speech may be found in prose as well as poetry, but the poets of Israel used imagery with an intensity and frequency not found in prose. Imagery, too, is a way to say much using few words. It also well illustrates the poet's ability to stimulate our imagination and arouse our emotions.

First, notice how an image captures our attention by telling us something that is literally false. In talking about God's past absence from Israel and his present appearance as a warrior on his people's behalf, Ps. 78:65 states:

> Then the Lord awoke as from sleep,
> as a man wakes from a stupor of wine.

It is simply not true that God sleeps (Psalm 121), especially a sleep deepened by heavy drinking. To unpack this image takes time and effort and illustrates that poetry in general must be read slowly and reflectively. The poet creates the association between God and a drunken person (the Hebrew word for "man" suggests a soldier) to emphasize only certain traits as illuminating the action of God. God does not literally drink or sleep, but the image does suggest God's profound absence from Israel followed by his angry, even irritable, action against their enemies. In short, here God acts like a drunk when wakened from sleep.

This somewhat shocking image illustrates how poetry works, even with other well-known images, such as God as a shepherd. We unpack the image by asking, How is God a shepherd? Even to begin to answer would require us to make many literal statements (God guides us, protects us, watches over us, provides for us . . .). In its ancient setting the shepherd is a frequent image for a king. Furthermore, the image not only provides intellectual content but also arouses comfort and communicates God's love to us. At a certain point, however, we may ask whether we have taken the comparison too far. There is no formula for determining this. Though images communicate adequately, they are also ambiguous, not precise. Since many Old Testament images are images of God (king, father, mother, warrior, spouse), they intentionally preserve the mystery of God. Images both reveal and conceal.

Another major characteristic of poetry in the Bible is **parallelism.** This term describes the echoing effect evident in the Psalms. The poet seems to say the same thing twice, only using different words:

A Why do the nations conspire,
B and the peoples plot in vain?
C The kings of the earth take their stand
D and the rulers gather together
E against the Lord
F and against his Anointed One.

(Ps. 2:1-2)

Notice that the poet is not saying the same thing twice, but rather adds new ideas in the second colon (B, D, F). There is continuity and progression from one line to the next. The example above has three bicola (two-line parallelisms). Note how colon B adds the idea of the meaninglessness of the plot against God; colon D emphasizes the alliance between the rebellious rulers, and colon F says that the plot is not only against the Lord but also against his anointed one (the king).

Terseness, imagery, and parallelism are the three most pervasive traits of poetry in the Old Testament. Countless other poetical devices occur less frequently, but to understand these three helps us gain appreciation and understanding as we read the poetry of the Bible.

Wisdom Literature

Wisdom in the Old Testament is much more than intellectual knowledge; it is applied intelligence. Indeed, it is fair to compare the biblical word "wisdom" (Heb. *hokmah*) with the idea of a skill, an ability to navigate through the obstacles that life presents. The wise know how to control their emotions, responding appropriately to the situation. They know the right time to say the right word and do the right thing. In the Old Testament there is a close connection between wisdom and creation. To live wisely is to live in harmony with the way God made the world.

Three Old Testament books articulate this idea of wisdom. The first is **Proverbs,** which states clearly its intention to impart "wisdom and instruction," or "discipline" (NIV), to its readers (Prov. 1:2). In large part, Proverbs does this by making observations and giving advice in pithy, two-line statements. An example of an observation is:

> A wise son brings joy to his father,
>> but a foolish son grief to his mother. (10:1)

An example of its advice is:

> Do not answer a fool according to his folly,
>> or you will be like him yourself. (26:4)

That these are not universally valid laws, but rather dependent on the situation, is well illustrated by the next proverb, which warns that the wise person should answer a fool to prevent that fool from thinking himself intelligent. The point is that the wise need to know what kind of fool they are dealing with!

Proverbs also confronts us with a less obvious but more fundamental teaching about wisdom. Wisdom is a skill to be sure, but at heart that skill is built on a relationship with God himself. It is possible to mimic the lifestyle of the wise person, but it is not possible truly to be wise without a relationship with God himself. Again, the book makes that clear right at the start:

> The fear of the Lord is the beginning of knowledge. . . . (1:7a)

In fact, the first nine chapters present the reader with a climactic choice. Throughout these chapters God's wisdom is personified as a woman named Wisdom, while the way of false gods is presented as personified Folly. In Proverbs 9 the reader must decide with which woman he will dine, and it is on this basis that he shows himself a wise person or a fool.

Both **Job** and **Ecclesiastes** function in large part to keep us from being overly optimistic about human wisdom. Ecclesiastes warns that under the sun even wisdom is meaningless

(Eccl. 2:12-16). Ultimately, the most important thing in life is to fear God and obey him (12:13-14). In Job, only the Lord speaks with wisdom, silencing the pretensions of Job and his friends, who claim knowledge on their own. Again, the message of the book is that wisdom is found only in relationship with God.

But it is also true that wisdom has an international setting. Even Solomon, the model wisdom figure of the Old Testament (1 Kgs. 4:29-34), is measured in the light of non-Israelite wisdom. Indeed, the wisdom books of Mesopotamia, Canaan, and especially Egypt have many formal similarities with biblical wisdom, but these similarities nearly dissolve in the light of the Bible's distinctive teaching that the fountainhead of all wisdom is one's relationship with the Lord, the God of Israel.

The Apocrypha contains two important books of wisdom. The first is known variously as **Ecclesiasticus,** the **Wisdom of Ben Sira,** or **Sirach.** It was originally written ca. 180 B.C. in Hebrew, though our present manuscripts are in Greek. It has clear relationships with the literary form and theology of Proverbs. The other book is the **Wisdom of Solomon,** written in Greek, sometime after the year 30. Along with Proverbs and Ecclesiasticus, it personifies wisdom as a woman. One of the book's primary purposes is to show that the Hebrews have true wisdom compared to the sophisticated Greeks. Christians of different communions differ over whether these books have canonical authority or are simply books that encourage and edify. In either case, they are worth reading.

Wisdom is a characteristic of other books of the Old Testament not usually called wisdom books. For instance, some would include the Song of Songs among the wisdom books. A broad definition that understands wisdom as applied knowledge, in this case to sexuality, would generously include it. Psalms contains a number of songs that share themes with the three core wisdom books (e.g., Psalms 1, 45, 119). The stories of Joseph (Genesis 37–50), Esther, and Daniel (1–6) recount the lives of wise men and women navigating the obstacles and threats of their times. They embody the principles of wisdom found in a book such as Proverbs.

The New Testament letter of James echoes the perspective of the wisdom tradition for a distinctly Christian context. Distinguishing between heavenly and earthly wisdom, James reflects the Christian's quest for understanding and insight for practical, ethical living.

It is important for Christian readers of the Old Testament to recognize that the New Testament presents Jesus Christ as the very embodiment of God's wisdom. He grew up in wisdom (Luke 2:40-51). Paul describes him as the one "in whom are hidden all the treasures of wisdom and knowledge" (Col. 2:2-3). To seek knowledge, then, for the Christian is to seek a deepening relationship with Jesus Christ.

TREMPER LONGMAN III

Job

The book of Job belongs to the genre of Wisdom literature and appears in the Writings division of the Hebrew Scriptures. Job's singular structure — a dialogue featuring Job, three friends, Elihu, and, in the end, God — and its distinctive theme — the suffering of the righteous — distinguish the book as unique. With the exception of a prose introduction (chs. 1–2) and epilogue (ch. 42), almost all of Job is poetic.

Content

The story of Job centers on a very righteous and, at the outset, very wealthy Edomite sheikh, who suddenly and for no clear reason suffers successive disasters that devastate his estate, his family, and his health. Job remains completely unaware that God has allowed an "adversary" to test through affliction the sincerity of his faithfulness to God. The afflicter wagers that, when Job's life turns sour, Job will curse his Maker.

But the sufferer disappoints his attacker. Initially, Job reacts with calm resignation to the loss of his family and fortune. Those who tout the "patience of Job," however, have only scratched the surface of his response, for after God allows the "adversary" to afflict Job's own body Job begins a vehement protest that charges God with a gross miscarriage of justice. Throughout most of the book, Job serves more as a model of protest than of patience.

Job's friends do not offer much help in his struggle with the timeless question of why the righteous suffer. The first three speakers even reject the premise that Job stands blameless. Substituting analysis for comfort, they try to make Job's particular case conform to their theology, which mandates the interpretation of suffering as punishment for sin. Then the brash young Elihu interprets affliction as a divine tool to prevent future sinning; by afflicting the innocent Job, God is doing him a favor.

Throughout the dialogue, Job defends his innocence, and he must deflect the "friends'" off-target sermons in his solitary struggle to make sense of his suffering. He lacks any hope that his misfortune will be set right after he dies. But to Job's credit, he allows his resultant despair, anger, frustration, and defiance to subject his theology to intense growing pains while the friends remain safely, though temporarily, barricaded in their theologically rigid box.

Job and his friends continue talking past one another until God breaks in and silences them all. He does not offer Job an explanation for his suffering, but the personal encounter expands Job's perception of God, puts his suffering in perspective, and results in Job's ceasing to struggle.

The book of Job does *not* teach that suffering never results from sinfulness, only that suffering does not always represent punishment for disobedience to God. So how should the innocent person react to suffering? God's ultimate approval of Job both in his patience and in his protest sanctions both responses, so long as the sufferer also follows Job's example of clinging to God in the midst of repentance *and* complaint.

Authorship and Date

Beyond the almost certain conclusion that an Israelite wrote the book of Job, guesses as to its author remain purely speculative. The mention of Job in Ezek. 14:14, 20 assumes him to be a well-known and greatly admired person whose life story probably became widely known through centuries of oral retelling. Most scholars believe that the present text represents the work of ancient editors throughout various stages of the book's written transmission.

Though Job contains allusions to other parts of the Old Testament (e.g., Genesis 1 and Psalm 8), the book lacks any reference to events or

Large encampment reminiscent of Job, the "greatest of all the people of the east," rich in flocks and progeny.
(Phoenix Data Systems, Neal and Joel Bierling)

institutions that would provide clues as to the date of the account's composition. The general picture of life and customs in Job seems to fit the patriarchal period; however, the story's historical setting does not necessarily indicate its time of authorship, just as its geographical setting (Edom) does not suggest its composition by anyone other than an Israelite. Modern scholars posit the book's commission to writing sometime in the 1st millennium B.C.

1–2 Tragedy Befalls a Righteous Man

This prose prologue confronts the reader with the age-old question, Why do the righteous suffer? The fact of their suffering flies in the face of a theology put forward throughout the Old Testament historical books and prophetic literature — the promise of blessing to the covenantally obedient and punishment to transgressors of divine law (e.g., Deuteronomy 28; 1 Chr. 28:8-9).

By ancient standards a wealthy man also blessed with ideal numbers of sons and daughters (seven and three; cf. Ruth 4:15), Job evidences all the expected rewards for leading a righteous life. In his homeland east of Palestine (Uz likely represents Edom; cf. Lam. 4:21), he even offers sacrifices for unknown sins that his children might have committed, just in case.

But a conversation between God and "the adversary" (also translated "the satan," but not meaning Satan himself) in the presence of the heavenly beings in God's court soon leads to the reversal of the unsuspecting Job's worldly fortunes and puts to the ultimate test his loyalty to God. In reality, the adversary's charge that Job's faithfulness hinges on his leading "the good life" represents a challenge not to Job but to God, and God allows the adversary to play out the contest on the human scene in a way that strikes the reader as arbitrary, unfair, and extreme.

In the space of one day, Job loses almost everything. Thanks both to supernaturally orchestrated natural disasters and to nomadic raiders from southwestern Arabia (Sabeans) and southern Mesopotamia (Chaldeans), Job's assets dry up, his workforce is trimmed to the bone, and the heirs to his former fortune precede him in death. Though impoverished and grieving, Job maintains an unshakably righteous posture toward God and without question accepts God's supreme right to curse him as well as to bless him. Note that Job rightly assumes God's ultimate responsibility for the calamities he has suffered (1:12; 2:3), but he does not presume to judge God by blaming him (1:21-22). Because of Job's faithfulness, the adversary has lost the first battle, but he will not surrender the war.

In a second heavenly court encounter, God grants the adversary added permission to afflict Job's own body, short of killing him, as a further test of the man's religious mettle. Covered head to foot with boils, Job separates himself from polite society by taking up residence on the local rubbish heap, replete with ashes associated in the ancient Near Eastern world with mourn-

Disease, Disabilities, and Healing

Health care refers to a system of institutions, personnel, and practices meant to maintain and/or restore health. Hunter-gatherers of the Paleolithic period probably already knew of the medicinal value of some plants and were probably engaging in simple healing activities. Survivable surgical procedures on the skull (trephination) began as early as the Neolithic period in ancient Syria-Palestine.

Public hygiene is part of any health care system, and sewage systems in some towns (e.g., Jericho and Tell Beit Mirsim in some periods) and private toilets in some dwellings (e.g., Jerusalem in the 7th-6th centuries B.C.) attest to the concern with public hygiene. The priestly tasks described in Leviticus 13–14 may also be seen as an effort in public hygiene. Despite several references to washing and related activities (Gen. 18:4; Ps. 60:8), it is likely that personal hygiene was generally poor in the absence of abundant water supplies. Ruth 3:3 indicates that even simple bathing was sometimes seen as a special or uncommon event.

The precise identification of most diseases in the Bible has been notoriously difficult, especially in cases of epidemics (Numbers 25; 1 Sam. 5:6-12). Researchers have established the probable existence of certain intestinal diseases (e.g., tapeworm and whipworm infections) in ancient Israel. The condition usually translated "leprosy" (Heb. *tsara'at*) receives the most attention (Leviticus 13–14), but it probably encompassed a large variety of diseases, especially those manifesting chronic discoloration of the skin.

The Hebrew Bible has at least two principal explanations for illness. One (Deuteronomy 28) affirms that health (Heb. *shalom*) encompasses a physical state associated with the fulfillment of covenantal stipulations that are fully disclosed to the members of the society, and illness stems from the violation of those stipulations. Therapy includes reviewing one's actions in the light of the covenant. The book of Job offers a contrasting, yet complementary, view: illness may be rooted in divine plans that may not be disclosed to the patient at all, and not in the transgression of published rules. The patient must trust that God's undisclosed reasons are just.

Disability, in modern terms, usually refers to a chronic condition that prevents a person from performing a role assigned by society. Accordingly, what a society deemed to be a disability may vary widely. In ancient Israel, infertility was viewed as an illness that diminished the social status of the afflicted woman (Gen. 30:1-20). Blindness (2 Sam. 5:8) and certain musculo-skeletal disorders would qualify as disabilities as well (9:3). An ill king, such as Uzziah (2 Chr. 26:20-21), could also be seen as unable to carry out his normal role.

Illness and healing rest ultimately upon God's control (Job 5:18). Since it was accessible and inexpensive, prayer was probably the most common option for medical consultation, and both petitions and thanksgiving prayers uttered from the viewpoint of the patient are attested (Isa. 38:10-20).

Illegitimate options included consultants designated as "physicians" (Heb. *rop'im;* 2 Chr. 16:12), pagan deities (2 Kgs. 1:2-4), and a large variety of "sorcerers" (Deut. 18:10-12). Warnings in the canonical texts, along with archaeological evidence for fertility cults, indicate that "illegitimate" options were used widely in ancient Israel.

Stories of healing miracles (e.g., 2 Kings 4, 8) may reflect an effort to promote the prophet as a legitimate consultant, and he was often in fierce competition with "illegitimate" options. His function was to judge the prospects of recovery (2 Kgs. 8:8) and intercede with God on behalf of the patient (5:11). Unlike some of the principal healers in other ancient Near Eastern societies, the effectiveness of the Israelite prophet resided more in his relationship with his god than in his technical expertise. The demise of the prophetic office in the early Second Temple period probably led to the widespread legitimization of the "physician" (cf. Sirach 38).

It is particularly difficult to identify and evaluate the therapeutic value of most specific treatments attributed to any of these consultants. Such treatments include the use of "balsam" from

Gilead (Jer. 46:11), "mandrakes" for infertility (Gen. 30:14), and "bandages" (Ezek. 30:21).

Another accepted option for dealing with some illnesses, particularly in the preexilic period, was the temple. In 1 Samuel 1 Hannah visited the temple at Shiloh to help reverse her infertility. 2 Kings 18:4 indicates that prior to Hezekiah the metallic serpent made by Moses (Num. 21:6-9) was involved in acceptable therapeutic rituals in the Jerusalem temple. Metallic serpents have been found in temples used for therapy during the 1st millennium B.C. (e.g., the Asclepieion at Pergamon).

By the postexilic period the Priestly Code severely restricted access to the temple for the chronically ill (e.g., "lepers," Leviticus 13–14; cf. 2 Sam. 5:8 on the blind and lame) because of fear of "impurity." The theology of impurity, as a system of social boundaries, could serve to remove socioeconomically burdensome populations from society, the chronically ill perhaps being the most prominent. In effect, the Priestly Code minimizes state responsibility for the chronically ill, leaving the eradication of illness for the future (Ezek. 47:12; cf. Isa. 35:5-6).

Thanksgiving or "well-being" offerings (Lev. 7:11-36) after an illness were probably always acceptable and economically advantageous for the temple. Offerings after an illness also may have served as public notice of the readmission of previously ostracized patients to society (Lev. 14:1-32).

The community responsible for the Dead Sea Scrolls added to the list of illnesses excluded from the normal community and expanded the restrictions for "leprosy," the blind, and the lame (1QSa 2:4-9). Socioeconomic reasons, as well as the fear of magical contamination, may be responsible for such increased restrictions.

During the 1st century A.D. a variety of health care systems were available in Palestine. These included those associated with the Egyptian goddess Isis and the Greek god Asclepius. In addition, there were secular Greco-Roman traditions associated with Hippocrates, Celsus, and other physicians.

Perhaps the most far-reaching consequence of the Priestly Code was the growth of chronically ill populations who were permitted little access to the temple. Much of the ministry of Jesus and his disciples appears to target these populations (Matt. 10:8; Mark 14:3), and an important focus of early Christianity may be seen as a critique of the Levitical health care system. Jesus demonstrated that travel to a shrine was not necessary for healing (Matt. 8:8), and he instructed his disciples to take no fees such as were charged in many Greco-Roman traditions (10:8). Likewise, he resisted legalistic restrictions on when healing could take place (Mark 3:2-5).

In the early Christian period illness was thought to be caused by numerous demonic entities, not always acting at Yahweh's command (Matt. 15:22; Luke 11:14), and not necessarily by the violation of covenantal stipulations (John 9:2). Illnesses mentioned include fevers (Mark 1:30), hemorrhages (Matt.

9:20), and what has been identified by some scholars as epilepsy (Mark 9:14-29). Emphasizing that the cure for illness may be found in this world, early Christianity preserved many older Hebrew traditions regarding miraculous healings (Acts 5:16; 9:34) and collective health (Jas. 5:16), though the influence of Hellenistic healing cults (e.g., the Asclepius cult) also may be seen.

In all biblical periods the family was probably the main caretaker of the ill (2 Sam. 13:5-6; Matt. 8:14). The best medical technology (e.g., scalpels, forceps, dental drills, and splints) may have helped only simple problems (e.g., extraction of lodged weapons). In general, trauma (from accidents or strife), malnutrition, and disease limited life expectancy to under 40 years throughout the biblical era.

For Further Reading

Avalos, Hector. *Health Care and the Rise of Christianity.* Peabody, Mass.: Hendrickson, 1999.

——. *Illness and Health Care in the Ancient Near East: The Role of the Temple of Greece, Mesopotamia, and Israel.* HSM 54. Atlanta: Scholars, 1995.

Kee, Howard Clark. *Medicine, Miracle, and Magic in New Testament Times.* SNTSMS 55. Cambridge: Cambridge University Press, 1986.

Twelftree, Graham H. *Jesus the Exorcist.* WUNT 54. Tübingen: Mohr, 1993.

Wilkinson, John. *The Bible and Healing: A Medical and Theological Commentary.* Grand Rapids: Eerdmans, 1998.

HECTOR AVALOS

ing. Job's wife, understandably bitter about the loss of her children and thus her social status (cf. Gen. 16; 29:31–30:24), challenges her husband to blaspheme by cursing God and thereby to hasten his own death.

Dismissing his wife's advice as unthinking foolishness, Job firmly maintains that God may do what he pleases. Job's commendable failure to "sin with his lips" proves wrong the adversary's claim that Job would curse God if physically afflicted. The phrase does not imply that he might have sinned in thought or deed.

When three of Job's friends hear about the personal disasters that have befallen their comrade, they travel to Job's home from areas in Arabia and Edom. The calamities have so transformed Job that they barely recognize him. They first mourn for him and then grieve with him for a full week. Their silence recognizes that words are inadequate to comfort their friend.

Despite Job's exemplary attitude, the sympathetic reader cannot help but ponder why God has allowed the assault on the blameless pawn in this spiritual power play. Ultimately, the book will teach that God alone is the source of wisdom and answers to no one.

3 Job Curses His Birth

Emotional frailty finally gets the best of Job, and he breaks the weeklong silence by cursing the day of his birth in terms that invoke the reversal of creation through a return to darkness and the absence of God (vv. 4-9; cf. Jer. 20:14-18). Job futilely enlists the cursing arts of magicians to make unlucky the day of his conception and thereby to prevent his parents from conceiving him. His current misery makes him forget about the blessed life he previously led so that he even wishes he had died at birth. In the book's first poetic speech, Job wonders why God withholds death from the sufferer and discloses that his worst fears have all come true.

4–5 Eliphaz Responds

Job's friend Eliphaz feels compelled to respond to Job's lament. He points out that Job has comforted many others through hard times,

but he gently chastises Job for impatience now that personal disaster has struck him. Speaking from the perspective of a theology of reward or punishment, Eliphaz concludes that suffering results from disobedience to God (4:7-9). Punishment even affects the offender's offspring, who cannot escape it at the city gate, where the ancients administered justice (5:4).

Eliphaz recounts a night vision, which reveals to him that not even the angels stand innocent before God. How much more impossible it is for humans, who bring trouble on themselves (5:7). Eliphaz admonishes Job to present his cause to God, who in supreme justice rewards good and punishes evil. Eliphaz sincerely believes that God is rightly disciplining Job for inevitable sin, yet he also reassures his friend that he is not among those whom God destroys for the concerted pursuit of wickedness. As a basically pious but imperfect man, Job should rejoice in his punishment and take comfort in the confidence that God will deliver him and make him secure once again. In this view, according to Eliphaz, lies the remedy for Job's impatience.

6–7 Job Protests

Job does not for a minute buy Eliphaz's argument. He maintains that his suffering far outweighs his sinfulness. He cannot understand why God suddenly treats him as an enemy. In the midst of his complaint that God has attacked him with poison arrows (6:4), Job wishes God would deal him the final blow (vv. 8-9). His only consolation is that he has not turned his back on God.

Job now focuses on his friends, who have failed him. He counted on their sympathetic support to keep him on the right spiritual path, but instead they have disappointed him much as a dried up riverbed (wadi) disappoints caravan traders emerging from the arid desert in search of life-sustaining water. Job's depression turns to anger. He accuses his friends of distancing themselves from him for fear that disaster will strike them too, and he challenges them to reveal the sin they claim he has committed.

Job determines to continue his complaint, unconvinced by Eliphaz's attempt to get him to recognize his guilt. In a parody of Psalm 8, which rejoices at the wonder of God's interest in humans, Job appears bitter that God watches him so closely (7:17-18). He protests that he cannot possibly represent the sort of threat posed by the legendary symbols of chaos, Sea and Dragon (cf. 3:8), and wishes God would leave him alone. Job complains that he cannot even find peace in sleep, for then dreams and visions torment him. "What have I done to deserve this?" Job asks God. "If sin is the problem, why don't you just grant me a pardon?"

8 Bildad's Admonition

So convinced of the relationship between sin and suffering on the one hand and righteousness and blessing on the other, the second friend, Bildad, chastises Job for questioning God's justice. He asserts that Job's sons must have sinned, and therefore God has punished them with death. Bildad remains convinced that if Job himself has lived a truly pure life, God will restore his fortunes. The obvious question for Bildad would be, Why did God punish a truly righteous person in the first place? Nevertheless, Bildad tells Job not to take his word for it, but instead to inquire into the theological discoveries of past generations. Above all, Bildad admonishes Job not to give up his confidence in God, for only the godless ultimately perish.

9-10 Job's Fatalism

In responding to Bildad, Job affirms God's ultimate justice (cf. 8:20). But Job also recognizes God's mysteriousness and therefore the futility of trying to prove his innocence to God. Job could never win a dispute against God; moreover, no one can thwart God's incomprehensible purposes. In this fatalistic approach to his plight, Job pictures God as exercising power over the universe in a way that cancels out the very order he has created.

Convinced of his own innocence, Job concludes that God does not regard righteousness as a reason for withholding judgment. Job has done all that he can do. God has declared him guilty and deserving of punishment anyway. He

would never get a fair trial against God, so why try any longer?

Yet Job cannot help but imagine the questions he would put to God in court. Why have you oppressed me, a man you know to be righteous and one whom you yourself have shaped? What charges do you bring against me? Why have I become such a prime target of your anger? Why did you bring me into the world? Finally, Job sinks into the depths of despair and wishes God would leave him alone, so that in dying he could return in peace to the darkness and gloom of primordial chaos.

11 Zophar's Accusatory Sermon

Zophar's frustration with Job's refusal to admit guilt has intensified by the time this third friend speaks, and he shows no sympathy for Job. In essence, Zophar asserts that Job should adopt a prayerful attitude, acknowledge his guilt, and turn away from his sin — in other words, repent — and then for Job life would be great again. Zophar ends with a warning that insinuates Job's guilt: death constitutes the only hope for the wicked, who will find no escape from God's judgment.

12-14 Job Lashes Out at His Friends

Job resents his friends for treating him as though his intelligence were inferior to their own. He sarcastically asserts that they possess a corner on wisdom (12:2). Then he contrasts their simplistic understanding with God's inscrutable wisdom, displayed in his upheaval of the stable order of nature for a purpose that only God understands. This reversal of theological order constitutes the circumstances in which Job now finds himself.

Job bitterly dismisses his friends as "worthless physicians" who would do better to listen in silence than multiply shallow words of explanation and advice. In trying to justify to Job God's actions against him, they have acted as false witnesses for God. Job knows the situation is not so simple, that a correct theology must make room for the suffering of a truly righteous person.

Job remains so convinced of his innocence that he turns from wishing that God would leave him alone (10:20-22) to initiating a dispute with God (contrast 9:3ff.). The undeserving sufferer resolves to pursue the clearing of his name despite God's seeming determination to slay him (13:15-18; contrast 2:6). Job finds it hard to believe that God would punish him so severely for the sins of his youth, and he cannot understand why he has suddenly become an enemy in God's eyes.

In chapter 14, Job philosophically reflects on humanity at large from the perspective of the turns his own life has taken. Surely insignificant, short-lived humans are not worth the intense pursuit to which God is subjecting Job. Verses 7-12 provide a rare glimpse into Old Testament views of the afterlife. Job contrasts humans, who die and stay dead (as far as Job knows), with felled trees, whose stumps revive and flourish with just a little water. Though Job appears not to believe in resurrection, he certainly seems to wish for it, for he wants Sheol (the Underworld, home to the dead) to serve as a hiding place from which he can return after God's anger fades away (cf. 7:9). Nevertheless, Job remains without hope for this eventuality, and he ends his speech feeling completely alone in his pain and grief.

15 Eliphaz Holds the Hard Line

Eliphaz scolds Job for his lack of verbal restraint. He considers Job's impassioned rhetoric as inane, irreverent, and obviously indicating guilt, without considering that Job might be speaking the truth. Then Eliphaz throws Job's sarcasm back on him by accusing Job of believing that he holds the corner on wisdom (v. 8; cf. 12:1). Failing to grasp that suffering teaches lessons otherwise incomprehensible, the insensitive friend wonders what Job knows that his friends do not.

To reassert Job's guilt, Eliphaz returns to the theme of humankind's inherent bent toward sinfulness (vv. 14-16; cf. 4:17-19). Then he details their miserable lives. Perhaps in the belief that Job needs spiritual disciplining rather than consolation, Eliphaz makes no mention of the hope for restoration that the righteous can expect.

16-17 Job Loses Hope of Being Cleared

Thoroughly disgusted with his "sorry comforters," Job gives up trying to convince them of his innocence. In this speech, he alternately addresses his friends and God, but sometimes no one in particular.

Job tells his friends that in their analysis of his situation they have taken the easy way out. Reverse the roles, and Job could just as simply sit in judgment over them. His protestations neither help nor hurt him. God has already mercilessly attacked him, and now his friends have teamed up against him, too. The metaphors Job uses to illustrate his point conjure up images of hand-to-hand combat and vicious attack by wild animals. Job affirms his innocence and his nonviolent posture, but he feels completely worn out.

In a cry that recalls Cain's murder of Abel, Job petitions the earth not to cover up the injustices done to him after his own death (16:18; cf. Gen. 4:10). The insinuation is that God is murdering him. Death maintains a psychological grip on Job, and he does not expect to live to see his innocence vindicated.

Job finds no one who will stand with him (17:10). That his innocence will die and descend with him to Sheol plunges him into further despair. Death offers no hope whatsoever.

18 Bildad Takes Offense

In a second attempt to break Job's unyielding insistence on his innocence, Bildad tells him to be reasonable. He takes offense at Job's rejection of the friends' counsel, and scornfully wonders why Job thinks that everyone else should change his theology to fit this supposedly unique experience.

Bildad's picture of the devastating life's end of the wicked includes several tactless parallels to the calamities that have befallen Job (vv. 13, 15, 19, 20). Though Bildad stops short of identifying Job himself as one of these deliberately wicked individuals, he implies that Job may suffer this end if he refuses to mend his unrepentant ways.

19 Job's Innocence versus God's Guilt

Job answers Bildad's question, "How long will you hunt for words?" (18:2), with one of his own: "How long will you torment me [with your own words]?" Job protests the friends' concerted effort to prove the justice of his disgrace by pointing out that even if he has sinned, he has not done so against them. Job's insistence that *God* is the one who has wronged *him* cuts short any attempt by the friends to claim an admission of guilt (v. 4).

Job then uses multiple metaphors to outline the ways that God has acted unjustly toward him: mugged townsman, traveler, deposed king, military enemy. In addition, God has stripped Job of support by his family, friends, servants, and associates and has made him offensive and abhorrent to them. God has made him a social outcast, for Job's community now view him as the sinner they never guessed he was.

Job wishes for a permanent written record of his defense, since he does not believe he will live to see his vindication. Once again, Job expresses the conviction that his avenger (often misleadingly translated "Redeemer") will ultimately clear his name (cf. 16:19). This avenger almost certainly does not refer to God, the opponent whom Job hopes to confront face to face in court (vv. 26-27).

Job ends his answer to Bildad with a warning to his three friends: beware of treating me unfairly, because your judgment will come too, and in the end you will pay for persecuting me with your accusations.

20 Zophar Warns Job to Repent

Insulted by Job's reproof, Zophar cannot resist responding. Using dramatic imagery, he echoes Bildad's belief about the fate of the wicked. Zophar notes that any good fortune — even exceptional achievement (v. 6) — enjoyed by the wicked will never last. Their accomplishments become their own undoing. The wicked cannot escape the sword of punishment. The heavens and the earth (often invoked as witnesses in ancient Near Eastern treaties; see Deut. 31:28) condemn them. Job must repent to avoid ultimate destruction as one of the wicked.

In the Hebrew text, Zophar's second speech is his last, while both Eliphaz and Bildad go on to deliver third sermons. Some scholars suggest that 27:13-23, which sounds more like the friends than Job, might actually represent a third speech of Zophar.

21 Job Contradicts Zophar

No longer content merely to deny his company's theological view of his suffering, now Job determines to "tell it like it is." He warns the friends that what he will say about the way God deals with the wicked and the righteous will shock them — he can hardly believe it himself. Job wants his friends truly to understand the perspective behind his thinking, for so far they have only heard his words.

Contradicting Zophar and Bildad, Job asserts that the wicked do indeed prosper. They lead long and charmed lives while displaying utter contempt for God. In contrast to his own agonizing and drawn-out road to death, the wicked die quickly and peacefully. They certainly do not reap what they sow, but this observation does not mean that Job wishes to follow in their footsteps (v. 16).

Job anticipates the friends' argument that God punishes future generations for the "sins of their fathers." But Job protests that Mosaic law prohibits fathers and sons from assuming punishment for the other's sin of murder (cf. Deut. 24:16). Job calls for the wicked to face their own music, but he observes that they do not. Instead, they die unpunished and are honored at their funerals. The friends' lying contradictions of the truth Job knows as fact offer him no comfort.

22 Eliphaz Invents Job's Sins

Until now the least caustic of the friends, Eliphaz here invents sins for Job to justify the conviction that God cannot be punishing Job for his piety. The unjustified oppression of others, including the poor and socially powerless, heads Eliphaz's list and echoes Zophar's description of the acts of the wicked (see 20:19; cf. Deut. 15:7-11). Sins of neglect appear in verses 7 and 9.

Eliphaz picks up on Zophar's accusation that

Job has committed "secret sins" (cf. 11:4-12) and charges Job with fooling himself into believing that he can get away with his wicked ways because his distant God cannot see them. If Job will only give up the charade, accept God's correction of him, and pursue a righteous life, he will find his fortunes restored. Job must make his treasure God rather than material wealth.

23–24 Job Holds His Head High

Because of Job's innocence, he can take a higher road than to waste his time defending himself against the specific sins of which Eliphaz falsely accuses him. Convinced that the righteous people present would support him and that God himself stands fully aware of his innocence, Job's thoughts return to his wish for a trial against his divine judge. But Job cannot find God, whom he has indeed made his treasure (23:12). Job despairs that despite his innocence, God will continue to treat him in what seems a completely arbitrary, unjust, and senseless way. Yet the innocent sufferer remains determined to speak in his own defense.

Job wanders outside his own misery to wonder why God does not hold regular court dates to judge the wicked. He acknowledges that the wicked do commit the social wrongs of which Eliphaz has accused him: oppression of the poor and needy; seizure of others' land by removing landmarks; and exacting pledges as securities against debt. Yet God ignores the cries of the wounded. He callously allows injustices to be committed.

Undoubtedly, Job includes himself among those who have spent time with the wicked but who have not followed in their footsteps. He concedes Eliphaz's point that the wicked believe they can hide their sins, but he denies that he stands among them. Job 24:18-21 sounds more like the friends' words than Job's, and some scholars posit that these verses originally belonged at the end of Bildad's third speech, recorded in the following chapter. Yet verses 22-25 seem to record a typical complaint by Job that God allows the valiant only a brief period of exaltation before dragging them off to ruin. Job ends by daring his friends to prove him wrong.

25 Bildad's Farewell

Bildad says scarcely anything new in his final speech. Here he acknowledges God's dominion and then echoes Eliphaz's point about the sinful nature of humans (v. 4; cf. 4:17). As the text stands, the three friends have run out of arguments, while Job has a lot left to say. But some scholars suggest problems in the historical transmission of the current text: some of the material credited to Job in the next six chapters sounds more like the friends; Bildad's third speech is so short; the text designates no third speech to Zophar (see 27:13-23); and Job appears to speak uninterruptedly for the next six chapters.

26–27 Job Shows the Courage of His Conviction

Job's sarcastic outburst in 26:1-4 may represent an interruption to Bildad's speech (ch. 25) and verses 5-14 that speech's conclusion. In describing the might and power God demonstrates in the universe, verse 6 refers to Abaddon, the "place of destruction" and counterpart to Sheol. In verse 14 the speaker notes the limited exposure to God's power that humans experience, and wonders at the impossibility of understanding the fullness of that power.

Chapter 27 opens with Job's most forceful declaration of his innocence and a refusal to perjure himself by embracing the friends' analysis of the reason for his suffering. Job's impeccably clear conscience affords him this privilege.

Because 27:13-23 contradict Job's previous position concerning the wicked, some scholars suggest that this speech may represent a third by Zophar — one that chapter 28 completes. They point out that Zophar's first speech (ch. 11) incorporates themes carried forward by 27:13–28:28: the fate of the wicked (27:13-23), God's hidden wisdom (28:1-27), and the folly of evil (28:28).

28 Human versus Divine Wisdom

Whether from the lips of Job or Zophar, or from the pen of a later editor, this "Hymn to Wisdom" demonstrates the difference between human know-how and divine understanding. The ancients thought of wisdom as a skill, and here human ingenuity in the technological enterprise of mining exemplifies the practical wisdom of humans, which sets them apart from the birds and the beasts. But the value of divine wisdom far exceeds that of the gains of human wisdom, here represented by the precious gems and metals recovered in mining. Inaccessible to humans and to what the ancients viewed as worldly powers — the sea (v. 14), Abaddon, and death (v. 22) — divine wisdom denotes God's unique understanding of how the universe operates. After all, God established wisdom and used it in creating the world (vv. 25-27).

As creatures made in God's image, humans must pursue divine wisdom by pursuing the only wise God. They do this by revering him through the shunning of evil — by leading a righteous life. Looking back to the opening chapters of the book, this practical approach to wisdom describes Job to a tee (1:1, 8; 2:3).

29–31 Job Summarizes His Case

Job thinks back to the "good old days" when God's watchful eye brought him blessing, not oppression (29:1-4; cf. 7:17-20). He waxes nostalgic over the days when his children surrounded him, life was easy, and he knew abundance (29:5-6). In those bygone times, men of all ages and stations in life respected him for his protection of society's weak and powerless and for his punishment of the wicked (contrast Eliphaz's accusations in 22:5-9). When Job spoke, everybody listened (29:21-25). Job assumed he would die at an advanced age in the peace and security that attended his righteous life (29:18).

But now God has completely turned the tables on Job. Even social outcasts disdain him, mock him, and profit from his downfall (30:1-15). God not only ignores Job's cries for help but also cruelly persecutes him. Job wonders what he has done to deserve such treatment (30:25-26). He helped others in need, and so he assumed he could expect the same treatment in return. But Job is not reaping what he sowed. No one comforts him. The sweet music of Job's life has transformed into the discord of grief (30:31).

Job's genuine surprise over the unexpected

disaster that has befallen him and his belief that the inheritance of the unjust is calamity (31:2-3) show that he subscribed to the retributive theology still advocated by his three friends. But personal experience has called his old thinking into question. He cannot believe that God does not recognize his innocence, and so he invites God to "weigh" his iniquity and remains convinced that the scales will bear witness to his integrity (31:6).

In protesting his innocence, Job touches on several areas that parallel prohibitions contained in the Ten Commandments: lying (31:5), adultery and covetousness (v. 9), idolatry (= nature worship, vv. 26-27), stealing (vv. 38-39).

Job adds to his defense that he has dealt fairly with the lesser members of his household — slaves whom he could have treated as mere possessions (31:13). He has acted generously toward the weak, the powerless, and the needy even when fellow community elders deciding cases at the city gate would have supported him against these disenfranchised elements of society.

Neither has Job found his security in material wealth rather than in God (31:24-25). Nor has he taken pleasure in the misfortune of his enemies. Job insists that he has not sinned and then tried to hide his iniquity, as Adam did (31:33; cf. the friends' accusations in 11:4-12), and he is prepared to sign a sworn statement professing his innocence. Job's closing addendum asserts his honest acquisition of his land, which represents the basis of his livelihood (31:38-40; contrast 24:2), and then he rests his case.

32–37 Elihu Speaks Up

A younger and until now silent fourth speaker, Elihu, suddenly and energetically interjects a long tirade lambasting both Job and his friends. Because of Elihu's unannounced entrance into the text and his absence from the epilogue, which mentions the three friends, most scholars believe that the Elihu material represents a later addition to the book.

In Elihu's attempt to succeed where Job and his friends have failed — in finding a satisfactory explanation for Job's suffering — the impassioned companion sometimes puts words into

Job rebuked by his friends; William Blake. *(The Pierpont Morgan Library / Art Resource, NY)*

Job's mouth or skews what Job has said earlier. Elihu's burning anger stems from two roots: his notion that Job considers himself more just than God, and his observation that the older friends have failed to defend God successfully against Job's specific complaints. Asserting that everyone has an equal capacity for wisdom, Elihu claims he will best his elders in imparting understanding on the subject of Job's affliction (ch. 32).

Claiming divine inspiration (33:4), the straight-talking Elihu first turns to Job, whose perspective he condemns (33:8-12). He wonders why Job thinks God owes him any justification for his actions (33:13). Elihu claims that as God afflicts people in dreams to turn them away from sin, so does he afflict people through physical suffering to stem the tide of transgression. Job's suffering does not represent punishment for sins Job has committed; rather, it constitutes discipline to prevent Job from sinning in the first place. In other words, God has afflicted Job for his benefit. In this way, Elihu seeks to preserve both Job's innocence and God's justice.

Next Elihu endeavors to instruct the friends in the correct response to Job's complaints. Job's

accusation that God has taken away his right constitutes a false charge and therefore puts Job in the company of the wicked. Elihu vigorously defends God's righteous integrity and denies that God ever perverts justice (34:10-15). He affirms that God repays people according to their deeds and chastises Job for his rebellious presumption that God should reward him on his own terms (34:33).

In chapter 35, Elihu charges Job with sulky navel-gazing. Job's complaint that his righteous conduct has done him no good demonstrates his failure to see the big picture. Elihu urges Job to address his complaint to God rather than whining in the wind. Job should abandon his death wish and focus on the lesson God is trying to teach him (36:20-23). Job should concentrate his energies on exalting God (36:24ff.).

Elihu ends his speech by stressing God's might and power over nature (particularly the elements) so as to emphasize God's inaccessibility and the insignificance to God of human wisdom (ch. 37). Job cannot expect an answer from such an exalted deity. Yet in the very next chapter God speaks through nature directly to his suffering servant.

38–41 God Answers without Explaining

Through a whirlwind, God delivers the final word that silences Job *and* his friends. God sarcastically challenges Job to teach him, since Job makes himself out to be so wise. Toward that end, God puts to Job a series of rhetorical questions that heighten Job's awareness of his limitations compared with the infinite nature and power of God, who exists and operates in a sphere that exceeds human understanding (chs. 38–39).

Where were you at creation, Job? Have you ever made the sun rise? Have you descended to the depths of the ocean? Do you understand just how expansive the world really is? Where do light and darkness come from? Can you direct the course of the constellations? Can you control the weather?

These questions, which highlight the complexity of the natural order and prompt Job to consider the parallel complexity of the moral order, humble Job enough to render him speechless. But God has not finished yet. He chastises Job for condemning divine actions to justify himself. If Job is so right and God so wrong, let Job do God's job. Let Job bear himself like a king, humble the proud, and trample and bind the wicked — then God will acknowledge Job's independent power to vindicate himself (40:10-14).

Then let him go on to deal with mighty mythical figures of chaos and evil (40:15–41:34). God's obvious implication consists in Job's inability to direct or control such forces. But God created everything and therefore controls and owns everything. Because no one can give to God anything that does not already belong to him, God owes to no one — including Job — anything. Not even an explanation.

42:1-6 Job's Retraction

Job responds to God's correction with appropriate humility. He acknowledges that he has issued his complaints without understanding the depths of God's purposes. Without asking for an explanation, Job "takes it all back," and he sincerely repents — not of some sin that has brought on God's punishment, but instead of his ignorant challenging of God's justice toward him. Seeing God, the prospect of which normally instilled fear for one's life (cf. Exod. 33:20), has not emboldened Job to argue his case, as he previously intended. Rather, the visual encounter with the awesome deity has helped Job to view his circumstances in the proper perspective (v. 5; cf. 19:26-27). He becomes content simply to recognize God's unfathomable greatness and to accept the vicissitudes of his life, whether or not he can make sense of them.

42:7-17 God Reprimands the Friends and Restores Job

God expresses to Eliphaz, the first of Job's visitors, displeasure with the three friends' misrepresentation of God, which stemmed from a rigid theological framework that set limits on divine nature and actions. Though God has just scolded Job for challenging his justice, here he affirms Job's honest search for truth (vv.

7-8). The previously proud but errant trio must humble themselves before Job, whose forgiveness and prayer on their behalf will effect God's forgiveness of them.

Despite affliction, Job has remained true to his inner nature. According to his lifelong practice of graciousness, he serves as champion for his friends, who have acted more as enemies. After Job accepts his suffering and forgives his friends, God clears him in the eyes of society by doubling his previous fortunes (v. 12; cf. 1:3). He provides Job with belated consolation and comfort from his siblings (contrast 19:13-19), who give him gifts betokening their renewed esteem. And God blesses Job with a second set of the perfect number of children (cf. 1:2). The adversary, whom God allowed to test Job through afflicting him, receives not so much as a passing mention. The dramatic demonstration of God's ultimate control over Job's fortunes takes center stage over against the foregone conclusion of the afflicter's defeat.

Evidently, Job now possesses so much wealth that his notoriously beautiful daughters receive shares in his estate along with their brothers.

The Lord answers Job out of the whirlwind; William Blake. *(The Pierpont Morgan Library / Art Resource, NY)*

Job's long life — also a sign of divine blessing — affords him plenty of time to delight in four generations of his descendants before he dies. But one might ask, "Doesn't God's restoration of Job's fortunes validate his three friends' theological system of rewards for righteousness and punishment for wickedness?" No, for the fact that Job suffered at all bursts this flimsy theological bubble.

Though in this account Job's suffering eventually ends in restoration, even exaltation, many "saints" throughout the centuries have not realized in this world the reward for their faithfulness. On the contrary, they have died in isolation, agony, and disgrace. Job learned the hard way about the mysteriousness of God's purposes, and he eventually accepted his lot without giving a thought to the possibility that God might repay him for doing so. Modern readers suffering the full range of afflictions must learn that same lesson, no divine strings attached.

Psalms

Psalms is a collection of 150 poem-songs stemming from worship in ancient Israel. Some psalms speak from the perspective of the individual, and others from the viewpoint of the congregation. Some woefully lament earthly circumstances, and others wonder at God's awesome power. Some emphasize God's saving faithfulness to his people, and others focus on God's just judgment of the wicked. Scholars classify particular psalms according to the overall sense of their content and/or structure under such headings as hymns of praise; royal or kingship psalms (which celebrate significant occasions in the life of the king); prayers of lament or supplication and of trust; and penitential, thanksgiving, and wisdom psalms.

Content

Often referred to as the Psalter, Psalms developed to become the hymnbook of the ancient Hebrews. Editorial doxologies added at the ends of Psalms 41, 72, 89, and 106 divide Psalms into five "books," with Psalm 150 comprising a doxology to the entire Psalter. The fifth of these divisions includes subgroups that represent once distinctly separate collections, such as the Hallelujah Psalms (111–118) and the Psalms of Ascent (120–136).

Titles

The traditional Hebrew titles ascribed to most of the poems in Psalms associate many of them with various individuals, who presumably authored or grouped the songs or to whom they were dedicated. The musically gifted shepherd-king David — by far the most frequently mentioned — appears in 73 of these headings (cf. 1 Sam. 16:17-23; 1 Chr. 25:1-8), but other names surface as well — Korah and Asaph, leaders in the musical service of the temple; Solomon; and even Moses. Some psalm titles relate the songs to specific historical circumstances or specify musical directions, such as prescriptions for instrumental accompaniment. While the Masoretic Text of the Hebrew Bible incorporates these ancient titles as the first verse of the songs they head, the titles do represent editorial additions, and some scholars question their historical accuracy.

The editorial notations "shiggaion," "miktam," "selah," and "maskil" may mark points of musical

Types of Psalms
Hymn of praise
Hallelujah
Royal psalm
Enthronement/coronation psalm
Royal wedding song
Prayer
Lament (personal/corporate)
Supplication (help/deliverance)
Song of trust/confidence
Prayer of assurance
Penitential psalm
Thanksgiving psalm
Wisdom psalm
Instruction
Song of Zion
Liturgical psalm
Processional song
Song of Ascent
Blessing/benediction
Prophetic liturgy
Covenant renewal
Pilgrim psalm
Oracle
Historical psalm

Music and Musical Instruments

Music is a vital part of all cultures past and present. Artifacts and ancient texts reveal that the people of ancient Israel/Palestine wove music into nearly every aspect of society. Worship, including sacrifices, and prophetic activity are among the primary occasions for which the ancients incorporated music.

Musical Instruments

Materials used in instrument construction — wood, animal viscera (strings) and skins (drum heads), and string — do not survive well in the archaeological record; thus physical data for instruments derive primarily from artistic depictions, partial instrument remains, and textual data. These sources provide information for classification and typology.

Chordophones are instruments in which strings constructed from various materials are stretched across a surface. When struck the strings vibrate to produce sound and may be amplified by a sound box or resonator. Chordophone examples from the Hebrew text and archaeology are lyres and harps *(kinnor, nebel)*. These instrument types appear in religious ceremonies and secular activities (1 Chr. 16:4-7; 1 Cor. 14:7).

Aerophones are wind-blown instruments. The player blows air across an opening in one end of the instrument, through a reed (single or double), or employs a mouthpiece (e.g., trumpet) to produce sound. Aerophones from Israel/Palestine include the *shophar*, flute, and double-pipe *(halil)* (Lev. 23:24; 1 Kgs. 1:40; Matt. 9:23).

Membranophones consist of a skin or membrane stretched across an opening; the surface is struck (e.g., frame drum). In the ancient Near East, the frame drum *(top)* was extremely popular. This membranophone played a major role in religious performance and victorious battle celebrations (Exod. 15:20; 1 Sam. 18:6-7).

Idiophones are self-sounding instruments, or instruments that produce sound from the instrument's material of construction (rattles, cymbals). Cymbals (metal) and rattles appear to have served in religious celebrations; rattles (clay) may have also functioned as children's toys (2 Sam. 6:5; 1 Cor. 13:1). Excavations have produced finds of both instruments dating to the Middle Bronze Age (ca. 2000 B.C. and later) in Israel/Palestine.

Musical Artifacts

Depictions of musicians often appear in plaque or mold-made figurines found in Israel/Palestine and the surrounding Near East. Plaques (ca. 4-6 in. in length) depict persons that appear to be women with frame drums (as found at Megiddo, Tel 'Ira). Many of the figurines date to the Iron Age (1200-586).

Line drawings found on ivory pieces, stone, and potsherds show persons with instruments and musical scenes (e.g., Kuntillet 'Ajrud). The artisans' iconographic representations include lyre players, flutists, and dancers. The context of each depiction is uncertain, but scenes display what appear to be the elite, with musicians and dancers involved in performance.

Several figurines in the round have been discovered depicting women with frame drums. Excavations in several of the coastal cities of Israel/Palestine (e.g., Shiqmona, Achzib) have produced excellent representations of

Bar Kokhba coins depicting trumpets and lyre.
(Richard Cleave, Pictorial Archive)

women with frame drums. Textual and archaeological data have demonstrated that women often played the frame drum in Israel/Palestine and surrounding Near Eastern cultures.

Stamp and cylinder seals throughout the Near East display images of musical scenes. Instrumentation includes chordophones, aerophones, and membranophones (e.g., Ashdod, Nebo).

Musical Performance

The earliest reference to performance in the Hebrew text mentions only two instruments: the *kinnor* (lyre) and *'ugab* (pipe) (Gen. 4:21). Nevertheless, data have shown that Israel/Palestine culture incorporated several instrument types. Men and women played instruments in various cultural contexts, and they also performed together on specific occasions (transporting the ark, advent of a new king, battle victories).

The Psalms in particular provide evidence of the role of music in worship (e.g., Ps. 150:3-5). Superscriptions to individual Psalms contain notations for liturgical use (Psalms 30, 70, 92, 100) and technical terminology referring to various types of music (45, 46, 56–60), perhaps including titles (cf. 8, 56, 76), and instructions for performance ("to the leader"; "Selah"; cf. Hab. 3) and instrumentation (4, 5, 76).

For Further Reading

Braun, Joachim. *Music in Ancient Israel/Palestine*. Grand Rapids: Eerdmans, 2002.

Smith, William S. *Musical Aspects of the New Testament*. Amsterdam: Ten Have, 1962.

THEODORE W. BURGH

and meditative interlude or give some direction as to the psalms' use. But the meanings of the words remain lost to us.

Date

The Dead Sea Scrolls, discovered at Qumran in 1947, have raised new questions concerning the date of the Psalter's completion. While some scholars believe that it reached its final form by the 2nd century B.C., others argue its completion did not occur until sometime during the 1st century, when the Essene sect, some of whose members separated themselves out as a monastic community at Qumran, met its end in the Jewish revolt against the Romans (A.D. 68). One Qumran manuscript includes an additional psalm (151), also found in the Greek version (Septuagint) and accepted as canonical by the Roman Catholic and Eastern Orthodox churches.

Background

The overall content of each of the five books in Psalms has led scholars to propose periods in Israel's history to which the books relate, although the dates of authorship for individual songs remain tenuous. The generally personal psalms in Book I focus largely on kingship and thus reflect the monarchic period from David to the destruction of the First Temple by the Babylonians (ca. 1000-587). Overall, the poems in Books II and III speak from the perspective of a nation subjected to exile as it anticipates the restoration of covenantal blessings (ca. 587-520). Books IV and V emphasize public worship and reflect the development of liturgy in the postexilic, Second Temple period, when Jews in the Diaspora made pilgrimages to Jerusalem to join the returnees living in Canaan under foreign rule (from ca. 520). While deeply rooted in the personal and national history of the ancient Hebrews, the Psalms reflect timeless joys and age-old struggles common to all humanity. Therein lies their enduring relevance for the worship of God even today.

Book I: Psalms 1–41

The Hebrew titles of most of these psalms associate them with David.

1 A Wisdom Psalm

Life's Two Paths Psalm 1 serves as an introduction to the book as a whole. It describes the one who is upright and celebrates the prosperity of the righteous (vv. 1-3; cf. Jer. 17:7-8), in contrast to the fate of the wicked, who falter in this life and ultimately perish (vv. 4-6). Thus the book of Psalms begins at a spiritual fork in the road that points out life's two possible paths, which lead to very different destinations. Wisdom dictates that the rewards of obedience to God are the obvious choice over the consequences of disobedience.

2 A Royal Psalm

A Warning to the Nations The psalmist points out the futility of foreign nations' schemes to defeat the king whom God has anointed and installed on Mount Zion, where stood the temple. In the immediate context, the chosen monarch, considered by God as a son, denotes David. The New Testament applies the reference to Jesus Christ, a descendant of David, who embodies the ultimate fulfillment of God's promise of a never-ending dynasty for the "man after his own heart" (v. 7; cf. Acts 13:33; Heb. 1:5; 5:5; see 2 Sam. 7:12-13). The psalm ends with a stern warning that failing to honor God will produce disastrous consequences.

3 An Individual Lament

A Cry for Divine Deliverance The Hebrew title credits the psalm to David on the occasion of his flight during his son Absalom's rebellion (2 Samuel 15). God's "holy mountain" (v. 4) refers to the post-Davidic temple constructed by Solomon. The titles of 13 other psalms link them to events in David's life.

Here the anointed king laments the erosion of his political support base and the multiplication of his enemies from within his own nation. The psalmist utters his cry for deliverance from his enemies with the confidence that God will fulfill the petition.

4 An Individual Lament

Confidence in God Brings Peace That God has relieved the psalmist's past distress provides the basis for the request that God answer his current prayer. The psalmist wonders at the opposition of his detractors, since God himself has set him apart, and he admonishes his adversaries to pursue a different course — righteousness. He finds great happiness and inner peace in the knowledge that God ensures his safety.

5 An Individual Lament

God as Defender of the Righteous The psalmist petitions the divine King to hear his morning prayer, which may accompany the morning sacrifice (cf. Lev. 6:12; 9:17). The poet affirms God's rejection of all wickedness and requests that God lead him in righteousness and judge his deceitful foes, whom he accuses of rebellion against God. Finally, the psalmist calls for God's gift of gladness to the righteous, whose reward is divine defense.

6 A Penitential Lament

A Cry for Mercy The first of seven "penitential psalms" (cf. Psalms 32, 38, 51, 102, 130, 143) poignantly expresses deep anguish in the midst of extended suffering and appeals for divine mercy in requesting God to rescue the psalmist. He reflects the Old Testament view that God is completely forgotten in Sheol, the silent abode of the dead, which seems the psalmist's imminent end. Weakened by illness of mind and body, the poet nevertheless ends with a vigorous cry for the departure of his foes in anticipation of God's answer to his prayer. With great confidence in God, he foretells the retreat and shame of his enemies.

7 An Individual Lament

A Plea for Vindication According to the Hebrew title, David has at least one of his Benjamite pursuers in mind when he calls for God's deliverance. Many Benjamites opposed the Judahite David's succession of their kinsman Saul to the kingship (cf. 2 Sam. 16:5-8, 13).

So confident of his innocence regarding his adversaries' charges against him, the psalmist calls on himself a curse if God finds him guilty. He prays for divine judgment against his enemies and for divine vindication of himself, and he portrays God as ready to battle to the death the unrepentant, who become victims of their own mischief and violence. The psalm ends with an offering of thanks and praise to God according to his righteousness. The poet does not claim sinlessness; rather, he pleads innocence of his enemies' charges.

8 A Hymn of Praise

Nature Displays God's Majesty The psalmist recognizes the wonders of the universe as displaying the great majesty of God's "name," which in ancient Near Eastern thought embodies the essence of one's being. To the poet, humans seem profoundly insignificant in comparison with the rest of the universe, so he celebrates their surprising elevation by God to a position of responsible dominance over all other earthly creatures (cf. Gen. 1:28; Heb. 2:6-9).

9 An Individual Lament

Thanksgiving for God's Justice Together, Psalms 9 and 10 appear to form the first, though imperfectly formed, acrostic psalm, in which the letters of the Hebrew alphabet begin in order the lines of this originally unified poem. The lines of Psalm 9 extend through the first half of the 22-letter alphabet (with one omission, *dalet*). The acrostic nature of Psalm 10 appears more garbled, but its lack of a Hebrew title — unusual for the psalms in Book I — supports its original attachment to Psalm 9.

The psalmist expresses his determination to devote himself to God in heart and deed. He ascribes the punishment of his enemies to God's righteous and thorough judgment, which abolishes their every trace — even the memory of them. In contrast, the psalm highlights God's eternity, celebrates the divine defense of the oppressed, and calls for the praise of God, who dwells in Zion (Jerusalem).

The psalmist requests God's graciousness in the face of affliction so that he might "advertise" God's acts. These acts include the defeat of wicked nations, whose downfall God has caused at their own hands. Those who forget God will themselves be forgotten in the silence of the shadowy underworld, Sheol (v. 17). But the needy and the afflicted will neither be forgotten eternally, nor will they perish forever. The psalmist calls for God to make known his power over mere humans.

10 An Individual Lament

A Prayer That God Overthrow the Wicked The psalmist charges that God is keeping his distance from the afflicted in their times of trouble. The wicked deny God's attention to their mistreatment of the oppressed and also God's very existence. But the poet affirms God's knowledge of their "mischief" and calls on God to raise his hand against the evildoers. God has helped the socially disenfranchised before, and the psalmist expresses confidence that God will vindicate them yet again.

11 A Song of Trust

The Triumph of the Righteous The righteous find secure refuge in God when attacked by the wicked. From his heavenly throne, God watches and tests humans. He discerns the wicked through their love of violence and rains down judgment upon them. In contrast, he loves those who uphold righteousness, and their reward consists in beholding God's face.

12 A Corporate Lament

God's Trustworthy Word The psalmist expresses distress over the lack of godly people and contrasts the deceit and flattery of humans with the pure and trustworthy declarations of God, who keeps his word.

13 An Individual Lament

Persevering Trust in God The psalmist again expresses the feeling that God remains distant during the time of trouble (cf. 10:1), and he wonders how long God will allow his enemy to prevail. Death and the ultimate triumph of his adversaries seem near. Yet God's past faithfulness provides the basis for his determination to continue trusting in God.

14 An Individual Lament

Human Folly in Spurning God The psalmist laments the foolishness of those who spurn God, whose unsuccessful search for those who seek him recalls his similar lack of success in finding a righteous remnant in Sodom and Gomorrah (cf. Gen. 18:16–19:29). Yet a righteous generation does exist, and its members take refuge in God. The psalm closes with an expression of hope for the restoration of the fortunes of Israel ("Jacob"; cf. Gen. 32:28).

15 A Processional Hymn of Praise

Requirements for Keeping Company with God This psalm outlines the requirements of righteousness for those who would seek to keep company with God on his "holy hill," Jerusalem (or "Zion"), where Solomon built God's temple. The characteristics of truthfulness, good neighborliness, fear of God, keeping one's word no matter what the personal cost, fair business dealings, and integrity toward the innocent stem directly from Mosaic law (e.g., Exod. 23:1, 7-8; Lev. 25:36; Deut. 16:19).

16 A Song of Trust

The Joyful Path of Life The psalmist takes refuge only in God and refuses to participate in the worship of other deities. The psalm celebrates the circumstances of his life and the joy and security that have come from obedience to God's counsel. In verse 10, the poet may be expressing confidence in God's protection from premature death as opposed to the joy and the eternal pleasures that attend him as he follows the "path of life."

17 An Individual Lament

Innocence as the Basis for Deliverance The psalmist's protest of religious innocence, which God himself has established through testing, provides the basis for his request that God protect him from the wicked enemies that surround him. He uses metaphors from the natural world to illustrate the divine protection of the righteous that he seeks. The "apple" of the eye refers to the vulnerable pupil, and the "shadow of your wings" portrays God as sheltering the psalmist from harm as a hen does her chicks (cf. Matt. 23:37). The poet petitions God for deliverance from his accusers, mere mortals whose rewards are limited to this life. He chooses a different path — righteousness, which brings the more satisfying reward of beholding God's face.

18 A Royal Davidic Thanksgiving Psalm

Celebrating Divine Deliverance The Hebrew title attributes this psalm to David on the occasion of his deliverance from his enemies and from Saul, who out of jealousy sought David's life (1 Samuel 18–26). The poem is preserved in almost identical form in 2 Samuel 22.

The psalmist declares his love for God, in whom he finds stability, strength, refuge, and deliverance. He pictures God as responding to his cry for help by snatching him out of the snares of death. God manifests his angry judgment of sinners in the natural phenomena of earthquakes, dark clouds, hail, brimstone, thunder, and lightning. He rides on a winged cherub, an ancient Near Eastern creature that guards holy places (cf. Gen. 3:24; Exod. 25:18-22).

God's deliverance out of "many waters" (v. 16) alludes to the waters of chaos, which are associated with death (cf. Ps. 69:1-2; Job 3:8; Rev. 18:21). The psalmist's acknowledgement of his inadequacy to prevail against his enemies strengthens the significance of God's able rescue.

Verses 20-29 demonstrate the prevalent Old

Testament perspective that righteous living earns divine reward. The psalmist defends the blamelessness of God, who equips the psalmist for victory in battle and establishes him as ruler over foreign peoples. God's faithfulness constitutes the basis for the psalmist's thanks and praise "among the nations."

19 A Hymn of Praise

The Heavens Declare God's Glory The psalmist draws attention to the glory of God attested by "the heavens." Throughout the day and night the world over, this expansive "tent" for the sun wordlessly declares through its courses the glory of its creator.

God's word — his law — goes further by testifying to his perfection, wisdom, righteousness, purity, and justice. The psalmist spells out the rewards that attend the person who obeys God: restoration of the soul, wisdom, heartfelt joy, and enlightenment. He asks for pardon from unrecognized sins and for aversion from willful transgression in his pursuit of blamelessness. Psalm 119 expands this theme by celebrating God's law as the expression of his will.

20 A Royal Psalm of Supplication and Trust

Faith as the Foundation for Confidence This psalm opens with a communal blessing invoking for the king God's help in preparation for battle. The psalmist's reply anticipates victory, and he affirms that the proper place for confidence lies not in the products of human ingenuity, but rather rests with faith in God.

21 A Royal Psalm of Thanksgiving

Praise for Answered Prayer The psalmist expresses praise to God for answered prayer and for abundant blessings. That God has granted to him life "forever and ever" represents the common overstated language found throughout Psalms, but it also points toward the eternal reign of Christ, the royal descendant of David, who represents God's fulfillment of his covenant promising an eternal Davidic dynasty (2 Sam. 7:8-16). The king's affirmation of his unshakable trust in God alludes to his confidence that God

will deliver him from enemies who manifest their hate for God by afflicting his anointed king.

22 A Lament and Thanksgiving

The Anguish of Divine Silence The psalmist alternates between anguish and trust as he laments God's silence and seeming distance in his time of need. Jesus quotes the deeply moving verse 1 as his despairing death cry on the cross (Matt. 27:46; Mark 15:34). The psalmist bolsters his confidence in God by recalling the divine faithfulness shown to his ancestors. Yet his current straits seem dire. People sneer at him much as those who mocked the crucified Christ (vv. 7-8; cf. Matt. 27:39-44). But the psalmist reminds himself that since his conception, he has come under God's care.

Now, however, God seems distant. The psalmist's enemies, portrayed as "bulls" from the Transjordanian cattle country of Bashan, have sapped his strength and courage. Since the foes anticipate his imminent death, they already draw straws to determine who will take home the dead man's clothes (cf. John 19:24).

The psalmist again draws on his knowledge of God's past aid to the afflicted to provide the foundation for his current, public praise of God and for his call to others to join him. He affirms God's universal rule both now and throughout the generations to come.

"The heavens are telling the glory of God" (Psalm 19).
(Richard Cleave, Pictorial Archive)

23 An Individual Thanksgiving Prayer of Confidence

God as the Good Shepherd In this beloved, best-known psalm, the poet uses the imagery of a good shepherd to illustrate God's physical and spiritual care of him (cf. John 10:11-16). The poignancy of the shepherd-sheep imagery emerges when one recognizes the great need of these helpless creatures (here, humans by inference) for an attentive and able shepherd (cf. Matt. 9:36). God's faithful care of his "sheep" testifies to his divinely faithful nature. Verse 4 pictures the shepherd leading his sheep through life-threatening terrain, but his protecting presence dissipates all fear on the part of his flock of one.

The imagery then shifts to a celebratory banquet in which the presence of the psalmist's enemies in no way deters God, the generous host, from honoring his befriended guest. The psalm ends with the poet's expression of confidence in his lifelong divine blessing and in his eternal presence with God.

24 A Processional Hymn of Praise

Worshipping the King of Glory David's transfer of the ark of the covenant to Jerusalem may provide the background for this psalm (cf. 2 Sam. 6:12-15). The poet acknowledges that the entire world belongs to God, its creator. Those who seek to worship him on the hill (Zion) made holy by his presence (via the ark) must demonstrate righteous conduct, pure motives, and honest dealings. The reward for such living consists in God's blessing. Verses 7-10 beckon the royal city to receive the mighty "King of glory."

25 An Acrostic Lament

An Appeal for Vindication, Guidance, and Forgiveness The poet opens this broken acrostic psalm (cf. Psalm 9) with an affirmation of trust in God, followed by an urgent request that God not let him down and by an expression of confidence that God will indeed vindicate him against his enemies. The psalmist displays a sincere desire to know and obey God's laws. An appeal that God in compassion forget the psalmist's youthful transgressions shifts into praise of God's goodness toward sinners and divine justice toward the humble.

Verses 12-15 demonstrate the poet's subscription to the expectation of divine reward for righteous conduct. Verses 16-22 return to the opening theme by outlining the psalmist's request for deliverance from his current trouble. The linking of this request with a petition for forgiveness from sins (vv. 17-18) suggests that he accepts the notion of divine punishment for transgression. The psalm ends with a general appeal that God "redeem" Israel from national affliction.

26 An Individual Lament

Innocence as the Basis for Vindication The psalmist offers evidence of his consistently upright conduct (though not moral perfection) as the reason he deserves divine vindication. He invites God to examine him and to test his claim. In verses 4-5, the poet's rejection of the company of the wicked recalls the theme of Psalm 1, and his general plea of "innocent" parallels the protests of the blameless sufferer Job. The psalmist's public washing of his hands to signify his innocence finds a parallel in Pilate's symbolic denial of personal responsibility for Jesus' death (v. 6; cf. Matt. 27:24; also Deut. 21:6-7).

The poet contrasts his hatred of "the company of evildoers" (v. 5) with his love for God's "house" (v. 8). Alarm at the notion that his lot might fall with that of sinners leads to the psalmist's request for God's gracious redemption and a pledge of continued righteous conduct and public worship of God.

27 An Individual Song of Petition and Trust

The Confidence to Wait For the psalmist, knowledge of God's faithfulness precludes fear even of a host of enemies. Their harmful intent and actions cannot shake the poet's confidence for his divinely protected welfare.

The psalmist's main goal throughout life has been seeking community with God, who provides protective shelter in the tabernacle (v. 4; cf. 23:6) and who honors the poet when enemies surround him (v. 6; cf. 23:5). He trusts in God's faithfulness even more than he trusts in parental support (v. 10). In the midst of trouble, his faith in God's goodness has warded off despair. The psalmist's reminder to "wait for the Lord" issues a profound admonition to modern society's quest for instant gratification as the means to fulfillment and happiness (v. 14).

28 An Individual Lament

Anticipating God's Answer The psalmist petitions God to hear and answer his cry for help and distinguishes him from the wicked (v. 2; cf. 26:9-10), against whom he calls down God's judgment for their evil deeds. The psalmist ends his prayer by blessing God in anticipation of the divine response to his plea. The shepherd imagery in verse 9 echoes 23:1-4.

29 A Hymn of Praise

The Power of God's Voice In its general theme and, at points, specific wording, this psalm displays parallels to Canaanite religious literature concerning the worship of the storm- and fertility god Baal. Yet the poem parodies Baal worship by declaring God as sole ruler over nature.

In this call to glorify God, the poet describes the divine voice in terms of the awesome phenomena of a storm. This evidence of the powerful nature of God's words recalls God's "speaking" the world into existence at creation (Genesis 1; cf. Ps. 33:6).

The divine voice even shatters the cedars of Lebanon, famous for their strength and beauty and used in Solomon's construction of the temple (1 Kgs. 5:8-10). God's voice also causes the earth to quake — even the 9000-ft. high Mount Hermon on the Israel/Lebanon border and the desert wilderness in Israel's southern extremity (= Kadesh, v. 8). This mighty, divine monarch presided over past events (v. 10), and his reign will never end.

30 An Individual Prayer of Thanksgiving and Supplication

God's Temporary Anger versus His Enduring Favor The psalmist offers praise to God for helping him in the midst of his trouble — in-

deed, for saving him from death (= "Sheol" or "the Pit," both the silent abode of the dead, v. 3). The psalmist contrasts the fleeting nature of God's anger and the resulting human sorrow with the enduring nature of divine favor and the accompanying human joy (v. 5).

The poet recalls the cycle of events through which he has just come: initial prosperity, subsequent adversity, and deliverance as a response to his supplication (vv. 6-11). The question addressed to God, "How will you profit if I die?" (v. 9), echoes the theme of 6:5. The poet's response to God's transforming his mourning into celebration is a pledge of perpetual thanksgiving.

31 An Individual Song of Petition and Thanksgiving

God's Goodness Stored Up for the Righteous In his plea for divine rescue, the psalmist expresses confidence that God will demonstrate faithfulness by providing guidance through a time of trouble (v. 3b; cf. 23:3). Jesus' dying words quote the psalmist's commission of his spirit to God (v. 5; Luke 23:46).

The psalmist attributes his devastated state to the consequences of sin (v. 10). His description of people's aversion to him recalls Job's rejection by family and friends (cf. Job 19:13-20). Calling for the shaming and death of his enemies (the wicked), the poet also hopes for divine blessing — the reward of the righteous that God "stores up" for those who fear him (v. 19).

32 A Penitential Wisdom Psalm

A Clear Conscience Generates a Light Heart The psalmist poignantly conveys his relief for God's forgiveness of his sin. When he maintained a stubborn, unrepentant spirit, he felt miserable. But after confessing his sin, God withdrew the weight of guilt (v. 4) that had sapped his strength. Relieved of his burden of conscience, the psalmist recommends the act of repentance to others (v. 6).

In verses 8-9, the voice of God pledges instruction and protection to the psalmist and warns against maintaining a posture of stubborn ignorance. The psalmist asserts that righteousness rooted in God brings true gladness, which emanates from a clear conscience and generates joyful abandon (vv. 10-11).

33 A Hymn of Praise

God's Direction of Human Affairs This psalm calls on the righteous to sing the praises of God, who spoke the world into existence (cf. 29:3ff.). The plans of entire nations will not prevail against this awesome God's sovereign direction of human affairs. From heaven, God watches the activities of all inhabitants of the world, and he understands everything they do. It is God, not mighty armies or war horses, who accomplishes victory in battle (cf. 20:7). God watches out for those who fear him. The psalmist petitions God for a reward according to the measure of hope that the righteous have demonstrated in their "waiting" for God with rejoicing and trust.

34 A Song of Corporate Thanksgiving

God's Unfailing Help through Times of Trouble The Hebrew heading dates this psalm to David's feigned madness before "Abimelech" (possibly King Achish of Gath; 1 Sam. 21:10-15). Using an alphabetical acrostic pattern (cf. Psalm 9), the psalmist praises God for deliverance from affliction. He asserts that those who "fear" (= revere) God lack nothing good. Fear of the Lord entails not merely refraining from evil but also doing good, seeking "peace" *(shalom),* the fruit of harmonious relationships with God and his creation. Similarly, the biblical notion of repentance conveys the idea of simultaneously turning away from sin and toward righteousness.

In verses 15-22, the poet acknowledges the abundant afflictions suffered by the righteous but emphasizes that God always delivers the righteous from their distress and never holds them guilty (does not condemn them), as he does the wicked.

35 An Individual Lament

The Anguish of Undeserved Opposition The poet here beseeches God to fight his battles for him

and claims that he has done nothing to deserve his enemies' attacks. On the contrary, by mourning for them in their time of need, he actually treated them as friends, even family (vv. 13-14). In contrast, they rejoice over his downfall, slander and jeer at him relentlessly, and repay him evil for good (v. 12).

The psalmist calls for God no longer to delay vindicating him by giving these backstabbers what they deserve (see "Israel and Its Enemies in the Psalms" [330]). The punishing angel of God (vv. 5-6; cf. Exod. 12:23) contrasts with the protecting angel of 34:7.

36 A Corporate Lament

The Fear of God as the Fountain of Life Verses 1-4 describe the appeal of wickedness to the ungodly, whose lack of fear (= reverence) for God leads them down the path of evil. In contrast, the righteous delight not in self-aggrandizing plans but in God's lovingkindness, faithfulness, and justice. The consequent blessing they receive is like drinking from abundant, life-giving water — a precious item in Canaan (cf. 23:2). The psalmist's petition for God's continued loving-kindness and prayer that God keep him from pride (vv. 10-11) receive God's assurance in verse 12 (cf. Prov. 16:18).

37 A Wisdom Psalm

The Righteous Ultimately Prevail The psalmist's observations over a long life provide the basis for his admonition not to worry about evildoers or to envy them, for their good fortunes will wither and fade quickly (vv. 2, 20). Rather than dwelling on the wicked ones' fleeting prosperity, one should remain faithful, trust in the Lord, and wait patiently (vv. 4-7; cf. 27:14). That God will give such a person the "desires of [his/her] heart" (v. 4) does not constitute a divine blank check for a personal wish list, but rather a promise of such blessings as a truly righteous person longs for.

The poet weaves through this alphabetical acrostic the ancient promise of land, progeny, and blessing (Gen. 12:1-3). The humbly patient righteous will "inherit the land" in place of the wicked (vv. 9, 11, 22, 29, 34). God ensures posterity for the blameless (v. 37). He prevents disaster from befalling the upright by holding their hand (v. 24) and never leaves them in need (vv. 25-26). Their "descendants are a blessing" (v. 26). In contrast, God will "cut off" the wicked and their posterity (vv. 9, 28, 38).

38 An Individual Penitential Prayer of Petition

Confession Breeds Confidence The psalmist sees his physical suffering as divine punishment for sin (vv. 3-4). Mental anguish accompanies the description of his humble state, which includes alienation from friends and family (v. 11; cf. 31:11-12). Turning a deaf ear to those who do evil against him, the psalmist confesses his sin with the confidence that God will respond by delivering him from his oppression.

39 A Lament

The Despair of Estrangement from God The psalmist tries to refrain from offending God with his sorrow and anger, but he wishes that God would end his life, which has become unbearable as a result of what he interprets as divine punishment for his sins (vv. 4, 7-11; cf. Job 10:18-22). He petitions God to listen to this prayer for mercy and to turn away the divine judgmental gaze so that he may realize some relief before he dies. The poet points out the insignificance of humans and the brevity of their lives (one handbreadth = ca. 3 in.), after which existence ceases (vv. 5, 11c, 13).

40 A Prayer of Thanksgiving and Petition

Delighting in Obedience to God The poet's despair in the previous psalm gives way to renewed joy as a response to God's deliverance. The psalmist declares God's wondrous works too numerous to count (v. 5). In the rejoicing over God's preference of obedience to various types of sacrifices, we hear echoes of Samuel's words to Saul (vv. 6-8; cf. 1 Sam. 15:22; Amos 5:21-24; Heb. 10:5-7). The psalmist finds the prescription for his conduct in the "scroll of the book" (v. 7), probably the Law in the Pentateuch.

The poet reminds God of his public outspokenness regarding God's faithful lovingkindness to him. Then he petitions God quickly to rescue him from his current affliction, which he traces to his innumerable sins (vv. 11-12). The psalm ends with a call for the humiliation of the poet's oppressors and the gladheartedness of those who share his pursuit of God. Psalm 70 repeats verses 13-17 almost verbatim.

41 An Individual Lament

An Everlasting Blessing on God, the Healer The psalmist confidently declares the faithful help of God for those who have shown kindness to others in need. The poet outlines his own straits, including harmful wishes against him by his enemies and betrayal by his friend, who violates the ancient code of friendship expressed in the sharing of a covenant meal (cf. John 13:18, 26).

Book I of Psalms closes with the poet's pronouncement of an everlasting blessing on God and a double "Amen," or "let it be so."

Book II: Psalms 42–72

The Hebrew titles of the psalms in Book II associate them with several sources: the Sons of Korah, assigned by David to perform the musical service of the temple (Psalms 42–49; 1 Chr. 6:22, 31); Asaph, leader of the Second Temple choir, to whom Book III ascribes additional psalms (50; 1 Chr. 6:39); David (51–65; 68–70); and Solomon (72).

Israel and Its Enemies in the Psalms

The Hebrew name of the book of Psalms is *Tehillim* ("Praises"), but the largest group of songs in the book are laments. Laments were sung or recited when life was hard and disappointing. Their presence in the Psalter shows that God invites our honest prayers, even when those prayers are sad, angry, or hate-filled. The Israelites' wilderness experience should have taught them that God dislikes it when his people complain about their lives and their God to a third party, such as Moses. He wants us rather to approach him directly with brutal openness in our prayers.

The laments of Israel name three main sources of trouble in life. The psalmists complain against their enemy, God, or even themselves, as Psalms 42–43, united in theme and by refrain, illustrate. Perhaps most difficult for the modern reader to understand is the unnamed enemy (cf. Ps. 42:3).

Why are the enemies unnamed? The psalms were written for use through generations, not for one specific historical occasion. The composer may have had a specific enemy in mind, but he left the name unspecified so later worshippers, experiencing a similar though not identical situation, could use the same psalm to appeal to God for help against their opponents (43:2).

But what about the anger and hatred vented against enemies in some Psalms? These prayers are filled with curses, sometimes referred to as imprecations (e.g., 58:6-9; 69:27-28). Christian readers remember that Jesus taught us to "turn the other cheek" and to love our enemies. Psalms is a model prayerbook or hymnbook, so what are we to do with psalms that contain these horrific curses?

It is quite wrong to say that they are simply the products of a primitive stage of religion or simply the expression of a wayward human voice. The Psalms are the word of God; however, the coming of Christ creates some break between our worship and that of the Old Testament people of God. We no longer offer sacrifices, not because sacrifices were wrong, but because Christ was the once-and-for-all sacrifice. We no longer wage holy war, not because Joshua or David were wrong — they were following divine instruction — but because Christ taught that warfare should engage spiritual enemies rather than ones of flesh and blood. This later discontinuity helps us understand the Old Testament imprecations as well as their proper use today. God directed Israel to be his instrument of judgment against specific, flesh-and-blood enemies. The psalmists, who have a keen sense of the violent injustice perpetrated by the enemy, call on God to come as judge and warrior to exercise his vengeance against these enemies.

During his life, Jesus himself embodied this type of vengeance against injustice, as when he cleansed the temple (John 2:12-25). Notably the context cites Psalm 69 to expose his motivation (John 2:17, quoting Ps. 69:9). The cross seems to mark a crucial moment of transition, however, from warfare against fleshly enemies to warfare against spiritual enemies. So, while we recognize the curses against the enemy as legitimate, Jesus' example teaches us not to pray these prayers toward our human enemies. Like his, our warfare engages the spiritual powers and principalities. We pray these prayers against Evil itself.

TREMPER LONGMAN III

42–43 An Individual Lament

The Longing for Renewed Communion with God Psalms 42–43 appear originally to have been one unified poem. They share the same theme of humble request and the same refrain (cf. 42:5, 11; 43:5).

The psalmist likens his thirst for renewed communion with God to the longing of a deer for brooks of water from which to drink. The picture is of the serene, pastoral calm of Israel's extreme northern territory in the vicinity of the Mount Hermon range and the headwaters of the Jordan River, where the poet finds himself in exile from the temple in Jerusalem (vv. 4, 6).

The psalmist recalls joyful times past, when he led public processions to the temple to celebrate religious festivals. From the depths of despair and feeling that God has forgotten him (v. 9), he musters hope that God will deliver him from the godless mockers who surround him so far removed from the central sanctuary in southerly Judah. He pictures God's light and truth as guiding him back to the temple, where he will offer praise with sacrifice and music. The perpetually burning oil lamps in the temple signified God's presence (cf. Exod. 27:20), and the bright pillar of fire guided the Hebrews on their exodus from Egypt (cf. Exod. 13:21).

44 A Corporate Lament

A Cry for Help Born of Bewilderment The congregation acknowledge God's acts in handing over the promised land to their ancestors. The people vow to trust in God to realize current victories for them. But bewildered, they complain that despite their faithfulness to God's covenant, he has allowed their enemies to triumph over them and to humiliate them.

In picturing the people's affliction, verse 19 conjures up images of lonely, uninhabited danger zones roamed by desert predators. The Apostle Paul quotes verse 22 in reference to persecution suffered by the early Christians (Rom. 8:36). The congregation calls on God to awaken himself (cf. 1 Kgs. 18:27) so he might "redeem" them (militarily and in reputation) to defend his kind and loving nature toward those who worship him alone (vv. 20-26).

45 A Royal Wedding Song

In Praise of the King and His Bride Unique in the Psalter as a primarily nonreligious poem celebrating the wedding of one of Israel's kings, this psalm shares the general theme of the Song of Songs. It also makes the royal marriage a metaphor for God's relationship with Israel and anticipates Jesus' relationship with his bride, the church (cf. Hos. 2:19-20; Isa. 54:5-8; Eph. 5:22-32; Rev. 21:1-2, 9).

The king may refer to Solomon, who married many foreign wives and easily could have taken a bride from Tyre (v. 12; cf. 1 Kgs. 11:1-3). Ophir, source of the gold of the bride's jewelry, probably lay in southern Arabia (v. 9; 1 Kgs. 9:28). Some scholars identify the king as Ahab, whose ivory-outfitted palace at Samaria accords with the reference of verse 8. Ahab's Phoenician princess bride Jezebel fits the description of verse 12.

46 A Song of Zion

Rest in Recognition of God's Sovereignty This psalm instills personal calm in the midst of apparent disaster by assuring the reader of God's immediate presence and protection, as well as of absolute control over his creation and human affairs. John echoes verses 4-5 in his visionary description of the apocalyptic holy city, the ideal realization of the psalmist's glad "city of God" (cf. Rev. 21:1-2).

47 A Hymn of Praise

God as King of the Earth The psalmist calls for the highest praise to God, whose sovereignty extends worldwide and who grants the promised "inheritance" (= Canaan; cf. Gen. 15:18-21) to Israel ("the pride of Jacob," v. 4) by subjecting to them the land's pagan predecessors. The poem foreshadows the everlasting, unopposed reign of God as King over all the earth (Isa. 45:23; Rom. 14:11; cf. Phil. 2:9-11).

48 A Hymn of Praise

The Awesome City of God The psalmist celebrates Jerusalem (Zion), God's high, mountain city

The Divine and Human Kings in the Psalms

The book of Psalms is largely a royal book. Modern readers often miss this important aspect of the Psalms because they themselves, not inappropriately, identify with the "I" who speaks in so many of these prayers. But one must take seriously the fact that when Psalm 131 begins, "My heart is not proud, O Lord," the title says that this is a psalm of the king, David. In a word, according to the canonical shape of the Psalter with its titles, much of it flows from the mouth of the king. In addition, many psalms have the human king as its subject. Psalms 20 and 21 are good examples, the first a prayer for the king before battle and the second after the battle, which begins:

> O Lord, the king rejoices in
> your strength.
> How great is his joy in the
> victories you give!
> (21:1)

Moreover, a number of psalms address God as king, not only of Israel but also of the entire universe. Psalm 47 describes the celebration as God ascends his throne as "King of all the earth" (47:7). A series of psalms (93, 95, 96, 97, 98, 99) all have some variation on the phrase "the Lord reigns" or "the Lord is king." Israel experienced God as their king long before they, at God's direction in reponse to their request (1 Samuel 8–12), appointed a human king over them. Indeed, in Israelite thought the human king was a representative of the divine king. The human king was an anointed one (Heb. *meshiah,* from which comes "messiah"), and both he and God deserved the praise of Israel. Indeed, the two are entwined in Psalm 2, a song that along with the first psalms was intentionally placed at the beginning of this great book as an introduction.

It is in this light that one understands why the New Testament so often quotes the book of Psalms in reference to Christ. Indeed, Christ himself indicated the close connection between his ministry and this book as he spoke to some confused disciples soon after his crucifixion: "This is what I told you while I was still with you: Everything must be fulfilled that is written about me in the Law of Moses, the Prophets, and the Psalms" (Luke 24:44). "Psalms" here surely refers at least to the book of Psalms and perhaps to the entire third part of the Hebrew canon, the Writings.

A handful of psalms are appropriately called "messianic." The New Testament quotes songs such as Psalms 2, 16, 22, 69, and 110, but more is intended by the term than this. Remember who Christ is. First, he is God himself. The praise and thanks that are directed toward God in the psalms are properly spoken to Jesus. Second, he is David's greater son. He fulfills the Davidic covenant (Rom. 1:3). In an important sense, Jesus is both the object of the praise of the psalms and also one who sings the psalms along with us (Heb. 2:12).

All the Psalms, even those quoted frequently in the New Testament, have a setting in the life of the Old Testament people of God. The anointed one in Psalm 2, for instance, is the human Israelite king; however, this human king was a reflection of the divine king, so when Jesus Christ — God in human flesh — came to establish God's kingdom, New Testament writers recognized him as the fulfillment of the psalms. The result is that they quote many psalms about him and also portray him as a psalm singer expressing some of his deepest feelings by himself quoting the psalms.

TREMPER LONGMAN III

made holy by his presence in the temple. Jerusalem sits in the central hill country of Judah ca. 2700 ft. above sea level. By depicting Mount Zion in "the far north," the poet probably intends a play between the Hebrew word for "north" *(zaphon)* and the Canaanite seat of the gods, Mount Zaphon, north of Israel in Lebanon. In such a wordplay, God would supplant Baal and his entourage of deities.

The mere sight of Mount Zion has instilled panic on the part of enemy kings and has caused the would-be attackers to retreat. God's breaking up of the "ships of Tarshish" (v. 7) refers to the Judahite king Jehoshaphat's failed attempt to revive the sea trade originally launched by Solomon (1 Kgs. 10:22; 22:48).

49 A Wisdom Psalm

The Certainty of Death and the Passing of Prosperity The psalmist beckons people of all classes to listen to his words of wisdom. Foolish people trick themselves into thinking their earthly prosperity will last forever; but ultimately, death will shepherd them to destruction in Sheol. Verse 15 may hold out a rare Old Testament hope for existence with God in the afterlife.

Verses 16-20 highlight the fleeting nature of earthly prosperity. The observation that the wealthy "can't take it with them" parallels Jesus' parable of the rich man (Luke 12:16-21; cf. Matt. 6:19-21).

50 A Prophetic Liturgy

The Inadequacy of Empty Ritual and Ignored Knowledge The first of the psalms of Asaph portrays God summoning heaven and earth (often invoked as witnesses in ancient Near Eastern treaties; see Deut. 31:28) to a public trial featuring himself as judge. The psalm issues a stern warning that sacrificial offerings do not in themselves satisfy God's hunger for his people's worship; rather, God requires the engagement of their hearts through thanksgiving and trust (cf. 40:6-8; 1 Sam. 15:22). The poet then indicts those who know God's laws well enough to recite them but who do the opposite of what the covenant requires.

51 An Individual Lament

A Pure Appeal for Divine Mercy According to the Hebrew title of this penitential psalm, it was composed after the prophet Nathan confronted King David following his adultery with Bathsheba (2 Samuel 12). The psalmist's request in verse 18 that God build the walls of Jerusalem may suggest that an editor added the final two verses sometime after the Babylonian destruction of Jerusalem (2 Kgs. 25:8-10).

In utter humility, the psalmist accepts full responsibility for his sin and offers no excuses for his transgression. In verse 5 he confesses his sinful nature, but the verse does not insinuate any fundamental sinfulness of childbirth or of sexual relations.

The psalmist throws himself on the mercy of God in seeking purification (v. 7; hyssop is the herb prescribed for ritual cleansing; Numbers 19) and in petitioning for divine forgetfulness. He seeks not only forgiveness but also renewal through the divine creation within him of a "clean heart," and he vows personally to convert sinners to God's ways.

In verse 14, the psalmist requests deliverance from "bloodguiltiness," which David incurred by arranging for the murder of Bathsheba's husband, Uriah (2 Sam. 11:14-17). The Israelite sacrificial system makes no provision for ritual purification from the sins of murder or adultery, both of which incurred the death penalty, and so the psalmist offers only his "broken spirit" and "contrite heart" in seeking divine mercy (see Deut. 19:11-13; 22:22).

52 A Lament

The Results of Self-Reliance versus Divine Trust The Hebrew title links this psalm to the betrayal of David to Saul by Doeg the Edomite (1 Samuel 22). The psalmist contrasts the foolishness of his enemy's self-reliance and pursuit of evil, which only earn divine retribution (v. 5), with his own unfailing trust in God, which makes him like a flourishing olive tree (v. 8).

53 An Individual Lament

Human Folly in Spurning God This poem is almost identical to Psalm 14.

54 An Individual Lament

Thanking God Up Front The Hebrew title associates this psalm with the betrayal of David's whereabouts to Saul by the Ziphites (1 Sam. 23:19ff.). The psalmist cries for divine help against those who seek his life. He expresses trust in God to punish the foes and pledges a freewill offering in anticipation of God's fulfillment of his request.

55 An Individual Lament

"Friendly" Betrayal versus Divine Faithfulness The poet's expression of anguish over the betrayal of a close friend recalls the defection of David's trusted friend and esteemed advisor, Ahithophel, to the revolt of Absalom (2 Samuel 15–17).

The psalmist expresses an inability to focus on anything but his opponents' angry grudge against him, which afflicts him emotionally, psychologically, and physically (vv. 4-5). He observes the uninterrupted scheming all around him but laments most the betrayal of his close friend, whose treachery he cannot bear (vv. 12-14).

The psalmist vows to call on God for help three times a day, during the regular times of prayer. The poem closes with an expression of confident expectation that God will punish the many godless traitors who deceitfully veil their malicious motives (vv. 19-23).

56 An Individual Lament

The Impotence of Humans against God The unrecorded occasion of David's capture in Gath by the Philistines provides the basis for the psalmist's expression of confidence in the face of immediate danger that, with God on his side, mere humans cannot prevail against him.

57 An Individual Lament

Songs of Praise through Perilous Times The poet pictures himself as taking refuge in the shadow of God's wings until danger has passed, just as David hid in Judean caves while Saul sought to kill him (cf. 1 Sam. 22:1; 24). Though life-threatening foes surround the psalmist, he remains so confident of divine protection that he can lose himself in songs of praise (vv. 7-11).

58 A Corporate Lament

Judgment on the Corrupt in Positions of Power The psalmist uses multiple metaphors in calling for divine judgment against powerful people who act on their evil motives. With graphic imagery that seems shocking to modern readers, the psalm portrays the undisputed conquest of the wicked as a reward for the righteous.

59 A Lament

Deliverance from Ambush Proclaiming his innocence, the poet protests the injustice of an intended enemy ambush (cf. David's declaration in 1 Sam. 24:11; the Hebrew title associates this psalm with Saul's dispatching henchmen to David's home to do him in; 1 Sam. 19:11-17). He likens his would-be attackers to hungry dogs that keep coming back (vv. 6, 14) and invokes divine judgment not only on them but also on "the nations" (pagan peoples, who also pursue deceit and wickedness). The poem ends with a confident expression of praise for God's lovingkindness.

60 A Corporate Lament

God's Sovereign Plan and Power The Hebrew title links this psalm with David's battles to Canaan's south in Edom and to its north in Mesopotamia (= Aram-naharaim) and Syria (Aram-zobah, north of Damascus). According to 2 Samuel 8, David realized victory over Edom, but when he marched opportunistically against the northern territories, the Edomites took advantage of his absence from Canaan and retaliated by invading across the valley of the Dead Sea. David's army commander, Joab, had to fight them off on his home turf.

The psalmist laments God's rejection of Israel, historically evidenced in the nation's (temporary) military defeat by the Edomites. He acknowledges God's sovereign plan and power to claim the promised land as his own. Verses 6-8 name Israelite cities and tribal territories both east (Succoth, Gilead, Manasseh) and west (Shechem, Ephraim, Judah) of the Jordan River, plus lands belonging to Israel's traditional enemies, the Moabites (east of the Dead Sea), Edomites (south of Moab), and Philistines (south-central Mediterranean coast).

61 A Royal Lament

Petition and Praise from Afar Far from home and faint of heart (v. 2), the psalmist cries to God for refuge. The image of God as a "tower of strength" derives from ancient city walls, which integrated fortification towers as lookouts and as stations for defensive troops. The psalmist anticipates that God will answer his prayer by prolonging his life, and he vows his perpetual praise.

62 A Song of Trust

God's Power to Protect The psalmist paints a picture of personal calm in the midst of a life-threatening situation. He expresses confidence in God's power to protect and implores his people to trust God as well. Verses 11-12 evidence the conviction that God bestows rewards and exacts punishments according to one's deeds.

63 A Song of Trust and Lament

The Thirst for Spiritual Satisfaction The Hebrew title connects this psalm with David's sojourn in the wilderness of Judah, to which he fled from the murder-bent Saul (1 Sam. 23:14). The "dry and weary" physical surroundings in which the psalmist finds himself contrast with the "fatness" of his spiritual satisfaction and joy born of his intimate relationship with God. The poet envisions a particularly humiliating fate for those who seek his life: in lieu of burial, the

exposure to nature of their corpses (v. 10; cf. 2 Sam. 21:1-14).

64 An Individual Lament

Evil Comes Back to Haunt the Evildoer The psalmist asks for divine rescue from those who plot against his life. He envisions their divinely orchestrated downfall as the turning on themselves of their own evil schemes (vv. 3-4, 7-8). Their punishment will serve as a public testament to God's vindication of the righteous.

65 A Corporate Thanksgiving Psalm

Reverence and Awe for the Sovereign God The opening verses set a tone of reverence for God as the congregation keeps silence before him, fulfills "the vow" (cf. Leviticus 27), and prays at the temple. The plea for God's attention in the psalms of lament here gives way to an affirmation that God does indeed "hear prayer" (v. 2). While the psalms usually speak of individuals' adherence to God's laws or of their outright rejection of his ways, here the psalmist notes God's initiative in choosing people to "bring near" to himself (v. 4). Reverence leads to awe (vv. 5-8) as the psalmist notes God's sovereignty over nature and humans. That the final verses focus on the divinely caused fertility of the earth suggests that this psalm may have figured in worship at the harvest festival (Leviticus 23).

66 A Thanksgiving Psalm

A Public Testimony to God's Awesome Deeds The psalmist breaks out in a global call for joyful praise of God, whose great power, evidenced in his awesome works, even inspires feigned obedience to him on the part of his enemies. The poet recalls as an example of God's "awesome deeds" his parting of the Red Sea for the Hebrews on their exodus from Egypt (v. 6; Exod. 14:21-22). Verses 8-12 note the "refining" hardships to which God has subjected his people. The psalmist recalls the vows he made while in distress (vv. 13-15) and publicly testifies to what God has done for him (vv. 16-20).

67 A Corporate Thanksgiving Psalm

Reverence and Praise as the Goals of God's Blessing The psalmist invokes God's graciousness and blessing on the congregation as witnesses to God's "way" and "salvation," so that all peoples will offer praise to God for his just judgments and guidance. The immediate evidence of God's blessing consists in the productive harvest, which also produces "fear" (= reverence) of God.

68 A Processional Hymn

God Takes His Seat in Jerusalem This "marching" song celebrates God's triumph over his enemies, his mighty works on behalf of his people, and his triumphant arrival in Jerusalem (cf. 2 Samuel 6). The account of the exodus from Egypt and the establishment of Israel in the promised land provides the historical framework for the thematic development of the psalm. God "marches through the wilderness" leading the former Hebrew "prisoners to prosperity" (v. 6; cf. Isa. 40:3). Verses 5-6 echo the Deuteronomic theme of God's concern for the least powerful members of society (cf. Deut. 10:17-19).

Verse 7 begins a summary of Israel's history and again pictures God as leading his people through the wilderness. His awesome presence at Mount Sinai, where he issued the Ten Commandments and established his covenant with Israel, caused the earth to quake (Exod. 19:18). Verses 11-18 recall the divinely accomplished "conquest" of Canaan. The mountain peaks in Bashan, northeast of the Sea of Galilee in today's Golan Heights, look enviously at Jerusalem (v. 16). Verse 18 pictures God's triumphal ascent to Jerusalem, his holy dwelling, Zion. He leads captive those who formerly threatened his people's very existence and receives tribute from his opponents. This God of deliverance bears his people's burden daily and ensures their vindication (vv. 19-23).

The procession includes the tribe of Benjamin, to which belonged Israel's first king, Saul. The tribe's southern neighbor, Judah — home to Jerusalem and Saul's successor, David — and two northern tribes, Zebulun and Naphtali, also receive mention to represent the 12-tribe nation as a whole. The temple, symbolic of God's

mighty power, inspires kingly gifts of tribute to God and efforts of prosperous foreign nations to make peace with him (vv. 29, 31). The psalmist calls on the "kingdoms of the earth" to praise God, the "rider of the heavens" (v. 33; cf. v. 4), for his strength and majesty.

69 An Individual Lament

An Urgent Call for Divine Rescue Drowning in his affliction by innumerable, powerful people who hate him without cause, the psalmist cries out for God to rescue him. His suffering, for no fault of his own but rather for his pursuit of God, includes estrangement from family, serving as the subject of gossip by community elders who administer judgment "in the gate," and even mockery by drunkards.

The psalmist will not allow his undeserved suffering to thwart his devotion to God (v. 13). He urgently petitions for a quick answer from God, who knows of the lonely straits in which the psalmist finds himself (vv. 14-19). In the bitter response of the poet's hoped-for companions, they offer "gall" and "vinegar" instead of sympathy and comfort (cf. Matt. 27:34, 48; Mark 15:23; Luke 23:36; John 19:28-30).

The psalmist calls down punishment on his persecutors even to the point of God's blotting them out of the "book of life" (cf. Exod. 32:32-33; Dan. 12:1; Phil. 4:3), mentioned in John's apocalyptic visions (e.g., Rev. 20:12). In contrast, the psalmist seeks God's salvation and vows an offering more pleasing to God than sacrifices — that of heartfelt worship (cf. 40:6-8). The poet envisions a divinely secured Judah and Jerusalem in which "those who love his name" dwell from one generation to the next (vv. 35-36).

70 An Individual Lament

A Cry for Hasty Vindication These verses represent an almost identical version of Psalm 40:13-17.

71 An Individual Lament

Past Experience Builds a Foundation of Hope Throughout his life, the poet has suffered "many troubles and distresses" from which

God has always "revived" him (v. 20). Now in his old age, he cries out for divine deliverance once again (vv. 9, 18). He couples his call for the dishonor of his adversaries with expressions of confidence in God's continued faithfulness (vv. 13-14, 22-24). The poet's "hope" — not a wish but an expectation — leads him to vow even greater acclamation of God in the midst of his suffering (vv. 5, 14).

72 A Royal Psalm

The Ideal Kingdom The Hebrew title associates this psalm with Solomon, and the poem's description of a peaceful, prosperous, and extensive kingdom certainly fits the Old Testament picture of Solomon's reign (1 Kings 10; 2 Chronicles 9). The psalm also anticipates the future, eternal kingdom ruled by the Messiah and characterized by divine justice and righteousness (cf. Isa. 9:6-7).

To rule successfully, the ideal human king needs divine righteousness and decision-making ability (vv. 1-2). That the king is responsible to defend the needy and afflicted (vv. 4, 12-14) echoes the Deuteronomic theme of God's concern for the socially powerless (e.g., Deut. 10:17-19). Verse 8 echoes the covenantal promise of Exod. 23:31 of an ideal empire from the Red Sea and the Mediterranean to the Euphrates River and the "ends of the earth." That kings from Tarshish (Tartessus in Spain?) and Sheba (probably in northern Arabia) bring gifts to the righteous king defines further the geographical influence of the ideal kingdom (vv. 10-11). The abundant fertility of the land parallels the widespread dominion that represents God's blessing of the king and his domain (v. 16).

The prayer for the king highlights the importance of the perpetuation of one's "name" (v. 17), which ensures continued participation in the covenantal promises. Other people's blessing by association with the king recalls the Abrahamic covenant (Gen. 12:3).

The crowning verses of the psalm focus not on the human king but on God, who alone can bring about this ideal kingdom (vv. 18-19).

Verse 20 appears to represent an editorial note originally designating the conclusion of an earlier collection of David's psalms.

Book III: Psalms 73–89

The Hebrew titles of the psalms in Book III associate them with several sources: Asaph, one of David's chief musicians (Psalms 73–83; 1 Chr. 6:39); the Korahites, assigned by David to perform the musical service of the temple (84–85, 87–88; 1 Chr. 6:22, 31); Heman the Ezrahite, leader of a guild of temple musicians (Psalm 88, also attributed to the Korahites; 1 Chr. 6:33); David (86); and Ethan the Ezrahite, leader of the second temple's choir (89; 1 Chr. 6:44).

73 A Wisdom Psalm

Worldly Prosperity versus Spiritual Fulfillment The psalmist affirms God's goodness to the "pure in heart" before recounting the moral lapse into which his temporary envy of the wicked nearly led him. The ease and prosperity of their life, characterized by a total disregard for God, caused the psalmist to question the point of his pursuit of righteous conduct, especially since it seemed to result only in hardship (vv. 1-14; cf. 10:3-11). A visit to God's "sanctuary" changed the psalmist's perspective, however, for the divine encounter led him to see the shaky position of the wicked and their ultimate end: destruction (vv. 17-20). Verses 21-22 testify to the internal havoc and irrational behavior that personal bitterness produces in the one who harbors it. Come what may, the psalmist's realization leads him to value "nearness" to God above all else.

74 A Corporate Lament

The Covenantal Curses Fulfilled The psalmist laments God's abandonment of his people and of his home on Mount Zion — evidenced by God's allowing the unchallenged assault on the temple, which symbolized his presence among his people. The poet's realistic description of the Babylonian destruction of the temple (587 B.C.) sounds like an eyewitness account (vv. 3-8). In verses 12-17, the psalmist remembers God's power, manifested in creation through his bringing order out of chaos, here depicted in terms reminiscent of ancient creation accounts. The psalm closes, as it began, by stressing that the opponents of God's people are opponents of God himself. Hence the psalmist pleads that God rescue himself by rescuing his chosen people (vv. 18-23).

75 A Corporate Psalm of Thanksgiving

In stark contrast to the previous psalm, this poem praises God for the "nearness" of his "name." In verses 2-5 God declares his supreme role as judge over all the earth and as humbler of the proud. The "cup" in verse 8 symbolizes God's wrath, even the dregs of which the wicked must drink (cf. Job 21:20). Lifting up the "horn" and "neck" symbolizes self-pride, which the righteous need not assert, for God will honor them (vv. 4-5, 10).

76 A Corporate Thanksgiving Psalm

The Invincibility of God The psalmist emphasizes God's unparalleled, victorious power. The futile enemy assault on Jerusalem ("Salem" and "Zion," v. 2) may represent the Assyrians' military failure recorded in 2 Kgs. 19:8ff. Here the majestic display of divine wrath, which instills universal fear, counterbalances God's purposeful inaction against the Babylonians, whose 6th-century destruction of Jerusalem Psalm 74 laments.

77 A Lament

Hope in the Midst of Despair In his dejection over God's current, seemingly endless rejection (either of the psalmist personally or of the Hebrew nation), the psalmist muses on bygone better days, when God worked wonders on behalf of his people and acted as their shepherd (v. 20a; cf. 23:1). The poet finds hope in recalling the exodus (v. 20), and his language reflects God's ordering of chaos at creation (vv. 16-19).

78 A Hymn of Praise

The Lessons of History Probably composed for recitation at communal festivals, this psalm takes seriously the divine directive to pass from one generation to the next the knowledge of God's covenant with Israel (vv. 1-8; cf. Deut. 11:18-19). The faithless behavior of the Ephraimites, the tribe from which Joshua hailed, serves as a negative example. Their forgetfulness of God's mighty deeds throughout Israel's history issued in military cowardice. (Verse 9 may refer to the Israelites' defeat under Saul at Mount Gilboa; 1 Sam. 31:1.) The psalmist remembers those mighty deeds of the exodus from Egypt and its ancient capital of Zoan (v. 12): the dividing of the Red Sea, guidance by the pillars of cloud and fire, provision of water from rocks in the desert, the "raining" of manna and meat from heaven.

Yet even the generation of "Jacob/Israel" (v. 21; both refer to the Hebrew nation as a whole) that experienced these mighty deeds did not demonstrate a lasting commitment to the covenant with their forgiving, compassionate God (vv. 34-39). God had displayed his mighty power in repeated punishments of their Egyptian masters (vv. 44-51), characterized as descendants of Noah's errant son, Ham (v. 51; Gen. 9:18-27); yet the rebellious people continued to "grieve" and "tested" God on their journey toward the promised land (vv. 40-41). Still, the divine shepherd led his flock onward, even as he engulfed their enemies in the (Red) Sea.

God brought his people to the "holy land" and delivered it over to them as their inheritance (v. 55). But because this second generation followed the rebellious example of their ancestors, God allowed his people's adversaries to prevail for a time, and he abandoned his tent-home in Ephraim's hill-country town of Shiloh, where the Hebrews pitched the tabernacle (v. 60; cf. Josh. 18:1), initially Israel's main sanctuary.

God's renewed action entailed not only driving back these temporarily successful adversaries but also rejecting the disobedient Ephraim as national tribal leader — a position the powerful tribe enjoyed through the period of the judges (v. 67). Judah emerged as Ephraim's divinely chosen replacement, with its mountain capital of Jerusalem ("Zion") and its God-fearing tribal son David, who represented God as human shepherd of the divinely chosen flock (vv. 70-72; cf. v. 52).

79 A Corporate Lament

A Petition for the Rescinding of Inherited Punishment The psalmist laments the 587 destruction of Jerusalem, the defilement of the temple, the humiliation of the Hebrew dead through exposure of their corpses, and the reproach of the divinely chosen nation among its scoffing, pagan neighbors (2 Kgs. 25:8ff.). The poet appeals to God's concern to defend the divine reputation in petitioning him to vindicate his chosen people rather than hold against them the sins of previous generations (vv. 9-10; cf. Num. 14:13-19).

80 A Corporate Lament

As in Psalm 79, the poet wonders how long God, the "Shepherd of Israel," will withhold his saving power from his afflicted people, who have become the laughingstock of their enemies. The psalmist's mention of the tribes of Ephraim, Manasseh (the two sons of Joseph who claimed their father's landed inheritance in Canaan), and Benjamin as those in need of help (vv. 1-2) may suggest the circumstances of the exiled northern kingdom before the fall of Judah (between 722 and 587).

In verses 8-16, the psalmist briefly summarizes the history of the Hebrew nation and likens it to a "vine" that sprawls toward Leba-

"Have regard for this vine; it is ravaged, cut down" (Psalm 80). *(www.HolyLandPhotos.org)*

non in the north and from the Mediterranean Sea to the Euphrates River. Stripped by God of its protective "hedges," however, the vulnerable vine has been reduced to food-for-the-taking (vv. 12-13). The psalmist promises the nation's steadfast obedience to God, if only he will "revive" the charred, hacked vine that he himself planted (vv. 14-19).

81 A Prophetic Liturgy

The Promised Blessings of Covenantal Obedience The first five verses summon Israel to a festival — probably the Feast of Tabernacles, the harvest festival commemorating the exodus (vv. 6-7) and featuring the reading of covenantal law (cf. Lev. 23:33-43; Deut. 31:9-13). The reference to "a language that I did not know" (v. 5) seems to indicate the foreign context in which the enslaved Israelites found themselves in Egypt (cf. Deut. 28:49; Ps. 114:1).

In verses 6-16 God speaks, emphasizing his wondrous works in Israel's exodus history, including the provision at Meribah of water from rocks (Exod. 17:6-7), establishment of the covenant with his people, and the promised blessings of obedience to his laws. Yet God laments his people's waywardness, by means of which they deny themselves these blessings. Still, it is not too late for God's people to reverse their fortunes. Obedience will result in divine punishment of their opponents and in abundant harvests for Israel.

82 A Prophetic Liturgy

God Judges the Gods In the divine assembly God appears as supreme judge of the heavenly beings who govern the earth (cf. Job 1:6-7). The reference may extend to the gods of other nations or to human rulers who exercise judgment over others (v. 6a; cf. John 10:34-36). God indicts these "gods" for their unjust judgments, which favor the wicked. He commands the rulers to aid the socially powerless and protect them from the wicked. The psalmist's invocation in verse 8 acknowledges God's worldwide, sovereign rule.

83 A Corporate Lament

A Historical Appeal for Present Deliverance The psalmist asks God to act on behalf of his people, whose geographically encircling enemies jointly aspire to wipe them out with the aid of the powerful Assyrians. Verses 6-7 probably comprise a list of Israel's traditional enemies, since not all the groups named are contemporaneous.

In invoking God's punishment of the adversaries, the poet appeals to God's past deliverances of his people (vv. 9-12; cf. Judges 4–5, 7–8). The psalmist calls for God to judge Israel's enemies as a demonstration of his worldwide sovereignty.

84 A Song of Zion

Reveling in Worship at the Temple The pilgrim psalmist celebrates the temple and the worship of God by portraying the spiritual journey of the godly, the "highways" of whose hearts lead them through arid "valleys" ("Baca" means "tears" or "balsam trees"; cf. 2 Sam. 5:22-25) to a blessed place of abundant "water" on their way to Jerusalem. (The "early rain" refers to the showers in October and early November that started the crops growing; v. 6.) The psalmist would rather live one day in the temple doorway than a lifetime in the household of the wicked (v. 10). The poet closes by expressing his absolute confidence in God's blessing of the upright (v. 11).

85 A Corporate Lament

Seeking Divine Forgiveness and the Glorious Life The psalmist acknowledges God's past forgiveness of his people (vv. 1-3) in preparation for a request that God forgive them once again (vv. 4-7). The restoration of "the captivity of Jacob (= Israel)" refers to God's freeing them from slavery in Egypt and bringing them to the promised land.

The poet anticipates a renewed peaceful relationship between God and Israel, who will not return to "folly" (covenantal infidelity, v. 8; the Hebrew is unclear). Harmony here on earth and also with God will characterize the resulting glorious life (vv. 10-11). The anticipated blessing of abundance from the land (v. 12) as the reward for a right relationship with the divine parallels a prominent theme in Canaanite religion, in which Baal and his wife, Asherah, represent gods of fertility.

86 An Individual Lament

The Goodness of the Only True God In petitioning God for deliverance from affliction, the psalmist asserts his own godliness and affirms God's goodness. He also certifies God's unique status as the only true God (vv. 8-10). The poet earnestly seeks divine teaching and guidance, and he pledges his thanks and praise for God's deliverance of his soul from the "depths of Sheol," the silent abode of the dead.

Verses 14-17 detail the type of trouble in which the psalmist finds himself and the kind of deliverance he seeks. Arrogant, violent, godless "ruffians" seek the psalmist's life. He asks for a sign for God's favor that will comfort him and shame those who hate him.

87 A Hymn of Praise

The Worldwide Citizenry of Zion This psalm looks forward to God's establishment of Jerusalem as the home of the worldwide elect. The exiles who returned with Nehemiah faced the challenge of proving their ancestral birthright to settle there (cf. Nehemiah 7), but by entering in a divine register the names of people from gentile nations, God will bestow birthrights confirming their legal residence. The poet's list of nations includes some of Israel's historic enemies, masters, and oppressors: "Rahab" (a poetical name for Egypt; cf. 89:10; Isa. 30:7), Babylon, Philistia, Tyre, and Ethiopia.

88 An Individual Lament

Hope against Hope for Relief In a gasp of desperation, the psalmist pleads for God's response to his constant cries for relief from divine affliction. He senses the nearness of death, and the absence of hope in the silent world of the dead (= "Sheol," "the pit," and "Abaddon," meaning "the place of destruction," vv. 3, 4, 11) offers no comfort. Indeed, others consider the strength-sapped poet as good as dead (v. 4). In verses 10-12, the psalmist's rhetorical questions imply that no benefit from his death would accrue to God (cf. 30:9). Verse 17 uses the image of water, often associated in the Bible with death, to picture the poet near to drowning from intense, divine affliction (cf. Ps. 69:1-2; Matt. 18:6; Rev. 18:21). Alienated as Job from friends, acquaintances, and those who love him, the dejected psalmist ends his prayer by lamenting God's rejection (cf. Job 19:13-19).

89 A Royal Psalm

The Davidic Covenant Invoked Verses 1-37 praise God for his promise of an everlasting dynasty to David and for his incomparable loyalty to that covenant. The powerful, divine conqueror of the sea, which in the Bible often represents chaos, also completely defeats the mighty Egypt, poetically called "Rahab," the mythological chaos monster defeated by Marduk prior to his creation of the world (cf. 87:4; Isa. 30:7; 51:9).

Verses 11-12 celebrate God's creation of the world and his power over it, represented by the mountains Tabor and Hermon. Verses 14-15 outline the divine attributes of righteousness, justice, loving-kindness, and truth. God's exaltation of the "horn" of the righteous, symbolizing their earthly strength, negates their need for self-promotion (vv. 17, 24; cf. 75:10).

Verse 19 may refer to the prophet Nathan's vision in which God outlined the Davidic covenant (2 Sam. 7:8-16). Here the psalmist elaborates the blessings, remembers the curses, and reasserts the divine promises of faithfulness to the covenant. But verses 38-45 comprise a lament accusing God of having broken the treaty by causing the defeat and shame of his "anointed" king.

The poem concludes with a prayer for deliverance that warns God against too long a delay in diverting his anger from the beleaguered psalmist, who, powerless to prevent his own death, shares with other humans a short life span. Without entertaining the thought that human disobedience might have triggered the divine withdrawal of covenantal blessings, the psalmist wonders what happened to God's commitment to the covenant (v. 49). The psalmist ends by petitioning for divine recognition of the widespread reproach he suffers at the hands of enemies he identifies not as his own, but as God's.

Verse 52 is a doxology marking the end of Book III.

Book IV: Psalms 90–106

Here only three psalms display titles that link them to specific individuals: Psalm 90, associated with Moses, and 101 and 103, attributed to David.

90 A Corporate Lament

The Eternal God and Transitory Humans The Hebrew title links this psalm with Moses, to whom it is probably attributed as the "man of God" par excellence. The poem begins by contrasting the eternal existence of God, for whom time is of no consequence, with the negligible life-span of humans, whose fleeting years are likened to new grass that sprouts in the morning but withers by evening. The psalmist moans that people live their lives under the judgment of God, from whom they cannot hide their "secret sins" (v. 8). After 70-80 years of labor and sorrow, life ends, so the poet makes a corporate request for wisdom to make the best use of time (v. 12). Further, he asks for the divine reversal of fortunes and as many days of gladness as the congregation has suffered affliction.

91 A Prayer of Trust

God the Protector of the Faithful The psalmist expresses his confidence in God's protection, which wards off not only imminent danger, expressed in terms of battle and deadly disease, but even the fear of it. Those who take refuge in God will remain immune to evil, while they watch the wicked get their due. The Devil quotes verses 11-12 when tempting Jesus in the wilderness (Luke 4:10-11). Verses 14-16 are an oracle of God's commitment to answer, accompany, rescue, honor, and bless with a long life those who love him.

92 A Hymn of Thanksgiving

The Enduring Nature of God and the Righteous After declaring the goodness of praising God, this psalm contrasts divine understanding with human senselessness and the transitory nature of the wicked with the eternal rule of God. The psalmist celebrates God's vindication of his anointed one (vv. 10-11). The righteous person flourishes like a palm tree, grows like a cedar of Lebanon, and thrives even into old age (vv. 12-14). Nourishment comes from being "planted in the house of the Lord" — the temple (v. 13). The tree imagery conveys the strength and endurance of the righteous, whereas the grass imagery of verse 7 contrasts the nature of the wicked.

93 A Hymn of Praise

God's Sovereign Rule This psalm confirms that God, regally robed with majesty and strength, has always reigned over the world (v. 2). The poem elevates God's might over that of the sea, which in the Bible often represents uncontrollable chaos, and acknowledges his ability to accomplish everything he desires to do (v. 5). Eternal holiness characterizes God's "house," the temple.

94 A Corporate Lament

Divine Vengeance Invoked This psalm calls on God as "judge of the earth" to exercise divine justice by exacting vengeance on the wicked. They flaunt their glee in afflicting God's people — even murdering society's weakest members (v. 6) — and foolishly deny that God pays any attention to their evil deeds (vv. 8-9). The poet's rhetorical questions communicate the inevitability of payback for the proud (vv. 9-10).

The psalmist affirms that God chastens the righteous for their own good and denies that divine discipline signifies abandonment by God (v. 12). An invitation to stand with the psalmist against evildoers (vv. 15-16) precedes the poet's expression of confidence in God's help when he and, by extension, the righteous are afflicted (vv. 17-19). In contrast, the wicked have only each other to lean on as they devise and carry out their murderous plans (vv. 20-21). God will see that they reap what they sow (v. 23).

95 A Hymn of Praise

A Call to Worship and Obey This psalm calls for the joyful praise and humble worship of the God of gods, who made and rules the earth and sea. The Old Testament does not deny the presence of other gods; rather, it affirms God's sovereign power, which renders the others nonentities (cf. 1 Sam. 5:1-5; 1 Kgs. 18:7-40). Verses 7-11 call for obedience by citing a negative example: the Hebrews' postexodus grumbling in the wilderness (Exod. 17:1-7) ultimately precluded an entire generation's entrance into the promised land.

96 A Hymn of Praise

God's Glory Inspires Joy and Reverence The psalmist instructs all the earth to praise the Lord with singing and to spread everywhere the word about his "salvation," "glory," and "marvelous works." While God created the heavens, the "gods of the peoples" lack not only power but, as "idols," lack even life itself. The psalmist prescribes the presentation of offerings and an approach to worship that displays respect and appropriate reverence for an unchanging, awesome God, the universal judge, whose justice, righteousness, and faithfulness give all creation reason to rejoice (vv. 9-13).

97 A Hymn of Praise

The Awesome Power of the Righteous God The theme of creation's gladness over the Lord's reign continues from the previous psalm (cf. 96:11-12). As in verse 2, the Old Testament often uses clouds to convey the presence of God (cf. Exod. 13:21; 19:16; 40:34; 2 Chr. 5:14; also Matt. 24:30; Acts 1:9-11; Rev. 1:7). This psalm also continues the themes of God's awesome power, which makes the earth tremble and the mountains melt like wax (vv. 3-5), and of his supreme divinity (v. 7). Hatred of evil and love of this righteous God go hand in hand (v. 10).

98 A Hymn of Praise

Righteous Judgment Elicits Joyful Praise This hymn calls for praise of God based on his wonderful deeds, which include making known his "salvation" (deliverance of the righteous, here probably through a military victory), revealing his righteousness to all, and remaining loving and faithful to the people of his covenant ("the house of Israel," v. 3). The psalmist pictures the natural world as a choir unable to hold back its expressions of joyfulness. The earth shouts and sings with accompaniment on the lyre, trumpet, and horn. For the righteous, anticipation of judgment by a righteous God represents not a threat but a saving event (v. 9).

Terra-cotta plaque from Petra showing two lyre players and one double-aulos player.

99 A Hymn of Praise

Humble Worship of the Holy God The psalmist emphasizes God's holiness, which effects fearful humility on the part of his creation (vv. 1, 5). God's enthronement above the "cherubim," guardians of holy places in ancient Near Eastern imagery, indicates his status as the supreme Judge-King, who carries out justice with fairness and righteousness "in Jacob" (= the nation of Israel). God's greatness in "Zion" refers to his rule from Jerusalem, the location of the "holy mountain" where the temple stood (vv. 2, 9). The psalmist cites the priestly exodus figures of Moses and Aaron as examples of faithfulness to God's laws and includes in their company the prophet Samuel, who performed certain priestly tasks (1 Sam. 9:1–10:16). Nevertheless, the moral transgressions of Moses and Aaron, to whom he spoke "in the pillar of cloud" (v. 7), necessitated the divine exercising of forgiveness and exacting of punishment (vv. 6-8; cf. Num. 20:1-12). God's forgiveness does not nullify the negative consequences of disobedience. Conversely, one's suffering of punishment does not indicate the divine withholding of forgiveness.

100 A Hymn of Praise

The Attitude and Aspects of Worship The worship of God includes not only singing his praises but also serving him with gladness in an attitude that acknowledges the subordinate and dependent relationship of humans to the Creator (v. 3). Thanksgiving, praise, and blessing constitute appropriate responses to God's goodness, everlasting loving-kindness, and perpetual faithfulness. God's "gates" and "courts" refer to the Jerusalem temple (v. 4).

101 A Royal Psalm

A Kingly Commitment to Righteousness Attributed to David, this psalm outlines the king's commitment to God. The psalmist promises to pursue blamelessness, conduct himself with integrity, hate religious faithlessness, divert his attention from "anything that is base" (worthless things), banish perverse tendencies, be a stranger to evil, silence slanderers, and refuse to tolerate the proud (contrast the description of corrupt leaders in 58:1-5). Further, and probably in reference to kingly administrative and judicial duties, he will welcome and employ the covenantally faithful but turn away the deceitful and silence the wicked to deny their access to Jerusalem (v. 8).

102 An Individual Lament

A Sufferer Pleads for His Life Wasting away from lack of appetite and suffering from insomnia, the psalmist petitions God for immediate attention to his cry for help. He feels completely alone and out of place (vv. 6-7). His reproachful enemies have made a fool of him. The ashes of mourning have become his bread and his tears his drink (v. 9). He sees his life slipping away because of God's rejection and wrath (vv. 10-11).

Verses 12-22 focus on the psalmist's expectation of divine compassion on Zion (Jerusalem), whose appointed time for favor has come (v. 13). He anticipates that national deliverance will trigger worldwide reverence toward God, even among contemporary kings, and cause for praise among future generations. All nations will gather together in the restored Jerusalem to worship God (v. 22). In verse 23, the psalmist returns to his own plight and petitions God not to cut short his life, which in its brevity and degeneration contrasts with God's eternity and unchanging nature (v. 27).

103 An Individual Thanksgiving

God's Mercies Enumerated With every fiber of his being (Heb. *nephesh,* "soul," vv. 1, 22), the psalmist blesses the Lord for the mercies he bestows: forgiveness, healing, redemption from "the pit" (Sheol, the abode of the dead), lovingkindness, compassion, and physical renewal (vv. 1-5). He then stresses God's gracious patience (vv. 8-9), restraint in exacting punishment (vv. 10-11), thorough forgiveness (vv. 12-13), and compassionate understanding of human frailty (v. 14). The psalmist goes on to contrast the temporary nature of humans with the everlasting love and faithfulness God shows them from generation to generation (vv. 15-18). The poem closes with a call for the hosts of heaven and all creation to ascribe blessing to the sovereign Lord (vv. 19-22).

104 A Hymn of Praise

In Praise of God, the Creator Alternately addressing God directly and referring to him in the third person, the psalmist celebrates the majestic Creator in a poem whose basic outline reflects that of Gen. 1:1–2:4. The poem also shows parallels to a 14th-century Egyptian hymn to the sun-god Aten. God's creation clothes, houses, and serves him (vv. 1-4). The "chambers on the waters" represent merely the subfloor of his heavenly home (v. 3; cf. Gen. 1:7). Verses 5-9 picture the irreversible separation of land and sea, followed by the divine provision of life-sustaining fresh water in verses 10-13. The earth's vegetation and formations provide food and lodging for humans, birds, and beasts, and the celestial lights govern their times of work and rest (vv. 19-23). Verses 24-26 summarize God's creation of the earth and sea and all they contain. Verses 27-30 highlight the utter dependence of all life on the Creator. The poem closes with the psalmist's blessing and praise of God and a call for the destruction of the wicked (vv. 31-35).

105 A Hymn of Praise

God Fulfills His Covenant The psalmist calls on God's chosen people (v. 6) not only to offer thanks and praise to the Lord, but also to acclaim him outside their ranks (v. 1), to "seek" him, and to "remember" what he has done for them (vv. 4-5). He recounts the history of Israel as a demonstration that God has fulfilled his promises to the nation's patriarchs, Abraham, Isaac, and Jacob/Israel. Verses 12-13 picture these ancestors' nomadic life as ethnic Mesopotamian sojourners in Canaan, and verses 14-15 allude to specific incidents when God protected them there (Gen. 12:17; 20:3, 7; 26:11; 35:5).

Verses 16-24 summarize the life of Jacob's son Joseph (Genesis 37–46), through whom the Hebrews came to live, multiply, and flourish in the "land of Ham" (Egypt). The next 12 verses review God's judgment of these jealous and oppressive hosts-turned-masters by means of punishments delivered by Moses and Aaron in which God destroyed the Egyptians' "vines and fig trees" (v. 33), a biblical expression meaning abundant prosperity. The Hebrews' divinely led exodus from Egypt and the miraculous provision of sustenance in the wilderness culminate in God's gift of the promised land to complete the fulfillment of the promises made to Abraham. The Hebrews' landed inheritance comes with both the freedom to worship God and the responsibility to keep his laws (v. 45).

106 A Corporate Lament

The Ungratefulness of the Hebrews Though this psalm begins with an expression of praise to

God (vv. 1-3), it quickly moves on to a brief personal petition for God's favor (vv. 4-5) and then a lengthy communal confession of national sin (vv. 6-46). The previous psalm recalls Israel's history as a demonstration of the covenantal faithfulness of God. This poem recounts many of the same events from the perspective of his people's repeated faithlessness and rebellion: their forgetfulness of divine deliverance from slavery (v. 7; Exod. 14:10-12); their desert cravings for the foods available in Egypt (v. 14; Numbers 11); Korah's rebellion (vv. 16-18; Numbers 16); worship of the golden calf at the foot of Horeb (= Mount Sinai; vv. 19-23; Exodus 32).

Verses 24-25 recall the Hebrews' faithless acceptance of the spies' majority report concerning the people's ability to take possession of the promised land (Num. 13:25–14:10). Influenced by the Moabites, the Hebrews again succumbed to idolatry, and only the actions of Phinehas curtailed the consequent divine punishment by plague (vv. 28-31; Numbers 25). Verses 32-33 blame on the people Moses' transgression at Meribah (Num. 20:2-13). Their covenantal disobedience continued in the promised land, where their failure to destroy the pagan inhabitants led to further idolatry and even to child sacrifice (vv. 34-39). Such deliberate infidelity resulted in a divinely orchestrated cycle of oppression by enemy nations and compassionate deliverance (Judg. 2:11-23), until God's judgment through their conquest by foreign powers became inevitable (vv. 40-46). The psalmist's petition in verse 47 reveals that he writes from the perspective of exile. The final verse represents a doxology that closes Book IV.

Book V: Psalms 107–150

Several groups of songs comprise this final book of the Psalter. Psalm 107 may serve as an introduction to Book V as a whole. The Hebrew titles of 15 of these psalms associate them with David (108–110, 122, 124, 131, 133, 138–145), while 127 is linked with Solomon. Psalms 111–118 are the "Hallelujah Psalms," the last six of which the Hebrews sang during the festivals of Passover, Weeks, and Tabernacles. Psalm 119 may introduce the "Psalms of Ascent," sung by pilgrims journeying to the hill-country capital, Jerusalem (120–134). The last five songs (146–150) conclude the Psalter by ascribing "Glory to God in the highest!"

107 A Hymn of Corporate Thanksgiving

God's Goodness to the Upright In calling for global thankfulness to God, the psalmist uses four metaphors to illustrate divine goodness, which he describes in terms of deliverance. The parched and hungry desert nomad finds sustenance in the city (vv. 4-9). The doomed prisoner gains freedom (vv. 10-16). The deathly ill receive healing (vv. 17-22), and the sailor tossed about by the sea reaches safe haven through divinely calmed waters (vv. 23-32). Verses 33-42 use the imagery of water to describe God's transformation of ideal circumstances into disastrous straits for the wicked and his redemption of potentially catastrophic situations for the needy upright. The wise person will take a lesson from these observations and live a life of righteousness, so as to enjoy God's everlasting lovingkindness (v. 43).

108 A Lament

Praise and Petition amid Peril Verses 1-5 repeat 57:7-11, and verses 6-13 repeat 60:5-12.

109 An Individual Lament

An Eye for an Eye Betrayal by those to whom the psalmist has shown love feeds his desire to see divine vengeance on his hateful adversaries. The poet details his hopes for their severe punishment in the judicial, spiritual, personal, familial, economic, and social realms (vv. 6-13). Finally, he calls for rescinding their participation in the covenantal blessings by "cutting off" their memory from the earth (vv. 14-15). The psalmist finds justification for his vengeance-bent request in the malevolent treatment his adversaries have dealt both to him and to others (vv. 5, 16-20).

Picturing himself as afflicted, needy, near to death, and reproached by others (vv. 21-25), the psalmist calls on God to demonstrate his power over the adversaries by causing his blessing to triumph over their curses (v. 28). The poem closes with an affirmation of confidence in God's deliverance of the needy, with whom the poet identifies.

110 A Royal Psalm

The Ideal Kingly Reign Possibly a coronation psalm used during the period of Israel's monarchy to portray the ideal kingly reign, this highly prophetic, alphabetical acrostic poem also foreshadows the reign of the Messiah. New Testament writers quote verse 1 more than any other Old Testament passage (e.g., Matt. 22:44; Acts 2:34-35; 1 Cor. 15:25; Eph. 1:20, 22; Heb. 1:3, 13). Verse 4 attributes to the king a priestly role, "according to the order of Melchizedek," the priest-king of Salem (Jerusalem) to whom Abraham gave one tenth of his battle spoils (Gen. 14:17-20). The author of Hebrews asserts not only the validity of the priesthood of Jesus, who was neither a descendant of Aaron nor even a Levite, but further, the superiority of the eternal priestly order to which he belonged — that of Melchizedek (Hebrews 7).

111 A Hymn

Divine Acts and Attributes That Inspire Reverence Each of the 22 lines of this acrostic hymn

— the first of the "Hallelujah Psalms" (111–118) — begins with a successive letter of the Hebrew alphabet. The various acts and attributes of God spelled out in verses 2-9 culminate in the poet's assertion that reverence for this awesome God is the beginning of wisdom (v. 10; cf. Prov. 1:7). Splendor, majesty, enduring righteousness, grace (= ill-deserved favor), compassion, covenantal faithfulness, truth, and justice characterize God and his works.

112 A Wisdom Psalm

A Portrait of the Reverent Person As with Psalm 111, 22 lines make up this acrostic wisdom psalm. Whereas the previous poem focuses on God and his works, these verses describe the acts and attributes of the person who reveres God and the blessings that ensue. Those rewards, reaped in the here and now in accordance with the Old Testament's grim view of the afterlife, include "mighty" descendants, wealth, an enduring reputation, honor (= the exaltation of "his horn," v. 9), and victory over adversaries (vv. 8, 10). The wise person's God-like characteristics include grace, compassion, righteousness, generosity, justice, and steadfast trust in the Lord.

113 A Hallelujah Hymn

Divine Compassion in Action The psalm calls for the eternal blessing of God's name, understood in ancient Near Eastern culture to define his very essence. In recognizing God's unique superiority over all creation (vv. 4-5), the hymn emphasizes his great humility in stooping to concern himself with the most desperate of human affairs. The psalmist gives two examples of God's active compassion: he elevates to a high social status the outcast mourning at the ash heap (cf. Job 2:8), and he blesses with children the socially shamed barren woman (e.g., Gen. 29:31–30:24; 1 Sam. 1:6). Today, many Jews sing Psalms 113 and 114 before the Passover meal and 115–118 after it.

114 A Hymn of Praise

A Covenantal Promise Delivered Here the Hebrews remember their deliverance from a foreign land (Egypt) and their establishment in the land of God's promise. Judah/Israel became home to the temple (v. 2) and a nation ideally under God's ultimate rule. Verse 3 remembers the divine parting of the Red Sea during the exodus and the supernatural stopping of the Jordan River while the Hebrews crossed from Transjordan into Canaan proper (Exodus 14; Joshua 3). Verse 8 recalls God's provision of water in the desert for the wandering Hebrews (Exodus 17; Numbers 20).

115 A Prayer of Assurance

Contrasting God and Idols This psalm contrasts God's omnipotence and goodness with the lifelessness of idol-gods made by humans. Confident in the Creator's blessing of lay and priestly Israelites (= the "houses" of Israel and Aaron, respectively), the poet encourages them to place their trust in the Lord. In affirming humans' status as stewards over God's earthly creation, verse 16 recalls Gen. 1:28. Verse 17 alludes to Sheol, the silent, shadowy abode of the dead. The psalm appears to reflect liturgical use and was perhaps sung antiphonally, alternating between a soloist or cantor (vv. 3-8, 14-15) and choir (vv. 1-2, 9-11) or congregation (vv. 12-13, 16-18).

116 A Thanksgiving Psalm

Divine Deliverance from Death The psalmist can hardly thank God enough for answering his prayer for deliverance from imminent death (v. 3). Wondering out loud how to demonstrate this thankfulness, he pledges to offer a "sacrifice of thanksgiving" (v. 17), which will include his drinking a cup of wine to represent his rescue from death — the "cup of salvation" (v. 13). On the poet's public payment of vows, see Leviticus 27.

The Psalms in Worship

The Psalms were written to serve the corporate worship of the people of God. They were the hymnbook of the temple, sung or recited by the faithful as they entered God's presence to praise the Lord and petition his help. This insight has bearing on how God's people should use this book today.

The original composition of a psalm apparently arose out of the personal experience of the author. Psalm 51, for instance, embodies the sentiments of a person who seeks forgiveness for a serious sin, and the title appropriately relates the composition to the time that Nathan confronted David concerning his sin of adultery with Bathsheba (2 Samuel 11–12). But the psalm itself says nothing that would specifically associate its contents with that historical occasion, and this seems intentional. The composers wrote not to memorialize an event (as does Exodus 15), but to give others after them words to express their own hearts to God in worship. The book of Chronicles gives us a glimpse of this process, reporting how David completed a song and then handed it to Asaph and the other musicians associated with the public worship of God at the sanctuary (1 Chr. 16:7).

In this way, the Psalms are very similar to our own hymns. Hymns often have stories behind their composition, but we still sing them without knowing their background. One well-known example is "Amazing Grace," by the Englishman John Newton (1779). Newton had been a slave trader, an exploiter of fellow human beings, when the spirit of God convicted him of his sin and turned him toward God. Newton wrote this hymn, inspired by the unexpected and undeserved transformation of his life. He did not intend us to sing it about his story, however — rather about our own. His song gave words for worship by all the generations of God's people. Through it we voice our overwhelming experiences of God's grace.

The book of Psalms has been the background of Jewish and Christian worship from time immemorial. The Old Testament amply evidences the use of the Psalms in corporate worship. The Song of Hannah illustrates their use in the private devotion of God's people as well. 1 Samuel 2:1-10 records her song of delight and praise at the birth of Samuel after a long period of barrenness. This song bears close similarity to Psalm 113. Similarly, rescued from the deep waters by the great fish, Jonah assembles a collage of psalms to express his thanks to God (Jonah 2).

The Dead Sea Scrolls provide early evidence for the use of the book of Psalms as an instrument of worship. Archaeologists have found more copies of Psalms at Qumran than of any other biblical book. Furthermore, the Qumran scribes composed new songs (known as the *Thanksgiving Hymns*) for their worship, drawing heavily on the canonical Psalter for their inspiration. Jewish liturgies for the Sabbath and other moments of traditional Jewish worship also show a rich use of Psalms.

Jesus, a Jew of the 1st century, was no exception. Indeed, when the Gospel writer reports that Jesus and his disciples "sung a hymn" on the eve of the Passover just before he was crucified, undoubtedly that hymn came from the great Hallel (Psalms 113–118) sung by Jewish people at that festival. And when the disciples raise their voices in Acts 4:24, they sing words from Ps. 146:6.

Significantly, the early Christian church understood that Jesus himself was both the fulfillment of the Psalms and the very person whom they praise. So from the earliest times until today the Psalms themselves and other songs inspired by that book enrich and deepen the corporate and private worship of God's people. As early as Athanasius (A.D. 297-373), the Psalms were said to be a mirror of the Christian's soul. That is, the Psalms gave insight as to whether one was moving toward God or away from God. And when we sing the popular hymn based on Psalm 23, "The Lord's My Shepherd," we rightly evoke memory of Jesus the Good Shepherd. The Psalms, thus, have always well served worship as the people of God enter into the presence of God.

TREMPER LONGMAN III

117 A Hymn of Praise

The Nations Called to Praise This brief call for universal praise of God for his great loving-kindness and everlasting truth reflects Psalm 87, which describes the gathering together in Jerusalem of the worldwide elect (cf. 102:21-22; Rom. 15:11).

118 A Thanksgiving Psalm

Celebrating National Deliverance The psalm calls for Israel's national thanksgiving for God's goodness and loving-kindness, demonstrated in his deliverance of them from enemy nations (vv. 1-4, 10-14). As in Psalm 115, the priestly "house of Aaron" receives special mention (v. 3). Here the poem elevates trust in God over trust in fellow humans — even socially powerful ones (vv. 8-9; cf. 115:3-8, which refers to lifeless idols). God delivers Israel from foreign nations with his "right hand," the preeminent symbol of strength and honor (vv. 15-16). The "gates of righteousness" (v. 19) reflects the temple, where offerings and sacrifices righted the imperfect Israelites' relationship with the holy God. The "stone that the builders rejected" (v. 22) refers to the nation of Israel, which God elevated above all the other nations (cf. the parable of the vineyard, where Jesus applies the metaphor to himself as the basis for Israel's forfeiture of its privileged position; Matt. 21:42; Mark 12:10-11; Luke 20:17; also Acts 4:11; 1 Pet. 2:7). Verse 27 suggests a festival use for this psalm. The "horns of the altar" — vertical projections from each of the altar's four corners, its most sacred parts — prevented sacrifices from falling off (v. 27); here the language may be symbolic.

119 A Wisdom Psalm

Delighting in God's Law In this longest of all the psalms, the acrostic literary style is fully developed. Twenty-two eight-verse stanzas, beginning with the letters of the Hebrew alphabet in order, comprise this meditation on God's law, also referred to by the psalmist as testimonies/instruction, precepts, statutes, commandments, ordinances/decrees, word, ways/paths, promises, and judgments/rulings. All but a few verses contain a reference to the Law. The wisdom theme emerges in the psalm's assertion that knowledge of God's commandments and obedience to him are the only means to true happiness and fulfillment (cf. Psalm 1; Prov. 1:7).

The psalmist regularly interjects prayers that ask for divine help in understanding the Law, spurning wickedness, and remaining faithful to God's commands. He expresses trust in the Lord and determination to obey him in the midst of affliction by wicked adversaries. Verse 71 interprets affliction in a positive light, and "salvation" in verse 81 refers to divine deliverance from persecution (cf. vv. 41, 123, 155, 174). The poet repeatedly professes his love for God's law, in which he "delights" and for which he daily praises God the ideal number of times — seven (v. 164). His recurring declarations of hatred for wickedness culminate in a closing confession of disobedience that reflects shepherd-sheep imagery (Psalm 23; Matt. 18:12-14; Luke 15:4-7).

120 An Individual Lament

Longing for Peace In this first of the Psalms of Ascent (120–134), which Hebrew pilgrims sang on their journeys to the hill-country capital, Jerusalem, for annual festivals, the poet petitions for divine deliverance from oppressors who afflict with their tongues through lies and deceit. To emphasize the extent of the hostile world he laments, the psalmist mentions regions well beyond the borders of Canaan (Meshech, a region in Asia Minor, and Kedar, in the Syro-Arabian Desert).

121 A Prayer of Confidence

The Traveler's Prayer Pilgrims to Jerusalem exposed themselves not only to the harshness of nature (v. 6) but also to mugging by bandits (cf. Luke 10:30ff.), who found especially good hiding places in the rocky hill country that characterizes the ascent to the capital. When the psalmist looks toward his mountain destination, he knows the potential peril that lies ahead. His expression of pure confidence in the protecting Creator pictures an ever-vigilant, all-powerful guardian.

122 A Hymn of Praise

Peace Sought for Jerusalem The joyful pilgrim has arrived in Jerusalem to participate in the celebration of an annual festival at the temple. For the sake of his kinfolk who live in Jerusalem and for the sake of its temple, the psalmist prays for the peace of the city and the prosperity of the national government seated there.

123 A Corporate Lament

Turning to a Gracious God The poet acknowledges the powerlessness of his people in relation to God, to whom they turn for gracious deliverance from materially well-off scoffers who hold them in contempt.

124 A Thanksgiving Psalm

Rescue against Unbeatable Odds The nation remembers their deliverance in the face of odds unbeatable apart from God's intervention. The psalmist portrays Israel's enemies as savage predators, drowning waters, and crafty trappers who fail in their quest against the Creator.

125 A Prayer of Trust

The Security of Divine Protection The poet cites the geographical permanence of the Temple

"Those who go out weeping shall come home with shouts of joy" (Psalm 126); Jericho road toward Jerusalem. *(BiblePlaces.com)*

Mount and the defensibility of its home, Jerusalem, to illustrate the security and protection of the righteous. He also foresees divine judgment on the disobedient.

126 A Corporate Lament

Seeking Continued Restoration This psalm may reflect the emotions of Jews who returned from captivity in Babylon, where Judah's inhabitants were exiled in the early 6th century. Their restoration to the promised land produced in them a dreamlike joy (vv. 1-3). Yet the practical outworking of renewing the land and/or nation raised a challenge for which they needed divine aid (vv. 4-6). The psalmist asks for abundant revival like the rebirth of the southern desert streambeds (wadis), which remain completely dried up for most of the year but turn into unstoppable torrents when the rains come.

127 A Wisdom Psalm

God's Essential Centrality in Human Endeavors The psalmist acknowledges the vanity of human endeavors apart from God. One aspect of divine blessing consists in the gift of children. In the ancient Near East, children helped work and manage the land and household. Sons, especially, held the key to the family's economic security and guaranteed its landed inheritance rights, which in turn ensured the family's continued participation in the covenantal blessings. They also provided supportive testimony for the family patriarch when enemies spoke against him in court sessions at the city gate (v. 5).

128 A Wisdom Psalm

Reverence Results in Blessing This psalm portrays the blessed life of the God-fearing from an ancient Near Eastern perspective: satisfaction with the results of his labors, a prolific wife and many children ("vine" and "olive shoots" signify prosperity, v. 3), and a long life ("seeing" his grandchildren, v. 6). The poet views Zion/Jerusalem (v. 5) as the place of origin for such God-given prosperity, since the temple stood there.

129 A Song of Trust

The Overthrow of Israel's Enemies In verse 1, the song leader issues an invitation to participate in a verbal remembrance of Israel's persecution (vv. 2-3). The "furrows" dug on their backs by the "plowers" refer to the cuts of whips ("cords," v. 4) lashed by taskmasters. Verses 5-8 call for punishment on the wicked, defined as haters of Zion/Jerusalem. The poet invokes their cursedness in agricultural terms picturing them as useless, quickly withering grass (sown randomly by the wind) that sprouted on the flat, mud-covered rooftops of ancient Near Eastern houses. They are like passersby who neglect to greet them with even a routine blessing, which would release a force more powerful than mere words (v. 8; cf. English "good-bye," "God be with you").

130 A Penitential Lament

Hope in the Forgiving, Redeeming God The poet acknowledges his sins, prays for divine forgiveness, and waits expectantly for signs of God's renewed loving-kindness and redemption (earthly blessing and deliverance from affliction). Based on his personal trust, the psalmist calls for national hope in the God who not only forgives but also redeems, that is, frees from earthly affliction and misfortune as the consequences of sin in Old Testament thought.

131 A Prayer of Confidence

Childlike Trust in God Through the poet's humble prayer, this psalm encourages childlike trust in God, portrayed here as a loving mother. "Hope" in verse 3 means not wishing but expectation.

132 A Royal Processional Hymn

The Davidic Covenant Remembered This psalm marks David's transfer of the ark of the covenant — the symbolic throne of God — to Jerusalem (2 Sam. 6:12-15). News of the transfer spread from Ephrathah (= Bethlehem, David's birthplace) to "Jaar" (short for Kiriath-jearim, home to the ark after its return by the Philistines; v. 6; 1 Sam. 4:10-11; 7:1-2). David's deter-

mination to build the temple ultimately found fulfillment in God's own choice of Jerusalem (Zion) as his dwelling-place (vv. 2-5, 13-14; cf. 2 Sam. 7:1-7). God trumped David's vow by promising a perpetual dynasty, which, despite the covenantal disobedience of David's successors, finds ultimate fulfillment in Christ (vv. 10-12, 17-18; cf. 2 Sam. 7:11-16).

133 A Wisdom Psalm

The Blessedness of Harmonious Community The psalmist celebrates the harmonious community of God's elect. He likens it to the holy oil of consecration used in anointing Aaron, the first high priest (Exod. 29:7), and to Jerusalem's blessing with the dew of the Hermon mountain range on Canaan's northern border, which enjoys more abundant fertility than the drier hill country of Judah and Jerusalem.

134 A Liturgy of Blessing

Evening Praise and Blessing In this last of the Songs of Ascents, the Jerusalem pilgrims call upon those who serve the temple by night, the priests and Levites, to praise God (vv. 1-2). In turn, the temple servants invoke the pilgrims' blessing by the Creator, who dwells in Zion (v. 3).

135 A Hymn of Praise

God's Goodness toward Israel The psalmist calls for the chosen nation Jacob/Israel to worship God in the temple (v. 4). He acknowledges God's goodness toward them (vv. 8-12) and asserts his omnipotence, demonstrated in his command over nature (vv. 6-7). Verses 8-9 remember the divine punishments on the Egyptians prior to the exodus (Exod. 6:28–12:36), and vv. 10-13 recall God's victories on the Hebrews' behalf on their way to the promised land (Numbers 21) and in Canaan itself (cf. Josh. 12:7-24). The belittling description of idols in verses 15-18 parallels 115:4-8. The psalm's closing call on Israel to "bless" the Lord singles out the Aaronites, the Hebrews' priestly line (Exod. 28:1), and the Levites, the other temple servants.

136 A Hymn of Thanksgiving

Israel's "Great Hallel" Israel sang this Great Hallel ("praise") at Passover in celebration of God's eternal, "steadfast love," proclaimed in each verse's refrain. "Hallelujah" comes directly from the Hebrew, meaning literally, "Praise the Lord." The psalm recognizes God's goodness, supremacy, uniqueness, wisdom demonstrated in creation (vv. 5-9; cf. Prov. 3:19-20), and power displayed in Israel's history (vv. 10-15; see Exodus 6–14; Numbers 21; Josh. 12:7-24; compare vv. 17-22 with 135:10-12). Verses 23-25 express thanks for God's deliverance of the lowly and his sustenance of humanity.

137 A Lament

The Exiles' Lament The psalmist expresses the deep sadness stemming from recollection of exile in Babylon, where the the Hebrew population had been deported in the 6th century (2 Kings 24–25). Back in their forefather Abraham's home country, the Hebrews find it painful to celebrate in song their memories of Jerusalem (= "Zion," v. 1). For the psalmist, pain turns first into determination not to forget the bygone capital and then into an angry call for divine vengeance against those who cheered its destruction (the Edomites, Israel's relatives through Esau and neighbors to Canaan's southeast; Obad. 8-14) and those who carried out the destruction. The shocking cry for vengeance (v. 9) fleshes out the call for the conquerors to reap what they have sown (v. 8) and exposes the cruelty of ancient warfare.

138 A Thanksgiving Psalm

God's Answers to Prayer That the psalmist vows to thank God "before the gods" (v. 1) evidences that Israelite religion did not deny the existence of other gods, though it did deny their power (cf. 95:3; 1 Sam. 5:1-5; 1 Kgs. 18:7-40). The poet views God's answer to his prayer as a testimony that will cause all earthly kings to sing the praises of God, who in his exalted state condescends to pay attention to human affairs and intervene in them (vv. 5-6, 7-8). Salvation for the psalmist means deliverance from his earthly enemies (cf.

119:81) and comes through God's "right hand," the symbol of strength and honor.

139 An Individual Thanksgiving

God's Omniscience and Omnipresence Personalized Verses 1-6 celebrate God's complete and intimate knowledge of the psalmist — both his actions and his thoughts. Verses 7-12 personalize for the poet God's presence everywhere, not only in the remotest places on earth (v. 9), but also in heaven and Sheol, the shadowy abode of the dead (v. 8). God can reach even into the deepest adversity to provide blessing (vv. 11-12). As divine Creator, God has knowledge of the psalmist from the very beginning (vv. 13-16). The psalmist's wonder at God's vast wisdom issues in a hateful outburst against God's enemies, whom the poet makes his own (vv. 17-18, 19-22). The tone of humility returns in the closing petition for divine soul-searching and correction (vv. 23-24).

140 An Individual Lament

Rescue from Danger The psalmist seeks protection from evil enemies who plot violence against him. Their wickedness goes clean to the heart and issues in hateful words and actions. The poet bases his call for judgment against the wicked on his personal history of divine help in similar situations (vv. 7-11). He closes with an affirmation of trust that God sides with the righteous afflicted (vv. 12-13).

141 An Individual Lament

Deliverance from Evil and Evildoers This psalm requests divine haste in answering the poet's prayer for protection from those who do evil and for resistance to temptation. Verse 2 parallels the prophet Samuel's assertion that God prefers obedience, which evidences a contrite heart, to routine sacrifice (1 Sam. 15:22; cf. Pss. 40:6-8; 50, esp. v. 23). Verses 3-4 preview the petition in the Lord's Prayer for "deliverance from evil" (Matt. 6:13). In verse 5, the likening of righteous correction to "oil upon the head" recalls the ceremony to purify Aaron for the priesthood (Exod. 29:7). Verses 6-10 shift the focus to the psalmist's present straits by asking God to protect him from hateful pursuers who have already killed companions of the poet (v. 7b).

142 An Individual Lament

Complaining with Hope The Hebrew title associates this psalm with the days when David, fleeing from Saul, hid in Judean desert caves (1 Samuel 22–24). Here the poet does not hesitate to complain to God about his circumstances. He feels alone, overpowered, and without an escape route. Yet neither does he complain for complaining's sake; rather, he expresses faith for his rescue by the God who knows his every move. He seeks deliverance not as an end in itself, but for the purpose of gaining the opportunity to recognize God with thanksgiving for reversing his fortunes.

143 An Individual Lament

A Desperate Plea for Rescue In this last of the seven "penitential" psalms, the poet bases his request for divine deliverance from dire straits not on any claim of personal righteousness, but on his service to God (vv. 2 and 12). He uses the words "life" and "soul" synonymously, and he views "judgment" in terms of affliction and death caused by human enemies, who have already all but killed him (vv. 3c and 7 refer to "darkness" and "the Pit," Sheol). The psalmist's recollection of God's past acts leads him to trust the Lord and long for his practical and spiritual guidance (v. 6; cf. 42:1-2).

144 A Royal Lament

Invoking a Divine Display of Power Praise of God for preparing David or his successor (see v. 10) for success in battle leads to wonder that the Lord bothers taking note of mere humans (vv. 3-4; cf. 8:4-8). The psalmist calls for a natural display of divine power (vv. 5-6; cf. Exod. 19:16-18) in delivering him from threatening "waters," often associated with death (cf. 69:1-2; Matt. 18:6). In anticipation of rescue from his enemies, the poet promises a musical offering of praise (v. 9).

Verses 12-15 seem out of place here and originally may have been part of another psalm. They picture the blessed life of the people of God in typical Old Testament terms — the earthly flourishing of family, fields, and flocks.

145 A Hymn of Praise

Defining God's Greatness This acrostic hymn heads the closing collection of songs in the Psalter — the hymns of praise represented in 145–150. Verses 1-7 announce the psalmist's vow to praise God perpetually and to witness publicly to his greatness and power. The rest of the hymn defines the nature of God's greatness by highlighting his goodness, mercy, and eternal dominion demonstrated in divine help to the needy, provision for all creatures, faithfulness to those who love and revere him, and judgment of the wicked. God metes out justice in accord both with his righteousness and with his lovingkindness (vv. 17-20).

146 A Hymn of Praise

The Divine Champion of the Oppressed "Hallelujah," Hebrew for "praise the Lord," begins the last five psalms. Here verses 3-9 contrast the folly of placing one's trust in humans with doing so in the Creator, whose help to the needy oppressed lasts forever. God's active concern for society's weakest members echoes a prominent theme expressed throughout the Bible and particularly emphasized in Deuteronomy (e.g., Deut. 14:28-29; 26:12-13; cf. Jas. 1:27; also Luke 4:18-19, quoting Isaiah 61).

147 A Hymn of Praise

The Unique Covenantal Blessings This hymn couples God's infinite wisdom and universal sovereignty with his active care for the afflicted. Verses 10-11 elevate human reverence for God over God-given strength (cf. 146:3-6).

The Greek Old Testament (Septuagint) designates verses 12-20 as a separate psalm. This section highlights the unique blessings enjoyed by the nation of Israel as a result of its divinely established covenant with God: national protection, symbolized by the strong defenses of its capital city and by the peacefulness of its borders; agricultural abundance; and knowledge of God's laws.

148 A Hymn of Praise

Heaven, Earth, and Israel This hymn begins with a call for the praise of God by heavenly beings and heavenly bodies created by his command (vv. 1-6). The "waters above the heavens" (v. 4) are the celestial ocean above the firmament, the source of rainfall (cf. Gen. 1:7; Ps. 104:3). Continuing to recall the creation account in Genesis 1–2, the psalm invokes praise of God by earthly creatures and nature, including the mythological "sea monsters," and ending with all humanity, regardless of status. The psalm climaxes by narrowing the focus on a call to praise by the chosen people, Israel, whom the uniquely exalted God (v. 13) has himself exalted (= "raised up a horn," v. 14).

149 A Hymn of Praise

In Celebration of Salvation The psalmist calls on Israel to praise its divine Maker and King with singing, dancing, and musical accompaniment to celebrate their divinely wrought deliverance from affliction. The "victory" (here the Hebrew word for "salvation") that "adorns" Israel refers to the divine judgment of its pagan oppressors through their military defeat and subjection (v. 8; cf. God's judgment of his own people by the Babylonians, 2 Kings 25). In the New Testament, the "two-edged sword," which cuts both ways, signifies the word of God, which brings salvation for the believing and damnation for the unbelieving (v. 6; cf. Heb. 4:12; Rev. 1:16).

150 A Hymn of Praise

An Orchestral Finale The song that closes the Psalter calls on every living creature to praise God, who dwells both in an earthly temple ("his sanctuary") and in the vast heavens (v. 1). His "mighty deeds" and "surpassing greatness" occasion this invocation of a loud, orchestral fanfare to honor the Lord (cf. 1 Chr. 13:8; 15:16, 28; 16:5-6).

Proverbs

A classic representative of the Wisdom literature of ancient Israel, Proverbs became an instruction book for the practical application of Israelite moral law to attitudes and everyday living. Though Proverbs shows parallels to ancient Egyptian and Mesopotamian wisdom writings, the book shows a distinct perspective consistent with the worship of Yahweh as directed in the legal tradition of the Pentateuch.

Literary Form

The Hebrew word for "proverb" *(mashal)* carries two meanings, which reveal the means and end of these pithy nuggets of wisdom: "to be similar to" and "to rule over." By means of comparison, a proverb aids the intellectual grasping of a truth and thereby allows a person to gain mastery over the principle that that truth implies (cf. the modern expression, "Knowledge is power"). Another characteristic typical of proverbs is generalization. For the most part, possessing knowledge positions a person for power, but possessing knowledge does not guarantee one will gain power. Similarly, Proverbs repeatedly asserts that the righteous will prosper, but the lives of many biblical figures, notably Job and Jesus, poignantly demonstrate exceptions to this general rule and distinguish it from a promise.

Occasionally, the mostly two-line, single-thought expressions in Proverbs appear in thematic clusters, but more often than not the text lacks progression of thought from verse to verse and jumps from one idea to the next with no apparent connection. Though the chapters of this book may seem disjointed, the brevity and poetic form of the proverbs offered the advantage of easy memorization in a time when oral tradition was the primary means of instruction. Proverbs also contains other, sometimes longer literary forms. For example, "sayings" offer observations about life but stop short of providing value judgments or advice for action. Admonitions/prohibitions, formulaic devices (e.g., "numerical sayings," ch. 30), and wisdom poems are additional teaching tools found in Proverbs, which throughout employs varying forms of poetic parallelism (see "Poetry and Wisdom Literature" [304]).

Content

Eight main sections make up the book of Proverbs. The first, chapters 1–9, offers a general introduction on wisdom by a parentlike teacher, who, in keeping with male-oriented ancient Near Eastern society, admonishes the student-son to shun Ms. Folly and pursue Woman Wisdom. The catchphrase "the fear of the Lord" emerges as the basis for a life characterized by wisdom (see 1:7). This "fear" (= reverence) means conduct that accords with Israel's legal tradition, and therefore "wisdom" primarily carries moral overtones, rather than defining a lofty level of intellectual ability. As the direct opposite of wisdom, "folly" or "foolishness" refers not to simple stupidity but to attitudes

---

Forms of Wisdom Literature

Proverb or aphorism

Admonition or prohibition

Instruction

Allegory

Riddle

Numerical saying

Hymn in praise of personified Wisdom

Disputation

Fable

Example story

Autobiography

List

and behavior that do not conform to Hebrew law. Six collections of proverbs and sayings appear in 10:1–31:9, and a complete acrostic poem (cf. Psalm 9) concludes Proverbs with a portrait of the "excellent wife," the perfect example of wisdom as developed through the book.

Proverbs restates a number of overarching themes in addition to wisdom/folly and its counterpart, righteousness/wickedness. Teaching concerning the use of words and the taming of the tongue; business, social, official, and family relationships; sexual restraint; the misuse of alcohol; and industriousness/laziness, with its counterpart, wealth/poverty, all find a prominent place throughout the book. The instruction contained in this ancient moral primer applies today largely because it recognizes and addresses universal factors that affect human behavior for better or for worse — pride and humility, anger, hopes and fears, joys and sorrows.

Composition

The literary collections in Proverbs originate from different periods in Israel's history. Themes that deal with familial and business relationships may have originated well before the monarchic period, and references to maternal instruction demonstrate that schooling in morality certainly occurred in the home (cf. 1:8b; 31:1-31). Certain proverbs and sayings, however, specifically address kings and court matters (e.g., the "Royal" collection, 16:1–22:16). That superscriptions heading a number of collections link them with various kings — in addition to Solomon — and that ancient evidence from Israel's neighbors, Egypt and Mesopotamia, shows the presence there of court and temple schools lead most scholars to view the bulk of Proverbs as having originated from the monarchic period to the exile (10th–6th centuries B.C.), with the final editing of the book occurring no later than the 2nd century. Though superscriptions name Solomon as author/compiler of the two longest collections (10:1–11:16 and chs. 25–29; cf. 1 Kgs. 4:32-34), finalization of the present form of the book appears to have come from later editors.

1:1-7 The Purpose of Proverbs

The introduction to Proverbs gives the purpose of the book: instruction, mainly but not exclusively for the young and naive, in wisdom, which results in appropriate behavior. Verse 3 links wise conduct with the divine characteristics of "righteousness, justice, and equity." To acquire knowledge, gained by instruction and issuing in wisdom, requires reverence (= "fear") of the Lord, a theme that occurs repeatedly throughout this book (v. 7). The "proverbs of Solomon," to which verse 1 refers, begin in chapter 10.

1:8-19 In Praise of Parental Instruction

The personal advantages of heeding the advice of one's elders, here described as the instruction of parents, stand over against the ultimate self-destructiveness of giving way to enticements by sinners, who claim that malicious crimes against the innocent pay and who promise criminal fellowship. "Sheol" and "the pit" (v. 12) refer to the silent, shadowy abode of the dead.

1:20-33 Woman Wisdom Prophesies

Personified as a woman, "Wisdom" laments her rejection by the simple and naive, whose fate for neglecting her instruction and correction consists in certain calamity. When it hits, their cries of distress will come too late. Those, however, who heed her advice by fearing the Lord from the start have no cause for fearing the disastrous consequences brought on by the pursuit of evil (cf. vv. 28-29 and 33). See also chapter 9, which pits substantive, trustworthy Woman Wisdom against loud-mouthed, ignorant Ms. Folly.

2 The Benefits of Pursuing Wisdom

Though Wisdom loudly and publicly announces her availability in 1:20ff., the search to find her requires attentiveness and concerted effort (vv. 2-4). The discovery of wisdom amounts to the discovery of God, who protects the pilgrim by keeping him on the paths of righteousness, with the result that he enjoys the covenantal blessing of life "in the (promised) land" (v. 21). In contrast, the consequence of following the "loose woman," whose road of marital and covenantal unfaithfulness leads to the same end as that of the thugs in 1:10-19, consists in forced relinquishment of that blessing (cf. 9:13-18).

The account of the fall provides the supreme example of unwise behavior and its consequences. Adam's and Eve's disobedience to God in choosing for themselves what constituted good and evil behavior (the meaning of "knowing" good and evil) resulted in their losing a life of paradise in the garden of Eden, not to mention the deadly effects of their transgression for the rest of humanity (Genesis 3).

3 Kindness, Truth, and Humility Characterize the Wise Person

Remembering instruction figures as importantly as initially accepting it (v. 1; cf. 2:1). A long life characterized by peace, prosperity, and peace of mind (*shalom,* the fruit of harmonious relationships with God and his creation) adds to the picture of the reward for pursuing wisdom (cf. ch. 2). While verses 2, 16-18, 23-24 describe such a life, verses 25 and 34 acknowledge the inevitable onslaught of "the wicked" and presuppose affliction even for the righteous, though God remains on their side (see vv. 33-35).

Kindness and truth characterize the life of the wise person. The admonition in verse 3 pictures the securing of these characteristics to one's body and, in doing so, parallels the similar command regarding the Torah in Deut. 6:8. Verses 27-31 describe the fleshing out of kindness and truth. Humility before God, defined as trusting in him and seeking his guidance, also marks a person as wise. Once again, Adam and Eve come to mind as the supreme examples of folly through their choice to disregard God's direction in favor of trusting their own judgment (contrast vv. 5-7 with Gen. 3:6). The promise in verses 9-10 of tangible reward for material generosity toward God fits with the Old Testament theology of this-worldly recompense for one's actions. The Old Testament often interprets such affliction as divine discipline, which Proverbs admonishes one to accept (vv. 11-12; cf. Heb. 12:1-13).

4 Avoiding Distractions

By remembering and passing on the instruction of his own father, the teacher demonstrates that he practices what he preaches (vv. 3ff.; cf. 3:1). Acquiring wisdom, which goes hand in hand with avoiding evil deeds and deceitful words, is the path to a blessed life. The Apostle Paul echoes the admonition to ignore distractions from the "upright path" when he urges the Philippians to follow his example of "forgetting what lies behind" and "pressing on toward the goal for the prize," the "upward call of God" (compare vv. 25-27 with Phil. 3:12-14).

"Listen, children, to a father's instruction, and be attentive, that you may gain insight" (Proverbs 4).
(Phoenix Data Systems, Neal and Joel Bierling)

5 Sexual Fidelity in Marriage

Wise behavior also includes the sexual fidelity of a husband to his wife. Not only should he resist the temptations of the sweet-talking adulteress, which will only produce a painful outcome, but he should also revel in his sexual relationship with his wife (cf. 7:6-27). Here, as throughout the book, Proverbs addresses its instruction to males, but it applies to women as well (cf. Deut. 22:22). Jesus affirms the validity of the Old Testament prohibition against adultery by intensifying its definition to include infidelity of thought (lust), not just action (Matt. 5:27-28).

The Hebrew word often translated here as "adulteress" means "strange woman" or "foreign woman" (cf. 2:16-17). The author's use of an alternative Hebrew word for "adulteress" heightens the sense of religious danger the loose woman poses through her added, inevitable temptations to the worship of "foreign" gods (cf. Numbers 25; 1 Kgs. 11:1-8).

6 Integrity in Work and Relationships

Verses 1-5 advise the financial guarantor stuck with a defaulter's debt to waste no time in diligently working off the unwisely acquired burden. Verses 6-11 cite the ant as an example of self-motivated industriousness in work. Emulating the insect will guard one from the clutches of poverty.

Again the teacher's attention turns toward the devious, deceitful person, who in the end will get his just deserts. As an aside, verses 16-19 list some of the evils that God hates: pride, lying, violence against the innocent, wicked plotting, quickness to do wrong, false witnesses, and those who pit friends and family members against each other (contrast 4:23-27). The formulaic language, "six things . . . yes, seven . . . ," marks the list as representative rather than complete (v. 16; cf. 30:15, 18, 21, 29).

Chapter 6 closes with more warnings about the consequences of sexual sins, including those with prostitutes, whom verse 26 mentions overtly for the first time in Proverbs. Batting eyes may look enticing (v. 25), but giving in to them is like embracing fire or walking on hot coals (vv. 27-28). The one foolish enough to commit adultery (v. 32) sustains the inevitable burns of permanent public shame and unrepayable debt to the personally and socially offended husband.

7 Adultery: A Case Study

The teacher metaphorically urges the student to marry Wisdom, the "wife" who will enable him to resist the smooth-talking adulteress (v. 4; "sister" conveys "bride"; cf. Song 4:9-12). Then the speaker describes the seduction of a naive young man by a married woman whose husband has temporarily left town. Before approaching the young man under cover of darkness, the adulteress makes alluring preparations for the enticement that reveal the degree to which she has planned her sexual transgression. Persuaded that he may "eat the forbidden fruit" discreetly, the youth walks straight into the bedroom trap, ignorant as a soon-to-be-butchered ox of the metaphorically mortal wounds he is about to sustain (cf. 2:16-19).

8 Wisdom Presents Her Resumé

In contrast to the secretive, scheming adulteress of chapter 7, Woman Wisdom loudly and publicly advertises her legitimate, universal availability at the city gate, where the ancients conducted their daily business. She proclaims the righteousness of her utterances and her unmeasurable value, which exceeds that of silver, gold, and jewels. She claims for herself godlike hatred of evil, power in human affairs, and the ability to grant desirable rewards. In verses 22-31, Wisdom states God's claim on her from before the creation of the world (cf. John 1:1-4, where the "Word" refers to Jesus). Verses 24, 28, and 29 remember day 2 of the creation account in Genesis 1; verses 25, 26, and 29 recall day 3; and verses 27 and 28 reflect day 1. By hating (rejecting) evil, Wisdom reveres God and loves (chooses) life (vv. 13 and 35). By default, then, the one who hates Wisdom (through neglect and rejection) loves (chooses) death, as did Adam and Eve at the fall.

9 Wisdom's Feast versus Folly's Fare

Chapter 9 closes the first main section of Proverbs by summarizing the message of chapters 1–8 in banqueting imagery. From her visually prominent, solidly built hilltop mansion, Woman Wisdom and her maidens universally summon houseguests to a life-giving feast featuring reverence for God as the course around which the rest of the meal revolves (cf. Jesus' parable in Matt. 22:1-14; Luke 14:16-24). In contrast, loud-mouthed but ignorant Ms. Folly lies in wait at her doorway, where she tempts well-intentioned passersby to depart from the straight and narrow path by sampling in secret her supposedly sweeter but actually fatal stolen fare (vv. 17-18; contrast John 4:14; 6:51). Woman Wisdom lays it on the line in verse 12: you determine your own fate through wise or foolish choices (cf. Psalm 1). The moral? Beware the false advertisements of Ms. Folly.

10:1–22:16 The Proverbs of Solomon

The short sayings that contain tidbits of wisdom for everyday living — the proverbs proper — begin in chapter 10, and they frequently take up specific points made in chapters 1–9 (compare 10:10 with 6:13; 10:12a with 6:19b). Three-hundred seventy-five proverbs attributed to Solomon extend from 10:1–22:16. While each verse in the rest of the book represents a distinct proverb, the sayings appear at least loosely grouped together according to similar themes, key words/phrases, or poetic style, such as the antithetic parallelism characteristic of chapters 10–15 in which a couplet uses contrasting images to present a single idea from opposite sides. The New Testament writers regularly echo the themes and language of Proverbs.

10

1 "Father" and "mother" do not represent contrasting interests here; rather, they form a word pair typical of Hebrew poetic parallelism (cf. 15:20; 17:25).

7 A person's "name" embodied his or her character and very being, and one's "memory" brought not only honor but a form of continued existence. Preserving both had great importance in ancient Israel.

12 On love's covering of transgressions, see 1 Pet. 4:8.

16 The Apostle Paul agrees that sin earns punishment, in the form of "death" (= damnation), but he asserts that God grants life ("eternal life") not as an earned wage but as a free gift (Rom. 6:23).

19 James also emphasizes the importance of a bridled tongue (Jas. 1:19; 3:1-12).

27 The blessedness signified by a long life in this world results largely from the Old Testament's undeveloped view of a robust afterlife.

30 On the exile of the wicked from "the land," see 2:22.

31 Ancient Assyrian texts abound with references to the cutting out of a person's tongue as a form of physical punishment for transgressions ranging from disobedience to parents to breaking a business contract to sacrilegious utterances. Mosaic law does not prescribe the practice.

11

1 Merchants weighed out goods on scales counterbalanced with objects of standardized weights (cf. Lev. 19:35-36).

4 Jesus' parable of the rich man and Lazarus illustrates the irrelevance of worldly riches in the afterlife (Luke 16:20-31). The proverb here comments on this-worldly circumstances.

24-31 Through generosity toward others, the giver also benefits; the miser's stinginess hurts him as much as anyone. Verse 15 has already warned against exercising benevolence imprudently.

12

4 Recall the examples of Esther and Vashti.

21 This generality, typical of proverbs (cf. 13:21), finds notable exceptions throughout the Bible.

26 Paul recognizes how individuals' actions influence the beliefs and behavior of others for good or for ill (1 Corinthians 8; 9:19-23).

13

8 Along with material wealth come problems about which the poor never have to worry.

9 The light, or lamp, signifies one's life.

13 "The word" and "the commandment" refer

to God's laws, the "respect" (or "fear") of which means following them.

24 This verse recognizes parental discipline as an act of love. Reacting to widespread, clear-cut cases of child abuse, modern Western society generally views as unacceptably harsh the use of a "rod" to punish one's children (by beating; cf. 10:13; 23:13-14). Proverbs views parental withholding of warranted, physically punitive "tough love" as a disservice to the child.

14

12 Paul echoes this truth in Rom. 6:21.

21, 31 On Mosaic law regarding treatment of the poor, see Leviticus 25; Deuteronomy 15; 24:6ff.

15

3 Job expressed conflicting sentiments about God's watchful eye (Job 7:17-20; 29:1-4).

8 Cf. 1 Sam. 15:20-22; Ps. 40:6-8.

11 "Sheol" stood for the abode of the dead, or sometimes simply the grave; "Abaddon" means "place of destruction" (cf. Ps. 88:3, 4, 11).

20 Cf. 10:1.

25 Lack of economic opportunities left widows among the least powerful members of society (cf. Deut. 14:28-29; 26:12-13; Jas. 1:27). The fairly wide age difference usually between wives and their older husbands resulted in widowed women making up a greater percentage of the population than today.

33 Cf. 16:18; 18:12 combines the two.

16

4 Here "evil" may mean disaster or trouble. The Old Testament repeatedly illustrates God's use of pagan nations to punish the wayward Hebrews (e.g., the Assyrians, who brought about the downfall of the northern kingdom in 722, and the Babylonians, who conquered the southern kingdom in 587/86; 2 Kings 17–18; 24–25).

12 Saul learned this lesson the hard way

through his disobedience concerning the Amalekites (1 Samuel 15, esp. vv. 22-28; cf. David's dying charge to Solomon, 1 Kgs. 2:1-4).

17

6 A large family signified God's blessing. Fathering male heirs ensured the family's continued participation in the covenantal promises, but in special circumstances the Mosaic law also provided for passing on family property to daughters (Num. 27:1-11; 36).

8 The proverb does not condone offering bribes but merely observes the apparent effectiveness of the practice as a means to selfish ends. Verse 23 overtly recognizes the goal of bribing as committing injustice.

13 Cf. Jesus' command to return good for evil (Matt. 5:38-48).

18 See 6:1-5.

18

10 The imagery of the "strong tower" comes from the well-fortified lookout towers built into the defense walls surrounding important ancient Near Eastern cities (v. 11).

18 Casting lots may strike modern Westerners as leaving a matter to chance, but ancient Near Easterners, including the Hebrews, relied on the practice to discover divine will (cf. Exod. 28:30; Esth. 3:7; Joshua 7; 18–19).

20 Cf. Deut. 8:3; Matt. 4:4.

19

5, 9 The Ninth Commandment prohibits bearing false witness (Exod. 20:16).

7 Cf. Job 19:13-22.

18 See 13:24.

20

9 John finishes this thought with a note of hope (1 John 1:8-10).

14 In many societies yet today, "bargaining"

often involves the buyer's pointing out imperfections in the goods she wishes to buy so that the seller will reduce the price. After the sale, the buyer may brag about the good deal she got.

16 See 6:1-5.

18 The proverb does not urge the making of war; rather, it prescribes entering into it only with wise counsel.

20 The proverb echoes the Fifth Commandment (Exod. 20:12).

22 See 17:13.

25 The proverb refers to making a sacrifice of something without verifying its ritual cleanness until after the fact.

28 See 16:12.

30 Cf. 13:24.

21
2 Cf. Matt. 6:1-18.

3 Cf. 15:8.

13 Deuteronomy shows particular concern for society's economically weak (cf. Matt. 25:31-46).

17 The proverb does not warn against taking time to enjoy life; rather, it observes that focusing on the pursuit (= "love") of pleasure leaves one a pauper. "Oil" refers to olive oil, a product put to a variety of uses in the ancient Near East (see Deut. 33:24).

22:1-16
4, 16 These generalities, typical of proverbs, find many specific exceptions in the biblical and modern worlds (cf. 3:9-10).

9 Cf. 11:24-31.

13 The sluggard claims a lame excuse for his laziness.

15 This viewpoint echoes 20:30 (cf. 13:24).

22:17–24:34 More Wise Sayings

The literary style of this section departs from the pithiness of Solomon's proverbs (10:1–22:16) and resumes the prosaic mode of expression characteristic of chapters 1–9. Here, distinct paragraphs conveying complete thoughts urge the avoidance or adoption of specific behaviors through a series of commands. Proverbs 22:17–24:22 closely parallels sayings in the 30-chapter "Teaching of Amenemope," a pre-Solomonic (before 960) Egyptian text that gives moral instruction to public servants. Most scholars agree that Proverbs has adopted and adapted sayings from this Egyptian text, rather than vice-versa. Attempts to divide this section into a parallel 30 paragraphs seem forced, though 22:20 refers to "30" sayings.

According to 22:17-21, heeding the "words of the wise" (v. 17) figures as the basis for a life of trust in God (v. 19). The rest of the chapter warns against oppressing the poor (vv. 22-23); being influenced by the hot-tempered (vv. 24-25; cf. 15:1, 18); becoming a guarantor for another (vv. 26-27; cf. 6:1-5); and seizing land (v. 28; cf. 23:10-12; Deut. 19:14).

Chapter 23 begins with warnings concerning the pursuit of upward mobility in the social and economic realms (vv. 1-9). On the prescription of harsh parental discipline in verses 13-14, compare 13:24. Mentoring advice follows, with encouragement to show consistent reverence for God, avoid keeping company with heavy drinkers and gluttons, and resist tempters to sexual transgression (vv. 15-28; cf. 6:24–7:27). The instruction concludes with a vivid and unattractive description of the dulled drunkard ruled by a self-destructive addiction to alcohol. Compare the deceptive appeal of strong drink (vv. 31-34) with the misleading promises of the wayward woman (7:6-23).

The first 14 verses of chapter 24 develop the contrast between wise and foolish persons. Strength, power, and mercy characterize the wise; but violence, scheming, and incompetence mark the foolish, who lack the skills necessary to conduct business and legal affairs "in the [city] gate." Verses 15-16 warn the wicked against trying to bring calamity on the righteous, but the instructions to the righteous in the next 13 verses begin with a warning that they not rejoice when calamity befalls their enemies (vv. 17-18). The prohibition against bias in judgment applies equally to the poor and the powerful (v. 23; cf. Lev. 19:15; Deut. 1:16-17). In the Golden Rule, Jesus gives a positive approach to the prohibition against "getting even" (v. 29; Matt. 7:12). The chapter closes similarly to chapter 23 by portraying the unenviable plight of a foolish person — here not the drunkard but the sluggard (vv. 30-34).

25–29 Additional Proverbs of Solomon

These five chapters contain 130 additional proverbs traditionally credited to Solomon (cf. 10:1–22:16). According to 25:1, the collection was compiled during the reign of Judah's righteous King Hezekiah, who reversed his royal predecessors' departures from the pure worship of Yahweh (2 Kings 18–20; 2 Chronicles 29–32). Pithy proverbs by comparison, replete with similes and metaphors drawn from nature and everyday life and often presented in pairs, predominate in chapters 25–27. Chapters 28–29 return to the antithetic parallelism characteristic of chapters 10–15.

25
6-7 Jesus' parable applies this principle of humility to the broader scope of human attitudes and behavior (Luke 14:7-11).

18 The Ninth Commandment prohibits bearing false witness (Exod. 20:16).

21-22 Treating one's enemies in a loving way issues in a dual result: blushing shame on the part of the enemy (or continued disfavor with God; cf. 24:17-18) and divine reward for the wronged (cf. Matt. 5:43-48). The Apostle Paul precedes his quotation of this proverb with a reminder from Mosaic law that God reserves vengeance for himself (Rom. 12:19-20; Deut. 32:35).

28 Perimeter walls played an important part in the defense system of ancient Near Eastern cities.

26
4-5 This contrasting pair of verses warns

against suspending one's wisdom by engaging in discussions one knows to be foolish; rather, one should use his wisdom to expose the foolishness and the fool for what they are.

8 To adhere the ammunition to the weapon represents the ultimate in foolishness.

13-16 Compare the reflection on the sluggard in 24:30-34.

17-28 James 3:5-12 also speaks of the problems caused by the "untamed tongue."

27
13 See 6:1-5.

20 Sheol is the grave, or the abode of the dead; Abaddon means "place of destruction" (cf. Ps. 88:3-4, 11).

23-27 The chapter ends with practical advice to a farming society, but the principle of prudent attentiveness to one's livelihood applies equally well today. Jesus bids his followers not to "worry" about tomorrow (Matt. 6:25-34).

28
4 Here and elsewhere in chapters 28–29, "law" refers to Mosaic law, the legal tradition of Israel set forth in the Pentateuch.

13 The New Testament concept of repentance includes both the confession of sins and the forsaking of them (1 John 1:9).

14 Here "fear" means "reverence," with the implied object being God.

17 For laws addressing manslaughter and murder, see Numbers 35.

20 The folly lies not in *being* wealthy but in pursuing schemes to "get rich quick" by cutting ethical corners (cf. Matt. 6:24).

21 On bribes, compare 17:8.

23 Cf. 9:7-9.

24 The Fifth Commandment mandates honoring one's parents (Exod. 20:12).

29

7 On Mosaic law regarding treatment of the poor, see Leviticus 25; Deuteronomy 15; 24:6ff.

9 Cf. 26:4-5.

14 See David's dying charge to Solomon (1 Kgs. 2:1-4).

15, 17 On parental discipline, see 22:15.

18 Divinely generated prophetic visions complement the Mosaic law through "special revelation," which is distinguished from God's "general revelation" of himself in the created order and the human conscience (cf. Rom. 1:18-32).

23 Compare 25:6-7; Luke 14:7-11.

25-26 Placing one's faith in human beings (= "fearing" them) and trusting in God stand opposite.

30 The Oracle of Agur

The names Agur and Jakeh (v. 1) do not occur elsewhere in the Hebrew Bible. That they do appear on South Arabian inscriptions and that "Massa" likely refers to a North Arabian (Edomite) tribe descended from Ishmael (Gen. 25:14; 1 Chr. 1:30) suggest that the sayings in this chapter originated outside Israel in an area renowned in ancient times for wisdom — "the east" (cf. Matt. 2:1). Agur assumes a posture of humility before sharing his insights in a way that often requires the reader to figure out the sayings' implications for wise behavior.

The "numerical sayings" in verses 15, 18, 21, 29 begin with a formulaic literary device that marks the lists they contain as representative rather than complete ("three things . . . , four . . ."; cf. 6:16-19).

4 The first of Agur's rhetorical questions finds an answer in the person of Christ (cf. Eph. 4:8-10).

11, 17 Old Testament law prescribes the death penalty for cursing one's father or mother (Exod. 21:17).

23 Cf. the desperation of the unloved Leah (Gen. 29:1–30:24) and the tension that developed when Hagar "supplanted" her mistress, "Sarah," by conceiving a child by Abraham (Genesis 16).

25 Cf. 6:6-11.

31:1-9 A Queen Mother's Advice to Her Son

We know nothing else of the non-Israelite (Massaite?) "king" Lemuel (cf. 30:1). His mother's seemingly corrective admonitions are our only available examples of the kind of maternal instruction referred to in 1:8b; 6:20. The account of the barren Hannah's vow regarding the son for whom she prayed helps explain the meaning of the last line in verse 2, where apparently the queen mother views Lemuel as the answer

"She opens her mouth with wisdom, and the teaching of kindness is on her tongue" (Proverbs 31). Wisdom is a concept personified in both Greek and Hebrew cultures in biblical times. *(Wikimedia Commons)*

to her prayers (cf. 1 Sam. 1:1-11). Her teaching echoes familiar warnings in earlier chapters about overindulgence in wine and women (v. 3; cf. Solomon's negative example, 1 Kgs. 11:1-13). Lemuel's position as king makes temperance in these areas particularly necessary for the competent and just fulfillment of his monarchical duties.

31:10-31 The Excellent Wife

In this complete acrostic poem, which may represent further advice to Lemuel, the "excellent wife" embodies the perfect example of the many qualities of wisdom, as defined in Proverbs. Proverbs 18:22 calls the finding of a wife "good," and 19:14 considers a prudent wife a gift from God. But the "excellent wife" — if one can find her — is the wise woman to marry (see 7:4)! The direct opposite of the adulteress and the sluggard, she is trustworthy and industrious (contrast 7:6-27; 24:30-34). She takes care of her household and takes economic initiative. She is strong, hard-working, and dignified. At the same time, she is compassionate, optimistic, and kind. She is a wise teacher. These qualities win her the respect of her husband and children, and the products of her labor earn for her public praise. No shrinking violet, no trophy wife, this "excellent" woman demonstrates the "fear" (= reverence) of God in practical, everyday life.

Proverbs thus comes full circle, with the "fear of the Lord" emerging not only as the beginning of knowledge, wisdom, and instruction, but also as the end result (1:7; 31:30).

Ecclesiastes

The Greek word *Ecclesiastes* translates Hebrew *Qoheleth,* a pen name associating the principal speaker in this unique piece of Old Testament Wisdom literature with King Solomon (cf. 1 Kings 8). The verbal root of the name means "to gather/assemble," and so English Bibles variously translate Qoheleth as "Teacher," "Preacher," or "Speaker" — one who addresses a group of people.

Content

In a manner similar to ancient "pessimism literature," which dates to 2000 B.C. in Egypt and Mesopotamia, Ecclesiastes presents the opposite of the black-and-white world portrayed in Proverbs. Abandoning that book's idealistic generalizations, Ecclesiastes reveals life for what it is, warts and all. The Teacher is scandalized by the unfairness of life: the wicked do not always perish and the righteous do not always prosper. Even worse, the wicked and the righteous share the same ultimate fate: death, which in the Old Testament view ends robust existence and the realization of rewards and punishments based on personal conduct. The Teacher's realism creates a crisis of fate, to which he responds pessimistically: "Enjoy life while you can." Nevertheless, the book ultimately expresses the faith that divine judgment will right life's wrongs, and so reverence for God and the keeping of his commandments set the bounds of the pleasure game.

Ecclesiastes includes sections written in narrative prose and groups of proverbs. The Teacher often appears to be confused, arguing with himself, or at least with the conventional wisdom of the day, in a struggle to reconcile the Hebrew belief in a just God with the unpredictable, often contradictory realm of human existence "under the sun." By denoting general knowledge about the world and nature in addition to moral discernment, the "wisdom" to which he appeals and refers carries a broader and more existential meaning than in Proverbs.

Authorship

Ecclesiastes' wider definition of "wisdom" fits the tradition of King Solomon (1 Kgs. 4:29-34), to whom the book alludes in 1:1, 12-18, though it stops short of claiming Solomonic authorship. The presence of two Persian loanwords puts the book's anonymous authorship or compilation at least four centuries after Solomon's reign. The insufficiency of other internal evidence (e.g., historical or political allusions) precludes a precise dating, but the discoveries at Qumran yielded fragments of the Hebrew text of Ecclesiastes indicating its existence by at least the mid-2nd century.

1–3 The Impermanence of Earthly Life Declared

The Teacher begins by declaring the impermanent, fleeting nature of life. The Hebrew word traditionally translated "vanity," "meaninglessness," or "uselessness" literally means "a puff of air," "a breath," or "nothingness," expressions that characterize life as brief, fragile, and devoid of lasting significance. But a number of the book's later comments make clear that life is not necessarily futile — perhaps thereby reflecting a "mature" teacher or the framework of a later narrator who has quoted and then provides a broader, more orthodox perspective on the words of the Teacher. The contrast between the repetitiveness and transience of human existence and the completeness and eternity of divine works produces human reverence for God (3:14).

The groundwork the Teacher lays for the centerpiece of his advice — "eat, drink, and be merry, for tomorrow we die" — does seem

Pool of Solomon, south of Bethelehem, "from which to water the forest of growing trees" (Eccl. 2:6).
(Phoenix Data Systems, Neal and Joel Bierling)

depressingly cynical if viewed from a Godless standpoint. In chapter 1, the Teacher observes that lessons from the past go unremembered, so human history only repeats itself in a wearisome "circle of life," just as the elements of nature go through their endless but progressionless motions (1:2-7). Universal forgetfulness creates only an illusion that anything new appears or happens "under the sun," a recurring phrase synonymous with "on earth" and "under heaven," all of which refer to the world of humans (1:9-11). The Teacher's own realization that at death he must pass on the achievements of his wisdom — perhaps to an incompetent fool — and his conclusion that neither people nor the products of their labor generate a lasting legacy leave him despairing of his earthly accomplishments (2:16-20).

In autobiographical style, the Teacher describes his pursuit of self-indulgent remedies for this perplexity: acquiring unprecedented wisdom (1:17-18; cf. Prov. 3:13-26); enjoying unbounded sensual and material pleasures; amassing unparalleled wealth and possessions; and engaging in physical labor. Though these activities brought him enlightenment and temporary pleasure, he acknowledges that none of them permanently cured his cynicism (compare 2:10, 12-14 and 2:17-18, 20). He is a confused wise man, constantly alternating between what

he knows from tradition (3:17; 9:1; 11:9) and what he sees in life.

Despite the inevitability and finality of death, the Teacher acknowledges the good that does come from God in this earthly life. All the ups and downs of life happen according to their divinely appointed times — even God's judgment of the righteous and the wicked (3:17). Humans may not fully understand God's works (3:11), but they might as well rejoice, do good deeds, and appreciate life as a gift from God — make the best of a bad situation.

4:1–11:6 Observations and Advice concerning Life "Under the Sun"

4 The situation is bad indeed. Observation of the earthly pain inflicted by powerful oppressors of the uncomforted leads the Teacher to consider the dead better off than the living, and the nonexistent the most fortunate of all. People's actions appear motivated only by "keeping up with the Joneses" (v. 4), and heirless workaholics engage in pointless self-denial of life's pleasures (v. 8). While Proverbs warns that a little "folding of the hands" renders one a pauper, the existentialist in Ecclesiastes touts leisure over work — better a little instant though temporary gratification than a lot of work for nothing that lasts (vv. 5-6; cf. Prov. 24:30-34).

Verse 9 introduces a proverbial style that punctuates the rest of the book with teaching and advice. The advantages of companionship form the theme of verses 9-12. In the realm of politics, wisdom trumps seniority, social status, and power (vv. 13-16), but the chapter ends on a familiar note of cynical resignation.

5-6 Despite his grim lament over the deficiencies of life, the Teacher assumes that his students will nevertheless pursue the worship of God, and he instructs them toward that end (5:1ff.). Practical fear (= reverence) for God involves approaching him in a posture of receptiveness, praying with careful deliberation, and keeping one's vows (cf. Deut. 23:21-23). The "house of God" (v. 1) refers to the temple. "Fools" — the wicked — offer insincere sacrifices, which they attempt to pass off as "mistakes," or unwitting sins (5:5-6; cf. Lev. 4:1–5:13; 6:24-30 for atoning sacrifices). Jesus' instructions on how to pray echo Ecclesiastes' warning against excessive wordiness with God (Matt. 6:7ff.).

Though the Teacher acknowledges that material wealth does not permanently satisfy, nevertheless he bemoans its loss, which at death leaves a rightful heir unsupported and returns one to the same humble, naked state in which he entered the world as a baby (5:10-17). This observation reinforces the Teacher's emphasis on the futility of pursuing impermanent fortune and fame (cf. 2:18-23). Once again, he concludes that a person must concentrate on the enjoyment of life, including finding delight in one's work. Enjoyment of the here and now offers the added benefit of preventing one from becoming too reflective (5:18-20). In fact, those who are stillborn are better off than even the most blessed person — here described in ideal ancient Near Eastern terms as a wealthy, long-lived father of many children, who likewise cannot both have his cake and eat it (ch. 6).

7 Here the Teacher's observations about life waver back and forth. On the one hand, he celebrates the end of life over its beginning. After all, death releases one from earthly ills: oppression, corruption, anger, nostalgic longing, adversity (vv. 1-14). Nevertheless, he considers wisdom advantageous in that it "preserves" one's life (v. 12). Then again, he recognizes the exceptions to this theological rule embodied by the short-lived righteous and the long-lived wicked (v. 15). The conclusion he draws addresses the natural human instinct to prolong life, despite his affirmation of death, and he speaks from a human perspective when he prescribes the avoidance of moral extremes to ensure longevity (vv. 16-18).

The modern cliché, "Don't believe everything you hear," echoes the meaning of verse 21. The speaker's quest for wisdom as an elusive woman reflects Prov. 31:10 (compare v. 26 and the description of seductive Ms. Folly in Prov. 9:13-18). The chapter closes with the Teacher's acknowledgment that humans have pursued moral mischief on their own initiative, in direct conflict with their divinely created condition (v. 29).

8:1–9:12 The Teacher commends the prudence of civil obedience for several reasons, including the keeping of one's divinely witnessed promise and the authority of the king to punish those he deems traitors (though the king's lack of authority over the divinely determined "day of death" strips him of control over the ultimate fate of his subjects; 8:2-9).

That neither the wicked nor the righteous get what they deserve disturbs the Teacher. The righteous suffer the just deserts of the wicked, while the wicked enjoy the rewards due the righteous. The fact that these injustices occur does not destroy the Teacher's faith that, ultimately, the tables will turn in favor of the righteous (8:12-13). But human incomprehension of why God allows this topsy-turvy situation to continue leads the Teacher to repeat his conclusion that pleasure is the only redeeming element of life.

The first half of chapter 9 reemphasizes the injustice that the righteous and the wicked share the same ultimate fate, with the only comfort for the wise/righteous consisting in their deeds' resting "in the hand of God" (9:1). Verse 2 refers to the "clean" and the "unclean," terms that relate to ritual purity. Verses 4-6, 10 reflect the Old Testament view that death brings a halt to any robust existence.

Once again, the existentialist's answer to this crisis of fate consists in maintaining a posture not of pouting but of perpetual celebration, signified by the prescribed white clothes and oil-anointed head (9:8), and in living life to its fullest (v. 10). Present reality is all there is, says the Teacher. Since life is not fair, since time and chance eventually catch up with everyone, and since death strikes at an unpredictable time, seize the day for pleasure and enjoy life while you can.

9:13–11:6 A military vignette that demonstrates the power of wisdom over might illustrates the higher value of wisdom but also comments on the social prejudice that cancels wisdom's reward for the wise but poor (9:13-18). A good number of the proverbs that follow contrast wisdom and folly, and several find expression in modern sayings. In the biblical world, the direction "right" — the direction in which the wise

Koheleth, "son of David, and king in Jerusalem"; engraving by Gustave Doré

turn in 10:2 — signified the good, the place of honor (cf. Matt. 25:31-46; Mark 16:19).

11:7–12:8 The Teacher's Conclusion

In his concluding remarks, the Teacher uses light and darkness in association with youth and old age (11:7-8; 12:2). He encourages the young to follow their dreams and pursue their desires during the prime of life, but he also counsels their remembrance of God and mindfulness of the ultimate certainty of divine judgment (cf. 12:13-14). A series of metaphors in 12:3-5 describes an elderly person with weakened limbs; idle, sparse teeth; dimmed eyesight; diminished hearing; light slumber; fear of heights and pedestrian road hazards; whitened hair; impaired ambulation; and sexual impotence. Two metaphors for death follow in 12:6. As the speaker ponders humans' return to the dust from which God formed them (12:7), he again emphasizes his opening declaration of the impermanence of this earthly life (v. 8) — a plausibly hopeful note, considering the litany of life's shortcomings laid out by the Teacher.

12:9-14 Postscript

This postscript presents the interpretive guide to the entire book, perhaps from the hand of a second wise man who has just quoted the confused, perplexed Teacher to his son. It affirms the limited truth of the Teacher's wisdom ("yes, life sucks and then you die — under the sun"), but points beyond. If the Teacher's preceding prescription, "Eat, drink, and be merry, for tomorrow we die," is the best medicine to suppress the symptoms of human cynicism, this concluding admonition represents the accompanying catalyst required to effect the medication's potency: "fear God and keep his commandments . . . because God will bring every act to judgment" (vv. 13-14).

Song of Songs

The Song of Songs, titled Song of Solomon in most English translations, concludes the collection of Wisdom literature in the Christian Bible. This poetic work focuses not on the religious beliefs or practices of ancient Israel, but on human love and lovemaking. Through the centuries, many Christians and Jews have sought to ease their discomfort with the inclusion in the biblical canon of this unashamedly sensual, openly erotic book by interpreting it as an allegory of Christ's relationship to his bride, the church, or of God's relationship to his chosen people, Israel. But even a cursory reading clearly reveals that these poems represent expressions of the very basic longings, fears, joys, and passions of a man and woman in love. Indeed, the Song of Songs contains not even one mention of God.

The Song approaches love and lovemaking from the standpoint of feelings and emotions, not technique or mechanics. Nevertheless, it contains timeless lessons for the lover. For example, compliments, not complaints, lead to sexually satisfying encounters. Verbal wooing generates sexual desire. Forcible intercourse becomes a nonissue in lovemaking done right. While the Song's presence in the Bible reaffirms the divine sanctioning of romantic love and sex between husbands and wives, this theme does not provide the framework for interpreting the rest of the Bible; nor does sexual fulfillment represent the ultimate goal of the human endeavor, contrary to the message of modern Western culture. Rather, the book's canonical setting invites us to say that the more we understand intimate love, the more we understand our relationship to God, often imaged as a marriage.

Literary Form

Scholars disagree on issues relating to the literary form of the book and the characters represented in it. Some see the work as a cohesive unit with a discernible progression of events leading up to and beyond a wedding night, while others view the poems as originally unrelated units strung together by an editor. Certain sections appear to feature a country girl and her beloved, a shepherd. Other poems identify a bride, at one point called the "Shulammite," and a groom, specified in one passage as King Solomon (3:6-11). Some scholars believe the book represents the thoughts and conversations of a single couple (the bride and groom); others who take the book as a unified whole see a country bride rejecting the advances of Solomon as she remains true to her shepherd-husband; and still others perceive multiple voices from different couples in a presumed collection of unrelated love poems. At several points, interjections by the "daughters of Jerusalem," brothers of the bride, and anonymous, secondary parties also surface.

Authorship

The opening verse of the Song identifies the work as Solomon's. Indeed, the book contains additional allusions to the king, and the likening of the woman in 1:9 to "a mare among Pharaoh's chariots" suggests Solomon's international commercial activities (cf. 1 Kgs. 10:28-29). Yet the title represents an editorial addition. Just as Ecclesiastes associates itself with the renowned wisdom tradition of Solomon although not claiming Solomonic authorship, so might the final editor(s) of the Song have sought to associate the work with the king famed for his love of women (cf. 1 Kgs. 11:3). Proposed dates of authorship for the Song range from ca. 950 to 200 B.C.

Interpreting the Song of Songs

The Song of Songs is one of the most perplexing books of the Old Testament and perhaps the most difficult to interpret. Several reasons account for the wide diversity of interpretations that have been proposed: (1) the lack of specific religious themes; (2) the erotic lines; (3) the vagueness of any plot; (4) the abundance of figurative language; and (5) the fact that the book is nowhere quoted in the New Testament so as to provide a guide for understanding it.

Six basic interpretations have been proposed. They are not necessarily mutually exclusive. (1) *Allegorical.* In this view, most prevalent throughout earlier church history, the literal details of the book are given an allegorical meaning. Thus the man is said to represent the Lord Jesus, and the bride his church, so that the real meaning of the book is Christ's love for his church. Those who took this approach felt the erotic details of the book were too "earthy" (and thus unspiritual) to be taken literally. Not surprisingly, the interpretation of details became quite diverse and fanciful. For example, the one who is brought into the king's chambers (Song 1:4) is said to be those whom Christ had wedded and brought into his church, and the two breasts in 4:5 are the Old and New Covenants. There were many subviews to the allegorical approach. For instance, some Roman Catholic scholars understood the extolling of the bride in 4:7 to have the Virgin Mary in view.

(2) *Typical.* Although similar to the allegorical view, it takes into account the historical setting of the book and is more restrained in interpretation. It is based on the idea in Scripture of Solomon as a type of Christ and the recognition that typology has a rightful place in the Bible. This would allow for understanding the book's message as a depiction of Christ's love for the church, but without pressing all the details for allegorical meaning.

(3) *Drama.* The first of two primary variations is the two-character drama, involving Solomon, or the man, and the Shulammite maiden, or the woman, in which the Song was originally meant to be acted and/or sung. A second variation is the three-character shepherd hypothesis, which proposes three primary characters to the drama: the man, the maiden, and a common shepherd. Supposedly, the maiden is really in love with the young shepherd, and the tension in the book stems from the man's efforts to win her away from him.

(4) *Mythological-cultic.* Certain critical scholars suggest that the Song derived from heathen cultic songs associated with pagan worship. Some take the view that the Song was really a celebration of the union of deities such as Ishtar and Tammuz, or perhaps associated with an ancient cultic funeral feast that extolled love as the only power greater than death (8:6).

(5) *Dream.* Here most, if not all, of the book's episodes are a reflection of the couple's feelings experienced in dreams (3:1-5; 5:2-8; and the refrains in 2:7 and 8:4). The characters are said to recall the early days of their married life together, though the woman struggles with insecurity and jealousy. Supposedly the book records the character and growth of the woman's love as a response to the purifying effect of the man's love.

(6) *Literal.* One of several different variations to this understands the book as primarily a celebration of the romantic and sexual relationship that God intended for a man and woman to have in a legal marriage sanctioned by God. One subview (the *anthology* view) understands the book to be a collection or anthology of love poems with no unifying thematic organization.

In another variation, the *literal-didactic* view, the Song is understood literally (thus underscoring the divinely intended beauty of God-ordained marriage), but the primary point of the book is found in the "moral lesson" that derives from the story, especially in the book's conclusion (8:5-14). The bride (who has carefully remained a virgin — 4:12; 8:8-10) feels insecure in their relationship precisely because the groom is a man of many lovers (6:8-9), and she yearns to be exclusively his (8:6-7). Thus the bride, the real heroine, delivers the great lesson of the book: there is a level of love far beyond sexual satisfaction, a love that is exclusive and possessive, and one that quite rightly feels jealous of all other intruders (2:15). Without such fidelity, the whole relationship is jeopardized, and the experiencing of love in its highest attainment is diminished.

J. Paul Tanner

1 The Best of Songs

This "best of songs" (the Hebrew is a superlative; v. 1) poetically expresses the mutual passion of a man and a woman in sensual terms. By itself, chapter 1 alludes to four of the five senses — touch, taste, smell, and sight — in conveying the emotional responses of people in love (for hearing, see 2:14). In verses 5-6, the woman defends her physical beauty despite being viewed by the shade-protected, urbanite "daughters of Jerusalem" as a lower-class working girl from the country. She compares her dark complexion to the black, goatskin tents of the nomadic Kedarites of the Sinai desert (v. 5) and attributes the neglect of her personal "vineyard" to her forcibly heavy workload. She has had neither time nor opportunity to take care of herself.

That the woman does not conform to ancient standards of beauty makes little difference to her man. He sees her through the eyes of love as "fairest among women" (v. 8), and he pays her the utmost compliment by likening her to his standout, chariot-pulling mare (v. 9). She answers by comparing him to a pouch of fragrant myrrh (an aromatic plant gum) suspended from her neck under her clothing. Women of means in the ancient Near East commonly wore such pouches in lieu of liquid perfume. The exchange of compliments continues as the man equates his beloved with the blossoms of the henna plant, used to manufacture a cosmetic dye, from En-gedi, site of a spring-fed oasis near the western shore of the Dead Sea and David's refuge during his flight from Saul (1 Samuel 24).

2 The Springtime Blossoming of Love

The beloved woman feels like a beautiful flower (v. 1), the "rose of Sharon" or crocus, one of the first flowers to bloom in the spring. Overcome with emotion, the woman longs for her lover's reclining embrace (v. 6). She pictures him running swiftly and agilely toward her and watching intently to spot her from a distance (vv. 8-9). She dreams of a private springtime rendezvous when he admires her appearance and revels in the sound of her voice. She censures all threats to the blossoming of their exclusive relationship (v. 15). Literally, "little foxes" did spoil vineyards (cf. Judg. 15:1-5; Samson accelerated their usual damage by using them to destroy Philistine fields). Verse 7 (also 3:5; 8:4) seems to acknowledge the need for love to blossom naturally and on its own (cf. 4:16; 7:10-13).

3 Manifestations of Love

Unable to tolerate another night of dreaming that she cannot find her beloved, the woman conducts a nocturnal search throughout the city. Once successful, she clings to him all the way home to her "mother's house," where the unwed woman would have lived and where the presence of a parental chaperone made it acceptable for the lovers to stay together (vv. 1-4).

Verses 6-11 describe the well-guarded wed-

"I am a rose of Sharon, a lily of the valleys" (Song 2:1).
(Wikimedia Commons)

ding procession of Solomon and liken the pedestrian caravan, which undoubtedly kicked up a good deal of dust, to columns of smoke rising up from the desert. David and Solomon used the famous cedar and cypress wood of Lebanon for their royal and religious building projects (2 Sam. 5:11; 1 Kgs. 5:1-10).

4:1–5:1 Portrait of a Wedding Night

The first six verses of chapter 4 take the form of a *wasf*, a convention of Arabic literature that uses metaphors from nature and craft to describe the human body (cf. 5:10-16; 6:4-7; 7:1-9). While visual comparisons normally dominate in the *wasf*, other senses also come into play, such as touch and taste. Today, Syrian weddings continue to incorporate the *wasf*.

In describing the dark locks of his bride's hair against the lighter background of her skin, the groom envisions from a distant perspective a flock of goats winding their way down Mount Gilead, an area of fertile pastureland east of the Jordan River. Newly shorn, freshly bathed, and therefore gleaming white ewes portray the bride's teeth, not one of which she has lost! For every tooth in the upper jaw, a matching "twin" corresponds in the lower (cf. 6:5b-7). Her "temples," likely her cheeks, remind him of the inside of a pomegranate because of their rosy color and the netlike shadow cast on them by her veil. He likens her regal, stately neck to the strong tower of David, a fortification structure in the defense wall around Jerusalem. The decorations on her elaborately ornamented bridal headdress, which would have hung down to cover her neck, remind him of military shields mounted on the city wall. He compares the feel of her breasts to that of fawns, which have soft hair and supple skin. He intends to make love to her all day (v. 6).

The smitten groom continues to excite the bride's sexual desire by extolling her complete appeal to him. Not only does she look and feel perfect, but she also smells and tastes wonderful. His references to Lebanon (north of Canaan), Amana (possibly a river in Syria), Senir, and Hermon (mountains on Canaan's border with Lebanon) summon her to leave all outside thoughts and fears behind as they enjoy each other's love. The groom calls his bride "sister," an ancient term of endearment (vv. 10, 12). He describes her virginity metaphorically as a "locked garden," inside which grow all manner of sensual pleasures (v. 12). Her sexual desire naturally and auspiciously aroused, she invites him to feast in the garden of her body, which she now calls his, and he satisfies himself liberally. The time for the ultimate expression of love has come to fruition. The last two lines of 5:1 represent the encouragement of the bride's and groom's mutual sexual enjoyment by knowing outsiders.

5:2–6:3 Departure and Pursuit

In a second bad dream, the man searches out the woman, who has already gone to bed. By the time she answers his knocking at the door, he has gone away. Emotionally frustrated, she pursues him on foot. After suffering blows from the night watchmen, she enlists the women of the city to communicate a message to her elusive beloved: she is sick with love for him. The *wasf* (see 4:1–5:1) resurfaces in verses 10-16 as she describes her one "among ten thousand": thick, curly black hair (v. 11); soft eyes that sparkle against their white background (v. 12); sweet-smelling cheeks and tasty lips (v. 13); a washboard abdomen (v. 14); and rock-strong legs (v. 15). He has the Midas look from head to toe (vv. 11, 14-15), and his physique, magnificent as the anciently famous cedars of Lebanon, makes him as wholly desirable to her as the bride in 4:7 is to the groom.

6:4-13 The Uniqueness of the Beloved

The groom compares the beauty of his bride to Tirzah ("pleasantness"), initial capital of the northern kingdom of Israel (1 Kgs. 16:23), and to Jerusalem, capital of the southern kingdom of Judah. When she looks at him, he can't think straight (v. 5a). The theme of the beloved's uniqueness reappears in verses 8-9, where for the groom neither queens nor concubines nor countless maidens can compare with his "perfect" bride (cf. 1:9; 5:10). Even the competition recognize her exceptional qualities (vv. 9-10) and find her beauty compelling (v. 13).

The identification of the woman as "Shulam-mite" (v. 13) is unclear. It should not be linked with the Shunammite beauty, Abishag, who nursed David in his old age (1 Kgs. 1:3-4). It may be a feminine parallel to the name Solomon or connote "peace" or "wholeness," from its Hebrew root *shalom*.

7 The Bride's Beauty Extolled Again

The groom further describes intimate features of the bride's body as he extols her beauty, again in *wasf* style. Curvaceous hips, a rounded belly, and a stately nose contribute to his ideal of the female form. Heshbon (v. 4) was the former Amorite capital in Transjordan (Num. 21:26). Carmel (v. 5), where Elijah challenged the prophets of Baal, refers to the range of mountains that rises eastward from the Mediterranean Sea in the area of modern Haifa. Likening his bride's hair to "purple" threads signifies a royal look.

The bride, who has saved her love for the groom, responds to his expressed desire by summoning him to the country, where she promises to give herself to him sexually. The springtime setting and the mention of the man-drake herb raise the notion of fertility (cf. Gen. 30:14-22).

8 The Compulsion and Discipline of Love

The bride knows that the social mores of her day prohibit the public display of affection be-tween spouses, but not between siblings; hence the wish that her husband were "like a brother" to her. She imagines an impromptu kiss leading to their reclining embrace in romantic privacy.

The groom recalls his "awakening" of the bride's love in the very location of her birth. She would not allow it to occur until the time was ripe (v. 4; cf. 2:7). The groom's admonition that she wear him as a "seal" over her heart expresses his desire for the unequivocal emotional bond with his bride and by extension for exclusive sexual intimacy with her. In antiquity, rings and cylinder seals, often hung on cords as necklaces, featured engravings of the owner's signature, initials, or other distinctive marks, the clay or wax impression of which identified the owner of the item bearing it (cf. Gen. 38:18). Verses 6-7 highlight the power of "love" in its broadest sense of total emotional and physical intimacy characterized by the same irresistible power as death and Sheol.

The bride's brothers chime in with a reflec-tion on their determination to guard their sister's virginity during her physically immature youth (v. 8), in antiquity an important element in preserving the honor of the entire family (cf. Genesis 34). Family leaders arranged marriages for their eligible members, hence the brothers' reference to the "day when she is spoken for."

In confirming her chaste behavior as an unmarried woman, the bride compares her breasts to defense towers incorporated into a fortification wall. Unlike the members of Solo-mon's harem (v. 11, "a vineyard at Baal-hamon"), which caretakers oversee, the bride is mistress of the vineyard of her own body.

This book of love poetry concludes with ur-gent expressions of desire by an eager husband and wife. He longs to hear her voice, and she beckons that he hurry to her for a passionate reunion (vv. 13-14).

The Prophets

Prophets

The prophetic movement in the Old Testament has its beginning with Moses. Even though Abraham is called a prophet because he prayed for Abimelech (Gen. 20:7), the more technical sense of the prophet as a divine spokesperson applies to Moses, who received, spoke, and explained God's word to Israel.

The Pentateuch sets Moses apart as the one who mediates between God and Israel, distinguished before Israel as God's servant to whom he spoke face to face (Num. 12:6-8; Exod. 33:11).

Deuteronomy contains Moses' final giving of the Law to Israel before his death. The book records the transition of leadership from Moses to Aaron, the elders, and the priests. Further, the book anticipates not only the rise of the monarchy in Israel (Deuteronomy 17), but also the rise of a prophet "like Moses" (ch. 18). The basic definition of the prophet (Deut. 18:15-18) specifies an Israelite sent by the Lord, with unique authority to which Israel must respond positively, while shunning the oracles and power plays of diviners and magicians (vv. 9-14). God's prophet is "like Moses," entrusted with the divine oracles, communicates them, and attests to them through signs even when this requires his own suffering for the purpose of bringing Israel back to the Lord (cf. Jeremiah).

The era after Moses and Joshua is characterized by the rare occasions when God spoke to his people (1 Sam. 3:1). It was not until Samuel that the prophetic voice was heard again throughout Israel (1 Sam. 3:20). Samuel truly was a prophet "like Moses" who left his mark on the history of Israel as a godly servant of the Lord (see 1 Samuel 12).

A radical change took place under Samuel, however. Israel demanded a king, and the Lord gave in. With the rise of kingship, the prophet turned to minister God's word from the people at large to the anointed king (Samuel to Saul, Nathan to David). The "court prophets" were consulted by the Israelite kings in order to determine God's will in battle (cf. 1 Samuel 28). The prophet was God's spokesperson as well as a royal advisor.

Kingship in Israel and Judah was generally corrupt, and gradually the prophet became

Statue of Elijah at Muhraka, highest peak of Mount Carmel, commemorating his victory over the prophets of Baal. *(Wikimedia Commons)*

the antagonist of the king. The stories of Elijah and Elisha illustrate the tensions between kings and prophets, which came to a peak during the ministry of Elijah (cf. his challenge of idolatry at Mount Carmel, 1 Kings 18). Then at Mount Horeb Elijah called on God to demonstrate his justice to unfaithful Israel (1 Kings 19). The prophet had become the "accuser" of God's people, *afflicting the comfortable."*

In response to Elijah's accusation, God proclaimed an oracle of judgment. The prophets' accusation and God's determination of judgment characterize the message of the *classical or literary prophets,* who, in the tradition of Moses and Elijah, serve as divine spokespersons as well as accusers. But also stemming from God's oracle to Elijah, the classical prophets *comfort the afflicted* or poor, who constitute the "remnant," and this is a major theme in the prophets. The nature of the God of Israel dictates judgment, even within Israel. It is also the basis of hope, as God's faithfulness to his promises is the sure foundation of the continuance of Israel.

The classical prophets, like their predecessors, are characterized by their relevance to the community to whom they minister God's word. They speak the language of the people and express themselves in rhetorical devices that reveal not only their mastery of the language but also the power of imagination. Through simile and metaphor, they appeal to their audience to "re-imagine" their relationship with the Lord. They refer to issues, political alliances, and circumstances that were relevant to their contemporaries. The prophets are first and foremost representatives of their own age and address God's word to their age. The language, images, references, and issues of the prophets communicate God's word in space and time; therefore, it is essential to know the background of the prophets and of their contemporaries: their social, political, and ethical world.

Prophecy

The *literary or classical prophets* are part of a movement that lasted for 300 years, from Amos (ca. 760 B.C.) to Malachi (ca. 450). This period includes the separate existence of the two kingdoms, the fall of Samaria (722), Judah's continuance for another century, the fall of Jerusalem (587), the exile, restoration (536), and the messages of hope (Haggai and Zechariah) as well as of doom (Malachi) given to the postexilic nation.

The prophetic movement differentiates itself through the distinctive contribution of each prophet and by the context of his ministry. The movement also reveals an inner, organic unity in the message of all the prophets. Understanding this dynamic interplay between the uniqueness of each of God's servants and the connectiveness of the prophetic message as a whole helps the modern reader better engage with the prophetic books.

The reader is best prepared to study the prophets by asking three sets of questions. First, what is the historical, social, religious, and political context in which *the prophet* spoke? Related to this is the chronological relationship among the prophets. Did the prophet live before, during, or after the Babylonian exile? If before the exile, is he primarily addressing Israel or Judah? If after the exile, what is his stance toward the new nation?

Second, how does *the book* unfold structurally the message of the prophecy? The prophetic speeches originated from the prophetic words spoken to a variety of audiences at different times throughout his ministry. The writing of the oracles into a book still reflects the prophet's speeches to particular audiences, but the composition and structuring of the messages in book form now address another audience, the readers, to whom God's word comes in a new historical context. The reader must connect the parts by understanding the literary genres, the literary and stylistic devices, and the distinctive literary features of the book, and the message of each part.

Third, what is the distinctive contribution of the prophetic book to the unfolding of the larger picture of *salvation history?* The answer requires a consideration of the message of the prophets, the relationship of the message of a given prophet to that of other prophets, how the prophetic message anticipates the message of the New Testament, and how the prophetic expectation is transformed in the light of the coming of Jesus Christ.

The prophetic message is a distinct *application of God's will* to a particular people living in a definite historical situation. The "predictions" of the prophets are not so much "foretellings" in a specific sense. Their words set into motion a course of events that begins with their own time and extends to the second coming of the Lord Jesus. The prophecies regarding the exile fold into the

Prophets of Israel
Prophets of Judah
Prophets of the Exile
Prophets of the Postexilic Period
Hosea
Amos
Jonah (?)
Isaiah
Jeremiah
Micah
Nahum
Habakkuk
Zephaniah
Jeremiah
Ezekiel
Daniel
Obadiah
Haggai
Zechariah
Malachi
Joel (?)

larger topic of the day of the Lord, as do the judgments on specific nations. There is no exhaustive fulfillment of God's word until the consummation. The imagery of particular judgments often has cataclysmic, cosmic, and universal dimensions. The message of judgment, while given in a definitive historical context, cannot be restricted to a particular era. The prophetic message of affliction and consolation is relevant as long as wicked people twist God's reign of justice and the righteous suffer. Similarly, the effective range of the oracles of salvation takes us from the days of the prophets to include the restoration of Israel after the exile, the first coming of Jesus, the age of the church, and finally the grand salvation of creation: the new heaven and earth.

The prophets are witnesses to the coming of the *kingdom of God* and to the fall of human powers. Their realistic portrayal of human corruption, oppression, limitations, and vulnerability is relevant for any age. But more than that, they witness to the inauguration of the kingdom of God that will bring about a radical transformation in human political, religious, economic, and social structures. Similarly, the prophets are candid critics of the descendants of David, many of whom have become corrupt and oppressive. The new age requires a new kind of spirit in the house of David. Many of the *"messianic"* prophecies speak directly to their current situation. Isaiah's prophecy of the child that will be born whose kingdom will be characterized by justice, righteousness, and peace is an implicit criticism of Ahaz (Isa. 9:6-7; cf. ch. 7). The presentation of Hezekiah (chs. 36–37) suggests that the prophecy of the child finds its realization in Hezekiah, but Hezekiah's reign was in the end also marred by political wranglings (ch. 39), and he too invites God's judgment (vv. 6-7). The fulfillment-in-time leads the reader to look for a reality in his own time. Several generations after Hezekiah's death, the godly looked at King Josiah as a potential candidate. But when Josiah died at a young age, he had not brought about the kingdom of justice, righteousness, and peace. None of his successors did, and then came the exile.

Each prophet contributes his own perspective to the message of human sinfulness and the need for the purification of humanity, the coming of the kingdom of God, the messianic age (with its justice, righteousness, and peace), and the remnant. Isaiah provoked Judah to jealousy by the image of Gentiles coming to Zion (Isa. 2:2-5) and thereby anticipates Paul's teaching on the inclusion of the Gentiles to stir the Jews to faith (Romans 9–11). The same prophet also presented the theme of Gentile inclusion in a variety of other ways (56:1-8; 61:5; 66:21). Other prophets (Zephaniah, Zechariah) made their own contribution to the theme or ignored it (Ezekiel). Yet all prophets are in agreement that the kingdom of God, the messianic kingdom, and the remnant distinguish themselves by the Spirit's transformation of a world characterized by justice and righteousness (Mic. 6:8; cf. Hos. 6:6).

Against the background of the Old Testament prophets, the reader will be better positioned to understand the message of the New Testament. Jesus summarizes the message of the Old Testament when he rebukes the Pharisees for having "neglected the weightier matters of the law: justice and mercy and faith" (Matt. 23:23). Jesus called on his contemporaries to prepare for the coming of God's kingdom (4:17), inviting the remnant to persevere, thirsting, hungering, weeping, and waiting (5:3). He taught them to pray for the kingdom (6:9) and to seek it (v. 33). Jesus connects the kingdom, himself, and justice and righteousness.

Jesus also corrects and transforms the expectations raised in the prophets. The prophets say little about angels, heaven and hell, or the resurrection. Jesus explains each of these topics. The greatest surprise is in his claim to be the King of Israel, the true Davidide. He teaches and heals, is humble and suffers abuse, and dies in the end. He has no army or political ambitions. Yet the Gospel writers witness to Jesus' claim that he is the true and only Messiah, with whom God is pleased. He has received authority over creation (John 13:3). No one can come to the Father except through Jesus Christ (John 14:6), who has received authority to judge and to save (5:26-27). Jesus is the Messiah (Acts 2:36), whose kingdom is not of this world. Nevertheless, he is the only legitimate ruler and will rule until all humans bow before him. The evidence of Jesus' messianic claims lies in his resurrection (1 Cor. 15:24-28).

The New Testament ends with the portrayal of Jesus' coming to vindicate the remnant and to avenge himself against their enemies (Revelation 19), as well as with the presence of God and the Lamb with the remnant in the New Jerusalem in the new creation (ch. 21). The blessing of Jesus rests upon them (Rev. 22:13-14).

The New Testament confirms rather than fulfills the message of the prophets (cf. 1 Peter 2). The prophets encouraged the godly to await the coming of the kingdom. This kingdom is confirmed in the exaltation of the Lord Jesus Christ at the right hand of the Father. Yet the members of his church still await the coming of the kingdom in glory and power, being assured that he who said "I am coming soon" (Rev. 22:20) will effect the transformation of all things. In this regard, the Old Testament prophets witness to a reality of God's kingdom in their time and beyond. So do Jesus and the apostles. The kingdom is here, but not yet here in its fullness. When the Scriptures are read in this manner, the message of the prophets connects with that of Jesus and the apostles. It is also transformed in the light of the coming of Jesus Christ.

FOR FURTHER READING

Blenkinsopp, Joseph A. *A History of Prophecy in Israel.* Philadelphia: Westminster, 1983.

Redditt, Paul L. *Introduction to the Prophets.* Grand Rapids: Eerdmans, 2008.

VanGemeren, Willem A. *Interpreting the Prophetic Word.* Grand Rapids: Zondervan, 1990.

Wilson, Robert R. *Prophecy and Society in Ancient Israel.* Philadelphia: Fortress, 1980.

WILLEM A. VANGEMEREN

Isaiah

The book of Isaiah heads the third major division of the Old Testament, the Prophets, containing books designated as "major" or "minor" based on their length. The prophets Isaiah, Amos, Hosea, and Micah lived in the 8th century B.C. Isaiah prophesied in his hometown of Jerusalem, and his prophetic career in the southern kingdom of Judah spanned over four decades.

Content

Chapters 1–39 of Isaiah include historical narratives, which proceed in roughly chronological order according to the man Isaiah's activities, prophecies of doom, and oracles of hope. Initial judgments against the hypocritical leaders in Jerusalem pave the way for oracles concerning the Syro-Ephraimite War during the rule of wicked King Ahaz and prophecies relating to the Philistine revolt against Assyria. This section ends by recording Isaiah's interactions with King Hezekiah during the Assyrian siege of Jerusalem. God's impending judgment constitutes the dominant theme of chapters 1–39, with the empire-building kingdom of Assyria constituting the threatened instrument of divine punishment.

By the beginning of chapter 40, however, Babylon has replaced Assyria as the dominant power in the ancient Near East. From here through the end of the book (ch. 66), the poetic oracles presuppose Judah's exile in Babylon, a period that started nearly a century and a half after Assyria's 722/21 conquest of the northern kingdom of Israel. In this last section of Isaiah, the theme of divine comfort for God's people takes over. Their time of judgmental punishment has passed, and restoration to the promised land via a "second exodus," this time from Babylon, holds for them a hopeful future. Some scholars believe that chapters 40–55 speak to the soon-to-be-released exiles in Babylon, while chapters 56–66 address the community of returnees in Judah/Jerusalem. In the New Testament, Jesus fulfills many of the prophecies of hope recorded in Isaiah.

Composition

Taken as an introduction to the book as a whole, Isa. 1:1 identifies the contents of the subsequent 66 chapters as the "vision" of 8th-century Isaiah. But modern scholars have challenged the traditional view that considers him the source of all the material contained in the book that bears his name. Though chapters 40–66 echo certain themes contained in chapters 1–39, they also contain specific, predictive prophecies that some scholars doubt Isaiah foretold. For example, they consider it unlikely that an 8th-century prophet not only predicted the 6th-century Persian king Cyrus's conquest of the Babylonian Empire but also named him specifically (see 44:28 and 45:1). Old Testament prophets normally directed their messages to contemporaries. For Isaiah to have directly addressed the Babylonian exiles (and perhaps returnees to Judah) pictured in chapters 40–66, his prophetic ministry would have to have extended well beyond the reign of Hezekiah (the last king mentioned in 1:1), and he would have to have lived for more than two centuries.

On the other hand, in this book God holds out his power to predict the future as proof of his divine supremacy (chs. 41, 44, 46, and 48). It is not unreasonable, therefore, to think that Isaiah mediated predictive messages as words from God and at times addressed audiences of future generations.

Those who do see multiple sources behind the text of Isaiah generally view the oracles in chapters 1–39 largely as originating with the prophet himself, while the narrative sections represent additions by later editors. Scholars suggest two general scenarios for the authorship of chapters 40–66: (1) A disciple of Isaiah ("Second Isaiah") authored chapters 40–66; (2) Second Isaiah authored chapters 40–55, and "Third Isaiah," perhaps a disciple of Second Isaiah, wrote chapters 56–66. Because Isaianic traditions characterize all these chapters, they became appended to the first part of the book and attributed to the 8th-century Isaiah much like Ecclesiastes and the Song of Songs became associated with King Solomon, who embodied their respective themes of wisdom and love.

1–39 Impending Doom

1 Confronting Judah with a Choice Verse 1 locates the man Isaiah in Judah during the period of its 8th- and early 7th-century kings; establishes him as a visionary prophet (cf. ch. 6); and confirms his Hebrew heritage as the son of Amoz (not the prophet Amos). Isaiah begins his address in typical ancient Near Eastern treaty style by invoking heaven and earth as witnesses to an indictment in which the overlord, God, states his case against his vassal, Judah, whose people have violated the moral covenant he established with them through Moses at Mount Sinai. The designation of God as the "Holy One of Israel" (v. 4) anticipates the prophet's visionary call (cf. 6:3); this name occurs almost exclusively in Isaiah.

The prophet zeroes in on the southern kingdom's desperate state after the Assyrian destruction of 46 of Judah's outlying fortified cities (vv. 7-9; cf. 2 Kgs. 18:13). The capital, Jerusalem ("daughter Zion," v. 8), stands isolated. The defeat of the northern kingdom by Assyria in 722 left Judah as sole survivor of the original 12 tribes, and Isaiah develops this "remnant" theme through the first major division of the book (v. 9). Yet Judah, whose extreme disobedience earns for it the nicknames "Sodom" and "Gomorrah" (v. 10; cf. 3:9), has failed to learn the lesson from the fate of the northern tribes. The hypocritical Judahite leaders sicken God by carrying out religious rites and ceremonies mechanically (vv. 10-15; cf. 1 Sam. 15:22). In spelling out the practical evidences of sincere repentance, Isaiah repeats the prominent

Deuteronomic theme of caring for society's disenfranchised, specifically orphans and widows (v. 17; contrast v. 23; cf. Deut. 14:28-29). The good news is that national repentance will effect divine cleansing of sins otherwise indelible (v. 18; "scarlet" and "crimson" dyes were colorfast). But continued rebelliousness will bring about violent devastation (cf. the covenantal curses in Deut. 28:15-68). God vows to purify the harlot city Jerusalem by crushing his enemies, who include unrepentant bribe-lovers (v. 23) and participants in Canaanite religious rites at pagan shrines in oak/terebinth groves (vv. 29-30).

2–4 The Purification Process and Its Peaceful Outcome Isaiah describes the outcome of the purification process by picturing Jerusalem ("the mountain of the house of the Lord," 2:2) as the multinational center of worship and government, ruled by God and characterized by everlasting peace (2:2-4; cf. the almost identical Mic. 4:1-3). The prophecy previews the formal incorporation of the Gentiles in the new covenant inaugurated by Christ (see Rom. 11:11-12).

God will humble his defiantly proud people to accomplish this ideal. They have violated God's laws by engaging in the magical arts, forbidden in Lev. 19:31, and by making alliances with foreigners, prohibited in Exod. 34:12-17 to prevent the Hebrews from slipping into the worship of false gods. They have amassed material wealth, multiplied war machinery (2:7), and made idols to worship (2:8). But they will run for cover at God's terrifying demonstration of majesty and power as he levels their pride, manifested ages before by the Tower of Babel and now embodied in symbols such as the famous cedars of Lebanon, which Solomon used in building the temple and royal palace (1 Kings 5; 7); the mighty oaks of Bashan, located in northern Transjordan; and the ships of Tarshish, which Solomon used to import gold and exotic goods (2 Chr. 9:21).

In chapter 3, Isaiah gives specific examples of how God will humble the disobedient. Famine, drought, incompetent leadership, and social strife will all contribute to the downfall of Judah's flagrantly wicked "Sodomites," who have brought their fate upon themselves (3:1-9).

Isaiah pictures a "world turned upside down" — women ruling over men and socially powerless children in the role of oppressors (3:12) — as God's judgment against leaders who have plundered the poor to become rich and thereby crushed the nation (3:13-15). God will reverse the fortunes of the haughty, seductive, elaborately adorned Jerusalemite women and the kingdom's mighty warriors alike. Judah's male population will be so severely depleted that women will compete to marry the same man in a desperate search for the social acceptance afforded by marriage (4:1).

A righteous remnant (the "branch of the Lord," 4:2) will survive the divine judgment (cf. 11:1). God will reverse his abandonment of the "house of Jacob" (2:6), and the Lord will signify his renewed residence among the remnant in Zion in a cloud cover by day, smoke and a fire by night (cf. Exod. 13:21-22; 19:16-18; 40:34-38); the dedication of the temple (1 Kgs. 8:10-12); and the second coming of Christ (see, e.g., Matt. 24:30; Luke 21:27; Rev. 1:7). Chapters 11–12 further develop the theme of the purged and peaceful kingdom introduced here.

5 A Prophetic Parable: The Song of the Vineyard

Verses 1-7 feature God as the "well-beloved" and the Hebrew nation as his "vineyard." (In v. 7 "the house of Israel" refers to the descendants of all 12 of Jacob's/Israel's sons; cf. Jesus' parable in Matt. 21:33-41.) God carefully prepares the soil, plants the choicest vines, makes provision for pressing and storing the wine, and anticipates a good harvest (righteousness). The vineyard, however, produces only worthless grapes (wickedness). God calls the "inhabitants of Jerusalem and people of Judah" to self-judgment ("What more could I have done to ensure a good crop?") and announces his plan to destroy the vineyard (contrast ch. 27).

Isaiah's prophetic woes (vv. 8-23) specify some of the nation's sins: appropriation of land (prohibited in Deut. 19:14), drunkenness, injustice, and pride. God's judgment will severely curb the fertility of the people's vineyards and fields, and Sheol, the abode of the dead, will swallow up the starved (v. 14). Judgment will also come in the form of exile. God will summon a swift, indefatigable, ever-ready predator, epitomized by the 8th-century Assyrian army (vv. 26-30), to carry out the covenantal curses (cf. Deut. 28:15-68).

6 Isaiah Responds to His Vision of God

The account of Isaiah's vision reveals the catalyst for his prophetic ministry: a religious conversion. As with other Old Testament figures, Isaiah's sight of God issues in fear for his life (cf. Exod. 3:6; 33:20), and the overwhelming holiness of God generates his confession of sin (cf. Job 42:5-6). Sanctification and forgiveness, mediated by heavenly beings called "seraphim" (mentioned in the Bible only here), issue in Isaiah's eagerness to volunteer for a prophetic mission, the seeming futility of which becomes immediately obvious (contrast Moses' reluctance in Exod. 3:10–4:17). Isaiah must deliver a message of impending disaster to his already doomed fellow Judahites, whose persistent hardening of heart has so dulled their moral sensitivity that nothing will prompt them to heed the warning (cf. Exod. 4:21; 7:3; 8:15, 32). Jesus quotes verses 9-10 when he explains to his disciples the reason for his use of parables (Mark 4:12-13). Judah's reason for hope does not completely fade away, however, for a "stump" refined by fire will remain (v. 13).

"My beloved had a vineyard on a very fertile hill" (Isa. 5:1). *(www.HolyLandPhotos.org)*

7–8 Isaiah Urges Faith but Predicts Doom

Shortly after Uzziah's death (ca. 736/35) and the call of

Isaiah, the prophet challenges to faith Judah's new king, Uzziah's grandson Ahaz, whose embrace of paganism went beyond even that of the northern kings (see 2 Kings 16; 2 Chronicles 28). Probably because Ahaz appeared to favor the Assyrians, Judah's neighbors to the north — Israel and Syria, whose geographical location made them more vulnerable than Judah to Assyrian invasion — jointly seek to overthrow the royal "house [dynasty] of David" represented by Ahaz and to place on the Judahite throne their man, "the son of Tabeel" (probably a Transjordanian who shared their opposition to Assyria). The coalition's attempt to take Jerusalem fails, but their military forces remain poised to attack Judah from within the territory of Ephraim, by then the most southerly of the northern tribes. God sends to the terrified Ahaz the prophet Isaiah, who delivers a message of reassurance and a challenge to be faithful to the Lord. Isaiah and his son Shear-jashub ("a remnant shall return") approach the king by the road to the Fuller's ("laundryman's") Field (7:3).

Isaiah's message is a divinely assured prediction that the coalition will fail to defeat Judah. Also, in the not too distant future "Ephraim" (7:8), here the entire northern kingdom, will itself fall. To ensure his security, Ahaz needs only to exercise faith in God rather than making alliances with foreign powers. In a clear show of false piety, Ahaz refuses God's offer to grant a sign of the king's choosing as a guarantee of the predicted outcome, for a sign would seal his obligation to faith (7:12; cf. Deut. 6:16). Ahaz then appeals to Assyria for help — a move that rid the southern kingdom of the immediate threat from Syria and Israel but at the same time severely limited Judah's independence by effectively subjecting the southern kingdom to Assyrian control (2 Kings 16).

God will not let Ahaz off so easily, however, and through Isaiah he provides an unsolicited sign, which will unfold over time: a "maiden" (the Hebrew word means merely a "young woman"; the Greek translation of the Old Testament, which Matthew quotes, indicates specifically a "virgin") will bear a son and call him Immanuel ("God with us"). The name will signify both God's initial protective presence with Judah and his eventual judgment of the southern kingdom (7:14). Before the boy can tell right from wrong, Syria and Israel will cease to exist as independent kingdoms. In fact, Syria fell to the Assyrians in 732; Israel's northern territory was occupied by the Mesopotamian superpower beginning in 734; and in 722 the northern kingdom crumbled completely. Like many other Old Testament prophecies, the divine sign carries a double meaning — one for the current day and one with future significance in the incarnate Christ (Matt. 1:23).

Isaiah goes on to predict bad times for Judah, too. Egypt and Assyria will humiliate and subordinate Judah — a fate signified by the shaving of the head, body, and facial hair (7:20). Briars and thorns will replace the kingdom's valuable vineyards. Ironically, Judah's impoverished, severely reduced population will enjoy more milk and honey than they can stomach, with these symbols of abundance constituting their *only* means of sustenance.

As with other Old Testament prophets, Isaiah's ministry involved symbolic actions in addition to oracles. Here he fathers a son by "the prophetess" (presumably, his wife) and gives him a name that predicts the doom awaiting not only Syria and Israel, but Judah, too (8:1-3). Again the Assyrians are the instrument of God's judgment, which neither human planning nor protective measures will thwart (8:6-10). The prophet pictures the invaders as an unstoppable flood of water overflowing the banks of the Euphrates River in contrast to the gently flowing "waters of Shiloah" (most likely an aqueduct outside Jerusalem). Isaiah's new son, "Mahershalal-hash-baz" ("swift booty, speedy prey"), becomes the inseparable twin of "Immanuel" in his representation of God's judging presence among his unfaithful people.

Isaiah instructs his students to preserve a record of his prophecy, which comes from God, and to resist seeking advice by occult practices. Still, he recognizes that God's judgment will not produce the chosen nation's immediate repentance. The famished but defiant people will gaze heavenward as if in prayer, but their parting communication before entering the darkness of exile will be cursing rather than remorse (8:21-22).

Nations, Peoples, and Empires (Part 1)

Ancient Israelites and Judahites encountered many nations, peoples, and empires throughout the course of their history. Four prominent groups affected the economic, political, religious, and social experience of the Hebrews.

Canaanites

Urban settlements along trunk highways and at ports on or near the eastern shore of the Mediterranean Sea were primarily inhabited by Canaanites, who often experienced Egyptian forced labor and taxation throughout the Late Bronze Age. Egypt's records seem to indicate that Canaan's principal eastern boundary was the Jordan River and that Transjordan was ordinarily not reckoned a portion of Canaan. Thus the term "Canaan" designated the combined territory of Phoenicia and Palestine west of the Jordan River, encompassing approximately modern Lebanon and Israel. The terrain of fertile valleys and plains between hills and mountains spawned a city-state form of government, with each urban fortification surrounded by smaller villages and the adjacent hinterland. Battered-earth ramparts characterized construction, as did gates designed with a smooth surface and a straight entrance to accommodate iron war chariots. (Canaan's monarchs and nobles evidently composed a military elite.) Underground drainage systems carried water away from not only these imposing gates but also palaces and temples. Canaanites produced pieces of jewelry from sheets and wires of gold and silver. Artisans carved ivory and bone for inlays in decorative furniture and further worked semiprecious gems. They sculpted both stone and metal into images of deities and guardian lions. Metallurgists cast bronze daggers, mirrors, swords, and tools. Potters made bowls, chalices, jars, jugs, and pots — besides figurines, incense burners, and masks used perhaps for spiritual purposes. Canaanites were enterprising traders and shippers, and they invented an alphabet that was destined to become the primary means of writing.

El was the supreme Canaanite deity, who created the planet and humans and begot gods and goddesses. Aged, he was noted for wisdom along with kindness and graciousness. El's wife was the holy Athirat, who conceived his children. Baal, clearly the most active deity in the Canaanite pantheon, brought rain plus lightning and thunder. He rather than his father, Dagon, was appointed king of the gods by grandfather El. Although Baal's chief consort was Anat, Astarte occasionally filled that role. Kothar-wa-Hasis, the divinities' artisan, built Baal's palace and made the magic clubs with which Baal defeated Yamm, god of the sea. The sun-goddess, Shapash, scorched the earth during the netherworld stay of Baal, who died and rose seasonally. Mot caused the temporary burial of Baal before his revival and

Astarte, Canaanite goddess of war and fertility and sometime consort of Baal, with her daughter; Iron Age I, ca. 1100 B.C. *(Richard Cleave, Pictorial Archive)*

was the primary death-god, but another named Resheph served as Shapash's porter at the time of her daily setting. Offerings to gods and goddesses included cattle, sheep, grain, wine, oil, and additional produce, considered food for the deities. Priests officiated over sacrifices held at temples. Canaanites prayed to communicate with the divine — Baal in particular being regarded an agent in history. The practice of divination involved inspection of livers and lungs, for example, and could be based on unnatural births of animals. Canaanites envisaged an existence after death, believing that the shades of the dead (or at least of deceased monarchs) were deified. While still alive, these rulers had the duty of protecting the poor, orphans, and widows and the requirement generally of maintaining a high ethical standard.

Egyptians

Located at Africa's northeastern tip, Egypt is sustained by the lushness of the Nile River and Delta, surrounded by desert on their east and west. Written on clay figurines in the shape of bound prisoners or on pottery bowls during the 12th Dynasty of the early 2nd millennium B.C., Execration Texts listed the names of various leaders and localities in Libya, Nubia, and Syria-Palestine and directed ritualistic curses against these foreigners. One hundred years afterward, Asiatic Hyksos infiltrators prospered and ruled as lords over Egyptian vassals. This occupation was a watershed in history, because until that point the Egyptians, despite periods of internal political chaos, had been free from invasion. The liberated 18th Dynasty's Amenhotep IV accompanied his indirectly expressed disdain for traditional cults by unquestionable signs of favor to the solar disk Aten alone. About 1350, he changed his own name to Akhenaten and, in Middle Egypt north of Thebes, established for his god a new worship center, Akhetaten (modern el-Amarna). Rather than attempting to annex property, the 10th-century Sheshonq I of the 22nd Dynasty preferred to despoil territories in Judah and Israel, an endeavor which had the advantage of providing needed booty in order to pay his army. A force of Jewish troops was maintained throughout the 5th century in the important garrison town of Elephantine at the First Cataract. They were absorbed into Egyptian society but also endured antagonism, which arose largely from local Egyptian resentment at the sacrifice of animals in Yahweh's shrine there.

The Egyptians organized their deities hierarchically, with the creator assuming the role of king of gods and goddesses. Likewise, the supreme god became a controller of time and human destiny. In theory the pharaoh (himself viewed as divine) was the sole liturgist in all sanctuaries, but in practice this position was delegated to priests functioning as royal deputies. The masses worshipped the deities of the state religion but additionally had minor patron deities not revered elsewhere. The last of the 10-day week in Egypt was a day off from work, thus offering an opportunity for common people to participate spiritually at a temple. In a more personal manner, the supernatural might become manifest through the medium of dreams. Individuals readily acknowledged that their bodily suffering could be due to a transgression against a god or goddess, to whom they begged for mercy. People had to live according to the concepts of justice and righteousness so they might be vindicated when standing before the heavenly tribunal for judgment, where their good qualities were weighed against their wrong behaviors. One aspect of the afterlife was the simple continuation of existence in the tomb, where family members left food and drink for the deceased's spirit. The soul could ascend to the sky and travel with the sun-god, or the ghost could exert influence upon a living human being.

Hittites

The Hittites were a people of Indo-european origin who penetrated into Anatolia probably before or around 2000 B.C. and became a great power of the ancient Near East in the following period. During the 13th century several battles with the Egyptians led to treaties and marriages as a diplomatic stabilization of the boundaries of their spheres of influence in Syria-Palestine. Although Hittites had put an end to the independent existence of the Hurrian kingdom of Mitanni a century earlier, their own empire collapsed merely 100 years later. Nevertheless, states particularly around northern Syria maintained Hittite traditions until the 7th century. The Hittite king was designated the governor of the storm-god, their pantheon's most important male figure. A clear relationship also existed between the queen and the sun-goddess, the leading female divinity and the storm-god's consort. When a king died, he became a god. As the land's supreme judge, the king invited persons who believed themselves unjustly treated in lower courts to appeal to his court, while serious cases (such as treason) which carried the death penalty were always referred there. In addition to the corpus of laws governing all citizens, there were rule books for the performance of every major governmental office. Prices and fines were measured in weights of silver. At least in theory, the law provided for periodic remitting of debts and manumitting of slaves. High esteem was attached to the ability to write; scribes are the only group of individuals aside from kings for whom genealogies were produced.

Every city and town in the

Hittite domains had at least one temple, served by both male and female cult personnel. Priests could marry and were exempted from many taxes and forced labor. Proper conduct of a cult was essentially conforming faithfully to carefully transcribed archaic ritual: a succession of acts at moments dictated by the liturgical calendar. The divine image to which worship was rendered could be a stela or a statuette (a bull for the storm-god, a deer for protector gods, a lion for war gods). Several Hittite rituals entailed lowering offerings for underworld deities

Sennacherib on his throne in camp, conferring with officials on the Assyrian conquest of Lachish; relief from his palace at Nineveh, 930 B.C. *(British Museum)*

into specially prepared pits in the ground. Other rites dispatched a small animal bearing away sin or impurity. While daily worship occurred at each of the temples, festivals were special times when the cult statue of the divinity was transported in procession through the streets; entertained with music, dancing, acrobatics, and athletic events; and offered a wide variety of sacrifices. The two main Hittite seasonal holidays marked the harvesting or planting of a crop and were celebrated for three to five weeks or longer in the spring and autumn. During these special occasions the king and queen visited sanctuaries in the capital and the most important nearby towns. With support from abundant clergy, both monarchs enacted worship on behalf of the gods and goddesses. The final religious season featured ceremonies on the winter solstice and the new year.

Mesopotamians

Mesopotamia sits within the boundaries of modern Iraq, straddling the Euphrates and Tigris rivers and their tributaries. The dwellers of the Babylonian plain in the south invented artificial irrigation systems in order to regulate the erratic water supply from rainfall and flooding so that crop production was possible. Mesopotamians bred horses from the middle of the 2nd millennium B.C. onward, and for swift communication the Assyrians in the north established a system of relay posts where fresh horses were kept at the ready 24 hours a day. In an emergency, messages could be relayed even faster by a system of observation towers and fire signals. Assyria also established a number of merchant colonies in Anatolia in order to promote trade. Mesopotamians eventually replaced their Akkadian language with Aramaic, which by the 1st millennium had been adopted throughout the entire Near East as the international tongue. In 853 a major Syro-Palestinian coalition including chariots and infantry from the kingdom of Israel confronted Assyria's Shalmaneser III at the battle of Qarqar on the Orontes River and in later years continued to resist his advances. Babylonia ultimately eliminated Assyria, defeated Egypt, and annexed Syria-Palestine ca. 600. Politically, Mesopotamian states were absolute monarchies, but had three checks to power: religion, legal precedent, and the attitudes of the nobility. Through his law code, the Babylonian Hammurabi, to whom any subject possessing a just grievance had access, typified the royal concern for justice. But all disputes (even homicide) were between private individuals seeking punishment and compensation, inasmuch as the state took no one to court. Only rarely did a woman act in a legal or business transaction on her own behalf, because she had virtually no rights as an individual. The art form most associated with Assyria is the bas-relief carving on slabs of stone, which were placed on edge to panel palace corridors and rooms. A Babylonian doctor could perform certain kinds of surgery, such as operations on the eye, and Babylonian scholars employed a system based on the number 60, which survives as hours with 60 minutes and circles with six times that many degrees.

The majority of chief deities of the pantheon were male (Adad, Ashur, Enlil, Marduk, Nabu, Nergal, Shamash, Sin), with the notable exception of Ishtar. By far the most important Mesopotamian festival was the New Year ceremony, including a coronation at which the right of the king to rule for another year was divinely confirmed and the princes and nobles renewed their loyalty oaths.

On this New Year holiday the high priest slapped the king's face and pulled him by the ears to remind the monarch that he was a humble servant of the deities, who were the sole guarantors of nature's renewal. Everyone, even the lowest slave, had a personal god or goddess, whose rank related directly to the human's rank. Death and what followed were very gloomy subjects in Mesopotamian thought, for there was no concept of a happy afterlife.

For Further Reading

Hoerth, Alfred J., Gerald L. Mattingly, and Edwin M. Yamauchi, eds. *Peoples of the Old Testament World.* Grand Rapids: Baker, 1994.

Sasson, Jack M., ed. *Civilizations of the Ancient Near East.* 4 vols. New York: Scribner's, 1995.

Wiseman, Donald J. *Peoples of Old Testament Times.* Oxford: Clarendon, 1973.

EDWIN C. HOSTETTER

9:1-7 The Future Hope Chapter 9 immediately moves us from the Immanuel of judgment to the Immanuel of hope, who transforms the dark days of exile into an eternity of light. Of the northern tribes, Zebulun and Naphtali fell first in the overwhelming Assyrian assault on Israel. The "Way of the Sea," an important ancient trade route connecting Egypt and Syria, passed through the territory of these tribes — the first to fall, but also the first to recover (v. 1). Isaiah compares the nation's future deliverance from divinely wrought oppression to the outnumbered Hebrews' Gideon-led victory over nomadic Midianite raiders (v. 4; see Judges 7).

The symbolism of a prophetic child carries over from chapters 7 and 8, now as a herald of hope for a coming kingdom of everlasting peace *(shalom),* which in Hebrew thought means not only the absence of war and strife, but also justice, righteousness, and covenantal blessings. The names of the eternal occupant of the revitalized Davidic throne indicate that he is none other than God himself (v. 6; cf. Luke 1:31-35).

9:8–10:4 Israel's Self-Inflicted Sentence The message of hope leaves off as quickly as it appeared. "Jacob" and "Ephraim and the inhabitants of Samaria," Israel's capital city, are terms for the entire northern kingdom, which has invited intensified divine judgment through its people's arrogant refusal to repent in the face of God's initial punishments (9:8-13). Isaiah condemns Israel's civic leaders and false prophets for leading the people astray, yet God holds even socially powerless individuals ("orphans" and "widows," v. 17) responsible for their godlessness and evil actions (9:14-17). The rampant wickedness in the northern kingdom has poised it to self-destruct in a frenzy of intertribal strife (9:18-21). In the coming "day of punishment," Israel's corrupt, oppressive leaders will find nowhere to run and hide (10:1-4).

10:5-34 Assyria Cut Down to Size God will show his anger with intense but measured punishment, which will leave a "remnant" of survivors (vv. 5-7, 20ff.). As the instrument of his wrath, however, the arrogant Assyrians will pursue a search-and-destroy mission that oversteps the bounds of the divine plan. Further, they will claim success for themselves, while discounting the God who ensures their victories. But Assyria will no more escape divine judgment for its haughty disregard of the Lord than will God's own people, whom he uses the Assyrians to punish (vv. 17-19, 34; cf. 37:36-38; 2 Kgs. 19:35-37).

The judgmental purge will produce a positive outcome as the righteous remnant of Israel returns, never again to rely on Assyria (vv. 21-23). In urging the southern kingdom to take courage, Isaiah alludes to the Hebrews' history of Egyptian slavery and divine deliverance (vv. 24, 26). Though Jerusalem's defeat by the Assyrians will appear imminent, God will stop them in their tracks. The hill-country cities listed in verses 28-32 occur in the order of a northern approach to Jerusalem from about 10 miles away. Actually, the oracle's purpose is symbolic and inspirational — Sennacherib and the Assyrian army marched on Jerusalem from the southwest (36:2).

11–12 The World Renewed Continuing with the theme of hope, Isaiah paints a picture of a renewed world order that recalls both the moral state of creation prior to the fall and the political state of the Hebrew nation during the height of the united monarchy (cf. 65:17-25; Revelation 21). In fulfillment of the Davidic covenant (2 Samuel 7), a spirit-endued descendant of Jesse, father of King David, will rule this new world with the ability to discern between good and evil) and with reverence for God, which produces righteous behavior. Appearances and hearsay will carry no weight in the court of this fair and faithful judge, to whom the nations will flock for justice (11:3, 10). In his kingdom, hatred will turn to harmony (11:6-9).

Isaiah portrays the renewal of the kingdom in political and geographical terms easily understandable to his audience. God will gather back to Canaan the remnant of his chosen people dispersed in far-off lands, from Ethiopia (Cush) and Egypt ("Pathros" refers to southern Egypt) to the southwest, Hamath to the north, and Mesopotamia (Assyria, Elam, and Shinar) to the northeast. The northern and southern tribes will reunite to reclaim the Philistine territory previously conquered by David and to repossess Transjordan. Neither the Sea of Egypt (possibly the Red Sea) nor the mighty Euphrates will hinder the exiles' homeward journey, which Isaiah likens to God's parting of the Red Sea during the exodus. The restored population's unbridled joy at God's deliverance will show itself in songs of praise and thanksgiving as a worldwide witness to God's greatness (ch. 12).

13–23 Oracles against the Nations These chapters contain a collection of oracles uttered at different times (e.g., 14:28; 20:1). Though at first glance they might suggest that God purposes permanently to punish the pagan nations, in part for their offenses against his chosen people, a closer look reveals that God ultimately intends to redeem for himself people of all nations and to restore universal peace to an entire world loyal to him alone (cf. 19:24-25). Ancient audiences probably found unimaginable the utter devastation of the overwhelmingly powerful nations whose demise the prophecies address.

13:1–14:23 (see also chs. 46–47) Babylon This oracle looks a century beyond the historical circumstances of Isaiah's day, when Babylon was still struggling to gain independence from the current Mesopotamian superpower, Assyria. Here, Babylon has already succeeded Assyria in that capacity, enslaved the Hebrews (14:1-3), and adopted the same self-sufficient posture that earned divine condemnation for the empire's prideful predecessor.

Isaiah portrays judgment day for the overconfident Babylonians as a battle scene, described as the foreboding "day of the Lord" (13:10). The divinely initiated purge will decimate the empire's population. In an indisputable demonstration of his sovereignty over the nations of the world, God will use Babylon's longtime allies, the Medes, as the instruments of his judgment. Cyrus's Medo-Persian army actually did overthrow the Babylonians in 539, the historical context of Isaiah 40–66. In 478 the Persian king Xerxes destroyed the city of Babylon, which had surrendered to Cyrus without a fight (cf. 13:19). In the 2nd century the complete desertion of Babylon by its few remaining residents would leave the formerly exquisite capital a ghost town inhabited by wild desert animals (13:17-22).

The taunt Isaiah scripts for the exuberant exiles, who return to the promised land as Persian subjects, personifies Sheol as a host eager to meet its Babylonian guests (14:9). Isaiah portrays Babylon as the morning star, which never fully rises (14:12). The lofty ambitions of Babylon, which parallel those involved in the building of the Tower of Babel, will sink to the depths of Sheol, "the pit" (14:13-14).

14:24-27 Assyria A fuller oracle concerning the future downfall of Assyria has already appeared in 10:5-34. The empire's divinely accomplished defeat in Judah, prophesied in verse 25 and recorded in 2 Kings 18–19/Isaiah 36–37, preceded their ultimate overthrow by the Babylonians.

14:28-32 Philistia The death of the pro-Assyrian Judahite king Ahaz should not occasion rejoicing on the part of the Philistines, who held the territory on Canaan's southern coast; for the long arm of Assyria — in effect, Judah's overlord at this time — still holds deadly cards. Nevertheless, the people of God will find refuge in Zion (= Jerusalem).

15-16 Moab The descendants of Abraham's nephew Lot populated Moab, the Transjordanian plateau east of the Dead Sea, but they enticed the Canaan-bound Hebrews to abandon their loyalty to Yahweh shortly before they entered the promised land (Numbers 25). As with Assyria and Babylon, Moab's failure to acknowledge the supremacy of Yahweh earns God's intense judgment, the foreshadowing of which gains Isaiah's sympathy (15:5). He foresees miserable Moabite fugitives seeking divinely sanctioned refuge in Jerusalem from the judgment that God will complete within three years' time. To pave the way for a welcome reception at the Judahite capital, the desperate Moabites send a lamb as tribute (16:1-5, 14).

This oracle, expanded in Jeremiah 48, names numerous sites in Moab, including Nebo, the mount from which Moses viewed Canaan (Deuteronomy 34); Medeba, a town at times controlled by the Israelites; Heshbon, seat of the Amorite king Sihon, who hindered the Hebrews on their journey from Egypt to Canaan (Num. 21:21-31); Zoar, to which Lot fled during the destruction of Sodom and Gomorrah (Gen. 19:18-30); Sela ("rock"), a name associated with the ancient Edomite fortress Petra; the Arnon, a deep "wadi" or gorge which at times marked the boundary between Moab and its northern neighbor Ammon and at the bottom of which flows the Arnon River; and Sibmah, famous for its wine and here a symbol of Moab's prosperity. The "temple" in 15:2 refers to a Moabite shrine, and the worshippers' baldness and beardlessness signify their state of mourning for Moab.

17 Damascus That the oracle against the Syrian city of Damascus (vv. 1-3) also includes a more extensive word against the northern kingdom of Israel (vv. 4-11) indicates that this prophecy relates to the alliance of the two powers against Judah in an attempt to stave off southwestern expansion by the Assyrians, whose fall Isaiah also foretells (vv. 12-14; cf. 10:5-34). The takeover backfired, for Judah's king Ahaz appealed to Assyria for aid, and the rising Mesopotamian superpower overran Damascus and eventually conquered the northern kingdom as well. The "asherim" of verse 8 refer to carved wooden images of the Canaanite fertility goddess Asherah. Verses 10-11 condemn the northern kingdom's religious compromising through political partnership with a pagan people — a situation forewarned in Exod. 34:11-16.

18 Cush/Ethiopia Ancient Cush encompassed the region south of Egypt and immediately east of the Red Sea (modern Sudan, Ethiopia, Eritrea, Saudi Arabia, and Yemen). The land "beyond the rivers of Cush" (v. 1) suggests specifically Ethiopia. Isaiah's description of the distant place as the "land of whirring wings" designates it as bug-ridden from the waters of the Nile River, on which the "papyrus vessels" travel and whose tributaries divide the land through which they flow (vv. 2, 7). The Nubian dynasty, based in Ethiopia, ruled Egypt from the mid-8th to the mid-7th century and thus spanned the heyday of Assyrian aggression and Hezekiah's reign in Judah. Isaiah's prophecy (v. 2) pictures a Judahite envoy making political overtures to the northern African kingdom, presumably to establish an alliance against the powerful invaders from Mesopotamia. God, however, calmly awaits the right time for "pruning" — meting out judgment on these smugly self-sufficient nations (vv. 3-6). As a result of God's judgment, the former *recipient* of the envoy from Judah will then *send* by envoys a "gift of homage" to Mount Zion, where the Jerusalem temple housed the "name" of the Lord.

19 Egypt In imagery reminiscent of the Canaanite storm (and fertility) god Baal, Isaiah pictures God riding on a cloud to bring judgment on Egypt (cf. Jesus' return, Mark 13:24-27; Matt. 24:28ff.; Rev. 1:7; cf. Dan. 7:13). The oracle foretells the disintegration of the Egyptian Empire from the inside out, beginning with internal strife (v. 2; cf. 9:19-21). Drought will devastate Egypt's economic lifeblood, its fishing industry and agriculture dependent on annual flooding of the Nile (vv. 5-10). Bewildered leaders will seek answers through the magical arts (vv. 3, 11-15) and abandon the nation's intellectually incapacitated advisors — the "princes" of Zoan (probably the delta city of Tanis) and Memphis, both former capitals of Egypt. Finally, poetic justice will come full circle as the former taskmasters of the Hebrew people themselves fall subject to a cruel king (v. 4).

The divine judgment of Egypt is punishment with a purpose, namely, God's revelation of himself to the Egyptian people, with the result that they swear allegiance to him even in Heliopolis ("City of the Sun," = On), Egypt's center of sun worship (v. 18). In a wordplay, the Hebrew alters the spelling of the city's name to make it read City of Destruction. God will "heal" the Egyptian people in response to their worship and cries for deliverance. In the end, Israel's greatest enemies — Egypt and Assyria — will join the Hebrew nation as equal partners in the worship of God, thus fulfilling God's promise to bless the nations of the earth through the descendants of Abraham (Gen. 12:2-3).

As history played out, the Assyrian army defeated Egyptian forces on Judahite soil in 701, though the Assyrian commander Sennacherib failed to conquer Jerusalem (2 Kings 18–19). When Assyria advanced on Egypt in the mid-7th century, the invaders sacked the capital of Thebes (Egyptian No-Amon, "City of [the god] Amun") and pillaged its temples, including modern Karnak and Luxor. Following the Babylonian defeat of Assyria and destruction of Jerusalem (587), influential Jewish colonies in Egypt and Assyria began to grow. Ultimately, however, Isaiah's prophecy anticipates not merely a regional spiritual renewal but a global one (vv. 16-21; cf. Rev. 20:11–21:8).

20 Egypt and Cush/Ethiopia In 713 the Philistine port city of Ashdod began a revolt against Assyria and eventually secured a pledge of support from Egypt and Cush. But the North African kingdoms left Ashdod in the lurch when the Assyrians arrived in 711 to quell the rebellion for good. By going naked and barefoot for three years, Isaiah publicly portrayed the role of a slave to warn of the humiliation awaiting Assyria's opponents (v. 2). A decade later, King Hezekiah of Judah wisely heeded Isaiah's counsel to rely on God, not Egypt, for deliverance from the Assyrians.

21 Babylon, Edom, and Arabia Verses 1-10 foretell the Medo-Persian conquest of Babylon (538), called the "wilderness of the sea [Persian Gulf]"

in verse 1 (cf. v. 9). Elam, between the Tigris River and Media, became a Persian satrapy, or province (v. 2). This second oracle against Babylon emphasizes Isaiah's personal distress over his vision of the devastation to come, even though the downfall of the Hebrews' exilic overlords means welcome relief for the captives (= the "threshed [people]," v. 10). Revelation 14:8; 18:2 take up the cry in verse 9 in recording the ultimate triumph of God over Satan.

The oracle concerning Dumah ("silence"), which the Septuagint changes to "Idumea" (= Edom), anticipates a temporary forestallment of judgment (vv. 11-12). Edom became home to Esau's descendants (Genesis 36).

Verses 13-17 foresee the impending fall of Arabia, conquered by Sargon of Assyria in 715. The oracle calls on the Dedanite merchants, who occupied an oasis in northwest Arabia, and the nearby inhabitants of Tema to shelter and care for their fellow Arabians, the powerful bedouin Kedarites, pictured as fleeing south from the front lines of battle.

22 Jerusalem, the Valley of Vision The first 14 verses use the past tense to convey certainty that divine judgment will not bypass Jerusalem. The 587/86 destruction of Judah's capital occurred a century after Isaiah's time at the hands of the Babylonian army, which included mercenaries from the outposts of Elam and Kir, inherited from the Assyrians (v. 6). The Jerusalemites armed themselves with weapons stored in the "House of the Forest" (the city's arsenal) and built up the water supply inside the city walls for sustenance against a siege. (In Isaiah's day, Hezekiah built the Siloam tunnel, which brought water into the city from a source outside the defensive walls; 2 Kgs. 20:20; 2 Chr. 32:30.) But their failure to place ultimate trust in God will lead to their defeat (v. 11). Instead of repenting of their sins, they partied on (vv. 12-13).

The remaining verses report God's replacing Shebna with Eliakim in a high position in Hezekiah's royal court (2 Kgs. 18:18ff.). But Eliakim will abuse his authority (v. 22), possibly by indiscriminately granting official favors to all manner of relatives (v. 24), and this action will undo him in the end (v. 25).

23 Tyre For centuries, extensive trade launched from the port cities of Tyre and Sidon, on the coast of today's Lebanon, established the Phoenicians as the dominant seafaring merchants in the eastern Mediterranean. Isaiah foresees the news of Tyre's destruction passing from the city's nearest colony on Cyprus to the far reaches of its sea-trade in Egypt and Tarshish (probably Tartessus in Spain, v. 6). In images borrowed from the birthing process and child-rearing, the sea itself bemoans the absence of her children, the Phoenician merchant ships (v. 4). Tyre earns the title "bestower of crowns" (v. 8) for its widespread establishment of colonies. The term "Canaan" (v. 11) included Phoenicia.

The prophecy envisions the "land of the Chaldeans" (Babylonia) as carrying out the destruction of Tyre (v. 13), after which the city goes unremembered for the span of a lifetime (70 years; v. 15). When Tyre does resume international trade, the material gains will benefit God's faithful (v. 18).

Assyria conquered and at least temporarily subjugated Tyre in 722/21. The decline of Assyrian power emboldened the city to reassert its independence, but the Babylonians recaptured it. The cycle of Tyre's resurgence and submission continued through its conquest by Greece under Alexander the Great (332) and beyond.

24–27 Global Judgment and Renewal
Sometimes called the "Isaiah Apocalypse," these four chapters contain a mixture of prophecies, prayers, laments, and songs of praise and thanksgiving, all of which revolve around God's judgment of the entire, corrupt world and renewal for the faithful remnant. By transgressing the "everlasting covenant" (24:5), usually understood as a reference to the promise to Noah (Genesis 9), humanity forfeits the promised blessings and becomes subject to the threatened curses. Only a few will survive the coming devastation, which will turn all human joy to gloom and from which not even kings can escape (24:6, 11, 21-22). The doomed "city of chaos," the "palace of aliens," represents the world gone morally wrong (24:10; 25:2; cf. 26:5; 27:10). The faithful remnant rejoices in God's display of righteous judgment (24:14-16), and the Lord's glory out-

Pool of Siloam, connected to Jerusalem's only perennial source of water, the Gihon Spring, by an underground tunnel constructed by Hezekiah.
(www.HolyLandPhotos.org)

shines the sun and moon (24:23; cf. Matt. 24:29; Rev. 6:12; 8:12).

The representative city that bears God's judgment stands in stark contrast to Jerusalem (Zion), where divine "salvation" will "swallow up" death and eradicate sadness and shame (25:6-12; cf. Rev. 21:4). The decisively humbled "Moab" represents all the unfaithful (25:10).

Jerusalem's gates open to welcome home the righteous (26:1-2). In the city's future lies divinely established peace, marked by God's blessing in all spheres of life (26:12). One of two clear Old Testament references to a bodily resurrection appears in 26:19 (cf. Dan. 12:2).

Isaiah borrows imagery from Canaanite myth in portraying God's cosmic victory over the forces of evil as the defeat of the mythical sea serpent "Leviathan" (27:1). Isaiah 27:2-6 recast the Song of the Vineyard in positive terms (cf. 5:1-7). Punished for unfaithfulness by exile (27:7-8), "Jacob" will receive full pardon by destroying the trappings of pagan religion (27:9). A trumpet blast will signal the start of the exiles' return from faraway Mesopotamia and Egypt (27:12-13; cf. Matt. 24:31).

28–31 Oracles against Israel and Judah
28 The Leaders of Israel and Judah Chapter 28 begins with an oracle against Israel prior to the

northern kingdom's defeat by the Assyrians in 722/21 B.C. The Israelite capital of Samaria lay in the tribal territory of Ephraim, which represents here the northern kingdom as a whole. The gluttony of Israel's civil and religious leaders make the kingdom morally ripe for judgment (vv. 3-4, 7). Verses 9-10 expose their prideful rejection of divine instruction, which they consider beneath their level of moral maturity. (Imitating the babbling of a child, the Hebrew in verse 10 uses words of one syllable to mock authentic prophetic warnings.) Since the Israelite leaders pooh-pooh prophetic instruction and refuse God's offer of "rest," the Lord will teach them through "a foreign tongue" — that of the Assyrians, who in 722 captured and deported the northern population (vv. 11-13). The "crown" of Israel will not completely disintegrate, however, for God himself will assume his rightful place as king over the surviving Israelite remnant (v. 5).

In verse 14 the focus shifts to the rulers of the southern kingdom of Judah. Isaiah ominously refers to their divinely prohibited alliance with Egypt against the Assyrians as a "covenant with death" and a pact with Sheol (v. 15). If the Judahite "scoffers" fail to heed prophetic warnings, they can expect God to reverse completely the victories he granted to King David (v. 21; cf. 1 Chr. 14:8-17).

The chapter ends with a parable. Just as for the farmer everything has a season, so God in his wisdom sends judgment or salvation as he sees fit (vv. 23-29).

29 Jerusalem

"Ariel" (v. 7), which sometimes means "Lion of God," can also mean "altar hearth" and here refers to the altar in the Jerusalem temple complex (cf. Ezek. 43:15). The envisioned siege found historical fulfillment in the Assyrian Sennacherib's divinely thwarted attempt to take the Judahite capital in 701 (see 2 Kgs. 19:32-37; Isa. 37:33-38).

The chosen people's spiritual blindness prevents them from understanding the divine instruction (vv. 9-10; cf. 6:9-10) and inclines them toward mechanical observance of religious ritual rather than heartfelt obedience (v. 13).

The spiritually dull conceal in the darkness their twisting of the truth (v. 15; cf. John 3:19-21).

They think they can achieve equality with God (v. 16; Gen. 3:5; cf. Rom. 9:20-21). But God the Creator can bring about true reversal in the world for the good of his people by opening their spiritual eyes and ears.

30 Judah's Foolishness

Isaiah pronounces woe on the defiant, faithless Judah for looking to Egypt for security (in the face of the Assyrian threat) rather than exercising trust in God. Egypt's inability to make good on any promise of military aid and the weakness of the kingdom's leaders will make the treacherous journey of Judah's envoys futile (v. 6). Egypt will be like "Rahab," the mythological chaos monster defeated by the god Marduk prior to his creation of the world (v. 7; cf. 51:9).

The prophet chastises the Judahites for actively suppressing divine truth (vv. 10-11). Since the divine rule that God established with his chosen people intertwined religion and state, the people's unfaithfulness invites both political and military disaster (vv. 12-14). God has urged his people to turn away from their sin and toward obedience to him (v. 15), but they have chosen military action rather than faith (vv. 16-17; cf. Matt. 26:52).

Verses 18-26 convey God's gracious longing to relieve the oppression through which he has taught his people a lesson and to restore to them unimaginably abundant blessings.

The concluding verses describe God's angry judgment against the pagan nations and single out the current power, Assyria. At Topheth ("place of burning," v. 33), located in the Hinnom Valley just south of Jerusalem (New Testament "Gehenna," a word for hell), human sacrifices were offered to the Ammonite god Molech. In the midst of this divine punishment, God's spiritually renewed people will worship him with songs, celebration, and gladness of heart (v. 29).

31 God's Supremacy over Egypt and Assyria

The Egyptian army is no match for God, who will protect Jerusalem despite his people's foolish hope in their southern neighbor. Even the mighty aggressor Assyria will panic in the encounter with God (v. 4; cf. the lion imagery applied to Assyria in 5:29-30). The chapter turns not on the theme of deliverance, however, but on the call to repentance and the pure worship of God, whose refining fire proves the righteous (vv. 6-7, 9).

32–35 A Brighter Future

32 A Righteous King and a Peaceful Future In a brief return to the theme of a future righteous king, Isaiah describes the renewed kingdom as populated by a morally enlightened people (vv. 3-4; contrast 6:9-10). Verses 6-8 reflect the Wisdom style of the book of Proverbs. Isaiah admonishes his female contemporaries, who are living the good life and lulled by a false sense of security, to put on mourning attire and lament the judgment that will precede this righteous reign, dominated by justice and peace.

33 A Prophetic Collage A variety of voices and poetic forms comprise this chapter. It begins with a prophetic woe against an unnamed "destroyer" (v. 1), followed by a prayer (vv. 2-4), a hymn (vv. 5-6), and a corporate lament that includes widespread geographic references (vv. 7-9). Prophetic threats against unspecified enemies and promises extend from verse 10 to the end of the chapter (the refining fire of God's judgment, vv. 14-15; the future, righteous king, v. 17; foreign oppressors, v. 19), with a hymn of confidence in verses 20-22. This chapter may have been used in worship, perhaps in times of national emergency, or later as a summary recollecting Isaiah's prophecies.

34 An Oracle against the Nations Verse 2 presents the future divine judgment of the nations as an accomplished fact. Their offenses against Zion (v. 8) earn them utter destruction in a final, bloody battle that ends in cosmic collapse (v. 4; cf. Matt. 24:29; Rev. 6:13-14). Edom, land of Esau's descendants and a constant thorn in Israel's side, will be a special target of God's wrath (vv. 5-7). God will carry out the devastation with chilling precision (vv. 11, 13-15).

The "book of the Lord" (v. 16) may signify the collection of Isaiah's prophecies. Elsewhere the "book" refers to the "book of life," which lists the saved (cf. Dan. 12:1; Mal. 3:16; Rev. 20:12).

35 A Preview of Renewal The idyllic renewal of the promised land and the joyful repopulation of Jerusalem stand in stark contrast to the intense devastation of pagan nations described in chapter 34. The barren southern desert (Heb. "Arabah") will blossom as gloriously as Canaan's densely vegetated north (vv. 6-7); spiritual and physical healing will abound (vv. 5-6; cf. Matt. 11:6); and God's redeemed will travel the perilless "Holy Way" to return to Zion, where they will find never-ending joy. This picture far surpasses Judah's actual restoration following the Babylonian exile and later that of the returned Diaspora. Ultimately, the prophecy anticipates the glorious final age envisioned in Revelation 21–22.

36–39 An Assyrian Siege and Hezekiah's Babylonian Blunder

A nearly identical textual twin of 2 Kgs. 18:13–20:19, these chapters bring to a climax Isaiah's preceding prophetic warnings by giving a prose account of the Assyrian king Sennacherib's siege of Jerusalem (chs. 36–37) and the visit of Babylonian well-wishers to the ailing Hezekiah (38:1-9; 39). Isaiah's account omits mention of Hezekiah's initial, fainthearted cowing to Sennacherib (2 Kgs. 18:14-16), which may have been a separate occasion.

The most obvious difference between the parallel chapters in Isaiah and 2 Kings consists in the addition of Hezekiah's poem in 38:9-20 expressing the ailing king's fear of an untimely death. Hezekiah nevertheless anticipates his recovery on the basis of Isaiah's prophetic assurances, backed up with a miraculous sign (38:5-8, 20).

40–55 Hope for Restoration

The transitional chapter 39 shifts attention away from the Assyrian threat, which provides the historical background for chapters 1–38, and toward Babylon, which overthrew Assyria, conquered Judah, and destroyed Jerusalem (587/86). Chapters 40–55, sometimes called "The Book of the Consolation of Israel," address the Hebrew exiles in Babylon. Here the hopeful theme of imminent restoration replaces the ominous message of impending doom that characterizes the first half of Isaiah. The New

Testament views the ultimate fulfillment of the prophecies in chapters 40–55 in eschatological terms.

40 On the Other Side of Punishment From chapter 40 on, the perspective in Isaiah changes dramatically. The political crisis threatened in chapters 1–39 is long gone, not because God's people have done a spiritual about-face in response to the harsh, prophetic warnings, but because he has punished them for failing to do so. Here God announces the end of the punitive period in a message of kindly comfort (vv. 1-2; cf. Deut. 30:1-10). The meat of this message, however, does not consist in a rehearsal of tangible, earthly blessings to which the Hebrews may look forward; rather, the message focuses on the greatness of God, who in his tireless, unfailing love, incomparable strength, and absolute sovereignty possesses the will and ability to effect his people's restoration to the promised land in a "second exodus" (cf. ch. 35).

In the context of the exiles' return from Babylon, verses 3-5 envisage the preparation of an easy route to Canaan through the desert, with God in the lead (cf. Exod. 13:17-22). The New Testament relates these verses to the ministry of John the Baptist as heralding the restorative mission of Christ (Matt. 3:1-3; Luke 3:1-6). In verses 11 and 12, the shepherd/sheep language of Psalm 23 balances God's ruling might with his nurturing care. The "span," or "half cubit," used metaphorically in verse 12, measured about 9 in.

Compared to God, the "[pagan] nations" aren't even a blip on the screen (vv. 15-17). Neither idols/graven images nor earthly rulers can compare to this sovereign ruler of the universe (vv. 18-26; compare v. 21 and Rom. 1:18-25). Finally, the chapter emphasizes the unfailing energy of God, who thoroughly reinvigorates the weary faithful (vv. 27-31).

41 The Power of God's Words God summons the nations to court for a hearing, at which he establishes himself without challenge as the one who puts into action the events that will lead to his people's release from bondage in Babylon, namely, the conquests of Cyrus the Persian (vv. 2, 25; 44:28). Cyrus's empire extended from the Persian Gulf and Caspian Sea in the east to the

Black Sea, due north of Canaan. Fearing the emerging power, the pagan peoples encourage each other in a futile attempt to resist. But now the politically powerless Hebrew exiles, who formerly ignored the prophetic call to exercise faith in God, will get a second chance to experience divine deliverance in the face of seemingly insurmountable odds. God will arm them with a divinely made "threshing sledge," a heavy, flint-studded, wooden beam dragged over harvested ears of corn to break them open. In subsequent winnowing (the tossing in the air of the threshed product), the wind blew away the inedible, lightweight husks — the easily disposed of "chaff" that serves as a metaphor for Israel's enemies (vv. 11-16). Verses 17-20 echo chapter 35 in previewing the abundant provisions God will grant to his afflicted people.

Verse 21 returns to the courtroom, where the inability of the pagan nations' gods to see the future disproves their divinity. Their silent impotence contrasts with God's power in speaking events into being (v. 25; cf. 40:8).

42 God's Servant and His Willfully Wayward People This first of what have traditionally been called "Servant Songs" (vv. 1-7) begins on a positive note: God's spirit-imbued servant will play a central role in establishing global justice and bringing about spiritual enlightenment among the pagan nations (cf. Gen. 12:3; 22:18). The grace of God in this new world order will extend even to Israel's former enemies (vv. 9-13). But their salvation will not be automatic. God's judgment for their idolatry will come first (vv. 14-17). Verses 10-12 constitute a victory hymn similar to those represented in Psalms 96 and 98.

Israel certainly has not demonstrated the capacity to fulfill such a servant role. The willful nation has turned a deaf ear and a blind eye to God's law and thereby rendered itself just as spiritually dull as the pagan nations. The chosen people have not even recognized God's judgment as punishment for their sin. Verses 18-25 constitute their wake-up call.

Three more "Servant Songs" appear in 49:1-13; 50:4-11; and 52:13–53:12, and the passages show a progressive development of the servant theme prominent in chapters 40–66. The New

Testament understands Jesus as the Suffering Servant, who on behalf of all humanity bears God's judgment for sin, mediates salvation, and returns to establish a just and righteous eternal kingdom (Matt. 12:15-21; Mark 10:45; Luke 4:16-21).

43 God's Loving Redemption and Israel's Rebuff Through Moses, God established a personal relationship with his people by revealing to them his name: Yahweh (Exod. 6:1-13). In ancient Near Eastern thought, a name served not merely as an identification label, but it actually conveyed the nature of its bearer — thus the importance of the prohibition against taking God's name in vain (Exod. 20:7). God's naming of the nation of Israel intensifies the intimate nature of their relationship and also establishes God's authority over his people (v. 1; cf. Gen. 2:19-20). He calls them "precious," declares his preferential love for them, and pledges to gather the scattered exiles from every direction of the compass (vv. 2-7).

Verses 8-13 return to the courtroom scene introduced in chapter 41, with God's calling Israel as witness to his unchallenged supremacy over the phony gods of pagan nations (v. 9; cf. 40:21-29). Verse 14 resumes the theme of Babylon's downfall, foreshadowed in 41:2, 25 by God's rousing of Cyrus the Persian. No longer should Israel look back to its ancestors' miraculous exodus deliverance through the Red Sea, for a new set of divine wonders awaits in a "second exodus" from captivity in Babylon (vv. 16-21).

Only God's determination to save his chosen people for the sake of his own name prevents defiant Israel from forfeiting all these plans for good (vv. 22-28). Fortunately for Israel, God's justified frustration with the nation does not cancel out his gracious forgiveness of their sins. These transgressions go all the way back to their "first ancestor" (v. 27), a probable reference to Jacob, renamed "Israel" and forebear of the 12 Hebrew tribes. Only through this ill-deserved pardon could Israel hope to escape God's total destruction (v. 28; cf. Joshua 6).

44–45 God's Singular Divinity Ensures Release, Renewal, and Restoration After summarizing the divine blessings in store for God's beloved servant "Jacob" (= Israel), also called by the poetic name "Jeshurun" (vv. 1-5), God repeats and intensifies his singular claims to divinity. His appeal to his chosen people as witnesses (44:8) resumes the courtroom metaphor (ch. 41; 43:8-13). These chapters extend the themes of God as sole Creator of the world, orchestrator of human affairs, redeemer and liberator of his chosen people, and forecaster of earthly events (chs. 40–43). Isaiah 44:9-20 develop in detail the contrast between this all-powerful God and utterly impotent, wooden idols, fashioned in human form by human hands.

The final verse of chapter 44 names Cyrus as God's instrument of restoration in Canaan (v. 28). Only rarely does the Old Testament specify future historical figures by personal name (cf. 1 Kgs. 13:2). Some believe these instances represent the work of authors/editors who lived after the events described. In chapter 45, God previews his orders to Cyrus, who despite his unfamiliarity with God, is nevertheless destined to do his bidding (v. 4; cf. Ezra 1:1ff.). In particular, the Persian king will release the captive Hebrews, whom the new conqueror will inherit from defeated Babylon, and rebuild Jerusalem and the temple (45:13; cf. 44:26-28).

Israel's divine reversal of fortunes will include commercial profit from Egypt and Cush/Ethiopia and voluntary subservience on the part of the Sabeans, nomadic raiders from southwestern Arabia (45:14). The courtroom hearing

"I will make a way in the wilderness and rivers in the desert" (Isa. 43:19). *(Richard Cleave, Pictorial Archive)*

resumes in 45:20 with God's reassertion to the pagan nations of his singular divinity. God's global offer of redemption to the penitent parallels the New Testament theme of the "ingrafting" of the Gentiles (v. 22; cf. Rom. 11:11-32). The Apostle Paul names Christ as the object of the universal allegiance to God foretold in 45:23 (Rom. 14:11; Phil. 2:10-11).

46 Contrasting Gods Chapter 46 sets in climactic contrast the Babylonian gods, whose motionless, unresponsive graven images their devotees must shoulder while marching into exile, and the vigorous God of Israel, who has "carried" his people from the beginning and will carry them back to Zion (vv. 1-7, 13). Bel, a title meaning "lord" (cf. the Canaanite Baal) and probably used here to refer to the Babylonian high god Marduk, appears in the name Belshazzar ("[May] Bel protect the king"; Dan. 5:1). The other principal Babylonian god, Nabu (Heb. "Nebo"), son of Marduk and god of learning, is represented in the name Nebuchadnezzar ("[May] Nabu protect my boundary stone," i.e., my borders). The sins of God's stubborn-minded Hebrew children will not deter him from granting their "salvation" — deliverance from affliction and oppression. The "bird of prey" from a distant, eastern country refers to Cyrus, whose Medo-Persian army defeated Babylon in 537 (v. 11).

47 A Taunt Song for Doomed "Queen Babylon" The taunting invitation to the city of Babylon (the "virgin daughter/fair maiden" and "daughter of the Chaldeans") to "sit in the dust" and "strip off the skirt" represents a summons for the capital city to mourn the inevitable fall of the Babylonian Empire, the idea of which the "queen" city never entertained (vv. 1, 7; cf. 32:11). Her haughty mistreatment of the Hebrew exiles has gone too far, and her lack of mercy is about to come back to haunt her as she finds herself relegated to slavery (vv. 2-6). The personification of Babylon continues in the picture of the city as a woman simultaneously widowed and deprived of her children (vv. 8-9). When it comes to thwarting the impending disaster, Babylon's magicians and astrologers will prove just as powerless as her gods, and even long-

time comrades will abandon the queen in her time of need (vv. 9-15).

48 A Sober Sendoff The focus shifts from Babylon to the Hebrew exiles, as God lectures the obstinate rebels for their arrogance. In the past, God announced in advance his actions to prevent his people from ascribing divine deeds to false gods (vv. 1-11). The Hebrews' "refinement" through exile in Babylon emerges as a purposeful, corrective punishment for their sin, not a disproof of God's sovereignty (vv. 9-11). In truth, God's "tough love" approach constitutes an act of grace (not merely *un*deserved favor, but *ill*-deserved favor), which saves his people from a worse fate — being "cut off" from their covenantal relationship with God. Yet God's primary motivation for restoring them is the vindication of his own name (v. 11; cf. 43:7, 25).

Verses 12-22 look to the future as they revolve around God's disclosure of his next move: the defeat of Israel's current captors, the Babylonians (= Chaldeans; vv. 14-16). The new, spirit-accompanied speaker in the last line of verse 16 may represent the prophetic author or the Servant of the Lord. With a final expression of frustration over the Hebrews' past, self-destructive disobedience, God drives the released captives out of Babylon to return to Jerusalem, where they may legitimately worship him in his chosen dwelling place (vv. 17-22). God charges them to proclaim their liberation in affirming his gracious redemption (v. 20). He reminds them of his historic, miraculous acts on behalf of their exodus ancestors (v. 21) but balances this reassurance with an ominous warning confirming that the old rules of punishment for disobedience still apply (v. 22).

49 New Children for Lady Zion In the second "Servant Song" (vv. 1-13), God's servant both *is* "Israel" and is *sent* to the people of Israel. Some scholars understand the nation of Israel as both conveying and receiving the message. Others see the messenger as an *individual* called Israel sent to minister to and on behalf of the nation of the same name. The poem stresses God's compassion for Israel and also commissions this servant to bring "light" to the pagan nations (cf. Gen. 12:2-3).

The bereaved Zion (= Jerusalem) — personified, like Babylon, as a woman (ch. 47) — receives comfort and the assurance that God has not forgotten her (vv. 14-26). The taunt song foretelling Babylon's bereavement and abandonment contrasts sharply with the impending reversal of fortunes for Lady Zion, who will soon welcome so many new children that she will lack room to house them all (vv. 14-23; contrast 47:9-15). While deposed Queen Babylon sits on the ground, foreign rulers will "lick the dust" of Zion's feet (v. 23; contrast 47:1). The doom of Israel's oppressors includes their having to resort to cannibalism (v. 26; cf. 2 Kgs. 6:24-30; Lev. 26:29; Deut. 28:53-55).

50 The Exile as Purposeful Punishment Verse 1 expresses the Hebrews' exile in the language of divorce. In Deuteronomy, the "certificate of divorce" required a husband to declare a valid reason ("some indecency") for dissolving the marriage (Deut. 24:1-4). Here it gives testimony that Israel's exile did not result from a lack of power on God's part; rather, God purposefully "sent [her] away" as deliberate punishment for unfaithfulness. Verses 2-3 offer further evidence against arguments that would deny God's absolute power.

The third "Servant Song" appears in verses 4-11. (Vv. 6-7 continue the "Suffering Servant" theme.) Despite intense affliction, the servant defiantly pursues his mission and expresses confidence in his divine vindication. The final two verses address the hearers of the servant: verse 10 calls the righteous to faith, while verse 11 prophesies the tormenting demise of the defiant.

51:1–52:12 Release and Restoration This section furthers the message to the righteous. God's provision of children to Abraham and his previously barren wife, Sarah, and the multiplication of their descendants provide the basis for the exiles' trust that God will make good on his promises to restore joy in the promised land and to establish for eternity global justice, righteousness, and deliverance from oppression (51:1-8). In 51:9-11, the prophet calls on God to awaken to this task. He affirms God's power to accomplish it by citing God's triumph over pre-creation chaos and parting of the Red Sea during the exodus (on "Rahab," see 30:7).

God speaks words of comfort to the soon-to-be-released captives. He points out the folly of fearing human oppressors instead of trusting in their vastly more powerful Creator God. The prophet interrupts (51:17-20), wanting to make sure the exiles hear the good news, which God restates in 51:22-23: their punishment has come to a permanent end. But that is not all, according to chapter 52. It is time to shake off the dust and chains of enslavement and prepare to return to the promised land. Isaiah 52:3 establishes the capture and release of the exiles as divinely accomplished feats, not humanly engineered business deals. The Assyrian and Babylonian deportations will end in a second exodus in which the ritually purified people will carry back to Zion the sacred temple treasures confiscated by the Babylonians (52:4-12; for the circumstantial contrasts between the two exodus events, compare v. 12 and Exod. 12:29ff.).

52:13–53:12 The Suffering Servant: Rejected by Humanity but Exalted by God This fourth, final, and best-known "Servant Song" develops the theme of the "Suffering Servant" to its greatest extent. The exaltation of the physically disfigured, humanly despised and rejected servant of the Lord will so surprise people that they will be rendered speechless (52:13–53:3). The poem makes clear that God himself causes the servant's intense suffering, not as a sign of *divine* rejection, but in order to effect spiritual healing from sins for "us all." A willing sacrifice unblemished by violence or deceit, the servant fills the role of a sacrificial lamb, which according to Mosaic law effected atonement for sins (53:7-9; cf. Leviticus 1; 5:14–6:13; John 1:29). The contrast between the servant's outward offensiveness and inner purity highlights the true measure of humanity: religious sincerity of spirit, which results in heartfelt obedience to God and by which he judges individuals (cf. 1 Sam. 16:7).

In the New Testament, Christ emerges as the ultimate Suffering Servant prophesied in Isaiah (Matthew 27; Rom. 5:6-9, 18-19; Phil. 2:5-11; 1 Pet. 2:21-24).

54–55 The Covenantal Blessings Revitalized and Enhanced As in 49:14-21, chapter 54 envisions the multiplication of inhabitants for the depopulated Zion, again portrayed as a wife socially disgraced because of her childlessness (the "barren one," v. 1). God, the husband who in 50:1 divorced his people for unfaithfulness, takes back his bride for good and vows never again to afflict her (cf. God's covenant with Noah in Gen. 9:11). Moreover, God promises to adorn her gloriously, to protect her unfailingly, and to provide for her abundantly and without charge (54:11-12). The reference in 55:3 to David likens the eternal nature of God's current promises to the covenant in which God pledged to establish a perpetual Davidic dynasty (2 Sam. 7:16), and 55:4-5 foresee the fulfillment of God's vow to Abraham that his descendants become a blessing to the nations of the earth (Gen. 12:3). Yet the road to such blessing is a two-way street. Repentance — the simultaneous abandonment of wickedness and "return" to the Lord — surfaces as the Hebrews' part of the bargain (55:6-7).

God's power to accomplish his superior purposes resides in his "word," which here proclaims the exiles' joyful return to a revitalized promised land restored for eternity (55:8-13). As in chapter 35, the picture of abundant, everlasting renewal painted here far surpasses the circumstances of Judah's restoration following the Babylonian exile and ultimately anticipates the global, final restoration envisioned in Revelation 21–22.

56–66 Reestablishing Righteousness

These last 11 chapters reassure the returned exiles, living in a still devastated Judah and Jerusalem, that in a future act of judgment God will root out the wicked from the promised land and reestablish righteousness in Zion.

56:1-8 God's Welcome to Foreigners and Outcasts The incorporation of converted social outcasts and foreigners into the Hebrew community began early in the nation's history with such individuals as the harlot Rahab and Ruth the Moabitess (Lev. 19:33-34; Josh. 6:22-25; Ruth 1:16). Verses 1-8 confirm the divinely sanctioned share of these converts in the religious life of the restoration community. Even converted eunuchs, who lack heirs to carry on their name and thus ensure their perpetual participation in the covenantal promises, enjoy primacy of place in God's scheme. Not surprisingly, however, these verses also emphasize the converts' obligation to observe covenantal law, especially by honoring the Sabbath. The "holy mountain" of Jerusalem, home to God's "house of prayer," thus begins to develop as the center of global worship envisioned in 2:2-4 (cf. Mic. 4:1-3; Psalm 87).

56:9–57:21 A Call to Contrition The ideal portrayed in 56:1-8 differs from reality, which this next section addresses. The blind watchmen and clueless shepherds of 56:10-12 represent Israel's corrupt, complacent religious and civil leaders. Death paves for the righteous the only path to peace (57:1-2), while the rebellious Hebrews never tire of engaging in pagan cult prostitution, brutal child sacrifice, and futile idol worship. God chastises the deceitful religious harlots for their wickedness, but so great is his desire to bestow on them the covenantal blessings that he calls them to contrition and pledges to heal them in response (57:11-21).

58 God Clarifies His Requirements This chapter exposes the Hebrews' obsession with religious ritual for the empty hypocrisy it is. The people's failure to recognize the sinfulness of their actions and intentions renders them unable to understand why God ignores their outward displays of piety (vv. 1-5). In verses 6-14, God corrects their understanding of what pleases him — sincere deeds of unselfish personal sacrifice, not false humility disguised by fasting (vv. 6-7; cf. Matt. 25:35-36).

59 God's Determination to Redeem Religiously fallen as God's people are, he still can save them. A litany of transgressions spells out the means by which the Hebrews have denied themselves communion with God and given birth to a depraved society: murder, lying, fraud, injustice, hastiness to do evil, and violence. God's displeasure with this appalling situation stirs him to "save" the repentant and punish the persistently wicked. Verse 20 anticipates Christ as the ultimate accomplisher of God's redemptive work. Paul borrows language from verse 17 in calling Christians to don the "full armor of God" (Eph. 6:11-17).

60 Jerusalem Rejuvenated The rejuvenation of Jerusalem, destroyed in 587/86 by the Babylonians, parallels the redemption of the people divinely designated to repopulate the holy city. Bathed in the light of God, Jerusalem stands out from the rest of the dark earth (vv. 1-13, 19-20; cf. Rev. 21:22-26; John 8:12). Foreign nations and kings flock to the radiant temple-city with riches to offer to God (vv. 4-9). God will guarantee the security of the rebuilt city (vv. 10-14), and its economic vitality, aesthetic beauty, structural strength, and peaceful atmosphere will surpass anything in its past (vv. 15-18). Verses 21-22 echo the divine promises of the "land" (= Canaan) and offspring (Gen. 12:1-3).

61 A Nation of Priests Some scholars view the speaker here as the Servant of the Lord first mentioned in 42:1 and so consider this poem a fifth "Servant Song." Others hear in these verses the voice of the prophet. Jesus publicly inaugurates his ministry by claiming the mission set forth in verses 1-2 (see Luke 4:16-21).

Verses 4-9 envision the entire nation of Hebrews serving as priests, with the peoples of foreign nations filling the secular roles assumed by Israel's non-Levitical tribes and providing their livelihood as prescribed by Mosaic law (cf. Exod. 19:6; Numbers 18). Firstborn sons normally inherited twice as much of their father's estate as younger male siblings, and here a divinely granted "double portion" replaces Israel's previous inheritance of humiliation-by-exile. A song of praise closes the hopeful chapter (vv. 10-11).

62 Jerusalem Essentially Changed The transformation of Jerusalem into a global beacon of righteousness will mean for the city an essential change of status (vv. 1-2). No longer called "Forsaken" or "Desolate," her new names will signal the renewal of her "marriage" to God and the newlywed delight he takes in his bejeweled bride (vv. 4-5, 12). Verses 6-7 call on watchmen,

posted on the defense walls of Jerusalem, vigilantly to hold God to his promise to exalt and protect the city, whose inhabitants will joyously welcome the returning exiles.

63:1-6 The Divine Avenger The divine bridegroom who delights in Jerusalem also avenges the city by punishing its enemies, here represented by Edom and its periodic capital, Bozrah (cf. 34:6). This homeland of Esau's descendants figures as a particularly appropriate representative for the pummeled peoples, whose blood has stained the garments of the divine avenger, for Edom means "red." These verses give a more graphic portrayal of the same event of judgment envisioned in 59:16-20 (cf. Rev. 19:11-16).

63:7–64:12 Lamenting the Present, Reminiscing about the Past The opening vow to praise God for his goodness to Israel launches a contrite rehearsal of the nation's rebellious history. This communal lament ends with a plea that God once again deliver them from the consequences of their sins. Verses 9-14 recall God's singling out the Hebrews as his chosen people, their rebellion, and Moses' role in mediating their deliverance from oppression in Egypt.

In 63:15–64:7, appeals that God renew his redemptive actions on Israel's behalf alternate with expressions of puzzlement over his neglect and despair at the plight of the nation so separated from God that even its founding fathers, Abraham and Israel (= Jacob, 63:16), cannot recognize it. The lament appears to lay at God's doorstep the blame for the nation's persistent religious rebelliousness (63:17; 64:7), but in actuality that is a path they have already determined to pursue. Decade after decade, the prophets delivered to Israel and Judah countless warnings to change course, which for the most part went ignored. Thus the Hebrews bore full responsibility for God's "delivering [them] into the hand of [their] iniquity."

The lament ends on a tone of utter humility by acknowledging God as sovereign "potter" over his people, the "clay" (64:8). Seeing no end to their punishment and bemoaning the devastation of their promised land, they plead for an end to their affliction. The basis of their hope for a reversal of fortunes lies in Deut. 30:1-10.

65–66 God's Double-Edged Answer God breaks his silence with a message of hope for the righteous and doom for the wicked. He begins by castigating his people as a whole for constantly rebuffing his overtures and flagrantly inflaming his anger by offering sacrifices at unauthorized locations, consulting the spirits of the dead, ignoring food laws, and communing with "Fortune" and "Destiny," the gods Gad and Meni (65:1-7, 11). Playing off the names of these Syrian deities, God declares that the "destiny" of the unfaithful lies in destruction, and their "name" leaves a legacy of cursedness (65:12-15).

But not all the grapes in the cluster of the chosen people are sour, and here the remnant theme developed in chapters 1–39 resurfaces as God vows to preserve and provide for the faithful. To signify their receipt of the promised inheritance of land, progeny, and blessing, their name will differ from that of the wicked (65:8-10, 13-25).

The utopian picture of the re-created world of human beings (the "new heavens" and "new earth," 65:17) includes for the inhabitants of the renewed Jerusalem perpetual gladness, longevity (an Old Testament sign of divine blessing), independence from overlords, enjoyment of the fruits of labor, intimacy with God, harmony in nature, and universally upright behavior (65:17-25; cf. 11:6-9; Revelation 21).

Chapter 66 continues to contrast the futures of the faithful and the wicked. In acknowledging the limitlessness of God, the opening verse echoes Solomon's prayer at the dedication of the first temple (1 Kgs. 8:27, 30). Verses 2-3 do not signal God's rejection of worship through the offerings and sacrifices legislated in Mosaic law; rather, they emphasize God's requirement of humble contrition as the necessary attitude for worship, because insincere ritual amounts to none other than abominable paganism (cf. 1 Sam. 15:22-23; Ps. 40:6-8).

In 66:5, hateful compatriots of the faithful discriminate against them. The taunting challenge of the skeptics echoes in the words of mockers at Jesus' crucifixion (Matt. 27:39-44).

Later, apocalyptic literature characterizes the events that precede the end times as the pangs of childbirth — language that here describes the rebirth of the nation of Israel from mother Zion (66:7-9; cf. Mark 13:8). Isaiah 66:13 likens God to a comforting mother and casts him in a maternal role.

According to 66:18-20, survivors of the destruction forewarned in verse 6 and described in verses 15-17 will proclaim God's glory in distant lands and usher back to Jerusalem the faithful who remain scattered abroad. The locations mentioned in 66:19 skirt the northern Mediterranean coast from Asia Minor as far east as Spain (Tarshish) and Put, which lies on the southern coast in the territory of modern Libya. From the ranks of the returning exiles, who represent a "grain offering," God will appoint priests and Levites, set apart for full-time sacred service in the enduring new world (66:20-22).

The final verses of Isaiah dramatically summarize the contrasting fates of the righteous and wicked. Those who recognize God's sovereignty will inherit an enduring legacy (66:23; cf. Phil. 2:9-11), and those who rebel will suffer deadly judgment (cf. Psalm 1; Rom. 6:23). The state of perpetual dying, pictured in 66:24 as the wages of the rebellious, offers a rare Old Testament hint at the afterlife.

Jeremiah

The second of the Major Prophets, Jeremiah addresses the southern kingdom of Judah during its last decades as an independent nation and then the Hebrew exiles deported by their Babylonian conqueror. 2 Kings 22–25 and 2 Chronicles 34–36 outline the historical circumstances of Jeremiah's prophetic activity. His late-7th- to early-6th-century-B.C. prophetic contemporaries include Habakkuk, Zephaniah, and the exiled Ezekiel.

Background

Jeremiah's call from God launched a prophetic career that lasted four decades and spanned the reigns of Judah's last five kings (627/26–587/86). This priestly descendant lived a century after Isaiah in a time when the crumbling Assyrian Empire lost out to a resurgent Egypt and an increasingly powerful Babylon, whose conquest of both of these major rivals solidified its position as the new ancient Near Eastern superpower. At first, Jeremiah concentrates on calling for repentance by Judah to avoid divine judgment of the kingdom. When national contrition does not follow, the prophet declares the certainty of Judah's punishment, to culminate in exile.

At least two historical phenomena contributed to the widespread rejection of Jeremiah's unpopular message. First, Jerusalem's century-old deliverance from defeat by the Assyrians, who succeeded in conquering the northern kingdom of Israel, undoubtedly reinforced the Judahites' belief that under no circumstances would God allow the overthrow of the capital, where lay his temple, or the disruption of God's promised perpetual Davidic dynasty seated there (2 Kings 18–19; 2 Sam. 7:16). Second, Jeremiah began prophesying during the reign of the righteous King Josiah, whose religious reforms began at least as early as the 621 discovery in the temple of the "book of the law" (2 Kings 22–23). Officially, Judah was moving in the right direction. But Jeremiah's insights penetrate the outward show of ritual reform and expose the insincerity and hypocrisy of Judah's religious and political leaders (except Josiah), who bear the responsibility for the spiritual shepherding of the people. The book of Jeremiah elaborates the intense physical affliction and emotional distress the prophet suffered by remaining faithful to his call. And like Job, Jeremiah freely complains to God about his plight.

After 22 years, the warnings of this prophet of doom started to materialize. The year 605 saw the beginning of the end for Judah, with conquering Babylon's initial exile of Judahites during the reign of the rebellious king Jehoiakim, followed by his successor Jehoiachin's surrender of Jerusalem in 597 and the deportation of Judah's elites (2 Kgs. 23:36–24:16). Jeremiah does not leave the exiled Hebrews hopeless, however. He proclaims the restorative purposes of their punishment and prophesies the eventual return of the Hebrew remnant to the promised land, where they will live under a new, permanent covenant (29:11).

Literary Form

Jeremiah contains a variety of literary forms in poetry and prose: laments and prophetic oracles of judgment and salvation, biographical vignettes from the life of the prophet, sermons, and a letter. That the book does not present this material in chronological order can make it difficult to follow. Generally, chapters 1–25 concentrate on prophecies against Judah and Jerusalem; chapters 26–45 contain biographical sketches that augment Jeremiah's prophetic message; chapters 46–51 present oracles against the pagan nations; and chapter 52 represents a historical postscript.

Authorship

Chapter 36 indicates that in 605/4 Jeremiah dictated to his personal scribe, Baruch, "all the words of the Lord that he had spoken to him." The resulting scroll covered the first 23 years of Jeremiah's 40-year prophetic career. The account also records King Jehoiakim's burning of the scroll and the subsequent re-creation and enhancement of the manuscript by Jeremiah and Baruch, who may have composed some of the material himself.

Text

The Hebrew (Masoretic) text of Jeremiah, on which translators base English versions, displays a long and complicated editorial history. Comparison of the Masoretic Text and the Septuagint (the Greek translation of the Old Testament) reveals that the Hebrew contains repetitions and additions in detail that the Greek omits. These omissions render the Septuagint's text approximately one-eighth shorter and strongly suggest that its translators worked from a briefer version of Jeremiah. A second significant difference between the Hebrew and Greek texts consists in the Septuagint's placement of the oracles against the nations (our chs. 46–51) immediately after the oracles against Judah and Jerusalem (chs. 1–25), rather than inserting the biographical material between the oracular sections. Chapter 52, which closely parallels 2 Kgs. 24:18–25:30, represents an editorial ending of the book that validates the whole of Jeremiah's message by demonstrating the historical fulfillment of his prophecy against Judah and Jerusalem.

1–25 Jeremiah's Call and Prophecies against Judah/Jerusalem

Jeremiah delivered the prophecies recorded in chapters 2–25 from 627/26–587/86, during the reigns of Judah's kings Josiah, Jehoahaz, Jehoiakim, Jehoiachin, and Zedekiah.

1 The Prophetic Call The opening verses of the book provide unusually detailed information about the prophet's pedigree and tenure. Jeremiah's hometown of Anathoth, set apart in Josh. 21:18 for Israel's priests, lay 3 miles northeast of Jerusalem. Called by God in the late 7th century (100 years after Isaiah), this priestly descendant prophesied during the reigns of Judah's last five kings.

As with other Old Testament prophets, Jeremiah's call and the accompanying visions confirm for his ancient audience the divine origin of his prophetic message. God's anointing Jeremiah as a "prophet to the nations" makes his call irresistible, despite Jeremiah's protest (vv. 6-8; cf. Exod. 3:11–4:17), based on his youth. God's promise to "be with" Jeremiah as he pursued his mission parallels the divine words of assurance given to Moses.

The power of God's spoken word is seen in verses 9-10, where Jeremiah receives the divine commission to overthrow and establish nations by means of his prophecies. Jeremiah's subsequent vision of an "almond tree" (Heb. *shaqed*) makes a wordplay with God's "watching" (*shoqed*) over his word to ensure its effectiveness.

Jeremiah's appointment accomplished, his assignment emerges in a second vision, one of a south-facing "boiling pot" — a metaphor for the impending divine judgment by military advances from Judah's north, from where such successively dominant kingdoms as Assyria, Babylon, and Persia ruled Canaan. During Jeremiah's career, it was Babylon that boiled over in judgment of Judah for her disobedience to God's covenant with the Hebrew people at Mount Sinai. God tells Jeremiah to get to work, warns him of the opposition he will face because of the unpopular message he must deliver, and promises deliverance from his adversaries (vv. 17-19).

2:1–3:5 Israel: Unfaithful Wife, Promiscuous Harlot Jeremiah's message to Jerusalem remembers a honeymoon version of the Hebrews' relationship with God during their journey from Egypt to the promised land (2:2-3). This exaggerated overstatement serves to emphasize the vast difference between the generally faithful days of yore and the thoroughly unfaithful present. A blessed life in the promised land has not resulted in Israel's appreciation to God for deliverance from Egypt, but instead in callous disregard of their faultless, divine benefactor, whom they have forsaken for the Canaanite storm and fertility god, Baal. The sovereign God declares it appalling that, from peon to prophet to priest, his people have rejected him, the "fountain of living water" (2:13), and embraced powerless foreign deities, when even pagan nations, represented by Kittim (= Cyprus) in the west and Kedar (in Arabia) in the east, remain faithful to their useless gods (= "broken cisterns").

Through this foolishness, the chosen people have brought disaster on themselves. The "lions," probably Assyria, conquered the northern kingdom of Israel a century prior to Jeremiah's time (2:15; cf. Isa 5:29-30; 31:4). The "people of Memphis and Tahpanhes" represent Egypt, whose army killed Judah's king Josiah in 609. Yet instead of relying on God, his people appeal to these very same foreign governments for political security.

The metaphors mount, beginning with Jeremiah's intensified portrayal of the unfaithful wife, Israel, as a religious harlot. "High hill" and "green tree" (2:20) refer to outdoor shrines, where pagan rites rivaled legitimate worship at the temple. Jeremiah's picture of Israel as a formerly "choice," now degenerate "vine" (2:21) recalls Isaiah's Song of the Vineyard (Isa. 5:1-7), but here the efforts of Jeremiah's audience to wash away the stains of sin prove futile (2:22). The sacrifice of human children in the Hinnom Valley (2:23) epitomized the depths of their undeniable faithlessness. The "trees" and "stones," worshiped as creator-gods by Israel's religious and civil leaders, refer to carved and sculpted idols (2:26-27; cf. 3:9).

God acknowledges that punishing his people has not brought about their repentance (2:30). Because they persistently refuse to admit wrongdoing in the midst of flagrant unfaithfulness, further judgment awaits them in the form of subjugation and deportation (2:37). Israel, despite her religious promiscuity, unrepentantly holds her head high in blatant denial of her religious adultery (3:2-5).

3:6–4:2 A Bright Future, Contingent on Repentance "Israel" here refers to the northern kingdom, whose fall to the Assyrians (722/21) preceded by over a century the Babylonian conquest of Judah (587/86). God through Jeremiah communicates divine disgust that Israel's affair with paganism became a way of life. Judah followed suit, and her halfhearted return to God (an allusion to Josiah's reforms; 2 Kgs. 23:1-30) constituted false pretense, not true penitence.

As deserving of punishment as Israel's faithlessness was, still it pales in comparison to the treachery of Judah, who failed to learn the lesson of her northern sister's fate. Nevertheless, Jeremiah envisions Israel's eventual repentant return to the Lord in terms of a future reunification of the exiled Hebrew nation, with godly leaders to "shepherd" the people in the way of righteousness (3:15-18). Jerusalem will be the seat of divine rule, although the ark of the covenant, once "the throne of the "Lord," has been lost and forgotten. The end result of Israel's repentance will consist not only in blessings for her but for "the nations" also (3:19; 4:1-23).

4:3-31 Judah's Urgent Need to Repent God offers the people of Judah and Jerusalem a chance to avert his wrath by "circumcising" their hearts, repenting with heartfelt sincerity, not merely outward ritual. To drive home the urgency of Judah's need to change, Jeremiah again warns of approaching destruction at the hands of the Babylonian army — the "lion" from the north (vv. 6-7), the "hot wind" from the wilderness (v. 11), the "besiegers from a distant land" (v. 16). Israel's northernmost tribe, Dan, which stands first in the Babylonian army's southward line of march, announces the advance of the oncoming invaders, who quickly proceed to the hill country of Ephraim, home to Jerusalem's defunct sister capital of Samaria (vv. 15-16).

Jeremiah is overwhelmed by the vision of utter disaster and the trumpet call to war (vv. 19-21). The extent of the coming destruction will stop just short of completely unmaking the earth, as the foreign nations, through whose alliances the seductive Judah continues to seek political security, turn on her with deadly intent (vv. 23-29).

5 Divine Restraint Holds Punishment in Check The unsuccessful search in Jerusalem for just one righteous person, whose identification would bring about God's forgiveness and avert the coming judgment, recalls Abraham's bargaining with God to save Sodom from destruction for the sake of 10 righteous inhabitants (vv. 1ff.; cf. Gen. 18:22–19:29). Evidently by overemphasizing the covenantal promises, discounting the curses, and underestimating their own responsibility to the covenant, the Hebrews cannot see their punishment coming (vv. 12-13). They ignore the warnings of the true prophets (v. 13), embrace the complacent message of the false prophets (v. 31), and pursue lives of selfish disregard for the socially disenfranchised (vv. 27-28). Even the priests have become a law to themselves (v. 31). The people have given up serving their God, so now they will have to relinquish the land with which God associates himself (v. 19). Yet their thorough wickedness contrasts with God's punitive self-restraint. The "devouring" nation he sends to judge his people nevertheless will not destroy them completely (vv. 10, 14-18; cf. the "remnant" theme in Isaiah).

6 The Siege of Jerusalem Foreseen Jeremiah calls on the members of his own tribe, Benjamin, to abandon Jerusalem, south of which trumpet blasts warn of the impending invasion from the north. The prophet satirically pictures the siege of Jerusalem in the peaceful, pastoral imagery of nomadic shepherds pasturing their flocks outside the city walls (v. 3). Yet the very next verse transforms the scene into one of destructive attack, launched unexpectedly in the heat of the day. All Jerusalem will bear the punishment of its morally calloused society (cf. 7:17-18), whose priests and prophets have failed to teach and admonish the people (v. 14) and whose hypocritical offerings of even the choicest imports God categorically rejects (vv. 10-20). The vain refining effort in verses 27-30 underscores the unsuccessful scouring of Jerusalem for a righteous person in 5:1ff.

7:1–8:3 Jeremiah's Sermon at the Temple To dispel the false notion that the presence of the temple in Jerusalem guarantees perpetual, unconditional divine protection, Jeremiah plants himself at the temple gates and declares the people's need to change their wicked ways (7:6). God may have saved Jerusalem and its inhabitants from the Assyrians in Isaiah's day, but the (presumed Philistine) destruction of Shiloh — original home of the temple's predecessor, the tabernacle — and the Assyrians' deportation of the northern kingdom (represented in 7:15 by its dominant tribe, Ephraim) demonstrate the potential for God to produce a very different outcome for persistently sinful Judah. In fact, her people's blatant, unabashed disobedience to the commandments given at Sinai invites a judgmental purge of the temple, where the Hebrews' hypocrisy reaches its height and transforms God's house into a robbers' den (7:11; cf. Matt. 21:13). In 7:9, Jeremiah accuses the Judahites of transgressing half of the Ten Commandments.

Incensed that the Judahites' worship of the "queen of heaven" (= Ashtoreth, a Canaanite consort of Baal) has become a family activity, God forbids the prophet to intercede for the people (7:16-20). Offerings and sacrifices garner God's favor only as sincere demonstrations of an obedient heart, which inspires righteous behavior outside the temple precincts (7:21-26).

God warns Jeremiah that no one will listen to his message, yet he must deliver it (7:27). His admonishment to Judah to "cut off your hair," a sign of mourning imposed by conquerors on subjugated rulers, anticipates the consequences of Judah's rejection by God (7:29). Indeed, his people rejected him first. Detestable idols defile God's temple, and the Judahites sacrifice children as burnt offerings to pagan deities just outside Jerusalem (Topheth means "place of burning"; cf. 19:5ff.). The Hebrews' dishonoring of God will be met with the dishonor of their own unburied corpses, which will lie exposed to the unhindered ravages of wild beasts (7:30-34; cf. Deut. 28:26). The exhumed remains of Judah's religious and civil leaders will suffer similar disgrace (8:1-2). Jeremiah's ominous prophecy concerning Judah's choice of "death" recalls the parting admonition of Moses, which has gone unheeded (8:3; cf. Deut. 30:15-20).

8:4-17 Thorough Wickedness, Certain Judgment God's greedy, deceitful, unrepentant people have bought the lies of professional interpreters of the Law ("scribes"), the bad advice of "wise men," and the comforting words of deceitful prophets and priests, who merely tell the people what they want to hear. The "serpents" of verse 17 symbolize the enemy army that God will use to judge Judah, and God provides no means of "healing" from their bite.

8:18–9:26 Circumcised in Body but Not Heart The speaker in this section alternates ambiguously between Jeremiah, God, and the Hebrew people, but determining who utters what remains a matter of interpretation, as reflected by the different translations. It does seem clear, however, that Jeremiah shares both God's anguish and anger over his people's unfaithfulness. There is no "balm in Gilead" — the Transjordanian region long famous for its healing ointment — that can restore moral health to Judah (8:22). Neither neighbors nor kin can trust each other. Without repentance, Judah calls on herself certain destruction, symbolically brought about by God's feeding her the bitter "wormwood" plant, which represents sorrow, and "poisoned" water. So inevitable is the coming judgment that God commands the summoning of professional mourners to lead the grieving over the devastation of Judah (9:17).

God delights in "loving-kindness, justice, and righteousness." God himself observes these principles and requires human beings to follow suit (9:24). Circumcision was a physical sign of the people's commitment to abide by such divine laws (Genesis 17) and symbolized an inward attitude that resulted in corresponding behavior not only in one's religious conduct but in the whole of one's life. But in the Judah of Jeremiah's day circumcision has taken on the same hypocritical characteristics as offerings and sacrifices (9:25-26; cf. 6:20). Thus Judah has become no different from the surrounding pagan nations.

10 The Folly of Fearing Scarecrow Gods As does Isaiah, Jeremiah exposes the utter stupid-

ity of worshipping man-made idols. Though elaborately decorated with silver from Spain (Tarshish probably refers to Tartessus) and gold from Uphaz (perhaps Ophir) and clothed in the colors of royalty (violet and purple), these wood-cored creations possess no more power than a scarecrow. In contrast, the unrivaled Creator of the world controls the "signs of the heavens," which terrify the nations (vv. 2, 12-13).

Verse 17 switches to a picture of imminent exile. Jeremiah bemoans this "injury," the pain of which he shares with his Judahite compatriots, whose godless "shepherds" (= leaders) receive the lion's share of the blame (vv. 19-21). Jeremiah humbly prays for God's just but merciful correction and also calls for judgment against the enemies of his chosen people, "Jacob."

11:1-17 Invoking the Covenantal Curses Jeremiah's undoubtedly unpopular message drives home that the impending devastation of Judah represents the legitimate, divine invocation of curses contained in the Mosaic covenant established at Mount Sinai and reaffirmed at the outset of Josiah's reforms (2 Kings 23). The curses are about to take effect because of a long history of the chosen people's covenantal transgressions, including their worship of the Canaanite fertility god Baal and other pagan deities. Once again God prohibits Jeremiah from vain intercession for the Judahites, metaphorically represented as an adulterous wife (v. 15) and as a beautiful tree about to be burned by the one who planted it (vv. 16-17).

11:18–12:17 Jeremiah Faces Death Threats and Blackmail God responds positively to Jeremiah's call for divine vengeance against those (probably priests and prophets) of his hometown, Anathoth, who have hatched plots to kill him and used blackmail to try to silence him (11:18-23). Understandably disturbed, the prophet presses the issue with God by complaining about the prosperity of the wicked, and he again calls for their destruction (12:1-2). But God responds: If you can't handle this challenge, how will you cope with the treachery of your own family (12:5-6)? In ancient times, densely vegetated banks, roamed by wild animals, flanked the Jordan River. This hazardous habitat, the "thickets of the Jordan" (12:5), symbolizes the perilous threat Jeremiah faces from his deceitful, malicious kin.

God understands betrayal, for his own "house" (Israel) has "roared" against him (12:7-13). Several other references to the Hebrew people reveal God's attachment to them, though their unfaithfulness has engendered divine "hate." Again, the "shepherd" leaders bear the responsibility for making Israel a moral wasteland (12:10-11).

Clearly judgment against Judah *and* her enemies is on its way (12:14). In harmony with Isaiah's vision of global reconciliation to God, however, hope for all peoples surfaces in the promise of divine restoration to their lands after punitive exile. But unless the restored peoples demonstrate that they have learned to obey God, they can anticipate repeated punishment.

13 Prophecies in Word and Deed God calls on Jeremiah to deliver his message with actions as well as words (cf. ch. 27; Isaiah 20; Ezekiel 5; Hosea 1). Here he instructs the prophet to purchase and wear a waistband and then bury it near "Perath" (the river Euphrates, or perhaps Parah, a town 4 mi. northeast of Jeremiah's hometown, Anathoth). As divinely directed, Jeremiah later returns to retrieve a rotted, useless piece of cloth. The literary allusion to the Euphrates as the place of the waistband's ruination portends the approaching devastation of Judah by an enemy from the north, or perhaps Judah's imminent exile in Babylon, through which flows the Euphrates.

In verse 12, Jeremiah's statement of the obvious provides a platform for characterizing the process of Judah's judgment as a divinely orchestrated, drunken family brawl. Light and darkness (vv. 15-17) stand for deliverance and judgment. The "king and queen mother" (v. 18) probably refer to Jehoiachin and Nehushta, whose exile to Babylon 2 Kgs. 24:8-16 records. The deportation cleans out even the cities of Judah's remote, barren south (v. 19). Jeremiah likens to the pangs of childbirth Judah's distress over her domination by former allies

(v. 21). The removal of Judah's "skirts" signifies her humiliation, and the exposure of her "heels" (in the Hebrew) represents her vulnerability (v. 22). Finally, God castigates Judah for her religious apostasy, portrayed in sexual terms, undoubtedly implying the Hebrews' participation in Canaanite fertility rites (v. 27). The Judahites' religiously adulterous worship of foreign gods renders the nation figuratively "unclean," while their engaging in pagan sexual rituals, such as cultic prostitution, makes them ritually unclean.

14:1–15:9 Judah Past the Point of No Return In ancient Israel, natural abundance signified God's blessing; so when in the Judah of Jeremiah's day severe drought dried up the water sources and life-sustaining vegetation needed by both humans and animals, the people understood the phenomenon as divine punishment. In these dire straits, they finally confess their sinfulness and plead for God's help, but it is too late. God refuses to listen to his people, rejects their offerings, and instructs Jeremiah not to intercede on their behalf (14:11-12; cf. 7:16-20; 11:14-17). The prophet tries in vain to make excuses for his compatriots by blaming their waywardness on false prophets, but God also rejects this argument and disowns those prophets as deluded soothsayers. Judah will reap what she has sown, and her violent reward will culminate in the inability of Jerusalem to bury her dead (14:1-18), a particular dishonor in the ancient Near East.

More confession and pleading follow (14:19-22), but God declares that not even the great prophets of old, Moses and Samuel, could change his mind (15:1). Again, the quintessentially unfaithful King Manasseh is blamed for ensuring Judah's eventual journey to exile (15:4; 2 Kings 21). A mother's bearing of seven sons represents complete blessing (cf. Ruth 4:15), so the "swooning away" of such a mother (15:9) epitomizes the absolute reversal of Judah's joy under the curse of God's unrelenting wrath.

15:10-21 Woe Is Me Apparently dejected by God's adamant rejection of Jeremiah's pleas on Judah's behalf and no doubt dreading having to deliver yet another oracle of woe to his compatriots, the prophet indulges in self-pity. He laments his birth and complains that everyone holds him in contempt, though he doesn't deserve it (v. 10). God answers that in the coming disaster Jeremiah's present persecutors will find themselves turning to the prophet for help (v. 11). The "your" of verse 11 refers to Jeremiah, whereas the "you/your" of verses 13-14 signifies Judah.

In verses 15-18, Jeremiah seeks divine vengeance on his "persecutors," whose hostility and alienation he blames on his pursuit of God's purposes. Recalling God's promise of "deliverance" at Jeremiah's call, noting the constancy of the opposition he faces, and perhaps anticipating intensified antagonism, the prophet expresses uncertainty about God's truthfulness and reliability (v. 18). God responds by restating the pledge he made at Jeremiah's commissioning and prods the prophet back to work (vv. 19-21; cf. 1:18-19).

16 No Family, No Sympathy, No Fun God's prohibition against Jeremiah's marrying and fathering children in Judah held greater significance in the prophet's culture than it does in modern Western society. While perhaps not an *outrageous* enactment of his prophetic message, Jeremiah's divinely mandated pursuit of the single life surely qualified as highly unusual behavior, since the means of ensuring the perpetual participation of one's family in the covenantal blessings consisted in the production of at least one heir. Indeed, God's withdrawal of "peace" *(shalom)* from his people signifies a disruption in (but not an irrevocable end to) the covenantal blessings (v. 5).

Jeremiah's ordered absence from both wakes and parties warns that widespread death will become the norm and gloom the prevailing mood in Judah prior to the ultimate punishment of exile (vv. 5-13). The prospect of a later "second exodus" that restores the Hebrews to the promised land offers a temporary psychological reprieve before God vows to hunt down his unfaithful people from their remote, secret hiding places (vv. 14-18). Responding with renewed faith, Jeremiah applauds the future global recognition of the one and only God (vv. 19-20).

17 A Mélange of Oracles The unifying theme of the distinct units in this chapter consists in the rewards of righteousness versus the penalties for wickedness. The opening oracle of judgment implies a contrast between the permanently sin-tainted tablet of Judah's heart and the stone tablets engraved with the Ten Commandments (vv. 1-4). By Jeremiah's day, forbidden worship before "Asherim" — carved wooden images of the Canaanite goddess of fertility — at outdoor, hilltop shrines called "high places" had become a regular practice throughout Judah (v. 2).

The following wisdom psalm uses metaphors from nature to contrast the person who trusts in fellow human beings and the one who trusts in God (vv. 5-8). Jeremiah has already chastised Judah for courting foreign, political alliances rather than turning to God for help (4:30-31). In verse 6, saltiness makes the land uninhabitable by rendering the water undrinkable.

Verse 10 emphasizes God's evaluation of human actions according to the attitudes that underlie them (cf. 9:25-26). Following the proverb in verse 11, Jeremiah offers a personal prayer in which he refers to the Lord as the "fountain of living water" (v. 13; cf. John 4:10-14) and rises to the divine challenge, given at his prophetic commissioning, not to flinch in the face of opposition (v. 18; cf. 1:17). His persecutors' question, "Where is the word of the Lord?" (v. 15), mocks the youthful Jeremiah, whose prophetic authenticity they doubt in view of his yet unfulfilled prophecies regarding the doom of Judah and Jerusalem.

In ancient Near Eastern cities, gates in the encircling fortification walls not only regulated coming and going but also served as focal points for commerce, judicial proceedings, and other official business. Thus Jerusalem's well-trafficked gates were an appropriate place for Jeremiah's admonition to heed the commandment to keep the Sabbath (vv. 19-27). The Jerusalemites' promised reward was the perpetuation of the Davidic dynasty, continual habitation of the city, and enduring visitation of its temple by worshippers from all regions of Judah.

"I went down to the potter's house" (Jeremiah 18); Moabite bowl, bottles, and pitcher, ca. 8th century B.C. *(Richard Cleave, Pictorial Archive)*

18 God as Sovereign "Potter" The making and remaking of a vessel by a potter become a metaphor for God's absolute right to plant and uproot kingdoms, including Israel. The "ancient roads" (v. 15) refer to Mosaic law, whereas the "bypaths" signify the road of disloyalty.

Malicious opposition to Jeremiah by socially powerful, back-stabbing priests, sages, and prophets — the objects of much of the prophet's criticism — stirs up his righteous indignation (vv. 18-23). The shockingly violent and unforgiving divine vengeance for which he calls parallels God's own punitive plans.

19:1–20:6 From Topheth to Temple Court Descending to the Hinnom Valley, site of pagan child sacrifice (see 7:31-32), Jeremiah smashes a pottery jar as a sign of the impending, irreparable destruction of rebellious Jerusalem. God's announcement that the Jerusalemites will cannibalize their children and compatriots (v. 9) is not a command, but instead a prediction of one of the most devastating consequences of covenantal transgression.

Jeremiah travels directly from the Topheth to the temple court — venues that should have stood at opposite ends of the religious spectrum. This time the prophet's summary oracle of doom earns him a beating and the humiliation of public display locked in stocks. At his release, the prophet pronounces judgment on his punisher, a priest whom Jeremiah renames "Terror on every side" (cf. 6:25) and whom he accuses of false prophesy.

20:7-18 Mingling Self-Pity and Praise Jeremiah's public boldness masks his private self-pity. He laments his lot as a prophet wounded by the derision of others when he speaks out but is unable to keep quiet. Even Jeremiah's trusted friends conspire revenge on account of his religiously and politically offensive message. Though the plotting and reproach do not cause the prophet to lose sight of his faith in the Lord as his avenging champion or the inner fortitude to sing God's praises, still his hope does not cancel his despair. Under what for Jeremiah is the almost unbearable distress of a life "spent in shame," he curses the day of his birth (vv. 14-18). But this strongest of Jeremiah's complaints is also the last to appear in the book.

21 Jerusalem under Siege With Jerusalem under siege by Nebuchadnezzar's Babylonian army (587), Judah's last king, Zedekiah, apparently remembers the capital's divine deliverance from the Assyrians over a century earlier (v. 2; 2 Kings 19). No doubt hoping for a similar outcome, Zedekiah seeks a reassuring word from Jeremiah, whose message until now has quite obviously not gotten through. The prophet could hardly have responded more harshly. Far from God's delivering Jerusalem *from* her enemies, he will deliver the city *to* them (v. 5). The Jerusalemites' only hope for survival lies in voluntarily surrendering themselves into the arms of the Babylonian army — a much-diminished "life" compared to what they could have enjoyed through obedience to their covenant with God (vv. 8-9).

22 Decrying Judah's Last Kings This chapter is a mixed collection of oracles against the three wicked Judahite kings who preceded Zedekiah and against the seat of the monarchy, Jerusalem. The first oracle (vv. 1-9) does not name a particular monarch but concentrates on the ground rules for the perpetuation of the Davidic dynasty (the "house of the king of Judah"): fidelity to the covenant through the pursuit of justice, righteousness, and care for the socially powerless (v. 3). The fertile fields of Transjordanian Gilead and dense cedar forests of neighboring Lebanon epitomized the lushness of nature, and their threatened transformation into "wilderness" dramatized the doom of a dynasty bent on disobedience (vv. 6-7).

Verse 10 introduces an oracle against Jehoahaz, or "Shallum." "The dead" probably refers to Jehoahaz's father, Josiah, whom Pharaoh Neco of Egypt killed in 609 (2 Kgs. 23:29-30). The one "who goes away," never to return, represents Josiah's immediate successor, Jehoahaz, who ruled for only three months before Neco captured him (cf. 2 Kgs. 23:31-33).

Jeremiah presents Josiah as a kingly model of justice and righteousness and paints his second successor-son, Jehoiakim, as the exact opposite — a lying, cheating, self-aggrandizing murderer, whose death no one will lament and whose body no one will bother to bury (vv. 13-19). A "donkey's burial" means a carcass left exposed to the elements of nature and ravages of wild animals — the ultimate dishonor (v. 19).

Verses 20-23 rail against the capital, Jerusalem. The city's crushed "lovers" refer to fallen foreign nations with whom Judah's kings repeatedly courted forbidden political alliances. Lebanon, Bashan, and Abarim (Moab) neighbor Canaan to the north, northeast, and east, respectively.

Nebuchadnezzar deposed and deported Josiah's grandson Jehoiachin ("Coniah") after he had occupied the Judahite throne for only three months (597; 2 Kgs. 24:8-17). Not a son but a Babylonian-appointed uncle (Zedekiah) succeeded Jehoiachin on the Judahite throne. Following the Persian conquest of the Babylonian Empire, Jehoiachin's grandson Zerubbabel served as governor in postexilic Judah, but an independent monarchy never revived.

23 Denouncing False Prophets Jeremiah's oracle blames Israel's morally errant civil and religious leaders for the "scattering" of the Hebrews in exile. A promise of hope, however, communicates God's plans to gather the dispersed "remnant" of his people back to the promised land, where they will flourish under the kingship of a just and righteous Davidic descendant (the "Branch," v. 5; cf. Isa. 11:1). This "second exodus" will replace the Hebrews' deliverance from Egypt as the standard-bearing attestation of God's faithfulness to his people.

Verses 9-40 castigate the false prophets of both the northern and southern kingdoms. "Adultery" in this context signifies religious disobedience, which undoubtedly included sexual sins involved in pagan fertility rites. The prophets of Samaria, the northern capital which has already fallen, spoke in the name of Baal, the Canaanite storm and fertility god. Jerusalem's prophets have helped mold a citizenry as offensive to God as Sodom and Gomorrah. God categorically disowns and vehemently opposes these fraudulent visionaries. God's nearness and omnipresence may be a comfort for the righteous, but the wicked — whether prophet, priest, or layperson — will not go unpunished.

24 The Good and Bad "Figs" Verse 1 summarizes 2 Kgs. 24:10-16, which records the surrender of King Jeconiah ("Coniah," more often called "Jehoiachin") and his deportation to Babylon along with the elite of Jerusalem (597). So far, Jeremiah's oracles have emphasized the inevitability of Judah's fall, and the prophet has informed the citizenry of Jerusalem that personal surrender to the besieging Babylonians (an indication of acceptance of God's punitive will) offers the only way to save themselves (21:8-10). Now, Jehoiachin's surrender represents an act of repentance that results in God's favorable plans for the future of the captives who accompanied the king into exile (the good "figs"). Jehoiachin's Babylonian-appointed successor, Zedekiah, and the remaining citizenry of Jerusalem, however, represent the unrepentant (the bad "figs") — the continuing object of God's righteous wrath. (In verse 8, the "remnant" designates those who *remain* in Jerusalem, whereas the term is normally reserved for the exiles.)

25 The Babylonians on the Move Reverting to the days of Jehoiakim, this account correlates the activities of Jeremiah with the rise of Nebu-chadnezzar. After defeating the Egyptians in 605 at Carchemish, the Babylonian king led his forces southwest through Syria to Judah's door-step. After 23 years of warning the southern kingdom about the coming judgment, Jeremiah finally sees it taking shape. He pronounces a 70-year sentence of servanthood to Babylon as punishment for the Judahites' failure to heed the prophets of God (v. 11).

A sweeping judgment of the pagan nations will accompany the punishment of Judah. (Expanded oracles against these nations appear in chs. 46–51.) Four of the five cities in the Philistine pentapolis (omitting Gath) are targets of God's wrath (v. 20). After dealing with Judah, God will punish the very instrument of his judgment — pagan Babylon ("Sheshach," v. 26), which Cyrus the Persian conquered in 539.

26–45 Vignettes from the Life of Jeremiah

The biographical sketches in these chapters skip chronologically forward and backward with frequency. Historical notations aid in navigating the changes in date.

26 Jeremiah's Death Sentence Overruled
This prose account records the events attending Jeremiah's sermon at the temple in the begin-ning of Jehoiakim's reign (609; 7:1-15). Verses 2-6 summarize the sermon, which urges reli-gious reform to avert the divine devastation of Jerusalem and the temple. On the fate of Shiloh, see chapter 7. God's potential "repenting" of the punishment he is planning against Judah (v. 3) demonstrates the biblical meaning of repen-tance as a deliberate about-face. The possibility that God may repent does not suggest his need for forgiveness from evil intentions toward Judah; rather, it demonstrates God's willingness to forgo justified judgment if Judah meets the moral demands of the covenant.

Jeremiah's message so angers the self-serving priestly and prophetic religious establishment that they arrest and try him. Their prescription of the death sentence follows the punishment required by Mosaic law for false prophecy (Deut. 18:20). But Judah's officials and general populace voice a different verdict, which rec-

ognizes Jeremiah as a true prophet of God. In protesting the prophet's execution, they cite Ju-dah's earlier response to the prophet Micah — a response that thwarted the destruction of Jeru-salem by the Assyrians (v. 18, quoting Mic. 3:12; cf. 2 Kings 19). Jeremiah evades death with the aid of Ahikam (v. 24), who had earlier helped the reformer, King Josiah (2 Kgs. 22:12ff.).

A prophetic colleague, who corroborated Jer-emiah's message of doom against Judah, lacked such influential connections, however. Fearing for his life, Uriah (not the Hittite husband of Bathsheba) fled to Egypt. Determined to silence the prophet permanently, King Jehoiakim sent henchmen to retrieve him for his execution.

27–28 Jeremiah Encourages Submission to Babylon
Jumping forward to the early years of Zedekiah's reign (594/93; see 28:1), God calls on Jeremiah to dramatize a message urging continued submission to Babylon by Judah and her Transjordanian and Phoenician neighbors, who were apparently plotting rebellion. Nebu-chadnezzar has recently forced the surrender of Jehoiachin (= Jeconiah, 27:20), whom he deported to Babylon along with many of the temple valuables, and appointed Zedekiah as a puppet-king in Jerusalem. Shackled as a slave to represent Judah, Jeremiah drives home to the new monarch that the kingdom's temporary submission to Babylon is part of God's plan — a plan being carried out by his "servant" Nebu-chadnezzar. Acceptance of Babylonian rule will avert the disasters of war, the destruction of Jerusalem, and subsequent exile for the remain-ing Judahites. Jeremiah urges Zedekiah to reject the advice of false prophets and sorcerers, who encourage defying the Mesopotamian overlord.

One of these prophets, Hananiah, takes on Jeremiah's challenge directly by predicting that Nebuchadnezzar will fall within two years. Since the events prophesied by both lie in the future, at present neither can prove the other wrong, but Hananiah seizes the public oppor-tunity to assert his prophetic superiority in a dramatic, symbolic act: he breaks the wooden yoke with which Jeremiah has shackled himself. But God then privately instructs Jeremiah to confront Hananiah with his fraudulently opti-mistic message. By misleading the people, the false prophet has made Judah's situation worse, and he will pay for the disservice with his life before the year's end. That this foretelling comes true confirms that Jeremiah is a true prophet of God — a proof not lost on the people of Judah.

29 Instructing the Exiles On the home front in Judah, Jeremiah urges submission to Babylon and by courier counsels the Judahites deported there after the surrender of Jehoiachin (597; 2 Kgs. 24:10-17). The prophet instructs the exiles to pursue a normal life in Mesopotamia, because doing so will demonstrate their contrite acceptance of God's punishment for their unfaithfulness. "Seventy years" as the length of the punitive period (v. 10; cf. 25:12) may simply mean "a very long time." Jeremiah also encourages the exiles with divine promises of eventual restoration to Judah and, rejecting the advice of the false prophets, warns against resistance by outlining the awful judgment in store for their defiant compatriots back home. When such a prophet, Shemaiah, discredits Jeremiah in a letter to the priests in Jerusalem, God pronounces a most severe punishment on him: the obliteration of his entire family line.

30–31 The Triumph of Divine Redemption The strikingly hopeful tone of chapters 30–33 represents a departure from Jeremiah's otherwise overwhelmingly gloomy message, and this section is often called the "Book of Consolation." Jeremiah's portrayal of the glorious future in store for both Israel and Judah far surpasses the optimistic picture generated in the immediately preceding chapters by his prophetic adversaries, Hananiah and Shemaiah, but the theology undergirding Jeremiah's vision contrasts with theirs by emphasizing punishment as a sure and necessary step to restoration (e.g., 30:11, 12-15). Jeremiah likens this punishment (exile and enslavement) to the pain of childbirth, relief from which will come in the form of release from foreign oppression and of return to the promised land, where the Hebrews will serve God under a Davidic ruler and live in peace and security. God's earnest concern for the welfare of Israel (= "Ephraim," the most prominent northern tribe, in whose territory the capital of Samaria lay) emerges in two metaphors. The first pic-

tures their relationship as father and firstborn heir (31:9) and the second as shepherd and flock (v. 10). Jeremiah links Jacob's wife Rachel with Ramah (5 mi. north of Jerusalem) because she died there. He pictures Rachel, a matriarch of the Hebrew nation, as mourning the loss of her children (her descendants) to exile (31:15). Jeremiah's visionary dream culminates in a call for the exiles to return to Canaan (31:21, 26).

The mostly prose remainder of chapter 31 outlines the new covenant under which the restored Hebrews will live. The current generation is complaining about bearing the punishment for their ancestors' sins (v. 29; cf. 32:18), but under the new covenant each individual will pay for his or her own transgressions (v. 30). The essence of this covenant's "newness" will consist in its divine inscription on people's hearts, so that obedience will flow naturally from within (31:33). God establishes this new covenant as everlasting by citing impossible conditions for ending it (31:36-37). The rebuilding of Jerusalem and the redemption of the adjacent Hinnom Valley — representing the worst of pagan worship as the site of human sacrifice — crowns Jeremiah's prophecy concerning the regeneration of the Hebrew nation. The New Testament, which means "new covenant," extends this vision of restoration beyond the historical and political context of Jeremiah's day by viewing the ultimate fulfillment of his prophecy as the redemptive work and final goal of Jesus Christ on behalf of all humanity.

32 The Certain Resumption of Normal Life The year 588 found Jerusalem besieged by the Babylonians for King Zedekiah's rebellion against Nebuchadnezzar and Jeremiah incarcerated for prophesying the fall of the capital, the exile of Zedekiah, and the futility of resisting the Chaldean (= Babylonian) combatants. Undoubtedly, the prisoner-prophet did not find making a real estate investment in his already captured hometown of Anathoth a priority until God instructed Jeremiah's cousin Hanamel to sell him the family field. Jeremiah's exercise of his "right of redemption" in purchasing the cousin's land guaranteed that it would remain "in the family," although now the Babylonians surely considered the property theirs (vv. 7-8). Ignoring this technicality, the kinsmen conduct the transaction and observe the proper legal procedures with the aid of Jeremiah's secretary, Baruch. The prophet announces that his dutiful purchase of the land symbolizes the Hebrews' eventual return to normal life in Canaan (v. 15). But Jeremiah then confesses God's might, summarizes his faithfulness to Israel and their ungrateful rebellion, and notes Jerusalem's deserved, imminent fall to the Babylonians, all leading to the lingering question on Jeremiah's mind: Did the purchase really have a point (vv. 16-25)? After all, Judah is as good as fallen.

God answers by confirming not only the certain fall of Jerusalem but also its destruction. He rehearses the long history of idolatry and unfaithfulness by the whole of Hebrew society, from the leadership on down, including their abominable pagan practices in the Hinnom Valley (v. 35). But God's unqualified resolve to return his people home and "restore their fortunes" after punishing them with exile justifies the soundness of Jeremiah's purchase. The people's future unwavering "fear" (= reverence) of God under a new and everlasting covenant will secure for them a life of resumed normalcy, symbolized by the buying and selling of land.

33 A Revival of Covenants Jeremiah remains in prison. The divine revelations he continues to receive there follow two biblical themes of redemption that began emerging immediately after the fall: the gracious initiative of God in salvaging sin-scarred humanity (vv. 6-9) and the divine goal of "recreating" a morally pristine world (vv. 7, 11).

In foretelling the appearance of the "Branch of David" (v. 15), Jeremiah envisions the reestablishment in Jerusalem of a perpetual Davidic dynasty (cf. 2 Sam. 7:12-16; 1 Kgs. 6:12). Jeremiah's oracle places politics and religion on equal terms by also recalling the divine pledge to Aaron's grandson Phinehas of an enduring Levitical priesthood (v. 18; cf. Num. 25:12-13). The impossibility of disrupting the regularities of nature exemplifies the unbreakable character of these revived covenants (vv. 20-21, 25-26). Verse 22 applies to David and the Levites the promise of innumerable progeny first made to Abraham (Gen. 15:5; 22:17). The two chosen but

rejected "families" of verse 24 most naturally refer to the descendants of David and Levi — the nation's political and religious leaders. Other possibilities include the northern and southern kingdoms of Israel and Judah, and the descendants of Jacob (the entire Hebrew nation) and David (cf. v. 26).

The Davidic monarchy never did revive as a political entity. According to the New Testament, however, Jeremiah's prophecies reach their fulfillment in Jesus, who embodies the ultimate and everlasting kingly "Branch of David" (Matt. 1:1-17) and trumps the Levites in his role as a priest according to the superior order of Melchizedek (Hebrews 7).

34 The Sabbatical Year Briefly Resurrected Zedekiah issues a hasty response to Jeremiah's prophecies concerning the success of the Babylonian siege and his own death in exile. The king, possibly to appease God and fend off his own downfall, reinstates the practice of releasing Hebrew unfortunates reduced to servanthood. But the desperate measure fails (perhaps because of the temporary withdrawal of the Babylonian army and the absence of an immediate threat) when masters soon re-enslave their fellow citizens. The Jerusalemites' mockery of God's law earns them the fate of a calf halved in a covenantal ritual to warn of the consequences of breaking the agreement (v. 18; cf. Gen. 15:9-11). Zedekiah will die in war, not peace (v. 21; contrast vv. 4-5). To see that he does, God will bring the Babylonian army back after it battles the advancing Egyptians (ch. 37).

35 Rechabite Faithfulness Puts Unfaithful Judah to Shame A flashback to the latter part of Jehoiakim's reign (609-597) finds the Rechabite clanspeople at the center of Jeremiah's prophetic attention. These members of an austere Yahwistic sect descended from Jonadab (Jehonadab), whom Jehu enlisted as a witness to his bloody purge of Baal-worshippers in Samaria some two centuries earlier (2 Kgs. 10:15-23). Now the avowed nomads have taken up temporary residence in Jerusalem for protection against the invading Babylonian army. Jeremiah escorts them to the temple, where he attempts to test their faithfulness to their vows. The Rechabites' obedience to a 200-year-old ancestral command to abstain from strong drink puts the Judahites to shame for their constant dismissal of God's laws and disregard of repeated prophetic calls to repentance. The faithfulness of the Rechabites earns God's promise that their family line will endure.

36 Jehoiakim Burns Jeremiah's Manuscript This episode of Jeremiah's life occurs in 605/4, in the first half of Jehoiakim's reign. With Jeremiah banned from entering the temple precincts (perhaps to appease his would-be executioners; cf. ch. 26) and his access to both religious and political leaders and large crowds of commoners severely limited, the prophet turns from orator to author. A year after beginning to dictate two decades' worth of oracles to his personal scribe, Baruch, Jeremiah orders the faithful secretary to read the manuscript at the temple, where an unusually large crowd is observing a fast. Having learned of the prophetic recitation, important officials summon Baruch for a second reading. After establishing the authority of the oracles as the words of Jeremiah, the fear-filled officials believe it urgent to alert Jehoiakim to Judah's dire situation. For a third time that day the scroll is read aloud, this time to the king in his winter home. Much to the alarm of the fretful temple officials, however, Jehoiakim reacts irreverently by shredding and burning up the scroll. This contrasts sharply with his father Josiah's contrite response to the long-lost "book of the law" (2 Kgs. 22:8-13).

Jehoiakim's defiance hurts only himself, for Jeremiah and Baruch rewrite the scroll, with additions that include a condemnation of the king. His successor-son, Jehoiachin, surrendered to Babylon after only three months on Judah's throne (2 Kgs. 24:8-17).

37–38 Jeremiah Imprisoned This vignette takes place in 588/87, toward the end of Zedekiah's reign. With the siege of Jerusalem temporarily lifted while the Babylonians concentrate on repelling Judah's military backup from Egypt, Zedekiah solicits Jeremiah's intercession for Judah, apparently in hopeful anticipation that the Babylonian withdrawal will remain permanent. But Jeremiah replies that they will return to de-

liver the deathblow to Jerusalem. Thus Jeremiah remains true to the divine prohibition against his praying on behalf of Judah (7:16; 11:14).

With the Babylonian army withdrawn, the prophet takes advantage of the opportunity to travel to and from Jerusalem. He sets out on a business trip, perhaps related to the later visit of his cousin recorded in chapter 32. But guards at Jerusalem's Benjamin Gate interpret Jeremiah's movements as an attempt to defect to the Babylonians — after all, the prophet had been openly urging surrender to them. Despite Jeremiah's protestations of innocence, the guards arrest, beat, and throw him into a makeshift jail, from which King Zedekiah frees him in hopes of coercing a positive word from God. For a second time, Jeremiah refuses to tell the king what he wants to hear.

Zedekiah, surely angered by the pessimistic prophet but still eager for his blessing, reimprisons Jeremiah in the court guardhouse. But the prophet continues to encourage surrender, and officials upset about the demoralizing effect on Jerusalem's defense forces call for his execution. They carefully lower Jeremiah into an empty, mud-bottomed cistern, where he will starve to death on his own, perhaps in their minds relieving them of the guilt of murdering God's prophet. A eunuch named Ebed-melech (literally, "servant of the king") pleads the prophet's case and with the king's approval rescues him from the cistern.

Again Zedekiah secretly requests a word from God, but the message of the reimprisoned prophet has not changed. Jeremiah pleads with the king to spare himself and his kingdom a worse fate than surrender will bring. The prophesied takeover of the king's harem signified particular humiliation (cf. 2 Samuel 16). To save his own neck, Jeremiah lies to the officials about his conversation with the king. He remains in prison until the conquest of Jerusalem.

39:1–40:6 Jerusalem Conquered An anticlimactic account of the long-anticipated but briefly summarized conquest and destruction of Jerusalem appears in 39:1-10 (cf. 52:4-16; 2 Kgs. 25:1-12). Here the record gives Babylonian names and titles of several of the conquering officials (vv. 3, 9, 13). Probably advised of Jeremiah's campaign for

Attempting to claim his share of property in Benjamin, Jeremiah is accused of deserting and is imprisoned in an unused cistern (Jeremiah 37–38); cistern at Beth-Shemesh dating from the time of the united monarchy. *(www.HolyLandPhotos.org)*

surrender (by Judahite defectors?), Nebuchadnezzar orders special treatment for the prophet. Freed and given the choice between a protected, probably privileged life in Babylon and a home among the nonexiled poorest of Judah's poor, Jeremiah elects to remain in his homeland, where he lives with the newly appointed Hebrew governor of Judah, Gedaliah — another member of the religiously upstanding (and evidently pro-Babylonian) family of Shaphan (40:4-6; cf. 36:9-26; 2 Kgs. 22:8-13). A preconquest oracle in 39:15-18 promises survival to the Ethiopian eunuch who rescued Jeremiah from certain starvation in a cistern (38:7-13).

40:7–41:18 Governor Gedaliah Murdered The seat of government in Judah moves several miles north of Jerusalem to Mizpah, site of a significant Israelite victory over the Philistines in the prophet Samuel's day (1 Sam. 7:3-17). Gedaliah urges submission to Babylon by the remaining Judahite military forces and encourages the pursuit of a prosperous postwar life. Returned Hebrew refugees from the Transjordanian regions of Ammon, Moab, and Edom contribute to a brief period of economic resurgence in Judah.

But one group also brings trouble. Gedaliah refuses to believe a warning about an imminent attempt on his life by an Ammonite prince. The surprise slaying, which also kills Babylonian soldiers, occurs while the two men and their associates share a meal — an event that in the ancient Near East normally symbolized the sealing of a friendship. To cover up his crime, the Ammonite assassin assumes Gedaliah's identity in welcoming to Mizpah 80 unsuspecting Israelite pilgrims. (Note that they mix pagan rituals — the shaving of beards and gashing of bodies — with prescribed Yahwistic practices — the offering of grain to God.) The attempted takeover continues with the slaughter of all but 10 of the pilgrims. A 400-year-old cistern dug by Judah's King Asa becomes a holding tank for the corpses, but loyalists of the late Gedaliah discover the treachery, rally their forces, and reclaim control at the pool of Gibeon, site of a bloody contest at the outset of David's reign (2 Sam. 2:12-17). The outnumbered Ammonites retreat, while the victimized Mizpahites set off toward Egypt for fear that the Babylonians will interpret the skirmish as Judahite rebellion and launch punitive reprisals.

42:1–43:7 An Ill-Advised Escape to Egypt While still in Judah, the fleeing Hebrew remnant asks Jeremiah to seek God's counsel concerning their departure for Egypt. The conquest and destruction of Judah has apparently freed the prophet to pray on behalf of the people (contrast 7:16; 11:14; 14:11). But their leaders, suspecting a conspiracy by Jeremiah and his scribe Baruch to betray them to Babylon, reject the prophet's warning to remain in Judah, where he claims they will prosper and enjoy divine protection from Babylonian retaliation. The roots of the leaders' skepticism probably lay in the preconquest, pro-Babylonian image the prophet projected by urging surrender to Nebuchadnezzar (ch. 36). The Judahite remnant proceeds to Egypt, despite the prophetic warning of Nebuchadnezzar's pursuit and destruction of them there. The people's preference of trusting foreign nations for protection still offends God (cf. 4:30-31; 22:20-23). No doubt reluctantly and perhaps forcibly, Jeremiah and Baruch go south with the group to the Egyptian city of Tahpanhes, in the eastern Nile Delta on the route to Canaan.

43:8–44:30 Apostasy in Egypt In Egypt, Jeremiah enacts his last recorded prophetic parable, which symbolically forewarns the extension of Babylonian rule there (43:8-13). Among the casualties of conquest, Jeremiah mentions four-sided stone pillars called "obelisks," which recorded royal and religious inscriptions and which likely originated in Heliopolis, the Egyptian center of sun worship (v. 13; cf. Isa. 19:18).

Jeremiah follows with a reminder to the Hebrews, now settled in different parts of Egypt, about their ancestors' disobedience and the resulting divine judgment. He is perplexed by the current generation's thick-headedness in ignoring the lessons of the past and denounces their present worship of foreign gods. The "queen of heaven" refers to the Canaanite goddess Ashtoreth, a consort of Baal (44:17-19). The people's idolatry only seals their doom, which Jeremiah predicted before their flight to Egypt (44:11-14; cf. 42:13-17). Only a negligible number of refugees will survive God's purge and return to Judah.

But the ever-defiant Hebrews categorically reject Jeremiah's correction. Failing to grasp the covenantal consequences of idolatry, they claim that when they abandoned the worship of Ashtoreth in the past (e.g., 2 Kgs. 23:1-30), they gained nothing but grief and disaster. Unable to penetrate their faulty reasoning, Jeremiah gives up.

In 588, Egypt's fledgling pharaoh Hophra tried to help Judah fend off the Babylonians. The attempt, though thwarted, spurred the temporary lifting of the siege of Jerusalem (37:5). Deposed nearly 20 years later (569), Hophra soon joined forces with Nebuchadnezzar in attacking Egypt, where enemies of the former monarch captured and executed him (44:30; on Zedekiah's compared fate, see 2 Kgs. 25:1-7). Though Hophra perished, Nebuchadnezzar emerged victorious. According to the Jewish historian Josephus, the Babylonian deportation of captives from Egypt included Hebrews

(cf. 43:11). Tradition maintains that Jeremiah remained in Egypt, where he was eventually stoned to death.

45 Assuring Baruch Recalling Baruch's intense scribal duties prior to the Babylonian conquest of Judah (ch. 36), this brief oracle scolds the secretary for his self-pity and selfish ambition and steels him for his shared task with Jeremiah. In an encouraging word, Baruch receives the divine promise that he will survive God's wrath in the imminent Babylonian onslaught.

46–51 Oracles against the Nations

The latter part of chapter 25 introduced in general God's coming punishment of the idolatrous non-Hebrew nations. In this last major section of Jeremiah, the oracles of judgment target every geographical region bordering Canaan, and then some.

46 Egypt Cf. Isaiah 19–20; Ezekiel 29–32.

Two oracles address separate victories over Egypt by Babylon — the initial instrument of God's judgment and its ultimate target (see chs. 50–51). The first oracle (vv. 3-12) speaks to the defeat of Pharaoh Neco at Carchemish (in northern Syria) in 605. Four years earlier, on the northward march through Canaan to assist the weakening Assyrians, Neco killed Judah's king Josiah, who tried to thwart the pharaoh's efforts at an alliance against Babylonian expansion (2 Kgs. 23:29-30). Verse 9 specifies the participation of mercenaries from various parts of the Egyptian Empire: Ethiopia (= Sudan), Put (= Libya), and Lud (possibly Lydia in west-central Turkey). The Transjordanian region of Gilead (v. 11) produced a healing ointment, or "balm," long famous in the ancient world.

The second oracle (vv. 14-26) expands the preview in 44:30 of Egypt's defeat during the days of Pharaoh Hophra, who hosted the fleeing Judahite remnant after the murder of Gedaliah (41:1–43:7). This Babylonian conquest of Egypt on her own soil occurred in 568 and resulted in the deportation of Hebrew refugees, who had established settlements in the Egyptian cities of Migdol, Memphis, and Tahpanhes (v. 14; cf. 44:1). In verse 18, the geographical prominence in Galilee of the isolated Mount Tabor, which rises steeply from the floor of the Jezreel Valley, and the Carmel range, which dominates the surrounding landscape southeast of modern Haifa, symbolizes the unopposable might of Babylon. Verse 21 pictures the doomed Egyptian mercenaries as "fattened calves," prepared for slaughter. The "daughter of Egypt" (v. 24) refers to Memphis (v. 19), then capital of the kingdom.

The oracle ends by casting in a hopeful light for the Hebrew remnant the divine judgment of Egypt, on whom the Israelites had disobediently and futilely relied for political security. When God restores the sufficiently punished people of Jacob (= Israel) to the promised land, no troubling Egyptian enemies will remain (vv. 27-28).

47 Philistia Cf. Isa. 14:28-32; Ezek. 25:15-17; Amos 1:6-8; Zeph. 2:4-7; Zech. 9:5-7.

Beginning in the 13th century, groups of Philistines migrated from Mycenae to Canaan's southern coastal plain, some by way of the island of Crete (= "Caphtor," v. 4). These indigenous Aegeans established five principal cities in Canaan: Ashdod, Ashkelon, Ekron, Gath, and Gaza. During the rise of David in the late 11th century, Philistine strength was waning, and the young David began subduing these adversaries of Israel well before becoming king. In the late 7th century, Egypt dominated the Philistine territory in southern Canaan; Pharaoh Neco already controlled Gaza when in 609 he set out for Carchemish (v. 1; 46:3-12).

Jeremiah's portrayal of the subsequent *northern* conquerors of Philistia (i.e., the Babylonians) as torrential floodwaters proves appropriate for these seafaring inhabitants of the coast, where the mostly flat terrain favored chariot warfare (vv. 2-3). The port cities of Tyre and Sidon, well north of Philistia on the Phoenician coast in Lebanon, forged economic alliances with their Philistine mariner-comrades (v. 4), but after Nebuchadnezzar's victory at Carchemish (605), Babylonian conquests southward along the eastern Mediterranean coast severely hampered the trade initiatives of these business partners.

48 Moab Cf. Isaiah 15–16; Ezek. 25:8-11; Amos 2:1-3; Zeph. 2:8-11.

A historic enemy of Judah, Moab encompassed the fertile plateau east of the Dead Sea and bordered Ammon to the north and Edom to the south. The tribe of Reuben received as its landed inheritance territory in the north of Moab (Numbers 32).

For its arrogance toward God, especially manifested in idolatry and the scorning of God's chosen people, Moab can expect the destruction of its cities, the devastation of its agricultural productivity, and the exile of its inhabitants. The combined disasters will humiliate the prideful people and produce nationwide mourning (cf. v. 37). Because worship at the illegitimate Israelite sanctuary at Bethel — rival of the Jerusalem temple — failed to save the northern kingdom from devastation by the Assyrians, Jeremiah compares Israel's shame of Bethel to the future Moabite shame of their chief god Chemosh, who will prove impotent to protect his worshippers (v. 13). The cutting off of Moab's "horn" (v. 25) symbolizes the sapping of the nation's strength. In the early 6th century, Moab participated in Judah's rebellion against Babylon, and Nebuchadnezzar's army defeated the Transjordanian troublemakers four years after its 587/86 destruction of Jerusalem (27:3). But the oracle ends on a hopeful note for Moab, whose fortunes God vows eventually to restore (v. 47).

The place names mentioned in this oracle cover Moabite territory from north to south. "Nebo" refers to the city, not the mountain from which Moses viewed the promised land (v. 1). During the Hebrews' postexodus journey toward Canaan, they defeated the Amorite army of King Sihon at Heshbon (v. 2; Deut. 2:26-37; cf. Num. 21:27-30). The east-west gorge cut by the Arnon River formed a natural geographical boundary in Moab; during the kingdom's periods of political and military weakness, the river marked Moab's northern border (v. 20). Kir-heres (modern Kerak in Jordan) probably served as the original capital of Moab (v. 31). Sibmah enjoyed ancient fame for the excellence of its wine (v. 32).

49:1-6 Ammon Cf. Ezek. 25:1-7.

Ammon, where the tribe of Gad settled, receives both a sentence and a promise similar to those of bordering Moab (ch. 48). The cities of Heshbon and Rabbah, located in territory alternately ruled by the Ammonites and Moabites, sat opposite Ai, with the Jordan River lying roughly halfway between. Here the fall of Ai portends an imminent invasion into Transjordan from over the river (v. 3). In the early 10th century, King David made a desperate attempt to cover up his adultery with Bathsheba by sending the doomed Uriah to the front lines of battle during Israel's siege of Rabbah (2 Samuel 11) — the ancient capital of Ammon and modern Amman, Jordan. "Milcom" names the Ammonite national god (vv. 1, 3). Solomon transgressed the covenant with Yahweh by worshipping the gods of Ammon and Moab (1 Kgs. 11:5, 7).

49:7-22 Edom Cf. Isa. 21:11-12; Obadiah; see also Isaiah 34.

The picture of devastation and desolation continues with Jeremiah's oracle against Moab's southern neighbor Edom, homeland to the descendants of Esau (Gen. 36:8). Teman, the name of a grandson of Esau, is used as a poetic equivalent for Edom and probably signifies a region in the south of the kingdom (vv. 7, 20). Dedan, an oasis inhabited by traveling merchants, lay in northwest Arabia (v. 8). Bozrah served as Edom's capital city (v. 22). Jeremiah invokes the memory of the divine destruction of Sodom and Gomorrah (possibly located in Edomite territory on the southeastern shores of the Dead Sea) to convey the totality of the coming devastation (v. 18). The picture of God as a lion attacking the "flock" of ineffectively shepherded Edomites (vv. 19-20) contrasts sharply with his image as the protective "good shepherd." Jeremiah projects that the outcry of the stricken Edomites will reverberate all the way to the Red Sea, some 200 miles southwest of Edom (v. 21).

49:23-27 Damascus Cf. Isa. 17:1-3; Amos 1:3-5; Zech. 9:1.

The smaller states of Hamath and Arpad lay well north of Damascus, but their defeat portended doom for Syria and its crowning city at the hands of southerly marching conquerors (v. 23). The Assyrians subdued this region more than a century before Jeremiah's day, and Syria continued to suffer under Babylonian domination. Several Syrian kings bore the throne name Ben-hadad (v. 27).

49:28-33 Kedar and the Kingdoms of Hazor Nomadic descendants of Ishmael's son Kedar occupied the Syro-Arabian desert region between Canaan and Babylon (note Jeremiah's references to their tents and unfortified settlements; vv. 29, 31). Leviticus 19:27 prohibits the trimming of beards, and the Kedarites' doing so marks them as covenantal outsiders (v. 32). The "kingdoms of Hazor" probably refers to seasonal settlements east of the impressively fortified stronghold in northern Galilee. Nebuchadnezzar conquered these independent desert peoples in 599/98.

49:34-39 Elam The introduction to this oracle dates it to 597, when Nebuchadnezzar exiled Jehoiachin and appointed Zedekiah as puppet king of Judah (v. 34; 2 Kings 24:17). Jeremiah gives no reason for God's judgment against Elam, a powerful kingdom bordering Babylon east of the Tigris River, but Nebuchadnezzar's takeover of this region to his rear undoubtedly strengthened his forward political and military capabilities in faraway Canaan. Thus the overthrow of Elam aided Babylon as the instrument of God's judgment against Judah. Jeremiah's oracle ends with a divine promise to restore the fortunes of Elam (v. 39). The Persian Empire, which in 539 succeeded Babylon as the reigning Mesopotamian superpower, established its winter capital at the Elamite city of Susa (Neh. 1:1; Esth. 1:2; Dan. 8:2).

50–51 Babylon Cf. Isaiah 13; 46–47.

In elaborating the doom of Babylon, these chapters provide great hope for the exiles by spelling out God's strategy for fulfilling the restorative promises of chapters 30–33. The concluding oracles also put the captives in Babylon on advance notice to abandon it while they can, once God sets in motion his plan for the destruction and desolation of their temporary habitation in Mesopotamia (51:6). In 539, the conquering Medo-Persian army of Cyrus earned Jeremiah's designation as destroyer from the north, which until now he had assigned to the newcomer's principal victim, Babylon. Much of the material in these chapters portrays the demise of the Babylonian Empire as accomplished fact — fulfillment of the prophetically symbolic act of Seraiah (brother of Baruch, Jeremiah's secretary) by his going to Babylon in ca. 594, between the first (597) and second (586) deportations of Judahites (51:59-64; 2 Kgs. 24:10–25:12).

Jeremiah expresses the defeat of the empire in terms of the proven impotence of its supposedly protective principal deities, the high god Marduk ("Merodach") and Bel ("lord"), a title that originally signified a separate god but eventually became identified with Marduk (50:2). Citing Babylon's arrogant irreverence for God and his chosen people as the root cause of its judgment, the prophet scorns the delight taken by the Babylonians in their punitive role against Judah and their presumption in pillaging the land God designated as the inheritance of the Hebrews (50:11). The example of Assyria, whom Babylonia defeated, should give fair warning (50:17-18).

Jeremiah envisions the exiles' return to Canaan (50:4ff.), which he repeatedly expresses as a command (50:8; 51:45-51). The northern kingdom, earlier conquered and exiled by Assyria, will also enjoy anew the abundance of its landed inheritance on both sides of the Jordan (Carmel and Ephraim in Canaan proper; Bashan and Gilead in Transjordan; 50:19). On the "everlasting covenant" (50:5, 20) that will govern the life of the reunited, pardoned remnant of Israel and Judah, see 31:31-34.

Jeremiah's prophetic command ordering the annihilation of the land and the inhabitants of "Merathaim" and "Pekod" (50:21), regions in southern Babylonia, plays on the meanings of these names: "Double Rebellion" and "Punishment," respectively. The oracle gives the Babylonians' 587/86 destruction of the Jerusalem temple as justification for the vengeful "utter destruction" of the entire "land of the Chaldeans," here represented by these regions (50:28).

The reference to the Babylonian fighting force "becoming women" (50:37) reflects the attitude of a patriarchal society. The terrible onslaught by the conquerors of Babylon will render even its king incapacitated (50:43).

"Leb-qamai" (51:1) is a code name for Chaldea ("Kasdim") that means "the heart of those who rise up against Me [the Lord]." The divine judgment of Babylon gives evidence that God has not forsaken his chosen, though guilt-ridden, people (51:5). Jeremiah pits the power over nature of the all-wise Creator against the impotence of mindless, man-made idols (51:15-19; cf. ch. 10). God himself constitutes the "portion of Jacob," the covenantal inheritance of the Hebrews (51:19; cf. Deut. 18:1-2; Josh. 13:33).

Jeremiah calls the nations to unite in devotion to judging Babylon, which built its empire by subjecting foreign kingdoms. He commands specific regions to join in the anti-Babylonian alliance: Ararat, Minni, and Ashkenaz (most likely the land of the Scythians), located from eastern Turkey to northwestern Iran, all of which fell under the control of the Medes, led by Cyrus (51:27). God will "dry up (the) sea" of Babylon, thereby devastating the Mesopotamian economy, which relied on an elaborate system of rivers and canals (51:36). That this same life-sustaining system of waterways will flood "Sheshach" (code name for Babylon, "Babel"; 51:41) represents waves of attackers. The ultimate disgrace of the empire comes with the picture of its sickened chief god, Bel (= Marduk), reduced to the indignity of vomiting (51:44). The oracles of Jeremiah end with chapter 51, but the New Testament book of Revelation recalls the fall of Babylon in symbolizing the final defeat of immorality at its worst (Rev. 14:8; 17:5; 18:2).

52 Jerusalem and the Temple: Destruction and Deportation

A historical postscript to the book of Jeremiah, chapter 52 closely parallels 2 Kgs. 24:18–25:30. Minor differences between the texts result from possible scribal errors and varying historical-theological emphases (e.g., Jeremiah's interest in Zedekiah). Jeremiah 52 omits the brief remarks about Gedaliah in 2 Kgs. 25:22-26, presumably because chapters 40–41 have already detailed the Babylonian-appointed Judean governor's short-lived political career and untimely assassination. Verses 28-30 specify three separate deportations of

Judahites to Babylon. The first took place in 597, when King Jehoiachin surrendered (2 Kgs. 24:10-16); the second occurred in 586, after the fiery destruction of Jerusalem and the temple (2 Kgs. 25:1-11); and the third came in 582/81, in response to the murder of Gedaliah (chs. 40–43). Daniel 1:1ff. records a prior deportation in 605, prompted by the rebellion of Judah's King Jehoiakim (cf. 2 Kgs. 24:1-3). See "Exile and Return" (281-83).

Lamentations

Five poems make up the book of Lamentations. They all deplore the ruination of early 6th-century-B.C. Jerusalem, including the temple, and the plight of the city's population. To the unexiled, rabble Hebrew remnant allowed to remain after the city's initial fall to Babylon in 597, the Babylonian conquerors' decimation of the former capital of Judah a decade later represented more than just a military victory. Theologically, the tragedy represented God's revoking of the covenantal blessings he had promised to his chosen people at Mount Sinai centuries earlier. The seeming finality of this judgment upended the Jerusalemites' falsely based confidence in God's *unconditional* protection of their city, which he had chosen as the site of his temple and the seat of an unending Davidic monarchy (2 Sam. 7:16).

Content

These poems trace the grieving process of the Hebrews, who despite repeated prophetic warnings remained stubbornly unpersuaded. Shock, desperation, and despair dominate chapters 1–2. Strong hope emerges in chapter 3, but chapter 4 puts the blame on former leaders. Chapter 5 ends the collection in a spirit of contrite resignation and hesitant faith for future restoration.

Literary Form

The poems display a funerary, dirge rhythm, and chapters 1–4 follow an acrostic pattern, in which each verse begins with a successive letter of the 22-letter Hebrew alphabet. (Chapter 3 devotes three verses to each letter.) Chapter 5 departs from the acrostic form, though its 22 verses maintain the parallel to the alphabet.

Authorship

The Septuagint, the 2nd–3rd century Greek translation of the Old Testament, names the prophet Jeremiah as the source of Lamentations, but the Hebrew text does not claim a particular author or authors. Some expressions in the book are similar to those of Jeremiah, but because of the long and complicated editorial history of that book, this similarity does not provide unquestionable evidence for Jeremiah's authorship. Nevertheless, the poems in Lamentations describe the devastation of Jerusalem in such personal terms as to suggest their authorship by an eyewitness or eyewitnesses to the 587/86 ravaging of the city. That the poems bewail the awful fulfillment of Jeremiah's prophecies against Judah makes appropriate their placement immediately after the book of Jeremiah.

The lost lament written by Jeremiah for the slain King Josiah (2 Chr. 35:25) does not appear in Lamentations. Since the destruction of the second temple in A.D. 70, the Jewish festal calendar has included the reading of this book on the anniversary of the 587/86 B.C. Babylonian assault on Jerusalem.

1 Lamenting the Demise of the Princess City

Verses 1-11 bemoan the reduction of personified Zion (= Jerusalem) to widowhood, slavery, and exile. Pilgrims no longer flood her streets at feast times; her friends have turned against her; and her enemies (the Babylonians) have become her masters. Famine threatens the few remaining inhabitants, who mourn the city's bygone better days. The poet acknowledges the punitive hand of God in humbling the former capital. The public nakedness of the divinely defrocked princess city brings such shame that she cannot even look at herself. Jerusalem lacked foresight by persisting in the sins that rendered her covenantally "unclean" and therefore deserving of punishment (v. 9). Worst of all, God's aiding the defilement of his temple by pagan invaders verifies the intentional withdrawal of his presence from Zion, whose inhabitants interject cries of affliction in verses 9c and 11c.

The city deplores her own plight in verses 12-22, with a bewailing interruption by the poet appearing in verse 17. Jerusalem, the "virgin daughter of Judah," protests her unparalleled pain. That God will similarly strike the enemies of Zion is the dearest wish of the despondent, self-pitying city — not to vindicate God's righteousness, but merely as revenge for herself and to gain company in her misery.

2 Jerusalem Hits Rock Bottom

This poem recognizes God as the author of Jerusalem's devastation and questions the extent of his punishment. God's "footstool" refers to the ark of the covenant, which contained a written copy of the now revoked Mosaic covenant (1 Chr. 28:2; Exod. 25:16). The patriarchal name "Jacob" (= "Israel"; cf. Gen. 32:28) refers to the entire Hebrew nation, and the "strongholds of daughter Judah" signify the fortifications of Jerusalem (cf. vv. 8-9). The "tent of daughter Zion" is the temple, God's home ("booth," "tabernacle"; vv. 4, 6). The enemies' celebration of capturing the temple makes God's rejection of his house all the more painful (v. 7). Verses 8-9 express God's demolition of Jerusalem as an architecturally calculated strategy (the stretching out of a line; cf. Amos 7:7-9) to collapse the city's defenses. The elders of fallen Jerusalem adopt the posture and practices of mourning (v. 10).

The most heart-rending result of God's wrathful display consists in the death of infants and children, some starving in their mothers' arms and others victims of cannibalism by the women who bore them (vv. 12, 20). The poet questions this slaughter of the defenseless, as well as the execution in the temple of priests and prophets (v. 20), whose failings he nevertheless recognized in verse 14. The poet approaches the depths of despair by portraying an utterly humiliated, divinely terrorized, survivorless Zion (vv. 15-22).

3 The Triumph of Hope

The book's central poem personalizes God's judgment of Jerusalem by portraying it from the perspective of an individual inhabitant of the city. The afflicted speaker bewails his physical deterioration, unanswered cries for divine help, and public humiliation. His eating of the bitter herb "wormwood" represents the sorrow-stricken nature of his graceless existence (vv. 15, 19; cf. Jer. 9:15). Physically and emotionally crushed, he nevertheless offers an inspiring declaration of faith in God's abiding love and compassion (contrast vv. 18 and 21ff.).

The speaker's acknowledgment of God as his "portion" (inheritance), demonstrates his appropriate assignment of priority to the Lord rather than to the covenantal promise of land and material blessing (v. 24). He contritely proclaims the virtue of accepting corrective punishment (the "yoke," v. 27) in the knowledge that God, who afflicts neither eagerly nor unjustly, will ultimately bestow love and compassion (vv. 26-33). Injustices do exist in the human sphere, but the "ill" that "goes forth" from God does not equate with those evils, and sinners have

Bittersweet wormwood, symbolic of utter calamity.
(Wikimedia Commons)

no grounds for complaining about suffering the adverse consequences of human transgression (vv. 34-39).

Verses 40-47 speak from a collective perspective, and the rest of the poem reads much like an individual psalm of lament. The poet pleads for God's attentiveness to his cry for help and expects God to judge the unrelenting oppressors. The invocation of their "anguish (= hardness) of heart" (v. 65) seeks to prevent their repentance and thus ensure their judgment (cf. Exod. 7:2-5).

4 Jerusalem's High Society Laid Low

This poem focuses largely on the humbling of Jerusalem's socially privileged but morally insensitive upper class, in whom the masses placed false hope. Like the temple treasures, they have lost their value and cannot even provide basic sustenance for the children of Jerusalem. The purple-clad people reared in royal circles now mourn in the ash pits of Zion (vv. 5, 7-8). Sin worse than Sodom's invited the degradation (v. 6). A quick slaying by sword would be a more fortunate end than this slow death by starvation and the horrors it provokes (vv. 9-10).

The fall of Jerusalem caught the world by surprise (v. 12). No one took seriously enough the covenantal requirement of righteousness to guarantee God's preserving the capital from assault (2 Sam. 7:1-17). Now the sinful prophets and priests, who bear the greatest responsibility for God's punishment of the misled masses, must publicly declare themselves ritually unclean as they flee into exile.

The reversal of fortunes prophesied in verses 21-22 injects a surprise ending of hope for demoralized Zion. Though at present the Edomite descendants of Esau gloat about the downfall of their historic Judean rival, Edom too will reap God's punishment.

5 Divine Restoration or Enduring Rejection?

In this final, communal plea for God to take note of his people's plight, the shock and desperation evident in chapters 1–4 give way to contrite resignation. The siege and conquest of Jerusalem have ended, but their memory and effects linger as the economically crushed Hebrew subjects of triumphant Babylonia deplore the loss of their landed inheritance, the ravishing of their women, the humiliation of their leaders, the forced labor of their children, and the joylessness of their existence (cf. Jer. 25:10). They have become a nation of widows and orphans — a socially and politically powerless people. The famine-stricken Judahites' life-risking forays to obtain food from the similarly subjected Egyptians and Assyrians reveals the extent of the Hebrews' dilemma (vv. 6, 9). Worn out from the struggle to survive, they admit their sinfulness — an extension of their ancestors' covenantal unfaithfulness, for which the current generation bears the punishment.

The Hebrews' only hope lies in the possibility of restoration and renewal by God. But unlike the optimistic individual in chapter 3, the collective community is not convinced that God will take them back (v. 22; cf. 3:21-25). Thus Lamentations ends with the gnawing question, "Is it too late for forgiveness?"

Ezekiel

A younger contemporary of Jeremiah, Ezekiel prophesied both before and after the fall of Jerusalem (587/86 B.C.). Whereas Jeremiah spoke from within Judah, and toward the end of his career from Egypt, Ezekiel delivered his oracles from Babylon, where he received his prophetic call several years after entering exile with the wave of Judahites deported by Nebuchadnezzar in 597. Ezekiel's career began over 125 years after the fall of the northern kingdom of Israel. His oracles targeted both his exilic companions and, probably by letter, the Hebrew community that remained in Jerusalem/Judah.

The Prophet

We know of Ezekiel from the biblical record only, and the book that bears his name gives little personal information about the prophet. He came from a priestly family and evidently figured among the elite of Jerusalem, since the first Babylonian deportation targeted the upper echelons of Judahite society (2 Kgs. 24:10-16). The sudden death of Ezekiel's wife (24:15-17) indicates that he was married, at least for a time. That the exiled Hebrew elders approached Ezekiel for consultations reveals their high regard for his prophetic credentials, despite his bizarre behavior. Judging from the prophet's assignment of very specific dates to many of his oracles, his career spanned at least a 22-year period, from 593 to 571.

Content

The book of Ezekiel represents a collection of independent oracles arranged for the most part in chronological order. Two recurring, introductory phrases alert the reader to the nature of the revelations that follow. "The hand of the Lord came upon me" introduces visionary revelations, four of which predominate: (1) Ezekiel's

prophetic call and his description of the cherub-driven chariot of God (chs. 1–3); (2) God's departure from the temple and Jerusalem (chs. 8–11); (3) the valley of dry bones (ch. 37); and (4) the restored temple and new Jerusalem (chs. 40–48). The more common phrase, "The word of the Lord came to me," introduces divinely communicated messages that Ezekiel must pass on to a particular audience, at times through shocking language and images. But Ezekiel also engages in a dozen attention-getting prophetic enactments — more than any of his fellow prophets.

The message of Ezekiel represents the two sides of one coin. First, the persistent religious and social sins of Judah and Jerusalem make inevitable their further punishment by God. The initial deportation by Babylon raised the theological question for the now geographically separated Judahites, "Which group constitutes the prophesied 'remnant' that will enjoy restoration by God — the exiles, or those whom God seemed to favor by allowing them to remain in the promised land?" Ezekiel answers that the exiles are favored, and time is running out for the unrepentant, overconfident escapees of the first judgment. The other, hopeful side of Ezekiel's message promises postjudgment restoration through the renewal of God's covenantal relationship with his people and their return to Canaan (see "Exile and Return" [281-83]).

Literary Form

The structure of the book reflects the above themes. In chapters 1–24, oracles of judgment against Jerusalem/Judah predominate. Chapters 34–48 carry primarily promises of restoration. Chapters 25–32 bridge these two sections with oracles against the pagan nations and share with chapters 1–24 the theme of judgment, which, when directed against the enemies of

God's people, indirectly promises hope for the Hebrews. The pivotal chapter 33 reports the fall of Jerusalem — the climax of God's judgment against his people — and thus inaugurates the shift in Ezekiel's prophetic emphasis.

The literary style of Ezekiel lays the foundation for apocalyptic (end times) literature, which the New Testament book of Revelation develops fully (see "The Beginnings of Apocalyptic Literature" [443-44]).

Authorship

Scholars generally agree that most of the early Old Testament prophets first transmitted their oracles orally. Only later did they and/or their disciples commit the revelations to writing. But Ezekiel seems to have communicated his oracles in written form from the beginning. Their complexity and length and the book's largely prosaic style support such an assumption, as does the text's picture of the prophet sequestered in his own home and struck dumb till the fall of Jerusalem. The autobiographical character of the book argues in favor of Ezekiel as the primary author, though he and/or his disciples probably edited the work (cf. 1:2-3). Ezekiel's flamboyant language gives color to the images and allegories of which he makes liberal use.

1 Ezekiel's Vision of God

The first three verses of Ezekiel provide most of the personal information we know about the prophet. A priest and son of a man named Buzi, Ezekiel lived among the exiles deported to Babylon after the surrender of King Jehoiachin in 597 (2 Kgs. 24:10-16). The "thirtieth year" (v. 1) may signify Ezekiel's age at the time of his visionary prophetic call, recorded in chapters 1–3. By relating this occasion to the year of Jehoiachin's exile, the editorial comments in vv. 2-3 clarify the year in question as 594/93. The river Chebar probably signifies the great canal that splits from the Euphrates River at a point north of Babylon and flows southeast past the city of Nippur, where some of the exiles settled (cf. 3:15).

Verse 4 begins a detailed description of Ezekiel's bizarre vision, sparked by the empowering "hand of the Lord" (v. 3; cf. Judg. 3:10). The prophet does his best to paint a verbal picture of the surreal revelation, and his language ("appearance," "as if," "[seemed] like/likeness") draws the reader into Ezekiel's own attempt to comprehend the images he sees. An ancient Hebrew would have understood that the initial picture of a storm — with wind, cloud, and lightning flashes — signified the presence of God (Exodus 19; Rev. 4:5), but by first elaborating the supporting characters and continuing to detail the heavenly set, Ezekiel builds suspense for the dramatic entrance of the focal point of his vision: God enthroned, whose recognition by Ezekiel culminates in sudden prostration by the prophetic inductee (vv. 26-28).

The four figures positioned below the throne of God display a highly embellished human form with angelic and animal features, and Ezekiel later identifies the beings as cherubim — guardians of holy places (cf. 10:15ff.; Exod. 25:18-22). The creatures stand wingtip to wingtip to form a square and uphold a platform, from the middle of which comes a fiery glow. The strange scene includes four eye-covered wheels-within-wheels (each pair set at right angles to each other), which allow the four-headed beings to dart in any of the four directions of the compass without turning, and which increase their ability to see everything at once. The awesome sound produced by their flapping wings is silenced by a "voice from above" — the voice of a radiant, enthroned, human-looking being, the glimpse of whose glory prompts Ezekiel to fall on his face, probably for fear of dying from having seen God, seated on his throne-chariot (cf. Isa. 6:5; Exod. 3:6).

Ancient Near Easterners associated deities with specific earthly homelands. Yahweh's temple-house in Jerusalem established his identity as the national God of Judah. So Ezekiel 1 leaves the reader wondering whether Yahweh's visionary appearance in Babylon portends good or ill for the exiles and the Hebrews who remain in Canaan. God's activity in Mesopotamia demonstrates the geographical limitlessness of his power, and Ezekiel will cite frequently his vision of God as proof of his prophetic call outside the borders of the promised land.

2–3 Ezekiel's Prophetic Commissioning

God addresses the prostrate Ezekiel as "son of man," which in his day simply meant "human being" but which in Daniel would take on messianic overtones (Dan. 7:13-14; cf. Matt. 8:20). The spirit facilitates the incapacitated Ezekiel's obedience to God's command, and this divine control becomes a model for a life in which Ezekiel embodies the message he proclaims in word and deed (2:1-2; cf. 3:23-24, 26-27).

God commissions Ezekiel to prophesy to a "rebellious people" (2:3), who, he knows in advance, will not heed his warnings (cf. Isaiah 6; Jeremiah 1). Ezekiel 2:6 foreshadows their hostile reaction to his message, but Ezekiel receives God's promise of strength and protection equal to their opposition (3:8-9). In this oracle, the anticipated rejection of Ezekiel's message overshadows its content, a warning against wickedness (3:17-21). Ezekiel's exilic audience probably viewed their judgment as a done deal, so for them the prophet's admonitions lacked urgency. The Hebrews left in Judah may have thought they had escaped God's judgment and so failed to take Ezekiel's warnings seriously.

Ezekiel repeatedly uses the double title "Lord God" (2:4) to communicate simultaneously God's personal relationship with the Hebrews (Lord) and his sovereign power (God). Ezekiel's first divinely commanded task consists in eating a scroll, unusual in that it contains writing not just on the inner surface but on both sides (perhaps to indicate completeness). By consuming the scroll, Ezekiel essentially *becomes* its message, and despite its bitter words of lament, mourning, and woe, the scroll satisfies his sweet tooth — perhaps an indication of the personal fulfillment generated by his prophetic role.

The exiles constitute the immediate audience to which Ezekiel must communicate the words on the scroll, and the spirit transports him to a community of Hebrews at the ancient Mesopotamian town of Tel-abib ("mound of the deluge," 3:14-15). Evidently filled with righteous anger at the anticipated rejection of his prophetic message, the stunned prophet sits idly for a week, after which God appoints him a "watchman" to his people (3:17; cf. 33:1-9). Like the lookouts stationed atop an ancient city's thick defense wall, Ezekiel must warn of impending attack; but the assailant in view is God himself, and the people's only defense consists in repentance and righteousness (cf. 18:19-29). Any failure by Ezekiel to reprimand the wicked brings down on him guilt for their death in sin. That 3:17-21 excludes the case of a wicked person who repents demonstrates that Ezekiel's ineffectiveness is a foregone conclusion, but still he must warn them.

Immediately after receiving this public commission, however, Ezekiel finds himself ordered to become a recluse, tied up and imprisoned at home by his opponents. Further, God vows to strike Ezekiel dumb. According to 24:27, the Lord did not "open" Ezekiel's mouth until the fall of Jerusalem seven years later, though the prophet begins issuing reproving oracles in chapter 4. Apparently he was unable to speak of anything but the fate of Judah and Jerusalem in that interval.

Colossal statue of a winged lion, Northwest Palace of Assurbanipal II, Nimrud. *(British Museum)*

Worshippers of Other Gods (Part 1)

The Old Testament contains a large body of material concerning non-Israelite religions. In fact, the Bible records that the ancestors of the Israelites worshipped many gods until Abraham (Josh. 24:2; Gen. 35:2), and the worship of other deities was outlawed only at the time of Moses (Exod. 20:3; 22:20). Israelites continued to worship pagan deities and perform pagan practices though condemned for doing so by the prophets. Because of this, the writer of Kings believed that the calamity that befell Israel and Judah was partly because of their clinging to pagan practices (e.g., 2 Kgs. 17:7-23).

Non-Israelite religions were not categorized separately in the Bible but were seen collectively as "religions of the nations" and were summarily condemned. Many deities of Syro-Palestinian origin are mentioned by name, including Asherah, apparently the name of both a goddess and a sacred pole (mentioned over 40 times; e.g., Deut. 16:21), Baal (the most frequently mentioned pagan deity; e.g., Judg. 2:13; 2 Kgs. 10:18-28), Milcom of Ammon (1 Kgs. 11:5, 33; 2 Kgs. 23:13; possibly the same as Molech), Chemosh of Moab (Num. 21:29; Jer. 48:46; also known from fragmentary Moabite inscriptions), and Dagon of Philistia (cf. 1 Sam. 5:1-7). Egyptian deities are sparsely mentioned, although in Exodus Pharaoh is described as a god of Egypt. Other Egyptian gods, such as Ptah, Amon, Bes, and Hathor, appear only indirectly in the Bible as part of personal or geographical names. Mesopotamian deities are also rarely mentioned, including Marduk (probably the Merodach of Jer. 50:2; called Bel in Jer. 51:44), and Nabu (Nebo; Isa. 46:1). Like some Egyptian gods, many Mesopotamian deities are represented in personal and geographic names (e.g., Sin the moon-god in the name of Sennacherib, king of Assyria; 2 Kings 18–19).

Many religious practices are described and condemned, including magic and divination (Deut. 18:10-14), cultic rites, worshipping on hills and under trees (2 Kgs. 16:4; Hos. 4:13), and child sacrifice (2 Kgs. 16:3). Though pagan magic was viewed negatively (Lev. 19:26, 31; 20:6, 27; Exod. 22:18), many Canaanite magical practices were observed during the divided monarchy, and a number of kings and queens practiced sorcery and divination (2 Kgs. 9:22; 21:6). The biblical writers did not equate magic with the worship of pagan deities, however, but seemed to acknowledge the reality of magical power (cf. 1 Samuel 28). Magic was considered evil because it unlocked divine secrets. The Israelites appear to have imitated some Canaanite magical practices, including the use of common items such as clothing (2 Kgs. 2:13-14), staffs (Exod. 7:9), hands (2 Kgs. 5:11), and hair (Judg. 16:17). But these materials probably only served as vehicles of expression to authenticate the prophet as a messenger of God. Many Israelite cultic and sacrificial rites must have appeared on the surface similar to Canaanite practices. For example, Jehu of Israel tricked local Baal worshippers into thinking he was devoted to Baal by correctly performing their sacrificial rituals (2 Kgs. 10:18-27).

Archaeological investigations since the early 19th century have uncovered a vast body of illuminating information on the religions of the ancient Near East. In Israel, the discovery of a number of figurines of nude females (probably of the Canaanite goddess Astarte) probably attest that at least some Israelites worshipped this deity in addition to Yahweh. Seal impressions that probably represent other deities and personal names with the element "Baal" found on ostraca from Samaria show evidence of Baal worship in the north. An 8th-century-B.C. inscription from Kuntillet ʿAjrud in northern Sinai refers to Yahweh of Samaria and an

Canaanite fertility figures, probably the goddess Astarte; limestone and clay tablets, ca. 1400 B.C.
(Richard Cleave, Pictorial Archive)

"asherah" (the Canaanite goddess Asherah or her image, a sacred tree). It may imply a popular level of polytheism involving Yahweh.

Much of Israelite religious architecture, hymnology, and language appears to compare closely to its Canaanite counterparts. Solomon's temple, built by Phoenician architects, has many structural similarities to the *bit hilani* temples found throughout northern Palestine and Syria in the late 2nd and early 1st millennia. A number of Israelite psalms have counterparts in the body of Canaanite hymnic material found in the coastal city of Ugarit (ca. 1400-1200), whose many myths and epics also illuminate our understanding of the Canaanite pantheon. Most striking is the

Bronze statue of Reshef, Canaanite god of pestilence; Syrian style, ca. 1400 B.C. *(Richard Cleave, Pictorial Archive)*

survival of Ugaritic themes in Psalm 29, suggesting that it may have had a foreign origin. Religious materials found at Emar, a 14th-13th century Bronze Age city on the Euphrates River, are similar enough to many Israelite rituals, religious calendars, and covenant formulas as to imply that the latter were not unique. For example, the Emar festivals have various requirements that compare to regulations in the book of Leviticus. Since the Israelites spoke "the language of Canaan" (Isa. 19:18), it is not surprising that recent studies conclude that biblical Hebrew is a dialect of Canaanite. Texts from Ugarit and elsewhere have cast new light on many obscure religious terms in the Bible. Furthermore, the massive corpus of cuneiform inscriptions discovered (in the hundreds of thousands) has provided a wealth of information concerning religious beliefs found in Syro-Mesopotamia, Anatolia, and Iran. Just as significant are the Egyptian funerary monuments and papyri that have illumined their religious practices.

It is difficult to generalize about the diverse religions of the "nations" of the ancient Near East, but they share a number of common features that distinguish them from the monotheistic religion of Israel. In general, they deified both animate and inanimate objects, had a belief in spirits and demons, and used incantations and magic. They believed that a primordial, chaotic realm existed prior to the gods, which was either darkness, water, spirit, or the sky. The gods were dependent upon this realm yet limited by it. Thus, not only were the gods not the source of all being, they were not eternal, omniscient, omnipotent, or omnipresent. According to one

Egyptian myth, Aten emerged out of the waters of Nun, the primeval ocean. In the Babylonian Creation Epic, the gods were created from the mingling of the primordial abyss and bitter waters. Marduk, the hero of the myth, fashioned the cosmos from preexistent matter but did not create it. Tiamat, a being shaped from the primordial mass, fought with her divine children. Many other myths show the tension between the gods and other forces of the universe. For example, Baal fought with Yamm ("Sea") in the Canaanite version. Since the gods originated in the world, there was no fixed boundary between them and the world of mortals.

The gods of the nations were portrayed primarily as having human characteristics (for a similar portrait of the God of Israel, cf. Genesis 18) and acted like superhuman creatures. They were male and female, desired to mate with each other, and had dysfunctional families. Similar to the gods of ancient Greece, they had reason, emotions, and even morals (and the lack thereof) like humans, only on a grander scale. They also inhabited and had jurisdiction over specific regions and lands, and only occasionally did they violate the space of another deity.

Even the gods needed to employ magical objects to obtain their own desires. They could acquire wisdom (i.e., they did not possess all-knowing power). The gods of Mesopotamia all desired to control the operable forces of the universe, personalized as the concept of Fate. Whoever possessed the Mesopotamian tablets of Fate had supreme authority in heaven.

MARK W. CHAVALAS

4–5 Ezekiel Enacts the Fate of Jerusalem

Ezekiel must have looked like a child playing war, when at God's command he set up a model siege of Jerusalem with stray building materials (a sun-dried mudbrick) and common kitchen utensils (an iron plate, used for baking bread). The prophetic enactment also involves Ezekiel's lying on his left side and then his right to symbolize his bearing the sin of first the northern kingdom (Israel) and then the southern kingdom (Judah; 4:4-6). The numbers of days that Ezekiel must lie down (390 for Israel; 40 for Judah) remains impossible to correlate exactly with periods in the histories of the kingdoms. In verse 5, the Septuagint reads 190, perhaps because the Greek translators wanted to approximate the 184-year period between the fall of the northern capital of Samaria (722/21) and the return of the exiles (538). Elsewhere in the Old Testament, the number 40 often represents one generation.

Ezekiel's diet also reflected the desperate conditions of the coming siege of Jerusalem. His daily ration of bread — made from a mix of whatever grains he could find — came to just eight ounces (4:10), washed down with about two-and-a-half cups of water. The prophet protests that God has gone too far in commanding him to fuel his bread-baking fire with human dung, which would make him, a priest, ritually unclean.

In the ancient Near East, military victors shamed defeated kings by shaving their heads. To symbolize the coming humiliation of Jerusalem and the mourning of her inhabitants, Ezekiel shaves his head and beard. His shorn locks represent the Hebrews still living in and around Jerusalem, one-third of whom the Babylonian army will kill outside the city; one-third of whom will die of disease and famine inside the former capital; and one-third of whom will scatter to pagan nations, where they will continue to suffer death and divine affliction. Only a meager remnant (the few "hairs" bound to the edges of Ezekiel's robes; 5:3) will survive God's anger over Jerusalem's idolatry and excessive wickedness.

6–7 Judah's Imminent End

Ezekiel's prophetic medium changes from deed to word, and his audience broadens from Jerusalem to all Judah. In addressing the "mountains of Israel" (6:2ff.), Ezekiel condemns the outdoor Canaanite shrines ("high places"), where the Hebrews practiced a mixture of covenantal Yahwism and pagan religious rites. God's slaying of the transgressors "in front of" their idols will demonstrate the powerlessness of false gods and the sovereignty of the Lord. The corpses encircling the smashed altars will defile the surrounding ground. To witness to God's supremacy, he will allow a remnant of Judahites to survive the deadly judgment. These exiled few will finally acknowledge their sinfulness. In the meantime, God will reduce the promised land to a barrenness even more desolate than the scarcely vegetated, sparsely populated southern wilderness (the Negev). The geographic references encompass the entire south-north extent of Canaan proper, the "four corners of the land" (7:2).

In chapter 7, repetition and redundancy intensify the sense of Judah's imminent end. The kingdom will soon reap the fruits of its pride and violence (7:10-11, 27). The reference to buyers and sellers (vv. 12-13) relates to Mosaic law regarding landed inheritance rights (cf. Leviticus 25). Fugitives of the divine judgment will don traditional mourning attire (sackcloth) and shave their heads to signify their shame. With food unavailable for buying, money will prove of no use in satisfying one's basic needs. Humiliated survivors will continue suffering disaster after disaster. Religious and civil leaders will become incapacitated. By these means will God enfeeble the Judahites for the "chain" of captivity (7:23).

8–11 Grounds for Desertion

Ezekiel's second vision of God occurs in September 592 (8:1).

8 Pagan Worship at the Temple In this revelation, a radiant being with a human appearance (God) grabs the prophet by the hair and transports him from his house to the northern gate of the temple court (cf. 1:26-28). As in his first vision, Ezekiel sees the glory of God *outside* the temple building. Here the Lord takes him on a tour of the sanctuary precincts that moves him ever closer to the temple itself, so that he witnesses God's grounds for deserting it. First the prophet sees that a pagan idol (possibly the Canaanite goddess Asherah) greets entrants to the grounds of God's house. But both here and with the production of each new piece of evidence, God tells Ezekiel that much more is to come. Next God shows his prophet a peephole to a secret room, into which Ezekiel digs his way. There he observes 70 Hebrew elders surreptitiously engaged in animal worship under the leadership of a member of the otherwise upright family of Shaphan. Carvings of "detestable" creatures adorn the walls of the darkened room (v. 10). Ezekiel's audience would have known of Tammuz (v. 14), the Mesopotamian fertility god who died at year's end and rose again each spring. Here the prophet observes Hebrew women publicly mourning the false deity's death in case he actually did control reproductive and agricultural processes. The most flagrant snubbing of God, however, takes place at the entrance to the temple itself. With backs turned to the ultimate symbol of his presence among his people, 25 men bow in worship of the rising sun. The people's public and private disregard of God indicates that the recently enacted religious reforms of Josiah did not take deep or abiding root among the people as a whole (cf. 2 Kings 22). Social sins abound along with the people's religious degeneration (v. 17), and the pervasive depravity invites God's unpitying judgment.

9 The Jerusalemites Judged God's case against Jerusalem proven, with Ezekiel as witness the visionary punishment begins. At God's summons, armed men approach from the north, from which direction came Babylon and earlier enemies of Israel. One of the contingent, clothed in traditional priestly linen, distinguishes with an ink mark the Jerusalemites who regret the city's covenantal transgressions, and the accompanying executioners kill everyone else (cf. Exod. 12:12-13; Rev. 7:3; 13:16-17). In Ezekiel's vision, judgment starts at the temple, whose courts the corpses of evil elders defile.

Ezekiel protests to God the comprehensiveness of the killing, but to no avail.

10–11 God Abandons the Temple and Exits Jerusalem Again Ezekiel sees the wheeling cherubim that appeared in his first vision (see ch. 1), but now their context becomes clear. They form a chariot-throne to carry the glory of God out of the temple before the destruction of Jerusalem by fire. To ignite the conflagration, God commissions the linen-clad scribe from the north to scatter over the city blazing coals taken from the midst of the cherubim. As elsewhere, a cloud represents God's glory (10:3-4; e.g., Exod. 40:34-38).

In Ezekiel's visionary exit from the temple precincts, he recognizes two leaders, against whom God commands that he prophesy for their misleading counsel. Evidently, they failed to take seriously the warnings concerning Jerusalem's inevitable judgment, for they forecast good times soon to come (cf. 13:10). Apparently, the leaders hedged their bets on the impregnability of Jerusalem, the protective "pot" of its "fleshly" inhabitants (11:3, 7, 11).

But the fortifications of Jerusalem cannot prevent God's judgment against the leaders (cf. 13:5). The immediate death of Pelatiah, one of Ezekiel's addressees, demonstrates the authenticity of the prophecy. Ezekiel repeats his concern that by destroying the Jerusalemites, God will eradicate the "remnant" of Hebrew heirs to the promised land. God responds that the exiles in Babylon are the true remnant — not the Jerusalemites (11:15-17). Ezekiel's prophecy concerning the new "heart" that God will give the restored remnant corresponds to Jeremiah's preview of the new covenant that will succeed the judgment of exile in Babylon (vv. 17-21; cf. Jer. 31:27-40). The visionary withdrawal of God from Jerusalem and the return of Ezekiel to Babylonia end the revelation, which the prophet details to the people in exile.

12 Enacting the Imminent Judgment of Judah

Even though the rebellious Hebrews persist as blind seers and deaf hearers (v. 2; cf. Isa. 6:9-10; Matt. 13:13-17), Ezekiel must continue prophesying to them — now by publicly acting out the coming deportation of Hebrews still in Jerusalem and the Babylonian-appointed puppet Zedekiah. Ezekiel calls Zedekiah the "prince" (vv. 10, 12) and reserves "king" for the exiled Jehoiachin, whose surrender to Nebuchadnezzar agreed with prophetic counsel (2 Kgs. 24:10-12). Ezekiel's enactment parallels Zedekiah's attempted escape when the Babylonian army breached the walls of Jerusalem — out the back door, under cover of darkness; he was blinded by his Babylonian captors and entered exile (2 Kgs. 25:1-7). The concluding oracle is a warning to the complacent, who, embracing the optimistic words of false prophets (v. 24), regard judgment as far in the future (vv. 22, 27) and so discount the prophecies of doom: God will delay judgment no longer (vv. 17-28).

13 Prophesying against False Prophets

Ezekiel now condemns the false prophets themselves for misleading the people with lies that have lulled them into a false sense of security. Like scavenging foxes, the charlatans prey off the desperation of the defeated Judahite people. Most vexing for God is the deceitful prophets' attributing to him their self-inspired misinformation. The account likens their advice to slapdash building repairs, where unsubstantial, plaster-patched walls are made to look good with a coat of whitewash but fail to make adequate battle fortifications (vv. 10ff.). These cosmetic efforts also represent the soothing words of the false prophets that will fail to withstand the divinely generated storm to come. These prophetic rivals have failed to warn the people of the coming judgment and the need to build protective "walls" through repentance. The oracle strips the impostors of their social status, ostracizes them from the Hebrew community, and bans them from the future restoration to Canaan (v. 9).

Ezekiel also condemns female diviners (vv. 18-23), whose main goal appears to have consisted in controlling the lives of others, possibly through the use of amulets or magical charms. That meager amounts of barley and bread sufficed as payment for the diviners' services testifies to the economic weakness of Judah at this time (v. 19).

14 Inescapable Punishment for Unfaithful Idolaters

The request by the Hebrew elders in exile that Ezekiel mediate a divine consultation demonstrates their recognition of his status as a prophet of God (cf. 20:1). But the only word God gives to the inquirers is a command to forsake their idolatry, lest he make examples of them. The prophet who mediates for them should also beware, for the guilt of his patrons also extends to him.

Four hypothetical situations emphasize God's certain punishment of the society that proves unfaithful to him (vv. 13-20). To dispel the notion that a community's righteous few ensure its sinful majority against divine devastation, the oracle cites the prophetic warnings of famine, ravage by wild beasts, war, and disease as judgments from which association with even the most revered of ancient Near Eastern heroes cannot provide escape. Ezekiel mentions three non-Israelites as examples of righteousness: Noah, Job, who remained faithful in the midst of great suffering, and Daniel, probably the wise ruler in the Ugaritic tale of Aqhat, but almost certainly not the biblical Daniel. Thus Ezekiel asserts that God reserves deliverance for the righteous and exacts punishment on the wicked, regardless of ethnicity.

Far from the exception to this divine rule, the Jerusalemites will become its prime example. God will spare a wicked few, not out of mercy, but as evidence of the appropriateness of his punishment through their persistently sinful conduct.

15 The Jerusalemites: Fuel for the Fire

The vine is often a positive symbol of life and fruitfulness (e.g., John 15:1-8). Here, however, Ezekiel emphasizes the inadequacy of vine wood as the raw material for useful items, and the charred remains of vine wood partially burnt as fuel are only fit for further consumption in the fire. The religiously unfaithful inhabitants of Jerusalem are like this wood. Some Jerusalemites have already "come out of the fire" (those exiled to Babylon in 597), but another fire will burn up the rest — a portent of the coming conflagration in 587/86.

16 Exposing Jerusalem as Total Adulteress

Having raised the issue of unfaithfulness, Ezekiel now details the evidence against adulterous Jerusalem, personified from infancy to adulthood. To intensify the audacity of her infidelity, Ezekiel rehearses the history of divine favor that boosted the city to preeminence.

The reference to Jerusalem's Canaanite parentage (v. 3) claims historical roots, for both the Hittites and the Amorites controlled Jerusalem at times before its conquest by the Hebrews. But the prophet also has the idolatrous religious ancestry of Jerusalem in view. Ezekiel likens Jerusalem to an unwanted newborn, not only neglected by midwife (v. 4) but discarded by parents and left to die through exposure (v. 5). God saved the rejected infant and caused her to thrive. When she reached sexual maturity, he committed himself to her in marriage by "covering" her with his "skirt" (cf. Ruth 3:9), which here symbolizes God's establishment of the covenant with the Hebrews at Sinai. God cleaned up his bride, lavished her with fine clothes and jewelry, and fed her delicacies, so that she became internationally famous for her beauty. But instead of responding in gratitude to her beneficent husband, she used her wedding gifts as bribes to seduce strangers — not out of material need, but purely from promiscuous desire. Jerusalem's unhidden harlotry refers to her covenantal transgressions in both the religious and political realms: indiscriminate idolatry, which included child sacrifice in imitation of her own rejection by parents (vv. 20-21) and the making of political alliances with foreign nations, forbidden in the covenant (Deut. 7:1-2). The city's brazen behavior makes even the pagan Philistines blush (v. 27). Mosaic law prescribed the death penalty for adulterers at the hands of the entire community (Deut. 22:22-24; cf. John 8:1-11). Here the spurning lovers of Jerusalem will execute her sentence — a presage of the merciless assault by Babylon in 587/86 (vv. 36-44).

Ezekiel accuses wicked Jerusalem of making her notoriously evil "sisters" look good (vv. 44-

52). This charge speaks volumes, for the Bible has nothing good to say about Samaria, the corrupt capital of the northern kingdom conquered by the Assyrians in 722/21, or Sodom, destroyed by God in Genesis 19.

Surprisingly, words of promised restoration for the city and her sisters close out the chapter. Their utter unfaithfulness stands in stark contrast to the determined covenantal faithfulness of God (v. 60). His gracious favor toward the undeservedly forgiven cities will surely silence them forever as he returns to them good for their evil (vv. 53-63).

17 The Allegory of the Eagles and the Vine

In this allegory, a great eagle (Nebuchadnezzar) plucks from Lebanon (Jerusalem) the topmost twig of a mighty cedar tree (King Jehoiachin, head of the Davidic royal family). The eagle removes the twig to a region known for its commerce (Babylonia, whose river system facilitated extensive trade). Back in Lebanon/Jerusalem, the eagle plants in fertile soil some of the native seed (Zedekiah, put in power over Judah by Nebuchadnezzar). The seed sprouts and flourishes, though as a low vine oriented toward the eagle (i.e., as a puppet to Babylonia). But along comes another eagle (the resurgent Egypt), whose nurture the vine solicits (Zedekiah's appeal for Egyptian aid in his treaty-breaking rebellion against Babylon; 2 Kgs. 24:20). The rhetorical questions in verses 9 and 10 leave no doubt as to the future of the vine: the first eagle will uproot it completely (the flight, capture, and deportation of Zedekiah in 587/86), so that it withers with the striking of the east wind (a mighty act of God).

But not even the mighty eagle Nebuchadnezzar will get the last word. God vows that he himself will take a sprig from the topmost branch of the cedar (i.e., a royal descendant of David) and cause it to flourish on "the mountain height of Israel" (i.e., revitalize the Davidic covenant in Jerusalem).

18 Reward and Punishment: Equity and the Individual

Ezekiel refutes the notion that people bear the punishment for the sins of their ancestors (cf.

33:10-20; Jer. 31:29ff.). The prophet's fellow exiles in Babylon were evidently citing the popular proverb of verse 2 to blame their situation on the wickedness of their forefathers. Ezekiel found precedent in Deuteronomic law forbidding fathers and sons to "stand in" for each other when either received the death sentence (Deut. 24:16). Against the current theology of his day, he asserts that God rewards and punishes people on the basis of their own behavior. Ezekiel's fellow Hebrews have only their sinful selves to blame for their exile in Babylon, and the prophet ends the chapter by charging them to repent (vv. 30-32).

Verse 4 repeatedly uses "soul" to mean simply "life" or "person," not a disembodied, spiritual component of one's "being." Accordingly, the reward of life and punishment of death refer respectively to physical existence and demise in the present world, not the afterlife. Throughout the Old Testament, long life symbolizes God's blessing, while untimely death signifies divine punishment. While Ezekiel makes it clear that God takes no pleasure in the death of human beings (v. 32), elsewhere he emphasizes the necessity of extreme punishment to allay God's righteous anger (e.g., 16:42).

Ezekiel refers to specific covenantal laws in defining the righteous person and the sinner (vv. 5-18). These regulations deal with theology and worship (esp. Exod. 20:1-17), ritual purity (Leviticus), and social justice (Deuteronomy). Many of the laws that comprise the prophet's legal litmus test derive from the book of Leviticus — not surprisingly, in view of Ezekiel's training as a priest.

Verses 19-29 anticipate the protest that God takes an unfair approach in rewarding the sinner who has only recently turned righteous and punishing one who had always done right but has now turned bad (cf. Matt. 20:1-16). Ezekiel defends God's absolute justice, which exceeds human ideas of fairness.

19 Mourning the Dying Davidic Monarchy

This allegorical lament mourns the imminent demise of the Davidic monarchy. In verses 1-9, the mother lioness represents Judah, for which the lion served as tribal symbol (Gen. 49:9). The

cubs are the pool of royal heirs to the throne. Ezekiel exaggerates the ferocity and power of the two Judahite kings to whom he specifically alludes: Jehoahaz (vv. 3-4), whom the Egyptian pharaoh Neco captured and deported to Egypt in 609 (2 Kgs. 23:30-34), and Jehoiachin (vv. 5-9), whom Nebuchadnezzar exiled to Babylon in 597 (2 Kgs. 24:10-15).

In verses 10-14 the imagery changes. The mother "vine" signifies the mountaintop capital of Jerusalem. The "east wind," often associated with events of divine origin (cf. 17:10), represents the Babylonian conquest of Jerusalem, the tearing off of whose "branches" recalls the deportation of the city's leading citizens (2 Kgs. 24:15-16). The replanting of the vine in a "dry and thirsty land" refers to Judah's exile in Babylonia (v. 13). The imagery describes not the land of the exile — a fertile region of Mesopotamia, veined with rivers and their tributaries — but its theological significance for the relocated Judahites, whose divine ousting from the promised land symbolizes their parched relationship with God. The "branch" from which goes out a destructive, spreading "fire" symbolizes Judah's last king, Zedekiah, whose rebellion against the superpower Babylon ended in the demise of the Davidic monarchy (v. 14).

20:1-44 God Breaks Communication with the Hebrew Elders

This oracle dates to July/August 591, during the seventh year of the Babylonian exile (v. 1). God again rejects the attempt of the Hebrew elders to consult him through Ezekiel (cf. ch. 14). The prophet's theologically interpretive rehearsal here of Israel's history explains God's response, spelled out in verses 30-31: The elders have personally perpetuated the rebellion and covenantal disobedience of their ancestors and thus have relinquished the privilege of communicating with God, who tolerates no rivals. The elders have embraced religious diversity, but the God of the Hebrews requires exclusive devotion (Exod. 20:3-5).

Ezekiel cites three cycles of divine charity toward the Hebrews, their response of disbelief and disobedience, and God's forgoing of their deserved destruction to prevent the defamation of his name among the heathen nations. Ezekiel first accuses the pre-exodus Hebrews of failing to heed God's prohibition against worshipping the gods of Egypt. He then convicts the exodus generation of transgressions against the covenant established at Sinai and, finally, charges the second generation of wilderness wanderers with sinning just like their parents. The Old Testament historical narratives do not indicate that God contemplated destroying the Hebrews for these instances of disobedience. The book of Exodus, however, does record two occasions on which Moses' appeals thwart God's determination to wipe out his chosen people: after their worship of the golden calf at Sinai (Exod. 32:1-14) and following their refusal to invade the promised land (Num. 14:1-20). Ezekiel has apparently applied this motif to the entire history of the Hebrew people, who continued to provoke God after they settled in Canaan. Yet they cannot escape the punishment of exile, decreed by God before the wayward Hebrews set foot in the promised land (v. 23) but earned by each generation of sinners, including the elders whom Ezekiel is addressing (vv. 30-31).

God's requirement that the Hebrews dedicate their firstborn offspring to God probably provides the background for verses 25-26 (cf. Exod. 22:29). Idolaters who burned their children as sacrifices to the Canaanite god Molech may have distorted this Mosaic law to justify their participation in the abominable rite. Exodus 13:11-13 and 34:20, however, stipulate the substitution of animals as "redemptive" sacrifices for human firstborn.

The Hebrews may determine to emulate the pagan nations by worshipping idols of wood and stone (v. 32), but God will prevent the ultimate success of their religious treachery against him. The exile will serve as a purging, wilderness experience to rout out the rebels and prepare the faithful for re-entry into the promised land (vv. 33-42) — a process pictured in the imagery of the shepherd's using his staff to sort out sheep for the slaughter (v. 37). Thus the oracle ends on a hopeful note for restoration of the repentant, but a note tempered by the deep sense of shame felt by this reformed remnant, who regret their iniquitous past (v. 43).

20:45–21:32 The Sword of Judgment Unsheathed

Chapter 21 interprets the allegorical oracle in 20:45-49, whose characterization of Canaan's barren southland (= "Teman," "Negev") as forested seems to puzzle even the prophet (20:49). Here the "South" probably represents the entire southern kingdom, whose total destruction will render it as bleak as its southernmost territory (cf. Babylonia in 19:13).

The fire that burns becomes the sword that slays — an omen of the decimation of Jerusalem and its population by the Babylonian army in 587/86. The text makes clear, however, that the judgment originates with God. In executing the divine plan, the "slayer" will use God's sword, ready for the indiscriminate slaughter of the righteous along with the wicked (21:4).

God calls on Ezekiel to go around moaning and groaning so that people, by asking him what's wrong, will unwittingly inquire about the oracle (21:6-7). When relating the coming devastation, the prophet must "cry out and wail," hit his thigh to mimic testing the sword (21:12-13), and clap his hands in symbolic initiation of the attack, which God also summons with a handclap (21:14, 17). God also instructs Ezekiel to draw (presumably in the dirt) two divergent roads and erect a signpost marking one road as the way to Rabbah, Transjordanian capital of the Ammonites (modern Amman, Jordan), and the other as the way to Jerusalem. The roads represent approach routes for the invading Babylonian army (21:19). Verse 21 pictures the king of Babylon using divination techniques to decide which destination to choose. Jerusalem comes up the winner (more appropriately, the loser) for breaking her treaty with Babylon under the soon-to-be-deposed puppet-king Zedekiah (21:23, 25-26). Verse 22 portrays the Babylonian army building earthen ramps for easier access of the attacking soldiers and their war machinery to the hilltop city's perimeter defense wall and entrance gates.

The chapter ends with an oracle against the Ammonites, who also embraced optimistic prophecies that gave them a false sense of security (21:29). Nebuchadnezzar did not attack the Ammonites during his 587/86 rampage against

Jerusalem, but the oracle warns of their future in oblivion (21:32).

22 The Indictment and Sentencing of Jerusalem

Here Ezekiel charges the inhabitants of Jerusalem, from the general populace up to religious and civil leaders, with sins against fellow humans and God. These transgressions, which have rendered the Hebrews "unclean" with regard to the covenant, include various kinds of social injustices, sexual sins, idolatry, and unethical business practices prohibited by Mosaic law. The eating of meat at mountain shrines (v. 9) refers to making a ritual meal of food sacrificed to idols. Verses 6-7 condemn Israel's rulers for their abuse of power; verse 26 highlights the failure of the priests to teach the Law to the laity; and verse 28 charges the prophets with fraud (cf. 13:8-16).

God vows to use the scattering of the Hebrews in exile as a means of purging his people of their uncleanness (v. 15), but first he will "smelt" them in the fiery destruction of Jerusalem. God's announcement that all the city's inhabitants have become junk "dross," however, forebodes grim prospects for recovering any refined "silver" (a surviving remnant) to banish in the first place (vv. 17-22). God himself had tried in vain to find even one righteous person to shield his people from his own destructive wrath (v. 30).

23 The Sinful Sisters Condemned

Ezekiel again uses graphic sexual imagery to portray the Hebrews' transgression of their covenant with God, especially through idolatry and the establishment of alliances with foreign nations. The oracle begins by introducing two sisters born from the united "mother" kingdom, which split after the death of Solomon (1 Kings 12). God marries both sisters (v. 4), and Samaria — the long defunct capital of the northern kingdom — becomes the measuring stick for the transgressions of her younger "sister" Jerusalem (cf. 16:44-63). But Jerusalem's iniquities far exceed the scale. The prophecy characterizes both cities as promiscuous adulteresses, whose religious harlotries extend back to the Hebrews'

days in Egypt (vv. 3, 8) and, in Jerusalem's case, carry forward to the present. Samaria's illicit treaty-making with Assyria led to her downfall in the 722/21 conquest of the northern kingdom (vv. 5-10). Now Jerusalem, who failed to learn from her sister's self-destructive, politically lustful folly, will collapse under the attack of her current lover, Chaldea/Babylonia, and cohorts Pekod, Shoa, and Koa (probably tribes on Babylonia's eastern border). Jerusalem will drink from the same "cup" of judgment as Samaria by suffering mutilation, humiliation, and slaughter (vv. 25-34). A closing indictment castigates the sister cities for simultaneously engaging in abominable pagan religious rites and worship at the temple. Ezekiel portrays the cities' multiple alliances with foreign nations as carefully planned orgies, participation in which earns the death sentence prescribed for adultery (vv. 40-47; Lev. 20:10).

24 The Final Siege Begins; Ezekiel's Wife Dies

God instructs the exiled Ezekiel to record the date on which he receives this oracle (usually understood as January 15, 588), for back home in Judah the forewarned judgment of Jerusalem has begun with the second and final Babylonian siege of the city (cf. 2 Kgs. 25:1; Jer. 52:4). The prophet re-employs negatively the imagery of Jerusalem as a "pot" that protects the inhabitants, its "fleshly" contents (vv. 3-13; cf. 11:3). The rebellious Jerusalemites have permanently stained their "pot" through sins (= "blood") for which they have failed to make atonement (placing blood on the "bare rock" rather than pouring it "on the ground, to cover it with earth," v. 7). Now the opportunity for ritual atonement has passed (v. 8), and the time for judgment has arrived. God will purify the city and her citizens by completely boiling Jerusalem's "flesh," burning up her "bones," and then melting by fire the rusted pot itself. The Babylonians' bloody conquest and fiery destruction of Jerusalem took place after an 18-month siege.

Ezekiel then receives an ominous but ambiguous divine word foretelling his imminent loss of someone he holds dear (v. 16). But God forbids the prophet to engage in normal mourning behavior (v. 17). Ezekiel communicates this prophecy to the people, and that evening his wife dies. The bereaved but obedient prophet's unusual public reaction to his loss leads the exiles to ask, "What does this mean for us?" whereupon Ezekiel prophesies the demise back home of what they cherish most: the temple and the kin left behind after the first deportation in 597. The reason for the people's failure to mourn these tragedies may lie in the deservedness of the punishment.

The destruction of Jerusalem in 587/86 constitutes the peak of Judah's punishment, and the "opening" of the prophet's mouth (v. 27; cf. 3:26; 33:21-22) on this day of judgment will mark the watershed event, which starts the Hebrews on the road to restoration.

25–32 The Nations Condemned

Cf. Amos 1–2; Isaiah 13–23; Jeremiah 46–51.

The Babylonians are besieging Jerusalem; Ezekiel is newly widowed as a sign of the city's imminent destruction; and the prophet's prospects of regaining his speech hinge on the occurrence of that tragedy. But the text now rails against the pagan nations, from whom God also demands good moral conduct.

25 Ammon, Moab, Edom, and Philistia Cf. Jeremiah 47–49.

Oracles against the three major Transjordanian regions begin with the northernmost, Ammon. By reacting to the downfall of Judah with ungodly rejoicing (cf. 18:30-32), the Ammonites invite their own punishment. Even their capital at Rabbah (modern Amman, Jordan) will become pastureland for the infiltrating "sons of the east" (nomadic tribes; v. 4). Moving south, Moab and Seir (the mountainous area of northern Edom, often named to represent the entire region) receive the same sentence for failing to recognize the uniqueness of Judah (and therefore of her God) among the nations. God also vows vengeance on Edom (land of Esau's descendants, doomed to perpetual conflict with the chosen line of Jacob; Gen. 25:23) and Philistia (the coastal region on Canaan's south-central coast, dominated by seafaring enemies of Israel) for taking their own vengeance against Judah (cf. Jer. 49:7-22; Obad. 1-14). The opportunistic

Edomites invaded southern Judah following the Babylonian destruction of Jerusalem (cf. ch. 35).

26–28 Tyre and Sidon Cf. Isaiah 23.

Three oracles condemn the prominent port city of Tyre, on the Phoenician coast roughly halfway between modern Beirut and Haifa (26:1–28:19). In the days of Israel's united monarchy (10th century), Tyre's King Hiram supplied Solomon with timber and skilled craftsmen for the construction of the Jerusalem temple and palace complex (1 Kings 5–7).

Tyre gained political power in the ancient Near East, not through military conquests but by dominating the world of commerce. The city boasted two harbors: one on the coast of the mainland, and the other at the offshore island on which the main city sat (26:5-6). The Phoenician inhabitants used their seafaring knowledge to trade a wide range of goods throughout the Mediterranean world and beyond. When Tyre's trading partners learn of her fall, they tremble, probably for fear of their own financial ruin (26:15-18). Because most of the major *land* routes ran through Canaan, the already rich Tyre recognized the economic opportunity opened to her by the fall of Jerusalem (26:2).

But Tyre's self-serving response to the political demise of Judah earns God's judgment (26:2). Ezekiel communicates the bad news in March/April 587/86, shortly after the Babylonian destruction of Jerusalem and just before Nebuchadnezzar, whom Ezekiel now names for the first time, comes knocking (26:1, 7). The siege of Tyre lasted 13 years, and the Babylonian assault was difficult (cf. 29:18), in part because of their target's island location. Nebuchadnezzar's army never did succeed in invading Tyre, though the standoff finally ended with her agreement by treaty to pay tribute to Babylon.

Chapter 27 metaphorically pictures Tyre as a magnificent vessel built of the best materials, sailed by a select crew, maintained by premiere repairmen, and loaded with the finest goods, but doomed to sink in the sea. The extensive geographical spread of Tyre's suppliers and trading partners testifies to the cosmopolitan nature of this ancient commercial hub: Senir (Canaan's Mount Hermon, 27:5); Bashan (northern Transjordan, v. 6); Elishah (probably Cyprus, vv. 6-7);

Sidon, Arvad, and Gebal (Greek "Byblos"; port cities on the Phoenician coast, north of Tyre, vv. 8-9). Persia, Lud (Lydia), and Put (Libya), from where Tyre drew its warriors, represent the whole of the ancient Near Eastern world, from well east of Tyre to the western extent of Mediterranean Eurasia to the North African coast west of Egypt (27:10). The place names in 27:12-25 represent Spain (Tarshish), Greece (Javan), Asia Minor (Tubal, Meshech), Armenia (Beth-togarmah), Arabia (Kedar and Dedan in the north; Uzal, Sheba, Canneh, and Eden in the south), neighboring Syria (Damascus) and Canaan (Judah, Israel), and Assyria (Haran, Asshur). The chapter closes with a lament describing the rituals carried out by Tyre's partners to mourn the sinking of the Mediterranean mother ship (27:30-32).

The long oracle in chapter 28 laments the rulers of Tyre, whose skill produced wealth leading to the overzealous pride that invited divine judgment (28:2-7). (On "Daniel" in 28:3, see 14:14.) Many of the metaphors here find general parallels in Genesis 2–3: the aspiration to achieve equality with God (v. 2); the initial Edenlike existence (v. 13); the cherub-guardian at the garden (v. 14); original moral innocence (v. 15); and expulsion as punishment for sin (v. 16). "Stones of fire" (vv. 14, 16) recall the fiery coals that ignite Jerusalem in the vision at 10:2. Since the Tyrians practiced circumcision, the rulers' sentencing to the "death of the uncircumcised" portended a humiliating end (28:10).

In the 9th century, King Omri of the northern kingdom of Israel forged an alliance with Phoenicia by arranging for his successor-son Ahab to marry the Baal-worshiping Sidonian princess Jezebel. Ezekiel attaches to the oracle against Tyre a word condemning her sister-city Sidon for "pricking" Israel with painful scorn (28:20-26). The oracles against Phoenicia result in a promise to the exiled Hebrews: God will restore them to the land of their inheritance, where they will pursue peacetime activities (building houses and planting vineyards) and enjoy political security (28:25-26).

29–32 Egypt Cf. Isaiah 19–20; and 46.

Ezekiel utters against Egypt his largest group of oracles directed at non-Hebrew nations. This kingdom that enslaved the Hebrews centuries before proved itself a fickle (and covenantally illegitimate) ally of Israel and Judah in their struggles against Assyria and Babylon. But Egypt's greater sin lay in opposing these nations that God appointed as instruments of his judgment against the wayward chosen people. The recurrent phrase, "Then they shall know that I am the Lord," makes clear the reason for God's punitive acts. The oracles in these chapters do not appear in chronological order, and only one lacks a date.

29:1-16 Pharaoh a Fish out of Water This oracle, dated to January 587, targets Pharaoh Hophra, who responded to the Judahite king Zedekiah's appeal for aid against the besieging Babylonians. Undoubtedly, Hophra considered Judah a crucial buffer that shielded Egypt from direct attack by Babylon. The pharaoh's attempt to save Jerusalem resulted in a short-lived reprieve for Judah's capital while Nebuchadnezzar's army withdrew to halt the advancing Egyptian relief forces. But the Babylonian siege resumed with a vengeance. Thus Ezekiel likens Egypt to a weak "reed," which when leaned on for support not only snaps but also results in injury to the leaner (vv. 6-7). Hophra's offense lay in considering himself divine (as did all the Egyptian pharaohs), as signified by his claim to have created the life-supporting Nile River (v. 3). Pharaoh may consider himself an invincible river "monster" (the Nile crocodile?), but God will fish him out and fling him into the waterless wilderness, where he will become carrion for birds of prey and scavenging beasts (vv. 3-5). Furthermore, God will devastate Hophra's entire kingdom, from north to south (Migdol, in the Nile Delta, to Syene/Aswan, on the border with Cush/Ethiopia; v. 10) and scatter its population in other countries. After it has lain desolate for 40 years (= one generation), God will repatriate the exiled Egyptians to "Pathros" (southern Egypt, v. 14). But the anemic nation of Egyptian returnees will never again embody for Israel a politically tempting ally (v. 16).

29:17-21 Wages for Nebuchadnezzar Ezekiel received this latest of his recorded words from

God on the Hebrew New Year's Day of 571. The Babylonian siege of Tyre had ended three years earlier, and this oracle publicizes Nebuchadnezzar's belated but forthcoming wages for doing God's work of judgment in Phoenicia: the conquest and plunder of Egypt. In verse 21, Ezekiel prophesies the simultaneous renewal of Israel's political strength, symbolized by the "horn."

30:1-19 Comprehensive Devastation in Store for Egypt and Her Allies This undated group of short laments elaborates the devastation of Egypt by the Babylonians and adds words of doom for Egypt's allies. Verse 5 names doomed nations to her south (Ethiopia/Cush), west (Put/Libya), north across the Mediterranean (Lud/Lydia), and east (Arabia). The ships bound for Ethiopia bearing God's messengers of doom travel upstream on the Nile (v. 9). Egypt's desolation "from Migdol to Syene/Aswan" covers the kingdom's north-south extent (v. 6). The cities named in verses 14-19 lie in the Delta region, except for Pathros and Thebes, in Upper (southern) Egypt.

30:20-26 A Broken-armed Pharaoh When Ezekiel uttered this oracle (April 587), Jerusalem had endured over a year of siege by the Babylonians. Pharaoh Hophra had failed to expel Nebuchadnezzar from neighboring Canaan. A broken-armed pharaoh is a metaphor for the defenselessness of the Egyptians against a divinely strengthened Babylonian conqueror.

31 The Example of Felled Assyria In June 587, Ezekiel delivers an extended allegory in which the fate of Assyria is an example of the future awaiting Egypt. Some English versions emend the Hebrew text of verse 3 to read "cypress" instead of Assyria, with "cypress" representing Egypt. This emendation renders the oracle more directly against Egypt but does not change the essential message to Pharaoh.

The allegory likens Assyria — the Mesopotamian superpower defeated by Babylon — to a vibrant and incomparable cedar of Lebanon that sustained and protected the nations over which it ruled. But Assyria's haughty pride prompted God to fell her, and now she and her allies, the formerly jealous "trees of Eden," lie in the "Pit"

("Sheol," the realm of the dead). The oracle closes with a taunting challenge that Pharaoh declare to which tree of Eden Egypt compares. But however great and glorious Egypt might be, she will share the fate of her predecessors to the Pit. Her consignment to lie unburied among the uncircumcised and murdered adds further insult (v. 18).

32:1-16 An Anticipatory Lament for Pharaoh When Ezekiel utters this lament for Pharaoh in March 585, Jerusalem has fallen and the Babylonians are besieging Tyre (chs. 26–28). This oracle anticipates the death of Pharaoh when Nebuchadnezzar focuses on Egypt. Again Ezekiel likens the Egyptian ruler to a sea monster that God will catch in a fishnet and abandon on land for birds and beasts to devour (cf. 29:1-16). The darkness that covers Egypt recalls the sign mediated by Moses prior to the exodus (vv. 7-8; cf. Exod. 10:21-23).

32:17-32 Egypt Condemned to the Nether World This oracle, also delivered in 585, parallels the allegory of Assyria (ch. 31) in condemning Egypt to the netherworld, where the kingdom will share a burial chamber with fellow oppressors who have already died a disgraceful death by murder. Awaiting Egypt are Assyria (defeated by Babylon), Elam (northeast of Babylon), Meshech and Tubal (minor kingdoms on Assyria's northern frontier), Edom (southeast of Canaan), the "princes/chiefs of the north" (presumably, city-states north of Canaan), and Sidon (the Phoenician port north of Tyre). Keeping company in death with the "uncircumcised" promises further humiliation.

33–37 Jerusalem Falls and Restoration Begins

The fall of Jerusalem inaugurates a new prophetic perspective for Ezekiel — one that emphasizes the promised restoration of the exiles to Canaan and God's renewal of their broken relationship with him.

33:1-20 Righteousness and the Watchman These verses draw together two themes presented earlier in the book: Ezekiel's duties as "watchman" for the "house of Israel" (vv. 1-9; cf. 3:17-21) and the righteousness of God's judgments (vv. 10-20; cf. 18:5-29).

33:21-33 Ezekiel Hears of Jerusalem's Fall When Ezekiel receives word of the fall of Jerusalem, he regains his speech (vv. 21-22; cf. 3:26-27; 24:27). The Hebrew survivors in Judah took their escape from the Babylonian sword as a sign that they constituted the remnant entitled to inherit the land God promised to Abraham — a misconception countered earlier in Ezekiel (11:15-17). But the prophet warns that their continued disobedience of the covenantal contract — by violating food laws, practicing idolatry, doing violence, and sinning sexually — cancels their legitimacy as rightful heirs. The judgment of the Judahites is not over yet.

At the same time, the urgent need for all Hebrews to repent still hasn't hit the true remnant — Ezekiel's fellow exiles in Babylon. They relish *hearing* prophetic pronouncements but fail to *heed* them (cf. 12:2; Isa. 6:9-10).

34 Culling a Remnant-within-the-Remnant Invoking the imagery of the shepherd and sheep, Ezekiel charges the Hebrew leaders with selfishness and with neglect and oppression of the people. Now God will step in to do their job by searching out the "lost sheep" and gathering them back to their own land, where he will provide sustenance, rest, and healing. But the great responsibility of the shepherds does not absolve the sheep of responsibility toward one another, and God will separate the good from the bad. A new David will shepherd this surviving remnant-within-the-remnant, and God will establish with them a new covenant that ensures harmonious relationships with God and creation (= *shalom,* "peace").

35:1–36:15 Contrasting the Fates of Edom and Israel Cf. Isa. 34:5-15; Jer. 49:7-22; Obadiah.

Chapter 35, which condemns Edom (represented by the Seir mountain range), forms a literary unit with 36:1-15, which prophesies contrasting blessing for the promised land (the "mountains of Israel"). Ezekiel cites several incriminating sins for which Seir and all Edom deserve judgment: everlasting "enmity" with the chosen line of Jacob (cf. Gen. 25:23); taking

advantage of their cousins' plight (v. 5); attempting to seize land in Israel and Judah (v. 10; 36:5); and rejoicing over their desolation (v. 15). Now having lived by the sword, Edom's inhabitants will die by the sword, and "the whole earth" will rejoice over Edom's desolation (v. 14; cf. 25:12-14).

Ezekiel's hopeful prophecy for Israel affirms the legitimacy of her punishment (v. 3) but promises that she will get the last laugh on Edom and the other opportunistic nations that sought to overtake Canaan (v. 5). God will turn the tables on them by restoring the vibrancy of the promised land. Crops will be more abundant than ever. God's people will return as permanent heirs to the land, where they will multiply and rebuild and populate the now decimated cities. And God will treat his people even better than he did before judging them (v. 11). The promise that the mountains will no longer bereave the nation of its children no doubt reflects the wartime perishing of many Hebrews in the mountainous regions that dominate much of Canaan's geography (vv. 12-14; cf. 39:1-4).

36:16-38 God Restores to Vindicate His Name Ezekiel explicitly applies to the Hebrew people the promises contained in 36:1-15. The prophet's introductory focus on their persistent and thorough sinfulness intensifies the gracious nature of God's future restorative acts. Yet here the emphasis lies not on God's grace (ill-deserved favor) but on his *motivation* for acting graciously toward his people, namely, the vindication of his name. The foreign nations of Ezekiel's day viewed the exile of the Hebrews as proof of the impotence of their God. God therefore determines to bring them home and restore their fortunes as a witness to his sovereignty. The promise of a "new heart" echoes Jeremiah's description of the new covenant (Jer. 31:31-34). Here God's gift of his spirit will enable the people to keep the covenant and thus ensure their enjoyment of the covenantal blessings, described largely in terms of renewed natural abundance and fertility. But the future, enabling gift does not cancel the people's immediate responsibility to repent. The offering of sacrifices surged during these times, as Hebrew pilgrims from all over Canaan flocked to the Jerusalem temple for communal celebration.

37 A Resurrected Nation In this allegorical vision, the spirit transports Ezekiel to a valley strewn with dry, disjointed bones. After taking the prophet on a tour of the area, God asks him whether the bones can ever live again. When Ezekiel cannot answer, God instructs him to

"O dry bones, hear the word of the Lord" (Ezek. 37:4); carved wood panel from the Church of St. Nicholas in Deptford, U.K.

tell the bones that they will indeed come to life. The bones respond to the prophecy in two stages: first they reassemble and reconstitute fleshly bodies, and then life enters the bodies through "breath" blown from the "four winds." The vision ends with the rising to its feet of a vast army of resurrected bodies. Verses 11-14 interpret the revelation. The bones represent the "whole house of Israel" (v. 11) — the exiles of both the northern and southern kingdoms. The revival of their hope involves divine removal from the "grave" of exile (= return to the "land of Israel") and imbuement with God's "spirit" — in Hebrew, the same word as "breath" and "wind."

But restoration does not stop there. A second,

enacted oracle prophesies the reunification of the southern and northern kingdoms, which developed separate monarchies after the death of Solomon. Ezekiel writes on separate sticks to represent Judah and Israel ("Ephraim," its most prominent tribe and name of one of Joseph's heirs to God's promise to Abraham; Gen. 48:1-5). Publicly, Ezekiel joins the sticks end to end to signify their restoration as a united nation. Further, he prophesies the rise of a new Davidic monarch to administer the eternal "covenant of peace" (cf. Isaiah 11) in a kingdom that enjoys God's renewed residence in its midst (cf. 10:1-5, 18-19).

38–39 Curses Bequeathed to Gog

In Ezekiel's prophecy against Gog — unknown historically but presented here as ruler of kingdoms in Asia Minor — God once again brings against his people invaders from lands north of Canaan (38:15). But he does so not to judge the Hebrews, as in the Assyrian and Babylonian conquests; rather, his purpose is to justify his name further among the nations by vanquishing the formidable but foredoomed combatants (38:15-16, 23; cf. 36:22-23). When God inspires Gog and his allies (38:5-6) to attack the restored Hebrew community, they are living in peace and security, as evidenced by the lack of defense walls surrounding their cities (38:8, 11). The Hebrews' spirit-empowered adherence to the new covenant ensures both their avoidance of forbidden alliances with foreign nations and divine protection as a promised blessing. So God arranges the defeat of unwitting Gog, whose stormy end Ezekiel describes in terms that echo the fate of the false prophets of preexilic days (cf. 13:11-13). Revelation 20:8 uses Gog and Magog to represent the multinational army of Satan, who leads them in a similarly doomed final attack on the faithful.

Chapter 39 further emphasizes Gog's inheritance of the judgment suffered by the formerly wayward chosen people. God vows to slay Gog's army on the "mountains of Israel" and give the invaders as food to predatory birds and beasts (39:4; cf. 14:15-16, 21; 36:12-14). Their feasting on the slain celebrates the slaughter as a sacrifice from God (39:17-20). Wholly depending on God for protection, the Hebrews will use as firewood the weapons confiscated from the fallen army, and the supply will last for seven years. It will take seven months to bury all the bodies, not to honor the foes but to "cleanse" the land from ritual defilement through contact with corpses. The number seven represents completeness and perfection. A summary of God's restorative acts toward his people closes the chapter (39:25-29).

40–48 Ezekiel's Vision of Jerusalem Restored

This longest and (except for 29:17-21) latest of prophetic visions in Ezekiel takes place in 573, over a dozen years after the destruction of Jerusalem and the temple. The oracle contains a mixture of symbolic description and practical directions for life centered on the worship of God in the rebuilt holy city, to which he and his people return. The challenge for the modern reader is to appreciate their abundant technical tedium as an integral part of the overall theological climax to which they bring the book.

40–42 Blueprint for a New Temple In a vision, God transports Ezekiel to the Temple Mount in Jerusalem, where a guide takes him on an architectural tour of a new temple complex. The guide instructs Ezekiel to concentrate on everything he sees and hears so that he can accurately report the details to his fellow exiles. In general, the tour proceeds from the perimeter of the complex to its center, all the way to the holy of holies, and back to the outside wall. The guide, outfitted with ancient versions of a tape measure and yardstick, takes detailed measurements of the architectural features. The purpose of this task consists in marking the boundaries between the sacred and the secular in anticipation of God's renewed residence there (cf. 43:7-9). The resulting blueprint differs significantly from those of the first and second (postexilic) temples (cf. 1 Kings 6–7; see also "The Temple"), and Ezekiel's own followers began early on to assign eschatological significance to the prophet's visionary description (cf. Rev. 21:1–22:5).

43 God Returns to the Temple Ezekiel gazes eastward to witness the approach of God's glory, which he beheld in previous visions (chs. 1, 10)

and which now re-enters and fills the temple. Once inside, God announces that he has come back to stay, and he charges Ezekiel with describing the temple to his fellows. After dictating the dimensions of a new altar, measured in "long cubits" (ca. 21 in.) and "spans" (ca. 8.75 in.), God gives instructions for its consecration by the priestly descendants of the Levite Zadok, whom Solomon appointed high priest.

44–46 Regulating Activities at the Temple These chapters weave together chastising reminders of the Hebrews' sinful history and regulations for activities at the new temple. The rules ban unconverted foreigners (44:7) from entry into God's house. The oracle blames the Levites' former religious waywardness for their relegation to menial work in the service of the temple and their prohibition from performing priestly duties. As reward for faithfulness, however, the Zadokite Levites inherit the honor of ministering as priests before God. Actually, the law of Moses established the functional distinction between Levites and priests (a Levitical subclass) at the outset of the Hebrews' covenantal relationship with God: only Levites in the lineage of Aaron, such as Zadok, could become priests. The sin offering required of priests defiled through contact with a corpse cleansed them from ritual impurity (44:25-27). Such contact constituted a covenantal transgression but not an act of immorality.

Chapter 45 addresses real estate allotments for the Hebrews' religious and civil leaders. The tribe of Levi did not receive a landed inheritance in Canaan (44:28), but Mosaic law required each of the other tribes to reserve certain of their cities exclusively for the Levites (Num. 35:1-8). This arrangement maintained a priestly presence throughout the kingdom. The Lord's own territorial allotment in restored Jerusalem provides living space for the landless Levites — the heirs of God himself (45:1-6). The designation of real estate for the Hebrew royalty is intended not so much to provide as to restrict. Not only must the civil leaders refrain from taking the property of commoners (45:7-9), but they must also use accurately calibrated weights and measures to collect taxes and supply the offerings for corporate sacrifices according to the festal calendar (45:10–46:15). The required return to the royal family of property bequeathed to servants maintains the long-term integrity of the family estate and accords with Mosaic law regarding the "year of jubilee" (46:16-18; cf. Lev. 25:10).

The continued requirement of sin offerings under the promised new covenant, in which God's spirit ensures the Hebrews' obedience, takes into account the inevitability of involuntary infractions of the Mosaic covenant (45:17-25; cf. Lev. 4:1–5:13).

47:1-12 The Life-Giving River After Ezekiel and his guide return to the central sanctuary, they wade almost waist high into an unfordable river flowing from beneath the temple. The river flows east to the Arabah, the rift valley in which the Dead Sea lies. The sea's excessively salty water, which supports neither plants nor creatures, turns fresh. Its new power to sustain marine life as varied as that of the "Great" Mediterranean Sea attracts anglers from "En-gedi to En-eglaim," on opposite sides of the Dead Sea and so representing its entirety.

47:13–48:35 The Division of Land The territory reapportioned to the tribes of Israel included land bounded by the Mediterranean Sea on the west, the "Eastern" or Dead Sea and Jordan River on the east, borders in modern Syria on the north, and the Brook of Egypt (whose fingers run deep into the Sinai Peninsula) on the south. Since the division of the land excludes the descendants of Levi, the splitting of Joseph's allotment between the descendants of his sons Ephraim and Manasseh boosts the number of tribal territories back to 12. Mosaic law provides for the incorporation into Hebrew society of foreign converts to Yahwism. The policy continues here with the entitlement of "aliens" to landed inheritances within the tribal allotments. Land given to the royal family surrounds the centrally located territory set aside for the Lord and extended to the priests and Levites. The overall picture of apportionment differs significantly from the original design laid out in Joshua 13–21. Here each tribe receives an equal allotment, and all tribes remain west of the Jordan (contrast Numbers 32).

The last six verses of chapter 48 return us to the holy city. Each of the 12 gates in its perimeter wall bears the name of a Hebrew tribe, including Levi and, therefore, Joseph (instead of Ephraim and Manasseh). The hopeful crescendo of chapters 40–48 reaches its climax in the final verse of the book, where Jerusalem receives for eternity a new name, "The Lord is there," which is itself prophetic.

Daniel

The Hebrew Bible groups Daniel with the Writings, where it appears after Esther and before Ezra-Nehemiah, whose historical accounts follow the chronological setting in Daniel. English Bibles that reflect the Christian tradition sandwich the book between the Major (Isaiah-Ezekiel) and Minor Prophets (Hosea-Malachi), thus following the order of the Greek Septuagint and reflecting the prophetic aspects of Daniel. Roman Catholic Bibles also adopt the Septuagint *version* of Daniel, which includes material lacking in the older Hebrew/Aramaic text. Protestant Bibles follow the shorter, Hebrew/Aramaic version and group the additional Greek sections among the Apocrypha (Deuterocanonical works).

The bilingual nature of the oldest extant manuscripts of Daniel testifies to the enduring importance of Hebrew for the postexilic Jewish community even as linguistically related Aramaic took over as the international, diplomatic language of the day. The book begins and ends in Hebrew, with 2:4b–7:28 written in Aramaic.

Content

Daniel divides into two major sections. Chapters 1–6 present biographical excerpts from the lives of Daniel and his three fellow exiles, best known by their Babylonian names, Shadrach, Meshach, and Abednego. The accounts extend from the deportation of the youths to Nebuchadnezzar's Babylon in 605 B.C. to the early years of Persian domination, which began in 539. The accounts portray Daniel the dream interpreter as a new Joseph (cf. Genesis 37–45) and relate humanly insurmountable predicaments faced by the faithful four to showcase the limitless power of God. Daniel and his friends become role models of covenantal fidelity amid dire circumstances created by a dominant, often hostile foreign culture, and God emerges as the universal Sovereign of all peoples.

The chronological setting of chapters 7–12 (544-536) overlaps the first half of the book, but the literary character of the two sections differs significantly. This second division details from an *auto*biographical perspective four visions that enlighten an elderly Daniel concerning the clash between good and evil in the supernatural sphere and played out in the world of human beings, where it moves toward the culmination of history. The revelations contain detailed historical allusions that parallel the religious persecution of the Jews in the early to mid-2nd century. In this regard, the material mirrors the realism of the prophets. But the bizarre imagery in the visions and their emphasis on the end times signal the infancy of a new type of literature, called "apocalyptic," which finds its fullest biblical expression in the New Testament book of Revelation (see "Beginnings of Apocalyptic Literature").

Date

Despite the 6th-century setting of Daniel and the autobiographical character of chapters 7–12, most scholars believe the book was composed some 400 years later by a devout Hebrew intent on inspiring faithfulness and hope for Jews suffering persecution by Antiochus IV Epiphanes, a 2nd-century Greek ruler of Syria. Allusions in Daniel to Antiochus's desecration of the Jerusalem temple in 167, its documented ritual cleansing three years later, and historically inaccurate descriptions of his demise (in late 164/early 163) suggest that the book of Daniel reached its final, written form sometime between the latter two events, or at least before the author learned of Antiochus's death. This approach to dating Daniel harmonizes with the primary role of

Beginnings of Apocalyptic Literature

Although apocalyptic literature is fully represented in the Bible only in Daniel 7–12 and the book of Revelation, it has important roots within the Old Testament.

An essential characteristic of this genre is *dualism,* which sees reality as determined by a struggle between two basic forces: forces that create order and give life, and forces that threaten that order. Elements of a dualistic worldview were present among Israel's ancestors and neighbors in Mesopotamia and Canaan. Their poets described, in rich *symbolic language,* the ongoing *divine combat* between the creator gods and the gods of chaos and death, often in the guise of a sea monster, serpent, or even the sea itself.

Ancient Israel strongly rejected this mythological worldview. The revelation that God is one ultimately eliminated notions of other gods either in league with or arrayed against the God of Israel, although remnants of this earlier view remained in Israelite poetry (cf. Psalm 82). God's conflict in the Old Testament was primarily on a historical plane against persons and nations that resisted God's rule.

The monotheistic and historical orientation of Old Testament faith did not, however, prevent Israel from adapting the symbolism of their wider cultural environment. Israel often described God's intervention in their history with poetic imagery from the divine combat narratives. In Exodus 15 and Psalm 114, the imagery of the Creator's primeval battle against the sea describes God's rescue of the Israelites from Pharaoh's army. Psalm 29 describes God's appearance in thunder and lightning, and Psalm 74 recounts God's victory over the dragons of the chaotic seas. Other texts describe God's reign over creation by means of a heavenly council (1 Kgs. 22:19-23; Isa. 6:1-13; Ps. 89:5-7). Although this symbolism was suppressed in much of the Old Testament, it reemerged with greater frequency in later apocalyptic literature.

Israel's faith in God as ruler of creation provided another essential element in apocalyptic literature, the concept of *eschatology.* Israel affirmed that God's conflict against rebellious persons and nations would not continue indefinitely, but rather was moving toward an ultimate end. Prophetic eschatology generally portrayed "the end" in historical terms as the resolution of a particular situation (e.g., the end of the northern kingdom, Amos 8:1-3). Isaiah 13:6-13 invokes "the day of the Lord," a time of cosmic judgment and calamity, to describe God's specific judgment of Babylon.

From the exilic period and after, God's final victory is described increasingly as an unspecified, even remote, future time. This literature employs poetic symbolism more frequently than historical references to identify God's ultimate enemies. Ezekiel 38–39 describes God's future battle against Gog and Magog, unknown nations symbolic of all God's enemies. Isaiah 24–27, often called the "Little Apocalypse," describes God's future victory over personified Death (25:7), as well as God's defeat of "Leviathan" (27:1). Zechariah 9–14 is a similar collection of oracles that describe the "day of the Lord" as an unspecified time when present reality would be transformed into a new order.

Late prophetic texts look increasingly toward the *heavenly realm beyond the existing world,* often expressed in visionary experiences (Ezekiel 1–3). Ezekiel 40–48 is a vision of a heavenly temple that was to serve as the pattern for a future temple for Israel. Zechariah is comforted regarding discouraging events in Jerusalem by visions of God's control exercised in the heavens (chs. 1–6). In Ezekiel and Zechariah, heavenly messengers or angels serve as mediators between the prophets and the heavenly world. As God seemed less directly engaged in earthly events and as they experienced increasing *alienation from the sources of power* over their communal destiny under Persian and later Hellenistic rule, the future time and transcendent realm of God's rule became more important within early Judaism. With the arrival of Hellenistic culture, with its cosmic speculation, philosophy of history, and heightened cultural conflict, the soil was fully prepared for the seeds of apocalypticism that would blossom in Daniel 7–12 and elsewhere.

For Further Reading

Collins, John J., ed. *The Origins of Apocalypticism in Judaism and Christianity.* Vol. 1 of *The Encyclopedia of Apocalypticism.* New York: Continuum, 1998.

Russell, D. S. *The Method and Message of Jewish Apocalyptic, 200 B.C.-A.D. 100.* OTL. Philadelphia: Westminster, 1964.

BARRY A. JONES

---

prophecy in the Old Testament, the addressing of contemporary issues and crises, but rejects the view that the Old Testament prophets also accurately predicted the future. Thus for the most part, the visions seen by Daniel become interpretations of past events that inspire moral courage on the part of the persecuted. An obvious challenge to this approach is to defend the author's reason for writing such a book *after* the period of persecution formally ended — an occurrence acknowledged in Daniel through allusions to the reconsecration of the temple.

Those who accept the principle of predictive prophecy generally argue for an earlier dating of Daniel. Their interpretations of the visions in chapters 2 and 7 claim certain historical advantages, though the inaccuracies concerning Antiochus IV's death remain a problem. Still others emphasize issues of content and literary style in arguing for an early composition of chapters 1–6 and a late writing of chapters 7–12; but the fact that both divisions of the book are bilingual presents problems for this view.

1–6 Daniel and Friends at the Babylonian Court

1 From Judahite Youths to Royal Consultants The account begins in 605 (1:1-2), the year the new King Nebuchadnezzar of Babylon defeated the Assyrians at Carchemish and then marched south through Canaan, where he besieged Jerusalem. Daniel's dating follows the Babylonian calendar (the Judahite king Jehoiakim's "third" year; cf. Jer. 25:1: "fourth" year, following the Hebrew calendar). The books of Kings and Chronicles record only the 597 and 587/86 Babylonian attacks.

Nebuchadnezzar adopts the ancient Near Eastern practice of training select foreigners for service in his court (cf. Moses in Exodus 2). Thus the promising Judahite youths Daniel,

Hananiah, Mishael, and Azariah find themselves displaced to Babylonia. Their Hebrew names associate them with the God of Israel. (The ending "el" comes from "Elohim" and "iah" from "Yahweh.") Their new, Babylonian names — Belteshazzar, Shadrach, Meshach, and Abednego — erase this connection. "Belteshazzar" (Daniel) refers to Bel, a title of the Mesopotamian high god Marduk (cf. 4:8).

As courtiers-in-training, Daniel and his friends pursue a three-year course of instruction in Chaldean (= Babylonian) language and literature, including magic and astrology. Mosaic law prohibited engaging in such practices, but the Hebrew youths committed no sin by simply studying these subjects. Daniel does believe, however, that eating food from the king's own, choice stores will ritually defile him (cf. Lev. 17:10-14) and/or put him in debt to Nebuchadnezzar. He petitions the king's commander for a diet of vegetables and water. Fearful of the king, the reluctant commander directs Daniel and his friends to test this new fare. When the lads prove healthier than those eating royal rations, they win the right to refuse the king's menu.

The observation that God gives to the youths broad knowledge and intelligence — and to Daniel, understanding of dreams and visions — implies that their obedience brought them divine favor. Nebuchadnezzar enlists the four to his personal service and holds their counsel in unrivaled regard. The parallels between Daniel and Joseph surface from the start. Daniel continued his service as a courtier till Babylon fell to the Persian king Cyrus, who allowed the Hebrews to return to Canaan (539; Ezra 1:1-4).

2 Daniel as Interpreter of Dreams Before Daniel and his companions finish their training, Nebuchadnezzar has a dream that leaves him anxious. He summons consultants skilled in the magical arts. ("Chaldeans," generally interchangeable with "Babylonians," is here used in its narrower sense, "master astrologers/magicians.") Nebuchadnezzar, refusing to describe his dream, insists that their ability to reveal its contents will prove their competence to interpret. Since none of them can deliver on the king's demand, he issues a death warrant for all the wise men of Babylon.

Even the four Judahite courtiers are included in this sentence, but Daniel's cool head, strong faith, and respectful manner with the head executioner win him an audience with the king. Nebuchadnezzar favorably receives Daniel's request for an opportunity to fulfill the royal demand. Daniel and friends pray that God will mercifully spare their lives by revealing the "mystery." God does so to Daniel, who first responds with a prayer of thanksgiving and praise and only then seeks a lifesaving, second audience with the king.

In a spirit of humility, Daniel gives God all the credit for revealing to him the dream and its interpretation. After announcing that the dream has to do with the future, Daniel describes Nebuchadnezzar's vision of a colossus resting precariously on partly clay feet. The golden head of the giant statue represents Babylon. Metals in descending order of value from torso to toes make up the rest of the body and represent the kingdoms that will succeed Babylon as reigning political powers. Though Daniel does not identify these kingdoms, the historical record suggests that they evolved as: Cyrus's empire of Medes and Persians (here viewed as a united political entity), Greece, and Rome. Scholars who favor a late (2nd-century) dating of Daniel must alter this scheme by considering the Median kingdom as the separate, less distinguished predecessor of the great Persian Empire; as a result the Greeks, not the Romans, round out the list. Thus Alexander the Great's four successors, who divided up the Greek Empire, become the partly iron, partly clay feet and toes of the colossus. A miraculously quarried stone that crushes these hybrid feet topples the entire monstrosity, which turns to dust. The stone grows into a mountain that overtakes the earth and represents the enduring, divine kingdom to end all human kingdoms.

Acknowledging the wisdom of Daniel and his God, Nebuchadnezzar bows before the Judahite youth, bestows on him lavish gifts, and promotes him to high positions in the government and court. At Daniel's request, the king also appoints the three friends to prominent administrative posts.

3 Daniel's Companions Tried by Fire Nebuchadnezzar commissions a 90-ft. high, 9-ft. wide golden "image" to be erected in the province of Babylon. That the king pursues this project subsequent to learning the meaning of his dream suggests to the reader that Daniel's astutely worded interpretation went to the king's visionary golden head. Though the text does not specify what or whom the image represents, the placement of this account following Daniel's dream interpretation suggests that the giant sculpture depicts Nebuchadnezzar — the king's version of his dream come true (cf. 2:37-38). His command that the royal bureaucracy "fall down and worship" the image further supports this assumption, for ancient Near Eastern monarchs commonly claimed divine status. The report that Shadrach, Meshach, and Abednego refuse to worship the statue enrages the king, who repeats the threat to throw those who do not obey into a "furnace of burning fire."

To Nebuchadnezzar's face, the young men confirm their resolve to remain faithful to the commandment requiring the worship of God alone (Exod. 20:3-5). Their stated confidence in God's *ability* to deliver them from the fiery furnace directly answers Nebuchadnezzar's challenge that no god could do so, but their steadfast obedience does not hinge on the expectation that God *will* rescue them. They obey God simply because it's the right thing to do.

Strong royal guards die casting the bound men into a furnace (probably a brick-baking kiln) heated to its maximum ("seven times hotter" than usual; "seven" in biblical usage implies completeness). But the faithful Hebrews remain unsinged, much to the dismay of Nebuchadnezzar, who observes a fourth, apparently angelic being walking among the flames with the now untied trio. At the summons of the astonished king, Shadrach, Meshach, and Abednego walk out of the furnace under their own power. Thus

God's proven ability to do whatever he wishes, in defiance of all human odds, emerges as the main message of the account. It verifies God's direct and unopposable authority over the Mesopotamian superpower — his instrument of judgment against Judah — embodied in its monarch. Though the deliverance of the Judahite trio leads to a royal edict requiring empire-wide respect for the God of the Hebrews, the miracle does not lead to Nebuchadnezzar's own conversion. Nevertheless, he honors the young men's courageous demonstration of religious conviction by ensuring their prosperity.

The book of Daniel uses several Old Persian words, including "satrap," a provincial governor. The use in this chapter of Greek words to name Mesopotamian instruments (e.g., "lyre"/"zither"; "trigon," a triangular lyre; and "psaltery," a type of harp; vv. 5, 7, 15) demonstrates the extent of cultural influences in Mesopotamia from Greece, which before Nebuchadnezzar's time began establishing geographically widespread colonies and supplying mercenaries to foreign armies. After verse 23, the Septuagint adds the Apocryphal/Deuterocanonical "Prayer of Azariah" and "The Song of the Three Children."

4 Nebuchadnezzar Goes Mad Having acknowledged, in a brief, psalmlike confession, God's enduring sovereignty (vv. 2-3; cf. 34-35), Nebuchadnezzar recounts the events that generated his humility. Another royal dream, which the court consultants again cannot interpret, leads him to call upon the superior gifts of Daniel.

Glazed brick wall relief of a lion, palace of Nebuchadnezzar II, Babylon. *(Oriental Institute, University of Chicago)*

This time Nebuchadnezzar willingly describes the dream, whose arbor imagery recalls Ezekiel's description of the flourishing and fall of prideful Assyria (Ezekiel 31). Reluctantly and regretfully, Daniel reports that the king's dream prophesies his temporary mental decline, but that the Babylonian king would come out of it better off. Nebuchadnezzar's refusal to turn over a righteous leaf would result in his divine transformation into a crazed "stump" of a man consigned to a beastly existence for "seven periods of time," until he acknowledged God as the source of all human power. Despite a yearlong opportunity to repent, the king's persisting pride triggers the onset of insanity. As prophesied, however, the humbling period of punishment ends in the restoration of Nebuchadnezzar's reason, which occasions his acknowledgment of God's supreme control over humanity. Thus Daniel's last picture of Nebuchadnezzar portrays him as the divinely reestablished Babylonian sovereign who serves as global witness for the God of the Hebrews.

5 The Writing on Belshazzar's Wall Belshazzar, son and coregent of Babylon's last king, Nabonidus, served as acting monarch during his father's 10-year sojourn in the northern Arabian oasis of Tema. Daniel 5 depicts Belshazzar's final, fatal fling on the eve of Babylon's downfall in 539. In the course of the party, the king decides to bring out goblets taken by his "father" (predecessor) Nebuchadnezzar from the Jerusalem temple. Raising the wine-filled sacred vessels, the guests toast their pagan idols. But merriment quickly turns to anxiety when a disembodied hand appears out of thin air and writes a message on the wall of the banquet hall. The fear-stricken Belshazzar quickly calls in the court magicians and astrologers to analyze the inscription, but despite the incentive of a royal appointment they are unable to decipher or interpret.

Once again, the stage is set for Daniel, who appears to have lost political status with the change in the royal administrations. (Nabonidus had apparently usurped the throne.) The queen mother enlightens the shaken king concerning the Judahite exile, now an octogenarian. In his apparently first and only audience with Belshazzar, Daniel rejects the king's generous offer of reward for his services. He reminds Belshazzar of his predecessor Nebuchadnezzar's humility-producing bout with insanity (ch. 4) and charges the king with prideful irreverence and willful disregard for God's sovereignty.

Daniel's explanation of the inscription, which simply lists three measurements of weight, appeals to the root meanings of the individual words to prophesy the imminent fall of Babylon. "Mene" (mina; from the verb "to number") says the days of Belshazzar's kingdom are "numbered." "Tekel" (shekel; from the verb "to weigh") condemns the "underweight" king for deficiency, presumably in righteousness. "Peres" (from the verb "to divide"), playing on the similar root for "Persia," prophesies the division of Babylonia between the neighboring kingdoms of Media and Persia.

Despite the bad news, Belshazzar awards Daniel with promotion. The irreverent king meets his death that night. The ancient historians Herodotus and Xenophon record a nocturnal conquest of Babylon, and Xenophon reports the slaying of Belshazzar by the triumphant Persians. "Darius the Mede," said here to have "received" Belshazzar's kingdom, goes otherwise unmentioned in the historical record and could not be Darius I, who ruled Persia from 522 to 486. "Darius the Mede" may be an alternative or throne name for Cyrus the Persian, who according to all available records conquered Babylonia and succeeded Nabonidus/Belshazzar (v. 31; cf. 6:28). Cyrus was about 62 when he conquered the capital.

6 Daniel Delivered from the Lions' Den The aged Daniel regains a position of political prominence in the new Persian administration. But the distinction he gains as a gifted administrator generates jealousy on the part of his two co-commissioners and the satraps (provincial governors) who report to them. Much as Esther's nemesis Haman, the conspirators devise a legal trap to get rid of their scrupulous colleague. Banking on Daniel's staunch devotion to God, they convince the king to sign a 30-day injunction prohibiting Persian subjects from petitioning any man or god, except the king. The decree

calls for throwing offenders to the lions, and no Persian law could be revoked.

As anticipated, the devout Judahite ignores the injunction and the threat of death, and he continues to pray openly to the "living God." The spying conspirators eagerly report this news to the king, who tries in vain to find a legal loophole. At the end of the day, the king dutifully entombs Daniel in the den, but not before expressing confidence that God will deliver his faithful servant from the beastly ordeal. The distressed monarch passes a sleepless night and at daybreak rushes to discover the fate of his inadvertent victim. From the would-be grave, Daniel reports that, in recognition of his innocence before God and the king, an angel ensured his safety by shutting the mouths of the lions (cf. the protecting angel in the fiery furnace, 3:25). The murderous plot backfires on Daniel's enemies when the king orders them thrown to the beasts.

The primary message here is not Daniel's deep devotion to God, or even faith, whose expression in this account comes from the Persian king (v. 16). Instead, the central point is God's supreme power in the world of human affairs. Once again, the acclamation of this divine Sovereign by the most politically powerful human monarch of the day reinforces the mandate for global honor of the God of the Hebrews (vv. 26-27).

7–12 The Apocalyptic Visions of Daniel

7 The Rise and Fall of the Four Beasts The book now turns apocalyptic, a term applied to literature that describes the "end times" and the age to come in visionary or prophetic revelations (see "The Beginnings of Apocalyptic Literature" [443-44]). Thus Daniel the dream *interpreter* becomes Daniel the *dreamer*. This first of Daniel's recorded visions occurs in 544, when Babylon's king Nabonidus began a decade-long sojourn in Arabia and left his son Belshazzar as acting monarch (cf. ch. 5).

Using different imagery to convey a similar message, this vision shows parallels to Nebuchadnezzar's dream of the composite "colossus on clay feet" (ch. 2). Here four "beasts," which rise out of a windswept cosmic sea, represent the four successive kingdoms. The symbolism may spring from ancient mythology, which features the sea monsters Rahab and Leviathan (cf. Job, Psalms, and Isaiah), but Daniel ties the message to human history. Scholars generally agree that the lionlike beast represents Babylon, but they variously identify the ravenous bear, four-headed leopard, and iron-toothed, multi-horned anomaly. The most widely adopted suggestions include their successive equation with the Medo-Persian Empire, Greece, and Rome (favored by an early dating of Daniel), *or* Media, Persia, and Greece (favored by a late dating of the book). Following the early dating, the leopard stands for the Greek Empire, split between Alexander the Great's four generals after his death, and the "little horn" stands for the Roman emperor Nero, infamous for his brutal persecution of Christians. For others, the antichrist of Revelation embodies the double fulfillment of the prophecy applied to Nero. With the late dating, the boastful, 11th horn of the fourth beast represents Greece's Antiochus IV, whose desecration of the second temple in Jerusalem sparked the Jewish "Maccabean" revolt in the 2nd century.

The appearance of the "Ancient of Days" (God), seated on a chariot-throne (cf. Ezekiel 1, 10), inaugurates judgment day for the beasts (v. 9; cf. Rev. 1:14). The court session commences with the opening of "the books," which record earthly deeds (v. 10; cf. Rev. 20:12). The multihorned beast suffers immediate death and destruction. Its reign of terror over the "saints" lasts "a time, times, and half a time," which some take to mean "a year, [plus two] years, [plus] half a year," that is, three and a half years (v. 25; cf. Rev. 12:14; but see 4:16, 25, 32, where "time" means an unspecified period). The intent of the boastful horn to "make war with the holy ones" illustrates its lust for divine status. The other beasts lose their power but receive a stay of execution (v. 12; cf. vv. 25-26). The imagery in Revelation 13 derives from this chapter. A humanlike being ("son of man"), who comes "with the clouds" (symbol of God's presence), receives from the Ancient of Days everlasting dominion over an eternal kingdom, which succeeds and subsumes the dominions of the deposed beasts (vv. 18, 27; cf. 2:34-35, 44-45).

8 The Ram and He-Goat Two years after Daniel's preceding revelatory dream, this second vision transports him to Susa, the winter capital of Persia, some 200 miles east of Babylon. Surveying his visionary surroundings, Daniel realizes that he has company — an unrivalled, two-horned ram (the Medo-Persian Empire; the longer horn represents Persia as the stronger of the two kingdoms). But invincibility eludes the ram when a hovering, single-horned he-goat (Alexander the Great) rushes it from the west (Greece) and shatters its horn-embodied power. At the peak of the he-goat's might, however, its horn is broken (Alexander's death at age 33), and four horns grow as replacements (the subsequent division of the Greek Empire into four parts: Egypt, Syria, Asia Minor, and Greece). One of these horns (Syria) sprouts an offshoot (the Seleucid ruler Antiochus IV) that grows like a weed toward the "Beautiful Land" (Canaan; Antiochus began southward invasions in 170). This growing horn claims equality with the Commander of the host (God, the "Prince of princes," v. 25); abolishes worship of God through sacrifice at his sanctuary (the second temple); and gains power over the sinful "host" (the chosen people of God; vv. 12, 24). These abominable circumstances will persist for "2300 evenings and mornings." If interpreted as 1150 12-hour evenings and 1150 12-hour mornings (2300 half days), this figure approximates the time between Antiochus's initial desecration of the temple (168/67) and its reconsecration after his death, commemorated by Hanukkah (165/64). The 1150 full days also fit with the interpretation of "time, times, and half a time" as "a year, [two] years, and half a year" (7:25).

In verses 15-26, the angel Gabriel interprets the vision. This identification by name of an angelic messenger of God marks the earliest such occurrence in the Bible (v. 16). Here the angel informs Daniel that his vision concerns the "time of the end," which lies "many days" in the future (vv. 17, 26). The allusions here appear tied to the particular historical period that extends from the supremacy of Persia through the death of Antiochus IV. Overcome by his visionary receipt of classified information concerning the future, Daniel takes some time to recover, but his subsequent resumption of regular responsibilities demonstrates an exemplary integration of his calling and "normal life."

9 Daniel's Prayer and Gabriel's Prophecy Daniel's reading of the prophecies of Jeremiah in 539 sparks a realization that the 70-year period of judgment against Jerusalem/Judah, which began with the Babylonian triumph over Assyria in 605, has almost ended (cf. Jer. 25:11-12). The realization moves Daniel to penitence, and he assumes the posture of a mourner (v. 3), offers a communal confession, and encourages God to spare Jerusalem from wrath — an implied request for restoration there. He laments that the city made holy by God's temple has suffered reproach from the pagan nations, who viewed its destruction and the exile of its people as

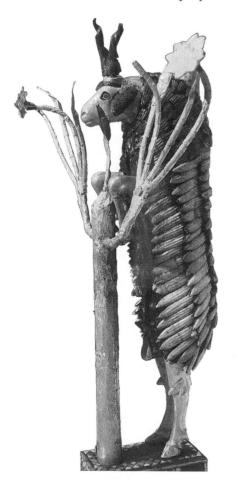

Statue of a male goat, which in Daniel's vision (ch. 8) represents Alexander, the "king of Greece"; Ur, ca. 2500 B.C.). *(British Museum; photo by Mitchell G. Reddish)*

proof of God's powerlessness to protect his homeland. This chastisement adversely affects God's own reputation, since both the city and the Hebrews bear his trademark name (v. 19; cf. Ezek. 36:16-38).

The angel Gabriel reappears to alert Daniel to troubles that lie beyond the period of judgment through exile. The "weeks" of verse 24 denote units of seven, which most interpreters understand as groups of seven years. A literal reading of the period under consideration would give 70 × 7 years = 490 years. According to verse 25, the time between the decree to rebuild Jerusalem and "the anointed prince" consists of (7 × 7 years) + (62 × 7 years) = 69 "weeks," or 483 years. Nehemiah 1:1–2:8 records the issuing of such a decree by the Persian king Artaxerxes I in 445. Working from that date, 483 years of lunar months (30 days each) would extend into one of the likely dates of Jesus' three-year public ministry. The "cutting off" of the Messiah in verse 26 would refer to the rejection and death of Christ. That this "cutting off" is said to take place "after the 62 weeks" (i.e., after the 69th week [7 + 62]) suggests to some scholars that an unspecified gap exists between this event and the beginning of the final seven-year "week," in which occurs the devastation described in the rest of the verse. This picture would fit with the great tribulation described in the book of Revelation. Verse 27 further describes the 70th "week," though obscurely. It remains unclear whether the covenant-maker refers to the Messiah or the destructive prince of verse 26. Those who accept the viability of predictive prophecy equate the destructive prince with the Roman emperor Nero and see the antichrist as embodying the double fulfillment of the prophecy. An alternative interpretation identifies the destroyer as Antiochus IV.

If one does not accept a literal interpretation of the numbers in 9:24-27, the beginning and ending dates of the 70 weeks can be tied to various historical events and periods that preceded the writing of Daniel. Viable alternatives to the identification of the "Messiah" (lit., "anointed one") would include Zerubbabel, the last legitimate descendant of David, who organized the rebuilding of the temple. The "cutting off" of the "Messiah/anointed one" might refer to the deposition of the Jewish high priest Onias III by Antiochus IV (2 Macc. 4:7). That in biblical usage the number seven indicates completeness or perfection may argue for chronological leeway in understanding Daniel's 70 weeks of 7.

10:1–11:1 A Vision, Visitant, and Revelation of the "Latter Days" This chapter sets the stage for the climactic revelation of the book. Three years into the reign of Cyrus and the restoration of the Hebrews to Canaan (536), Daniel, who has remained in Babylon, pursues a three-week period of mourning. At the end of this time, he sees in a vision a man clad in linen, the fabric of priestly garments (cf. Exod. 28:39-42). Though Daniel's companions fail to see the vision themselves, a feeling of fear overtakes them. They desert the drained Daniel, who swoons when the visionary being begins to speak.

An unnamed angel resuscitates the frightened seer. The divine messenger reveals that a battle in the spiritual realm against the patron angel ("prince") of Persia delayed him from coming to Daniel's aid for three weeks until help came from Michael, his sole ally (10:21) and the archangelic defender of God's people (cf. Jude 9; Rev. 12:7). Daniel's heavenly visitor, who resembles a human being, announces that he has come to enlighten Daniel concerning the fate of his people in the "latter days," according to the "book of truth" — the divinely prewritten record of human history (10:14, 21). The angel's anticipated struggle against the supernatural patron of Greece gives a first hint about the events to come (10:20).

11:2-45 Canaan Caught in the Crossfire Daniel's angelic visitor interprets the events pictorially portrayed in previous visions (esp. chs. 7–8). Verses 2-19 recount the Greek period from the time of Alexander the Great (the "warrior king" of v. 3) to the defeat of Antiochus III by the Romans in 190 (vv. 18-19). Verse 2 summarizes the Persian monarchy from Cyrus to Xerxes, the "fourth" king, whose failed invasion of Greece in 480 signaled the transfer of ancient Near Eastern power to the Macedonians. Verse 4 highlights the division of Alexander's empire between his four generals, two of whose dynasties played prominent roles in the history of the Jews in Canaan: Ptolemy I ("king of the south") and his descendants ruled Egypt from 304-30, while Seleucus I ("king of the north") and his successors governed Syria during roughly the same period. Because Canaan constituted the only viable land bridge between the two kingdoms, their interest in dominating this geographical buffer zone loomed large, and future rivalry between them would eventually involve the Hebrew bystanders.

Verse 6 alludes to the temporary alliance of Egypt and Syria forged by the marriage of the Ptolemaic princess Berenice to Antiochus II (grandson of Seleucus I). Their divorce and the subsequent murder of Berenice sparked a revengeful invasion of Syria by her brother Ptolemy III (v. 7), now the Syrian ruler, and the three kings who succeeded him perpetuated the feud with incursions that reached as far south as Raphia (20 mi. south of Gaza; vv. 9-13). Jewish militants, intent on shedding Egyptian domination, joined with the third of these Seleucid rulers (Antiochus III) in attacking Egypt (vv. 14-15). The allied success resulted in another failed marriage alliance between the Ptolemies and Seleucids (v. 17), and Antiochus's subsequent military campaigns in Asia Minor and Greece met with humiliating defeat by the Romans (vv. 18-19).

Verse 20 briefly acknowledges the relatively short-lived career of the next Syrian ruler, Seleucus IV, who oppressed the "jewel of the kingdom" (probably a reference to Jerusalem and the temple) by raising taxes, no doubt to replenish the royal treasury bankrupted by his predecessors' constant military campaigning. The assassination of Seleucus (175) paved the way for a takeover by his brother, the villainous Antiochus IV, whose "contemptible" behavior concerning the chosen people and their religion constitute the focus of verses 21-39. The first of two invasions by Antiochus into Egypt met with at least temporary success, thanks to the murder of his rival ruler, Ptolemy VI, by Egyptian insiders (173; v. 25). Antiochus returned to Syria by way of Jerusalem, where with a "heart . . . set against the holy covenant" he slaughtered 80 thousand Jews. In 168 he again attacked Ptolemaic Egypt, now recently allied with Rome, whose naval backup fresh from Kittim (Cyprus) forced the enraged Antiochus to turn back. The retreating Syrian ruler found in Jerusalem a convenient outlet for his anger (vv. 29-30). With the aid of Jews sympathetic to Hellenization, he desecrated the temple by erecting in it an altar to Zeus (the "abomination that makes desolate," v. 31) and by using the altar of burnt offering to celebrate pagan religious rites. Antiochus won some of the Jews over to his program of sacrilege, but those who stood their ground with respect to the covenant suffered widespread slaughter at his command (vv. 32-35). For the faithful, "a little help" (v. 34) came in the form of a successful revolt led by the Maccabee family, and in 164 Antiochus abandoned his persecution against the faithful followers of Hebrew religion and turned his attention eastward to Persia.

Verses 36-45 prophesy the "end" in Canaan of a "king" who considers himself divine, but the historical record indicates that Antiochus died in Persia by early 163. Some scholars view the historically accurate verses 1-35 as prophecy after-the-fact, with verses 36-45 predicting Antiochus's inevitable doom, though the prophecy did not pan out in historical detail. Some identify this "king" as an evil antichrist struggling in vain and alone in the end times (cf. 8:19-25). From a literary standpoint, the historical allu-sions to Antiochus combine with eschatological foreshadowing to link the past events of 11:2-35 with the future foreseen in chapter 12.

12 Awakening the Dead to Eternity The archangel Michael prophesies the final rescue of God's faithful from unprecedented persecution. Verse 2 contains the most explicit Old Testament reference to resurrection by foreseeing the restoration to life of all the dead, some of whom attain "everlasting life" and the rest of whom inherit "everlasting contempt" (cf. Isa. 26:19).

Two witnesses to Daniel's vision of the angel appear on each flank of the Tigris River, over which the angel hovers (cf. 10:4). One asks when the prophesied end will come and receives the standard answer, "a time, times, and half a time" (cf. 7:25). Verses 11-12 may specify numbers of days that approximate the nearly three-and-a-half year period between the defilement of the temple by Antiochus IV and its cleansing in 164.

When Daniel asks for clarification as to the outcome of the end-time events, the angel refuses to give details. Instead, he instructs Daniel to live out his life in the knowledge that one day, he will rise from death to receive his ultimate inheritance.

Hosea

The book of Hosea heads the Minor Prophets, in the Hebrew Bible the Book of the Twelve. Hosea is the only prophet from the northern kingdom of Israel whose words have survived in a book of the Bible that bears his name. His prophetic contemporaries of the 8th century B.C. included the southern "writing prophets" Isaiah, Micah, and Amos (who prophesied *to* the north but hailed from Judah). Hosea's career spanned the last three decades of Israel's existence as an independent political entity. The end came in 722/21 when Assyria conquered Samaria, the kingdom's northern capital.

Message

Hosea's basic message aims at communicating God's steadfast love for Israel (often referred to as "Ephraim") despite her persistent disobedience; his determination to punish the kingdom, failing her repentance; and his promise to restore her to a right relationship with him. The prophet chastens Israel for two covenantal violations in particular: fraternizing with foreign nations (specifically, Assyria and Egypt, the dominant political powers of the day), and idolatry. The geography of the northern kingdom made straying in these ways easier. Major ancient roadways connecting Egypt with Phoenicia, Asia Minor, and Mesopotamia passed through the heart of Israel and thus exposed her to a wide range of influences from foreign cultures. Also, since the rich farmland of the northern kingdom nurtured an agriculturally based economy, the Hebrews determined it wise to broaden their worship to include Baal, the fertility god of the native Canaanites, whom the Israelites failed to drive out (Num. 33:50-56).

In the first three chapters, the prophet enacts his message. He takes a "wife of harlotry," and their marriage becomes an illustration of God's relationship with covenantally unfaithful Israel.

Chapters 4–14 consist of prophetic speeches by Hosea that alternately warn of judgment and offer hope for restoration. These speeches abound in metaphors that portray the God of judgment as a lion, leopard, and bear and the God of restoration as a loving husband, father, and healer.

Composition

Undoubtedly, Hosea originally communicated his prophecies orally over his 30-year career. The book of Hosea represents the work of the prophet, his supporters, and/or later generations in committing at least some of his prophecies to writing. That the book includes brief addresses to Judah suggests to some scholars that a Judean editor played a role in shaping the present text. Others believe that Hosea may have spent some time in Judah; thus his concern for the southern kingdom, too.

1–3 Portrait of a Prophetic Family

1:1–2:1 Hosea and His Family of Harlotry Though Hosea hailed from the northern kingdom and pursued his prophetic ministry there, verse 1 first sets his activity in context by naming the four 8th-century southern (Judahite) kings during whose reigns he prophesied. The last strong northern king, Jeroboam II, ruled Israel for much of this time (ca. 785–745), but the verse makes no mention of the rulers who followed him in rapid succession until the fall of the northern kingdom to Assyria in 722/21.

Hosea's first prophecy consists in an extended enactment that portrays the relationship of God and Israel in marital and familial terms. Hosea plays the part of God. Gomer, the "wife of harlotry" whom he marries, represents Israel, whose adulterous worship of gods other than Yahweh violates the covenantal obligation of exclusive faithfulness (Exod. 20:3-5; cf. Ezekiel 16). The children born to Gomer become living prophecies through their names, beginning with the eldest son, Jezreel — site of the bloody excesses of Jeroboam II's grandfather Jehu in fulfilling the command to wipe out the line of the wicked King Ahab (1:4; cf. 2 Kings 9–10). The overenthusiasm of Jehu invited God's destruction of the northern kingdom (1:4-5). The name "Not Pitied" *(Lo-ruhamah)* for Hosea's second child, a daughter, reveals that the opportunity has passed for Israel to receive God's compassion and forgiveness. Judah's time has not yet run out, but later prophets also rebuke the southern kingdom for squandering her chance to repent. The name of the second son, "Not My People" *(Lo-ammi)*, symbolizes the "divorce" of God and Israel. Initially, God claimed the Hebrew people through the promise to Abraham (Gen. 12:2), and he proclaimed his identity as their God at Sinai (Exod. 20:2). But their rejection *of* God has led to rejection *by* God. Nevertheless, restoration of the relationship will ultimately win out, with God once again claiming Israel as "My people" *(Ammi)* to whom he has shown "compassion" *(Ruhamah;* 2:1). The prophecy concerning innumerable descendants for Israel echoes God's elaboration of the promise in Gen. 22:17 (1:10). Hosea 1:11 prophesies the reunification of Israel and Judah as the good result of the punishment awaiting Israel on the "day of Jezreel" (cf. 1:5).

2:2-23 The Remaking of God's Marriage to Israel Through the children, Hosea calls on Gomer to abandon her harlotry. The challenge represents God's threat-laden appeal to wayward Israel (cf. Jer. 2:1–3:5; Ezekiel 16).

The fertile northern kingdom erroneously attributed her agricultural abundance to her illicit "lover" Baal, the Canaanite fertility god. God's plan to strip the northern kingdom of the gifts of nature for which she credited the pagan deity paves the way for God to restore these blessings in showing that they originate with him (vv. 8-13, 14-23). His tender wooing of Israel following her punishment will restore their "marriage," which God will reinvigorate through a covenant that ensures Israel's harmonious relationship with nature and neighboring peoples. "Jezreel" (1:11; lit., "God sows"), the

cradle of Canaan's agricultural abundance, now becomes a positive symbol of Israel's future prosperity. The similar transformation of the valley of Achor ("Trouble"; cf. Joshua 7) to a "door of hope" signals renewal for Israel, who will abandon even the allusion to Baal by referring to her husband/God as *'ishi* ("my man/husband"), rather than the usual *baali* ("my lord/master/husband"; 2:15-16). In verse 23, God and Israel claim each other in "marriage" vows that reverse the mutual rejection of 1:9.

3 Discipline and Deprivation Though verse 1 does not specifically name Gomer, most scholars interpret this account as Hosea's buying back his adulterous wife from her latest lover. The prophet's action symbolizes God's enduring love for Israel despite her worship of "other gods," as seen in her eating "raisin cakes" as part of pagan rites. Hosea pays a ransom roughly equivalent to the price of redeeming a female dedicated to God (cf. Lev. 27:4), and he then imposes on the adulteress a program of sexual abstinence comparable to God's depriving the northern kingdom of political and religious institutions (v. 4). During this time of punishment, Israel will renew her appetite for God and governance under the legitimate Davidic monarchy, to be seated in the southern kingdom, Judah.

4–14 Oracles of Judgment and Promise

The rest of Hosea consists of oracles that both foretell Israel's judgment and engender hope for post-punishment restoration. The political fortunes of the Hebrew people depend, as always, on their conduct in the religious sphere.

4 God's Lawsuit against Israel God brings a lawsuit against Israel for her breach of covenant. Verse 2 charges the kingdom with transgressions against five of the Ten Commandments (Exod. 20:13-17). The infractions have wreaked havoc on all earthly creation — the land, its inhabitants, and their habitations.

Verses 4-10 blame the waywardness and coming judgment of Israel on her priests, who have failed to teach God's laws. Instead, they have made their living promoting paganism.

Soon priest and people alike will find that their sinful indulgences get them nowhere.

Verses 11-14 vividly describe pagan ritual practiced in Israel. Cult prostitution (intended to influence fertility gods to enhance production and reproduction), drunkenness, idol worship, and divination all violated Mosaic law, and the offering of sacrifices at pagan shrines flaunted the people's unwitting infractions.

Israel's figurative and literal harlotry sound a cautionary note for Judah (v. 15). Gilgal and Beth-aven ("house of evil" — an intentional revision of "Bethel," "house of God") were major worship centers in the southern part of Israel (cf. Gen. 28:10-22; Joshua 4; 1 Sam. 7:16; 11:14-15). These rivals to the temple offered relatively easy access by bordering Judahites. Drunken and licentious "Ephraim" (v. 17), the dominant tribe in the northern kingdom, is a poetic equivalent for stubborn "Israel," on whom the divine shepherd has given up (v. 16). Verse 19 pictures the divinely abandoned kingdom as swept away in a whirlwind, surrendered to the shameful disobedience she loves.

5 Judah Enters the Indictment Hosea widens the circle of responsibility for Israel's judgment to include her political leaders. Mizpah and Tabor shared respectable reputations in the history of the Hebrew people. The prophet Samuel judged legal matters at Mizpah, and the team of Deborah and Barak won a decisive victory over the Canaanites at Mount Tabor (1 Sam. 7:16; Judges 4). But apparently Israel's leaders now have established pagan shrines there. Ephraim/Israel's spirit of religious harlotry penetrates deeper than merely outward acts (cf. 4:17). Pride perpetuates her stumbling in sin. Her unrepentant attitude makes a mockery of sacrifices to God, so he refuses to meet Israel in worship (v. 6). The "illegitimate children" (v. 7) are the Israelites, who have not been taught the laws of God and so, in their ignorance, betray the Lord by participating in pagan rites (v. 7).

The revelation that Judah has similarly stumbled (v. 5) receives elaboration in the rest of this chapter. Hosea calls on three Benjamite religious centers between Israel and Judah to sound the alarm for the southern kingdom (v. 8), whose leaders cannot wait to grab terri-tory in the soon-to-be-conquered north (v. 10; cf. Deut. 19:14). In verse 11 he indicts both kingdoms for seeking political security from foreign powers rather than relying on God (cf. v. 13; the "great king," probably the 8th-century Assyrian monarch Tiglath-pileser III). For both Israel and Judah, the best hope for help rested in God, but their bypassing of his protection invited both subtle and overpowering attacks by God until their affliction would prompt repentance and a sincere search for him (vv. 12, 14).

6 Reliable versus Fleeting Faithfulness The opening verses 1-3 envision the fulfillment of 5:15, as God's wounded people seek God's healing. "Two" and "third" (v. 2) function as a poetic pair to symbolize the renewal of life for the Hebrew nation (cf. 1 Cor. 15:4). Verse 3 likens the reliability of God to daily and seasonal certainties of nature: the dawning of each new day and the arrival of the spring rains. In contrast, the short-lived faithfulness of Ephraim/Israel and Judah compares to morning clouds and dew, which disappear with the warmth of the rising sun.

God speaks events into happening (e.g., Genesis 1; John 1:1-3); therefore, the judgment of the Hebrews decreed "by the words" of God through the prophets is taken as accomplished fact (v. 5). God's preference of loyalty over sacrifice recalls Samuel's chastisement of the disobedient King Saul (1 Sam. 15:22; cf. Matt. 9:13). Verses 8-10 charge Israel and its priests with violence and apostasy on both sides of the Jordan. The picture of murders, possibly of religious pilgrims, by priests on the road to Shechem makes the indictment particularly poignant, for it was at this city in the hill country of Ephraim that the Israelites reconfirmed their covenant with God under Joshua (Joshua 24). Again, "harlotry" refers to religious disobedience in general and cult prostitution in particular.

7 Israel's Royalty Epitomizes Her Depravity God wants to "heal" unfaithful Israel/Ephraim, but the kingdom keeps to her sinful ways. Her royalty set a tone of moral depravity through lying, adultery, drunkenness, and conspiracy fanned to flames by anger. Verse 7 alludes to the multiple, mid-8th-century Israelite kings, most of whom murdered their predecessors only to fall victim to the next power-hungry usurper of the throne (cf. 2 Kgs. 14:23–17:41). By ignoring God and seeking political security from foreign nations such as Egypt and Assyria, which levied on them heavy tribute, Israel has unwittingly grown weak. The kingdom wails her woes to God, but he sees through the false repentance and recognizes her ulterior motive of gaining divine assurance of a good harvest (v. 14). Israel has returned to God evil for his good and so has sealed her doom. Divine inaction is not an option.

8 Summing Up Israel's Sins Hosea calls for a trumpet to warn of the coming attack against Israel as punishment for her transgressions. Here the "house" of the Lord refers to his household, his chosen people (v. 1). Though in their distress they claim fidelity to God, their actions prove otherwise. Without God's approval, they have established their own monarchy, which rivals the divinely sanctioned Davidic dynasty in Judah. They have crafted idols, which at best compete with God for worship. The "calf of Samaria" recalls the two golden calves set up by Israel's first king, Jeroboam I, at the southern and northern extremes of the kingdom (Bethel and Dan) to discourage pilgrimages to the Jerusalem temple (vv. 6-7; cf. 1 Kgs. 12:26-30). The bull-calf represented the Canaanite fertility and storm-god Baal, and Israel's homage to this image testifies to the adoption of foreign religious practices by the breakaway northern tribes. Worship of Yahweh has thus been compromised, so Israel's offerings fail to atone for her people's sins (vv. 11-13; cf. Exod. 20:3-5). Rather, this sin earns the kingdom the punishment of "return to Egypt" — ejection from the promised land and dominance by a foreign nation (v. 13).

The kingdom's alliance-making with foreign nations is again pictured as sexual promiscuity (vv. 8-10). Ironically, Israel's lover Assyria will soon become the vulture-like enemy that swoops down on the northern kingdom (vv. 1, 9). Self-reliant forgetfulness of God on the part of Israel and Judah will result in God's destruction of the bastions of their supposed strength (v. 14).

9 Israel's Regress Religious festivals that celebrated agricultural blessings often took place at local threshing floors and wine presses, where farmers processed harvests of grain and grapes (Leviticus 23). Hosea's charge concerning Israel's harlotry "on every threshing floor" refers to participation in pagan religious practices at such celebrations. Instead of acknowledging and ensuring divine blessing, these tainted rites call down famine and drought. Even worse, Ephraim/Israel will no longer be able to celebrate the festivals once God exiles them to a foreign land — Assyria — as long ago in Egypt (vv. 3, 5-6). Because the unclean sacrifices that the exiles will be able to offer will fail to please God, the sacrificial meals will generate grief instead of joy. The people will die in spiritual and material poverty, and even their corpses will remain outside the promised land. Memphis, the sometime capital of Egypt that boasted great tombs, symbolizes Israel's graveyard in exile (v. 6).

Because Israel has dived so deeply into sin, she cannot recognize the truth of prophetic pronouncements. Hosea alludes to the abuse of the Levite's concubine (the "days of Gibeah") to represent the depths of Israel's moral depravity (v. 9; cf. 10:9; Judges 19). Similarly, he likens Israel to her unfaithful ancestors, who worshipped the fertility god Baal of Peor

Bull-calf, symbol of the Canaanite fertility- and storm-god Baal; silver figurine and ceramic shrine, Ashkelon, 1600 B.C. *(Israel Antiquities Authority)*

while camped in Transjordan prior to entering the promised land (v. 10; cf. Numbers 25). Now God, who caused the Hebrews to flourish in the barren wilderness, will diminish the population of Israel in a land of abundance. The punishment reverses God's promise to Abraham of innumerable descendants, a sign of divine blessing (vv. 11-17). In Hosea's day, Gilgal (v. 15) served as an Israelite center of worship — a northern rival to the Jerusalem temple. There Samuel had publicly inaugurated Saul as the first king of a united Hebrew nation, but through disobedience to God at Gilgal Saul later lost his divine appointment (1 Sam. 11:14-15; 15).

10 Anticipating Israel's Just Deserts God complains not that Israel is not religious enough, but rather that she misdirect her worship. The more abundance she receives, the more thanks she gives — not to the Lord, but to pagan fertility gods, worshipped at outdoor altars and sacred pillars. Thus her outward piety only demonstrates her inward faithlessness to God (vv. 1-2).

Hosea now anticipates the fall of the northern kingdom through the Assyrian capture of her capital and the death of her king in 722/21. Stripped of king and the trappings of religious ritual, the people recognize that the end of the monarchy results from their lack of reverence for God (v. 3). But instead of turning to God in repentance, they mourn the deportation of their forbidden idol, the "calf of Beth-aven" (vv. 5-6; cf. 4:15; 8:6-7; on the "great king," see 5:13). Fallen into disuse, the high places of "Aven" ("evil"), where Israel multiplied her sins, will beg to be covered up, presumably so judgment will end. On the "days of Gibeah" (v. 9), where abuse led to a civil war that nearly wiped out the tribe of Benjamin, see 9:9. Now foreign nations will finish off Israel for her "double guilt" of idolatry and alliance-making with foreign nations.

God had made life relatively easy for Israel — as easy as threshing (dragging a sledge over grain stalks to separate the kernels from the chaff) for a young cow. But he is about to fit the Hebrews with a heavy yoke and put them to the hard task of plowing for themselves (v. 11; "Jacob" is a poetic equivalent for "Judah").

Hosea calls his people to righteousness (v. 12); nevertheless, severe judgment for their wickedness lies before them (vv. 13-15). "Beth-arbel" probably refers to a Transjordanian city of Gilead, which the Moabite king Salamanu invaded during Hosea's day, or perhaps to a site by the Sea of Galilee, associated with one of the Assyrian kings who invaded Israel: Shalmaneser III (mid-to-late 9th century) or Shalmaneser V (late 8th century).

11:1-11 God, the Loving Parent God struggles with the full range of emotions over the punishment of his stubborn child. In verses 1-4, he laments Israel's ungrateful response to his tender care from their infancy. The more God beckoned his people through the prophets, the more they turned toward pagan deities (v. 2). Divine anger predominates in verses 5-7, which convey God's determination to punish Israel with conquest by Assyria and exile there. God can hardly believe the severity of the punishment he has just determined to inflict on Israel (v. 8; Admah and Zeboiim are linked geographically with Sodom and Gomorrah, "cities of the valley" annihilated by God; cf. Gen. 10:19). God does not take back his threat of judgment; rather, he decides not to destroy Israel completely, vows to restore to the promised land the people whom he punishes, and determines to ensure their future fidelity so that they will never again earn annihilation (vv. 9-11).

11:12–12:14 Blind to Sin Hosea returns to the present reality of the chosen people's unruliness. Israel/Ephraim has violated the covenant by establishing treaties with Assyria, from where the "east wind" blows, and Egypt, to whom they pay oil as tribute (12:1). The prophet's summary of the doggedness of the patriarch Jacob (here a poetic equivalent for "Judah"), from his contentious infancy to his wrestling with the angel of the Lord, exemplifies the determined fidelity to God to which Hosea urges a return (vv. 2-6).

Israel's blindness to her sin, represented by her use of dishonest business practices, makes unlikely such a return (vv. 7-8). So God determines the kingdom's punitive return to more humble conditions — a tent-dwelling life reminiscent of the Hebrews' days as wanderers in the wilderness, a period they were to commemorate by living in tents during the Feast of Tabernacles (v. 9; cf. Lev. 23:33-43). Divine messages delivered by the prophets have failed to get Israel to see her sin, but sinful she remains (vv. 10-11).

Verse 12 cites again the personal history of Jacob, renamed Israel after working for 14 years as a shepherd in Haran, in the far north of "Aram" (Syria), and gaining Leah and Rachel as wives (Genesis 29; 32:28).

13 Ephraim: The Exalted Tribe Laid Low

Here "Ephraim" refers to the tribe in particular, not the entire northern kingdom. Through the worship of Baal and handmade idols, this most prominent of the northern tribes has invited its death, pictured in metaphors from nature (v. 3; cf. 6:4). The chosen people's obligation to worship God exclusively recalls the first of the Ten Commandments (v. 4; Exod. 20:2-6). He met their needs, but the comforts of abundance led to their abandonment of the Giver, who will now punish them as a predator (vv. 5-8; cf. 5:14). Their king will prove powerless to defend them, for God, who at the request of his people established the monarchy, retains control over this institutional symbol of the Hebrews' rejection of him (vv. 10-11; cf. 1 Sam. 8:4-22).

Verse 13 pictures Ephraim as a baby who resists being born. The metaphor communicates the foolishness of Ephraim in delaying repentance from "stored up" sins (v. 12). That in verse 14 Hosea seems to summon a stinging death for Ephraim suggests that the first two lines of the verse are rhetorical questions: "Shall I ransom them from the power of Sheol [the Underworld]? Shall I redeem them from death?" with the implied answer being, "No," for "Compassion will be hidden from My sight."

In 12:1, the "east wind" that Israel/Ephraim pursues for treaties is Assyria. That same "east wind" will sweep through Israel with devastating effects (v. 15; cf. 2 Kgs. 17:1-6).

14 Wooing Israel to Repentance

Hosea ends with a pressing appeal that Israel repent from the two violations of the covenant that concern the prophet most: trust in foreign nations, evidenced by Israel's treaty-making with Assyria, and idolatrous worship of foreign gods, a by-product of such misplaced trust (cf. 5:11). The kingdom's repentance involves her acknowledgment of God as the source of help for the helpless. Politically, Israel surely assumed powerless "orphan" status in comparison to the growing Assyrian Empire.

The God intent on devastating Ephraim in chapter 13 now promises to a repentant Israel healing, love, renewal, and renown (vv. 4-7). From fertile Lebanon, famed for its mighty cedars, come images from nature that depict the high standard of God's promised blessing.

Hosea closes with an editorial word to the wise (v. 9), but still Israel failed to heed the prophet's urgings. The Assyrians invaded in the late 8th century, conquered Samaria in 722/21, deported the Hebrew population of the northern kingdom, and repopulated the territory with conquered peoples from Mesopotamia.

Joel

The book of Joel portrays the devastation wrought by a plague of locusts as a foreshadowing of God's judgment on the approaching "day of the Lord." Thus Joel ("Yahweh is God") urges his Judahite audience to sincere repentance, which might yet reverse their fortunes. Whereas 1:1–2:27 dwell on the current circumstances of the Hebrew community, 2:28–3:21 look toward a final day of judgment, when God sentences "the nations" and establishes forever the kingdom of the repentant elect.

Date

The book offers insufficient data for pinpointing the precise time of the prophet's ministry. Joel demonstrates familiarity with the 8th-century-B.C. prophets Isaiah and Amos and also the 6th-century prophet-in-exile, Ezekiel. References to slave trade between the Phoenicians and Greeks support a postexilic setting, and scholars have suggested dates of composition that extend into and even beyond the 4th century. The prophet's call to weep "between the vestibule and the altar" (2:17) reflects features of the second temple, built after the Hebrews' return from exile in Babylon (see Ezra).

1 A Plague of Locusts: Portent of Worse to Come

Joel summons the attention of his fellow Judahites, from drunkards to farmers to priests, to awaken their realization that the current stripping of the local vegetation by a swarm of locusts portends the judgmental "day of the Lord." Throughout history, and even within the last century, winds from the Arabian Desert have driven swarms of locusts west into Canaan/Israel. Modern research reveals that swarms contain up to 10 billion individual locusts, which can travel as many as 3000 miles during their lifetime. A swarm can consume in a single day enough food to feed 40 thousand people for one year. So Joel's audience would have had little trouble realizing the severity of the forewarned day of the Lord. Joel likens the locusts' attack to an overpowering military invasion (v. 6).

The frequent biblical pairing of the fruitful "vine" and "fig tree" represents abundant prosperity. Their devastation (v. 7) symbolizes total agricultural catastrophe.

Joel's concern in admonishing the people to mourn the situation lies not so much with the personal hardships it presents but with the interruption of daily offerings at the temple for lack of grain, wine, and oil (vv. 8-10). He calls for a national day of fasting and communal prayer at the temple to lament the coming day of the Lord (v. 14). With devastated crops and pastures, empty storehouses, and an accompanying drought, Judah's future looks terribly bleak (vv. 16-20).

2:1-11 The Overwhelming Day of the Lord

Joel uses the recent invasion of Judah by locusts as a springboard to warn of impending attack

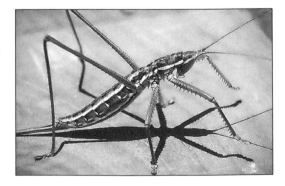

The cutting, hopping locust, whose swarms symbolize destruction. *(Phoenix Data Systems, Neal and Joel Bierling)*

by a punishing army, commanded by God (v. 11; some scholars interpret this passage as referring to the onslaught of the locusts only). The priests' blast of the ram's horn in Zion (= Jerusalem) warns of imminent danger (vv. 1, 15). Joel describes the overwhelming invasion in language that recalls the plague of locusts sent on Egypt (v. 2; cf. Exod. 10:14). Verses 3-9 picture an innumerable army, characterized by strength, endurance, agility, energy, discipline, and skill. These mighty invaders penetrate every corner, and nothing escapes them. They send people into panic and intimidate all creation (vv. 6, 10).

2:12-17 A Way Out?

The situation is not without hope. Repentance might yet save the day. But people of all ages and statuses must gather at the temple to cry for mercy (v. 16). Yet Joel's charge to "rend your heart and not your clothing" calls the Hebrews to mourn their sins with inward sincerity, not merely outward show (vv. 12-13). The priests are to pray that God will honor his covenant and preserve his people (v. 17).

2:18-27 Envisioning a Reversal of Fortunes

Joel envisions God as ousting the "northern" invaders and throwing them into the "eastern" and "western" seas (the Dead Sea and Mediterranean). Most conquerors of ancient Israel/Judah came from areas north-northeast of Canaan (e.g., Assyria and Babylonia). But Joel portrays the results of sincere repentance as not only averting disaster but also restoring divine blessings that obtain from covenantal obedience (cf. Deut. 28:1-14). For Joel's famished audience, the most desirable of these blessings was surely bountiful supplies of food. This reversal of Judah's punishment represents God's positive response to the petition that he spare his people from shame and thereby defend his reputation (vv. 26-27; cf. v. 17).

2:28-3:21 Looking Farther Ahead

Joel looks even farther into the future to a time when God bestows his spirit on not only prophets and priests but all people. Peter quotes Joel when announcing the fulfillment of this prophecy on the day of Pentecost (Acts 2:17-21).

The prophet describes a final day of the Lord on which the penitent elect obtain deliverance from divine judgment (2:30-31). The subsequent reversal of the *ill* fortunes of Judah and Jerusalem involves the reversal of the *good* fortunes of the oppressive foreign nations, which have prospered at the expense of God and his chosen people. "Jehoshaphat," the valley courtroom to which God gathers these nations, means "Yahweh judges"; some translations call it "Valley of Judgment" or "Valley of Decision" (3:2). Seafaring peoples in the Phoenician ports of Tyre and Sidon and the "regions of Philistia," on the southern coast of Canaan, engaged in international commerce throughout the Mediterranean world (3:4). By selling Judahites into foreign slavery, the merchant mariners have written their own sentence: enslavement of their descendants to the Sabeans, renowned traders of Saba/Sheba in southwest Arabia (3:8). In warning the nations to prepare for their day of judgment by transforming tools into weapons, Joel reverses the hopeful words of global peace in Isa. 2:4.

Joel 3:18-21 elaborates the restoration of Judah's fortunes announced in 3:1. The promises include abundant crops, perpetual habitation, and divine vengeance against her enemies. On the "spring" flowing from the temple (3:18), cf. Ezek. 47:1-12; Rev. 22:1-2. Finally, Joel singles out for condemnation two more regions: Egypt, which once enslaved the Hebrew people, and Edom, home to the adversarial descendants of Esau.

Amos

Despite its relative brevity, the book of Amos continues to pack a major punch against the very social injustices that persist in modern times. While Mosaic law legislated the rituals of Hebrew religion, the code also mandated righteous behavior in practical living; therefore the economic oppression, judicial unfairness, and dehumanizing policies of the temporarily resurgent northern kingdom in the early 8th century B.C. constituted moral violations of the covenant. The Judahite lay prophet Amos ventured north into Israel to announce her inescapable punishment for these callous and flagrant transgressions. Amos's contemporaries included the southern prophets Isaiah and Micah and the northern prophet Hosea, on the heels of whose career came the forewarned fall of Israel at the hands of the Assyrian army (722/21).

1–2 A Prophetic Setup

The opening verse of Amos identifies the prophet as a shepherd from the Judean town of Tekoa, 12 miles south of Jerusalem. That this southerner prophesies against the northern kingdom of Israel intensifies the insult of his reproving message. The reigns of Judah's King Uzziah and Israel's King Jeroboam II overlapped from ca. 767-753, and most scholars assign Amos's prophetic activity to ca. 760. In 759, a severe earthquake rocked the region around Jerusalem, and this tremor may constitute the quake to which v. 1 dates Amos's oracle.

God's lion-like "roaring" (1:2) signals the imminence of his punitive pounce on the object of his judgment (cf. 3:4). His roaring "from Zion" emphasizes that he lives in Jerusalem — not Bethel or Dan, the centers of northern worship set up as rivals to the temple (1 Kgs. 12:25-33). From the mountaintop capital of Judah, God's voice carries all the way to the peaks of Carmel, the highest mountain range in the northern

kingdom. This coastal region of abundant rainfall and lush pastureland dries up at the sound of God's roar.

The literary formula "For three . . . and for four" (1:3–2:6) means "over and over again." Thus Amos charges various groups with innumerable and repeated sins, first against humanity (1:3–2:3), then God (2:4-5), and then both (2:6-8). Beginning with Damascus, capital of Israel's immediate neighbor to the north, the prophet slowly tightens the geographical noose around the neck of the unsuspecting northern kingdom. Amos pictures in agricultural terms ("threshing" with "sledges of iron") the military violence of Damascus against "Gilead," the Transjordanian region south of Syria (1:3). "Hazael" murdered "Ben-hadad" to seize the throne in Damascus (1:4; 2 Kgs. 8:7-15). Tiglath-pileser III of Assyria conquered Damascus (732) and exiled its inhabitants to "Kir," the Syrians' original Mesopotamian home (1:5; 2 Kgs. 16:9).

To Israel's southwest (1:6-8), Gaza (and then the Phoenician port of Tyre, vv. 9-10) earns condemnation for selling people as slaves to Edom, homeland of Esau's descendants (Genesis 36). Three other cities of the Philistine pentapolis (Ashdod, Ashkelon, and Ekron), established on the southern coast of Canaan beginning in the late 13th century, are indicted.

The prophet condemns unforgiving Edom, to the southeast, for violence against "his brother" (the Hebrews, descended from Esau's brother Jacob; 1:11-12). Ammon (north of Edom, across the Jordan River from the hill country of Ephraim) unmercifully acted for selfish gain, and Amos's judgment focuses on her capital, Rabbah (modern Amman, Jordan), and her king (vv. 13-15). Moab, east of the Dead Sea, separated Edom from Ammon (2:1-3). The desecration of a corpse by the residents of the fortified city "Kerioth" exemplifies the region's crimes against humanity.

Amos then pronounces judgment against the southern kingdom Judah for transgressions of the "Law" (the covenant mediated through Moses at Mount Sinai) and proclaims the coming destruction of the political and religious capital, Jerusalem (2:4-5).

No doubt pleased with the prophet's condemnation of their immediate neighbors, the Israelites have been set up for Amos's most comprehensive condemnation yet — that of the northern kingdom itself (2:6-8). Amos castigates Israel for sins against humanity, as he did her pagan neighbors, *and* against God, as he did Judah. He charges Israel with social injustices in the marketplace, the court, and the cult (2:6-8). For humanitarian reasons, Exod. 22:26-27 commands the return before nightfall of "garments taken as pledges." The disobedient Israelites use them to make comfortable beds with cult prostitutes (2:8).

In 2:9-11, God gives a historical summary of his actions on behalf of the Hebrews. Here "Amorite" encompasses a range of ethnic groups that inhabited Canaan when the Hebrews entered the promised land under Joshua. Numbers 6 details the regulations of the Nazirite vow, to which Samson's mother bound her son (Judges 13). Israel met the goodness of God with an ungrateful response — disobedience and the gagging of God's prophets (2:12). The heavy wagonload of Israel's sins invites harsh divine judgment, prophesied as military defeat (2:13-16).

3 Driving Home Israel's Doom

Amos accuses Israel of abusing the beneficent and exclusive relationship God established with the Hebrew people (v. 2). The rhetorical questions in verses 3-6 prepare his audience to agree with his prophetic perspective in applying to Israel the theme of imminent calamity developed there (vv. 7-8).

That the prophet accords pagan Ashdod and Egypt the moral superiority to serve as character witnesses against Israel reveals the depths to which the northern kingdom has sunk (v. 9). Just as a shepherd was required to show proof that a wild beast killed a member of his employer's flock, so guarding against animal thievery

(cf. Gen. 37:29-33), the postjudgment remnants of Samaria will give evidence of the northern kingdom's fall. The "house of Jacob" refers to the Hebrew nation (v. 13). The illegitimate "altars of Bethel" accommodated sacrifices to a golden calf set up by the renegade Jeroboam I, first ruler of the breakaway northern kingdom (v. 14; 1 Kgs. 12:25-33). Ancient Israelite altars included "horns," vertical projections from each of four corners, which prevented sacrifices from falling off the altar and also allowed a fugitive who grabbed hold of them to gain legal asylum from murder-bent pursuers. The cutting off of these horns (v. 14) symbolizes the complete absence of sanctuary when divine judgment rains down on Israel. The prophesied destruction of the "winter house," "summer house," and "houses of ivory" portends the economic downfall of the affluent, condemned in 2:6-8 for getting rich at the expense of the poor (v. 15; cf. 1 Kgs. 22:39; excavations at Samaria have unearthed hundreds of carved ivory fragments).

4 God's Warnings Ignored

Amos's addressing of the rich wives of Samaria as "cows of Bashan" is not in itself an insult. The sleek cattle that pastured in this fertile region of northern Transjordan received the best of care, and the prophet's comparison highlights the similarly privileged status of these well-off women. But Amos immediately condemns them for their oppression of the poor. On the "hooks" used to lead them into exile (v. 2), cf. 2 Kgs. 19:28. Amos sarcastically emphasizes the emptiness of the Israelites' outward display of religiosity at the kingdom's central worship sites, which included Bethel and Gilgal (vv. 4-5), for God requires inward devotion.

Amos accuses Israel of ignoring divine warnings meant to effect the kingdom's collective repentance. "Cleanness of teeth" denotes famine (v. 6). The withholding of the latter (autumn) rains would have devastated unripe crops (v. 7). Drought (v. 8), blight (v. 9), and plague (v. 10) round out the list of warnings, whose combined effect on land and people Amos likens to God's fiery destruction of Sodom and Gomorrah. But Israel fails to repent, and Amos reintroduces his audience to the God they have forgotten — the creator of the world and sovereign over humanity and nature (v. 13).

5 Justice Served against Unjust Israel

So certain is Israel's doom that Amos writes a funeral song in advance of her demise. His portrayal of Israel as a dead virgin communicates particular tragedy, since the bearing of children constituted a woman's crowning achievement (cf. Judg. 11:37). Verse 3 pictures the death of Israel as devastating military defeat — a 90 percent reduction in the kingdom's fighting force.

Israel can still steer off her fatal course (vv. 4-7). She must seek God through heartfelt commitment to the covenant, not through rituals at illegitimate centers of worship. The northerners must not even "cross over" into Judah to worship at Beersheba, whose pagan "high place" the reforming King Josiah later destroyed (2 Kgs. 23:8). Verse 6 calls Israel the "house of Joseph," since from Joseph's sons Ephraim and Manasseh came the largest and most powerful of the northern tribes.

Verses 8-9 reiterate the sovereignty of God over his orderly creation (cf. 4:13). The constellations of the Pleiades and Orion marked distinct seasons, as darkness and light mark night and day.

Attention returns to the social injustices perpetrated in Israel, specifically, corruption in the judicial system (v. 10) and economic oppression of the poor by the rich (v. 11). The judicial atmosphere has become so degenerate that the wise know to keep a low profile (v. 13). God will deny wealthy oppressors opportunity to enjoy gain gotten at the expense of the poor. Verses 14-15 hold out the possibility that a moral about-face in Israel might win divine grace. But Amos gives no guarantees. In fact, God will respond with chastisement and disgust to the anticipated kingdom-wide wailing (vv. 16-17). Amos exposes the foolishness of Israel's longing for the "day of the Lord." She thinks religious rituals will make her acceptable to God, but Amos warns that God "hates" this empty display (vv. 21-23). Amos charges that Israel's two-faced religiosity, now shown in their worship of the Assyrian gods Sakkuth and Kaiwan, associated with Saturn (vv. 25-26), began as early as

Ivory carving of a sphinx in a thicket, representing the wealth and luxury assailed by Amos (3:15; 6:4).
(Israel Antiquities Authority)

the wilderness wanderings. So judgment day for persistently unfaithful Israel will not bring divine vindication against her enemies, but conquest by them.

6 Humbling the Self-Reliant Hebrews

Amos lumps the Judahite leaders of Jerusalem/Zion with the Israelite elite of Samaria and condemns the lot, whose self-sufficiency fools them into thinking they will escape God's judgment. The prophet cites Philistine Gath and the Syrian cities of Calneh and Hamath as ominous examples of fallen prosperity. Because in their self-indulgent lifestyle they have forgone sincere grief over the ruination of their nation, they have assured that they will be the first of Israel to be exiled.

The arrogance of Jacob/Israel has manifested itself in the perversion of justice, the suppression of righteousness, and self-reliance, exemplified in the nation's claim to have conquered the Transjordanian towns of Lo-debar and Karnaim without divine help (vv. 8, 12-13). God will punish the prideful Hebrews, from the greatest to the least, with military conquest by a foreign nation, whose domination will surpass the full north-south extent of the promised land (vv.

9-11, 14). Israel met Assyrian conquest in 722/21, and Babylonia defeated Judah in 587/86.

7–9 The Visions of Amos

In a series of visions God reveals the divine plans to destroy Israel (7:1-3, 4-6, 7-8; 8:1-3; 9:1-4).

7 Israel Fails to Measure Up Amos fulfills the prophetic role of intercessor by pleading with God not to carry out his plans to destroy Israel by famine (caused by locusts) and fire as threatened (7:1-3, 4-6). God relents, but the northern kingdom strikes out when she fails to measure up to God's standards (vv. 7-8). Amos singles out for attack the intertwined institutions of religion ("high places," "sanctuaries") and monarchy (the "house of [King] Jeroboam").

Amaziah, priest of the illegitimate royal sanctuary at Bethel, feels endangered by Amos's prophecy, so he informs Jeroboam of Amos's threats against the monarchy and kingdom. Then Amaziah tells the prophet (= "seer") to return home to Judah and prophesy there. But Amos responds that he is not a professional prophet — he was sent by God with a mission (vv. 14-15). Amos meets the priest's attempt to silence him with a condemnation that spells utter personal disaster: Amaziah's wife will disgrace him through unfaithfulness, his heirs will all be murdered, his landed estate will be divided up, and he will die on the ritually "unclean soil" of a land tied to pagan gods — in other words, in exile (v. 17). Amaziah's attempt to squelch the prophet's message will fail to thwart God's punishment of Israel. The entire kingdom will suffer exile.

8 A Famine of God's Words The fourth vision further confirms the doom of the northern kingdom. A Hebrew wordplay connects the envisioned "basket of summer fruit" *(qayits)* with the "end" *(qets)* for Israel. She will perish quickly, just as summer fruit does.

Israel earns this sentence through false piety, greed, and social injustice. The Israelites see their meticulous observance of religious rituals, such as the new moon and the Sabbath, as only interrupting their number one priority: profit-making. Their greed leads merchants to balance their scales with an underweight shekel and so sell less for more money. They knowingly give credit to people who cannot afford to pay and enslave the unfortunates when they default on the debt (v. 6). They even sell the husks of wheat so as not to miss an opportunity to make a buck.

Amos describes two "acts of God" that will accompany God's judgment for these social sins: an earthquake, which will simulate the undulating waters of the Nile River (cf. 1:1), and a solar eclipse (vv. 8-9). The prophet likens the intensity of the Israelites' grieving over their judgment to mourning for an "only son," whose death in a patriarchal society spelled doom for the family legacy (v. 10).

An even greater famine, the absence of any word from God, will run the entire north-south extent of Canaan (vv. 11-14). Although they now ignore Amos's prophecy, when they do decide to listen to God, he will not speak.

9 The Illusion of Immunity In Amos's fifth and final vision (vv. 1-4), God metes out judgment at the altar of the temple. The proper offering of sacrifices at that altar effected atonement for sins (Leviticus 1–7), but because of Israel's misuse of religious rituals the altar becomes for her a symbol not of pardon but of inescapable punishment. Verses 2-4 reinterpret in threatening terms the omnipresence of God (contrast Ps. 139:7-12). He retrieves fugitives from Sheol, the underworld abode of the dead; above the earth in heaven; atop the highest mountains (the "summit" of the Carmel range); within the deepest depths of the sea; and in foreign "captivity."

Verses 5-6 reinforce God's dominion over the created order, with the rising and subsiding of the earth alluding to earthquakes (v. 5; cf. 8:8) and the "vaulted dome" referring to the sky. On the "upper chambers" of God's heavenly abode (v. 6), cf. Ps. 104:3.

Amos does not contradict his previous affirmation of Israel's unique relationship with God (v. 7; cf. 3:2); rather, he asserts, her divinely orchestrated exodus from Egypt and establishment in Canaan does not mean that her salvation is any more certain than is God's transplanting of the nonelect Philistines and Syrians in the same geographical region a guarantee of theirs ("Caphtor" = Crete; "Kir" = a country in Mesopotamia). While God's work on behalf of Israel does not imply her national immunity from divine judgment, he will nevertheless execute it only against the sinners of the northern kingdom who continue to deny this truth. God will catch each one in his filtering sieve (vv. 8-10).

Amos anticipates the restoration of the "booth of David" — possibly the breakaway northern kingdom, which established a non-Davidic monarchy after the death of Solomon (1 Kings 12); the southern kingdom of Judah (cf. 2:5); or the entire nation of Hebrews rejoined as a united kingdom. Amos describes the restoration in terms that recall the blessings of the Mosaic covenant: political strength, which extends over the elect Gentiles (cf. Acts 15:16-17); crops so abundant that farmers will not be able to process the harvest of one season before it is time to sow for the next; and permanence in the promised land. In verses 14-15, Israel's promised enjoyment of the fruits of her labor reverses the sentence delivered in 5:11.

Obadiah

Other than naming Obadiah, this shortest of Old Testament books offers no personal information about the prophet whose oracle against Edom the work records. The long history of strife between the Edomite descendants of Esau and the Hebrew descendants of Jacob provides the background against which Obadiah's prophecy stands. But the centuries-long period spanned by the conflict makes it difficult to pinpoint the particular historical circumstances that sparked Obadiah's oracle. Similarly, it proves difficult to place the prophet in time, though his apparent awareness of events surrounding the fall of Jerusalem to the Babylonians in 587/86 B.C. suggests that he prophesied after that disaster (vv. 10-14).

Verse 1 introduces the divine revelation to Obadiah (= "servant of Yahweh") as a "vision," but the 21-verse book takes the form of an oracle. In this context "vision" carries a wider meaning: general prophetic perception, which encompasses both visual and verbal revelations.

As elsewhere in the Old Testament, "Esau" serves as the poetic equivalent of "Edom" (cf. also "Teman," probably an area of southern Edom; v. 9), and "Jacob" stands for Israel.

Edom Pays the Price of Arrogance

Obadiah announces that God is mustering the nations for battle against Edom, the historic enemy of the Hebrews. The rocky, mountainous terrain of northern Edom, which overlooked the southern end of the Dead Sea from the east, offered the Edomites countless naturally defensible positions (v. 3). Their capital, Sela ("Mount Esau," vv. 8-9, 21), became in the 3rd century the site of the impregnable Nabatean fortress of Petra, in modern Jordan. But Edom's defensive strength generated in it a sense of national invincibility. This political and military arrogance resulted not only in Edom's sins of omission against its neighboring cousins but also in gloating over the misfortune of Jerusalem/Judah and even in inhumane opportunism at the Hebrews' expense (vv. 10-14). Obadiah's description of Edom's sins against the southern kingdom recall the events surrounding the Babylonian destruction of Jerusalem in 587/86, after which the Edomites invaded southern Judah (cf. Ezek. 35:1-15).

In its self-serving pride, however, Edom failed to consider the sovereignty of God, who now determines to punish the nation at the hands of her own allies (v. 7; the eating of bread denotes the sharing of a meal to seal a covenant). The Edomites will reap what they have sown (v. 15). Their arrogance will lead to national humiliation (v. 2). These looters of Jerusalem will themselves suffer a ransacking that exceeds the plundering of thieves, who take only what they want, and the gleaning of harvesters, required by Mosaic law to leave portions for the underprivileged (v. 5). The merciless Edomites who murdered fugitives from Judah will suffer slaughter by the Hebrew survivors on Mount Zion (= Jerusalem). In verse 18, the "house of Jacob" denotes the southern kingdom of Judah, and the "house of Joseph" stands for the coalition of the 10 northern tribes dominated by Ephraim and Manasseh.

The resurgence of the Hebrews will involve wiping out not only Edom, but also the nations, who have joined Edom in drinking to the misfortune of Judah. The revelers will now get drunk on the destructive cup of God's wrath (v. 16), while the Hebrews take over their territory. Verses 19-20 foresee the repossession of the promised land by Hebrew exiles returned from distant locations: Zarephath, on the Phoenician coast north of Israel, and Sepharad, probably Sardis in far western Asia Minor. The judgment of Edom emanates from Mount Zion/Jerusalem, home to the temple and center of God's rule over his reestablished kingdom (v. 21).

Jonah

The account of Jonah is set in the days of the Neo-Assyrian Empire (ca. 911-612 B.C.). The mention of the prophet Jonah in 2 Kgs. 14:25 identifies him as an Israelite from a town in the territory of Zebulun and links him with Jeroboam II, who ruled the northern kingdom from ca. 785-745. Though during these years Assyrian weakness allowed for Israel's temporary resurgence, the Mesopotamian superpower recovered and conquered the northern kingdom in 722/21. Just over a century later, the Babylonians took over by sacking Nineveh, Assyria's last and greatest capital city (704-612) and the divinely decreed destination of Jonah.

The Bible makes Jonah famous not for his faith but for his failings. Initially, he rejects his prophetic mission to the enemies of Israel. Given a second chance to obey, Jonah does his duty but begrudgingly. He becomes angry when God shows mercy toward the penitent Ninevites. Yet he himself expects mercy from God's display of control over nature — even though he doesn't deserve it. He would rather die than see God's point.

Model of a Phoenician "Tarshish-type" merchant ship, 13th century B.C. (Richard Cleave, Pictorial Archive)

Message

Though the miraculous events portrayed in Jonah have sparked much debate over the historicity of this account, the lessons of the book do not hinge on whether Jonah actually spent time in the "belly of the whale" or whether the "gourd" really grew overnight. The main concern of the book does not lie in proving God's ability to intervene in creation. Rather, through the negative example of Jonah, it illustrates God's preference of grace over judgment; asserts his sovereign right to exercise mercy; and affirms his care for the nonelect — here, the pagan enemies of the chosen people. And by implication the book poses the question, "Do any of us really want what we deserve?"

Composition

The author of Jonah goes unidentified, and textual clues remain insufficient for determining the book's date of composition. Thematically, Jonah's psalm of thanksgiving in 2:2-9 parallels prayers throughout the book of Psalms.

1:1-16 Jonah on the Run

The prophet Jonah receives divine instructions to preach in wicked Nineveh, capital of the enemy Assyrian Empire, which conquered the northern kingdom of Israel in 722/21. But instead of heading northeast to Mesopotamia, Jonah boards a westbound ship sailing from the Mediterranean port of Joppa (near modern Tel Aviv) toward Tarshish (= "open sea," possibly Tartessus in Spain). In ancient Near Eastern thought, deities resided in geographically defined territories, in which their power was concentrated. But if by leaving the promised land Jonah thinks he can escape God's authority, a violent storm at sea forces him to abandon that notion. Roused from slumber by the ship's desperate captain, Jonah joins his shipmates in recognizing the tempest as a sign of divine anger. When a roll of the dice (the casting of "lots," v. 7) points to disobedient Jonah as the root of God's wrath, the prophet offers his own sacrifice in the sea as the means of placating the Lord and saving his shipmates. Though rightfully upset with Jonah for bringing danger upon them, the pagan crew initially resists the temptation to toss him overboard because they fear further enraging his powerful God for murdering a man who may actually be innocent. After valiant but vain efforts to row to safe haven, however, they utter a hopeful prayer and heave Jonah into the swell. The Lord stops the storm, and the crew pay homage to Jonah's God.

1:17–2:10 Jonah's Ordeal at Sea

In the meantime, Jonah enters the stomach of a "large fish" ordained by God to swallow him up. The point of 1:17 lies not in the science of Jonah's ordeal but in its miraculous nature. By stating that the prophet remained at sea (often associated with death), inside the fish, for "three days and three nights" — the time the ancients thought it took for a soul to travel to the afterworld — the account implies that Jonah should have been good and dead (cf. Matt. 12:40). But instead we find him praising the Lord for bringing him back from the brink of death. Having already descended to the "depth of Sheol" (abode of the dead; "the Pit," 2:2, 6), Jonah felt his life fading away when he "remembered the Lord" and prayerfully renewed his commitment to faithfulness — though notably, without repenting of his disobedience. God completes the miraculous "deliverance" of Jonah by expelling him from his watery tomb and returning him to dry land.

The episode emphasizes that God desires obedience, not sacrifice — especially not human sacrifice. Jonah's death would have freed him from going to Nineveh, but it would not have satisfied God, whose mission for Jonah the mercifully unsuccessful fugitive will not thwart.

3 Jonah Gets a Second Chance

The second time Jonah hears God's call to prophesy in Nineveh, he obeys. In portraying the Ninevites' repentance as universal and their presumably populous city (and/or surrounding region) as vast, the account accents the magnitude of Jonah's success. Fasting, wearing sackcloth, and sitting on piles of dust or ashes constituted mourning rituals that were also signs of penitence (vv. 5-6). God responds favorably to the Ninevites' contrition and withholds the punishment he had planned for them.

4 An Object Lesson for a Begrudging Missionary

Now the reader learns why Jonah had tried to evade his mission to the Ninevites: he begrudged them God's mercy. When Jonah sees that they will not get the punishment they deserve, he complains to God. He had done his duty, but evidently in hopes that God would enact the threatened judgment (3:4). Now that God has taken compassion on the Ninevites, Jonah would rather die than accept God's way.

For a second time God denies Jonah his death wish. Caught without a valid response to God's challenge that his anger is unfounded, the prophet goes off by himself to watch and wait. God takes this opportunity to give Jonah an object lesson, which again demonstrates the Lord's power over creation. First God shows compassion on his sullen servant by providing him shade from a quick-growing plant. But just when Jonah gets comfortable, the Lord causes a worm to attack the plant, so that it withers as fast as it grew. Having stripped Jonah of the short-lived source of shelter, God now afflicts him with a desert-hot wind, which combined with the sun's heat reawakens Jonah's desire to die. When the sun-stroked prophet protests the justice of his anger over the loss of his ill-deserved gift of shade, God points out the far greater justification he legitimately claims for sparing himself the loss of the Ninevites. For though they do not number among God's chosen people — and so lack the the Mosaic law to guide them — the Ninevites are counted among God's creatures, and he cares about them, too (cf. Ezek. 18:21-32; Matt. 5:43-48).

Micah

Among the Minor Prophets, the book of Micah shows thematic parallels with Amos. Both 8th-century prophets castigate the Hebrews for social injustices that violate the covenant God established with them at Sinai. But unlike Amos, Micah does not narrow his focus on a northern audience; rather, he indicts the capitals of both Israel and Judah for transgressions that invoke the covenant curses (Deut. 28:15-68). The condemnation of Samaria and Jerusalem dominates chapters 1–5. But in the last two chapters (6–7), Micah issues oracles of hope, which envision restoration for a "remnant" of Hebrews — a theme developed in Isaiah 1–39. This hope emanates from faith in the forgiving nature of the ever-loving God, who makes good on his historic promises. Micah's name (= "who is like Yahweh") expresses the wonder of this God, who delights not in punishment but in compassion.

Background

During Micah's lifetime, Assyria posed the greatest threat to the divided Hebrew kingdoms. By sacking Samaria in 722/21 B.C., Assyria sealed the conquest of the northern kingdom. In 701, Judah narrowly escaped the same fate when the Assyrian siege of Jerusalem failed (2 Kings 18–19).

Composition

The stringing together of originally independent oracles has left abrupt transitions that make for Micah's rather jerky literary style. Scholars generally agree that Micah uttered the oracles in chapters 1–3. Debate continues concerning the source and original audience of chapters 4–7, which refer to events that may more closely reflect the Babylonian assault on Jerusalem in the early 6th century.

1 Samaria and Jerusalem Put on Alert

Verse 1 identifies Micah as a Judahite whose hometown lay ca. 25 miles southwest of Jerusalem. References to the reigning kings of Judah locate him in the 8th century (cf. Jer. 26:18), when his prophetic contemporaries would have included Hosea, Amos, and Isaiah. Micah's prophecies, which welded divinely communicated words and visions, targeted the capitals of both the northern and southern Hebrew kingdoms — Samaria in Israel and Jerusalem in Judah.

Micah's opening oracle warns all the world of its imminent upheaval by God as punishment for his people's sinful rebellion, perfected in Samaria and exported to Jerusalem. "Jacob"/Israel may stand for the northern kingdom or the nation as a whole (v. 5). Outdoor pagan shrines were called "high places," and identification of Jerusalem as the "high place of Judah" makes a derogatory play on the city's mountain elevation and its inhabitants' religious disloyalty (v. 5). With the charges leveled and the evidence stated, verses 6-7 declare the sentence: the smashing of Samaria, source of the sin. Her "harlot's earnings" refer to illegitimate gains from cult prostitution, which commonly attended pagan worship.

Micah describes his public lamentation of the devastation to come, yet he does not want word of the disaster to reach neighboring Philistine Gath, likely to gloat over the misfortune of its enemies (vv. 8-9). Verses 10ff. contain a series of puns on place names to portend the doom of nearby Judahite cities and towns. For example, the inhabitants of the "House of dust" (Beth-leaphrah) will roll in the dust — a sign of mourning; those who live in "Going out" (Zaanan) will lack an escape route; the "House of removal" (Beth-ezel) will have its support removed; the inhabitants of "Possession" (Mareshah) will find it possessed by an invader.

The fortified city of Lachish receives singular blame for adopting the sins of Israel and spreading them to Jerusalem, "daughter Zion" (v. 13). Adullam, a Canaanite city in Judah, will inherit Israel's glory, while the Hebrews shave their heads to mourn the departure of their exiled children (vv. 15-16).

2 Poetic Justice for Oppressors

Here the emphasis on injustices perpetrated by the rich and powerful parallels Amos's focus on social sins. Proclaiming the poetic justice of God's threatened judgment, Micah warns that calamity is coming for those who bring disaster on others. Mosaic law forbade the confiscation of land, which embodied a family's participation in the covenantal promises. Because land also provided the basis for one's livelihood, preserving its apportionment helped ensure an equitable distribution of wealth. In Micah's oracle, law-breaking confiscators of their fellows' land will lose their own land, and God will reapportion it to nonbelieving outsiders (vv. 1-4). The former land-grabbers will go unrepresented for marking out new territorial claims (v. 5).

Micah exposes the efforts of the socially powerful to silence the reproaching prophets of God (vv. 6ff.). The abusive elite, who rob unsuspecting fellow citizens and evict women and children, would rather listen to the lies of false prophets who tell them what they want to hear (cf. v. 11, "wine and liquor," symbolizing wealth and prosperity). Micah orders the merciless evictors to get out of town themselves (v. 10).

The prophet foresees a future in which God reassumes his position as champion of his people (vv. 12-13). The oracle may relate to the Assyrian siege of Jerusalem in 701, when according to 2 Kgs. 19:35 God saved the penned-up inhabitants of the great walled city by slaying the besiegers overnight (cf. 5:1-6; 2 Kings 18–19).

3 An Undaunted Micah Tells It Like It Is

Micah continues to castigate evil-loving leaders by grotesquely portraying their social oppression in cannibalistic terms (vv. 2-3). Just as they had ignored the needs of the unfortunate, now God will refuse to hear their own cries for help (v. 4).

Micah exposes the corrupt prophets who align themselves with the wealthy and comfort the rich with what they want to hear in exchange for their own economic advantage (v. 5). Justice for these false prophets will consist in "darkness," the inability to receive revelation from God (vv. 6-7).

In contrast, Micah declares his empowerment by God's spirit to seek justice and to expose the nation's sins (v. 8). The prophet upbraids both secular and religious leaders — politicians, judges, priests — all of whom presume God's unconditional protection (vv. 9-11). God's judgmental ruination of Jerusalem, home to his temple, rests on the heads of these corrupt covenant-breakers (v. 12).

4 No Pain, No Gain

In language nearly identical to Isaiah's, Micah describes the future restoration of Jerusalem to an exalted position in a world of peaceful nations (vv. 1-3; cf. Isa. 2:2-4). To epitomize the reversal of fortunes enjoyed by the Hebrews in these "last days," Micah pictures individuals sitting under their "vines" and "fig trees" — a symbol of prosperity. The power of God's spoken word ensures the fulfillment of the prophecy (v. 4). This divinely afflicted but preserved remnant will return to Zion to be transformed into a "strong nation" under God's rule (vv. 6-8). "Tower of the flock" and "hill of daughter Zion" (v. 8) refer to Jerusalem (Mt. Zion), the center of God's rule.

Micah interprets the coming judgment as the painful, purgative precondition for Zion's ultimate exaltation (v. 9). Micah's contemporaries may assume that expulsion from the promised land signifies abandonment by their divine King and Counselor, but the prophet views the inevitable exile as an integral trial in the plan of their very-much-engaged God. Verse 10 anticipates the Babylonian exile of the 6th century, though in Micah's day (8th century) Assyria posed the current Mesopotamian threat (5:5-6). Eventually, God will equip the redeemed remnant to judge the unjust nations. Threshing (vv. 12-13) involved trampling grain stalks to dislodge the kernels from the chaff. Horns of iron and hoofs of bronze ensure the success of Zion's "threshers."

5 Anticipating a Davidic Deliverer

This chapter weaves together oracles addressing present circumstances and prophecies concerning the future. Verse 1 appears to have in view the 701 Assyrian siege of Jerusalem (the "judge of Israel" referring to King Hezekiah). The next three verses anticipate a future deliverance of Judah by a ruler in the tradition of King David: a "shepherd" from the king's hometown of Bethlehem (v. 2; cf. Matt. 2:1-6). In verses 5-6, the current Assyrian invasion becomes a symbol of the future attack from which this Davidic shepherd-ruler delivers his people. The pairing of "seven" and "eight" is a literary device meant to communicate not literal numbers of subordinate leaders but a number "sufficient" to finish vanquishing the enemy. "Nimrod," a royal city of Assyria, serves as a poetic equivalent for the empire.

Verses 7-9 envision the "remnant" of the chosen people as pervading the nations, where their presence brings both blessing and judgment (cf. Gen. 12:3; also 4:9-13). God will match the fierce judgment of the people's enemies by purging them of their own military might and the trappings of pagan religion (vv. 10-15).

6 God's Lawsuit against His People

This chapter takes the form of a covenantal lawsuit, to which God calls witnesses from nature (vv. 1-2; cf. Deut. 4:26). God begins by citing from his people's history evidence that proves his own covenantal fidelity (vv. 3-5). After God establishes his faithfulness as fact, he sets forth the core legal, ethical, and religious requirements of the covenant: righteous conduct rather than lavish ritual (vv. 6-8; cf. 1 Sam. 15:22). Verse 7

alludes to the pagan practice of sacrificing one's firstborn child to placate the gods — a practice at times carried out even by the Hebrews (2 Kgs. 17:17-18).

God specifies several breaches of contract committed by his people: dishonest business practices, violence, lying, and deceit (vv. 9-12). The chapter closes with the sentencing of God's people (vv. 13-16). Dissatisfaction and futility will characterize their lives, as reward for their following the example of the wicked northern kings Omri and Ahab.

7 Light at the End of the Tunnel

Micah bewails the thorough moral bankruptcy of his society. With corrupt political and judicial decision-makers, money talks. People with influence work deals with those in power. Trying to keep them honest only risks retaliation. A person can't trust anyone — neighbors, friends, even family members (cf. Matt. 10:34-39).

But Micah maintains hope in the midst of this moral darkness. He recognizes the justice of God's present punishment without losing sight of a future characterized by divine vindication of the chosen people at the expense of their enemies. God will set things right by action portrayed as miraculous military triumph covering the whole of the ancient Near Eastern world, from Egypt to Assyria and the Euphrates River, and will instill the fear of the Lord among the pagan nations, which will slither forth in surrender (vv. 12, 16-17). In contrast, Micah paints a peaceful, pastoral picture in petitioning his Shepherd-God for a return of the Hebrew flock to fertile fields. Micah's hope for the restoration of his people to a position of divine favor, in accordance with God's promises to the patriarchs, rests with his faith in the forgiving nature of God and in his "unswerving loyalty."

Nahum

The book of Nahum provides a fitting follow-up to Micah. There the 8th-century-B.C. aggression of Assyria provides the historical backdrop and threatens the means by which God will mete out judgment on his unfaithful people. Whereas Micah ends with a hopeful prophecy that anticipates the postpunishment restoration of a Hebrew remnant, Nahum announces the catalyzing event for its fulfillment: the divinely orchestrated downfall of Nineveh, last capital of the oppressive Assyrian Empire. Though for a time employed by God as the instrument of his judgment, Assyria pursued violence to excess (2:11-12; 3:10), and Nahum holds nothing back in describing the reciprocal judgment of God against Nineveh, the center of Assyrian power. Whereas the book of Jonah illustrates God's eagerness to extend grace to the Ninevites, Nahum reveals the consequences of their persistence in overstepping the moral laws of the Lord. Nahum's portrayal of an intensely vengeful God takes for granted the righteousness of his anger and the justice of his punishments.

Date

References to two historical events bracket the time period during which Nahum delivered this prophecy: the sacking of Thebes (Heb. No-Amon, 3:8) by the Assyrians ca. 661 and the fall of Nineveh in 612. Thus Nahum appears to have ministered after the Assyrian conquest of Samaria/Israel (722/21 but before the ultimate fall of Judah with the Babylonian destruction of Jerusalem in 587/86.

1 The Prophetic Finger Points at Nineveh

Nahum received both oracular and visionary revelations (1:1). Proposed locations for Nahum's hometown of Elkosh include sites ranging from Judah to Assyria, where conceivably the Hebrew prophet could have landed after deportation from the fallen northern kingdom. But the uncertain identification of Elkosh and the lack of further personal information about Nahum render such suggestions speculative.

While the reader knows from the start that the book points a prophetic finger at Nineveh, the oracle does not name the city until 2:8. The prophecy begins with an ominous emphasis on the punitive vengefulness of God, who though "slow to anger" eventually wreaks havoc on his enemies. Indeed, God's thorough judgment of his adversaries constitutes one element of his goodness toward "those who take refuge in him" (v. 7; cf. vv. 14-15). By outlining the power of God over nature, Nahum sums up God's ability to accomplish his will (cf. Mic. 1:4). Verse 4 alludes to the parting of the Red Sea at the exodus and to the stopping up of the Jordan River when the Hebrews entered Canaan. The Transjordanian area of Bashan, the Carmel mountain range of Canaan, and Lebanon to its north boasted the region's best forests; so their "withering" takes on greater significance. The destructive "rushing flood" (v. 8) parallels the breaching of Nineveh's walls by floodwaters in 612, which allowed the joint Medo-Babylonian army to conquer the capital (cf. 2:6).

Divine sovereignty extends over humanity, too (vv. 9ff.). Wickedness will not prevail. Verse 11 probably refers to an Assyrian king — perhaps Sennacherib, who besieged Jerusalem in 701. Verse 14 sentences the idol-worshipping Assyrian king to historical oblivion — a fate worse than physical death. His demise bodes well for Judah by freeing her inhabitants to resume their covenantal activities in peace.

2 The Attack Envisioned

This chapter vividly describes the devastating assault on Nineveh. Within the city, chaos and confusion rule the streets. From outside, war machines equipped with battering rams ("mantelets") knock breaches in the fortification walls. Water from the Tigris River floods the city, perhaps through canals whose opened gates allow the uncontrolled flow to wash away the palace (v. 6). The fleeing citizens leave behind a wealth of plunder. The end has come for the heretofore impregnable Nineveh, characterized as a lions' den in which the Assyrian predators took refuge while they devoured their prey of conquered peoples.

3 Celebrating the Death of Assyrian Tyranny

The most graphic portrayals of Nineveh's fate appear here: piled-up corpses left by the attack, the city's shameful exposure and humiliation for international "harlotry" (garnering political support for a price). Nahum ominously invites Nineveh to compare herself to another city with natural water defenses and foreign military support: the sometime Egyptian capital of Thebes, bounded by her allies, Ethiopia, Lubim (Libya), and Put (probably Somalia).

The Assyrians knew all too well the fate of mighty Thebes, for they themselves sacked it (ca. 661). Verse 10 recalls Assyria's practice of exiling indigenous populations (cf. 2 Kgs. 17:5-6), her gruesome practice of "dashing to pieces" the children of conquered peoples (cf. Hos. 13:16), and her merciless humiliation of their leaders. Such barbarism explains the universal rejoicing at her demise (v. 19) and justifies the reciprocal punishment of the excessively violent city.

Nahum's taunting tone is clear in verses 13-18. His derisive characterization of the Ninevite population as "women" grows out of a patriarchal society that did not train females as warriors and so expected them to flee in the face of danger. And flee the fainthearted Ninevite warriors will — like a swarm of innumerable locusts that are here one minute and gone the next. Verses 18-19 warn the Assyrian king that his officials ("shepherds") are dead, and the breakdown of his kingdom has passed the point of healing. Nahum closes by sanctioning human approval of God's just judgment against the wicked.

Habakkuk

The defining function of the biblical prophets was to serve as mediators between God and human beings. While the Bible most often records divine messages delivered by prophets to people, Habakkuk exemplifies the prophetic role of presenting human concerns to God.

Like Job, Habakkuk struggles with the earthly success of the godless and the ill-fortune of the God-fearing. He holds nothing back in complaining against the seemingly unjust ways of the Lord. In the end, however, he surrenders his call for God to explain himself, acknowledges God's sovereignty, and affirms his unqualified faith in God (3:16-19).

Date

Habakkuk's oracle anticipates the invasion of Judah by the Babylonians, who crushed the Assyrian competition by conquering its capital, Nineveh, in 612 B.C.; defeated an alliance headed by the Egyptian army (deployed to Carchemish) and thus inherited Judah as a dependent state in 605; besieged Jerusalem for Judean resistance in 598; and finally put an end to the rebellious southern kingdom by destroying Jerusalem in 587/86. Most scholars date Habakkuk's oracle to the dozen years preceding the first Babylonian siege of Jerusalem, during which time Jeremiah also prophesied.

1 Habakkuk's Problems with God

The revelations to Habakkuk are a combination of oracles and visions (v. 1). His opening question complains against the apparent blind eye God turns to the triumph of the wicked over the righteous. God responds not with a disclaimer but by declaring his personal responsibility (vv. 5-11). God himself has orchestrated the growing political and military dominance of the Chaldeans (= Babylonians), whom no one can

stop. Though God vows to hold guilty for their wrongs these self-idolizing, Mesopotamian powermongers, Habakkuk finds little comfort in the promise.

In fact, this response does not fit Habakkuk's understanding of God's purity and justice. "How can a righteous God use the worst people to punish those who, by comparison, are not so bad? How can God let the Chaldeans drag everyone into their net and then revel in their own self-sufficiency? Will God never stop them from grabbing everything they want at the expense of others?" challenges the incredulous prophet.

2 The Prophet Awaits a Reproving Response

Expecting but not fearing divine reproof for his bold questioning of God's ways, Habakkuk assumes a sentry-like lookout and awaits an answer (cf. Ezek. 3:17). The reply comes in a vision, which God instructs the prophet to record on "tablets," much as the Babylonians wrote on clay, ivory, and wood. The additional instruction that Habakkuk "wait" for fulfillment of the vision generates hope for the satisfaction of his righteous sensibilities. The rest of the chapter explains the ways in which God will fulfill his vow to hold the proud Chaldeans accountable for their guilt, manifested in an appetite for imperialistic expansion as insatiable as Sheol's (the Underworld's) for the dead. The international crimes committed by the Chaldeans will come back on them in the form of punishment: looting, slaughter, humiliation (vv. 15-16), and the devastation of natural resources. Vain worship of lifeless, handmade images will profit them nothing. The speechlessness of their idols contrasts with the creation-wide silence commanded by God's mere presence in "his holy temple."

"Write it plain on tablets" (Habakkuk 2); an inscription from Tel Dan mentioning the "House of David." *(Israel Antiquities Authority)*

3 Faith Defies Fear

Because of the independent heading and conclusion of chapter 3, some scholars believe that it originally circulated as an independent unit. The psalm, which reflects in style and language the oldest poetry in the Bible, is labelled "Shigionoth" (v. 1), related to an Akkadian word meaning "song of lament." "Selah," another obscure, psalmic notation, punctuates this piece (vv. 3, 9, 13). The psalm concludes with a dedication to "the choirmaster" (presumably of the Jerusalem temple) and a note prescribing accompaniment on stringed instruments. Some take these elements as evidence that Habakkuk came from the tribe of Levi and served as a temple musician, or at least that this prayer functioned as part of the temple liturgy.

The tension between Habakkuk's desire for divine justice in the world and divine mercy toward the judged emerges in the opening line (v. 2). In describing God's arrival for action, verses 3-7 use language reminiscent of his presence at Sinai and his activity during the events leading to and following the exodus. Other Old Testament books associate Mount Sinai with the land of Edom, for which the regional name "Teman" frequently serves as a poetic equivalent, and Mount Paran (Deut. 33:2; Judg. 5:4-5). On the natural phenomena attending God's appearance (vv. 4, 6), compare the theophany on Mount Sinai in Exod. 19:16-20. "Pestilence" and "plague" (v. 5) recall the divine punishments sent on the Egyptians prior to the exodus. Verse 7 mentions two nomadic tribes from south of Canaan, one of whose defeat by the wandering Hebrews the book of Numbers records (Numbers 25, 31).

Verses 8-15 portray God as the chariot-riding, spear-wielding divine warrior who defeats the nations of the world to "save" his people from oppression. Water imagery calls to mind the creation; the flood; the crossing of the Red Sea and the drowning of the Egyptian army during the exodus; and the crossing of the Jordan River on the Hebrews' entry into Canaan as demonstrations of God's control over the unpredictable, uncontrollable "sea" — ancient Near Eastern symbol of chaos.

Just thinking about the invasion of Chaldeans (1:5-11) causes Habakkuk to tremble (v. 16). But the devastation envisioned by the prophet fails to weaken his faith or dampen his praise. Trusting in the demonstrated strength of his God, Habakkuk faces the future with unwavering confidence.

Zephaniah

The period of Judah's history reflected in the book of Zephaniah slightly precedes the time of Habakkuk's oracle. The long career of Jeremiah spanned the ministries of both of these 7th-century-B.C. contemporaries.

Zephaniah prophesied during the last period of political resurgence in Judah. Assyrian decline and Egyptian anxiety over the growing power of Babylon temporarily diverted the attention of the major powers in the ancient Near East and thus opened the way for Judah to expand her territory and flourish economically. But this period of opportunity followed on the heels of the kingdom's appalling moral decline, cultivated by the wicked kings Manasseh and Amon (2 Kings 21). No wonder, then, the intensity and scope of the judgment forewarned by this outspoken servant of God.

1 A Dark Day Coming

Verse 1 traces Zephaniah's genealogy back to "Hezekiah," possibly the pious Judahite king whose 29-year reign began ca. 715 (2 Kings 18–20). This introductory verse places Zephaniah's prophetic ministry during the similarly lengthy reign of Hezekiah's great-grandson Josiah (640-609), best remembered for his religious reforms following the discovery ca. 621 of the long-forgotten covenantal law code (2 Kings 22–23). Since Zephaniah blames a sinful Judah for provoking God's imminent and universal judgment of the world, some scholars argue that Zephaniah prophesied during the first half of Josiah's reign, before the sweeping reforms enacted by the king. But at least at the grassroots level, religious unfaithfulness no doubt persisted despite the official successes of this conscientious monarch; so Zephaniah might just as reasonably have mediated messages of condemnation against Judah during the "reforming" half of Josiah's rule (cf. Jer. 3:6–4:2).

The prophet wastes no time in announcing the divine plan to destroy all the creatures of the earth (v. 2). Zephaniah lists in reverse order of their recorded creation the doomed mammals and marine animals. The reason for God's universal judgment is Judahite idolatry. Centuries before Zephaniah, God designated the Hebrews as the people through whom he would redeem sinful humanity. But instead of "following the Lord," who demands exclusive fidelity, Judah worships the Canaanite fertility god Baal, the "host of heaven" (sun, moon, and stars), and the Ammonite god Milcom. Ritual homage to these pagan gods included forbidden "sacred" prostitution and child sacrifice. Now God is making a sacrifice of the Judahites — not to please or appease himself, but to punish them for their willful and persistent disobedience (vv. 7ff.).

Judgment starts with the Judahite royalty and religious leaders. Punishment infiltrates the walled city of Jerusalem from the usual approach of attacking armies — the north, probable location of the Fish Gate. The "Second Quarter," north of the temple, and the "Mortar," or market area, name the districts of Jerusalem in which the divine searchlight will first expose complacent inhabitants destined for an unexpected reversal of their good fortunes (v. 13; cf. Amos 5:11). All who thought of God as a disengaged deity had another thing coming.

In light of the Mosaic covenant, which outlined blessings for obedience and curses for transgression, the judgmental "day of the Lord" could spell good for the Hebrews by bringing punishment on their enemies. Zephaniah, however, warns that the day will bring certain judgment on Hebrew and heathen alike (v. 18).

2 A Ray of Hope

At the end of chapter 1, all hope seems lost. But now Zephaniah issues an urgent call to eleventh-hour repentance. Even now the pursuit of righteousness and humility might "hide" the humble from the divine wrath to come (v. 3; Zephaniah = "Yahweh hides/protects").

The succeeding oracles against enemy kingdoms that surround Canaan assume the preservation of a Judahite remnant, which will inherit the territories of the divinely judged foreign adversaries. Verses 4-7 warn of the bleak fate of the Philistines, who controlled the south-central Mediterranean coast west of Judah (v. 4; missing is Gath, which after its conquest by the Assyrians in 712 disappears from the historical record). Some of the Philistines came to Canaan from Crete, thus their designation as "Cherethites" (v. 5).

Zephaniah likens the futures of Moab and Ammon to the divine desolation of Sodom and Gomorrah (vv. 8-11). The overarching sin of these distant cousins of the Hebrews across the Jordan River Valley (Gen. 19:30-38) consists in their arrogant taunting of God's elect.

In Zephaniah's time, an Ethiopian ("Cushite") dynasty ruled Egypt, the Hebrews' historic southern adversary (v. 12). From the north, Assyria — which had already conquered the northern kingdom of Israel — threatened the survival of Judah, too. Similarly to Moab and Ammon, however, Assyria has earned divine judgment for her self-sufficient pride. Zephaniah dooms the populous Assyrian capital of Nineveh to habitation by wild animals — a fate that symbolizes the divine dismantling of the entire empire.

3 A Bright Future

The hopeful note for the Hebrews sounded at the beginning of chapter 2 and the subsequent oracles against the encircling enemies of Judah, climaxing with condemnation of the Assyrian capital, would have been well received by Zephaniah's audience. But without warning, the urban object of Zephaniah's wrath has changed from Nineveh to Jerusalem (vv. 1-7). Caught by surprise, the prophet's audience faces a choice: either take back support of his indictment or admit its validity.

Zephaniah characterizes Jerusalem as covenantally rebellious and morally unteachable. He portrays her political and judicial leaders as ravenous predators, her prophets as reckless traitors, and her priests as abusers of the Mosaic law. God lives in the midst of this moral decay but remains uncompromisingly righteous. The people, though shamefully exposed by the light of his purity, fail to repent — even after the Lord makes instructive examples of other sinful nations. To purge the world of sin, God will carry out global judgment, but he will leave a remnant who, purified of pride and deceit, will never again profane Jerusalem, the mountain city made holy by the Lord's presence in the temple (v. 11).

If Zephaniah begins on a note of utter despair, the book ends with great hopefulness. The prophet calls Zion/Jerusalem to joyful celebration as he portrays the redemptive purge as accomplished fact. The restoration will consist in God's gathering of the exiles and returning them home, where they will command global admiration. All who humbly turn toward God, Hebrews and Gentiles (v. 10), the weak and the "outcast," will find a welcome reversal of fortunes (vv. 19-20).

Haggai

The last three Minor Prophets — Haggai, Zechariah, and Malachi — address the community of Hebrews reestablished in Jerusalem following the Babylonian exile. The book of Ezra credits Haggai and Zechariah for motivating the Hebrews to complete reconstruction of the temple (Ezra 5:1; 6:14), and Haggai's very name (= "festal," from the Hebrew word for the annual pilgrimages to Jerusalem) may reflect this concern. Ezra 4:24–6:15 covers the periods of their recorded prophetic activities.

1 Rebuild the Temple!

Verse 1 dates Haggai's first prophecy to 520 B.C., year 2 of the Persian monarch Darius I (522–486) — great-grandson of Cyrus, whose decree 18 years earlier freed the Hebrew exiles to return to Jerusalem and rebuild the temple (Ezra 1:1-4). Haggai addresses the senior leaders of the returned Hebrew remnant: Zerubbabel, a descendant of David and civil governor of the now truncated Persian province of Judah, and the high priest Joshua ("Jeshua" in Ezra).

Through Haggai, God complains that the Hebrew returnees have put off rebuilding his temple (cf. Ezra 4). God's complaint that his house still lies desolate while his people enjoy shelter in well-appointed homes (v. 4) contrasts with his initial response to the temple-building intentions of King David — but for good reason. In 2 Samuel 7, this monarch of an ascendant Hebrew kingdom regrets living in a sturdy cedar structure while God stays in a tent (the tabernacle, which housed God's throne — the ark of the covenant). In contrast to the Hebrew community of David's day, however, the meager group of returnees to Judah lacked political distinctiveness and national identity. As Persian subjects, most of whom were probably born and raised in Persia, they needed a physical symbol that represented the uniqueness of their community, differentiated it from other groups, and thereby helped save it from assimilation into the dominant culture(s) of the day. Since the Hebrews derived their communal identity primarily from their worship of Yahweh, his temple embodied that symbol. The rebuilt temple would make possible God's return to Jerusalem, signify his presence among the returned Hebrew remnant, and unite them in centralized worship. In addition, the sanctuary would witness to God's enduring power and vindicate his name among detractors, who viewed the exile of the Hebrews as evidence of God's impotence (cf. Ezek. 36:16-38).

Behind Haggai's urgent call to rebuild the temple lies a concern with the religious and cultural survival of his people. But how can he get them to resume work on the abandoned reconstruction? What the returnees want most at the moment are the blessings of the covenant made at Sinai — especially agricultural prosperity and economic well-being (cf. Deut. 28:1-14). In order to experience these blessings, says Haggai, they had better make among them a home for the One who grants the blessings. Work on the temple resumes three weeks after Haggai's initial urging.

2 On the Road to Restoration

After a month of labor, the second temple doesn't come close to matching the splendor of Solomon's magnificent sanctuary, destroyed by the Babylonians some 70 years earlier. But God encourages the people by confirming his presence in their midst and promises eventually to make the new temple more glorious than the first. To fulfill this pledge, God will exert his sovereignty over all creation and overthrow the present international political and economic order. Judah will be elevated and the temple enriched (vv. 6-9).

The interactive oracle in verses 10-19 calls for priestly answers based on the ritual purity laws stipulated in Leviticus. Haggai's point is that physical contact with the temple, by means of rebuilding it, does not make the people holy. Touch communicates ritual defilement, but not ritual purity. Nevertheless, the returnees' work has demonstrated an attitude of heart that implies their intention to live by the covenantal laws; so God promises to reverse the deprivation they have so far suffered. The divine vow comes three months after the temple construction began.

The final oracle, addressed to Governor Zerubbabel, predicts God's overthrowing of foreign nations and implies that God will ensure the political security of the community of Hebrew returnees. The impression of a "signet ring," or "seal," identified the owner of the item bearing the mark or verified the authority of the docu-

Signet ring, a symbol of political authority, used to seal and authenticate official documents. *(Richard Cleave, Pictorial Archive)*

ment to which the seal adhered. God's making Zerubbabel into a "signet ring" represents the designation of this Davidic descendant as the divinely appointed political authority, though Haggai stops short of calling Zerubbabel a king (cf. Jer. 22:24-30).

Zechariah

Zechariah ("Yahweh remembers") prophesied from 520-518 B.C., quite likely after having returned to Jerusalem with the group of Babylonian exiles that accompanied Zerubbabel in 538. Along with his contemporary, Haggai, Zechariah urged the rebuilding of the temple.

Zechariah contains the greatest percentage of visionary material of any prophetic book of the Bible. In the first major section (chs. 1–8), the writer reports eight visions, interspersed with related oracles. The second section (chs. 9–14) contains two extended oracles representing an early stage of apocalyptic thought.

Composition

Largely because of literary differences between the first and second parts of Zechariah, and their concentration on concerns that seem to reflect different periods in the history of the Hebrews restored to Canaan, most scholars believe that the last six chapters of the book came from an author later than Zechariah — most probably an individual living in the 5th or 4th century. Some see a connection between Zechariah 9–14 and the book of Malachi, whose opening words parallel the superscriptions of Zechariah 9:1 and 12:1. Nevertheless, the ancient manuscripts we have group together all 14 chapters that in modern Bibles make up the book of Zechariah.

1:1-6 Learn from the Past

Zechariah's recorded prophetic ministry began two months after Haggai delivered his first oracle (v. 1), during the reign of the Persian king Darius I. The account traces Zechariah's ancestry back two generations to Iddo, quite possibly the priest named in Neh. 12:4 among the exiles who accompanied Zerubbabel on his return to Judah from Babylon.

In exhorting the Hebrews to learn from the past, verses 1-6 give a brief historical introduction to the circumstances in which the community of returnees in Jerusalem now find themselves. Here Zechariah's primary purpose consists in urging his people not to repeat the mistakes of their ancestors, who failed to heed the warnings of earlier prophets concerning the need for repentance and thus had to experience the covenantal curses (cf. Deut. 28:15-68).

1:7–8:23 Eight Visions and Related Oracles

1:7-17 Vision 1: God's Horsemen Darius I developed throughout the Persian Empire a system of roads then unrivalled in the ancient Near East. Like the mounted "police" who patrolled these roads, four riders appointed by God to patrol the earth report peace throughout. (If the colors of the horses originally conveyed special meanings, they elude us today [v. 8].) But the angel accompanying Zechariah bewails this peace, for it signifies divine inaction toward restoring Judah and Jerusalem. The angelic reminder stirs God to compassion for Jerusalem/

Known as the Tomb of Zechariah, this freestanding monument was carved out of the bedrock on the lower slope of the Mount of Olives in the second century B.C., well after the Old Testament period.
(www.HolyLandPhotos.org)

Zion and fuels his anger at the foreign nations, who have taken too far their mandate to punish God's people. The Lord vows to return to Jerusalem, cause his temple-home to be rebuilt, and have Jerusalem surveyed in preparation for her rebuilding.

1:18-21 Vision 2: Four Horns Four animal horns (symbolizing strength, aggression, and/or pride; cf. Ps. 75:4-5; Dan. 8:3-9) represent powerful foreign nations that have overdone their duty as instruments of God's judgment against Judah/Jerusalem. "Four" seems not to refer to particular nations but to convey the idea of completeness and thereby to encompass all foreign oppressors of the Hebrew people. Similarly, an adequate number of "blacksmiths" ("four") will hammer out God's righteous anger against the excessively hostile nations.

2:1-5 Vision 3: Interrupting the Survey of Jerusalem An angelic messenger interrupts a surveyor's measuring of Jerusalem to stress that the city will not need new defense walls. Seventy years earlier, the Babylonian army broke down the walls as part of the punitive destruction of the Judahite capital (2 Kgs. 25:10). But God himself will serve as Protector of the restored city, whose boundless population stone walls would only cramp. Thus the survey for which God calls in 1:16 must here measure not the city's limits but its limitlessness. The point here is the realization of Jerusalem's promised restoration, not a prohibition of the literal rebuilding of the walls.

2:6-13 Summoning the Exiles Who will fill the restored Jerusalem envisioned in verses 1-5? — the exiles, here summoned back from Babylon, the "land of the north." Though Babylon lay due east of Canaan, the intervening Arabian Desert prohibited a direct, westward approach to the promised land. Instead, pilgrims, merchants, and armies all skirted the Fertile Crescent and entered Canaan from the north, through Syria and Lebanon; hence the Old Testament's designation of Babylon and other Mesopotamian invaders as northern lands or enemies.

But Zechariah does not simply invite the exiles home; rather, he urges them to escape while they can, for God will soon judge the oppressive nations in which many of the exiles have chosen to remain. The tables will soon turn: the exiles ("slaves") will "plunder" the nations that have been plundering them (v. 9; cf. Exod. 12:35-36). Zechariah calls on Jerusalem (= "daughter Zion") to rejoice that the Lord is coming home to stay (v. 10). Verse 11 anticipates the conversion of all nations to the worship of Yahweh.

3 Vision 4: Ritual Cleansing and a Clean Slate The high priest Joshua stands before the "Adversary/Accuser" (the meaning of "Satan") in the divine courtroom (cf. Job 1–2). Joshua's filthy clothes represent his guiltiness of sin. But instead of condemning Joshua, God commutes his sentence ("a brand plucked from the fire," v. 2). After summarily rebuking the Adversary, God orders clean clothes for the high priest to signify his cleansing from sin and his suitability for conducting priestly activities in the soon-to-be-rebuilt temple. God's priestly charge to Joshua promises rewards for righteous conduct: authority in the temple and free access to the heavenly courtiers (v. 7). "My servant the Branch" (v. 8) refers to Zerubbabel, the civil governor descended from David; but the designation carries messianic overtones that anticipate the coming of Jesus Christ, who ushers in the kingdom of peace and prosperity signified by neighborly repose beneath "vines" and "fig trees" (v. 10; cf. Isa. 11:1-5). In the enigmatic verse 9, the "seven facets" on the stone set before Joshua may represent an all-seeing, all-knowing jewel, with the number seven signifying completeness. The inscription engraved on the stone grants to the restored kingdom a clean slate for a new start with God.

4 Vision 5: A Lampstand and Two Olive Trees An oracle to Zerubbabel interrupts Zechariah's fifth vision. In verses 1-5, the prophet sees a golden lampstand with a topmost central bowl, which presumably channels fuel oil to seven spouted lamps (cf. Exod. 25:31-40) representing the globally vigilant eyes of the Lord (vv. 10b-14; their number, seven, indicates that God sees all; cf. 3:9). Two oil-producing olive trees flank the lampstand and represent the two "anointed ones" — Joshua the high priest and Zerubbabel the governor, respectively appointed by God as leaders in the religious and political spheres.

Verses 6-10a interject an oracle emphasizing to Zerubbabel that credit for his forthcoming accomplishments (and those of Joshua) belongs to God. The "top stone" (v. 7) refers to an essential architectural feature of the second temple, such as a keystone centrally placed at the top of an arch to prevent its collapse. Zerubbabel began and supervised this construction project, and here he receives divine confirmation that he will finish the job (cf. Ezra 5:2; 6:15). The "day of small things" likely refers to the local opposition that caused the initially enthusiastic returnees to abandon their rebuilding efforts (Ezra 4). Zerubbabel's resumption of the work, signified by his possession of a "plumb line," or "plummet stone," for sighting the straightness of walls, brings gladness to the all-seeing eyes of God.

5:1-4 Vision 6: A Gigantic, Flying Scroll Zechariah envisions a 30-foot-long, 15-foot-wide flying scroll (one cubit = 18 inches). This document represents the curses contained in the Hebrews' covenant with God (Deuteronomy 28). One side of the scroll carries punishment for stealing (Exod. 20:15); the other side brings judgment for taking God lightly (Exod. 20:7). The first transgression represents all the covenantal laws that deal with sins against fellow human beings (commandments 5 through 10), and the second stands for all the laws that address sins against God (commandments 1 through 4). The airborne scroll seen by Zechariah purges the community of returnees by afflicting evildoers with the consuming curses of the covenant.

5:5-11 Vision 7: Wickedness Whisked Off Woman Wickedness embodies the sin of the covenantal people (contrast Woman Wisdom in Proverbs). Packed for shipping in a lead-lidded bushel basket, Wickedness is whisked off to the land of the exile (Shinar = Babylonia) by two stork-winged women riding the wind. This permanent exiling of Wickedness, signified by her relocation to a Mesopotamian temple built just for her, completes the purge of the restored Hebrew community in Canaan.

6:1-8 Vision 8: Charioteers Eager for Action Zechariah's last vision answers the question raised in the first one (1:7-17): how long will God go without bringing restoration to Jerusalem and Judah? The approach of four chariots speeding from God's presence through a bronze mountain pass portends a military strike (vv. 1, 5; contrast 1:8-11). The four chariots patrol the entire earth and presumably rout out all elements of opposition to God's restorative purposes for his people. In particular, Zechariah specifies the two directions from which enemies entered Canaan — north, from which direction came most of the invaders, and south, from where the Egyptians advanced. God will be particularly satisfied with the punitive mission to the "north" (= Babylonia; cf. 2:6-13).

As in chapter 1, the significance of the horses' colors eludes us. The bronze of the mountains probably represents strength (cf. the colossus in Dan. 2:31-35).

6:9-15 Crowned Priest and Consecrated Politician In Ezra 7:11-28, the Persian king Artaxerxes grants the Hebrews permission to return to Jerusalem with as many valuables as they can glean in Babylon. Verse 10 names several of these wealth-laden returnees. Zechariah must use some of their silver and gold to make a crown for the head of the high priest, Joshua. Then Zechariah must address the priest with a prophecy concerning "Branch" — the governor, Zerubbabel — which confirms his building of the second temple and his shared authority with Joshua over the restored Hebrew community (cf. 3:8). That the high priest wears the crown while the governor attains priestly status symbolizes the leaders' functional equality, which produces peace between the temple and state by nullifying their competition (vv. 11, 13). Though Zechariah portrays Zerubbabel enthroned as a monarch (v. 13), the prophet stops short of calling him a "king" in accordance with Jeremiah's prophetic termination of the dynasty of Jehoiachin, Judah's last king and possibly an ancestor of Zerubbabel (Jer. 22:30; cf. Hag. 2:23; also Heb. 3:1; Matt. 21:1-9). The rebuilding of the temple by returned exiles will confirm the divine origin of Zechariah's prophecy, but its fulfillment requires the Hebrews' complete obedience to God (v. 15).

7:1–8:23 Long Answer to a Short Question The oracles in chapters 7 and 8 date to 518 — two years after the opening oracle of the book, and two years prior to the completion of the second temple (1:1; Ezra 6:15).

Zechariah speaks these oracles in response to an inquiry of representatives sent to Jerusalem from Bethel, a major religious center established by the northern kingdom's breakaway monarch, Jeroboam I, to rival Jerusalem and the temple (1 Kgs. 12:25-33). The visitors ask whether they should continue to observe the mourning fast of the "fifth month" (7:3), which apparently commemorated the Babylonian destruction of the temple in 587/86. Now that many of the exiles have returned and are rebuilding the temple, the Bethelites' question seems reasonable.

Zechariah acknowledges the visitors' dutiful observance not only of the fifth month's fast but that of the seventh month also, in commemoration of the murder of the preexilic, Babylonian-appointed governor Gedaliah (2 Kgs. 25:25). But the prophet charges the Bethelites with selfish, insincere motives for keeping the fasts. He notes that the preexilic prophets chastised their well-off audiences for the same kind of false piety (e.g., Amos 8) and then admonishes the inquirers to practical righteousness, as required by the Mosaic law (e.g., Deuteronomy 22; cf. Matt. 7:12). The negative example and fate of the preexilic Hebrews show the consequences of disobedience to God (7:11-14).

Yet condemnation does not come for the Bethelites; rather, God in his mercy announces his determination to return to Zion/Jerusalem, establish it as the center of truth and righteousness, and make it a city in which the elderly can find tranquility and children can express youthful exuberance (8:1-8). This promise should inspire moral courage for the returnees engaged in rebuilding the temple (8:9). Though before the period of judgment God made life hard for the defiant Hebrews, he now plans to bestow on the restored remnant the blessings of the covenant, peace, and prosperity (8:10-12). Verse 13 anticipates the fulfillment of God's promise to make his people a blessing to the nations. A

glorious future lies before the Hebrew remnant — but they must treat each other well. God's righteous sensibilities demand honesty and judicial fairness in all their dealings (vv. 16-17).

At the end of chapter 8, Zechariah finally addresses the question put to him in 7:3: Should the Bethelites continue to observe the mourning fast? His answer draws on the preceding picture of the Hebrews' imminent reversal of fortunes: Soon joy will so obliterate sorrow that fasting will turn into feasting and mourning into celebration. (The fasts in the 4th and 10th months commemorated the Babylonians' breaching of the wall of Jerusalem [Jer. 39:2] and the beginning of the city's siege by Nebuchadnezzar [2 Kgs. 25:1-2].) The Hebrews' great good fortune will attract to the worship of the Lord people from many nations who want to experience God's favor as his people do. The foreigners' eager attachment to the Jews will give evidence that indeed the chosen people have become a blessing to the nations (8:22-23; cf. v. 13).

9–14 Broadening the Scope

The last six chapters of Zechariah show similar concerns as chapters 1–8, but the scope of the prophecies broadens by giving greater attention to the non-Hebrew nations and to the end toward which history is moving. The same introductory superscription precedes the two extended oracles that make up this section (chs. 9–11; 12–14; cf. Mal. 1:1).

9 Foes Vanquished and Transformed The purge prophesied in chapter 9 envisions not just the perishing of powers traditionally antagonistic toward the Hebrews but also the transformation of their enemies into friends and the incorporation of non-Hebrews into the community of the chosen people. The oracle predicts this future for certain cities in and around Canaan: Hadrach, in far northern Canaan; Hamath and Damascus, in Syria; Tyre and Sidon, prominent seaports on the coast of Phoenicia; and Gaza, Ekron, Ashkelon, and Ashdod, the four remaining Philistine cities on the south-central coastal plain of Canaan. When God causes the Philistines to start observing the Hebrew food laws (v. 7a), these foreigners will become incorporated into the Judahite community of the chosen people, as had the Jebusite inhabitants of Jerusalem conquered by David (v. 7b). The ruler of this eclectic kingdom will not need a war horse as a mount, but only a young donkey, for worldwide peace will take hold. (Matt. 21:5; John 12:15 quote v. 9 in reference to Jesus.) The "seas" in v. 10 refer to the Mediterranean Sea on the west and the Dead Sea on the east; the "River" denotes the Euphrates, in Mesopotamia.

The rest of the oracle addresses the Hebrews. The "blood" of the covenant recalls the sacrificial rites performed in ratification of the agreement made at Sinai (v. 11). The picture of the Hebrews as freed from imprisonment in a "waterless pit" (a dry cistern or well) communicates their divine rescue from certain death (cf. Gen. 37:18-36; Jer. 38:1-13). The writer portrays the southern kingdom of Judah as God's bow and the northern kingdom of Israel ("Ephraim," its largest and most prominent tribe) as the arrows he will use in defending the Hebrews against Greece, the reigning regional power following Alexander the Great's defeat of the Persians in 333. (Some scholars take this reference to Greece to indicate that an author who lived long after Zechariah's time [late 6th century] wrote chapters 9–14.) The military victory envisioned in vv. 15-17 appears so complete that God's people will revel in celebration. The "bowl" of v. 15 refers to a large, usually stone tub that held water for ritual bathing before performing religious rites.

10 The Exiles Come Home   The prophet implores the people to turn to God for the rain that ultimately produces food and drink (10:1; cf. 9:17). Instead, the people wander about like stupid sheep because of the scarcity of decent "shepherds" (leaders) to guide them, theologically or politically. They take the word of household idols ("teraphim," which cannot speak) and garner false hopes from fortune-tellers, who purposely lie.

God determines to "save" his people by strengthening them for victorious battle over their foreign oppressors and by bringing them back from exile. God will summon the remnant back from far-flung countries, such as Egypt, to

which some of the Judahites fled from the Babylonian army in the early 6th century, and Assyria, to which the Israelites ("Joseph"/"Ephraim") were deported after the fall of the northern kingdom in 722/21. The restored throng will sprawl beyond their previous borders into fertile Gilead in Transjordan and lush Lebanon (vv. 10-11). Verse 11 describes the homeward journey of the exiles in images reminiscent of the crossing of the Red Sea during the exodus (Exod. 14:21-22).

11 The Short-Term Shepherd and His Foolhardy Flock   The homeward march of the exiles and their settlement in and around the promised land proper spell defeat for the antagonistic neighbors bordering Canaan. Verses 1-3 portray their ruination as the destruction of their symbols of strength: the stately cedars of Lebanon, the mighty oaks of Bashan (northern Transjordan), and the densely vegetated banks of the Jordan River.

The shepherd imagery resumes in verse 4 with God's instruction that the prophet "pasture" the oppressed, foredoomed flock of Hebrews. His two staffs (v. 7) symbolize the favor of God and the political unity of the chosen people. But the shepherd soon abandons his task, and the sheep prefer to be exploited. (The identification of the "three shepherds" annihilated in "one month" remains uncertain; v. 8.) The prophet gives notice by breaking his staff "Favor" — an act that symbolizes God's revoking of the covenantal blessings — and by requesting payment for his prophetic act. The "flock" insult him with the "lordly price" of 30 shekels of silver, the price of a slave (Exod. 21:32; cf. Matt. 26:15; 27:3-5) and apparently not worth keeping. The prophet's breaking of his other staff, "Unity," signifies dissension between the northern Hebrews and their southern kin. In verses 15-17, God gives the foolhardy flock what they want: a coldhearted shepherd who devours his own sheep.

12 Nationwide Remorse   The first nine verses of this section promise the divine defense of Judah and Jerusalem against attacking nations. Jerusalem is a "cup of reeling" (v. 2) that sends enemy heads spinning. Verse 3 pictures the Judahite capital as a heavy stone, injurious to anyone who tries to lift it. A flaming Judah burns up the wood and sheaves that come too close (v. 6)

The Davidic monarchy figures prominently from 12:7 to 13:1. This "house of David" bears the responsibility for causing nationwide mourning. (In the Hebrew text, the object of "pierced" can read either "the one," perhaps the Messiah or a prophet, or "me," God himself; cf. John 19:34-37.) The intensity of the remorse comes across in the bitter weeping over the death of an "only son" and a "firstborn," who in patriarchal society embodied the all-important perpetuator of the family line and the primary heir to the family estate. An allusion to a communal, pagan ritual of mourning for the pagan fertility-god Hadad-rimmon (believed to die and rise with the seasons, v. 11) may convey the great scope of the people's grief. The Hebrews' private mourning conveys the depth and sincerity of their remorse (vv. 12-14). The grieving of the royal line of David and the priestly line of Levi, and the families of their sons Nathan and Shimei, conveys that the sorrow permeates the political and religious spheres and extends beyond generational lines.

13 Purifying a Remnant God responds to the Hebrews' genuine remorse by opening a "fountain" that will wash away their sin (v. 1). The image relates to the practice of ritual bathing, which brings about ceremonial purification to prepare a person for participation in religious rites, such as the offering of sacrifices. In the New Testament, John the Baptist's baptism by immersion symbolizes not only the washing away of one's sins but also that person's dying to sin and rising to new life in Christ.

Cleansing in Judah comes by way of God's eradication of idolatry and false prophecy. The false prophets will be so ashamed that they will no longer attempt to present themselves as legitimate by wearing "a hairy mantle in order to deceive" (v. 4; cf. Elijah, 2 Kgs. 1:8), and they will lie about the origin of their body scars, inflicted from gashing themselves in frenzied efforts to communicate with the gods (v. 6; cf. 1 Kgs. 18:28).

Verses 7-9 resume the shepherd-sheep imagery of chapters 10 and 11. Here the striking of God's shepherd-associate (cf. 12:10) initiates the process of purifying the flock, which involves scattering the sheep and then singling out one-third of them for refinement (cf. Mark 14:27). Once purified, this remnant becomes fit for a renewed relationship with God (cf. Jer. 31:31-34).

14 The Battle That Ends All Battles The closing chapter of Zechariah describes a climactic battle against Jerusalem. God initiates the assault by gathering the city's foes against her, but then he defends Jerusalem against the attackers. A mountain-splitting earthquake forms an escape route for the city's inhabitants. (The Mount of Olives runs for 2½ miles in a north-south direction on the east side of Jerusalem.) The accompanying extinguishing of the heavenly luminaries is another natural phenomenon typical of biblical end-times imagery (cf. Joel 2:30-32; Rev. 6:12-14). On the "living waters" that constantly "flow out of Jerusalem," see Ezek. 47:1-12 (cf. Rev. 22:1).

Verses 9ff. presume the triumph of God over the nations he stirred up against Jerusalem. The victory establishes him as "king over all the earth" and ensures the security of the now global capital, from which God lifts the curses for disobedience to the covenant. The flattening of the rugged hill country surrounding Jerusalem echoes Isaiah's call for the preparation of a smooth highway to facilitate God's approach to the city (Isa. 40:3-4), and the abiding mountain elevation of the city itself remembers the prophet's last-days description of Jerusalem as "highest of the mountains" (Isa. 2:2).

Verses 12-15 elaborate the plague sent to punish the nations that have mounted the failed assault on Jerusalem. The poetic justice of verse 1 triumphs in verse 14, which describes the Judahites' plundering of their attackers — nations that no doubt previously plundered the Hebrews. Survivors of the plague must make an annual pilgrimage to Jerusalem to worship God and to celebrate the Feast of Tabernacles (Booths), which commemorates the Hebrews' wandering in the wilderness after their exit from Egypt (vv. 16ff.; Lev. 23:33-36). Failure to honor God in this way will result in devastating drought for the homeland of any offenders. The prophetic warning singles out Egypt, whose reluctant release of the enslaved Hebrews launched them on their 40-year trek through the barren desert.

The last two verses of Zechariah picture an ultimate Jerusalem wholly dedicated to God. Exodus 28:36-38 gives instructions for affixing the inscription "Holy to the Lord" on the head-piece of the high priest; in the New Jerusalem, even horses wear this mark of consecration for service to God. Ordinary cooking pots become as sacred as bowls that hold offerings presented at the altar. In verse 21, a Hebrew word that can be translated either "Canaanites" or "traders" strengthens the message: the absence of both types of people from the ideal temple signifies the absolute purity of the religion practiced there (cf. Matt. 21:12-13; Acts 21:27-29).

Malachi

Malachi, the last book of the Old Testament, reflects the situation of the Hebrew community in Judah some 80 years after the ministries of the other postexilic "minor" prophets, Haggai and Zechariah. "Malachi" may represent not a personal name but a title or pen name meaning "My messenger." The book reinforces the requirements of covenantal fidelity on the part of 5th-century-B.C. Hebrew priests and laypeople, who have grown morally and ritually lax while awaiting the glorious future promised by earlier prophets.

Message

Malachi opens with a word of encouragement that confirms God's continued love for his people and closes by restating that the day of judgment, which brings punishment on the nations and "salvation" (deliverance) for the disillusioned Hebrews, will indeed come. But the core of the book takes on the flavor of rebuke. Presented as six "disputes" in question-and-answer style, Malachi reveals God exposing the false assumptions and thoughtless behavior of his faltering flock.

Malachi reminds us that God requires unconditional fidelity to him. The obligation to live up to God's standards does not hinge on whether God "answers" our prayers, acts on our timetable, or administers justice in line with our expectations. God required of the 5th-century Hebrews fidelity with no contingencies, a faithful walk of faith, and he requires it of us today.

1:1-5 Dispute 1:
I Have Loved You

The returned exiles' complaint that God does not love them stems from their unfulfilled expectation of a glorious life back in Canaan. Indeed, the earlier postexilic prophets nur-

tured this expectation. But God insists that he *has* demonstrated his love for the chosen (= "loved") line of Jacob. If they want proof, they should compare their fortunes to those of their cousins in Edom, the "hated" (= nonelect) descendants of Esau, whom the Babylonians also overran but whose kingdom God will not allow to be rebuilt.

1:6–2:9 Dispute 2:
You Priests Have Despised Me

If God starts on the defensive side of the dispute (1:1-5), he quickly moves to the offensive by charging the Hebrew priests with dereliction of duty. He observes that sons and servants honor their human fathers and masters; therefore, God, as father and master of his chosen people, rightly expects honorable treatment by their priestly leaders. But the priests show only disdain for the Lord. They neglect their duty to control the quality of sacrifices presented to him. They would not dare to offer such imperfect gifts to the Persian governor — yet they do so to the God whom even foreign nations fear! God would prefer that the temple close for business rather than to have mockery of the sacrificial system continue.

If the priests have not taken God seriously till now, they had better start. If they don't quit defiling his altar, the Lord will render them ritually unclean for priestly service by smearing their faces with dung (2:3). God had long ago set apart the tribe of Levi for full-time service to him. Their job included teaching God's laws to the laity by word and example (2:5-7). But far from equipping people to uphold God's laws, the priests of Malachi's audience have promoted the waywardness of others through their own unfaithfulness and false teaching. Their corruption of the covenant, designed to produce peace between a holy God and his beloved but sinful people, has invited on them a punishment that parallels their demonstrated disdain for God: disdain for them by the people they lead.

2:10-16 Dispute 3:
You People Treat Each Other Treacherously

The covenantal failure of the priests has led to the breakdown of the Hebrew community as a whole. Men's divorcing their wives in order to intermarry with worshippers of pagan gods compromises the community's covenantal fidelity, breaks apart the family of God, and threatens the religious distinctiveness of the next generation of Hebrews. Their forsaking of the marriage covenant and dismissal of the matrimonial rules — and the disregard for their Father-God that such behavior betrays — cause God to reject their sacrifices, as with the irreverent priests (1:6–2:9). Deuteronomy 24:1-4 addresses divorce from the perspective of Mosaic law, and Ezra 9–10 and Nehemiah 13 deal with the problem of interfaith marriage during the same period addressed by Malachi.

2:17–3:5 Dispute 4:
You Question My Justice

For the returnees to Judah, disappointment with the less-than-ideal circumstances of life in postexilic Canaan has developed into a cynical view regarding the justice of God. The covenant promised tangible blessings — abundant crops, economic prosperity, political security — and the prophets foretold a Day of the Lord on which the divine judgment of the enemies of the Hebrews would secure for them these rewards. But for years now, the deprived community of the chosen people has seen everyone else enjoy the prosperity they expected for themselves. They blame it all on God, never stopping to ponder that their own unfaithfulness to the covenant precludes their enjoyment of its blessings.

The announcement that God is sending his messenger to prepare the way for the promised judgment day should teach them to be careful what they ask for, because God's moral smelting will extend to the Hebrews as well as to the heathen. Hebrews who transgress the Mosaic law

"The sun of righteousness shall rise" (Malachi 4). Winged sun disk, Chorazin synagogue.
(www.HolyLandPhotos.org)

(cf. 3:5) will one day find out that their membership in the community of the chosen does not make them immune from the dark side of God's justice.

3:6-12 Dispute 5:
You Rob Me of My Tithe

Haggai had blamed the delay of God's blessings on the Hebrews' failure to finish rebuilding the temple (Haggai 1). That project completed, Malachi blames the continued deprivation on their failure to tithe their crops and animals in support of the temple and the Levites — an obligation not just for times of plenty but also times of scarcity. This snubbing of God's laws is nothing new (v. 7), nor is the promised reward that awaits the chosen people who live according to God's laws (vv. 10-12). By robbing God of the token return on what he has given them in the first place, they forfeit the even greater blessings for obedience and thus rob themselves more than God.

3:13–4:3 Dispute 6:
You've Given Up on Me

The Hebrews' disappointment had led to cynical complaining (cf. 2:17), which now turns to blasphemous arrogance. Seeing no profit from their service to the Lord, they declare it useless. They give up on God and turn an envious eye toward evildoers who, in their shortsighted view, appear to get away with their wickedness.

But not all the returnees disparage God, and he enters the names of the faithful in a "book of remembrance" to ensure their sparing come judgment day (3:16-18). That event will restore the recognizable distinction between the wicked, hopelessly doomed to destruction like chaff set ablaze, and the righteous, restored to youth by the healing warmth of the sun and employed by God in the judgment of evildoers. The image of the sun god as a winged disc in Persian and Egyptian art may lie behind Malachi's reference to the "sun of righteousness" rising with "healing in its wings" (4:2).

4:4-6 Elijah's Return Augurs Judgment Day

This postscript to Malachi ends the Old Testament with an admonition to remember the covenantal starting point of Hebrew history, the laws God established for his people through Moses at Mount Sinai (= Horeb). The promise that prior to the day of judgment God will ensure the covenantal purity of his people through a returned Elijah provides a natural transition to the New Testament. Clad in clothing similar to his prophetic predecessor, John the Baptist "cleansed" his followers with the baptism of repentance; therefore, Jesus identified him as the second Elijah anticipated by Malachi (Matt. 11:14; 17:10-13).

Apocrypha/Deuterocanonical Books

The term *Apocrypha* means "hidden" and refers to a collection of Jewish books that variously date from the 3rd century B.C. to the 2nd century A.D. The alternative label *deuterocanonical,* meaning "secondarily canonical," indicates that these works are of secondary status compared with the other canonical books of the Bible.

Since the time of Luther, Protestants have adopted the contents but not the order of the Hebrew Bible of Judaism for their Old Testament. As a result, they have either completely excluded the Apocrypha from their Bibles or grouped the books together after the Old Testament. Reflecting the practice of some early manuscripts, the Roman Catholic Church and some other Christian denominations include the apocryphal works as an integral part of the Old Testament.

The size of the Apocrypha varies among denominations, largely for historical reasons. Roman Catholic, Slavonic, and Greek Bibles all include the books of Tobit, Judith, Wisdom of Solomon, Sirach, Baruch, the Letter of Jeremiah (often as ch. 6 of Baruch), 1 and 2 Maccabees, as well as the additions to Esther and Daniel. In addition, the Greek and Slavonic Bibles include 1 Esdras, the Prayer of Manasseh, Psalm 151, and 3 Maccabees, and the Slavonic Bible also includes 2 Esdras (as does the Latin Vulgate appendix). Some important early manuscripts of the Greek Bible also include 4 Maccabees.

Diversity is the hallmark of the collection: it comes from various places and times, is made up of several different literary genres, and, as noted, is presented by different Christian groups in various forms. To appreciate their significance more fully, the books of the Apocrypha need to be associated with other Jewish writings from the period between the Bible and the Mishnah (ca. 200 B.C. to A.D. 200): (1) the Dead Sea Scrolls, sectarian and other nonbiblical Jewish compositions found in the Judaean wilderness, which show that Jewish literature in this period was very extensive. Copies of Tobit and Sirach have been found among the Scrolls, as also have Psalm 151 and possibly the Letter of Jeremiah; (2) Jewish compositions called the Pseudepigrapha ("falsely attributed writings," e.g., the Testament of Moses), some of which (e.g., some of the writings of Enoch) have also been found among the Dead Sea Scrolls. In a strict sense, the Wisdom of Solomon, Baruch, the Letter of Jeremiah, the Prayer of Manasseh, and 1-2 Esdras are all pseudepigrapha, since it is widely agreed that they were not written by those whose names they bear; (3) the writings of Philo and Josephus. Philo's philosophical and exegetical works are not unlike the Wisdom of Solomon in certain respects; Josephus relies heavily on 1 Esdras and 1 Maccabees for a large part of his work. All these Jewish writings provide valuable information about the variety of Judaism and about the Palestinian setting both of emerging rabbinic Judaism and also of Jesus and the early Christian communities.

Narratives

The book of **Tobit** takes its name from a pious Jew who was supposedly taken into exile when the kingdom of Israel fell in 722 B.C. Tobit's many acts of charity include the burial of fellow Jews. Struck with blindness and poverty, Tobit sends his son Tobias to recover the family fortune left in Media. The story turns into a romantic quest. Tobias is accompanied by the angel Raphael ("God heals"), whose true identity is revealed only at the end, and by his dog. (Hence, even today many dogs are called Toby.) On the journey he stays with relatives in Ecbatana (Persia) and marries Sarah, the daughter of the house, from whom he exorcises the demon Asmodeus on their wedding night. The money is recovered, and on his arrival home Tobias heals his father's sight. This popular tale about life in exile shows how God answers the prayers of the righteous, even if they are temporarily afflicted with troubles.

The book of **Judith** is in two parts. Chapters 1–7 describe all the mighty exploits of Nebuchadnezzar's army; on its way to Jerusalem the army is encamped outside the unknown small town of Bethulia in Samaria. Chapters

Judith with the Head of Holofernes; **engraving by Jacob Mathan, after Hendrik Goltzius.** *(Cooper-Hewitt, National Design Museum, Smithsonian Institution / Art Resource, NY)*

8–16 contain the story of Judith, who shames the terrified men of Bethulia by using her piety and sexuality to overthrow the general Holofernes. He loses his head to her twice: once through infatuation so that he admits her to his tent and once when she executes him there! Though set in the 6th century, the story almost certainly reflects events in the 2nd century

when Judas Maccabeus took on the might of the Syrian army and its general Nicanor. The story shows how God, who is far greater than any human king, delivers and protects his people in unexpected ways.

The **Additions to Esther** were probably composed by several authors. Overall they give the narrative of Esther an explicitly religious character by including a God-given dream and its interpretation, the prayers of Mordecai and Esther that are answered, reference to dietary laws, and disparaging comments about the Gentile way of life. The Additions suggest that some Jews outside Palestine deliberately adjusted the book of Esther to support the identities of their own communities.

The three stories of **Susanna, Bel,** and **the Dragon** are exciting narrative additions to the book of Daniel that show Daniel's wisdom and tenacious faithfulness.

3 Maccabees, which has deuterocanonical status in Eastern churches, has nothing to do with the Maccabees but is a 1st-century-B.C. historical novella designed to encourage Jews in Egypt to avoid the threats of their Gentile overlords. By the end of the story the Gentile king has become the patron of the Jews.

Wisdom

Probably from late 1st-century-B.C.-Alexandria, the **Wisdom of Solomon** has three parts. The first contains a sustained argument for immortality; only that way can the righteous who receive no reward on earth stand vindicated before God. The second features a magnificent poetic description of personified wisdom as the mirror of the divine. The third section is a set of illustrations from history of the saving power of wisdom.

Sirach (the Greek title), the **Wisdom of Jesus Ben Sira** (Hebrew), or **Ecclesiasticus** (Latin) was composed in Jerusalem in the early 2nd century B.C. Like Proverbs, Sirach contains collections of sayings on all aspects of daily life and teaches forcefully that God will reward everyone as they deserve. Like the later Wisdom of Solomon, Sirach extols the personified figure of wisdom and famously identifies her with the law.

4 Maccabees is an attempt to demonstrate in philosophical terms the supremacy of religious reason based on the Law over emotions of any kind. The martyrs of the Maccabean period are one of the positive examples used to prove the thesis. Because of its remarks on the inviolability of the temple (4 Macc. 4:5-14), the book is commonly dated to the time of Caligula (A.D. 37-41), but that may be too precise.

Historiography

1 Maccabees reliably covers events from just before the Maccabean Revolt (167-164 B.C.) to the end of the reign of John Hyrcanus (104). In effect, however, the book is propaganda dressed up as history. Its aim is to preach against cultural assimilation and to celebrate Jewish independence, thereby securing the place of the Maccabee brothers and the dynasty they established as the rightful rulers of Judea.

2 Maccabees covers much of the same ground as 1 Maccabees 1–8, and Judas Maccabeus remains the hero of the work. But the temple and those who are prepared to be martyred for all that it represents take the foreground. The book provides innovative teaching on resurrection (chs. 7–8) and creation out of nothing (7:28).

1 Esdras reproduces much of 2 Chronicles 35–36, Ezra, and Nehemiah 7–8 and is probably an early alternative translation into Greek of those chapters. It also contains the memorable story (chs. 3–4) of the contest concerning what is the strongest thing on earth.

Poetry

Much of **Baruch** is poetry. Probably written in the early 1st century B.C., though set in the 6th, the work contains a corporate confession of sin, a hymn in praise of wisdom, and material on Jerusalem that echoes the language of Isaiah 51 and 54. The **Letter of Jeremiah** consists of an introduction and 10 stanzas that preach against idolatry.

The **Prayer of Azariah** and the **Song of the Three Young Men** are two extensive poetic additions to Daniel 3; perhaps they were designed for audience participation as the story of Daniel was read.

The **Prayer of Manasseh** is a 1st-century-B.C. penitential psalm put into the mouth of the wicked king Manasseh (2 Kgs. 21:1-18). **Psalm 151** has a complex textual history but is now also known among the Dead Sea Scrolls; in it David speaks in the first person of his childhood and divine selection.

Apocalypse

2 Esdras (**4 Ezra** in the Latin tradition) is the only apocalypse among the books of the Apocrypha. From the late 1st century A.D., its Jewish author in the guise of Ezra struggles with the theological problems arising from the destruction of the temple in 70. In the first part an angel attempts to answer some of the author's questions, while in the second the author is reassured in three grand visions of the impermanence of Rome, of the promise of the Messiah, and of the authority of Israel's holy Scriptures.

Further Reading

Harrington, Daniel J. *Invitation to the Apocrypha.* Grand Rapids: Eerdmans, 1999.

Metzger, Bruce M. *An Introduction to the Apocrypha.* Rev. ed. New York: Oxford University Press, 1977.

Detailed commentaries on individual books are published in the Anchor Bible series (New York: Doubleday): Carey A. Moore, *Tobit* (1996); *Judith* (1985); *Daniel, Esther, and Jeremiah: The Additions* (1977); David Winston, *The Wisdom of Solomon* (1979); Patrick W. Skehan and Alexander A. Di Lella, *Sirach* (1987); Jonathan A. Goldstein, *I Maccabees* (1976); *II Maccabees* (1983); Jacob M. Myers, *I and II Esdras* (1974).

GEORGE J. BROOKE

Nations, Peoples, and Empires (Part 2)

Alexander and the Spread of Hellenism

The face of the classical world was radically transformed through the vision and skills of two men: Philip, the king of Macedonia, and his son, Alexander. Philip and his armies succeeded in unifying the independent city-states of Greece (including Athens, Thebes, and Sparta) under his rule before his untimely death in 336 B.C. His son had received a thoroughly Greek education, being tutored by Aristotle himself, and determined to forge an empire built upon Greek institutions and culture.

Alexander led the armies of Greece and Macedonia through Asia Minor, Syria, and Palestine, defeating all opposition along the way. In Egypt he was welcomed as a new pharaoh and a son of the god Ammon. Alexander made plans for a new city strategically placed where the Nile pours into the Mediterranean. This city, Alexandria, was to become one of the most important centers of commerce, learning, and art in the ancient world — and, significantly, the largest center for Jews outside Palestine. Alexander continued to expand his empire eastward, conquering Persia and eventually

pressing as far as the Indus River. Here his troops, weary of war and its diminishing returns, refused to continue, so that Alexander would have to be content with an empire that stretched from Greece to Egypt and through what is now Iran.

In the wake of Alexander's conquests came hellenization (from Greek *hellēnizein,* "to imitate the Greeks"), the importation of Greek language, education, culture, and governance into the conquered territories. Alexander either remade existing cities after the image of the Greek city-state or created new ones, and these became the administrative, commercial, and cultural centers of his empire. Essential buildings would include the gymnasium, where young men were trained in Greek language, logic and rhetoric, ethics, as well as physical skills, and where the temples, theaters, and arenas featuring Greek piety, drama, and athletic competitions found a home. Palestine was not exempt from this influence, as the emergence of Greek cities throughout the region shows. Native populations began to learn Greek alongside their native languages in order to communicate and do business with the new powers. This widespread adoption of a common, second language was probably the most significant result of Alexander's career. It brought Greek philosophy and ethical theory to the world, but the removal of language barriers

Alexander the Great attacking Persian king Darius; mosaic from the House of the Faun, Pompeii. *(Erich Lessing / Art Resource, NY)*

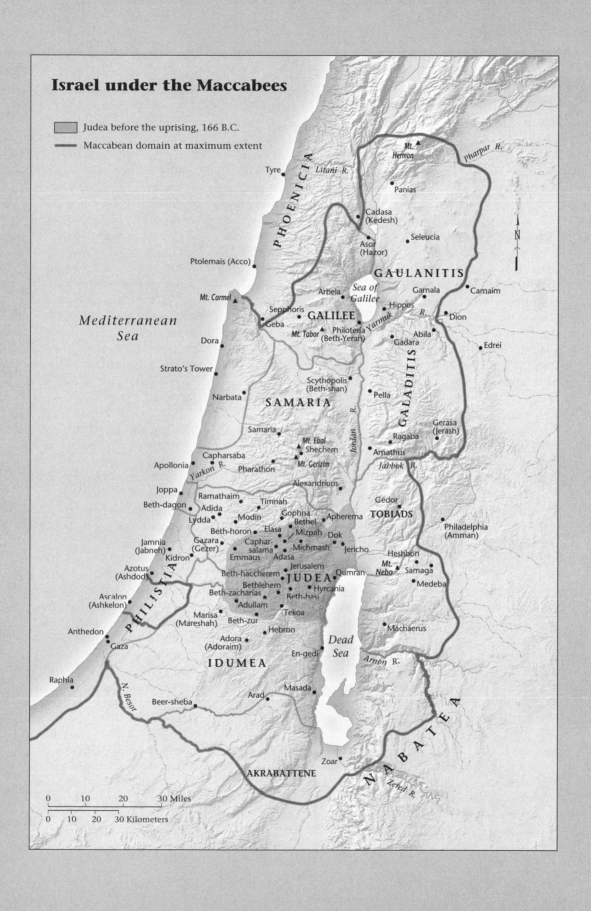

Israel under the Maccabees

Judea before the uprising, 166 B.C.
Maccabean domain at maximum extent

Mediterranean Sea

PHOENICIA

Tyre
Litani R.
Pharpar R.

Mt. Hermon

Panias

Cadasa (Kedesh)

Seleucia

Asor (Hazor)

GAULANITIS

Ptolemais (Acco)

Arbela
Sea of Galilee
Gamala
Carnaim

Mt. Carmel

Sepphoris
GALILEE
Hippos
Dion

Geba
Mt. Tabor
Philoteria (Beth-Yerah)
Gadara
Abila
Edrei

Dora

Yarmuk

Strato's Tower

Scythopolis (Beth-shan)
Pella
GALADITIS

Narbata

SAMARIA

Samaria
Mt. Ebal
Shechem
Jordan R.
Amathus
Gerasa (Jerash)

Capharsaba
Mt. Gerizim
Ragaba

Apollonia
Yarkon R.
Pharathon
Jabbok R.

Joppa
Alexandrium

Beth-dagon
Ramathaim
Timnah
Gophna
Gedor

Adida
Modin
Bethel
Apherema
TOBIADS

Lydda
Beth-horon
Elasa
Mizpah
Dok
Philadelphia (Amman)

Jamnia (Jabneh)
Gazara (Gezer)
Caphar-salama
Michmash
Jericho
Heshbon

Kidron
Emmaus
Adasa
Mt. Nebo
Samaga

Azotus (Ashdod)
Beth-haccherem
Jerusalem
Qumran
Medeba

Ascalon (Ashkelon)
Bethlehem
JUDEA
Hyrcania

PHILISTIA
Beth-zacharias
Beth-basi

Anthedon
Adullam
Tekoa
Machaerus

Gaza
Marisa (Mareshah)
Beth-zur
Hebron

Adora (Adoraim)
Dead Sea

Raphia
En-gedi
IDUMEA
Arnon R.

Masada

Beer-sheba
Arad

N. Besor
Zoar

AKRABATTENE
NABATEA
Zered R.

0   10   20   30 Miles
0 10 20 30 Kilometers

also enabled the rapid spread of "native" ideas and movements.

The Hellenization Crisis and Hasmonean Revolt

Alexander's world empire was short-lived. In 323, at age 33, Alexander died, leaving no viable heir. His four generals divided up his empire, fighting among themselves until only two prominent rulers were left — Seleucus I, who held Syria, Asia Minor, and Babylon, and Ptolemy I, who held Egypt and Palestine. These kings and their successors continued to vie with each other for territory, particularly Palestine, the strip of land sandwiched between the "kings of the north" (Seleucus's dynasty) and the "kings of the south" (Ptolemy's line). The Ptolemies held Palestine until 198, when Antiochus III was finally able to drive Ptolemy V's forces back into Egypt.

Antiochus III continued the Ptolemies' policy of allowing the Jews to govern themselves and observe their ancestral customs. Many elites in Judea had already accepted Greek as a second language and recognized the economic and political advantages of assimilating to the dominant Greek culture, at least as far as their religion would permit. Within Jerusalem, however, a large portion of the aristocracy (including priestly families) favored a more radical policy of hellenization. With their support, a priest named Yeshua, who took the Greek name Jason, offered vast sums of money to Antiochus IV Epiphanes for the privilege of refounding Jerusalem as a Greek city. Antiochus was always looking for funds with which to finance his campaigns

against Egypt or pay his annual tribute to the Roman Republic (already a major power in the Mediterranean). Additionally, he welcomed any local initiative to adopt the Greek way of life, since that brought greater coherence to his empire. Antiochus therefore deposed the more conservative Onias and appointed Jason as high priest.

Jason set aside the Torah as the law of the land in favor of a Greek constitution, enrolling all his like-minded compatriots as citizens of the new "Antioch-at-Jerusalem." A gymnasium and other Greek institutions were built. Jason himself was replaced by Menelaus, who gave Antiochus a larger bribe and continued hellenization in even more radical terms, polarizing the population. In 167, when Antiochus was embroiled in a campaign against Egypt, Jerusalem fell into chaos as the supporters of Jason, the supporters of Menelaus, and the more conservative Jews all took up arms against one another. Antiochus, thinking Jerusalem was rebelling against him, marched on the city, slaughtered thousands, and enslaved many more. Sensing (or being informed) that religion was the source of the discontent, he turned the temple into a pagan shrine, made Torah observance a capital crime, and began a harsh persecution of those who would not give up their ancestral way of life. Daniel 8 and 11 are cryptic but rather accurate narrations of the history of the Hellenistic kingdoms from Alexander to Antiochus IV, written especially to encourage fidelity to Torah at this time of severe repression.

Antiochus might have succeeded, but for the skills and ener-

gies of a priest named Mattathias and his five sons, John, Simon, Judas Maccabaeus, Eleazar, and Jonathan. (1 and 2 Maccabees tell the story of the crisis they reverse and their ongoing successes.) These organized the refugees who had fled Jerusalem for the countryside into a guerrilla army, which grew as they achieved victory after victory over both apostate Jews and the Syrian armies. By 164, they had retaken Jerusalem and reconsecrated the temple, a triumph commemorated in the festival of Hanukkah. Although Judas's forces were eventually driven from Jerusalem by Syrian armies, no further attempts were made by the successors of Antiochus IV to suppress Torah observance or disturb the temple.

After Judas died in battle, Jonathan led the resistance. Because a series of rivals laid claim to the Syrian throne and each wanted the support of the Judean armies, Jonathan was able to extract concessions by diplomacy that could not be won by military force. He was eventually appointed high priest and governor of Judea by a Seleucid king. His brother Simon succeeded to these offices after Jonathan's death, and under him the last of the Syrian forces were removed from Jerusalem and peace was restored.

The Growth and Decline of the Hasmonean Dynasty

Simon's son John Hyrcanus I and grandson Alexander Jannaeus expanded the territory of the Hasmonean state to include all the lands once held by Solomon. Although Israel was once again an independent nation and had regained its former stature, the Hasmonean leaders fell from popular favor. Looking and acting more like the Seleucid kings than pious high priests, they even took the title of "king," a title many Jews felt should be reserved for the house of David. After Alexander Jannaeus's death his two sons, John Hyrcanus II and Aristobulus II, divided Jerusalem in their contest for the crown and high priesthood. They both appealed to the Roman general Pompey, who had been expanding the Roman Republic's territories eastward, delivering the death blow to the Seleucid dynasty in 64 B.C. Pompey's intervention resulted in a siege of Jerusalem in 63, the imprisonment of Aristobulus II, the conferral of the high priesthood and oversight of Judea to Hyrcanus II (without the title "king"), and the removal of Samaria, Galilee, and Transjordan from Hasmonean hands into Roman jurisdiction. The Hasmonean dynasty came thus to an abrupt end, and a new Gentile master appeared on the scene.

DAVID A. DESILVA

The New
Testament

The World of the New Testament

Shortly before the advent of Jesus Christ, the Roman Empire had already become the ruling power over Israel.

Hasmonean Rule, 143-63 B.C.

After the demise of the Persian Empire, Alexander the Great defeated the Persians in Asia Minor in 334-333 B.C., Israel in 332, Egypt and Mesopotamia by 331. After the death of Alexander in 323, his kingdom was eventually divided among four generals, two of which affected Israel. Israel came under the Ptolemies of Egypt from 301 to 198 and under the Seleucids from 198 to 143. It remained somewhat independent under Hasmonean rule from 143 to 63, at which time the political leader and high priest were combined in one person, Alexander Jannaeus. But when Jannaeus died in 76 B.C., the political leadership was continued by his wife, Salome Alexandra, and their son Hyrcanus II became the high priest. When Salome Alexandra died in 67, Hyrcanus became political leader and continued as high priest with the support of the Pharisees. Three months later, Hyrcanus's brother Aristobulus II, who sided with the Sadducees, seized control and became king and high priest. Hyrcanus was willing to accept this, but the Idumean Antipater II (son of Antipater I, who had been appointed governor of Idumea by Jannaeus), father of Herod the Great, had other plans for him. Antipater convinced Hyrcanus that he had been wronged, for he was the legitimate ruler. It is at this juncture that Rome stepped in.

The Roman general Pompey advanced eastward by capturing Damascus in 64 and proceeded to Israel, where both rivals, Hyrcanus II and Aristobulus II, appealed to him to be the rightful ruler. After some delay, Pompey sided with Hyrcanus II. Then he captured Jerusalem, entered the temple's holy of holies without plundering it, and reinstated Hyrcanus II as high priest. The political leadership was given to Scaurus, whom he made legate of the province of Syria (63). This marked the end to 80 years (143-63) of independence of

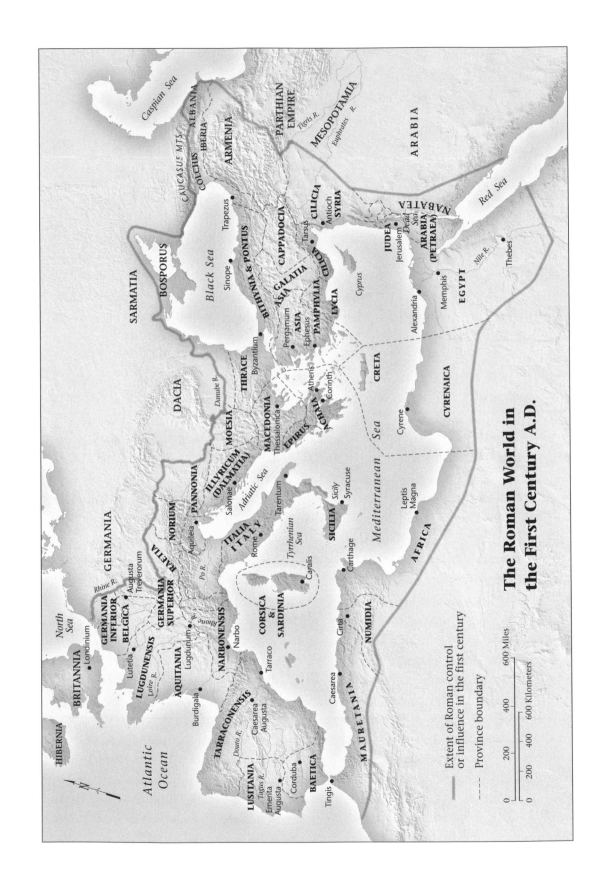

The Roman World in
the First Century A.D.

— Extent of Roman control
  or influence in the first century

- - - Province boundary

| 0 | 200 | 400 | 600 Miles |
| 0 | 200 | 400 | 600 Kilometers |

Atlantic Ocean

HIBERNIA

BRITANNIA
• Londinium

North Sea

Rhine R.

GERMANIA
GERMANIA INFERIOR
BELGICA
• Augusta Treverorum
GERMANIA SUPERIOR
• Lutetia
RAETIA
NORICUM
LUGDUNENSIS
• Lugdunum
Loire R.
AQUITANIA
NARBONENSIS
• Narbo
• Burdigala
Rhône

TARRACONENSIS
• Tarraco
• Caesarea Augusta
Douro R.
LUSITANIA
• Emerita Augusta
Tagus R.
• Corduba
BAETICA
• Tingis

MAURETANIA
• Caesarea

NUMIDIA
• Cirta

AFRICA
• Carthage

CORSICA & SARDINIA
• Caralis

Po R.
• Aquileia
ITALIA
ITALY
• Rome
Tyrrhenian Sea
• Tarentum
SICILIA
Sicily
• Syracuse

Mediterranean Sea

• Leptis Magna

AFRICA

RAETIA
NORICUM
PANNONIA
Danube R.
DACIA
ILLYRICUM (DALMATIA)
• Salonae
Adriatic Sea

SARMATIA

BOSPORUS

Black Sea
• Trapezus
• Sinope

MOESIA
THRACE
• Byzantium
MACEDONIA
• Thessalonica
EPIRUS
ACHAIA
• Athens
• Corinth

CRETA

CYRENAICA
• Cyrene

CAUCASUS MTS.
ALBANIA
COLCHIS
IBERIA
ARMENIA

PARTHIAN EMPIRE
MESOPOTAMIA
Tigris R.
Euphrates R.

ARABIA

BITHYNIA & PONTUS
ASIA
GALATIA
CAPPADOCIA
• Pergamum
ASIA
• Ephesus
PAMPHYLIA
LYCIA
CILICIA
• Tarsus
Cyprus

SYRIA
• Antioch
NABATEA
JUDEA
• Jerusalem
Dead Sea
ARABIA (PETRAEA)

Red Sea

EGYPT
Nile R.
• Alexandria
• Memphis
• Thebes

Caspian Sea

the Jewish nation as well as the end of the Hasmonean house. Hyrcanus became merely a vassal of the Roman Empire.

Roman Rule, 63 B.C.–A.D. 70

Hyrcanus II, 63-40 B.C. Although Hyrcanus II was reappointed high priest, Antipater II was the power behind the throne. Antipater proved himself useful to the Romans officials and in their operation against the Hasmoneans.

The Roman Republic was plagued with problems. In 49 B.C. Julius Caesar waged war against Pompey, and Antipater appeared with troops to help Caesar. Antipater knew whose side to be on. After the victory over Pompey (in Egypt) in 48, Caesar confirmed Hyrcanus as high priest and also gave him the title of ethnarch of the Jews. Further, in appreciation for Antipater's services, Caesar made him a tax-free Roman citizen and procurator over Judea. Although Antipater was of lower rank than Hyrcanus, he continued to wield power by appointing his oldest son, Phasael, governor of Jerusalem and Herod, his second son, governor of Galilee in 47.

After Cassius, Brutus, and their followers murdered Julius Caesar in 44, Cassius went to Syria. Needing to raise certain taxes required by Cassius, Antipater selected Herod, Phasael, and Malichus (a Jewish noble) for the job. Because of Herod's success in this endeavor, Cassius appointed him governor of Coele-Syria. Herod, an Idumean, became betrothed to Mariamne, granddaughter of Hyrcanus II and daughter of Aristobulus's son Alexander, and thus a niece to Antigonus, Herod's rival. Herod's position was strengthened, and as a result he became regent when the aging Hyrcanus died.

When Antony defeated Cassius in 42, the Jewish leaders accused Herod and Phasael of seizing the power of the government, leaving Hyrcanus with only titular honors and no real authority. Herod's defense nullified these charges. Antony asked Hyrcanus who would be the best qualified to rule, and Hyrcanus chose Herod and Phasael. Antony appointed them as tetrarchs of Judea.

Antigonus, 40-37 B.C. The Parthians, who lived south of the Caspian Sea, appeared in Syria to deliver it from Roman power. Antigonus, son of Aristobulus II, asked them to help remove Hyrcanus, eliminate the Idumean Herod, and restore the Hasmonean monarchy. Antigonus was able to control Jerusalem and much of the countryside. Herod, his family, and his troops moved to Masada and then to Petra. Antigonus was made king and cut off Hyrcanus's ear to prevent the possibility of his restoration to the high priesthood.

Meanwhile Herod went to Rome, where Antony, Octavius Caesar, and the Senate designated him King of Judea. In late 40 or early 39, Herod returned to Israel, and with the help of Antony's legate Sossius was able to recapture Galilee. It was before attacking Jerusalem that he married Mariamne, a Hasmonean, which consolidated his acceptance by the Jews but may also have served to spite Antigonus, Mariamne's uncle. Herod then laid siege to Jerusalem, which finally fell in the summer of 37. Antigonus was beheaded, marking the end of Hasmonean rule. Herod became king.

Herod the Great, 37-4 B.C.

Consolidation, 37-25 B.C. Having won over Antigonus, Herod needed to gain the loyalty of his subjects and to eliminate those hostile to his rule. He severely punished the Pharisees and others who opposed him and rewarded with favors and honors those who were loyal to him. Herod also executed 45 of the wealthiest among the aristocracy and confiscated their properties. In an attempt to diminish Hasmonean influence, he appointed the Aaronic Hananel as high priest to replace the mutilated Hyrcanus. But Herod's mother-in-law Alexandra pressured to have her 17-year-old son Aristobulus become high priest. Aristobulus was well liked by the populace, but Herod contrived to have him "accidentally" drowned in a pool at Jericho. Meanwhile, Octavius defeated Antony in the battle of Actium (30). Herod successfully convinced Octavius that he would be loyal, and Octavius confirmed his royal rank. The following year Octavius returned to him Jericho and added Gazara, Hippos, Samaria, Gaza, Anthedon, Joppa, and Straton's Tower.

Prosperity, 25-14 B.C. Herod proceeded to build theaters, amphitheaters, and a race course, all in violation of Jewish law. About 24 he built a royal palace and built or rebuilt many fortresses and Gentile temples, including the rebuilding of Straton's Tower, which he renamed Caesarea. His greatest achievement was the rebuilding of the Jewish temple in

Herodium, mountain palace-fortress of Herod the Great. *(Phoenix Data Systems, Neal and Joel Bierling)*

Jerusalem, begun ca. 20. In 23/22 Octavius, now named Augustus, gave Herod Trachonitis, Batanea, and Auranitis and, in 20, Zenodorus. Herod remitted one-third of the taxes to bring goodwill among his subjects, and later in 14 he reduced taxes again by one-fourth.

Domestic Troubles, 14-4 B.C.   Herod had married 10 wives, and this led to domestic infighting. During this time he drew up six wills. In the fifth (5 B.C.) Antipas was to succeed as king, but only days before his death Herod drew up his sixth will, whereby Archelaus was to succeed as king, with Antipas and Philip as tetrarchs. Although this last will was disputed, it remained intact, except Archelaus was named ethnarch rather than king. Herod, nearly 70 years old, died a very sick man in the spring of 4. Shortly before Herod's death are set the visit of Jesus by the magi, the journey of Joseph, Mary, and Jesus took to Egypt, and Herod's massacre of all the male children of Bethlehem two years and under (Matt. 2:1-16).

Archelaus, 4 B.C.–A.D. 6   Archelaus (born ca. 22 B.C.), the son of Herod the Great and Malthace (a Samaritan), was made ethnarch over Idumea, Judea, and Samaria with the promise that he would be made king if he ruled with prudence. But his rule was disastrous and short-lived. He deposed two high priests, divorced his wife, and married Glaphyra, who had been the wife of Alexander, the half-brother of Archelaus, thus violating ancestral law. An unlikely delegation of Jews and Samaritans complained to Augustus about Archelaus's brutality and tyranny, indicating the seriousness of the complaint. Archelaus's brothers Antipas and Philip also went to Rome to complain about him, and as a result Archelaus was banished in A.D. 6 to Vienna in Gaul.

Archelaus's brutal treatment of the Jews and Samaritans is in keeping with Matthew's report that Joseph heard that Archelaus was ruling Judea and was afraid to go there. Being warned in a dream on his return from Egypt, he took Mary and Jesus to Nazareth in Galilee (Matt. 2:22-23).

Pontius Pilate, A.D. 26-36   With Archelaus deposed, his territories of Idumea, Judea, and Samaria were retained by the Roman government and were ruled by 14 different governors from A.D. 6 to 41 and from 44 to 66 (Herod Agrippa I was given these territories in 41-44), with Pilate the most notable. (Felix and Festus are mentioned in Acts 24–26 in connection with Paul's imprisonment in Caesarea.) Pilate was appointed prefect through the influence of his mentor Sejanus, commander of the praetorian guard, who was known to be anti-Semitic. According to Josephus and Philo, Pilate was greedy, inflexible, cruel, and resorted to robbery and oppression. He exhibited this behavior shortly after his arrival in Judea in 26, when he introduced into Jerusalem Roman standards with embossed figures of the emperor, arousing the indignation of the Jews. He also seized funds from the sacred treasury, Corbanas, in order to construct an aqueduct. Luke 13:1 mentions a cruel incident in which he mixed the blood of the Galileans with their sacrifices. Pilate is most notable for his trial of Jesus in 33.

Here he is portrayed as weak and willing to comply with the wishes of the Jewish leaders rather than enact his own desires — just the opposite of his portrayal in Josephus and Philo. The Jews, having learned that Pilate's mentor Sejanus had been recently executed by Tiberius, cleverly used this to threaten Pilate by declaring that a refusal to release Jesus to them would signify that he was not Caesar's friend (John 19:12). Pilate realized, however, that the Jews might also accuse him of still being a friend of Sejanus or friendly toward his policies, which Tiberius had now refused to accept. Pilate was deposed at the end of 36 or the beginning of 37 due to a Samaritan complaint to Vitellius, prefect of Syria.

Herod Antipas, 4 B.C.–A.D. 39 Herod Antipas (born ca. 20 B.C.), the younger brother of Archelaus, was made tetrarch of Galilee and Perea, the territories where both Jesus and John the Baptist concentrated their ministries. He rebuilt Sepphoris (ca. A.D. 8-10), the largest city in Galilee and, until he built Tiberias, capital of his territories. Joseph, living in Nazareth only 4 miles SSW of Sepphoris, may well have used his carpentry skill (Matt. 13:55; Mark 6:3) during its rebuilding. Antipas also rebuilt Livias (or Julias) in Perea (ca. 13) in honor of Augustus's wife Livia and built the new city of Tiberias on the Sea of Galilee (ca. 25) in honor of the emperor Tiberius.

In the eyes of Rome Antipas was a good ruler. In A.D. 6 he, along with his half-brother Philip the tetrarch and a Jewish and Samaritan delegation, had his brother Archelaus deposed. Antipas hoped he would receive the title of king, but Tiberius allowed him only the dynastic title of Herod. In the Gospels Herod Antipas is best known for his imprisonment and beheading of John the Baptist (Matt. 14:3-12; Mark 6:17-29; Luke 3:19-20), who had criticized Antipas's marriage to Herodias because her former husband was still alive. In 33 Antipas was involved with the trial of Jesus (Luke 23:6-12). Three years later Antipas's former father-in-law Aretas attacked and defeated Antipas to avenge Antipas's treatment of Aretas's daughter when he fell in love with Herodias. The Jews saw this defeat as divine punishment on Antipas for killing John the Baptist. In 39 Antipas and Herodias were banished to Lugdunum Convenarum (now Saint-Bertrand de Comminges) in the foothills of the Pyrenees in southern France, and his territories were given to Agrippa I, Antipas's nephew and brother-in-law.

Philip the Tetrarch Philip the Tetrarch (born ca. 22/21 B.C.) was the son of Herod the Great and Cleopatra of Jerusalem. Augustus appointed him tetrarch over the northern part of Herod the Great's domain: Gaulanitis, Auranitis, Batanea, Trachonitis, Paneas, and Iturea. It was in his territory that Jesus most likely fed the 5000 and later the 4000, and where in Caesarea Philippi Peter confessed Jesus' messiahship and received the revelation of the formation of the church (Matt. 16:13-20; Mark 8:27-30). Philip, well liked by his subjects, married Herodias's daughter Salome, whose dance led to the execution of John the Baptist. When Philip died in 34, Tiberius annexed his territory to Syria, and in 37 Caligula gave this territory to Agrippa I.

Herod Agrippa I Agrippa I (born 10 B.C.) was the son of Aristobulus (son of Herod the Great and Mariamne) and Bernice (daughter of Herod's sister Salome and Costobarus). His sister was Herodias. Agrippa, who was schooled in Rome and had indulged in careless and extravagant living, was considered the black sheep of the Herodian family. When Caligula became emperor (A.D. 37), he gave Agrippa the territory of Philip the Tetrarch along with the title of king, which Herod Antipas had coveted. In late summer 38, Agrippa went to Israel to see the land he would govern. This roused Antipas's jealousy, and he along with Herodias went to Rome to request a new title. Instead, Caligula banished them to France and Agrippa acquired Antipas's territories of Galilee and Perea. In 41 Agrippa was in Rome when Caligula was murdered, and he helped Claudius ascend to the throne. Claudius confirmed Agrippa's rule and added Judea and Samaria to his domains, meaning that he ruled over all the territory of his grandfather Herod the Great.

Agrippa I is known in the New Testament for his persecution of the early church in order to curry the favor of the Jews (Acts 12:1-19). He killed James the son of Zebedee and imprisoned Peter. Agrippa died in 44 at Caesarea (Acts 12:20-23).

Herod Agrippa II Agrippa II (born A.D. 27) was the son of Agrippa I and Cypros, daughter of Phasael (Herod the Great's nephew) and Salampsio (Herod's daughter). He was too young to succeed his father immediately, but in 53 Claudius finally granted him Philip the tetrarch's territory plus the tetrarchy of Abilene (or Abila) and the town of Arca at the northern extremity of the Lebanon range. In 54 Nero added to his realm portions of Galilee and Perea. When Festus became procurator of Judea (59-62), Agrippa II, in company with his sister Bernice, went from Caesarea Philippi to Caesarea to welcome him to his new office. There he heard Paul's case (Acts 25:13–26:32). In the war of 66-70, Agrippa II openly sided with the Romans, giving allegiance to Vespasian and joining with Titus in the triumph over his own people. Agrippa was rewarded by further increase of his kingdom.

FOR FURTHER READING

Bond, Helen K. *Pontius Pilate in History and Interpretation.* SNTSMS 100. Cambridge: Cambridge University Press, 1998.

Bruce, F. F. *New Testament History.* Garden City: Doubleday, 1969.

Hoehner, Harold W. *Herod Antipas.* SNTSMS 17. 1972; repr. Grand Rapids: Zondervan, 1980.

Schürer, Emil. *The History of the Jewish People in the Age of Jesus Christ (175 B.C.–A.D. 135),* vol. 1. Rev. and ed. Geza Vermes, Fergus Millar, and Matthew Black. Edinburgh: T. & T. Clark, 1973.

Schwartz, Daniel R. *Agrippa I: The Last King of Judaea.* Texte und Studien zum Antiken Judentum 23. Tübingen: J. C. B. Mohr (Paul Siebeck), 1990.

HAROLD W. HOEHNER

Worshippers of Other Gods (Part 2)

Introduction

Even a cursory reading of the literature of the Roman Empire impresses one with the importance and pervasiveness of religious worship. The traditional Roman city would have sanctuaries erected to numerous gods, such as Jupiter (Zeus), Juno, Minerva (Athena), Mercury, Isis and Serapis, Apollo, Mars, Venus (Aphrodite), Artemis (Diana), and Hermes. It is said that the city of Philippi in Macedonia had a mix of Greco-Roman gods numbering more than two dozen, while the coins of the city of Nicomedia in Bithynia indicate that more than 40 deities were worshipped in that city. The Apostle Paul explains this proliferation of gods and goddesses as the result of the ungodliness and unrighteousness of people who knew God through the witness he had left of himself in the natural world, yet ignored him and exchanged the glory of the incorruptible God for images made in the various forms which appear in the worship of the ancient world: humankind, birds, animals, and reptiles (Rom. 1:18-23).

Lystra

The striking story of Acts 14:8-13 reports an event that occurred in the city of Lystra. God had used Paul to heal a man crippled from birth, with the result that the priest of Zeus, the major deity of that city, prepared to lead the people in worship of Barnabas and Paul, saying they were Zeus and Hermes who had become like men and come to earth. The crowd's use of Lycaonian, a language apparently unknown to Paul's company, explains why Paul and Barnabas did not grasp what was afoot until the preparations to pay them divine honors were well advanced.

A story told by Ovid may have played a part in the reaction of the crowd. In his *Metamorphoses* Ovid tells of an aged couple, Philemon and Baucis, who entertained Zeus and Hermes unaware and were rewarded for their hospitality. Additionally, Zeus and Hermes are mentioned in statue and altar dedications at a town near Lystra by men with Lycaonian names. Zeus, worshipped by the people of Lystra, was known as the highest god, the strongest god, the constantly victorious god who was father of gods and men. He was named by Aeschylus as all-powerful, all-accomplisher, cause of all, and thus was worshipped everywhere. So it is not surprising to find his sanctuary "before the city" or facing the city gate of Lystra, or to find that he is accompanied in worship by Hermes, the swift messenger of the gods, whose work involved successful communication with enemies and strangers.

Athens

Given the proliferation of polytheism, it is understandable that the Apostle Paul, while touring the city of Athens, was "deeply distressed to see that the city was full of idols" (Acts 17:16), or that his first words addressed to the rulers of the city were, "I see how extremely religious you are in every way." The apostle mentioned only one of those objects of devotion, however: an altar "to an unknown god." Paul used this inscription as an introduction to his proclamation of the living God, who was unknown to his hearers. While some have doubted this characterization of an Athenian god, the Greek traveler Pausanias (ca. A.D. 150) notes that near Athens there were altars of gods both named and unknown. Tertullian and Jerome also mention an altar to unknown gods.

Corinth

While the "many gods and many lords" (1 Cor. 8:5) of Corinth are not named in the biblical text, the Apostle Paul makes it very clear that there were pagan sanctuaries in Corinth. Archaeologists report that they included kitchen and dining areas that were set apart for the worship of pagan deities, places where religious and social life were joined in sharing the sacrificial meat that had been offered to the idol. Paul warns believers against joining the real devotees of the gods in the deity's temple grounds to share in the celebrations. He reminds his readers that while an idol is nothing, what the Gentiles sacrifice is sacrificed to demons, and "you cannot partake of the table of the Lord and the table of demons" (1 Cor. 10:20-21). Corinth was the center of the worship of Aphrodite, the goddess of love, whose temple was situated on the Acrocorinth that rises 1900 feet above the city. The city's reputation for sexual promiscuity has often been related to her temple, said to have been staffed at one time by a thousand female slaves, and gives background for the various admonitions against unchastity in Paul's Corinthian letters.

Ephesus

That the city of Ephesus was involved in the worship of other gods is powerfully seen in two major events: first, many believers who had practiced magic — an effort to manipulate and master the spirits by magical incantations — burned their books, valued at 50 thousand pieces of silver, in the town square (Acts 19:18-19). Second, the name, glory, and temple of the goddess Artemis whom "all of Asia and all the world worship" were perceived to be threatened by the powerful ministry of Paul. Also threatened

was the livelihood of the silver artisans who made shrines of Artemis — apparently likenesses of the temple with the image of the many-breasted goddess within — for deposit in her temple (Acts 19:27). Artemis had been worshipped in Ephesus since before 1000 B.C., and her temple was considered to be one of the seven wonders of the ancient world. It is no wonder that the populace grew angry with Paul and sought to silence him with the chant, "Great is Artemis of the Ephesians."

For Further Reading

Arnold, Clinton E. *Ephesians: Power and Magic.* 1989; repr. Grand Rapids: Baker, 1992.

Bruce, F. F. *The Book of the Acts.* NICNT. Rev. ed. Grand Rapids: Eerdmans, 1988.

———. *Paul: Apostle of the Heart Set Free.* Grand Rapids: Wm. B. Eerdmans, 1977.

Burkert, Walter. *Greek Religion.* Cambridge, Mass.: Harvard University Press, 1985.

Deissmann, Adolf. *Light from the Ancient East.* Rev. ed. 1927; repr. Grand Rapids: Baker, 1978.

MacMullen, Ramsay. *Paganism in the Roman Empire.* New Haven: Yale University Press, 1981.

Marshall, I. Howard. *The Acts of the Apostles.* 1980; repr. Grand Rapids: Eerdmans, 1996.

WAYNE S. FLORY

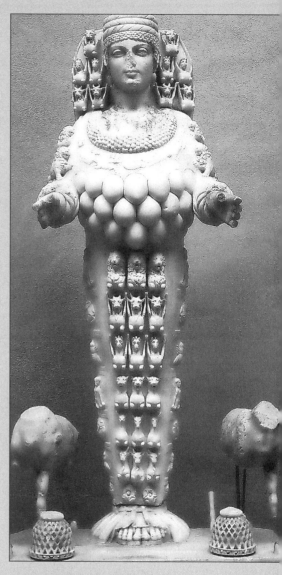

Statue of Artemis of Ephesus, goddess of fertility and patron of the city; 2nd century A.D.
(www.HolyLandPhotos.org)

Judaism in the Time of Jesus

Judaism in the time of the New Testament was marked by its variety and vitality. Two major historical events at the close of the Old Testament period set the stage for subsequent centuries: the return of some of the Jewish exiles to the land of Israel and the rebuilding of the temple in Jerusalem. While the Jewish people enjoyed a measure of religious freedom, external political domination (Persian, Greek, and Roman) characterized much of the next 500 years. The day-to-day struggles of life under foreign occupation in Judea exerted tremendous influence on the shape of religious attitudes and concerns in the postexilic period.

Scripture

Political turmoil and pressing spiritual challenges (idolatry, intermarriage, ritual purity) required attention. It is during this period that the Jewish community achieved some general consensus regarding which ancient writings should be considered authoritative — the Hebrew Bible, Christianity's Old Testament canon. At the beginning of the postexilic period the Mosaic law (Pentateuch) was already universally recognized. Later in the 2nd century B.C. the Jewish scribe Jesus ben Sirach suggests that a collection he calls "the Prophets" — the composition of which he leaves undefined — is likewise suitable for "wisdom and instruction" (Sirach Prologue 7). Scholarly debate continues concerning the time of the eventual inclusion of the third component of the canon, the Writings. In any regard, its acceptance is not later than the council of Jamnia in A.D. 90.

Since for much of this period the book of Malachi was regarded the last writing that could claim prophetic inspiration, contemporary authors sought other ways to strengthen the authority of their message. They resorted to writing under the pseudonyms of heroes of the biblical past (e.g., Abraham, Enoch, Moses). This literature was marked by its interpretive freedom to reshape well-known biblical stories in order to address the specific challenges facing the Jewish nation in the Hellenistic and Roman periods. Overall, it also often possessed a pronounced pessimism toward current events that in turn gave rise to apocalyptic speculation. The writers held out little hope that the course of history could be salvaged. Instead, they hoped God would intervene to re-create a new heaven and a new earth, devoid of sin and suffering.

Redemption

From the golden age of Israel's monarchy, political rule was understood to be the covenantal right of David's descendants (2 Sam. 7:16). During the postexilic period the limits of political power created a vacuum that was filled from necessity by the high priest. This shift toward political power-sharing may already be signaled in Zechariah's vision of the two olive trees (Zech. 4:1-14). The Jewish revolt (167-164 B.C.) against the Seleucids led by the Hasmoneans, a priestly family from Modiin, culminated in a dynasty of ruler-priests.

The traditional separation of powers between the political and cultic spheres prevented these priests at first from assuming the title "king." Soon, however, their inhibitions waned. Coins minted during the reign of Alexander Jannaeus (103-76) ascribed to him the title in Hebrew "Yehonathan the King" together with its Greek equivalent, "King Alexander." Josephus further reports that the father of Jannaeus, John Hyrcanus (134-104), was "thought worthy by God of three of the greatest things: government of his people, the priestly honor, and the gift of prophecy" (*J.W.* 13.299-300). Josephus's testimony is evidence of the first occasion in Jewish tradition that a single individual assumed the offices of "the three crowns" (prophet, priest, and king). This fusion of biblically distinct roles would later prove fertile ground for early Christian Christology.

The changes in political power likewise influenced Jewish ideas regarding the identity and future role of the hoped-for Redeemer. Both Jewish Pseudepigrapha (T. Levi 18:1-14; T. Jud. 17:5-6) and the Dead Sea Scrolls (CD 12:23; 14:9; 20:1) suggest belief among some in two messiahs, one royal and one priestly. Nevertheless, while the assumption of political power by the Hasmonean priests may have proven a catalyst for belief in a priestly Messiah, disillusionment with their rule also revived renewed expressions of the traditional hope for a Davidic Messiah (Pss. Sol. 17:6, 21).

Temple

The temple played a central role in Jewish life during the New Testament period. The most prominent demonstrations of this were the annual pilgrimage feasts (Passover, Feast of Weeks, Tabernacles) centered at the temple and public participation in the sacrificial system. The annual temple tax — obligatory for all Jewish males, whether they lived in Judea or abroad — helped to unify the Jewish people. According to Josephus, "In no other town may there be an altar or a temple, because God is one and the Hebrew race is one" (*Ant.* 4.20). The influence of the temple was felt in daily life, especially in areas of ritual purity (Acts 21:26). Practices of ritual washing that earlier were limited to the temple precincts became expected custom elsewhere (Matt. 15:1-2). So important was the temple to Jewish spirituality that eschatological expectations were even defined in terms of hope for a heavenly temple "not made with hands" (4Q174 3:2-6; cf. Mark 14:58; Tob. 14:5).

Although scholarship has sometimes suggested intrinsic tension between the temple, with its Sadducean priesthood, and local synagogues, which served as the focal point for Pharisaic learning, there is no record of institutional incompatibility in the literary sources (cf. *m. 'Abot* 1:2). Recent archaeological excavations in Jerusalem accord with the testimony of Jewish literature to numerous synagogues in Jerusalem (*y. Meg.* 3:1:73[d]). According to these sources, some were even within the temple precincts themselves. Moreover, 1st-century synagogues were oriented toward the temple in Jerusalem, as were public daily prayers.

Synagogue

Inscriptional evidence from mid-3rd century-B.C. Egypt suggests that the synagogue was already an established institution. The time and purpose of its origins are unknown. Rabbinic tradition reports that the exiled King Jehoiachin (2 Kgs. 24:10-15) took stones from the destroyed Solomonic temple to build synagogues for the community in Babylonian exile (*b. Meg.* 29a). The implication is that these served to replace the first temple, but we have no other literary or archaeological evidence to corroborate this notion.

Philo, Josephus, and the New Testament describe synagogues in 1st-century Judea and abroad (*Embassy* 132, 156, 311; Mark 1:21; Acts 14:1; 17:1). While prayer would become a focal point of Jewish gathering, we have no mention of corporate prayers in Jewish synagogues prior to the destruction of the temple in A.D. 70. Instead, they served as venues for the Jewish community to meet, particularly for reading and teaching the Scriptures (Luke 4:16-20; Acts 13:15; *m. Sotah* 7:7-8; *m. Yoma* 7:1; *Ant.* 4.209; *Good Person* 81–82).

Jewish Sects

In his report about the Hasmonean period (164-40), Josephus first mentions three Jewish philosophic groups: the Sadducees, Pharisees, and Essenes (*Ant.* 13.171-73). While other groups find mention in 1st-century witnesses, these parties represent the three broadly divergent streams of Jewish piety during the days of the Second Temple. The stark scarcity of our historical sources limits our certainty regarding both the date and circumstances surrounding the origins of each movement.

Baram synagogue in the Upper Galilee. *(Wikimedia Commons)*

Sadducees Of the three Jewish philosophies mentioned by Josephus, we know the least about the Sadducees. Indeed, we have not a single page penned by a Sadducean hand. Moreover, the reliability of what information we do have is tempered by the fact that it has come to us through the hands of their detractors. The Sadducees are first mentioned in the 2nd century B.C. According to uncertain rabbinical tradition (*'Abot R. Nat.* 5), the name for the sect is derived from Zadok, a student of Antigonus of Socho, who taught: "Be not like servants who serve the master for condition of receiving a reward, but be like servants who serve the master not upon condition of receiving a reward" (*m. Abot* 1:3). Zadok misunderstood this to suggest that there would be no eternal reward (resurrection). We hear elsewhere that the Sadducees did not believe in the resurrection, nor the immortality of the soul (Matt. 22:23; Acts 23:8; *J.W.* 2.162-63; *Ant.* 18.16). It is likely they founded their doctrine upon a very rigid, narrow reading of the Mosaic law. Unlike the Pharisees, who maintained the continuity of divine revelation in the literature of the Law, Prophets, Writings, and even later teachings (oral law) of Israel's sages, the Sadducees insisted that doctrine should be derived from the written Scriptures alone (*Ant.* 13.297; 18.16).

A second tradition regarding the origin of the Sadducees is that they were descendants of another Zadok, the high priest in the time of David (2 Sam. 8:17) and Solomon (1 Kgs. 1:34ff.). In Ezekiel, the family of Zadok is entrusted with control of the temple (Ezek. 40:46; 43:19; 44:15). Regardless of the origin of the Sadducees, by the New Testament period they are closely identified with the temple establishment in Jerusalem. They were predominated by aristocratic priests who controlled the temple and the Sanhedrin. The longest family dynasty of high priests during the period of the Second Temple is that of the Sadducee Annas (Luke 3:2). It is his family that the New Testament identifies by name as the primary opponents of Jesus (Luke 19:47) and who are responsible for his transfer into Roman hands (John 18:13, 24; Luke 23:10). They also opposed Jesus' followers after his death and resurrection (Acts 4:6).

Essenes The Essenes in recent scholarship have been closely identified with the Qumran congregation. Among all the 1st-century Jewish sects, the reports about the Essenes in classical literature (Josephus, *J. W.* 2.119-61; Pliny, *Natural History* 5.73; cf. Philo, *Contempl. Life* 25) approximate most closely the doctrine and practices of the Dead Sea sect. For example, they advocated an extreme opinion regarding divine predeterminism: ". . . Fate is mistress of all things, and nothing befalls men unless it be in accordance with her decree" (*Ant.* 13.171). Although Josephus couches his report in Greek philosophical vocabulary that would have been familiar to his Roman readers, his portrayal of the Essene view of divine predeterminism mirrors the faith of the Dead Sea sect: "From the God of Knowledge comes all that is and shall be . . . it is in accord with his glorious design that they accomplish their task without change" (1QS 3:15-16).

The Essenes shared all their possessions within a highly structured communal setting (*J. W.* 2.122; 1QS 6:18-23). Moreover, according to Josephus, they lived in strict observance of the Torah and were punctilious about ritual purity (*J. W.* 2.129). Their uncompromising demands for doctrinal correctness put them at odds with the temple establishment (CD 6:11-13; 4:15-18; 5:6-7) and eventually resulted in their separation from the temple and the mainstream of Jewish religious life. These separatist tendencies were reinforced by a spiritual dualism that divided humanity into two camps (1QS 3:17-18) and led to an ethic of hatred toward those outside their movement: "that they may love all that he has chosen and hate all that he has rejected" (1QS 1:3-4; 9:21-22; cf. Matt. 5:43-44).

Pharisees The Pharisees are the Jewish group most frequently mentioned in the New Testament. Accounts of pointed exchange between Jesus and the Pharisees likely reflect the dialectical method of learning so indicative of the Pharisaic style of study. Josephus records that "the Pharisees had passed on to the people certain regulations handed down by former generations and not recorded in the Law of Moses" (*Ant.* 13.297). His statement attests to their role in the development of the oral law — the interpretation and practical application of the written Scriptures. Jesus also speaks of this role and its authoritative place in Jewish society: "The Pharisees sit on the seat of Moses (the seat of instruction in the synagogue). Do what they say . . ." (Matt. 23:2).

Josephus reports that in contrast to the harsh and sometimes precipitous rulings of the Sadducees, the Pharisees were more lenient in judgment (*Ant.* 13.294; 20.199). Indeed, it is within this stream of Jewish piety — reflected also in proto-Pharisaic Judaism and its successor, Rabbinic Judaism — that we hear increasing emphasis upon the intrinsic value of the human individual: "The world was created through a single man to teach that if any man has caused a single soul to perish, Scripture imputes it to him as though he had caused a whole world to perish . . ." (*m. Sanh.* 4:5; cf. Matt. 12:6; Luke 6:9).

Likewise, we hear concern among the sages about the frailty of the human condition in bearing the sometimes difficult precepts of Scripture. For example, concerning the challenge of Sabbath observance the guiding was, "the Sabbath is given to you but you are not given to the Sabbath" (*Mek. Exod.* 31:14; cf. Mark 2:27). The scope and impulse of Pharisaic Judaism are epitomized in the threefold imperative enunciated by the men of the Great Synagogue: "Be humane in judgment, raise up many disciples, and make a hedge for the Torah" (*m. Abot* 1:1).

R. STEVEN NOTLEY

The Use of the Old Testament in the New Testament

The Old Testament, especially the books of Isaiah, Deuteronomy, Psalms, and Zechariah, resonates throughout the pages of the New Testament. The citations can serve to validate an event (Matt. 4:15-16) or discussion (Rom. 3:10-18), provide an example or an illustration (Gal. 4:21ff.), or they may simply be included because the words are familiar and part of the language of early Christianity. There are two key elements to understanding early Christian Old Testament interpretation. First, what God accomplished in Jesus was decisive in salvation history and served to mark a shift in the ages. The mystery hidden from the beginning of time had been revealed in the coming of the long-awaited messianic redeemer, and salvation history had reached its culmination in him. Second, the early Christians firmly believed that they were now living in the end of times.

The citations are of two general types: explicit quotations and allusions. Quotations, whether word for word or a paraphrase, are often preceded by a formula and break into and disrupt the text (e.g., Mark 1:2). Allusions to the Old Testament can be more difficult to trace (e.g., Revelation 1) as they do not generally disrupt the text. An allusion is a reference to a text that may occur without explicitly quoting it or the source. It is assumed that the audience will pick up on the allusion, although this depends upon the individual's familiarity with the sources. One ought not polarize these two categories, but instead consider them as two points on a continuum.

The context in which to understand the use of the Old Testament in the New Testament begins with ancient Judaism. The Scriptures, as the divine Word, were central to Jewish life, and *midrash* (exegesis) was key to understanding the Scriptures. As such, Scripture played a crucial role in shaping the Jewish identity, belief system, theology, eschatology, and ethics. Furthermore, the public reading of Scripture and its use in liturgy and the synagogue ensured that the language and imagery found therein was familiar to most Jews and Gentile sympathizers. Yet the shared Scriptures also became the locus for disagreements. Divergent movements within Judaism sought to validate beliefs and ideologies through the "correct" interpretation of the text. A variety of approaches and exegetical methods were employed (literalist, midrashic, allegorical, and pesher) which prevented interpretation from becoming purely arbitrary and subjective.

A careful comparison of the New Testament and ancient Jewish usage of the Old Testament reveals a fundamental continuity. The authors of the New Testament also viewed the Scriptures as divine revelation and maintained that they were applicable to life's present circumstances. They employed the same exegetical methods. Particular similarities exist between the New Testament authors and the Qumran community. Both embraced a revelational model of interpretation and had a strong eschatological orientation. And both had a leader whose interpretation of the Old Testament shaped their respective movements — the Teacher of Righteousness in Qumran and Jesus in early Christianity. Jesus was himself engaged in the interpretation of the Old Testament, often in conversation with the Jewish religious leadership over issues related to the Law. His fresh, authoritative teaching was grounded in his eschatological and revelational approach to the text.

Early Christian exegesis seems to have gained impetus as followers of Jesus were confronted by the need to understand and explain the life, death, and resurrection of Jesus, the Messiah, in the light of Jewish expectations and the broader scope of salvation history. It is difficult to say whether the exegetical enterprise began as part of a defensive apologetic, an aggressive evangelistic/missions campaign, or out of a need to shore up inner support within their community. Certainly, it was part of the process of legitimation, similar to that which occurred in Qumran, as the early Christians first struggled and then parted ways with Judaism. During this process there would have been the need to reformulate numerous issues pertinent to their communities. A reconsideration of issues such as the role of the Law, identity of the people of God, means of salvation, Christology, *theo*logy, ethics, and eschatology was ultimately validated by Old Testament texts.

The text-form of the Old Testament quotations offers further clues for understanding its use in the New. The text-form in Judaism was somewhat fluid during the period of the composition of the New Testament documents, and adjustments were made to the Old Testament text in light of the usage. While it is somewhat true that the Bible of the early Christians was the Septuagint, there is evidence that some authors of the New Testament used additional Hebrew or mixed text-form manuscripts. Employing Jewish exegetical models, translators and interpreters would make slight adjustments to the text to support their argument. Thus the theology of the scribe/community is at times encoded within the text itself (e.g., Matt. 4:15-16; 12:18-21).

The enigma of and fascination with the use of the Old Testament in the New Testament lies in attempting to describe each occurrence. There are numerous theories. It has been argued that the New Testament authors are proof-texting, meaning that a passage is removed from its context and employed with a different meaning in a new context. While there appear to be some examples of this in the New Testament (e.g., Matt. 2:15 = Hos. 11:1), this explanation is considered too simplistic to account for the majority of Old Testament uses. Other scholars have countered that there is a demonstrated concern for the original context. Some have argued that there is evidence of a typological usage, in which historical events in Israel's past are thought to prefigure the greater event in the New Testament. More recently, an emphasis has been placed upon the exegetical enterprise within early Christianity, suggesting that the New Testament authors were not merely citing the Old Testament; rather, they were drawing upon exegetical work that was ongoing within the various Christian communities.

In the Old Testament citations in the New Testament, we have a deposit of early Christian exegesis. The sustained emphasis upon various Old Testament passages related to Christology and messiahship (e.g., Isa. 7:14; 9:2-7; 11:1-6; 42:1-4; 53; Psalm 2; Num. 24:17; Zechariah 9–14) found throughout the New Testament and especially in John, Matthew, and Hebrews provides evidence of a much larger enterprise. Similarly, Paul's use of the Old Testament in Romans and Galatians, which together contain half of the Old Testament references of Paul's letters, is diverse both in its usage and content. See, for example, the series of passages in Rom. 3:9-20 used to demonstrate that all humanity is under the power of sin, Paul's midrashic use of the Abraham tradition in Romans 4, and the allegorical treatment of Sarah/Hagar narrative in Galatians 4. Revelation provides another distinctive example. It is shaped by constant interaction with the Old Testament text by way of allusion, not direct quotation. The Old Testament reverberates throughout the New Testament for those who have ears to hear.

FOR FURTHER READING

Beale, G. K., and D. A. Carson. *Commentary on the New Testament Use of the Old Testament.* Grand Rapids: Baker, 2007.

Hubner, Hans. "New Testament Interpretation of the Old Testament." In *Hebrew Bible/Old Testament: The History of Its Interpretation.* Vol. 1/1: *From the Beginnings to the Middle Ages (until 1300),* 332-72. Edited by Magne Sæbø. Göttingen: Vandenhoeck & Ruprecht, 1996.

Longenecker, Richard N. *Biblical Exegesis in the Apostolic Period.* Grand Rapids: Eerdmans, 1975.

Vermes, Geza. "Bible and Midrash: Early Old Testament Exegesis." In *Cambridge History of the Bible.* Vol. 1: *From the Beginnings to Jerome,* 199-231. Edited by Peter R. Ackroyd and Craig F. Evans. Cambridge: Cambridge University Press, 1970.

RICHARD BEATON

The Gospels and Acts

The Gospels appear first in the New Testament. This is not because they were written first, but because their subject matter is of first importance. They bear witness to the priority of the life, death, and resurrection of Jesus to the entire witness of the Bible. Each in its own way, they help us to understand that the story of the Bible is only one story, which runs with essential continuity from the story of ancient Israel to the story of the early church. This is God's story, and God's story cannot but pivot around the good news of the advent of Jesus as God's Son and Messiah.

What is a "Gospel"? Originally, these four books (and others like them) are unlikely to have been known by this name. In fact, the unadorned titles of these books as they appear in Greek would be "According to Mark," "According to Matthew," and so on. At a basic level, there is only one "Gospel," who is Jesus Christ, and these books are simply different ways of portraying him. Placing these four books side by side in the New Testament, the ancient church bore witness to the fundamental unity of their focus and subject, Jesus, while at the same time allowing that Jesus' significance could be faithfully rendered in more than one way.

Scholars now largely agree that the Gospels are most like examples of the ancient genre of "biography." The ancient philosopher and biographer Plutarch (ca. A.D. 45-125) wrote of his biographical approach: "As portrait painters work to get their likenesses from the face and the look of the eyes, in which the character appears, and pay little attention to other parts of the body, so I must be allowed to dwell especially on things that express the inner character of these men, and through them portray their lives." This description helps us to understand why we have four Gospels and why they do not agree on all of their particular elements. Like Plutarch, those who wrote the "lives" of Jesus we now know as "Gospels" were like portrait painters who selected what they regarded as most important about him. Often drawing from the same reservoir of episodes and traditions about Jesus, they chose the material and placed it within a narrative framework that helped to highlight what they regarded as most significant about Jesus. Like Plutarch's biographies, the Gospels are not mere chronicles and are not concerned with telling us everything just as it actually took place.

What can we expect of the Gospels, if they belong to the family of Roman biography? (1) They will focus on Jesus' public life as an adult. (2) They will demonstrate why Jesus was so important as to have merited treatment in a biography. (3) The episodes they report will not be fictional accounts but will be interpreted in sometimes fresh ways by their inclusion in a narrative representation of Jesus' life. (4) They will present Jesus as an example worthy of emulation — as one who embodies the values and commitments of those for whom the Gospels were first written.

This last point encourages us to regard the Gospels as written first and foremost for Christians. In fact, each of the Gospels opens in a way that assumes on the part of its readership a belief that Jesus is God's agent of salvation. This assumption is not likely to have been granted, and certainly not shared, by nonbelievers reading the first column of a Gospel scroll in the ancient Roman world.

Of course, the analogy with Plutarch's approach should not be pushed too far. This is because biographies in Roman antiquity emphasized the life, virtues, and accomplishments of their subject, whereas biographical material in the Old Testament and in Jewish writing roughly contemporary with Jesus highlighted instead God's call on the lives of persons, on the character of their divine mission, and on how that mission was accomplished. Clearly, the Gospels share these emphases with Israelite biography. From the perspective of the Gospels, a narrative of the life of Jesus belongs to a much larger story, which is nothing less than the story of God's creating and redeeming purpose.

Telling a story is always difficult in this way. "How far back in the story must I go in order to make sense of the story itself? Where shall I begin?" we ask. The Gospel of **Matthew** begins with a genealogy — a very important point of beginning in Matthew's world, though not necessarily so today. In many times and places, including the context of the Old Testament and the Roman world of the 1st century, the status of one's ancestors determined one's status within the community. The question, "Who am I?" could be addressed in terms of one's ancestral heritage. Thus Matthew claims that the story of Jesus cannot be understood apart from an initial understanding of his parentage, and especially his relationship to Abraham and David. Having established this, Matthew is in a position to begin his account of Jesus' birth, which is seasoned generously with affirmations of divine intervention and direction and scriptural fulfillment.

Matthew proceeds from these beginnings to explore more fully in his narrative the vital relationship between Jesus' life and the history and hope of God's engagement with Israel. It is within this relationship that Matthew develops his concern with the church. Among the Evangelists, Matthew alone employs the Greek word for "church," *ekklēsia* (Matt. 16:18; 18:17), and one finds in the pages of this Gospel heightened concerns with church discipline, liturgical practices, and mission (e.g., 6:9-13; 18; 26:26-28; 28:16-20). Here the Evangelist has brought the traditions about Jesus to bear on the needs of still-youthful Christian communities struggling with important issues of power and authority, identity and witness, and so, of internal behavior and relations. Insisting on the church's roots in the mission and message of Jesus and its continuity with historic Israel, Matthew works to aid his readers as they endeavor to find their way as a new religious movement in the Mediterranean world of the 1st century.

Mark's approach is somewhat different, but the effect he achieves is similar. **Mark** mentions nothing of Jesus' birth and says nothing of Jesus' family until Jesus returns to his hometown to preach (Mark 6:1-6). Where does Mark begin? As his opening citation of Isaiah 40 makes clear, for Mark the beginning of the Gospel is in Israel's hope for the coming of God to bring consolation to Israel. Opening his narrative in this way, Mark claims that the coming of Jesus is nothing less than the coming of God to bring salvation.

This opening emphasis on Jesus' identity is crucial to a Gospel where the identity of Jesus seems often to be in question. Numerous characters make inquiries about Jesus' identity, and the Gospel as a whole turns on the question Jesus himself raises at its midpoint, "Who do you say that I am?" (Mark 8:29). Mark is not concerned with Jesus' identity for speculative reasons, however, but so that he can develop a perspective on God's work and on authentic discipleship that will address the realities of the lives of those who seek to follow Jesus, and who experience suffering because of it.

Luke takes a still different approach. Unlike Mark, he devotes a great deal of attention to the birth of Jesus — tying it, first, into his account of the birth of John the Baptist, and, more profoundly, into God's promises to Abraham, now coming to fruition (Luke 1:5–2:52). For Luke, then, the story of Jesus cannot be understood apart from its location at the center of God's ancient purpose to bring salvation to the whole world through the people of Abraham. The narrative Luke weaves is fundamentally oriented around the theme of salvation — not as a merely spiritual or primarily future matter, but as a matter that embraces life in the present. Salvation signals the restoration of the integrity of human life and the commissioning of the community of God's people to put God's grace into practice among themselves and toward ever-widening circles of outsiders. Early on, Jesus is identified as savior (2:11), and in this role he communicates the presence of divine salvation for those who dwell on the outward bounds of acceptable society. Luke's Gospel is thus concerned with the history and practices that define the community of God's people, and with the invitation to participate in God's redemptive project.

John initiates his narrative of Jesus' adult life and ministry by tracing Jesus' beginnings neither to his baptism nor birth, nor even to scriptural promise, but to the eternal past. Echoing the words of Genesis, John writes, "In the beginning . . ." (John 1:1), then affirms that the Son of God, God's own Word, was God's agent of creation and, indeed, was God. For John, then, the mural of Jesus' life is not complete unless it is set in relation to all eternity and the whole cosmos.

Readers who expect Gospels to center on the life, death, and resurrection of Jesus may be puzzled by the beginning of the Gospel of John, with its commentary on the creation story of Genesis 1. This beginning does not segregate Jesus from concerns with the people of God in the 1st century A.D., however. In fact, throughout the Gospel, Jesus is shown to be superior to Jewish ancestors in the faith (John 4:12; 6:32; 8:35-38) and to replace by his own person both Jewish feasts and Jewish institutions (2:1-11, 19-22; 6:32-41; 7:37-39). What we learn, rather, is that the significance of Jesus cannot be contained in such disputes, and

Apostles gathered at the Last Supper; fresco from rock-carved church at Göreme, Turkey.
(© Gilles Mermet / Art Resource, NY)

that the good news is for all times and places. Near the end of the Gospel of John we find a purpose statement: "Now Jesus did many other signs in the presence of the disciples, which are not written in this book. But these are written so that you may come to believe that Jesus is the Christ, the Son of God, and that through believing you may have life in his name" (20:30-31). Those first disciples in whose presence Jesus performed signs are thus distinguished from those who would come later and who did not witness his earthly ministry. John is clear. Even if these later disciples do not witness the ministry of Jesus firsthand, they do have the Gospel and, just as Jesus' significance cannot be relegated to the annals of 1st-century Palestine, so their faith and discipleship cannot be dismissed as second rate.

Plainly, the New Testament Gospels orient us to the significance of Jesus' life in different ways, but all of them situate him squarely within the purpose of God and present Jesus as the fulfillment both of Israel's hopes and of God's plan to bring salvation.

Thus far, we have discussed the Gospel of Luke alongside the books of Matthew, Mark, and John. This is justifiable in that, for the New Testament, these four have served as "the fourfold Gospel canon." Indeed, together these four books comprised one of the first collections of Christian literature that circulated in the early church. Its particular relation to the **Acts of the Apostles** nonetheless gives to the Gospel of Luke a special character apart from the other Gospels.

At the onset of Acts we read, "In the first book, Theophilus, I wrote about all that Jesus did and taught from the beginning until the day when he was taken up to heaven, after giving instructions through the Holy Spirit to the apostles whom he had chosen" (Acts 1:1-2). This provides an obvious bridge back to the beginning of the Gospel of Luke, which likewise contains a dedication to Theophilus (Luke 1:1-4). If Matthew, Mark, and John are most reminiscent of the traditions of biography in Israel and in Roman antiquity, Luke, now bundled together with Acts, is most related to traditions of history-writing, or historiography, in ancient Greece, Rome, and Israel. As history-writing, the Gospel of Luke and the Acts of the Apostles, or Luke-Acts, would have functioned above all to tie the story of Jesus' life, death, and resurrection into the story of the early church, and both into the ancient and eternal story of the outworking of God's purpose in and through people who have oriented their lives radically in relation to him. Read together, Luke and Acts are focused on the invitation to participate faithfully as God's people in God's redemptive purpose.

If Luke and Acts are two parts of the same story, why are they separated in the New Testament? On the one hand, this is because of the striking similarity among the Gospels, and especially among the Gospels of Matthew, Mark, and Luke. Other reasons have to do with the particular role of Acts in the New Testament. Located between the Gospels and the collections of letters in the New Testament, the book of Acts serves two immediate functions. First, it provides a bridge from Jesus to church, showing how the movement initiated by and surrounding Jesus in Palestine developed into communities of believers throughout the Roman Empire. This "bridge" supports the spread of the good news to the Gentiles throughout the world. Second, the chronology of Acts provides an outline on which to hang the people, places, and events of the New Testament era. Without Luke's historical narrative, we would know little of the chronology and progression of the Pauline mission, and we would grasp less fully the role of Peter the apostle and James the brother of Jesus in the earliest days of the Christian movement.

JOEL B. GREEN

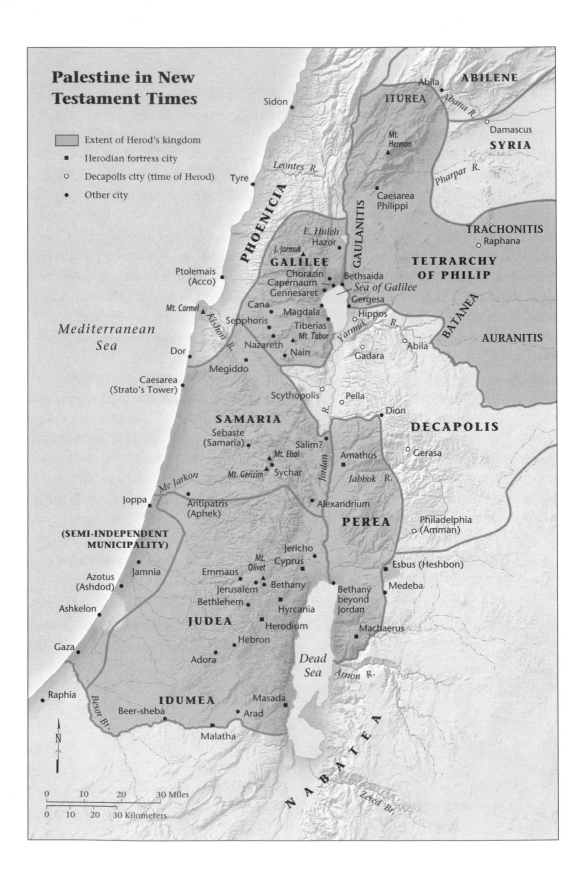

Palestine in New Testament Times

Extent of Herod's kingdom
■ Herodian fortress city
○ Decapolis city (time of Herod)
● Other city

ABILENE
Abila
ITUREA
Damascus
SYRIA
Mt. Hermon
Sidon
Abana R.
Pharpar R.
Leontes R.
PHOENICIA
Caesarea Philippi
Tyre
GAULANITIS
TRACHONITIS
Raphana
E. Huleh
Hazor
TETRARCHY OF PHILIP
J. Jarmuk
GALILEE
Chorazin
Bethsaida
Ptolemais (Acco)
Capernaum
Sea of Galilee
BATANEA
Gennesaret
Gergesa
Mt. Carmel
Cana
Magdala
Hippos
Sepphoris
Tiberias
Yarmuk R.
Mediterranean Sea
Kishon R.
Nazareth
Mt. Tabor
Nain
Abila
AURANITIS
Dor
Gadara
Megiddo
Scythopolis
Pella
Dion
Caesarea (Strato's Tower)
SAMARIA
DECAPOLIS
Sebaste (Samaria)
Salim?
Amathus
Mt. Ebal
Gerasa
Mt. Gerizim
Sychar
Jordan R.
Jabbok R.
Joppa
Me Jarkon
Antipatris (Aphek)
Alexandrium
PEREA
Philadelphia (Amman)
(SEMI-INDEPENDENT MUNICIPALITY)
Jericho
Esbus (Heshbon)
Azotus (Ashdod)
Jamnia
Emmaus
Mt. Olivet
Cyprus
Medeba
Jerusalem
Bethany
Ashkelon
Bethlehem
Hyrcania
Bethany beyond Jordan
JUDEA
Herodium
Gaza
Hebron
Machaerus
Adora
Dead Sea
Raphia
IDUMEA
Masada
Arnon R.
Beer-sheba
Arad
Malatha
NABATEA
Besor Br.
Zered Br.

0   10   20   30 Miles
0   10   20   30 Kilometers

Matthew

Often described as the canonical Gospel with the most Jewish flavor, Matthew is a natural bridge between the Testaments by showing how Christianity grows out of and fulfills the history of redemption initiated in the Hebrew religion of the Old Testament. The connection between Christianity and Judaism emerges in the very first verse, which establishes Jesus as a direct descendant of David, forefather of the prophesied Messiah, and of Abraham, forefather of the entire Hebrew nation (see Isa. 9:6-7; 11:1-10; Gen. 17:1-8). The Gospel portrays Jesus as the new and greater Moses who not only upholds the validity of the Hebrew law but actually intensifies it. At the same time, Jesus redefines the contemporary Jewish understanding of the Messiah and his kingdom. The kingdom of God that Jesus ushers will not liberate the Jewish people from oppression by the Roman government but will make possible their rescue from the eternal consequences of sin. In addition, Matthew includes elements that stress the universality of the ospel — the widening of the door of salvation to allow unfettered access to the Gentiles — culminating in the Great Commission (Matt. 28:19-20).

Composition

Most of the Gospel of Mark appears in Matthew, worded in a way that aids Jewish understanding. (Mark appears to address a Gentile audience.) Matthew prefaces the Marcan material with birth and infancy narratives about Jesus and weaves in lengthy didactic discourses (five in all, to parallel the Five Books of Moses, Genesis through Deuteronomy). Some of these discourses grow out of shorter teaching sections in Mark. Order and symmetry characterize the literary structure of Matthew both in detail and overall arrangement.

Authorship and Date

Scholars refer to the writers of the Gospels as "evangelists" — lit., "proclaimers of the good news." As with most books in the Bible, the text of Matthew does not identify its author, but in the early history of the church the book became attributed to the relatively obscure apostle Matthew (called "Levi" in Mark and Luke), a Jewish tax collector for the Roman government prior to answering Jesus' call to discipleship. The 2nd-century church father Papias says that Matthew wrote "oracles" (in context, most naturally understood as a "Gospel") in Hebrew or Aramaic. But careful study of the Greek text argues against its having been translated from a Semitic original. So either Matthew wrote in both a Semitic and the Greek language, or he wrote in a Semitic style of Greek.

Our earliest indication of the existence of Matthew's Gospel comes from Ignatius, bishop of Antioch (A.D. 98-117). The early migration to Antioch of Christian disciples fleeing persecution suggests that the Gospel may have been written in or near this Syrian city (see Acts 11:19-27). Matthew almost certainly used Mark as a source, and the proposed dates for composition of this Gospel range from ca. A.D. 75 to 90.

1:1-17 Jesus, the Messianic Heir of David

Cf. Luke 3:23-38.

Matthew's genealogy of Jesus emphasizes his legitimacy as heir to King David (promised a perpetual dynasty in 2 Sam. 7:12-16) and his embodiment of the Messiah promised by the Old Testament prophets (e.g., Isaiah 11). The Gospel writer presents the genealogical list in three parts, beginning with Abraham as father of the Hebrew nation (Gen. 12:1-13). Each section includes 14 generations. (The final group counts both Jesus' adoptive father Joseph and his biological mother Mary.) This arrangement accommodates Matthew's purpose of highlighting Jesus' Davidic ancestry. The initial group ends with David in the final, emphatic position (vv. 2-6a). Also, Hebrew consonants represented not only sounds but numbers, too, and the numerical values of the consonants in David's name add up to 14 (d = 4, v = 6). The 14 generations that make up each of the last two groups of Jesus' ancestors give a numerical reminder of his Davidic descent. The "deportation to Babylon," highlighted by its position at the end of the second group (v. 11), marks the end of the monarchy in Judah. The mention of this event also anticipates the promised resumption of the Davidic dynasty in the person of Jesus Christ, who ends the third group and culminates the entire genealogy.

The incompleteness of the genealogy, which portrays general ancestor-descendant relationships in specific father-son terms, is not unusual in the Bible (see 1 Chronicles 1–9), but the inclusion of women is. Also, Matthew includes Gentile women and some that had "reputations": Tamar, who committed incest with her father-in-law (Genesis 38); Rahab, the harlot rescued from Jericho (Joshua 2); Ruth, the Moabite convert to Yahwism; and the adulterous Bathsheba, the "[wife] of Uriah," a non-Hebrew. Thus Matthew announces Jesus' messiahship for all people — Gentiles as well as Jews, women as well as men, sinners as well as saints (contrast Tamar, Rahab, and Bathsheba with Ruth and Mary; the "bad" Davidic kings Ahaz, Manasseh, and Amon with "good" kings Asa, Jehoshaphat, Hezekiah, and Josiah).

By emphasizing Jesus as the Davidic Messiah prophesied in the Old Testament, Matthew plays into the expectation that deliverance from foreign oppression and a resurgence of the Judahite monarchy lies in the near future (see Zechariah). The rest of the Gospel will demonstrate how Jesus' life and ministry redefined these expectations in spiritual terms.

1:18-25 Marriage, Birth, and Adoption

Cf. Luke 1:26-38; 2:1-21.

In New Testament times, Jewish engagement and marriage were equally binding, and breaking an engagement required getting a divorce. Engagement did not obtain the sexual privileges of marriage, however. To avoid shaming Mary, the honorable and compassionate "husband" Joseph determines to divorce his pregnant fiancée on the quiet. But a visionary angelic messenger clues Joseph in to the divine origin of Mary's conception, the divine nature of the son she will bear, and the redemptive purpose of his life in fulfillment of prophecy (v. 23 quotes Isa. 7:14). Joseph marries his bride, but he abstains from sexual relations with her until after she gives birth (ca. 6 B.C.). That the official marriage publicly masked Mary's miraculous conception by the Holy Spirit becomes known during Jesus' adult ministry, when his fellow Nazarenes still consider him the son of Joseph (13:54-56).

In naming Jesus, Joseph again demonstrates obedience to the angel's instruction (v. 21) and confirms his adoption of Jesus as his son-an adoption that establishes legally Jesus' Davidic descent and thereby his legitimacy as dynastic heir (v. 20, "Joseph, son [= descendant] of David . . ."). Since "Yahweh [the Lord] *is* salvation" (the meaning of Hebrew "Joshua," for which "Jesus" is the Greek equivalent), Jesus saves his people by embodying God in their midst — "Immanuel" (= "God with us").

2 Magi, Murder, and Migration

David hailed from Bethlehem, and Jesus' birth there reinforces his embodiment of the Davidic Messiah promised by the prophets (e.g., Mic. 5:2, quoted in v. 6). "Herod the king" (v. 1) refers to Herod the Great, an Idumean (= Edomite, and therefore a descendant of Esau [Genesis 36]) who ruled Palestine under the authority of the Roman government (see "World of the New Testament" [499-506]). The "magi," not kings but members of a caste reputed for their knowledge of astrology, medicine, and natural science, probably came from Persia or perhaps from Babylonia. Matthew does not indicate how many magi asked Herod for help in locating the infant whose "star" (a long-tailed comet?) they pursued. Their calling him "King of the Jews" threatens the unpopular Herod, so that he starts gathering intelligence for a secret mission to murder his perceived rival. Based on prophetic

The Temptations of Jesus

Matthew, Mark, and Luke all portray Jesus as tempted (or "tested"; the Greek allows either translation) for 40 days after his baptism (Matt. 4:1-11; Mark 1:12-13; Luke 4:1-13; cf. Heb. 2:18; 4:15). During the course of Jesus' ministry, adversaries and even allies continued the tempting/testing begun by Satan in the wilderness (see Mark 8:11-13, 32-33; 10:2; 12:13-17 par.), so that at the end Jesus could say to the disciples, "You are those who have stood by me in my trials" (Luke 22:28). In the garden on the night he was arrested, Jesus warned his disciples to pray that they might not enter into temptation/testing (Mark 14:38 par.), even as he himself struggled to prepare for his most daunting trial, his passion and death (vv. 33-36 par.; cf. Heb. 5:7-9). On the cross, bystanders tempted him with painkilling wine (Mark 15:23) and mocked him in terms reminiscent of both Satan's wilderness temptation (15:29-30; cf. Luke 4:9) and scriptural portraits of righteous sufferers (Mark 15:26-32; cf. "psalms of the righteous sufferer," the Isaian Servant Songs, and esp. Wis. 2:12-24). Jesus' "cry of dereliction" (Mark 15:34; Matt. 27:46) marks the pinnacle of all Jesus' trials and probably reflects ancient belief that God may temporarily "hide God's face" from the righteous in order to test the content of the heart (2 Chr. 32:31; T. Jos. 2:4-7). The cry echoes Ps. 22:1 and addresses God as "my God": Jesus has not "lost faith" but has

Traditional Mount of Temptation near Jericho. (*Richard Cleave, Pictorial Archive*)

endured his trials to the end. He is "tried and true" (Heb. 2:10, 17-18; 5:8-9; 13:12).

The trials of Jesus need to be seen against the backdrop of conventional Jewish and Christian traditions about temptation or testing. Biblical and postbiblical authors took for granted that trials of faith are inevitable in the life of the righteous (Sir. 2:1; Jdt. 8:25-27). The agent could be God, as so often in the Hebrew Bible (e.g., Gen. 22:1; Exod. 16:4; Deut. 8:2-5; Ps. 66:10), Satan (under various aliases) or his human agents (e.g., T. Job; Jub. 17:15-16; 1 Cor. 7:5), or human passion (Jas. 1:12-15). In trials of seduction ("temptations") the tempter makes a deceptive offer of benefit or pleasure (Luke 4:3, 6-7; 1 Tim. 6:9). In trials of af-

fliction ("tests") the agent causes pain or suffering that tempts the afflicted to abandon faith (1 Thess. 3:5; 1 Pet. 4:12; 5:8-9; Rev. 3:10). But the two sorts of trial blur, and in Greek both are designated with the single word *peirasmos*. New Testament views of temptation/testing are influenced by the apocalyptic expectation that the end will be preceded by a time of eschatological affliction (Gk. *thlipsis*) or testing (Mark 13:19; Rev. 3:10; cf. Dan. 12:1). The appropriate response to temptation/testing is always endurance (Gk. *hypomonē*; Rom. 5:3-4; Jas. 1:3-4).

Jesus' endurance of his testing is held up as a model for Christians to emulate (1 Pet. 2:21; 4:1), and proclaimed the basis for his empathy for his disciples whenever they are tested (Heb. 4:15). Paul holds that Jesus' "faith" or "obedience unto death" is the very grounds for our salvation: by it Christ reversed the effects of Adam's disobedience (Rom. 5:19). There are hints in Mark and Hebrews that it was on account of Christ's endurance of testing that God accepted his death as the perfect sacrificial offering, able to atone for sin (see esp. Heb. 5:8-9). Outside the New Testament, such a connection between endurance and redemptive sacrifice is attested in Wis. 3:5-6; 4 Macc. 17:21-22; and some early Jewish interpretations of the sacrifice of Isaac (e.g., *Bib. Ant.* 40.2, 5-6). The conviction of New Testament authors is that Christians should pray to avoid trial but need not fear it, for they need not rely on their own power alone. Christ opens blind eyes, so that the tested may view their trials in the proper light and follow Jesus in the way (Mark 10:46-52). He gives power to conquer the weakness of will that is otherwise our human lot (Rom. 7:24-25). Like the strengthening angel who helped Christ in the garden (Luke 22:43), the Holy Spirit stands ready to help those in need (Mark 13:11; Rom. 8:1-27). With the testing, God will provide the way out (1 Cor. 10:13).

Bibliography

Garrett, Susan R. *The Temptations of Jesus in Mark's Gospel.* Grand Rapids: Eerdmans, 1998.

Gibson, Jeffrey B. *The Temptations of Jesus in Early Christianity.* JSNTSup 112. Sheffield: Sheffield Academic, 1995.

SUSAN R. GARRETT

information gleaned from the religious leaders of Jerusalem, Herod points the magi toward Bethlehem with orders to report back when they find the infant-king, ostensibly so Herod can worship him too. The star that guided the magi to Palestine leads them directly to Jesus, to whom they present gifts befitting a king. ("Myrrh" was an expensive perfume.) Herod's attempted trickery fails when, at God's visionary prompting, the magi slip home by an alternative route so that they do not have to reveal the baby's whereabouts to his would-be murderer.

Joseph's response to another angelic warning further ensures Jesus' survival. He moves his family to Egypt, outside the range of Herod's rule. Thus Matthew reapplies to Jesus the prophecy of Hosea commemorating God's calling his "son," the Hebrew nation, out of Egypt (Hos. 11:1; cf. Exod. 4:22ff.). Outmaneuvered by the magi but apparently unaware of Jesus' escape to Egypt, an angry Herod slaughters all Bethlehem's baby boys in an attempt to kill the perceived threat to his throne. In describing the mournful results of Herod's brutality, Matthew refers to Jeremiah's portrayal of weeping Hebrew mothers separated from their exiled children (v. 18; Jer. 31:15).

Two more dreams give further guidance to Joseph. The first reveals that Herod's death (4 B.C.) has made it safe to take Jesus back to Palestine. The second keeps the family moving north to Galilee on account of the succession of Herod's son Archelaus to power in Judea (where Bethlehem lay). Note that another son assumed rule over Galilee — Herod Antipas, regretful beheader of the John the Baptist. By highlighting Jesus' residency in Nazareth, Matthew associates him with the messianic "branch" of Old Testament prophecy (e.g., Isa. 11:1).

3 John and His Baptism of Jesus

Cf. Mark 1:2-11; Luke 3:1-22.

Sometime during Jesus' residency in Nazareth, his relative John begins calling the

The Jordan River near Yardenit, traditional site of Jesus' baptism. *(Richard Cleave, Pictorial Archive)*

Jews to repentance to make them fit for the soon-to-arrive "kingdom of heaven" — a phrase unique to Matthew. (The other evangelists use the synonymous "kingdom of God"). Matthew identifies John as the forerunner of the Lord prophesied in Isa. 40:3. John's hairy garb and mission of spiritual cleansing (through baptism in water) make him the Elijah-like prophet foretold in Mal. 4:5-6 (cf. 2 Kgs. 1:8). Like the second Elijah, John uses several metaphors to convey the coming judgmental day of the Lord.

John's baptism grows out of the regular practice of ritual bathing, mandated by Mosaic law (e.g., Exod. 29:4). But the baptism of John suffices for a lifetime, since it signifies purification not of the body but of the heart — cleansing from the inside out. John, the desert-dwelling nonconformist, sees through the false piety of the Hebrew religious establishment, epitomized in the Sadducees, who dominated the high priesthood, and the more numerous Pharisees, who over time came to be associated with strict adherence to the Law. John preempts their claim to spiritual security as members of the chosen line of Abraham and refuses to baptize the false penitents.

John tries to refuse to baptize Jesus, too. Having acknowledged Jesus' superiority (v. 11), John protests that it is he himself who needs baptism by Jesus (v. 14). But Jesus insists on setting an example for his followers, whose emulative cleansing will "fulfill all righteousness" (v. 15). Jesus' baptism inaugurates his formal, three-year ministry. His visible empowerment by the Holy Spirit and the audible approval of God the Father equip him for his mission.

4:1-11   Jesus Dismisses the Devil's Dares

Cf. Mark 1:12-13; Luke 4:1-13.

By passing three tests of obedience to laws God established through Moses, Jesus proves his worthiness for the difficult task ahead (see "The Temptations of Jesus" [525-26]). His success in defying the Devil ("accuser"), whose purpose is to gather condemnatory evidence against Jesus, is made even more significant by his suffering the privation of creature comforts, human companionship, and food for 40 days. Jesus first resists the temptation to use his power to put first the satisfaction of his own physical needs and desires (v. 4; cf. Deut. 8:3). The second test anticipates his crucifixion: he refuses publicly to prove his divine Sonship by invoking the power of God the Father to save him from certain, physical death (vv. 6-7; cf. Deut. 6:16). The Devil even quotes Scripture (Ps. 91:11-12) in an attempt to get Jesus to doubt God's affirmation at his baptism (compare v. 6 and 3:17). The "holy city" (v. 5) refers to Jerusalem. Scholars have suggested several identifications for the "pinnacle of the temple." Finally, Jesus refuses to compromise his faithfulness to God for the promise of selfish gain (vv. 9-11; cf. Deut. 6:13; Exod. 20:3-5). The Devil suggests that the "kingdoms of the world" are his to give, but his obedience to Jesus' order, "Begone, Satan!" betrays his subordination. In verse 11, angels minister to Jesus not to fulfill a dare by the Devil (v. 6) but to reward Jesus for his steadfast obedience to God.

4:12-25   Jesus' Ministry Begins

Cf. Mark 1:14-39.

Learning of the arrest of John the Baptist, Jesus withdraws to Galilee. Capernaum becomes the base for his ministry — another development Matthew sees as fulfilling Old Testament prophecy (vv. 14-16; cf. Isa. 9:1-2). Concentrating Jesus' activities in "Galilee of the Gentiles ['nations']," inhabited by a mixed population of Jews and non-Jews, anticipates the application of the new covenant to all peoples.

With John in prison, Jesus carries forward the call to repentance (v. 17; cf. 3:2). Recruiting helpers proves an easy task: the fishing teams of brothers Simon Peter and Andrew and then James and John join Jesus without delay. Teaching, proclamation of the kingdom, and healing characterize the rapidly growing ministry. The spread of Jesus' reputation north into Syria, east to Transjordan (where most of the 10 autonomous, Greek cities of the "Decapolis" lay), and south to Jerusalem and Judea attracts to him a multitudinous following.

5–7 Teaching the Multitudes: The Sermon on the Mount

5:1-16 The Beatitudes and the Cost of Discipleship Cf. Luke 6:20-23; 14:34-35.

Like an ancient rabbi, Jesus teaches his followers from a seated position. He opens his mouth to speak the life-giving "word that proceeds out of the mouth of God" (cf. 4:4). With nine "Beatitudes" (from Latin *beatus,* "happy, blissful, blessed") Jesus congratulates the discouraged, mournful, meek, persecuted, and others deemed weak by worldly standards but righteous by God. "Blessed be" does not mean that such people should be happy with their current circumstances; rather, the declaration promises them heavenly reward (v. 12).

Nevertheless, the *goal* of moral goodness lies not in the receipt of personal reward but in public witness that directs others to the worship of God (cf. 6:1). Jesus instructs his followers that, unlike the pure salt used to season food today, the salty mix of minerals used to fertilize the fields of 1st-century Palestine could lose its taste and effectiveness.

5:17-48 Intensifying the Law Cf. Luke 6:27-36; 12:57-59; 16:18.

Jesus corrects any misconception that his

The traditional location for the Mount of Beatitudes on the northwestern shore of the Sea of Galilee, between Capernaum and Gennesaret. (Richard Cleave, Pictorial Archive)

emphasis on attitude of heart negates the requirements expressed in the Old Testament "Law" (Genesis through Deuteronomy) and "Prophets" ("Former Prophets," Joshua–2 Kings; "Latter Prophets," Isaiah–Malachi, excluding Daniel). On the contrary, the demands of Jesus' teaching *fulfill* the Law — not by expanding its outward rituals, nor by protecting it from transgression with a "fence" of auxiliary rules, but by requiring a holistically righteous approach to life, from which the keeping of God's law flows naturally. This concept does not originate with Jesus, for it permeates the Old Testament prophetical books (e.g., see Jeremiah 31, esp. vv. 31-33; contrast Amos 8). Average Jews of Jesus' day admired the Pharisees for their meticulous observance of the Mosaic law aided by the "scribes," who interpreted it. The charge to outdo them in righteousness surely seemed an impossible task (v. 20), but not for the righteous of heart, a characterization that did not fit the micromanaging religious leaders (cf. 12:34-35).

Yet Jesus' looking beyond the letter of the Law actually intensifies its requirements! Murder earns judicial condemnation, but now judgmentalism warrants damnation. Having sex with someone else's spouse breaks the Law, but now lustful looking counts as an adulterous act. The Law requires punishment to suit an offense (see Exod. 21:23ff.), but now the victim must forgo recompense *and* volunteer for further mistreatment. The Law mandates neighborly love between Hebrew compatriots (Lev. 19:18), but now the Jews must also love their foreign enemies and even pray for their persecutors. Thus Jesus defines the fulfillment of the Law not as adherence to a set of rules but as conduct that demonstrates a state of being — Godlike moral perfection, which he demands of his followers (v. 48).

Jesus acknowledges that Mosaic law permits a man to divorce his wife (vv. 31-32). The "certificate of dismissal" protects the divorcée from the false charge of deserting her husband, but she still needs a means of support, almost always provided by a male in that patriarchal society. Jesus teaches that remarriage by or to a divorcée spells adultery, and he considers the divorcing husband responsible for her economically necessitated transgression.

In New Testament times, traveling Romans (especially soldiers) routinely conscripted Jews as pedestrian porters, and this practice lies behind Jesus' instruction to "go the extra mile" (v. 41).

6:1-18 Secret Goodness Cf. Luke 11:2-4.

At first glance, Jesus' warning against public displays of piety (6:1) seems to contradict the instruction to let the light of one's good works shine (5:16). But 5:16 advocates public righteousness to stimulate praise of God, whereas 6:1 prohibits public righteousness to generate praise of oneself — hypocrisy. Jesus expounds his instruction from three commonly abused practices of piety: almsgiving, prayer, and fasting — duties that "the hypocrites" make a great show of fulfilling. Pious showiness earned a person the respect of his peers, but Jesus announces that it gets one nowhere with God. Humility in faithfulness does.

Verses 9-13 comprise "The Lord's Prayer." In our oldest and best manuscripts of Matthew, verse 13 lacks the traditional ending, "For thine is the kingdom. . . ." "Debts" (v. 12) refer to moral debts to God (i.e., sins), though the forgiven "debtors" may include those released from financial obligations in the Year of Jubilee (Lev. 25:8-55). Deliverance from evil — more accurately, the "evil one," Satan — means empowerment to resist temptation (cf. 4:1-11).

6:19-34 Treasure Leads the Heart Cf. Luke 11:34-36; 12:22-34; 16:13.

What makes a heavenly reward better than an earthly one? Jesus moves from the abstract (respect, esteem, honor) to the concrete: mammon (Aramaic for "wealth"). Heavenly treasures trump earthly ones because no one can steal them, and they do not decay. Only if a person's heart lies in heaven can he outdo the scribes and Pharisees in righteousness and thus enter God's kingdom (see 5:20). Wealth keeps the heart earthbound. A "clear" (generous) eye, unclouded by riches, illuminates the whole body for good works. A bad (stingy) eye, blinded by wealth, handicaps the rest of the body for righteousness (cf. 20:15). Jesus' assertion that service to riches and service to God are mutually exclusive reinforces his warning against

amassing wealth (vv. 22-24; cf. 19:16-24). This teaching upended the Jews' understanding of material wealth as a sign of blessing from God (e.g., Job 1–2; 42:10-17).

Jesus also recognizes the anxieties of everyday existence, so he encourages his followers to trust God to meet their basic needs, of which he is already aware (cf. vv. 8, 32). God's observable care of the rest of creation should inspire this trust, especially in light of the superior worth of human beings, made in God's image. Besides, worrying cannot lengthen one's life by even a bit. Better to focus on pursuing God's kingdom (by living righteously; 5:17ff.) and seeking the care and rewards of his righteousness (cf. 5:6). Set your priorities straight, and rest assured that God will supply your needs (v. 33).

7:1-12 Proper Treatment of Professing and False Disciples Cf. Luke 6:31, 37-42; 11:9-13.

Jesus' command not to "judge" is not a general prohibition against criticizing others; rather, it instructs Jesus' followers not to question each other's profession of discipleship, for only God knows true disciples from false ones. Instead, a person should first practice moral self-criticism and self-correction, then compassionately help restore others to complete moral health.

But nonjudgmentalism within the community must not result in its indiscriminate inclusion of those who do not even profess discipleship, lest they destroy the community from within. Jesus likens these false disciples to "dogs," who scavenged the streets for food. A scrap of sacrificed meat ("what is holy," v. 6) kindly tossed their way only invites their ravenous attack for more. Similarly, giving "swine" what they fail to value only asks for trouble.

Jesus' comments regarding "asking," "seeking," and "knocking" should be read in the light of his teaching in 6:19-34. God's granting of requests does not apply to acquiring material wealth but to benefiting from his righteous acts (cf. 6:19, 33) — empowerment to live a righteous life and entry into God's kingdom. Receipt of these good gifts from God generates the responsibility to treat others with goodness. In the "Golden Rule" (v. 12), Jesus sums up and affirms the Old Testament principles governing communal relationships.

7:13-29 Take the Hard Road Cf. Luke 6:43-49; 13:23-24.

The elusive "narrow gate" to eternal life stands for the Godlike perfection demanded in Jesus' teachings (5:48). The easily accessed wide gate and broad road, which attract the masses to a different destination — destruction! — represent the lax standards forwarded by false prophets and followed by false disciples (cf. Jeremiah 27–28). Their disregard of the demands of righteousness invalidates their claim of service to God.

Jesus instructs his followers not to let false prophets lull them to destruction down the road of indiscipline and denial; rather, they must exercise wisdom by obeying his teachings. For if they "build their house on the rock" (obey his words), they will weather the storms of persecution and at the last judgment gain eternal life. Persecution will destroy their moral backbone, and they will collapse in a heap before reaching the narrow gate to life (cf. 25:3-46).

Matthew adds to Jesus' sermon an editorial postscript that notes the multitude's amazement at the distinctively authoritative way Jesus taught (vv. 28-29). The scribes interpreted the Old Testament law, but Jesus perfected it (see 5:17).

8:1-9:8 Miracles Augment Jesus' Teaching

Cf. Mark 2:1-12; Luke 5:12-26; 7:1-10; 9:57-60.

The good fruit of Jesus' ministry authenticates his service to God, his Father, and the miracles he performs demonstrate his divine power in the physical, natural, and spiritual realms. In extending a healing touch to the untouchable "leper" — socially ostracized and prohibited from entering the temple to offer sacrifices (Leviticus 13–14) — Jesus shows compassion as well as power. He could have healed the man with just a word, as he subsequently does from a distance the servant of a centurion. This demonstration of faith by the Roman official occasions Jesus' announcement that believing Gentiles will enter the company of the elect (who feast with the Hebrew patriarchs in the kingdom of heaven), whereas the "chosen" but faithless will perish. As further examples of Jesus' fulfillment of Old Testament prophecy, Matthew records various healings, including that of Peter's mother-in-law, and exorcisms (vv. 14-17).

When a man from the educated class of scribes volunteers to follow Jesus, he makes clear that discipleship entails more than faith alone. Another disciple requests permission to fulfill important filial duties to his father first, but Jesus disallows the delay and dismisses the social obligation as insignificant compared to following him. (The request may have been to deposit the bones of his father's corpse into an ossuary, a secondary burial box, to make room in the family tomb for the next member who dies — thus Jesus' reference to letting the dead bury their own dead, v. 22.)

Some scholars take Jesus' reference to himself as the "Son of Man" (lit., "human being"; see Ps. 8:4) as carrying messianic overtones (cf. Dan. 7:13).

In ancient times as today, the winds of northern Palestine intensified as they channeled through deep gorges opening out to the Sea of Galilee. One such violent storm arose during Jesus' retreat from the pressing crowds. The terror and desperation of Jesus' comrades at sea contrast with his oblivious slumber on board. In response to their pleading, he calms the storm with a word, and their fear turns to awe as they contemplate what kind of man could possess such power over nature.

The seafaring ordeal ends near Gadara, a city in the Transjordanian Decapolis, and here Jesus conquers violence in the spiritual realm. The demons that possess two men (Mark and Luke mention only one) recognize Jesus as the "Son of God" and realize that his presence spells their punishment by exorcism before "the time" of final judgment (cf. Mark 5:1-20; Luke 8:26-39). At the demons' request, Jesus orders them into a herd of pigs, which rush to their death in the sea. The Gentile swineherds report the exorcism and the economically disastrous loss of the pigs, thus prompting the townsfolk to beg Jesus to leave the area for fear of what other miracles he might work there.

Traversing the Sea of Galilee from southeast to northwest, Jesus returns to "his own city" of

Capernaum, the base of his ministry (4:13). By proclaiming forgiven the sins of a paralyzed man (according to popular belief the cause of his physical condition; cf. John 9:1-3) — Jesus sparks in some onlooking scribes the unspoken charge of blasphemy. They fail to recognize his authority to grant such forgiveness. Jesus then heals the paralysis to show that he does, in fact, possess the unseen power to forgive sins.

9:9-17 Celebrating with Sinners

Cf. Mark 2:13-22; Luke 5:27-39.

When Jesus beckons Matthew, who collected Roman taxes at a profit, the man follows without question or delay (contrast 8:21-22). But when an entire crowd of religious undesirables joins Jesus for a meal, the purity-conscious Pharisees question the company he keeps. Jesus cites God's preference of compassion over sacrifice (Hos. 6:6) and thus clarifies his mission of mercy toward acknowledged sinners as opposed to unsullying association with self-professed saints (such as the Pharisees).

Disciples of the imprisoned John the Baptist pose their own question: "Why do Jesus' followers fail to fast?" Jesus replies that fasting would signify mourning, but the presence of Jesus the celebrated bridegroom precludes their gloom. In a foreshadowing of his death, Jesus says that one day his disciples will fast for good reason (v. 15), but for now such behavior does not fit the circumstances.

9:18-34 Still More Miracles

Cf. Mark 5:21-43; Luke 8:40-56.

Jesus' mission of mercy continues with the healing of a ritually unclean woman who in faith touches the fringe of his cloak (see Leviticus 12); the resuscitation of a child in the company of disbelieving, derisive mourners and musicians, customarily hired to play dirges at the home of the deceased; the simultaneous granting of sight to two blind men, who appeal to Jesus as the promised Davidic heir; and an exorcism that enables the de-possessed demoniac to speak.

9:35-10:42 Instructing the Apostles for Missionary Work

Cf. Mark 6:6b-13; Luke 9:1-6; 10:1-12; 12:2-9, 51-53; 14:26-27.

In Matthew's second "teachings" section, Jesus' compassion for the needy multitudes sparks his commissioning of 12 disciples as apostles ("messengers") to expand his ministry and spread the word about the arrival of the "kingdom of heaven." Corresponding in number to the 12 tribes of Israel, these "harvesters" represent the beginnings of a new community of God that will grow out of their missionary work, first among Jews (10:5-15) and then among Gentiles (vv. 16-42).

Jesus grants to the apostles power to exorcise demons, heal physical ailments, and raise the dead. The duty of verbal proclamation accompanies these acts of mercy. The itinerant ministry foreshadowed in 8:20 becomes a prescription for the apostles' mission in 10:9ff. Jesus instructs the apostles not to accumulate money or material possessions (see 6:19-21) but validates their right to practical support by those who benefit from their ministry.

Jesus gives advance warning that the work of harvesting will not be easy. The apostles will become targets of persecution, from which they should flee (10:23). Nevertheless, they must pursue their mission with fearless determination. Trust in God should supplant anxiety (vv. 19-20) and embolden them to spread widely the message Jesus gives them to proclaim (v. 27). That he too endures persecution provides moral support for their mission (v. 25). But he warns that denial of Jesus in order to avoid *physical* martyrdom will result in his disowning the denier before his Father in heaven and thus incur the denier's eternal punishment of body *and* soul (vv. 28, 32-33).

Jesus acknowledges the divisive destiny (not purpose) of his mission (10:34-36, quoting Mic. 7:6). The family strife he foretells arises not from personality conflicts or interpersonal power plays but from discipleship, which invites persecution by unbelieving relatives. To follow Jesus requires making secondary even the most fundamental human emotions and inclinations (10:37; cf. 8:21-22). Still, he shows supportive solidarity with his disciples by putting their treatment on equal terms with his own (10:40-42).

11 John's Questions, Jesus' Confidence

Cf. Luke 7:18-35; 10:13-15, 21-22.

Before his imprisonment, John acknowledged Jesus as the One whose coming he heralded (ch. 3). Perhaps John expected that the "Coming One" would use such power to liberate his faithful forerunner. Jesus answers John's doubts by sending back his emissaries as eyewitnesses to Jesus' fulfilling of Old Testament prophecies (Isa. 35:5; 61:1). Jesus confirms the Baptist's embodiment of the prophesied messenger who prepares the way for God's coming, the second Elijah whose work allays God's judgment (Mal. 3:1; 4:5-6).

Contemporaries of Jesus and John, however, fail to appreciate either one. "This generation" (v. 16) refers to the skeptical scribes and Pharisees, who label the bohemian Baptist a demoniac but condemn the socially engaged Jesus as a hedonistic reprobate. Just as unresponsive to Jesus' ministry are the cities north of the Sea of Galilee (including his home base of Capernaum), where he has performed most of his mighty works. He banishes them to Hades and compares them to the materially rich but morally bankrupt Phoenician port cities Tyre and Sidon (v. 21; cf. Isaiah 23) and to Sodom (v. 24), ancient epitome of evil.

At the conclusion of the chapter, Jesus confidently articulates his unique relationship to God the Father. Jesus' singular position qualifies him to give "rest" to the spiritually "weary and heavy-laden." The offer comes not from a relaxation of God's moral requirements, but from Jesus' partnership with them under the same "yoke."

12:1-14 Lord of the Sabbath

Cf. Mark 2:23–3:6; Luke 6:1-11.

When on a Sabbath day's walk Jesus' hungry disciples grab handfuls of wheat, the Pharisees call the action "work" (harvesting and threshing) and cry "infraction of the rules!" Jesus corrects their compassionless legalism by appealing to Mosaic law, which allows priests to work in

the temple on the Sabbath and thus break it (cf. Num. 28:9-10), for the temple (made for God) supersedes the Sabbath (made for humans' physical and spiritual well-being). As "God with us," Jesus supersedes even the temple and therefore certainly the Sabbath (vv. 7-8; cf. Hos. 6:6). Jesus continues to elevate compassion over legalism when at the Sabbath synagogue service he heals a man's withered hand. This act of mercy only cements the resolve of the hardhearted Pharisees to "destroy" Jesus.

12:15-37 The Source of Jesus' Power

Cf. Mark 3:7-30; Luke 6:17-19; 11:14-23.

Jesus flees, not from fear of the malice-bent Pharisees, but so he can further his ministry, in fulfillment of prophecy (vv. 18-21; cf. Isa. 42:1-4). But when he heals a person who is blind and mute, the Pharisees charge that his power *over* the evil thought to cause this condition itself derives *from* evil. Their charge amounts to denial of the Holy Spirit — a sin that God cannot forgive because it seals shut the door to repentance and belief. For words express the attitude of the heart and so shape how a person lives — and in the end this either justifies or condemns him before God.

12:38-50 Jesus Refuses to Offer Proof

Cf. Mark 3:31-35; Luke 8:19-21; 11:24-32.

If the scribes and Pharisees have not grasped Jesus' identity by observing the miracles he has worked, he is not about to accommodate them with a command performance to prove himself. The only sign he will give lies in the future: his three-day entombment, which parallels the prophet Jonah's seafaring sojourn in the belly of the sea creature (Jonah 1:17). The repentant inhabitants of Nineveh, the objective of Jonah's mission, and the wisdom-seeking Queen of Sheba are unlikely models of righteousness compared to the spiritually stubborn religious establishment of Jesus' day.

Verses 43-45 warn that half-baked religiosity makes a recipe for spiritual disaster. Those who respond to Jesus' activity but fail to rearrange their lives wholeheartedly will be worse off than had they never believed.

When members of Jesus' biological family approach him for a word, he identifies his disciples — willingly committed to God, his Father — as his true family. Thus Jesus follows his own requirement of subordinating biological bonds to spiritual commitments (see 10:37).

13 Jesus Teaches in Parables

Cf. Mark 4:1–6:6a; Luke 4:16-30; 8:4-19; 10:23-24; 13:20-21.

Parables comprise this third "teachings" section in Matthew. Jesus attracts such a large beachside crowd that he must board a boat and deliver his discourse anchored just offshore. Like an ancient rabbi, he sits down to teach, using stories from everyday life that carry a deeper, spiritual meaning. He explains that parables obscure his teachings for those who are not open to his message and have already dulled their spiritual senses, but parables impart greater understanding to true disciples, whose receptive eyes and ears render them ready to learn (vv. 10-17).

Jesus begins with the parable of the Sower (vv. 3-9), which illustrates the variety of responses his message will bring (vv. 18-23). Six more parables about "the kingdom" appear in verses 24-50. The wheat and the tares (vv. 24-30) teaches the coexistence of true and false disciples till the last judgment (the "harvest"; vv. 36-43). The mustard seed (vv. 31-32) and the leaven (v. 33) emphasize the amazing growth of the kingdom. The hidden treasure (v. 44) and the valuable pearl (vv. 45-46) stress the supreme worth of the kingdom. The dragnet (vv. 47-50) reiterates the different fates of true and false disciples, separated at the last judgment.

The parable of the believing scribe concludes the discourse (v. 52). The scribe's "new" treasure represents understanding gained from Jesus' teaching, and the old treasure stands for his still valuable knowledge of the Law (cf. 5:17-19).

When Jesus returns to Nazareth, the hometown crowd reacts skeptically to his teaching and miracles (vv. 53-58; cf. Mark 6:1-6), thus failing to recognize him as the Son of God. By limiting his miracle-working in this city of doubters, Jesus models his own instruction not to "throw pearls before swine" (7:6).

14 John's Death; Cause for Wonder

Cf. Mark 6:14-56; Luke 9:7-17; John 6:1-21.

Herod Antipas, ruler of Galilee, mistakes Jesus as John the Baptist come back from the dead. Herod had recently beheaded the imprisoned Baptist to please his dancing stepdaughter Salome, whose vengeful mother put her up to the grisly request. Scandal, lust, malice, and manipulation characterize the circumstances leading to John's decapitation, and he becomes the first martyred disciple of Jesus (vv. 1-12).

Responding to news of John's murder, Jesus seeks solitude (cf. 4:12). But soon the crowds find him, and he resumes his compassionate miracle-working. Five loaves of bread and two fish prove sufficient to feed 5000 men plus women and children, with a basketful of leftovers for each of his 12 disciples (vv. 13-21; cf. Mark 6:30-44; Luke 9:10-17; John 6:1-14).

Dismissing the disciples and the crowd, Jesus finally finds time alone to pray. In the morning he catches up with the storm-tossed Twelve by walking to their battered boat, now far from shore. Peter's faith prompts him to mimic the feat, but Jesus must rescue him from drowning when that faith wavers in the wind. The episode inspires the disciples' confession of Jesus' divinity.

After landing at Gennesaret, near Capernaum, Jesus continues healing the sick, often through their simply touching his cloak (cf. 9:20-22).

15:1-20 Redefining Defilement

Cf. Mark 7:1-23; Luke 11:37–12:12.

Religious leaders accuse Jesus' disciples of failing to observe the dietary law of washing hands as dictated by rabbinic tradition (Mark adds vv. 3-4 as an explanatory note for Gentile readers), but Jesus responds concerning their own mere lip service to the Law of God. Addressing the surrounding multitude, Jesus perfects their understanding of "defilement": outward observation of the dietary laws does not make a person righteous, but evil speech, which betrays the state of the heart, reveals inward uncleanness. Jesus writes off the Pharisees as spiritually "blind guides of the blind" headed for the "pit" of God's judgment (v. 14).

In Parables

Parables are extended analogies that function like lenses to enable people to see and understand. Similarly to a mirror, a parable forces people to see how truth functions in a parallel arena and then urges them to transfer that insight to their own lives. For example, the parable of the unforgiving servant tells of a magnanimous king who forgives but also expects his servant to show the same graciousness to others. The parable is a lens through which we see the character and expectations of God. Except for the example stories (see below), parables are stories with two levels of meaning, the story level through which one sees and the reality level being portrayed.

Jesus told parables to *prompt thinking and stimulate response* in relation to God. They demonstrate what God is like and what humans are to become. Parables often use both explicit and implicit questions, forcing listeners to decide about the circumstances of the parable and apply the conclusions to their own lives. Sometimes this results in self-condemnation (cf. David's response to the story of the ewe lamb, 2 Sam. 12:1-9), but more often it entails a new understanding of the character of life with God. Nearly all Jesus' parables in some way urge reception of the gospel message and obedience to the Father's will, for his parables are primarily about the kingdom of God and discipleship.

Depending on how one defines "parable," approximately one-third of Jesus' teaching in the synoptic Gospels is in parables, with no parables in the Gospel of John or the rest of the New Testament. If a parable is understood simply as a story with a moral, the Gospels contain about 40 parables. But if one includes illustrative sayings such as Jesus' teaching that one remove the beam from one's own eye before removing the speck from another's (Matt. 7:3-5), there are at least 65. The Gospel writers arranged the parables according to subject (the kingdom, Israel, future judgment, lostness, money, prayer), with most of them appearing in Matthew 13, 18, 20–22, 24–25; Mark 4, 12; and Luke 7–8, 10–20. Context, if given, is important for interpreting the parables, but with some of the parables no specific context has been preserved.

Jesus' parables are brief and symmetrical. They are quite diverse in form, length, and function. Some are addressed to the crowds generally, some to the religious authorities opposing Jesus, and some to the disciples. They feature normal aspects of Palestinian life such as family, master–servant relations, and workers. They use everyday features, but the are *not* everyday occurrences. They are more pseudorealistic than realistic, often having elements of exaggeration or surprise (e.g., a debtor owes $10 million and in the end is given over to torturers; Matt. 18:24, 34). Parables often were intended to shock, for Jesus sought to stop the nation of Israel in its tracks, make people aware of the judgment they faced, and call them back to God — messages still as relevant as ever.

Different kinds of parables are evident:

1. Similitudes, shorter, explicit comparisons using "like" or "as" and describing typical or recurring events (e.g., the parable of the leaven, Matt. 13:33);
2. Narrative parables, comparisons based on narratives describing *specific* events (e.g., the parable of the banquet, Luke 14:15-24);
3. Example stories that present a positive or negative character (or both) to imitate or to reject. Only four example stories, all in Luke, appear in Jesus' teaching: the good samaritan; the rich fool; Lazarus and the rich man; and the parable of the pharisee and the tax collector.

Some scholars would add allegories as a fourth category. An allegory is usually defined as a series of related metaphors with the result that each (or most) of the elements in the narrative correspond to some feature in reality (as in the parable of the Sower). Contrary to those who argue that parables have only one point, many parables have several points of contact between story and reality. Allegory is best seen not as a separate category but as a way of thinking. Stories with related metaphors, such as the parable of the Sower, are still narrative parables.

For centuries Christians

assigned theological significance to elements in the parables that had little to do with Jesus' intent. They made Jesus' parables mirror their own theology point for point, as though they were theology set to story, somewhat like *Pilgrim's Progress.* At the end of the 19th century Adolph Jülicher argued that Jesus' parables were not allegories, did not have allegorical correspondences, and made only one general point. These limitations are as wrong as the church's theological readings. The key in interpreting the parables is determining how Jesus' analogy works in his context, not in finding correspondences. Nearly always that key will occur at the end of the parable and often will require a reversal of expectations (e.g., the toll collector is shown to be in the right, not the Pharisee; Luke 18:9-14).

For Further Reading

Blomberg, Craig L. *Interpreting the Parables.* Downers Grove: InterVarsity, 1990.

Snodgrass, Klyne R. *Stories with Intent.* Grand Rapids: Eerdmans, 2008.

Stein, Robert H. *An Introduction to the Parables of Jesus.* Philadelphia: Westminster, 1981.

KLYNE SNODGRASS

15:21-39 Jesus Reaches Out to Gentiles

Cf. Mark 7:24–8:10.

Traveling north to the Phoenician seaports of Tyre and Sidon, Jesus encounters a Canaanite woman who begs him to heal her demon-possessed daughter. By addressing Jesus both as "Son of David" and "Lord," the non-Jew recognizes both Jesus' Jewish messiahship and his deity. Initially insistent on limiting his mission to the Jews, Jesus refuses the woman's petition (cf. 10:5-15). But the faith evidenced by her humble persistence changes his mind (v. 28).

Literary context suggests that Jesus returned to the predominantly Gentile western side of the Sea of Galilee, where he healed great throngs (vv. 29-32). Again, he miraculously provides food for a hungry multitude (vv. 29-39; cf. 14:13-21), this time numbering 4000 men plus women and children (cf. 16:9-10; Mark 6:30-44; 8:1-10).

16:1-12 Signs and Evil "Leaven"

Cf. Mark 8:11-21.

The ultraconservative Sadducees join forces with the Pharisees in hounding Jesus to prove his identity with a miracle on demand (cf. 12:38ff.). Jesus dismisses the challenge by castigating them for their failure to recognize him from the miracles he has already worked (the "signs of the times," v. 3). On the "sign of Jonah" (v. 4), see 12:39-41.

Jesus seizes the disciples' concern for bread to warn against the "leaven" of the Pharisees' hypocritical teaching, which crowds out faith (vv. 5-12).

16:13-28 Correctly Identifying Jesus and His Mission

Cf. Mark 8:27–9:1; Luke 9:18-27.

In the vicinity of Caesarea Philippi, the northernmost area of Jewish settlement, Peter confesses Jesus as the messianic Son of God. This confession contrasts with the mistaken identification of Jesus by others, who variously view him as John the Baptist, Elijah, Jeremiah, or another prophet. Jesus' calling Peter "Bar-jona" ("son of Jonah") associates him with the previously promised "sign of Jonah," which will consist in Jesus' death, burial, and resurrection (cf. v. 4; 12:39-41). In verse 18, Jesus plays on the meaning of "Peter" (Greek for "rock") to communicate the strong foundation on which Jesus will build "his church" (cf. Acts 2-5). The change of address from "you . . . Peter" to "this rock" makes it likely that Jesus has in mind his *teaching* as the sure foundation of the church. Peter receives the "keys to the kingdom" as indication of his pivotal role in forming the church (v. 19). "Binding" and "loosing" represent rabbinic authority to interpret the Law; Jesus authorizes Peter (and later the disciples) to maintain discipline in the church (cf. 18:18).

Now that the disciples have recognized Jesus' true identity as the Messiah, he begins to prepare them for his suffering, death, and resurrection. Jesus takes Peter's protest as a fourth temptation, so he calls the disciple "Satan" and orders him back to his position as a follower ("behind").

Then Jesus reiterates to the disciples the self-denying requirements of discipleship and the superior worth of eternal life over worldly gain (cf. 10:28, 38-39). Verse 27 predicts his second coming at the last judgment.

17:1-23 Jesus, the New Moses

Cf. Mark 9:2-32; Luke 9:28-45.

Jesus chooses Peter, James, and John — three of the first four disciples he had called (4:18-22) — to accompany him up an unidentified "high mountain," where they witness his "transfiguration." The event recalls Moses' encounter with God atop Mount Sinai (Exod. 34:29-30). But Jesus embodies the new and greater Moses who perfects the Law, so his transfigured face shines "like the sun," and even his garments become "dazzling white." Moses and Elijah accompany him as witnesses to his authority. God again declares Jesus his "beloved Son" (cf. 3:17).

On descending the mountain, Jesus instructs the disciples not to report this event until after his death and resurrection (v. 9). He explains that John the Baptist embodied the second Elijah, forerunner of the Messiah as foretold in Mal. 4:5-6.

Jesus uses the disciples' inability to cure an epileptic child to challenge them to greater faith (vv. 14-20). Their anticipatory grieving over Jesus' suffering and death, for which he continues to prepare them, shows that they understand the awful future (vv. 22-23).

17:24-27 Paying the Temple Tax

All Jewish males over the age of 19 had to pay an annual tax for the upkeep of the Jerusalem temple. The two-drachma tariff amounted to two days' wages for the average worker. Jesus clarifies for Peter that as members of the royal family of God, the Owner of the temple, they (and the other disciples) enjoy exemption from the temple tax. But so as not to offend their fellow Jews, they pay it voluntarily. The miraculous provision of the stater (= four drachmas) means that God himself pays the housekeeping bills incorrectly addressed to his "sons."

18 Obligations within the Christian Community

Cf. Mark 9:33-45; Luke 9:46-48; 15:3-7; 17:1-4.

In this fourth "teachings" section, Jesus expands his concern for the "least in the kingdom of heaven" in a discourse on Christian community (cf. 11:11). Entry into the kingdom requires repentance and childlike humility, an acknowledgment of dependence on God. Membership in the kingdom carries the responsibility of nurturing children in faith. The person who causes another to "stumble" (by forsaking his faith) is better off dead (vv. 8-9).

Verses 15-17 prescribe spiritual correction within the Christian community. One-to-one reproof of the sinning member should start the process. If this action fails to effect changed behavior, the reprover should try again in the presence of one or two other people, the required number of witnesses to convict an accused criminal. As a last resort, the rebuke should go public within the church. If the sinner still refuses correction, he forfeits treatment as a member of the community (vv. 18-20).

All this talk about sinning prompts Peter to ask about the limits of forgiveness within the Christian community. Jesus' answer, "70 times seven" (alternatively translated "77 times"), draws on the number seven, which represents completeness and perfection, and thus implies limitless forgiveness of fellow Christians.

The slave (= sinner) in Jesus' parable owed as much as he could possibly owe. The sale of his wife (a transaction forbidden by Jewish law), his children, and his possessions would not come close to commanding enough money for repayment of the debt — the equivalent of 15 years' wages for a manual laborer — and the slave could never repay the full amount, even if granted the "patience" for which he begs. But his failure to act mercifully toward his own debtor (= fellow Christian), who owes him a relatively minor amount (3-4 months' wages), betrays his lack of heartfelt appreciation for the king's (= God's) graciousness. The king hands the slave over to "torturers" till the ingrate pays up — no more possible for him to do than before (= eternal punishment). The parable teaches that the Christian's receipt of God's gracious forgiveness for unrepayable debts of sin obligates him to limitless forgiveness of fellow believers (cf. 6:12).

19:1-12 Jesus on Divorce, Remarriage, and Celibacy

Cf. Mark 10:1-12; Luke 16:18.

When Jesus heads south from Galilee to the Transjordanian region east of Judea, Pharisees test him concerning the legality of divorce. Jesus points out that from the beginning God established the marital relationship as an unbreakable union. Moses merely permitted divorce to regulate what the hard-hearted Hebrews were already doing. His "command" that rejected wives receive a certificate of divorce protected them from the false charge of desertion and discouraged pettiness on the part of disgruntled husbands (Deut. 24:1-4). Jesus teaches that divorce, though a practical fact, does not in reality obliterate the marriage, so remarriage after divorce constitutes adultery. "[Sexual] immorality" *violates* the marriage bond, but Jesus does not teach that the violation *nullifies* that bond, nor that biblically allowed divorce on account of infidelity nullifies it (v. 9; 5:31-32).

The disciples react by doubting the worth of assuming the risks in such a permanent commitment. Jesus acknowledges the greater difficulty of the alternative — becoming "eunuchs" (cf. 1 Cor. 7:1-16). Thus Jesus reserves sex for marriage.

19:13-30 The Requirements and Rewards of Discipleship

Cf. Mark 10:13-30; Luke 18:15-30.

When the disciples try to block the bringing of children to Jesus for a blessing, they display their failure to grasp the Lord's teaching in 18:1-5. Children may rank lowest in status in 1st-century Palestine, but Jesus boosts them to the top in the kingdom of heaven (vv. 13-15).

A young ruler, whose great wealth represented to his contemporaries a divine reward for righteousness, by human standards stood first in line to inherit eternal life. But only by humbling himself — becoming materially dependent on God by selling all of his possessions — can he "mature" to the childlikeness that

Jesus requires for discipleship. Jesus' recognition of the difficulty for the rich to enter the kingdom of heaven joins his similar statements about the Pharisees and other religious leaders in contradicting popular understandings of those qualified for admission.

Peter's question (v. 27) contrasts the disciples' response to the call of Jesus with that of the rich young ruler (vv. 21-22). For their obedience, Jesus pledges them positions of prominence in the coming kingdom, with the promise of heavenly reward for all who have met the demands of discipleship (v. 29; cf. 10:37-39).

20:1-16 Parity in the Kingdom

Cf. Mark 10:31; Luke 18:30.

Through the parable of the Workers in the Vineyard, Jesus teaches the ungrudging acceptance of Gentiles into the kingdom. The "first" represent the Jews, to whom Jesus ministers initially but who in the parable receive their "wages" last, so that they know how much the Gentiles are paid. The "last" represent the Gentiles, who, though second to receive Jesus' invitation into the kingdom, receive their reward first. The "third hour" means 9 a.m. — three hours after dawn, when the sunup-to-sundown workday began. Thus the workers who sign on later in the day — some not till the final, "eleventh hour" (5 p.m.) — receive a full day's wage for only a partial day's work. God's policy of equal pay puts the Gentiles on par with the Jews.

20:17–21:17 Suffering and Servanthood

Cf. Mark 10:32–11:11; Luke 18:31-43; 19:28-46; 22:24-27; John 2:13-22; 12:12-15.

Jesus now predicts his passion for a third time (20:17-19). Unaware of the private conversation between Jesus and the Twelve, the mother of James and John makes a bid that her sons receive privileged positions in Jesus' kingdom (cf. 18:1). Jesus emphasizes first that those given such positions must be able to suffer ("drink the cup") as he soon will, and second that the appointments are not his to make. He holds up his example of servanthood as the means to greatness. By giving his life Jesus will make obsolete the Jewish sacrificial system, which provided for forgiveness of sins via the substitutionary offering to God of a slain animal. Jesus' death is a "ransom for many" (20:28), rather than "all," not because his sacrificial death cannot atone for the sins of all humanity, but because it effects atonement only for those who become his true disciples (cf. 26:28; John 1:11-12).

Jesus exemplifies his admonition to servanthood by continuing to work miracles of mercy as he approaches and enters Jerusalem (20:29-34; 21:14).

Old Testament quotations and Jesus' acclamation by "children" in the temple underscore his entry into Jerusalem as fulfillment of prophecy (18:1-6; 19:13-15; cf. Mark 10:13-16). His gentleness, which accords with his teaching on servanthood, does not prevent him from exercising his authority as the messianic king (signified by his mounted entry to the city; cf. Zech. 9:9) or casting opportunistic businessmen out of the temple (21:12-13; cf. Isa.56:7; Jer. 7:11). The merchants were selling offerings for a profit, and Jewish pilgrims bringing foreign currency from outside Palestine faced an additional money-changing fee for their price-inflated purchases.

21:18-22 Jesus Curses the Fig Tree

Cf. Mark 11:12-14, 20-24.

The fruitless fig tree, doomed by Jesus to remain barren, represents the Jewish leaders, betrayed by the "bad fruit" of their reaction to Jesus and destined for destruction (cf. 3:7-10). Jesus uses the incident to underscore the power of faith, coupled with prayer (cf. 17:20).

21:23–22:14 The Church of the Chosen Replaces the Chosen Nation

Cf. Mark 11:27–12:12; Luke 14:16-24; 20:1-19.

When Jesus returns to the temple, the religious officials demand to know who gave this outsider authority over their turf. Jesus responds by asking them the source of John's baptism. The unwillingness of the priests to answer justifies his refusal to respond directly, but the three parables that follow ensure that they do not miss the implication of his question.

In the parable of the Two Sons (21:28-32), the first son (representing the Jewish leaders) feigns respect for his father (God) but fails to deliver on his promise of cooperation. The second, disrespectful son (symbolizing the tax collectors and prostitutes) regrets his initial defiance and demonstrates his changed attitude with action (repentance). This time, the chief priests and elders do answer Jesus' question, but in doing so they condemn themselves.

In the parable of the Vineyard (21:33-44), the landowner represents God, the vineyard the Mosaic covenant established at Sinai (Exodus 19ff.), and the vinegrowers the chosen nation of Israel. The slaves sent to collect the landowner's dues symbolize the prophets who preach repentance, and the son whom the tenant farmers kill stands for Jesus himself. The temple officials sign their own sentence when they predict a "wretched end" for the vinegrowers and their replacement by honorable tenants (the church, made up of Jews and Gentiles). The religious leaders of Jerusalem understand Jesus' meaning all too well, but they refrain from arresting him for fear of his multitudinous supporters.

The third parable (22:1-14) likens the kingdom of heaven to a wedding feast given by a king (God) for his son (Jesus). The summoning slaves stand for the prophets, and the unresponsive invitees represent the chosen people. The expansion of the guest list signifies the opening of the kingdom to the Gentiles; the evil and good guests represent false and true disciples (both Jews and Gentiles), distinguished from one another by their clothing; and the king's inspection symbolizes the last judgment.

22:15-46 Jesus Dumbfounds His Detractors

Cf. Mark 12:13-37; Luke 20:20-44.

The Jerusalem Pharisees and supporters of Herod (the "Herodians," v. 16) challenge Jesus with a question that mixes politics and religion in a thinly veiled attempt to cause him trouble with Rome (vv. 15-22). Jesus' failure to incriminate himself by advocating tax evasion in the name of religion robs the Pharisees of an opportunity to accuse him of inciting civil disobedience (cf. 17:24-27). The silver denarius bore the image of Tiberius Caesar.

Next the Sadducees, who control the high

priesthood, test Jesus with a question that takes the laws regarding "levirate marriage" to an absurd, hypothetical end in the afterlife (vv. 23-33; see Deut. 25:5-10). Jesus points out the Sadducees' failure to understand the nature of resurrected life and bases his answer on the Torah (Exod. 3:6), the only Scripture they accepted.

The Pharisees launch a second offensive (vv. 34-40) by enlisting a specialist in Mosaic law to force Jesus into elevating one of its 613 commandments above all the rest. Quoting from Judaism's central prayer, the Shema (Deut. 6:4-5), and from Lev. 19:18, Jesus obliges his antagonists by naming not only the foremost command — total love of God — but also its corollary — genuine love of others (cf. the Golden Rule, 7:12). Then by affirming that these two laws govern "the whole Law and the Prophets," Jesus upholds the entire Old Testament legal system and leaves the opponents no fault to find with him.

Finally, Jesus poses his own challenge (vv. 41-46). But the Pharisees' inability to understand the Messiah in heavenly terms, not just human ones, makes the question an unanswerable riddle for them. Shamed by their speechlessness, they give up for good the attempt to trap Jesus with his own words.

23–25 Jesus' Fifth and Final Discourse

23 Warning and Woe Cf. Mark 12:38-40; Luke 11:37-52; 13:34-35; 20:45-47.

Having silenced the Jewish leaders, Jesus instructs his listeners to follow the law as expounded by the scribes, who teach while seated in the "chair of Moses" in each synagogue. But Jesus warns his audience not to follow the example of the status-seeking religious leaders, who fail to practice what they preach. His disciples must show humility and shun honorific titles. Jesus alone is their Teacher ("rabbi," lit., "my great one"), and they may refer only to God as "Father."

Jesus denounces the scribes and Pharisees in a series of woes that contrast with the Beatitudes of ch. 5 (vv. 13-36). Here the overarching sin of the religious establishment consists in hypocrisy, both nurtured and masked by their legalism. Swearing by the temple or by an of-

fering left on the altar means holding up these items as collateral against a debt (vv. 16-22), but which items a creditor could confiscate in the event of the creditor's defaulting since technically they belonged to God. The leaders' unremarkable tithing of common garden herbs (vv. 23-24) parallels the relatively petty pains they take to strain out tiny gnats from their wine to avoid ingesting the ritually unclean insects. But their noteworthy neglect of more important responsibilities — justice, mercy, and faithfulness — is tantamount to swallowing an unclean camel. Whitewashing tombs prevented accidental contact with the dead, which rendered a Jew ritually unclean (v. 27).

Jesus charges the religious leaders with self-deception in considering themselves morally superior to their ancestors (vv. 29-30). Their abuse of the current servants of God makes them heirs to their forebears' guilt for murders of the innocents, from Abel (in Genesis) through the priest Zechariah (in 2 Chronicles, the last book in the Hebrew Bible) and all those in between.

The desolation of the "house" (v. 38) signals Jesus' imminent departure from the temple (24:1) and perhaps also its coming destruction by the Romans (A.D. 70). The prophesied acclamation of Jesus by the Jerusalemites recalls the cry of the multitudes when Jesus entered the city (see 21:9) and previews his warm welcome at the second coming.

24–25 The Surprise End Cf. Mark 13; Luke 12:39-46; 17:23-37; 19:12-27; 21:5-33.

On leaving the temple Jesus prophesies its destruction, which prompts from his disciples questions about the future, particularly the end times. Jesus cites phenomena that will lead up to the actual end: the appearance of false messiahs; the occurrence of wars and natural disasters; the persecution of Christians (a theme developed eschatologically in 24:15-28); apostasy, betrayal, and hatred within the Christian community; the rise and success of false prophets; and, as a positive consequence, the worldwide preaching of the gospel.

Jesus speaks of a "desolating sacrilege" (24:15; cf. Dan. 11:31) that will precede the destruction of the temple. Many scholars consider the erection of Roman standards in the temple in A.D. 70 as an abomination similar to that caused by Antiochus IV Epiphanes in 167 B.C., especially since the Romans followed up their takeover of the sanctuary by destroying it along with the rest of Jerusalem. Flight on the Sabbath would force the transgression of the Law's distance restrictions on Sabbath travel, deprive fugitives of roadside services suspended on the day of rest, and put lone fugitives in danger of attack by highway bandits (cf. the parable of the Good Samaritan, Luke 10:25-37).

The worldwide "elect" are those followers who "endure to the end" (24:13) of the shortened period of "great tribulation" (vv. 21-22) and whom Jesus at the second coming gathers from "the four winds" (v. 31). Throughout the Bible, the darkening of the heavenly luminaries, the appearance of clouds, and the loud call of a trumpet signal the presence of God (24:29-31; cf. Exod. 19:16; 40:34-38; Rev. 6:12-17). The 1st-century fulfillment of "all these things" (24:34) would culminate in the Romans' destruction of the temple, with the ultimate fulfillment of the prophecies at the "end of the age" (see Revelation, esp. 1:7; 7:1ff.).

Short parables that urge readiness for the end while pursuing the normal activities of life (eating and drinking, marrying, working) appear in 24:32–25:46. The secret timing of Jesus'

return, known only by God, necessitates constant personal preparedness for the final judgment. The devastating consequence of moral nonchalance — eternal punishment — is shown in the fate of the unfaithful slave (24:45-51); the five foolish bridesmaids (25:1-13); the lazy slave (vv. 14-30, where "talent" names the highest monetary unit in 1st-century Palestine); and the uncaring "goats" (vv. 31-46), all of whom represent false disciples. In contrast, the respective counterparts of the doomed inherit eternal life: the faithful slave; the five wise bridesmaids; the industrious slaves; and the compassionate "sheep" — all true disciples. The parable of the Sheep and Goats addresses the ways people receive Jesus' message and apply it in love toward their neighbors.

26:1-5 Conspiracy and Cowardice

Cf. Mark 14:1-2; Luke 22:1-2.

With Passover just two days away and the disciples fully aware of Jesus' coming crucifixion, the Jewish leaders of Jerusalem gather in the courtyard of the high priest Caiaphas and conspire to kill Jesus. In front of the multitudinous pilgrims that swell the capital city for the festival, he has humiliated the religious establishment by exposing their hypocrisy and has stupefied them with his superior insight into the Scriptures (see esp. chs. 22–23). But Jesus' popularity with the grass roots prompts the cowardly, power-hoarding plotters to go underground with their murderous scheme.

26:6-16 Jesus Anointed for Burial

Cf. Mark 14:3-11; Luke 22:3-6; John 12:1-8.

Meanwhile, at Jesus' lodgings in Bethany (see 21:17), a woman pours a whole bottle of costly perfume on Jesus' head as he reclines (on his side, propped up by an elbow) at mealtime. The disciples protest the act as wasteful, but Jesus recognizes it as a preparatory anointing for his burial — in Jewish practice a most honorable deed (cf. Luke 7:36-50). Burial practices involved covering corpses with spices and perfumes to mask the stench of rotting flesh (cf. Luke 24:1).

Jesus' sanctioning of the woman's act

The transfiguration of Jesus; 6th-century mosaic, Monastery of St. Catherine, Sinai. (Richard Cleave, Pictorial Archive)

prompts Judas to turn traitor. He offers his services to the chief priests, who advance him "30 pieces of silver" to orchestrate a sting that targets Jesus.

26:17-29 The Last Supper

Cf. Mark 14:12-25; Luke 22:7-23; John 13:1-30.

In contrast to Judas's individual treachery, the disciples as a group demonstrate their allegiance to Jesus by obeying his instructions regarding Passover preparations in Jerusalem. During dinner on Passover eve, Jesus announces his betrayal by one of the Twelve, who are all partaking from the common bowl with him. Jesus does not single out the traitor, but his response to Judas's feigned ignorance about the treachery clearly implies that he can identify his betrayer. Judas shows himself a false disciple by hypocritically addressing his victim with the honorific title "Rabbi" ("my great one"), and Jesus lets Judas's words stand as a self-condemnation.

In the ancient Near East, the sharing of a meal sealed a treaty, or covenant (e.g., Gen. 26:30; Exod. 24:3-11). The Last Supper seals in advance the new covenant established by the imminent sacrifice of Jesus, the ultimate Passover lamb (see Exodus 12). He commands the disciples to eat bread and drink wine representative of his body and blood, the offering of which effects not the temporary covering up of sins (as with animal sacrifices under the old, Mosaic covenant), but their permanent remission or removal (v. 28; cf. 20:28).

26:30-56 Jesus Arrested

Cf. Mark 14:26-52; Luke 22:39-53; John 13:36-38; 18:1-11.

On the way to Gethsemane, located on the Mount of Olives opposite the Temple Mount, Jesus warns the disciples that they will all desert him "this night." Peter declares his loyalty to the point of death, but Jesus predicts that Peter will deny him three times before the first light of day, announced by a crowing cock.

As at the transfiguration, Jesus shows a particular bond with Peter, James, and John, in whom he confides his grief of soul (cf. 17:1ff.).

Jesus asks them to stay awake with him and pray and himself prays that he might avoid the "cup" of suffering in store for him; but he also expresses his willingness to accept "No" for an answer (vv. 39, 42, 44). After each of his three private prayer sessions, Jesus returns to his disciples only to find them fast asleep. Peter's three failures to pray leave him without the spiritual steeling he needs to resist the three temptations to deny Jesus later that night. In contrast, the prayerful Jesus receives strength to endure his arrest in the garden (vv. 47-56) and the events that follow.

Arriving at Gethsemane and backed by an armed mob, Judas addresses Jesus as "Rabbi" (cf. v. 25) and heightens his hypocrisy by greeting him with a kiss of betrayal. Jesus' ironic acknowledgment of Judas as "Friend" exposes him as a false disciple, like the inappropriately clad guest in the parable of the Wedding Feast (22:12). Jesus exemplifies his admonishment to meekness when he halts a disciple's violent resistance to the arrest and refrains from calling for overpowering angelic protection (6000 troops made up a Roman "legion"). The desertion of the disciples fulfills the prophecy Jesus uttered just hours before (v. 31), and together the events fulfill Hebrew prophecy concerning the Messiah.

26:57-68 Trial by the Sanhedrin

Cf. Mark 14:53-65; Luke 22:63-71; John 18:19-24.

The trial of Jesus by the Jewish council ("Sanhedrin," made up of 71 aristocrats and presided over by the high priest) proves bogus from the start. It takes place in the middle of the night and on the eve of the Sabbath — practices forbidden in later rabbinic regulations — and lacks any witnesses for the defense. Bent on the single purpose of obtaining capital evidence against Jesus, the council pins its hopes on willing perjurers, but to no avail. When two witnesses claim that Jesus threatened to destroy the temple, the high priest tries forcing Jesus to defend himself against this charge of sedition. But only when Caiaphas queries Jesus about his divine, messianic status does he open his mouth — not to give a direct answer (consistent with his own teaching, he refuses to be put under oath; v. 63; cf. 23:16-22), but instead to turn Caiaphas's command into a confession (v. 64; cf. Jesus' response to Judas in v. 25). With incriminating evidence nowhere to be found and the high priest unintentionally acknowledging Jesus' divinity and messiahship, Jesus voluntarily hands the Sanhedrin the excuse they seek: he voices his equality with God, no doubt fully aware that the unbelieving councilors will consider the claim blasphemy — according to Jewish law, punishable by death. Their immediate declaration of a sentence violates the Law, which sought to thwart impulsive judgments by delaying pronouncement of a verdict till the day after a trial.

26:69-75 Peter Denies Knowing Jesus

Cf. Mark 14:66-72; Luke 22:54-62; John 18:15-18, 25-27.

As members of the Sanhedrin physically and verbally assault Jesus (vv. 67-68), Peter shows the courage-sapping effects of prayerlessness (see vv. 30-56). Retreating from his courtyard seat near the proceedings, he thrice denies any association with Jesus. Challenged as an outsider because of his Galilean accent, he swears to his truthfulness. (Contrast Jesus' refusal to take an oath in v. 63.) The crow of the cock sparks his remembrance of Jesus' forewarning (vv. 33-34), as well as bitter remorse (see 10:32-33).

27:1-26 Judas's Suicide and Pilate's Self-Exoneration

Cf. Mark 15:1-15; Luke 23:1-5, 17-25; John 18:28–19:16.

Though Jewish law stipulated capital punishment for certain religious crimes, in New Testament times the Roman government reserved the sole right of execution. So the Sanhedrin takes its case against Jesus to Pontius Pilate, the Roman prefect (governor) of Judea; tells him that Jesus claims to be "King of the Jews"; and hopes that Pilate finds him guilty of treason.

Meanwhile, a deeply regretful Judas, powerless to undo his treachery, flings his blood money into the temple and goes off to commit suicide (cf. Acts 1:16-20). Forbidden to use ill-gotten gains for sacred purposes, the chief priests purchase a burial ground for foreigners with Judas's silver.

Pilate questions Jesus to see whether the prisoner poses a threat to Rome. Jesus tacitly accepts from Pilate the designation "King of the Jews" by replying "You say so"; thus the governor unwittingly becomes a co-confessor with the high priest, Caiaphas (cf. 26:63-64). Nevertheless, Pilate senses no political threat from Jesus; but the dynamics of the trial clarify for him the source of the Jewish leaders' malice: jealousy. So he leaves it to the Jewish crowd to decide Jesus' fate. Manipulated by their leaders, the people prefer a convicted murderer named Barabbas (Mark 15:7) to the miracle-working Galilean, whose execution as a criminal they demand. Pilate acts on his wary wife's dream-inspired confession of Jesus' righteousness and his own verdict of "innocent" by literally washing his hands of the Jewish matter (cf. Deut. 21:1-9). The riot-inclined mob accept for themselves and their children full responsibility for taking Jesus' life. The Romans customarily flogged the condemned before their execution.

27:27-66 Jesus' Crucifixion and Burial

Cf. Mark 15:16-47; Luke 23:26-56; John 19:17-42.

Roman soldiers stationed at Pilate's headquarters (the Praetorium) intensify the abuse of Jesus begun by the Sanhedrin (cf. 26:67-68). Little do they realize the irony of the mock coronation they stage.

In the Roman period, a person sentenced to crucifixion customarily carried the horizontal bar of his cross to the execution site. Matthew notes the conscription of a man from Cyrene (home to a thriving Jewish colony on the Libyan coast) to take up the task for Jesus. In the environs of Jerusalem, Golgotha served as a regular place of execution.

The ridicule continues at Golgotha with the relentless berating by onlookers, including the Jewish leaders and the criminals crucified beside him. The publication of his crime on a placard ironically proclaims his kingship (cf. v. 11). But ominous signs surface at noon, the "sixth hour" from dawn. Three hours of inexplicable darkness fall, and at about 3 p.m. Jesus, crying out to God, quotes Ps. 22:1 in Aramaic.

Some bystanders mistake the address, "Eli" ("My God"), as a shortened form of "Elijah" and think that Jesus might be appealing to the prophet for help in coming "down from the cross," as challenged (v. 49; cf. v. 42).

The relatively brief time Jesus hangs on the cross before dying, the physical strength evidenced in his final, loud outcry, and his taking the initiative to "yield up" his spirit indicate that he — not his executioners — occupies the position of power in the matter of his death (cf. 26:64). The remarkable phenomena that attend his expiration confirm the divine hand in Jesus' self-sacrifice. The spontaneous rending of the temple "veil," which separated the holy place from the holy of holies, signifies the immediate obsolescence of the old, Mosaic covenant. The raising of deceased saints foreshadows Jesus' resurrection and inspires death-defying courage on the part of persecuted disciples. The awesome events make believers out of the Gentile guards, but not the Jewish leaders (vv. 63-64). Pilate continues to let the Jews decide what to do with Jesus (cf. v. 24). He allows a disciple to dignify Jesus' corpse with a proper burial (rather than tossing the body into a mass grave), but on the Sabbath Pilate sanctions the posting of a guard by the Pharisees, who fear that Jesus' followers will steal the corpse to inspire popular belief in his resurrection — a "deception" they consider worse than belief in Jesus as the divine Messiah.

28 The Risen Christ

Cf. Mark 16; Luke 24:1-12; John 20:1–21:2.

Unlike the skittish apostles, several of Jesus' female followers remain on the scene. These observers of the crucifixion and mourners at Jesus' burial return to his tomb at daybreak on Sunday (v. 1). An angel — whose fearsome arrival has made the grave guards faint — greets the women, announces Jesus' resurrection, and invites them to see the opened, empty tomb for themselves. On the way to tell the disciples the good news, the women encounter Jesus himself, and their grasping of his feet in worship confirms his physical reality. He repeats his intention of reuniting with the disciples in Galilee and sends the women to summon the Eleven northward (see 26:32). Since the testimony of women counted for little in the ancient court system, the appearance of Jesus first to these female witnesses affords them a noteworthy reward for their faithful ministry to the persecuted Messiah.

Meanwhile the revived guards report their ordeal to the chief priests, who have a vested interest in keeping the disappearance of the body quiet (cf. 27:63-64). Both the guards and the Jewish leaders have something to lose, so they strike a bargain: the guards take a big bribe to lie that the disciples stole Jesus' body — a "deception" that would squelch belief in his resurrection — and the leaders promise to keep the guards out of trouble with Pilate for having failed at their guardpost.

The disciples catch up with Jesus in Galilee, perhaps on the Mount of Beatitudes (v. 16; cf. 5:1). His universal authority justifies his commissioning them to a worldwide ministry; the baptism of disciples in his name, along with those of God the Father and the Holy Spirit (cf. their presence at Jesus' baptism in 3:16-17); and the teaching of followers to observe all of his commands (the Great Commission). That Jesus himself has endured persecution and conquered death strengthens for these first missionaries the impact of his promised presence through the tribulation-laden "end of the age" (cf. ch. 24 and Jesus' instructions for missionary work in 9:35–10:42).

Mark

The Gospel of Mark, though coming second in the New Testament canon, appears to have come first in order of composition. All but four paragraphs in Mark find parallels in Matthew or Luke, or in both of these other Gospels, which with Mark comprise what scholars call the "Synoptics." Despite their close literary relationship, however, the synoptic Gospels display individual characteristics. For Mark, the overarching distinctive consists in the portrayal of Jesus as a man of action. In Mark, things are always happening "immediately"; Jesus' teachings take a back seat to detailed accounts of his miracles; and his actions attract a constant throng, often because of people's repeated disobedience to his orders not to tell anyone about his miracle-working.

The omission of birth and infancy narratives about John the Baptist and Jesus helps make Mark the shortest of the canonical Gospels. Mark starts with the activities of John and proceeds in a generally chronological order through Jesus' ministry, passion, and resurrection. In some sections, however, chronology gives way to thematic arrangement, as with the episodes evidencing Jesus' authority in 2:1–3:6.

The translation in Mark of expressions from Aramaic (a Semitic language related to Hebrew) suggests that the book addresses a non-Jewish audience — probably Roman, since Mark substitutes Latin terms and expressions for their Greek equivalents. That a number of early church fathers place the presumed author, John Mark, in Rome with Peter and Paul offers external evidence favoring this view.

Authorship and Date

The text of Mark does not name the book's author, but the title eventually assigned to this Gospel reflects both the tradition of authorship perpetuated by the early church fathers, beginning with Papias in the 2nd century A.D., and the implications of textual evidence from Acts and the New Testament epistles. In those books, John Mark (respective Hebrew and Latin names) appears as a missionary companion of Paul, Barnabas, and Peter. Papias indicates that Mark served as Peter's interpreter in Rome and committed to writing an account of Jesus' life and ministry. Slightly later than Papias, the church father Irenaeus says that Mark based his account on the preaching of Peter — an eyewitness to Jesus' ministry, unlike Mark, and one of Jesus' closest earthly companions. The writings of Clement of Alexandria, Origen, and Jerome further support this tradition.

Scholars dispute the date of authorship for the book of Mark, with proposals ranging from as early as the mid-40s to soon after 70. In 13:14, Jesus refers to the "desolating sacrilege," a phrase that most scholars take to refer to the Roman desecration of the temple in 70 — more than three decades after Christ's ascension to heaven. Earlier dating of the Gospel would view this statement as predictive prophecy. If Jesus' statement refers to a past desecration of the temple (such as that by Antiochus IV Epiphanes in 167 B.C.) or is an editorial composition put in Jesus' mouth after the fact, authorship of Mark sometime after A.D. 70 is possible. Since Luke appears to have used Mark as a source for writing his Gospel, the dating of the two-part work Luke-Acts also affects the dating of Mark. Most scholars today date Mark in the late 60s.

1:1-11 John's Baptism of Jesus

Cf. Matthew 3; Luke 3:1-6, 15-18, 21-22.

Mark begins with a declaration of purpose: to relate the beginning of the "good news" of Jesus Christ. The opening quotation ties the "good news" to Isaiah's prophecies, which greatly influenced the composition of Mark's

Gospel. The author omits an account of Jesus' birth and ignores his human ancestry in favor of getting right to the genealogical point: Jesus is the Son of God, as proclaimed from heaven at his baptism (v. 11). The rest of Mark's Gospel provides the proof. (Note, however, that a considerable number of ancient manuscripts omit "Son of God" from 1:1.)

1:12-13 Satan Tempts Jesus in the Wilderness

Cf. Matt. 4:1-11; Luke 4:1-13.

Mark notes that Jesus' temptation in the wilderness lasted 40 days (= "a long time"), but he does not give any details of the Devil's demands or Jesus' refusal to give in. As in Matt. 4:11, angels minister to Jesus in this time of testing.

1:14-39 Jesus Begins His Ministry

Cf. Matt. 4:12-25; 7:28-29; 8:14-17; Luke 4:14-15, 31-44.

Following his baptism, Jesus goes to Galilee to begin his ministry, which he declares to represent a decisive moment appointed by God (v. 15, "the fulfillment of time").

All Jewish men held the right to expound the Hebrew Scriptures in synagogue services, but from the start the authoritative nature of Jesus' teaching distinguishes it from that of the "professional" interpreters of the Law.

Jesus exorcises a demon (vv. 21-28), which identifies him by name probably to try to repel Jesus' power, since ancient Near Easterners believed in the potency of names. The Saturday sunset marks the end of Sabbath, and most people wait till then to approach Jesus for a miracle (v. 32); but by curing the demoniac in the synagogue and Simon's mother-in-law (Mark calls Peter by his Hebrew name, vv. 29ff.), Jesus has already exercised his lordship over this holy day (cf. Matt. 12:1-14).

1:40-45 Jesus Heals a "Leper"

Cf. Matt. 8:1-4; Luke 5:12-16.

After curing a man with a chronic skin disease (not leprosy in the modern sense), Jesus instructs him to keep the miracle quiet. But the "leper" disobeys and Jesus becomes an instant

celebrity, mobbed by crowds of people (e.g., see 2:1-12; 3:9-10; 6:53-56). Jesus' desire for secrecy may have sought to avoid such crowds as well as messianic expectations that he was a political-military deliverer.

2:1-12 Jesus Heals a Paralytic

Cf. Matt. 9:1-8; Luke 5:17-26.

Mark (as Luke) details the means by which the friends of the paralyzed man gain him access to the hemmed-in Jesus: digging a hole through the flat, mud-plastered roof of the house (accessible by an outside staircase) and lowering the man down through the opening.

2:13-22 Celebrating with Sinners

Cf. Matt. 9:9-17; Luke 5:27-39.

Jesus now calls another disciple, a customs official or tax farmer despised by his fellow Jews because of his employment by the Gentile bureaucracy. Mark and Luke call him Levi, either the original name of Matthew as he is called in Matthew's Gospel or his second name (cf. Simon Peter).

Jesus further antagonizes the religious establishment by attending a banquet in Levi's home along with other social outcasts. This action underscores his mission to the least and lost, a foretaste of opportunity for all in the coming dominion of God.

2:23–3:6 Lord of the Sabbath

Cf. Matt. 12:1-14; Luke 6:1-11.

Controversy arises when Jesus' disciples help themselves to grain while walking through a field on the Sabbath. The Pharisees take this action as a violation of Jewish law, but Jesus responds that even priests were permitted to satisfy their hunger on the Sabbath. He reminds them that David and his men took the holy bread of the Presence kept continually in the temple, an offering which could be eaten only by the priests (1 Sam. 21:1-6). Thus Jesus makes the point that he inaugurates a new day — the old rules no longer apply.

Mark notes the unlikely collaboration of the Pharisees with the "Herodians" — Jewish sup-

Miracles

The Gospels are emphatic that Jesus' mighty deeds were an essential part of his mission. They offer some 35 distinct accounts plus references to healings and exorcisms in numerous summaries. Much of Jesus' fame derives from them (Mark 1:45), and even his enemies admitted his powers (Matt. 9:34). Intriguingly, while many of Jesus' healings have parallels in the Greco-Roman world, the Gospels have no counterparts to pagan healings of extended pregnancies, baldness, headaches, infertility, gout, and worms, of tattoo-removal, or restoration of broken pottery. What are we to make of this selectivity, especially in light of the repeated statements that Jesus healed all who beseeched him (Matt. 4:24; Luke 6:19)?

Since Jesus cannot properly be understood apart from Israel's story, it is necessary to go back to the very beginning and the creation of humanity in God's image. Image language was not new. Pagans made images of their gods, ritually "opening" their eyes, ears, and mouths and "mobilizing" their limbs before placing them in temples. The biblical story takes up but reverses this activity. It is God who makes us in his image (Gen. 1:26-27). He gives us sight, speech, and hearing (Exod. 4:11) and places us in his "palace" (cf. Isa. 66:1; Job 38:4ff.; Isa. 40:2; 45:18). This pattern is echoed in the Exodus, when God formed Israel, his "son," to bear his image as a new humanity

in a new "Eden" (Exod. 4:22; Isa. 43:1; Lev. 19:2).

But Israel, like Adam, rebelled and were likewise expelled from their paradise-land. God executed their sentence by ironically re-creating his people in the image of the idols they worshipped (Isa. 6:9-10 [note the temple setting]; Ps. 115:4-8; 135:15-18). "Blind" and "deaf," they would stumble into the death of exile (Isa. 29:9-14; cf. Ezekiel 37). But God also promised that he would have compassion on them (Isa. 49:13; 54:10). He would bring them out of exile in a new creational new exodus, restoring sight, hearing, and speech, healing the lame, raising the dead (Isa. 26:19; 35:5-6; 61:1; Ezekiel 37), and granting superabundance to the land (Isa. 51:3). They were thus to prepare the way for his coming (Isa. 40:3), when he would bind "strong man" Babylon (Isa. 49:24-25) and bring his captive people safely home.

With this in mind, Jesus' response to John the Baptist — "the blind see, the deaf hear, the dead are raised" (Matt. 11:3-6 par. Luke 7:20-23, citing Isa. 26:19; 35:5-6; 61:1) — makes perfect sense. These were all signs that the promised new creational new exodus, which John himself earlier announced (Isa. 40:3 in Matt. 3:3 par. Luke 3:4), had come. When challenged over his exorcisms, Jesus again alludes to Isaiah's promised deliverance (Mark 3:27; Isa. 49:24-25). This time, however, the ultimate oppressor and strong man is not Babylon and its idols but Satan and the demons (cf. 1 Cor. 10:20).

Jesus' power over the sea, the drowning of demonic "legion" (Mark 4:35–5:20), and the feedings in desert places (Matt. 14:15-21; John 6:1-15) also echo Yahweh's mighty deeds at the first exodus (Exodus 14–16). And astoundingly, who else if not God himself walks

Pavement mosaic commemorating the miracle of the loaves and fishes; mid-5th century, Church of the Multiplication, et-Tagbah. (*Wikimedia Commons*)

on the waters (Matt. 14:25; cf. Job 9:8)? In healing fevers, dropsy, the hemorrhaging woman, and lepers, Jesus as Israel's healer reverses Deuteronomy's exilic curse (Exod. 15:26; Deut. 28:16ff.). He is thus also shown to be Isaiah's servant who effects the new exodus redemption of unclean and leprous Israel (Isa. 1:6; 53:4; Matt. 8:17). The astonishing catches of fish (John 21:1-14; Ezek 47:9-10) and his turning of water into wine (John 2:1-11; cf. Amos 9:13; Joel 3:18) similarly announce the blessing of the land with extraordinary abundance. This is why the Gospels speak not of miracles but "mighty deeds," "signs," and "works" — the terminology of the exodus (Deut. 3:24; 4:34; Ps. 44:1; 106:8) and creation (65:6; 102:25).

At the same time, the drowning of the swine (associated with idolatry, Isa. 65:4) and the cursing of the fig tree (a symbol of leafy but budless and fruitless Israel, Jer. 8:13) indicate that this new exodus also entails judgment if rejected (Mal. 4:6).

Why did neither John nor Israel grasp the significance of Jesus' mighty deeds? Probably because the Messiah was not expected to heal, and these prophecies were largely understood in metaphorical terms, that is, as healing those who were "blind and deaf" to the Law (CD 1:9ff.; Tg. Isa. 42:14-24). So not only were these healings signs indicating the need to believe in Jesus as the ultimate expression of God's will (cf. John 9), but they were also powerful declarations of God's commitment to restore his creation and our bodies, as Jesus' resurrection testifies.

Jesus' mighty deeds were both the sign and demonstration that Israel's longed-for deliverance had come. They announce and constitute the beginning of the new creation and the restoration of the image of God in humanity. And if for Israel, then also for the whole world, to whom Israel was to be a light and whose only hope was in God's justice (Isa. 42:4-6).

RIKKI E. WATTS

porters of Herod Antipas, ruler of Galilee — as witness to the intensity of their hatred for Jesus.

3:7-30 Jesus Calls the Disciples

Cf. Matt. 10:1-4; 12:15-37; Luke 6:12-19; 11:14-23.

"Idumea" refers to the area south of Judea. Tyre and Sidon, on the coast of modern Lebanon, were prominent port cities established by the Phoenicians and important centers of maritime trade in New Testament times.

All 12 disciples appointed by Jesus as apostles hail from Galilee, with the possible exception of his betrayer, Judas Iscariot, who may come from the town of Kerioth in Judea. Two pairs of fraternal fisherman — Simon Peter and Andrew, James and John — followed Jesus first. Matthew, also called Levi, shed his career as a tax collector in the service of the Roman government to answer Jesus' call. Simon in verse 18 is called "the Cananaean," from an Aramaic word meaning "Zealot," perhaps related to a Jewish guerilla group that sought to oust the occupying Romans during the First Jewish Revolt (66-74). Luke refers to Thaddaeus as "Judas son of James," while Bartholomew may be the "Nathanael" of John 1:45ff.

Mark notes the efforts of Jesus' family to protect him from people who think he is insane (3:21). But Jesus' comments about the "eternal sin" of blasphemy against the Holy Spirit show that those who write him off as an instrument of Satan have already blasphemed their way out of the kingdom of God (vv. 29-30).

3:31-35 Jesus Identifies His True Family

Cf. Matt. 12:46-50; Luke 8:19-21.

When Jesus' biological relatives approach, he makes clear that natural ties of kinship or friendship provide no special advantages in the coming kingdom. Instead, a new and broader understanding of "family" accepts anyone who does the will of God.

4:1-34 Jesus Teaches in Parables

Cf. Matthew 13; Luke 8:4-18; 13:18-19.

In this first major account of Jesus' teachings, Mark emphasizes that not everyone can grasp the importance of Jesus' ministry or his role in bringing about God's kingdom. These seemingly simple stories will be heard in a variety of ways, and only true disciples will grasp their deeper ("secret") meaning. The method fulfills

Synagogue at Capernaum, a richly ornamented basilica with gabled roof; 4th century A.D. *(David Shankbone, Wikimedia Commons)*

the Old Testament prophecies contained in Ps. 78:2 and Isa. 6:10.

Only Mark records the short parable comparing the kingdom of God to the mystery of a growing seed (vv. 26-29). The farmer represents Jesus and his disciples, who sow the seed of the kingdom; but God controls its fruition.

4:35–6:6a Demonstrating His Power

Cf. Matt. 8:18-34; 9:18-26; Luke 8:26-56.

In the account relating the healing of the demoniac (5:1-20), the country of the Gerasenes (Matt. 8:28, "Gadarenes") designates the largely Gentile area southeast of the Sea of Galilee. Mark gives details of the healing not mentioned in Matt. 8:28-33 (which indicates two afflicted men), including the name of the demoniac ("Legion") and the number of swine (about 2000) into which Jesus sends the "unclean spirits." The "Decapolis" (5:20) refers to 10 autonomous Greek cities, most of which lay east of Galilee in Transjordan.

In the report of Jesus' revival of a little girl (5:21-43), Mark gives her father's name as "Jairus." As at the transfiguration and in the garden of Gethsemane, Peter, James, and John emerge as Jesus' inner circle of disciples (5:37;

cf. 9:2; 14:33). Jesus issues his resurrecting command in Aramaic — a language related to Hebrew, used as the international language throughout much of the 1st millennium B.C., and spoken widely in Jesus' day.

6:6b-13 Commissioning the Apostles for Missionary Work

Cf. Matt. 9:35–10:1, 9-14; Luke 9:1-6.

Jesus sends the disciples in pairs so their testimony to the gospel will hold up as valid according to Mosaic law (cf. Deut. 19:15). The disciples anoint the sick with olive oil, used for medicinal purposes in addition to others (v. 13).

6:14-56 John Beheaded; Five Thousand Fed; Jesus Walks on Water

Cf. Matthew 14; Luke 9:7-17; John 6:1-21.

Herod had married his brother's wife, Herodias. She resented John the Baptist for criticizing the relationship and, with her daughter's aid, coerced Herod to have him beheaded (vv. 17-29).

Mark's version of the feeding of the 5000 is the most detailed among the four Gospels (vv. 30-44). The disciples complain that buying bread for the crowd would require seven months' worth of wages for the average day laborer, who earned one denarius per day. It is the disciples' own food that provides the basis for the miraculous bounty.

Seeing the disciples struggling to row against a strong wind, Jesus walks across the water, enters the boat, and the wind calms (vv. 45-52). In Mark's account Peter does not try to mimic the miracle.

7:1-23 The Limits of Tradition

Cf. Matt. 15:1-20.

Jesus' opponents criticize the disciples for failing to observe ritual cleansing prior to preparing and consuming food. Mark clarifies that Jesus' teaching nullifies the food taboos dictated in Mosaic law (v. 19; cf. Leviticus 11). Jesus counters that the Pharisees violate the spirit of the Law when they withhold support from their parents; claiming that the funds are earmarked

Jesus' Teachings

The focus of Jesus' teachings was not on himself but on the reign of God (the "kingdom of God") and on the redemption of Israel, a redemption with profound significance for all humanity.

The fundamental element of Jesus' teaching was his proclamation of the reign (or kingdom) of God (Mark 1:14-15), by which he meant the powerful presence of God. This proclamation reflected the vocabulary and imagery of the book of Isaiah. Passages such as Isa. 40:9 ("herald of good news . . . say to the cities of Judah, 'Here is your God!'") and 52:7 ("who brings good news . . . who announces salvation, who says to Zion, 'Your God reigns!'") provide the scriptural backdrop to Jesus' proclamation. Isaiah 61:1-2 ("The Spirit of the Lord God is upon me, because the Lord has anointed me . . . to bring good news . . .") identifies proclamation of the good news of God's reign as the specific task of the Lord's anointed one (or Messiah). These prophetic passages provided the elements out of which Jesus shaped his proclamation.

Appealing to these very passages, Jesus reassures an imprisoned and discouraged John the Baptist that he is indeed the "one who is to come," for "the blind receive their sight, the lame walk, the lepers are cleansed, the deaf hear, the dead are raised, and the poor have good news brought to them" (Matt. 11:5 par. Luke 7:22). He is God's Messiah, whom, in the words of one of the Dead Sea

Scrolls, "heaven and earth will obey."

Like other Jewish teachers of his day, Jesus is called "rabbi" or teacher (Mark 4:38; 9:17; 10:17; 12:14, 19). He teaches as opportunities arise, seated in the presence of his disciples and crowds, whether outdoors or in someone's home (Matt. 5:1; Mark 12:41; Luke 5:3). At other times he teaches in more formal settings, such as the synagogue (Mark 1:21; 6:2; Luke 4:20). Although not a professional scholar, Jesus appealed to and interpreted Scripture to address

"When Jesus saw the crowds, he began to speak and taught them" (Matthew 5). *(Richard Cleave, Pictorial Archive)*

people's specific needs and experiences (e.g., Isa. 6:9-10 in Mark 4:12; Jer. 7:11 in Mark 11:17; Isa. 5:1-7 in Mark 12:1-9; Ps. 118:22 in Mark 12:10-11).

The arrival of the reign of God escalated the war between God

and Satan. We are told that Satan has fallen from heaven (Luke 10:18), his allies are now being trodden upon by Jesus' followers (v. 19), and he himself has been bound by the "stronger" Jesus (Mark 3:27; cf. 1:7), who is now setting free those held captive by unclean spirits (Luke 13:16). It is for this reason that Jesus saw his ministry of exorcism as tangible evidence of the reality of the presence of God's reign (Luke 11:20) and that his contemporaries, who did not separate Jesus' words from his acts of power, referred to his

exorcisms as "teaching" (Mark 1:22, 27).

Closely following the proclamation of the reign of God was the hope for the redemption and restoration of Israel. We find this in the call throughout for Israel to repent

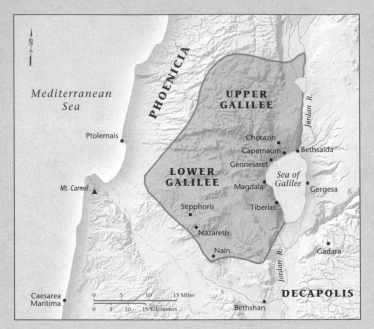

Galilee at the Time of Jesus

(Mark 1:15; 6:12; Matt. 11:21 par. Luke 10:13), in the appointment of the Twelve and their commission to proclaim the kingdom and to cast out evil spirits (Mark 3:15; 6:7), and in the promise that when the kingdom comes in its fullness the Twelve will rule over the 12 tribes of Israel (Matt. 19:28; Luke 22:28-30).

Jesus also proclaims the compassion and goodness of God. He teaches that God is ready and eager to receive repentant sinners (Luke 15:11-32), that he is a God who answers prayer (Matt. 6:5-13; Luke 18:1-7), rewards faithfulness (Matt. 24:45 par. Luke 12:42), and expects his people to be, as he is, compassionate (Luke 6:36; 10:37) and forgiving (Matt. 6:12-15; 18:21-22). Above all, God is a personal God who knows humanity's needs, even to minute details (Matt. 6:25-34; 10:30 par. Luke 12:7); therefore,

people are to have faith in God (Mark 2:5; 5:34, 36; 11:22, 24; Luke 7:50).

Jesus is also a teacher of wisdom and ethics, all of which must be understood in the light of the coming judgment. Like Dame Wisdom herself (Prov. 9:1-6), Jesus urges his hearers to come to him and to take upon themselves his yoke (Matt. 11:28-30), even claiming that someone greater than Solomon is present (Matt. 12:42 par. Luke 11:31). Jesus urges humility, warning that those who exalt themselves will be humbled, while those who humble themselves will be exalted (Mark 9:35; Luke 14:11). Jesus expects his followers to help the poor (Mark 10:21; Luke 14:13) and not assume that the sick and downtrodden are worse sinners than anyone else (Luke 13:1-5; 16:19-31; John 9:1-3).

Jesus' teachings of the end

times crystallized after entering Jerusalem. He warned of a coming fearful judgment if God's message and Messenger were not received. The temple has become fruitless, its purpose left unfulfilled (Mark 11:15-19). The ruling priests, God's stewards over his temple and people, will lose their authority because of theft and murder (Mark 11:17; 12:1-12). Indeed, the days will come when Jerusalem will be besieged, her inhabitants will be dashed to the ground, and not one stone of the city will be left upon another (Luke 19:41-44). Even the beautiful temple complex will be completely demolished (Mark 13:1-2). These terrible events will be preceded by signs, but the final events will unfold so swiftly that few will be prepared and many will perish (Mark 13:3-37). Jesus warns his disciples to be alert and faithful.

For Further Reading

Borg, Markus J. *Conflict, Holiness, and Politics in the Teachings of Jesus.* Harrisburg: Trinity Press International, 1998.

Chilton, Bruce D. *A Galilean Rabbi and His Bible: Jesus' Use of the Interpreted Scripture of His Time.* Good News Studies 8. Wilmington: Michael Glazier, 1984.

————. *Pure Kingdom: Jesus' Vision of God.* Studying the Historical Jesus. Grand Rapids: Eerdmans, 1996.

McKnight, Scot. *A New Vision for Israel: The Teachings of Jesus in National Context.* Studying the Historical Jesus. Grand Rapids: Eerdmans, 1999.

CRAIG A. EVANS

as an offering to God, they nevertheless continue to use them for their own purposes.

7:24–8:10 Jesus Reaches Out to Gentiles

Cf. Matt. 15:21-39.

Traveling north to Tyre, Jesus is implored by a Greek woman of Syrophoenician nationality to exorcise a demon that is is tormenting her daughter. Jesus declines (7:26) on the grounds that Jews ("children") have prior claim to his mighty works ("crumbs") than Gentiles ("dogs"). But when she acknowledges him as "master," which in common usage meant "benefactor," he relents in recognition of her faith.

Mark presents a detailed account of Jesus' curing of a deaf man with a speech impediment (7:31-37). Jesus' use of spit to heal the man stems from the ancient belief in the curative power of saliva. Again Jesus uses the Aramaic language to command the man's wellness (cf. 5:41).

8:11-21 On Evil "Leaven"

Cf. Matt. 16:1-12; Luke 11:16; 12:1.

The Pharisees demand a sign from heaven to clarify the source of Jesus' power in performing miracles, but he refuses to be tested. He warns the disciples of the corrupting influence ("yeast") the Pharisees' teaching has on true faith (v. 15). Mark lumps Herod together with the Jewish religious leaders as threats to Jesus' life and mission. When the disciples bemoan their lack of bread, Jesus laments that they have missed the point of the miraculous feeding of the multitudes.

8:22-26 The Blind Man of Bethsaida

This miracle goes unreported in Matthew and Luke, but Matthew may have summarized and combined this healing with that of Bartimaeus (10:46-52; cf. Matt. 20:29-34; Luke 18:35-43). Again, Jesus applies his own, healthy spittle to cure the sensory organs of another (7:31-37).

8:27–9:1 Identifying Jesus and His Mission

Cf. Matt. 10:32-33; 16:13-28; Luke 9:18-27.

In the villages surrounding Caesarea Philippi, Herod Philip's district capital some 25 miles north of the Sea of Galilee, Jesus' ministry takes a bold turn. At Jesus' prompting, Peter recognizes him as the Messiah (in Greek, the Christ). But Jesus warns them against publicly identifying him as such, since even those close to him will have difficulty grasping what this means.

Jesus then begins to prepare the disciples for the persecution and death that lie ahead. When Peter resists, Jesus charges that his objection serves human interests, not those of God (8:33). Jesus instructs the crowd and the disciples that any who would be his followers must face these trials. How a person accepts Jesus and his ministry now will determine his or her own fate at the final judgment (8:38).

9:2-32 Jesus, the New Moses

Cf. Matt. 17:1-23; Luke 9:28-45.

Jesus invites three of his inner circle to accompany him up a mountain, where he becomes "transfigured." In an event resembling the theophanies of the Old Testament, Jesus is clothed in unearthly brilliance and accompanied by none other than Moses and Elijah. Thinking that this marks Jesus as one of the greatest prophets, Peter suggests erecting booths or tents as dwellings for the three divine beings. The event may foreshadow Jesus' second coming.

While Matthew makes Jesus' curing of an epileptic child a miraculous healing of a medical condition, Mark's more detailed account portrays it as an exorcism that hinges on the faith of the boy's father.

9:33-50 Christian Obligations and Behavior

Cf. Matt. 5:13; 18:1-9; Luke 9:46-50; 14:34-35; 17:1-2.

Discussion among the disciples about rank among the followers shows that they have missed the point of Jesus' announcement concerning his own self-sacrifice (vv. 30-32). The talk provides him opportunity to teach concerning the "greatest" and the "least." Believers must humble themselves in service even to those considered least important by society.

In verses 38-41, Jesus sanctions the perform-

Caesarea Philippi, capital of the tetrarch Herod Philip on the southern slope of Mount Hermon. Here Peter recognized Jesus as the Christ. *(Richard Cleave, Pictorial Archive)*

ing of exorcisms by an outsider, who cannot long resist conversion in the face of the irresistibly convincing miracles he performs in Jesus' name.

The picture of hell/Gehenna in verse 48 (duplicated in vv. 44 and 46 in some manuscripts) recalls the Hinnom Valley, the worm-infested, perpetually smoldering garbage pit of ancient Jerusalem. Salting with fire (vv. 49-50) refers to moral judgment.

10:1-12 Marriage and Divorce

Cf. Matt. 19:1-12.

As Jesus heads from Galilee to Judea by way of Perea, the region east of the Jordan, Pharisees again test him on points of the Law. At issue are differing rabbinical interpretations — one that allows a man to divorce his wife for even the most minor of reasons, and another that permits the dissolution only in the case of moral misconduct on her part. Unlike Gentile women, Jewish wives did not have the right to initiate a divorce. Jesus' concern is for marriage as created by God, and the interference of another person in that union, either through infidelity or remarriage, constitutes adultery.

10:13-31 The Requirements and Rewards of Discipleship

Cf. Matt. 18:3; 19:13-30; Luke 18:15-30.

Despite the disciples' resistance, Jesus welcomes those who present little children for his blessing. This move further demonstrates his concern and compassion for the most vulnerable members of society and provides a model for how one should receive the gift of God's kingdom.

The rich young man learns that he must abandon his reliance on mammon (wealth) and become dependent on God, and the vignette adds new insight into Jesus' teaching on earthly treasure in Matt. 6:19-24. Salvation comes only as a gift from God. On verses 29-30, compare the rewards realized by Job for faithfulness in the face of extreme adversity (see Job 42).

10:32–11:11 Suffering and Servanthood

Cf. Matt. 20:17–21:17; Luke 18:31-43; 19:28-46; 22:24-27.

James and John petition Jesus for positions of honor in his kingdom (10:33-40; in Matthew their mother issues the request; cf. 9:33-37). But they do not yet grasp what lies ahead. The "baptism" to which Jesus refers means suffering, as connoted also by the "cup." He explains that the leaders in his kingdom will not wield earthly authority but be servant and slave to all (10:42-45).

As Jesus and the disciples leave Jericho, a blind beggar named Bartimaeus (Aramaic for "son of Timaeus") cries out for Jesus to heal him. His use of the title "son of David" suggests that Jesus' identity as the Messiah has become public knowledge (10:48).

That Jesus enters Jerusalem riding a colt (the Hebrew term can designate the young of many types of animals) suggests the humble royal mount prophesied in Zech. 9:9. He is greeted with shouts of "Hosanna" ("save, we pray, now"), a standard word of praise used to glorify God.

11:12-26 Jesus Curses the Fig Tree and "Cleanses" the Temple

Cf. Matt. 6:14; 21:12-22; Luke 19:45-48.

Upon entering the temple courtyard, Jesus immediately begins to cleanse God's "house." He throws out those selling and buying animals for sacrifice and those who charged a fee for currency exchange, and he halts people using the precincts as a thoroughfare for transporting sacrificial paraphernalia (11:15-17). The religious authorities are incensed, partly because these actions impinge on their authority and perhaps cut into their revenue.

Mark surrounds this event with his account of Jesus' cursing of the fig tree (vv. 12-14, 20-24), which illustrates God's judgment on Jerusalem and its temple. The mention that "it was not the season for figs" (v. 13) makes this action even more surprising.

11:27–12:12 The Church Replaces the Chosen Nation

Cf. Matt. 21:23-27, 33-46; Luke 20:1-19.

A delegation representing the leaders of the Sanhedrin, the supreme religious council, challenge Jesus' authority for his disruptive "cleansing" of the temple. He turns the question back on them, asking why they had not objected to John's activity, which Jesus considers to have laid the foundation for his own ministry (11:30).

Mark's version of the parable of the Vineyard (sometimes called the "Wicked Tenants"; 12:1-12) recounts God's dealing with Israel (the vineyard). In the past, the religious authorities ("tenants") have rejected and abused his prophets ("slaves"), and will soon do likewise with God's "beloved son" (12:6). God will cast out the wicked tenants and replace them with new ones, followers of the "cornerstone" (v. 11).

12:13-37 Jesus Outsmarts His Detractors

Cf. Matt. 22:15-46; Luke 20:20-44.

Jesus' religious and political opponents join forces in an attempt to trap him into saying something offensive to the authorities or at least damage his reputation among the masses. Asked whether it is proper for Jews to pay the Roman poll tax, he risks being seen either as treasonous or disloyal to his people and faith. Jesus' answer is that in the long run what is really important belongs to God.

The Sadducees' question about the nature of resurrection is meant to ridicule Jesus' teaching. Instead, he forcefully shows that they are ignorant of both the Hebrew Scriptures (cf. Exod. 3:6) and the power of God.

Recognizing Jesus' careful response to these questions, one of the scribes asks which, of all the commandments in Scripture, he regards as most important. In verses 32-34, Mark adds the legal expert's enthusiasm for Jesus' answer, showing his grasp of the nature of the coming kingdom of God.

12:38-40 A Warning against Hypocrisy

Cf. Matt. 23:1-7; Luke 20:45-47.

Jesus condemns as bad examples those who concentrate on outward piety. The scribes' "devouring of widows' houses" (foreclosure on their property; v. 40) violates Mosaic law, which mandates special care of society's weakest members (see, e.g., Deuteronomy 26).

12:41-44 A Poor Widow Models Charity

Cf. Luke 21:1-4.

In this account, omitted in Matthew, a widow contributes her last cent to the temple treasury. In ancient times, widows lacked the economic opportunities available to men and therefore made up some of the poorest of Palestine's poor. Jesus pronounces this widow's ostensibly meager gift greater than the larger sums given by the rich, who hold back for themselves plenty of money to live on.

13 The Coming Destruction

Cf. Matt. 10:17-21; 24:1-36; 25:13; Luke 21:5-33.

In this longest block of his teaching in Mark, Jesus lays out for the disciples the earthshaking events that lie ahead. In terms much like those of the prophets of old, he foretells the coming destruction of the temple and widespread social and political upheaval (vv. 1-8). Just as Jesus himself is the "stone" that will be rejected, so too will the disciples experience persecution and judgment before the religious and governmental authorities (vv. 9-13). Nevertheless, he assures them that both he and they will be vindicated, and those who have judged them will themselves be judged when the Son of Man returns (vv. 24-27). In the meantime, they must remain faithful and strong (vv. 32-37).

14:1-2 Conspiracy

Cf. Matt. 26:1-5; Luke 22:1-2.

The chief priests and scribes decide that the only way to silence Jesus is to kill him, but realizing his popularity among the people, they are forced to do it on the sly. For fear of provoking a riot, they determine to wait until after the "festival," which by Jesus' day combined the Feast of Unleavened Bread and Passover.

14:3-11 Jesus Anointed for Burial

Cf. Matt. 26:6-16; Luke 7:36-50; John 12:1-8.

Again Jesus' participation in a meal departs from Jewish custom. The setting is the home of Simon, a leper and so ritually unclean, and normally a woman would not enter the hall where men were feasting. Mark defines the monetary worth of the ointment as more than 300 denarii (the equivalent of a year's wages for the common laborer), an indication of both the woman's wealth and her devotion to Jesus.

In Mark's account, Judas receives only a promise of money to betray Jesus.

Olive trees in Gethsemane, the place of Jesus' betrayal and arrest. *(www.HolyLandPhotos.org)*

14:12-25 The Last Supper

Cf. Matt. 26:17-29; Luke 22:7-23; John 13:1-30.

Jesus instructs the disciples on finding an upper room where they are to prepare for the Passover meal. The man they were to meet would have been easy to spot, for normally women carried water jars (v. 13).

During the meal, Jesus announces his betrayal (vv. 17-21) and predicts that he will drink "the fruit of the vine" in the coming kingdom of God (v. 25). He breaks bread, representing his body, and passes a cup, symbolizing his blood, "poured out for *many*," an inclusive term in Semitic usage indicating all humanity. From the early years after Jesus' death and resurrection, followers of Christ have commemorated the Last Supper by celebrating the Lord's Supper or Eucharist ("Thanksgiving").

14:26-52 Jesus in Gethsemane

Cf. Matt. 26:30-56; Luke 22:31-34, 39-53; John 13:36-38; 18:1-11.

Leaving the upper room for the Mount of Olives, Jesus realizes that the disciples will abandon him in his time of trial and death. Despite the protests of Peter, Jesus knows that he too will disown him.

When praying in Gethsemane, Jesus assumes childlike subordination to God by addressing him as "Abba," the intimate Aramaic word for "Father" (v. 36). It is with a kiss of greeting, a sign of affection, that one of his own disciples singles him out as a "bandit" to the armed crowd accompanied by the religious leaders (themselves called "robbers" by Jesus in 11:17-18). Only Mark notes the naked escape of Jesus' unnamed follower (vv. 51-52).

14:53-65 Jesus before the Sanhedrin

Cf. Matt. 26:57-68; Luke 22:63-71; John 18:19-24.

By highlighting the Sanhedrin's failure to garner corroborating testimony against Jesus from two witnesses (the minimum number required by Mosaic law), Mark shows the inadmissibility of the evidence against Jesus, as well as its falsehood (v. 59; cf. Deut. 19:15). In Mark,

Jesus confesses his messiahship outright (v. 62; cf. Matt. 26:64; Luke 22:70).

14:66-72 Peter's Denial

Cf. Matt. 26:69-75; Luke 22:54-62; John 18:15-18, 25-27.

Pressed by one of the high priest's female servants who recognizes Peter as one of Jesus' companions, the disciple emphatically denies their association. Mark separates the two crows of the cock (see v. 30), the second of which triggers Peter's memory of Jesus' prediction that the disciple would deny him three times that night.

15:1-15 Jesus Appears before Pilate

Cf. Matt. 27:1-2, 11-26; Luke 23:1-5, 17-25; John 18:28–19:16.

Because only the Romans could apply the death penalty, the Jewish council turn Jesus over to Pontius Pilate, the fifth Roman procurator of Judea (A.D. 26-36), for judgment. Pilate addresses the charge that Jesus claimed to be "King of the Jews" and so posed a threat to Roman authority (v. 2). (In the religious trial, the issue was Jesus' messiahship; 14:61.) Jesus' answer, "You say so," makes Pilate appear to affirm Jesus' kingship.

Following the custom of granting amnesty to a Jewish prisoner during religious festivals, Pilate presents to the crowd the choice of releasing Barabbas, a convicted revolutionary and murderer, or Jesus, the peace-loving Messiah. The mob, stirred up by the chief priests, demands that Jesus be crucified, and Pilate gives in.

15:16-47 Crucifixion and Burial

Cf. Matt. 27:27-61; Luke 23:26-56; John 19:17-42.

In the courtyard of the governor's palace, Jesus is surrounded by a chorot (600 men) of Roman soldiers. They clothe him in royal garb and a crown crafted of thorns; mock him as "King of the Jews"; and even send him to carry his wooden cross to the place of crucifixion outside the city walls.

Some among the onlookers offer him wine mixed with bitter-tasting gall to ease the pain, but Jesus refuses the drink, perhaps to experience fully the agony of crucifixion or to refrain from postponing his death. (A crucified person might take several days to die; not so with Jesus. See Pilate's apparent surprise in v. 44.) At noon, three hours after Jesus' nailing to the cross (v. 25), the skies darken, and three hours later he dies.

Mark identifies by name individuals unmentioned or anonymous in Matthew, including Alexander and Rufus (sons of Simon of Cyrene, v. 21) and Salome (wife of Zebedee; cf. Matt. 27:56). Joses is a variant of the name Joseph (v. 40).

That the women who witnessed Jesus' burial "saw where the body was laid" (v. 47) becomes important when on the next day they return to the tomb and see that the corpse no longer lies where they know it had been placed (16:6).

16:1-8 The Risen Christ

Cf. Matt. 28:1-10; Luke 24:1-12; John 20:1-18.

Expecting Jesus to be dead, the women bring spices to the tomb to anoint the body, but they realize that they have forgotten to bring help in rolling away the stone that blocks the entrance. In Mark's account, the angel ("a young man, dressed in a white robe") sits inside the open, empty tomb. Instructed to inform the disciples of Jesus' resurrection, the female visitors are too stunned by the news to do more than flee and keep the angelic announcement to themselves.

16:9-20 A Late Conclusion to Mark's Gospel

Cf. Matt. 28:16-20; Luke 24:13-53; John 20:19–21:14.

The last dozen verses of Mark represent a late, editorial conclusion to the book and do not appear in the oldest extant manuscripts. These verses summarize Christ's postresurrection appearances; his giving of the Great Commission; his ascension into heaven; and the apostles' fulfillment of the commission by proclaiming the gospel worldwide.

Luke

As the most comprehensive of the synoptic Gospels, Luke is also the longest book in the New Testament. Luke gives a fuller account of the nativity of Jesus than does Matthew; uniquely recounts the birth of John the Baptist; alone describes Jesus' ministry in the Transjordanian region of Perea; records well-known parables of Jesus that appear nowhere else (e.g., the Good Samaritan, Rich Fool, Prodigal Son, Rich Man and Lazarus, Pharisee and Tax Collector); gives more and different details regarding Jesus' resurrection; and supplies the only record of Jesus' ascension to heaven.

In Luke, Jesus associates with all kinds of people, from Pharisees to social outcasts. But whether among the self-righteous or "sinners," he maintains his moral purity, demonstrates prayerful piety, and consistently abides by both religious and civil law. Other distinctive characteristics of Luke include the frequent mention of the Holy Spirit and the role of women in Jesus' ministry. Thus the universal message of the gospel embodied by Jesus emerges as universally appealing, especially to the cosmopolitan Gentile audience toward which Luke appears slanted.

Authorship and Date

Scholars deduce the authorship of Luke from its literary relationship to the book of Acts and from a comparison of the "we" sections of Acts (which depict the travels of Paul and his missionary companions) with the itineraries of the missionaries as recorded in the New Testament letters of Paul. The conclusion that the same author wrote Luke and Acts stems from the introductory dedication of both books to a man named Theophilus; the reference in Acts 1:1 to the "first account" (the preceding, companion volume); and the similarities of thematic interest and writing style. Luke is singled out as the

author of Luke-Acts because of the impossibility of harmonizing the geographical movements of Paul's other missionary companions, as recorded in his epistles, with the itineraries in the "we" sections of Acts. That Paul calls Luke "the beloved physician" (Col. 4:14) supports his authorship of this Gospel, since at a number of points it pays unique attention to medical detail (e.g., the naming of diseases; cf. 14:2). Support for Luke's authorship from outside the Bible comes from early church tradition and later Christian writers. The linguistic refinement of the Greek text of Luke is paralleled in the New Testament only by the book of Hebrews.

Luke reveals his use of sources to write his account (1:1-4). Since 65 percent of the material in Mark also appears in Luke — sometimes word for word — it seems obvious that Mark was one of Luke's sources. That Luke also includes material found in Matthew but not in Mark has led scholars to suggest a now lost source used by Matthew and Luke and referred to as "Q" (from German *Quelle,* "source"). The composition of Luke must therefore come after Mark and possibly also Matthew, if only slightly. Luke 21:20 quotes Jesus as referring to the siege of Jerusalem, carried out by the Romans from A.D. 67-70, so either Jesus predicted this event or Luke wrote after it took place. Presumably, Luke wrote Acts after writing his Gospel account. He accompanied the Apostle Paul to Rome and may have written his Gospel there, though early traditions also support its being written in Greece.

1:1-4 Luke's Purpose for Writing

Luke acknowledges the existence of other Gospel accounts written by eyewitnesses to the events of Jesus' life and ministry. The Gospel of Mark, from which Luke draws much of his material, represents one such record. Luke's

Jesus and History

Attitudes toward the historical reliability of the Gospel narratives have shifted since the early part of the 20th century, even among those who do not see the New Testament as inspired. In part, the increased optimism comes with a shift in the way moderns define history. History is a way we arrange the events of the past so that they are meaningful, or memorable, or inspiring, or instructive. History — not just past events, but also what we write about them — is not repeatable in the way a mathematical equation is, and historians sifting the same sources will not construct the same picture of the past. Once we recognize this, we stop looking for certainty and begin looking for what is probable or plausible. With that as our goal, there is much that one can say about Jesus.

The new confidence is also partly the result of a new approach to our sources of information about Jesus. In the past some scholars mostly looked for what was distinctive about Jesus. If material attributed to Jesus was different from what 1st-century Palestinian Jews and early Gentile Christians would have said or done, then they felt it must have come from Jesus (e.g., the saying "let the dead bury their dead"). This approach yields only small amounts of data, and the picture of Jesus that results is of a man disconnected from his environment.

A more profitable approach is first to look for multiple independent testimony to the words and deeds of Jesus, and second to look for what fits within a 1st-century Palestinian Jewish environment but goes against the grain of the beliefs and practices of early Christians. We have several independent early sources for what Jesus said and did. Most New Testament scholars believe that Matthew and Luke used both Mark and another source commonly called "Q" (from German *Quelle,* "source"). Most, as well, hold that John was written independently of Mark and Q. Paul also gives independent testimony, although his letters contain only a few sayings of Jesus and no stories about what Jesus did. The 1st-century Jewish historian Josephus included a short paragraph about Jesus in his *Jewish Antiquities,* and although his text was expanded by Christian copyists, most scholars believe that we can be confident with his description of Jesus as a teacher and a miracle worker who attracted great attention and was crucified by Pilate. Another account is the Gospel of Thomas, written in Greek probably in the 1st century but mostly preserved in Coptic. Some scholars believe this Gospel depends on one or more of the New Testament Gospels; others hold it to be independent of them, making it another valuable source for the historical Jesus.

If three independent witnesses are enough to count something to be a historical "fact," then we can be certain that:

- Jesus healed and cast out demons;
- he preached and taught about the coming and present kingdom of God;
- he called disciples and appointed 12 of them to special roles;
- he predicted the destruction of the temple in Jerusalem;
- he was seized by the temple authorities and handed over to Pilate, who crucified him.

Eleven sayings or parables are triply attested, appearing in Mark, Q, and Thomas. By these rules, we can be certain that:

- Jesus explained his ministry by talking about John's baptism;
- Jesus sent his disciples on a mission to the towns of Galilee, telling them to heal, to cast out demons, and to rely on the hospitality of the townspeople for their sustenance.

We can be certain, also, that Jesus told his disciples that:

- they should let their lights shine;
- they should ask and receive;
- none who blasphemed the Holy Spirit would ever be forgiven;
- the kingdom was like a mustard seed;
- hidden things would be revealed;
- if they wanted to be his disciples, they would need to bear their own cross.

The second method looks for what fits within 1st-century

Palestinian Judaism but seems at odds with the beliefs and practices of the early church. Many features of Jesus' life and ministry can be demonstrated this way. For example, we can be certain that Jesus was baptized by John. Since the church believed Jesus to be the sinless Son of God, they would not have invented a story that puts him going into the waters as though he were a sinner. Likewise, the episode when Jesus entered the temple and turned over the tables is the single event that makes him look dangerous to the Romans, and it seems unlikely that the church, who believed Jesus died an innocent man, would have invented this.

Most who write about the historical Jesus would agree with most of the "facts" listed above. But history is more than facts; history tries to put facts together into a coherent story and to draw cause-and-effect connections between facts. Here are a few currently influential reconstructions of Jesus.

- "Jesus the Apocalyptic Prophet" This view suggests that Jesus was motivated by his sense that the end of the present age was close. He preached, healed, and cast out demons to spread this message and to ask people to commit themselves to it. He predicted the destruction of the temple, and his entry into the temple was less a cleansing than an acting out of his prophecy. The temple leaders arrested him for disturbing the peace during a festival, and the Romans gladly crucified him because he talked about a kingdom.
- "Jesus the Peasant Cynic Sage" Jesus did not expect the end of all things but believed that

God's reign began as people gathered into Jesus' new communities. He healed and cast out demons to attract people to hear him, and then he taught them to share their food and their homes and to treat all as equals, no matter what their social status. He acted out his prediction of the temple's destruction because he felt the temple leaders were crushing the poor. They seized him and gave him to the Romans, who crucified him.

- "Jesus the Agent of God's Restoration of Israel" The way we construct Jesus must explain the phenomenon of the early church. Here Jesus preaches apocalyptically but does so metaphorically rather than literally as a way of speaking about the coming disaster with the Romans and the salvation he was providing. Jesus knowingly sacrifices himself for the sins of the world.
- "Jesus the Marginal Jew" Jesus believed both in the coming end of the age — as with the "apocalyptic prophet" view — but also believed that the kingdom had begun in his ministry. Jesus probably did not reject the purity codes and probably baptized those who accepted his message. Thus Jesus taught a specific way to practice Judaism in the light of the present/coming kingdom.

Some New Testament scholars suggest that the quest for the historical Jesus has nothing to do with faith or living the Christian life; it is strictly an academic exercise and one Christians should not worry about. It is true that the rules of evidence given above yield

much less than the contents of the canonical Gospels. A story that appears only once and fits well with the teaching of Jesus' followers — e.g., the woman caught in adultery (Matthew) or the birth stories in Luke — cannot be absolutely proven by these rules. Yet they are part of our faith; we believe them, even if we cannot prove them historically. If that be true, why bother with a historical search, since the result can only be a shadow of the composite picture of all four Gospels?

Christians, gratefully, do not have to choose between the reconstructed historical Jesus and the Jesus whom we know through the whole New Testament and the traditions of the Christian church. Believing in the latter does not rule out the search for the former. Careful study of the New Testament will show that the way Matthew describes Jesus is very similar to, but also significantly different from, the way Mark, Luke, and John describe him. Our faith, embodied in hymns and confessions and creeds and catechisms and all sorts of church traditions, blends together all these different elements into one portrait. That is good, because it helps us to center ourselves, to focus our lives on the one Lord the church confesses. But behind the unified picture of the creeds are the diverse portraits of the New Testament. Without the historical Jesus — the one man who lived in a very particular time and place — we have a hard time explaining why the central documents of our faith tell the stories in different ways. Discovering the historical Jesus, then, is a historical-theological task for the church — historical, because it operates by the rules of history, and theological, because it aims at making the Jesus who is responsible for the diverse portraits of the New Testament available for those who love him now.

For Further Reading

Crossan, John Dominic. *The Historical Jesus: The Life of a Mediterranean Jewish Peasant.* San Francisco: Harper & Row, 1991.

McClymond, Michael J. *Familiar Stranger: An Introduction to Jesus of Nazareth.* Grand Rapids: Eerdmans, 2004.

Meier, John P. *A Marginal Jew: Rethinking the Historical Jesus.* 4 vols. New York: Doubleday, 1991-2009.

Sanders, E. P. *The Historical Figure of Jesus.* New York: Penguin, 1995.

Wright, N. T. *Christian Origins and the Question of God.* 2 vols. Minneapolis: Fortress, 1992-96.

RICHARD B. VINSON

particular contribution consists in giving a chronologically sensitive history of the Gospel events and demonstrating their historical reliability. His immediate purpose consists in enlightening Theophilus ("loved by God"; perhaps Luke's literary patron or a potential or recent convert) concerning the "truth" of the gospel teaching he has received.

1:5–2:52 The Birth and Childhood of John and Jesus

Only Luke recounts the events surrounding the birth of John the Baptist, and only Luke and Matthew write about the nativity and childhood of Jesus. Luke gives a fuller historical account of Jesus' birth, whereas Matthew concentrates on establishing Jesus' Davidic descent and messiahship (see Matthew 1–2).

1:5-25 A Father-to-Be Struck Speechless Verse 5 dates the events of the nativity to the reign of Herod the Great, an Idumean who under the authority of the Roman government ruled Palestine during the last half of the 1st century B.C. Next Luke introduces the priest Zechariah, who along with the other priests in his division is performing one of his two annual weeks of service at the Jerusalem temple, and his wife Elizabeth, whose ancestry traces back to Aaron, the brother of Moses and first high priest (see Exodus 28). The barrenness of Elizabeth parallels that of the Old Testament matriarchs Sarah, Rebekah, and Rachel, as well as of Hannah, who bore Samuel, and the mother of Samson. The advanced age of the priestly couple recalls the elderly Abram and Sarah and underlines the intervention of God in Elizabeth's ability to conceive.

The ancient Hebrews used lot-casting (similar to our drawing of straws) to determine the will of God (e.g., Josh. 14:1-2). So when Zechariah gains by lot the honor of burning incense in the temple, it isn't just a lucky break for him. His solitary presence in the sanctuary occasions the appearance of the angel Gabriel (cf. Dan. 8:16; 9:21), who tells Zechariah that he and Elizabeth will become the parents of a son. Gabriel instructs Zechariah to name the boy John, informs the father-to-be that the boy will follow the requirements of a Nazirite vow by abstaining from the consumption of alcohol (Num. 6:1-4; cf. Samson, Judges 13), and describes John's future work in terms that parallel Malachi's prophecy of the returned Elijah (Mal. 4:5-6).

Ancient Near Eastern cultures viewed childlessness as a sign of divine disfavor (v. 25), and Zechariah, no doubt delighted at the angel's news, asks for a sign to dissolve his doubt about the truth of the announcement. Gabriel grants the request, but in a way that disciplines Zechariah for his disbelief: the priest will remain mute till Gabriel's words come to pass. Soon Elizabeth becomes pregnant, but her husband remains tongue-tied till after she gives birth (vv. 57ff.).

1:26-38 Gabriel's Message to Mary With Elizabeth in her sixth month of pregnancy, Gabriel makes an even more surprising announcement to her relative Mary, namely, that the engaged but unwed virgin will conceive a son by the Holy Spirit. Again Gabriel dictates the name of the child — Jesus — and describes him in terms that echo the Old Testament — here God's promise to David of a perpetual dynasty and prophecies foreshadowing the promised Messiah (cf. 2 Sam. 7:1-17; Dan. 7:13-28). Mary expresses her voluntary submission to God's will by calling herself his "servant." Mary's acceptance took courage, since pregnancy out of wedlock invited scandal and jeopardized her impending marriage to Joseph (cf. Matt. 1:18-25).

1:39-56 Mary Visits Elizabeth Having learned from Gabriel of Elizabeth's pregnancy (v. 36), Mary travels south, from Nazareth to Judah, and stays with her relative for the last three months before John's birth. Mary's greeting to Elizabeth sparks her baby to leap for joy in the womb and occasions Elizabeth's filling with the Holy Spirit, which leads her to perceive that Mary will become the mother of the Lord. Elizabeth pronounces on Mary a blessing, after which Mary offers a song of praise to God, termed in Latin the "Magnificat" (cf. the song of Hannah, 1 Sam. 2:1-10).

1:57-80 Elizabeth Gives Birth and Zechariah Speaks On the eighth day after Elizabeth delivers, she and Zechariah follow the Mosaic law by presenting their baby boy for circumcision (cf. Gen. 17:12-14), at which time his official naming takes place. Much to everyone's dismay, both parents insist on calling their son John, a name nowhere represented in his ancestry. The act of obedience to the angel Gabriel's command loosens the tongue of Zechariah, and the unusual events make the family the talk of the

Shepherd with flock. *(BiblePlaces.com)*

region. Filled with the Holy Spirit, Zechariah utters a prophetic song of praise, known as the "Benedictus." The prophecy exudes hope for the fulfillment of Old Testament promises of divine salvation (= deliverance) from Israel's oppressors. This hope rests on God's promise to Abraham (Gen. 12:1-3) and a continuation of the Davidic dynasty (= "house," v. 69). Zechariah sees his son as the one ordained to "clear" the way for the Lord, as prophesied in Mal. 3:1 (v. 76). John lives in the desert till he begins his adult ministry.

2:1-20 The Birth of Jesus The census ordered by the emperor Caesar Augustus (v. 1) may refer to one taken not for purposes of taxation but for determining allegiance to Rome. The historical record documents well his taxation censuses of Roman citizens in 28 B.C., 8 B.C., and A.D. 14. The Greek of verse 2 may indicate that the census occurred *before* Quirinius became military governor of Syria in A.D. 6.

Hebrew custom in 1st-century Palestine considered engagement to be as binding as marriage; indeed, engaged couples were called husband and wife, though conjugal rights applied only after their official marriage. So when in compliance with the emperor's decree Joseph "goes up" to the Judean hill country from Nazareth (70 mi. *north* of Bethlehem but far *lower in elevation*), he takes with him his betrothed, Mary, whose miraculous pregnancy has reached nearly full term. Thus Bethlehem, birthplace of Joseph's royal forefather, becomes the birthplace of Jesus, whose Davidic ancestry through his adoptive, human father legitimates him as the rightful heir to the throne.

Yet the circumstances of Jesus' birth prove far from regal. Overcrowding from the influx of homecomers to Bethlehem has forced Joseph and Mary to take lodging apparently on the lower floor of a private home, where many 1st-century households kept their livestock. Mary employs the animals' feeding trough (manger) as a bed for her newborn son. Luke records the angelic announcement of Jesus' birth to local shepherds, whose profession parallels that of Jesus' monarchic predecessor David, the shepherd-king. The shepherds visit the stable and thus become eyewitnesses to the truth of the revelation concerning the Savior (see vv. 10-12).

2:21-40 Simeon and Anna Recognize the Messiah
Mary and Joseph follow the Mosaic law by having Jesus circumcised on the eighth day after his birth, they officially name him at that time (cf. 1:59ff.), dedicate him to God at the temple after the period of ritual purification, and offer the required sacrifice (cf. Leviticus 12; Exod. 13:2, 12-13). The Holy Spirit leads the righteous Jerusalemite Simeon to the temple, where as divinely promised he encounters the Christ child. Simeon's prophecy foresees a fundamental change in God's covenantal relationship with humanity. Jesus' ministry will widen the offer of salvation to Gentiles; but salvation for the chosen people of the old covenant, the Jews, will now depend not on their ancestry but on their acceptance or rejection of Jesus as the Messiah. Simeon's ominous words to Mary that a "sword will pierce [her] soul" find fruition in Jesus' crucifixion and burial. The elderly prophetess Anna also recognizes Jesus as the Christ, and her testimony at the temple reinforces the witness of Simeon.

2:41-52 Jesus Stays Behind
Luke provides our only window into the childhood of Jesus. Here the 12-year-old Jesus and his family join with relatives and friends in the annual pilgrimage to Jerusalem for the Passover festival (Lev. 23:3-8). When the caravan sets out on the return trip to Nazareth, Jesus' parents assume that their son has stayed with the group. But failing to find him at the end of the first day's journey, they go back to Jerusalem, where after three days of searching they finally locate Jesus in the temple. With his reckoning as an adult set to occur within the year (at age 13), Jesus finds himself at home in the house of God, his Father, where his interaction with the teachers of Hebrew religion fosters and furthers his growth in wisdom. By stressing Jesus' continued "obedience" to his parents back in Nazareth and by commenting on his intellectual, physical, spiritual, and social growth, Luke portrays Jesus as the ideal child who develops into an ideally well-rounded adult (v. 52).

3:1-22 The Ministry of John the Baptist

Cf. Matthew 3; Mark 1:2-11.

Luke sets the ministry of John at ca. 27-29, in the reign of Herod Antipas, a son of Herod the Great during whose rule Jesus was born (v. 1). The regions of Galilee, Ituraea, Trachonitis, and Abilene all lay well north of Judea and Jerusalem. During John's ministry, Caiaphas served as high priest (A.D. 18-36), but the lasting influence of his predecessor and father-in-law Annas (A.D. 6-15) leads Luke to mention the priests as a pair (v. 2).

Luke's quotation from Isa. 40:3-5 extends the offer of salvation to all humanity (vv. 4-6; cf. Matt. 3:2). Verses 10-14 note practical implications of righteousness: generosity, honesty, justice, and contentment.

In Luke's account of Jesus' baptism, the Holy Spirit descends on the Lord while he prays, and the Spirit alights in the physical form of a dove (cf. "like a dove" in Matthew and Mark).

3:23-38 The Genealogy of Jesus

Cf. Matt. 1:1-16.

In Luke's Gospel, the genealogy of Jesus introduces the account of his public ministry, which he begins at 30 — the age when Hebrew priests assumed their duties (Num. 4:2-3). Luke traces Jesus' ancestry through his human father, Joseph, to establish Jesus as the legitimate heir to the Davidic throne (v. 31). That the genealogy extends back to Adam makes Jesus the Savior not just of the Jews but of all humanity (cf. Matt. 1:2, where Jesus' lineage starts with Abraham, forefather of the Hebrew people).

4:1-13 Temptation in the Wilderness

Cf. Matt. 4:1-11; Mark 1:12-13.

Full with the Holy Spirit, Jesus fasts for 40 days. Although "famished," he resists the Devil's command to turn stones to bread. Luke reverses Matthew's order of the remaining temptations and ends them at Jerusalem, where Jesus' ministry will culminate.

4:14–9:50 Jesus' Ministry in Galilee

4:14-30 Hometown Rejection Cf. Matt. 4:12-17; 13:54-58; Mark 1:14-15; 6:1-6a.

Filled and led by the Holy Spirit, Jesus exits the wilderness and heads home to Galilee, where he begins his public ministry and his reputation grows (cf. v. 23). Though widely praised throughout the region, Jesus prophesies and experiences rejection in his hometown, Nazareth. From his boyhood, Jesus has recognized his sonship to God (cf. 2:49), but his townspeople see him only as the offspring of a familiar carpenter (v. 22). At the local synagogue, Jesus declares himself the embodiment of Isa. 61:1-2a — the Spirit-empowered preacher of the gospel, deliverer of the oppressed, and healer of the blind (cf. Matt. 11:2-6). Jesus stops just short of Isaiah's reference to the "day of vengeance of our God," meaning judgment day. From the beginning of his Gospel, Luke emphasizes the offer of salvation to Gentiles and the condemnation of unbelieving Jews (cf. 2:32ff.; 3:4-6). The examples Jesus cites from the ministries of the prophets Elijah and Elisha illustrate this reversal of Jewish expectation and enrage the hometown crowd (1 Kgs. 17:9-16; 2 Kgs. 5:1-14). Expelled from the city by a mob bent on stoning him for blasphemy, Jesus nevertheless escapes unharmed to carry on with his mission.

4:31-44 Favorable Reception Cf. Matt. 7:28-29; 8:14-17; Mark 1:21-38.

The amazement with which the residents of Capernaum receive Jesus' authoritative teaching contrasts with the skepticism of his hometown crowd. The miracles he performs in Capernaum provide tangible reasons for their faith. Jesus' demonstration of authority in the spiritual and physical realms validates the authority of his teaching, and the receptive Galilean multitudes will not let him go (contrast vv. 29 and 42).

5:1-11 Jesus Catches Some Fishermen Cf. Matt. 4:18-22; Mark 1:16-20.

A multitude of eager listeners backs Jesus up to the shores of Lake Gennesaret, another name for the Sea of Galilee. The availability of a fishing boat belonging to Simon Peter affords Jesus the opportunity to continue addressing the crowds while anchored just offshore. He follows up his teaching with another miracle, this time directing Simon Peter toward an unmanageable catch of fish after he and his partners have seen nothing but empty nets all night long. The awesome demonstration of Jesus' power heightens Simon's sense of sinfulness and stirs his fear. Jesus meets the amazement of the fishermen with an irresistible call to discipleship.

5:12-26 Jesus Heals a Leper and a Paralytic Cf. Matt. 8:1-4; 9:1-8; Mark 1:40-45; 2:1-12.

The advanced disease of the man "full" of leprosy (an unspecified skin disease making him ritually impure and a social outcast) and the immediacy of the paralytic's restoration underline Jesus' unlimited power to heal. Recognizing the latter man's faith, Jesus forgives his sins, believed by his contemporaries to be the cause of his affliction.

By noting Jesus' solitary withdrawal to the wilderness for prayer, Luke shows that Jesus has not let popularity diminish his piety (v. 16; cf. 3:21; 6:12; 9:18, 28; 11:1).

5:27-39 Feasting with Levi and Company Cf. Matt. 9:9-17; Mark 2:13-22.

Jesus enlists an unlikely candidate for discipleship — a tax collector named Levi whose occupation carried the stigma of dishonesty and complicity with the Roman establishment. Levi immediately repents ("leaves everything") to join Jesus' cause. Jesus further alienates the guardians of religious orthodoxy by joining Levi's celebratory banquet, where he mingles with people considered outside the fold.

The question then arises as to why Jesus' followers do not fast, as do the Pharisees and even the disciples of John the Baptist. Jesus answers that a new age is at hand, one marked by repentance and hope and therefore a time for celebration. Pointing ahead to his own death, he remarks that there will yet be plenty of time for mourning and preparation for the final days.

6:1-11 Sabbath Law vs. Legalism Cf. Matt. 12:1-14; Mark 2:23–3:6.

Jesus runs afoul of the Pharisees' interpretation of the Law when his disciples grab handfuls of grain while passing through a field on the

Sabbath. Rubbing the heads of wheat between the hands separates the edible grain from the inedible chaff (v. 1), which the religious legalists consider to be labor. In his account of Jesus healing on the Sabbath, Luke notes that the man had a withered *right* hand — presumably the one whose loss of use caused the greatest handicap (v. 6). Luke also addresses this issue in 14:1-9, where Jesus heals a man with dropsy.

6:12-16 Jesus Appoints Twelve Apostles Cf. Matt. 10:1-4; Mark 3:13-19.

After a night of prayerful consideration, Jesus singles out a dozen of his disciples (followers in general) for the special role of apostle (vv. 12-13). These 12 would comprise his authorized representatives in ministry and his closest companions.

Luke reports that it was Jesus who gave Simon the new name Peter (v. 14). Another of the Twelve, also named Simon (v. 15), is called "the Zealot," possibly indicating his religious devotion (cf. Acts 22:3) or perhaps association with a party of Jews opposed to the Roman occupation. Judas Iscariot is identified as the one who would become a "traitor" (v. 16; cf. Matt. 10:4; Mark 3:19, "who betrayed him").

6:17-49 The Sermon on the Plain Cf. Matthew 5–7.

A great throng of listeners and miracle-seekers awaits Jesus, accompanied from his mountain retreat by the 12 apostles. Matthew and Mark make general statements similar to vv. 17-19, which note the spread of Jesus' reputation and the multitudes who come to him for healing (see Matt. 4:23-25; Mark 3:7-12). Chapter 6 encapsulates much of the teaching in Matthew 5–7, the Sermon on the Mount.

Luke's congratulatory "beatitudes" focus on hardships familiar to Jesus' audience: poverty (of goods, not spirit as in Matthew), hunger, sorrow, and persecution (vv. 20-23; cf. Matt. 5:3-12). The succeeding, antithetical woes ("but woe . . .") appear only in Luke and warn of future ill fortune for those who lead the good life now, namely, the persecutors of Jesus' disciples (vv. 24-26).

Jesus then teaches his followers how to respond to their lot in life, and particularly to their antagonists: in a nutshell, overcome evil with good. They must go beyond merely fulfilling the requirements of the Law by loving their enemies and exhibiting Godlike mercy. Generally, verses 27-36 parallel Matt. 5:38-48, and verses 37-49 parallel Matt. 7:1-27. As introduction to his warning against judging others, Jesus offers a proverb questioning the blind leading the blind (v. 39). Compare v. 45 with Matt. 12:34-35.

7:1-10 Jesus Heals a Centurion's Slave Cf. Matt. 8:5-13.

In keeping with his emphasis on the inclusion of non-Jews among the elect, Luke details the worthiness and humility of a Roman centurion who requests healing for his slave (vv. 4-5, 7). In Luke's account, the officer sends "Jewish elders" (v. 3) and "friends" (v. 6) to intercede with Jesus, who dares to violate Jewish sensitivities by entering the Gentile's house.

7:11-17 A Widow's Son Revived The account of this miracle in Nain (7 mi. southeast of Nazareth) appears only in Luke, who shows particular concern for the poor and oppressed. Already husbandless, the bereaved mother faces certain economic devastation with the death of her only son, since in her society men supported women. Jesus' compassion for the widow leads him to resurrect the young man, and the astounded eyewitnesses recognize God's hand in the event, though they see Jesus himself as only a "great prophet."

7:18-35 Jesus Answers John with Action Cf. Matt. 11:1-19.

When John the Baptist learns of Jesus' miraculous healings, he sends two messengers to investigate. Jesus sends them back to report that these deeds fulfill what had been prophesied by Isaiah and represent what Jesus claims as his mission (cf. Isa. 61:1; Luke 4:16-21). The raising up of the dead (v. 22) recalls the immediately preceding episode at Nain (7:11-17).

Jesus' contemporaries fail to understand either John or Jesus or their ministries. Luke emphasizes the difference between those who accept and those who reject John's invitation to baptism (and the underlying call to repentance) and thus their reaction to God's plan of salvation (vv. 29-30). The "children" of wisdom (v. 35) are the repentant "tax collectors and sinners" in contrast with those of the religious establishment who resist spiritual renewal.

7:36-50 Gratitude Proportionate to Forgiveness This account describes a separate occasion from the episode recorded in Matt. 26:6-13; Mark 14:3-9. Here an "immoral woman" crashes a dinner party given for Jesus by a Pharisee named Simon. As a matter of courtesy, Simon should have provided his guests with water to wash the dust off their sandaled feet and with anointing oil to make their faces shine with the joy of the occasion. But at least for Jesus the host has done neither. As per custom at the dinner table, Jesus' legs undoubtedly stretched behind him at an angle as he reclined on one side, propped up by an elbow. Thus the uninvited woman gains easy access to his feet, which she washes with tears of repentance, dries with her loose locks of hair (worn in the style of a prostitute), kisses unceasingly, and bathes in expensive perfume. Jesus' holier-than-thou host objects, for if Jesus were really a prophet he would know not to let this sinner touch and thus ritually defile him. Jesus turns the occasion into a lesson on forgiveness. Simon and his self-righteous Pharisee friends feel no need for God's forgiveness, but this woman recognizes the great depth of her sinfulness, and her behavior shows her gratitude. Jesus declares her sins forgiven, but the pronouncement prompts the ever-skeptical Pharisees to wonder just who Jesus thinks he is.

8:1-21 Fruitful Seed and True Family Cf. Matt. 13:1-23; 12:46-50; Mark 4:1-25; 3:31-35.

Luke uniquely notes the practical support of Jesus' ministry by women and names three who accompanied Jesus and the itinerant Twelve (vv. 1-3). Mary Magdalene (not the woman of 7:36-50) and Joanna will witness the empty tomb on the morning of Jesus' resurrection (24:10). Herod in verse 3 is Herod Antipas, ruler of Galilee (3:1).

The women who support Jesus' ministry and the fruitful seed in the parable of the Sower (vv. 4-15) exemplify the true family Jesus claims for himself — those who accept his teaching and

willingly commit themselves to God, his Father (v. 21).

8:22-39 Jesus Stills a Storm and Calms a Wild Man Cf. Matt. 8:23-34; Mark 4:35–5:20.

The winds of northern Palestine intensify as they channel through deep gorges opening into the Sea of Galilee, the world's lowest freshwater lake (ca. 680 ft. below sea level), and churn up the waters of this 13 × 7–mile natural bathtub. Jesus encounted just such a storm as he left the pressing crowds and crossed this sea. The fear of Jesus' companions contrasts with his peaceful slumber on board (cf. Jonah 1:4-5). In response to their panic, Jesus calms the storm with a word, and they are awestruck at his power over nature.

Luke's account of the healing of the Gerasene demoniac closely parallels that of Mark 5:1-20. By exorcising the demons that had long afflicted the man, Jesus again demonstrates power over chaotic forces. Though Lev. 11:7 prohibits Jews from eating pork, the largely Gentile population east of the Sea of Galilee commonly raised swine, and into such a herd Jesus transfers the evil spirits. (The "abyss" of v. 31 denotes the watery chaos under the earth.). Fearing Jesus' divine power, the local people implore him to leave, but the healed demoniac has been spiritually transformed and now proclaims God's mighty acts through Jesus.

8:40-56 A Hemorrhage Healed and a Child Resurrected Cf. Matt. 9:18-26; Mark 5:21-43.

In contrast to the Gerasenes' begging Jesus to leave their area, a welcoming crowd awaits him on the other side of the Sea of Galilee. Jairus, a leader of the synagogue and thus an important person in the religious community, implores him to minister to his dying daughter. But Jesus first attends to a woman chronically afflicted with hemorrhages, a condition that marks her as ritually unclean. Luke's account includes wording that highlights the clairvoyance of Jesus (vv. 46-47a). Jesus then revives Jairus's daughter but instructs the parents not to publicize the miraculous healing.

9:1-17 The Apostles Carry Out Their Mission; Five Thousand Fed Cf. Matt. 10:1-14; 14:1-2, 13-21; Mark 6:6b-16, 30-44; John 6:1-14.

Now the disciples become active agents of Jesus' mission in their own right. Luke pits Herod's puzzlement over this ministry against the power of the apostles, who derive their authority from Jesus. Despite his desire for respite from the crowd, for prayer and reflection with his disciples, Jesus abandons his need for privacy in order to minister to the needy multitudes.

9:18-27 Jesus Clarifies His Mission as Messiah Cf. Matt. 16:13-28; Mark 8:27–9:1.

In a quiet time of prayer with his disciples, Jesus asks who people think him to be. It is Peter who confesses him to be the Messiah. Immediately afterward, Jesus predicts his suffering, death, and resurrection, which for the faithful will effect deliverance from the eternal consequences of sin. Thus Jesus corrects the Jewish expectation of a messianic revolutionary who would bring deliverance from political oppression in the here and now — a notion based on prophecy and postponed by Jesus till his second coming (cf. Isa. 9:1-7).

9:28-45 Jesus Transfigured Cf. Matt. 17:1-8; Mark 9:2-32.

Consistent with Luke's portrayal of a pious Jesus, his transfiguration takes place while he prays (v. 29). In contrast to Jesus, the disciples' succumb to slumber, which occurrence points out their comparative weakness but also tempers the obtuseness of Peter's offer to make booths for Jesus, Moses, and Elijah (v. 33; cf. 22:39-46). Luke's approximation, "eight days," may reflect a Roman week (v. 28).

As Jesus descends from the mountain, a man in the awaiting crowd implores him to exorcise a demon from his only son. Despite the seriousness of the affliction, here graphically described, a mere word from Jesus restores the boy's health, thus testifying to the power of God (vv. 37-43).

9:46-50 Lessons in Humility and Tolerance Cf. Matt. 18:1-5; Mark 9:33-41.

Concerned about rank among themselves, the disciples have failed to understand Jesus' teaching about humility. Giving an object lesson, he proclaims a socially lowest-ranking little child as equal to himself in God's view. Even one as far beyond the bounds of Jesus' circle as an unnamed exorcist (vv. 49-50) might contribute to his mission.

9:51–19:27 Jesus' Journey to Jerusalem

Much of this section contains material unique to Luke's Gospel. Here Jesus' teachings dominate the narrative, punctuated by relatively few accounts of miracles.

9:51-62 Resolve to Carry On Jesus knows that great suffering awaits him in Jerusalem, and it takes determination to head that way (v. 51). His rejection en route by Samaritan villagers gives only a hint of worse to come, and the restraint he shows toward them foreshadows his forgiving spirit on the cross (23:34). The *region* of Samaria, as distinguished from the capital city of the former northern kingdom of Israel, lay between Galilee to the north and Judea to the south. After the Assyrians conquered Israel in the late 8th century B.C., they deported much of its Hebrew population and resettled the area with conquered Gentile foreigners (2 Kings 17). The Samaritans were offspring of marriages between these Gentiles and the remaining Hebrews. Their establishment on Mount Gerizim of a central sanctuary that rivaled the temple in Jerusalem fueled a mutual hatred between the Samaritans and Jews — thus the Samaritan villagers' refusal to host Jesus and his fellow Jewish pilgrims to Jerusalem, and the eagerness of James and John (nicknamed the "Sons of Thunder"; Mark 3:17) for revenge (vv. 53-54).

Although the Samaritan inhospitality left Jesus no choice but to move on, the urgency of proclaiming the gospel "everywhere" required a roving ministry (vv. 57-60; cf. Matt. 8:19-22). Jesus' warning of would-be followers not to "look back" parallels his own resolve to "plow" forward to Jerusalem (v. 62).

10:1-24 The Commissioning of Apostles Cf. Matt. 9:35–10:15, 40; 11:20-27; 13:16-17; Mark 6:6b-13.

As Jesus proceeds toward Jerusalem, where his ministry will culminate, he appoints a team to pave the way for his arrival, which he equates with the arrival of the kingdom of God.

The number of messengers — 72 (70 in some ancient manuscripts) — corresponds to the count of nations derived from Genesis 10. Thus the mission of the apostolic deputies becomes worldwide evangelization, in accord with Jesus' command in 24:47.

The instructions given to the 72 expand Jesus' directives to the Twelve in 9:1-6. The nearness of the kingdom requires that the apostolic deputies focus intently on their mission without wasting precious time on practical preparations for their journey, small talk along the way, or bettering their food and lodging arrangements at their destinations. Here the standard Hebrew greeting, "Peace" *(shalom),* conveys not just a casual "hello" but extends wishes for the blessings of God's kingdom (v. 5). Judgment will come on those who reject the messengers and thus reject Jesus and the kingdom (v. 16).

Verse 17 moves directly from the commissioning to "mission accomplished," as the 72 report back to Jesus. Satan's "falling from heaven" refers to the messengers' breaking of his power through their divinely granted authority over the forces of evil. Jesus redirects the missionaries' delight in this power to delight in the joy of their eternal salvation. (On the "heavenly record" of v. 20, cf. Mal. 3:16; Rev. 3:5.) Jesus models his instruction in a prayer of rejoicing that expresses his exclusive relationship to God (vv. 21-22; cf. John 1:14, 18). The "wise and intelligent" are the self-reliant religious establishment, learned in the Mosaic law, with the "infants" in learning (the apostles) recalling the humble multitudes who like children acknowledge their spiritual inadequacy (cf. 7:29-30).

10:25-37 Neighborliness and the Good Samaritan The parable of the Good Samaritan, unique to Luke's Gospel, comes in response to the testing of Jesus by an expert in the Mosaic law (vv. 25-27; cf. Matt. 22:34-40). First, Jesus gets the lawyer to answer his own question about how to inherit eternal life — love God and neighbor. Seeking to save face, the lawyer presses Jesus on a technicality: "Who *is* my neighbor?" Jesus' answer transforms the question into a call to action: "Whom can I be a neighbor to?" That Jesus makes two religious professionals — a priest and a Levite — the bad examples in the story

surely surprises the lawyer, but the real shock comes when a Samaritan turns out to be the hero (for the enmity between Jews and Samaritans, cf. 9:51-56). Narrowly focused on following the letter of the Law (avoiding ritual defilement through contact with what might be a corpse), the religious professionals fail to carry out its selfless spirit. Not so with the Samaritan, whose natural love for himself spills over in acts of mercy toward the mugged wayfarer everyone else has left for dead. A manual laborer commonly received one "denarius" (worth 18 cents in silver) at the end of each workday (v. 35). Here the Samaritan advances two denarii to the innkeeper — enough to support a single individual for two weeks.

10:38-42 Mary and Martha When Jesus comes to town, Martha plays the part of a good, ancient Near Eastern hostess, while Mary takes the position of a student — a role traditionally reserved for men. Jesus' word to Martha implies that simple hospitality was sufficient, and by defending Mary's right to learn from him, he shows that women were welcome as his disciples. John 11 reveals that Martha and Mary lived in Bethany (a town several miles southeast of Jerusalem) with their brother Lazarus, whom Jesus raised from the dead.

11:1-13 Jesus Teaches How to Pray Cf. Matt. 6:9-13; 7:7-11.

The prayerful Jesus portrayed throughout Luke now instructs his disciples on what and how to pray. Luke's summary version of the Lord's Prayer includes the main points of the longer rendering in Matthew: ascribing honor to God's name, which embodies his character; anticipating God's supreme rule on earth; asking for daily sustenance; petitioning for pardon from sins; and requesting resistance to temptation.

The hypothetical situation in verses 5-13 teaches persistence in prayer. The midnight insistence of a host needing to borrow a meal's worth of provisions for an unexpected guest derives from the ancient Near Eastern code of hospitality. The neighbor's getting out of bed and unbolting the door would wake the children, since Palestinian families slept close together in one room. More than any good earthly father, God will certainly grant through the power of the Holy Spirit the valid requests of his earthly "children" (disciples).

11:14-23 The Source of Jesus' Power Cf. Matt. 12:22-30; Mark 3:22-27.

Luke's version of this account has Jesus healing a demon that is mute. The Pharisees insist that his power to exorcise comes from Beelzebul, another name for Satan, the "ruler of the demons." Jesus responds that he is stronger than the evil forces and empowered "by the finger of God" (cf. Exod. 8:19).

11:24-26 The Return of the Unclean Spirits Cf. Matt. 12:43-45.

Jesus warns that God's kingdom requires firm commitment. A person who fails to respond wholeheartedly is like someone who escapes one demon only to fall victim to a whole host of them.

11:27-28 Jesus Passes the Blessing Here as elsewhere in his gospel, Luke shows his unique interest in reporting the response to Jesus of women. When a female from Jesus' crowd of followers calls out to him a blessing, he revises it to say that the truly blessed are the obedient hearers of God's word.

11:29-32 The Sign of Jonah Cf. Matt. 12:38-42; Mark 8:11-13.

Those who continue to question Jesus' role demand a spectacular sign from heaven as proof of his credibility. Luke identifies the sign as Jonah himself and his prophetic message. Jonah's warning of impending judgment led the Ninevites to repent, and Jesus is even greater than Jonah.

11:33-36 The Parable of the Lamp Cf. Matt. 5:15; 6:22-23.

In ancient thought, the eye was the source of light that made seeing possible. Jesus' point calls for repentance and obedience. What is truly important is whether a person is good or bad "inside."

11:37–12:12 Jesus Warns against Hypocrisy Cf. Matt. 15:1-20; 23:1-39; also 10:26-33; 12:31-32.

Invited to dine with Pharisees, Jesus gets grilled for what they consider as his indifference to rituals of purification before eating. He counters by elevating a person's attitude of heart, which governs behavior, over outward rituals (11:39-41). In a series of six "woes" (vv. 42-52) Jesus contrasts concern for social honor and religious status with faithfulness and witness to God's salvific project through compassion and ethical behavior.

He warns his disciples and the larger crowds against hypocrisy. Then, focusing on what lies ahead for himself and his followers, Jesus implores them to remain faithful, even in the face of persecution (vv. 4-12).

12:13–13:9 Urging a Heavenly Perspective Through exhortation and encouragement, Jesus urges his disciples to look beyond the finite world and adopt an eternal outlook on life.

12:13-21 The Rich Fool This parable, which appears only in Luke, illustrates the eternal poverty of the person absorbed in pursuing materialistic goals and living the good life. Compare the account of the rich young ruler seeking to be a disciple and Jesus' comments on the peril of wealth in Matt. 19:16-30.

12:22-34 Stop Worrying, Start Trusting Cf. Matt. 6:19-34.

Recognizing the anxieties of everyday life, Jesus instructs his followers to trust God to meet their basic needs. Just as God cares for the rest of creation, so will he care for humans, made in God's image. Rather than worrying about such mundane matters, as do the Gentiles, Jesus' followers should adjust their priorities and focus on pursuing God's kingdom through righteous living. Unburdened by material pursuits, they can expect God's greater gift.

12:35-48 Alertness and Best Behavior Cf. Matt. 24:42-51.

Jesus cautions his followers to be prepared for his final coming, an event that is certain but whose precise timing cannot be predicted. The literal translation "let your loins be girded" (v. 35) refers to tucking the hem of one's tunic into the belt around the waist to allow the legs greater and more spontaneous freedom of movement (cf. rolling up your sleeves to do a job). The imagery of the wedding feast (v. 36) recalls the parable of the Ten Bridesmaids (Matt. 25:1-13). Verse 48b encapsulates the message of the parable of the Talents (Matt. 25:14-30).

12:49-59 Distinguishing Disciples Cf. Matt. 5:25-26; 10:34-36; 16:2-3.

Jesus characterizes his earthly ministry as a fire that will separate disciples from non-disciples (cf. Zech. 13:7-9). The process will require Jesus' own "baptism" of suffering (cf. Mark 10:38-39). His exhortation to "settle out of court" advises repentance and discipleship before one appears before the divine Magistrate, who sentences to debtors' prison (= hell) the morally shortsighted (vv. 58-59).

13:1-9 Nationwide Need for Repentance When Jesus hears about a Roman slaughter of Galilean pilgrims worshipping at the temple in Jerusalem, he quickly corrects any misconception that the victims so suffered because of sinfulness greater than that of their fellow Jews. Neither did the 18 people who died in the collapse of the Siloam tower (in the wall of Jerusalem) receive this awful fate over equally deserving Jerusalemites. Jesus' exhortation to repentance, however, does not promise escape from physical death; rather, the threat of "perishing likewise" warns of dying without having settled up with God before appearing before the divine Magistrate for judgment (cf. 12:58-59). The parable of the fruitless Fig Tree given a date with an axe illustrates the limited time a person has opportunity to repent. By absorbing more than their fair share of nutrients from the soil, fig trees deprive neighboring plants of needed nourishment; thus the owner's unwillingness to let his unproductive tree continue "wasting the soil."

13:10-21 Setting Things Straight on the Sabbath Luke ties Jesus' teaching about the Sabbath to his freeing from the bonds of sickness a woman long doubled-over (cf. 14:1-6; Matt. 12:9-14; Mark 3:1-6). (Current thinking attributed physical diseases to the forces of evil; v. 11.) Jesus answers the protests of the religious legal-

ists by insisting that their fellow descendant of Abraham deserves at least the standard of care that they themselves give their farm animals.

The short parables of the Mustard Seed and the Leaven encourage the crowd of believers by picturing the rapid growth of the kingdom of God (cf. Matt. 13:31-33; Mark 4:30-32).

13:22-35 Getting into God's Kingdom Cf. Matt. 7:13-14, 21-23; 8:11-12; 23:37-39.

As Luke's travelogue resumes, a follower asks Jesus whether only a few people are gaining salvation. Jesus' indirect response intensifies the seriousness of his appeal that disciples strive to enter the kingdom through the "narrow door" — both hard to find (cf. Matt. 7:14) and, once found, difficult to get through. Since God shuts out "evildoers" (v. 27), the key to gaining entry becomes clear: doing good. But Jesus' response does not teach that a person *earns* salvation through good works; rather, good works *identify* the person sincerely striving to enter the kingdom (cf. Phil. 2:12; Jas. 1:22-25; 2:14-26). In the final judgment, faithful obedience will matter more than who comes "last" or "first" in the current world order (cf. Matt. 19:30–20:16).

In an apparent effort to shame Jesus in front of his following, some Pharisees try to scare him into leaving town by telling him that Herod Antipas is out to kill him (as Herod had John the Baptist; 9:9). But Jesus transforms the (false) dilemma into an opportunity to show his bravery (cf. 9:51). He dismisses his supposed assailant as an inconsequential vixen (the Greek word for fox is feminine) and defiantly refuses to budge until he is ready. He will die in Jerusalem, the historic killing ground of the prophets, and will go there on his own timetable.

14:1-24 Humility Earns Honor On the Sabbath-day healing of a man with dropsy (a disease that causes swelling and pain from pockets of collecting fluid), cf. another such healing recorded in 13:10-17. Here the miracle takes place during a meal hosted by a prominent Jewish leader — apparently a member of the Jewish court, the Sanhedrin — and attended by his cronies, who "watch" Jesus closely to see how carefully he will follow the Sabbath rules. Rather than being caught in what looks like a setup, Jesus asks the legal experts present whether it is legal to heal on the Sabbath. *He* knows that *they* know the Mosaic law nowhere prohibits the practice — only later did the rabbis define healing as work and so make laws that limited its exercise on the Sabbath to life-and-death cases.

After silencing his opponents and exposing their hypocrisy (v. 6), Jesus shames them by pointing out the foolishness of their quest for social status and admiration by others (vv. 7-11). Jesus warns his fellow guests that presuming to grab places of honor (seats nearest the head of the table) only risks humiliation (here a forced, public march to an assigned seat farthest from the host). The real way to ensure honor is to take last place first — from there, the only way to go is up! The tone of Jesus' advice reflects the ancient literary genre called "Wisdom," epitomized in the Old Testament book of Proverbs, which aims at equipping people for successful, godly living.

By advising his host to throw parties for the destitute, rather than for those who have the means and feel the need to reciprocate, Jesus again counsels selfless behavior that ultimately benefits the benefactor. In Jesus' culture, the offer of hospitality creates a dilemma for the intended guest: refusing the invitation insults and dishonors the hopeful host, but accepting it obligates the guest to return the favor lest he dishonor himself. Jesus' solution to this rotating social debt that traps hosts and guests in a financially draining cycle of alternating roles is to show hospitality to people who cannot repay you. Not only do you look good (earn honor) without incurring unending social or financial debt, but you receive an eternal payback in recognition of your righteousness. Everybody wins.

Jesus brings this teaching home in the parable of the Great Banquet (vv. 15-24; cf. Matt. 22:1-14). Read in light of the preceding three verses, the first-invited guests (the Jews) send their regrets, not just because they are too busy to come, but also because they want to avoid the obligation to reciprocate with the host (God). Their passing up of the invitation (rejection of the old covenant) amounts to slapping the host in the face, and his compelling the poor and handicapped (Gentiles) to fill up the banquet hall (the kingdom of God) both does them a favor and preserves his honor.

14:25-35 Calculating the Cost of Discipleship Cf. Matt. 5:13; 10:37-38; Mark 9:50.

Luke uses stronger language than Matthew in communicating the self-sacrificial requirements of discipleship. Here even one's natural love for family and self must display itself to such a lesser degree than one's love for Jesus so as to seem like "hatred" in comparison.

The parables of the Tower Builder (vv. 28-30) and the Warring King (vv. 31-32) caution that followers should calculate the cost of discipleship and consider the risks involved before committing to the cause. The discarding of the "salt" that degenerates to "tastelessness" metaphorically portends a sorry future for the halfhearted disciple (cf. 9:57-62).

15 Three Parables of the Lost and Found That Jesus associates with unscrupulous governmental employees and religiously lax Jews ("sinners"), just as he does with the religiously meticulous Jewish leaders (cf. 14:1-24), catches the critical eye of the Pharisees and scribes. Jesus responds to their grumbling with three parables that illustrate the spontaneity and propriety of unbridled joy over the salvation of the spiritually lost — his mission as stated in 5:29-32.

Jesus uses the parable of the Lost Sheep retrieved by its owner (vv. 4-7) to convey great heavenly rejoicing over the single "lost" sinner who repents and returns to God (cf. Matt. 18:12-14). Jesus sarcastically refers to the Pharisees and scribes as the "ninety-nine righteous persons who need no repentance." In fact, they do need repentance but are too self-righteous to see it (cf. 7:29-30 for their refusing the baptism of John).

The parable of the Lost Coin (vv. 8-10) conveys the joy of God, surrounded by the angels, when a sinner repents. The woman's 10 coins may refer to those that decorate her wedding headdress; so her intense effort to find the lost coin would correspond to a modern woman's scouring the house for a diamond missing from her engagement ring. The joy on finding the coin stems not only or even primarily from its monetary worth (one day's wages), but mainly from its sentimental value. Thus the parable pictures the emotional investment of God in individual human beings. His persistent pursuit of the lost flows not from determined tyranny but from heartfelt attachment.

The longer parable of the Prodigal Son (vv. 11-32) comes even closer to the point by making a person the "lost" element in the story. The impatient second son, who stands to inherit much less than his firstborn elder brother, wants to collect right now. After converting his inheritance to cash (v. 13), he travels abroad, leads a wild life, and runs through his money. A famine in the now penniless prodigal's new country of residence makes food scarce for the scavenger. So he takes a job as a swineherd — an especially detestable job for a Jew (cf. Lev. 11:7) — but still the boy goes hungry. That he longs to eat the carob pods fed to the pigs shows the depths of his destitution. Having hit bottom, he resolves to return home and repentantly throw himself on his father's mercy by forfeiting his sonship and requesting servanthood on his father's estate. But on recognizing the returning prodigal in the distance, the father does the forfeiting — he sheds his dignity as patriarch by running to greet his still-beloved son. The prodigal launches into his confession of sin and acknowledgment of unworthiness, but his father stops him short. He covers the repentant renegade's rags with the best robe available; gives his son a signet ring, a symbol of his restored position in the family; puts sandals on his feet to distinguish him from the barefoot servants; and throws a welcome-home party, at which he even serves meat (not a regular part of meals in ancient Palestine) — the calf he has been fattening up for a special occasion! Such is the father's overwhelming joy on reunion with the son he presumed gone for good (cf. Gen. 46:29-30).

Although this story makes the same essential point as the preceding two parables, here Jesus surprises his audience by inserting them into the story. The dutiful oldest son, who so resents the celebration of his wayward sibling's return that he resists joining the party, represents the exclusivistic scribes and Pharisees miffed about Jesus' mixing with those considered less than holy. The father's reminding his eldest that he

stands to inherit the entire estate chides these law-abiding listeners for pouting about the good fortune of their repentant neighbors. Jesus leaves his audience to decide whether they will add to their strict obeying of the Law repentance from the sins they overlook and compassion for the boldly sinful who forsake their wicked ways.

16:1-18 The Shrewd Steward In this parable (vv. 1-13), Jesus goes beyond prescribing compassion for penitent sinners (15:11-32) to advising his disciples (the "children of light," v. 8) to learn lessons from people who are clearly unrighteous. The steward, given notice on suspicion of mismanaging his master's estate, puts his street smarts into action before turning over the balanced books. By giving unauthorized discounts to his master's debtors, the steward indebts them to himself and so stockpiles credits on which he can collect during his impending unemployment. The master discovers the ruse and praises the steward for his shrewdness, though not for his trickery. Then Jesus commends the steward's earthly good thinking as applicable to the eternal sphere. The "dishonest wealth" (v. 9; Greek *mammon*) means wealth so greatly loved that it leads to unrighteous behavior (cf. 1 Tim. 6:10, "all kinds of evil"). Here Jesus appears to be teaching financial charity toward others as a way to make friends with God, the divine Gatekeeper who in 13:22-30 opens up only to sincere seekers of the kingdom identifiable by their "good deeds." Financial faithfulness (charitable giving) shows a person worthy of the true riches of God's kingdom by demonstrating that person's love of God, not money (vv. 10-13; cf. 12:33-34; Matt. 6:19-24).

The scoffing of the Pharisees leads Jesus to observe that, though they enjoy the admiration of their fellow Jews (for outwardly appearing to follow the Law to the letter), God finds them inwardly detestable. Citing a common practice of the Pharisees — namely, remarriage by and of divorcées, which results in forbidden adultery — Jesus exposes their violation of the very "Law" on which they stake their religious claim to fame (cf. Matt. 5:32). By upholding the validity of the Law even now that the preaching of the gospel has begun, Jesus refuses to let the

Pharisees off the hook. These hypocrites stand in contrast to the sinners who are finding favor with God ("forcing their way" into his kingdom through repentance).

16:19-31 The Rich Man and Lazarus The parable of the Rich Man and Lazarus illustrates the fate of people who fail to make friends with God by exercising charity toward others — that is, people who do not practice Jesus' teaching in 16:1-13. The "rich man," whose self-importance shows in his wearing of clothes fit for royalty ("purple and fine linen"), stands for the self-righteous Pharisees. Diseased and famished Lazarus, who lies helpless at the rich man's gate, stands for the needy, whom the Pharisees completely ignore. Even the dogs that lick Lazarus's sores (saliva was believed to have medicinal value) treat him better than the rich man does.

Overlooked in his life on earth, however, Lazarus receives heavenly charity in death. (The Greek name "Lazarus" comes from Hebrew "Eleazar," "God is [his] help.") Angels whisk the deceased pauper off to Abraham's side: the "bosom of Abraham," which likely pictures a heavenly banquet where Lazarus reclines in the place of honor — immediately in front of and to the right of the forefather of the Hebrew nation (cf. 14:7-11).

Meanwhile the rich man also dies and goes to Hades, the shadowy world of the dead. Now he is the one longing for help, and by addressing Abraham as "father" (= forefather) appeals to his Hebrew ancestry for some measure of relief from the flames that torment him. But kinship cannot bridge the chasm between Hades and heavenly bliss; and Lazarus, who in life didn't get a crumb from the rich man, could not now give him a drop of water even if he were willing. Neither will Abraham grant the alternative request to "resurrect" Lazarus to the rich man's brothers and shock them into repentance (here, helping the poor) to avoid an afterlife of torment. If "Moses and the Prophets" (the laws and prophecies contained in the Hebrew Scriptures) cannot move them, neither will a man's rising from the dead — a foreshadowing of the death and resurrection of Jesus.

17:1-10 Duty within the Christian Community Cf. Matt. 18:6-9, 15-22; Mark 9:42-48.

Jesus now turns from addressing the Pharisees to teaching his disciples. In Luke, his summary of duty within the Christian community warns members against causing others to abandon their faith, mandates both rebuke for sinfulness and unlimited forgiveness ("seven" symbolizes perfection and completeness, so v. 4 indicates an unlimited number of times), and points out that only a small amount of faith is necessary to carry out these commands. Jesus also admonishes his followers not to expect special treatment from God for fulfilling their Christian duties (vv. 7-10).

17:11-19 A Samaritan Models Thankfulness On the way to Jerusalem, 10 men, afflicted with some variety of skin disease, approach Jesus but, obediently following the Mosaic law, keep their distance while begging for merciful healing (Lev. 13:45-46; Num. 5:2-4). Jesus commands that they show themselves to the priests to be declared healed and thus fit for reentry into mainstream society. The actual healing takes place when the lepers demonstrate their faith by setting off to obey Jesus' command. But the miracle moves only one of the 10 to give thanks — notably, a "foreign" Samaritan (cf. 9:51-56). Jesus' disappointed surprise at the neglectful nine points out the contrast between God's rightful expectation of thanks for his acts of mercy toward humans and our errant expectation of congratulations for dutiful obedience to him (cf. vv. 7-10).

17:20-37 The Current Kingdom and the Second Coming Cf. Matt. 24:26-44; 10:39.

The Pharisees expect the kingdom of God to manifest itself in political, revolutionary terms: the overthrow of the Roman government. Jesus corrects this mistaken notion by declaring that the kingdom "is in your midst." In other words, Jesus represented that kingdom; threatening Rome was not his mission.

The Pharisees have failed to recognize Jesus as the current embodiment of the "kingdom," but the unmistakable signs that will immediately precede and accompany his future return (signs that occur during the "days of the Son of

Man" and on "his day") will rule out any question in the last days. Jesus tells his disciples not to follow false leads in watching for his second coming to satisfy their wishful thinking — "you will know it when you see it" (cf. 2 Thess. 2:1-12; 3:1-15). He must endure suffering and rejection before "his day" comes. Just as Lot's wife should have focused on fleeing from destruction rather than fatally turning her head to watch (Gen. 19:24-26), so his followers should continue to fulfill their duties to fellow believers (vv. 1-10) and to God (vv. 11-19; cf. 9:61-62).

18:1-8 Pray without Ceasing The parable of the Widow and the Unjust Judge applies Jesus' teaching about persistence in prayer to future petitions for his second coming, at which time he will "grant justice to his [persecuted] chosen ones" (vv. 7-8). In ancient Palestine, widows made up a large class of society, since as young teenagers most girls married much older men. Widows lacked social power and financial opportunity, and the widow in Jesus' story can only hope to influence the unfair, unsympathetic judge through persistent pleading. Eventually exasperated, he executes justice for the widow just to get rid of her. But beyond the comparison to God's certain and speedy exercise of justice for his chosen ones, the question lingers, will they lose faith that Jesus will return to deliver on the promise? In other words, when he does come again, will any faithful people be left to execute justice for? This question assumes a significant, troubled interval of time between Jesus' departure and return — one that challenges his disciples to persevere.

18:9-17 Humble Prayer, Certain Justification A second lesson on prayer teaches humility before God as the requirement for justification. The falsely pious prayer of the Pharisee who touts his moral superiority actually condemns him as a hypocrite. Jesus has earlier exposed the Pharisees' commission of the very sins represented by the people with whom the Pharisee in the story contrasts himself (on justness, 11:37–12:12; on adultery, 16:14-18). Nevertheless, the Pharisees' observable acts of piety, such as fasting on Mondays and Thursdays and donating a tenth of all of their possessions, won them the admiration

of the Jewish masses — but not Jesus. In his day, the financially opportunistic tax collectors were looked down on in the public eye; so the current parable catches the attention of Jesus' ancient audience by making the respected Pharisee the loser and the universally despised tax collector the winner (cf. the parable of the Good Samaritan, 15:11-32). The depth of the publican's humility even prevents him from adopting the normal posture of prayer: face lifted heavenward, with eyes open (v. 13). The story also spells out in spiritual terms the contrasting results of humility and self-exaltation illustrated in the social sphere by Jesus' teaching in 14:7-11.

Luke here adds a note about Jesus' welcome reception of children, for in ancient Palestine they completely lacked social power and thus, by default, embodied humility (vv. 15-17; cf. Matt. 18:3; 19:13-15; Mark 10:13-16).

18:18-30 The Requirements and Rewards of Discipleship Cf. Matt. 19:16-29; Mark 10:17-30.

The difficulty of implementing Jesus' teaching on charity becomes painfully obvious in his encounter with the rich ruler. More than simply fulfilling all the commandments, to attain the kingdom of God a person must reorder his or her priorities, including sacrifice on behalf of the poor and marginalized. The disciples' example enacts this teaching.

18:31-34 Jesus Details His Nearing Passion Cf. Matt. 20:17-19; Mark 10:32-34.

Jesus has already predicted his suffering, death, and resurrection both in general (5:35; 12:50; 13:32-33; 17:25) and specific terms (9:22, 43-45). Here the emphasis lies on his passion as fulfilling Old Testament prophecy. The incomprehension of the Twelve in Luke contrasts with their understanding in Matthew (cf. Matt. 17:1-23).

18:35-43 A Blind Man Receives Sight Cf. Matt. 20:29-34; Mark 10:46-52.

The parallel account of this healing in Mark gives the blind man's name as "Bartimaeus" (cf. also Mark 8:22-26). As with the Samaritan leper, Jesus commends the blind man's faith as making his healing possible (17:19).

The Last Supper

The first three Gospels contain accounts of a meal held by Jesus with his closest followers in Jerusalem shortly before he died (Matt. 26:17-29; Mark 14:12-25; Luke 22:7-38). Paul gives a brief account of the central event in the meal when he is trying to encourage a proper attitude to the celebration of the Lord's Supper in the church at Corinth (1 Cor. 11:23-26).

The meal was held in the upper room of a house and took place in the evening as the main meal of the day, but no explicit reference is made to what was consumed, other than bread and

meal, perhaps with something of the Passover atmosphere already present). A Passover meal would have included hors d'oeuvres and a main course of roast lamb and the ritual drinking of wine at four points in the meal. It was customary to interpret the various dishes as symbols of different aspects of the original Passover and the liberation from Egypt recorded in Exodus. It fits in with this custom that Jesus is recorded as having given a new interpretation to the bread and to one of the cups of wine. In both cases he gave thanks to God (as Jews did at every meal)

ingly in our sources. Common to all four are the words, "This is my body," to which Luke and Paul add, "which is [Luke: 'given'] for you. Do this in remembrance of me." But as regards the cup there is less agreement. Mark and Matthew have, "This is my blood of the covenant which is poured out for many [Matthew: 'for the forgiveness of sins']"; whereas Luke and Paul have, "This cup is the new covenant in my blood [Luke: 'which is poured out for you']." There is no agreement among scholars as to the precise original wording or how the variants in the wording arose. It would not be surprising if early Christians paraphrased or added to the original wording in order to bring out its implied meaning more specifically. It seems certain that Jesus identified the bread as a symbol of his body and the cup of wine as representing either his blood or what was effected by his blood. The reference to blood points unmistakably to death and probably to death by violence. The reference to his body is less clear, but the Lucan/Pauline phrase "which is [given] for you" and the parallelism with the blood combine to suggest that here also is symbolism for the death of Jesus. Whether the expression "which is . . . for you/many" is attached to the bread or the cup saying, it indicates that what Jesus is doing with his body and blood is somehow for the benefit of the participants. The reference to the (new) covenant (cf. Jer. 31:31-34)

The Upper Room (Coenaculum) in the Crusader-era Church of the Apostles on Mount Zion. *(Richard Cleave, Pictorial Archive)*

wine. According to the Evangelists, however, the meal was in fact a Passover meal (although John appears to date the meal a day earlier, in which case it would have been an ordinary evening

and then distributed the food and passed the cup so that all the participants shared together.

The precise details of what Jesus said with respect to the bread and the cup vary surpris-

must be understood as a contrast to the "old" covenant that was established in the wilderness shortly after the Passover in Egypt and sealed by the offering of an animal whose blood was smeared on the people and objects associated with the covenant that God was making with them (Exod. 24:1-8). The use of "for many" points to the vicarious suffering of the Servant of Yahweh described in Isa. 53:11-12. Jesus' sharing of the bread and the common cup to be consumed by the guests at the meal suggests some kind of union created by the common act of eating and drinking both among the guests and between them and Jesus.

John 13 also has an account of the meal that contains none of this description and surprisingly focuses on the footwashing performed by Jesus on the guests. John has already provided teaching in which, first, Jesus himself is said to be the bread that bestows life on those who eat it; and, second, it is necessary to eat the flesh of the Son of Man (Jesus) and drink his blood in order to have eternal life and remain in union with him. The bread is identified as the flesh of Jesus given for the life of the world (John 6:32-58). All this is a development of key thoughts in the other Gospels.

In 1 Corinthians a traditional account of what Jesus did is cited as a guide to how Christians should celebrate their regular congregational meals. By their nature the symbolic actions at the meal are a means of proclaiming the death of the Lord Jesus that was intended to continue as a solemn way of remembering him and maintaining unity in the body of the church.

For Further Reading

Marshall, I. Howard. *Last Supper and Lord's Supper.* Grand Rapids: Eerdmans, 1981.

I. HOWARD MARSHALL

19:1-10 A Rich Man Gains Salvation The response to Jesus by Zacchaeus, Jericho's chief tax collector grown rich by fleecing his fellow Jews, contrasts with the response of the rich ruler in 18:18-25 and shows that "what is impossible for mortals is possible for God" (18:27). To gain entry into the kingdom, both men need to demonstrate their love of God, not of money, by sharing their material wealth with the poor. Zacchaeus spontaneously vows his generous charity and also pledges to pay back far more than Mosaic law required for financial fraud (cf. Lev. 5:16). Zacchaeus's promises do not buy him salvation; rather, they identify him as a humbly repentant seeker of the kingdom (cf. 13:22-35; 16:1-18). On Jesus' mission of seeking and saving the lost (v. 10), see chapter 15.

19:11-27 The Parable of the Pounds Cf. the parable of the Talents in Matt. 25:14-30.

The crowd around Jesus apparently still thinks about his kingdom in political terms. Perhaps they draw parallels between Jesus' journeying to the Judean capital of Jerusalem and the traveling to Rome of aspiring local rulers seeking imperial support for their political ambitions back home. But Jesus will make Jerusalem his point of departure for heaven, and this parable is a kind of prophetic autobiography, with the exacting nobleman and his departure for a distant country representing Jesus and his postpassion ascension. The nobleman's reception of a kingdom signifies Jesus' heavenly exaltation by God (cf. Acts 2:29-36). The slaves left behind stand for Jesus' followers, entrusted with carrying out the "business" of the kingdom during his absence from earth. The hateful, pursuing citizens represent the Jewish leaders, who reject Jesus' authority (vv. 39-48). The return of the nobleman signifies Jesus' second coming. The summoning of the slaves to give an account stands for the last judgment, and the execution order for the hateful citizens portends the final punishment of the Jewish leaders, though not of the slave who held onto his pound (Gk. *mina,* three months' wages for a laborer). The severe but not fatal punishment of this unproductive disciple illustrates that fear of God must issue in risk-taking action, not cautious incapacitation.

19:28–21:38 Jerusalem and the Temple

19:28-48 Popular Acclamation vs. Official Opposition Cf. Matt. 21:1-17; Mark 11:1-19.

Only Luke records the Pharisees' protest over the popular acclamation of Jesus (v. 39); his reply that in the event of the disciples' silence the stones would take up the cry (v. 40); and the lament of Jesus over Jerusalem, which the Romans would overrun in A.D. 70 (vv. 41-44). Much to the chagrin of the malice-bent religious leaders, popular support for Jesus intensifies as daily he teaches at the temple. Thus it is their resistance to Jesus that brings the downfall of Jerusalem (v. 44).

20:1-19 The "Wicked Tenants" Question Jesus' Authority Cf. Matt. 21:23-27, 33-46; Mark 11:27–12:12.

Jesus presents a parable to "the people," but it is really addressed to the religious leaders who oppose him. Expecting the "tenants" to return their share of the produce, the "landlord" (God) finds his slaves/messengers (prophets) scorned, so he sends his principal heir. When the "beloved son" receives the same brutal treatment, the landlord breaks the lease and turns over the vineyard as a gift to new tenants. When the scribes and chief priests realize that it is they who have been characterized as the offenders, their immediate impulse is to do away with Jesus. But sensing the growing acceptance of Jesus' messsage, they refrain (v. 19).

20:20-44 Jesus Cannot Be Trapped Cf. Matt. 22:15-33, 41-46; Mark 12:13-27, 35-37a.

The Pharisees and Herodians (supporters of Herod) are unlikely allies in an attempt to stir up trouble for Jesus. Luke explicitly details their evil intentions (v. 20). Knowing that he will not hold back the truth, they expect that he will offend either the religious or political authorities, or both. The denarius (v. 24) bore the image of the emperor and the inscription "Tiberius Caesar, son of the divine Augustus."

Jesus paints a picture of life in the age to come far greater than that rejected by the Sadducees. The dead are "children of God," "children of the resurrection," and so no longer burdened with earthly concerns for marriage and bearing offspring (vv. 35-36).

The Messiah had long been expected to be a descendant of David. Jesus now proclaims that the "son" will be greater than David (vv. 41-43; cf. Ps. 110:1).

20:45-21:4 A Widow's Offering Cf. Mark 12:41-44.

Jesus contrasts the pious display of the theologians (20:45-47), as well as the comparative ease of the rich (21:1), with the example of a poor widow who gives generously of her limited resources. Particularly forceful is Jesus' charge that the religious leaders (and by extension the temple system itself) have contributed to the desperate plight of widows and other dispossessed persons in Judean society (20:47).

21:5-38 Forecast of Destruction Cf. Matt. 10:17-21; 24:1-22, 29-36; Mark 13:1-20, 24-32.

In this "little apocalypse," Jesus details "signs" that will precede the destruction of Jerusalem. Luke substitutes a reference to "Jerusalem surrounded by armies" (v. 20) for Matthew's and Mark's "abomination of desolation," probably since his Gentile audience would not have understood the distinctively Jewish terminology (cf. Matt. 24:15; Mark 13:14). The fulfillment of "the times of the Gentiles" (v. 24) refers to their role in the coming upheaval and the eventual proclamation of the good news among them.

Verses 34-38 prescribe constant, sober alertness for the end so that the devastating events that precede it do not take Jesus' followers by surprise and weaken their faith. Maintaining moral readiness becomes the key not to "escaping" the bad times themselves but to resisting the temptations to abandon faith in the midst of those times. Only by remaining faithful will a person be able to "stand before the Son of Man" at the last judgment. The crowds find Jesus' teaching so compelling that they get up early to hear him.

22:1-6 Conspiracy and Betrayal

Cf. Matt. 26:1-5, 14-16; Mark 14:1-2, 10-11.

Stymied in their desire to do away with Jesus, the religious leaders find unexpected assistance from one of Jesus' own disciples. Luke blames the treachery solely on the satanic possession of Judas, who conspires to aid the scribes and temple police while avoiding the crowds gathered for the great pilgrimage feast.

22:7-23 The Last Supper

Cf. Matt. 26:17-29; Mark 14:12-25; John 13:1-30.

Uniquely in Luke, Jesus brings up the need

to prepare for the Passover meal, and so he emerges as a model of compliance regarding Jewish law (v. 8). Luke's account of the Last Supper begins with Jesus' expression of gladness to be celebrating the Passover meal with the apostles, followed by his announcement that he will not partake of it again until the arrival of God's kingdom (vv. 15-18). The closing revelation that his betrayer is sharing this last meal, under pretense of table fellowship, casts the betrayal in the worst possible light (vv. 21-23). Nevertheless, verse 22 clarifies that Jesus' "going" (to endure his suffering [v. 15]) has been predetermined (by God), so that even his betrayal by Judas falls under the ultimate control of God.

22:24-30 Leading by Serving

Cf. Matt. 20:25-28; 19:28; Mark 10:42-45.

The apostles' attempt to identify the traitor among them leads to a dispute over which of them is the greatest. In line with his previous admonitions on humility, Jesus takes the opportunity to point out his personal example of leading by serving. The apostles, who themselves have served Jesus in standing by him during his trial-fraught ministry, need not worry about chasing after greatness. Their servant-Lord Jesus — to whom God the Father has awarded a kingdom in the age to come — has already appointed them to positions of honor and authority in that kingdom.

22:31-34 Jesus Foretells Peter's Denials

Cf. Matt. 26:33-35; Mark 14:29-31.

Jesus' addressing Peter by his old name, Simon, anticipates the apostle's coming denials of association with him (vv. 54-62). That Peter later denies knowing Jesus but does not deny him as the Christ, however, demonstrates the efficacy of Jesus' prayer that Peter's faith not fail (as a result of the imminent ordeal). As with Judas, Luke lays the blame for the denials on Satan, whose demand to "sift all of you like wheat" (= shake the apostles' faith) will prove Peter vulnerable but ultimately not defeated, for Jesus gives him the assignment of strengthening his fellow apostles after he reclaims his moral courage ("turn[s] back," vv. 31-32).

22:35-38 Back to Normal

Jesus instructs the apostles to resume their normal practice of preparedness for a journey by taking money ("purse"), a bag (for clothes and supplies), and a sword (for self-defense against bandits). The reversal of his earlier command to leave such supplies behind (9:1-6; 10:1-16) signals the end of an era, for Jesus' own earthly ministry will soon come to an end.

Jesus' dying the death of a common criminal (crucifixion) will fulfill the prophecy of Isa. 53:12 (v. 37). The apostles take the directive to acquire swords as a call to arms in defense of Jesus, but he quiets their enthusiasm for armed resistance (v. 38; cf. vv. 50-51).

22:39-53 Betrayal and Arrest

Cf. Matt. 26:30, 36-56; Mark 14:26, 32-52.

Luke gives a more condensed version of the arrest of Jesus than do Matthew and Mark. He does not name Gethsemane as the specific location of Jesus' arrest on the Mount of Olives, and he reports only one episode in which the disciples fall asleep while Jesus goes off to pray. Before Jesus does so, therefore, he instructs the apostles to pray also — not for him, but for their own strength to resist the temptation to abandon their faith, as he has petitioned for Simon Peter in verse 32.

Verses 43-44 do not appear in some of the oldest manuscripts of Luke, and many scholars believe a scribe added them later. The often misread verse 44 does not say that Jesus' sweat drops *of* blood but that his sweat became *like* drops of blood — he sweat profusely, as though he were bleeding.

Luke excuses the apostles' slumber on their sorrow (over Jesus' fate). Judas approaches Jesus to deliver a kiss, but Jesus stops him short with a rhetorical question that exposes the ostensibly friendly greeting as a betrayal (v. 48; cf. vv. 21-23). Because the apostles have brought two swords, which they are willing to use to defend Jesus (v. 38), it comes as no surprise when one of them attacks a member of the entourage of arresters. Jesus' immediate rebuke for the assault and his healing of the wound (which only Luke records) underscore his opposition to armed resistance of the coming ordeal (vv. 37-38). His comment that the current "hour" and "the power of darkness" belong to the arresters highlights the evil origin of the events set in motion by the betrayal (v. 53).

22:54-62   Peter Denies Knowing Jesus

Cf. Matt. 26:57-58, 69-75; Mark 14:53-54, 66-72; John 18:15-18, 25-27.

Luke places Peter's denials of Jesus before his account of the trial by the Sanhedrin. Thus the denials fall directly on the heels of Peter's failure to stay awake and pray for moral courage (vv. 40, 45-46). Despite the lapse of time between challenges, Peter's resistance only heightens (vv. 58-59). When the cock crows, Jesus casts a knowing glance at Peter (v. 61; cf. v. 34).

22:63-71   Jesus before the Council

Cf. Matt. 26:57-68; Mark 14:53-65; John 18:19-24.

According to Luke, Jesus' appearance before the Sanhedrin takes place come daylight, after a night of mockery, slander, and abuse by his guards (vv. 63-65). Luke gives a condensed version of the trial, in which Jesus refuses to answer outright the questions of his accusers but volunteers statements that imply his equality with God (sitting at God's right hand [v. 69; cf. Ps 110:1] and tacitly accepting the designation "Son of God" [v. 70]) — statements the council take as blasphemy, punishable by death according to Jewish law. The literal translation of Jesus' response in verse 70 reads, "*You* say that I am [the Son of God]," an answer that turns the council's question into an inadvertent confession of his divinity (cf. Matt. 26:64).

23:1-25   Verdict: Innocent — Sentence: Death

Cf. Matt. 27:1-2, 11-26; Mark 15:1-15; John 18:28-40.

By adding the Sanhedrin's false accusation that Jesus has been fomenting tax revolt among the Jews, Luke intensifies the council's portrayal of the supposedly self-proclaimed king of the Jews as a threat to Rome. In fact, Jesus has done just the opposite: he has supported paying taxes to Caesar, has not once called himself the

Christ, and has forbidden the disciples to advertise him as such (20:21-26; 9:20-21).

Pilate is not convinced of the ploy against Jesus, but overwhelmed by the persistence of the chief priests and the size of the crowd, he seizes the opportunity to push the case off onto the regional ruler of Galilee, Herod (Antipas), who happens to be visiting Jerusalem at the time and under whose jurisdiction the Nazarene prisoner falls. Herod, though happy finally to meet Jesus (cf. 9:9), cannot get an answer out of him. In Luke, the continued mockery and abuse of Jesus take place under Herod's watch, not Pilate's (v. 11; cf. Matt. 27:27-31; Mark 15:16-20).

The reaching of concurring verdicts by Herod and Pilate repairs their relationship, puts an exclamation point on the innocence of Jesus, and makes the people's call for his crucifixion all the more unjust.

23:26-56   Jesus Crucified and Buried

Cf. Matt. 27:32-66; Mark 15:21-47; John 19:17-42.

Luke continues to give unique attention to the women who support Jesus and his ministry. The public lamenting of the "daughters of Jerusalem" over Jesus' imminent crucifixion shows them courageous dissenters to the death sentence demanded by the majority of the Jewish leadership. Jesus selflessly turns the lamentation back on the women (cf. 11:27-28) in anticipation of the awful events that will attend the (Roman) destruction of Jerusalem, which he prophesied in 19:41-44; 21:5-6. Jesus ominously warns that if gross injustice, such as that now being done to him, can happen in the "green wood" (the times of peace under Roman rule), just imagine what will happen in the "dry [tree]" (the coming Roman assault on Jerusalem, 70).

In Luke, Jesus' crucifixion between two "criminals" (lit., "doers of evil") fulfills the prophecy of Isa. 53:12, which Jesus cites in 22:37 (cf. Matt. 27:38; Mark 15:27). His call for the forgiveness of his crucifiers appears only in Luke (v. 34), as do the rebuke of the one criminal by the other for blaspheming Jesus (vv. 40-41) and Jesus' affirmation of salvation for this one who recognizes his innocence (v. 43).

Consistent with Luke's emphasis on Jesus' prayerful piety, rather than crying out in agony

The risen Jesus appears on the road to Emmaus; bronze relief at the Callisto Catacombs, Rome.

Jesus utters a prayer immediately before expiring on the cross. His voice remains loud, however, in evidence of his physical strength even in death, and the wording of his prayer makes the moment of his dying a purposeful event over which he maintains control (cf. Matt. 26:51-54). The nature of his death and all that surrounds it cause the onlooking centurion to confess Jesus' righteousness (v. 47; not his divinity, as in Matt. 27:54; Mark 15:39).

Luke presents Joseph of Arimathea as a good and righteous dissenter to the plans and actions of his fellow council members regarding Jesus (vv. 50-51). By laying Jesus' body in a brand new tomb, Joseph treats the corpse with special respect. In ancient Palestine, rock-hewn tombs normally accommodated generations of family members. These burial caves featured a raised platform for laying out the body of a newly deceased person and a large, disk-like stone door that rolled sideways to seal off the entrance. After the flesh of a corpse decayed, the skeletal remains were transferred to an ossuary, or secondary burial box, to clear the platform for the body of the next relative who died.

The "day of Preparation" refers to Friday before sunset, by which time must cease all the work of preparing for the Sabbath day of rest

(v. 54). The women from Galilee have remained loyal disciples to the end and beyond (vv. 49, 55-56).

24:1-12 The Empty Tomb

Cf. Matt. 28:1-10; Mark 16:1-8.

Two dazzlingly clad men (angels; cf. v. 23) appear to the women who return to the tomb to perfume Jesus' corpse, and the double witness to his resurrection satisfies the legal requirement for judicially valid testimony (Deut. 19:15; contrast the single angel in Matthew and Mark and its dramatic descent from heaven, attended by an earthquake, in Matthew). Only Luke relates the disbelief of the disciples on hearing the report of the women. (In referring to the apostles as "the eleven," Luke allows his audience to assume the obvious absence of Judas, though he does not report the traitor's demise until Acts 1:15-19; cf. Matt. 27:5.) Peter, however, demonstrates his having "turned back" from his denials (22:31-34) by running to the empty tomb to see for himself (v. 12).

24:13-35 Eyewitnesses to the Resurrection

Reported only in Luke, two of Jesus' disciples, a number of whom have evidently spent the Sabbath in Jerusalem with the now 11 apostles, leave the group of mourners on Sunday to go to the nearby town of Emmaus. Luke records personal and place names and notes the length of the day's journey, thus providing circumstantial details supporting the validity of the reported encounter that follows. The two travelers (again a sufficient number to give legally valid testimony) find themselves joined by the resurrected Christ but do not recognize him. They relate to their seemingly uninformed traveling companion the recent fate of the one on whom they had pinned their messianic hopes and the reports of his now empty tomb. The disciples' disappointment that Jesus did not "redeem" Israel or "set it free" shows they are still thinking of the Messiah in political terms (v. 21). Their comment that it was the "third day" since the events culminating in Jesus' crucifixion reflects the 1st-century Jewish belief that the soul departed from a person three days after physical death,

The Trial, Death, and Resurrection of Jesus

Why did Jesus have to die? This is one of our most crucial questions for understanding the significance of Jesus' identity and mission. First, the Gospels themselves, our most important witnesses to Jesus' life and ministry, devote an inordinate amount of space to the predictions and plots that anticipated Jesus' execution and to their narratives of his suffering and death. For them, the character of Jesus' life and the manner of his death are inseparable realities. Second, Paul, Peter, and other New Testament writers clearly represent the cross of Christ as central to the gospel. Third, among the events of Jesus' life, none is more historically certain than his crucifixion at the behest of the Roman governor Pontius Pilate — an event noted by ancient Jewish, Roman, as well as Christian sources. Fourth, under Roman rule, crucifixion as a mode of execution was reserved for enemies of the Roman political order. Jesus' crucifixion thus begs an important question: How could Jesus' ministry have led anyone to the conclusion that he posed a political risk to imperial Rome?

Key to answering this question are the Gospel reports of hearings (Luke 22:66-71; cf. John 11:47-53) and trials (Matt. 26:57–27:31; Mark 14:53–15:20; Luke 23:1-25; John 18:13–19:16). In John 11, the Jewish leaders in Jerusalem recognized the potential of Jesus' popular following to jeopardize the uneasy balance that characterized Rome-Jerusalem relations. More explicit are the charges brought against Jesus in Luke 23:1-5. There Jesus is discredited as a false prophet leading God's people astray (Matt. 27:63; cf. Deuteronomy 13) and presented to Pilate, the Roman governor, as a threat to Caesar. Opposing the payment of taxes to Caesar, as one part of this indictment has it, would have had immediate economic repercussions. Far more significantly, refusing to pay taxes and urging others to do the same would have symbolized a rejection of the political jurisdiction and imperial authority of Rome over Jewish people and Jewish affairs. A similar political note is sounded in John 19:12, 15, where the dominion of Caesar is contrasted with that of Jesus.

Why would the Jewish elite have presented Jesus to Rome's agent of governance in these terms, and sought the death penalty in this case? The Gospels record Jesus' numerous infractions of Jewish legal practices, including his characteristic overruling of Jewish laws related to food and table companions, as well as his practice of healing on the Sabbath. More pointedly, according to the Gospel records of Jesus' initial trial before the Jewish council in Jerusalem (the Sanhedrin), Jesus was charged with blasphemy. From their perspective, his speaking and acting against the temple (Matt. 21:12-17; Mark 11:11-19; Luke 19:45-48) amounted to profaning the God of the temple. His claim regarding his forthcoming presence and rule at the right hand of God (Matt. 26:64; Mark 14:62) was particularly blasphemous. In all likelihood, the Sanhedrin, though powerful in so many affairs of Jewish life, probably did not possess the authority to decide for and carry out the death penalty. Jesus, viewed as a false prophet and blasphemer, was clearly deserving of death in their view, so he was handed over to the Roman legal system for trial, sentencing, and execution.

Why did Jesus have to die? From a historical perspective, the answer is clear, even if it is multilayered. Put simply, too many Jewish and Roman leaders opposed his mission and message as dangerous. The law of Moses called for the removal of his person and influence on account of its harmful effect on God's people. And the law of Rome required that he (and others like him) be made an example so other would-be pretenders to the throne might be reminded of the fate of those who incited rebellion against the empire.

This is not the whole story, however. Of this we are reminded by the close association of cross and resurrection in Gospel narratives and creedal statements. Through Jesus' own predictions of his suffering and death, and his insistence that these were "necessary" in God's redemptive design, and through the generous use of the Scriptures in the Gospel records of the events leading up to Jesus' death, we learn that more than human forces were at work in Jesus' execution. As Luke records it, Jesus anticipates his death with the words, "the Son of Man is going as it has been determined [by God]" (Luke 22:22; cf. Isaiah 53). In short, the cross was neither an accident of history nor a surprise to God, but was actually central to God's eternal purpose.

This means that the resurrection of Jesus cannot be viewed as "overturning" the cross or "in spite of" the cross. Viewed consistently as God's powerful act, the resurrection of Jesus from the dead is God's vindication of Jesus' person, mission, *and death.* If the heinous reality of Jesus' execution on a Roman cross calls into question his status as God's Son, Lord, and Messiah, the resurrection is irrefutable proof that Jesus is all these and more. If Jesus' execution seems to prove that the interpretation of the Scriptures and view of God paraded by the Jewish elite in Jerusalem were valid, and that Rome's authority in human affairs was absolute, the resurrection is irrefutable proof that neither of these affirmations was true. If Jesus' death on a Roman cross portrays Jesus as a political threat, this is because he did, indeed, pose such a threat, since the coming of the rule of God into the world cannot but call into question all other rulers and all other ways of exercising power. The resurrection of Jesus is thus the historical ground of the theological affirmation that in Jesus' person and work we see the revelation of God's character and purpose.

The unanimous witness of the New Testament writings is that Jesus was resurrected from the dead and is alive, but no one actually witnessed the resurrection event itself. Does this mean that we lack any evidence for Jesus' resurrection? No, but it does mean that the evidence available to us is less direct. Most interesting in this regard is the tradition of the empty tomb, witnessed in each of the Gospels (Matt. 27:62–28:15; Mark 16:1-8; Luke 24:1-12; John 20:1-18). Since women in antiquity were generally not recruited to provide legal testimony, it is astonishing that, according to the unified testimony of the Gospels, the first witnesses of the empty tomb were women. It is highly unlikely that early Christians would have invented stories of the empty tomb in which women were the key figures (cf. Luke 24:11).

With regard to this same tradition, it is also interesting that nothing in the New Testament indicates that anyone doubted testimony that the tomb was empty. Matthew's Gospel observes that, when the tomb was discovered to be empty, plans were concocted and guards bribed in order to spread the story that Jesus' body had been stolen by his disciples (Matt. 27:62-66; 28:11-15). Rather than denying the empty tomb, here was an attempt to explain it away.

The New Testament contains repeated assurances that people experienced encounters with the risen Lord and that this experience utterly changed their lives. Indeed, *something* must explain the transformation of the disciples that occurred so quickly following the crucifixion — this transformation from a disheartened, fractured company to the cohesive, hopeful, and purpose-driven band of followers. What the New Testament relates is consistent with what we know of beliefs regarding the resurrection among Jews in this period. Resurrection hope was deeply embedded in a constellation of hopes regarding God's restoration of Israel and the ushering in of God's dominion. The proclamation of the fulfillment of precisely these hopes among those first Christians speaks to their belief that the long-awaited resurrection had actually begun with God's powerful act in raising Jesus from the dead. That the good news be grounded in the historical reality of the resurrection of Jesus from the dead was therefore nonnegotiable.

JOEL B. GREEN

Tomb with rolling stone outside Jerusalem; 1st century A.D. *(Phoenix Data Systems, Neal and Joel Bierling)*

so that by now Jesus should be really dead. Jesus walks his traveling companions through the Old Testament prophecies concerning the Christ to correct their understanding of the nature of his messianic mission (v. 27).

At the end of the journey, the three travelers share fellowship over a meal, and the disciples finally recognize Jesus (compare vv. 16 and 31). Some scholars see the meal at Emmaus as a eucharistic celebration reminiscent of the Last Supper (compare v. 30 with 22:19), though Luke commonly uses the terminology of "breaking bread" to describe ordinary meal-taking (e.g., Acts 2:42; 20:7; 27:35). In any case, Jesus' vanishing at the point of recognition prompts the disciples to exchange notes about the emotional sensation generated in them by his exposition of the Scriptures — an inward feeling that helps them believe what they have just seen and propels them back to Jerusalem to give eyewitness testimony of the resurrected Christ to the apostles and company. Upon returning, they learn from the Eleven that Jesus has already appeared to Simon Peter (cf. 1 Cor. 15:5).

Several features of Luke's account combat any skepticism that the reports of Jesus' postresurrection appearances constitute fabrications born of the wishful expectation of his followers: the disciples' initial disbelief of the report by the women who discover the empty tomb; the nonrecognition of Jesus by the two disciples on the road to Emmaus; and the doubt of the disciples in whose midst Jesus now appears. Indeed, Christ's coming back to life catches even

his disciples by surprise, and he has to convince them of his physical existence by showing them his flesh, inviting them to touch him, and eating food in front of them. Yet his sudden vanishing and materializing hint at elemental differences between his pre- and postresurrection bodies (vv. 31, 36).

24:44-53 Jesus' Final Instructions and Ascension

Having convinced the disciples of his fleshly reality, Jesus helps them to understand the prophecies concerning the Messiah that he had explained to them before his crucifixion but that they failed to grasp. He recommissions the disciples with the task of proclaiming repentance for the forgiveness of sins (vv. 47-49; cf. 9:1-6; 10:1-16). The proclamation comes in Jesus' name, since his sacrificial death has made forgiveness possible (cf. the Great Commission in Matt. 28:18-20). His command that the disciples stay in Jerusalem till they are "clothed with power from on high" (v. 49) anticipates their filling with the Holy Spirit on the day of Pentecost (Acts 2:1-4).

Luke ends his Gospel with the ascension of Jesus into heaven and the joyful and obedient response of his disciples, who remain eyewitnesses till the end of his earthly sojourn (v. 51; cf. Acts 1:9-11). Verses 13-53 represent a telescoping of events, since Acts 1:3 reports that Jesus made postresurrection appearances over a period of 40 days before ascending to heaven.

John

In complementing the synoptic Gospels, the Gospel of John shows both subtle similarities to its literary relatives and striking differences from them. John's portrayal of Jesus as an initiative-taker accords with Mark's picturing him as a man of action. But in Mark Jesus repeatedly commands others to keep his messianic identity a secret, while in John Jesus offers frequent evidence of his messiahship. John's inclusion of lengthy discourses by Jesus parallels a similar distinctive of Matthew, but the style of Jesus' speech in John differs significantly (perhaps due to John's paraphrasing or interpretation of the material). Further, Matthew's emphasis on the "kingdom of God" gives way to John's focus on eternal life. John provides a selective account of Jesus' ministry and teaching to show his role as a Messiah who was both human and divine, whereas Luke aims at a consecutive, seemingly more comprehensive, record. The stated purpose of John's Gospel, found almost at the end (20:30-31), shapes its profoundly theological emphases.

Nevertheless, John's greater attention to theology than biographical details does not necessitate viewing his account as unhistorical. Indeed, John adds much to our knowledge of Jesus' activities and teaching by emphasizing his ministry in Judea, especially in and around Jerusalem, whereas prior to the passion narratives the Synoptics concentrate on events in Galilee. John does not include the parables but provides the otherwise unrecorded reports of Jesus' turning water into wine at a wedding in Cana; his encounters with Nicodemus and with the Samaritan woman at the well; the allegory of the Good Shepherd; the raising of Lazarus from the dead; Jesus' washing of the disciples' feet at the Last Supper; the refusal of Thomas to believe in the resurrection without seeing and touching Jesus for himself; and Peter's three professions of love for the resurrected Christ over a beachside breakfast at the Sea of Galilee. Moreover, John's mention of three, possibly four separate Passover festivals, as opposed to the one Passover of Jesus' passion reported in the Synoptics, clarifies that Jesus' public ministry took place over a period of at least two and perhaps as long as three-and-a-half years.

Themes

Because of John's interest in the theological significance of Jesus' actions, he always refers to the miracles as "signs" or "works." Jesus' discourses explain the symbolic meaning of his deeds, and often the words used in his explanations carry a double meaning. For example, Jesus refers to his crucifixion as a "lifting up," which conveys the physical elevating of his body on a cross and also the spiritual glorification he receives from God the Father for exercising the authority to lay down his life (10:18). John's generous use of double entendre fits well with the frequent irony that punctuates the book (e.g., 4:10-11).

Theological themes include the revelation of God by Jesus, the divine, incarnate "Word" (Gk. *logos*), the filial relationship of Jesus to God the Father, and the messiahship of Jesus. His "I am" statements, distinctive to John, unpack these themes by symbolically conveying his unique qualification to provide eternal life. Here Jesus calls himself the "Bread of life," "Light of the world," "Door," "Good Shepherd," "Resurrection and the Life," "Way, the Truth, and the Life," and "True Vine." In using "I am," without predicate, Jesus identifies himself as God, who first revealed his name to Moses as "Yahweh" ("I am"; Exod. 3:14). Another distinctive of John is its emphasis on the "Paraclete," or Holy Spirit, whose sending by God the Father follows Jesus' postpassion ascension to heaven.

The Johannine Writings

Five books — the Gospel of John, the three epistles of John, and the book of Revelation — make up the "Johannine writings" in the New Testament, so named because their authorship is traditionally assigned to the Apostle John. The Gospel of John actually does not name its author, although it implies that the "beloved disciple" is responsible for the Gospel (John 21:24-25). According to some early church traditions, this disciple is John, the son of Zebedee, but the Gospel itself does not make this identification. 1 John is said to be written simply by "the elder." 2 and 3 John are anonymous, but 2 John especially is closely related to 1 John. In the book of Revelation, "John" is named as author, although not specifically identified as John the Apostle. By identifying all these figures with each other, the conclusion emerged that John the Apostle, the son of Zebedee, wrote these five books. Hence, together they are called the "Johannine writings."

The conclusion that all five books were authored by John was not, however, universally accepted in the ancient church, nor has it received universal acceptance today. Matters such as the authorship of ancient documents are not easy to settle, and the testimony of the early church fathers shows that there were differences of opinion regarding the authorship and origin of these documents. For example, Dionysius, the bishop of Alexandria (3rd century A.D.), disputed the Johannine authorship of the

Revelation, based on matters such as style, vocabulary, and thought. But his reservations may also have been influenced by his desire to squelch increasing belief concerning a final "millennium." The rise of Montanism, a late 2nd-century prophetic movement centered in Phrygia, may also have led to anxiety regarding claims to have and speak by the inspiration of the Spirit.

The genre of these five documents — gospel, letters, and apocalypse — varies significantly. The **Gospel of John,** while displaying significant differences from the other three Gospels, nevertheless provides a narrative of Jesus' life that includes his teaching, miracles, calling of disciples, death, and resurrection. According to 20:30-31, the purpose of the Gospel is to present Jesus as the Messiah, the Son of God. Moreover, the hidden identity of Jesus is revealed to the reader in the opening verses of the Gospel, which identify him as "the Word" (1:1), who became flesh (v. 14) and embodied the fullness of divine revelation (vv. 17-18). Jesus is presented primarily with respect to his Jewish identity, and the feasts and rituals of Judaism (Passover, Tabernacles, temple) and the imagery of the Scriptures (temple, shepherd, lamb, King, prophet, Son of Man, water, life, Law, wisdom, Moses, Jacob, Abraham, and so on). The Gospel points to disputes about Jesus' identity and comments that there was a "division" among the people as to who he was

(7:40-42). The Gospel also hints that there would come a time when Jesus' followers would leave the synagogue (9:22; 16:2), and thus a deeper rift among the Jews would develop with respect to identifying Jesus as the Messiah, the Son of God.

While the Gospel has its eye primarily on the identification of Jesus with respect to the institutions, feasts, and Scriptures of Israel, the **epistles** address a situation of a divided Christian community (1 John 2:19). Now the division is not between church and synagogue, but within the church itself. The issues that divided these early Christian congregations are not explicitly spelled out but seem to have involved the reality of Jesus' incarnation (1 John 4:2-3; 5:6-8; 2 John 7), the problem of sin and the continued need for atonement (1 John 1:8–2:2; 3:4-10), and competing claims to prophetic inspiration and to deeper understanding of God's revelation (1 John 2:20, 27; 4:1; 2 John 5-6, 9). The epistles insist on the genuine incarnation and real flesh of Jesus, the ongoing need for atonement, even for believers, and the continuity of the truth first revealed through and in Jesus with the teaching of the Holy Spirit in the life of the church. Each of these themes can be found in the Gospel of John as well. The need for correction of false beliefs suggests that different members of the early Christian community understood certain fundamental affirmations of the faith, such as the incarnation and the role of the Spirit and inspiration, very differently.

According to church tradition, these documents come from the same general area, Asia Minor, and are all dated toward the end of the 1st century. Typically the letters are dated after the writing of the Gospel, since the letters are taken to deal with problems that arose in a somewhat established group of Christian congregations. The book of **Revelation** is most commonly thought to be written under the rule of the Roman emperor Domitian (81-96). Certain Roman writers disparaged Domitian as arrogantly seeking divine honors and referring to himself as "Lord and God." Such a situation would undoubtedly have threatened early Christian monotheistic commitments, and the book of Revelation gives evidence of the threat from the imperial cult in the eastern part of the empire. But Thomas's confession of Jesus as "My Lord and my God!" (John 20:28) is an implicit admission of the singular authority of the risen Lord.

Similarly, a number of like thought patterns unite these books, particularly the Gospel of John and Revelation. First, these books distinctively share similar descriptions of Jesus Christ. Jesus is designated as the "Word of God" (John 1:1, 14; 1 John 1:1; Rev. 19:13), and the books share the description of him as "the beginning" or the one who was "in the beginning" (John 1:1; 8:25; 1 John 1:1; Rev. 3:14; 21:6). He is referred to as a "lamb" (John 1:29, 36), and specifically as the "Lamb of God who takes away the sin of the world." "Lamb" frequently designates Jesus in the book of Revelation (e.g., Rev. 5:6, 8, 12, 13; 6:1, 16, 7:9), with particular emphasis falling on the universal redemption effected through the death of the Lamb. In 1 John, Jesus' death avails for the sins of the whole world (1 John 2:2). While a lamb, Jesus is also characterized as a shepherd (John 10:11-18; Rev. 7:17). Jesus speaks majestically in revelatory "I am" statements, which make his identity known (Rev. 1:8, 17-18; 22:13). He is the enthroned Son of Man of Daniel 7 with the authority to judge (John 5:22, 26-27; Rev. 1:13; 14:14-20). In Revelation, he has a throne alongside the throne of God (e.g., Rev. 3:21; 22:1, 3), and in the Gospel he is addressed by his own disciples as "My Lord and my God" (John 20:28). His status and role as King and Messiah feature prominently (e.g., John 1:49; 12:13; 18:33, 37, 39; 19:3, 12, 14, 19, 21).

Other symbolism and language are common and important to two or more of these books. In both the Gospel and Revelation, Jesus is described as the source of living water (John 7:37-39; Rev. 7:16-17; 22:1), who provides spiritual nourishment and refreshment for his people (John 6:35; Rev. 7:16-17). Similarly, he is portrayed as light (John 8:12; Rev. 21:23-24).

The temple becomes unnecessary and is replaced either by the risen Jesus (John 4:21) or the presence of God (Rev. 21:22). Language of "witness" and "testifying" figure throughout John, the epistles, and Revelation, as does an emphasis on what can and was seen by the eyewitnesses. Both John and Revelation especially emphasize the importance of worship (John 4; Revelation 5–6). And John, 1 John, and Revelation lay particular emphasis on the role of the Spirit in prophecy and testimony, and the problem of false prophets.

In short, the traditions of the early church and certain patterns in the use of language and thought suggest a link between these documents. A "Johannine circle" or "school" may have emerged that cherished the living memory of the Apostle John and wrote down his teachings in the form of the Gospel. The epistles were then written by his students or coworkers, who preserved the apostolic witness to the "Word of life." Their testimony provided guidance for proper understanding of the Gospel and interpretation of the traditions deemed to come from John. While Revelation seems to stand apart in terms of genre, nevertheless, its traditional ascription to the Apostle, setting in Asia Minor, and themes and imagery suggest some points of contact with the Gospel.

MARIANNE MEYE THOMPSON

Authorship and Date

Early church tradition assigned authorship of this Gospel to the Apostle John, who was closely associated with Peter and in the later years of the 1st century A.D. lived in Ephesus in Asia Minor. The earliest witness to John's authorship comes from Irenaeus, a student of John's own disciple Polycarp. But the author of the book calls himself only "the disciple whom Jesus loved" (21:24; cf. v. 20), a self-designation meant to generate trust in his testimony as a confidant of Christ. The author characterizes himself as an eyewitness to Jesus' ministry (19:35), and the style and content of the book substantiate that claim by detailing weights and measurements, distances, personal names, and features of the topography of Jerusalem before its destruction by the Romans in 70.

Most scholars consider John the latest Gospel, written in the last third of the 1st century. The Rylands Fragment of John dates to ca. 135, and its discovery in Egypt requires that the manuscript must have entered circulation several decades earlier to allow time for it to reach North Africa.

1:1-18 The Word Enfleshed

Matthew and Luke begin their Gospels by recounting Jesus' miraculous conception, but John begins with a reference to Christ's preexistence. As the divine Word, present with and distinct from God the Father, the Word served as the agent of creation and the source of both physical and spiritual life (= "light"; vv. 1-4; cf. Genesis 1, where God "speaks" the world into existence, with "light" coming first). Verses 6-8, 15 summarize the role and ministry of John the Baptist as a witness to the "light" of Christ, whom the world (= "darkness") nevertheless failed to comprehend. In fact, the chosen nation of his fellow Jews ("his own") did not "receive" (believe in) him; but individual Jews and Gentiles who did receive him through faith gained spiritual rebirth (by "the will of . . . God") and thus status as children of God, regardless of human ancestry (vv. 9-13; cf. 3:1-15).

Verses 14-18 highlight the uniqueness of the Word both in relation to God the Father and to humanity. The Word, God's speech or revelation, becomes incarnate ("enfleshed") by taking on human form in the person of Jesus Christ. That Christ "dwelt among us" robs humanity of any excuse for failing to know ("see") God (vv. 5, 10). The theme of the "new and greater Moses," developed in Matthew, emerges in verse 17, where the grace (= ill-deserved favor) and truth imparted by Christ supersede the previous word, the Law given by God through Moses at Mount Sinai (cf. Matt. 17:1-13). This new Word is none other than the only Son of the Father, a designation that further underscores his unique identity and status.

1:19-34 The Witness of John the Baptist

In this Gospel, the primary importance of John the Baptist is his witness to the identity of Christ. When emissaries of "the Jews" (here the Pharisees; see v. 24) question John concerning his own identity, he first tells them who he is not — not the Messiah, a second Elijah, or the eschatological prophet anticipated by the Jews (cf. Mal. 4:5-6; throughout this Gospel, "the Jews" can refer to the religious authorities, the Pharisees, or the general populace — which included Jesus and the disciples). Rather, John claims identity as merely the prophesied "voice" whose testimony prepares the world for the arrival of the superior Word. On seeing Jesus, John acknowledges him as the "Lamb of God," who will atone for the sins of the entire world. The title and image grow out of the Jewish sacrificial system, which prescribes the slaying of lambs and other animals to effect atonement from sin (cf. Leviticus 1). The Baptist's identification of Jesus as the preexistent, divine redeemer of the world receives validation from John's witnessing the visible descent of the Holy Spirit on Jesus (cf. Luke 3:22). The Spirit's remaining "upon" Jesus ensures his baptism of others "with" the Holy Spirit — a baptism superior to the water baptism of John.

"Bethany beyond the Jordan," where John first carried out his ministry, names an unknown location in Perea (Transjordan, east of Judea), not the town outside Jerusalem where Jesus raised Lazarus and lodged prior to his passion.

1:35-51 Jesus' First Disciples

The effectiveness of John the Baptist's "voice" becomes apparent when two of his own disciples hear his confession of Jesus as the Lamb of God and leave John to follow him. The followers include Andrew, who also enlists his brother Simon, and an unnamed person. From Luke 5:10 we know that the fraternal team of John and James cooperated with Simon (and presumably Andrew) in a fishing business on the Sea of Galilee, though here the four accompany John the Baptist in Perea. Jesus gives Simon a new name: "Cephas" in Aramaic, "Peter" in Greek, both of which mean "stone."

Next a fellow townsman of Andrew and Peter joins Jesus' ranks — Philip from Bethsaida, a fishing village on the northeastern end of the Sea of Galilee. Recognizing Jesus as the fulfillment of prophecy, Philip summons Nathanael, whose initial skepticism that anything good could "come out of Nazareth" undergoes a complete reversal in response to a second display of prophetic knowledge by Jesus. (Nathanael does not appear in the synoptic Gospels' lists of the Twelve, unless he is the same as Bartholomew.) Jesus responds to Nathanael's acknowledgment of his identity with a picture of himself as the means for God's revelation (v. 51; cf. v. 18; Gen. 28:12). Jesus may have taken the designation "Son of Man" from Dan. 7:13.

2:1-12 Wine for a Wedding

When the wine runs out at a friend's wedding celebration at Cana in Galilee (Nathanael's hometown, 4 mi. north of Nazareth; cf. 21:2), Jesus' mother informs her son of the embarrassing situation in which their host, the bridegroom, finds himself. Though Jesus lets Mary know that his purposes differ from hers, he transforms the water into wine — not to protect the honor of the groom, but to symbolize the presence in Jesus of the messianic age of abundant blessing (cf. 1:16). This "sign" is Jesus' first recorded miracle, a religiously symbolic deed.

On a number of occasions subsequent to this one, Jesus will repeat the observation that his "hour" (or "time") has not yet come (v. 4), by which he means that the week of his death and resurrection lie further in the future.

The town of Capernaum, to which Jesus travels next, sits beside the Sea of Galilee, well north and east of Cana. That Jesus goes "down" to Capernaum refers to its lower elevation relative to Cana (cf. 4:46-47, 49; cf. v. 13, where he goes "up" to the mountaintop city of Jerusalem).

2:13-22 Jesus the New Temple

Cf. Matt. 21:12-17; Mark 11:15-18; Luke 19:45-47.

The significance of Jesus' cleansing the temple in Jerusalem goes beyond a righting of the improper, unethical use of the building to convey that the risen Christ will replace the temple as the dwelling of God (cf. 1:14). Whereas in the synoptic Gospels the Jewish leaders ask by what authority Jesus overtakes their turf, in John they demand from him a "sign," which Jesus promises through his passion but which the Jews mistakenly take as a threat against the Jerusalem temple. That temple may no longer have existed when John was written, and here the emphasis falls on Jesus as the Messiah who does not build but instead embodies a new temple.

In John, that this encounter takes place at the first of three (possibly four) Passover festivals reported in the Gospel suggests that Jesus' ministry lasted between two-and-a-half to three-and-a-half years. Since the synoptic Gospels mention only the Passover of passion week, they locate Jesus' cleansing of the temple at the close of his ministry, rather than at its outset. Note also in John's account the more comprehensive and aggressive nature of Jesus' actions (making a whip, driving out the animals as well as the sellers, spilling their coins), which trigger the disciples' memory of the "zeal for [God's] house" in Ps. 69:9.

2:23–3:21 Enlightening Nicodemus

Nicodemus, a member of the ruling Jewish council, the Sanhedrin, now approached Jesus. Nicodemus comes under cover of darkness, which may serve as a foil to Jesus' "enlightening" of him. Jesus indicates that enlightenment can come only with (spiritual) rebirth (by "water [a symbol of the Holy Spirit] and the Spirit"). By taking Jesus' words as a reference to physical rebirth, Nicodemus demonstrates that he has not yet experienced spiritual rebirth, despite his belief in Jesus' divine mission. And no wonder, for the windlike Holy Spirit exercises sovereign, unpredictable control in the realm of spiritual rebirth (v. 8).

Jesus notes that people talk about what they know and observe (vv. 11-13). He himself knows not only about earthly phenomena but also and uniquely about heavenly matters. So if Nicodemus fails to believe Jesus concerning earthly phenomena (water and wind), how will he believe Jesus concerning heavenly matters, about which he has no independent knowledge? Jesus bridges this gap by likening his coming crucifixion, resurrection, and exaltation (the triple meaning of his "lifting up") to the erection of the bronze serpent during the Israelites' wandering in the wilderness (Num. 21:8-9). Just as snake-bitten Israelites could save themselves from physical death by looking at the serpent, so will individuals save themselves from spiritual death by believing in Jesus.

The word "so" in the much-loved verse 16 communicates not the greatness of God's love for the world but the *way in which* God loved the world — by giving his only Son to bring eternal life to human beings. Jesus' mission does not consist in judging humanity in the sense of condemning it; rather, Jesus comes as a "light" that illuminates for the entire world the way to eternal life: belief in him. But light also exposes everything around it, and so judgment by the Light of Jesus happens in the sense of showing people for what they are — practitioners of the "truth" (such as Nicodemus, who has come to the Light), or darkness-loving doers of evil.

3:22-36 John Delights in Jesus' Success

Even after Jesus begins his ministry, his herald, John, continues to baptize the repentant till the ruler of Galilee, Herod Antipas, throws him in prison (Mark 6:17-29). But unlike the Jewish religious leaders, who resent Jesus' activities at the temple (2:18), John derives joy from the increase of Christ's following even at the expense of his own. John reiterates his former testimony to the superiority of Jesus (1:19-36), and verses 31-36

add confirmation of Jesus' words to Nicodemus (compare vv. 31-32 with 11-13; vv. 35-36 with 15-18).

4:1-42 Acceptance in Enemy Territory

Jesus then heads toward Galilee (cf. Matt. 4:12, where Jesus goes north to avoid persecution after the manner of John the Baptist's recent imprisonment). A Jew would normally avoid going through Samaria because of the centuries-old history of hatred between the Jews and Samaritans (cf. Luke 9:51-56). But God's love for the world (3:16-21) propels Jesus through enemy territory, where he takes the initiative in striking up a conversation not just with any Samaritan, but with a Samaritan woman (note her surprise in v. 9 and that of the disciples in v. 27). The encounter takes place at 6 p.m. (the sixth hour from noon) beside "Jacob's well," located between Mounts Ebal and Gerizim, where on initially entering Canaan the Israelites ratified the covenant given at Sinai (Josh. 8:30-35). Jesus' request that the woman draw him a drink of water quickly turns into an offer to her of "living water." He explains that this "water" consists in salvation, eternal life — far superior to the "well water" of Judaism, which requires repeated "drinking," namely, repeated sacrifices to atone for sins.

Again John stresses Jesus' omniscience by showcasing his independent knowledge of the woman's marital history (v. 18; cf. 1:42, 47-48; 2:24-25). She responds by identifying Jesus as a prophet and inquiring about the proper locale of worship. "This mountain" (v. 20) refers to Mount Gerizim, site of the Samaritan temple, which before its destruction in the late 2nd century B.C. competed with the temple in Jerusalem. But Jesus makes irrelevant the issue of earthly location by announcing the imminent elevation of worship to the spiritual plane — worship in "spirit [= the Holy Spirit] and truth" (cf. 14:6). Jesus' words spark the woman's confession of belief in the coming Messiah, and Jesus identifies himself to her as such (cf. Mark 8:27-30; contrast Mark 1:34, 40-45).

While the woman runs to relate her amazing encounter with Jesus, the disciples, concerned to provide him with physical nourishment,

Jacob's Well at Shechem, where Jesus offered the Samaritan woman "living water" (John 4). *(Phoenix Data Systems, Neal and Joel Bierling)*

learn that what really sustains him is working out God's will. The spiritually ripe woman and her Samaritan townsfolk exemplify the "fields . . . ripe for harvesting," which the disciples must "reap" through evangelism. Here Jesus' experience of Samaritan acceptance contrasts with his rejection by Samaritans during his last journey to Jerusalem in Luke 9:51-56.

4:43-54 Jesus' Word Brings Life

The observation that "a prophet has no honor in his own country" reminds readers that Jesus has left Judea to avoid oppression by the Jewish leaders of Jerusalem, who should have eagerly ushered the Messiah to that religious center (cf. vv. 1-3). As in Samaria (vv. 39-42), Jesus receives a warm reception in Galilee, Galileans having already witnessed his first "sign" at Cana and his activities in Jerusalem during the Passover pilgrim feast (2:1-13). While in Cana Jesus effects his second sign — healing a boy at the point of death. The miracle is fulfilled at the mere word of Jesus and in Capernaum, some 20 miles away, thus highlighting his great power and strengthening the reason to believe in him (v. 48). The child's father has already shown faith by walking a day's journey to summon Jesus to save his son (v. 47). He shows greater faith by heading home unaccompanied after Jesus' "word" assuring the boy's healing (v. 50).

5 Like Father, Like Son

Another, unnamed feast draws Jesus back to Jerusalem, where he performs a third sign. The pool of Bethesda (called in some ancient manuscripts "Bethsaida" or "Bethzatha") attracted the physically afflicted, for popular belief held that the pool had curative powers. Jesus singles out for healing a man whom he recognizes has suffered a long time. The curing occurs on a Sabbath, when Jewish law permits healing only in life-threatening cases. The man's long-standing ailment does not qualify as such. By slipping away anonymously, Jesus at least temporarily eludes persecution by the Jewish religious leaders for "working" unnecessarily on the day of rest and for instructing the healed man to work, too, by carrying his mat. Later, Jesus encounters the man in the temple and prohibits him from sinning — thought to cause physical ailments (cf. 9:1-2) — so he will avoid an even worse future, namely, eternal damnation (v. 14). Persecuted by the religious authorities for breaking the Sabbath, Jesus claims that his actions emulate God's own, for God is a life-giving God (vv. 17, 19-21). The leaders' malicious intent intensifies when he calls God his "father" — a declaration of equality with God, which they view as blasphemy, a capital crime (cf. 8:58-59).

Jesus' explanation of his sonship to God the Father in apprentice-mentor terms demonstrates both his equality with and obedience to God. The Father delegates authority to the Son, but the Son commands equal honor, and dishonoring the Son means dishonoring the Father. Jesus' singular authority to "judge" (reward "believers" with eternal life [v. 24] and condemn evildoers [v. 29]) is nevertheless inextricably tied to the directives of the Father (v. 30). The dual testimony of Father and Son validates Jesus' judgments as just (cf. Deut. 19:15). Additional though inferior validation comes from the testimony of John the Baptist, and Jesus' own "works" witness to his divine apostolicity (vv. 33-36).

Verse 37 restates the claim of 1:18 that no mere human being has seen God the Father. Here Jesus uses the observation both to contrast his uniquely intimate relationship to the Father with the Jewish leaders' lack of knowledge of

Steps leading down to the southern pool of Bethesda, associated with healing in biblical times. *(www.Holy-LandPhotos.org)*

God and to accuse them of failing to recognize Jesus as the one prophesied in the Scripture — evidence of their spiritual dullness (v. 38) and testimony to their disbelief of Moses, the ascribed author of the Law (Genesis-Deuteronomy). How then will they ever believe Jesus himself (cf. 3:12)?

6 The Bread of Life

Cf. Matt. 14:13-36; Mark 6:30-52; Luke 9:10-17.

John's associating of the feeding of the 5000 with Passover underscores Jesus' self-characterization as the "bread of life." Here Jesus himself takes the initiative in anticipating the need to feed the hungry throng, for he has a symbolic purpose in mind, whereas in the synoptic Gospels the disciples raise the issue from a purely practical standpoint (cf. Matt. 14:15; Mark 6:35-36; Luke 9:12). Compare the complete satisfaction of the multitude's hunger (v. 11) with the perpetual satisfaction of believers, who gain eternal life (v. 35), and the saving of all the leftover bread (v. 12) with Jesus' certain success in bringing salvation (vv. 37-39).

The multitude responds to the miraculous

multiplication of the loaves and fish by identifying Jesus as "the prophet," presumably on the order of Moses as promised in Deut. 18:15. But Jesus eludes their efforts to force him into a political role that accords with their expectations of a messianic revolutionary. Miraculously walking on the Sea of Galilee under cover of darkness, he rejoins the Twelve, who have rowed nearly halfway from Tiberias (on the western shore of the Sea) to Capernaum (the base of Jesus' ministry, on the northern shore).

The multitude persists in tracking Jesus, who sees their enthusiastic pursuit as merely a desire to fill their stomachs. When they request a faith-inspiring sign (v. 30), he has to explain the miraculous feeding of the previous day, which symbolizes the eternal life–producing satisfaction that comes from belief in him (vv. 32-40).

The Jewish leaders focus on Jesus' claim to have "come down out of heaven" (v. 38; cf. 5:18). Jesus' additional equation of his "flesh" with the heavenly bread, which produces eternal life, seems preposterous, for cannibalism repulses them, and their own Scriptures forbid drinking blood (Lev. 17:10-14). They fail to understand "eating" and "drinking" as metaphors for believing in the power of his sacrificial death. "Taking in" Jesus through such belief results in Jesus' and the believer's "abiding" in each other; and because Jesus lives eternally, those who abide in him — and he in them — live eternally, too (vv. 56-57). Neither the manna in the wilderness nor the "manna" of the Passover ritual can compare (vv. 49-50, 58).

Jesus' shocking symbolism trips up more than the Jewish leaders — many of his followers abandon their discipleship. Peter speaks up for the Twelve in professing the loyalty of the hand-picked apostles, but Jesus again displays his prophetic knowledge in foretelling his betrayal by one of them (vv. 70-71).

7:1-13 Now Is Not the Time

Even Jesus' brothers (cf. Matt. 13:55) want to make him a public figure (cf. the attempt of the multitude to make him king; 6:15). But Jesus, who receives glory from God, does not seek glory from any human being, let alone from the "world" of evildoers who hate him because he exposes their unrighteousness (cf. 5:41, 44). He refuses to put himself on display in Judea during the most popular Jewish festival, the autumn Feast of Tabernacles, for he knows that the time is not yet ripe for his self-sacrifice at the hands of the religious leaders who seek his life.

But after his brothers leave for Judea, Jesus also goes up (in elevation) from Galilee to Jerusalem to attend the festival inconspicuously. While the Jewish leaders wonder where he is, the multitudes whisper assessments of his character and ministry, apparently unaware that Jesus just might be listening in.

7:14-52 Conflicted Crowds and Frustrated Pharisees

When Jesus finally does appear at the temple halfway through the Feast of Tabernacles, he does not announce his presence by performing impressive miracles, as his brothers urged (vv. 3-4); rather, he goes there to teach. But even his teaching makes people marvel, especially since he lacks rabbinic training. The wonder of the audience occasions Jesus' declaration that his teaching comes from God — a claim verifiable by people truly devoted to doing God's will.

When Jesus mentions the Judean leaders' plot to kill him, the multitude, which includes many Galilean pilgrims, displays its ignorance of the effort. Jesus challenges that the catalyst for the conspiracy — his "one deed" of restoring a man to health on the Sabbath (5:1-18) — merits more than the Jews' injuring of bodies on the Sabbath through circumcision. That practice also violates Mosaic law, even while complying with it. (Leviticus 12:3 requires circumcising boys on the eighth day after birth, with no alternative arrangements if that day falls on the Sabbath.)

Jerusalemites who hear Jesus' defense, however, recognize that he is the target of the murderous plot. Some of the people already recognize that Jesus is the Messiah, and the failure of the religious leaders and their lackeys to act against him suggests that some of them also suspect he is such. But two traditions about the Messiah make others question Jesus' messianic status. One tradition holds that no one will know the Messiah's origin. The other recalls Mic. 5:2 in asserting the Messiah's known Davidic ancestry and native claim to Bethlehem. The Jews' assumed knowledge that Jesus hails from Galilee argues against both traditions, betrays a general ignorance of his nativity in Bethlehem, and most significantly in John demonstrates their failure to recognize his heavenly origin.

As usual in John, however, Jesus elevates the earthbound discussion to the heavenly plane. Verse 28, normally translated as an affirmation that the crowd knows from where Jesus comes (Galilee), can just as easily be taken as a question challenging their presumed knowledge of his origin and the resulting disbelief in his messiahship. Since Jesus is thinking in heavenly terms, the implied answer is "No" (cf. 8:14). He tells them directly that he comes from God (v. 29) and will return to God (vv. 33-36). As usual, the people misunderstand, and they wonder whether he plans a teaching mission to the Gentiles living side-by-side with those Jews dispersed outside Palestine.

Verses 37-38 resume the theme of the "living water," which Jesus offered to the Samaritan woman (4:1-15). On each morning of the weeklong festival (Tabernacles), Jewish priests entered the temple and presented to God an offering of water from the Pool of Siloam. On the climactic day of the celebration, Jesus proclaims himself the ultimate libation (v. 37; cf. Isa. 55:1). His self-sacrifice will eliminate the need for repeated religious rituals by obtaining for believers a self-sustaining source of spiritual life, the indwelling Holy Spirit.

Nicodemus, who earlier came to the Light under cover of darkness (3:1-15), shows his growing spiritual enlightenment by speaking up for Jesus before fellow Pharisees. They immediately reprimand him for suggesting that they not condemn Jesus before hearing direct testimony from him and sarcastically denounce the worth of any prophet from Galilee (v. 52; cf. 1:46).

7:53–8:11 The Pharisees Foiled Again

The story of the woman caught committing adultery does not appear in the earliest and best manuscripts of John. Later manuscripts insert it at various places (also following 7:36 or 21:24; cf. after Luke 21:38).

The account describes another failed attempt by the Pharisees to trap Jesus between the civil law of the ruling Romans, who reserved the right of capital punishment, and the religious law of the Hebrew Scriptures, which required the execution of adulterers by their fellow Jews. But Jesus presents a countercharge, and the woman's would-be executioners can only walk away. Customarily, the oldest man cast the first stone in execution by stoning. But Jesus makes sinlessness a condition for that act, and a claim to sinlessness would amount to the capital crime of proclaiming equality with God. The Jewish leaders have already accused Jesus of such blasphemy (5:18) and dare not indict themselves for the same offense. Jesus, whose sinlessness uniquely qualifies him to stone the woman (v. 46), graciously dismisses her instead, but not before admonishing the abandoned adulteress to abandon her sinning.

8:12-59 The Light of the World

Despite mocking Nicodemus's proposal (7:50-52), the Pharisees find themselves hearing testimony from Jesus, though they are inclined reject its validity. As with Jesus' calling himself the "living water," his calling himself the "light" stems from a ritual performed during the Feast of Tabernacles. Four immense candelabra burn continually at the temple to remind the Jews of the pillar of fire by which God guided and protected their ancestors during their wandering in the wilderness after escaping bondage in Egypt (Exod. 13:21). As the "light of the world," however, Jesus shines not only for the Jews but also for the Gentiles. And as the "light of life," he illuminates the way out of the path of "darkness" — a biblical symbol of death — to the ultimate promised land of eternal life (v. 12).

Mosaic law required at least two witnesses to establish the validity of any testimony (Deut. 19:15). Since Jesus' contemporaries fail to recognize God's testimony to Jesus as his Sender, they consider Jesus' testimony to himself as unfounded bias. They keep querying him about his identity, but remain clueless and close-minded about his answers. In verse 22, the Jews speculate that Jesus intends to commit suicide, but in verse 28 he foretells his death at their hands. There "lifting up" weds the image of Jesus' humiliating elevation on a cross with the seemingly contradictory result of his exaltation by the Father.

In the following discussion of freedom from enslavement to sin, Jesus' countrymen again display their shallow understanding of Jesus' teaching and of their own history. They understand enslavement purely in socio-political terms. Even so, their denial of having ever been enslaved fails to acknowledge their current subordination to Rome and to previous political powers, not to mention their ancestors' past enslavement in Egypt — freedom from which spawned the events commemorated by the festival they are currently celebrating! Addressing spiritual enslavement in terms of the culture of his day, Jesus pictures the Son of God's freeing people from sin as growing out of the inherent authority of a son, an heir who enjoys permanent status in the family (= household), to free a family slave.

The Jews claim Abraham as their father. But Abraham obeyed God, whose message Jesus brings. That the Jews seek to kill Jesus, therefore, exposes them as false descendants of Abraham, in the spiritual sense. Their rejection of the truth imparted by Jesus betrays them instead as children of the Devil, the father of lies (cf. Matt. 3:7-10; Luke 3:7-9). The Jews then charge Jesus with demon-possession, thereby proving his point that they ignore the truth. Jesus' declaration that obedience to his "word" brings about eternal life seals their disbelief. His concluding claim to have existed before Abraham and to embody the divine "I am" — the personal name by which God identified himself to Moses (Exod. 3:14) — prompts them to try stoning him for wrongly attributed blasphemy.

9 Sin and Sight

In the 1st century, physical ailments were thought to be punishment for sin. Faced with a man blind from birth, the disciples ask the cause of the condition: his parents' sin or the man's sin while still an infant in the womb. Jesus' granting of sight to the man both symbolizes Jesus' role as the universal Light of eternal life and evidences the truth of his claim to be that Light (cf. 8:12). By sending the blind man to wash in the Pool of Siloam (= "Sent"), Jesus makes the man's obedience necessary for the healing, much as Jesus' own obedience to his

Jesus the Good Shepherd, who "lays down his life for the sheep" (John 10); marble statue, 3rd century, Catacomb of Domitilla. *(Scala / Art Resource, NY)*

heavenly Sender is required to bring about spiritual healing for humanity.

Although some witnesses view this miracle as testimony to Jesus' righteousness, the Pharisees charge that its performance on the Sabbath disproves his claim to come from God. The newly sighted man thinks Jesus is a prophet, but his parents, fearful of ostracism by the Pharisees, avoid the question (cf. 7:13). The Pharisees attempt to force the healed man to condemn Jesus as a sinner, but instead he delivers a sermon, exposing their blindness to the obvious truth of Jesus' heavenly origin, attested by the sign under scrutiny. The man's expulsion from the synagogue by the affronted Pharisees propels him out of the "darkness" and prompts Jesus, the Light, to search him out and elicit his confession of faith. The entire episode illustrates "judgment" as the result of Jesus' mission. Belief enables a person to "see" his or her inherent sinfulness so that repentance and forgiveness follow. In contrast, the self-sufficiency of spiritual blindness prevents repentance and dooms a person to die in a sinful (unforgiven) state.

10:1-21 The Good Shepherd

The allegory of the Good Shepherd explains through pastoral imagery familiar to Jesus' listeners the significance of the immediately preceding events. In the opening parables (vv. 1-5), the sheep represent the formerly blind man, representative of those who believe in him; the thieves and robbers stand for the Pharisees; and the shepherd represents Jesus. At night, flocks of sheep slept protected in low-walled enclosures, with a hired doorkeeper guarding the gate. A thief would hop the wall and hoist the sheep out individually, rather than overwhelming the porter and herding the flock out the entryway, so causing the sheep to panic and scatter. In contrast, sheep naturally followed their shepherd, whose familiar voice and kind ways kept the flock calm.

Jesus' also calls himself the "gate" of the sheepfold, the open door through which his flock may find freedom and sustenance in God's "pasture" (vv. 7-10). He "lay[s] down his life" like a "good shepherd" who sleeps in front of the gate of the sheepfold as guard. In Jesus' case, endangerment for the sake of the sheep means certain death, but one through which he exercises authority in surrendering himself to being killed (cf. 19:30) and in subsequently reclaiming his life (cf. 20:6-9). Whether Gentile (the "other sheep," v. 16) or Jew, the sheep know their shepherd, whose voice and teaching they readily recognize and willingly follows (v. 14; cf. 7:17).

10:22-42 Conflict with the Jewish Authorities

The scene switches to a different, winter festival — the Festival of Dedication, known today as Hanukkah or Lights, which celebrates the rededication of the temple after its desecration by Antiochus IV Epiphanes in 167 B.C. (Dan. 11:21-39). John's repetition of the sheep-shepherd imagery associates this account with the preceding allegory.

The Jews encircle Jesus and demand a straight answer to the question of his messiahship. Their urgent interest stems from the expectation that the Messiah would provide politico-military leadership in shedding foreign (here Roman) domination (cf. 1:19-28; 11:48). Jesus asserts that he has already answered their question (cf. 5:45-47; 7:25-44), and rather than take on the connotations that come with the term "Messiah," declares his unity with God the Father (v. 30; cf. 8:19). The declaration prompts another attempt by the Jews to stone Jesus for blasphemy (cf. 5:18). But he uses their Scriptures to indict them (vv. 34-36). According to Ps. 82:6, God himself has set the precedent that validates the incarnate Jesus' self-designation as the Son of God. Jesus' "sanctification" (v. 36) refers not to purification from sin but to the only, first-born Son as set apart by the Father for service in the world.

Evidence of the truth of Jesus' claim to deity comes when he eludes the encircling Jews armed to stone him. He revisits Perea (east of the Jordan River), where in contrast to the Jews many people believe in him (v. 42; cf. vv. 25-26).

11:1-53 Lazarus Lives Again

While in Transjordan, Jesus learns that a close friend is terminally ill — Lazarus, who with his sisters Mary and Martha lives in Bethany, 2 miles southeast of Jerusalem. Verse 2 points ahead to the anointing of Jesus' feet by Mary (12:1-8; see also Luke 10:38-42).

To his companions, Jesus seems to minimize the gravity of Lazarus's condition. He gives the impression that the sickness is not fatal (v. 4), and he delays leaving for two days after receiving the sisters' cry for help (vv. 3, 6). When Jesus finally goes to Bethany, in close proximity to the Jewish leaders seeking his life, the disciples show understandable concern. All along Jesus has meant that the death resulting from Lazarus's illness will not end the episode but instead will occasion an act of divine redemption that brings glory to God (cf. the sign in 9:1-3).

Jesus arrives in Bethany one day after the death of Lazarus. Grief-stricken Martha and Mary express their faith that if Jesus had come sooner he could have prevented Lazarus's death, though Christ's curing, in absentia, the failing son of the royal official has already demonstrated that Jesus need not have been physically present (4:46-54). As also in that instance, however, a confession of faith by the pleading party (here Martha) precedes Jesus' performance of a sign that strengthens faith and convinces others to believe in him.

The power of the Word to speak Lazarus back to life parallels Jesus' authority to "lay down" his own life and to "take it up again" (cf. 10:18) and certifies his raising to life on the last day believers who have died (vv. 25-26; cf. 1 Thess. 4:16-17). The raising of Lazarus attracts record numbers of believers in Jesus and so seals the resolve of the Jewish Council (Sanhedrin) to destroy him for fear that the Roman government, envisioning a political threat from the fast-growing, grassroots movement, will put an end to Jewish national interests. The current high priest, Caiaphas, unwittingly prophesies the spiritual significance of Jesus' death for the universal church, comprised of Jews and Gentiles (vv. 49-53).

11:54–12:11 An Ominous Anointing

Cf. Matt. 26:1-13; Mark 14:1-9; Luke 7:36-50.

The third Passover mentioned in John finds pilgrims to Jerusalem abuzz about Jesus, who after raising Lazarus back to life withdrew to a town a dozen miles north of Jerusalem. Would Jesus come for the festival, with a warrant out for his arrest? Heading south and skirting the wilderness side of the hill country, Jesus barely bypasses Jerusalem to revisit Mary, Martha, and Lazarus in nearby Bethany. During supper, Mary uses a large amount of costly, exotic perfume to "wash" Jesus' feet and uses her hair as a towel to dry them. Ancient Near Eastern hosts normally provided their guests with water for foot-washing, a courtesy made necessary by sandaled feet and dusty roads. Further, not hosts but slaves performed the service. So Mary's hospitality, which cost not only her dignity but also considerable wealth (nearly a year's salary for the average manual laborer), far surpasses a host's obligations, and her extravagance draws criticism by Judas Iscariot, the less-than-trustworthy treasurer of the Twelve. Jesus, however, approves Mary's act as an appropriate anointing of him for his impending burial (cf. 12:23-24).

News of Jesus' presence in Bethany spreads fast, and crowds sweep in to see both Jesus and Lazarus. As the ultimate embodiment of evidence certifying Jesus' claims about himself, the re-enlivened Lazarus attracts believers in Jesus. So the Jewish leaders see that they will also have to kill Lazarus to squelch the people's growing enthusiasm for Jesus.

12:12-50 Jerusalem Welcomes Jesus

Cf. Matt. 21:1-11; Mark 11:1-10; Luke 19:29-40.

Jesus' arrival in Jerusalem turns into a welcome parade, with crowds lining the streets and acclaiming him king of Israel. Palm branches symbolized military victory, but Jesus triumphs peacefully, conveyed by his riding on a young donkey, not a seasoned warhorse. The effort of Gentile followers ("Greeks," v. 20) to gain an audience with Jesus confirms the Jews' fear that he has won over "the whole world."

Jesus' announcement that the hour of his glorification has arrived marks a turning point in his public ministry. He uses imagery familiar to his audience in likening his coming death, burial, and resurrection to the sprouting of a grain of wheat — a process which works on the principle that things have to get worse (death, burial, and isolation) before they get better (bearing fruit). The necessity for disciples of Jesus to follow and stay with him (v. 26; cf. 13:36; 14:3) contrasts with the impossibility of these pursuits for the unbelieving religious leaders (7:34; 8:21).

For the first time in John, we hear God's voice from heaven. The declaration offers support for Jesus' witness about himself (v. 28) — not to reassure Jesus but to help the people understand that he has come from God (v. 30).

Jesus continues to cast his passion in a positive light and explains it as a dramatic reversal of the current world order. The demeaning torment of his crucifixion will be a charismatic "lifting up" for glorification (vv. 31-32). Jesus multiplies his claims to deity by declaring that seeing and believing in him will mean seeing and believing in his Sender, God the Father (vv. 44-50). Jesus' mission involves declaring God's "commandment" of eternal life. This commandment requires Jesus' self-sacrifice on the cross — an act to bring about salvation, not condemnation (= judgment). On the theme of light versus darkness (vv. 35-36, 46), cf. 1:4-5; 3:1-21; 8:12.

13:1-20 The Last Supper

In John's account of the Last Supper, Jesus' eternal love for "his own" (all who believe; cf. 6:37-39) prompts him to teach servanthood by example (cf. Luke 22:24-27; Matt. 20:26-28). Jesus' washing the feet of the apostles signifies their cleansing from sin, which his death will accomplish. (Judas, however, remains "unclean"; vv. 10-11.) By dressing as a slave and assuming a duty reserved for slaves, Jesus the Master makes humility a must for his disciples. If he washes their feet, who are they not to wash each other's feet? But the extent of the humility modeled by Jesus goes even deeper; for though slaves had to wash the feet of others, and disciples had to perform for their rabbis the duties of a slave, neither slaves nor disciples had to stoop so low as to wash the feet of their own masters (lords) or teachers. So the Lord and Teacher Jesus does for his disciples what they would never be expected to do for him.

13:21-30 Jesus Confronts His Betrayer

Cf. Matt. 26:20-25; Mark 14:17-21; Luke 22:21-22.

Jesus offers a further example of the humility he requires when he awards his known betrayer, Judas Iscariot, a morsel of bread dipped in the common bowl — a token customarily handed by the host to the honored guest. That Satan "enters" Judas only after Jesus hands him the bread demonstrates Jesus' control over Satan, Judas, and the treachery to come, in accordance with Jesus' authority to lay down his life and to take it up again (cf. 10:18). His honorific gesture also betrays the betrayer to the "beloved" disciple, reclining immediately in front of Jesus, and no doubt the news spreads quickly around the table. But evidently the disciples either fail to grasp the immediacy of Judas's treachery or they cannot conceive that Jesus would order Judas to initiate the betrayal, for no one opposes his exit. That Judas executes his dastardly deed only at the command of Jesus, and that Judas leaves "immediately" on Jesus' order to make it quick underscore Jesus' control over his self-sacrifice (vv. 27, 30). Judas forsakes Jesus, the Light, to enter the darkness of night (cf. the symbolism of light and darkness in John).

13:31-38 Love Demands the Ultimate

To the remaining 11 disciples, Jesus declares his betrayal by Judas a glorification of the Son by the Father (cf. 12:28). This glorification, symbolized by his "lifting up" on a cross to die, will consist in the conquest of sin and death through his resurrection. The new era thus ushered in calls for a new commandment to distinguish God's people, a commandment governed by the rule of love as modeled by Jesus, not the dictates of law as communicated through Moses. The love of Jesus for his disciples has recently been demonstrated in his example of servanthood to them (vv. 1-20), and that same love is about to lead him to his death on their behalf. If he

will die for them, they must risk their own lives for each other (cf. 15:12-13). Peter sincerely but mistakenly thinks he is ready to lay down his life for Jesus right now, but his coming denials of association with Jesus (18:15ff.) testify to the obvious: If Peter isn't ready to risk it all for Jesus, then he is surely not ready to die for his fellow disciples. The new commandment of love does not relax the requirements of discipleship; rather, it intensifies them (cf. Matt. 5:17-48).

14 Promising a Home and a Helper

Immediately after foretelling Peter's denials, Jesus encourages the disciple with a comforting answer to his question, "Where are you going?" (13:36). Jesus is going to his Father's already spacious house to prepare rooms for the disciples to inhabit. Symbolically, this language communicates membership in the "household" or family of God, similarly to Jesus' dwelling in the Father and the Father in him (v. 10) and to the mutual indwelling of Jesus and the disciples through the Holy Spirit, the Helper ("Advocate") who will never leave them (vv. 16, 20). But the metaphor grows out of the physical "house of the father," the family dwelling to which the patriarch kept adding rooms to accommodate an ever-growing extended family. Sons, slated to inherit the estate, normally brought their wives to live in the family home and raised their own children there.

The very purpose of Jesus' departure ensures his return to take the disciples to their new home. Jesus reminds them that, in the meantime, they know both where he is going and how to get there, namely, believing in him (v. 6). Why would they want to join Jesus as members of God's household ("come to the Father")? Because membership means eternal life, gained through release from sin and death by the truth, the "way" which Jesus uniquely reveals and thus embodies (cf. 8:12, 24, 31-36).

Jesus' promise to do anything the disciples ask in his name (v. 14) does not grant them — or modern Christians — carte blanche in prayer to God (cf. 15:7, 16); rather, the promise ensures the disciples' accomplishment of the "greater works" foretold in verse 12. Physical restrictions will not apply when the limitless Holy Spirit empowers the multiple disciples after Jesus' leaves, so they will be able to do more works over a wider geographical area.

Jesus ends this final discourse by stressing his love for God the Father demonstrated by obedience to the Father's "commandment," namely, that Jesus sacrifice himself on the cross to save humanity (v. 31; cf. 10:18). Jesus will put his words into action by going to Gethsemane for his arrest, arranged by the "ruler of this world" (Satan) in the person of Judas Iscariot (cf. 13:27). By obeying his beloved Father, Jesus models his teaching that the disciples demonstrate their love for him by keeping his commandments to them. In John, Jesus has given only one, the commandment of self-sacrificial love for fellow believers (13:34) — the direct parallel of the commandment Jesus received from the Father.

15 The True Vine

In calling himself the true vine, Jesus declares that he replaces the chosen nation of Israel, characterized in the Old Testament as the vine planted in the promised land by God (cf. Isa. 5:1-7). Here the language of "abiding" parallels the language of "indwelling" in chapter 14, and "branches" that abide in Jesus, the Vine, become not just members of the new nation of God's elect but integral parts of it. Abiding in Jesus means not just staying attached to him but actually being an extension of him. Branches that fail to "bear fruit" (false disciples who fail to keep Jesus' commandment of self-sacrificial love; vv. 8, 10) are surgically removed and thrown away by the Divine Vinedresser, who also "prunes" (lit., "cleanses") the branches that do bear fruit so they will produce even more.

The difficult path of true discipleship will surely necessitate such cleansing, for Jesus' sincere but imperfect "friends" expect to suffer the same hatred and persecution that the world has inflicted on him. The world's rejection of Jesus, who came to save the sinful from automatic condemnation (cf. 12:47), both fulfills the Hebrew Scriptures (v. 25; cf. Ps. 35:19; 69:4) and leaves the disbelieving doomed by inexcusable guilt (cf. 8:24; cf. Rom. 1:18-23). With the help of the Holy Spirit, the disciples will spread the message of God's revelation, embodied in Jesus and made known to the disciples as "friends" because they love him (vv. 15, 26-27; cf. 14:21).

16 Witness of the Spirit and Joy

The inevitable persecution the disciples will suffer after Jesus leaves could easily cause them to lose faith ("stumble"). But by giving them advance warning, Jesus makes their future suffering a fulfillment of prophecy that should strengthen rather than weaken their faith. The example of ostracism from the synagogue (v. 2) issues a challenging reminder of the backbone shown by the formerly blind man (9:24-34), and the coming opportunity ("hour") for misguided religious zealots to kill Jesus' followers anticipates Paul's confession (v. 4; Acts 22:3-5; 26:9-11).

Jesus takes up the positive result of his departure, namely, its sparking the sending of the "Helper" (Holy Spirit). The Helper will compel the world to recognize the sin of disbelief in Jesus, the righteousness of Christ attested by his return to God the Father, and the condemnation of Satan sealed by Jesus' death, resurrection, and ascension (vv. 8-11; cf. 1:10-11). As with Jesus, the Spirit-Helper will not speak on his own initiative but will impart "whatever he hears," meaning the truth from God.

The disciples fail to understand Jesus' figurative language in foretelling his death, sorrow over which his resurrection will translate into joy. His explanation in plain speech draws their confession of belief in his divine origin, but he knows that, like Peter, they are not yet willing to lay down their lives for him, as he will soon do for them (vv. 29-32; cf. 13:37-38; 15:13). The "peace" (not simply inner calm, but spiritual well-being born of abiding in Jesus) amid "tribulation" that Jesus makes available to the disciples comes from the expectation of their suffering (v. 4) combined with his triumph over the "world" through the condemnation of its ruler, Satan, at the cross (v. 33; cf. v. 11). So certain is this triumph that Jesus casts the imminent victory as a past event.

Jesus, His Disciples, and the Christian Today

The term "disciple," from Latin *discipulus,* means "pupil." It is related to Hebrew *talmid* ("pupil"; 1 Chr. 25:8). In the Greek world *mathētēs* usually implied a school of "learners" gathered around a "teacher" *(didaskalos).* Most Greek philosophers developed a teacher–learner relationship with followers, who by listening and in "dialog" with the teacher hoped to advance to teachers themselves.

The Old Testament reflects very little of such a teacher–disciple idea because of the biblical concept of revelation as a direct communication from God to a prophet or leader. Indeed, Greek *mathētēs* does not appear in the Septuagint, though 1 Chr. 2:55 (family of scribes) and Isa. 8:16 may hint in that direction. Prophets might be part of a guild (2 Kgs. 6:1), and they often had assistants or servants, for example, Elijah (Elisha), Elisha (Gehazi), and Jeremiah (the scribe Baruch). But the basic role of these assistants was to serve and explain the words and actions of the prophets, not to learn the prophet's traditions in order to become prophets or teachers themselves.

Rabbinic Tradition

That situation changed in the rabbinic period (postexilic) when the emphasis was placed on learning the precise requirements of the Torah (Law) and the strict legal tradi-

tions of the oral interpreters. Male followers of a *rab* (rabbi) joined him in order to hear and learn his interpretations for keeping the Law (both written and oral).

Accordingly, much like the Greek disciples, these *talmidim* would apprentice themselves to a skilled rabbi in the study of Torah in order to become rabbis themselves. They were not only expected to recite verbatim the opinions of their *rab,* but also to learn how to counter opposing opinions of other rabbis. The Mishnah (the codification of the oral Law) includes the opinions of various revered rabbis. The students were also expected to assist their *rab* in some general duties associated with living. But the student was not expected to perform menial tasks, such as washing or touching the feet of the teacher (contrast Jesus the teacher in John 13:5ff.).

New Testament

In the New Testament the term "disciple" *(mathētēs)* appears only in the Gospels and Acts. It is used not only in reference to the disciples of Jesus but also concerning the disciples of John the Baptist and of the Pharisees (e.g., Mark 2:18). Note the claim in John 9:28 that the Pharisees were disciples of Moses, a conveniently constructed legend of succession to legitimize their rabbinic views.

The Early Disciples of Jesus It seems that a personal "call to follow" was regarded by the Evangelists as a basis for the earliest discipleship with Jesus (Luke 5:27). Implied within that call were not merely a summons to learn and obey his teaching (cf. John 15:10) but also to believe or accept him as God's only incarnate self-disclosure (1:1-18) or personal agent on earth (5:30).

Although Jesus was called "Rabbi" in the Gospels (Mark 9:5; 10:51; John 1:38), they are clear that Jesus was not merely expounding some teaching or doctrine, but that he embodied a new sense of authority in all he said and did (Mark 1:27). Thus, according to Mark, the people were repeatedly shocked by Jesus (e.g., 1:27; 4:41). Likewise in the the Sermon on the Mount Jesus lumps together all the opinions of the rabbis concerning the Law, and by announcing "but I say to you" (Matt. 5:22, 28, 32, 34, 39, 44) he challenges his followers to become more radical in their commitments to him and God's "righteousness" than all the scribes and Pharisees (5:20).

Authentic discipleship for Jesus meant consistency of commitment even to the point of persecution and death (John 16:2). Some turned back (John 6:66), but then those disciples were unfit for the kingdom of God (Luke 9:62). Jesus equated the cost of discipleship with taking up the cross (Luke 9:23; 14:27). Moreover, losing one's life for the gospel would be gain (Mark 8:34-35). Thus the "volunteers" for Jesus scarcely realized what discipleship actually meant.

The Twelve Just as adding three and four equals seven and often symbolizes divine perfection, multiplying those numbers frequently symbolizes the people of God, most clearly in the 12 sons/tribes of Israel and the original followers of Jesus (cf. Rev. 7:4-8; 21:12-14).

The lists of the original Twelve in the synoptic Gospels and Acts are slightly different, but they apparently represent three subgroups, with Peter, Philip, and James the son of Alphaeus leading the subgroups. Judas, the traitor, is always last until he is replaced by Matthias (Matt. 10:2-4; Mark 3:16-19; Luke 6:13-16; Acts 1:13-14). Although Judas was replaced (Acts 1:20-26), no effort was made to choose a successor for James the brother of John when he was killed (12:2). The Twelve are together symbolic representatives of Jesus' disciples. A specific line of succession is not envisaged. Moreover, Jesus' disciples must not be limited to 12. They encompassed others such as the "Seventy" (Luke 10:1) and included women (Luke 8:1-3; 23:49; cf. Acts 9:36, where Tabitha is called a *matheria*).

Relation to Apostle The term "apostle" in the Gospels also can refer to one of the Twelve (Luke 6:13). It is from Greek *apostolos*, meaning a "sent one" (cf. English "missionary," from the Latin participle *missus*, "sent"; Heb. *shaliach*, "agent" or "representative").

Among the Old Testament figures who were "sent" *(shalach)* to speak for God are Moses and Isaiah (Exod. 3:10; Isa. 6:8). This Hebrew verb is rendered as *apostellein* in the Septuagint.

In the fourth gospel Jesus is the Father's special agent or Sent One (John 5:30; 6:57; cf. 1 John 4:9; Gal. 4:4, 6), and he sends his followers into the world to represent him (John 20:21). "Apostles" in Acts seems to be a technical term for the Twelve who accompanied Jesus from the beginning and were witnesses to his resurrection (1:22). They are contrasted to the elders and other disciples (15:2, 22).

Paul consistently asserted his apostleship in his letters (Rom. 1:1; 11:13; 1 Cor. 4:9; Gal. 1:1) and refused to be ranked lower than the original apostles (1 Cor. 9:1-5; 15:9-10; 2 Cor. 11:5; 12:11). He regarded James the brother of Jesus as an apostle (Gal. 1:19) but does not refer to Timothy or others of his recent associates as apostles. Paul asserts that seeing and being called by the risen Lord were crucial for his apostleship (e.g., 1 Cor. 9:1; 15:8).

Disciples as Obedient Learners Christian discipleship involves more than quoting the teacher. Like the rabbinic *talmidim*, Christians are to take Jesus' yoke upon them and learn of him (Matt. 11:29). Indeed, they are to obey (keep) his commandments (John 8:51; 14:15), just as Jesus kept his Father's commandments (15:10). Such learning and obedience involve far more than words because they are a way of life. That is why early Christians adopted the concept of "walking"

(peripatein, John 8:12; 2 Cor. 5:7; Gal. 5:16) in the "way" (John 14:6; Acts 9:2). This idea is similar to the rabbi's concept of *halak* ("walk"), but the rabbis focused upon legal prescriptions *(halakah).* Instead, followers of Jesus' way are to keep his "commandment" of love. They are thereby known as his disciples (John 13:35) and evidence the lifestyle of the Holy Spirit (14:15; Gal. 5:22; cf. 1 John 3:7-21).

Disciples Today

Being disciples of Jesus is still very relevant for our modern world, which considers that it does not matter what a person believes as long as he or she is serious. Disciples of Jesus must understand that there are many teachers and opinions in the world, but there is only one "Rabbi" who has the authority of God and calls disciples to follow him. Such following demands consistency of lifestyle, even to the point of death. Some today may turn back and find they are not fit for the kingdom of God in Christ (Luke 9:62; John 6:66). But failure does not necessarily mean exclusion if we confess our sinfulness, because God is able to renew us (John 1:9). God expects us to learn from the "way" of Jesus, to accept unconditionally Christ's lordship over our lives (e.g., Col. 1:10; 2:6), and to show love toward God and others.

Like early Christians, disciples today live in anticipation of the return of Jesus in the Parousia, praying *Maranatha*, "Our Lord, come!" (1 Cor. 16:22; Matt. 6:10; Rev. 22:20).

GERALD L. BORCHERT

17 Jesus Prays for Glorification and Care

Now Jesus turns from addressing the disciples to praying for them. But first he prays for the mutual glorification of the Father and the Son, which the climactic events of his passion will accomplish (cf. 13:31-32). From the beginning of history, the goal of human redemption has consisted not in saving humanity for humanity's sake, but in glorifying God by demonstrating the failure of evil to thwart his ultimate purposes for creation. Jesus' prayer holds up that goal as the central purpose of his earthly mission.

Jesus cites the disciples' faith as the basis for the Father's guarding them in the face of persecution by a hostile world after Jesus leaves them (v. 8; cf. 16:30). His petition applies beyond the circle of apostles to all the faithful (vv. 6, 20), but the prayer does not extend to the "world" of evildoers who have not believed in him (v. 9). Protecting them "in your [God's] name" (v. 11) equips Jesus' followers to "abide" in him and thus to "be one" with him as he is with the Father (vv. 22-23; cf. 15:4ff.). Jesus' prayer that God "sanctify" the disciples asks that he set them apart for ministry in the evil world, to which from the standpoint of their spiritual renewal they do not belong (cf. Phil. 2:15). Jesus' closing expression of desire that the disciples join him to behold his glory anticipates the fulfillment of his promise to prepare for them dwelling places in the "house" of the Father (v. 24; cf. 14:2-3).

18:1-12 Jesus Insists on Arrest

Cf. Matt. 26:30-56; Mark 14:26-52; Luke 22:39-53.

Finally, Jesus and his disciples leave the supper table. They cross the Kidron Valley, which separates Jerusalem from the Mount of Olives to the east, and enter a familiar "garden" — Gethsemane, according to Matthew and Mark. In John, Jesus has already prayed extensively in the upper room, and his prayer has invoked his glorification through suffering (17:1) rather than wished for a way out of his passion (cf. Matt. 26:39 par.). Judas and company arrive immediately, and the arrest proceeds at once (cf. Matt. 26:36-46 par.). Since Jesus is acting on the Father's command that he lay down his life (cf. 10:18), he presents himself to the arresters,

rather than allowing his betrayer to do so (cf. Matt. 26:48-49 par.). By declaring "I am [he]," Jesus corrects the arresters' shallow understanding of his identity and origin: Jesus is not just a man from Nazareth — he is the incarnate Word from God (cf. 1:1; 16:30). This powerful declaration so astounds the adversaries that Jesus must, in effect, insist on their arresting him (vv. 6-8). By stopping Peter's attempt to thwart the arrest through armed resistance, Jesus further demonstrates his purposefulness in "drinking" the God-given "cup" of suffering (v. 11).

18:13-27 Denial by Peter and Trial by the Sanhedrin

Cf. Matt. 26:57-75; Mark 14:53-72; Luke 22:54-71.

The lasting influence of the former high priest Annas, who had vacated the post nearly two decades earlier, shows in the delivery of Jesus to him for trial, instead of to the current high priest, Annas's son-in-law Caiaphas. The accompaniment of Peter by another, known disciple makes Peter's denials of discipleship a demonstration of his unreadiness to follow Jesus' requirements of self-sacrificial love for fellow followers of Christ (cf. 13:31-38).

Knowing that the religious leaders have already denied the validity of Jesus' witness concerning himself (cf. 8:13), Jesus commends to the high priest the testimony of the disciples (perhaps the two present, Peter and presumably John), in keeping with the rules of fair trial. But the court takes this suggestion as contempt, and Annas, unable to wrench incriminating evidence out of Jesus himself, passes the prisoner and the problem to Caiaphas. With the tide turning against Christ, Peter twice more denies association with him, and the cock crows as Jesus had predicted (cf. 13:37-38).

18:28–19:16 Pilate's Predicament

Cf. Matt. 27:1-26; Mark 15:1-15; Luke 23:1-5, 17-25.

Passing over the details of Jesus' appearance before Caiaphas, John moves straight to the Roman trial by Pilate, which takes place at the governor's official residence in Jerusalem (the Praetorium) in the early hours of the morning.

The Jewish leaders remain outside the palace to avoid ritual defilement and so disqualification from eating the Passover meal that evening. When Pilate asks the Jews for a specific charge on which to try Jesus under Roman law, he comes up empty-handed. But on learning of his subjects' intense desire to execute Jesus, Pilate questions him with an eye toward a charge of sedition, for which for Rome alone could carry out the death penalty. Jesus' explanation that his kingship is not of earthly origin convinces Pilate of the prisoner's innocence, however. So at noon on the "day of Preparation for the Passover" (v. 14), the day on which the Jews sacrificed their Passover lambs and roasted them for the evening meal, Pilate publicly pronounces Jesus guiltless and thus presents to the Jews the perfect sacrifice, who at their unwitting insistence is about to become the ultimate, atoning sacrifice for the entire world (cf. Caiaphas's prophecy, 11:49-52).

John's account emphasizes the attempt of the Roman governor to avoid executing an innocent man; his fear of divine retribution for mistreating an unrecognized deity in the face of Jesus' self-designation as the Son of God; his frustration over Jesus' refusal to defend himself; his false sense of authority (in fact, Jesus occupies the position of power by exercising his God-given authority to lay down his life and take it up again); and his buckling under pressure from the chief priests, who by professing their exclusive loyalty to Caesar make Pilate look disloyal if he fails to sentence to death the "King of the Jews."

19:17-37 Jesus Lays Down His Life

Cf. Matt. 27:27-56; Mark 15:16-41; Luke 23:32-49.

In John's account, that Jesus himself carries his cross to the site of the crucifixion emphasizes his initiative in laying down his life. Pilate refuses to change the wording of the inscription mocking the crucified Jesus as "King of the Jews," and his repeated pronouncement of Jesus' innocence makes the title a statement of truth. Further, the universality of Jesus' atoning sacrifice receives symbolic emphasis from the three languages used in the inscription: Hebrew, probably meaning Aramaic as spoken by the Jews; Latin, the official language of the ruling Romans; and Greek, used in commerce throughout the Roman Empire.

John interprets the division of Jesus' outer garments among four Roman soldiers and their lot-casting for his seamless undergarment as a fulfillment of Ps. 22:18. The beloved disciple, included here among Jesus' family, stands as a foil to Jesus' unbelieving biological brothers, whose absence from this humiliating public scene clashes ironically with their earlier, unfulfilled urgings that he show himself in public (7:2-5).

Just as on the first Passover, the Israelites used bunches of the hyssop plant to apply to their doorposts blood from a sacrificed lamb, so at Jesus' crucifixion the use of hyssop in extending to him a drink of sour wine adds to his identification as the ultimate Passover lamb (cf. Exod. 12:22-23). Death does not happen to Jesus; rather, he makes it happen. Jesus the Word declares his mission of salvation accomplished (v. 30; cf. v. 28). He bows his head in a physical laying down of his life. His release of his spirit separates it from his physical body and marks the finality of death. Jesus, who understands from the start the Father's command, does not on the cross question his faithfulness (cf. 10:18; Luke 23:46; contrast Matt. 27:46; Mark 15:34).

Breaking the legs of a crucified person (v. 32) hastens death, for without the torso's support by the legs, the chest of the person hanging by outstretched arms cannot expand to allow adequate air into the lungs. With Jesus already dead, a Roman soldier spears his side instead (vv. 33-34). The blood that gushes out symbolizes the atonement for sins effected by Jesus' death, and the water represents the living water of eternal life.

19:38-42 Converted Councilors Bury Jesus

Cf. Matt. 27:57-66; Mark 15:42-47; Luke 23:50-56.

John reports that Joseph of Arimathea and Nicodemus, both members of the Jewish ruling council (Sanhedrin), together bury Jesus. Joseph now casts aside fear of his fellow Jews and acknowledges his discipleship. The anointing of Jesus' corpse with a king-befitting 75 pounds of perfume and spices further emphasizes his glorification (cf. 17:1, 5, 22; see also his anointing by Mary, 12:1-8).

20 Jesus Takes His Life Up Again

Cf. Matthew 28; Mark 16; Luke 24:1-12.

Mary goes to Jesus' tomb in the darkness of early morning, and the resurrected Jesus appears to her as the Light of eternal life (contrast Matt. 28:1; Luke 24:1-2; cf. 1:5; 8:12). Peter and the "other" disciple run to the tomb, not to verify his resurrection (cf. v. 9) but to confirm Mary's report that someone has stolen his corpse (v. 2). (For the other disciple, seeing is believing; v. 8.) But a grave-robber would hardly have unwound the linen wrappings binding the body, let alone have taken the time to roll up the facecloth and store it separately. Though the disciples have not yet understood the truth, the scene reveals that Jesus has deliberately taken his life up again, according to God's command (cf. 10:18).

When Jesus appears to Mary Magdalene, she mistakes him for the gardener. Though blinded by her tears, this faithful follower nevertheless recognizes the voice of her "Teacher" (Aramaic *Rabbouni*) and attempts to "hold on" (or "cling") to him. Jesus must shake her off in order to ascend to his Father (v. 17).

Perhaps out of fear of reprisal by the Jewish leaders, the congregated disciples barricade themselves behind closed doors. But unhindered by the barrier, the ascended Christ revisits his faithful followers, commissions them as apostles ("sent ones"; cf. Matt. 10:1; 28:18-20; Mark 3:13-15; Luke 9:1-2), and empowers them for mission by breathing on them the Holy Spirit, the promised Helper (14:16-17, 26; 16:7-13). They are to preach repentance and the forgiveness of sins in preparation for the rule of God (cf. Jesus' mission of "judgment"; 3:17-19).

The refusal of the absentee Thomas to believe the report of his fellow disciples without seeing and touching for himself Jesus' healed-over wounds makes his eventual confession of belief all the more forceful (v. 28). Jesus' words to the "doubting Thomas" in verse 29 encourage the late 1st-century readers of John to believe despite lacking the benefit of personal encounter with the resurrected Christ. Indeed, inspiring belief in Jesus as "the Christ, the Son of God" is the evangelist's purpose in recording the resurrection and the other signs that appear in this Gospel, for such belief leads to eternal life (vv. 30-31).

21 An Encounter in Galilee

For other accounts of postresurrection appearances by Jesus, see Matt. 28:16-20; Mark 16:9-20; Luke 24:13-53.

The epilogue to John's account finds seven of the apostles fishing on the Sea of Galilee, called in John's day the Sea of Tiberias, after the lakeside city named for the Roman emperor Tiberius. Not until Jesus instructs the unsuccessful fishermen where to cast their nets do they recognize him.

The charcoal fire around which the group eats breakfast recalls the setting of the fireside denials of Jesus by Peter (18:15-27). Here his three professions of love for Jesus make amends for the three denials, and Jesus charges him with pastoral care over the "flock" of the faithful (cf. Luke 22:31-32). In 13:37, Peter proclaimed his readiness to "lay down his life" for Jesus. Now the Lord describes Peter's death as fulfillment of that earlier claim. Not only will Peter die for Christ, he will die in the same manner, with hands outstretched on a cross (v. 18), and with the same result of glorifying God (v. 19). Jesus dismisses as irrelevant Peter's curiosity about the fate of the beloved disciple, the author-apostle who in the last verse of his Gospel account finally refers to himself as "I."

Acts

Acts forms a sequel to the Gospel of Luke and narrates the evangelistic activities of the apostles during the 30-year period following Jesus' ascension to heaven. The book's position between the Gospels and the Epistles makes thematic sense by emphasizing the apostles' carrying out Christ's Great Commission through the power of the Holy Spirit (John 16:7ff.) and by introducing the widespread Christian congregations, the letters to which elaborate Jesus' teachings.

Content

The first dozen chapters of Acts track the birth of the Christian church and the spread of the gospel among the Jews, first in Jerusalem and throughout the surrounding territory of Judea (chs. 1–7), and then northward to Samaria and neighboring regions (chs. 8–12). The Apostle Peter occupies the most prominent leadership role in these efforts. The rest of the book (chs. 13–28) traces the northwesterly spread of the gospel mainly among the Gentiles in Syria, Asia Minor, and Greece through the missionary journeys of Paul, whose continued preaching in Rome while a prisoner awaiting trial ends the account. Written primarily for a Gentile audience, as was Luke, Acts portrays Christianity as fulfilled Judaism. The Roman government of the 1st century A.D. declared legal the religions of the nations it conquered. Judaism fit this category, so certifying the mother-daughter relationship of Judaism and Christianity became especially urgent for Christianity. And since social unrest arose wherever the gospel took root, Acts takes particular pains to portray Christianity as nonthreatening to Rome, possibly to assure Roman citizens that nothing should prevent their participation in the Christian community.

Authorship and Date

The same author who wrote the Gospel of Luke also wrote Acts. Both books are dedicated to a man named Theophilus. Acts 1:1 refers to the "first account" (the preceding, companion volume), and both works display similarities of thematic interest and writing style. The "we"-sections of Acts reveal that on Paul's second missionary journey Luke accompanied him as far as Philippi (in Macedonia) and rejoined the apostle for the return trip to Palestine at the end of his third evangelistic tour. Likely, Luke relied on his own memory of eyewitnessed events and gleaned additional information from Paul and his other traveling companions (e.g., Barnabas, Silas, and Timothy), from Christians in Jerusalem, Antioch (Syria), and elsewhere, from the administrator-evangelist Philip, and from written documents such as the decree of the Jerusalem Council (15:23-29) and the letter of Claudius Lysias (23:26-30). Because Luke does not record Paul's trial by Emperor Nero, Nero's persecution of Christians (which began in 64), or the Jewish Revolt of 67-70, some scholars date Acts to the early 60s. Since, presumably, Luke wrote Acts after writing his Gospel account, most scholars propose a later date in the 80s.

1:1-11 Reviewing the Facts

As a sequel to Luke, Acts begins by recapping the last 40 verses of the Gospel. Those verses recount Jesus' postresurrection appearances, instructions to the apostles, and ascension to heaven (vv. 3-12; cf. Luke 24:13-53). When in anticipation of the day of Pentecost Jesus foretells the apostles' baptism in the Holy Spirit, they wonder aloud about the imminence of the messianic kingdom, which the Old Testament associates with an outpouring of God's Spirit

Acts and History

Unlike the modern sense of history as a record of names, dates, and events in the past, in the ancient world history writing often represented a chronicle or journal of current or recent happenings and the author's impressions. Approaches to understanding the type of history represented in Acts include reading the book as either Acts *of the Apostles* or as Acts *of the Holy Spirit*. While both readings offer useful perspectives, neither is altogether sufficient as a lens through which to read the entire set of events depicted in the book. Only certain apostles — notably Peter and Paul — receive significant narrative focus, and the pivotal role of the Holy Spirit is mentioned infrequently (e.g., 8:29, 39; 10:19; 13:2, 4). A more comprehensive view is to understand Luke-Acts as the story of how God's promise to Abraham was connected to the life, death, and resurrection of Jesus (cf. Luke 1:5; 24:49). Specifically in Acts, the work of Jesus is understood as directly connected to fulfillment of promise (cf. 1:4; 2:33, 39; 7:17; 26:6-7). Indeed, in the introduction to his two-volume account of the beginnings of the Christian movement (the Gospel and Acts), Luke sets forth to present "an orderly account of the events that have been fulfilled among us" (Luke 1:1-4).

Perhaps the best way to discern what the book of Acts is essentially about is to compare the composition of the Christian community at the beginning of Acts and at the end. At the beginning, the community is comprised primarily of Jews. At the end, it includes persons from a wide range of ethnicities. In fact, this transformation of the community of believers is the result of the living out of the promise. In Acts, the historical movement is toward inclusion of all nations and away from a perspective that made the law of Moses a necessary requirement for Christian faith. It is no surprise that Paul, in the course of his work among Gentiles, relied quite heavily on the promise to justify the inclusion of non-Jews (e.g., Rom. 4:14-16; Gal. 3:14-19).

Given this combination of enactment of the promise and of communal growth in Acts, an examination of the story-telling process embodied in Acts will prove illustrative.

Twelve to Seven to Paul

The reorganization of the Twelve in chapter 1 foreshadows how they will be characterized throughout the narrative. Luke portrays them as ones who are concerned to maintain a powerful Jewish cultural symbol: the Twelve. By chapter 6, Luke has transformed the Twelve. Here they are portrayed as having instituted a communal hierarchy with them at the top, and the community's division of labor is based upon this hierarchy (cf. 6:1-6). Luke depicts the Twelve as believers in Jesus who occupy a position of authority, based upon both their knowledge about Jesus and their Jewish heritage (1:15-22). Their primary focus is on Jews, although those non-Jews who submit to the law of Moses may be included (e.g., 6:5). After chapter 6, the Twelve, as a group, are not mentioned again in Acts.

In chapter 6, the Seven are introduced (v. 5). Notably, here also a major shift occurs regarding who addresses the Jerusalem Jewish council on behalf of the faith. Previously in Acts, only Peter — a member of the Twelve — has spoken on behalf of the faith. Now a series of events occur that place Stephen — a member of the Seven — before the council. His remarks include references to Abraham (7:2, 8, 16, 17, 32) and lead to a general persecution of believers, which causes the movement to expand into the regions to which the Christians are fleeing. Only the Twelve are left in Jerusalem (8:1). Narrative focus remains on the ministry of the Seven until Saul — later called Paul (13:9) — comes to accept Jesus (9:1-9).

Transformation of Paul

We are introduced to Saul as Stephen is being killed. Luke characterizes Saul as a "young man." He is Jewish and has animosity for Jewish Christians (8:1; 9:1-2). In Acts, Saul begins as an upholder of the authority and worldview of the Jerusalem temple authorities. A transformation toward acceptance of the fulfillment of the promise takes place when Jesus confronts Paul (9:5). Paul's worldview became flexible. He is successful in negotiating the boundaries of a variety of cultures but only after his transformation. This experience was radical, and so is his ability to move cross-culturally to carry out the promise.

Transformation of Peter

Peter is introduced as a leader among the Twelve. As Luke portrays the events, under Peter's leadership the movement did not move beyond the geographical bounds of Jerusalem. Peter and John went to Samaria, but only in response to the missionary activity of one of the Seven, Philip (8:14-25). After this, Peter is depicted away from Jerusalem, but only among Jews and possibly Samaritans (8:25; 9:32-43). At this point he has not expanded his own worldview to include the "ends of the earth."

Chapter 10 depicts the process of transforming Peter. On a rooftop in Joppa, Peter has a vision and is challenged to forgo the restrictions of Mosaic law (v. 15). In Luke's account, a vision, a conversation with a divine voice (vv. 13-16), and a visit from the Spirit (vv. 19-20) occur to encourage Peter to see the implications of the promise.

The Spirit sends Peter to Cornelius, a centurion in the Roman army. Peter goes to Cornelius's house out of obedience to the Spirit, but he does not know what he is expected to do once there (10:28). Here Luke portrays explicitly Peter's unchanged worldview. He is a believer in Jesus whose acceptance of Mosaic law forbids interaction with non-Jews. After hearing Cornelius's account of how God had instructed him to send for Peter, Peter exclaims: "I truly understand that God shows no partiality, but in every nation anyone who fears God and does what is right is acceptable to God" (10:34). In fact, it is the transformed Peter who speaks on behalf of non-Jewish inclusion at the Jerusalem council that convenes to discuss Jewish and Gentile community rules (15:7-11).

Conclusion

Acts is history that incorporates an emphasis on the transformational impact of the promise. Persons, institutions, and the world are being transformed to conform to the embodiment of the promise in history. Believers today are the heirs to this work.

COTTREL R. CARSON

---

and characterizes as a worldwide phenomenon with Israel at the fore (e.g., Isaiah 11–12). But Jesus redirects the apostles' attention to their immediate mission of evangelizing the world (v. 8; cf. Luke 24:47). His admonition to ignore distracting interests and instead to focus on fulfilling the Great Commission, plus the emphasis on the enabling Holy Spirit, make for a fitting transition from the Gospel of John, which stresses both themes in its later chapters (e.g., John 14:16ff.; 16:7ff.; 20:22; 21:18-22). The Bible regularly associates clouds with the presence of God, thus the incarnate Christ's conveyance to heaven in a cloud and his angelically foretold return "in the same way" (vv. 9-11; cf. Exod. 13:21; 40:34; Rev. 1:7).

1:12-26 Obedience and Prayerful Preparation

The apostles (less the late traitor, Judas Iscariot) demonstrate their obedience to Christ's command "not to leave Jerusalem" (v. 4) by returning to the city from the site of Jesus' ascension, the Mount of Olives ("Olivet"), which rises up from the Kidron Valley east of Jerusalem's Temple Mount. A "Sabbath day's journey" equals three-fifths of a mile, the maximum distance allowed by Jewish law for travel on the day of rest. The devotion of the apostles to prayer, their unity of mind, and their inclusive association with other believers, including women (to whose voice the Gospel of Luke gives unique prominence), show the fledgling church as a model community.

Beginning in verse 15 and continuing through chapter 12, the Apostle Peter takes the lead in "shepherding" the Christian flock and furthering the mission to the Jews (cf. John 21:15-17). His first initiative consists in identifying a replacement for Judas. The disciples nominate two men whose faithfulness during Jesus' earthly ministry parallels that of the apostles, from their favorable response to the baptism of John up to the present moment. Lots are cast to determine God's will, and Matthias emerges as the candidate of divine choice.

2 The Holy Spirit Rushes In

The day of Pentecost — the Feast of Weeks, which concludes the grain harvest — falls on the 50th day after Passover and the immediately succeeding, weeklong Feast of Unleavened Bread (Lev. 23:15-21). It is the first Jewish festival after Jesus' passion and ascension, and the celebration sees Jerusalem swelling with pilgrims, both Jews living outside Palestine and Gentile converts who speak a wide array of foreign languages (vv. 8-11).

The manifestation of the Holy Spirit as a "rushing wind" plays on the words for "spirit" and "wind" in both the Aramaic spoken by first-century Jews and Greek, in which Acts was written. The "tongues, as of fire," that rest on each of the apostles signify the Holy Spirit's enabling them to speak in foreign languages and thus to communicate "God's deeds of power" (the gospel) to the pilgrims present in the Judean capital.

The Jerusalemites, to whom the foreign languages sound like unintelligible babble, dismiss the Galilean apostles as drunk already at 9 a.m. But Peter explains the occurrence as satisfying the prophecy of Joel concerning the outpouring of God's Spirit. Peter's sermon proclaims the crucified, resurrected, and ascended Christ as embodying the ultimate heir whom God promised to David (2 Sam. 7:12-16). The apostle points out the responsibility of his audience in putting Jesus to death, and some 3000 people respond by accepting baptism to demonstrate repentance. In turn, they receive the Holy Spirit, thus signifying their forgiveness. Together the Christians pursue communal living characterized by corporate learning, prayer, and worship and the sharing of meals, property, and possessions. The apostles perform miracles ("wonders and signs"), and new converts join the Christian community daily.

3 Peter Heals and Preaches

Peter's healing of a man lame since birth provides an example of the "wonders" performed by the apostles. The lame beggar sits outside the temple gate because his condition makes him ritually unfit to approach God's holy sanctu-ary. His physical exuberance over having been healed and enabled to enter the temple precincts on his own two feet catches the attention of other worshippers. Peter gives all the credit to Christ, reminds the awestruck onlookers that out of ignorance and in fulfillment of God's purposes they put Jesus to death (cf. the "Suffering Servant" of Isaiah 42–53), gives eyewitness testimony to his resurrection, and urges the crowd to repent of their sins. The promise of divine "refreshment" and "restoration" after "returning" to God recalls the assurance of Isaiah 54–55. Peter's observation that God raised up his "Servant" for the Jews "first" notes the initial offer of salvation to them (cf. Matt. 10:5-15; Rom. 1:16).

4:1-31 Peter and John Arrested

The Sadducees, who deny any resurrection from the dead at all, try to stop Peter's proclamation of healing in the name of the resurrected Christ. But the arrest of Peter and John fails to diminish the effect of the apostles' evangelistic efforts.

Peter turns the hearing before the Jewish leaders into an opportunity to proclaim Christ as the only way of salvation (v. 12; cf. John 14:6), but despite acknowledging the "notable sign" they refuse to believe. The failure of the religious rulers to find a legitimate charge against the apostles, along with popular knowledge of the healing, leaves the leaders no recourse save prohibiting Peter and John from further public proclamation of Christ. The apostles counter that by preaching they are only doing the will of God.

When the larger Christian community hears about the ordeal of Peter and John, they petition God for continued "signs and wonders" in the name of Christ and like boldness to proclaim the gospel. In ancient Palestine, freed slaves became bondslaves by voluntarily submitting to a lifetime of servanthood to the master who emancipated them; thus the Christians consider themselves "bondservants" of the Lord, who frees them from sin (v. 29).

4:32–5:11 Sharing Goods

The convert Barnabas exemplifies the communal practices of the early Christians by donating to the group the proceeds from his sale of land. Later in Acts, Barnabas surfaces as a missionary associate of Paul. Ananias and Sapphira also sell some land and give a portion of the money to the apostles, while claiming to have donated the full amount from the sale. Peter discovers the lie, separately reprimands husband and wife — not for keeping some of the money but for lying about it — and both die on the spot. The swift and severe divine punishment for attempted deception of the Holy Spirit strikes fear into the hearts of all who hear and shows that participation in the Christian community is a serious commitment.

5:12-42 The Apostles Undeterred

In the temple precincts the apostles continue their ministry of healing and evangelism. The rapid multiplication of believers becomes too much for the Sadducees, who dominate the high priesthood. They again arrest the apostles out of jealousy and a reasonable fear that the increasingly numerous Christians will retaliate against the Jewish leaders, whom the apostles continue to blame for Jesus' death.

But during the night the apostles miraculously escape from the public jail and return straight to the temple to teach. The perplexed Jewish leaders usher them to a hearing before the Sanhedrin, whose members complain that the apostles have ignored the previous order not to speak in Christ's name (4:18). Peter repeats their obligation to obey God, not human beings. When Peter preaches the exalted Christ before the Sanhedrin, they plan to silence the apostles permanently. But one of their prominent members — Gamaliel, a rabbi who taught the Apostle Paul (22:3) — persuades the Council to drop the matter in hope that the Christian movement will simply fade away.

After receiving further threats and yet another flogging, the undeterred apostles celebrate their suffering for Jesus' sake by preaching both in the temple and door-to-door.

6:1-7 A Practical Problem Fairly Addressed

Jewish Christians from outside Palestine (Greek-speaking Hellenists) complain that their widows aren't getting a fair share of the communal food rations. Native Palestinian converts agree to appoint Hellenistic believers (indicated by their Greek names) to ensure fair distribution of food among all the Christians. The 12 apostles "lay hands on" the seven men to signify agreement with the congregation's choice of administrators. The group includes Stephen, the record of whose martyrdom immediately follows (6:8–8:1a).

6:8–8:1a The Lynching of Stephen

Like the apostles, Stephen performs miracles that reveal God's power and follows up with masterful arguments defending the Christian faith. But Stephen runs up against some determined opponents from a synagogue established by one-time Jewish deportees, who after release by their foreign captors returned to Jerusalem from areas around the Mediterranean. Unable to refute Stephen fairly, the Freedmen foment antagonism toward him by pressuring witnesses to testify that he blasphemes God, the temple, and the Mosaic law.

Stephen's extended self-defense rehearses the history of the Hebrew people, beginning with Abraham's migration from Mesopotamia and

Herod the Great's palace by the sea and amphitheater at Caesarea Maritima. *(www.HolyLandPhotos.org)*

Paul's Cities

Paul spent his lifetime as a Christian missionary travelling to almost 50 cities of the Roman Empire, proclaiming his message of salvation to Jews and Gentiles through the promise God made to Abraham. Although he would have preached wherever he found receptive audiences, whether in the countrysides or small villages, he concentrated primarily on larger important cities such as Antioch of Syria, Jerusalem, Caesarea Maritima, Athens, and others to which most of his preserved letters to churches were written — Rome, Corinth, Philippi, Thessalonica, Colossae, and Ephesus.

Paul's letters bear the imprint of that Greco-Roman-Jewish cultural amalgamation that occurred in what he called "the fullness of time" (Gal. 4:4). Nowhere was the culture of the ancient world more evident than in its large metropolises. It was to these that Paul persistently made his way, seeking out those cities with significant Jewish populations that would catapult his cross-cultural work into a new geographical area.

Paul's missionary method involved giving the gospel in each new city "to the Jew first and also to the Greek [= Gentile]" (Rom. 1:16; Acts 13:46). He sometimes passed through significant sites without stopping to preach, such as the island of Samothrace, and the cities of Neapolis, Amphipolis, and Apollonia in Macedonia, in none of which any evidence of Jewish population has been found.

Tarsus

Paul was born and spent his earliest years in the Diaspora, the dispersion of Jews outside the borders of the Holy Land. He was "a Jew, from Tarsus in Cilicia, a

The Bema, a marble platform for public oration and the administration of justice in the agora at Corinth. Here Paul addressed the Corinthians. *(www.HolyLandPhotos.org)*

citizen of no ordinary city" (Acts 21:39), whose population has been estimated at half a million. The city lay on the Cydnus River, ca. 10 miles north of the southeastern coast of Turkey (ancient Asia Minor).

A great international highway, connecting the west coast of Asia Minor to Syria-Palestine and points east, ran through Tarsus, passing north of the city through the narrow Gates of Issus in the Taurus Mountains. It was the most important city of Cilicia, which was made a province under Pompey in

67 B.C. Eastern Cilicia was joined to Syria ca. 25, and throughout Paul's lifetime Tarsus was a part of the province called Syria-Cilicia (cf. Gal. 1:21).

When Julius Caesar visited Tarsus in 47, the residents called it Juliopolis (the City of Julius) in his honor. After defeating Brutus and Cassius, leaders in the assassination of Caesar, Mark Antony spent time in Tarsus and in 41 had a rendezvous with Cleopatra, the Egyptian queen, who was rowed up the Cydnus River dressed as the goddess Aphrodite.

Tarsus was an important educational center. Strabo, the 1st-century geographer, wrote that its citizens were fervent in the pursuit of culture and that most of its university students were from Tarsus itself (unlike Athens and

Alexandria, which drew students from throughout the empire), so there probably was not as much cross-cultural activity in Tarsus as in these other university cities. Nevertheless, it did provide Paul with an educational setting in which to spend his early years. His later writings are saturated with images from the Greco-Roman world, and these play an important role in Paul's communication and interaction in his Jewish-Gentile environment.

Antioch of Syria

Antioch of Syria, one of the largest cities in the Roman Empire with a population of 300 thousand, contained the mother church of Paul's work, sponsoring his missionary journeys, and, more than any other in the empire, became identified with the early Jewish Christian outreach to the Gentile world. It was the "headquarters" of earliest Gentile Christianity and, next to Jerusalem, was undoubtedly the most important base of missionary work in the history of the early church. Here the disciples of Christ were first called "Christians" (Acts 11:26).

Jerusalem

Jerusalem was the most important city in the history of the Jewish people, their capital city, where God had the temple erected and where Jesus the Messiah was crucified, buried, and resurrected. Portions of some of the walls, streets, pools, gates, and buildings from the 1st-century city have been excavated in modern times.

Paul first saw Jerusalem as a young boy when sent there to study under the noted Pharisee Gamaliel I (Acts 22:3). He lived in Jerusalem until his conversion to Christ and his call to become an apostle to the Gentiles. He ended his third and last recorded missionary journey by taking a large monetary contribution to the needy church in Jerusalem.

The Old City, in the southern part of modern Jerusalem, lies north and west of the Temple Mount, surrounded by a wall 2.5 miles long. This was also the location and extent of the city in the time of Paul. Its population numbered between 25 and 40 thousand.

Major Port Cities

During his travels Paul visited a number of major port cities in the Mediterranean world. Caesarea Maritima was the most important center of commercial and political influence in Israel, housing the governor Pontius Pilate, named in an inscription found near the theater, and the later governors Felix and Festus, under whom Paul was imprisoned in Caesarea for two years. A mosaic inscription from the floor of Festus's reception hall has recently been discovered. The Jewish king Herod the Great built the harbor city, which included one of his palaces also recently discovered near the theater. Other harbor cities visited by Paul included Assos and Miletus in modern Turkey, and Nikopolis on the western shore of Greece.

Ephesus

Paul spent three years in Ephesus, on the western coast of Asia Minor and with a large harbor now filled with silt. Ephesus housed the temple of Artemis (Roman Diana), one of the seven wonders of the ancient world. It was the largest city in the Roman province of Asia, with a population of 200 thousand, and contained the most important church in the area, the first of the seven to which the book of Revelation was addressed. The theater in Ephesus (Acts 19:29) is still standing.

Philippi

Philippi was probably not a large or impressive city at the time of Paul's visit. It had been ravaged by a brutal battle between the forces of Octavian and Brutus only a few decades earlier (42 B.C.) and was repopulated as a Roman colony by the authority of Octavian and Mark Antony. Later, in 30, after Octavian defeated Antony's revolt, he forced some of Antony's troops to leave Rome and settle in Philippi. Of the several cities known to be Roman colonies in the New Testament (Philippi, Pisidian Antioch, Lystra, Troas, Corinth, and Ptolemais), Philippi is the only one specifically so designated (Acts 16:12). The international east-west Egnatian highway passed through the city. On the Sabbath Paul went to the riverside, where he "supposed there was a "place of prayer" (= synagogue; Acts 16:13, 16).

Thessalonica

When Paul and his companions left Philippi, they "passed through Amphipolis and Apollonia" and came to "where there was a synagogue of the Jews" (Acts 17:1).

Thessalonica (modern Thessaloniki) is located on the eastern coast of Greece in the northern province of Macedonia. Built into the western slope of Mount Khortiatis on the bay of Salonika, at the head of the Thermaic Gulf, the city lies in a natural amphitheater. Since the 2nd century B.C., Macedonia had been divided into four smaller districts for administrative purposes, and Thessalonica was made the capital of the second district. Luke refers to officials of the city as *politarchs* (Acts 17:6); 19 inscriptions containing this term have been found in Thessalonica, three from the 1st century.

Athens

Another harbor city in the southeastern coastal area of Greece visited by Paul was Piraeus, which served as the harbor for the better-known city of Athens nearby. Athens was an internationally known educational center more concerned with ideas than commerce. It, too, housed one of the seven wonders of the ancient world, the temple of Athena, also known as the Parthenon. A city of about 25 thousand people, Athens was so filled with statues, altars, and temples of pagan gods that Petronius, a Roman satirist, said it was easier to find a god than a man in Athens.

Corinth

Paul's limited success in Athens prompted him to move on to Corinth, 50 miles southwest. Unlike Athens, where classical Greek culture was predominant, Corinth was a Roman colony. In the 1st century B.C. it had a population numbering 300 thousand, with an additional 500 thousand slaves. Its Jewish population dated to the reign of the Emperor Caligula in the 1st century A.D. The city derived its name from the currant and was a wealthy commercial center of agriculture, famous for its vineyards and the production of wine. The temple of Aphrodite on the adjacent Acrocorinth was renowned as a center of prostitution long before Paul's arrival. Immorality was so prevalent there that the expression "to Corinthianize" meant "to be immoral." The officials of the famous Isthmian Games were headquartered in Corinth.

Rome

Unlike most of the cities visited by Paul, the church in Rome had evidently been established by "visitors from Rome, both Jews and proselytes" (Acts 2:10) who had been converted in Jerusalem during the Feast of Pentecost and returned to the capital with their new faith. Rome, the capital of the Roman Empire, was built on seven hills along the east bank of the Tiber River, 22 miles from its mouth. It was the official residence of the emperor and the senate, the political powers that governed the known world at that time. The city, whose population in the 1st century is estimated at between 600 thousand and one million, was filled with arches, streets, and aqueducts and was crowded with buildings constructed on Greek architectural orders. The Pantheon, one of the best-preserved buildings from the Roman Empire, still stands in the heart of the city. It was a temple dedicated to all the gods, built by the Emperor Augustus, and completely rebuilt by Hadrian between 120 and 125. The Mammertine Prison, where Paul and Peter may have been imprisoned before their martyrdom, still exists beside the Roman Forum.

For Further Reading

Blaiklock, E. M. *Cities of the New Testament.* Westwood, N.J.: Revell, 1965.

Hawthorne, Gerald F., Ralph P. Martin, and Daniel G. Reid, eds. *Dictionary of Paul and His Letters.* Downers Grove: InterVarsity, 1993.

McRay, John. *Archaeology and the New Testament.* Grand Rapids: Baker, 1991.

Murphy-O'Connor, Jerome. *St. Paul's Corinth.* 3rd ed. Collegeville: Liturgical, 2002.

———. *Paul: His Life and Teaching.* Grand Rapids: Baker, 2003.

JOHN MCRAY

Cleopatra's Gate at Tarsus, also called the Sea Gate, leading to the Cydnus River. *(www.HolyLandPhotos.org)*

including Joseph's success in Egypt, the raising up of Moses to deliver the enslaved Hebrew people, their worship of the golden calf at Sinai, and the building of the temple by Solomon. Appealing to the prophet Isaiah (7:49-50; Isa. 66:1-2), Stephen charges the Jewish leaders with following in the spiritually misplaced footsteps of their forefathers. They themselves violated the Mosaic law by murdering the "Righteous One" (Jesus) prophesied in it. Thus their accusation against Stephen returns to them as an indictment.

Taking as blasphemy Stephen's description of the exalted Jesus, the angry hearers disregard civil law by seizing the right to exact capital punishment — the penalty for blasphemy, according to Mosaic law, but the meting out of which the governing Romans reserved for themselves. The dying Stephen's commendation of his spirit to Jesus and his forgiving prayer for his executioners parallel Jesus' words on the cross (Luke 23:34, 46). At Stephen's stoning, a young man named Saul lends a hand, and the incident seems to whet his appetite for persecuting Christians (8:3; 9:1-4).

8:1b-40 Spreading the Gospel

The stoning of Stephen sparks a Jerusalem-wide persecution of believers by Jews who reject Jesus as Messiah. Saul personally imprisons all the Christians he can. But instead of stamping out Christianity, the intimidation encourages believers who flee the capital to spread the word into the surrounding territory of Judea and north into the region of Samaria. Their preaching is bolstered by the exorcisms and miracles of the evangelist Philip.

A Samaritan local named Simon has been astonishing his townsfolk with magic, but the wonders worked by the Christian evangelist outstrip the magician's tricks. So much greater prove the miracles of Philip that they amaze even Simon into belief in Jesus. When word reaches the apostles in Jerusalem that the Samaritans are being baptized, Peter and John set out to impart to them the Holy Spirit, so signifying the Samaritans' full Christian equality with their traditional enemies, the Jews. Simon mistakenly thinks he can buy apostolic

authority, but Peter's rebuke shows the apostles immune to bribes.

When the apostles head back to Jerusalem, the Lord diverts Philip southwestward. The Holy Spirit leads him to a Gentile God-fearer (or perhaps full convert) returning home to Ethiopia and his job as royal treasurer after a pilgrimage to Jerusalem. The Ethiopian's eagerness to understand the prophetic words of Isaiah allows Philip to explain how Jesus fulfills them. When the travelmates happen on a pool of water, the new believer jumps at the opportunity to be baptized. The homebound Ethiopian takes the gospel deep into Gentile territory, while Philip, miraculously transported to the southern Palestinian coast, preaches Jesus to the Jews, from Azotus (Philistine Ashdod) north to the provincial capital of Caesarea-by-the-Sea.

9:1-31 Saul's Conversion

Back in Jerusalem, Saul plans to expand his persecution of those belonging to the "Way," the term used to designate the community of believers. Armed with letters of authorization from the high priest in Jerusalem, Saul heads for Damascus, Syria, to arrest and extradite believers in Jesus. Near the city, however, a dramatic encounter with Christ completely changes Saul's course. From a flash of blinding light, Jesus voices solidarity with his disciples by questioning Saul's persecuting him through them. Reduced to dependency on his traveling companions, the visually incapacitated Saul spends the next three days sitting dumbstruck in Damascus.

There the Lord convinces a certain Ananias to heal the infamous Way-hater. Ananias lays hands on "Brother" Saul, thereby renewing his sight and imparting to him the Holy Spirit. Saul responds by accepting baptism, fellowshipping with the Damascene disciples, and vigorously proclaiming Jesus as the Son of God.

Saul's newfound enthusiasm causes the unbelieving Jews to plot against him. Supporters help Saul escape by lowering him in a basket through the window of a home built into the city's encircling fortification wall. Successfully reaching Jerusalem, where he had originally persecuted Christians, the enthusiastic convert meets with a chilly reception by the understandably suspicious disciples there. But Barnabas befriends the unlikely "brother" and promotes Saul's acceptance by the community of believers. When Greek-speaking Jews plot to murder Saul, the disciples whisk him from the hill country down to the coast and set him sailing from Caesarea to his hometown of Tarsus, in southeastern Asia Minor (22:3).

9:32–11:18 Welcoming Gentile Believers

Once again Peter ventures from Jerusalem toward the Mediterranean coast. Stopping at the town of Lydda, situated beside the main east-west highway connecting the Judean hill country to the seaport of Joppa (modern Tel Aviv), Peter heals a paralytic and thus turns the region's inhabitants to belief in Christ.

Summoned to Joppa by disciples mourning the death of their beloved Christian sister Tabitha, Peter performs another miracle (cf. Jesus' raising Jairus's daughter; Luke 8:40-42, 49-56 par.). The lodging of Peter with a tanner shows his Christlike willingness to associate with the socially marginalized, for Jewish regulations on ritual purity rendered tanners untouchable by virtue of their constant contact with corpses. The mention of Peter's housing arrangements hints at the apostle's readiness to respond open-mindedly to further relaxation of Mosaic rules for the sake of welcoming Gentiles into the Christian community.

The challenge comes when a vision from the Lord prompts a devout, God-fearing Gentile named Cornelius to summon Peter north to Caesarea. Before receiving the call to the home of this Roman military man, Peter himself sees a vision, in which God commands him three times to kill and eat creatures declared unclean by Jewish food laws (Leviticus 11). As a result, Peter does not hesitate to disregard the ritual taboos attached to associating with Gentiles. To the audience gathered at Cornelius's home, Peter proclaims God's impartial welcome of people from "every nation" (Gentiles as well as Jews) who accept forgiveness from sin through belief in the crucified and resurrected Christ, the "Lord *of all*." The Holy Spirit's "falling on" the Gentile hearers signals their saving belief

and demonstrates to the "circumcised believers" present (the Jewish Christians who accompanied Peter from Joppa) God's full acceptance of Gentiles without their having to submit to circumcision after having already received the Holy Spirit. The new believers' submission to water baptism upholds the importance of the rite as a demonstration of membership in the Christian community.

11:19-30 Christianity Takes Root in Antioch

Through believers fleeing persecution in Jerusalem and missionaries from points west (Cyrene, on the northern African coast, and the Mediterranean island of Cyprus), Christianity continues to spread northward. In the Syrian provincial capital of Antioch — outstripped in population only by Rome and Alexandria — the gospel takes root among both Jews and Gentiles. The church in Jerusalem initiates a sister relationship with the Antiochene congregation by sending Barnabas to encourage the church there. Barnabas goes on to Tarsus to retrieve Saul (9:27-30), and the two return to Antioch, where they conduct a yearlong teaching ministry among the city's "Christians" — a term coined there, possibly derisively. The Syrian Christians demonstrate concern for the church in Jerusalem by sending back Barnabas and Saul with economic relief against the "worldwide" famine that hit Palestine ca. 46/47 (Claudius reigned 41-54).

12:1-24 Herod Struck Down

The events related here predate Barnabas's and Saul's mission to Jerusalem (11:27-30). In 41, Claudius awarded to Herod Agrippa I rule over all the domains of Palestine formerly governed by his grandfather Herod the Great. To curry political favor with the Jewish leadership antagonistic to Christianity, Agrippa perpetrates further persecution of the church. James, brother of John, suffers martyrdom at the hands of Herod, who during the Passover festival imprisons Peter with a view toward killing him too. But an angel of the Lord secretly breaks the bound and heavily guarded Peter out of jail (cf. 5:17-20). John Mark, at whose mother's house the local disciples have been praying, later becomes a missionary companion of his relative Barnabas (Col. 4:10) and Paul (13:5) and composes the Gospel of Mark. Peter instructs the prayer group to send word of his release discreetly to James — presumably the brother of Jesus.

Representatives of Tyre and Sidon, which had fallen from favor with Agrippa, appeal to him for reconciliation in the hope of restoring access to sources of food. They acclaim him as a god, whereupon the Lord inflicts on Herod a severe intestinal disease (peritonitis? roundworms? cancer?). He dies (44), and the gospel continues to spread.

12:25–14:28 Paul's First Missionary Journey

Barnabas and Saul return to Antioch, having completed their mission to Jerusalem and enlisted John Mark to journey with them. The rest of Acts will detail the westward spread of the gospel through Asia Minor, across the water to Greece, and eventually to Rome through the efforts of Saul, called from 13:9 on by his Roman name, Paul.

The church in Antioch commissions Barnabas and Saul, who sail from Seleucia (the nearest Mediterranean port) to Cyprus, Barnabas's home. The irrepressible Paul establishes an evangelistic strategy that becomes the format for all of his missionary trips. Following the example of the Twelve, who centered their evangelistic efforts at the heart of Judaism, the temple, Paul and Barnabas preach at local synagogues in urban areas. As the synagogue floor remained open to all qualified speakers, these settings expose the gospel to mixed crowds of Jews, Gentile God-fearers, and Gentile converts to Judaism. From the very start, a pattern develops in which Gentile enthusiasm for Christianity generates Jewish jealousy that causes the missionaries to abandon the synagogue setting and pursue evangelism exclusively among area Gentiles. Persecution by persistently hostile Jews eventually causes the evangelists to flee to the next town, where the cycle repeats. In this early stage of the church's development, the Roman government still views Christianity as a form of Judaism, and Rome's toleration of the

established religions of its conquered populations postpones official persecution until the empire perceives Christianity as a new religion, distinct from Judaism.

In the port of Paphos, at the end of their trek through Cyprus, Paul and Barnabas meet an influential Gentile — the Roman proconsul (ruler of the senatorial province) Sergius Paulus. The missionaries also encounter Elymas, an antagonistic magician who, for fear of losing the proconsul's business, tries to thwart his conversion to Christianity. But Paul's striking Elymas blind demonstrates to Sergius Paulus the gospel's superiority over magic and so seals his faith.

After sailing to the region of Pamphylia, along the south-central coast of Asia Minor, John Mark leaves Paul and Barnabas to return home to Jerusalem. In 15:38-39, Paul calls him a deserter, but Barnabas shows him the same generosity of spirit from which the newly converted Paul himself benefited (9:26-27).

Paul and Barnabas penetrate the interior of Asia Minor by going north to Antioch, near the region of Pisidia. Paul's first recorded sermon, given in the synagogue there, reviews the history of the Hebrew people and proclaims the resurrected Jesus as the culmination of salvation history (cf. 7:2-53). Paul also proclaims the availability of forgiveness and freedom from sin made possible by Christ's sacrificial death and offered on the basis of belief alone — "justification by faith," which Paul elaborates in his letters (esp. Romans). The Gentile hearers welcome Paul's proclamations gladly, but the Jewish aristocracy force the evangelistic duo to abandon their cause in Antioch (13:51; cf. Matt. 10:14).

After similar successes and persecution in Iconium, the missionaries land in Lystra, home of Paul's later traveling companion, Timothy. Paul's miraculous healing of a man lame from birth reminds locals of a legend according to which the disguised Greek gods Hermes and Zeus earlier visited an elderly Lystran couple. The townsfolk quickly equate Paul and Barnabas with those deities, but the apostles tear their robes to mourn their misidentification and rush to prevent worship of themselves.

Persistent Jews from Antioch and Iconium

catch up with the two in Lystra, stone Paul, and leave him for dead. But the apostle revives and takes off for Derbe, final stop for this first missionary journey. On the return to Syrian Antioch, Paul and Barnabas backtrack through the same cities and towns, but rather than speaking publicly they concentrate on strengthening the faith of the believers made on their outbound trip and on appointing elders to lead each local congregation. Back in Antioch the apostles report their success among the Gentiles, perhaps blissfully unaware of the controversy brewing among Judean Judaizers over the spiritual status of uncircumcised Gentiles.

15:1-35 The Jerusalem Council

Gentile males who converted to Judaism had to undergo circumcision, in compliance with the Mosaic law. Some Jews and Gentile converts believed the rite should likewise apply to Gentiles who converted to Christianity. When such "Judaizers" from Judea push this doctrine in Antioch, Paul and Barnabas argue against the position, aware that the requirement will discourage conversion by Gentiles, who view circumcision as a mutilation that mars the Greek ideal of male physical beauty, and will foster fundamental differences in the form of Christianity practiced by Jews and by Gentiles who do convert. So the Christians in Antioch send Paul and Barnabas to Jerusalem to settle the issue with the apostolic Twelve and the elders of the mother church.

Peter opposes some fellow disciples converted from Pharisaic Judaism when he denies the necessity for Gentile Christians to observe Mosaic law, which even Jews have found unbearable. Peter's argument appeals to his vision in chapter 10, according to which God's repealing of the kosher food laws symbolizes his cancellation of the entire Mosaic law, and to the subsequent reception of the Holy Spirit by uncircumcised believing Gentiles in the ritually unclean home of a Roman! Peter deduces that Jews and Gentiles alike receive salvation solely through God's grace.

Jesus' brother James bolsters Peter's position with quotations from the prophets Amos and Isaiah that support the salvation of Gentiles apart from observance of the Law. But James suggests the Gentile Christians in Antioch voluntarily forgo Greek practices that will hamper their social interaction with Jewish Christians: eating food sacrificed to idols, marrying close relatives, and eating the meat of strangled animals undrained of their blood. With a united voice, the Jerusalem church composes a letter outlining the conclusions expressed by Peter and James and sends it to the Christians at Antioch by Judas Barsabbas and Silas, leaders of the Jerusalem congregation.

15:36–18:23 Paul's Second Missionary Journey

Paul's desire to check on the churches established during his first missionary journey sparks a second trip through Asia Minor and beyond.

15:36–16:5 The Team Splits Paul's disagreement with Barnabas over whether to give John Mark a second chance at accompanying them causes the team to split up (13:13; cf. Col. 4:10; 2 Tim. 4:11; Phlm. 24). Barnabas sails home to Cyprus with his relative Mark, while Paul and his fellow Roman citizen Silas (15:22ff.) take the land route back to Asia Minor. In Lystra Paul also teams up with Timothy, a half Jew/half Greek who undergoes circumcision to avoid distracting disputes among Jews over his status with regard to Mosaic law.

16:6-40 On to Macedonia The Holy Spirit prevents both the missionaries' preaching in "Asia," a western Roman province of Asia Minor, and movement into areas along the region's northern coast. So the evangelists travel northwest to the port city of Troas, where in a vision Paul sees a man beckoning them across the water to Macedonia. Luke now includes himself as one of Paul's companions (v. 10). The travelers end up inland at Philippi, a colony established for Roman veterans. Pious Jews prove scarce in Philippi, which apparently lacked the minimum of 10 Jewish men to form a synagogue; for on the Sabbath Paul and Silas find gathered at the river a prayer group composed only of women. One of them, a businesswoman named Lydia, becomes the first recorded European convert to Christianity.

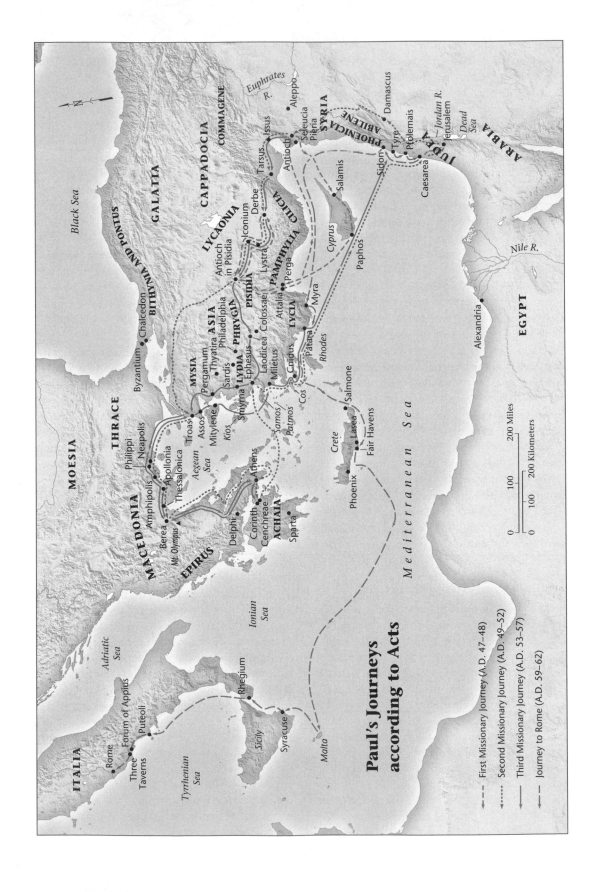

Paul's Journeys according to Acts

- - - - First Missionary Journey (A.D. 47–48)
········· Second Missionary Journey (A.D. 49–52)
———— Third Missionary Journey (A.D. 53–57)
– – – Journey to Rome (A.D. 59–62)

0   100   200 Miles

0   100   200 Kilometers

ITALIA

Rome
Forum of Appius
Three
Taverns
Puteoli

*Tyrrhenian
Sea*

Rhegium

Sicily
Syracuse

Malta

*Adriatic
Sea*

*Ionian
Sea*

MOESIA

THRACE

MACEDONIA
Philippi
Neapolis
Amphipolis
Apollonia
Berea   Thessalonica
Mt. Olympus

EPIRUS

ACHAIA
Delphi
Corinth
Cenchreae
Athens
Sparta

Byzantium
Chalcedon

BITHYNIA AND PONTUS

Black Sea

GALATIA

CAPPADOCIA

COMMAGENE

*Euphrates
R.*

Aleppo

SYRIA
Issus
Seleucia
Pieria
Antioch
Tarsus

CILICIA

LYCAONIA
Derbe
Iconium
Antioch
in Pisidia
Lystra

PISIDIA

PHRYGIA

ASIA
Pergamum
Thyatira
Philadelphia
Sardis
Smyrna
Ephesus
Laodicea
Colossae
Miletus

MYSIA

LYDIA

Troas
Assos
Mitylene
Kios

*Aegean
Sea*

Samos
Patmos

Cos

Cnidus

PAMPHYLIA
Attalia
Perga
Myra
Patara

LYCIA

Rhodes

Salmone
Lasea
Fair Havens
Crete

Phoenix

Cyprus
Salamis
Paphos

Sidon

PHOENICIA
Tyre
Ptolemais
ABILENE
Damascus
Caesarea

Jordan R.
Jerusalem
Dead
Sea

JUDEA

ARABIA

Mediterranean Sea

Alexandria

Nile R.

EGYPT

The Course of Paul's Ministry

Any discussion of the course of Paul's ministry is largely dependent on Luke's portrayals in Acts. While Paul's letters provide firsthand information about his theology, pastoral counsel, and relations with various churches, they generally lack a great deal of historical information about the course of his ministry.

There were certainly differences between Paul's purposes in writing his letters and Luke's purposes in writing Acts, and undoubtedly differences between Paul as represented in his own letters and as portrayed by his "biographer." But we must not drive too large a wedge between them, for both contribute what little we know about the course of Paul's ministry and of the history of the early church in general.

Encounter by Christ and Early Ministries

When Saul the Pharisee was encountered by Christ on the Damascus road (Acts 9:1-19; cf. 22:6-16; 26:12-18), a number of realizations must have almost immediately become fixed in his consciousness:

(1) Despite his zeal and sense of doing God's will, his previous life and activities in Judaism lay under divine rebuke. A voice from heaven had corrected him, and there was nothing more to be said.

(2) Jesus of Nazareth, whose followers he had been persecuting, was alive, exalted, and in some manner associated with God the Father, whom Israel worshipped. So he had to revise his whole estimate of the life, teaching, and death of Jesus, for God had vindicated him.

(3) If Jesus is Israel's Messiah and the fulfillment of the nation's ancient hope, then traditional thinking of the goal of life, rather than merely dwelling on the future, must be revised to emphasize what has been realized and inaugurated with Jesus of Nazareth and to focus on the personal and transcendent instead of just the legal and historical.

(4) The question from heaven, "Why do you persecute me?" signaled something of the indissoluble unity that exists between Christ and his followers.

(5) He had a mandate to minister to Gentiles on behalf of Jesus, Israel's Messiah and the nations' Lord. Later, he would come to understand that mission as involving the equality of Jews and Gentiles before God.

Immediately following that Damascus road encounter, Saul began proclaiming Jesus as the Son of God and the Christ (Messiah) in the Jewish synagogues of Damascus (Acts 9:19b-22). Then he took up residence in Arabia for three years (Gal. 1:17), during which time he evidently reevaluated his theology in the light of his Christian experience. After that he returned to Damascus (2 Cor. 11:32-33; Acts 9:23-25) and then to Jerusalem, where he ministered to Hellenistic Jews and Jewish believers in Jesus (Gal. 1:18-20; Acts 9:26-29). Subsequently, he traveled to Caesarea and Syria, and then back to his hometown of Tarsus in Cilicia (Gal. 1:21-24; Acts 9:30).

Some of the afflictions and hardships enumerated in 2 Cor. 11:23-27 may have occurred during those days in Tarsus, perhaps in retaliation for an attempted mission to Gentile proselytes within the Jewish synagogues of Cilicia. It may also have been during this period that he began to experience the loss of all things for Christ's sake (cf. Phil. 3:8), perhaps being disinherited by his family, as well as having the ecstatic experience mentioned in 2 Cor. 12:1-4.

Barnabas brought Saul to Antioch of Syria, where he successfully ministered for one year (Acts 11:25-26). Here this group of Jewish and Gentile believers were derisively called "Christians" ("Followers of Christ"), for many viewed such a ministry to Gentiles and the fellowship of Jewish and Gentile believers as going beyond what was usually permitted within Judaism.

First Missionary Journey and the Jerusalem Council

Paul's activities at Syrian Antioch were evidently confined to believers associated with the synagogue, both Jews and Gentiles. The conversion of Gentiles who had come under the ministry of Judaism before they believed in Jesus would not have seemed exceptional.

During the missionary journey reported in Acts 13–14, however, Barnabas and Saul were providentially directed into a radically new policy for their mission to Gentiles — the legitimacy of a direct approach to Gentiles, with no prior commitment to Judaism required, and of Gentile believers expressing their faith in Jesus apart from any distinctive Jewish practices. Paul's acceptance of this new policy is signaled by the change of his name henceforth in the record from Saul to Paul (13:9) and by his listing first among the missionaries (v. 13a) — with John Mark evidently registering his objection by leaving the group (v. 13b). The implications appear in the typical pattern of Paul's ministry at Pisidian Antioch and every city thereafter with a sizable Jewish population: an initial proclamation in the synagogue to Jews and Gentile adherents, and then, when refused an audience in the synagogue, a direct ministry to Gentiles.

Until now, Gentiles who had come to acknowledge Jesus as Messiah had been either full proselytes or "God-fearers" (Cornelius was an exception; cf. 10:1–11:18). Preaching to Gentiles directly, however, begun by Paul in his mission on Cyprus and continued throughout southern Asia Minor, was a matter of far-reaching concern at Jerusalem — especially in view of the tensions arising within Palestine after the death of Herod Agrippa I (A.D. 44).

Paul's new approach to Gentiles, despite his claims of divine sanction, must have seemed to many Jewish believers in Jesus to threaten the ministry of the Jerusalem church and to raise grave suspicion among other Jews. It was apparently at this time and in this context that Paul wrote to his converts in southern Galatia, who were being influenced by Jewish Christians from Jerusalem.

At the Jerusalem Council (Acts 15:1-29), however, the gospel was set free from any necessary Jewish rituals and practices (v. 19) — except for those measures intended to engender harmonious relations between Jewish and Gentile believers (vv. 20-21). In effect, Paul was left free to reach Gentiles directly, apart from any Jewish teaching or prerequisites, and to integrate them as believers in Jesus into "the body of Christ," apart from any Jewish regulations. This was an important turning point in the course of Paul's ministry.

Further Missionary Journeys

Acts 16:6–19:20 portrays the working out of this new Gentile policy through two further missionary journeys of Paul throughout the eastern Roman Empire from 49 to 56. An extraordinary combination of strategic planning and sensitivity to the guidance of the Holy Spirit enabled Paul to establish churches in western Asia Minor, Macedonia, and Greece. Paul's ministries at such cities as Troas, Philippi, Thessalonica, Athens, Corinth, and Ephesus focused on God's direction in and supervision of the gospel's outreach, Christianity's right to be considered a "legitimate religion," and Paul's circumstantial proclamation.

During this period Paul wrote 1-2 Thessalonians, 1-2 Corinthians, and Romans. A major concern of Paul throughout the period, but particularly in the later years, was the collection of money from his Gentile churches for impoverished Jewish believers at Jerusalem (1 Cor. 16:1-4; 2 Cor. 9:1-15; Rom. 15:25-32). This was not only an act of love, but also a symbol of unity that would help his Gentile converts realize their debt to the mother church at Jerusalem and give Jewish believers an appreciation of the vitality of the Christian faith in the Gentile churches. Paul seems to have felt it necessary to present the gift personally to the Jerusalem church so that it would be viewed as a true symbol of Christian unity, and not as a bribe — though he feared both opposition from the Jews and rejection by the Jewish Christians there (cf. Rom. 15:30-31).

Imprisonments, Defenses, Ministries, and Martyrdom

Acts 19:21–28:31 sets out Paul's somewhat circuitous final journey to Jerusalem, his arrest and defenses there and imprisonment at Caesarea, and his voyage to Rome and ministry there. Inherent in Luke's narrative are three major themes: (1) Paul's relations with the Roman provincial government in Judea ended with an acknowledgment of his innocence (cf. 25:25; 26:31); (2) even though the Jewish high priests and Sanhedrin opposed Paul, the Jewish king Agrippa II agreed with a verdict of innocence (cf. 26:32); and (3) Paul's innocence was demonstrated before Roman and Jewish rulers and also publicly (25:23).

At Rome, despite being under house arrest, Paul was free to receive visitors, including the leading Jews of the city (Acts 28:17-28; cf. v. 30). Despite all the difficulties encountered, Paul continued "proclaiming the kingdom of God and teaching about the Lord Jesus Christ with all boldness and without hindrance" (28:31).

Some argue that Luke did not speak of Paul's execution because that would have ruined his portrayal of the triumphant advance of the gospel. Others propose that Paul's case never came to trial because his accusers failed to appear within the statutory 18-month period and so Paul was released. It seems likely that Luke intended his readers to infer that Paul's case — whatever its outcome — did, in some manner, come before the imperial court for judgment.

We are forced to look elsewhere for further information about Paul's Roman imprisonment, his trial in Caesarea, and its aftermath. Accepting the so-called Prison Epistles (Philippians, Colossians, Philemon, and Ephesians) as having been written during Paul's Roman imprisonment, we may surmise that Paul fully expected to stand before Caesar's court — and, while he could not be certain, he also expected to be released (cf. Phil. 1:19-26; Phlm. 22). There is little reason to doubt his intuition, and such a release may be dated ca. 63.

Accepting the Pastoral Epistles (1-2 Timothy, Titus) as genuine — whether written directly by Paul himself, penned by a secretary at Paul's direction, or coauthored by someone such as Silas — we may believe that after Paul's release from this Roman imprisonment he continued his evangelistic work in the eastern portion of the empire, at least in lands surrounding the Aegean Sea. Perhaps after that he even fulfilled his long-cherished desire to visit Spain (Rom. 15:23-24; cf. 1 Clement 5). Since 2 Tim. 4:6-18 speaks of an approaching second trial, we may conclude that Paul was rearrested ca. 67 and, according to tradition, beheaded at Rome by order of the Emperor Nero.

For Further Reading

Brown, Raymond E. *An Introduction to the New Testament.* New York: Doubleday, 1997, 428-37.

Gorman, Michael J. *Apostle of the Crucified Lord.* Grand Rapids: Eerdmans, 2004.

Longenecker, Richard N. "Acts." *The Expositor's Bible Commentary,* ed. Frank E. Gaebelein. Grand Rapids: Zondervan, 1981, 9:205-573.

——, ed. *The Road from Damascus: The Impact of Paul's Conversion on His Life, Thought, and Ministry.* McMaster New Testament Studies. Grand Rapids: Eerdmans, 1997.

Puskas, Charles B., Jr. *The Letters of Paul: An Introduction.* Good News Studies 25. Collegeville: Liturgical, 1993, 20-34.

Ramsay, William M. *St. Paul the Traveller and the Roman Citizen.* Rev. ed. Grand Rapids: Kregel, 2001.

RICHARD N. LONGENECKER

In Philippi, Paul exorcises a spirit from a female fortune-teller, whose masters resent their lost means of income and falsely charge Paul and Silas with public disturbance and infringement on the rights of Roman citizens. Ironically, the local authorities strip, beat, jail, and shackle Paul and Silas in violation of their right as Roman citizens to a proper trial! The evangelists witness to their fellow prisoners till a midnight earthquake shakes them free. Presuming that all the inmates have escaped, the distraught jailer attempts suicide to avoid execution for failure at his post, but Paul intervenes. In response, the jailer begs to know how to become saved and then takes Paul and Silas to his own home for first aid and food. When on the next morning the local authorities order the evangelists released, Paul and Silas reveal their Roman citizenship and refuse to go without an apology for their illegal treatment.

17:1-15 Paul at Thessalonica When the missionaries depart Philippi for Thessalonica, Luke no longer refers to the group as "we." The "we"-narrative resumes when Paul returns to Philippi, thus indicating that Luke stayed there, perhaps to pastor the fledgling Philippian church (20:6).

In the seaport city of Thessalonica, capital of Macedonia, the familiar pattern resumes: Paul's success with the Gentiles, then antagonism from the Jews, and finally flight from persecution. That "God-fearing Greeks" and "leading women" embrace the gospel casts Christianity in a good light, but jealous Jews' rousing of "wicked men" to plague Paul with mob violence makes disbelieving both irrational and unrespectable. In nearby Beroea, that "noble-minded" Jews prove to themselves the truth of the gospel by examining the Hebrew Scriptures, and that "prominent" Greeks also accept the faith, makes converting to Christianity the right and reasonable thing to do. When Thessalonian troublemakers hound Paul, their persecution ironically helps spread the word by propelling Paul to Athens, with Silas and Timothy soon to follow.

17:16-34 Proclaiming the Unknown at Athens By the time Paul visits Athens, the thousand year-old city exhibits a high degree of intellectual,

cultural, and religious pluralism. There the disturbing abundance of idols provokes Paul to proclaim publicly "Jesus" and the "resurrection," which Epicurean and Stoic philosophers understand as heretofore unheard-of deities. The materialistic Epicureans held the pursuit of pleasure as the highest ideal, while the rationalistic Stoics prized steadfastness in the face of adversity. The curiosity of these high-minded philosophers gets the better of them, and they seek further interpretation of Paul's teaching. Given a platform at the "Areopagus" — either Mars Hill or the council that met there — Paul draws on the diverse richness of Athenian culture to fill the gaps in its religious poverty. He reveals to them the "unknown god" to whom they have dedicated an altar and quotes from the Greek poets Epimenides and Aratus in focusing his attack on idolatry (v. 28). Having made the case for the Creator-Sustainer God for whom all humanity "gropes," Paul foretells the final judgment by the resurrected Christ.

Some Greek philosophical schools tentatively taught the immortality of the soul, but the idea of bodily resurrection repelled the population as a whole, for the Greeks believed that the body only encumbered the superior soul. But Paul's knowledge that God created humans as a union of a tangible body and an intangible soul makes the bodiless existence of the soul an incomplete and imperfect notion, and he remains firm on Jesus' bodily resurrection. Unconvinced skeptics write him off, and others reserve judgment till they hear more. But a few believe, including the council member Dionysius and a woman named Damaris. Their high social standing bolsters the good image of Christianity repeatedly emphasized by Luke, especially in the record of this second journey.

18:1-17 Tentmaking in Corinth The association of Paul with fellow Jewish tentmakers Aquila and Priscilla starts in Corinth, some 50 miles west of Athens. The former residents of Italy had fallen victim to the A.D. 49/50 ousting of Jews from Rome by Emperor Claudius for rioting over the preaching of "Chrestus" (probably a form of Latin *Christus,* "Christ"). Paul's supporting himself economically while carrying on his evangelistic activities has spawned the modern designation of self-supporting missionaries as "tentmakers."

In Corinth, Luke emphasizes the rejection of the gospel by Jews, Greek God-fearers, and proselytes to Judaism. Their vehement resistance steels Paul's resolve to abandon their evangelization and take the gospel to the area's as yet unbelieving Gentiles. When the synagogue leader Crispus converts, however, others follow suit, and Paul settles in for an 18-month mission among the Corinthians.

When the Jewish opposition complains before the Roman proconsul Gallio that Paul's preaching violates Jewish law, Gallio dismisses the charge as insignificant and irrelevant to his judicial purview. The frustrated prosecution pounces on the new synagogue leader, Sosthenes, perhaps because they blame him for losing their case. Gallio's disinterest in the religious dispute allows the spread of the gospel throughout Achaia (= Greece). 1 Corinthians 1:1 reveals that the pummeled Sosthenes followed his predecessor, Crispus, by becoming a Christian.

18:18-23 Back to Antioch The vow Paul takes in Cenchreae, port for points east of Corinth, may express his thankfulness for past blessings, petition protection for his return voyage, or express a specific religious commitment. Aquila and Priscilla accompany Paul as far as Ephesus, provincial capital of Asia to which he pledges to return. Paul's homeward sail ends at the Palestinian port of Caesarea, from where he goes "up" to greet the church in Jerusalem and then "down" from the Judean hill country, northbound to Antioch, where the journey originated.

18:24–21:16 Paul's Third Missionary Journey

18:24–19:41 Upheaval in Ephesus Paul now retraces his route through the regions of southern Asia Minor called Galatia and Phrygia, in which lay the previously evangelized cities of Derbe, Lystra, and Iconium, with Pisidian Antioch not far north (chs. 14, 16). While Paul makes his way eastward toward the coastal capital, Ephesus, an eloquent orator from Alexandria, Egypt, arrives in the coastal capital. Well educated in

The Areopagus (Mars Hill), the rocky outcrop overlooking Athens, where Paul revealed the "unknown god" and called the Athenians to repent (Acts 17). (www.HolyLandPhotos.org)

the Hebrew Scriptures and a believer in Jesus, Apollos no doubt honed his rhetorical skills in his hometown, renowned in the ancient world as a bastion of learning. But Priscilla and Aquila must inform the well-meaning Apollos concerning the baptism of Jesus, which supersedes that of John.

After Apollos leaves for Corinth, Paul becomes the main teacher in Ephesus. First he rebaptizes those whom Apollos had baptized with John's baptism of repentance, and their speaking in tongues and prophesying confirm their reception of the Holy Spirit.

Paul's two-year, self-appointed tenure at a local lecture hall (during siesta time at the "school of Tyrannus") enables Ephesian converts and visitors traveling to the provincial capital to spread the gospel throughout Asia Minor. The apostle's healings and exorcisms underscore his teachings about Jesus. Paul's abilities outshine those of the seven Sceva brothers, sons of a self-styled high priest (perhaps not even Jewish), who attempt to perform their own exorcisms by using the name "Jesus." When a demoniac attacks two of these magicians, many Ephesians come to believe in Jesus. They make public the supposedly secret rituals and incantations and burn textbooks containing magical formulas.

When a local idol-maker, Demetrius, recognizes the economic implications of

Daily Life in New Testament Times

Daily life was hardly uniform among the various residents of the early Roman Empire. An urban craftsman in Ephesus experienced life much differently from a tenant farmer in rural Galilee or a Roman magistrate in Philippi. Men and women also generally undertook distinct roles and responsibilities. The most profound differences in quality of life, however, existed between elites and nonelites.

Occupations

The Roman Empire was a preindustrial, agrarian society with an underdeveloped economy. Elites controlled much of the landed wealth, and they typically viewed manual labor of any kind as incompatible with their social status, instead exalting leisure as the goal of the good life. The labor force consisted of nonelites (slave and free), the majority of whom worked in agriculture (grain, olives, and grapes) and lived at a subsistence level. Although we have evidence for the continued existence of small landholders during the imperial era, nonelites more often worked as tenants on large landed estates owned by the urban-dwelling aristocracy. The pastoral images of the Gospels (esp. the parables portraying agricultural day-laborers and tenant farmers; Matt. 13:24-30; 20:1-16; Mark 12:1-8) reflect these realities.

Other occupations included fishing, leather-working, pottery-making, and various crafts. Jesus is identified as a *tekton,* a term used to refer to craftspersons who do hand fabrication, usually of some complete product such as a plow or a table. In no case should these artisan occupations be viewed in terms of the modern "free enterprise" system. The fishing industry around the Sea of Galilee, for example, was controlled by local ruling elites who sold fishing rights to brokers ("tax collectors"), who in turn contracted with local families who fished the lake. Given the location of his toll office in Capernaum, Matthew may have served as just such a broker of Galilean fishing rights on behalf of the ruling tetrarch Antipas (Matt. 9:9).

Education

Education in ancient Mediterranean society finds its origins in classical Greece and, except for the addition of Latin to the general curriculum during the Roman era, schooling remained remarkably uniform throughout the Hellenistic world. The threefold division of primary, secondary, and higher education will be familiar to modern readers. Less familiar will be the centrality of physical training and the general restriction of higher education to elite males.

Primary schooling was widespread and included children of both genders and nearly every social class. Beginning at age seven, children attended the reading school and the *palaestra,* which focused, respectively, on elementary reading/writing skills and physical training. Memories of primary education preserved in ancient literature paint a rather dark picture of brutality at the hands of underpaid and socially despised instructors. Elites generally trained their children at home under the care of slave tutors.

Secondary education led students on to grammar school, where they studied the classics and, to a lesser extent, mathematics, music, and astronomy. Homer, Euripides, Menander, and Demosthenes were favored Greek authors; Virgil, Terence, and Cicero represented the Latins. Studies ranged from the careful copying of texts to discussions of a work's contribution to the moral life. The culmination of secondary education found students producing an original composition, typically in Attic Greek, on an assigned theme.

Higher education was the province of elites, who typically attended the *ephebeia,* an exclusive male institution associated with the municipal *gymnasium,* where future aristocrats spent a year or two in a program that was primarily physical and only secondarily academic in nature. The gymnasium contained a stadium and sand-covered courtyard for physical exercises, along with baths and a lecture hall. Activities included wrestling and related contact sports, as well as running, long-jumping, and discus throwing. Completion of the course of study at the *ephebeia* qualified young males for full social and political acceptance into the small circle of powerful elites found in each of the cities of the Greco-Roman world. More serious academic pursuits at the third and final level of training included the study of rhetoric or, for a smaller percentage of the population, philosophy.

Many Jews also received a standard Hellenistic education, as surviving evidence from the Jewish community at Alexandria clearly indicates. Other Jews attempted to insulate their children from pagan influence by focusing on Scripture and Jewish tradition rather than the Greek classics. Formal Hebrew schools, patterned after the three-stage model, appear well after the establishment of the Hellenistic schools. Late evidence for Jewish primary schools (early 2nd century A.D.) suggests that much early training was done, according to the biblical mandate, in the home (Deut. 4:9; 6:7). Jewish boys clearly learned to read well enough to participate in synagogue readings and exposition (Luke 4:16-20). Debate in later rabbinical works suggests that at least some girls also studied Torah.

Housing and Life in the Ancient City

Ancient cities were smaller than the large urban centers familiar today. Rome, with ca. one million residents, was by far the largest, and most municipalities were probably less than a tenth this size. Population density, however, guaranteed that urban dwellers in the cities in which early Christianity took root endured uncomfortable crowding at home (200 persons per acre).

Extensive open space and attractive public facilities offered some consolation for crowded living conditions, and life was lived mostly in public — on the streets and sidewalks, in the market-places, and in public squares.

One of several pools at the gymnasium in Sardis *(www.HolyLandPhotos.org)*

Privacy was rare, and few events in the neighborhood would escape the attention of local residents. Persons of common ethnic origin (a number of ancient cities had a Jewish quarter), or families who shared the same trade (e.g., the "Portico of the Perfumers" in Rome), would live and work in close proximity. While Paul was in Corinth he had no difficulty locating a couple who shared both his Jewish ethnicity and his craft (Acts 18:1-3).

Urban housing always presented a challenge, and nonelites generally occupied small rented apartments carved out of poorly designed buildings. These dwellings were typically cramped, cold, and dark.

The elites who owned these apartment buildings generally lived elsewhere. Large Roman villas, familiar from excavations at Pompeii, housed a number of the empire's wealthier persons. These larger homes, along with their extended households, became an important component in the social life of the early Christians. The few elites who joined the Christian movement ("not many," writes Paul, but some; 1 Cor. 1:26) served as patrons of their local communities. The whole church in Corinth, for example, enjoyed the hospitality of a certain Gaius (Rom. 16:23), a gathering that could hardly occur in a cramped urban apartment. Phoebe apparently played a similar role in the Greek city of Cenchreae (Rom. 16:1-2).

Joseph H. Hellerman

Harbor Street leading to the theater at Ephesus.
(www.HolyLandPhotos.org)

Christianity's growing popularity at the expense of paganism, he stirs up trouble. Many Ephesian merchants sold goods relating to the Greek goddess of the hunt, Artemis (Roman Diana), whose "image" (evidently a meteorite thought to represent her) stood in the city's temple — one of the seven wonders of the ancient world. Demetrius weds business concerns with religious fervor for the local goddess in stirring up antagonism against the "Way." The Ephesians drag Paul's Macedonian companions to the theater, which accommodated 25 thousand people, but most in the raucous crowd are unaware of what the fuss is about. Jews in the audience, fearing they would be identified with the Christians, thrust a certain Alexander to the fore to offer their defense. But only the town clerk can quiet the crowd, persuade them to see reason, and break up the disorderly assembly, which risks reprisal by the Roman authorities.

20:1–21:16 Farewell to Ephesus The near riot in Ephesus marks the end of Paul's 27-month sojourn in that city. With representatives from several Gentile churches in Asia, Paul moves on to Macedonia and Greece (Achaia). There, according to Paul's letters, the Christian congregations entrust to the apostle relief aid for the church in Jerusalem, where he determines to

arrive in time for Passover (24:17; Rom. 15:25-27; 1 Cor. 16:1-5; 2 Cor. 8–9). That Paul is forced to take the land route back through Macedonia allows Luke to rejoin him at Philippi ("we"-section beginning in v. 6). Returning to Asia Minor, Paul fellowships with Christians in the port of Troas, where his long, late-night Sunday sermon lulls young Eutychus to sleep. Paul either revives or resurrects Eutychus from his seemingly fatal fall from a third-floor window. Meeting up again at Assos, Paul and his companions island-hop their way south to Miletus, for bypassing congregations on the western coast of Asia Minor allows them to make speedier progress toward Jerusalem (20:16).

Paul's long stay in Ephesus led to particularly close relationships with fellow believers, and his knowledge that he will never again see his Ephesian friends prompts him to summon the city's church elders to meet him in Miletus for a final farewell. Paul emphasizes to them the boldness of his preaching in the face of persecution, the uncertainty of the fate that awaits him in Jerusalem, and his determination to complete his missionary task. After warning the elders to guard against influences that would weaken belief, the apostle assures them of the sufficiency of God's gracious word to give them the promised "inheritance" (i.e., eternal life). Paul's closing admonition that they follow his example of working hard and helping the weak precedes his final, impassioned parting from them.

More island-hopping finally lands Paul and company back in Palestine. At the Syrian port of Tyre, Christians warn the apostle against

Remnant of the Roman road north of Tarsus.
(www.HolyLandPhotos.org)

Travel in the Roman Empire

The New Testament relates how a singular message of good news to humanity was carried across the vast expanse of the Roman Empire. Part of the preparation for the spread of that message can be credited to Caesar Augustus, who had earlier undertaken for the empire's strength and stability certain measures to ensure an unhindered peace, good communication, and a reliable coinage. These measures began a two-centuries-long period of peace that ancient writers such as Philo and Plutarch came to call the "peace of Rome" (pax Romana). Cleared of pirates, the growing network of Roman roads and seaways thronged with merchants, government officials, those seeking medical treatment, pilgrims to sanctuaries and holy festivals, holiday-makers, sightseers, teachers of various kinds, and students seeking an education. Conditions could not have been more favorable for spreading the gospel "to the ends of the earth" (Acts 1:8; Matt. 28:19-20) by missionaries and their converts who were a part of that increased traffic.

Overland Travel

Travel in antiquity was a much slower affair than today. The most speedy but least common form of land transport was by horseback. The only explicit New Testament reference to travel by horseback is Paul's hurried night trip under military escort to Caesarea (Acts 23:23-24). His earlier persecuting mission to Damascus was probably on foot — unable to see, the persecutor had to be led "by the hand" (Acts 9:8). Ancient sources report that, in very exceptional circumstances, a courier or dispatch rider on urgent official business might cover between 100 and 150 miles in a day. This amounts to ca. 10 to 12 miles an hour. Distances of ca. 50 miles per day were much more the norm.

Donkey and mule transport were the more widespread forms of animal transport. A laden animal might make no better time than a walking man (Mark 11:1-11; Luke 13:15); an animal-drawn cart was only slightly faster (Acts 8:27-29, 38). But the modest gain in speed was more than offset in carrying power. A pack mule could carry a 250-lb. load, and an animal-drawn cart between two and four times that. These options in transport were quite costly.

The most common and slowest traffic on Rome's highways and byways was pedestrian, and this would have included most Christian travelers. A normal day's journey by foot was ca. 20 miles (Acts 10:23-24, 30), though crises might call for covering much longer distances (23:23, 31-32).

Travel over land was also subject to the seasons. Many would avoid the dangers of travel during the winter months (early November to early March) and the discomforts and risks of the fall wet season and the spring runoff. There were, however, professional travelers who were prepared to undertake the risks of travel in the "off seasons" for profit, as well as government and military travelers on urgent official business. Paul and other missionaries were probably among these more intrepid professionals (Acts; 2 Cor. 11:26-27).

Except where one was entitled to requisition transport and hospitality (Matt. 5:40-41; Mark 11:3-6; Acts 27-28) or could count on the help of family or friends (27:3; 28:14), the average traveler had to fend for him- or herself by sleeping rough or by putting up in a boarding house or inn. Wayside facilities were of generally poor quality and often rather nightmarish.

The genius of the call to Christian hospitality was that not only did it ensure close-knit local communities, it was also the means to a more vigorous Christian mission. Jesus instructed his disciples that they were to receive the hospitality of those who accepted their message on the way (Luke 9:3-4; 10:1-7). Hospitality to travelling missionaries (Acts 16:11-15; 1 Cor. 9:4-6; 3 John 5-8) and their letter-carrying associates (Rom. 16:1-2; 1 Cor. 16:10-11; Col. 4:7-9) reflected well on the Christian community because it was an expression of love and helped spread the good news about Jesus throughout the empire. Where hospitality was denied (Luke 9:5; 10:10; 3 John 9-10), the progress of the gospel might be hindered.

**Prominent Roads and Ship Routes
of the Eastern Roman Empire**

Trapezus

Euphrates R.

Sinope

SYRIA

Damascus

Antioch

Orontes R.

Jerusalem

Hebro R.

CAPPADOCIA

Parnassus

Archelais

Tarsus

Sidon

JUDEA

GALATIA

Ancyra (Ankara)

Caesarea
Maritima

Heracleia

Antioch
in Pisidia

Sebaste

Black
Sea

Byzantium

Egnatian Way

ASIA

Pergamum

Colossae

Myra

Cyprus

EGYPT

Memphis

Troas

Ephesus

Alexandria

THRACE

Nile R.

MACEDONIA

Aegean
Sea

Athens

Crete

Philippi

Thessalonica

Corinth

Sparta

Delphi

ACHAIA

Mediterranean
Sea

Egnatian Way

Dyrrachium

Brundisium

Cyrene

CYRENAICA

Adriatic
Sea

Appian Way

Tarentum

Rhegium

Syracuse

ITALIA

Messana

Malta

Rome

Tiber R.

Tyrrhenian Sea

Sicily

N

200 Miles

100

100

200 Kilometers

100

100

0

0

——— Prominent Roads

- - - Ship Routes

Travel by Sea

In the century before Christ, the Romans had vigorously engaged in clearing the Mediterranean of pirates. This ensured a more regular and safer flow of maritime traffic and trade in foodstuffs, building products, metals, and a wide variety of exotic goods. Grain, however, was arguably the most critical transport commodity on the Mediterranean. Failure in its sufficient production and regular supply raised the double threats of inflation and hunger. The emperors were keenly aware that discontent among the Roman population was a risk to political stability. Among other strategies, they offered significant inducements to shipbuilders and merchants to transport a significant volume of grain — even during the risky season.

Paul and his associates book passage on trading vessels to and from the island of Cyprus and to and from various points along the northern and western coastlines of the Mediterranean on their missionary labors (Acts 13:4, 13; 16:11; 18:18, 21-22; 20:6, 13-16; 21:1-3, 6). Later, Paul and the rest of the prisoner detail are transported to Rome aboard a coastal trader (27:1-5) and two Alexandrian grain carriers (vv. 6-44; 28:11-13). The first such carrier mentioned in Acts, bearing cargo and 276 passengers and crew, was certainly not the largest of its kind plying the open waters of the Mediterranean. Paul and the other passengers would have stayed on deck, bringing their own food and shelter (27:3). The description of the ship, the conditions it met, and the manner of its sailing at Acts 27 match well what we know from both ancient maritime sources and archaeological artifacts.

Ancient writers such as Vegetius Renatus, Pliny the Elder, and Tacitus indicate that from the end of May to mid-September conditions generally favored maritime travel; from early November to early March seaboard travel was extremely dangerous. The rest of the year was risky. The temptation of riches and the risk of a sudden change in weather could be a lethal mix for merchants and traders. First-century authorities and modern maritime archaeology indicate that shipwreck on the Mediterranean was far from uncommon. In fact, the remains of ships and their cargoes at some wreck sites lie pancaked one atop the other.

That Paul was also a seasoned maritime traveler seems to be the case from his knowledgeable advice at Acts 27:9-10 and the fact that three times previously he had experienced shipwrecks and on one of those occasions had spent a night and a day clinging to wreckage out in the open sea (2 Cor. 11:25). The first Alexandrian grain carrier on which the prisoner Paul traveled was making a "dangerous season" run (Acts 27:9). It was also carrying a dangerous cargo. If not sacked or binned, grain can "flow" in rough seas, threatening breach or capsize. If it gets wet, it will expand and can split a ship's hull. The nautically responsible efforts to undergird the hull of the ship (Acts 27:17), to lighten it by dumping cargo and tackle (vv. 18-19), and to drop four anchors to control its shoreward progress (vv. 29, 40) all failed. Driving shoreward, the ship became stuck on a sandbar just off the coastline of the island of Malta *(Melite Africana)* and was broken up by the surf.

One might wonder why Luke would include such an extended description of Paul's shipwreck. Luke's object, from the divine assurance given to Paul at Acts 27:23-24, is to demonstrate that the Lord Jesus provides for his prisoner witness so that his mission will succeed. Nothing — not storm, shipwreck, or snakebite — can stand in the way of the progress of the gospel to the capital of the empire and its sovereign (cf. Acts 19:21; 23:11).

For Further Reading

Casson, Lionel. *Ships and Seamanship in the Ancient World.* 1971; repr. Baltimore: Johns Hopkins University Press, 1995.

———. *Travel in the Ancient World.* 1974; repr. Baltimore: Johns Hopkins University Press, 1994.

Rapske, Brian M. "Acts, Travel and Shipwreck." In *The Book of Acts in Its Greco-Roman Setting,* ed. David W. J. Gill and Conrad Gempf. The Book of Acts in Its First Century Setting 2. Grand Rapids: Eerdmans, 1994, 1-47.

Throckmorton, Peter, ed. *History from the Sea: Shipwrecks and Archaeology.* London: Mitchell Beazley, 1987.

BRIAN M. RAPSKE

going to Jerusalem, and further south in Caesarea Agabus predicts Paul's arrest in the Judean capital (21:11).

21:17–23:11 Paul Imprisoned

The Christians in Jerusalem, including Jesus' brother James, give Paul a warm welcome. But a rumor is circulating that Paul instructs Jewish Christians outside Palestine not to observe the Mosaic law — a teaching utterly intolerable to legal loyalists in the religious capital. To discredit the rumor, Paul shows his respect for Jewish law by voluntarily undergoing prescribed purification rites along with four other Jewish Christians. Their ritual defilement while fulfilling a Nazirite vow necessitates a week of "cleansing" before resuming the obligations of the vow, which ends in shaving the head and presenting offerings at the temple. But Paul's well-intentioned demonstration backfires when Jews from western Asia Minor spy Paul in the inner court of the temple and assume that he has brought to this sacred place of sacrifice his Gentile companion Trophimus, from Ephesus. Jewish law allowed Gentiles to enter the outer court, but their entry into its inner court warranted the death penalty.

The mob drag Paul to the outer court, where Roman troops intervene to prevent his being beaten to death, but the unruliness of the crowd necessitates removing Paul to the adjoining Fortress of Antonia. The din prevents the soldiers from determining why their prisoner has caused such uproar. Evidently the commanding officer (Claudius Lysias) wonders whether Paul might be the Egyptian Jew who three years earlier convinced revolutionaries to join him in standing watch on the Mount of Olives (opposite the Temple Mount to the east) till the walls of Jerusalem collapsed at his command, and then help him liberate the city from the Romans. Have the Jews recognized Paul as that escaped leader of the Sicarii ("Assassins"), on whom they now seek revenge for fostering false hopes? But when Paul identifies himself as a Cilician Jew, Lysias grants the chained apostle permission to address his antagonists from a perch on the staircase.

When Paul speaks in Aramaic ("the Hebrew dialect"), a hush comes over the crowd. He identifies himself as one of them: a fellow Jew reared in Jerusalem, a disciple of the respected Pharisee, Gamaliel (the Sanhedrin's voice of restraint in 5:34-40), and a strict adherent of the Law. In fact, his Judaistic zeal drove him to persecute the followers of Christ ("this Way") after approvingly witnessing the stoning of Stephen, the first Christian martyr. Thus the drama and surprise of Paul's unlikely conversion to Christianity, which he publicly recounts, appear all the more intense. In describing the restoration of his sight by Ananias, Paul shows his conversion was sanctioned by a Jewish Christian who measures up to Mosaic standards and enjoys a good reputation among the Jews of Damascus.

When the apostle mentions his commission to the Gentiles, however, the Jews of Jerusalem resume their uproar, and the Roman military whisk Paul to the barracks for a torturous interrogation. Victims of a Roman scourging often died from their wounds, made worse by the bits of metal and bone embedded in the leather thongs of the wooden-handled whip. Just in time, Paul identifies himself as a Roman citizen — as such he would avoid a scourging even if tried and found guilty. The revelation strikes fear into Lysias — who bought his Roman citizenship (perhaps with a bribe) in contrast to Paul's superior citizenship-by-birth — for he himself could be severely punished just for chaining the uncondemned Roman without a fair trial, much more for scourging him.

Paul spends the night in protective custody, but in the morning, with Lysias still wondering why the Jews harbor such intense antagonism toward the prisoner, the Roman commander summons the 71-member Jewish Council (Sanhedrin) for a hearing. The high priest Ananias takes as blasphemous Paul's claim to have a "perfectly good conscience before God" (with regard to keeping the Law), so he orders the apostle slapped on the mouth. Ignorant of Ananias's identity, Paul reprimands him for breaking the Mosaic requirements of justice in judgment and restraint in punishment, but Paul immediately apologizes on becoming aware of Ananias's status as a religious "ruler," even though the high priest made the first wrong move. Then thinking on his feet, Paul takes control. He tells the Sanhedrin (and the listening Lysias) what the complaint against him is: his belief in the resurrection of the dead. Paul believes that the resurrection of Jesus makes possible this "hope" (not a wish but a certain expectation), but he refers to resurrection only in general terms so as to pit against each other the Sanhedrin's Sadducees, who deny the bodily resurrection and the spiritual world, and his fellow Pharisees, who believe in both, though not in the resurrection of Jesus. Thus the apostle garners partisan support, the infighting ends the hearing, and Paul retains protection by the Romans. That night God informs him of his upcoming mission in Rome — a destination already on Paul's mind (cf. 19:21).

23:12-35 Paul Sent to Caesarea

When Paul's nephew overhears his uncle's enemies hatching a plot to murder him, the young man relays the news first to Paul and then to Claudius Lysias. The Roman commander, no doubt glad for an excuse to dissociate himself from the situation and the personal risk involved, assembles a 270-strong military escort to usher Paul out of Jerusalem in the middle of the night. Regional unrest may have necessitated the large contingent, though its size might reflect overcompensation for the previous day's mistakes, strategically glossed over in Lysias's explanatory letter to his superior — the Judean governor Felix, to whom Paul is now passed. By bringing to the fore his discovery of Paul's Roman citizenship, Lysias presents himself as Paul's protector from start to finish (contrast v. 27 with 22:27-29). When Paul and his military escort reach the coastal plain at Antipatris (ancient Aphek, rebuilt and renamed by Herod the Great), the flat terrain enables a swift, 30-mile horseback ride northwest to Caesarea, accompanied only by the 70 cavalrymen. Felix houses Paul in the official governor's residence — the palatial Praetorium, built by Herod the Great — while awaiting the arrival of Paul's accusers.

24 Paul's Case Unresolved

Though Paul retracted his reprimand of the high priest (23:1-5), the mistake makes leveling charges against Paul a matter of honor for Ananias, and the foiling of the plot to murder the apostle further injures the high priest's pride. Instead of sending to Caesarea the Asian Jews who stirred up trouble for Paul in the temple (21:27-29), Ananias himself takes to the governor a contingent of Jewish elders and a skilled orator-attorney (Tertullus) to act as prosecutor. Tertullus starts with the standard compliments to Felix and then states the charges against Paul: he is an agitator who tried to desecrate the temple. Roman tyrants used the first, catchall charge as a political weapon of terror. With no eyewitnesses present, the prosecution's second, false accusation amounts to hearsay, as Paul points out (vv. 18-20). The Jewish leaders' claim to have arrested Paul certainly stretches the truth, for the crowd's near lynching of him necessitated involvement by the Romans.

Paul denies the charges against him and points out the lack of supporting evidence. He admits as a member of the Way (a Christian) to serving the same God as his Jewish accusers, believing their Scriptures, expecting the resurrection of the dead (as does the Pharisaic component of the Jewish leadership), and striving to live a religiously and civilly righteous life. To that end, he ritually purified himself before peacefully bringing alms and sacrifices to the temple. But Felix delays deciding the case — supposedly till Lysias can come and clarify the facts. In the meantime, he treats his teenaged, Jewish wife, Drusilla, to an audience with Paul. But the fact that Felix had coaxed this third wife away from her Syrian husband makes Paul's talk of righteousness, self-control, and future divine judgment too close for comfort, and the governor cuts the encounter short.

Lysias never makes it to Caesarea to follow up on Paul's case. Interest in Paul's preaching and persistent hope for a bribe (v. 26) lead Felix to keep Paul in custody indefinitely, though his granting to Paul limited freedoms belies any suspicion of his guilt. When after two years a new administration in Rome relieves the ineffective Felix of his duties, the outgoing governor knows that his political career hangs in the balance. Leaving Paul in prison means leaving on a good note with the Jews, who might otherwise complain to the new administration about

Felix's multiple former offenses against them — offenses that go unmentioned in Luke.

25:1-12 Paul Forced to Appeal

Festus, the new governor of Judea, wants to start off right with the Jews, so three days after his arrival in Caesarea he heads for the region's religious capital, Jerusalem, to meet with the Jewish rulers. Two years have not tempered the Sanhedrin's grudge against Paul, and in Festus's play for their favor they see a chance to revive their conspiracy to murder his inherited prisoner. They request that Festus send for Paul, whom they plan to ambush en route. Festus refuses on account of the brevity of his visit to Jerusalem, but he invites Paul's accusers to Caesarea for a hearing. Though they cannot prove their allegations, Festus wants to please the Sanhedrin, so he proposes returning to Jerusalem to try the case.

But Paul senses trouble and knows his rights. Since the charges concern Jewish law, he may fear that Festus will relinquish the case to the Sanhedrin, whose opposition to him precludes the possibility of a fair trial. He evades the clutches of the Jewish Council by exercising his right as a Roman citizen to appeal his case to the emperor — by now Nero, who only later initiated his intense persecution of Christians (ca. 64).

25:13–26:32 Paul's Defense before Agrippa

Festus receives an official welcome from a regional ruler more experienced in matters of Jewish law and religion — Herod Agrippa II, brother of the ex-governor's Jewish wife Drusilla and great-grandson of Herod the Great, an Idumean (Edomite) descendant of Esau. Agrippa's younger sister Bernice accompanies him from Caesarea Philippi, his capital 30 miles north of the Sea of Galilee. Festus seizes the opportunity to get Agrippa's expert advice about Paul's case, for Festus knows that the Jews' theological opposition to Paul does not by Roman law warrant execution.

In defending himself before Agrippa, Paul emphasizes his upbringing as a strict Pharisee and details his intense persecution of Jesus'

followers under the authority of the Jewish chief priests. He credits the irresistible intervention of God that brought about his belief in the resurrected Christ as fulfillment of Jewish prophecy and as an event that required his obedient preaching of the gospel to Jews and Gentiles alike. Other than the Sadducees, Paul's fellow Jews believe in the resurrection of the dead, so his belief in the bodily resurrection of Jesus should not call for his execution. Nor should his belief that through Christ their own Scriptures find fulfillment. For the Gentile Festus, however, the idea of physical resurrection seems preposterous, so he accuses Paul of insanity. Paul appeals to Agrippa for backing. Agreeing with Paul means contradicting in public the politician to whom he is paying official respects; but disagreeing with Paul offends the listening Jews by belittling the Hebrew Scriptures. So Agrippa evades the question with a quip about Paul's attempt to convert him and quickly signals the Roman adjudicators to adjourn for consultation. Agrippa's verdict accords with the assessment of Felix and Festus: Paul has committed no crime, religious or civil. He does not even deserve imprisonment, much less execution. But Paul cannot take back his appeal to the emperor, so off to Rome he must go.

27–28 Paul's Passage to Rome

That Luke accompanied Paul to Rome shows in the detailed report of the 2000-mile voyage, which takes several stages and three seafaring vessels to complete. Harsh weather in the Mediterranean region required suspending the sailing season during the winter months, beginning in mid-November. When Paul and company reach Crete — not quite halfway to Rome — it is time to drop anchor, for it is already past "the fast" (the Day of Atonement), which comes in October. Paul prophesies disaster if they put out to sea, and when the crew tries skirting the coast to find safe harbor for the winter a northeaster sweeps in. The crew can only hope to hold the vessel together till the storm lets up. They load the lifeboat out of the water, encircle the ship's hull with supporting cables, drop a drift anchor (or take down the top sails) to avoid entrapment in the whirlpools and sandbars off the North African coast, and toss overboard the tackle and cargo. Lacking compasses, 1st-century sailors steered their course by the sun and the stars, which the crew of Paul's ship cannot see for the storm, and after 11 days of cloud cover, the seasick sailors have no idea where they are. When their hope hits bottom, however, Paul encourages them with a reassuring vision from God that promises the survival of all on board. The two-week ordeal ends with the sighting of an unfamiliar island (Malta). The ship breaks apart after getting stuck in a reef off the bay, and all 276 voyagers swim and paddle ashore.

The warm hospitality of the Maltese people turns to reverence for Paul when he survives unharmed a deadly snakebite. During the next three months, Paul heals the father of the island chieftain and the area's other ill. The people show their gratitude by donating supplies for the last leg of the sail to Italy, taken on an Egyptian ship bearing figureheads of the "Twin Brothers" — the Roman deities Castor and Pollux, protectors of sailors. The refreshingly uneventful cruise to Sicily and on to the Italian mainland ends at Puteoli, some 120 miles south of Rome. The welcome of fellow Christians along the land route from there to Rome bolsters Paul's courage. Once in the capital, it takes the apostle just three days to summon the city's Jewish leaders to his quarters, which he shares with a single Roman guard. Paul wants the opportunity to tell his story face-to-face

and to show that his Christianity does not make him anti-Jewish. Although they claim ignorance about his case and feign only cursory knowledge of Christianity, several factors cast doubt on such claims: by this time, a Christian community already existed in Rome, as evidenced by Paul's writing Romans before he journeyed there as a prisoner, and Paul's reputation precedes him among believers stationed close to the city (cf. 28:15). Nevertheless, in a subsequent forum with "large numbers" of local Jews, Paul explains to them the gospel. After quoting Isaiah's prophecy that foretells their disbelief, Paul announces God's extension of salvation to the Gentiles.

Acts closes by noting the evangelistic freedom enjoyed by Paul during two years under house arrest in Rome. The long delay in his appearance before Emperor Nero may have resulted from the loss at sea of the list of charges against him plus the necessity of waiting for prosecutors to arrive from Palestine. Luke probably does not relate the occurrence or outcome of Paul's trial because it had not yet taken place when he wrote Acts. By starting with the birth of the Christian church in Jerusalem and ending with Paul's ongoing evangelism in Rome, center of the entire inhabited world in the 1st century, Luke portrays the early Christians' obedience to Christ's commission that his followers globalize the gospel — a task that requires fulfilling by subsequent generations of believers to the present day and beyond (Luke 24:47; cf. Matt. 28:19-20).

Christianity in the Eyes of Non-Christians

Since information about the earliest stages of Christianity comes mostly from the New Testament itself, determining how outsiders viewed the fledgling movement proves difficult. The earliest New Testament writings, the letters of Paul, which were written to Christians as they struggled with doctrinal and behavioral issues within the church, only occasionally grant a glimpse of how outsiders viewed the church. Likewise, the Gospels and other writings that were written in the decades after Paul reveal more about how the early Christians saw themselves than about how non-Christians viewed them. When the New Testament does speak to the matter of outsiders' perceptions of the church, it speaks with an insider's voice; the voices of the outsiders themselves remain silent or muted.

The Gospels all depict Jesus and his followers operating within the context of 1st-century Palestinian Judaism. Jesus preached in towns and villages that were characteristically Jewish rather than in the larger cities of Galilee with significant Gentile populations. His movement would most likely have been seen as an attempt to reform Judaism from within, and his questioning of traditional beliefs and practices aroused the concern and opposition of some Jewish leaders. Indeed, Jesus' interruption of proceedings in the Jerusalem temple seems to have solidified the opposition of the Jewish establishment. His execution by the Romans, however, seems to have resulted from their perception that he represented a threat to security and stability.

According to the book of Acts, Jesus' followers continued to participate in regular Jewish activities, visiting the temple and attending synagogue meetings, much as a local synagogue community would have. But their teaching about the resurrection of Jesus alienated them from other Jews, leading to occasional riots or hearings before Jewish authorities. Their eventual openness to non-Jewish members, which led to their being known derisively as "Christians" (Acts 11:26), also caused tension with other Jewish groups. Disruptions of the peace brought them to the attention of Roman officials, who nevertheless determined that they were no tangible threat to law and order. In fact, perhaps for apologetic reasons, Acts portrays the Roman officials as generally sympathetic to the movement.

Paul's letters also indicate that relationships with Gentile outsiders was overall positive. He expressed concern that Christians behave as good citizens (Romans 13), as did the author of 1 Peter, and that their worship be orderly so as not to disturb outsiders (1 Corinthians 14). Paul also addressed the growing tension within the church and between Christians and non-Christian Jews concerning observance of the Mosaic law.

In the period when the Gospels were written (A.D. 70-100), tensions between church and synagogue grew more acute, due in part to the different routes taken by Jews and Christians after the Roman destruction of the temple (70). Matthew's vilification of the Pharisees in particular and John's castigation of "the Jews" indicates the depth of the division. Luke's portrayal of the church as the true Israel and Revelation's designation of Jews as the "synagogue of Satan" (Rev. 2:9) further speak to the division, while showing that Christianity affirmed its Jewish roots but dismissing Jews as an illegitimate branch.

The separation of Christianity from Judaism was clearly final by the middle of the 2nd century, as Justin Martyr's "Dialogue with Trypho (the Jew)" and Marcion's rejection of the Jewish Scriptures and their God confirm.

If the tradition that Gamaliel II (80-115) introduced into synagogue worship the "benediction of the heretics" is valid, and if it referred to Christians, then rabbinical Judaism was also consciously distancing itself from the church by the end of the 1st century. Information from Jewish sources about Jewish perceptions of Christianity during the first few centuries is practically nonexistent, however, since traditions reflecting the division come from after the compilation of the Mishnah (ca. 200). Talmudic stories about Jesus and his followers, which generally discredit his character and teachings, serve mainly to reinforce the view from Christian sources that animosity toward the other existed in both camps.

The earliest information from Gentiles about their perceptions of Christianity come from the early 2nd century. Around 110 Pliny the Elder was appointed governor of the Roman province of Bithynia-Pontus in Asia Minor. According to one of his letters to the emperor Trajan, sometime in 112 he encountered there a problem involving a religious group known as Christians. Upon investigation, Pliny concluded that their faith was *superstitio* — a designation Romans gave to religions they considered strange and non-Roman. The influence of the movement had sometimes led to the neglect of traditional religious

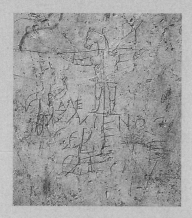

Alexamenos grafitto (with tracing) from Rome depicting a crucified figure with the head of a donkey. *(Wikimedia Commons)*

observances. A few years later, the Roman Tacitus, in his *Annales,* succinctly described the brief persecution of the Christian *superstitio* that had occurred in Rome under Nero. This *superstitio* was "deadly," Tacitus wrote, because of its "hatred of mankind." Writing a few years later, Suetonius also commented briefly on this episode in discussing Nero's reign in his *Lives of the Caesars:* "Punishment was inflicted on the Christians, a class of men given over to a new and mischievous *superstitio.*"

In short, while the New Testament suggests that Roman officials were curious about and sympathetic to Christianity, Roman sources from the early 2nd century indicate that the movement was seen as dangerous. Followers of such *superstitio* were a threat to the empire's welfare because they ignored and even challenged the traditional piety toward the gods, as expressed in rituals and observances intended to guarantee the

well-being of the state and society. Tacitus, as well as Plutarch, saw Judaism also as a perverse *superstitio.* But Christians, as Pliny observed, carried their *superstitio* to "extravagant lengths." Thus their religion was more dangerous than that of Jews.

The evidence of the New Testament and of later sources, then, indicates that the movement begun by Jesus aroused concerns about its threat to traditional observances. The tension between Christianity and its Jewish origins, which eventually led to the break between church and synagogue, and the suspicions that Christianity subverted the traditional order of society are both reflected in the New Testament. Later Roman evidence reveals that those suspicions became a standard component of Roman perceptions of Christianity.

R. Scott Nash

Bust of the young Nero
(www.HolyLandPhotos.org)

The Letters

Twenty-one of the 27 books of the New Testament are in the form of letters, with letters also appearing in Acts 15:23-29 and Rev. 1:4–3:22. The 21 separate epistolary writings have traditionally been divided into two major groups: (1) 13 Pauline letters, which were early recognized by the church as a distinctive body of writings, and (2) eight other sermons, tractates, and letters, all of which are generally set out in epistolary form, claim in seven instances to represent the teachings of various early Jewish Christian leaders, and evidently circulated at first mainly within Jewish Christian circles — only becoming generally known and accepted within the Gentile church of the western Roman Empire in the 3rd and 4th centuries A.D.

The Pauline Letters

The Pauline letters are pastoral instructions, rebukes, and encouragements to churches or groups of churches within the orbit of Paul's mission to Gentiles in the Greco-Roman world and to certain individuals associated in some manner with the apostle in his ministry. Most of the addressees were evangelized by Paul himself or one of his converts — the letter to Christians at Rome being the notable exception.

External Evidence Surprisingly, Luke's second volume, the Acts of the Apostles, reflects no knowledge of Paul's letters. This may be interpreted as evidence for Luke's chronological distance from the events he narrated, either later or before Paul wrote.

2 Peter 3:15b-16, however, indicates an early collection of Paul's letters that were being widely read and considered on the same level as "the other Scriptures." But 2 Peter says nothing about the extent of the Pauline collection, and there is debate about the authorship and date of 2 Peter itself. 1 Clement (ca. 96) and the seven letters of Ignatius (ca. 110) refer to Paul's letters and so testify to the early collection, circulation, and authority of Paul's writings. But neither Clement nor Ignatius evidences any awareness of 2 Corinthians.

Marcion, a prominent (though heretical) Christian teacher of northern Asia Minor and later Rome, argued ca. 140 for a canon of 10 letters of Paul (minus 1-2 Timothy and Titus) and the Gospel of Luke, all of which he purged or altered to suit his own understanding of the gospel. It is uncertain whether Marcion did not know about the Pastoral Epistles or deliberately rejected them because they spoke in opposition to his thesis. The Muratorian Canon or "Fragment" (ca. 180-200) lists the full complement of the 13 Pauline letters as accepted by the church of its day. Church fathers such as Irenaeus of Asia Minor and Gaul (France), the most prominent Christian theologian of the latter 2nd century, and Tertullian of North Africa, the most prolific Latin Christian of the early 3rd century, not only knew of Paul's 13 letters but also used them extensively in their writings.

Contents **Galatians** may be the first of Paul's extant letters, although many date it between 2 Corinthians and Romans. It was probably written ca. 49, just after the first missionary journey (Acts 13–14) and before the Jerusalem Council (Acts 15). It is a *"rebuke and request"* letter in which Paul confronts the teaching of some Jewish Christians that Gentile believers in Jesus must keep the Mosaic law in order to be both justified by God and live a truly Christian lifestyle. With impassioned eloquence, Paul defends the legitimacy of his own apostolic authority and message, proclaims that righteousness is by faith alone, sets out the true function of the Mosaic law, and argues for the pivotal importance of the Spirit and love in the Christian life.

1-2 Thessalonians were written in the early 50s, probably from Corinth shortly after Paul's proclamation of the gospel at Thessalonica on his second missionary journey and the establishment of a group of new believers there (Acts 17:1-9). In the first letter Paul commends his addressees for their reception of the gospel and their growth, zeal, and fidelity; encourages them in the face of persecution; defends his motives and conduct and those of his companions; teaches regarding holiness of life; instructs regarding the coming of the Lord; and exhorts steadfastness and patience. The second letter clarifies his converts' misunderstanding about the coming day of the Lord, insisting that they must remain steadfast and persistent.

1 Corinthians was written in the mid-50s during Paul's extended ministry at Ephesus on his third missionary journey (cf. Acts 19:1-10). In this letter of *"response and instruction"* Paul addresses a number of concerns and issues within the Corinthian church — divisions and problems within the Corinthian community (chs. 1–6) and questions that believers there had asked in a previous letter (chs. 7–14). In addition, he gives instructions regarding the resurrection of believers in Jesus, which his converts at Corinth seem to have regarded as somewhat inconsequential (ch. 15), and their lethargic response to the collection from the Gentile churches for Jewish believers at Jerusalem (16:1-4). Paul concludes with statements about his own travel plans and those of Timothy and Apollos, further instructions and greetings, and a typical closing.

2 Corinthians was evidently written during the last half of the 50s. There is little doubt about its authorship, for it certainly reflects the style and concerns of Paul. There are, however, several places within the letter where the topic, tone, and rhetoric suddenly change, which has raised concerns about whether it is one letter or several letters brought together.

Chapters 1–9 are conciliatory and apologetic, while chs. 10–13 are severe and harsh, even sarcastic. Also, several references to events in Paul's life seem to suggest various times for his writing of these materials (cf. 13:1), and some allusions to the reactions of believers at Corinth to his person and ministry seem to suggest various incidents or times in their relationships. Most scholars today conclude that 2 Corinthians is composed from two or three letters — all authored by Paul himself, but at different times and responding to differing circumstances in the church at Corinth.

Romans is a "letter essay" that sets out in a protreptic rhetorical style a four-part "word or message of exhortation" set in an epistolary frame. Paul wrote to Christians in Rome who were not his own converts but whom he considered to be within the orbit of his Gentile ministry (1:1-15; 15:15-22). It was written at the end of his missionary activities in the eastern Roman Empire, probably in the spring of 57 or 58 — before his final visit to Jerusalem to present the collection from the Gentile churches and further evangelization in the western regions of the empire (15:23-29). Paul's purposes in writing were primarily twofold: to share with Christians at Rome the nature of his preaching among the Gentiles (1:11) and to enlist their support for the furtherance of such a Gentile mission in Spain. He may also have wanted to defend himself against certain criticisms, to counsel the Christians at Rome concerning their responsibilities to the secular authorities, and to speak to existing divisions between the various house churches at Rome.

Romans has often been read as a compendium or comprehensive statement of Paul's teaching — and so the first systematic theology of the early church. Though it is the longest of the apostle's surviving letters, however, it lacks a number of subjects that seem from his other letters to be absolutely essential to his thought and proclamation — most obviously, the omission of any discussion of the resurrection of believers, which has such an important place in his earlier letters (cf. esp. his earlier letters; 1 Thessalonians 4–5; 2 Thessalonians 2; 1 Corinthians 15). Throughout the past two centuries, however, Romans has increasingly been seen in the context of a real, historical, and/or polemical situation, and so to reflect the occasional character of a real letter and the dialogical nature of its circumstances.

The **Prison Epistles** — Philippians, Colossians, Philemon, and Ephesians — are somewhat difficult to place historically. While all indicate that they were written from prison (Phil. 1:12-26; Col. 4:3-15; Phlm. 9-13, 23; Eph. 3:1, 13; 4:1; 6:19-20), the question remains: Were they written from imprisonment in Ephesus (perhaps ca. 53-57), Caesarea (ca. 58-59), or Rome (ca. 60-62)? Issues regarding provenance and date usually concern the number and nature of the journeys between Philippi and Rome reflected in the Philippian letter; the tone and temper of these letters compared to Paul's other letters, particularly Galatians and 2 Corinthians; and the theological statements of these letters compared to Paul's other letters, particularly Galatians, 1 Corinthians, and Romans. Whatever is accepted regarding the origins of these letters has a profound effect on how one relates their themes, rhetoric, and language to the other Pauline letters. Nonetheless, Roman provenance for all four still remains most probable. For while Paul in Philippians, for example, is awaiting a judgment that could issue in either life or death — and while he hopes for a judgment in his favor — his words also reflect a realization that he is at a point where no higher appeal can be made (Phil. 1:20-30), which would have been true only at Rome.

Philippians is a letter of *"praise, thanksgiving, and instruction"* addressed to one of Paul's best churches. It urges its readers to hold fast and reaffirm their Christian commitment in light of apparent opposition, persecution, and internal strife at Philippi. Intertwined throughout the letter are ethical teachings for Christians who find themselves in a hostile environment (1:27–2:18; 3:12–4:9) coupled with statements about Christian teachers there who opposed Paul (1:15-18; 3:2-11). Paul bases his pastoral instructions on the Christ-hymn of 2:6-11. In all of their thinking and actions, they are to follow the pattern set by Christ in his incarnation (2:6-8), which will lead to God's vindication (vv. 9-11) — a pattern expressed by Timothy and Epaphroditus (vv. 19-30) and accepted by Paul himself (3:4-14, 17).

Colossians and Ephesians are often viewed as pseudepigraphical writings (perhaps by disciples of Paul) because of their distinctive vocabulary and style, absence of some themes found in such earlier Pauline letters as Galatians and Romans, and developments in Christology, ecclesiology, and ethics. See "The Question of Pseudepigraphy" (685-86).

Colossians was written to a church founded by Epaphras, one of Paul's converts (1:7; 4:12). It speaks against some type of "deceptive philosophy" advocated by someone within the Colossian congregation (2:8) and counters that teaching, which in effect relegated Christ's work to only some first stage of God's redemptive activity. The letter defuses and "re-baptizes" many of the gnostic expressions used by the false teacher himself and/or the worldview that he espoused (cf. 1:15-20).

Ephesians was probably originally written as a *homily* or *tractate* to be sent out widely to churches in western Asia Minor — with the copy delivered to Ephesus preserved in the early Christian canon. Its language is very similar to that of Colossians, and so these two writings must always be related. In Ephesians, however, the language, themes, and theology are directed more to universal teaching — Christ's victory over the evil powers, overcoming the separation between Christians and Jews — rather than simply countering some false teaching.

Philemon is a personal *letter of recommendation* on behalf of the slave Onesimus, who had become a Christian through Paul's ministry while in prison. It is associated with Colossians by its closing greetings (vv. 23-24; Col. 4:10-14). The letter eloquently expresses an important facet of the social dimension of Paul's proclamation of new life and freedom "in Christ" — asking that Philemon receive back his runaway slave Onesimus as both "a person" and "a believer."

The **Pastoral Epistles** — 1-2 Timothy and Titus — are commonly identified as New Testament pseudepigraphy. Yet assuming the release of Paul from an earlier imprisonment at Rome, his further ministry in the eastern Roman Empire, and his final imprisonment and martyrdom at Rome — and allowing for greater freedom on the part of his secretary

— these letters can be credited to Paul and dated somewhere in the mid-60s. **1 Timothy** and **Titus** are probably to be compared to letters from a ruler or senior official to a newly commissioned delegate and the community to which he is dispatched. The instructions regarding worship and exhortations regarding ethics are evidently applications of the gospel message directed against a particular opposition encountered later in the church's history. **2 Timothy** is primarily a *farewell discourse* with epistolary features.

The Jewish Christian Epistles

The remaining New Testament letters are Hebrews and the seven **Catholic or General Epistles,** so identified first by Eusebius (ca. 325) on the assumption that they were addressed to a more "universal" audience than Paul's letters. While these eight writings are basically epistolary in form, some are probably better understood as sermons or homilies with appended epistolary features, others as tractates or teaching epistles, and in only a few cases as true letters.

It is probably truer to say that Paul's letters, though addressed to specific churches and particular individuals, had a wide circulation within the Western church, which was almost entirely Gentile, whereas Hebrews and the Catholic Epistles circulated primarily within the more limited circles of Jewish Christians — as well as, to some extent, in certain areas of the Eastern church of Gentile Christendom. The latter seven were probably viewed among Jewish Christians as expressing the characteristic teachings of the earliest leaders of the Jerusalem church, similar to the Jewish practice of compiling the teachings of important rabbis. At any rate, they seem to have been largely unknown among Gentile Christians of the Western church during the first two or three centuries.

External Evidence Marcion's canon (140) makes no reference to these epistles — probably no surprise in view of his antagonism to everything Jewish. The Muratorian Canon (ca. 180-200), while mentioning "an epistle of Jude" and "two ascribed to John" as "accepted in the Catholic church," does not mention Hebrews, James, 1-2 Peter, or 3 John. This may be because the Muratorian Canon is fragmentary, defective at both its beginning and end, but it is inconceivable that these books would have been listed before the Gospels. Nor would they have been mentioned after the writings of such heretical teachers as Arsinoes, Valentinus, Metiades, Basilides, and Assianus, with which the fragment ends.

Hebrews was known and attributed to Paul in the Eastern church from at least the late 2nd century. Its Greek style, syntax, and vocabulary, however, were early recognized to be non-Pauline, and so usually treated as "translation Greek" by someone other than Paul. Eusebius accepted Hebrews as canonical, even though he acknowledged that the Roman church denied Pauline authorship. So did the canons of Cyril of Jerusalem (350), Athanasius (367), and Gregory Nazianzus (400). In the Western church, however, the omission of Hebrews in the Muratorian Canon is continued in the Latin list of canonical writings in Codex Claromontanus (300) and the African canon (360). Hebrews finally won a place in Western Christendom through the efforts of Hilary, Jerome, and Augustine, and so appears in the canonical lists of the councils of Hippo and Carthage in North Africa and was accepted by the Syrian church.

The first Jewish-Christian letters to receive general acceptance within the entire church were 1 John and 1 Peter. Both seem to have been known by Papias in the early 2nd century. Jude appears in the Muratorian Canon as the first of three Catholic Epistles accepted by the church at the end of the 3rd century, together with two letters of John. James was known by Origen's time, but we do not know when it was first considered canonical. Irenaeus cites 2 John, and the Muratorian Canon evidently refers to 1 and 2 John. But there is no evidence for the early circulation of 3 John. While 2 Peter is acknowledged as extant by Origen's time, Origen himself is quoted by Eusebius as saying that Peter left "one acknowledged epistle and possibly two, although this is doubtful."

The situation in the early church was similar to that within Second Temple Judaism in determining the canon of the Jewish Scriptures. Whereas the Law and the Prophets had early fixed status, the closing of the canon with respect to the Writings continued to be debated throughout the 1st century A.D. Likewise, whereas the Gospels and Pauline corpus early took their place as authoritative, Hebrews, the Catholic Epistles, and the Johannine Apocalypse (Revelation) continued to be disputed in many quarters of Christendom until the 4th century. The uncertainty was finally settled in the Eastern church only by Athanasius's 39th Easter Festal Letter (367), which presented a firmly delineated New Testament canon that included these books — with that canon then accepted within the Western church through the efforts of such leading Latin church fathers of the late 4th and early 5th centuries as Hilary, Jerome, and Augustine.

Contents Other than a standard epistolary subscription or closing (13:22-25), **Hebrews** is in form a *homily or sermon.* It argues that Jewish believers in Jesus are to recognize the superiority of Jesus over angelic mediation, the Mosaic law, the land of Palestine, the Aaronic priesthood, the Melchizedekian priesthood, the tabernacle in the wilderness (and so the Jerusalem temple), the Old Testament sacrificial system, and even God's covenant with his people — now fulfilled in Jesus' relations with God's people. Believers in Jesus are to be people of faith prepared to suffer persecution, not just to hold on to past traditions and seek freedom from opposition. They must focus on Jesus and "the city to come" and be ready to move forward with God, rearranging their commitments in terms of the superiority of Jesus and leaving, if need be, their former situations of security. Obviously the writer felt at home in the Scriptures, particularly the Pentateuch and Psalms. From the Pentateuch he drew the basic structure of his thought regarding redemptive history, while from the Psalms he derived primary support for his Christology.

James consists of various *pastoral admonitions,* mainly ethical in nature. These seem to be grouped into longer and then shorter sets, interspersed at times with individual sayings. The writing begins with a salutation but does not include any other features typical of ancient letters. Rather, it appears to be a compendium of sermonic material or an ethical tractate, taken to be representative of James, the leader of the Jerusalem church — and so sent out to Jewish believers in Jesus scattered throughout the Jewish Diaspora but considered an extension of the ministry of the Jerusalem church.

1 Peter is a *homily* in letter form. It speaks of suffering as a possibility (1:3–4:11) and a present condition (4:12–5:11). Probably the first section should be seen as a compilation of Petrine sermonic and catechetical material, to which has been added a salutation (1:1-2), exhortations regarding the present suffering (4:12–5:11), and a closing personal subscription (5:12-14). In the form sent out to believers in the five provinces of northern Asia Minor and preserved in the New Testament, the work is genuinely a letter. But in that it incorporates earlier material representative of Peter's preaching and teaching — perhaps even an early baptismal hymn (3:18-22), it also has the character of a sermon or tractate.

1 John is not in the form of a letter but instead appears to be a *tractate*. **2 and 3 John,** however, exhibit the usual features of an ancient letter. Probably 1 John should be viewed as a compendium of Johannine teaching, with 2 and 3 John serving as letters addressing two specific situations.

Both 2 Peter and Jude exhibit features associated with ancient letters. **2 Peter** is a *farewell discourse* with epistolary features. Its theological warnings and literary style evidence decided differences from what appears in 1 Peter. Many of those differences may be explained by the fact of Silas's having aided in the composition of 1 Peter (cf. 5:12), while 2 Peter makes no such suggestion and may only indicate how Peter himself wrote without secretarial help. **Jude,** "a servant of Jesus Christ and brother of James," was also a leader in the Jerusalem church, so there would have been a desire among Jewish Christians to have also a *collection* of his preaching and teaching. His concerns are very much like those of 2 Peter, with both letters evidencing a great deal of nonconformist Jewish thinking that had been taken into the writers' new Christian commitments.

FOR FURTHER READING

Brown, Raymond E. *An Introduction to the New Testament.* New York: Doubleday, 1997, 383-772.

Kümmel, Werner G. *Introduction to the New Testament.* Rev. ed. Nashville: Abingdon, 1975, 247-452.

Metzger, Bruce M. *The New Testament: Its Background, Growth, and Content.* 3rd ed. Nashville: Abingdon, 2003, 249-301.

Moule, C. F. D. *The Birth of the New Testament.* 2nd ed. London: A. & C. Black, 1966, 178-209.

Murphy-O'Connor, Jerome. *Paul, the Letter-Writer.* Collegeville: Liturgical, 1995.

Puskas, Charles B., Jr. *The Letters of Paul: An Introduction.* Good News Studies 25. Collegeville: Liturgical, 1993.

RICHARD N. LONGENECKER

Ancient Letter Writing

Study of the 21 New Testament letters in the light of the practice of letter writing in the 1st century A.D. enhances our ability to understand the structure and meaning of these texts. One way to categorize 1st-century letters is to distinguish between real, private, personal letters and artificial, public, literary epistles. Real letters were written to specific people in response to specific occasions. Many volumes of Hellenistic papyrus letters provide ample illustrations of real letters in the New Testament era. Ancient handbooks on epistolary theory also provide descriptions of a wide variety of specific types of letters, such as letters of friendship, recommendation, rebuke, request, information, instruction, consolation, thanksgiving, apology, introduction, and invitation. Artificial letters were written as literary essays for the general public. The epistolary forms attached to these essays function merely as external brackets and are not integrally related to the content of the essays. The literary epistles of Plato, Cicero, and Seneca are examples of philosophical and moral essays with epistolary forms tacked on. Recognizing these two categories of ancient letters, real letters and essay letters, helps us to categorize the New Testament letters along the same lines.

The 13 Pauline letters can be categorized as real letters, since they were written in the context of very personal relationships in response to specific occasions. In some ways, Paul's letters differ from other 1st-century letters: most ancient letters are addressed to another individual and are relatively short; the letters of Paul addressed to churches are more public than private and are extended by autobiographical and theological excursions. Nevertheless, Paul's letters are remarkably similar to different types of ancient letters. Although Paul's letters are not pure models of the letter types described in the handbooks and illustrated in the papyri, it is enlightening to observe the similarity of 1 Corinthians to a letter of response and instruction; of Galatians to a letter of rebuke and request; of Philippians to a letter of friendship and thanksgiving; and of Philemon to a letter of recommendation.

With significant adaptations and additions, the form of Paul's letters is similar to the conventional form of ancient letters. The basic elements of the standard form and the common Pauline modifications are as follows:

The *salutation* includes the name of the sender, the name of the recipient, greetings, and usually a good health wish. Paul usually inserted titles for himself (apostle, servant) and for his readers (saints, in Christ, church). Short theological additions telegraph the emphasis of the letter. For example, mention of liberation from the present evil age (Gal. 1:4)

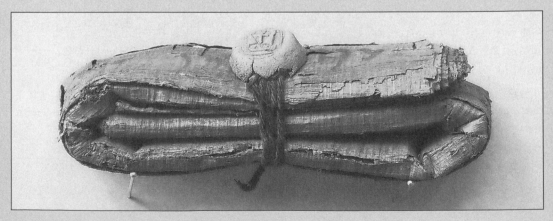

Rolled and sealed papyrus letter. *(bpk, Berlin / Aegyptisches Museum, Berlin / Art Resource, NY)*

Ceramic inkwell from Qumran; ca. A.D. 50. *(Richard Cleave, Pictorial Archive)*

points to the theme of freedom in Christ. Paul always combined the usual Greek greeting with a common Jewish greeting in his benediction of "grace and peace."

The *body* of the letter is introduced and structured by the use of standard formulas. Paul altered the typical Greek custom of beginning a letter with a thanksgiving to the gods by expressing his thanksgiving to God the Father of Jesus Christ for his readers. Paul's thanksgiving paragraphs introduce the main themes of the letter. Paul omitted any thanksgiving but used a common expression of rebuke to begin his letter to the Galatians. Some kind of disclosure formula ("I want you to know") usually signals the transition to the main body of the letter. Other conventional statements found both in ancient letters and Paul's letters include an expression of joy or grief, a request, a notification of a coming visit, a reference to writing, and an expression of reassurance or responsibility. Such statements indicate transitions in the body of the letter. Paul introduced his ethical instruction with a traditional request formula, such as "I beg of you" (Rom. 12:1).

The *closing* of the letter expresses greetings to individuals other than the addressees, a health wish, a final prayer, or farewell. Often Greek papyrus letters ended with a subscription written in the author's own hand, distinguished from the hand of the amanuensis (secretary), to summarize the main point of the letter. Paul employed this common practice as well (Gal. 6:11).

Besides the Greek letter tradition, Paul's letters include many other literary traditions, such as diatribe, hymns, household codes, creedal confessions, and benedictions. But the basic form of his letters is derived from the form of real, personal ancient letters. In addition to Paul's letters, 2 Peter, 2 and 3 John, and Jude may also be included in the category of real letters.

Hebrews, James, 1 Peter, and 1 John are essays, not real letters. Some features of letters may be found in these books, such as the final greetings in Hebrews and the opening greetings in James and 1 Peter. But these books should be classified as representative samples of the preaching and teaching of the early church. Revelation contains letters, but the book as a whole is an apocalypse, not a real letter.

For Further Reading

Aune, David E. *The New Testament in Its Literary Environment.* LEC 8. Philadelphia: Westminster, 1988.

Deissmann, Adolf. *Light from the Ancient East.* Rev. ed. 1927; repr. Grand Rapids: Baker, 1978.

Doty, William G. *Letters in Primitive Christianity.* Guides to Biblical Scholarship. Philadelphia: Fortress, 1973.

Stirewalt, M. Luther, Jr. *Paul, the Letter Writer.* Grand Rapids: Wm. B. Eerdmans, 2003.

Stowers, Stanley K. *Letter Writing in Greco-Roman Antiquity.* LEC 5. Philadelphia: Westminster, 1986.

White, John L. *The Form and Function of the Body of the Greek Letter.* SBLDS 2. Missoula: Scholars, 1972.

——. *Light from Ancient Letters.* Philadelphia: Fortress, 1986.

G. WALTER HANSEN

Romans

In general, Paul's letters to churches (Romans through 2 Thessalonians) appear in descending order of length without regard to the likely order in which the apostle wrote them. The same holds true for the letters to individuals (1 Timothy through Philemon). Paul probably composed Romans from the Greek city of Corinth ca. A.D. 57 or 58, before starting the return trip to Palestine during his third missionary journey (cf. Acts 20:1-3).

The Church and Paul's Message

Most of Paul's letters address specific situations of churches he established on his evangelistic tours of the Roman Empire. Though at the time Paul writes Romans he has not yet visited the imperial capital, much less established the church there, his letter to the Christians of Rome shows his awareness of tensions between the city's Jewish and Gentile believers (chs. 11, 14), paralleled in the relationship between the church in Jerusalem and the predominantly Gentile congregations established by Paul (see Acts 15). The importance of Christian unity leads Paul to highlight the sinfulness of all humanity as the universal leveler that necessitates for Jew and Gentile alike justification by God's grace (ill-deserved favor) through faith in Jesus Christ and that precludes judgmentalism within the church (ch. 14).

While the genesis of the Roman church remains uncertain, it could well have originated with Jews and Gentile converts returned to Rome after having made a pilgrimage to Jerusalem at Pentecost, when they heard and believed the gospel (Acts 2:1-11). Having expressed his desire to visit the Christians in Rome (Acts 19:21; cf. 23:11), Paul reveals his plan for a layover there on his way to Spain. The epistle alerts the congregation to his upcoming visit, provides a firsthand introduction to his theology, and offers a taste of how in person he will further strengthen them in their faith.

1:1-17 Paul's Mission and Message

In ancient Palestine, freed slaves became bondslaves by voluntarily submitting to a lifetime of servanthood to the master who had released them. Paul calls himself a "bondservant" of Christ, whom he serves as an apostle ("one sent") bearing the message of the gospel (vv. 2-5). His greeting to the Christians in Rome acknowledges the Jewish roots of Christianity and its relevance for all people. By using both the Greek and Hebrew words of greeting — "grace" and "peace" — Paul suggests that Gentile and Jewish "saints" (Christians) enjoy equal standing in the church. "Grace" reminds his audience of the ill-deserved favor God grants to sinners who trust in Christ. "Peace" is not merely the absence of strife but the active enjoyment of divine blessing.

Though Paul has yet to visit Rome, he knows by reputation the faithful Christian community there. He reveals two reasons for his longstanding desire to meet them in person: their mutual enlightenment in the Christian faith, and his desire to collect from them financial support for his mission to Spain.

In verses 16-17, Paul states his theme: salvation through faith. The priority of Jews over "Greeks" (= Gentiles) concerns who first heard the message, not their spiritual quality. Jesus commanded proclaiming the gospel to the Jews first and then to the Gentiles, and the book of Acts illustrates the outworking of this principle (Matt. 10:5-15, 16-42). The quotation from Hab. 2:4, "the righteous will live by faith," does not command how to live one's earthly life; rather, Paul is asserting that one gains *eternal* life by exercising faith in the message of the gospel (cf. 3:30).

Paul's Gospel

Paul understood his vocation as an apostle to be, above everything else, a call to preach what he called "the gospel of God" (Rom. 1:1; 1 Thess. 2:2, 8-9; cf. 1 Tim. 1:11) or "the gospel of Christ" (Rom. 15:19; 1 Cor. 9:12; 2 Cor. 9:13; Gal. 1:7; Phil. 1:27; 1 Thess. 3:2; cf. 2 Thess. 1:8). The proclamation of this gospel was to Paul a compulsion prompted by God, and to be deprived of the ability to carry out this calling would be worse than death (1 Cor. 9:16). Paul's life was bound so tightly to the gospel that to speak of his own affairs was inevitably to speak of the advancement of the gospel in those affairs (Phil. 1:12). When Paul spoke of "my gospel" (Rom. 2:16; 16:25; 2 Tim. 2:8), therefore, he did not mean that his gospel differed from that of other Christians, but that he felt an enormous personal responsibility for promoting the gospel.

What was this gospel? The noun "gospel" (Gk. *euangelion*) referred essentially to "good news" of any sort, and the verb "preach the gospel" *(euangelizō)* meant telling this good news to others (1 Thess. 3:6). The ancient Greek translators of Isaiah used the verb to refer to the future proclamation in Judah of the "glad tidings" that the punishment of God's people for their sins had ended and that God would rescue Judah from exile (Isa. 40:9; cf. 52:7; 61:1-2). Jesus understood his ministry to be the fulfillment of such prophecies (Luke 4:16-21), and so it was

natural for early Christians such as Paul to think of their proclamation of Jesus as the "good news of God, which he promised beforehand through his prophets in the holy scriptures" (Rom. 1:1-2; cf. 10:15-16).

More specifically, Paul understood the gospel to be the account of Jesus, the Messiah, Son of David, and Son of God (Rom. 1:1-3) who died to atone for a sinful people (1 Cor. 15:1-3; cf. 1:18) and who was raised from the dead (Rom. 1:4; 1 Cor. 15:4-8; cf. 2 Tim. 2:8). Paul's gospel also included many theological and ethical applications derived from these fundamental historical truths (e.g., 2 Cor. 9:13; Gal. 2:14). As a result, his preaching of the gospel to a single group might extend over a long period of time (1 Thess. 2:9) and, after his absence, require the additional efforts of one of his co-workers (1 Thess. 3:2).

The fullest exposition of Paul's gospel appears in his letter to the Romans, and this letter's thematic statement (1:16-17) sums up Paul's gospel. Echoing Ps. 98:2-3, he describes the gospel as the ultimate revelation of God's "righteousness" or saving power for everyone who believes, not only Jews but non-Jews also. Receiving God's powerful, saving righteousness is not a matter of belonging to the right nation but of faith.

The rest of the letter clarifies that "faith" does not mean a vague trust in something transcendent. It refers specifically to the convic-

tion that God atoned for human sin through the sacrificial death of his Son on the cross and, by this death, reconciled a rebellious people to himself (Rom. 3:25; 5:6-11; 8:3; cf. 1 Cor. 1:17-18). To use the language of the courtroom, God justified, or acquitted, the ungodly on the basis of Christ's death (Rom. 3:24). This was an act of God's free grace, unprompted by any deserving conduct or attractive quality in the ungodly people who received it (1:18–3:20; 4:4-8; 5:6-8; 11:6; cf. 1 Cor. 1:26-31).

Paul's letter to Rome also demonstrates that for Paul the gospel had ethical implications. Paul tells the Roman Christians that he is eager to come to Rome to reap some fruit among them by the proclamation of the gospel there (Rom. 1:13-15). Although his readers are already believers (1:12; 15:14), they need to hear the gospel again. Their church is divided along ethnic lines (14:1–15:13), but the gospel's offer of salvation to *everyone* who believes implies that such divisions are inappropriate (1:16; 3:29-30; 4:11-12; 10:12-13; 15:7-12).

Paul drew this same ethical conclusion from the gospel in his letter to the Galatian churches. Here he describes how he once accused Cephas, certain people from James, and Barnabas of not "acting consistently with the truth of the gospel" because they were excluding Gentile Christians from table fellowship in Antioch (Gal. 2:11-14; cf. v. 5). If all are sinners and all who have faith in Christ will stand acquitted in God's eschatological court, Paul reasoned, then the question of whether one would or would not follow the Jewish food laws should be irrelevant to Christian fellowship (2:15-21).

To believe the gospel, therefore, was to embrace it not merely with the head but also with the heart. It was not simply to be rescued from final judgment but also to live in the present in "a manner worthy of the gospel of Christ" (Phil. 1:27).

The gospel was not, however, a fixed body of doctrinal and ethical principles. Paul believed that it was alive with God's gracious, saving power (Rom. 1:16) — that it was the instrument through which Christ Jesus "abolished death and brought life and immortality to light" (2 Tim. 1:10). When Paul preached the gospel, he did not simply speak common words but delivered a message that was accompanied by power and by the presence of the Holy Spirit (1 Thess. 1:5; Rom. 15:19). This power was evident in the change that the gospel brought to those who heard and responded to it (1 Thess. 1:6-10). Despite the unsophisticated rhetoric of the preacher (1 Cor. 2:3-4), the unimpressive social status of those who heard the message (1:26-31), and the socially unacceptable content of the message itself (vv. 17-25; 2:6-16), God called out a people for himself through the preaching of the gospel (1:26a).

Paul could speak with conviction about the gospel's power because he had personally experienced its power. Outside the gates of Damascus God had overwhelmed him with the truth of the gospel by revealing Jesus to him (Gal. 1:11-12). There he saw "the light of the gospel of the glory of Christ, who is the image of God" (2 Cor. 4:4) and received God's commission to preach this gospel among the nations (Gal. 1:16). From that point, Paul was consumed with the pursuit of this divine vocation (1 Cor. 9:16). He considered the gospel a God-given trust (Gal. 2:7; 1 Thess. 2:4; 1 Tim. 1:11) — a precious treasure (2 Cor. 4:7) that he should defend, confirm, and strenuously contend for in adversity (Phil. 1:7, 16, 27; 4:3; cf. 2 Cor. 4:8-12). Above all, it was something that he should preach as far and wide as he could, whether in Jerusalem, Illyricum, Rome, or Spain, whether in plenty or famine, in honor or dishonor (Rom. 15:19, 24, 28; Phil. 4:12; 2 Cor. 6:8). Famine and dishonor predominated (1 Cor. 4:9-13; 2 Cor. 6:4-10; 11:23-33), and Paul had a profound sense of his own insufficiency in the face of the task God had given him (2:16). Even so, Paul considered his call to preach this gospel an act of God's mercy and did not lose heart despite his sufferings, for through his preaching he saw God's Spirit give people life, remove the veil of spiritual blindness from their eyes, and begin to transform them into God's image (2 Cor. 3:6, 16-18; 4:1, 12).

For Further Reading

Barnett, Paul. *Paul: Missionary of Jesus.* Grand Rapids: Eerdmans, 2008.

Dunn, James D. G. *The Theology of Paul the Apostle.* Grand Rapids: Wm. B. Eerdmans, 1998, 164-69.

Fitzmyer, Joseph A. *To Advance the Gospel.* 2nd ed. Biblical Resource Series. Grand Rapids: Wm. B. Eerdmans, 1998, 149-61.

O'Brien, Peter T. *Gospel and Mission in the Writings of Paul.* Grand Rapids: Baker, 1995.

Stuhlmacher, Peter. "The Pauline Gospel." In *The Gospel and the Gospels.* Grand Rapids: Wm. B. Eerdmans, 1991, 149-72.

FRANK THIELMAN

1:18–3:20 Salvation Open to All

To establish the necessity of the gospel for salvation, Paul indicts humanity for its inexcusable corruption, caused by the deliberate suppression of God's obvious self-revelation through the human conscience and the natural order. Verses 26-31 spell out the consequences of disregarding God. On God's "giving up" the unrighteous to their depravity (v. 24), compare his hardening the heart of Pharaoh for refusing to obey God's commands through Moses (Exodus 4–14).

Paul cautions against "judging" fellow humans, that is, writing them off as eternally damned. To do so is to condemn one's own, equally sinful self (2:1; itemized for the Jew in vv. 17-23). Just as the eternal benefits of the gospel apply to Jews and Gentiles alike, so also do the eternal consequences of stubborn unrepentance. For the Jew, the Mosaic law sets the standard of measurement for righteousness of the heart. The Gentile displays righteousness not by obeying the Law's peculiarly Jewish features (circumcision, food laws, sacrifices) but by obeying its universal moral principles (2:29; cf. 1 Sam. 15:22; Ps. 40:6-8; Isa. 1:11-20). Both Jews and Gentiles must meet the requirement of righteousness, but the means of their demonstrating it and of God's evaluation differ.

Beginning with Abraham God made circumcision a sign of membership in the covenantal community (Gen. 17:10-14). But Israel's history illustrates that physical circumcision apart from obedience to the Law does not guarantee salvation; otherwise, Christ need not have died on the cross. Conversely, righteousness demonstrated by obedience to God's fundamental laws does obtain salvation for the physically uncircumcised. The gospel defines "Jewishness" and "circumcision" — indicators of election by God for salvation — in terms that go beyond physicality, namely, as attitudes of the heart.

Nevertheless, the availability of salvation to Gentiles does not cancel the historically privileged relationship with God enjoyed by the Jews. Their covenantal failures may contrast with the faithfulness of God, but this neither legitimates continued sinning nor renders Jews morally superior, despite their unique role in salvation history.

3:21–5:21 Becoming Right with God through Faith

Paul announces the good news, the manifestation of *God's* righteousness "apart from law." The prophesied Christ embodies the perfect righteousness of God, gained through faith by the sinner, whose "justification" (restoration to a right relationship with God) results from God's free gift of grace. The idea of "redemption," which Christ achieves for sinners, recalls the substitutionary "buying back" of a person or item set apart for a particular purpose (cf. Exod. 13:1-16). The sin of humankind evokes the righteous anger of God and sets humanity apart for eternal death. On behalf of doomed humanity, Christ "propitiates" (appeases the anger of) God by dying on the cross. By dying as a substitute for sinful humans, Christ pays for their redemption. But sinners cannot claim this redemption by working for it; rather, they become redeemed

Panoramic view of the interior of the Colosseum, or Flavian Ampitheater, at Rome. *(Wikimedia Commons)*

Jews and Gentiles in the Church

Acts 10 is the first recorded conversion to Christ of a "full-blooded" Gentile, Cornelius. That the Jewish believers in Jerusalem debated their response to this event (Acts 11:1-18; cf. 15:1-29) is hardly surprising. Judaism had always encompassed contradictory and competing attitudes toward Gentiles. The opposing attractions of universalism and exclusivism, of approach and avoidance, repeatedly pulled Israel toward and then away from the Gentile world. Both unfavorable and favorable views of Gentiles are amply represented in the Hebrew Bible. The conquest narratives commend the wholesale elimination of the native Canaanite populations (note the frequent use of the phrase "utterly destroy" in Josh. 2:10; 8:26; 10:1; 11:21), while passages such as Exod. 22:21; Lev. 19:10; Deut. 10:19 demand the fair, even compassionate treatment of "resident aliens."

Particularly instructive are the nearly opposite responses to the trauma of the exile. Prominent Jewish leaders reacted to the deportation of their ancestors to Babylon as punishment, especially for idolatry, by calling for strict separation. The books of Ezra and Nehemiah require, among other things, that Jewish men divorce their non-Jewish wives. Many intertestamental writings reinforce the demand for segregation, not only in marriage (Tob. 4:12-13) but also in matters such as eating and hospitality (e.g., 1:10-11; Sir. 11:34). An entirely different response is evident in Ruth and Jonah, which encourage a more inclusive attitude toward Gentiles. Undoubtedly, the most important "pro-Gentile" voice was that of Isaiah, who saw Israel not as a walled-off sanctuary but as a "light to the nations" (Isa. 42:6; 49:6; 60:3). Several passages speak of God's universal salvation (42:1-9; 49:1-26; 60:1-22). The expectation is that postexilic Israel would be restored, and that this faithful people would include believing Gentiles (2:2-4; 11:1-16; 55:1-5; 66:18-23). One implication is that the Messiah, through whom God would renew Israel, is also the one through whom the Gentiles would be brought to faith (9:1-7; 11:10-16).

At the time of the founding of the Christian church, the admission of Gentiles was already realized as a Jewish impulse, especially in the context of a messianic community that believed in the present dawning of God's reign on earth. Gentile inclusion, then, was less an "if" than a "when" and a "how." How much had already changed because of Christ, and how much remained to be changed? At one end of the spectrum were those who thought that little had altered in the human situation; Gentiles would enter Israel as they always had, through proselytism into Judaism (e.g., the position of the "false believers"; Gal. 2:4). At the other end stood Paul, who believed that God had already created a new people without distinction between Jew and Gentile (Gal. 3:28). This meant, practically, that the laws that had once separated the two groups (e.g., those compelling circumcision and regulating food) were now optional, even for Jews (1 Cor. 9:19-23). In between were perhaps the majority of Jewish Christian leaders, such as Peter and James (and quite likely Barnabas), who accepted uncircumcised Gentiles into the church but who did not believe that such acceptance signaled the end of the present age and its Law. After all, Israel itself had not yet been restored; therefore, while the reign of God might be anticipated by the presence of believing Gentiles, it is not yet fully realized. Paul got around this difficulty by arguing that Jewish unbelief had necessitated a reversal of the prophetic timetable. Now is the moment of Gentile ingathering, after which "all Israel will be saved" (Rom. 11:25-32; cf. Acts 1:6-7). The present mission to the Gentiles is not foreshadow; it is substance, fueled for Paul by Gen. 12:3 and Isaiah (cf. Rom. 15:12, 21).

Gentile inclusion was neither a uniquely Christian innovation nor the dominant controversy within 1st-century Christianity. The more persistent Christian dispute concerned Jewish — not Gentile — legal obedience (e.g., the eating of certain foods by Jews; Gal. 2:11-14; cf. Matt. 15:1-20; Mark 7:1-20). Paul was accused not of preaching Christ to Gentiles, but of teaching disobedience to Jews (Acts 21:17-

26). In short, it appears that Jewish Christians could agree to admit uncircumcised Gentiles while still disagreeing as to the meaning and implications of that action. Practically, the phenomenon of shared meals in mixed churches required a decision: either Jews had to disobey the Law, or Gentiles had, at least on these occasions, to eat kosher.

Early Christianity should not be viewed in terms of the "Gentile question," nor should Judaism be regarded primarily as an obstacle overcome by true 1st-century believers. Controversy over Gentiles (and, as a consequence, over the Law) in the 1st-century church developed only gradually and never included a wholesale repudiation of Judaism, even by Paul. The decisive event was the Jerusalem Council (ca. A.D. 50, 20 years after the founding of the church; Acts 15:1-29; Gal. 2:1-10), at which the leaders in Jerusalem agreed formally to the admission of uncircumcised Gentiles. For his part, Paul continued, however grudgingly, to recognize the validity and authority of the Jerusalem apostles (even in Galatians, e.g., 2:2).

Over time, the Christian mission to the Gentiles succeeded, while the Jewish mission faltered (Rom. 9:1-13). With the destruction of Jerusalem in 70, the center of Jewish Christianity was forever lost. The church was well on its way to becoming a Gentile institution. This earthshaking shift moved Christianity at least part way off its Jewish foundations, encouraging it to see Christianity as superseding Judaism, and opening it increasingly to anti-Jewish theological perspectives (e.g., Marcion and other gnostics). Ironically, it was Gentile — especially Gentile Christian — attitudes toward Judaism, and not the reverse, that soon would become the more historically important and morally urgent question.

CRAIG C. HILL

only by exercising faith in the work of *Christ* on the cross. The continuing value of the Law lies in its use as a vehicle for expressing the fundamental requirements of righteousness (cf. Matt. 5:17-48).

In cementing the case for justification by faith apart from works, Paul goes back to Abraham — long before the time of Moses and the Law. God reckoned Abraham righteous on the basis of his belief in God's promises. That he first exercised this faith before he became circumcised (as the sign of the covenant; Genesis 17) makes him the spiritual ancestor of the Gentiles. That he continued to exercise this faith by and after becoming circumcised makes him not only the physical ancestor of the Jews but their spiritual ancestor too. Just as Abraham's exercise of faith made him "right with God" before he received the sign of the covenant and before the Mosaic law even existed, so now does the exercise of faith in Jesus justify Jews and Gentiles alike after the giving of the Law and apart from obedience to it.

Paul now lists the benefits of justification: peace with God, hope (expectation) in God's glory (the second coming), and joy in persecution. Paul proclaims the wonder of Christ's dying — not for friends (John 15:13), nor even for good people — but for sinners. His ultimate sacrifice for them guarantees salvation (eternal life) for the justified — those who receive reconciliation with God through Christ's death on the cross.

In 5:12-21 Paul compares and contrasts the responsibility for initiating sin and righteousness through Adam and Christ, respectively. The sin of one man, Adam, morally tainted all humanity; the death of one man, Christ, justifies all people. Adam's initial act of sin inaugurated the reign of death and earned condemnation for humanity; Christ's one act of grace justifies multitudinous transgressors and initiates the reign of eternal life. The more sin, the greater God's grace.

6 Dying to Sin, Rising to Righteousness

Paul rejects the argument that a believer ought to continue sinning to multiply the grace of God (cf. 3:1-8; 5:19-21). Identifying with Christ through baptism means dying to sin, which he conquered through his death, and then rising to eternal life, symbolized by submersion and rising out of the baptismal water. The Christian should use one's mortal body as an "instrument of righteousness" rather than obeying bodily "lusts" — a warning no doubt clear to those living in morally decadent Rome.

The apostle also contradicts the argument that believers need not worry about sinning since God's grace will cover any penalty earned by unrighteous conduct. Emancipation from sin does not allow the believer to do whatever he or she pleases. Rather, slavery to sin (which earns eternal death) is exchanged for slavery to righteousness (with the free gift of eternal life and "sanctification" — being made godly).

7–8 Freed for Obedience

Christ's death also releases believers from the obligations of the Law, just as the death of a marital partner releases the surviving spouse from the bond of marriage. Paul attributes to the Law responsibility for arousing the fleshly passions that *lead* to sin. He distinguishes the Law *from* sin, defends the inherent goodness of the Law, and explains its noble function, namely, of awakening human beings to their sinfulness (through failure to follow the Law perfectly) and to the realization that they must rely on God's grace for salvation. Paul's self-analysis in 7:9-11 parallels the account of the fall of Adam and Eve (Gen. 2:15-17; 3).

To illustrate that the Law itself is not sin but creates the opportunity for sin, Paul cites his personal struggles. He wants to obey God's law — which amounts to a confession of its goodness — but in fact does the opposite, so demonstrating his enslavement to sin against his will. Paul does not place the blame else-where (7:17), nor does he consider the flesh inherently evil, as do the Greeks. Rather, he highlights the tyrannical nature of sin's rule over his body. His helpless, hopeless plight makes his and all humanity's moral emancipation by Christ all the greater cause for celebration. That in the flesh Christ defeated the ruler over the flesh seals the decisiveness of his victory and renders irreversible the condemnation of Tyrant Sin. Identifying with Christ transforms a condemned prisoner of sin into a fellow victor over sin (8:1). The believer's dwelling "in Christ" combines with indwelling by the Holy Spirit to enable "walking" in ways that bring the mortal body back to moral life (cf. John 14–15).

Paul enhances the attractiveness of exchanging slavery to sin for slavery to righteousness (cf. 6:15-23) by observing that believers, though still slaves, do not receive a "spirit of slavery," which results in relating to God from an attitude of fear. Rather, they obtain a "spirit of adoption," which prompts relating to God as "Abba" ("Father"). Unlike slaves, children enjoy inheritance rights, and the "glorification" willed by God to believers/heirs promises an eternal life so wondrous as to render their earthly sufferings a paltry price to pay. All creation, which suffers the fallout of human sinfulness, aches for the birth of redeemed humanity — which will also free creation from corruption (8:18-25).

Paul encourages believers by observing that the Holy Spirit represents (intercedes for) them before God the Father, that God "works

Panoramic view of the Roman Forum, the oldest of Rome's public squares, a complex of open spaces and government buildings, temples, and shops. *(Wikimedia Commons)*

all things together for good to those who love him," and that his elect can rest assured of their resurrection and eternal life (8:26-30). Verses 29-30 summarize the doctrine of "predestination," God's foreordination of individuals for eternity. Chapter 8 closes by celebrating the unbounded love of God, whose holiness uniquely qualifies him to condemn sinful humanity but who instead sacrificed his own Son to redeem it. No circumstance, no power, no distance can ever separate us from a love so great (cf. Ps. 139:7-12).

9–11 The Inscrutable Ways of God

Paul laments the broken relationship between God and the Hebrew people, God's first elect. But he acknowledges that physical descent from Abraham does not guarantee salvation. That the line of Esau (the Edomites) legitimately claims Abraham as a forefather but falls outside the covenantal promises, reserved for the descendants of Esau's twin brother Jacob, illustrates Paul's point. It is not for humans to question their Creator's fairness in designating some for election but not others, for none *deserve* his mercy — neither the Jewish "remnant" nor Gentiles. As a nation the Hebrews sought to *earn* salvation by obedience to the Law instead of fulfilling its mandated works of righteousness through faith in God's redemptive promises. Christ's victory over sin and death releases Jews from the obligations of the Law and makes salvation available to Jews and Gentiles on the same terms: faith alone. People need to know of the availability of salvation, so Paul stresses the urgency of proclaiming the gospel (cf. Matt. 28:19-20).

Lest his audience think that God's enabling salvation for the Gentiles indicates his rejection of the Jews, Paul offers himself as proof that God has saved a Hebrew remnant. The offer of salvation by faith to the Gentiles instills jealousy in the Jews, which leads some of them to salvation by faith, too. For Paul, the Jewish apostle to the Gentiles, the prospect of indirectly leading some of his kinsmen to saving faith lends even greater significance to his ministry.

Nevertheless, Paul warns Gentiles against arrogance toward the Jews, whose role in the history of redemption functions as the root system supporting the salvation of those "grafted" on. If God cut off the natural branches from the tree (the unbelieving Jews from the promises of the covenant), he will not hesitate to cut off wild ingrafts. Nor is he unable to reintroduce the natural branches into the tree. In fact, he plans to do just this. The Jews' partial "hardening" (rejection of the gospel) buys time to ensure the salvation of all the Gentile elect (11:25). But in the end God will purify the Jews, too, according to his promise. In closing (vv. 32-36), Paul recognizes God's ultimately merciful purpose in *allowing* human sinfulness in order that he might show his faithfulness.

12:1–15:13 Practicing the Christian Faith

12 Relating to Friends and Foes Here Paul gives specific exhortations for the practical outworking of the Christian faith. The admonition to present one's body as a living sacrifice (12:1) flows from his discussion of dying to sin and rising to righteousness (ch. 6), his personal battle with mind over matter (7:14-25), and the victory won by Christ over sin. This victory enables the Christian's renewed mind to govern the behavior of the body and frees the flesh from imitating the sinful actions of nonbelievers (conformity to "the world").

Humility and mutual regard must characterize relationships among Christians, with believers exercising their varied gifts to support the functioning of the church, the "body" of Christ. Sincere love, abhorrence of evil, mutual devotion and respect, diligence in service, joy, perseverance, prayer, charitable support of fellow Christians, and hospitality comprise the particulars of Paul's prescription for relationships within the church. Toward non-Christians — even persecutors — believers must demonstrate a forgiving spirit, empathy, sympathy, nonvindictiveness, even hospitality, so that good gets the upper hand. Leaving vengeance to God prevents the Christian from being consumed by evil.

13 The Christian and Law When Paul exhorts Christians to obey the "governing authorities," put in place by God, he assumes the proper exercise of justice by those authorities — praising citizens for right conduct, punishing people for evil actions — and their devotion to serving God as rulers (vv. 3-4, 6). Insofar as they pursue these goals, they deserve financial support for their administrations, obedience to their laws, and moral support for their policies (cf. Matt. 22:15-22; Luke 20:21-25). The principle of love sums up the obligations of the Mosaic law and governs Christian conduct. The Law's prohibitions against harming others get intensified by Jesus, who prescribes taking neighborly initiative to ensure the welfare of anyone in need (cf. Luke 10:25-37). The surprising nearness of Jesus' return (= "salvation," v. 11) should rouse Christians to proper behavior, characterized by sobriety, sexual discipline, and relational harmony. The admonition to "owe nothing to anyone" does not prohibit taking out a loan or borrowing from a friend; rather, it prohibits defaulting on one's debts (v. 8).

14:1–15:13 Freedom and Responsibility Loving one's neighbor (13:10) may require the Christian to forgo personally acceptable practices to avoid influencing a fellow believer in ways that go against his conscience and thus for him constitute sin. When Paul discusses eating "anything" versus eating "only vegetables," and regarding "one day to be better than another," he appears aware of dissension between Jewish and Gentile Christians over the obligation to observe food laws and the Sabbath. That in large measure meat for sale in the Roman market came from animals sacrificed to pagan gods doubtless complicated for many Christians the question of acceptable fare (cf. 1 Corinthians 8). In the interest of harmony within the church, Paul prescribes gracious self-denial for Christians who *can* relax Mosaic rules without violating their consciences, and he forbids judgmentalism by all parties. In other words, follow your conscience, but unselfishly adjust your behavior to build up the faith of others, not tear it down; and leave the judging to God. Paul holds up Christ as the ultimate example of self-denial for

the sake of others (15:1-13). His was a complete self-sacrifice for the sake of all.

15:14-33 Paul's Calling

In closing, Paul notes that he has preached the gospel from Jerusalem all the way to Illyricum (on the eastern shore of the Adriatic Sea opposite Italy), reiterates his plans to visit the Roman church on his next intended missionary journey (to Spain), and talks ominously of his immediate trip to Jerusalem to deliver to its poverty-stricken church relief aid from the Christians of Greece (Macedonia and Achaia). Acts 21–28 tell how Paul got to Rome in a way unforeseen at the time he wrote Romans.

16 Greetings and Benediction

Phoebe, who may have carried Paul's letter to Italy, hails from the port city servicing Corinth, where Paul is composing his letter. His commendation of Phoebe to the Roman church suggests that she is moving to the imperial capital or visiting it. Paul met and worked with fellow tentmakers Prisca (short for Priscilla) and her husband Aquila during the apostle's second missionary journey (Acts 18). They had settled in Corinth after Claudius ousted Christians from Rome, but evidently they returned after the emperor's death. Paul's extensive missionary journeys throughout Palestine, Syria, Asia Minor, and Greece brought him into contact with residents and no doubt fellow travelers from all over the empire, perhaps including some or all of the other Christians of Rome to whom he sends greetings.

Paul inserts a final exhortation to ignore wily troublemakers who try to disrupt Christian unity. He also conveys greetings from Timothy, the beloved coworker who joined Paul during his second journey (Acts 16:1-3; cf. the apostle's mentoring relationship with Timothy as indicated in 1-2 Timothy). Tertius identifies himself as the "writer" of Romans — not the author but the secretary (v. 22). A closing benediction returns the reader's attention to glorifying the eternal, revealed, and only wise God.

1 Corinthians

During his second missionary journey the Apostle Paul made his way to southern Greece (Achaia), where he established the church in Corinth — a cosmopolitan center of commerce and trade located on a narrow isthmus between the Aegean and Adriatic seas (Acts 18:1-17). Sailors often avoided the perilous waters south of Greece by dragging their ships over the strip of land separating the seas — a time-consuming shortcut that took them past Corinth.

The City and the Church

As a stopover for travelers of widespread geographical origins and destinations, Corinth offered nearly limitless opportunities for exporting Christianity throughout the ancient world. But the cultural diversity of the transient population also fostered an atmosphere of religious pluralism dominated by flourishing paganism, epitomized in the abundance of "sacred" prostitutes working for Aphrodite (the Greek goddess of love) on the city's acropolis. No wonder, then, the variety and vulgarism of the problems characterizing the ethnically mixed but mainly Gentile Corinthian church. Paul's correctives address issues ranging from church unity to sexual morality to practical matters of religious practice to theological foundations of faith in Christ.

The Letter

Actually, 1 Corinthians constitutes the second letter of Paul to the church in Corinth. The first letter (5:9) remains lost to us. The apostle now writes from Ephesus while on his third missionary journey. He plans to revisit Corinth, for he has already become aware of disturbing problems in the church there, by means of a letter and a delegation soliciting Paul's judgment on a number of issues. The problems prove too pressing to postpone responding till he arrives in person. Evidently the apostle dictated his letter to a secretary, but by signing off in his own handwriting, Paul makes sure the Corinthians know that the letter carries authority and that he means business.

1:1-9 A Positive Opening

Paul's opening words of encouragement foster receptiveness to the stern exhortations that dominate this letter. Acts 18:17 identifies Sosthenes (v. 1) as a leader of the synagogue in Corinth; his mention as co-author of 1 Corinthians suggests that he had become a Christian. Paul touts the benefit of "sanctification" (being made godly, v. 2) in Rom. 6:15-23. By using both the Greek and Hebrew words of greeting ("grace" and "peace," v. 3), Paul regards Gentiles and Jews as equal in the church. In chapter 12, he elaborates the spiritual "gifts" alluded to in verse 7. The "revelation of our Lord Jesus Christ" refers to his second coming, and his "day" to the final judgment, when confirmation in blamelessness (the result of sanctification) ensures for the Christian eternal life.

1:10–4:21 Divisions and Foolishness

Oral reports from "Chloe's people" (probably slaves) prompt Paul's initial exhortation against divisions within the church. The apostle chastises the cliquish Corinthians claiming spiritual superiority by association with wrongly idolized heroes of the faith — Paul himself, who established the city's church, the eloquent Alexandrian orator Apollos (Acts 18:24-28), and the Apostle Peter (Cephas), especially renowned in Jewish circles (Acts 1–12). Paul expresses relief that he did not baptize many of the Corinthians, not because he considers the rite unimportant but because he does not want the focus to be on him. He counters the Christians' exalted claims by characterizing the gospel they received as "foolishness" in the eyes the world. The heart of this gospel — the death and resurrection of Jesus — is a "stumbling block" to the Jews, who on the whole reject Christ's messiahship, and "foolishness" to the Gentiles, who regard crucifixion (inflicted on common criminals) as the most shameful of executions. God's provision of salvation through such a humbling means rules out religious pride by making humility a requirement for saving belief.

Paul had gone to Corinth after the intellectual elite of Athens rejected his gospel-laden message (Acts 17:15–18:1). Here he elaborates the difference between human wisdom manifested in persuasive speech, such as that of the Greek rhetoricians undoubtedly esteemed by the people of cosmopolitan Corinth, and the otherworldly, age-old wisdom of God uniquely imparted by the Holy Spirit to believers but incomprehensible to unspiritual ("natural") hearers. Paul exposes the persistent spiritual immaturity of the Corinthian Christians evidenced in their "fleshly" (sinful) squabbling (cf. Rom. 7:14–8:17). The apostle uses examples from agriculture and architecture to illustrate the relationship of Christian leaders and the church to God. No growth occurs without God; no structure stands without a foundation — for the church, Jesus Christ. Paul equates the church with the temple of God, made holy by the indwelling of his Spirit, and warns destroyers of the church (false teachers) that God will destroy them.

Finally, Paul points out the illegitimacy of bragging about salvation, since it comes as a gift. Though he rejects being idolized by Corinthian believers, he does not relinquish fatherly authority over this congregation. Rather, Paul exhorts them to imitate his Christian conduct, sends a tutor (his beloved protégé, Timothy) to foster their spiritual maturation, and alerts them to his coming visit.

5 Incest Necessitates Ostracism

While the Corinthian cliques claim spiritual superiority, the church as a whole tolerates incest in its ranks! Even secular Roman law prohibited sexual relationships between a man and his "father's wife" (= stepmother). Paul chastises the church fellowship for failing to ostracize the sinning husband (apparently, the only believing partner). His wickedness threatens to corrupt the whole church, as a little yeast leavens an entire lump of dough. The Corinthian church needs to clean house, not cut itself off from the secular world, as they mistakenly interpreted Paul's earlier instruction. "Handing over" the sinning man to Satan suggests expulsion from the Christian community to prompt repentance for salvation at the final judgment.

In 4:5, Paul prohibits judging other Christians, but here he orders it. The universal moral principles of God make obvious the boundaries of holiness — a characteristic required of the church as God's temple (cf. 3:16).

6:1-11 Settling Internal Disputes Internally

Paul's teaching on lawsuits seems to interrupt his exhortations to sexual morality, which continue in 6:12-20. Perhaps the case of incest addressed in chapter 5 was fueling legal action that goes unspecified here. In any case, Paul expresses disapproval that Corinthian Christians have been suing each other in secular law courts presided over by non-Christian judges. They should be addressing internal disputes within the church, or better yet wronged believers should simply absorb brotherly offenses rather than seek retaliation and recompense (cf. Matt. 18:21-35). In the end, worldly judges will not judge the world; rather, sanctified, justified Christians will (cf. Matt. 19:28). In the meantime, the sinners-turned-saints of Corinth should settle internal disputes internally.

6:12-20 More on Immorality

When Paul says, "All things are lawful for me," he is claiming freedom from the peculiarly Jewish features of the Mosaic law, not freedom to violate God's universal moral principles. He clarifies the point by prohibiting sexual immorality, because for the Christian it unites the sacred, bodily "temple of the Holy Spirit" with sin.

7:1–11:1 Questions from the Corinthians

Paul now answers questions put to him by the Corinthian church in a letter lost to us.

7 Sex and Marriage In response to the Corinthians' questions on marriage, the apostle commends celibacy, for it maximizes the time and energy a Christian can devote to spreading the gospel. Nevertheless, he recognizes celibacy as a uniquely bestowed, divine "gift." Marriage, however, provides the right context for satisfying sexual desire and the means for avoiding sexual immorality. That no inherent evil attaches to sex itself shows in Paul's commands that husbands and wives satisfy each other sexually and that widows remarry if they lack sexual self-control.

Paul echoes Jesus' instruction when he prohibits Christian couples from divorcing, disallows remarriage with a different partner (while the first partner remains living), and counsels the reconciliation of separated spouses (vv. 10-11; cf. Matt. 5:32; 19:3-9). Through his own authority as an apostle, Paul faces an issue unaddressed by Jesus: marriages between Christians and non-Christians. He exhorts Christians to remain with their non-Christian spouses, since by the influence of the believer "sanctification" rubs off on the entire family and may result in their salvation. Divorce initiated by the unbelieving partner, however, frees the Christian ex-spouse from the "bondage" of seeking reconciliation, though Paul leaves unclear whether this freedom includes the right to remarry within the Christian community, as widows obtain (cf. v. 39).

Verses 17-34 extend Paul's commendation of celibacy and elaborate the distractions of marriage, though without characterizing marrying as wrong. Indeed, marriage constitutes no sin (vv. 36-38). Widows should be allowed to remarry "in the Lord," that is, within the Christian community (v. 39).

Paul's counsel does not equate with a purposeless approach to life; rather, he cautions against being preoccupied with seeking to escape one's plight in life (v. 21). His sense of urgency in securing the Corinthian Christians' "undistracted devotion to the Lord" may derive from an expectation of the Lord's impending return suggested by the "present crisis" of the times (vv. 26, 35).

8:1–11:1 Sacrifices to Idols Because most of the meat for sale in the markets of Corinth comes from animals sacrificed to pagan idols, the city's Christians wonder whether they should eat it or abstain. Paul understands the issue as a matter of ritual propriety, not morality, and approves in principle the eating of such meat, for the deities to which it has been sacrificed do not really exist. But the less "knowledgeable" Christian, who still believes in the reality of gods other than the Lord, sins by eating the dedicated meat, because for him the act means participating in a pagan rite and violates his conscience.

Paul resolves the question by applying the law of Christian love, which requires self-imposed limits on legitimate personal freedoms: more "knowledgeable" believers should not eat the meat if doing so might cause "weak believers" to sin by following suit or might give a wrong impression to non-Christian observers (cf. Rom. 14:1–15:13). For the same reasons, Paul forbids eating at pagan feasts (v. 10; cf. 10:1-13). Paul highlights the incompatibility of participating in such feasts and partaking of the Lord's Supper (10:14-22). He declares as sin against Christ himself the heedless tripping-up of weaker-conscienced fellow Christians.

Paul supports his exhortations by appealing to his own example of voluntarily giving up personal rights, such as marriage and material support, for his work as an apostle — rights legitimately exercised by the other apostles (9:5, 14). For Paul, the opportunity to offer the gospel free of hindering cost and to win all types of people to Christ trumps exercising his rights and personal freedoms. He likens such self-discipline to that of an athlete training to win first prize — a familiar metaphor to the Corinthians, since every three years their city hosted the Isthmian Games, outranked only by the Olympics. Isthmian competitors trained for 10 months, and event winners won a perishable pine wreath crown. Thus Paul urges Christians to live lives worthy of an "imperishable wreath," eternal life. He summarizes these instructions in 10:23–11:1.

The Holy Spirit in the New Testament

A significant difference in turning to the New Testament from the Old is the much more central role the Holy Spirit plays in the ongoing biblical story. This is related both to the early Christians' *experience* of the Spirit as now "poured out upon all people" (Acts 2:17, fulfilling Joel 2:28) and to their own *expectations* regarding the coming messianic age and God's establishing his people anew on the basis of a new covenant (Jer. 31:31-34; Ezek. 37:26-27). Thus their experience of the outpoured Spirit, and their later reflections about Jesus as the long-awaited Messiah, caused them to see these realities in the light of certain Old Testament passages that looked forward to a time when God's Spirit would be especially on the Messiah (Isa. 11:1-2), but also available to all God's people, so causing them to live (Ezek. 37:14). The fact that prophecy played such a predominant role in the life of the early church also caused them to see themselves in continuity with the Old Testament prophetic tradition.

We meet the Holy Spirit (a name derived from Isa. 63:11) at the very beginning of the Story as the one who impregnated Mary with the child Jesus (Matt. 1:18; Luke 1:35), the Jewish Messiah. The Gospel writers, especially Luke, thus attributed Jesus' earthly ministry not to his deity but to the anointing of the Spirit at his baptism (Luke 3:22). Led by the Spirit for testing in the desert (4:1), he returned to Galilee "filled with the power of the Spirit" (4:14).

His first recorded public act was to declare in his home synagogue that the prophecy of the Spirit's anointing the Messiah for mighty deeds was now being fulfilled (4:18-21). Thus Peter explains "how God anointed Jesus of Nazareth with the Holy Spirit and with power, how he went about doing good and healing all who were oppressed by the devil, for God was with him" (Acts 10:38).

Jesus himself promised that the same Holy Spirit would come upon his followers so that they would bear effective witness to him (Acts 1:5, 8), which happened at Pentecost (2:1-41), after Jesus, "exalted at the right hand of God," had "received from the Father the promise of the Holy Spirit" and "poured out this that you both see and hear" (v. 33). The rest of Acts tells how this Spirit-empowered people took the good news about Jesus from Jerusalem as far as Rome.

The Gospel of John both elaborates several aspects of the Spirit's ministry on Jesus and shows interest in the Spirit's activity in the ongoing church. The Son, therefore, is the one to whom the Father has given the Spirit without limit (John 3:34), and he in turn breathes the Spirit on his disciples (20:22), to whom the Father and Son will send the Spirit as Advocate after Jesus has returned to the Father (14:15-18; 15:26; 16:12-15). Because the Father himself is Spirit, his true worshippers worship him in the Spirit and truth (4:23). So the Spirit indwells the believer as a "fountain of life" (4:14; 7:37-39).

Revelation and 1 John then provide evidence of the ongoing work of the Spirit in the Johannine churches. Believers have received the true "anointing" of the Spirit (1 John 2:20), and in Revelation the Spirit is the source of John's visions (Rev. 1:10) and thus the one who speaks to the churches (e.g., 2:7, 11). His present ministry is envisioned as the seven eyes of the Lamb, the "seven spirits of God (= the sevenfold Spirit; cf. Isa. 11:2; Zech. 4:6, 10), sent out into all the earth" (Rev. 5:6).

The Spirit is also a part of the experience and theology of the author of Hebrews (Heb. 2:4; 6:4; 10:15) and Peter (1 Pet. 1:2, 12; 4:14). But it is the Apostle Paul who presents the most thoroughgoing understanding of the Spirit in the New Testament. The Spirit is the renewed presence of God, who creates and indwells the new temple (1 Cor. 3:16-17; 2 Cor. 6:16; Eph. 2:22), the Spirit of the Son (Gal. 4:6; Phil. 1:19) as well as the Father, who is the key to the ongoing life of the believing community. Christian conversion comes by the Spirit (1 Cor. 6:11; 2 Thess. 2:13; Tit. 3:6). He is the "down payment," the evidence and guarantee of the final glory (Eph. 1:13-14), The Spirit inhabits the community of faith and ministers in their midst with gifts, including signs and wonders, prophetic speech, teaching, and singing (1 Cor. 12:8-11; 14:1-33; Rom. 15:19). Moreover, the Spirit enables Christian living (Gal. 5:16-25; Rom. 1:1-18), thus fulfilling the righteous

Dove with olive branch; detail of funerary stone of Titzanus, Early Christian Necropolis Museum, Tarragona. *(Phoenix Data Systems, Neal and Joel Bierling)*

requirement of the Law (Rom. 8:4). It bears fruit in the believing community so that believers bear God's likeness (Gal. 5:22-23) as they are being conformed into the image of the Son (Rom. 8:29)

Both the personal nature of the Spirit and his intimate relationship with the Father and the Son in both Paul and John, plus the many Trinitarian passages in the New Testament, led the later church finally to articulate its belief in God as Trinity: One God in three divine persons.

GORDON D. FEE

11:2-16 Head Covering and Prayer

Biblical scholars have offered wide-ranging interpretations of Paul's instructions concerning the covering of one's head for prayer. Does "head" imply authority or origin (v. 3)? Is head covering a piece of cloth or long hair, hanging in loose locks or gathered and arranged on top of the head? Does the "symbol of authority" on a female pray-er's head *give* her authority to pray and prophesy in public, or does the covering symbolize a man's authority over her (v. 10)? Paul is certainly prescribing an observable distinction between male and female prayers, but the broader question concerns whether his specific instructions relate simply to his own culture or apply universally today. At minimum, the passage teaches that men and women should not dishonor the gospel by presenting themselves for public prayer in a way that offends the sensibilities of other people.

11:17-34 The Lord's Supper

Paul chastises the Corinthian church for making a mockery of the Lord's Supper by maintaining disunity even in their congregational gatherings. The apostle has already corrected them for theological divisions (1:10ff.), and now he adds an indictment for practical separateness in a forum meant to foster fellowship. Early comers to Corinthian church meals are consuming too much food and drinking till drunk, without leaving enough to nourish later arrivers who keep longer working hours. Paul exhorts the reverent observation of the Lord's Supper — a communal commemoration of Christ's death, not a feast to satisfy the stomach. He warns that approaching the Lord's table too casually, without self-examination for repentance from sins, invites divine judgment on the partaker. The words of institution quoted by Paul and attributed directly to Christ come from a tradition that predates the formulas recorded in the synoptic Gospels (vv. 24-25; cf. Matt. 26:26-28; Mark 14:22-24; Luke 22:17-20).

12–14 Spiritual Gifts

Paul's emphasis on Christian unity and fellowship continues in an extended discussion of abilities endowed by the Holy Spirit to individual Christians for the common good of the church as a whole. Paul likens the necessary church unity of variously gifted Christians to the many-membered human body, made up of functionally different but all essential parts. Spiritual gifts (12:8-10) include wisdom (the practical application of moral law for success in life), knowledge (the intellectual grasping of truth); faith (beyond belief in Christ for salvation); healing (in the holistic sense); miracles

Early Christian Churches and Their Worship

The various churches described in the New Testament are seen as worshipping communities of men and women and their families assembled in the homes of Jesus' followers. From the gatherings after Pentecost in "homes" and "upper rooms" (Acts 2:46; 5:42; 12:12; cf. 20:7-8) to Paul's writing to congregations meeting in believers' homes (e.g., Rom. 16:23; 1 Cor. 16:19; Col. 4:15; Phlm. 2) we learn that the courtyard of fairly well-to-do members provided a venue for the practice of worship. Earlier associations with the Jerusalem temple (Acts 3:1) and more importantly the Jewish synagogue (13:13-47) offered patterns of worship the early believers as messianic pietists followed, adding such distinctive elements as a convivial meal in celebration of the risen Lord, whose presence was expected and experienced. The prayer call *Marana tha*, "Come, our Lord" (1 Cor. 16:22; Didache 10:6), is evidence of this vivid awareness of the Lord's coming to meet his people (Matt. 18:20) who gathered in his name and at a time of table fellowship. Other loanwords in Aramaic or Hebrew such as "Amen," "Abba," and "Hallelujah" carry us back to the earliest Jewish Christian followers, with a sample of their table "prayers over food" preserved in Didache 9–10.

Other aspects of worship in the original Jewish Christian community are attested in Acts (baptism in the name of Jesus, teaching the basic "apostolic" beliefs [2:42], a common fund for the relief of those in need [cf. 1 Tim. 5:3-16], and united praying using the language of the Psalms and often directed to specific objectives [12:12]).

A debated issue involves the invocation of and prayer to Jesus as Lord, ranking him as the exalted one who shared the glory of the Father (Acts 7:54-60; cf. the pre-Pauline hymn incorporated into Phil. 2:6-11) as worthy of worship. The canticles of the nativity (Luke 1–2) are further evidence of the intimate association in worship of the Messiah with Israel's covenantal God. This paved the way for an enriched monotheism in which God and Jesus are co-sharers of the divine throne (Rev. 3:21; 22:3) and equally hailed as worthy to receive the church's and all creation's homage (4:11; 5:9, 12-14) with no sense of rivalry or displacement of belief in the "one God" of the synagogue's creed, the Shema (Deut. 6:4; cf. 1 Cor. 8:6).

These are the earliest roots of worship traced to the Jesus movement and its followers in Jerusalem, as recorded in Acts. If the letter of James comes from or at least mirrors this period, some features are confirmed. The practice of psalm-singing (Jas. 5:13) and the role of the teacher (3:1-12) are clear examples, with added items such as recourse to corporate prayer in time of sickness (5:13-16) with an invocation of Jesus as Lord, whose "excellent name" (2:7) suggests baptism and a high status (v. 1).

Paul

Paul's correspondence with the church at Corinth opens a window on one company of first-generation Christians in a Greco-Roman cultural setting. The phrase "when you come together" (1 Corinthians 12–14) points to the assembled people as they meet for worship "on the first day of every week" (16:2), or Sunday, then known as the Lord's day (Rev. 1:10; Didache 14:1).

Paul's consideration and critique of how the Corinthians evidently described their worship gatherings is one of the fullest accounts on record. They are acknowledged to be spiritually gifted (1 Cor. 1:7; 14:12) with an excess of vitality and dynamism, associated with "power" and "spirit." Coupled with their exploiting of "freedom" and "knowledge" (all Corinthian watchwords), their worship was in danger of getting out of control. By way of corrective, Paul's summary conclusion (14:40) makes this point: "let all be done [in worship] decently and in order."

Part of their problem may be a native Hellenistic desire to express their worship in exuberant ways (1 Cor. 14:12: they are "eager for spiritual gifts"). They also exhibit a faulty belief that the kingdom had already come in its fullness and they were sharers in the heavenly life and worship now (4:8), hence their practice of "the tongues of angels" (13:1).

Paul sensed that this situation needed to be firmly kept in check. While lifting up the charismatic expressions in word, hymn, and prayer (1 Cor. 14:15), he entered some cautions. Worship should be intelligible, hence the need for interpretation of glossolalia (speaking in tongues) and the role of the prophet (v. 3) in upbuilding the community (12:7; 14:26). Unbelievers and ungifted members should not conclude (14:23) that they are demonized (12:1-3, reflecting their Hellenistic background) but rather should be able to enter into the meaning of God's immediate presence and be impressed by God's truth (14:25), uttered by true prophets (male and female, 11:2-16; 14:33b-36 suggests women prophets who claimed to communicate a message at variance with God's word through Paul, and are rebuked to silence).

In all, the stress falls on the need for good order (1 Cor. 14:33, 40) and intelligible worship accessible to all. All gifts, motivated by love (ch. 13), should serve one purpose: edification of the community, which is Paul's key word. To that end, he appeals for a "reasonable worship" (Rom. 12:1), both well thought out and inspired by the Holy Spirit, with no distinction between "mind" and "spirit" (1 Cor. 14:15).

Asia Minor

Worship in Asia Minor is represented by the later (or post-)

Pauline letters to the Colossians and Ephesians along with 1 Peter, which is an independent witness. Churches on the Pauline foundation in Ephesus and further afield show clear signs of a developing liturgical tradition. There are still features that hark back to the earlier period, such as baptisms, prayers, hymns, and praises — all attributed to the Spirit (Eph. 5:19-20 par. Col. 3:16-17). But some notable and spontaneous expressions of worship (cf. 1 Corinthians) are absent, and the emphasis falls on the ministries of teaching and instruction, with the employment of set patterns under the direction of appointed leaders. Here the data in the Pastoral Epistles show how the churches are becoming organized and regulated with officeholders and the transmission of traditional teaching forms. Discipline and repelling deviance from the apostolic-Pauline standards by promoting sound doctrine and conducting worship in a proper manner are the call to Timothy (1 Tim. 4:11-16). False ideas are exposed and denounced by Timothy's recourse to the church's confession of faith and creedal formulas (3:16; 2 Tim. 2:11-13).

Worship functions in the pastors' congregations as a stabilizing, boundary-fixing marker. Its effect is to close ranks and define the church not so much as a charismatic community of the Spirit awaiting the imminent end time, but as a settled institution with a future here on earth, adapting to the needs of Christians in society and the family and accepting their role and station as citizens in the empire.

1 Peter handles the tension of the pilgrim people living in the world in a unique way. It pictures the church as God's worshipping temple (1 Pet. 2:1-10), yet not in any fixed way since they are "aliens and exiles" in the Dispersion (1:1; 2:11). Their worship, harking back to baptism (3:21) and enlightenment in the new birth (1:23-25), is controlled by the thought of the new Israel, God's servant and elect people (2:9-10). This same emphasis permeates Hebrews, a rhetorical sermonlike document that is part hortatory, part polemical. Throughout it uses the cultic idioms of the tabernacle

Peter's house at Capernaum, later the location for a house church.
(Wikimedia Commons)

Orant — a figure with bent arms raised in a posture of prayer — from the catacomb of Priscilla in Rome. *(Scala / Art Resource, NY)*

and the sanctuary to portray the finality and sufficiency of Christ's self-offering and sacrifice. Jesus is both victim on the earth and high priest in the heavenly sanctuary, where he continues his ministry (Heb. 7:25; 9:24; 13:10), calling his pilgrim people to engage with him in the worship of his Father. He is the model worshipper leading God's family in their hymns (2:11-12; 13:12-16).

Johannine Communities

The communities associated with John and his followers in Asia are a distinct group, as the Fourth Gospel, the Johannine letters, and the Apocalypse (Revelation) reveal. Threatened by false teachers, both Jewish and protognostic or docetic, they offer a defensive reaction to what looks to be an increasing formalizing of worship in the churches of their day at the turn of the century. Individual and personal participation in worship is the key to Johannine spirituality. Worship is not tied to sacred places and spaces; it is "in spirit and truth" (John 4:20-24) and largely independent of outward forms, locations, and ceremonials. While Jesus is baptized and endorses baptism indirectly (4:2), there is no command to incorporate baptism into the Johannine community. What matters is baptism in the Holy Spirit (1:33). Likewise, there is no institution of the Last Supper, though Jesus does share a meal. Rather, he discourses on the bread of life at Capernaum (ch. 6), just as he had spoken of the living water to the woman at the well (ch. 4). This governs John's concept of worship as individualized communion with the living Lord, irrespective of outer forms. It is the reality behind the outward pattern that John accentuates (1 John 4:7-12).

Such a variety of worship styles and practices can hardly be systematized into a set pattern. The churches adapted their worship to the cultural and theological needs of the hour, and there is development within the canonical record and beyond. Yet certain "constants" remain to be observed: the living Lord is at the heart of all worship, whether in adoration, petition, or devotion, as well as ceremonial practices such as initiation into his death and resurrection (Rom. 6:1-14) or taking bread and cup in remembrance of his death and victory in the coming kingdom (1 Cor. 10:16; 11:23-26). The role of the Holy Spirit is central both to check excesses and to activate and enliven all the exercises of public worship. The keynote, if one such emphasis may be said to predominate, is that of celebration in joyous acknowledgment of the Redeemer's coming from God as God to die on the cross and be elevated to the Father's presence. Then in anticipation of God's future triumph the church in worship reaches out to embrace that future and bring it near.

For Further Reading

Bauckham, Richard. "The Worship of Jesus." In *The Climax of Prophecy*. Edinburgh: T. & T. Clark, 1994, 118-49.

Bradshaw, Paul F. *The Search for the Origins of Christian Worship*. 2nd ed. New York: Oxford University Press, 2002.

Dugmore, C. W. *The Influence of Synagogue on the Divine Office*. 1944. Repr. Westminster: Faith, 1964.

Hurtado, Larry W. *At the Origins of Christian Worship*. Grand Rapids: Wm. B. Eerdmans, 2000.

———. *One God, One Lord*. Philadelphia: Fortress, 1988.

Martin, Ralph P. *Worship in the Early Church*. Grand Rapids: Wm. B. Eerdmans, 1975.

———. "Patterns of Worship in the New Testament Church." *JSNT* 37 (1989): 59-85.

RALPH P. MARTIN

(lit., "acts of power," particularly in the spiritual realm, such as the performance of exorcisms), prophecy (words of God for specific situations), spiritual discernment ("distinguishing" between the forces of good and evil), tongues (the ability to speak in unlearned human languages, not ecstatic utterances), and interpretation of tongues ("translation," necessary for personal and communal edification). Hierarchically ordered gifts include apostleship (being "sent" by God for a specific mission), prophecy, teaching (in religious and spiritual matters), miracle-working, healing, helps (supporting tasks), administration, and tongues (12:28).

The apostle encourages the prayerful pursuit of spiritual giftedness but elevates love as the overarching principle that gives spiritual gifts their value, that should govern their exercise, and that will outlast them in the end. Paul's profile of active love describes what it does and does not do, not how it does or does not feel (13:4-8). These verses make clear that love takes the initiative to overcome feelings when necessary for righteous behavior.

Paul devotes most of chapter 14 to comparing the communal benefits of tongues and prophecy. He commends prophecy as the superior gift because of its greater capacity for corporate enlightenment, exhortation, consolation, and witness to unbelievers (vv. 3, 24-25). Since the Christian community can benefit from tongues only through an interpreter, and since the purpose of spiritual gifts consists in the common good of the church (12:7), Paul limits the public exercise of tongues to occasions on which an interpreter is present to assist the congregation in understanding. Further guidelines ensure orderliness so that all in attendance can hear and thus worship in *mind* as well as in spirit. (Verses 34-35 appear to address a specific problem in the Corinthian church, perhaps women interrupting worship with questions; cf. 11:5.)

15 The Nature of Resurrection

Paul's last major corrective to the ethnically mixed Corinthian church takes up the issue of resurrection of the body, in which most Jews believed but most Gentiles did not. Paul summarizes the gospel with emphasis on the bodily resurrection of Jesus confirmed by his postresurrection appearances to a great many people, a number of whom Paul names and most of whom are living witnesses at the time Paul writes. The apostle's own eyewitnessing of the resurrected Christ lends firsthand credibility to his claims.

Paul points out the futility of faith in Christ apart from belief in the resurrection of the dead — not only Christ's resurrection, but also that of believers. The goal of salvation history has consisted in reversing the fatal effects of sin; so if death gets the last word for believers in Christ, they have exercised faith for nothing. Paul stresses, therefore, that the resurrection of Christ to eternal life represents not a unique event but a preview of what is in store for believers. Therein lies the hope of the gospel. The death sentence earned by Adam for all humanity is reversed in renewal for eternal life made possible by Christ's self-sacrificial conquest of death.

"Baptism on behalf of the dead" (vv. 29-34) may mean that Christians were undergoing baptism on behalf of loved ones who died as unbelievers in order to achieve salvation for them after death and/or to make reunion with them possible in the afterlife. Whatever the underlying reason for the practice, Paul mentions it not to evaluate its effectiveness but to expose its incompatibility with disbelief in bodily resurrection. Corinthian Christians who deny

Marketplace (agora) at Corinth, showing a number of small shops with the Acrocorinth beyond.
(www.HolyLandPhotos.org)

the resurrection are acting irrationally by getting baptized "for" the dead. Further, Paul's own self-endangerment to spread the gospel constitutes irrational behavior if no resurrection will occur. He and the rest of humanity might just as well enjoy this one-and-only life while they can.

The apostle answers with an analogy from nature persistent skeptics insistent on knowing the mechanics of resurrection and the characteristics of the resurrected body. As a mere seed dies before transformation into a flourishing plant, so the earthly human body dies before transformation into a superior, resurrected "spiritual" body — still physical, as with the resurrected Christ, but with a "heavenly image" suited for immortality (v. 49). Yet the perishable bodies of believers living at the time of Jesus' second coming will undergo this essential change without dying (vv. 51-52). Paul's denial that mortal "flesh and blood" can inherit the eternal kingdom of God only makes sense; thus the necessity of believers' resurrection in immortal, imperishable bodies. By robbing death of ultimate victory, resurrection affirms the value of putting faith into practice in this earthly, mortal life.

16 Closing Instructions and Greetings

Paul closes the letter with practical instructions and greetings. On the eastward trek from Syrian Antioch through Asia Minor, the apostle has been collecting relief funds for the impoverished church in Jerusalem, and he instructs the Corinthians to start saving their contributions before he arrives for an extended visit. Paul's post-Pentecost exit from Ephesus will follow an itinerary through Macedonia (northern Greece), where he earlier established churches in Philippi and Thessalonica, and on to Corinth in southern Greece.

In case Timothy gets there first, Paul exhorts the Corinthians to treat his pastoral protégé right. Apollos's delayed return to Corinth may relate to the church conflicts described in 3:1-9.

Paul's commendation of the "household of Stephanas" recognizes this Corinthian family as the first Christian converts in southern Greece (cf. 1:16). In passing on greetings from his fellow Jewish tentmakers Aquila and Prisca (short for Priscilla), who landed in Corinth after being ousted from Rome (Acts 18:1-3), Paul reveals that the couple has moved to Ephesus, where they host a church in their home.

The penning of the greetings in Paul's "own hand" (v. 21) authenticates the letter, mostly written down by a secretary — apparently Sosthenes (1:1). The apostle's use of "Maranatha," Aramaic for "O [our] Lord, come!" testifies to the early acknowledgment of Christ's deity among Aramaic-speaking Christians.

2 Corinthians

More than a year after composing 1 Corinthians, Paul writes 2 Corinthians from Macedonia. In the interim he has made a second trip to Corinth, but the problems in the church persisted. After returning to Ephesus he wrote a third, now lost letter expressing sorrow over that visit and the strained relationship between church founder and congregation (2:1-4; 7:8). 2 Corinthians is his fourth letter to this fellowship of Christians.

Background

The events leading to Paul's composition of 2 Corinthians involve his coworker Titus, who has recently delivered to the congregation Paul's "sorrowful letter" prescribing church discipline for his primary opponent (2:5-10). Paul finds it impossible to remain in Ephesus awaiting Titus's report on the Corinthians' response, so he leaves for the Asian port city of Troas to intercept the emissary on his return trip. But Paul finds it impossible to remain in Troas too, so he sails to Macedonia (northern Greece), where he finally meets up with the returning Titus.

The Letter

Titus's report of Corinthian compliance with Paul's instructions brings great joy and relief to the apostle and occasions this emotion-laden letter, which poignantly reveals Paul's feelings about himself, his ministry, and his relationship with his church "children." In anticipation of his upcoming, third visit to Corinth (12:14; 13:1-2), Paul also gives instruction for the church's contribution to his relief fund for the impoverished church in Jerusalem.

Because the last four chapters of 2 Corinthians display an overall change in tone, from joy and relief to a defense of Paul's apostolic authority, some scholars consider chapters 10–13

at least a part of the lost "sorrowful letter." More probably, here Paul targets a different contingent of the Corinthian church — the minority who persist in opposing him.

1:1-14 Celebrating Comfort after Affliction

Paul names as his coauthor Timothy, whom he recruited for ministry during the previous missionary journey (Acts 16:1-5). The "saints throughout Achaia" include converts in Athens, Cenchreae, and perhaps other cities of southern Greece in which Paul pursued evangelistic activities (Acts 17:16–18:23). His signature greeting, "Grace and peace," strikes a chord with ethnically mixed audiences of Gentiles and Jews.

Paul begins by celebrating the comfort of God, which counterbalances afflictions endured for the sake of Christ and enables him to comfort others who are suffering. The greatness of Paul's joy over such comfort stems from the seriousness of the life-threatening afflictions he and his companions have recently experienced in the province of Asia. The leaders' upstanding conduct through such trials gives good reason for the Corinthian church to take pride in their association with Paul and company, as the evangelists also take pride in the spiritually maturing congregation at Corinth.

1:15–2:11 Repairing Strained Relationships

The painful nature of Paul's second visit to Corinth assumed in chapter 2 — an apparently unsuccessful attempt to correct problems in the church — caused Paul to cancel a planned, subsequent trip so as to spare the Corinthians further hurt stemming from their then-strained relationship with him.

Paul also refers to a now-lost "sorrowful" letter giving the same reason for keeping his distance — his love for the disaffected Corinthians. But the church's disciplining of Paul's primary (unidentified) opponent has sufficiently repaired their relationship; so Paul urges the majority to emulate his own forgiveness by reincorporating the offender into their community. Such forgiveness robs Satan of the advantage inherent in fractured Christian fellowship.

2:12-17 Anxiety Relieved

Paul recalls the intensity of his anxiety over his previously strained relationship with the Corinthian Christians, his impatience in awaiting news from his assistant Titus, sent to Corinth to deliver the sorrowful letter (vv. 12-13), and his joyous relief at the positive report (vv. 14-17; cf. ch. 7). The image of participation in a divinely led triumphal procession stems from the parading of victorious Roman generals through the streets of Rome with captives trailing behind and incense perfuming the air in thanks to the gods. To unbelievers, bearers of the gospel represent an aroma "from death to death" (as the smell of incense reminded captives of death in battle and the end of life as they knew it), for rejection of the message by people spiritually dead in their sins seals their death for eternity. Conversely, those who accept the gospel become spiritually enlivened now for eternal life.

3 Unveiling Salvation

Just as Paul and the Corinthian church have good reason for mutual pride, so also does each party embody a living letter of recommendation for the other — letters written by none other than Christ himself (vv. 1-3; cf. 1:14). The imagery contrasts with Moses' receipt of the Law on tablets of stone — a contrast Paul develops further by asserting the superiority of the new covenant based on its permanence, as opposed to the impermanence of the old covenant symbolized by the fading of glory from Moses' face (Exod. 34:29-35). Paul refers to the Mosaic law as the "ministry of death" and the "ministry of condemnation" because it awakens the human conscience but cannot elicit perfect obedience for salvation. Getting a clear look at the glory of the Lord through the Holy Spirit, instead of a veiled impression of righteousness through

the Law, transforms the beholder into the Lord's glorious image. Thus the "ministry of righteousness" brings freedom from the Law.

4:1–7:16 Ministry and Motivation

Paul and his companions persevere in their ministry despite the rejection of the gospel by people whose minds "the god of this world" (Satan) has blinded to its "light" and despite the subjection of their mortal bodies ("earthen vessels") to all kinds of affliction. The apostle characterizes the evangelists' ministry as one of voluntary service to Christ and describes their spirits as indomitable. In fact, the entrusting of the gospel "treasure" to mere mortals ensures that the glory for its eternal life–producing success gets credited to God alone (4:7). Paul's confidence in the resurrection (cf. 1 Corinthians 15) provides the basis for his discounting temporary earthly afflictions in expectation of an incomparably glorious eternity (4:14, 17-18).

The ancient Greeks disparaged the body as a burden for the soul (Acts 17:16-34). In chapter 5, Paul disparages the *mortal* body ("earthly tent") but celebrates the eternal, heavenly body believers will inherit when resurrected. He says the soul need not get naked but only change clothes. Resurrection promises this better body, but the final judgment requires pleasing of God while still "clothed" in the mortal one.

All believers, while still in their mortal bodies, enjoy inner re-creation resulting from their restoration to a right relationship with God ("reconciliation") through the substitutionary, sacrificial death and resurrection of Christ. Paul urges the re-created Corinthians to repay this ill-deserved favor (= grace) of God by behaving in ways that do not discredit the ministry to which they have responded — a ministry that continues to entail affliction and hardship for their long-suffering spiritual fathers, the apostle and his associates.

The "discrediting" conduct prohibited by the apostle seems to center around forging ties with unbelievers for purposes Paul leaves ambiguous (6:11–7:1; cf. 1 Cor. 8:9-13). Paul preempts the complaint that his instruction is restrictive by characterizing the Corinthians' lingering affection for worldly associations as the real restrainer, for partnering with pagans hinders the Christian's progress toward holiness (cf. 1 Cor. 5:9-13). "Belial" (6:15), a mythological term later identified with the Devil, usually represents "wickedness" in biblical usage.

In chapter 7, Paul celebrates his relief at the restoration of his relationship with the Corinthians as reported by Titus. The comforting news makes the apostle a joyful sufferer in ministry and reverses his initial regret over sending to the Corinthians a now lost letter, which first caused them sorrow but ended by evoking their repentance.

8–9 Funds for the Mother Church

The apostle's restored confidence in the Corinthian congregation emboldens him to announce a financial challenge: match the Macedonian churches in joyful and generous donations to the relief fund he is collecting for the mother church in Jerusalem. The Macedonian congregations, which include Philippi, Thessalonica, and Berea, have given "beyond their means." Although the Corinthians' year-old commitment to contribute has been an inspiration, Paul emphasizes an even stronger foundation for charitable giving: the example of Christ, who impoverished himself by coming in human form and giving himself on the cross for the eternal enrichment of humanity. Paul further points out that the Corinthians might someday need similar aid from Jerusalem (8:14). What the Corinthians "sow" they will "reap" in blessing (9:6).

Paul promises to the generous and cheerful giver "abundance in every good work." He is sending to Corinth an advance team including Titus and Christian "brothers" from Macedonia to help the church complete its fund drive before he arrives. The handling of the money by fellow workers protects the apostle from the appearance of extortion (evidently charged by his opponents; cf. 11:7-15, 20) and suspected embezzlement (cf. his defense in 12:16-18). Thus he will avoid even the appearance of evil (8:20-21).

10–13 Stern Words to Persistent Critics

Paul now takes a dramatically different tone, probably because he is targeting a different audience — his opponents, not his supporters as in chapters 1–9. Unmistakable sarcasm and irony pepper this forceful apology of his ministry.

10 Countering False Charges By characterizing Christ himself as meek and gentle, Paul turns into a compliment the complaint of his opponents that he is meek in person but bold "when absent" (in his letters). Paul's previous lack of success apparently led to the charge of cowardice by his critics. Paul denies the charge by asserting his readiness to "punish" them if he must (v. 6), preferring to exercise his apostolic authority to enlighten rather than reprimand, refusing to ignore their criticism (v. 8), and claiming that he is the same in word and deed (v. 11). For now, he cares only for God's ap-

Temple of Apollo at Corinth; 6th century B.C. *(www.HolyLandPhotos.org)*

proval. Self-commendation counts for nothing (v. 18).

11 Winning at a Fool's Game Paul expresses his fear that the Corinthians are falling easy prey to preachers of an unorthodox version of the gospel — "super-apostles," whose claims to superiority Paul rejects. His observation that his "untrained" speech does not betray a lack of knowledge warns the Corinthians against forsaking his pure and simple gospel for the seemingly supercharged versions of apostolic frauds. Thus the battle for Christian "purity" rages over the mind, not just the body.

Paul confronts the criticism that he would not accept wages for his ministerial work (vv. 7-11). The Corinthians have taken offense at his determination not to burden them financially (cf. 1 Cor. 9:11-18). They assume he loves the Macedonians more because he took their money. The outrageous assumption only steels Paul's resolve to maintain his distinctiveness from false apostles, who take advantage of the Corinthians without their even noticing. Paul sarcastically admits his weakness in perpetrating such offenses (v. 21). But he will engage the false apostles in a round of their foolish boasting game — and will play to win! If they claim an impeccable pedigree, so does he. If they claim servanthood to Christ, he claims superior servanthood, not by virtue of his accomplishments but by way of his weaknesses: the quantity of his afflictions, the intensity of his sufferings, the gravity of his endangerment, the comprehensiveness of his perils, and the constant weightiness of his concern for his converts.

12:1-13 Boasting at Arm's Length The necessity of Paul's profitless boasting stems from his Corinthian opponents' unfavorable comparison of him to the self-promoting superapostles. In verses 1-7 he recounts a past vision to prove his apostolic competitiveness — even his superiority (v. 7) — in the arena of revelations. His being caught up to the "third heaven" signifies being conveyed to the very presence of God. But since the transport to paradise shows him divinely favored rather than humanly fragile, he down-

plays the ecstatic experience in several ways: he speaks of himself only in the third person, emphasizes that the event took place a long time ago, dismisses the question of whether the revelation occurred in or out of body, and follows up the report with an immediate mention of his "thorn in the flesh," sent to keep him humble. The ambiguous affliction, which God thrice refused to remove, serves as a constant reminder to Paul that his apostolic strength lies in his human frailty, which unlike overconfidence does not downplay the power of God. Thus he establishes firm ground for refusing to boast, save in his weaknesses.

Paul ends his fool's speech by asserting that the signs, wonders, and miracles he performed among the Corinthians should have convinced them of his apostolic authenticity (v. 12). He reprimands his opponents for compelling him to brag when he had already proven worthy of their commendation, and he sarcastically requests their forgiveness for failing to charge money for his ministry.

12:14–13:13 Concern for Corinth Claiming responsibility for the welfare of the Corinthian Christians, Paul warns that he will not accept communal strife and unrepentance — which he as their spiritual parent will find personally humiliating. By appealing to the Mosaic requirement of two or three witnesses to establish legal truth (Deut. 19:15), Paul characterizes this visit as the final witness to the sincerity of the Corinthians' Christian commitment. He is prepared to do whatever necessary to punish persistent sinners, but would prefer using his God-given apostolic authority for its intended purpose of enlightenment. Let the Corinthians worry less about the spiritual condition of Paul and more about their own (v. 5).

In closing, Paul returns to the theme of taking comfort (v. 11; cf. 1:3-7). Against the Corinthians' inclination to cliquishness, he encourages like-mindedness and Christian unity (cf. 1 Cor. 1:10–4:21), demonstrated in their greeting each other with a "holy kiss" and grounded in their fellowship in the Holy Spirit. The last verse — 13:13 — is the only biblical benediction that includes all three persons of the Godhead.

From Jesus to Paul

Jesus taught and acted with messianic authority that led his hearers to pay attention. The need to memorize and spread his message began during his own ministry, when he sent out the Twelve and the Seventy with the good news of the kingdom. The presence of Greek-speaking members in the church at Jerusalem ("Hellenists"; Acts 6) meant that traditions about his words and deeds had to be translated into Greek very soon after Pentecost. The continuing presence of apostles in Jerusalem ensured the preservation and a measure of control of these traditions.

We do not know whether Paul ever heard Jesus speak, but he had many opportunities to learn about him. As a Pharisee, Saul of Tarsus would have heard of his teachings through the Pharisaic "grapevine" and from the testimonies of Christians he persecuted. After his encounter with Christ on the Damascus road (probably less than two years after the crucifixion), Paul presumably would have wanted to discover all that he could about him (Phil. 3:8, 10). As a new Christian, joining in worship with Christians at Damascus he would have shared his own story and heard the stories of others. Paul lived and taught for at least a year in Antioch, where refugees from Jerusalem had been among the first preachers, bringing with them the message of Jesus (Acts 11:19-26). His visits to Jerusalem enabled him to learn firsthand from Peter,

James, and others (Gal. 1:18-19; 2:9). Finally, his close association with people such as Barnabas, Silvanus, and John Mark, who knew the traditions from Jerusalem, would have given Paul many occasions to deepen his knowledge of the earliest Christian beliefs.

Some have argued that Paul was so passionate about the Christ he knew by faith that he had little interest in the Jesus of history. They note that Paul rarely alludes to Jesus' teachings and says nothing of his miracles or parables. On this view, the apostle was only interested in the powerful, risen Christ that would appeal to Gentiles rather than the Jesus depicted in the synoptic Gospels who taught more explicitly about the kingdom than about himself.

But Paul shows no evidence of a distinction between the risen Christ and the pre-Easter Jesus. Instead of viewing the crucified Christ in a worldly way, believers are to understand the significance of the cross by the Spirit (cf. 2 Cor. 5:16). Before coming to faith in him, Paul believed Jesus could not be the Messiah because he was a criminal, under the curse pronounced in the Old Testament on anyone hung on a tree; now Paul saw that the curse was part of God's plan of salvation and worthy of the resurrection (Deut. 21:23; Gal. 3:13).

In Galatians, Paul emphasized that his gospel came through revelation from God because at stake was his insistence that

Gentiles need not become Jews to be members of God's people. His authority was being questioned by people who asserted that non-Jews had to be circumcised and keep the food laws and calendar in order to be true Christians (Gal. 1:6-9; 2:11-14; 6:12-13; Acts 15:1-5). Apart from this issue, Paul's gospel was the same as that of those who believed before him (Gal. 1:23; cf. 1 Cor. 15:11). Writing to the Corinthians, Paul describes his gospel of the death and resurrection of Christ as a tradition he had received and passed on (1 Cor. 15:3-7). Other than not requiring Gentile Christians to take on the distinctive Jewish customs, there is no evidence that Paul's gospel differed from that preached by the most conservative Jewish Christians in Jerusalem.

The rarity of direct references to traditions about Jesus in Paul's letters is actually characteristic of all New Testament epistles and most apostolic fathers until the middle of the 2nd century. We find very few direct quotations of Jesus, few references to his deeds, and no mention of his parables in any of the earliest Christian writings apart from the Gospels, yet we know that these Christians treasured the stories and sayings of their Lord. So Paul is not unusual in this regard. His letters, like those of other early writers, are full of echoes of Jesus' teachings (cf. Rom. 12:14; 13:8-10; 14:14). He simply does not identify them as such.

Paul and other apostles presupposed that the recipients of their letters already knew basic traditions about Jesus (cf. Rom. 6:17). Their epistles were not sent to establish the fundamentals of the Christian faith, but to address specific pastoral issues and needs. Speaking with apostolic authority and an awareness that the Spirit of Jesus spoke through them, the apostles apparently felt no need to refer to Jesus' teachings to underscore their exhortations. Furthermore, Christ's death on the cross and his resurrection eclipsed in significance any particular act of mercy or miracle prior to his passion. So it is perhaps not so surprising to see early Christian writers pointing to these crucial events rather than to lesser deeds. That is not to say that the sayings and ministry of Jesus were unimportant to them, only that letters were not the place to convey these traditions. Paul and other early Christians emphasized the person of Jesus even more than his teachings because the resurrection had vindicated him as Messiah, who brought salvation through his death on the cross. Thus the Proclaimer became the Proclaimed.

For Further Reading

Barclay, John M. G. "Jesus and Paul." In *Dictionary of Paul and His Letters,* ed. Gerald F. Hawthorne, Ralph P. Martin, and Daniel G. Reid. Downers Grove: InterVarsity, 1993, 492-503.

Kim, Seyoon. "Jesus, Sayings of.". In *Dictionary of Paul and His Letters,* ed. Hawthorne, Martin, and Reid, 474-92.

Still, Todd D. *Jesus and Paul Reconnected.* Grand Rapids: Eerdmans, 2008.

Wenham, David. *Paul: Follower of Jesus or Founder of Christianity?* Grand Rapids: Wm. B. Eerdmans, 1995.

———. *Paul and the Historical Jesus.* Cambridge: Grove, 1998.

MICHAEL B. THOMPSON

Galatians

Originally, "Galatia" referred to an area of north-central Asia Minor settled by three Celtic tribes. The province of Galatia established by the Romans grew to include adjacent territory to the south and extended almost to the Mediterranean coast. In the book of Acts, Luke records Paul's establishment of Christian churches in four cities of or near southern Galatia during his first missionary journey (Acts 13:14–14:23). On the apostle's second journey he might have traveled to northern Galatia too, but Luke does not specify any north Galatian cities visited by Paul.

Background

Paul's letter to the Galatians addresses multiple church congregations under pressure by "Judaizers," who were preaching the need for Gentile Christians to observe the Mosaic law specifically with regard to circumcision — the central issue addressed by the Jerusalem Council in Acts 15. In Galatians Paul vehemently opposes the Judaizers, but nowhere does he invoke the momentous decision of the Council in support of his message of salvation solely by God's grace through faith in Jesus Christ. The omission seems odd if Paul wrote the letter after the meeting occurred; therefore, many scholars believe he composed Galatians after his first journey ended but before the Council met, and that his visit to Jerusalem recorded in chapter 2 corresponds to the famine relief visit of Acts 11:27-30. Since Paul began his second missionary journey only after the Jerusalem Council took place, this epistle must address churches in southern Galatia only. Other scholars point to the striking thematic parallels between Galatians and Romans (written a dozen years after the Council) to argue for a later dating of Galatians, which allows for an audience that includes Christians in the northern part of the

province. In this case, Paul's visit to Jerusalem in chapter 2 takes place at the time of the Council (ca. A.D. 49).

Message

The questions of date and audience, however, in no way obscure the clear message of this epistle: the redemptive work of Christ on the cross nullifies for Jew and Gentile alike any partially works-based program for salvation and renders equally redeemed all who exercise faith in Jesus. That this freedom from religious legalism does not give license for moral abandon shows in Paul's exhortations to Spirit-led conduct and Christian unity.

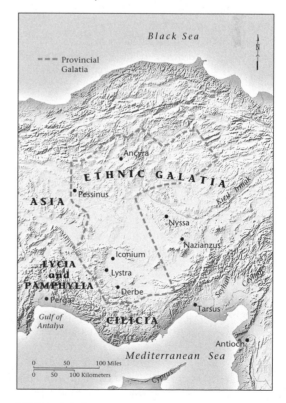

The Two Galatias

1–2 Paul Establishes His Authority

Forgoing his typical greeting of thanksgiving, Paul wastes no time in asserting his divine appointment as an apostle and establishing the authority of the gospel as preached by him. His urgency stems from his audience's acceptance of a distorted version of the gospel, which renders it void of its meaning, "good news." So strongly does Paul oppose the misrepresentation that he invokes a curse on the perpetrator, hypothetically includes himself in the curse, and repeats the invocation. The reason for Paul's rhetorical questions concerning from whom he seeks approval, God or human beings (1:10), becomes clear in 6:12 and 6:17: those preaching the distorted gospel do so to avoid persecution by otherwise disapproving *people,* while Paul bears on his body the scars of persecution that prove his effort to please *God* by preaching the pure gospel, whatever the personal consequences. The apostle's self-designation as a "bondservant" of Christ acknowledges his voluntary subservience to the master who freed him from sin.

To establish the authenticity and authority of his gospel message, Paul cites his past persecution of believers and his zeal for Judaism as evidence that his unlikely apostleship originated with God, not humans. Paul did not learn the gospel from his colleagues in Jerusalem; rather, God gave the gospel to him, beginning with a conversion-generating revelation of Jesus (Acts 9:1-9). His limited contact with only Cephas (the Aramaic equivalent of "Peter") and James, the brother of Jesus, seals the divine origin of Paul's message. That believers in Judea knew the apostle to the Gentiles only by reputation yet celebrated his evangelistic activity in Syria and Cilicia (Paul's native territory in southeastern Asia Minor) supports the divine bestowal of his apostolic authority.

Only after 14 years (either from his conversion or his initial trip to visit Peter) did Paul return to Jerusalem and share with the city's leading Jewish Christians the particulars of his gospel for the Gentiles. The refusal of the Jewish believers to require the circumcision of Paul's Greek associate Titus and the mention of Christian liberty under threat (2:3-4) combine to suggest the issue at stake: whether conversion to Christianity by Gentiles requires their obedience to the Mosaic law (as did conversion to Judaism). Paul's preaching among the Gentiles has already answered an emphatic "No!" That the leading Jewish Christians of Jerusalem did not require him to alter his message ("contributed nothing") shows their support, and the extension of the "right hand of fellowship" by the apostolic "pillars" of the Jewish Christian church (2:9) shows them opposed to the "Judaizing" crowd.

Peter's joining with Gentiles in table fellowship during a visit to Antioch (Acts 10) supports Paul's advocacy of Christian freedom from the Law — even for Jews. But Peter's recoiling from the Gentiles on the arrival of other Jews from Jerusalem (possibly Judaizers themselves) drew public reproval from Paul for hypocrisy. His sermonic rebuke asserted believers' justification (consideration as righteous) by God's grace (ill-deserved favor) apart from works of the Law, solely because they exercise faith in Christ, who fulfilled the righteous requirement of the Law on their behalf. Adding obedience to the Law as a requirement for salvation denies the sufficiency of Christ's atoning work on the cross — which alone achieved what the Law could not.

3–4 Faith over Law

Paul reminds the Galatians that they received the Holy Spirit — the sign of their salvation — by exercising faith in Christ, not by performing works of the Law. "Ending with the flesh" (seeking salvation through the Law) amounts to foolishness. The apostle's position is not some current theological fad; rather, it originates with Abraham, the forefather of the Hebrew nation. More than four centuries before giving the Law through Moses, God made his promise to Abraham, who himself was not righteous but whose faith God regarded as righteousness. Inheriting the promised blessings, therefore, does not depend on biological descent from Abraham; instead, the promises pass to his only truly righteous descendant, Jesus Christ, and to people who exercise Abraham-like faith in him. Till the coming of Christ, who through his own death killed the curse that doomed humanity, the Law served as a temporary guardian to expose our inability to obey God perfectly and thereby earn salvation even in part (3:23-24). Rather than nullifying the faith-based covenant with Abraham, the Law itself is relieved of its role by emancipating faith in Christ, the necessity of which the Law points out and the availability of which extends to all people indiscriminately.

Paul extends the metaphor of the Law as guardian of spiritual minors, whose moral immaturity postpones the receipt of their rightful inheritance and thus relegates them to the practical status of a slave (4:1-11). Like the date set by a father for his heir's coming of age, so came the "fullness of time," when through the redemption from the Law effected by Christ God made possible our adoption as mature heirs qualified to receive the covenantal promises through faith. Why are the Galatians reverting to an inferior status by re-enslaving themselves to the "elemental" principles of the Law, including the observation of Jewish feasts and festivals (4:10)? Let them embrace his current admonition with the same enthusiasm they showed at their conversion.

Paul ends his argument with an allegory from the very Law to which the Galatians are returning. Hagar, the slave of Abraham's wife, represents the covenant made at Mount Sinai, headquartered at the Jerusalem temple, and perpetuated by Hagar's descendant "slaves" of the Law — left out of the covenantal will. The "free woman" (Abraham's wife, Sarah) represents Christianity, the covenant of faith headquartered in the "Jerusalem above" (heaven). Sarah's free heirs, though now persecuted by their Law-enslaved kin, will alone inherit the promises made to Abraham because of his faith.

5–6 Fleshing Out Christian Freedom

For a Gentile male, the first step in conversion to Judaism was circumcision as the initial act of obedience to the Law. The Jewish Christian "troublers" of the Galatians are pushing circumcision as a requirement for conversion to Christianity too; so Paul warns that saying "yes"

to circumcision implies the obligation of keeping the entire Law. To submit to circumcision, therefore, means choosing a life of "slavery" to the Law and rendering personally irrelevant the redemptive work of Christ, which inspires Spirit-led obedience to the "law" of love (cf. 6:2, "the law of Christ"). Paul's ire at the Judaizers surfaces in his wish that they castrate themselves (instead of preaching circumcision to the Galatians, whose Greek way of thinking viewed circumcision as a mutilation that marred the ideal of male physical beauty; 5:12). The "works of the flesh" (5:19-21) and the contrasting "fruit of the Spirit" (vv. 22-23) emphasize behavior that respectively fractures and fosters Christian unity (cf. vv. 15, 26). To "live" by the Spirit (5:25) means to gain eternal life; to "walk" by the Spirit (v. 16) means to respond to the promise of eternal life with Spirit-led conduct during one's earthly life.

Christian community requires the gentle correction of "transgressors" (those who carry out "deeds of the flesh," as in 5:19-21) to restore them to fellowship and the communal bearing of "burdens" (hardships) now in the knowledge that each individual will answer for his or her individual conduct at the final judgment (6:2, 5). The obligation to provide economic support for teachers of the gospel surfaces in 6:6. Paul adds these ethical admonitions to correct the misimpression that Christian freedom from the Law equals license for lack of personal restraint.

Paul endorses the letter as an authoritative document by finishing it off in his "own hand" after having dictated it to a secretary. He underscores his stance against the gospel-damaging propaganda of Judaizers motivated by self-protection and self-promotion. Fearing their own persecution, they inflict on the Galatians the mark of slavery to the Law (circumcision). That Paul's priority is not his personal, physical welfare but the religious welfare of his spiritual children shows in the marks of Christian freedom he bears on his body — scars of persecution that prove the purity both of his motives and his message.

Ephesians

Ephesians appears as the first of the three Prison Epistles, so called because their claimed author, Paul, was imprisoned at the time of writing, probably in Rome (Acts 28:30-31). Thematically, Ephesians closely parallels Colossians in developing the metaphor of Christ as the head of his body the church, thus stressing the churchly unity of Gentile and Jewish believers. Paul may have written the letters around the same time and had his colleague Tychicus deliver them on the same trip to western Asia Minor (cf. 6:21-22; Col. 4:7-9).

Background

Ephesians targets a primarily Gentile audience, but the letter gives few clues as to what prompted its composition. Most of Paul's letters to churches deal with specific issues of Christian belief and practice facing particular congregations. But Ephesians displays a general, theologically reflective character that dominates even the exhortations of chapters 3–6, and the epistle appears not to address any single church congregation, let alone its current problems. That the oldest and best manuscripts of Ephesians lack the geographical designation "at Ephesus" (1:1) combines with the apparent personal unfamiliarity of Paul and the audience (who have only "heard of" each other; 1:15; 3:2) to suggest that the letter did not specifically address the church in the Asian provincial capital of Ephesus — a church founded, nurtured, and intimately known by the apostle himself (Acts 19; 20:17-38). Instead, Ephesians probably served as a circular missive (like Galatians) passed between churches not founded by Paul in the vicinity of Ephesus, to which city Tychicus may have taken the original copy of the letter.

Authorship

Because Ephesians differs distinctively from Paul's other New Testament epistles not only regarding occasion and audience but also literary style, many modern scholars believe that a disciple or admirer of Paul authored the epistle pseudonymously. Although the letter clearly claims authorship by the apostle (1:1), and early church tradition corroborates the claim, the common and accepted ancient practice of ascribing authorship to a prominent figure leaves open that possibility.

1 Celebrating God's Grace

In introducing himself to an ethnically mixed but mostly Gentile audience, the majority of whom he has probably never met, Paul identifies himself solely in terms of his apostleship to Christ. His signature greeting, "Grace and peace," strikes a chord with both Gentile and Jewish "saints" (Christians).

Paul celebrates salvation for eternal life as initiated by the extravagant grace (ill-deserved favor) of God the Father, mediated by the redemptive self-sacrifice of Jesus Christ, and guaranteed by the gift of the Holy Spirit to believers (vv. 3-14). Their receipt of "every spiritual blessing in the heavenly places" (v. 3) emphasizes the immediacy of their sharing in the exaltation of the ascended Christ, while the serving of the Holy Spirit as a "pledge of our inheritance" promises the full fruition of redemption (ransom) in the form of eternal life. Mosaic law provided for redemption from sins through the sacrifice of animals, the spilling of whose blood (representing life) substituted for forfeiting the sinner's life. The rite prefigures God's ultimate redemption of morally doomed humanity through Christ's self-sacrifice, which suffices once and for all. The doctrine of "election," God's singling out individuals for salvation, emerges in verses 4-5, 11 but does not of necessity rob elect individuals of their free will or cancel their responsibility to respond to the gospel with faith (v. 13). On God's adoption of believers as heirs (v. 5), cf. Gal. 4:1-7.

The apostle expresses thankfulness for his audience of believers (vv. 15-23). Spiritual wisdom (the practical outworking of moral knowledge) and understanding form the core of Paul's intercessory prayer for these Christians. He encourages them with assertions of the great power of God conveyed to believers through the resurrection, ascension, and exaltation of Christ, who rules supremely and for eternity. The church as his "body" shares in that rule (cf. Rom. 12:1-8; 1 Corinthians 12).

2 Salvation by Grace

Paul showcases the spiritually enlivening grace of God, motivated by his love for humanity and facilitated by his merciful character. Moral deadness — the condition of humans resulting from the initial transgression of Adam — enslaves every person to sin and subjects them to the "ruler of the power of the air" (Satan). Because of people's "disobedience [to God]" by automatically indulging their sinful inclinations, all deserve God's righteous "wrath" — ultimately, consignment to eternal death. Yet in exchange for faith alone God bestows on doomed sinners the gift of spiritual enlivenment and exaltation with the resurrected and ascended Christ — the very gift of which sinners' actions prove them not just *un*deserving but actually *ill* deserving, and a gift whose acceptance obtains for them eternal life. While their deeds do not earn for them this ill-deserved favor (grace), their gratefulness results in good works. Note that the *ultimate* goal of God's graciousness consists not in benefiting humanity but in demonstrating his own exaltedness (v. 7).

The gift of God's grace should make a particularly deep impression on Gentiles, for whom the self-sacrifice of Christ widened the door to salvation (vv. 11ff.). Though the Old Testament demonstrates that Gentiles could participate in the covenant established through Moses at Mount Sinai, their membership was not automatic (v. 12; cf. Lev. 19:33-34; Josh. 6:22-26; Ruth). Since before Moses, male circumcision distinguished the chosen Hebrews as the heirs of God's promises to their forefather Abraham (Gen. 12:1-3; 17:9-14). By rendering obsolete the exclusive Mosaic covenant, however, the "blood of Christ" (on the cross) gives Gentiles (the "uncircumcision") equal status as members of "God's household" and therefore equal entitlement to inherit his promises. In the temple precincts, a dividing wall separated the outer court of the Gentiles from the inner court, immediately adjacent to God's dwelling place and admissible only to Jews; "breaking down" this wall by Christ brought Gentiles "near" to God (vv. 13-14). Paul further pictures the unity of Gentiles and Jews who exercise faith in Christ as the building blocks of a holy temple (the church) founded on the apostles and prophets, themselves linked by Christ, the pivotal cornerstone (cf. Isa. 28:16).

3 Persecution a Privilege

Paul acknowledges his current imprisonment as part of his apostolic privilege. As the apostle to the Gentiles, he celebrates their newly enabled participation in the promises of the gospel through the previously veiled "mystery" of Christ, God's plan to redeem through him Gentiles as well as Jews (vv. 3-6). So Paul's suffering for the sake of the Gentiles' salvation should not spawn in them discouragement but celebration (v. 13; cf. 1 Cor. 1:23-24). The apostle's petitionary prayer for his audience concentrates on their grasp of the limitless love of God (vv. 14-18). The closing "Amen" means, "Let it be so."

4:1-16 Unity of the Body

By recounting his imprisonment in the service of the Lord, Paul cultivates in his audience a sense of responsibility to honor through their Christian conduct his suffering for their sake. That he lacks a founder's authority (though not apostolic authority) over his target congregations may lead him to frame his exhortations as a plea (v. 1). The fact of Christian unity (vv. 4-6) provides the basis for acting accordingly (vv. 2-3). The task of the church as a whole consists

Women in the Early Church

Attitudes toward women in the 1st-century church were heavily influenced by two major sources — the history of Judaism and the example of Jesus. Jewish Christians knew, and Gentile Christians were quickly taught, the major themes of the Old Testament. On the one hand, God had created man and woman alike in his image to rule over the rest of creation (Gen. 1:26-31) and had created Eve to be a suitable helper for Adam (2:18), an expression that suggests equality more than subordination. On the other hand, the first couple fell into sin, after which God promised the woman, "your desire shall be for your husband, and he shall rule over you" (3:16). No debate surrounds the fact that after this point gender relations throughout the Old Testament were highly patriarchal.

But Jesus came to reverse the effects of the fall, and his teaching and example regularly challenged the conventions that had come to characterize 1st-century Judaism. He regularly treated women with a dignity that surprised or upset men in his culture. Perhaps the two most dramatic examples involved his conversation with the Samaritan woman at the well (John 4:1-42) and his acceptance of Mary of Bethany in the role of a rabbi's disciple (Luke 10:38-42). Jesus risked the perception of scandal by allowing women to travel with him and his disciples (and to support them financially; Luke 8:1-3), and one of these, Mary Magdalene, for-

merly demon-possessed, became the first witness to the resurrection and an "apostle to the apostles" (John 20:1-2, 18). Still, Jesus did not choose a woman among his 12 closest followers, though the significance of this observation remains disputed.

The book of Acts contains no instructions regarding gender roles, but it does present a significant number of examples of women in prominent positions. Women as well as men prophesy (Acts 2:17-21), Priscilla (with her husband Aquila) teaches Apollos "the Way

Mosaic of Saint Perpetua from the Euphrasius basilica in Poreč, Croatia. *(Wikimedia Commons)*

of God more accurately" (18:26), and Paul is willing to preach to an all-female assembly, from which the first European convert, Lydia, emerges (17:11-15). From the epistles we learn of numerous other prominent women leaders in the church and coworkers with Paul during this first Christian

generation: Phoebe is a deacon and a patron (Rom. 16:1-2); Junia is an apostle, in the broader sense of missionary or church planter (v. 7); Chloe and Nympha and their (apparently fatherless) households figure prominently (1 Cor. 1:11; Col. 4:15); and Euodia, Syntyche, and others are fellow laborers in the gospel whom Paul values (Phil. 4:2-3; cf. Rom. 16:6, 12).

Paul does continue to command women to submit to their husbands, not simply as a vestige of the old order but comparable to the church's submission to Christ (Eph. 5:22-24; Col. 3:18). But he also commands mutual submission (Eph. 5:21) and radically redefines male authority as not greater privilege but greater responsibility (vv. 25-33). The most probable interpretation of Peter's reference to married women as "weaker vessels" (1 Pet. 3:7) highlights their greater vulnerability in their voluntarily adopted role of subordination. On the other hand, 1 Cor. 12:7, 11 makes clear that God's Spirit gives his gifts as the Spirit determines, none of which appear to be gender-specific. Galatians 3:28 clearly declares that in Christ "there is neither Jew nor Greek, slave nor free, male nor female." At the very least, these texts suggest that men and women, as in creation, are equally valuable in God's eyes; neither is inherently inferior to the other.

Whether Paul means more than this and is in principle abolishing all role differentiation in the church remains debated. At least in his world, he never takes this step. He commands women to cover their heads as a sign of respect in worship (1 Cor. 11:3-16). He assumes that women may pray and prophesy in church (11:5), but instructs that they should refrain from specific kinds of speech (14:33b-38) — perhaps asking questions during the evaluation of prophecy or expressing views contrary to his own. "Prophecy" in ancient Jewish and Greco-Roman contexts could refer to spontaneous utterances of messages believed to be from God (or a god) but also to thoughtfully prepared addresses equally attributed to the divine. Apparently Paul allowed women to do what today would be called preaching.

In the most scrutinized text of all, Paul forbids women from teaching or exercising authority over men (1 Tim. 2:12). But the grammatical construction used here, coupled with the observation that teaching and exercising authority are two distinctives of the office of elder/overseer in 1 Timothy (3:2; 5:17), suggest that Paul is merely prohibiting women from the single office of elder or overseer. A discussion of the criteria for overseers and deacons immediately follows, with probable references to women deacons but not to women elders (3:1-13). Nevertheless, the word for having authority in 2:12 is found nowhere else in Scripture and in other Greek literature can mean "to domineer," so perhaps Paul is prohibiting only an overly harsh use of authority, especially in light of the false teaching with which Timothy's church in Ephesus was infected.

Debate also continues over Paul's reasons for his various prohibitions. On the one hand, he regularly refers to the order of creation to buttress gender role distinctions, suggesting that his teaching cannot be dismissed as limited to his time and culture (1 Cor. 11:8-9; 1 Tim. 2:13; cf. 1 Cor. 14:34). On the other hand, it is possible that new creation in Christ goes beyond even original creation (Gal. 3:28), so the question of contemporary application is by no means settled.

For Further Reading

Beck, James R., and Craig L. Blomberg, eds. *Two Views on Women in Ministry.* Grand Rapids: Zondervan, 2001.

Belleville, Linda L. *Women Leaders and the Church.* Grand Rapids: Baker, 2000.

Piper, John, and Wayne A. Grudem, eds. *Recovering Biblical Manhood and Womanhood.* Wheaton: Crossway, 1991.

CRAIG L. BLOMBERG

in growing up theologically for effectiveness in further building itself up (vv. 13-16). Leaders and laypeople share responsibility for this task as they perform their variously vital ministerial functions (vv. 11-12). On believers' receipt of spiritual gifts after Christ's ascension to heaven (vv. 7-10), compare the advantage of the Holy Spirit cited by Jesus to comfort the apostles concerning his imminent departure from earth (John 15:26–16:13).

4:17–5:20 Christian Conduct

Paul disparages the spiritually unenlightened, "impure" behavior of non-Christian Gentiles (4:17-19) and exhorts his audience of believing Gentiles to abandon their own similar, preconversion conduct. The renewal of their minds should issue in actions characterized by Godlike righteousness and holiness. The practical specifics of such living include telling the truth; getting properly angry (at unrighteousness) without letting such anger fester and lead to sin; working hard and sharing with the needy the fruits of one's labor, instead of stealing; refraining from vulgar talk, and instead uplifting others with one's speech (4:29; 5:4, 19-20); shedding divisive feelings and conduct toward fellow Christians and instead extending to them Godlike kindness and forgiveness; filling one's heart with the Holy Spirit rather than overindulging in alcohol (as typical during Hellenistic religious orgies; 5:18) — in short, imitating God as children do their parents. Paul warns against the foolish notion that sinners who persist in their disobedience to God will inherit eternal life anyway. On the contrary, they will incur his wrath — incentive enough to "awake" from spiritual deadness (5:14) and "live as children of light," not "darkness." Behaving wisely means translating one's moral knowledge into action and requires making the most of one's time to do so (5:15-16).

Agora of Ephesus, a large square marketplace bordered on three sides by a vaulted colonnade and shops. *(www.HolyLandPhotos.org)*

5:21–6:24 Mutual Subjection

Reverence for Christ requires of his followers their mutual subjection. Paul approaches the idea of subjection not from an authoritarian, top-down platform, but from the standpoint of the subject's voluntary compliance in a hierarchy of authority — one that demands showing mutual respect across the board. The metaphor of Christ as the head of his body, the church (described in bridal terms; 5:26-27), provides the model for marital relationships, in which husbands and wives similarly become "one flesh." Paul's admonition that wives subject themselves to their husbands, as required of the church toward Christ, carries no more or less weight than the exhortation that husbands treat their wives with self-sacrificial love, as Christ did by dying for the church. Thus for husbands and wives mutual subjection takes different forms of the same command.

The principle holds true in the relationships of children with their parents and slaves with their masters. Paul does not aim at evaluating the moral justice of slavery, practiced throughout biblical history, but at addressing the relationships resulting from the existing practice. Contemporary society can apply Paul's instruction to the relationship of employees and employers. Children should obey their parents simply because it is the right thing to do. Fathers should treat their children reasonably and rear them according to biblical principles. Slaves or servants should obey their masters as a sincere offering of service to God, the impartial heavenly Master and Rewarder of all. Overbearing human masters had better take note.

Paul weaves throughout this section some of the benefits of voluntary subjection in its various forms. A husband does himself a favor by treating his wife in a loving way (5:28-29). Children obtain divine blessing by obeying their parents (6:2-3). Slaves store up heavenly reward by rendering their service to please God (6:7-8). But note that Paul assumes individual obedience to his instructions, reward or no reward. He attaches no conditions for compliance with them, and he does not consider the possibility of Christian relationships that lack mutual subjection. The implication? Just do it.

Nevertheless, Paul is no fool. He knows that his exhortations are hard to take and his instructions difficult to obey, for the Devil directs a host of spiritual forces focused on preventing Christian conduct. So perhaps with the living reminder of Roman soldiers in and around his place of imprisonment, Paul commends to his audience their preparation to the hilt with the spiritual armor that will keep them alive in the battle for their obedience.

In closing, Paul requests prayer on his behalf, but prayer petitioning his boldness in spreading the gospel while a prisoner, not the alleviation of his troubles. Instead, by sending his colleague Tychicus to deliver the letter and give a verbal report concerning Paul's personal circumstances, he takes the initiative to allay the anxieties of his audience.

Philippians

The Roman colony of Philippi, which lay along the main east-west highway stretching from Byzantium through northern Greece (Macedonia) to Brindisium (Italy), boasted the first church founded by Paul on the European continent (Acts 16). From the start, this loyal congregation sent regular gifts of support to the apostle as he pursued his missionary activities (4:15-20). The delivery of such a gift by the Philippian believer Epaphroditus and his imminent return home occasion this most personal of Paul's letters to a church.

Background

Writing from prison, Paul characterizes his life as hanging in the balance regarding his upcoming trial. Likely he is awaiting judgment directly by Caesar in Rome, where for more than two years under house-arrest he has enjoyed considerable freedom to preach the gospel to a wide variety of visitors (Acts 28:30-31). Alternatively, Paul may write Philippians during his immediately preceding imprisonment in Caesarea (Acts 24:27) or during a possible incarceration in Ephesus, where on his third missionary journey he ministered for over two years despite intense opposition (Acts 19).

Message

In addition to thanking the Philippians for their most recent gift, Paul urges by example a joyful perspective on the uncertainties of life as they relate to personal Christian faith and the furtherance of the gospel; admonishes Christian unity; and warns against those who insist on inflexible adherence to the Law. Chapter 2 describes the "self-emptying" of Christ, and chapter 3 contains Paul's religious autobiography, which serves to illustrate the supremacy of salvation by grace through faith alone.

1:1-11 A Heartening Greeting

Paul cites his colleague Timothy as coauthor (perhaps secretary) of the letter. Timothy had joined Paul toward the start of his second journey, during which the evangelistic team (including Silas, Luke) founded the church at Philippi. Service to Christ (v. 1) conveys a voluntary, lifelong commitment to laboring for the gospel. "Saints" simply means Christian believers. The mention of "overseers" and "deacons" testifies to the organized administration of the Philippian church (cf. Acts 14:21-23).

Contemplation of the Philippians' ready acceptance of the gospel and their perseverance in the Christian faith causes Paul joy — an overarching theme of this letter. He prays for their continual increasing in Christian love, informed by mature knowledge and guided by discernment. The resultant filling with the "harvest of righteousness" (righteous thinking and behavior) will present them blameless at the second coming of Christ, when the last judgment takes place. But the Philippians' righteous fruitfulness does not produce their ultimate blamelessness, which rather results from their acceptance of God's grace (v. 7).

1:12-26 Perspective

The apostle demonstrates his personal commitment to the teaching that "all things work together for good to those who love God" (Rom. 8:28) by reflecting on the positive outcomes of his current imprisonment with respect to the furtherance of the gospel. Not only have the Roman soldiers guarding the governor's palace gained exposure to the good news, but also local Christians have become emboldened to proclaim it. Good results even from those who preach from impure motives (e.g., competing with Paul), so redeeming those motives (cf. Mark 9:38-40).

Paul expresses trust for his release from prison but welcomes whatever fate awaits him — physical life or death (vv. 19-26). His eagerness to remain alive stems from wanting to help the Philippians grow in their faith. His welcoming of death grows from the personal benefit of presence with Christ in heaven.

1:27–2:18 Unity and Discipleship

Paul calls the Philippians to exemplary Christian conduct in preparation for his anticipated return visit (1:27; cf. 2:24). If his plan fails, their good reputation will encourage him from a distance. That the Philippians need this encouragement becomes apparent in Paul's reference to their persecutory "opponents," such as those under whom the apostle continues to suffer (1:27-30).

Paul bases on the example of Christ an impassioned admonition to Christian unity, achieved through unselfish consideration of fellow believers. The ancient world did not prize humility, but despised it, so this teaching runs counter to the culture of the day. The *"kenosis"* (Greek for "making empty") passage of 2:5-11, which elaborates Jesus' humility in "emptying" himself, may quote an early hymn of praise to Christ. Did Jesus, who existed before becoming human (John 1:1-18), shed certain divine attributes, such as omnipotence and omniscience? The Gospel accounts repeatedly show Jesus to possess such powers. Did he simply shirk divine status, though not divine nature? Or does the emptying refer to his giving up of his spirit on the cross (Luke 23:46; John 19:30; cf. Isa. 53:12)? Here Paul describes the possibility of his own death as a sacrificial "pouring out" (2:17).

That salvation solely by God's grace does not free believers for morally irresponsible behavior shows in Paul's urging to "work out your own salvation with fear and trembling" (2:12). Christians must through their actions shine as "stars in the world" (2:15), giving witness to the gospel, belief in which leads to eternal life.

2:19-30 Visitors

Accompanied by the Philippian native Epaphroditus, Timothy will carry the letter to Philippi, convey news of Paul's condition, and return to the imprisoned apostle, hopefully with a glowing report about the beloved congregation. Epaphroditus had taken gravely ill while or shortly after traveling to see Paul, probably to deliver the final installment of a financial pledge from the Philippian church. His return to Philippi alive and well will relieve both the church's anxiety over him and Paul's worry over the anxious church.

3 Breaking with the Past

Fresh reflection on a threat to the predominantly Gentile church in Philippi prevents Paul from prematurely ending the letter. Judaizing Christians (both Jewish and Gentile) sought to impose on Gentile converts observance of Jewish laws, of which circumcision constituted the first work. Paul calls the Judaizers "dogs" and "evil workers" who "mutilate the flesh" (3:2), thus reflecting the Greek notion that circumcision mars the ideal of male physical beauty and Paul's view that the Judaizers' insistence on circumcision mars the truth of salvation by grace through faith alone. "True" circumcision is circumcision of the heart (cf. Jer. 4:4; 9:25-26), validated by the Jerusalem Council, which upheld Gentiles' freedom from the Law (Acts 15).

Paul defuses the charge that he opposes the Judaizers out of defensiveness for his personal deficiency with regard to the Law. As a member of the tribe that produced his namesake, the first Hebrew king, Saul, the apostle comes from prominent Jewish stock. His circumcision on the "eighth day" fulfilled to the letter the Mosaic mandate (Gen. 17:12; Lev. 12:3), and his status as a Pharisee — thus one of the strictest observers of the Law — evidences his superior legal status, which he translated into action by zealously persecuting Christians before becoming one himself (Acts 9). But Paul's legitimate claims to legal blamelessness are all "rubbish" to him now. Vainly striving for righteousness according to the Law cannot compare to gaining righteousness through faith in Jesus Christ. Nevertheless,

Paul does not boast having attained righteous perfection. He has left the past behind, but his faith-inspired future requires continued growth. Freedom from the Law does not absolve Paul (or Christians) of moral responsibility; it rather spurs him (and them) to ever greater responsibility in pursuit of the prize of resurrection to eternal life.

A final note asserts the end of the Judaizers as "destruction" (damnation) because they cannot perfectly observe all the outward requirements ("earthly things") of the Law, despite their strict observance of its dietary regulations (making a god of their "appetite," or "belly") and proud exposure to undergo circumcision ("glorying" in their "shame"; v. 19). Since the Philippian population consists primarily of transplanted citizens from Rome, Paul makes the point that Christians owe their heavenly citizenship and so their ultimate allegiance to a Sovereign who lives elsewhere, not to the Law.

4 Exhortation and Acknowledgment

The importance of Christian unity prompts Paul to urge the resolution of tensions between two apparently prominent women in the Philippian church. The divine roster of the eternally saved ("the book of life, v. 3) appears first in Exod. 32:32-33 and frequently in Revelation.

Paul's final exhortations mandate rejoicing in the Lord (a deliberate act); publicly displaying patience while awaiting his return; prayerfully petitioning God to meet personal needs and thanking him in advance for doing so, rather than worrying; and filling one's mind with honorable thoughts. The reward for such Christian

Traditional site of Paul and Silas's imprisonment at Philippi (Acts 16). *(Phoenix Data Systems, Neal and Joel Bierling)*

discipline is a divinely granted peace of mind and heart that inexplicably persists even amid adverse circumstances (vv. 11-13).

In closing, Paul thanks the Philippians for their most recent gift of support, delivered to the imprisoned apostle by their own Epaphroditus. Paul celebrates the gift not because of its material benefit to him, since his contentment does not depend on his material welfare (vv. 6-7); rather, he rejoices in its enhancement of the Philippians' eternal treasure. The description of the Philippians' gift as a fragrant aroma pleasing to God reflects the Israelite sacrificial system (v. 18; Leviticus 1–7).

Paul's closing greetings make special mention of the believers of Caesar's household, Roman Christians in the emperor's employ.

Colossians

The town of Colossae, neighboring the more prominent cities of Laodicea and Hierapolis, lay 100 miles east of Ephesus, capital of the Roman province of Asia. Colossians addresses a primarily Gentile audience, as evidenced by the references to their fleshly uncircumcision (2:13) and their pre-Christian alienation (1:21) — language that parallels the specifically Gentile address of Eph. 2:11-13.

Authorship

Several factors support Paul's composition of this "Prison Epistle" during his house arrest in Rome: the presence with him of Onesimus, a runaway slave from Colossae, whose anonymity would be guaranteed in the distant, populous imperial capital; Paul's freedom to receive visitors other than personal friends; and the presence of Luke, who accompanied him to Rome (Acts 27–28).

The site of ancient Colossae, a thriving commercial center at the junction of the main route from Ephesus to the Euphrates until the road to Pergamum was moved to the west. (www.HolyLandPhotos.org)

Colossians shares striking literary parallels with Ephesians. Some verses and passages appear nearly word for word in both letters. Each epistle expounds the metaphor of the bodily unity of Christ and the church, with Colossians emphasizing the preeminence of Christ as its head. Scholars who question Paul's authorship of these letters generally credit the composition of both to a single associate of the apostle well versed in his theology.

The Letter

At the time of writing, Paul has never visited the church in Colossae, but its founder, Epaphras, has brought him news about the congregation. Epaphras may well have embraced Christianity during Paul's evangelistic sojourn in Ephesus (Acts 19); so here Paul, as spiritual grandfather of the Colossian church, exercises his apostolic authority to teach and admonish its members. Apparently a mix of heresies devaluing Christ threatens orthodox belief and practice among the Christians of Colossae (esp. 2:8-23).

1:1-12 Celebrating the Colossians' Faith

Paul names as his coauthor Timothy, recruited toward the beginning of the apostle's second missionary journey (Acts 16:1-5). The "saints" (Christian believers) of Colossae, whose faith Paul celebrates and supports in prayer, comprise a church founded by Epaphras, a missionary associate possibly converted during Paul's Ephesian ministry and now working with the incarcerated apostle (4:12). He calls Epaphras a "bondservant" to convey his voluntary, lifelong dedication to serving Christ (v. 7). Paul appears not to know personally the recipients of his letter, but only to know them by reputation (vv. 4, 9; 2:1). "Spiritual wisdom," which he prayerfully seeks for the Colossians, means the practical outworking of moral knowledge, as summarized here in the description of leading lives that please the Lord: doing good, remaining faithful, displaying patience, maintaining joy, and giving thanks to God. His qualification of believers to "share in the inheritance" evokes the metaphor of adoption into his family of "saints" slated to gain eternal life (v. 12; cf. Eph. 1:5; Rom. 8:15-17; Gal. 4:1-7).

1:13-23 Christ Outranks Creation

As "light" equals salvation (1:12), Paul now equates "darkness" with condemnation — a prominent theme in the Gospel of John. These verses summarize the Gospel in terms of Jesus as the "Light of the world" by emphasizing the universal preeminence of Christ as foundational for the redemption of creation he made possible through his death on the cross. In the Old Testament, "redemption" encompasses the substitutionary payment of financial and moral debts and the fulfillment of obligations on behalf of another person (Exod. 13:11-16; Lev. 25:25-49; Ruth 4:4-6). As used by Paul, redemption refers specifically to the self-sacrificial death of Christ to pay on behalf of believers their moral debt of sin (v. 14). On the visible revelation of God in Christ (v. 15), cf. John 1:14, 18. The designation of Jesus as the "firstborn" of all creation does not refer to the account of creation, but conveys in culturally relevant terms his unique status as the privileged heir of God the Father. In verse 18, "firstborn" status with respect to resurrection from the dead accords to Christ universal supremacy. Note God's selfless initiative in providing redemption *through* his firstborn heir, whereas in the Law God mercifully provided for the redemption *of* the firstborn heirs of his chosen people (Exod. 13:15). The "fullness" indwelling Christ affirms the totality of his divine nature (v. 19; 2:9).

1:24–2:7 Christian Suffering

To make redemption possible, Jesus suffered persecution in its ultimate form — execution. But making the availability of redemption known entails suffering by proclaimers of the

gospel such as Paul. His suffering does not help Christ redeem human beings, as though Jesus' work on the cross fell short of that task; rather, Paul's suffering represents the continuing consequences of helping to fulfill the ascended Christ's ongoing, earthly mission of redemption, namely, proclaiming its universal availability — the newly unveiled "mystery" that spells good news for Gentiles. That Paul does not bemoan, but, rejoices in his sufferings on behalf of the Colossians and their fellow Christians in neighboring Laodicea (2:1) should bolster their faith, against the arguments of false teachers pushing perversions of the truth about Christ (2:4). Underlying Paul's comments is his denial that the suffering of Christians betrays weakness on the part of their Lord. In fact, it is precisely his divine preeminence that qualified him for *supreme,* substitutionary suffering, rather than freeing him from it (cf. 1:13-20).

2:8-23 Countering Heresy

Paul counters the so-called "Colossian heresy," which elevates the rule-oriented teaching and tradition of mere human beings over the spiritual freedom enabled by the fully divine Christ. A mix of Judaistic legalism (vv. 16, 21), asceticism (self-abasement), and angel worship (v. 18) threatens the religious re-enslavement of Colossian believers. Paul exposes the ineffectiveness of such practices for salvation and proclaims the nullification of the Law by the crucified Christ, who actualizes the hope of salvation held out by the Law but unattainable through it (v. 17). Baptism (v. 12) symbolizes the believer's unity with Christ. Being made "alive together with him" includes symbolic circumcision of the heart, which eliminates the need for physical circumcision as the indicator of true membership in the community of God's elect. Freedom from the rules of Judaism, however, does not license Christians for moral abandon.

3:1–4:6 New Life in Christ

Unity with Christ involves both dying to sinful behavior and rising to righteous conduct, facilitated by the heavenward focus of the mind. Death to sin includes abandoning such vices as Paul lists in 3:5-9; resurrection to righteousness includes pursuing such virtues as appear in verses 12-17. Between these lists, the apostle highlights one of his favorite themes: Christian unity, brought about by inner renewal that obliterates ethnic, ritual, cultural, and socio-economic barriers (3:11). ("Scythians" here designates a group of ancient, nomadic tribes considered the most barbarous of barbarians.) Paul's exhortations to mutual subjection and respect between members of a household (3:18–4:1) parallel his admonitions in Eph. 5:22–6:9. In 4:3-6, the apostle urges the Colossians to pray for his wisdom in preaching the gospel and for their own wisdom in witnessing by word and deed. Gracious speech, "seasoned with salt," means speech unspoiled by the kinds of vices listed in 3:8.

4:7-18 Concluding Remarks and Greetings

Though a prisoner, Paul enjoys freedom to communicate through correspondence. Presumably, he sends his letter through his coworker Tychicus, apparent courier of Ephesians also (Eph. 6:21-22). His traveling companion, the homeward-bound slave Onesimus, features as the subject of Philemon.

Paul concludes by conveying greetings from the only Jewish Christians (coworkers "of the circumcision") currently with him. Evidently Epaphras also evangelized in nearby Laodicea and Hierapolis. Luke joined Paul during his second missionary journey. The "letter from Laodicea" (v. 16) may refer to Ephesians, probably a circular epistle intended for churches in the vicinity of Ephesus. Archippus appears to have inherited from Epaphras leadership of the Colossian church. By penning the closing greetings himself, Paul endorses the contents of the entire letter.

1 and 2 Thessalonians

Composed by the Apostle Paul only two decades after the crucifixion of Jesus, 1 and 2 Thessalonians join Galatians as the earliest writings of the New Testament. The Thessalonian epistles, best known for their teaching on the second coming of Christ and related events, comprise one of the three major prophetic portions of the New Testament, along with Jesus' Olivet discourse (Matthew 24; Mark 13) and the Apocalypse of John (Revelation).

Background

During Paul's second missionary journey, he and his companions traveled to the free Greek

Triumphal arch of the emperor Galerius on the Via Egnatia, Thessalonica, glorifying the Roman victory over the Persians. (*www.HolyLandPhotos.org*)

city of Thessalonica, capital of the Roman province of Macedonia (Acts 17:1-15). This urban hub enjoyed commercial advantages owing to its naturally protected port on the Aegean Sea and its location at the midpoint of the Egnatian Way, the major east-west road connecting Rome with Byzantium (modern Istanbul). Jews and Gentiles made up the mixed population of Thessalonica, and though Paul and company seem to have realized most of their evangelistic success with the city's Gentiles, unbelieving Jews emerged as persecutors against both Paul and the Thessalonican converts to Christianity. An attack by antagonists targeting Paul prompted the members of the fledgling church to protect the apostle by sending him on his way after only about a month of ministry among them.

Paul's deep concern for the new believers persisted as he made his way to Athens. When Timothy joined up with him in the Achaian capital, Paul commissioned him to return to Thessalonica and check on its church. By the time Timothy returned to southern Greece, Paul had moved on to Corinth, where Timothy caught up with his mentor. The good report of the Thessalonians' perseverance in the faith despite continued persecution occasioned Paul's writing of 1 Thessalonians. Apparently soon thereafter, fanaticism based on the expectation of Christ's imminent second coming seems to have taken root in the church. Hope for relief from persecution may have spawned the false teaching, or at least its embracing by some believers. Paul writes 2 Thessalonians to correct their wishful thinking and reverse its unproductive outcomes for practical life. Noting the difference in tone between the two letters, some scholars date 2 Thessalonians somewhat later and posit its writing by a disciple of Paul in the apostle's name.

1 Thessalonians

1–3 Celebrating the Faith of a Fledgling Church

Paul composes this letter in the first person plural to acknowledge the part played by his missionary companions Timothy and Silvanus (the Latin form of Silas) in establishing the church at Thessalonica (Acts 15:36–16:3; 17:1-15).

Paul encourages the Thessalonians by commending their acceptance of the gospel despite attendant tribulation and their exemplary tenacity to the Christian faith reputed throughout Greece. In 1:3-5 Paul cites the three primary Christian virtues: faith, love, and hope, with hope denoting not wishfulness for Christ's return but confident expectation of it — an expectation essential for the faithfulness of a church under persecution (cf. 5:8; 1 Corinthians 13). Further encouragement comes from Paul's recognition that God marked the Thessalonian believers for salvation, as sealed by their receipt of the Holy Spirit (1:4-6). That for the Thessalonians conversion to Christianity meant abandoning idol worship (1:9) identifies them as Gentiles, at least predominantly.

The overview of the missionaries' caring, diligent, sensitive ministry among the Thessalonians (2:1-12) climaxes in a celebration of the fruits of the evangelists' labor — the Thessalonians' proper reception of the gospel (vv. 13-14). On the beating and imprisonment of Paul and company at Philippi (2:2), which propelled them on to Thessalonica, see Acts 16:19-40. Paul professes the purity of his message and motive (2:3-6), enhanced by the missionaries' practice of working for their keep while carrying out their ministry (2:9).

Paul likens the plight of the persecuted Thessalonian believers to that of the first Christians in Judea — Jews who comprised the mother church in Jerusalem despite harsh treatment by their unconverted kin (2:14-16). The apostle's castigation of his compatriots in 2:15 recalls Matt. 23:37-39, where Jesus laments the Jews' rejection of God by killing the prophets and anticipates his own death at their hands. Paul sees his team of evangelists as the inheritors of such expected persecution (2:15-16; 3:3-4), which forced them to leave Thessalonica all too soon and hindered their return (Acts 17:1-15). Eventually, Paul's anxiety concerning the spiritual welfare of the Thessalonians made it worth the risk to send Timothy back for a visit. His good report to Paul comforts the apostle and sustains his intense desire to return to Thessalonica for further ministry.

4–5 Exhortation and Clarification

Paul ends the letter with exhortations regarding practical and theological issues on which the Thessalonian believers need instruction and correction. Note his psychologically astute coupling of praise for their Christian progress with admonition to greater growth (4:1, 9-10). The apostle urges sexual purity as an important component of "sanctification" (being made godly). Honorable sexual behavior will distinguish the Thessalonian Christians from their unbelieving fellow Gentiles (4:5). The apostle's urging to diligence in self-supporting manual labor may counterbalance the Thessalonians' temptation to abandon their jobs (4:11-12; cf. 2:9; 2 Thess. 3:10-12) in the expectation of Christ's imminent return.

The apostle assures his audience that deceased fellow Christians will not miss out on the joyful occasion of Jesus' second coming (4:13-18; 5:10). God will raise them from the dead, just as Jesus himself rose from death, and will unite them with those Christians still alive in the "catching up" of believers to meet Jesus as he descends from heaven. Though Paul has just tempered Thessalonian expectations of an imminent return of Christ, he nevertheless urges constant readiness for the event. In 5:4-5, "darkness" signifies both ignorance and evil, while "light" symbolizes knowledge and righteousness. In Eph. 6:10-17, Paul elaborates the theme of the "armor of God," briefly introduced in 5:8.

In closing, Paul exhorts the healthy Christian community to appreciate church leaders, confront wrongdoers, support the weak, show patience toward all, forgo revenge, and seek the common good.

2 Thessalonians

1 Eternal Relief from Earthly Affliction

The greeting of verses 1-2 matches almost word for word the opening verse of 1 Thessalonians. The letter then commends the persecuted Thessalonians for their perseverance in the faith and assures them that in the end God will make it right by punishing the persecutors for eternity, while the Thessalonian believers gain eternal relief from affliction. Their current suffering does not indicate divine disapproval; rather, their endurance prompts God to consider them worthy of entering his kingdom (v. 5).

2 The Day of the Lord

Paul now warns the Thessalonians against false hopes that their glorious future is already at hand. Verse 2 suggests that the desperate believers have accepted false doctrine attributed to Paul and announcing the arrival of the end times. He reminds the church of his previous (but undocumented) teaching on what must happen before Christ's return: the seizing of God's seat in the Jerusalem temple by a self-proclaimed but false "god," who acts by the power of Satan and wins to himself the wicked, already doomed to judgment for their rejection of the gospel. Restrained for now (by what or whom Paul does not say here; v. 6), the deceptive leader of the unfaithful will meet a quick end on the arrival of Christ. Paul's "man of lawlessness" parallels the "antichrist" of 1 John 2:18-25 and the "beast" of Revelation 13.

The chapter ends with words of encouragement confirming the Thessalonians' election by God for salvation (cf. 1 Thess. 1:4). The reminder should strengthen their tenacity to orthodox Christian teaching and comfort them with the expectation of eternal relief from persecution.

3 Warning against Idleness

In soliciting the prayers of the Thessalonian believers for the successful spread of the gospel, Paul subtly reminds them that he too suffers persecution. He ends the letter with a final, extended exhortation to keep working (cf. 1 Thess. 4:11-12). Some have abandoned their jobs, perhaps in expectation of Christ's imminent return. Paul bases on his own example of economic self-support the command that people pull their own weight by working. He prescribes social ostracism and Christian admonishment as the proper tools for prodding the undisciplined back to a productive life.

The invocation of inner "peace" (v. 16) must have carried special meaning to the persecuted Thessalonian believers (cf. Phil. 4:7).

To confirm the authenticity of this letter, Paul draws attention to his handwriting, displayed in the closing greeting. As per custom, he often employed a secretary to write down the bulk of his letters. Validating the contents of this epistle looms especially important for Paul as he combats false doctrine, perhaps contained in documents that fraudulently bear his name (cf. 2:2).

1 and 2 Timothy

Called the "Pastoral Epistles" because they address young ministers, 1 and 2 Timothy along with Titus are the latest of the New Testament letters claiming authorship by the Apostle Paul. The books contain instructions on matters of church administration, such as the appointment of leaders and the ousting of the unrepentant, warnings against false doctrine, guidance on dealing with fellow Christians of different age groups and sexes, and admonitions to exemplary personal conduct. 1 Timothy and Titus, probably authored contemporaneously, show the closest literary and thematic parallels.

Background

Timothy hailed from Lystra, in southern Asia Minor. Paul visited this town on his first missionary journey, when his ministry may have resulted in Timothy's conversion to Christianity (Acts 14:23ff.). When Paul returned to Lystra during his second evangelistic tour, he enlisted Timothy as an itinerant missionary companion and pastoral protégé (Acts 16:1-3). Timothy's subsequent activities included consolidating the church in Beroea, checking on the church in Thessalonica, mediating corrective measures in the Corinthian church, and overseeing ecclesiastical matters in Ephesus — his assignment at the time Paul writes these letters.

Authorship

Strong and early church tradition supports the claim of Pauline authorship made in all three Pastoral Epistles. Nevertheless, the question of their authorship has generated more debate among scholars than any of the other New Testament letters traditionally attributed to the apostle. Those who reject Paul's writing of the Pastorals cite their differences in vocabulary and grammatical style as compared to the apostle's other, uncontested letters. They also note the impossibility of harmonizing the geographical movements of Paul, Timothy, Titus, and Demas with the record of their travels in Acts and other Pauline epistles. Many who deny Paul's authorship of these books view them as the 2nd-century effort of a pseudonymous author to combat the rise of Gnosticism, a heresy that characterized the spiritual world as good and the material world as evil. See "The Question of Pseudepigraphy" (685-86).

Scholars who accept Paul's authorship of the Pastorals stress that the different purpose, subject matter, and target audience of these epistles naturally call for different vocabulary and grammatical style, and they note Paul's likely employment of secretaries, who through the years exercised differing degrees of literary freedom in penning his dictation. A tenable explanation of differing geographical data includes the apostle's possible release from the Roman imprisonment recorded at the end of Acts (anticipated in Phil. 1:19, 25; 2:24); his resumption of an itinerant ministry, during which he wrote 1 Timothy and Titus; and his rearrest and imprisonment in Rome, when in anticipation of his execution he wrote 2 Timothy (2 Tim. 4:6-8).

The Question of Pseudepigraphy

"Pseudepigraphy" (lit., "false writing") has come to mean a writing falsely ascribed to a particular author ("falsely named"). Many writings from classical antiquity and the Greco-Roman world were pseudonymous. Most scholars have concluded from this that the early Christians must also have accepted pseudonymity as a legitimate literary practice, and they so classify such New Testament letters as 2 Thessalonians, Colossians, Ephesians, 1-2 Timothy, Titus, James, 1-2 Peter, and Jude — as well as perhaps the Johannine Apocalypse (Revelation). Others argue that the early Christians would have been alert to such a practice and repelled by it.

Questions regarding pseudepigraphy are not necessarily the same as for an author's use of an amanuensis (secretary) or an anonymous writing later ascribed to someone. Pseudepigraphy has to do with a writing whose author is "falsely named" in the composition itself.

The key difficulty in studying New Testament pseudepigraphy is the lack of direct evidence, and so scholars have had to look more widely to practices in Greco-Roman and Jewish writings. But many argue that early Christianity had a uniqueness that renders invalid comparisons with other writings of the day. Questions regarding literary genre also arise; for example, can Jewish apocalyptic writings be compared to Christian letters?

Only two early Christian texts speak directly to the question of pseudepigraphy. The writer of 2 Thessalonians acknowledges the existence of reports that were being falsely attributed to him (2 Thess. 2:1-3), refers to a forged letter (2:15), and expresses concern for authenticity of authorship — even setting out a test for authenticity: his own handwriting in the subscription (3:17). Evidently he wants his readers to understand that authorship is important for both authenticity and authority.

Tertullian (ca. 145-220 A.D.) in his treatise *On Baptism,* written toward the end of the 2nd century, asks whether women in the church can baptize others (ch. 17). He notes that some in his day were citing the precedent of the godly woman Thecla, who, in effect, baptized herself by throwing herself to her death into a water pit (Acts of Paul and Thecla 34). Tertullian could have pointed out that such a "baptism" should hardly be taken as a precedent. For while Thecla taught Christian doctrine and performed miracles, she never baptized others — only herself, and that as a final act of martyrdom. Instead, Tertullian attacked the authorship of Acts of Paul and Thecla, arguing that the writings were wrongly ascribed and its author was removed from his place/office. Tertullian clearly considered the authorship of a text to be important for its authority, and he expected his readers to do so as well.

Eusebius of Caesarea (ca. 260-339), theologian, bishop, and church historian, refers to the words of two 2nd-century church leaders that have a bearing on the question of pseudepigraphy. He quotes Dionysius, a bishop at Corinth, as complaining about those who have adulterated his writings (*Ecclesiastical History* 4.23.12). Just what others "exchanged" or "added" in Dionysius's letters we are not told, but he resents these matters going out under his name. He further notes "the sacred writings of the Lord" as having also been adulterated, probably meaning Marcion's treatment of the New Testament. Eusebius also cites a writing by Serapion, bishop of Antioch in Syria ca. 200, which argues that the *Gospel of Peter* is heretical (*Eccl. Hist.* 6.12.3-6). More importantly, however, Serapion wants his readers to understand that authorship is important for authenticity and authority. If the text were indeed by Peter, he would accept it — but, in fact, it is not.

The Muratorian Canon, an 8th-century Latin manuscript translated from an original Greek text dated ca. 180-200, evidently represents the views of the Western church at the end of the 2nd century regarding the books to be included in the New Testament canon. After setting out those works to be received as canonical, it addresses other extant writings. Acceptable to be read in the church are the epistle of Jude and two ascribed to John, the apocalypses of John and Peter, and the Wisdom of Solomon, but not the epistles to the Laodiceans and the Alexandrians pseudepigraphically attributed to Paul. The canon appears to view authorship as the most important criterion for accepting or rejecting the authenticity and authority of a text.

The earliest extant evidence, therefore, suggests that Christians of the first two centuries did relate authenticity and authority to questions about authorship and did not view pseudonymity as an acceptable literary technique. Many of the matters of content, style, structure, and vocabulary that have led scholars to propose pseudonymity for various New Testament writings can better be explained in terms of diverse settings in differing circumstances, the use of assistants as amanuenses, and our own lack of understanding regarding resemblances and differences in the writings under consideration.

For Further Reading

Aland, Kurt. "The Problem of Anonymity and Pseudonymity in Christian Literature of the First Two Centuries," *JTS* 12 (1961): 39-49. Repr. in *The Authorship and Integrity of the New Testament*. London: SPCK, 1965, 1-13.

Collins, Raymond F. *Letters That Paul Did Not Write*. Wilmington: Michael Glazier, 1988. Repr. Eugene: Wipf and Stock, 2006.

Ellis, E. Earle. "Pseudonymity and Canonicity of New Testament Documents." In *Worship, Theology and Ministry in the Early Church*, ed. Michael J. Wilkins and Terence Paige. JSNTSup 87. Sheffield: Sheffield Academic, 1992, 212-24.

Goodspeed, E. J. "Pseudonymity and Pseudepigraphy In Early Christian Literature." in *New Chapters in New Testament Study*. New York: Macmillan, 1937, 169-88.

Guthrie, Donald. "The Development of the Idea of Canonical Pseudepigrapha in New Testament Criticism," *Vox Evangelica* 1 (1962) 43-59. Repr. in Aland, *The Authorship and Integrity of the New Testament*, 14-39.

Metzger, Bruce M. "Literary Forgeries and Canonical Pseudepigraphy," *JBL* 91 (1972) 3-24. Repr. in *New Testament Studies: Philological, Versional, and Patristic*. Leiden: Brill, 1980, 1-22.

RICHARD N. LONGENECKER

1 Timothy

Cf. the parallels with Titus.

1 The Church Scene in Ephesus

In standard, 1st-century practice, the letter begins with identification of the writer and the intended recipient. "Grace and peace" form the signature greeting in most of Paul's letters, and here "mercy" is an added invocation of God's blessing on his "loyal child" (convert) in the faith (cf. 2 Tim. 1:2).

Timothy is currently overseeing the church in Ephesus, where Paul ministered for more than two years during his third missionary journey (Acts 19). Timothy's mission is to squelch unorthodox doctrine, fruitless philosophical speculation, and misleading instruction in the Mosaic law by unqualified teachers. Paul affirms the goodness of the Law when applied properly, not as a works-based way to obtain salvation but as a means of convicting people of their sinfulness (cf. specific examples in vv. 9-10) and thus their need for the gospel. By deploring his own preconversion transgressions and identifying himself as "foremost" of sinners, Paul shows that rather than standing in judgment over the wicked, he fully appreciates their urgent need for God's mercy and grace. He charges Timothy to cling to his faith and conduct himself accordingly so as to keep a clean conscience, in contrast to two spiritually "shipwrecked" apostates mentioned by name. Paul's enigmatic announcement that he has "turned [them] over to Satan" probably means that he has ejected them from the church and so subjected them to the source of worldly suffering (cf. 1 Cor. 5:5).

2 Prayer and Propriety

Paul's pastoral instruction to Timothy begins with the directive to pray for the salvation of all people, especially governmental authorities, whose salvation would ensure for Christians a peaceful life. God "desires" the salvation of all but recognizes Jesus as the sole mediator, whose giving of himself as a "ransom for all" makes possible the salvation of all humanity; but individuals must respond to Christ's offer by recognizing "the truth" of the gospel (v. 4).

The directives to women in vv. 9-15 fit the cultural norms of the 1st century A.D., but modern readers should not dismiss this teaching as culturally irrelevant today. Because women at that time typically lacked a formal or religious education, the apostle prohibits their exercise of authority over men and in matters of church and faith (cf. 1 Cor. 14:34-35, directed to women whose talkativeness during church services detracts from reverent worship). The apostle's comments in verse 15 do not make childbearing the means by which women attain salvation; rather, they assure sincere Christian women of their salvation despite the great pain that attends giving birth.

3 Qualifications for Church Leaders

From the first of his missionary journeys, Paul appointed leaders in the local churches that he founded (Acts 14:21-23). Here he outlines the qualifications for "bishops" ("overseers," essen-

Temple of Hadrian at Ephesus, commemorating his visit in A.D. 128. *(Richard Cleave, Pictorial Archive)*

tially synonymous for Paul with "elders") and for "deacons" ("helpers," who assist the overseers in the distribution of charity and other practical matters). Paul requires overseers to demonstrate irreproachable character through upstanding personal conduct that commands recognition even outside the church. Overarching temperateness, a well-managed household (vv. 4-5), and spiritual maturity qualify candidates for church leadership. Possible interpretations of the directive that leaders "be husbands of [only] one wife" include the disqualification of bigamists or remarried divorcées and widowers (vv. 2, 12). "Lovers of money" (v. 3) are prey to competing priorities (cf. 6:9-10). Deacons must measure up to a similar set of standards. Verse 11 states requirements either for female deacons (deaconesses) or the wives of male deacons. Verse 16 quotes a hymnic or creedal confession that summarizes the earthly career of Christ, from his incarnation to his postresurrection return to heaven.

4   Pastoral Encouragement

Paul instructs Timothy to educate the Ephesian church about satanically inspired doctrines that stress self-deprivation of legitimate pleasures (e.g., marriage and food) and distract Christians from the pursuit of true godliness (cf. Acts 20:28-31). He encourages Timothy in overcoming the authoritative handicap that attends his relative youth in a society that values wisdom gained by years. He must vigorously pursue his ministry of teaching and exercise his spiritual gift as conferred by the church elders.

5:1–6:2   Correction and Care

Timothy should not, however, overcompensate for his youth by rigidly exercising pastoral authority. When correcting individual believers, he should treat them as he would members of his family by showing respect for his elders, sensitivity to his peers, and purity of intentions toward the opposite sex. Paul pays specific attention to widows, a significant component of the 1st-century population owing to the typical marrying of girls in their early teens to older men. Destitute upon their husbands' death,

many in Ephesus resorted to cult prostitution at the temple of Artemis (cf. Acts 19:24-41). Paul's program for widowed Christian women aims largely at preventing their moral descent through providing for their economic welfare.

Paul calls "real widow" one who forfeits remarriage to concentrate on spiritual devotion (5:3, 5, 16). Descendants of such widows should assume responsibility for their support (v. 8), and widows at least 60 years old who have led commendable Christian lives should receive support from the church. Young widows should remarry not only to recoup economic support but also to legitimate acting on their natural sexual desires and to resume responsibilities that make for a productive life (v. 14). A Christian woman with dependent widows (v. 16) might include a mother-in-law charged with supporting the wives of her deceased sons (cf. Ruth 1).

Church leaders who are especially competent deserve double compensation ("honor"; vv. 17-18). To protect the high profile elders — often the favorite targets of false accusers — the apostle charges Timothy to require testimony from at least two witnesses before acting on a charge against them (cf. Deut. 19:15). The apostle recommends public rebuke as a deterrent against persistent sinning. Rather than hastily ordaining candidates for church leadership, Timothy should take ample time to observe their behavior in the light of the requirements elaborated in chapter 3.

Paul admonishes slaves to act respectfully toward their masters and work extra hard for those who are fellow Christians (6:1-2; cf. Eph. 6:5-9).

The apostle interjects sound medical advice in 5:23. Timothy's drinking of unpurified water was causing problems for his sensitive stomach. Imbibing a mixture of water and wine would help alleviate the symptoms, since the alcoholic component of the wine would counteract the offending impurities in the water.

6:3-21   Final Instructions

For the third time Paul warns against false doctrine (vv. 3-5; cf. 1:3-7; 4:1-8). He also restates the merits of pursuing godliness and good works versus amassing material wealth (vv. 6-10, 17-19; cf. 3:3; 4:7-8; Phil. 4:11-12). Paul challenges Timothy to persevere in working out his personal Christian faith and commends him for his "good confession" that Christ is

Lord (vv. 11-14; cf. John 18:33-37). A final, fourth warning against falling prey to false doctrine drives home the essentialness of intellectual discipline to maintaining one's Christian faith (vv. 20-21).

2 Timothy

1:1–2:13 No Reason for Timidity

The first hints that Paul expects soon to die surface immediately. His greeting to Timothy mentions the promise of "life and immortality" (1:10). The apostle's fatherlike affection for his protégé appears in the reflective designation of Timothy as his "beloved" child in the faith, whose tears at their last parting Paul recalls and whom he longs to see one more time. Sure of God's forgiveness, Paul confirms his clarity of conscience and his certainty of salvation in the face of impending death (1:3, 12; cf. 1 Tim. 1:16). As he anticipates passing the apostolic baton, Paul exemplifies his charge that Timothy meet courageously the challenges of the Christian calling (cf. 4:6-8). He directs attention to Jesus, who showed exemplary courage by enduring the agony of crucifixion — reason enough for Timothy not to be ashamed of the gospel or of Paul's suffering in its service, and not to be timid in ministry. A reminder of his empowerment by the indwelling Holy Spirit assures Timothy that he can fulfill Paul's charge.

At the time of writing, Timothy is still overseeing the church in Ephesus, capital of the Roman province of Asia. So as a warning by negative example, Paul cites his forsaking by Asian Christians ashamed of his imprisonment. In contrast he blesses the Ephesian native Onesiphorus, who on visiting Rome sought out the incarcerated apostle. Timothy should emulate his moral courage by finding strength in the "grace" of Christ. Paul also commands

the entrusting of the gospel message to faithful people who will perpetuate the ministry he has so publicly pursued (2:2). Examples of the diligent soldier, athlete, and farmer challenge Timothy to focus attention and energy on his ministerial task (2:3-6). Paul's own focus — the sharing of believers in the resurrection and eternal reign of their faithful Lord, Jesus Christ — likely stems from his current circumstances as a condemned prisoner. Far from shaking his faith, his ominous earthly fate has bolstered his confidence for eternity — an emboldening example for Timothy.

2:14–4:8 The Mentor's Final Charge

Timothy knows well Paul's teaching with regard to the gospel (2:2, 8; cf. 3:14-15); so Paul reminds him to shun and squelch quarrelsome religious speculation and false doctrine, which prove unprofitable at best and spiritually destructive at worst (cf. 1 Tim. 1:3-7; 4:1-8; 6:3-5; Tit. 1:10-16; 3:9). Instead, the apostle commends the pursuit of godliness evidenced by good works (cf. Titus 2; 3:8). He instructs Timothy to demonstrate kindness, patience, and gentleness when correcting opponents, with the ultimate goal of bringing about their repentance for salvation. Nevertheless, such beneficent Christian meekness should not be confused with unconstructive timidity.

In chapter 3, Paul's prediction of the end times cautions Timothy to hold firm to orthodox doctrine, as taught by the apostle and in the

Hebrew Scriptures (vv. 14-16), and to persevere amid inevitable persecution. Extrabiblical texts identify Jannes and Jambres as the magicians of Pharaoh who opposed Moses (Exodus 7), and Paul cites the ultimately unsuccessful pair to foretell the failure of learned fools who oppose the "truth" of God — specifically, the truth of the gospel (v. 8). The reminder that Timothy has previously witnessed God's deliverance of Paul from dire circumstances gets Timothy to expect persecution but also reassures him of God's continued presence and supreme power (vv. 10-12; cf. Acts 13–14; 16:1-5). Verses 16-17 instruct Timothy to use the God-inspired Scriptures as his manual for ministry.

A final charge stresses Timothy's primary ministerial duties and steels him for the difficulties he will face in fulfilling them (4:1-5). Timothy remains in the race; but Paul has successfully "finished the course" (cf. 1 Cor. 9:24-27). He faces his imminent death with honesty about the present (4:6), peace of mind about his past (v. 7), and confidence about his future, which holds an eternal reward (v. 8). His self-characterization as a "libation" (4:6) recalls the Israelite sacrificial system, in which a liquid offering often accompanied the presentation of a grain offering or animal sacrifice (e.g., Lev. 23:13, 18, 37).

4:9-22 Last Requests and Final Instructions

Practical matters come last in the apostle's final letter. Luke, the physician-author of Luke-Acts and frequent missionary companion of Paul, attends the imprisoned apostle in Rome (v. 11).

Paul urges Timothy to visit him soon — before winter, when stormy weather prevents safe seafaring from Asia Minor to Italy, and before Paul's "departure" (execution; vv. 6, 21). He also summons John Mark, the author of the gospel of Mark and the cousin of Barnabas whose desertion of Paul during his first missionary journey caused a relational rift (Acts 15:36-41). Apparently Titus has completed his work in Crete (Tit. 1:5). Tychicus served as a courier of earlier Pauline epistles, and perhaps Paul has sent him to Ephesus to fill in for Timothy while he visits Paul in Rome. The apostle appears particularly keen on retrieving certain "parchments" — documents that contain information valuable enough to record on the expensive material. The farewell request that Timothy bring his mentor's cloak (v. 13) conjures the image of the falling of Elijah's mantle to his prophetic successor, Elisha (2 Kgs. 2:13).

After warning Timothy to watch out for "Alexander the coppersmith" (cf. 1 Tim. 1:20), Paul voices Christlike magnanimity toward those who deserted him (v. 16; cf. Luke 23:34). His rescue "from the lion's mouth" (v. 17) implies extreme danger, but verse 18 makes clear that ultimately Paul does not define divine deliverance as immunity from harm, but, rather, as safe passage to eternal salvation on the other side of affliction.

Greetings to the fellow tent-making couple with whom Paul lived and worked at Ephesus (Prisca, the shortened form of Priscilla, and Aquila) head the list of closing notes. Verse 21 mentions Roman Christians who remain loyal to Paul.

Titus

As with 1 and 2 Timothy, the Pastoral Epistle to Titus instructs a young minister on matters of church administration, doctrinal purity, and personal conduct. The close thematic parallels of 1 Timothy and Titus suggest their contemporaneous authorship, presumably by their common mentor Paul, as claimed in the opening of both letters. Apparently, Titus (an uncircumcised Greek Christian) is attending to ecclesiastical affairs among his ethnic kin on the island of Crete while Timothy (a circumcised Christian of Jewish and Greek parentage) is overseeing the church at Ephesus, where the need exists to foster the unity of Jewish and Gentile Christians.

Though Titus goes unmentioned in the reports of Paul's missionary journeys in Acts, Paul himself refers to him in his letters to the Galatians and Corinthians (Gal. 2:1-3; 2 Cor. 2:13; 7–8; 12:18). Toward the end of Paul's life, Titus has moved north to Dalmatia, opposite Italy on the eastern side of the Adriatic Sea (2 Tim. 4:10).

1:1-4 Greeting

Paul identifies himself as God's bondservant to communicate his voluntary assumption of lifelong service to the master who freed him from slavery to sin (cf. Rom. 1:1), and as Christ's "apostle" (one sent), to acknowledge his commissioning for the evangelization of people "chosen" by God for faith leading to eternal life (cf. 1 Thess. 1:4-6). Evidently Titus, whom Paul calls his "true child" in the faith, converted to Christianity through Paul's ministry, as did Timothy (cf. 1 Tim. 1:2). On Paul's signature greeting, "grace and peace," see Rom. 1:7.

1:5-16 Elders and False Teachers

The close literary relationship between Titus and 1 Timothy becomes evident from the start. Paul left Timothy to oversee ecclesiastical matters in Ephesus, and he left Titus to do the same on Crete, where earlier as a prisoner Paul put into port on the way to Rome (Acts 27:7-13). In Titus, instructions on the appointment of church elders come first (vv. 5-9; cf. 1 Tim. 3:1-13). Warnings against false doctrine follow (vv. 10-16; cf. 1 Tim. 1:3-11; 4:1-5; 6:3-10). "Those of the circumcision" (v. 10) refers to Jews, for whom the rite constituted the sign of belonging to the chosen community of God. The ethnic slur that "All Cretans are liars" (v. 12) is attributed to the 6th-century-B.C. philosopher Epimenides. The islanders' natural bent for falsehood makes it all the more important that Titus steer them clear of false teachers and the untruths they propagate.

2 Faith Made Practical

Paul outlines proper conduct for Christians of different ages and social positions and for Titus himself (cf. 1 Tim. 4:12–6:2). Sensible, godly living and the denial of worldly desires form the overarching principles of Paul's instruction, and the expectation of Christ's return (the "blessed hope") provides the basis for their practical application (vv. 12-13).

3 Humility and Conviction

Whereas in 1 Timothy Paul urges prayer for rulers and authorities, in Titus he prescribes subjection and obedience to them (v. 1; cf. Rom. 13:1). The urgent need for the freely bestowed favor of God obliges the believer to treat all people with consideration (cf. 1 Tim. 2:1-7).

In conclusion Paul restates his

commendation of godly behavior and admonition to shun false doctrine (vv. 8-9). Persistent troublemakers are to be ousted from the church (vv. 10-11; cf. 1 Tim. 1:19-20). Closing greetings identify the Macedonian port of Nicopolis as the location of Paul's intended wintertime sojourn and name current associates of the apostle, including his sometime courier Tychicus (Acts 20:4) and the eloquent Alexandrian Jew Apollos, who converted to Christianity and preceded Paul at Ephesus (Acts 18:24-28).

Philemon

As the shortest of Paul's epistles, Philemon appears last among them. Paul's coworker Tychicus served as courier of this "Prison Epistle" and traveling companion of the runaway slave whose conversion to Christianity and return to his master occasions Paul's cover note.

A Request Hard to Refuse

The imprisoned Paul acknowledges his longtime ministerial protégé Timothy as coauthor (perhaps secretary) of this very personal letter. Archippus (v. 2), addressed in Col. 4:17, is the leader currently in charge of the congregation Colossae where Philemon appears to live and host a house church. Since Paul neither founded the church in Colossae nor visited the town, it seems likely that Philemon encountered him and embraced the Christian faith during Paul's more-than-two-year ministry in Ephesus, some 100 miles west (see the Introduction to Colossians [678]; Acts 19). The opening celebration of Philemon's faith resembles the apostle's joyful praise of the Philippian Christians (vv. 4-7; cf. Phil. 1:3-11).

While a prisoner, Paul has met and converted to Christianity Philemon's runaway slave, Onesimus ("whose father [in the faith] I have become"). Paul wants to retain him as a colleague in ministry and believes he has the apostolic authority to mandate Philemon's compliance (v. 8). But instead he sends Onesimus home and challenges Philemon to take some Christian initiative. Such initiative involves receiving the returning slave as a spiritual brother on par with Paul himself, when the usual response called for the slave's punishment or even execution. Christian renewal enables the formerly "useless" Onesimus to live up to his name, which means "useful, profitable" (cf. v. 11). By expressing confidence that Philemon will go the extra mile in honoring Paul's "request" (v. 21), the apostle might also be hinting that Philemon lend Onesimus for ministerial service (v. 13) or perhaps set the slave free altogether. That elsewhere Paul assumes the continuation of slavery in his teaching on Christian relationships might argue against the suggestion that he has the liberation of Onesimus in mind (Eph. 6:5-9; Col. 3:22–4:1; 1 Cor. 7:21-24). Yet the immediacy of the situation with the runaway slave may form the backdrop for the apostle's comments on master-slave relationships in Ephesians and Colossians, probably written contemporaneously with Philemon.

That Paul handwrites this promise to pay any debts Onesimus owes to Philemon makes it all the more difficult for the slaveowner to refuse the apostle's request. The reminder of Philemon's own spiritual indebtedness to Paul (v. 19) and the prospect of hosting the apostle as a houseguest (v. 22) increase the pressure. Naming Epaphras, founder of the church in Philemon's hometown and current coworker with the imprisoned apostle, first on his list of well-wishers suggests his endorsement of Paul's request.

Hebrews

Although Hebrews lacks the opening greetings typical of ancient letters, the book includes the expected closing. It appears to constitute a letter written in sermonic style, similarly to 1 John. The general address, "To the Hebrews," leaves questions as to the specific destination of this letter, but its contents strongly support the tradition that Jewish Christians comprised the originally intended audience. The overarching purpose of Hebrews emerges as an effort to prevent the addressees from abandoning their Christian faith to return to Judaism, and the persuasive strategy employed by the author makes Mosaic institutions the basis for demonstrating the superiority of Christ. As the perennially sufficient redemptive sacrifice and the exalted high-priestly mediator between humans and God, Christ perfects the provision of salvation, of which goal the Old Testament priesthood and sacrificial system fell short. By frequently quoting the Septuagint (the Greek translation of the Hebrew Old Testament), the author invokes the Old Testament itself to support the superiority of the new covenant of grace established by Christ over the old covenant of law mandated through Moses. The use of the Septuagint may suggest a Greek-speaking Jewish Christian author and/or an original audience of Greek-speaking Jewish Christians.

The author of Hebrews appears well acquainted with the spiritual and social circumstances of the addressees. They have suffered persecution; at least some have quit attending Christian gatherings for fellowship and worship (perhaps to avoid persecution); and the halt to their maturing as Christians threatens to undo their spiritual progress thus far. So the author both challenges and inspires them with exhortation and encouragement, which climax in chapters 11 (frequently hailed as the Bible's great chapter on faith) and 12.

Authorship

Even in the oldest manuscripts of Hebrews its author remains anonymous, and the early church reached no consensus regarding authorship. Proposed authors have included the Apostle Paul, whose influence permeates the book but whose direct authorship scholars seriously doubt, largely because the rough literary style evident in Paul's other letters contrasts with the polished Greek of Hebrews. Further, Paul often backs up his teaching by appealing to his apostolic authority, but Hebrews relies on the authority of others. And Paul identifies himself in his other letters and declares his mission as one to the Gentiles (cf. Rom. 11:13; Acts 13:44-52).

Other suggestions include Apollos, the eloquent Alexandrian Jew taught in Ephesus by Paul's fellow Christian workers Priscilla and Aquila (Acts 18:24-28). That translators produced the Septuagint in Alexandria supports this suggestion, as do his reputed linguistic refinement, his ethnicity, and his familiarity with the teaching of Paul. Priscilla, a one-time Roman exile, might have authored Hebrews and purposely left the letter anonymous to preclude gender-based objections to her teaching. Greetings from fellow Italian Christians (13:24) could accord with this suggestion and might indicate that Hebrews was written for wavering believers in Rome, where Christian persecution became imperial policy during the reign of Emperor Nero. Barnabas represents another plausible candidate. Personal training with Paul on his first missionary journey and Barnabas's own Levitical background favor his intimate knowledge of Pauline doctrine and Old Testament law, both of which Hebrews reflects.

Date

Despite uncertainty over authorship, the early church knew and used the letter as authoritative Scripture in a writing as early as A.D. 95 (cf. 1 Clement). That Hebrews contains such abundant comparisons between Christ and the Old Testament priesthood and sacrificial system, centered in the Jerusalem temple, but does not mention the destruction of the temple by the Romans in 70, seems strong evidence for the book's authorship prior to that event.

1 Christ Superior to Prophets and Angels

Ultimately, the supremacy of Christ rests in his divinity. Christ is the Son of God the Father, heir to "all things" (the created world as his kingdom) and agent of their creation, embodiment of God's glory and nature, and sustainer of creation. God sustains the world by the same powerful "word" with which he created it, the "Word" Jesus Christ (Genesis 1; John 1:1-3), thus establishing Christ as superior to the Old Testament prophets, through whom God spoke to the Hebrew ancestors.

The Redeemer's having "sat down" in the heavenly seat of honor at the "right hand" of God shows his authority and confirms his superiority over angels. They are created servants of God who themselves worship his "firstborn" Son, the doubly-blessed heir.

In support of the assertions about Christ that appear throughout the book, the author quotes from the Greek Septuagint. Translating into English from the Septuagint rather than from the original Hebrew and Aramaic texts (on which both the Septuagint and modern translations of the Old Testament are based) produces slightly different wording, though only in minor detail and without changing their essential meaning. Compare verse 6 with Ps. 97:7; verse 7 with Ps. 104:4; verses 8-9 with Ps. 45:6-7; verses 10-12 with Ps. 102:25-27; 2:5-8 with Ps. 8:4-6.

2 Taking Salvation Seriously

The preeminent position and role of Christ constitute good reason for a warning against apostasy. The "message declared through angels" refers to the Mosaic law (cf. Acts 7:38, 53), transgression of which brought punishment for the Hebrews (v. 2; cf. 3:16-19 and the covenantal curses in Deuteronomy 28). Since Christ supersedes the angels, his way of salvation supersedes the mode of salvation mediated through them and requires even more careful heeding. For "signs and wonders, . . . miracles, . . . and gifts of the Holy Spirit" as witnesses to the salvation announced and provided by Christ (v. 4), see Acts 2. The rule of Christ over his kingdom has begun, but only in part (v. 8).

Christ's sinless suffering as a human being and his triumph over death (the consequence of sin) through resurrection "perfected" him for crowning as the appeaser of God's anger against sinful humanity and as the empathetic mediator between God and humans (cf. 4:14–5:10). His becoming human made him "lower than the angels," but only temporarily, without reducing or suspending his divinity, and with the purpose of his ultimate and eternal exaltation by God the Father (v. 9).

3:1–4:13 More Authoritative than Moses

As the way of salvation provided by Christ supersedes the Mosaic law, so also does the person of Christ, the Son of God, supersede the man Moses, a servant of God, as the moral authority over the church — "holy partners in a heavenly calling" (3:1). The Gospel of Matthew, also written for a primarily Jewish audience, portrays Jesus as the new and greater Moses. A second warning against abandoning the faith admonishes Christians to learn from the disobedient Hebrews of the exodus, whom Moses led but whom God denied entry into the promised land because of their failure to trust him (Num. 13:17–14:45). Apostasy from the Christian faith threatens worse consequences: denial of entry into Christ's eternal, heavenly kingdom (3:7-11, 15; cf. Ps. 95:7-11).

Mere knowledge of the gospel is not enough to effect salvation (4:1ff.). The obedient exercise of faith must follow hearing the gospel for one to gain the ultimate Sabbath rest of God. The possibility of falling short of entering this rest (through apostasy) accords with Paul's admonition to "work out your own salvation with fear and trembling" (Phil. 2:12) and to "press on" diligently (3:12-14; 1 Cor. 9:24-27; cf. Jas. 1:4). The mention by Moses' successor, Joshua, who led the postexodus generation into the promised land, of a future rest for God's chosen people provides the parallel for the promised, ultimate rest of Christ's eternal kingdom.

4:14–5:10 Jesus, the Supreme High Priest

Now the writer elaborates Jesus' role as high priest — in Judaism, the mediator of a right relationship between the holy God and his chosen but sinful people. The incarnation of Christ enables his full understanding of human weakness, evidenced through his tearful pleading with God in the garden of Gethsemane (5:7). Christ's complete ability to sympathize with human weaknesses and his appointment by God to the office of high priest put him at least on par with Aaron, the first Hebrew high priest (Exodus 28). But the sinless Christ's submission to the will of the Father by his self-sacrificial death on the cross makes him an even better high priest than Aaron, because his obedience completely qualified him as the source of eternal deliverance from slavery to sin. Aaron and his successors had to offer sacrifices repeatedly to atone for their own recurring sins and those of their compatriots.

5:11–6:20 The Risk of Falling Away

Failing to progress toward spiritual maturity by re-embracing "elementary," Law-driven Judaism opens one to the risk of eventually abandoning the faith, an irreversible trend that precludes gaining eternal salvation. An analogy from agriculture (6:7-8) contrasts Christian growth with apostasy and parallels Jesus' parable of the Sower (Matt. 13:3-9, 18-23; Luke 8:5-15).

Following this warning comes encouragement (6:9-12). The writer expresses confidence in the potential of his addressees, confirms God's faithful remembrance of their past progress in the faith, urges them to diligent perseverance, and reminds them of the salvation it promises. This assurance comes from God himself, whose having made good on his covenant with Abraham (Gen. 12:2-3) demonstrates the absolute

reliability of his word, as certified by sealing the promise with a vow ("two unchangeable things," 6:18; cf. 7:21). Thus the "hope" of eternal salvation constitutes not wishful thinking but certain expectation, mediated by Jesus the eternal high priest in the "inner shrine" (holy of holies) of the tabernacle (cf. Exod. 26:31-35).

7–8 Christ's Superior Priesthood

Chapter 7 establishes the superiority of Christ's priesthood, "according to the order of Melchizedek" (6:20), over that of the Levites — the Hebrew tribe within which God set apart Aaron and his male descendants for priestly service (Numbers 18). The biblical portrayal of Melchizedek ("my king is righteous"), the priestly type of the Messiah (Ps. 110:4), suggests several parallels with Christ: Melchizedek's dual role as king and priest; his claim (in name) to righteousness and peace (the active experience of divine blessing); and his symbolic eternality (7:3).

Verses 4-10 show the superiority of Melchizedek (and therefore of Christ) over the Levitical priests, descendants of Abraham. That this patriarch of the priestly line tithed to Melchizedek and was blessed by him demonstrates his inferiority to Melchizedek, thus the inferiority of Abraham's priestly descendants to Melchizedek's priestly successor, Christ.

Verses 11-26 establish the need for a priesthood superior to that of the Levites and then outline the advantages of Christ's superior priesthood. The Mosaic law, practically mediated by the Levites, is inadequate to justify sinful human beings, for they cannot follow it perfectly (cf. Rom. 3:20; Gal. 2:16). A Jewish audience might well object to the notion of a non-Levite as their high priest, but the writer of Hebrews turns the problem into an advantage by asserting that the different ancestry of Christ (a Judahite) automatically necessitates new rules for salvation (grace through faith in Jesus). The Levites became priests by mere physical descent, and their priesthood lasted only for a lifetime; but Christ became a priest by divine oath, and his immortality guarantees his perpetual priesthood, his eternal role as mediator of salvation for "those who approach God through him." Furthermore, the Levitical priests had to offer sacrifices repeatedly, for their own sins and those of their fellow Hebrews. Not so Jesus, whose very sinlessness qualified him to be the one-time offering sufficient to appease God's anger against the sins of all humanity.

Chapter 8 demonstrates the inferiority of the imitative, earth-bound priestly service to its heavenly fulfillment, accomplished by the ascended Christ who sits in the place of highest honor, at God's right hand in the sanctuary that he himself built. The earthly ministry established through Moses represented a mere hint of the promises contained in the new and better covenant foretold by the prophet Jeremiah (8:8-12; cf. Jer. 31:31-34).

9:1–10:18 The Ultimate Sacrifice

Here Hebrews elaborates the comparisons between the earthly religious ritual of the first covenant and the ultimate provision of salvation by Christ. Chapter 9 outlines the floor plan and furnishings of the tabernacle, the movable tent that first served as God's sanctuary and after which Solomon modeled the first temple (cf. Exod. 25:1–27:21). Verses 6-10 point out the functional differences between the tabernacle's holy place, where the priests performed daily religious rituals, and the holy of holies, entered only by the high priest once a year to offer an animal sacrifice in atonement for the sins of the nation. The rites performed in the tabernacle purified the body, but not the conscience (vv. 9-10). They served as a stopgap till the coming

of Christ, uniquely qualified to enter the heavenly holy of holies as both high priest and sacrifice to bring about eternal redemption through the cleansing of human consciences (vv. 11-14). Thus the priestly work of Christ renders the old rituals irrelevant for obtaining eternal life.

"Redemption" (9:15-22) is the substitutionary payment of debt — moral or material — on behalf of another (cf. Exod. 13:11-16). In the Old Testament, moral redemption required the shedding of blood, which symbolized the essence of life, and the righteous anger of the holy God against disobedient sinners demanded their death. God's gracious provision in the Hebrew sacrificial system for death-by-substitute showed his great mercy. Similarly, the ratification of a covenant often required the offering of animal sacrifices, thus the shedding of blood (v. 20; cf. Exod. 24:3-11). The supreme demonstration of God's mercy, motivated by his limitless love for humans, was the giving of his own Son as the ultimate redemptive sacrifice, the shedding of whose blood seals the new covenant and guarantees forgiveness for the inheritance of eternal life.

Verses 23-28 reiterate the superior priesthood of Christ, emphasizing the perennial sufficiency of his one-time self-sacrifice. While the Hebrew high priests had to return annually to the holy of holies to make atonement for sins, Christ returns to usher in ultimate "salvation" for the "many," redeemed through their faith (v. 28).

The sacrificial system prescribed in the Law is inadequate to justify ("perfect") humans

Christ in majesty; mosaic in Hagia Sophia, Istanbul. *(www.HolyLandPhotos.org)*

before God (10:1). The Law served its purpose of making people aware of their sins (Rom. 3:20), but only the self-sacrifice of Christ can redeem them. His accomplishment of the redemptive will of the Father brings about the new covenant that offers not just temporary atonement (through works of the Law) but eternal forgiveness (by grace through faith in Christ). No more sacrifices are needed.

10:19-39 Knowledge Increases Responsibility

Jesus' continuing priestly role as mediator between God and humans enables us to "draw near" to him with full assurance that our faith in Jesus justifies us (renders us morally pure) in the eyes of God. The writer of Hebrews expresses these truths as exhortations to unwavering Christian commitment and mutual encouragement in the practical outworking of the faith. Verse 25 highlights a vital ingredient for fulfilling these admonitions: regular participation in corporate fellowship and worship.

Christ's second coming (the "day" that draws near; 10:25) will bring salvation for the faithful (9:28) but judgment for those who reject the gospel (vv. 26-31). Knowing the truth of the gospel makes a person responsible to live by it. If condemnation comes to knowing transgressors of the Law, it will certainly come, and with eternal consequences, to people who offend God by purposely refusing his free gift of grace.

Having incited fear to urge his readers to faithfulness, the writer offers encouragement (vv. 32-39). Recognizing that the addressees had previously weathered persecution well, he or she observes that now they need only endurance and the determination not to let their progress in the faith go to waste. For "shrinking back" leads to destruction, but continuing in faith results in the reward of eternal life.

11:1–12:11 Models of Faith

The writer defines faith and illustrates its outworking by citing from biblical history figures who proved their faith true by translating it to action. Faith means confident belief in "things not seen," which lack empirical proof. The addressees themselves show such faith by believing that God created the world (11:3). Retracing biblical history, the writer groups for commendation: Abel (Genesis 4), Enoch (5:21-24), Noah (6:13-22), Abraham (12:1-8), and Sarah (17:19; 21:1-2). These individuals demonstrated their conviction that God's promises find their true fulfillment in a world that transcends the present, earthly one. Their lifelong pursuit of a "heavenly" country through continued obedience to God's commands sets the standard for persevering in the Christian faith as opposed to falling away or reverting to Judaism (cf. 5:11–6:20; 10:26-39).

The roster resumes with the example of Abraham, whose faith in God's ability "even to raise someone from the dead" enabled the aged patriarch's obedience in offering as a sacrifice Isaac, the promised heir of God's covenant (11:17-19; Gen. 17:15-21). Abraham "received back" his son, as though from death, by God's last-minute sparing of the boy (Gen. 22:1-19). In ancient Near Eastern society, fathers near death pronounced blessings on their sons, the heirs to the family estate. Normally, the eldest son received a double portion of the inheritance. God's covenantal promises to Abraham passed to his descendants through a chosen line of heirs that sometimes deviated from the system: Isaac (younger than his half-brother Ishmael), Jacob (the younger twin of Esau), and Joseph (the second youngest son of Jacob) through his sons Ephraim and Manasseh, whose descendants' dual receipt of tribal territories in the promised land constituted the double portion of inheritance allotted to the chief heir. The accounts of Moses' birth, solidarity with his fellow Hebrews, and leadership in delivering them from slavery in Egypt are detailed in the book of Exodus.

After 40 years of wilderness wanderings, the Hebrews entered Canaan under Moses' successor, Joshua. Their first conquest occurred at Jericho, home of Rahab the harlot and an ancestress of none other than Jesus himself (11:30-31; Joshua 2; 5:13–6:27; Matt. 1:1-16, esp. v. 5). Between the death of Joshua and the rise of the prophet Samuel, various "judges" rose to leadership among the Hebrews, including Gideon (Judges 6–8), Barak (4–5), Samson (13–16), and Jephthah (10:6–12:7). 1 and 2 Samuel detail the activities of the prophet Samuel and King David. Unnamed models of faith (11:33-38) include Daniel and his companions Shadrach, Meshach, and Abednego, who "quenched raging fire" (Daniel 3; 6); Elijah and Elisha, who revitalized the dead (1 Kings 17; 2 Kings 4); Jeremiah, who suffered beatings and imprisonment (Jeremiah 38). According to tradition, Isaiah was "sawn in two," and Zechariah was stoned to death (2 Chr. 24:15-22).

Recounting the terrible tribulations endured by these well-known figures fosters in the afflicted addressees of Hebrews an identification with their ancestors in faith (11:35-38; cf. 10:32-34). The amazing successes of these ancestors inspire perseverance in faith (11:33-35; cf. 10:35-36). God's delay in fulfilling his promises to the ancestors actually benefits the addressees of Hebrews (and by extension future generations of the faithful) and assures them of their great worth in the eyes of God (11:39-40).

Finally, the writer offers Jesus himself as the ultimate example of faithful endurance, which resulted in his exaltation (12:1-3). A footracing strategy underlies the exhortation to "look to Jesus": contestants run straight by focusing on a specific point directly ahead (cf. 1 Cor. 9:24). The exhortation continues by downplaying the severity of the addressees' suffering for their faith (12:4ff.). Their comparatively light hardships to date represent God's discipline, which shows them to be true children of a divine Father acting in their best interest (cf. Prov. 13:24). The supporting quotation in 12:5-6 comes from Prov. 3:11-12. The ultimate exaltation of the unjustly persecuted Christ undergirds the assertion that in the end discipline produces good results (12:2, 11).

12:12-29 Divine Grace Mandates Active Appreciation

The writer exhorts pursuing peace with all people (afflicters included), but not at the expense of maintaining righteous conduct. Esau's irreversible error in selling his birthright (the superior blessing bestowed on the eldest son) is an example of godlessness, because by doing so he spurned the blessings of the Abrahamic covenant, which would have passed to him (cf. Gen. 25:27-34; 27:30-40). Sanctification is the process of being made holy; it must govern personal conduct for the common good (vv. 14-15). Not to pursue holiness risks falling short of God's grace. In other words, humans bear responsibility, not for earning God's grace, but for responding to it appreciatively with appropriate actions. Verses 18-29 contrast the former unapproachability of God, as illustrated at Mount Sinai, with the access to God enabled by Jesus. Mount Zion — the mountaintop in Jerusalem on which the temple sat — represents here the "heavenly Jerusalem," where the spirits of the privileged heirs (the "firstborn") of the new covenant claim their inheritance: "perfection," completion in righteousness. Verses 25-29 preclude presuming that God's provision of humanity's access to him involves a reduction in his holiness or its demand for obedience. Indeed, God is love, but God is still a "consuming fire," and his absolute holiness requires reverence and awe.

13 Summary and Conclusion

Miscellaneous exhortations comprise the bulk of this chapter. Active love toward fellow Christians requires hospitality to strangers (cf. Genesis 18; 19), intercessory prayer for afflicted members of "the body" (the church), sexual faithfulness in marriage, material contentedness, emulation of and obedience to faithful Christian leaders, and resistance to false teaching. Verses 9-15 discourage spiritual reversion to the constraints of the Law, whose food laws and animal sacrifices proved inadequate to effect salvation. The mandate to burn animals sacrificed as sin offerings "outside the camp" addressed the situation of the nomadic Hebrews of the exodus; the suffering of Jesus "outside the city gate" refers to his crucifixion outside the walls of Jerusalem (vv. 11-12). Jesus' all-sufficient sacrifice eliminates the need for animal sacrifices, and the writer admonishes that Christians respond by offering to God a sacrifice of praise.

Hebrews ends with closing greetings typical of other New Testament letters (vv. 18-25). Verse 23 notes the release from prison of Timothy, Paul's ministerial protégé and the addressee of 1 and 2 Timothy. The passing of greetings from "those from Italy" may indicate that the writer remains in the company of fellow Christians from Italy or writes this treatise from there (v. 24).

James

Unlike the letters of Paul, named for their addressees specified by locality, James and the other Catholic or General Epistles (1-2 Peter; 1-2-3 John; Jude) take their names from those traditionally credited with authoring them, for these books address diverse groups of Christians spread throughout the Roman Empire. James appears to target Jewish Christians (1:1), as supported by the book's dominantly Jewish flavor both in literary style and subject matter. Numerous allusions and parallels to the sayings of Jesus recorded in the Gospels — particularly the Sermon on the Mount in Matthew 5–7 — permeate the book, which, though introduced as a letter, develops more like a manual for Christian conduct. Early on, the heavily practical tone of James and its relative lack of doctrinal teaching combined with questions concerning its authorship to pose hurdles for the book's acceptance into the canon. James's insistence on goods works as the necessary outcome of genuine Christian faith guards against misconstruing the Pauline doctrine of justification through faith alone as a license for unrestrained freedom (2:14-26).

Authorship and Date

The New Testament mentions more than one James (Greek for Hebrew "Jacob"), including the apostle and brother of John martyred by Herod Agrippa I (Acts 12:2), and the half-brother of Jesus who became a leader in the Jerusalem church after Christ's resurrection and ascension to heaven (Acts 15:12-21; 21:18; 1 Cor. 15:7; Gal. 2:9, 12). The Jewish features of the book and its similarities to the speech of the James in Acts 15 support the epistle's authorship by this initially unconvinced but ultimately converted James the half-brother of Jesus. On this assumption, the martyrdom of James in A.D. 62 (according to the Jewish histo-

rian Josephus) dates its writing to the mid-1st century.

1 Wisdom from Head to Toe

As with Paul, James identifies himself as Christ's "bondservant" to indicate his voluntary servitude to the master who freed him from slavery to sin (cf. Rom. 1:1). He names as his audience the "twelve tribes" of the Dispersion — Jewish Christians living outside Palestine. Originally, "Dispersion," or "Diaspora," designated Jews deported to Mesopotamia after the Babylonian conquest of Judah in 587/86 B.C. Contrast the probably metaphorical use of "Dispersion" in the epistolary greeting of Peter, who appears to be addressing Gentiles and not Jews, whom the Babylonian exile cured of idolatry (1 Pet. 1:1; 4:3).

James begins with five subsections reminiscent of the Old Testament's "wisdom" sayings (cf. also Jesus' Sermon on the Mount in Matthew 5–7). James gives a Christian perspective to the application of Israelite moral law to attitudes and everyday living. He extols Christian maturity as the perfect result of enduring trials and the basis for rejoicing in them (vv. 2-4); commands asking God for wisdom (the ability to translate moral knowledge into practical action) but decries doubt-tainted petitioning (vv. 5-8); exposes the folly of pursuing fleeting, material wealth (vv. 9-11; cf. Isa. 40:8); defends God as the giver of good gifts only and not the source of temptations to evil (vv. 12-18); and commends obedience to the "Word" (= Christ) in word and deed as the evidence of genuine "religion" (vv. 22-27). Elaborations of these opening themes punctuate the rest of the book.

James emphasizes the importance of controlling one's speech here (vv. 19-20, 26) and in 3:1-12; 4:11, because what comes out of the mouth reveals the state of the heart (cf. Matt. 15:18-20).

Society in New Testament Times

Broad Social Values

Mediterranean antiquity exhibits a set of social values that differ markedly from modern Western culture.

Social Stratification Western culture exhibits little social stratification compared to preindustrial antiquity. Equality before the law and equal opportunity for all are deeply held values that generally find expression in daily life. The world of the New Testament was, in contrast, a highly stratified society, with a social pecking order that asserted itself everywhere Rome ruled. Basically, the empire had no middle class. It was a two-class society in which a small percentage of wealthy elites (3 percent at most) controlled both the means of production — land, in an economy based on farming — and the legal system. Control of the courts guaranteed the elites that the distribution of landed wealth would remain in their favor from generation to generation. The great majority of the population, in contrast, consisted of humble, nonelite free persons and slaves.

Preoccupation with social distinction is vividly reflected in the relentless quest for acquiring and preserving public honor on the part of the empire's elite males. Even within the two broad classes of elite and nonelite we find numerous expressions of further stratification. Elites subdivided into three aristocratic orders: senators, equestrians, and local municipal decurions. Among senators, those who could claim consular ancestry, designated *nobiles,* stood out from newcomers to the senatorial class. Certain equestrians further separated into three ranks, roughly translated "excellent," "most accomplished," and "most renowned." Nonelites were divided between slave and free and, among the free, citizen and noncitizen.

A consuming passion to identify persons publicly according to social status found expression everywhere in the ancient world. Clothing, for example, was a constant reminder of rank on the part

Roman high official wearing a toga; mosaic tombstone of Optimus, Early Christian Necropolis Museum, Tarragona. *(Phoenix Data Systems, Neal and Joel Bierling)*

of the elites. Only the senatorial class could wear the toga with a broad purple stripe. Equestrians were assigned the toga with a narrow stripe, along with gold rings on their fingers. Attempts by nonelites to usurp the right to wear gold rings in public encountered firm resistance from imperial authorities. Emperor Claudius responded to infractions against laws that reserved the *tria nomina* ("three names") and the toga for Roman citizens alone. Noncitizens who claimed for themselves these public expressions of rank were swiftly and decidedly censured.

Seating at public events similarly mirrored the social hierarchy. In Rome, Augustus confirmed the existing practice of reserving the front row of stalls at every performance for senators. Soldiers were separated from civilians, and special seats were assigned to married commoners, boys not yet come of age, and, close by, their tutors. Seating according to social status was also observed throughout the various municipalities of the empire, and enormous fines were imposed for violation. Jews in Palestine engaged in similar practices. At Qumran, for example, sitting according to rank was strictly enforced at the community's daily meal.

Moreover, different standards of justice were variously applied to persons depending on their social standing in the Roman world. In the early empire, only those with citizen status enjoyed legal protection against flogging, torture, and certain kinds of execution (e.g., crucifixion). By the early 2nd century A.D. the distinction between citizens and noncitizens had evolved into a legal distinction between elites *(honestiores)* and nonelites *(humiliores),* and cruel penalties once limited to slaves now applied to the humble free. Such inequities in the legal system appeared perfectly reasonable to ancient elites.

Relationship of the Individual to the Group Anthropologists categorize modern America as a distinctly individualistic society, where personal fulfillment, the achievement of life goals, and one's rights as an individual take priority over commitment to any social group to which a person might belong. Such was decidedly not the case in Mediterranean antiquity, where loyalty to one's dominant group took priority over individual desires and, in turn, conditioned nearly every aspect of life. People had a strong sense of group identity, along with clear distinctions between groups and clear group boundaries. Individuals were fiercely loyal to the group and found their identity primarily in belonging to a group. For this reason, characters in ancient narratives are typically introduced in relation to the family ("John the son of Zebedee"), village ("Jesus of Nazareth"), or social group ("a man of the Pharisees named Nicodemus") to which they belong.

Persons in these strong-group societies socialized their offspring not to become independent of their families of origin but, rather, to be reintegrated into family and village life as young adults (typically formalized through some act of initiation at or near puberty), where they would remain emotionally and economically interdependent with parents, siblings, and fellow villagers. In the ancient Mediterranean world, an individual would feel responsible primarily to the group for his or her own actions, destiny, career, development, and life in general. The good of the whole was of foremost concern.

Such values greatly influenced the relationship of individual Christians to their local churches in the Roman world (e.g., "Give *us* this day *our* daily bread"). This is not to rule out completely concern for individual identity and self-awareness. But we must become sensitive to group-oriented values if we wish to understand the New Testament world. For example, in prophesying in his role as high priest that "It is better for you that one man die for the people than that the whole nation perish" (John 11:50), Caiaphas was reflecting a deeply ingrained cultural value — the group comes first.

Early Church Social Values The equitable distribution of landed resources, along with equal treatment before the law, represent values that were part of Israel's heritage as a people, as reflected in the teachings of the Torah. Israel had begun to depart from these practices long before the Babylonian captivity, however, and during the New Testament era Roman Palestine exhibited the same social stratification as the rest of the empire.

In harmony with the ideals of their Israelite heritage, Jesus and his followers vehemently challenged the emphasis on rank and privilege so prevalent in the world in which they lived. Both Jesus' life (Mark 10:35-45) and death (Phil. 2:6-11) served vividly and prophetically to rebuke those aspects of culture that valued and rewarded people differently according to social status. Jesus' example soon found expression in the theology (Gal. 3:28) and teaching (Jas. 2:1-7) of the early church, whose egalitarian orientation was so countercultural to the world of their day.

Although Jesus and his followers rejected the rigid social stratification of their world in favor of the more egalitarian orientation of their local communities, they clearly embraced ancient society's emphasis on the group. The modern emphasis upon Jesus as personal savior would have been, at best, secondary to early Christianity's view of Jesus, where Jesus was understood primarily as the savior of a group. This is easily demonstrated from the language of the New Testament itself. For example, Paul uses the term "Lord" with a first-person possessive pronoun 54 times in his letters — 53 times in the plural — "*our* Lord" (Lord of a group).

Not to be overlooked is the New Testament use of the surrogate family (believers as "brothers and sisters," God as "Father") as the central metaphor for the Christian church. The patrilineal kinship group (see below) was the primary focus of relational loyalty for persons in Mediterranean antiquity. This made "family" the ideal metaphor for a new community (the church) that would command ultimate allegiance of its members.

Family in the Ancient World

Marriage Strategies Nowhere is the contrast between the ancient and modern worlds more apparent than in the respective marriage strategies of the two cultures. Marital goals in modern, individualistic societies relate foremost to the mutual fulfillment and satisfaction of the two parties involved, since there a person's spouse ideally functions as his or her central locus of relational loyalty and primary source of emotional and material support. In the world of the New Testament, however, marriage is a legal and social contract between two families, intended solely to promote the status of each and preserve the family as a whole. The concern is to produce legitimate offspring and so preserve and transfer property to the next generation. An arranged marriage could augment the extended family's wealth and social status. Feuding clans might intermarry in order to avoid future bloodshed by building an alliance. In each case, it is the good of the group — the extended family — that is in view in the arrangement. Although these social contracts might result in mutually satisfying marriages, the relational satisfaction and compatibility of the bride and groom are decidedly not a primary consideration.

Family Membership These rather utilitarian marriage strategies arise from the manner in which Mediterranean persons viewed family membership. Ancient family systems were lineage groups whose members shared a common blood ancestry (consanguinity), traced solely through the male line. Those who participated in the patriline (bloodline) were family. Those who did not remained outsiders. Family membership was, therefore, reckoned by blood, not marriage.

According to this view, a husband and wife do not belong to the same kinship group, since they originate from two different patrilines. Consequently, a person seeks his or her primary source of relational support and encouragement not from the spouse but, rather, from the members of the blood family. Marriage is therefore viewed in contractual rather than relational terms. These values are particularly apparent in times of conflict. Whenever, due to some unresolvable dispute, a person is forced to choose between loyalty to one's spouse and loyalty to the patriline, the individual generally sides against the spouse and with the blood family.

Priority of the Sibling Bond

Among the members of one's patriline no family bond exhibits a greater degree of interpersonal solidarity than the relationship between siblings. The tightest unit of loyalty and affection in the New Testament world is the lineage group of brothers and sisters. The emotional bonding modern Westerners expect as a mark of a healthy husband-and-wife relationship is there normally characteristic of sibling relationships.

The New Testament bears witness to the enduring value of sibling solidarity. Jesus, for example, places the act of leaving one's siblings at the forefront of the relational sacrifices made by some of his followers (Mark 10:28-30). In Matt. 10:21 Jesus lists the inevitable relational chaos that will result from his call to radical discipleship. Since the most important relationship in Jesus' world is the bond between blood brothers, it only follows that discord between siblings is the worst family tragedy imaginable (cf. the numerous Old Testament narratives detailing various incidents of brother betrayal).

The centrality of brother-and-sister relations to ancient Mediterranean family values explains why Jesus chose the sibling bond to define the quality of interpersonal relationships he envisioned for his community of followers (Matt. 23:8). The New Testament metaphor of "brothers and sisters in Christ" would have strongly resonated in the ancient world.

For Further Reading

DeSilva, David A. *Honor, Patronage, Kinship and Purity: Unlocking New Testament Culture.* Downers Grove: InterVarsity, 2000.

Garnsey, Peter, and Richard Saller. *The Roman Empire: Economy, Society and Culture.* Berkeley: University of California Press, 1987.

Hanson, K. C., and Douglas E. Oakman. *Palestine in the Time of Jesus.* Minneapolis: Fortress, 1998.

Jeffers, James S. *The Greco-Roman World of the New Testament.* Downers Grove: InterVarsity, 1999.

Malina, Bruce J. *The New Testament World.* 3rd ed. Louisville: Westminster John Knox, 2001.

Osiek, Carolyn, and David L. Balch. *Families in the New Testament World.* Louisville: Westminster John Knox, 1997.

JOSEPH H. HELLERMAN

Throughout the Bible orphans, who lacked inheritance rights, and widows, who generally lacked opportunities for self-support, epitomize the socially powerless and economically destitute. The Mosaic law mandated special protections for these poorest of the poor, but for believers James translates that legal obligation into the moral obligation of taking compassionate Christian initiative toward society's neediest members (v. 27).

2:1-13 No Favorites

Revisiting the subject of material wealth (cf. 1:9-11), James stresses the moral rightness of treating others with respect irrespective of their economic status. More importantly, the poor enjoy wealth of faith and share in the inheritance of God's eternal kingdom, while the rich perpetuate oppression. James's reasoning from the Mosaic law (vv. 8-11) targets his Jewish audience and sets up a foil for his admonition to live instead by the "law of liberty," the "royal law" of God's kingdom as spelled out in Jesus' teaching, which brings liberation from slavery to sin. Mercilessness toward others invites judgment on oneself (v. 13; cf. Jesus' parable of the Unforgiving Servant, Matt. 18:21-35).

2:14-26 Works Prove Genuine Faith

At first, James may seem to contradict Paul's teaching on justification (restoration to a right relationship with God) through faith apart from works (adherence to the law of Moses; cf. Rom. 3:21–5:21). But James encourages "good works" of Christian charity as evidence of salvation (v. 18). While Paul denies works of the Law as a necessary means of salvation (but cf. Rom. 2:13; Gal. 5:13-14, 19-23; Eph. 2:10), James insists that good works result from salvation and prove genuine faith. Faith without works is useless not only for those who truly need the practical help promised in pious pronouncements, but also for professing believers who fail to produce the fruit of their faith. As actions speak louder than words, faith that does not issue in good works is mere belief, and even demons believe in God (v. 19).

Both Paul and James appeal to the ex-ample of Abraham to support their teaching on justification (v. 23, quoting Gen. 15:6). But Paul focuses on the faith exercised by Abraham prior to undergoing circumcision and so faith apart from works of the Law (Romans 4). James insists that good works necessarily follow from genuine faith; therefore he emphasizes Abraham's obedience to God as a necessary outcome of his justification by God. James sees no contradiction between his assertion that Abraham was "justified by works" (v. 21) and the Old Testament's assertion that Abraham was justified because he "believed God" (v. 23). He also cites the example of Rahab the harlot, whose justification is shown by her incorporation into God's chosen community (v. 25; cf. Joshua 2; 6:22-25).

3:1-12 The Power of the Tongue

James holds teachers of the gospel to a stricter standard of behavior, presumably because of their high profile as knowledgeable practitioners of the faith after whom other Christians model their own behavior and in response to whose example nonbelievers either embrace or reject the gospel. Control of one's speech becomes the focal point, for the main activity of the teacher consists in talking, and the tongue can do just as much damage as good. But James commends controlled speech not just for teachers but for all Christians, for it enables controlled behavior (vv. 3-4). The observation that the tongue "stains the entire body" (v. 6) echoes the teaching of Jesus in Matthew 15, where he chastises the Pharisees for hypocrisy through their simultaneous lip-service to God and dishonoring of their parents. Similarly, James points out the hypocrisy of blessing God but cursing fellow humans, made in God's image (vv. 9-10).

3:13–4:10 Resisting Worldly Wisdom

James pits worldly wisdom, manifested in selfish ambition, against the "wisdom from above." Divine wisdom shows in generosity of spirit, specifically characterized in verses 17-18.

Envy — the root of selfish ambition — gives birth to strife and sin and prompts improper requests that God will not fill. For members of the church (the bride of Christ), friendship with the "world" (the domain of Satan) constitutes religious adultery. James does not mean that Christians should refrain from associating with unbelievers; rather, Christians should not adopt the attitudes and lifestyles of those not spiritually reborn (cf. 1:27). The antidote to worldly wisdom and its awful manifestations consists in mourning one's desire for worldly pleasures, resisting evil, and drawing near to God in an attitude of genuine humility. True humility disallows slander against fellow Christians, for slander equals judgment, not only of the person slandered but also of the law of love (cf. 2:8). God alone stands above the Law, so he retains the sole right of judgment and the unique power to grant eternal salvation or condemn for eternity.

4:13–5:12 A Day of Reckoning

Mortality is real. Control is illusory. James exposes the folly of ignoring these facts and pursuing material gain instead of following one's conscience (4:13-17).

In a style reflecting the Old Testament prophets, James portrays as accomplished fact the future demise of the rich and the rotting of their material treasure (5:1-6). The ultimate and eternal fate of rich oppressors spells hope for the poor oppressed and gives them reason to wait patiently for Christ's return and the final judgment. In biblical times, manual laborers received wages at the end of each workday. Mosaic law prohibited employers from delaying payment (Lev. 19:13) and promised punishment to transgressors on God's hearing the cries of the defrauded (cf. Deut. 24:15). James portrays the pursuers of wealth as fools indeed through imagery borrowed from the Israelite sacrificial system: by leading a lifestyle focused on gaining pleasure, they give God good reason to condemn them (5:5). The next verse, which intensifies the accusation in 4:2, exemplifies the frequent biblical equation of the rich with the unrighteous and the poor with the righteous (for James, oppressed believers). The selfishly ambitious do not just murder — they murder the righteous!

James cautions Christians to remain patient as they eagerly anticipate judgment day, for the same Judge of the unrighteous rich will also judge believers (cf. 4:11-12). The Hebrew prophets and Job exemplify patient endurers of suffering to whom God ultimately showed mercy (5:10-11). Christians must not slander each other (5:9) or take oaths; rather, they are simply to tell the truth (v. 12; cf. Matt. 5:34-37).

5:13-20 Responsibilities of the Community

James addresses the issue of Christian community from the standpoint of solidarity in prayer and mutual confession of sins. The sick should summon church elders to pray for healing. The accompanying "anointing with oil" may prescribe the administration of medicine, for olive oil was considered a general curative (cf. Luke 10:34). Physical ailments were thought to result from particular sins, so to healing promised in response to prayer James attaches an affirmation of forgiveness (v. 15). To encourage the practice of prayer, James cites the example of Elijah, whose earnest petitioning produced dramatic effects in nature (1 Kgs. 17:1; 18:1).

James ends on a positive yet urgent note: reversing a wayward Christian's course toward apostasy (sinning that ends in rejecting the faith) saves his or her soul from eternal death and achieves for that person forgiveness of sins so as to gain eternal life.

1 and 2 Peter

The New Testament canon groups 1 and 2 Peter with the General Epistles, so called because they do not specify individual Christians or particular church congregations as the original addressees. Both letters claim authorship by Peter, the prominent apostle who after Jesus' resurrection took the lead in evangelism among the Jews (Acts 1–12).

1 Peter

In A.D. 64 — during the reign of the Roman emperor Nero and at the outset of his empire-wide persecution of Christians — Peter suffered martyrdom in Rome, from where he appears to write 1 Peter (5:13). Since much of the letter addresses Christian persecution from the standpoint of local social harassment, not official political oppression, Peter probably wrote this epistle during the years immediately preceding his death. In it he exhorts believers to righteous conduct for future, eternal salvation despite consequent earthly persecution by unbelievers. Peter's ethical admonitions parallel those of the Apostle Paul, with whose teaching Peter may have become familiar through their common associates Silvanus (Silas) and Mark (5:12-13). Similarities in the teaching of Peter and Paul may also indicate that they drew from a common corpus of oral or written instruction.

2 Peter

2 Peter addresses a different threat to Christian faithfulness: false teachers infecting the church with heresies. Against false doctrine, Peter affirms true Christian knowledge. He shows particular concern to counter the denial of Christ's return by the heretics, who used their skepticism as an excuse for lack of moral restraint. More than half the Epistle of Jude parallels in whole or in part the wording of 2 Peter.

Authorship

Scholars have questioned Peter's authorship of both letters, and especially 2 Peter. The acceptance of the letters into the New Testament canon by the early church, which applied strict rules for canonicity and excluded books authored pseudonymously, supports the letters' claim to authorship by the apostle. Literary links between 1 and 2 Peter and the sermons of Peter in Acts further support his authorship of both letters, as do 1 Peter's multiple allusions to activities and teachings of Jesus in which Peter figures prominently in the Gospels. The noticeably different vocabulary and style of 2 Peter may stem from its different subject matter or Peter's employment of different secretaries, who according to custom exercised varying degrees of literary freedom in penning dictation. Also, the reference to Paul as "our beloved brother" in 2 Pet. 3:15-16 and the characterization of his teaching as hard to understand sound like contemporary references to an apostolic colleague, not remembrances of a pillar of the faith by a pseudepigrapher.

1 Peter

1:1-2 Greetings

In the style of ancient letters, 1 Peter begins by identifying the author, the Apostle Peter, and intended audience. The "exiles of the Dispersion" (v. 1) refers here to Christians scattered throughout the Roman Empire and living as cultural aliens in a society antagonistic to Christian beliefs and practices (cf. Jas. 1:1). The Roman provinces specified here span the northern half of Asia Minor. On the doctrine of election, briefly bridging verses 1 and 2, see Rom. 8:29-30; 9:19ff.

The Christian's sprinkling with Jesus' blood to "sanctify" (= make holy) obedience to him parallels the literal dabbing of Hebrew priests with the blood of a sacrificial animal during the ceremony of priestly consecration (Exod. 29:19-21).

1:3-12 Emphasizing Eternity

Opening with praise to God, the letter succinctly summarizes the gospel and focuses on its eternal reward for believers: by the death and resurrection of Jesus Christ, God's mercy makes possible our "rebirth" for the "imperishable" inheritance of eternal life. The "last time" (v. 5) is the return of Jesus, when the final judgment brings salvation (eternal deliverance from oppression) for believers. Although comparatively insignificant (v. 6), earthly trials serve a useful purpose, the purifying of faith, as with precious metals in a refiner's fire (v. 7). The letter commends oppressed Christians who believe in Jesus and love him without the benefit of having seen him (v. 8; cf. Thomas in John 20:24-29). Hearing the Spirit-inspired gospel is a uniquely human privilege (vv. 10-12).

1:13-25 A Call to Holy Living

The promise of eternal salvation does not relax the requirements of personal morality, as made clear in the exhortations that dominate the rest of 1 Peter. The call to Godlike holiness means abandoning "former desires" (sexual, material, social) characteristic of a lifestyle pursued out of ignorance of the gospel (cf. 2:16, 24; Rom. 6:15-23). "Fear of," or reverence for, God (v. 17) and a keen comprehension of the significance of Christ's substitutionary, or redemptive, death — like the atoning sacrifice of an unblemished lamb in Israelite sacrifices — should motivate the Christian for holy living and issue in genuine, active love for fellow Christians born into God's family through the living, imperishable Word of God, Jesus Christ.

2:1-10 Building on the Cornerstone

Christian growth, or "growing into salvation," requires nurturing a newbornlike longing for pure, spiritual sustenance. Prophecies concerning the messianic "cornerstone" provide the

The crucifixion of Peter, upside-down; etching by Jan Luiken (1649-1712).

framework for the exhortation that Christians join themselves to Jesus by embodying "living stones" comprising the spiritual temple of God (Isa. 28:16; Ps. 118:22). Originally, the texts quoted in verses 9-10 uniquely addressed the chosen Hebrew people, but Peter applies them more universally because of Christ's widening the door of salvation for the Gentiles.

2:11–4:19 A Righteous Response to Persecution

For the Christian living among unbelievers (generalized as "Gentiles"), excellent behavior characterized by "honorable deeds" invites present slander but will ultimately result in the unbelievers' glorifying God when Christ returns "to judge" (2:11-12). The injunction to obey political authorities assumes their just exercise of power (cf. Rom. 13:1-7). Christian freedom does not release believers from legal obligations; rather, it intensifies their responsibility for ethical behavior by requiring their voluntary servanthood as "servants" to righteousness (2:16).

Peter prescribes for the Christian slave the proper response to unfair treatment: follow the example of Jesus, the epitome of the unjust sufferer (cf. Eph. 6:5-9; Col. 3:22–4:1). The instructions to wives and husbands assume the social hierarchy of 1st-century Palestine, characterized by patriarchal authority and power (socially, economically, religiously, politically); however, the commendation of meekness (not weakness or timidity), chasteness, respectfulness, and beauty of character crosses all cultural and temporal boundaries. Husbands must treat their wives as equal heirs of eternal life (3:7). The principles of Christian behavior in the husband-wife relationship also apply communally within the fellowship of believers (3:8-12).

In dealing with people outside the Christian fellowship, gentleness and reverence are the rule, but not timidity. Christians should behave righteously so as to keep a clean conscience, stand up for their good behavior, and refuse to be intimidated from exercising right conduct. Current, temporary suffering for doing right is far better than future, eternal suffering for doing wrong (3:17). The imprisoned spirits who failed to thwart God's redemptive plan in Noah's day learned this truth from Christ, who between his death and resurrection descended to hell in disembodied form and proclaimed his victory over evil (3:19-20). Christ's vindication before those demons previews the final salvation of believers. Demonstrating the genuineness of one's repentance from sin by being baptized ensures ultimate deliverance through the resurrected and ascended Christ, whose exaltation by God the Father makes him sovereign over all heavenly and earthly powers (3:21-22). But the baptismal waters themselves do not wash away sins from the outside; rather, the sinner's inward repentance and faith bring about their remission (3:21).

The sinless Jesus' physical suffering provides the example for his followers, who should expect not praise but persecution by unbelievers for forsaking a sinful life of moral abandon and idolatry (4:1-6). The unbelievers' offense at "feeling judged" foreshadows their real and final judgment by God. Christian martyrs "judged in the flesh" (persecuted to death) by earthly afflicters have already received the reward of heavenly life "in the spirit" (4:5-6). In the meantime, believers must fulfill the law of Christian love by bolstering each other with practical support and nurturing spiritual unity within the Christian fellowship. Peter's exhortation to joy in suffering accords with Paul's attitude toward his persecution as a minister of the gospel (4:12-19; cf. 2 Corinthians 4; Ephesians 3). The Christian must not sin in response to suffering but instead glorify God by persisting in the righteous behavior that spawns the suffering (4:15-16, 19).

5:1-11 Tend the Flock

Peter exhorts Christian leaders to render voluntary, unselfish, and eager service to their "flocks" in an exemplary, nonauthoritarian manner. He prescribes humility for all Christians, anxiety-free trust in the caring Lord (v. 7), alertness to the ever-present danger of spiritual attack, and resistance to the Devil. For the persecuted Christian, comfort comes from recognizing that other believers are suffering, that earthly suffering is temporary, and that suffering ends in eternal reward from God.

5:12-14 Closing Notes

Peter names as courier and/or secretary of this letter his Christian "brother" Silvanus (Latin for the Aramaic "Silas," probably the Silas who accompanied Paul on his second missionary journey; Acts 15:40–18:5). Most likely, "she who is in Babylon" refers to the church in Rome (cf. Rev. 17:5, 18). In their heydays, both imperial capitals represented the apex of idolatry, but in New Testament times Babylon lay nearly uninhabited. Peter further characterizes Mark (probably John Mark, former missionary companion of Paul) as his "son" in the faith.

2 Peter

1 Knowledge Necessitates Action

2 Peter opens with a more specific claim to authorship by "Simon Peter" and a less specific identification of the intended addressees. By qualifying as "truth" the divinely imparted knowledge of God, Peter lays the groundwork for his warnings against "false" prophets and teachers in chapter 2. Because the true knowledge of God makes believers partakers of the uncorrupt divine nature, they must conduct themselves uncorruptly. Knowledge must lead to corresponding action (cf. Jas. 2:14-26; Eph. 4:17–5:20). Peter's perception of his imminent death (v. 14) motivates this reminder.

Since it is the incarnate Christ who reveals to humans the knowledge of God, establishing the historical truth of Christ's identity becomes the top priority; so Peter gives firsthand testimony of Jesus' transfiguration, when God's own declaration of the divine sonship of Christ verified his fulfillment of prophecies concerning the Messiah conveyed and interpreted by the Holy Spirit through humans, as with all true prophecy (vv. 16-21). Peter alludes to his apostolic companions as fellow witnesses of the transfiguration (v. 18), since both Israelite and Roman law required at least two witnesses to validate testimony (Deut. 19:15).

2 The Fate of False Teachers

Cf. Jude 4-16.

Just as there had always been false prophets, so now there are false teachers, against whose "destructive opinions" (or "heresies") Peter warns (cf. Col. 2:8-23). Peter castigates these self-serving false teachers, who earn divine condemnation in line with the false prophets of former times. Old Testament examples of God's condemnation of the wicked and rescue of the righteous form the basis for Peter's assurances of God's continuing power to exercise judicial control in the world till he judges it finally (vv. 5-9; cf. Genesis 6–10; 13; 18–19). The corrupt defiance of intractable false teachers exposes the untruth of their teaching (vv. 10-17; cf. the insincerity of the prophet Balaam, Numbers 22–24; 31:8, 16). In contrast, the morally excellent conduct of true Christians demonstrates the genuineness of their sharing in the divine nature (cf. 1:4-11). The false teachers' suffer wrong as the "wages" of their wrongdoing (v. 13; cf. Rom. 6:23). A person's enslavement by what overcomes him parallels Jesus' teaching on treasure leading the heart and Paul's teaching on freedom *from* sin *for* slavery to righteousness (v. 19; cf. Matt. 6:21; Rom. 6:16-20). It is ultimately worse for a Christian teacher to abandon the faith than never to have known the "Way" (vv. 20-22).

Heresies

"Heresy" derives from a Greek word meaning "selection, choice." In its first theological sense, "heresy" meant a chosen pattern of belief and practice that differs from that of others in the same religious community. Acts 5:17 refers to the "heresy" of the Sadducees, and 15:5; 26:5 to that of the Pharisees; yet both had their place within Judaism. Christianity, too, appears as a "heresy" within Judaism (Acts 24:5, 14; 28:22).

"Heresy" can also refer to divisions seemingly devoid of differences in belief and practice (Gal. 5:20; 1 Cor. 11:19; cf. 1:10-12; 11:18). But the term can also refer to differences so serious that from the writer's standpoint they rule the heretics out of his religious community (Tit. 3:9-11; 2 Pet. 2:1). Paul pronounces the Judaizing heresy — the false teaching that

Christians, particularly Gentile believers, must keep the law of Moses to maintain their salvation — a "different" or nongospel and designates its proponents as "dogs," "evil workers" who should be "accursed" (Gal. 1:6-9; Phil. 3:2). He turns Hymenaeus and Alexander over to Satan because they "rejected conscience" and "suffered shipwreck in the faith" (1 Tim. 1:19-20). Thus "heresy" comes to mean a divergence from correct belief ("orthodoxy") and practice ("orthopraxy"), though these two aspects are so closely linked that the New Testament hardly distinguishes the two. English translations render the Greek term variously with "dissension, division, schism, sect," as well as "heresy."

2 Peter 2–3 describes heresy of the most serious sort as "destruc-

tive" and attributes it to "false teachers" who "deny the Master [Jesus] who bought them" and scoff at his coming again (contrast the erroneous teachings that he had already returned [2 Thess. 2:1-3] and the resurrection had already taken place [2 Tim. 2:17-18]). They introduce their false teaching sneakily, lure their listeners with deceitful flattery and boastful bombast (cf. Rom. 16:17-18; 2 Tim. 4:3; Jude 16), exploit them financially, tarnish the way of truth with their morally unrestrained behavior (cf. Jude 4, 18; contrast the opposite error of asceticism; Col. 2:16-23; cf. 1 Tim. 4:1-5), and speak and act as though demonic forces have no power over them. Paul adds that false teachers ("super-apostles") prey on those who already believe in Christ rather than evangelizing unbelievers (2 Corinthians 10–11).

Whereas a denial of Jesus' return in judgment gave a feeling of moral freedom to the heretics attacked in 2 Peter, a claim of superior knowledge did so to those attacked in 1 John. Hence we call them "gnostics," from Greek *gnosis,* "knowledge." According to their "falsely called knowledge" (1 Tim. 6:20-21), they do not belong to the inferior world of flesh, infected as it is with evil; therefore, they "hate" true believers and claim sinlessness for themselves (1 John 1:8, 10) even though they break Jesus' commandments (2:4). In their view, their bodies do not represent their essential

Zodiac with the sun-god Helios surrounded by astrological symbols; floor mosaic in the synagogue at Sepphoris. *(Wikimedia Commons)*

identity, so that the satisfaction of fleshly lusts does not incur guilt. Thus also, they say that Jesus Christ only seemed to have a body of flesh ("Docetism"), or they distinguish a Jesus of flesh from a Christ of spirit and say that the spiritual Christ descended on the fleshly Jesus not till his baptism and ascended from him before his crucifixion ("Cerinthianism"). They deny the incarnation and death (and therefore also the bodily resurrection) of Christ as God's Son.

1 John counters these "antichrists" by affirming a unique Jesus Christ as God's Son, whose body was both seen and touched and not only passed through the water of baptism but also bled in death. The author denies believ-ers' sinlessness but affirms that as believers they cannot practice sin. He demands love of other believers and assures believers that they already have knowledge and therefore do not need to imbibe the gnostic heresy.

The New Testament treats heresy as intolerable and heretics as outlaws (cf. Rev. 2:2, 6, 14-15, 20-25). Some scholars think the descriptions of heretics' immorality to be overdrawn, but the temptation of accommodation to immorality in the pagan environment should not be underestimated. Some also think that Christianity started as a potpourri of differing factions without a common core of belief and practice, so that the distinction between heresy and correct belief/practice did not emerge till one faction became dominant over weaker factions. But at the very earliest, Paul gives the impression of a gospel held in common with Jesus' original disciples and based on tradition (1 Cor. 15:1-11).

For Further Reading

Brown, Harold O. J. *Heresies.* Garden City: Doubleday, 1984.

Turner, H. E. W. *The Pattern of Christian Truth: A Study in the Relations between Orthodoxy and Heresy in the Early Church.* London: Mowbray, 1954.

Robert H. Gundry

3 The Promised Day

Mindful of the nearing end of his earthly life (cf. 1:14), Peter completes this letter with a sermonette on the end times. He briefs his audience about mockers who, believing that the promised return of Christ will never come, pursue moral laxity in the meantime (cf. Jude 17-18). Peter revisits the example of Noah (2:5) to forewarn that the ungodly elements of the postflood world will also and certainly suffer destruction by their Creator, not through water but "fire" (cf. 1 Pet. 3:20). The delay in Christ's return proves the patience of the eternal God in providing ample opportunity for human repentance out of the Father's desire not to condemn.

Nevertheless, the time will come when God does purge the world of evil and inaugurate the reign of righteousness. The unpredictable arrival of Christ's return (the "day of the Lord," v. 10) makes it imperative for Christians to persist in godly living, so that the final judgment brings them salvation rather than condemnation. In support of his teaching, Peter cites the writings of the Apostle Paul and notes the distortion of his doctrine by false teachers (v. 16; cf. 2 Thess. 2:1-12). The falling away of false teachers from orthodox Christianity (2:20-22) forewarns Peter's audience to take seriously his admonition that they guard their own faith against the corruptive influences of "lawless" people. A closing exhortation to grow in the "knowledge" of the Lord returns readers to Peter's opening theme (cf. 1:3-11).

1, 2, and 3 John

1 John

1, 2, and 3 John are included among the General Epistles. 1 John lacks features typical of other New Testament letters, namely, identifications of the author and addressees and opening and closing greetings. It may reflect a different form of 1st-century letter or may represent one written in sermonic style and intended for circulation to various churches, as with Paul's letter to the Ephesians. Early church tradition credits the Apostle John with authorship of this anonymous letter, and its literary style and thematic emphases compared to the Gospel of John support the tradition. Tradition also asserts that toward the end of John's life he lived in Ephesus. These traditions combine with the intimate tone of 1 John to suggest that it addresses groups of Christians personally known by John in the area around that city.

Written toward the end of the 1st century A.D., 1 John combats the growing heresy of Gnosticism (from the Greek for "knowledge"), which was drawing some away from the orthodox Christian faith. Broadly speaking, Gnosticism viewed the spiritual world as good and the physical world as evil. The distinction carried deep implications for Christian belief and practice, particularly regarding the incarnation of Christ, the relationship of his divine and human natures, and the moral conduct of Christians. One form of Gnosticism, Doceticism, sought to protect the pure goodness of the divine Christ by denying his real humanity. Cerinthianism (after the gnostic leader Cerinthus) asserted that the divine spirit (in the form of a dove) came on the human Jesus at his baptism and left immediately before his crucifixion. The independence of the physical and spiritual meant that immoral conduct could not taint spiritual purity, so Christians could feel free to sin. Against this teaching, 1 John confirms the real humanity of the divine Jesus Christ, declares righteous conduct as the evidence of genuine faith, and prescribes as its necessary outcome active love for fellow believers.

2 and 3 John

2 and 3 John exhibit the features typical of New Testament letters. They identify their author as "the elder," whom early church tradition equated with the Apostle John. 2 John addresses a church, and 3 John addresses an individual. Both elaborate themes in 1 John. 2 John warns against false doctrine and teachers and admonishes active love toward fellow Christians. 3 John details examples of loving and unloving behavior.

1 John

1:1-4 Eyewitnesses to the Word

The opening verses emphasize the testimony of multiple eyewitnesses to the earthly life of Christ. The addressees would recognize such testimony as valid under both Roman and Israelite law, and their acceptance of the testimony (against contemporary gnostic heresies) would unite them in Christian fellowship with the author and his fellow proclaimers of the gospel and thus complete their joy.

From the beginning, 1 John exhibits striking literary resemblances to the Gospel of John (John 1:1-18), and the similarities support the view that the same author wrote both books. In their prologues, the most obvious parallels include the general emphasis on eyewitness testimony to the earthly life of Christ (vv. 1-3; John 1:14-15); the allusion to Christ's eternal preexistence (v. 1; John 1:1); the reference to Jesus as the "Word" (v. 1; John 1:1); the Word as the source of eternal "life" (vv. 1-2; John 1:3-4); the earthly "manifestation" (incarnation) of the Word (v. 2; John 1:14); and Christ's preexistence with God the Father (v. 2; John 1:1-2).

1:5–2:17 Walk in the Light

The symbolic language of John's Gospel resurfaces in the language of "light" and "darkness," representing good and evil (vv. 5ff.; cf. John 1:4ff.; 8:12). Since God is pure light, true fellowship with him precludes walking in darkness (sinning). When we do what is right, we enjoy fellowship with other Christians and spiritual "cleansing" from past sins through the substitutionary sacrifice of Jesus. Claiming sinlessness is self-deception, but confession of sins brings God's forgiveness and his reckoning of the repentant sinner as righteous (cf. Rom. 3:21–5:21).

"My little children" (2:1) identifies the addressees as the writer's subordinates in (and perhaps converts to) the Christian faith (cf. 1 Tim. 1:2; 2 Tim. 1:2; 1 Pet. 5:13). He aims to steer his spiritual children clear of sinning. Anticipating their moral imperfection, however, he encourages their confession of sins by portraying Christ as the righteous Advocate who represents them before God the Father and who has already appeased his just anger over the sins of all humanity (cf. Rom. 8:33-34). Nevertheless, the availability of God's grace does not reduce the importance of obedience to him. In the truth-test of 2:3-6, the author asserts that knowing Christ necessarily results in keeping his commandments (cf. 3:23-24) and walking in the light (cf. 1:6-7). Similarly, "abiding in the light" necessitates following the law of Christian love, commanded by Christ (2:9-11); and abiding in the love of God precludes loving the "world," the domain of Satan characterized by carnality, greed, and pride (2:15-17; cf. 5:19). The commendations in 2:12-14 show the aim of the letter as one of encouragement, not castigation.

2:18-28 Cling to the Truth

Now the author elaborates the assertion that the world of evil is "passing away" because the "true light" of righteousness is already shining (cf. 2:8, 17). False disciples, "antichrists," are forsaking the church — an indication of the nearing end times and the appearing of the ultimate Antichrist. The addressees with their sincere belief in Jesus as the Messiah contrast with the deserters who deny that truth, and the author urges them to cling to the teaching they originally received. He warns against deceptive false teaching, which diminishes Christ. Their divine "anointing" from God — their receipt of the indwelling Holy Spirit — ensures their perception of the truth about Christ apart from explanations by a human teacher. Holding on to that truth will make them confident encounterers of Christ at his second coming.

Library of Celsus, Roman senator and governor of the province of Asia, at Ephesus; 2nd century A.D. *(www. HolyLandPhotos.org)*

2:29–3:10 Deeds Reveal Your Identity

Spiritually reborn "children" of God act as he does — righteously. Children of the Devil act like the Devil — they sin. The writer does not deny that true Christians can and do sin (see 1:8-10). Nor does he say that non-Christians never do good. Rather, overall righteous conduct characterizes the lives of genuine believers, who when they do fall into sin lose fellowship with God temporarily. Similarly, sinfulness characterizes the lives of unregenerate non-believers, who do not know God himself, as revealed in Christ. According to the gnostic heresy combated in this letter, the essential purity of the Christian spirit went unsullied by sins committed in the flesh. But Christ came to eradicate the "works of the Devil" (3:8) — not some metaphysical idea of evil but its earthly outworking.

3:11-24 Love Brings Salvation

Active love for fellow believers assures the Christian's deliverance from "death" (eternal condemnation as the wages of sin) to eternal "life." Hating a fellow Christian is equal to the crime of murder (v. 15). Verse 16 reiterates the

self-sacrificial demand of Christ's law of love (cf. John 15:12-13), which requires not only right conduct but a right attitude of the heart (vv. 17-18). The promise of receiving from God "whatever we ask" (v. 22; 5:14-15) recalls Matt. 7:7-8. Behind the caution against surprise at the hatred of Christians by the "world" (v. 13) lie Jesus' words in John 15:18-25.

4:1-6 Confessing the Incarnation

Neither Hebrew nor Christian thought sanctions indiscriminate religious belief. The Old Testament offers guidelines for discerning between true and false prophets (e.g., Deut. 18:14-22), and here 1 John instructs Christians to discern between true and false teachers, distinguishable by their confession or denial of the incarnation of Jesus Christ. First-century gnostic heretics accepted the divinity of Jesus but denied his full humanity. 1 John attacks the false doctrine at its roots — it stems from the spirit of the "antichrist" (lit., "against Christ").

4:7–5:3 God's Exemplary Love

Active love comes from God and characterizes Christian conduct toward fellow believers. God himself epitomized this love by sending his Son as a sacrifice to appease his own righteous anger against sinful humans. The self-giving, initiative-taking love God showed for humanity obligates Christians to act accordingly toward each other. Christians can see from their own acts of love toward fellow believers that they "abide in God" (cf. John 15:1-11; 17:20-26) and thus can rest assured of avoiding punishment at the final judgment. Both 4:15 and 5:1 make clear that orthodox Christian belief includes confessing the divinity of Jesus as well as his humanity.

5:4-21 Faith for Life

Overcoming the world — gaining victory over evil and sin — necessitates exercising faith in Jesus as the Son of God. Verses 6-8 speak of Christ's coming "by water and blood" — likely references to his baptism and death as witnesses to his divine sonship and true humanity. The addition of a third witness — none other than the

Holy Spirit — seals the validation of Jesus' identity (cf. John 8:12-18). Believing in Jesus equals recognizing the truth of this testimony and obtains for the believer eternal life; disbelieving in Jesus equals calling God a liar and leaves the disbeliever devoid of eternal life (vv. 9ff.).

Verses 16-17 distinguish between "mortal" sin that does lead "to death," and sin that does not. Without specifying the particular sin or sins meant, the writer prescribes intercessory prayer only for fellow Christians committing sins not leading to death, whether physical death as a natural consequence of sin or perhaps more likely eternal condemnation, such as that earned by unforgivable blasphemers of the Holy Spirit. By denying the truth of God's witness concerning the identity of his Son, Jesus, false disciples commit such blasphemy, thus revealing their anti-Christian attitude of heart, and sealing their ultimate fate.

1 John ends on a dual note of encouragement concerning the spiritual safety of true disciples in a world ruled by Satan, and of exhortation that they guard against idolatry (vv. 18-21). Verse 20 restates the main objective of the letter: to reinforce correct belief about Jesus as the incarnate Son of God, who enables humans to realize the truth that leads to eternal life.

2 John

Guarding the Faith

An elder statesman of the church at large, "the elder" writes to a particular but unidentified congregation of Christians addressed symbolically as the "elect lady" (the congregation as a whole, chosen by God for salvation) and her "children" (its individual members); (cf. 1 John 2:1). The opening emphasis on "truth" sets the stage for a warning against falling prey to gnostic heretics who deny the full humanity of Christ. As a safeguard, the elder prohibits the church from welcoming such false teachers into their "house." This welcoming includes practical hospitality (providing food and lodging), for in the 1st century churches met in private homes, and housing false teachers would give them a forum for preaching their heresy. The elder also forbids "greeting" false teachers — acknowledging them as true believers, as fellow Christians commonly did with a "holy kiss" (cf. Rom. 16:16; 1 Cor. 16:20) or "kiss of love" (1 Pet. 5:14). Before the warnings, however, comes an exhortation to active Christian love within the fellowship of true believers, in accordance with Christ's command (John 13:31-38). In closing, the author expresses the hope of visiting his addressees and conveys greetings from the members of a "sister" church — likely his own local fellowship.

3 John

Fostering Christian Fellowship

As in 2 John, the author refers to himself as an elder statesman of the church at large. Whereas 2 John prohibits fellowship with false teachers, 3 John commands the Christian welcome of true believers. This letter addresses Gaius, whom "the elder" commends for welcoming fellow Christians he has sent, evidently to carry out an itinerant teaching ministry. In contrast, the author criticizes Diotrephes for spurning apostolic authority, failing to receive the missionaries, and opposing church members who show them hospitality. That Christian love does not equal spinelessness shows in the writer's threat to confront Diotrephes in person (cf. 1 Cor. 4:21). Diotrephes' deeds qualify as evil, for they fail to follow the law of Christian love (cf. 2 John 5-6). The author's mention of having written "something to the church" (v. 9a) may refer to 2 John, and the exposure of Diotrephes' recalcitrance (v. 9b) may directly attack the man's rebellion against that exhortation to Christian love. Alternatively, the reference may relate to 1 John, which repeatedly commands Christian love, or to another, lost letter. Demetrius probably carries the letter to Gaius. The elder recommends the courier to ensure his proper reception.

Jude

Jude appears last among the Catholic or General Epistles. Thematically, the book closely parallels 2 Peter (esp. ch. 2) in warning against heretics infiltrating the 1st-century church. 2 Peter may expand Jude, or Jude may condense 2 Peter, or both books may draw from a common source. Of all the canonical writers, only Jude employs Jewish apocryphal stories in support of his teaching (vv. 9 and 14).

Unlike 2 Peter, Jude does not specify the nature of the heresy infecting the church, but the book's condemnation of false teachers appears no less forceful, largely by piling up examples that illustrate God's past punishment of his opponents. Thus emerges the message, "Do not bond with the heretics — they are doomed!" On the positive side, Jude urges steadfastness to standard Christian belief and practice.

1-25

Cf. 2 Peter 2–3.

In writing to his contemporaries "called" to the Christian faith, the relatively obscure Jude (Aramaic for the Greek for "Judas") identifies himself first and foremost as Christ's "bondservant" (voluntary servant for life) and second as the brother of James — possibly the leader of the Jerusalem church and a half-brother of Jesus.

Having intended to write an upbeat letter in celebration of salvation, Jude has found it necessary to change his focus. Ungodly individuals who deny the lordship of Christ have infiltrated the church unnoticed, and they threaten the steadfastness of Jude's audience. In warning against the corrosive influence of such persons, Jude recalls instances of God's punishment of his opponents: the "destruction" (physical death) of a generation of Hebrews who distrusted God despite their divine deliverance from slavery in Egypt (v. 5; Numbers 14); the eternal imprisonment of fallen angels (v. 6; cf. 2 Pet. 2:4); and the fiery destruction of Sodom and Gomorrah (v. 7; cf. 2 Pet. 2:6-8; Genesis 18–19). Through licentious living, rejection of authority, and ignorant arrogance, these "intruders" perpetuate the pattern of disobedience to God exemplified by Cain, who out of jealous revenge murdered his brother Abel; continued under the misleading prophet Balaam; and pursued by the mutinous family of Korah, who sought to usurp the Hebrew priesthood (Genesis 4; Numbers 22–24; 31:8, 16; Numbers 16).

Alternately with the Old Testament allusions, Jude weaves two stories from ancient Jewish pseudepigraphal literature. The first comes from the Assumption of Moses, which reports a dispute between the Devil and the archangel Michael, come to claim the body of Moses for burial. Instead of presuming his own authority to rebuke the Devil, Michael invokes the right of God to do so (v. 9). The story provides a stark contrast to the arrogance of ignorant but dangerous infiltrators of the church — spiritually empty shells (vv. 12-13) who flout the seriousness of Christian "love feasts" (the common meal accompanying the Lord's Supper; cf. 1 Cor. 11:17-29). Jude then quotes 1 Enoch to foretell the condemnation of the self-interested infiltrators (vv. 14-15).

Jude reminds his audience that the earlier warnings of the apostles should alert them against mockers of the faith. The church should persist in orthodox belief and practice, foster communal unity and edification through prayer and the extension of mercy, and wait eagerly for the second coming of Christ.

Revelation

The last book of the Bible is perhaps also the most perplexing. Called "Revelation," it is often read as a blueprint of the catastrophes of the end times. But the book's full title, "The Revelation of Jesus Christ," makes clear that the preeminent figure in this work is Jesus Christ, the Lamb of God, King of Kings and Lord and Lords, whose victory is won through the blood shed on the cross, not the battlefield (5:8-14). In the meantime, the church suffers harassment, persecution, alienation, and even martyrdom as it awaits the return of the Lord. And for these difficult times, the church needs the encouragement that God will ultimately triumph over all the forces of evil, oppression, and injustice. Revelation provides such a reminder.

The book of Revelation has the characteristics of three genres, including epistolary, prophetic, and apocalyptic literature. In many ways it functions as do the **letters** of the New Testament. Its recipients are "the seven churches that are in Asia" (1:4), and chapters 2–3 contain a specific letter to each of these churches. John, the author of Revelation, knows about their specific circumstances and writes words of comfort and exhortation to call them to obedience and faithfulness in the face of various threats. Some of the churches (Ephesus, Laodicea) are referred to elsewhere in the New Testament (Acts 18–19; Ephesians; Col. 4:15), and others (Smyrna, Philadelphia) are known from the writings of early church fathers such as Ignatius (ca. A.D. 110).

The author also refers to his writing as a **prophecy** (1:3; 22:6-7, 18-19) and warns that the words of the book are to be *kept.* While Revelation discloses and prophesies judgment and salvation, it is above all a book which, like the writings and words of all the biblical prophets, intends to admonish, correct, and encourage its readers. It calls for repentance, obedience, faithfulness, and perseverance. Revelation is not a code that needs to be cracked but a proclamation that must be heard and obeyed.

Revelation also belongs to a genre of ancient Jewish and Jewish Christian literature designated by modern scholars as **apocalyptic.** The most common interpretive errors are to take the symbolism literally and to confuse the symbols of the book with its message. John was not predicting a time when, one by one, these symbols would "come to life" and begin to be realized in historical events. Instead, he was using symbols from his time and place to depict the Roman Empire as a beastly threat to the church. Revelation does not predict wars on the battlefield but conflicts that occur daily and repeatedly as the church struggles to bear faithful witness in a hostile environment.

Revelation has been subject to a wide variety of interpretations. The *preterist* approach suggests that the book be read entirely against its 1st-century backdrop, taking into account specific historical figures and events, and stressing what is known about the situation of the church in the Roman Empire toward the end of the 1st century. *Historicist* interpretation thinks of Revelation as a symbolic presentation of church history from apostolic times until the return of Christ. Such an approach has allowed the identification of the antichrist with a variety of historical figures, including Islam, the pope, and Hitler. There is virtually no way to validate such interpretations, for they change as world history changes. *Futurists* find in the book a message primarily, if not exclusively, for the final generation of Christians. Not surprisingly, virtually every generation of believers has had some who thought they were the "last" generation. And those who adopt a thoroughly *symbolic* (or *idealist*) reading interpret Revelation as a graphic description of conflict between good and evil, God and Satan, throughout all of history.

The Aegean island of Patmos, a place of exile for Roman political prisoners. *(www.HolyLandPhotos.org)*

John likely wrote Revelation during the rule of the Roman emperor Domitian (A.D. 81-96). Rome's military victories had brought it enormous wealth, power, and influence, but John calls the church to see through the veneer of worldly success to the corrupt empire beneath. One of the most graphic — and, for the church, threatening — demonstrations of Rome's corrupting power was the spread of state-sanctioned cults of the deities of the empire and its tolerance of the cult of the emperor. In 64-65, Emperor Nero tortured and crucified Christians in Rome. Christians were singled out as scapegoats, deemed by some as both antisocial and atheistic for their refusal to honor the gods of the Roman state. Toward the end of the century Domitian began to exhibit tendencies that led John to see him as a second Nero. In Revelation, John portrays the conflict of the church with a beastly, corrupting empire and self-glorifying emperor, anticipating both great suffering or tribulation as well as the ultimate victory of Jesus Christ.

Marianne Meye Thompson

The Churches of 1 Peter and Revelation

Revelation

Revelation derives its title from Greek *apo-kalypsis,* "uncovering." This prophetic record foresees the final fulfillment of salvation history, initiated by God immediately after the fall of Adam and Eve, and so forms a fitting climax not just to the New Testament but to the entire Bible. Revelation also comprises the Bible's most fully developed form of "apocalyptic" literature, a genre that prophesies cataclysmic events that culminate in the eternally decisive triumph of good over evil (cf. Daniel 7–12; Matthew 24–25). Apocalyptic literature flourished in the ancient world from ca. 250 B.C. to A.D. 250, a period during the middle of which grew the widespread persecution of Christians through-out the Roman Empire. Revelation emerged primarily as an exhortation that Christians resist conformity to the pagan secularism of Rome. The impetus for the exhortation may draw on Emperor Nero's past persecution of Christians to prevent their giving in to worldli-ness when threatened by future tribulation and martyrdom. Revelation assures Christians that resisting conformity to the world ensures their inclusion in the eternal kingdom of Christ, who at his second coming will crush and confine for good the forces of evil, including unrepentant humanity.

Modern readers often find understanding Revelation a daunting task at best because of the book's pervasive symbolism, frequent flashbacks, flash forwards, and unannounced switches between heavenly and earthly scenes. These features, combined with the temptation to assign symbolic meaning where it does *not* belong, make the interpretation of Revelation a matter that requires close attention and careful study. Keeping in mind the style of the book, its origi-nal purpose, and a general outline of its contents facilitates an understanding of this eternally con-sequential and universally relevant message. See "The Use of Imagery in the Apocalypse" (733-34).

Content

Chapter 1 explains the origin and nature of the book as a record of visionary messages imparted by Christ to the author, named John. Chapters 2–3 contain separate messages of ex-hortation and/or encouragement targeting each of seven churches, to which John addresses the entire book. Chapters 4–5 describe the vision-ary appearance of Christ in the heavenly court to claim his rightful inheritance of the world from God the Father. The cataclysmic events of the tribulation predominate in chapters 6–19; and the book culminates in chapters 20–22 with a description of the millennial (1000-year) rule of Christ, the last judgment, and the new Jerusalem.

Authorship and Date

The author reports his name as John. Since the writing style differs significantly from those of the Gospel and Letters of John, some scholars doubt that the same man wrote Revelation. The book does show certain thematic similarities with the Gospel (emphasis on witness/testimo-ny), and reasonable explanations for the stylistic differences include the book's unique subject matter and prophetic character, the "ecstatic" or visionary nature of its origin, and the author's probable lack of a secretary while writing from exile on the island of Patmos for preaching the gospel. Early tradition favored John the apostle as the author and during the latter part of his life locates him in Ephesus, where he would have gained firsthand knowledge of the Ephesian church and had opportunity to visit the other six churches addressed in Revela-tion (1:11). Scholars generally agree that John wrote Revelation during the last third of the 1st century, most likely during the reign of the Ro-man emperor Domitian (81-96), as attested by

Apocalyptic Literature in Judaism and Christianity

The book of Revelation has many features of a kind of ancient Jewish and Jewish-Christian literature designated by modern scholars as *apocalyptic literature,* which flourished particularly between 250 B.C. and A.D. 250. "Apocalyptic" comes from Greek *apokalypsis,* which means "disclosure" or "revelation." The word is found in the opening words of Revelation: "The revelation of Jesus Christ" (1:1). The transliterated form of the word has given us the English term *apocalyptic.*

An *apocalypse* is a literary work. It is typically a prose narrative written in the first person. As the meaning of apocalypse (disclosure, revelation) suggests, the work focuses on the disclosure of things that are currently unknown or hidden. In this work, the narrator records a series of revelations, reported to have been received either through visions, journeys to heaven, or both. The seer is guided by a heavenly escort, usually an angel, who serves as interpreter of these visions and experiences. These visions and journeys disclose transcendent realities to the "seer," who may then record them and their interpretation for others to read and ponder. The secrets that are made known typically take the form either of a historical narrative that leads to the present and foreshadows God's assured future salvation, or of heavenly myster-ies currently unavailable to human beings.

Apocalypses have a number of other features in common. They depend heavily on imagery and motifs from the *Old Testament.* They use *symbolism* of numbers, colors, and animals, particularly fantastic or mythical beasts, all of which must be interpreted for the seer. Apocalypses are generally written under a *pseudonym* of a worthy ancient figure, such as Adam, Abraham, Moses, Enoch, or Ezra. Christians also adopted the strategy of pseudonymous writing. Christian apocalypses appeared under the name of ancient prophets, such as Isaiah, and the apostles, including Peter, Thomas, and Paul. The notable exception is the book of Revelation, written by John, a well-known figure in the 1st century. Pseudonymity allowed otherwise unknown authors to claim the authority of a revered religious figure for their work. It also al-lowed the actual author to write of contemporary events under the guise of predictive prophecy. Apocalypses tend to have in common a similar worldview, known as *apocalypticism.* Apocalypti-cism is typically sharply dualistic, describing what goes on in the world in terms of conflict and even combat between good and evil or, more specifically, between God and his angels on the one hand and the Devil and demons on the other. In Jewish and Christian apocalypses, this conflict is not open-ended, but will end in God's decisive intervention to overthrow evil and vindicate righteousness. In spite, then, of the suffering and ills of the present life, a recurring theme of apocalyptic literature is the expectation that God will vindicate his faithful saints, punish the disobedient and apostate, and triumph over all powers of evil.

Although not all apocalypses have to do with the end times, many include or focus on speculation regarding the end of the present course of human history. *Apocalyptic eschatology* refers to the expectations surrounding the end as found in apocalyptic literature. These include beliefs that the end will be foreshadowed by various eschatological signs, particularly in the natural realm; that these will include or culminate in a cosmic catastrophe or series of cataclysms; that the end is near; and that a redeemer figure of some sort, such as the Son of Man in 1 Enoch or the mysterious "Melchizedek" in one of the Dead Sea Scrolls, will arise to bring God's deliverance.

Ancient Jewish apocalypses include 2 Baruch, 4 Ezra, and 1 Enoch. In addition to the New Testament book of Revelation, there are other Christian apocalypses from the 1st and 2nd centuries. These include The Ascension of Isaiah, The Shepherd of Hermas, and The Apocalypse of Peter. This last work, written in the 2nd century under

the name of Peter, describes a journey through hell and heaven and the torments and blessings to be experienced in each of these

realms. It subsequently influenced Dante's *Divine Comedy*.

MARIANNE MEYE THOMPSON

the early church father Irenaeus. Some would date the book to the reign of Nero, who began wide-scale persecution of Christians after the burning of Rome in 64, or Titus, who succeeded Nero but ruled for only two years (79-81).

1:1-8 Introduction and Greetings

The first three verses characterize this mainly visionary record as a prophecy originating with God the Father, given to Christ for his "bondservants" (v. 5), and mediated through a heavenly messenger to John, an eyewitness to the earthly ministry of Jesus, the "Word" of God (cf. John 1:1). The nearness of the "time" (the return of Christ, v. 3; compare v. 7 with Dan. 7:13; Zech. 12:10) drives home the urgency for every generation of Christians to heed this message, for "nearness" calculated according to God's timetable could mean any time soon in human terms (cf. 3:3; 1 Thess. 5:2; Ps. 90:4-6).

John greets his audience in ancient epistolary form (vv. 4-7). He addresses seven churches in Asia (a Roman province covering western Asia Minor), including congregations in the provincial capital of Ephesus and the less prominent towns of Thyatira and Laodicea (v. 11). The salutation "Grace . . . and peace" imitates the signature greeting of Paul (cf. Rom. 1:7), which pairs the usual Greek and Hebrew words of greeting and conveys the respective meanings of ill-deserved divine favor and abundant blessing. On the eternality of God heralded in verse 4 (see also v. 8, where "Alpha" and "Omega" name the first and last letters of the Greek alphabet); cf. John 1:1-2. "Seven spirits" before God's throne probably denotes the many aspects of the one Holy Spirit fully imparted to each of the seven churches (cf. 4:5; Isa. 11:2). Christ as the "firstborn of the dead" (v. 5) celebrates the victory accomplished by his resurrection (cf. Col. 1:15-18).

1:9-20 John's Initial Vision

Verses 9-10 summarize the circumstances of John's initial vision, which spans 1:11–3:22. His preaching of the gospel has landed him in prison on Patmos, an Aegean island off south-central Asia Minor. One Lord's day (Sunday), while in a state of prophetic ecstasy, he received a revelation from God. In highly symbolic language John describes his vision of Christ surrounded by seven churches, represented as golden lampstands. To John, Christ looks like a formidable human being ("Son of Man") clothed in priestly garments and displaying snow-white hair indicative of his eternality; fiery eyes that penetrate the darkest corner; hot and heavy bronze feet for stomping his foes in judgment; a voice as loud as whitewater rapids; razor-sharp words that cut both ways (for judgment and salvation); and a shining face, the intense brightness of which indicates his absolute righteousness. John faints at the awesome appearance of Christ (v. 17) but revives at his reassuring declaration of power over death and "Hades," in Hellenistic thought the scene of eternal torment.

2–3 Seven Messages for Seven Churches

Seven individualized messages to the churches named in 1:11 follow the same overall pattern: an address to the church's "angel" (a heavenly representative or guardian of the church (cf. 1:16, 20); an identification of Christ the speaker in terms excerpted from John's vision of 1:19-20 as applicable to the specific situation of the church; a summary of the church's circumstances and spiritual health; an exhortation to perseverance and/or repentance; and a promise to "conquerors," Christians who by their conduct prove themselves as true disciples of the ultimate conqueror, Christ (cf. 5:5).

The Goal of Faith

The belief that God is at work in human history and the hope that God's purposes ultimately will prevail are basic to Christianity, as they already were to Judaism. The origins of these ideas are complex but intelligible. Of particular importance are the covenantal traditions of Israel, which included promises for the future. In Genesis, Abraham and Sarah are pledged a multitude of descendants (Gen. 15:5), land (vv. 7, 18-21), prosperity, and blessing (22:18). Thus the expectation was fostered that God will act over time to fulfill God's promises. Similarly, the covenant at Sinai included pledges of deliverance, land, and divine revelation (Exod. 3:7-10; 6:2-8). The blessings of this covenant were conditional, to be bestowed or withdrawn based upon Israel's covenantal loyalty or infidelity. The coupling of faithfulness and fate led to the convictions that Israel's tragedies were divine punishments and that corporate repentance would lead to national restoration, both important ideas in later eschatological preaching.

The covenant with David (2 Samuel 7) also played a significant role in later eschatological expectation. God's promise to David of an everlasting throne contributed to the hope of Israel's renewal following the exile (Jer. 23:5-6; 33:14-26). Moreover, it became the basis for belief in a kingly Messiah who would rule eternally (Mark 11:10; Matt. 12:23).

Eschatology is a theological response to the existence of evil, a belief that, despite present appearances to the contrary, God will win. One might say that eschatology is theology projected forward: if God is such a God, then the future is such a future. For that reason, the experience of the exile was crucial to the development of biblical eschatology. Jerusalem lay in ruins. Had God abandoned Israel? Was there "a future with hope" (Jer. 29:11)? Yes, answered prophets such as Jeremiah and Ezekiel, both of whom had earlier warned of Israel's destruction. God has not abandoned the covenant. The people will return to the land, the temple will be restored, and the children of Israel equipped by the Spirit to obey the law "written on their hearts" (Jer. 31:33).

The expectation of a glorious future became increasingly pronounced in the writings of the exilic and then postexilic prophets (Ezek. 34:25-31; 36:8-12, 29-30). This trend is most evident in apocalyptic literature, which came into being at this time. Apocalyptic writings stress the imminent and direct intervention of God to destroy evil and establish everlasting peace. The apocalyptic chapters of Daniel (7-12) were especially influential, in particular, the vision of the coming heavenly Son of Man who would judge and rule eternally over the earth (Dan. 7:13-14), a complex of ideas that were taken up both by Jesus and the early church.

By the 1st century A.D., there existed in Judaism a diversely constructed but widely held belief that God would act decisively to fulfill Israel's expectations of restoration and glory. So when, according to Mark 1:15, Jesus began his ministry by preaching that "The time is fulfilled, and the kingdom of God has come near," his words were certain to cause a stir. His actions, too, spoke powerfully of the approaching reign of God. In Luke's Gospel, Jesus explicitly identifies his work with the eschatological program of Isa. 61:1-2 (Luke 4:18-19).

It is evident from the Gospel record that Jesus disappointed the expectations of most of his fellow Jews. His was not the messiahship popularly anticipated. In particular, he did not seek to gather an army and lead them against the Romans. Instead, he appears to have thought that God would act directly to bring the "peaceable kingdom" to earth. Moreover, he accepted his impending death at the hands of the Romans, believing that both he and his message would be vindicated beyond the grave.

Despite differences with his contemporaries, Jesus' expectations for the future were thoroughly Jewish. God's reign would come to earth, inaugurated by the Son of Man (Mark 8:38; 13:26-27). The first petition of the Lord's Prayer asks, "Your kingdom come, . . . on earth as it is in heaven." The earthliness of Jesus' hope is underscored by descriptions of God's dominion that include such mundane activities as eating and drinking (Matt. 8:11; Mark 14:25; Luke 22:28-29). Another link to Jewish expectation is to be found in the calling of the 12 disciples, which likely has in view the much anticipated restoration of the 12 tribes (cf. Matt. 19:28).

Jesus' teaching about God's reign emphasized reversal. The tables will be turned; those who are on the inside now will be on the outside then, and vice versa (Mark 10:31). This view is exemplified in the Beatitudes (Matt. 5:3-5)

Jesus not only anticipated this reversal; he enacted it. He was notorious for accepting the company of the unacceptable. He touched lepers and healed demoniacs, welcomed prostitutes and ate with tax collectors, approached women with respect and treated the poor with dignity.

In this as in many other cases, Jesus appears to have believed both that God's reign was still coming and that it was already demonstrated in his ministry. The distinction between what God has already done (or is now doing) and what God has yet to do is often characterized as the difference between "realized" and "future" eschatologies. The tension between these perspectives is especially pronounced in the case of the early Christians, who looked back on the work *already* completed by Jesus (such as his victory over sin and death in his crucifixion and resurrection) and also looked forward to his coming in glory.

In many important ways, the New Testament church's expectations mirrored those of Jesus. Both looked forward to the coming of God's great final victory. Both anticipated the arrival of one who would fulfill the role of Daniel's Son of Man. The early church unambiguously identified Jesus with that figure, now vindicated and enthroned in power. So the prediction of the coming of the Son of Man in Matthew (24:30-31) becomes a promise of the Lord's return in Paul (1 Thess. 4:15-18).

That is not to say that there were no differences, developments, or disagreements in Christian eschatology. In particular, the passage of time encouraged new perspectives. Many of the later New Testament writings demonstrate a shift toward a more realized eschatology. Mark, probably the earliest Gospel, has a largely future eschatological orientation; John, the latest Gospel, has by a considerable margin the most realized eschatological perspective. (Only in John is "eternal life" a present possession of believers; cf. John 3:36; 5:24; 6:47.) Other changes included the tendency to exalt the church and depreciate Israel in Christian thinking. Doubtless, the rancorous divorce between Judaism and Christianity stands behind this move toward the idea that the church had superseded or taken the place of Israel.

The move away from Israel, especially understandable in an increasingly Gentile church, fits hand in glove with a move toward a more heavenly and less earthly eschatological expectation. The "restoration of Israel" was less concrete expectation and more spiritual metaphor as time went by. The recovery of the 12 tribes became a nonissue, as did the repossession of the land. Altogether, there was more talk of heavenly and less talk of earthly paradise, although the latter did not disappear entirely (cf. Revelation 21).

Both biblical Testaments end on a note of hope (Malachi 4; Revelation 22), a fact which perfectly exemplifies the eschatological character of Judaism and Christianity. The expectation of God's final victory is not only at the conclusion of both Testaments; it is at the very heart of biblical faith.

For Further Reading

Hill, Craig C. *In God's Time: The Bible and the Future.* Grand Rapids: Eerdmans, 2002.

CRAIG C. HILL

2:1-7 To Ephesus The visionary Christ commends the Ephesian Christians for upholding high moral standards within their community. They share his abhorrence of the Nicolaitans, a Christian sect that permitted participation in the local pagan cults. But in the commendable effort to maintain religious purity, the Ephesians have forsaken acts of Christian love for one another (cf. 1 John 4:7–5:3). Only repentance — here, the resumption of loving acts — will avert God's punishment. The tree of life initially planted in the garden of Eden becomes for Christians a symbol of eternal life made available through the resurrected Christ, exalted to the heavenly "paradise of God" (v. 7).

2:8-11 To Smyrna Christ reassures his spiritually rich followers in the coastal town of Smyrna by stating his awareness of their material poverty and religious persecution. By foretelling their intensified but temporally limited suffering, he prepares them to heed his exhortation that they cling to their faith even in the face of death. Such faithfulness will seal their receipt of the "crown" of eternal life and ensure their protection from the "second death" (v. 11) at the final judgment (cf. 20:14-15).

2:12-17 To Pergamum Pergamum served as the regional center of Roman emperor worship and maintained on its acropolis an enormous altar to Zeus ("Satan's throne," v. 13). Christ commends the church as a whole for faithfulness in this pagan, pluralistic, anti-Christian atmosphere. But the community's failure to correct those who abandon orthodox doctrine and practice (vv. 14-15) has invited his punishment, and he exhorts them to repent and to correct wayward members. The promised "hidden manna" (v. 17) symbolizes eternal life and recalls the food miraculously given to the Israelites of the wilderness wanderings. The inscribed white stone, representing a favorable vote in 1st-century legal and business practices, constitutes a ticket to eternal life for the faithful.

2:18-29 To Thyatira In contrast to the situation at Ephesus, acts of Christian love have increased at Thyatira, but Christians there tolerate a false prophetess and teacher ("Jezebel"; cf. 1 Kings

Asklepion (healing sanctuary) at Pergamum, a city among "the seven churches that are in Asia." *(Richard Cleave, Pictorial Archive)*

16–21) who has pursued and encouraged participation in immoral and idolatrous practices, perpetuated at pagan festivals sponsored by the city's numerous trade guilds. For refusing to mend her ways she incurs a curse from God — good reason for her wayward companions to repent and for others to persist in orthodox belief and practice. In verses 26-27, the promise given to the faithful recalls Ps. 2:8-9. Thyatira was the hometown of Lydia, Paul's first-recorded convert in Europe (Acts 16:14).

3:1-6 To Sardis The church in Sardis enjoyed a reputation for Christian vitality, but John's vision exposes the truth of its spiritual apathy. Unless Christians there soon demonstrate their faith with action, Christ's return will catch them off guard, and they will come up short on judgment day. The few who remain faithful receive Christ's assurance of eternal life and the promise of "white garments," symbolizing justification (consideration by God as righteous; cf. v. 18). The metaphor carried special significance in view of the city's wool-dyeing industry.

New Testament Attitudes toward the Roman State

New Testament views of Rome range from affirmation of its authority to guarded acknowledgment of its power to negative assessment of state power as demonic.

Several epistles urge a positive approach toward the Roman state. Titus 3:1 encourages peaceful behavior by reminding Christians "to be subject to rulers and authorities, to be obedient." Similarly, 1 Tim. 2:1-2 urges the reader to pray "for kings and all who are in high positions," again so Christians may live in peace under rulers who strive to secure peaceful conditions. Likewise, 1 Pet. 2:13-14 advocates obedience to state authority "for the Lord's sake." The purpose here, however, is more directly to silence criticism of the church. Christians are to prove by their obedience to the state that they are good citizens and no threat.

In Rom. 13:1-7 Paul provides Christians in Rome with specific instructions on how to relate to the Roman state. They are to "be subject to the governing authorities," recognizing that ultimately all authority comes from God, who uses even Roman officials as instruments of peace. Possibly writing with a view to the edict of Claudius in A.D. 49 that had expelled Jews from Rome for rioting and Nero's probable recent rescinding of that edict early in his reign, Paul urges the Roman Chris-

tians, both Jew and Gentile, to live together in peace so no repetition of the earlier disorder might occur and adversely affect the church in Rome. In Rom. 13:6-7 Paul specifically urges Christians to pay their taxes. Josephus indicates that nonpayment of taxes was already advocated at that time by Zealots in Judea (*J.W.* 2.118), and Tacitus notes that Romans themselves were complaining about the practices of tax collectors (*Ann.* 13.50-51). Paul's strong affirmation of Roman authority is aimed at stemming unrest that could lead to disastrous consequences for Christians in Rome.

Luke-Acts reflects a more guarded acceptance of Roman authority. Luke 2:1-5 depicts Jesus' parents complying with a state-ordered census. In Luke 20:25, Jesus allows paying taxes to Rome, but again ultimate loyalty must be to God. Throughout Acts Paul enjoys the privilege of Ro-

man citizenship and appeals to Roman authority for protection. Paul and other Christians who are investigated by Roman officials are exonerated by them. The same respect does not hold for Jewish authorities ruling with Roman support. When ordered by the council convened by the high priest to stop their preaching, Peter and John assert that one must obey God rather than any human authority whenever their commands conflict with one another (Acts 5:29). In Acts 12, Herod is guilty of abusing his power by persecuting the church. Luke's apologetic concern allows him to portray Jewish authorities ruling under the Romans in a negative light, but he refrains from criticizing the Romans themselves.

Jesus' word about paying taxes (Luke 20:25; cf. Matt. 22:21; Mark 12:17) reflects caution about complete acceptance of Roman authority. As long as the Roman state

Bronze prutah of the Roman procurator Pontius Pilate, with inscriptions "of Tiberius Caesar" (left) and "year 18" (right); minted in Judea, A.D. 31. *(Richard Cleave, Pictorial Archive)*

abides by its God-given mandate to maintain the peace, it should be supported. State authority, however, is limited to the political realm; the state has no jurisdiction in "the things that are God's."

Revelation 12–13 and 17 express a negative rejection of state power when that power has overstepped the boundary between the political and the religious. Generally understood to refer symboli- cally to Rome and the cult of the emperor, to which residents of the empire were expected to show devotion, Revelation portrays the Roman state as demonic. In this, the book expresses an attitude toward Rome found in other early Christian writings of the period (cf. Epistle of Barnabas 2:1; 4:3-5; Sibylline Oracles 8:65-72). Possible persecution of the church by Ro- man officials has here altered the relative tolerance toward the state implied in earlier New Testament books. As long as the state fulfills its role as peacekeeper, Christians are urged to recognize its authority and to support it with prayers and taxes. When it conflicts with the ideals of religion and punishes those who cannot compromise their loyalty to the higher authority of God, it is to be resisted.

R. SCOTT NASH

3:7-13 To Philadelphia Only encouragement and promise come to the relatively small but commendably steadfast church in Philadelphia, persecuted by Jewish rejecters of the gospel. Christ, who as the heir of David keeps the key to the messianic kingdom (cf. 2 Samuel 7; Matt. 1:1-17), reassures them of their salvation.

"Pretribulationist" interpreters take the promise in verse 10 to "keep you from the hour of trial" as an indication that God will remove true Christians in a "rapture" before the great tribulation. "Posttribulationists" believe the phrase promises Christ's faithful protection on earth *during* the final display of divine judg- ment (cf. John 17:15).

3:14-22 To Laodicea The relatively easy life enjoyed by Laodicean believers bred spiritual apathy. This self-sufficient city had grown so wealthy from banking and industry that it needed no aid from Rome for reconstruction af- ter a destructive earthquake in 60. Likening the temperature of the church to Laodicea's water supply, turned tepid while flowing by aque- duct from a nearby hot spring, Christ calls the congregation good for nothing and threatens metaphorically to spit the lukewarm Laodiceans out of his mouth.

Residents of this renowned center for medical studies used a Phrygian eye-powder acclaimed for its curative powers and wore distinctive garments made from the wool of the region's sheep, famous for their jet-black coats. But Christ exposes the physically healthy and well-clothed Laodicean Christians as spiritu- ally blind and naked. He exhorts them to "buy" from him heavenly treasure (by putting their faith into action), don the "white" garments of righteousness (cf. vv. 4-5), and gain spiritual eyesight from him. Note Christ's assurance that his continued love for the lackadaisi- cal Laodiceans motivates his reproval (v. 19). His knocking on the door to the hearts of the spiritually calloused Laodiceans (v. 20) invites them to join the messianic banquet and renew their covenant with him. Assuring to those who respond a royal seat with the resurrected, ascended, and exalted Christ promises them eternal life in the messianic kingdom (v. 21).

4 John Visits Heaven

In a new vision, Christ invites John to enter heaven and learn of future events on earth. There he sees God the Father enthroned in splendor and surrounded by 24 similarly en- throned "elders," clothed in white (symbolizing righteousness) and crowned with gold (their heavenly treasure). These elders may represent the true church, comprised of the new Israel (drawn from the 12 Hebrew tribes) and the apostolic church (born from the ministry of the 12 apostles; cf. 7:5-8; 21:12, 14). Others interpret the elders as individuals, namely, the 12 patri- archs and the 12 apostles. The attendant thunder and lightning evidence the presence of God (cf. 11:19; Exod. 19:16). In front of the throne appears the Holy Spirit, manifested as seven burning lamps corresponding to the seven churches (cf. 1:20). A crystalline sea and four creatures, rep- resenting all earthly beings, complete the scene. As the creatures continually confess the holiness of the almighty, eternal God, the elders prostrate themselves in worship before the Creator.

5 The Seven-Sealed Scroll

God holds a scroll inscribed on both sides but unreadable because seven seals secure its outer edge. The scroll represents the deed to the created world, the inheritance reserved for a worthy recipient (vv. 9-10). When no viable candidates emerge, John weeps. But a deserving heir does appear: the Lion of Judah, descended from David, who through resurrection overcame death as the ultimate sacrificial Lamb that now intercedes between his faithful followers and God his Father (cf. Heb. 4:14–5:10). In the Bible the number seven represents perfection or completion, and here the seven horns of the Lamb represent his supreme power, as the seven eyes stand for the Holy Spirit sent to all believers after Jesus' ascension to heaven (cf. John 14:16; 16:7-14). The Lamb's taking of the scroll prompts universal worship that acknowledges his worthiness to inherit the messianic kingdom.

6–16 The Seven Seals, Trumpets, and Bowls

John sees three groups of ultimate catastrophes, initiated by the breaking of seals. Tragedy intensifies as the tribulation wears on.

6:1–8:1 The Seven Seals The disasters represented by the seals focus on war and its fallout.

6 Militarism Spawns Martyrdom By breaking the seals on the scroll, the Lamb asserts his right to rule the world. But chaos abounds, and the world becomes temporarily worse before Christ makes it eternally better. Militarism tips the first domino in a series of disasters: war, famine (flour for a couple of loaves of bread costs an entire day's wage, v. 6), death, persecution and martyrdom, and worldwide fear inspired by natural disasters that presage the second coming of Christ (cf. Matt. 24:29-30; Mark 13:24-26; Luke 21:25-27).

But the destruction intensifies at the authoritative direction of the supreme God, who judges the world even as he goes about redeeming it.

Christians who suffer increasing persecution undergo the testing of their faith, martyrs for which receive the heavenly rewards of rest and a "white robe" signifying justification (cf. 2:10 and God's hardening of Pharaoh's heart to the ultimate advantage of the chosen Hebrews; Exod. 4:21). Indeed, completion of God's plan requires filling up the ranks of predetermined martyrs, so that their deaths become not simply tragic consequences but redemptive triumphs paralleling the victory over death won by Christ (6:10-11; cf. Heb. 11:32-40).

7:1–8:1 Protecting the Elect Next John sees four angels restraining the "winds" of destruction on earth. The angels may represent the four horsemen given authority to wreak the havoc (v. 2; cf. 6:2-8). Before the devastation starts, a fifth angel marks for protection from divine wrath 12 thousand saints from each of 12 Hebrew tribes, for a total of 144 thousand. The "seal" stamped on their foreheads indicates ownership and provides protection (cf. 14:1). The pervasive symbolism in Revelation supports interpreting the 144 thousand saints as representative of the *last generation* of the church, comprised of both Jews and Gentiles proven true by persecution in the great tribulation (v. 14). The number 144 thousand may derive from 12 (the patriarchs or tribes) × 12 (the apostles) × 1000 (perhaps representing the "great multitude," v. 9; cf. the "thousands of thousands" of worshippers in 5:11). The posttribulational multitude "standing" before the throne of God answer the question in 6:17 of who will receive divine protection to withstand the final "wrath of the Lamb." The characterization of the group in purely Jewish terms (vv. 4-8) allows a parallel with the faithful remnant in Isaiah 24–27 (the "Isaiah Apocalypse"), a prophecy rooted in the promised restoration to Canaan of Jews exiled to Babylon (compare v. 17 and Isa. 25:8).

The scene in vv. 9-12 describing universal praise of God parallels that in 5:9-14. But the breaking of the final, seventh seal freezes even that awesome activity as complete silence permeates heaven in recognition that the end has come.

8:2–11:19 The Seven Trumpets Ancient Near

Eastern armies began battles in response to the blast of a trumpet. In Revelation, seven trumpets sound to activate plagues and punishments that give humanity a warning taste of the nearing last judgment of God.

8:2-13 Natural Disaster Strikes Before the disasters fall, an angel reinforces the prayers of saints (5:8; cf. 6:10) "sealed" for protection in chapter 7. The natural disasters delayed in 7:3 and now launched by the first four trumpets recall several of the plagues inflicted on Egypt (compare v. 7 with Exod. 9:22-35; v. 9 with Exod. 7:20-21; v. 12 with Exod. 10:21-29). The growing intensity of the final catastrophes becomes evident in the increased percentage of people afflicted: from 25 percent by the seal-judgments (6:8) to 33 percent by the trumpet-disasters (vv. 7-12), with worse to come foredoomed in verse 13. Nevertheless, God remains in control of the world and continues to set limits on its devastation (cf. ch. 6).

9 Release the Demons! With the sounding of the fifth trumpet, Satan (the "fallen star") releases demons (represented as locusts) empowered to torment unbelievers who have not been sealed. This trumpet-disaster is the first to target human beings directly. The names of Satan in verse 11 mean "Destruction/Destroyer."

The "first woe" (v. 12; cf. 8:13) refers to the events recorded in vv. 1-11. The second woe (vv. 12-21) starts at the sounding of the sixth trumpet, when four angelic cavalry commanders are ordered to kill one-third of humankind. The deadly judgment seems intended by God to prompt repentance by the wicked survivors, though they ignore the warning (vv. 20-21).

10 The Seven Thunders Sealed Up The merciful interlude between the sounding of the sixth and seventh trumpets parallels the delay before the breaking of the seventh seal. Here the sealing up or calling off of seven peals of thunder, which portend seven more disasters, spares the entire world (land and sea). Contrast in chapters 6–7 the launching of disasters by "unsealing" the scroll and the sparing of Christians by "sealing" (marking) them for protection.

The "little scroll" (cf. ch. 5) held by the "mighty angel" (Christ? cf. 1:13-16; 7:2) and eaten by John tastes sweet because it represents sweet relief for believers (God's word). But once in his stomach the book nauseates John, for that message means divine judgment for the unrepentant.

11 The Two Witnesses This passage invokes a number of images from the Old Testament. Compare John's visionary measuring of the temple and altar with Ezekiel 40–42; the two olive trees and two lampstands with Zechariah 4 (esp. vv. 11-14); and the calling of the "great city" "Sodom" and "Egypt," symbolizing depravity and oppression. The Law required "two witnesses" to confirm testimony (Deut. 19:15).

The measuring of the *earthly* temple appears to set the boundaries of protection for true believers during the tribulation. The 42 months given to the nations to trample the city made holy by the presence of the temple equal the 1260 days (42 months of 30 days each) during which the "two witnesses" (Moses and Elijah? the true, witnessing church of the tribulation?) prophesy doom, as indicated by their dress as mourners. Eventually slain by the "beast" of the abyss, the demon king of 9:11, their bodies lie unburied and exposed — the ultimate dishonor — while their human enemies celebrate. But three and one-half days later God rewards the martyred witnesses with resurrection and ascension to heaven in full view of their foes.

The "third woe" (vv. 15-19) comes with the seventh trumpet, heralding the inauguration of Christ's eternal rule over the messianic kingdom, and the 24 elders introduced in 4:4 summarize and praise his final victory. The awesome display of nature that attends the opening of the heavenly temple bespeaks the presence of God, for whom the long-lost ark of the covenant will again serve as throne (cf. Jer. 3:16).

12 Signs of the Times Chapters 12–14 portray the last ditch efforts of a desperate Satan to dominate the world. Ousted from heaven and aware that his days on earth are numbered, he tries to take the faithful down with him. But even the earth itself works against him (v. 16).

Here Satan is a great, red dragon, the "ancient serpent," deceiver of the whole world, and perpetual "accuser" of believers. By contrast Christ, the sacrificial "Lamb" (v. 11), is the advocate of his followers in the heavenly court (1 John 2:1). The archangel Michael (v. 7), commander of the heavenly army that evicts the satanic forces from heaven, figures in Dan. 12:1 as guardian of the Hebrew people.

The identity of the woman who gives birth to a son remains less clear. Some interpreters see her as the Hebrew nation, which gave birth to the Messiah (v. 5) and ultimately to the church (her persecuted offspring, v. 17). Others interpret her as Jesus' first disciples, who "cried out" in grief at his death (the "birth" of salvation, v. 2; cf. John 16:20-22) and established the church after his ascension to heaven (v. 5). The woman's finding refuge in the wilderness parallels the Hebrews' deliverance from Egyptian oppression (v. 14). The period of her temporary respite — a "time" (one year), "times" (two years), and "half a time" (half a year) — corresponds to the three and one-half years granted to the nations for trampling the holy city and to the two witnesses for prophesying (cf. 11:2-3; Dan. 7:25; 12:7).

13 The Beast and Its Brand A blasphemous beast emerges from the sea (symbol of uncontrollable chaos), derives power and authority from the dragon of chapter 12, inspires worldwide worship of itself by recovering from an apparently mortal wound to one of its heads, persecutes Christians, and acts in defiance of God for 42 months (cf. 11:2-3). Only true believers, whose names appear in Christ's book of eternal life, refuse to worship the beast. Another beast, in sheep's clothing, comes forth from the earth (v. 11) and executes the orders of the first beast by performing miraculous signs that trick people into worshiping it, slaying resisters, and branding compliers with a mark that licenses them alone to go about normal life. The mark, 666 — called a human number since repeated sixes never reach seven, the Bible's numeric symbol for perfection — represents the antithesis of the seal received by the 144 thousand saints of chapter 7. People branded with the mark of the beast enjoy immunity from its punishments but lie exposed to divine wrath, while true believers bearing God's seal stand

protected from his wrath but invite persecution by the beast.

The beast may embody at once the four, successive world empires of Daniel 7, with the Roman Empire representing the beast. The revitalization of the slain head of the beast may reflect the suspicion that Nero did not die in 68, as reported, but would return and revive the empire (Nero *redivivus* [returned to life] myth). The second beast (the "false prophet" of 16:3; 19:20) would stand for imposed emperor-worship. An alternative interpretation identifies the figures as the antichrist and his top aide, who as head of the state cult compels worship of the emperor (cf. 19:20, which portrays the beast and the false prophet as individuals, not institutions).

14 The Lamb and the Redeemed John now envisions a posttribulational celebration. Zion names the Temple Mount in Jerusalem (alternatively, the heavenly Zion), where Christ, the Lamb, appears accompanied by the 144 thousand saints. "Redeemed" through Jesus' death on the cross, they are a faithful ("not defiled") sacrifice ("firstfruits") consecrated to God and celebrate having survived the tribulation without bowing to the false prophet or the antichrist (13:14-15).

Verse 6 returns to the tribulation, when prophesying angels warn of God's impending eternal judgment against people who join the cult of the beast. John's audience would have understood "Babylon" (v. 8) to symbolize Rome. Both empirical capitals epitomized moral decadence. The fall of seemingly invincible Babylon makes certain the fall of the current (and future) political centers of godlessness; and so the prophecy of verse 8 is expressed as accomplished fact.

Verses 14-16 describe the "reaping" of the saints — the reward apparently celebrated in verses 1-5. That the crowned reaper sits on a cloud (an indicator of divinity), looks like the "Son of Man" (Jesus' favorite self-designation, meaning simply "human being"), and responds to orders originating in the temple (which houses the throne of God) paints a picture of Christ's second coming.

Verses 17-20 describe the outpouring of

The Use of Imagery in the Apocalypse

Symbols convey meaning to people's rational, emotional, or perceptive dimension and include various numbers, colors, places, objects, and beings. Though scholars debate the interpretation of these elements, it is certain the original audiences understood the images they portrayed.

Numbers were used to express quantities and/or symbolic meanings and were derived through a variety of means, including *gematria,* the application of the numerical value of alphabetical letters. The number *three* often symbolizes completeness. The Trinity is portrayed as Father, Son, and Holy Spirit; likewise, the dragon, the beast from the sea, and the beast from the earth represent an unholy trinity (Rev. 12:9; 13:1-11). *Four* can indicate boundaries, as in the four living creatures surrounding God's throne (4:6-7; 15:7; 19:4) and the four horsemen of the apocalypse (6:1-8). *Six* can refer to humankind. It is used in a multiple number 666 (13:18) and interpreted by some in a reverse form of gematria with reference to an individual or as the unholy trinity. *Seven* is used literally with reference to the seven churches of Asia (2:1–3:22) and symbolically to indicate perfection or completion. The most powerful anti-Christ beast has seven heads (17:3, 7). The restoration of the earth takes place during the seventh seal, and the seventh trumpets occur after the seventh plague (11:14-19). *Ten* may also indicate completion and derives

its significance from the 10 fingers of a hand. Ten also draws on the combination of three and seven (completion). Scholars interpret the 10-day imprisonment of the faithful of Ephesus as literal (2:10). The symbolic/literal interpretation of the 10 horns of the great red dragon (12:3); the 10 horns of the

beast out of the sea (13:1); and the scarlet-colored beast with 10 horns (17:3, 7, 12, 16) is debated. *Twelve* represents order and derives attention from the 12 tribes and the 12 apostles. The New Jerusalem has 12 gates and 12 foundations (21:12-14, 21), and the tree of life yields 12 kinds of fruit (22:2).

The woman and beast in the wilderness and the fall of Babylon; woodcut by Martin Gräff, 1502.

Revelation contains multiples of 12: the 24 elders around God's throne (4:4); the 144 thousand composed of 12 thousand from 12 tribes (7:4); and the New Jerusalem measuring 12 stadia (21:16). *Thousand* represents a large number: Satan's being bound for a thousand years (20:3, 7), and the thousand-year interval between the first resurrection and the second death (20:6). Likewise, multiples of a thousand represent an uncountable number: the 10 thousand times 10 thousand, and thousands of thousands praising God in heaven (5:11).

Revelation contains vivid *colors. White* can have a literal interpretation and also symbolize purity and conquest. It describes Christ's hair (1:14); the stone given to the overcomer (2:17); the garments of God's servants (3:4-5, 18; 7:9); the clothing of the 24 elders (4:4; 7:13); horse(s) (6:2; 19:11, 14); the robes of the martyrs (6:11); robes made white by the blood of the lamb (7:14); a cloud (14:14); the army from heaven robed in white (19:14); and the great white throne (20:11). *Red* symbolizes slaughter/bloodshed: the red horse (6:4) and a great red dragon (12:3). *Black* is often associated with famine and scarcity: the black horse (6:5). *Ashen/pale* represents death, the color of a corpse: the ashen/pale horse (6:8).

Beings can be used symbolically: *angels* range from messengers (1:1; 2:1, 8, 12, 18) to celestial beings (5:2; 7:2; 14:6, 8-9, 15, 17-19). The *lamb* symbolizes the crucified Christ (5:6, 8, 12-13; 12:11; 21:9, 14, 22-23). Other beings include the seven *spirits,* interpreted as angels or the Holy Spirit (4:5); the four *living creatures* around the throne (4:6). The *woman with child* represents Israel (12:1-2), but the *son* is Christ (12:5). The *dragon* is Satan (12:3-4, 7, 9, 13, 16-17; 20:2); the *beast from the sea* represents world empires (13:1); and the *beast from the earth* has secular power and gives religious sanction for its injustice (13:11).

Symbolic *objects* include a variety of items. *Names* can be literal (3:5, 8; 13:6, 8, 17; 19:12) or offer a symbolic description of a person's character (3:1; 9:11; 15:2; 17:5; 19:13). The *bow* (6:2) and the *crown* (2:10; 6:2; 12:1) symbolize conquest and victory. The *scales/balances* symbolize a time of scarcity (6:5). The *measuring rod* represents God's care and protection of his people (11:1; 21:15). *Horns* symbolize power: the slain lamb with seven horns (5:6); four horns of the golden altar (9:13); the great red dragon with 10 horns (12:3); the beast from the sea with 10 horns (13:1; 17:12, 16); the beast from the earth with two horns as a lamb, symbolizing harmlessness (13:11); the scarlet beast with seven heads and 10 horns (17:3, 7). *Diadems* are the insignia of royal authority (12:3; 19:12). *Lightning and thunder* are visible and audible portrayals of God's power and majesty (4:5).

Places and *people* are described symbolically. Babylon is the symbolic name for Rome (14:8; 16:19; 18:2, 10, 21). God's people are described as Israel (7:4) and the beloved city (20:9).

Revelation is unique to the New Testament in style but not in perspective, for it presents the exalted Christ. One must use discernment in interpreting this book. Some passages call for a literal interpretation, while some are figurative. The multiplicity of symbols demonstrates John's vividness in presenting Revelation and the rich experience of God's people.

For Further Reading

Aune, David E. *Revelation.* 3 vols. WBC 52. Waco: Word, 1997-98.

Butler, Trent C., ed. *Holman Bible Dictionary.* Nashville: Holman, 1991, *s.v.* "Imagery," 689; "Number Systems and Number Symbolism," 1029-31; "Symbol," 1310-11.

Clouse, Robert G., ed. *The Meaning of the Millennium: Four Views.* Downers Grove: InterVarsity, 1977.

Koester, Craig R. *Revelation and the End of All Things.* Grand Rapids: Eerdmans, 2001.

Mounce, Robert H. *The Book of Revelation.* NICNT. Grand Rapids: Wm. B. Eerdmans, 1977.

STEVEN L. COX

God's wrath on worshippers of the beast, as warned in verses 6-11. There the "cup of his anger" contains the "wine" of his wrath (v. 10). These final four verses describe the production of this wine as the trampling of human "grapes" ripened by godlessness for divine judgment. Dealing with sin "outside the city" keeps the city from defilement (cf. Lev. 4:21; 24:23). Verse 20 may foreshadow the battle of Armageddon (16:12-16) or symbolize the global nature of God's judgment against sinful humanity.

15–16 The Seven Bowls The plagues poured out from seven bowls display God's wrath against the unrepentant and come rapid-fire at the end of the tribulation (15:1; 16:17). Resisters of the beast, the saints marked with the seal of God, enjoy immunity from these divine punishments, which largely parallel the trumpet-disasters and/or recall plagues inflicted on Egypt. The saints celebrate deliverance by singing the "song of Moses," which recalls safe passage through the Red Sea (15:3-4; Exod. 15:1-8; Deut. 32:1-43). Other Old Testament allusions include the heavenly "tent of witness," reflecting the tabernacle housing the ark of the covenant (15:5; Exodus 24–27); the priestly robes of the angels (15:6; cf. Exodus 28); and the smoke filling the temple as indication of God's glory (15:8; cf. Exod. 40:34-38).

The first bowl-plague causes "painful sores" reminiscent of the boils inflicted on the Egyptians (16:2; cf. Exod. 9:9-11). The second and third plagues putrefy fresh- and saltwater sources so both land and sea creatures die, and the fifth plague darkens the earth. All three duplicate earlier trumpet-disasters (compare 16:3-4 with 8:8-11; Exod. 7:20-21; 16:10 with 8:12; Exod. 10:21-29). The pouring out of the seventh bowl creates an unprecedented storm even more devastating than the hailstorm rained on the Hebrews' Egyptian oppressors (compare 16:17-21 with Exod. 9:22-35).

The initial bowl-plagues appear divinely intended to prompt repentance by worshippers of the beast (16:9-11), but as with Pharaoh their persistent recalcitrance eventually seals their fate. Thus the drying up of the Euphrates River in 16:12 promises not deliverance but doom (contrast Exodus 14). In the 1st century, the Euphrates delimited the civilized world, so

in John's vision the barbaric armies to the east answer the satanic summons to "Harmagedon" (Hebrew for Mount Megiddo, Armageddon), for all-out battle against God. Megiddo, which guards a strategic east-west pass through the Jezreel Valley in Galilee, was the site of countless armed engagements since ancient times and had become a symbol of military conflict. The final battle in John's vision (elaborated in 19:11-21) ushers the fulfillment of 14:8 by felling "Babylon the great" (16:19).

17:1–19:4 The Fall of Rome

As noted, "Babylon" refers to Rome, the city built on seven hills (17:9) and 1st-century champion of apostasy and immorality (cf. 14:8). The lengthy description of Rome's religious harlotry (ch. 17) and materialistic pursuit of pleasure (ch. 18) makes God's annihilation of the self-secure superpower a necessary act of divine vengeance and justifies the saints' celebration of her demise (19:1-4). The couching of her wickedness in sexual terms reflects the language of the Hebrew prophets (cf. Isa. 1:21; 23:15-18; Jer. 2:1–3:5; Ezekiel 16; 23). The "adultery" of Rome stands in contrast to the "chastity" of the saints in 14:4 and the portrayal of the church as the pure bride of Christ in 19:7. Interpreters view

The mound of Megiddo (Hebrew "Harmagedon" or Armegeddon), where John envisioned the final battle between the forces of God and the forces of evil.
(Richard Cleave, Pictorial Archive)

the beast-serving kings of 17:9-18 variously as specific Roman emperors or symbolically succeeding world empires.

19:5-21 The Marriage Banquet

The heavenly banquet celebrating the marriage of Christ, the Lamb, and his bride, the true church, fulfills the prophetic parables about the messianic wedding feast recorded in Matt. 22:2-14; 25:1-13; Luke 14:15-24 (cf. Matt. 8:11; Luke 13:29). Verses 11-21 describe a different kind of feast — the bloody banquet of Armageddon, when evil gets devoured by the army accompanying Christ at his second coming (cf. 16:17-21).

20 The Binding of Satan

With his servants, the beast and the false prophet, defeated at Armageddon and consigned to the "lake of fire" (19:20), the dragon (Satan) himself receives a 1000-year sentence to the "pit" (cf. 9:1-11). Meanwhile, faithful Christians who have died come to life in the "first resurrection" and reign with Christ (during the "millennium"). ("Amillennialists" view this period as symbolic of Christ's rule at God's right hand and in the hearts of true believers, rather than as a posttribulational era.) But the saintly reign does not effect universal conversion, and when Satan is released he leads the innumerable holdouts of the earth in a final failed revolt, after which he is sent to the place of eternal torment to join his already condemned associates. "Gog and Magog" (v. 8) represent all nations gathered for war against Israel (cf. Ezekiel 38–39). In a second resurrection, the rest of the dead rise to life for the final judgment, when God reviews the written record of their earthly deeds and checks it against the list of the elect inscribed in the book of (eternal) life. Condemnation falls on the wicked unbelievers, who in the "second death" join Satan and his beastly aides for eternity (cf. 21:8).

21:1–22:5 The New Jerusalem

The eternal imprisonment of evil coincides with the eternal renewal of the world, now free of chaos (symbolically, the "sea"; 21:1). In contrast to the harlot Babylon (17:1–19:4), the "new Jerusalem" constitutes the true church, described as an urban utopia built of jewels and called the "bride" and "wife of the Lamb," whose marriage to Christ heaven celebrates in 19:7-9. "Entrance" into the city is through gates inscribed with the names of the 12 Hebrew tribes (21:12; cf. Ezek. 40:30-34), and the names of the apostles appear on the foundation stones of the city wall (21:14). God's dwelling among the saints obviates the need for a physical tabernacle/temple (21:3, 22), and their having been made holy by Christ's paying their debt of sin allows them unhindered fellowship with God as intended from creation. The precious stones that adorn the city recall those of the high-priestly garments (Exodus 28) and suggest that every new Jerusalemite enjoys access to God apart from human intermediaries. The measurements of the city symbolize perfection.

The perpetual daytime that characterizes the new Jerusalem represents its righteous purity, embodied by the eternal Illuminator in whom "there is no darkness at all" (1 John 1:5-7). The Edenic tree of life grows alongside the life-giving water flowing from the throne of God. Sustenance from them reverses the curse of death, handed down to humanity through the disobedience of Eve and Adam. The entire scene blends the characterizations of Jesus as the light of the world, the true vine, and the source of living water.

22:6-21 Closing Exhortations and Encouragement

John's angelic guide confirms the truth of the visionary messages; John verifies witnessing them; and Christ affirms his near return to weigh the deeds of humans and compensate them accordingly and irreversibly for eternity. Christ's identity as the promised Messiah, the "root and the descendant of David" (v. 16), ensures his power and authority to fulfill his word — encouraging news for the clean-robed repentant and fair warning for the persistently sinful, who, to chart the good course for eternity, need only drink the "water of [eternal] life," offered by Christ as a gift (v. 17).

So serious is the message of Revelation that John calls curses on anyone who amends his record. A final benediction invokes divine favor ("grace") on the saints to whom John addresses the book (cf. 1:11).

John's record ends with the opportunity Christ offers to humanity for irreversible reinstatement from the consequences of sin spawned in the garden of Eden (Gen. 3:22-24). But every individual must decide between Christ's promise of eternal restoration and never-ending suffering under the curse of sin. The invitation is simple: "Come." And eternity beckons a response.

The Bible and the Church

The Guide for Christian Faith

From the earliest days of the church's history, Christians have made the journey from Scripture to theology. Diverse methods for connecting the written word of God in the Bible with Christian teachings or doctrines have been developed throughout many different historical periods. Modern Western scholars label the study of this subject as *theological hermeneutics,* the theory of interpretation (hermeneutics) related to language about God (theology). Let us first consider what Christian doctrine is and does, and then briefly examine some of the principal ways Christians have journeyed from Bible to doctrine, exploring problems encountered along the way and theological responses.

The Nature and Function of Christian Doctrine

Basically, Christian doctrine is simply the teachings of the Christian faith. For some Christians who hold a high view of church authority, Christian doctrine may be defined as the official, definitive teachings of the church. In any case, although based upon and tested by Scripture, Christian doctrine is more than repetition or reorganization of the words of Scripture. We cannot simply "collate the data" from the Bible to make the doctrines of the faith.

Christian communities engage in critical self-examination of the language they use to speak of the mystery of God. This critical reflection upon the day-to-day or "first-order" language of the faith means that theology (language about God) is the next step, or "second-order" language. So a more precise definition of Christian doctrine would be the use of second-order religious language by members of Christian communities to describe basic teachings of their faith in the most coherent way possible. For many Christians these basic teachings are first of all derived from the Bible. The traditions of Christian communities (including their surrounding cultures) and the personal experience of Christians also shape doctrine. For example, the doctrine of the Trinity is not fully developed in the

Bible. Rather, the doctrine's biblically warranted formulation resulted from a centuries-long historical process in the early church.

The theologian George Lindbeck has described three different approaches to doctrine in recent Christian theology. The "cognitive-propositional" approach views doctrines as providing information and making truth claims about objective realities in the external world. The "experiential-expressive" approach interprets doctrines as symbolizing inner feelings and experiences. The "cultural-linguistic" approach understands doctrines as rules, which work something like grammar, guiding the ways Christians speak of their faith.

Examining doctrines based upon their function as rules, rather than defending them as propositional explanations of reality or expressed symbols of inner experiences, provides a way to account for doctrinal development and change. For example, using Athanasius's rule that "whatever is said of the Father is said of the Son, except that the Son is not the Father," one might trace doctrinal development of the Trinity across the first four centuries.

Scripture as the Norm of Doctrine

The inspiration and authority of Scripture have evoked much debate and controversy among Western Christians in the modern era. Much effort has been expended in proposing and defending various theories regarding the nature of the Bible and diverse ways Christians understand its authority as Holy Scripture. Despite continuing differences over the status of the so-called apocryphal (deuterocanonical) books, the major Christian traditions agree that both the Old and New Testaments make up the *canon*, the rule that governs the teachings of the faith.

Christians believe God has spoken and continues to speak in a unique way through the particular books that constitute the canon of Scripture. Theological statements about the Bible's inspiration may be understood as human efforts to explain the practical reality that God spoke and still speaks to the people of God through these writings. When recognized and read as Holy Scripture, the Bible becomes uniquely authoritative for Christian belief and practice. Scripture also serves as an inexhaustible source of guidance for the people of God.

One valuable way theologians describe the Bible's special authority is to characterize Scripture as the "norm-making norm" or "rule-making rule" of the faith. In other words, the Bible is the rule on which all other traditions of Christian faith depend and against which they are tested. For evangelical and other biblically centered Christian traditions, this view describes all other sources of religious authority as subordinate to and evaluated by Scripture.

Given the Bible's rich diversity, merely using verses of Scripture as prooftexts for

Christian doctrines is an inadequate way to connect Bible and doctrine. Even a beginning student of the Bible can recognize that citing verses out of context has been used to endorse such sinful practices as burning witches (Exod. 22:18) and rationalizing slavery (Eph. 6:5). Instead, discovering the *patterns* of Scripture offers deeper understanding of the Bible's authority as the norm of doctrine than prooftexting can provide. A few highlights from the history of biblical interpretation can assist us in the journey from Scripture to theology.

Methods in the History of Interpretation

Among various interpretive methods used by early Christian writers, typology and allegory in particular were extensively developed. Typology identifies a correspondence between a person or event and a "similar situation" in the biblical text. So one person or event becomes a "type" of another. Typology assumes some sort of historical connection between the two parts of the correspondence. One biblical example is Paul's description of the relationship between Christ and Adam (Rom. 5:12-21). Adam is "a type of the one who was to come [Christ]" (v. 14).

Allegory also interprets a "similar situation" between someone or something in the text and another person or thing. The correspondence may involve persons, groups, events, or even material objects. The explanation of Jesus' parable of the Wheat and Tares (Matt. 13:36-43) provides a biblical example. Unlike typology, no historical connection is necessarily assumed to exist between the two parts of the correspondence. This lack of restriction eventually leads to loss of hermeneutical control, resulting in allegorical flights of fancy. For example, Origen, the master of allegory, once interpreted the kidneys of a sacrificial calf to represent the soul of Christ (*Homilies on Leviticus* 3.5).

Despite these difficulties, the allegorical method eventually became the dominant interpretative method until the Reformation of the 16th century. Various systems of interpretation with complex levels of meaning developed. The most common was the "fourfold sense" of Scripture with four interpretive levels : (1) historical or literal, (2) allegorical, (3) moral or tropological, and (4) mystical or anagogical. Theological interpretation of Scripture likewise moved through four temporal levels: (1) the past, (2) the connection of past and present, (3) what shall be done in the present or immediate future, and (4) the future of eternity. Interpreting the word "Jerusalem" in a biblical text provides a simple example. The literal level refers to the historical city of Jerusalem. The allegorical level symbolizes the soul's quest for salvation. The moral level interprets the church's struggles against sin in the world (the "church militant"). The mystical level points to the heavenly Jerusalem. During the high Middle Ages this elaborate system of interpretation of the "sacred page" became closely allied with scholastic theology.

This system's complexity created many opportunities for interpretive elaboration, rationalization, and abuse, which caused the Reformers to reject allegory. Following the watchword of "Scripture alone" *(sola Scriptura),* they instead favored a simpler method of interpretation, closely tied to Scripture's literal sense.

Pressured by both experimental science and the Enlightenment, much Protestant theology moved toward a "flat Bible" approach. Some theologians understood the Bible as a collection of divinely given truths or even facts, guaranteed by inspiration. Theology was to organize and systematize "scientifically" all the truths or facts of the Bible. Responding to the challenge of historical-critical method, more sophisticated versions of biblical theology (e.g., history of salvation) located Scripture's truth in reconstructed historical events "behind the text." Across the theological spectrum of modern Protestantism the doctrine of revelation came to occupy a key place in connecting Scripture with other doctrines.

Revelation and Theology

The doctrine of revelation was a secondary issue in Christian theology before the 18th century. Theologians commonly understood revelation as communication of information about a God who was knowable. Sin blinded people from knowing God, but through the gift of God's grace, knowledge of God was available to humanity. Theologians *assumed* the availability of knowledge of God; it was a background belief that did not need explicit proof.

The Enlightenment challenged traditional Christian theology, undermining the belief that God could be known through human reason. Immanuel Kant (1724-1804) argued that realities transcending time and space were not knowable by pure reason. Traditional "philosophical proofs" of God's existence were invalid, since God could not be known rationally, but only through faith. Religion was limited to practical truths of the moral law, established by the voice of conscience.

Theologians who responded to Kant's claims about the limits of rational knowledge could no longer *assume* the availability of knowledge of God as a gift of grace. Instead, they thought they needed to demonstrate the *plausibility* of knowledge of God. Even if they could not rationally prove that knowledge of God was available to humanity, they sought to show that it was *reasonable* to hold this belief. Establishing the possibility of knowledge of God was a prior task to the question of salvation. Theology's first question was no longer "How can we be saved?" but "What knowledge do we possess to proceed?"

Modern theologians, both liberal and conservative, developed elaborately argued doctrines of revelation in their quest to establish philosophical foundations or rational grounds for Christian beliefs. Revelation was no longer a secondary doctrine, but instead the first doctrine for theology to consider, even before discussing the doctrine of God. Revelation became an "umbrella concept" to cover all God's dealings with humanity.

Elevating the doctrine of revelation made it vulnerable to serious criticism during the second half of the 20th century. Biblical scholars pointed out that this expanded view of revelation does not reflect the specialized way the Bible speaks of revelation — as "uncovering" a mystery or prophecy to God's people (e.g., Matt. 10:26). Focusing on the Bible's status as revelation often ignores what the Bible actually says about revelation and its limits. Philosophical critiques examined difficulties with the special categories of knowing that theologians created for knowledge deriving from revelation. Also, the cultural shift from modernity to postmodernity rendered suspect all forms of knowing that claimed to rest upon universal philosophical foundations. Finally, pastoral critiques highlighted dangers of shifting theology's emphasis from God's saving grace to the doctrine of revelation itself. Theological conflicts over worship and the replacement of theological language with psychological language in ministry reflected the separation between theology and pastoral ministry.

Recent Theological Responses

Among many diverse responses to the problem of revelation in contemporary theology, three promising approaches can be highlighted. First, theology might be reorganized to begin with basic Christian convictions and practices, rather than contemporary difficulties in knowing God. Pastoral approaches to Christian doctrine, which emphasize Christian practices, build bridges between theology and daily life in Christian communities.

Second, narrative approaches use "story" as a master concept for theology. Narratives of individuals and communities are connected with "the master story" found in Scripture and the story of Christianity.

Finally, canonical approaches emphasize the historical and theological process through which the Bible is read holistically as authoritative Scripture. A postcritical canonical approach, which accepts yet moves beyond historical-critical and controlled typological approaches, offers a method of theological reflection attuned to the patterns of Scripture.

The journey from Scripture to theology continues in our day to explore old and new ways in which the Bible serves as the guide for Christian faith.

FOR FURTHER READING

Grant, Robert, and David Tracy. *A Short History of the Interpretation of the Bible.* 2nd ed. Philadelphia: Fortress, 1984.

Scalise, Charles J. *From Scripture to Theology: A Canonical Journey into Hermeneutics.* Downers Grove: InterVarsity, 1996.

Thiemann, Ronald F. *Revelation and Theology: The Gospel as Narrated Promise.* Notre Dame: University of Notre Dame Press, 1985.

CHARLES J. SCALISE

The Guide for Christian Living

With the psalmist, the people of God proclaim, "Your word is a lamp to my feet and a light to my path." In Psalm 119, the writer gratefully recognizes that God's word guides his steps and shapes his life. Living in and by this word brings delight, elicits love and wonder, and increases wisdom and hope. God's word is a gift whose study brings joy and understanding to the person who is in relationship with the giver.

This word is both light and delight, says the psalmist, for those who wholeheartedly seek God and earnestly desire to perform God's will. Its guidance is available to persons who come to it in a posture of humility and trusting in God's steadfast love. Such a divinely provided resource draws responses of praise, gratitude, and obedience from those who love God.

In the New Testament, we read that the "sacred writings" (2 Tim. 3:15), the "God-breathed" Scriptures, instruct us "for salvation through faith in Christ Jesus" (John 5:39). The Bible bears witness to Jesus; it points readers to him. The stories and signs of Jesus were written down, John's Gospel explains, "so that you may come to believe that Jesus is the Messiah, the Son of God, and that through believing you may have life in his name" (John 20:30-31).

The Bible is a guide for Christian living because through it we encounter the work and character of the living God that culminates in the story of Jesus' life, death, resurrection, and ascension. We see God's purposes for Israel and for the church being worked out. Through direct teaching and through the stories of men and women who have been God's friends, we discover what it means to walk with God. God's qualities of love, righteousness, mercy, holiness, and justice become the basis and model for our decisions and dispositions. Within the pages of Scripture, we learn of Jesus' character and ministry, are invited to follow him, and are called to be like him. We read of the gift of the Holy Spirit, who brings understanding and power for response.

Our Christian moral identity is formed in response to the character and activity of God revealed in the Scriptures, as well as in the church, the world, and our own lives. But most importantly, it is formed in response to the love God has shown us in Christ. The Scriptures live in us as we read them, reflect on them, live with them, and hide them in our hearts. But, in a sense, we also come to live inside the Bible, as its stories become our stories, as they begin to describe reality for us, and as we imagine ourselves present to some of the events we read about. In this way, our character and identity are gradually shaped; our loves, loyalties, preferences, dispositions, and motivations are transformed.

While Christians sometimes think that Scripture guides us primarily through specific rules about what we should and should not do, its more formative impact is related to how it shapes our total selves. This happens over the long term, through our exposure to the Bible in study, Christian liturgy, and prayer. It occurs as we hear sermons and interpret parables and as the Scriptures shape the life of a community of faith. And if we are faithful in the process, God's word "reads" us; it challenges and convicts us, and gradually we are shaped and formed into particular kinds of persons that embody the gospel, the good news. Our way of life becomes "worthy of the gospel of Christ" (Phil. 1:27).

As we read the Scriptures, we also learn to read the world in a distinctive way. The Bible's perspectives on the value of life and the power of human sinfulness help us to interpret events, cultural values, and societal practices. We learn to view persons and situations through a lens shaped by God's word and purposes. As we dwell in the Scriptures, they begin to affect what we care and worry about and whom we notice. But we need a community of faith to do this well; we need sisters and brothers to help us see insights and emphases in the Bible that we would miss on our own, or that we might deliberately avoid.

Finding in Scripture a guide for Christian living requires that we engage in several other related practices. Through regular prayer and dependence on the Holy Spirit, the texts of Scripture come alive and God speaks to our lives. We are formed by Scripture as we study it on our own and in community.

Although Christians often read the Bible quite individualistically, its words were originally addressed to communities. Scripture is so rich that the individual can find treasures within it daily, but its wisdom and truth are most available in the context of a believing community that is historically rooted, presently engaged in God's work in the world, and guided by the Holy Spirit.

The church, both through its tradition and in a local congregation, helps us to deepen our individual understandings of Scripture and to check the accuracy of our personal interpretations and applications. Especially when it is made up of people quite different from ourselves, the church helps us to understand the Bible's narratives and teachings more fully. Because our own experiences and social location affect what we see and pay attention to, believers from other socioeconomic and cultural backgrounds can open our eyes to new insights as well as help us to see our own blind spots.

As Christians grow in faith and discover the increasing significance of the Scriptures for our lives, we rejoice that "All scripture is inspired by God and is useful for teaching, for reproof, for correction, and for training in righteousness, so that everyone who belongs to God may be proficient, equipped for every good work" (2 Tim. 3:16-17). We affirm that Scripture is normative or authoritative for our lives and that "whatever was written in former days was written for our instruction, so that by steadfastness and by the encouragement of the scriptures we might have hope" (Rom. 15:4).

Because the Bible is richly multifaceted, how it is normative is a fairly complex question. Scripture speaks to all areas of life, but it does not speak in a single mode. In it we find specific "instruction," but we also find much more. The Bible is made up of wonderful and disturbing stories, poetry and laments, prophecy and parables, commandments, history, proverbs, direct teaching, and apocalyptic visions. While we might be persuaded that these passages are inspired by God, it is not always immediately clear how they might be authoritative or life-giving to us today.

It is not only the diversity of biblical genres that challenges us in seeing portions of the Bible as our guide to Christian living. The texts emerged from, and were originally addressed to, communities of believers whose life situations, social and cultural contexts, and economic and political circumstances were quite different from ours. When we read these ancient texts, we bring our own presuppositions, values, needs, and experiences, shaped not only by the Scriptures but also by the contemporary world. While some of our questions transcend culture and time, others are rooted in assumptions and frameworks quite alien to the biblical writers.

In addition, we bring to the texts our sinfulness. It is difficult to be guided by Scripture when we pick and choose what portions we take seriously, when we exempt our own lives from its scrutiny, or when we soften its demands toward us as we hold others strictly accountable to the letter of the law. In our self-serving sinfulness, we eagerly seek out verses that will legitimate our strongly held opinions, whether or not those opinions were shaped by biblical concerns and commitments.

In fact, our use of the Bible for guidance is sometimes shaped by our own peculiar needs and prejudices. We refer to the parts that we like and quietly ignore sections that are inconvenient or troublesome. When we view Scripture primarily as a law book, we assume that if an issue is not addressed, then the Bible has nothing to say about it. As a result, certain areas of our lives are completely unaffected by the biblical witness. Since the Bible says nothing specific about reproductive technologies, speed limits, or insider trading, we assume that our behavior in those areas is subject to another law, or to none at all.

But if God's purposes are to form us to holiness and that we be conformed to the image of Christ, then every area of our lives comes under God's scrutiny, and God's word provides necessary and relevant guidance. When a topic is not addressed directly, there are often larger principles that can guide us, such as the preciousness of human life, God's concern for the weak, the commandments to love neighbor, stranger, and enemy, or God's concern for truthful speech. In other cases, we can apply biblical texts "analogically"; for example, the parable of the Good Samaritan can be a window for us on how to understand race relations, or ancient Israel's practical responsibility for sojourners can suggest ways a local church might respond to migrant workers in its community.

Scripture guides our Christian living when we handle a particular passage with respect, seeking to understand what the text means in its literary and social context, what the author intended, and what it meant to the original recipients. The Bible is a grace- and truth-filled guide when we are careful that our interpretations and applications are true to the genre in which a text is written. For example, we will be wary of turning narrative accounts into rules or poetry into scientific claims. Commandments and principles that recur throughout the Scriptures provide some of the most fundamental and authoritative structuring for the Christian life.

When we look into God's word for guidance on a particular matter, we sometimes find specific relevant texts. It is rarely the case, however, that such texts are the only way in which Scripture addresses the issue. Individual passages are part of a larger whole, and the guidance process involves bringing a particular text into conversation with the full canon. This helps us to discern whether a particular teaching is central or peripheral, universal or specific to a single occasion.

We need also to examine the ways biblical themes and theological concepts might inform our search for guidance. For example, if we are seeking scriptural wisdom on divorce, Jesus' teaching on the subject is central, but the Bible's many passages on marriage and covenant are crucial as well. In fact, some of our most basic guidance comes through struggling with the implications of central theological themes and concepts in and derived from Scripture — concepts such as creation, love, and justice.

While for the people of God, the teachings of Scripture should never be considered apart from our relationship with God, there are ways in which the Bible's guidelines and commandments have also affected the larger society. In the West, understandings of justice, equality, and civil law have been shaped profoundly by the Bible. Through the Decalogue, in particular, Scripture has provided important boundaries for social life. Although the Bible's impact is less evident today, the adequate functioning of Western institutions continues to depend on observing these boundaries and on persons shaped by basic biblical values and commitments.

In the Bible, God has provided practical wisdom for living, commandments to guard our integrity and well-being, and numerous testimonies to the dangers of unfaithfulness and to the joys of living by the word. But even more, in Scripture God has given us a story to be lived out, owned, and appropriated by all who hunger for the life it promises.

FOR FURTHER READING

Birch, Bruce C., and Larry L. Rasmussen. *Bible and Ethics in the Christian Life.* Rev. ed. Minneapolis: Augsburg, 1989.

Fowl, Stephen E., and L. Gregory Jones. *Reading in Communion: Scripture and Ethics in Christian Life.* Grand Rapids: Wm. B. Eerdmans, 1991.

Hays, Richard B. *The Moral Vision of the New Testament*. San Francisco: HarperSanFrancisco, 1996.

Mulholland, M. Robert. *Shaped by the Word*. Rev. ed. Nashville: Upper Room, 2000.

Spohn, William C. *What Are They Saying about Scripture and Ethics?* Rev. ed. New York: Paulist, 1995.

Verhey, Allen. *Remembering Jesus: Christian Community, Scripture, and the Moral Life*. Grand Rapids: Wm. B. Eerdmans, 2002.

CHRISTINE D. POHL

Glossary of Terms

acrostic A poetic form in which the initial letters of each line, couplet, or stanza read in succession spell out a name or alphabetic pattern

apocalyptic Relating to the literary genre "apocalypse" (from Greek for "revelation"), characterized by visions, vivid symbolism, otherworldly creatures, and cataclysmic, cosmic events

Apocrypha Fifteen books or parts of books found in the Greek Septuagint but not in the Hebrew Bible, accepted as canonical by the Roman Catholic and Orthodox churches; also called "deuterocanonical"

apology A statement supporting or in defense of a belief or doctrine

apostasy The act or process of falling away from or abandoning the faith; rebellion against God; breaking the covenant

assumption The taking up of a person bodily into heaven

atone To make one; **atonement** Reconciliation with God ("at-one-ment") through the cancellation of sin

ca. *Circa;* about, approximately

Catholic Epistles The seven "General" New Testament letters (James, 1-2 Peter, 1-2-3 John, Jude) circulated among a number of churches or intended for the church at large

Christology Theological understanding of the person and nature of Christ

circumcision Removal of the foreskin as a symbol of covenant with God

cosmos The world or universe as an orderly, harmonious system

covenant A solemn agreement between two or more parties, including God and humans, made binding by an oath

cult The system or practice of worship, including personnel and paraphernalia

Decalogue The Ten Commandments

Deuteronomistic Relating to the history of Israel recorded in the books of Deuteronomy–2 Kings; the perspective that God's judgment on Israel was due to the people's sins

Diaspora The geographical and cultural dispersion of the Hebrew people and their religion beyond the borders of Palestine after the Babylonian exile

eschatology Beliefs or expectations concerning the end time

expiation The restoration of the relationship between God and humans through the removal of sin, involving an act of sacrifice

grace The undeserved favor of God toward humans

Hellenistic The period and culture marked by the influence of Greek thought and institutions following the conquests of Alexander the Great (336-323 B.C.)

incarnation God's taking of human form as Jesus of Nazareth to redeem humankind

intertestamental period The era of postexilic Judaism from the completion of the book of Malachi to the destruction of the Jerusalem temple in A.D. 70

monarchy The period in Israelite history from the reign of Saul through the fall of the kingdom of Judah in 586 B.C.

monotheism The belief that there is only one deity

Parousia The divine presence; in the New Testament, the future or second coming of Christ

patriarchs The male heads of ancient Hebrew families and clans, specifically the four generations of Israelite founders recorded in Genesis 12–50 (Abraham, Isaac, Jacob and his 12 sons)

Pentateuch The first five books of the Old Testament (Genesis–Deuteronomy)

pilgrimage Travel to a holy site, referring especially to festivals celebrated at the Jerusalem temple

polytheism Belief in the existence of more than one god

postexilic Relating to the period or events following Israel's Babylonian exile (after 539 B.C.)

preexilic Relating to the period or events before the exile (before 587 B.C.)

providence God's loving care and protection of the world; a benevolent and purposeful ordering of history

Pseudepigrapha A collection of noncanonical writings "falsely ascribed" to biblical figures to lend them theological authority

redemption Release from legal obligation or bondage; deliverance from desperate circumstances; ransom

retribution Recompense or payment for what one deserves, either for good or evil

sanctification Making something or someone clean or holy to God; consecration

Second Temple The postexilic period of Judaism (516/15 B.C.–A.D. 70), i.e., after the Babylonian exile

Septuagint The Greek translation of the Hebrew Bible (Old Testament), made in the 3rd–2nd centuries B.C. in Alexandria, Egypt; abbreviated LXX

superscription A heading or title added to a psalm or other text

Synoptic Gospels The Gospels of Matthew, Mark, and Luke, so named because of the similarities of structure, perspective, and contents

theocracy Government under God's direct guidance or by officials regarded as ruling with divine authority

theophany An appearance of God to humans, often recorded with vivid descriptions of natural phenomena or supernatural imagery

transcendent God's unique mode of relationship with the world, "going beyond" the boundaries separating his holiness or otherness and the realm of finite being

Who's Who in the Bible

Aaron Brother of Moses and first high priest of Israel

Abdon A minor judge of Israel

Abednego A companion of Daniel, exiled to Babylon

Abel Second son of Adam and Eve

Abiathar Priest at Nob and later joint high priest during David's reign

Abigail Wife of Nabal and later David

Abihu Son of Aaron, stricken dead for offering improper sacrifice

Abijah Son of Jeroboam I of Israel whose death was a sign of divine displeasure

Abijah, Abijam Son of Rehoboam and king of Judah

Abimelech 1. King of Gerar who took Sarah as his wife 2. Son of the judge Gideon; king and destroyer of Shechem

Abiram A Reubenite who conspired against Moses and Aaron

Abishai Nephew of David who avenged his brother Asahel's death by murdering Abner

Abner Commander of Saul's army

Abraham, Abram Patriarch of Israel, "the father of many nations and faiths"

Absalom Son of David who led a rebellion against his father

Achan A Judahite, stoned for taking booty after the fall of Jericho

Achish King of Philistine Gath to whom David fled

Adam The first human

Adonijah Son of David who attempted to succeed him

Adoni-zedek Amorite king of Jerusalem

Adoram, Adoniram Taskmaster over forced labor during reign of Solomon

Agabus NT prophet who predicted famine and Paul's arrest

Agag Amalekite king killed by Saul

Agrippa 1. Agrippa I, ruler over Judea who persecuted the early Christians 2. Agrippa II, last Herodian ruler, before whom Paul was tried at Caesarea

Agur Author or collector of proverbs

Ahab Omride king of Israel, husband of Jezebel and opponent of Elijah

Ahasuerus King of Persia who took Esther as queen

Ahaz King of Judah and father of Hezekiah

Ahaziah 1. King of Israel, son and successor of Ahab 2. King of Judah, succeeded by his mother Athaliah

Ahijah Prophet from Shiloh who foretold Jeroboam's demise

Ahimaaz Son of the high priest Zadok who informed David during Absalom's revolt

Ahimelech Priest at Nob, killed for aiding David

Ahinoam Wife of Saul and later David

Ahithophel David's trusted counselor who directed Absalom's revolt

Alexander 1. Alexander the Great, Macedonian king whose conquests throughout the ancient Near East made possible the spread of Hellenism 2. Son of Simon of Cyrene

Amasa Commander of Absalom's army, killed by Joab

Amaziah 1. King of Judah, son of Joash and father of Azariah 2. Priest of Bethel at the time of Jeroboam II and Amos

Amnon Son of David who raped Tamar and was killed by Absalom

Amon King of Judah, son of Manasseh and father of Josiah

Amos Eighth-century Judahite prophet who addressed the northern kingdom

Ananias Christian in Jerusalem accused of withholding funds from the apostles

Anath Canaanite goddess of war

Andrew One of the 12 apostles, brother of Simon Peter

Anna Prophet in the Jerusalem temple when the infant Jesus was presented

Annas High priest in Jerusalem, father-in-law of Caiaphas

Antiochus Antiochus IV Epiphanes, Seleucid ruler who imposed Hellenistic institutions on Jerusalem

Apollos Alexandrian Jew and influential preacher to the church at Corinth

Aquila Husband of Priscilla and Christian associate of Paul

Araunah Jebusite who sold David his threshing floor, later the site of Solomon's temple

Archippus Leader of the church at Colossae

Artaxerxes I King of Persia at the time of Ezra's return and Nehemiah's governorship

Artemis Anatolian mother goddess, patron deity of Ephesus

Asa King of Judah who reformed worship in Jerusalem

Asahel Nephew of David, killed by Abner

Asaph Leader of David's temple singers

Asenath Egyptian wife of Joseph

Asherah Canaanite goddess, consort of Baal

Ashtoreth Canaanite goddess Astarte, consort of Baal

Asmodeus Demon in Tobit who killed Sarah's seven husbands on her wedding night

Astarte Alternative form of the name Ashtoreth

Athaliah The only ruling queen of Judah, daughter of Ahab and Jezebel

Augustus Octavian, called Augustus Caesar, first emperor at Rome

Azariah, Uzziah Eighth-century king of Judah

Azariah Hebrew name of Abednego

Azazel Male goat that bore Israel's sins into the wilderness on the Day of Atonement

Baal Canaanite storm- and fertility-god

Baal-berith "Baal of the Covenant," worshipped at Shechem

Baal-zebub God of Philistine Ekron

Baasha Third king of the northern kingdom

Balaam Mesopotamian prophet summoned by Balak to curse Israel

Balak King of Moab who sought supernatural protection against the Hebrews

Barabbas Prisoner released at Passover instead of Jesus

Barak Israelite commander enlisted by Deborah

Barnabas Senior partner in mission with Paul

Bartholomew One of the original 12 disciples

Bartimaeus Blind beggar healed by Jesus

Baruch Scribe of the prophet Jeremiah

Barzillai Gileadite who brought provisions to David during Absalom's revolt

Bathsheba Wife of Uriah and later David, mother of Solomon

Beelzebul Greek pun on the name Baal-zebub

Bel A name of the Babylonian god Marduk

Belial A name of Satan

Belshazzar King of Babylon at the time of Daniel

Belteshazzar Hebrew name of Daniel

Benaiah Commander of David's bodyguards and chief of Solomon's army

Ben-hadad Dynastic name of the kings of Damascus

Benjamin Youngest son of Jacob

Ben Sira, Jesus Author of the apocyphal book of Sirach (Ecclesiasticus)

Bernice Sister of Agrippa II who heard Paul's defense

Bezalel Craftsman chosen to construct the tabernacle, its furnishings, and the ark of the covenant

Bildad One of Job's three friends

Bilhah Servant of Rachel, mother of Dan and Naphtali

Boaz Landowner in Bethlehem who married Ruth

Caesar Title of Roman emperors, Augustus in the Gospels, Claudius in Acts

Caiaphas High priest at the time of Jesus' Jewish trial

Cain Eldest son of Adam and Eve

Caleb Head of a Kenizzite clan in Judah, one of the 12 sent to spy out Canaan

Cambyses Cambyses II, Persian king, son and successor of Cyrus II

Cephas Aramaic nickname or surname of Simon Peter

Chemosh National god of Moab

Chileab Son of David and Abigail

Chilion Younger son of Elimelech and Naomi

Chloe Wealthy woman whose people informed Paul of dissension in the Corinthian church

Claudius Fourth Roman emperor

Claudius Lysias Commander of the Roman cohort in Jerusalem who took Paul into custody

Coniah Alternative name of Jehoiachin, king of Judah

Cornelius Roman centurion at Caesarea, first Gentile convert to Christianity

Crispus Ruler of the synagogue at Corinth, baptized by Paul

Cyrus Cyrus II, Persian king who authorized the

Jews' return from exile and the rebuilding of the Jerusalem temple

Dagon National god of the Philistines

Damaris Athenian woman converted by Paul

Daniel Jewish youth exiled to service in the Babylonian court

Darius 1. Darius I, king of Persia who reaffirmed Cyrus's permission to rebuild the Jerusalem temple 2. Darius the Mede, known only from the book of Daniel

Dathan Reubenite who with his brother Abiram rebelled against Moses in the wilderness

David Successor of Saul, who established capital of United Monarchy at Jerusalem, father of Davidic dynasty, traditional author of many canonical psalms

Deborah Judge and prophet of Israel

Delilah Philistine woman who betrayed Samson

Demas Gentile coworker imprisoned with Paul

Demetrius Silversmith at Ephesus who provoked riot against Paul

Dinah Only daughter of Jacob, raped by Shechem

Dionysius the Areopagite Member of the Athenian council converted by Paul

Diothrephes Leader of a house church denounced by John

Doeg Edomite servant who informed Saul of Ahimelech's aid to David and then executed 85 priests of Nob

Eglon King of Moab assassinated by Ehud

Ehud Benjamite judge who delivered Israel from Moabite rule

El Generic Semitic word for "god," including a name of the God of Israel

Elah Fourth king of Israel, assassinated by Zimri

Eleazar Son of Aaron in charge of the tabernacle

Elhanan Bethlehemite who killed a Philistine giant; perhaps David's personal name

Eli Priest of the Shiloh sanctuary

Eliakim Son of Josiah, installed by Pharaoh Neco as king of Judah and renamed Jehoiakim

Eliashib High priest at the time of Nehemiah

Eliezer Servant of Moses, adopted as his heir

Elihu Last of Job's comforters

Elijah Israelite prophet during the reigns of Ahab and Ahaziah

Elimelech Bethlehemite who with Naomi moved their family to Moab

Eliphaz "The Temanite," first of Job's friends

Elisha Prophet of the northern kingdom, disciple of and successor to Elijah

Elizabeth Mother of John the Baptist and relative of Mary

Elkanah Father of Samuel and husband of Hannah

Elohim Most common generic name for God in the Old Testament

Elon A minor judge of Israel

Elymas Jewish magician who opposed Paul on Cyprus

Enoch Descendant of Seth and father of Methuselah who because of his great piety did not die

Epaphras Founder of the church at Colossae

Epaphroditus A Christian sent by the Philippian church to aid the imprisoned Paul

Ephraim Second son of Joseph and ancestor of an Israelite tribe

Ephron Hittite who sold Abraham the cave of Machpelah

Er Son of Judah and deceased husband of Tamar

Esarhaddon King of Assyria, son and successor of Sennacherib

Esau Older son of Isaac and Rebekah who lost his birthright to his younger twin Jacob

Eshbaal Original name of Ishbosheth, son and successor of Saul

Esther Jewish woman in Ahasuerus's harem, elevated to queen, whose intervenion thwarted a plot against the Jews in the Persian empire

Ethan Leader of the Second Temple choir

Eutychus Youth who fell from window during Paul's preaching at Troas

Eve The first woman

Evil-merodach, Amel-marduk Third king of Babylonia, son and successor of Nebuchadnezzar II

Ezekiel A Jerusalemite, major prophet of the exile

Ezra Priest and scribe commissioned to lead the return from exile, reestablish the Law, and rebuild the temple and walls of Jerusalem

Felix Antonius Felix, Roman procurator of Judea who kept Paul imprisoned at Caesarea

Festus Porcius Festus, Roman procurator of Judea who sent Paul to Rome for trial

Gabriel Archangel who revealed mysteries to Daniel and announced the births of John the Baptist and Jesus

Gad 1. Son of Jacob and Zilpah 2. Prophet during

David's reign 3. Syrian deity, often translated "Destiny" or "Fate"

Gaius The recipient of 3 John

Gallio Proconsul of Achaia

Gamaliel Gamaliel I the Elder, influential member of the Sanhedrin and teacher of the Law

Gedaliah Governor of Judah under Babylonian rule

Gehazi Servant of the prophet Elisha

Gershom Son of Moses and Zipporah

Gershon Eldest son of Levi, head of a Levitical family

Geshem Arab who opposed Nehemiah's efforts to rebuild the walls of Jerusalem

Gideon Israelite judge who repelled Midianite invaders

Gog An apocalyptic foe of Israel

Goliath Philistine giant slain by David

Gomer Wife of Hosea

Habakkuk Prophet whose book questions God's use of the Chaldeans to punish Israel

Hadad Edomite king and enemy of Solomon

Hadad-rimmon A West Semitic deity

Hagar Egyptian servant of Sarah, mother of Ishmael

Haggai One of the 12 Minor Prophets

Ham Son of Noah, ancestor of the Canaanites

Haman Persian prime minister who plotted against the Jews

Hanani Brother of Nehemiah

Hananiah Prophetic opponent of Jeremiah

Hannah Mother of Samuel

Hanun Ammonite king whose insult to David's envoys led to war

Hazael King of Damascus, assassinated Ben-hadad and usurped the throne

Heman Leader of a guild of temple musicians

Hermes Messenger of the Greek gods

Herod 1. Herod I the Great, founder of Herodian dynasty 2. Herod Antipas, tetrarch of Galilee and Perea

Herodias Daughter of Aristobulus and Berenice, manipulated the execution of John the Baptist

Hezekiah King of Judah, reformer at time of Assyrian siege of Jerusalem

Hiel Rebuilder of Jericho

Hilkiah High priest during Josiah's reign

Hiram 1. Hiram I, king of Tyre who supplied materials for the temple and traded with Solomon 2. Artisan from Tyre, sent to provide bronze work for the temple

Hobab Father-in-law of Moses

Holofernes Chief general of Nebuchadnezzar's army

Hophni A son of Eli

Hosea Eighth-century prophet to the northern kingdom

Hoshea Last king of Israel

Huldah Prophetess consulted by Josiah

Hur A leader during the wilderness wanderings

Huramabi Tyrian craftsman who produced metalwork for the temple

Hushai Adviser to David during Absalom's revolt

Ibzan A minor judge from Bethlehem of Zebulun

Ichabod Son of Phinehas and grandson of Eli

Iddo Ancestor of Zechariah

Immanuel Name of child representing God's presence, foretold by Isaiah

Isaac Son of Abraham and Sarah, father of Jacob and Esau

Isaiah Judahite prophet in the latter 8th century

Ishbaal, Ishbosheth, Ishvi Youngest son and successor of Saul

Ishmael Son of Abraham and Hagar

Israel 1. Later name of Jacob 2. Name of northern kingdom after united monarchy split under Rehoboam

Ithamar A son of Aaron

Jabin Canaanite king of Hazor defeated by Deborah and Barak

Jacob Younger twin son of Isaac and Rebekah, ancestor of the 12 tribes of Israel

Jael Kenite woman who killed Sisera with a tent peg

Jair A judge from Gilead

Jairus Synagogue ruler whose daughter Jesus restored to life

James 1. Son of Zebedee, one of the first disciples 2. Half-brother of Jesus

Japheth Youngest son of Noah

Jason High priest at the time of Antiochus IV Epiphanes

Jeconiah, Jechoniah Alternative names of King Jehoiachin of Israel

Jeduthun A Levitical musician in the tabernacle and temple

Jehoahaz 1. King of Israel, son and successor of Jehu 2. King of Judah, deposed by Pharaoh Neco II

Jehoash King of Israel at the time of Elisha's death; also called Joash (different from the Judahite King Joash/Jehoash)

Jehoiachin King of Judah exiled by Nebuchadnezzar, also called Coniah

Jehoiada Priest who led coup against Athaliah and installed Joash of Judah as king

Jehoiakim King of Judah installed by Pharaoh Neco to replace Jehoahaz

Jehoram King of Judah, succcessor of Jehoshaphat; also called Joram

Jehoshaphat King of Judah, son and successor of Asa, allied with Ahab of Israel through marriage

Jehu King of Israel who usurped the throne from Joram

Jephthah Gileadite judge who liberated Israel from Ammonite dominance

Jeremiah Judean prophet from Anathoth at the time of Jerusalem's fall to Babylon

Jeroboam 1. Jeroboam I, first king of the northern kingdom, Israel 2. Jeroboam II, son and successor of Joash whose reign was prosperous

Jerubbaal Alternative name of the judge Gideon

Jeshua Priest who returned from exile with Zerubbabel

Jesse Father of David

Jesus Christ See Index of Subjects

Jethro A priest in Midian, father-in-law of Moses

Jezebel Queen of Israel, Phoenician wife of Ahab

Joab Commander-in-chief of David's army

Joanna A woman who accompanied and aided Jesus and the disciples

Joash King of Judah, son of Ahaziah and Athaliah, who repaired the temple; also called Jehoash (different from the Israelite King Jehoash)/Joash)

Job Righteous man of Uz whose suffering is debated in the book of Job

Joel The second of the Minor Prophets

John One of the inner circle of 12 apostles, son of Zebedee and brother of James, and traditional author of the Revelation, Gospels of John, and 1-3 John

John Mark Companion of Barnabas, Paul, and Peter; author of the Gospel of Mark

John the Baptist Forerunner of Jesus the Messiah

Jonadab, Jehonadab Ancestor of the Rechabites

Jonah Eighth-century Israelite prophet

Jonathan 1. Firstborn son of Saul and Ahinoam, friend of David 2. Leader of Jewish resistance following the death of his brother Judas Maccabeus

Joram King of Israel, son of Ahab and successor to his brother Ahaziah; also called Jehoram

Joseph 1. Son of Jacob and Rachel, ancestor of an Israelite tribe 2. Husband of Mary the mother of Jesus 3. Joseph of Arimathea, member of the Sanhedrin in whose tomb Jesus was buried

Joshua Successor to Moses who led Israel into the promised land

Josiah Seventh-century king of Judah who reformed worship in Jerusalem

Jotham 1. A son of Gideon 2. King of Judah, son of Azariah and father of Ahaz

Judah 1. Son of Jacob and Leah, ancestor of the tribe and nation 2. Name of the southern kingdom after united monarchy split under Rehoboam

Judas Iscariot Disciple and betrayer of Jesus

Judas Maccabeus Leader of the Jewish revolt against Antiochus IV Epiphanes

Jude Author of one of the General Epistles

Judith Heroine who delivered Jerusalem from Nebuchadnezzar's army and killed the general Holofernes

Kaiwan Babylonian name for the planet Saturn

Keturah Wife or concubine of Abraham

Kohath A son of Levi and grandfather of Moses, head of a Levitical family

Korah Head of a Levitical family who led a revolt against Moses and Aaron

Laban Brother of Rebekah and father of Leah and Rachel

Lamech A descendant of Cain

Lazarus Brother of Mary and Martha whom Jesus raised from the dead

Leah Elder daughter of Laban, Jacob's first wife

Lemuel King of Massa

Levi 1. A son of Jacob and Leah, ancestor of the tribe of priests and cultic personnel 2. Hebrew name of the disciple Matthew

Leviathan Mythological sea monster

Lot Nephew of Abraham who settled in the Jordan plain

Luke A physician and companion of Paul, author of a Gospel and Acts

Lydia Trader of purple cloth and Paul's first-recorded European convert to Christianity

Maacah Daughter of Absalom and wife of Rehoboam

Magog Ancestor of Anatolian peoples, leader of apocalyptic battle

Maher-shalal-hash-baz Symbolic name of Isaiah's third son

Mahlon Husband of Ruth

Malachi Author of the last of the Minor Prophets

Manasseh 1. Son of Joseph and Asenath, ancestor of an Israelite tribe 2. King of Judah, son of Hezekiah, whose long reign is condemned as the most evil

Manoah Father of Samson

Mara Name taken by Naomi, "Bitter"

Mark John Mark, companion of Paul, Barnabas, and Peter, author of the second Gospel

Martha Sister of Mary and Lazarus

Mary 1. Mother of Jesus 2. Mary Magdalene, follower of Jesus 3. Sister of Martha and Lazarus

Mattaniah Last king of Judah, installed by Nebuchadnezzar and renamed Zedekiah

Mattathias Priest who with his five sons revolted against Antiochus IV Epiphanes

Matthew Tax collector, one of the original 12 disciples

Matthias Disciple chosen to replace Judas Iscariot

Melchizedek King of Salem and priest of God Most High

Melqart God of Tyre

Menahem King of Israel who overthrew Shallum

Menelaus High priest during the reign of Antiochus IV Epiphanes

Meni "Destiny," a pagan deity

Mephibosheth Grandson of Saul and son of Jonathan

Merab Elder daughter of Saul

Merari Ancestor of a Levitical family

Merib-baal Original name of Mephibosheth, Jonathan's son

Merodach Hebrew form of Marduk, chief god of Babylon

Merodach-baladan Two-time king of Babylon who as chief of the Bit-yakin tribe sought Hezekiah's support

Mesha Ninth-century king of Moab who revolted against Israel

Meshach Babylonian name given to one of Daniel's companions

Micah 1. Ephraimite who hired a Levite as priest for his personal shrine 2. Micah of Moresheth, Judahite prophet

Micaiah Ninth-century prophet of the northern kingdom

Michael An archangel, guardian of Israel

Michal Daughter of Saul and wife of David

Milcom National god of the Ammonites

Miriam Prophet and sister of Moses

Mishael Hebrew name of Meshach

Molech A Canaanite deity to whom children were sacrificed

Mordecai Uncle of Jewish Persian Queen Esther

Moses Israelite liberator and lawgiver

Naaman Aramean commander cured of leprosy by Elisha

Nabal Wealthy Calebite, husband of Abigail

Naboth Jezreelite killed by Ahab to aquire his vineyard

Nadab 1. A son of Aaron 2. King of Israel, son of Jeroboam I

Nahum Seventh-century prophet of Judah

Naomi Mother-in-law of Ruth

Nathan Prophet in David's court

Nathanael A disciple, possibly the same as Bartholomew

Nebo Nabu, a principal Babylonian god

Nebuchadnezzar Nebuchadnezzar II, longest-reigning and most powerful Neo-Babylonian king

Neco Neco II, Egyptian pharaoh

Nehemiah Governor of Jerusalem, a leader of the return from exile

Nicodemus Pharisee and teacher who came secretly to Jesus

Noadiah A prophetess

Noah Son of Lamech, principal figure in the Flood account

Obadiah 1. Steward of King Ahab's household 2. Sixth-century prophet against Edom

Obed-edom Head of a Levitical family charged to guard the temple

Oholah, Oholibah Sisters personifying Samaria and Jerusalem in Ezekiel's prophecy

Oholiab Craftsman responsible for construction of the tabernacle

Omri Founder of a 9th-century dynasty of the northern kingdom

Onan A son of Judah

Onesimus A slave, subject of Paul's Letter to Philemon

Onesiphorus Christian from Ephesus who aided the imprisoned Paul

Onias High priest deposed by Antiochus IV Epiphanes

Ornan Alternate form of Araunah

Orpah A Moabite daughter-in-law of Naomi

Osnappar Assyrian king who resettled conquered peoples at Samaria

Othniel Israelite judge who captured Debir

Paul Apostle to the Gentiles, credited with writing 13 New Testament letters

Pekah Eighth-century king of Israel

Pekahiah King of Israel who briefly succeeded his father Menahem

Pelatiah A corrupt leader in Jerusalem during the exile

Peninnah A wife of Elkanah

Perez A twin son of Tamar

Peter Simon Peter, one of the 12 disciples and a leader of the early church

Pharaoh Title of the kings of Egypt

Philemon A resident of Colossae, owner of the slave Onesimus

Philip 1. Apostle and evangelist 2. King of Macedonia, father of Alexander the Great 3. Herod Philip, tetrarch of Ituraea

Phinehas 1. Priest, grandson of Aaron 2. Younger son of Eli

Phoebe Leader and deacon of the church at Cenchreae who delivered Paul's letter to Rome

Pontius Pilate Roman procurator and governor of Judea

Potiphar Officer of Pharaoh who purchased Joseph and in whose house he served

Prisca, Priscilla Teacher and missionary coworker of Paul, wife of Aquila

Pul Nickname of Tiglath-pileser III

Qoheleth Principal speaker in the book of Ecclesiastes

Queen of Heaven A goddess worshipped at the time of Jeremiah

Quirinius Governor of Syria

Rabshakeh Assyrian emissary sent to Hezekiah

Rachel Younger daughter of Laban, a wife of Jacob

Rahab 1. Prostitute who aided Joshua's spies at Jericho 2. Mythological chaos monster

Raphael Angel who accompanied Tobias

Rebekah Wife of Isaac and mother of Jacob and Esau

Rehoboam Son and successor of Solomon whose harsh rule brought the end of the united monarchy

Reuben Firstborn son of Jacob and Leah, ancestor of an Israelite tribe

Rezin King of Damascus who revolted against Assyria

Rizpah A concubine of Saul

Ruth Moabite widow, ancestor of David and Jesus

Sakkuth Assyrian deity associated with Saturn

Salome 1. Step-daughter of Herod Antipas who requested the head of John the Baptist 2. Wife of Zebedee, mother of James and John

Samson Last of the great judges

Samuel Judge and prophet who anointed Israel's first two kings

Sanballat Governor of Samaria, opponent of Nehemiah's rebuilding of Jerusalem

Sarah, Sarai 1. Wife of Abraham, mother of Isaac 2. Wife of Tobias

Sargon II King of Assyria

Satan The "Adversary" or Devil

Saul 1. First king of Israel 2. Saul of Tarsus, Hebrew name of the Apostle Paul (his Roman name)

Sceva Jewish high priest, father of seven exorcist sons

Sennacherib King of Assyria who invaded Judah during the reign of Hezekiah

Sergius Paulus Proconsul of Cyprus converted by Paul

Seth Third son of Adam and Eve

Shadrach Babylonian name of Hananiah, one of Daniel's companions

Shallum Alternative name of Jehoahaz, king of Judah

Shalmaneser V Assyrian king who laid siege to Samaria

Shamgar Israelite judge

Shaphan Scribe who brought the book of the law to King Josiah

Shear-jashub A son of Isaiah

Sheba Benjamite who led a second revolt against David

Sheba, Queen of Sabean queen who visited Solomon

Shebna Court official during Hezekiah's reign

Shelah A son of Judah

Shem Eldest son of Noah

Shemaiah False prophet at the time of Jeremiah

Sheshbazzar First Babylonian governor of Jerusalem

Shimei Benjamite who cursed David at the time of Absalom's revolt

Shishak Sheshonq I, Egyptian pharaoh who invaded Palestine during Rehoboam's reign

Sihon Amorite king of Heshbon

Silas, Silvanus A leader of the Jerusalem church, companion of Paul

Simeon 1. Second son of Jacob and Leah 2. Devout man present when the infant Jesus was brought to the temple

Simon 1. Simon Peter, most prominent of the 12 disciples 2. Simon the Cananaean, also called the Zealot, one of the 12 disciples 3. Simon the Leper, in whose home Jesus was anointed for burial 4. Simon of Cyrene, forced to carry Jesus' cross 5. A Pharisee who invited Jesus to dinner 6. A magician in Samaria 7. Brother of Judas Maccabeus, succeeded his brother Jonathan as high priest

Sirach Jesus Ben Sira, author of the apocryphal book of Sirach

Sisera Canaanite commander defeated by Deborah and Barak

Solomon King of Israel's golden age, son and successor of David

Sosthenes Ruler of a synagogue at Corinth

Stephanas Paul's first convert in Corinth

Stephen A leader of the Jerusalem church and the first Christian martyr

Susanna Heroine of the apocryphal book of Susanna

Tabeel Father of the unnamed person whom the Syro-Ephraimite coalition sought to put on the throne of Judah

Tabitha Aramaic name of Dorcas, a Christian at Joppa noted for her good works

Tamar 1. Daughter-in-law of Judah 2. Daughter of David and Maacah

Terah Father of Abraham

Tertius Secretary of Paul who transcribed his letter to Rome

Tertullus Prosecutor of Paul at Caesarea

Thaddaeus One of the 12 disciples

Theophilus Person to whom Luke addressed his Gospel and Acts

Thomas One of the 12 disciples

Tiberius Emperor of Rome during Jesus' ministry

Tiglath-pileser III, Tiglath-pilneser King of Assyria who captured Galilee and Gilead

Timothy Coworker of Paul

Tirhakah King of Egypt who aided Hezekiah during Sennacherib's campaign

Titius Justus Host of a house church at Corinth with whom Paul lodged

Titus Coworker of Paul

Tobiah Ammonite opponent of Nehemiah

Tobias Son of Tobit

Tobit Pious exile whose blindness was cured by the archangel Raphael according to the apocryphal book of Tobit

Tola A minor judge

Trophimus Ephesian Christian who accompanied Paul to Jerusalem

Tychicus Messenger for Paul

Tyrannus Teacher at Ephesus in whose hall Paul lectured

Uriah Elite Hittite warrior whose death David arranged, husband of Bathsheba

Uzzah Man of Kiriath-jearim killed for touching the ark of the covenant

Uzziah Azariah, king of Judah and father of Jotham

Vashti Persian queen deposed by King Ahasuerus

Xerxes Xerxes I, king of Persia, called Ahasuerus in the Bible

Yahweh The God of Israel

Zacchaeus Chief tax collector of Jericho

Zadok High priest under David and Solomon

Zebedee Galilean fisherman, father of James and John

Zechariah 1. King of the northern kingdom, son of Jeroboam II 2. Postexilic prophet, one of the Minor Prophets 3. Priest, father of John the Baptist

Zedekiah Last king of Judah, installed by Nebuchadnezzar to replace the exiled Jehoiachin

Zelophehad Man of Manasseh whose daughters petitioned for his inheritance

Zephaniah Minor Prophet during the reign of Josiah

Zerah A twin son of Tamar

Zerubbabel A leader of the return from exile

Zeus Chief god of the Greek pantheon

Ziba A steward of the household of Saul

Zilpah Servant whom Leah gave to Jacob, mother of Gad and Asher

Zipporah Midianite wife of Moses

Zophar One of Job's comforters

Nations and Peoples

Amalekites Nomadic or seminomadic people associated with Edom, descendants of Esau and traditional enemies of Israel

Ammonites Sedentary people E of the Dead Sea and Jordan Valley with their capital at Rabbah (modern Amman). Descendants of Lot, they briefly subjugated Israel, were defeated by Jephthah, slaughtered by Saul, and conquered by David. Solomon's marriage to the Ammonite Naamah produced Rehoboam.

Amorites A Semitic-speaking population of Canaan, especially Transjordan, prior to the period of the judges

Anakim A tall people ("giants") who occupied southern Canaan, especially around Hebron, before the Israelite conquest

Arabs Nomadic and sedentary inhabitants of the Arabian Peninsula, in biblical usage including at times the N Syrian desert, Sinai, and generically all desert E of Israel

Arameans Peoples inhabiting most of Syria in the 2nd millennium and speaking various Semitic dialects of Aramaic. The Aramean states of Zobah, Damascus, Beth-rehob, Geshur, and Maacah were important in the history of biblical Israel.

Asaphites Postexilic guild of temple singers

Assyria One of the major empires of the ancient Near East, located around the upper Tigris River in northern Iraq. Originally a series of autonomous cities during the 3rd millennium B.C., Assyria first came to prominence as a state and empire in the 2nd millennium. During the Old Assyrian period Semitic-speaking Amorites entered Mesopotamia and established Assyrian trading colonies in Anatolia. In the 14th century Assyria became an international power under the Middle Assyrian Empire. Extensive military campaigns under the Neo-Assyrian Empire (934-609) brought Assyria into direct contact with Israel, particularly under kings Tiglath-pileser III, Shalmaneser V, Sargon II (whose capture of Samaria in 722 ended the northern kingdom), Sennacherib, and Esarhaddon. Revolts in conquered territories weakened Assyria, and by 609 its territory was under the control of the Chaldeans (Babylonia) and Medes.

Babylonia Mesopotamian civilization and empire occupying much of southern Iraq. In the 3rd millennium B.C. the area was divided politically into two kingdoms, Sumer in the S and Akkad in the N. A massive influx of Amorite peoples ca. 2000 established dynasties at Isin and Larsa. Best known of the Early Babylonian kings was the Amorite Hammurabi of Babylon, who gained control over all southern Mesopotamia and demonstrated a concern for justice through his famed law code. Weakened by the invasion of Indo-European peoples and then Assyrian control, Babylonia next came to prominence under a Chaldean dynasty founded by Nabopolassar. This Neo-Babylonian Empire (626-539) brought the demise of Assyria (605) and eventually Judah, when Nebuchadnezzar II laid siege to Jerusalem (597), destroyed the temple, and deported the Hebrews (586). In 539 Cyrus II captured the capital, Babylon, and the land came under Persian control.

Canaanites Inhabitants of Palestine, Phoenicia, and southern Syria in the 2nd millennium B.C. The area encompassed a range of politically independent city-states united by a common culture and religion. Dialects of the Canaanite language include Phoenician, Ugaritic, and Hebrew.

Chaldeans Loose confederation of Semitic-speaking peoples in southern Babylonia. In 626 they captured Babylon and established a new dynasty that brought about the Neo-Babylonian Empire. In the Bible Chaldea is synonymous with Babylonia.

Cherethites Mercenary group, originally from Crete and living in Philistia, that served as David's bodyguards

Dedanites Merchants from northwestern Arabia

Edomites Southern neighbors of the Moabites, located S and E of the Dead Sea. Descendants of Esau, they were regarded with animosity by Israel despite their close relationship.

Egypt Ancient and highly developed civilization along the lower (N) Nile River whose political and military power influenced much of Israel's history. Politically unified from the end of the 3rd millennium B.C. under the first, "Proto-dynastic" kings, Egypt came to prominence under the 3rd through 8th Dynasties, during the Old Kingdom period (ca. 2700-2130) with its massive royal temples and the first pyramids. Following a century of competing local dynasties, Egypt was reunified in the 21st century B.C.. During this Middle Kingdom period Egypt expanded commercial and military contact with Syria-Palestine. In the 18th century, a second "intermediate" period brought an influx of Semitic peoples from the E. Again reunited under the New Kingdom (ca. 1539-1075), Egypt gained great power throughout the Levant. By the beginning of the 1st millennium, Egypt's grandeur was past. Despite occasional attempts at conquest, Egypt came increasingly under control by the Persian, Hellenistic, and Roman empires.

Gentiles Non-Jewish persons, reflecting religious, political, and/or territorial affiliations

Greece, Greeks Inhabitants of the Greek peninsula and Greek settlements in western Asia Minor, the Greek islands, and coastal Italy. In the NT, the name was used for Hellenized or Greek-speaking persons and often generically for Gentiles. Adoption of the Phoenician alphabet, formation of city-states (the *polis*), and increased trade characterize the Archaic Age of Greece (800-500 B.C.). Having repelled Persian invasion, Greece reached its political and cultural height during the Classical Period (450-323). Disunity reigned following the defeat of Athens by Sparta in the Peloponnesian War, until Philip II of Macedonia consolidated power. His son, Alexander the Great, conquered territory as far E as India, bringing radical political and cultural change to the Mediterranean world. Though Rome gained control over Greece in 146 B.C., Greek cultural influence prevailed.

Hittites Indo-European-speaking but ethnically diverse people whose empire centered in eastern Anatolia extended from the Aegean to the Euphrates and the northern Levant during the 2nd millennium B.C. OT references to Hittites in Palestine designate Canaanite descendants of Seth.

Hivites Pre-Israelite, non-Semitic inhabitants of Canaan

Horites Semi-nomadic inhabitants of Seir prior to the Edomites, not to be identified with the Hurrians

Hurrians An ethnic group attested throughout the ancient Near East in the 3rd-2nd millennium B.C., founders of the powerful Mitanni kingdom. Cuneiform texts from Nuzi in northern Iraq shed light on common Mesopotamian and biblical legal practice.

Hyksos Asiatic "rulers of foreign countries" who dominated Egypt during the 15th and 16th Dynasties of the Second Intermediate Period

Idumeans Postexilic and Hellenistic successors of the Edomites who resisted the Nabatean influx and moved W to southern Judea and the northern Negev

Indo-Europeans Peoples speaking various representatives of the linguistic family encompassing most of the languages of Europe-Anatolia and many languages of southwestern Asia and India

Ishmaelites Nomadic merchants from Arabia, also called Midianites

Izharites A major division of the Kohathite family of Levites

Kedarites Confederation of tribes based in the northern Arabian Desert

Kenites Pre-Israelite inhabitants of the southern Canaanite wilderness near Sinai, renowned for metalworking

Libnites A division of the Gershonite family of Levites

Massaites Northern Arabian tribe of the 8th-7th centuries

Medes Indo-Iranian people who formed an empire in Persia and Asia Minor in the 7th-6th centuries B.C. Media allied with the Babylonians to overthrow the Neo-Assyrian Empire in 612.

Conquered by Cyrus II, the Medes remained a major component of the Achaemenid (Persian) Empire.

Meunites A Transjordanian people, neighbors of the Moabites and Ammonites

Midianites Confederation of tribes located in southern Transjordan and the northwestern Arabian Peninsula

Moabites Inhabitants of a small Iron Age kingdom in Transjordan, bordered by and closely related to Ammon and Edom. The Moabites had frequent and generally hostile contact with Israel.

Nabateans Arab kingdom of the Hellenistic and early Roman periods centered at Petra, amalgamated with and successors to the Edomites

Nephilim A people of the pre-Flood generation, offspring of divine beings and human women. Israelite spies identified "gigantic" inhabitants of Canaan as Nephilim.

Parthians Iranian tribe from northeastern Iran who overthrew Seleucid rule in the mid-3rd century B.C. and formed an empire that rivaled Rome in the Near East until the 3rd century A.D.

Pelethites Mercenaries, probably of Aegean origin, part of David's personal bodyguard

Perizzites Pre-Israelite inhabitants of Canaan, inhabitants of unwalled towns in the central highlands

Persia Indo-European people who overthrew the Medes and conquered Babylon in 539 B.C. to form an empire that reached from Ionia to India until its conquest by Alexander the Great in 330. Cyrus II established the Achaemenid dynasty and allowed the captive Jews to return to Jerusalem.

Philistines An Aegean people, part of the Sea Peoples, who migrated to the southern coast of Palestine (derived from their name) in the 13th-12th centuries B.C., becoming a principal rival of Israel under the judges and the early monarchy. Their settlements included a league of five major cities.

Phoenicians Seafaring peoples whose independent city-states along the northern Canaanite coast, principally Tyre and Sidon, engaged in commerce and colonization in northern Africa, southern Spain, and the Mediterranean islands.

Rechabites Followers of the Kenite Jehonadab who supported Jehu, noted for religious conservatism

Rephaim 1. The dead, inhabitants of Sheol 2. A pre-Israelite populace of Canaan, giants or warriors

Rome City on the Tiber River and the republic and massive empire that embraced much of Europe and the Mediterranean world and Mesopotamia. Rome was settled as early as the 10th century B.C. and ruled by kings from the 8th century. In 509 monarchy was replaced by the Republic, governed by annually elected consuls and the Senate, and domination was extended to the entire peninsula and through colonization beyond Italy. Following the assassination of Julius Caesar, Octavian (Augustus) ruled as *princeps,* inaugurating the Roman Empire (27 B.C.– A.D. 476).

Sabeans Tribe and kingdom in southwestern Arabia

Samaritans In the OT, residents of the district of Samaria, including Mesopotamian colonists settled there by the Assyrians. In the NT and elsewhere, members of a Hebrew religious sect tracing descent from the tribes of Ephraim and Manasseh and claiming to preserve the true Mosaic faith.

Sea Peoples Various Aegean and North African groups that invaded Egypt and the eastern Mediterranean in the 13th-12th centuries B.C. Those who settled on the coastal plain of Canaan became the Philistines.

Semites Peoples sharing a common linguistic rather than ethnic heritage, including the Akkadian, Ugaritic, Hebrew, Aramaic, Phoenician, and Arabic languages

Shulammite Inhabitant of Shunem

Sumer First major civilization in Mesopotamia, located in the alluvial plain between the Tigris and Euphrates in southern Babylonia. The Sumerian language, written in cuneiform, is attested by the late 4th millennium B.C. City-states flourished in the early 3rd millennium, including Uruk, Lagash, Nippur, and Kish, unified under central rule by the 3rd Dynasty of Ur (2050-1950). Sumer gave way to the Old Babylonians under Hammurabi in 1750.

Syrians Peoples associated with Damascus and its environs, in biblical usage Aram.

Gazetteer of Places

Abaddon Place of the dead, Sheol

Abarim Mountain range E of the Dead Sea and opposite the Judean wilderness, overlooking the Jordan Valley

Abilene Region in the eastern Anti-Lebanon range

Achaia Roman province encompassing southern Greece, ruled from Corinth

Achor, Valley Valley on the Judah-Benjamin border

Achzib Port city on the border of Asher, N of Acco

Adam City in Transjordan where the Jordan River was blocked, allowing the Israelites to cross

Aegean Sea A northern bay of the Mediterranean Sea

Ai Canaanite town just E of Bethel, a major conquest of Joshua's second campaign

Aijalon Valley Important trade route through the original, central hill country territory of Dan

Alexandria Mediterranean seaport in the western Nile Delta, capital of Egypt under the Ptolemies and a major Hellenistic cultural center

Amana Mountain peak in the Anti-Lebanon range

Ammon Transjordanian kingdom at the headwaters of the Jabbok River, in the area of modern Jordan

Amphipolis Macedonian city on the northern Aegean coast

Anatolia Asian portion of modern Turkey, the peninsula bounded by the Black, Aegean, and Mediterranean seas.

Anathoth Levitical city in the tribal territory of Benjamin, home of Jeremiah

Antioch 1. Antioch of Pisidia, a city on the Anthius River in the southern part of the Roman province of Galatia, central modern Turkey 2. Antioch of Syria, a city on the Orontes River, capital of the Roman province of Syria

Antipatris City rebuilt by Herod the Great on the site of Aphek

Aphek City-state controlling the Via Maris, just above the source of the Yarkon River

Apollonia Macedonian town on the Via Egnatia, the major E-W road from Asia to Italy

Aqabah, Gulf of Northeastern arm of the Red Sea, E of the Sinai Peninsula

Arabian Peninsula Large, mostly desert peninsula between the Red Sea on the W, the Indian Ocean to the S, Iraq and the Persian Gulf on the E

Arad City in the Negev, ENE of Beer-sheba

Aram Important state in southern Syria with its capital at Damascus, rival to Israel for control of the Levant

Ararat Assyrian Urartu, mountainous country in eastern Asia Minor around Lake Van (southeastern Turkey and Armenia into northwestern Iran)

Areopagus Mars Hill, near the Acropolis and marketplace of Athens

Ariel Poetic name for Jerusalem

Armageddon Location of the final battle between the forces of good and evil, from Hebrew "mountain of Megiddo"

Arnon River Major perennial stream in Transjordan, flowing into the eastern side shore of the Dead Sea at its midpoint, boundary between Amorite territory and Moab

Arpad City-state in northwestern Syria, N of Aleppo

Arvad Northernmost Phoenician city-state, a small island off the Syrian coast

Ashdod Philistine city, N of Ashkelon on the Via Maris

Asher Tribal territory in the western Galilee highlands

Ashkelon Large Philistine seaport N of Gaza

Ashkenaz Kingdom near Armenia, identified with the Scythians

Asia Roman province covering western Asia Minor

Asia Minor The Anatolian Peninsula, bounded by the Black Sea on the N, the Aegean on the W, and the Mediterranean on the S

Asshur Capital of Assyria

Assos Strategic city on the Gulf of Adramyttium on the eastern coast of the Aegean Sea

Assyria A major empire of ancient Mesopotamia, centered in northern Iraq around the upper Tigris River

Athens Major cultural and political city-state of Greece on the peninsula of Attica

Auranitis Transjordanian province under Herod the Great, earlier known as Hauran

Avaris Hyksos capital in the eastern Nile Delta

Azotus Greek name of Ashdod

Baal-peor Site in Moab, cult center of idolatrous worship

Baal-perazim Mountain NW of Jerusalem, location of David's first victory after being crowned king of Judah and Israel

Babel, Tower of City and tower in the plain of Shinar (Babylonia)

Babylon Region and its capital on the Euphrates River SW of Baghdad

Bashan Fertile plateau of upper Transjordan, E of the Sea of Galilee and N of the Yarmuk River

Batanea Name of Bashan in the Graeco-Roman period, one of four divisions of Herod the Great's kingdom

Beer-sheba Major city in the northern Negev, southern extreme of Israelite territory

Benjamin Tribal territory in the southern Judean highlands, central ridge between Jerusalem and Bethel

Beroea Macedonian city in the foothills of Mount Bermion, W of Thessalonica

Bethany Village on the lower slope of the eastern ridge of the Mount of Olives

Beth-aven Benjamite city near Ai and Bethel

Bethel Important sanctuary town at the Ephraim-Benjamin border, near Ai on a crossroads of the N-S mountain road N of Jerusalem

Bethesda Pool by the Sheep Gate in Jerusalem

Beth-ezel City in southern Judah

Beth-leaphrah Small town in Judah, S of Jerusalem

Bethlehem Town in the Judean hill country just SSW of Jerusalem, home and first capital of David, birthplace of Jesus

Beth-millo Fortress in the region of Shechem

Beth-shean Town at the junction of the Jezreel and Jordan valleys, strategic location at E-W and N-S trade routes

Beth-shemesh City in the Sorek Valley, SW of Jerusalem

Beth-togarmah A place N of Israel, probably in Armenia

Bethulia City in Samaria, setting for the apocryphal book of Judith

Bezek Canaanite city, defeated by Judah and Simeon

Bitter Lakes Two connected lakes E of Goshen, between the northern tip of the Gulf of Suez and the Mediterranean Sea

Bochim Place W of the Jordan River near Gilgal and Bethel

Byblos Canaanite and Phoenician port N of Beirut, ancient Gebal

Caesarea 1. Caesarea Maritima, a major Roman seaport on the eastern coast of the Mediterranean, N of Tel Aviv, capital of the Roman government in Palestine 2. Caesarea Philippi, capital of the Roman tetrarch Herod Philip, on the southern slope of Mount Hermon near one of the sources of the Jordan River

Calneh A city at the northern end of the Orontes River in Aram-naharaim, capital of the Neo-Hittite state of Unqi

Cana Village in Galilee, NE of Nazareth

Canaan The land along the eastern shore of the Mediterranean occupied by the Israelites, encompassing most of Palestine W of the Jordan as well as modern Lebanon and part of southern Syria

Canneh Northern Mesopotamian city that traded in textiles with Tyre

Capernaum City on the northwestern shore of the Sea of Galilee, center of Jesus' ministry

Caphtor Place of origin of the Philistines, usually identified as Crete

Carchemish City in Syria near the prime ford of the Euphrates, N of Aleppo near the border of Turkey

Carmel Fertile, forested mountain range along the northern coast of Israel, from Mount Carmel at the bay of Acre to the plain of Esdraelon

Cenchreae Eastern port of Corinth on the Saronic Gulf

Chaldea Region in southern Babylonia bordering the Persian Gulf, biblical name for Babylonia

Chebar Mesopotamian canal running E from Babylon

Chinneroth/Chinnereth/Kinneseth, Sea of Sea of Galilee

Cilicia Roman province on the southeastern coast of Anatolia

Colossae Important city in the upper Lycus River valley of central Asia Minor

Corinth City controlling the isthmus connecting mainland Greece and the Peloponnesian Peninsula

Crete Largest and southernmost of the Greek islands

Cush Area S of Egypt and W of the Red Sea, encompassing parts of modern Sudan, Ethiopia, Eritrea, Saudia Arabia, and Yemen

Cyprus Island in the eastern Mediterranean, an important stop for traders from Anatolia and the Levant

Cyrene Capital of the North African Roman province of Cyrenaica (modern Libya)

Dalmatia Roman province on the northeastern coast of the Adriatic Sea

Damascus Capital of Aram in southern Syria

Dan City on the northern border of Israel, in the Huleh Valley at the foot of Mount Hermon

David, City of Oldest part of Jerusalem on the Ophel ridge between the Kidron and Tyropoeon valleys, captured by David from the Jebusites

Dead Sea Large salt lake at the southern end of the Jordan River

Decapolis Group of 10 Hellenistic cities in Transjordan, E of Samaria and Galilee

Dedan Oasis in northwestern Arabia

Derbe City in the region of Lycaonia in southwestern Galatia

Ebal, Mount Mountain N of Shechem, across the valley from Mount Gerizim

Ebenezer Site near Aphek S of Gilgal where the Philistines captured the ark of the covenant

Ecbatana Capital of the Median Empire, between Tehran and Baghdad in the Zagros mountains of northwestern Iran

Eden Idyllic garden in which God placed the first man and woman

Edom Mountainous region S and E of the Dead Sea, bounded on the N by Moab

Egypt One of the earliest and greatest civilizations of the world, situated along the lower Nile River

Egypt, Brook of Seasonal stream that formed the south border of Canaan and Judah

Ekron A city of the Philistine pentapolis, on the eastern edge of the Shephelah, the frontier between the Philistines and Israel

Elam State and region E of the Tigris River in highland Iran

Elath Harbor city at the head of the Gulf of Aqabah

Elim A campsite of the Israelites after crossing the Sea of Reeds

Elishah A name for Cyprus

Emmaus Village near Jerusalem where the risen Christ appeared to disciples

Endor Canaanite town in northwestern Manasseh, SW of Mount Tabor

En-eglaim Site on the western shore of the Dead Sea

En-gedi Oasis on the western shore of the Dead Sea, SE of Hebron

En-rogel Spring near Jerusalem, on the boundary between Judah and Benjamin

Ephesus Large port city in Ionia on the southwestern coast of Asia Minor

Ephrathah A name for Bethlehem or the surrounding area

Esdraelon Western section of valley and plains separating Galilee from Samaria, often used interchangeably with Jezreel

Etham First stopping place after departing Succoth during the exodus, near the eastern Nile Delta

Ethiopia Ancient name of the Nile Valley region S of Egypt, modern Sudan, also called Cush

Euphrates River Longest and most important river of southwestern Asia

Ezion-geber Edomite town on the Gulf of Aqabah

Fertile Crescent Semicircular strip of land arching between Palestine and the Persian Gulf

Gad Tribal territory in the Transjordanian highlands, between the Jabbok and Arnon Rivers

Gadara City of the Decapolis SE of the Sea of Galilee

Galatia Region and Roman province in north-central Asia Minor

Galilee Northern region of Palestine between the Jezreel Valley and the Litani River, location of much of Jesus' ministry

Gath A city of the Philistine pentapolis on the coastal plain S of Ekron

Gaza Philistine coastal city on the southern border of Canaan

Geba City near the N border of Benjamin, guarding the Michmash pass N of Jerusalem

Gebal Canaanite and Phoenician seaport on the Mediterranean, called Byblos by the Greeks

Gehenna Hinnom Valley, a ravine S and SW of Jerusalem

Gennesaret Coastal plain NW of the Sea of Galilee, also another name for the Sea

Gerar City on the southern border of Canaan near Gaza

Gerizim, Mount Mountain NW of Shechem opposite Mount Ebal

Gethsemane Garden E of the Kidron Valley near the Mount of Olives where Jesus prayed before his betrayal and arrest

Gezer City overlooking the Aijalon Valley at the junction of the northern Shephelah and Judean foothills

Gibeah Benjamite city N of Jerusalem, home and headquarters of Saul

Gibeon Important Benjamite city NNW of Jerusalem

Gilboa, Mount Mountain opposite the Hill of Moreh which together guard the eastern pass from the Esdraelon Plain into the Jezreel Valley

Gilead Transjordanian region between Bashan and Moab

Gilgal Place E of Jericho where the Israelites encamped after crossing the Jordan, later a cultic center

Golan Heights Transjordanian plateau E of the Sea of Galilee, from the Yarmuk gorge to the slopes of Mount Hermon

Golgotha Place of Jesus' crucifixion outside Jerusalem

Gomorrah One of the five Cities of the Valley, near the southern end of the Dead Sea

Goshen Fertile region in the eastern Nile Delta where the Hebrews settled

Greece Major ancient civilization centered on the southern end of the Balkan Peninsula

Hades Greek name for the underworld, abode of the dead

Hadrach City in northern Syria on the Orontes River between Hamath and Damascus

Hamath City and district on the Orontes River between Damascus and Aleppo, ideal northern boundary of Israel

Haran Cosmopolitan Mesopotamian city N of the confluence of the Euphrates and Balikh rivers to which Terah and his family migrated

Hatti Non-Indo-European kingdom in central and eastern Anatolia, displaced by the Hittites

Hazor Major fortified Canaanite and Israelite city in northern Galilee at the southwestern corner of the Huleh Plain and N of the Sea of Galilee

Hebron City SSE of Jerusalem on the crest of the Judean mountain ridge, burial place of the patriarchs and capital of Judah under David

Heliopolis On, Egyptian center for worship of the sun-god

Hermon, Mount Three-peaked summit at the southern end of the Anti-Lebanon range, highest in the Levant

Heshbon City of northern Moab, capital of the Amorite king Sihon

Hinnom Valley Narrow gorge W and S of Jerusalem, Gehenna

Hor, Mount Mountain on the border of Edom near Kadesh

Horeb A name for Mount Sinai

Hormah City in the Negev of Judah near the border with Edom

Huleh Northernmost and smallest of three lakes along the course of the Jordan River

Iconium City in south-central Asia Minor, in NT times part of Galatia

Idumea Greek name for Edom

Illyricum Large, mountainous Roman province in the northwestern Balkan Peninsula

Israel 1. Nation comprising the 12 tribes 2. The northern kingdom during the divided monarchy

Issachar Tribal territory between the eastern Jezreel and Jordan valleys

Italy Boot-shaped peninsula bounded by the Tyrrhenian, Adriatic, and Ionian seas and extending N to the Alps

Ituraea Area of the Beqa' Valley N of the Sea of Galilee ruled by the tetrarch Herod Philip

Jaar A name for Kiriath-jearim

Jabbok River One of four major streams of Transjordan, a major tributary of the Jordan

Jabesh-gilead City in northwestern Gilead

Javan A name for Ionia, a region of Greek settlement in southwestern Asia Minor

Jazer Amorite town in central Transjordan, later a Levitical city

Jebel Musa Traditional site of Mount Sinai

Jericho Town N of the Dead Sea, the first conquered after Israel entered Canaan

Jerusalem Primary city of ancient Israel, capital of Judah and the united monarchy

Jeshurun A poetic name for Israel

Jezreel Eastern section of the broad valley separating Galilee from Samaria

Joppa Mediterranean harbor just S of modern Tel Aviv

Jordan 1. Largest and most important river in Palestine, flowing S from Mount Hermon to the Dead Sea 2. Rift Valley between modern Israel and Jordan

Judah 1. Tribal territory in the central hill country, between but not including Jerusalem and Hebron 2. The southern kingdom during the divided monarchy, tribal territories of Judah and Benjamin

Judea Postexilic Greek name for Judah

Kadesh, Kadesh-barnea Site in northern Sinai where the Israelites encamped before entering Canaan

Karnaim Fortress city in Gilead

Kerioth Fortified city in Moab

King's Highway Major international route between Damascus and the Gulf of Aqabah

Kir City in southern Mesopotamia to which Tiglath-pileser III deported captives from Damascus, original home of the Arameans

Kiriath-jearim Hill-country city on the border of Judah, Benjamin, and the original territory of Dan

Kittim A name for Cyprus, later all the coastlands of the eastern Mediterranean

Lachish Prominent fortified Canaanite and Israelite city in the foothills of Judah SW of Jerusalem

Laodicea Prosperous commercial city in the Lycus River valley of southwestern Phrygia, W of Colossae

Lebanon Mountainous region N of Israel noted for its cedar forests

Lebo-hamath City on Israel's northern border

Levant Name for the lands of the eastern Mediterranean, primarily Syria-Palestine and Anatolia, but often also the coastlands from Egypt to Greece

Libnah City in the Shephelah conquered by Joshua

Lo-debar City-state in northern Transjordan above the Yarmuk River

Lud A name for Lydia

Lydda City SE of Joppa, also called Lod

Lydia Region and kingdom in western Asia Minor, whose capital was Sardis

Lystra Town in the region of Lycaonia in south-central Anatolia

Macedonia Region and kingdom between the Balkans and the Greek peninsula

Machpelah Field and cave in Hebron, burial site of the patriarchs

Madeba, Medeba Moabite city in the Transjordanian highlands S of Heshbon

Mahanaim City in Gilead along the Jabbok River

Makkedah City in the Shephelah of Judah E of Lachish

Malta Ancient Melita, largest of the Maltese islands, S of Sicily

Manasseh Tribal territory immediately S of the Jezreel Valley and between the Yarmuk and Jabbok rivers in Transjordan

Marah Israelite encampment in the wilderness of Shur

Mareshah Fortified town in the southern foothills of Judah

Massa, Meribah Oasis in Sinai, site of Israelite rebellion during the wilderness wanderings

Media Kingdom in northern Iran, later a province of the Persian Empire

Mediterranean Sea Large sea bounded by Europe, North Africa, Asia Minor, and Syria-Palestine

Megiddo City in northwestern Palestine strategically located at a pass from the coastal plain into the Jezreel Valley, along the Via Maris connecting Egypt to Damascus and Mesopotamia

Memphis Capital of Egypt during the Old Kingdom, on the western bank of the Nile S of Cairo

Menzaleh, Lake Saltwater lagoon E of the Nile Delta, separated from the Mediterranean by a narrow peninsula

Merathaim Southern region of Babylonia where the Tigris and Euphrates rivers empty into the Persian Gulf

Merom Spring S of the Canaanite frontier of Upper (northern) Galilee

Meshech Region in eastern Asia Minor, possibly Cappadocia

Mesopotamia Area roughly between the Tigris and Euphrates rivers and their tributaries

Michmash Town near the boundary of Benjamin and Ephraim NE of Jerusalem

Midian Region in the northeastern Arabian Peninsula, E of the Gulf of Aqabah

Migdol Place representing the northern boundary of Egypt

Miletus Large port with four harbors at the mouth of the Meander River on the western coast of Asia Minor

Millo A structure in the City of David

Minni Small state S of Lake Urmia in northern Iraq

Mitanni Hurrian confederacy in northern Mesopotamia and Syria during the late 2nd millennium

Mizpah Mizpah of Benjamin, important military and cultic city on the border of Judah and Israel

Moab Kingdom immediately E of the Dead Sea, bordered by Ammon on the N and Edom on the S

Moriah, Mount Site of the temple in Jerusalem

Nahor City in northwestern Mesopotamia, SE of Haran

Nain Town on the N slope of the Hill of Moreh, SE of Nazareth

Naphtali Northern tribal territory W of the Sea of Galilee, bounded by Asher on the W and Zebulun and Issachar on the S

Nazareth Town in central Galilee just N of the Jezreel Valley, hometown of Jesus

Neapolis Seaport of Philippi

Nebo, Mount Mountain from which Moses viewed the promised land, E of the Dead Sea and mouth of the Jordan River

Negev Arid southern region of Palestine

Nicopolis City on the isthmus of the Bay of Actium in northwestern Greece

Nile The great river of Egypt, flowing N from Lake Victoria to the Mediterranean Sea

Nimrod Calah, Assyrian capital under Assurbanipal II

Nineveh Last capital of the Assyrian Empire

Nob City in Benjamin N of Jerusalem, religious center after the destruction of the Shiloh sanctuary

Olives, Mount of Central peak of the N-S ridge just E of Jerusalem, across the Kidron Valley from the temple

Olivet A name for the Mount of Olives

On City in N Egypt, center for sun worship, Heliopolis

Ophir Maritime city famed for its gold

Orontes River Main river of western Syria

Paddan-aram Area around Haran in northern Mesopotamia

Pamphylia District on the southern coast of Asia Minor bounded on the W by Lycia, on the N by Pisidia and the Taurus Mountains, and on the E by Cilicia

Paran Desert region south of Judah, W of Edom and N of the wilderness of Sinai

Pathros Upper (S) Egypt, south of Memphis and the Nile Delta

Patmos Aegean island off south-central Asia Minor

Pekod Region E of the lower Tigris River

Pentapolis League of five Philistine cities

Penuel City on the Jabbok River where Jacob wrestled with God

Peor Mountain in northwestern Moab

Pergamum City in western Asia Minor N of Smyrna, one of the seven churches of Revelation

Persia Late 1st-millennium empire, stretching at its height from Ionia to India

Persian Gulf Arm of the Arabian Sea between southwestern Iran and Arabia

Petra Capital of the Nabatean Empire, SSW of the Dead Sea

Philadelphia City in the Roman province of Asia, ancient Lydia

Philippi Roman colony in northeastern Greece at the border of eastern Macedonia and Thrace

Philistia Coastal plain of Palestine controlled by the Philistines, from Raphia to Joppa

Phoenicia Greek name for ancient Canaan, coastal region of southern Syria, Lebanon, and Israel

Phrygia Territory of west-central Asia Minor, between the northern Aegean Sea and Halys River

Pisgah Mountain in northwestern Moab near Mount Nebo

Pisidia Mountainous region in southwestern Galatia

Pithom Egyptian store-city built by Hebrew laborers

Put Region in Africa, possibly in Libya

Puteoli Port W of Naples

Qarqar City in the Orontes River Valley of Syria near Hamath, site of a battle between the Assyrian Shalmaneser III and a coalition including Ahab of Israel

Qumran Settlement on the northwestern shore of the Dead Sea S of Jericho that produced the Dead Sea Scrolls

Rabbah Capital of Ammon, modern Amman

Ramah Ramah of Benjamin, a town N of Jerusalem on the Judah-Israel border, hometown of Samuel

Rameses Store-city in the Nile Delta built by the Hebrews

Ramoth-gilead Levitical city in eastern Gad

Raphia City SW of Gaza on the Palestine-Egypt frontier

Red Sea Northwestern arm of the Indian Ocean S

of the Sinai Peninsula, separating Africa from the Arabian Peninsula

Reeds, Sea of Body of water E of the Nile Delta associated with the exodus

Rehob 1. Place in extreme northern Canaan near the entrance to Hamath 2. Town in the Plain of Acco

Reuben Tribal territory in Transjordan, S of Gilead and N of the Arnon River

Riblah City on the eastern bank of the Orontes River S of Kedesh

Rift The Jordan River Valley

Rome City on the Tiber River, capital of the Roman Empire

Saba Kingdom in southern Arabia

Salem City where Melchizedek was king, identified with Jerusalem

Samaria Capital of the northern kingdom, Israel, and later name for a region in the central hill country

Samothrace Mountainous island in the northeastern Aegean Sea

Sardis Capital of Lydia, one of the seven cities of Revelation

Seir 1. High hilly plateau within Edom and another name for Edom, also called Mount Seir 2. Mountain on the northern border of Judah

Sela Edomite fortress city

Seleucia Port city of Antioch in Syria

Senir Amorite name for Mount Hermon

Sepharad Place where exiles from Jerusalem were resettled, possibly Sardis

Sheba Saba, country in southwestern Arabia that traded with Solomon

Shechem City in the heartland of the Ephraimite hill country, in the pass between mounts Ebal and Gerizim, first capital of the northern kingdom

Sheol The netherworld, abode of the dead

Shephelah Lowland region between the coastal plain and the Judean hills

Sheshach A cryptogram for Babylon

Shiloah Pool and aqueduct in Jerusalem, part of the Siloam water system

Shiloh Ancient holy site in northern central Ephraim N of Bethel

Shinar A name for Babylonia

Shunem Town in the hill territory of Issachar guarding the pass to the Jezreel Valley at the foot of the Hill of Moreh

Shur Desert region in northeastern Sinai

Sibmah Moabite town near Heshbon

Sidon Phoenician metropolis and harbor N of Tyre

Siloam System that conducts water from the Gihon Spring in the valley E of the City of David to the pool within its southeastern corner

Sinai 1. Peninsula between Egypt and Palestine 2. Wilderness area and the mountain where Moses received the Law

Sirbonis, Lake Mediterranean gulf E of the Nile Delta

Smyrna Harbor on the western coast of Asia Minor, modern Izmir, Turkey

Sodom City at the southern end of the Dead Sea, one of the five Cities of the Valley

Succoth Location of the first encampment of the Israelites during the exodus

Suez, Gulf of Northwestern arm of the Red Sea between Egypt and the Sinai Peninsula

Susa Capital of Elam in southwestern Iran

Syene City on the eastern bank of the Nile at the southern border of Egypt

Syria Aram, areas associated with the city-state of Damascus

Syria-Palestine Geographic region encompassing the coastal plain of the eastern Mediterranean, the fringes of the Syrian Desert, and the double mountain chain from the central steppe, including Aram, Phoenicia, and biblical Israel

Taanach City on the southwestern edge of the Jezreel Plain SE of Megiddo

Tabor, Mount Isolated mountain in the northeastern Plain of Esdraelon

Tahpanhes Egyptian outpost bordering Sinai in the northeastern Delta

Tappuah City on the Ephraim-Manasseh border

Tarshish Unidentified seaport distant from Palestine

Taurus Mountains Southern mountain range of Turkey parallel to the Mediterranean Sea

Tel-abib Mound of ruins in Babylon

Tema City in northern Arabia

Teman Region in and name for Edom

Thebes Capital of Egypt in the Middle Kingdom and again in the New Kingdom, located in Upper (southern) Egypt

Thebez City in Ephraim NE of Shechem

Thessalonica City in Macedonia on the Thermaic Gulf

Thyatira Commercial and industrial city in Lydia on the road between Pergamum and Sardis

Tigris River Major river which, with the Euphrates to the W, created the fertile floodplain fostering ancient civilization in southern Mesopotamia

Timnah City on the northern border of Judah between Beth-shemesh and Ekron

Tiphsah City destroyed by Menahem, possibly Tappuah

Tirzah City in the hill country of Samaria NE of Shechem, capital of the northern kingdom under Jeroboam I

Topheth Place in the Hinnom Valley S of Jerusalem where children were sacrificed to Molech

Trachonitis Region in northern Transjordan, the northeastern extent of Herod the Great's kingdom, also called Hauran

Transjordan Region E of the Jordan River, from Mount Hermon to the Gulf of Aqabah

Troas Principal Aegean seaport in Mysia, SSW of Troy

Tubal Nation in eastern Asia Minor, possibily Cilicia

Tyre Principal Phoenician seaport S of Sidon, an island connected to the mainland by causeway since the time of Alexander the Great

Ugarit Capital of 2nd millennium Canaanite city-state, modern Ras Shamra

Ur Ancient Sumerian capital W of the Euphrates, ancestral home of Terah and Abraham

Uz Homeland of Job, possibly located in Edom or Aram

Uzal Place possibly identified with modern Sanʿaʾ, capital of Yemen

Yehud Persian district of Judah in the postexilic period

Zaanan A town in the Shephelah of Judah

Zagros Mountains Major system of parallel mountain ranges in western Iran, boundary between Assyria and Media

Zarephath Phoenician port between Sidon and Tyre

Zebulun Tribal territory in the highlands of south-central Galilee

Ziklag Town at the southern edge of the Shephelah, given to David by Achish king of Gath

Zion A name for Jerusalem, the Temple Mount, Judah, and the entire ancient country of Israel

Ziph A town in the hill country of Judah S of Hebron

Zoan A city in the eastern Nile Delta, early 1st-millennium capital of Egypt

Zoar Southernmost city in the Valley of Jericho, one of the five Cities of the Valley

Zorah Town in the Sorek Valley, NE of Beth-shemesh and W of Jerusalem

Index of Subjects

afterlife. *See* death; heaven; hell

Alexander the Great, 391, 445, 448-50, 492, 494, 499, 753

altar, 124-27, 161, 227-28, 486; built by Abraham and others, 85, 90, 94, 97, 239; in Ezekiel's vision, 440, 731; for foreign gods, 255, 451, 506, 618, 727; "horns" of, 119, 227-28, 349, 461, 734; of incense, 120, 135; unique location of, 153, 158, 180-82, 274, 287, 510

Amarna Age, 84

angel, 148, 456, 679, 695, 717; communicates with people, 91-94, 97, 184-91 passim, 198, 443, 448-51, 479-80, 491, 524-26, 543, 555, 559-61, 578, 723, 732, 736; destroys enemies, 256, 328, 731; protects God's people, 121, 239, 328, 445, 447, 450, 611, 730; strengthens Christ, 526-27, 545. *See also* archangel

Antiochus IV Epiphanes, 442, 444, 448, 450-51, 494, 540, 544, 593, 754

apocalyptic, 283, 400, 424, 443-44, 479, 525, 685, 723-24, 748, 751; Daniel as, 442, 447-51, 725; and Jesus, 558; Revelation as, 176, 331, 336, 719, 722

Apocrypha, 19-20, 305, 489-91, 717, 742, 751

apostles: in Acts, 602-29; commissioned by Jesus, 531, 547-48, 565-66, 576, 601; as foundation of the church, 671

Aramaic, 26, 31, 285-88, 386, 442, 600, 605, 626, 656, 660; in the Gospels, 523, 529, 542, 544-54 passim, 586, 601; in the Persian Empire, 34, 169, 256

archangel, 450-51, 717, 732, 755

ark of the covenant, 130, 139-40, 144, 163, 193, 203, 230, 403, 421, 477, 731, 735; construction of, 118, 135, 231, 256; David transports it to Jerusalem, 76, 167, 218, 232, 266-67, 326, 351; at Jericho, 165, 171, 174-75; Solomon installs it in the temple, 234, 264, 271

Asherim (Asherah), 188-89, 237, 254-58, 340, 389, 407, 426-27, 429, 754. *See also* idols, idolatry

Aten, 344, 385, 427

Atonement, Day of, 67, 120, 130, 132-37, 154, 628, 754

Atrahasis Epic, 83, 84, 86

baptism, 552, 568, 656, 659, 679, 708; with the Holy Spirit, 585, 602, 658; of Jesus, 525-27, 543, 545, 561, 654, 658, 711-12, 714; by John the Baptist, 484, 488, 526-27, 538, 544, 557, 561, 564, 569, 619; of new disciples, 543, 605, 610-11, 647

Beatitudes, 528, 539, 543, 563, 726

Bible: and archaeology, 46-55; composition of, 18-24; as divine and human, 15-17; interpretation of, 35-38; as literature, 43-45; significance of, 3, 741-50; story of, 4-8; transmission of, 25-30

blessing: children as, 202, 360, 406; of children, by Jesus, 537, 552; as God's covenantal promise, 90, 107, 114, 138, 152, 356; long life as, 318, 342, 432; of the nations, through Abraham, 74-76, 92, 105, 162, 398, 482; obedience leads to, 201, 272-74, 307, 318, 674; of the patriarchs, 91, 95, 97-100, 107; in the Psalms, 325-29, 336-37, 340, 344, 346-47, 350-52

blood: on the altar, 119, 124, 126; atoning role of, in sacrifices, 125, 130, 670, 697; of Christ, significance of, 128, 130, 134, 541, 554, 573, 600, 671, 697, 707, 719; eating/drinking of, proscribed, 85, 131, 158, 209, 589, 613; at the Passover, 113, 133, 574, 600; on the priests and people, 118, 120, 144, 707; of revenge/avenging, 151, 159, 180, 189, 217, 224, 252; water turned to, 109, 112

Book of Life, 121, 336, 393, 677

call of: Abraham, 75-76, 89, 91, 95; Ezekiel, 423-24; Isaiah, 254, 277, 381-83; Jeremiah, 401-2, 407; Jesus, to discipleship, 523, 537, 547, 562, 597, 703; Jonah, 467; Moses, 108, 188; Paul, 608, 643-44; Samuel, 201, 203

canon: Christian, 16, 20-25, 369, 520, 544, 636, 638, 684-85, 700, 706, 742, 749; Jewish, 20-22, 25, 153, 282, 332, 369, 508, 638; of Marcion, 633, 637; Muratorian, 633, 637-38, 685

census: by David, 167, 225, 230, 268, 269; in Pentateuch, 138-40, 149; Roman, 69, 560, 728

children: as blessing of God, 129, 347, 350; of the Devil, 591, 714; of God, 7, 575, 585, 714; to honor their parents, 160, 674; promised to Abraham,

Ramesses II, 108, 110, 172

redemption, 5-7, 82, 142, 509, 523, 599, 752; as God's pledge and act, 152, 344, 395-96, 411; in Jesus' life and teaching, 549, 593; need of, 78, 127; in Paul, 128, 142, 392, 645, 649, 669-70, 679

remnant, 376-79, 649, 730; in Ezekiel, 423, 428-29, 433-34, 438; in Isaiah, 381-83, 387-88, 391-92, 400, 404; in Jeremiah, 401, 409, 415-16, 418; returned from exile, 285, 290, 295; saved in the flood, 84-85, 156

repentance, 134, 204, 268, 273, 381, 410, 536; in Corinth, 652, 655, 663, 725, 735; in Isaiah, 381, 383, 393, 398; in Jeremiah, 401, 403, 405, 410, 413; in Jesus' teaching, 527, 536, 538, 562, 567-71, 581, 601; in John the Baptist's teaching, 527, 564, 619

restoration: of David's house, 206, 464; from exile, 163, 259, 271, 280, 292, 294, 321, 350, 377-80, 393-98, 406, 411, 430-39 passim, 469-70; with God, 164, 453, 645, 662, 704; to the image of God, 7, 547; in Jubilee year, 68, 137

resurrection, 6-8, 127-28, 490, 517-21, 634-35, 652, 689, 695, 730; assurance of, for the elect, 649, 662; bodily, in the Old Testament, 391, 451; nature of, 659-60; predicted by Jesus, 565, 572, 587, 594-95; as proof and vindication of Jesus' person and mission, 379, 580, 666; Sadducees' disbelief in, 511, 553, 605, 627; women as first witnesses to, 543, 555, 564, 578, 601, 672

return, from exile, 163, 281-83; and Cyrus, 280, 286; and Ezra, 288, 290; and Joshua (high priest), 477, 480-81; and Nehemiah, 291-95; and Zerubbabel, 285-88, 295, 409, 449, 477-81

revelation, 7, 17, 515; Jesus incarnate as the fullness of, 583, 585, 596; to Moses, 153, 282; and theology, 744-45; through visions and dreams, 105, 423, 447, 471, 473, 724

Rome, 445, 448, 621, 648, 650, 662, 706, 720, 728-29, 735-36, 763; Christians in, 609, 635, 642, 694, 722; Jesus' relation with, 538, 542, 571, 577, 579, 600; Paul in, 602, 616-17, 625, 628-29, 636, 670, 676, 678, 684, 690; ruling Israel, 501-5, 560, 591

Sabbath, 67, 120, 132-33, 513; as day of rest, 115, 156, 695; and disputes with Jesus, 532, 562-63, 568-69, 579, 588, 590, 592; Jesus as the lord of, 532, 545; observance commanded, 121, 143, 407

Sabbatical Year, 158, 163, 294, 412

sacrifices and offerings, 123-30, 146, 150, 158, 231-32, 278, 290, 400, 486-87, 653, 696-97; by Solomon,

228, 234, 271. See also altar; priests; tabernacle; temple

Sadducees, 499, 510-12, 527, 535, 538-39, 553, 575, 605-6, 627-28, 710

salvation, 15-16, 354, 518-20, 662, 695, 714; based on faith, not works, 91, 568, 647, 649, 667-69, 671, 687, 698; history of, 118, 377, 514-15, 612, 645, 659, 722; as open to all, 174, 561-62, 607, 613, 629, 645, 649, 708. See also exodus; grace

Sanhedrin, 511, 541-42, 553-54, 568, 577, 579, 586, 593, 599, 600, 606, 616, 626-28

scribes, 26-29, 32-33, 288, 385, 528-32, 539, 553-54, 569-70, 575; Baruch as, 402, 413, 414, 597; Ezra as, 285, 288, 291

Second Temple, 262, 282-83, 287, 308, 321, 329, 420, 448, 458, 477, 481-82, 510-11, 638, 752

Seleucus, Seleucids, 448, 450, 494-95, 499, 509. See also Antiochus IV Epiphanes

Septuagint, 19-21, 26, 127, 165, 201-2, 226, 240, 296, 321, 402, 420, 442, 515, 597, 694-95, 752; readings of, 184, 353, 390, 428, 446, 598

sermon, 156, 633, 637; Hebrews as, 638, 657, 694; of Jeremiah, 401, 404, 410; of Jesus, 528, 530, 563, 592, 597, 700; of Job's "comforters," 306, 311, 313; of Paul, 612, 622, 668; of Peter, 605, 639, 706, 709

Seti I, 172

sexual relations, 127, 131, 149, 210, 221, 333, 357, 370, 524, 652

shepherd, sheep: David as shepherd, 201, 339, 561; God as Shepherd, 303, 326-27, 338-39, 394, 417, 454, 470; imagery of, 5, 326, 349, 394, 438, 483-84, 593; Jesus as the Good Shepherd, 348, 582, 584, 592-93

signs: by the apostles, 605, 654, 664; by Jesus, 520, 546-47, 582, 601, 746; of Moses, before Pharaoh, 109, 111-14; of the times, 535, 731; in writing systems, 28, 33-34

sin, 5, 591-92; of Adam and Eve, 77, 81-821, 120; atonement for, 118-19, 128-30, 147, 278, 397, 463, 585, 600, 697; and guilt, 126, 147, 159, 413, 430, 456; offering, 125, 129, 140, 440-41, 699; punished, 6, 120-21, 155, 164, 180, 193, 220-24, 306, 329, 436, 591. See also holiness, holy; repentance; sacrifices and offerings

slaves/servants, 642, 701-2; of God, 475, 539, 605, 674, 695; Israelites as, 68, 105, 111, 114, 131, 234; in Jesus' parables, 61, 538, 540, 553, 574-75; laws concerning, 117, 137, 158, 160, 162, 293, 385

Son of Man, 530, 554, 574-75, 580, 583-84, 586, 723-26, 732; in Daniel 7, 175, 448, 726 spirit: of the dead, 265, 385; evil/unclean, 167, 189-90, 210, 548-50, 564, 567, 618. *See also* Holy Spirit

suffering: for Jesus, 519, 596, 606, 667, 689, 699, 708, 727; of Jesus, 527, 535-37, 541, 565, 568, 572, 576, 579, 599, 695, 699, 708; in the Psalms, 322, 329, 336-37, 343; of the righteous, 306-18 passim; of the "Suffering Servant," 395, 397, 574, 605

synagogue, 154, 510-13, 545, 608, 656; and church, 630-31, 646-47; Jesus teaches and heals in, 532, 545, 549, 562, 654; Paul preaches in, 610, 616. *See also* temple

tabernacle, 74, 134-36; God's presence at, 140, 147, 163, 203, 233; instructions for building and setting up, 118-22; Levites maintaining, 139, 178, 268. *See also* temple

Tabernacles, Feast of, 67, 118, 132-34, 234-35, 237, 271, 294, 339, 346, 457, 484, 509, 583, 590-91

Tammuz, 68, 132, 370, 429

tax: collectors, 523, 534, 538, 547, 556, 562, 572, 574, 620, 726, 728; for the temple, 509, 536; by the Romans, 553

temple, 231-33, 509-10; church as, 136, 652, 657, 707. *First Temple:* building of, 107, 157, 225-26, 230, 271; cleansing of, 258, 279; dedication of, 126, 234, 271, 400; destroyed, 168, 175, 321, 418-22; God's presence in, 233-34, 476; preparations for, 230, 268; sacrifices and services at, 124-25, 219, 319. *Second Temple:* building of, 169, 280-82, 286-88, 419, 477-82; cleansing of, 133, 330, 451, 494, 553, 586; destroyed, 27, 491, 539-40, 544; worship at, 199, 287, 329, 340

temptation, 81, 189, 237, 268, 352, 467, 529, 535, 541, 566, 575-76, 625, 682, 700, 711; of Jesus, 118, 525-26, 545, 561-62; to worship false gods, 158, 183, 358

Ten Commandments. *See* Decalogue

thanksgiving: offering of, 87, 125-26, 129, 309; in Paul, 641, 668; psalms, 111, 270, 302, 323-29, 335-38, 342, 344, 346-50, 352-53, 466. *See also* worship

tithe, 192, 264, 278, 294, 539; in Pentateuch, 98, 125, 137, 147, 150, 158, 161; in the Prophets, 487

transfiguration, 536, 540, 548, 551, 565, 709, 724

Unleavened Bread, Feast of, 111, 113, 118, 132-34, 236, 278-79, 288, 554, 605. *See also* Passover

Urim and Thummim, 119, 154, 179, 209, 286

vine, vineyard, 160, 246, 339, 345, 350, 537; and Isaiah's Song of the Vineyard, 382, 391, 403; in Jesus' parables, 349, 537, 538, 553, 575; of Naboth, 240, 252, 758; in the Prophets, 403, 430-32, 436, 458, 469, 480; in the Song of Solomon, 371, 373

vows, 366, 413; by God, 220, 381, 398, 400, 407, 417, 425, 431, 434-35, 439, 453, 456, 473, 480; in Pentateuch, 137, 150, 160; of the psalmists, 333-36, 347, 352

war: civil (Israel-Judah), 12, 166, 182, 193, 216-17, 222, 236, 238, 273, 456; holy, 142, 173-74, 180, 211, 220, 273, 330; pagan gods of, 148, 187, 384, 386; spiritual, 176, 307, 674

wealth, 314-15, 317, 347, 700, 705; in Jesus' teaching, 529, 552, 567, 570, 574; of the patriarchs, 90, 99, 105; in the Prophets, 381, 469, 481; of Solomon, 228, 230, 235, 270; in Wisdom literature, 283, 356, 359, 366-67

Weeks, Feast of, 118, 132-34, 154, 196, 232, 235, 274, 346, 509, 605

wisdom, 301-5, 393, 569, 700; personified, 359, 363, 550. *See also* poetry

wise men, 102, 305, 405, 445. *See also* magi

works, 595-96, 688-89, 700, 704; vs. faith, for salvation, 91, 568, 647, 649, 667-69, 671, 687, 698; of God, 177, 238, 329, 335-36, 339, 343, 347, 365-66, 648-49; of Jesus, 532, 547, 551, 582, 588

worship: of Baal, 149, 156, 185, 189, 226, 239, 257-58, 405, 426, 452, 457; at Bethel and Dan, 157, 237, 253, 416, 460-61; calendar of, 132-34; centralized in Jerusalem, 138, 153, 158, 160, 226, 228, 234, 279, 381; David organized, 219, 266-68; in early Christian churches, 656-58; of golden calf, 117, 120, 146, 157, 345, 433, 461, 610; psalms in, 348. *See also* feasts and festivals; sacrifices and offerings; thanksgiving

Index of Scripture and Other Ancient Sources